BBC
PRONOUNCING DICTIONARY
OF BRITISH NAMES

BBC
Pronouncing Dictionary
of British Names

SECOND EDITION

Edited and Transcribed by
G. E. POINTON

Oxford   New York
OXFORD UNIVERSITY PRESS
1983

Oxford University Press, Walton Street, Oxford OX2 6DP

London Glasgow New York Toronto
Delhi Bombay Calcutta Madras Karachi
Kuala Lumpur Singapore Hong Kong Tokyo
Nairobi Dar es Salaam Cape Town
Melbourne Auckland

and associated companies in
Beirut Berlin Ibadan Mexico City Nicosia

Oxford is a trade mark of Oxford University Press

First edition 1971
Second edition 1983

British Library Cataloguing in Publication Data

British Broadcasting Corporation
The BBC pronouncing dictionary of British names.
—2nd ed.
1. Names—Great Britain—Dictionaries
2. Names—Pronunciation
I. Title   II. Pointon, G. E.
421'.55   PE1660
ISBN 0–19–212976–7

Typeset by Gloucester Typesetting Services
Printed in Hong Kong

PREFACE

ELEVEN years have passed since the publication of the first edition of this dictionary, edited by Miss G. M. Miller, and the BBC's Pronunciation Unit has been continuing its work throughout that time. A lot of new information has come to light, concerning personal and place names which had not previously been recorded by us and also names which were already part of our collection. This new information has been incorporated where appropriate in the second edition.

Some minor changes have been introduced in the lay-out: most importantly, each place name is now identified by its county, or in Scotland its region. This is in order to show at a glance which place is intended. There are many names which occur in more than one county, and the BBC has established the pronunciation only of those whose county is stated. Other places whose names are identically spelt may be differently pronounced.

Secondly, there is no longer any typographical distinction between personal and place names. The addition of county and region names has rendered the previous practice superfluous.

The bracketing of both IPA and Modified Spelling has been discontinued without, we hope, giving rise to any ambiguity.

I have included on another page the names of members of the Pronunciation Unit, past and present. If there are any omissions, they are not intentional, as all my fellow-workers in the Unit are responsible for some part of the material in this book.

Those who have helped in the revision of the work are too numerous to mention by name, and include many people in public libraries, post offices, police stations, and elsewhere, who remained anonymous. I am grateful to them all for the time they gave me as well as for the information. BBC staff around the country, in local radio stations and regional headquarters, were also very helpful and deserve my thanks. Special mention must be made of two people, however: Miss Nia Rhosier, who

Preface

ot of time and effort to helping me with the
atries, and Mr Gregory James, lecturer in the
Language Centre at the University of Exeter, who
checked many of the entries for Devon and Cornwall.
My thanks go also to Miss Alexandra Bejda who prepared much of the typescript for this edition, and to
Betty Palmer and Ena Sheen of the Oxford University
Press for their help in seeing the work through to
publication.

The responsibility for any errors which may remain
lies entirely with me.

G. E. POINTON

Broadcasting House
London W1A 1AA
August 1982

PREFACE TO THE
FIRST EDITION

IN this book the BBC has gathered together the fruits of more than forty years of research into the pronunciation of proper names in the United Kingdom. The book was compiled primarily for the use of members of staff, but the BBC hopes that it will prove useful to many other readers. Here they will find the pronunciation which as nearly as possible represents the usage of the inhabitants of the place or of the family bearing the name listed. Although the BBC does not, and never did, impose pronunciations of its own on English words, the myth of 'BBC English' dies hard. It owed its birth no doubt to the era before the Second World War, when all announcers and perhaps a majority of other broadcasters spoke the variety of Southern English known as Received Pronunciation, which is the type of English spoken by those educated at public schools; but there was nothing esoteric about this way of speaking, nothing exclusive to the BBC, and in its pre-war setting it came to be accepted as the natural mode of communication over the air. Even today, when a much wider variety of voices is heard, the old style is still regarded as having an important place in broadcasting. The good announcer remains, as far as the BBC is concerned, the pleasant, unobtrusive speaker who does not distract attention from his subject matter by causing embarrassment, unwitting amusement, or resentment among intelligent listeners. He is the mouthpiece for the BBC's official pronouncements, the man who links programmes, announces concerts, narrates opera scripts, reads bulletins prepared in the newsroom, and generally undertakes the exacting task of interpreting other people's work, only occasionally displaying his own versatility by taking part in particular programmes.

In the early 1960s, the BBC felt that it would be more realistic to throw the stage open to the men behind the scenes, so that news men participated personally in news broadcasts, meteorologists gave us our weather forecasts, policemen enlisted our aid direct from Scotland Yard, and the BBC Motoring Unit kept us hourly aware of traffic problems. This created a greater sense of immediacy between the listener and those at the heart of the event. Naturally, there was no longer insistence on purely southern usage, as these experts are likely to be drawn from all parts of the country. Their prime advantage is that they are informed and articulate on their own subject, and consequently easy to follow. They hold the interest and sympathy of the listener because of their expertise. At the same time, a more colloquial element has been introduced, which has disposed even further of a sense of formality. Individual departments are of course responsible for avoiding the pitfall of employing the man who is patently neither adequate speaker nor expert. In both radio and television, News Division has experimented widely. London television presentation announcers, on the other hand, continue to be drawn from the ranks of RP speakers, while domestic radio presentation has extended its range to take in several Commonwealth announcers. In the BBC's European and World Service English language broadcasts, understandably, Southern English RP remains the accepted norm for all announcers, both in news bulletins and in programmes. As well as the need to overcome the occasional vagaries of short-wave reception, there is the consideration that to a very large number of listeners English is a foreign tongue, and a stable style of pronunciation greatly helps intelligibility. It is also appreciated by the world-wide followers of BBC English by Radio programmes.

There is one sphere, however, in which the BBC expects conformity from all its official broadcasters, and that is in the treatment of British proper names. It is felt that, as a matter of courtesy, the bearer of a name or title should be referred to by the pronunciation which he himself prefers; and that place names should be pronounced as they are locally, with perhaps rare exceptions where there is a recognized 'national' pronunciation. A name is usually a matter of vital moment to those closely and often emotively concerned with it, and unfavourable reaction to a mispronunciation, with all the lack of interest and care that the latter implies, is immediate. On the BBC's part, the size of the Pronunciation Unit's telephone bills must be considered one small testimony to its endeavour to keep in close touch with personal and local usage. It is this Unit, which emerged as the direct heir to the BBC's Advisory Committee on Spoken English in 1939, that continues to carry out the Committee's far-sighted recommendations in regard to both English and foreign language problems. It is worth pausing for a moment to study the calibre of the Committee itself, which was set up in 1926 by the Director-General, Mr. J. C. W. Reith, later Lord Reith. Foremost among its members were four linguistic specialists—Arthur Lloyd James, Professor of Phonetics at the School of Oriental and African Studies in the University of London, who acted as honorary secretary to the Committee and linguistic adviser to the announcers; Daniel Jones, Professor of Phonetics at University College London, a phonetician of world repute, whose close association with the BBC continued until his death in 1967; H. C. Wyld, Merton Professor of English Language and Literature in the University of Oxford; and Harold Orton, later to become Professor of English Language and Medieval Literature in the University of Leeds. Among the members of the main Committee over the years were the Poet Laureate Robert Bridges, Sir Johnston Forbes-Robertson, George Bernard Shaw, Sir Julian Huxley, Lord David Cecil, Sir Kenneth Clark, Lady Cynthia Asquith, Rose Macaulay, and many others of distinction. After some early lively battles on matters of principle, the members settled down to collecting information for inclusion in a successive range of booklets covering the pronunciation of English, Scottish, Welsh, and Northern Irish place names, and of British family names and titles. All their findings, published before 1939, have been incorporated in this present book, together with much evidence acquired since that time.

I wish to acknowledge my indebtedness to Professor A. Lloyd James and Professor Daniel Jones, who were responsible for the inception of this collection and for the principles on which it is based, and with whom I had the constant pleasure of working during their years as the Corporation's Linguistic Advisers; to my colleague, Elspeth D. Anderson, who has not only collaborated closely throughout the preparation of the dictionary, but who did much of the research over a long period of years; to R. L. W. Collison, formerly BBC Librarian and now Professor of Library Service in the University of California, Los Angeles, who advised on the more intricate aspects of indexing; to Dr. Aled Rhys Wiliam, formerly of the BBC in Wales and now Director of Audio-Visual Media at the University of Salford, whose scholarly yet practical knowledge of his country and its language, enhanced by his broadcasting experience, has left him singularly well equipped to advise on Welsh names; to Arthur G. Kent of Jersey and Frank Falla of Guernsey, who undertook the difficult task of indicating by pen rather than by word of mouth the pronunciation of Channel Islands names, and whose wishes I hope I have interpreted successfully; to A. C. Gimson, Professor of Phonetics in the University of London, who has been unfailingly swift and generous with advice on general and specific points whenever this was sought; to J. Windsor Lewis, Lecturer in the Department of Phonetics in the University of Leeds, for accepting the arduous assignment of proof-reading, in the course of which he has offered much constructive criticism and valuable guidance on phonetic problems, particularly in relation to Welsh names; and to numerous BBC colleagues in London and the Regions.

G. M. MILLER

Broadcasting House,
London, W.1.
December 1970

INTRODUCTION

A CURIOUS witness to the remarkable diversity of provenance of the inhabitants of the British Isles is the fact that the first entry in this dictionary should be *Aagaard* and the last *Zabiela*—names more immediately suggesting an affinity with Scandinavia and the Iberian Peninsula. Here, however, the recording of pronunciations rather than research into historical origins has been the aim. The book includes titles, family names (i.e., surnames), certain Christian names (or personal first names), place names, those of institutions and societies, and adjectival forms of proper names, drawn from England, Wales, Scotland, Northern Ireland, the Isle of Man, and the Channel Islands—the last appearing in a separate appendix. Some names, like that of *Yehudi Menuhin*, appear because their owners, although not technically of British nationality, have made their homes here and are very much a part of the British scene. It is not an exhaustive collection, and not every pronunciation of every name is represented; only those for which satisfactory evidence was available have been included. Local clergy, town clerks and their staff, postal and police officials, and many private citizens have contributed—sometimes very extensively—to the information on place names. Advice on personal names has been most carefully sought from the individuals concerned, or from members of their families or other sources close to them. Although it is naturally outside the scope of the book to record the many popular versions of pronunciations used by those professing no local or personal knowledge of the names, there are cases, like those of *Carlisle* and *Newcastle*, in which an accepted 'national' pronunciation has been recorded, even though it is not necessarily the most general one among the educated local population. Many historians, artists, musicians, scientists, and others have been consulted about present-day spoken forms of historic names. Descendants of historical personages, too, have sometimes provided interesting information about past and present usage. For entries like *Wriothesley*, where evidence was elusive, various written sources were also consulted.

Spellings

For place-name spellings, the authorities accepted have been the Handbook entitled *Post Offices in the United Kingdom* published by the Post Office in November 1974, the *Census 1971, England and Wales, Index of Place-names*, the *Ordnance Survey Gazetteer of Great Britain*, the *Gazetteer of Welsh Place-Names*, and Bartholomew's *Survey Gazetteer of the British Isles* and *Gazetteer of Britain*. Spellings of titles were verified in Debrett.

Titles

The pronunciation of a title has been linked, according to its origin, sometimes with a family name and sometimes with a place name. In the case of an historic hereditary title where the line of succession has come to an end, or the title is in abeyance, and the last holder's pronunciation is known to us, this has been recorded, as appropriate, as a *dukedom, earldom, viscountcy,* or *barony*. Likewise, the term *barony* appears in association with certain family names to record the specific pronunciation of one who has been a life peer. However, no mention is made of the large majority of life peers whose title is identical with their family name and whose pronunciation is in no doubt. A place name has sometimes been retained in a title, not because it is an integral part of the title, but because of its pronunciation interest. This situation arises when the place name, in this particular form, appears only in the title and is not to be found elsewhere, e.g., *Viscount Greenwood of Holbourne, Baron Tedder of Glenguin*. The opportunity to record the pronunciation might otherwise be lost. There are titles, on the other hand, where the territorial designation is included as a matter of course because it is an essential distinguishing feature of the title, e.g., *Baron Balfour of Burleigh, Baron Balfour of Inchrye*.

County names

The names of counties, or in Scotland regions, have been included for each place name recorded. Many place names occur in more than one county or region. In such cases only those counties have been included for which satisfactory evidence of the pronunciation has been obtained by the Pronunciation Unit. For instance, Bartholomew's *Survey Gazetteer of the British Isles* records 48 places called *Broughton*, but for those in counties not named in the dictionary, we have not had occasion to verify the pronunciation. When a river flows through more than one county, those counties have been identified.

Indexing

Names of the same spelling appear in the sequence of Christian name (i.e., personal first name), family name (i.e., surname), and place name. A title, if isolated, precedes all of these, but titles generally are associated with particular family or place names. Otherwise names are in strict letter-by-letter alphabetical order. Where the same sequence of letters appears twice, as a single word and as a group of two or more words, the single word is given precedence, e.g., *Vandyck*, *Van Dyck*.

All names beginning *Mac-*, *Mc-* or *M'-* have been treated as beginning with *Mac-*, and placed accordingly. Optional ways of writing this initial syllable, according to family preference, are exemplified in the name *MacGregor, Macgregor, McGregor, M'Gregor*.

St., the standard abbreviation of *Saint* in family and place names, is treated for alphabetical purposes as if it were written in full. In general, the names of saints associated with these islands occur, as do other Christian names, in their due alphabetical places throughout the book. Certain of them, however, having come to the notice of the BBC in the form of names of individual churches or hospitals, have found their place alphabetically under *St.*, intermingled with place names and family names.

Unless otherwise stated, it may be assumed that the ordering of variant pronunciations within an entry is as follows for place names: the first entry is that preferred by the local educated population, and is recommended to BBC announcers. Local dialectal pronunciations are given last if at all. Between these two extremes are given, in descending order of frequency heard (in so far as we can judge) any other variant pronunciations we have been made aware of.

All entries under a place name refer to one specific place. Family names with variants must be understood differently: some bearers of the name prefer one pronunciation, others prefer another. Thus *Kenneth Alwyn* (conductor) is ˈɔlwɪn, áwlwin, while *William Alwyn* (composer) is ˈælwɪn, álwin, and to refer to them otherwise would be, at the least, discourteous, if not completely wrong. Even so, in a very general way, the first pronunciation given is normally that for which we have the most evidence, and subsequent ones are in an approximate order of decreasing frequency.

Welsh names

Those who are already aware of the complex linguistic situation arising from the differing pronunciations of North and South Wales on the one hand, and from the existence of a demotic and a classical language on the other, will appreciate that the BBC's need to adapt individual pronunciations still further to the speech of English announcers must inevitably produce different solutions from those which might appear in a work of exclusively Welsh interest. It can be taken for granted, however, that a BBC announcer is expected at least to distinguish between *l* and *ll* in those Welsh names in which these consonants would be differentiated by local educated speakers of English. Professor A. Lloyd James, whose comprehensive collection of Welsh names and their pronunciations was published by the BBC in 1934 in *Broadcast English IV*, found it necessary to recommend considerably anglicized versions for the use of announcers in London and the rest of the country. In the present work extensive advice on the adaptation of these names and many others has been given by Dr Aled Rhys Wiliam, Mr Jack Windsor Lewis, and Miss Nia Rhosier; if there has been any failure to adopt their recommendations, the fault is certainly not theirs. Orthography was checked largely against *A Gazetteer of Welsh Place-Names* prepared by the Language and Literature Committee of the Board of Celtic Studies of the University of Wales, but in cases where this was at variance with *Post Offices in the United Kingdom* the final decision was allowed to rest with the latter, as it is the forms used there which are most likely to appear in national newspapers and in BBC news bulletins. Nevertheless, the Committee's admirable principle of making stress patterns clear by the use of hyphens has been followed wherever possible. In Welsh names stressed at the regular penultimate syllable no hyphens are necessary. The appearance of a hyphen before the final syllable, however, reveals that stress falls on that syllable, e.g., *Troedrhiw-fuwch*. The practical benefit of the system is perhaps most evident in two-syllable names which, in North Wales, tend usually to be stressed on the first (or penultimate) syllable, whereas in the South their counterparts are often stressed on the second (or final) syllable, thus, *Penrhos* in Gwynedd, but *Pen-rhos* in Gwent and Powys. Hyphens are in general also used before and after the definite article in three-syllable names where the stress falls on the last syllable, as in *Pen-y-bank*, *Pen-y-fan*, *Pont-y-clun*.

KEY TO PRONUNCIATION

Two systems have been employed to indicate pronunciation, one for the benefit of those acquainted with the International Phonetic Association's method of symbolizing sounds and the other for the general user. In the IPA system, a 'multiliteral' transcription has been used, with the addition of italicized [ə], [h], [r], [p], [d], to indicate variant pronunciations. For the second method an English modified spelling system has been used which, after its explanations have been studied, should be immediately obvious to most English speakers. The systems have been adapted to Received Pronunciation, which is familiar alike to BBC announcers and to listeners and viewers in this country and overseas, whether it happens to be their own type of speech or not. The only exception to this is that orthographic *r* is acknowledged in both pronunciation systems. In those cases, however, in which it is in general omitted by Southern English speakers, it it written as italicized [*r*] in the IPA version.

Vowels

IPA symbol	English modified spelling	Words containing sound
i	ee	see
ɪ	i	pity
e	e	get
æ	a	hat
ɑ	aa	father
ɒ	o	not
ɔ	aw	law
ʊ	ŏŏ	book
u	oo	food
ʌ	u	but
ə	ă, ĕ, ŏ, ŭ	*about*, butt*er*
ɜ	er, ur, ir	f*er*n, f*ur*, f*ir*
	ö	*is used to indicate this same centralized vowel sound in cases where there is no 'r' in the original spelling*, e.g.

Beinn Laoigh ben 'lɜɪ, ben lö-i

De Veulle də 'vɜl, dĕ völ

Des Voex deɪ 'vɜ, day vö

Exotic vowels

		More or less as in French
æ̃	a*ng*	vin
ɑ̃	aa*ng*	banc
õ	õ*ng*	bon
ɛ:	e	fèvre
y	ü	du

Diphthongs

eɪ	ay	day
aɪ	ī	high
ɔɪ	oy	boy
oʊ	õ	no
aʊ	ow	now
ɪə	eer	here
ɛə	air	there
ʊə	ōŏr	poor

Consonants

p, b, t, d, k, m, n, l, r, f, v, s, z, h, w are used in both transcriptions with their customary English values.

Otherwise the symbols are:

g	g	get
x	<u>ch</u>	Scottish *loch*
tʃ	ch, tch	church
dʒ	j	jet
n̩	n	see note on syllabic n
ŋ	ng	sing
l̩	l	see note on syllabic l
ɬ	<u>hl</u>	Welsh *llan*
θ	th	thin
ð	<u>th</u>	there
ʃ	sh	shut
ʒ	<u>zh</u>	*s* in *measure*
r̩	r	is used in French-type pronunciations to denote devoiced, non-syllabic r following p, t; e.g., **Earl of Ypres** ipr̩, eepr
hw	wh	where
j	y	yes

Stress symbols

In the IPA transcription main stress is indicated by the symbol ['] preceding the stressed syllable, and secondary stress by the symbol [ˌ]. In modified spelling, secondary stress is not shown, but main stress is indicated by an acute accent '´' above the syllable. Thus:

Aberdeen *Grampian*, ˌæbər'din, abbĕrdéen

Use of hyphens

The use of hyphens in the IPA script has been kept to a minimum, but hyphens have been introduced to avoid the ambiguity which might arise when [ɪə] and [ɔɪ] are employed not as diphthongs but in each case as two distinct vowels. *Flawith* makes the point particularly well, as its pronunciation allows two such variants: 'flɔ-ɪθ, fláw-ith; flɔɪθ, floyth. In modified spelling hyphens are used more frequently, and generally for obvious reasons. A less obvious treatment becomes necessary in a name like the Welsh *Dewi*, where the use of open [e] 'e' before [w] 'w' constitutes a sound sequence unfamiliar to most users of the Received Pronunciation of English, and where the pronunciation ['dewɪ] has been written 'dé-wi'. Similarly, the Irish name *Mulcahy*, pronounced [mʌl'kæhɪ] with *a* as in 'cat', has been written 'mulká-hi'.

The two systems

In the text, the IPA transcription precedes the modified spelling, the two being separated by a comma. Where more than one pronunciation is shown, a semi-colon keeps them apart. The two methods are systematically related, although the precision of the IPA system cannot be quite matched by the other, and certain concessions have had to be made in the modified spelling system in order to avoid misinterpretation. For example, the sound corresponding to [ju] appears as 'yoo' at the beginning of a pronunciation, as in **Udall** 'judɔl, yoodawl, but in all other cases as 'ew'; that corresponding to [ɔr] is generally written 'or', but before another vowel, or following 'w'. it becomes 'awr', so that **Dorey**

ˈdɔrɪ, dáwri may not be mistaken for ˈdɒrɪ, dórri, and that the initial syllables *Ward-*, *Wark-*, and *Warm-*, pronounced [wɔrd-], 'wawrd-', [wɔrk-], 'wawrk-', [wɔrm-], 'wawrm-', should not be confused with the English words *word*, *work*, and *worm*. A convention of the modified spelling is that it is in general related to the original spelling of the name, so that *Burghersh* is written 'búrgersh', although the two vowel sounds are the same. Wherever they occur, the modified spellings 'ăr', 'ĕr', 'ŭr' are merely different representations of the same sound. A double consonant, or in appropriate cases 'ck', is used to make the open nature of the preceding vowel more obvious, as in **Debenham** ˈdebənəm, débbĕnăm, **Brecon** ˈbrekən, bréckŏn.

Unstressed syllables

In many names, unstressed syllables have alternative forms whose vowels may be transcribed in the IPA system in the one case as [ə] and in the other as [ɪ]. To include both of these in all entries would have increased greatly the bulk of the dictionary. Consequently a simplified solution has been found: both pronunciations have been shown where the traditional orthography spells the unstressed vowel *a*, *i*, or *y*, while for such names with *e* in the traditional orthography the IPA transcription uses [ɪ], but the Modified Spelling has 'ĕ', which may be interpreted by the reader as either [ə] or [ɪ].

Exotic vowels

As the key to pronunciation shows, the nasalization of a vowel in IPA script is indicated by the use of a tilde [~] over it; in modified spelling, it is shown by writing an italicized '*ng*' after the vowel. Of the nasal vowels the first, [æ̃] 'a*ng*', is related to the [æ] 'a' of English *hat*; the second, [ɑ̃] 'aa*ng*', to the [ɑ] 'aa' sound of English *father*; and the third, [õ] 'ō*ng*' to the close *o* used by many Scots, Irish, and Welsh speakers in the word *no*. The vowel [ɛː]—the only instance in which the IPA length mark [ː] has been used, incidentally—is a lengthened version of the first vowel in English *ever*. In Southern English usage [eɪ] 'ay' is generally substituted for this sound, but there are names in which a closer approximation to the foreign sound is usual.

Syllabic *l*

In the numerous cases in which final syllables spelt *-al*, *-all*, *-el*, *-ell*, *-il*, *-ill*, *-ull* are pronounced as a syllabic *l*, no indeterminate vowel has been introduced into either system of pronunciation and they are written simply as *l*, e.g., **Dougall** 'dugl, doŏogl; **Mitchell** 'mɪtʃl, mítchl; **Sempill** 'sempl, sémpl; **Minshull** 'mɪnʃl, mínshl. When a syllabic *l* occurs in the middle of a word, however, it becomes necessary to introduce a syllabic mark, [ḷ], in the IPA script, and to use a hyphen in an appropriate place in the modified spelling. Thus, **Chittlehamholt** 'tʃɪtḷəmhoʊlt, chíttl-ăm-hōlt, to suggest that, in the more careful pronunciation at least, the *l* would constitute a syllable in itself.

Syllabic *n*

There is a good deal of variety in the treatment of final unstressed syllables in which the following consonants are preceded by a vowel, and followed by another vowel plus *n*: [t] 't', [d] 'd', [s] 's', [z] 'z', [ʃ] 'sh', [ʒ] 'zh'. Although the majority usually in relaxed speech make the *n* syllabic, some endeavour, even in informal speech, always to retain the indeterminate vowel, and this has been indicated by writing (ən) with an italicized, alternative [ə] in IPA script, and 'ăn', 'ĕn', 'ŏn', 'ŭn', not merely 'n', in modified spelling, e.g., **Beaton** 'bitən, béetŏn; **Rowden** 'raʊdən, rówdĕn. Occasionally, on the other hand, it becomes necessary to accommodate a syllabic *n* in the middle of a name, and this is done by writing [ṇ], with a syllabic mark, in IPA script and using a hyphen to show the suitable break in modified spelling, e.g., **Aldenham,** Baron 'ɔldṇəm, áwldn-ăm.

Italicized [ə] in IPA transcription

Although the use of italicized [ə] in the IPA transcription has been restricted largely to endings where syllabic *n* may occur, it could feasibly be extended to cover such further possible variants as [-bərə], [-bərɪ], [-dʒəm],

[-ʃəm], [-rəm], [-rən], [-wəl]. This would not in most cases affect the present modified spelling renderings.

Italicized [r] in IPA transcription

The decision to acknowledge orthographic *r* in all positions in both pronunciation systems leads to its italicization in the IPA transcription in the following positions:

(1) before consonants, e.g., **Parnell** pɑ*r*nel, paarnéll

(2) in final positions, e.g., **Grosvenor** ˈgroʊvnə*r*, gróv-nŏr, except when this is a linking *r*, as mentioned below.

It is not italicized

(1) in initial positions, e.g., **Renwick** ˈrenɪk, rénnick

(2) after consonants, e.g., **Franklin** ˈfræŋklɪn, fránklin

(3) as linking *r* between two words, where the second word begins with a vowel, e.g., **Over Alderley** ˈoʊvər ˈɔldərlɪ, ŏvĕr áwldĕrli.

The devoiced [ɹ̥] 'r', used in the *Earl of Ypres* and similar names, occurs only after the unvoiced plosives *p*, *t*. It is employed to guard against the possible interpretation of the single-syllable [ipɹ̥], 'eepr' as two syllables, [ˈipər], 'éepĕr'.

Initial orthographic rh

Rh occurs particularly at the beginning of Welsh names and is generally an indication that the *r* is a strong voiceless sound in the Welsh language; but, as this is a pronunciation not usually employed by non-Welsh speakers, it has not been shown in the modified spelling pronunciation. Its presence in Welsh, however, is acknowledged by writing [*h*r] in IPA script, so that *Rhos*, for example, appears as [*h*roʊs], 'rōss'.

Orthographic rhiw

This root may occur initially, medially, or finally in Welsh place names. To pronounce it as one syllable, [*h*rju], 'rew', is normal in Welsh, but not in RP usage, and it has in general been treated as [*h*rɪ'u], 'ri-óo', with [ˌ*h*riu], 'ree-oo' occasionally when it is initial.

Initial orthographic wh

While most southern speakers, at least, habitually make no distinction in pronunciation between such pairs of words as *Wales* and *whales*, others regularly do. It is a matter of usage in particular regions or speech groups. Allowance has been made for both schools here by writing [ʍw] in IPA script, and by showing 'wh' in modified spelling, e.g., **Whitefield** ʹʍwaɪtfild, whítfeeld. In those cases in which there has been no evidence of the existence of a pronunciation with [ʍw], no [ʍ] has been shown. A further possible treatment of the spelling occurs in the name **Whewell**, pronounced ʹhjuəl, héw-ĕl.

Final orthographic -ian, -ien, -ion, -ear, -ier, -iour, -iel, -iol

In all cases where the pronunciation of these syllables has been indicated in IPA script as [-ɪən], [-ɪər], [-ɪəl], it can be taken for granted that the alternatives [-jən], [-jər], [-jəl] are acceptable variations, e.g., **Fabian** ʹfeɪbɪən, fáybi-ăn; **Collier** ʹkɒlɪər, kólli-ĕr; **Baliol** ʹbeɪlɪəl, báyli-ŏl can also be ʹfeɪbjən, fáyb-yăn; ʹkɒljər, kól-yĕr; ʹbeɪljəl, báyl-yŏl.

Attributive stress

An aspect of stress to be remembered is that, although a two- or three-syllable name may be stressed on the final syllable when used in isolation, more often than not the stress moves to the first syllable when it is used attributively. For example, *Thorness* is pronounced θɔrʹnes, thornéss; but *Thorness Bay*, in the natural rhythm of the English language, becomes ʹθɔrnes ʹbeɪ, thórness báy. This point has not been elaborated in individual cases, but taken for granted, and the stress shown is that which would apply if the name were used in isolation.

Initial Dun- and Strath- in Celtic names

The unstressed initial syllables *Dun-* and *Strath-* in Scottish and Northern Irish names have been shown in this book only as [dʌn-], 'dun-' and [stræθ-], 'strath-', which is the way in which they are pronounced in careful speech; but in colloquial use they are just as often pronounced [dən-], 'dŭn-' and [strəθ-], 'străth-', and a footnote to this effect appears on the relevant pages.

ABBREVIATIONS

County and region names

Beds.	Bedfordshire
Berks.	Berkshire
Bucks.	Buckinghamshire
Cambs.	Cambridgeshire
Ches.	Cheshire
D. & G.	Dumfries and Galloway
Derby.	Derbyshire
Glos.	Gloucestershire
Gtr. M'chester	Greater Manchester
H. & W.	Hereford and Worcester
Hants	Hampshire
Herts.	Hertfordshire
H'land	Highland
Lancs.	Lancashire
Leics.	Leicestershire
Lincs.	Lincolnshire
Northants.	Northamptonshire
Northd.	Northumberland
Notts.	Nottinghamshire
Oxon.	Oxfordshire
Salop	Shropshire
S'clyde	Strathclyde
Staffs.	Staffordshire
Wilts.	Wiltshire
Yorks.	Yorkshire

Other abbreviations

admin. dist.	administrative district
anc.	ancient
A.-S.	Anglo-Saxon
Assoc.	Association
c.	century
cf.	compare
C.n.	Christian name
Co.	County
Coll.	College

div.	division
f.n.	family name
HRH	His *or* Her Royal Highness
I.	Isle, -s
mt.	mountain
nr.	near
q.v.	which see
Rt. Revd	Right Reverend
St.	Saint *or* Street
Univ.	University

WORKS OF REFERENCE
CONSULTED

Bardsley, C. W. (1901): *A Dictionary of English and Welsh Surnames*. Henry Frowde, London.

Bartholomew, J. (1951): *Survey Gazetteer of the British Isles*, 9th edition. Bartholomew, Edinburgh.

Davies, E. (ed.) (1958): *A Gazetteer of Welsh Place-Names*, 2nd edition. University of Wales Press, Cardiff.

Gimson, A. C. (ed.) (1977): *Everyman's English Pronouncing Dictionary*, 14th edition. Dent, London.

Hudson, E. (ed.) (1958): *Commercial Gazetteer of Great Britain*. Geographia, London.

Lloyd-James, A. (1936): *Broadcast English II: Recommendations to announcers regarding the pronunciation of some English place-names*, 2nd edition. BBC, London.

—— (1932): *Broadcast English III: Recommendations to announcers regarding the pronunciation of some Scottish place-names*. BBC, London.

—— (1934): *Broadcast English IV: Recommendations to announcers regarding the pronunciation of some Welsh place-names*. BBC, London.

—— (1935): *Broadcast English V: Recommendations to announcers regarding the pronunciation of some Northern-Irish place-names*. BBC, London.

—— (1939): *Broadcast English VII: Recommendations to announcers regarding the pronunciation of some British family names and titles*. BBC, London.

Mason, O. (1977): *Gazetteer of Britain*, 1st edition. Bartholomew, Edinburgh.

Montague-Smith, P. (ed.) (1979): *Peerage, Baronetage, Knightage, and Companionage*. Debrett's Peerage, London. Earlier editions also consulted.

Reaney, P. H. (1961): *A Dictionary of British Surnames*. Routledge and Kegan Paul, London.

Thorne, J. O. (ed.) (1963): *Chambers's Biographical Dictionary*, new edition 1961, revised 1963. Chambers, Edinburgh.

Townend, P. (ed.) (1971): *Peerage, Baronetage and Knightage*. Burke's Publishing, London. Earlier editions also consulted.

Withycombe, E. G. (1950): *The Oxford Dictionary of English Christian Names*, 2nd edition. Oxford University Press. Oxford.

Census 1971, England and Wales, Index of Place-Names (1977). HMSO, London.

Concise Dictionary of National Biography Part I (1953). Oxford University Press, Oxford.

Crockford's Clerical Directory (1979). Oxford University Press, London. Earlier editions also consulted.

Ordnance Survey Gazetteer of Great Britain (1969). HMSO, London.

Post Offices in the United Kingdom (1974). HMSO, London.

Webster's Pronouncing Biographical Dictionary, 2nd edition (1961). Bell, London.

Who's Who 1981. Black, London. Earlier editions also consulted.

MEMBERS OF THE
BBC PRONUNCIATION UNIT
SINCE ITS INCEPTION

Miss G. M. Miller, MBE, *Pronunciation Assistant 1939–71*
Mrs C. H. M. Langlands, *Pronunciation Assistant 1971*
Mrs H. C. Wright, *Pronunciation Assistant-in-Charge 1971–78*
Mrs S. E. Fairman, *Acting Pronunciation Assistant-in-Charge 1978*
G. E. Pointon, *Pronunciation Adviser 1979–*

Miss E. D. Anderson
Miss P. O. Blyth
Miss J. Brennan
Miss L. A. Broome
Mrs A. C. Chappell
Miss K. C. Coombe
Miss M. G. Cooper
Miss M. T. Edmond
Miss H. D. Fairbank
Miss P. M. Hurst
Miss M. Lane
Miss F. Liddle
Miss H. Likeman
Mrs L. L. S. Montague
Miss A. C. Mylod
Miss M. Slowey
Mrs M. Spearman
Mrs E. A. Terry
Miss J. M. Wilson

A

Aagaard, *f.n.*, ˈeɪɡɑːd, áygaard
Aan, River, *also spelt* **Aven**, *Grampian*, ɑːn, aan
Aaronovitch, *f.n.*, əˈrɒnəvɪtʃ, áronnŏvitch
Aarvold, *f.n.*, ˈɑːvoʊld, áarvōld
Abady, **Temple**, *composer*, ˈtɛmpl ˈæbədɪ, témpl ábbădi
Abaty Cwmhir *Powys*, əˈbætɪ kʊmˈhɪər, ăbátti kōōm-heer. *Welsh form of* **Abbeycwmhir**, *q.v.*
Abberley *Wilts.*, ˈæbərlɪ, ábbĕrli
Abbeycwmhir *Powys*, ˈæbɪ kʊmˈhɪər, ábbi kōōm-heer. *English form of* **Abaty Cwmhir**, *q.v.*
Abbey St. Bathans *Borders*, ˈæbɪ snt ˈbæθənz, ábbi sĭnt báthănz
Abbiss, *f.n.*, ˈæbɪs, ábbiss
Abbots Bromley *Staffs.*, ˈæbəts ˈbrɒmlɪ, ábbŏts brómli
Abbotsham *Devon*, ˈæbətsəm, ábbŏtsăm
Abbotsinch *S'clyde*, ˈæbətsɪnʃ, ábbŏtsinsh
Abbotskerswell *Devon*, ˈæbəts-ˈkɜːzwəl, ábbŏtskérzwĕl
Abbs, *f.n.*, æbz, abz
Abdela, *f.n.*, æbˈdelə, abdéllă
Abel, *f.n.*, ˈeɪbl, áybl
Abelard, *f.n.*, ˈæbəlɑːd, ábbĕlaard. *Appropriate also for the* ~ *Music Ensemble.*
Abelard-Schuman, *publishers and printers*, ˈæbəlɑːd ˈʃuːmən, ábbĕlaard shōōmăn
Abelé, *f.n.*, ˈeɪbəlɪ, áybĕli
Aberaeron, *also spelt* **Aberayron**, *Dyfed*, ˌæbərˈaɪrən, abbĕríron
Aberafan *W. Glam.*, ˌæbərˈævən, abbĕrávvăn. *Welsh form of* **Aberavon**.
Aberaman *Mid Glam.*, ˌæbər-ˈæmən, abbĕrámmăn
Aberangell *Gwynedd*, ˌæbərˈæŋɛɬ, abbĕráng-e‌hl
Aberarth *Dyfed*, ˌæbərˈɑːθ, abbĕráarth
Aberavon *W. Glam.*, ˌæbərˈævən, abbĕrávvŏn
Aberayron *see* **Aberaeron**
Aberbargod *see* **Aberbargoed**
Aberbargoed, *also spelt* **Aberbargod**, *Mid Glam.*, ˌæbərˈbɑːɡɔɪd, abbĕrbaárgoyd; ˌæbərˈbɑːɡɒd, abbĕrbaárgod; ˌæbərˈbɑːɡɔd, abbĕrbaárgawd
Aberbeeg *Gwent*, ˌæbərˈbiːɡ, abbĕrbeeg

Aberbig *Gwent*, ˌæbərˈbiːɡ, abbĕrbeeg. *Welsh form of* **Aberbeeg**.
Aberbran *Powys*, ˌæbərˈbran, abbĕrbraan
Abercairney *Tayside*, ˌæbərˈkɛərnɪ, abbĕrkáirni
Abercanaid *Mid Glam.*, ˌæbər-ˈkænaɪd, abbĕrkánnīd
Abercarn *Gwent*, ˌæbərˈkɑːn, abbĕrkaárn
Aberchalder *H'land*, ˌæbər-ˈxɔldər, abbĕrcháwldĕr
Aberchirder *Grampian*, ˌæbər-ˈxɜːrdər, abbĕrchírdĕr
Aberconway, Baron, ˌæbərˈkɒn-weɪ, abbĕrkónway
Aberconwy, *Gwynedd*, ˌæbər-ˈkɒnwɪ, abbĕrkónwi
Abercorn, Duke of, ˈæbərkɔːn, ábbĕrkorn
Abercraf *Powys*, ˌæbərˈkrɑːv, abbĕrkraáv. *Welsh form of* **Abercrave**, *q.v.*
Abercrave *Powys*, ˌæbərˈkreɪv, abbĕrkráyv. *English form of* **Abercraf**, *q.v.*
Abercregan *W. Glam.*, ˌæbər-ˈkrɛɡən, abbĕrkréggăn
Abercrombie, *f.n.*, ˈæbərkrʌmbɪ, ábbĕrkrumbi; ˈæbərkrɒmbɪ, ábbĕrkrombi. *The first is appropriate for Sir Patrick* ~, *architect, and Lascelles* ~, *poet.*
Abercwmboi *Mid Glam.*, ˌæbər-kʊmˈbɔɪ, abbĕrkōōm-bóy
Abercynon *Mid Glam.*, ˌæbər-ˈkʌnən, abbĕrkúnnŏn
Aberdare *Mid Glam.*, ˌæbərˈdɛər, abbĕrdáir. *Appropriate also for Baron* ~.
Aberdaron *Gwynedd*, ˌæbərˈdærən, abbĕrdárrŏn
Aberdeen *Grampian*, ˌæbərˈdiːn, abbĕrdeén
Aberdeen and Temair, Marquess of, ˌæbərˈdiːn ənd tɪˈmɛər, abbĕrdeén änd tĕmáir
Aberdonian, *native of Aberdeen*, ˌæbərˈdoʊnɪən, abbĕrdŏniăn
Aberdour *Fife, Grampian*, ˌæbər-ˈdaʊər, abbĕrdówr
Aberdovey *Gwynedd*, ˌæbərˈdʌvɪ, abbĕrdúvvi
Aberdulais *W. Glam.*, ˌæbər-ˈdɪlaɪs, abbĕrdílliss
Aberedw *Powys*, ˌæbərˈeɪdu, abbĕráydoo

Abererch *Gwynedd*, ˌæbərˈɛərx, abbĕráirch

Aberfan *Mid Glam.*, ˌæbərˈvæn, abbĕrván

Aberfeldy *Tayside*, ˌæbərˈfeldɪ, abbĕrféldi

Aberffraw *Gwynedd*, əˈbɛərfrau, ăbáirfrow

Aberffrwd *Dyfed*, ˌæbərˈfrud, abbĕrfroód

Abergavenny, Marquess of, ˌæbərˈgenɪ, abbĕrgénni

Abergavenny *Gwent*, ˌæbərgəˈvenɪ, abbĕrgăvénni

Abergele *Clwyd*, ˌæbərˈgeleɪ, abbĕrgéllay

Aberglaslyn Pass *Gwynedd*, ˌæbərˈglæslɪn, abbĕrglásslin

Abergorlech *Dyfed*, ˌæbərˈgɔrləx, abbĕrgórlĕch

Abergwessin *Powys*, ˌæbərˈgwesɪn, abbĕrgwéssin

Abergwili *Dyfed*, ˌæbərˈgwɪlɪ, abbĕrgwílli

Abergwynfi *W. Glam.*, ˌæbərˈgwɪnvɪ, abbĕrgwínvi

Abergynolwyn *Gwynedd*, ˌæbərˈgʌnʊlwɪn, abbĕrgunólwin

Aberhafesp *Powys*, ˌæbərˈhævesp, abbĕr-hávvesp

Aberkenfig *Mid Glam.*, ˌæbərˈkenfɪg, abbĕrkénfig

Aberlady *Lothian*, ˌæbərˈleɪdɪ, abbĕrláydi

Aberllefenni *Gwynedd*, ˌæbərɬəˈvenɪ, abbĕrhlĕvénni

Aberlour *Grampian*, ˌæbərˈlauər, abbĕrlówr

Abermorddu *Clwyd*, ˌæbərˈmɔrðɪ, abbĕrmórthi

Abermule *Powys*, ˌæbərˈmjul, abbĕrméwl

Abernant *Dyfed*, ˌæbərˈnænt, abbĕrnánt

Abernethy *H'land, Tayside*, ˌæbərˈneθɪ, abbĕrnéthi. *Appropriate also for Lord* ∼.

Aberpedwar *Powys*, ˌæbərˈpedwər, abbĕrpédwăr

Aberporth *Dyfed*, ˌæbərˈpɔrθ, abbĕrpórth

Abersoch *Gwynedd*, ˌæbərˈsoux, abbĕr-sóch

Abersychan *Gwent*, ˌæbərˈsʌxən, abbĕr-súchăn

Abertay, Barony of, ˌæbərˈteɪ, abbĕrtáy

Aberthaw *S. Glam.*, ˌæbərˈθɔ, abbĕr-tháw

Abertillery *Gwent*, ˌæbərtɪˈleərɪ, abbĕrtiláiri

Abertridwr *Mid Glam., Powys*, ˌæbərˈtrɪduər, abbĕrtríddoŏr

Abertysswg *Mid Glam.*, ˌæbərˈtʌsʊg, abbĕrtússoŏg

Aberuchill *Tayside*, ˌæbərˈʊxɪl, abbĕroŏchil

Aberuthven *Tayside*, ˌæbəˈrɪvən, abbĕrívvĕn

Aberystwyth *Dyfed*, ˌæbərˈɪstwɪθ, abbĕrístwith; ˌæbərˈʌstwɪθ, abbĕrústwith

Abineri, *f.n.*, ˌæbɪˈneərɪ, abbináiri

Abinger *Surrey*, ˈæbɪndʒər, ábbinjĕr. *Appropriate also for Baron* ∼.

Abinger Hammer *Surrey*, ˈæbɪndʒər ˈhæmər, ábbinjĕr hámmĕr

Abington *Northants., S'clyde*, ˈæbɪŋtən, ábbingtŏn

Abington Pigotts *Cambs.*, ˈæbɪŋtən ˈpɪgəts, ábbingtŏn píggŏts

Abley, *f.n.*, ˈæblɪ, ábbli

Aboyne *Grampian*, əˈbɔɪn, ăbóyn. *Appropriate also for the Earl of* ∼.

Abra, *f.n.*, ˈeɪbrə, áybră

Abrahams, *f.n.*, ˈeɪbrəhəmz, áybră-hămz

Abram *Gtr. M'chester*, ˈæbrəm, ábrăm

Abridge *Essex*, ˈeɪbrɪdʒ, áybrij

Abse, *f.n.*, ˈæbzɪ, ábzi

Aby *Lincs.*, ˈeɪbɪ, áybi

Acaster Malbis *N. Yorks.*, əˈkæstər ˈmælbɪs, ăkástĕr málbiss

Achanalt *H'land*, ˌæxəˈnælt, achănált

Achany Glen *H'land*, ˈæxənɪ, áchăni

Acharacle *H'land*, əˈxærəkl, ăchárrăkl

Acharn *Tayside*, əˈxɑrn, ăcha'arn

Achdalieu *H'land*, ˌæxdəˈlu, achdáloŏ

Acheson, *f.n.*, ˈætʃɪsən, átchĕssŏn

Achillini, *f.n.*, ˌækɪˈlinɪ, ackilléeni

Achmore, *also spelt* **Auchmore,** *Central*, ˈæxˈmɔr, ách-mór

Achmore *H'land*, ˈæxˈmɔr, ách-mór

Achmore *W. Isles*, ˈæxmɔr, ách-mor

Achnacarry *H'land*, ˌæxnəˈkærɪ, achnăkárri

Achnasheen *H'land*, ˌæxnəˈʃin, achnăsheén

Achonry, *f.n.*, ˈækənrɪ, áckŏnri; əˈkɒnrɪ, ăkónri

Achray, Loch *and* Forest, *Central*, əˈxreɪ, ăchráy

Achurch *Northants.*, ˈeɪtʃɜrtʃ, áytchurtch

Ackrill, *f.n.*, ˈækrɪl, áckril

Ackroyd, *f.n.*, ˈækrɔɪd, áckroyd

Acland, *f.n.,* 'æklənd, áckländ

Acle *Norfolk,* 'eɪkl, áykl

Acol *Kent,* 'eɪkɒl, áykol

Acomb, *f.n.,* 'eɪkəm, áyköm

Acomb *Northd., N. Yorks.,* 'eɪkəm, áyköm

Acontius, Jacobus, *Elizabethan philosopher and engineer,* dʒə-'koubəs ə'kɒntɪəs, jăkốbŭss äkóntiŭss; ə'kɒnʃɪəs, äkónshi--ŭss. *He hailed from the Tirol and was originally Jacopo Aconzio,* 'jækəpou ə'kɒntsɪou, yáckŏpŏ äkóntsiŏ.

Acott, *f.n.,* 'eɪkɒt, áykot

A'court, *f.n.,* 'eɪkɔrt, áykort

Acraman, *f.n.,* 'ækrəmən, áckrämän

Acrefair *Clwyd,* ˌækrɪ'vaɪər, ackrĕvír

Acrise *Kent,* 'eɪkrɪs, áykreess; 'eɪkrɪs, áykriss

Acton Burnell *Salop,* 'æktən bɜr-'nel, ácktŏn burnéll

Acutt, *f.n.,* 'eɪkʌt, áykut

Adair, *f.n.,* ə'dɛər, ădáir

Adam, *f.n.,* 'ædəm, áddăm

Adare, *f.n.,* ə'dɛər, ădáir. *Appropriate also for Viscount* ∼.

Adbaston *Staffs.,* 'ædbəstən, ádbästŏn

Adburgham, *f.n.,* æd'bɜrgəm, adbúrgăm

Adcock, *f.n.,* 'ædkɒk, ádkock

Addlebrough *N. Yorks.,* 'ædlbərə, áddlbŭră

Addlestone *Surrey,* 'ædlstoun, áddlstŏn

Adeane, *f.n.,* ə'din, ădeén

Adel *W. Yorks.,* 'ædl, áddl

Adeney, *f.n.,* 'eɪdnɪ, áydn-i; 'eɪdnɪ, áyd-ni

Ades, *f.n.,* 'ædɪs, áddiss

Adey, *f.n.,* 'eɪdɪ, áydi

Adeyfield *Herts.,* 'eɪdɪfɪld, áydi--feeld

Adgie, *f.n.,* 'ædʒɪ, ájji

Adie, *f.n.,* 'eɪdɪ, áydi

Adisham *Kent,* 'ædɪʃəm, áddi-shăm

Adlam, *f.n.,* 'ædləm, ádlăm

Adlard, *f.n.,* 'ædlərd, ádlaard

Adlestrop *Glos.,* 'ædlstrɒp, áddl--strop

Adley, *f.n.,* 'ædlɪ, ádli

Adorian, *f.n.,* ə'dɔrɪən, ădáwriăn

Adrianssens, *f.n.,* 'eɪdrɪənsənz, áydriănssénz

Adshead, *f.n.,* 'ædzhed, ádz--hed

Adur, River, *W. Sussex,* 'eɪdər, áydŭr. *Appropriate also for the administrative district, which takes its name from the river.*

Adversane *W. Sussex,* 'ædvər-seɪn, ádvĕrssayn

Advie *H'land,* 'ædvɪ, ádvi

Adwalton *W. Yorks.,* ˌæd'wɒltən, adwáwltŏn. *A local pronunciation,* 'ædərtən, áthĕrtŏn, *derives from Heather Town, an old name for the area.*

Adwick-le-Street *S. Yorks.,* 'ædwɪk lɪ 'strit, ádwick li stréet

Adwick upon Dearne *S. Yorks.,* 'ædwɪk əpɒn 'dɜrn, ádwick ŭpon dérn

Ady, *f.n.,* 'eɪdɪ, áydi

Adye, *f.n.,* 'eɪdɪ, áydi

Ae *D. & G.,* eɪ, ay

Aehron, *f.n.,* 'ɛərən, áirŏn

Aelred, *C.n.,* 'eɪlred, áylred

Aeolian Hall *London,* i'oulɪən, ee-óli-ăn; eɪ'oulɪən, ay-óli-ăn

Aeronwy, *C.n.,* aɪə'rɒnwɪ, ïrón--wi

Affleck, *f.n.,* 'æflek, áffleck

Afford, *f.n.,* 'æfərd, áffŏrd

Affric, Loch *and* River, *H'land,* 'æfrɪk, áffrick

Aflalo, *f.n.,* ə'flɑlou, äflaálŏ

Afon, River, *Mid Glam.–W. Glam. boundary,* 'ævən, ávvŏn

Afon Wen *Gwynedd,* 'ævən 'wen, ávvŏn wén

Afton, *f.n.,* 'æftən, áftŏn

Agar, *f.n.,* 'eɪgər, áygăr; 'eɪgɑr, áygaar

Agate, *f.n.,* 'eɪgət, áygăt; 'ægət, ággăt

Agen Allwedd *Powys,* 'ægen 'æɪwəð, ággen áhl-wĕth. *Said to be the longest cave in Britain, part of the* **Dan yr Ogof** *cave system (q.v.).*

Ager, *f.n.,* 'eɪgər, áygĕr; 'ædʒər, ájjĕr; 'eɪdʒər, áyjĕr

Aggett, *f.n.,* 'ægɪt, ággĕt

Aghacully *Co. Antrim,* ˌæxə'kʌlɪ, a<u>ch</u>ăkúlli

Aghaderg *Co. Down,* ˌæxə'dɜrg, a<u>ch</u>ădérg. *Another form is* **Aghaderrick,** *q.v.*

Aghaderrick *Co. Down,* ˌæxə-'derɪk, a<u>ch</u>ădérrick. *See also* **Aghaderg.**

Aghadowey *Co. Derry,* ˌæxə'duɪ, a<u>ch</u>ădoʹo-i

Aghagallon *Co. Antrim,* ˌæxə-'gælən, a<u>ch</u>ăgálŏn

Aghalane *Co. Fermanagh,* ˌæxə-'leɪn, a<u>ch</u>ăláyn

Aghalee *Co. Antrim,* ˌæxə'li, a<u>ch</u>ălee

Aghanloo *Co. Derry,* ɒn'lu, aanloʹo; ˌæxən'lu, a<u>ch</u>ănloʹo

Agharan *Co. Tyrone,* ˌæxə'ræn, a<u>ch</u>árán

Aghavea *Co. Fermanagh*, ˌæxə-'veɪ, a<u>ch</u>ăváy

Aghyaran *Co. Tyrone*, ˌæxɪ'ɑrn, a<u>chi</u>-aárn

Agius, *f.n.*, 'eɪdʒəs, áyjūss

Agivey *Co. Derry*, ə'gɪvɪ, ăgívvi

Aglionby, *f.n.*, 'æglɪənbɪ, ággli-ŏnbi

Agnellus, *C.n.*, æg'neləs, ag-néllŭss

Agnew, *f.n.*, 'ægnju, ág-new

Ago, *f.n.*, 'agoʊ, aágō

Agoult, *f.n.*, 'ægult, ággoolt

Agrell, *f.n.*, ə'grel, ăgréll

Aguilar, *f.n.*, ə'gwɪlər, ăgwíllăr

Agutter, *f.n.*, 'ægətər, ággŭttĕr ə'gʌtər, ăgúttĕr

Aherne, *f.n.*, ə'hɜrn, ăhérn

Ahoghill *Co. Antrim*, ə'hɒxɪl, ăhó<u>ch</u>il

Aichroth, *f.n.*, 'eɪtʃrɒθ, áytch-roth; 'eɪkrɒθ, áykroth

Aikman, *f.n.*, 'eɪkmən, áykmän

Aileen, *C.n.*, 'eɪlɪn, áyleen; 'aɪlɪn, fleen

Ailesbury, Marquess of, 'eɪlzbərɪ, áylzbŭri

Ailort, Loch *and* River, *H'land*, 'aɪlərt, fílŏrt

Ailsa, Marquess of, 'eɪlsə, áylssă

Ailsa Craig, *S'clyde*, 'eɪlzə 'kreɪg, áylză kráyg

Ailwyn, Baron, 'eɪlwɪn, áylwin

Aimers, *f.n.*, 'eɪmərz, áymĕrz

Ainge, *f.n.*, eɪndʒ, aynj

Ainley, *f.n.*, 'eɪnlɪ, áynli

Ainscough, *f.n.*, 'eɪnzkoʊ, áynzkō

Ainscow, *f.n.*, 'eɪnzkoʊ, áynzkō

Ainsley, *f.n.*, 'eɪnzlɪ, áynzli

Ainslie, *f.n.*, 'eɪnzlɪ, áynzli

Aintree *Merseyside*, 'eɪntrɪ, áyntri

Aird, *f.n.*, ɛərd, aird

Airdrie *S'clyde*, 'ɛərdrɪ, áirdri

Airds, The, *S'clyde*, ɛərdz, airdz

Aire, River, *N. Yorks.*, ɛər, air

Airedale, Baron, 'ɛərdeɪl, áirdayl

Airey of Abingdon, Baroness, 'ɛərɪ əv 'æbɪŋdən, áiri ŏv ábbingdŏn

Airlie, Earl of, 'ɛərlɪ, áirli

Airor *H'land*, 'ɛərər, áirŏr

Airthrey Castle, *also spelt* Airthrie, *Central*, 'ɛərθrɪ, áirthri

Aish *Devon*, eɪʃ, aysh; æʃ, ash. *Appropriate for both places of the name in Devon.*

Aisher, *f.n.*, 'eɪʃər, áyshĕr

Aiskew *N. Yorks.*, 'eɪskju, áysskew

Aislaby *N. Yorks.*, 'eɪzlbɪ, áyzlbi. *Appropriate for both places of the name in North Yorks.*

Aisthorpe *Lincs.*, 'eɪsθɔrp, áyss-thorp

Aistrop, *f.n.*, 'eɪstrɒp, áysstrop

Aitchison, *f.n.*, 'eɪtʃɪsən, áytchis-sŏn

Aithrie, Viscount, 'eɪθrɪ, áythri

Aithsting *Shetland*, 'eɪθstɪŋ, áyth-sting

Aitken, *f.n.*, 'eɪtkɪn, áytkĕn; 'eɪkɪn, áykĕn

Aitkenhead, *f.n.*, 'eɪkənhed, áykĕn-hed

Aitkin, *f.n.*, 'eɪtkɪn, áytkin; 'eɪkɪn, áykin

Aked, *f.n.*, 'eɪkɪd, áykĕd

Akeld *Northd.*, 'eɪkəld, áykĕld

Akeman St. *Tring* (*Herts.*), 'eɪkmən, áykmän

Akerman, *f.n.*, 'eɪkərmæn, áykĕr-man; 'ækərmən, áckĕrmän

Akers, *f.n.*, 'eɪkərz, áykĕrz

Akery, *f.n.*, 'eɪkərɪ, áykĕri

Akhurst, *f.n.*, 'ækhərst, áck-hurst

Akister, *f.n.*, 'eɪkɪstər, áykistĕr

Akroyd, *f.n.*, 'ækrɔɪd, áckroyd

Akst, *f.n.*, ækst, ackst

Alan, *C.n. and f.n.*, 'ælən, álän

Alanbrooke, Viscount, 'ælənbrʊk, álänbrŏŏk

Alarcon, *f.n.*, æ'lɑrkən, alaárkŏn

Alasdair, *C.n.*, *also spelt* Alastair, Alistair, 'ælɪstər, álistĕr

Alastair, *C.n. see* Alasdair

Albany, *f.n.*, 'ɔlbənɪ, áwlbăni

Albemarle, Earl of, 'ælbəmɑrl, álbĕmaarl

Alberbury *Salop*, 'ɔlbərbərɪ, áwlbĕrbŭri

Alberry-Speyer, *f.n.*, 'ælbərɪ 'speɪər, álbĕri spáy-ĕr

Albery, *f.n.*, 'ælbərɪ, álbĕri. *Appropriate also for the ~ Theatre, London.*

Albiston, *f.n.*, 'ɔlbɪstən, áwlbis-stŏn

Albon, *f.n.*, 'ælbən, álbŏn

Albourne *W. Sussex*, 'ɔlbɔrn, áwlborn; 'ælbɔrn, álborn

Albrecht, *f.n.*, 'ɔlbrekt, áwlbrekt

Albrighton *Salop*, ɔl'braɪtən, awlbrítŏn. *Appropriate for both places of the name in Shropshire.*

Albu, *f.n.*, 'ælbju, álbew

Albury *Herts.*, *Oxon.*, *Surrey*, 'ɔlbərɪ, áwlbŭri

Alby *Norfolk*, 'ɔlbɪ, áwlbi

Alby Hill *Norfolk*, 'ɔlbɪ 'hɪl, áwlbi híll

Alce, *f.n.*, æls, alss

Alcester, *f.n.*, 'ɔlstər, áwlsstĕr

Alcester *Warwicks.*, 'ɔlstər, áwlsstĕr

Alciston *E. Sussex*, 'ɔlsɪstən, áwlssistŏn

Alcock, *f.n.*, 'ælkɒk, álkock; 'ɔlkɒk, áwlkock. *The first was*

the pronunciation of Sir John ~, airman, and of Sir Walter ~, organist and composer.
Alconbury *Cambs.*, 'ɔlkənbəri, áwlkŏnbŭri; 'ɔkənbəri, áwkŏnbŭri
Alcorn, *f.n.*, 'ɔlkɔrn, áwlkorn
Aldborough *Norfolk, N. Yorks.*, 'ɔldbərə, áwldbŭrā
Aldbourne *Wilts.*, 'ɔlbɔrn, áwlborn
Aldbrough *Humberside*, 'ɔlbərə, áwlbŭrā
Aldbury *Herts.*, 'ɔldbəri, áwldbŭri
Alde, River, *Suffolk*, ɔld, awld
Aldeburgh *Suffolk*, 'ɔlbərə, áwlbŭrā; 'ɔldbərə, áwldbŭrā. *Home of the ~ Festival.*
Aldeby *Norfolk*, 'ɔldəbi, áwldĕbi
Aldeguer, *f.n.*, 'ɔldigər, áwldĕgĕr
Aldenham, Baron, 'ɔldnəm, áwldn-ăm
Aldenham *Herts.*, 'ɔldənəm, áwldĕnăm
Alder, *f.n.*, 'ɔldər, áwldĕr
Alderbury *Wilts.*, 'ɔldərbəri, áwldĕrbŭri
Aldergrove *Co. Antrim*, 'ɔldərgroʊv, áwldĕrgrōv
Alderley, Nether *and* Over, *Ches.*, 'ɔldərli, áwldĕrli
Aldermaston *Berks.*, 'ɔldərmastən, áwldĕrmaastŏn
Alderney, Viscount, 'ɔldərni, áwldĕrni
Aldersey *Ches.*, 'ɔldərsi, áwldĕrssi
Aldershot *Hants*, 'ɔldərʃɒt, áwldĕr-shot
Alderson, *f.n.*, 'ɔldərsən, áwldĕrssŏn
Alderton, *f.n.*, 'ɔldərtən, áwldĕrtŏn
Alderwasley *Derby.*, 'ɔldərwɒzli, áwldĕrwozli
Aldham, *f.n.*, 'ɔldəm, áwldăm
Aldhelm, *C.n.*, 'ɔldhelm, áwld-helm
Aldington, Baron, 'ɔldɪŋtən, áwldingtŏn
Aldous, *f.n.*, 'ɔldəs, áwldŭss
Aldred, *f.n.*, 'ɔldrəd, áwldrĕd; 'ɒldrəd, ól-drĕd
Aldreth *Cambs.*, 'ɔldrəθ, áwldrĕth
Aldridge, *f.n.*, 'ɔldrɪdʒ, áwldrij
Aldringham *Suffolk*, 'ɔldrɪŋəm, áwldring-ăm
Aldwark *Derby., N. Yorks.*, 'ɔldwɔrk, áwldwawrk
Aldwick *W. Sussex*, 'ɔldwɪk, áwldwick
Aldwinckle, *f.n.*, 'ɔldwɪŋkl, áwldwinkl

Aldwych *London*, 'ɔldwɪtʃ, áwldwitch
Aled, *Welsh C.n.*, 'æled, áled
Aleksic, *f.n.*, ə'leksɪk, ălécksick
Alençon Link, *Basingstoke*, 'ælɑ̃sõ, álaangssŏng
Alethea, *C.n.*, ælɪ'θɪə, alĕthée-ă; ə'liθɪə, ălĕethiă
Alethorpe *Norfolk*, 'eɪlθɔrp, áyl-thorp
Alexa, *C.n.*, ə'leksə, ălécksă
Alexander, *C.n. and f.n.*, ælɪg-'zandər, alĕgza'andĕr; 'elʃɪndər, él-shindĕr. *The second is a Scottish pronunciation.*
Alexander of Tunis and Errigal, Viscount, ˌælɪg'zandər əv 'tjunɪs ənd 'erɪgɔl, alĕgza'andĕr ŏv tewniss ănd érrigawl
Alexandre, *f.n.*, ælɪk'sandər, alĕksa'andĕr
Alfold *Surrey*, 'ɔlfoʊld, áwlfōld; 'ælfoʊld, álfōld; 'əfoʊld, aáfōld
Alford, *f.n.*, 'ɔlfərd, áwlfŏrd
Alford *Grampian*, 'æfərd, áffŏrd
Alford *Lincs.*, 'ɔlfərd, áwlfŏrd
Alford *Somerset*, 'ɒlfərd, ólfŏrd; 'ælfərd, álfŏrd
Alfoxton Park *Somerset*, æl'fɒkstən, alfóckstŏn
Alfreda, *C.n.*, æl'fridə, alfreédă
Alfreton *Derby.*, 'ɔlfrɪtən, áwlfrĕtŏn; 'ɒlfrɪtən, ólfrĕtŏn; 'ælfrɪtən, álfrĕtŏn
Alfriston *E. Sussex*, ɔl'frɪstən, awlfrístŏn
Algar, *f.n.*, 'ælgər, álgăr
Algarkirk *Lincs.*, 'ɔlgərkɑrk, áwlgärkirk; 'ɔldʒərkɑrk, áwljärkirk; 'ɒldʒkɑrk, áwlj-kirk; 'ældʒərkɑrk, áljärkirk
Algeo, *f.n.*, 'ældʒɪoʊ, áljiō
Aline, Loch *and* River, *H'land*, 'ælɪn, álin
Alington, *f.n.*, 'ælɪŋtən, álingtŏn. *Also appropriate for the Barony of ~.*
Alistair, *C.n. see* **Alasdair**
Alkborough *Humberside*, 'ɔlkbərə, áwlkbŭrā
Alker, *f.n.*, 'ɔlkər, áwlkĕr
Alkham *Kent*, 'ɔlkəm, áwlkăm; 'ɔkəm, áwkăm
Alkin, *f.n.*, 'ælkɪn, álkin
Alkington *Glos.*, 'ɔlkɪŋtən, áwlkingtŏn
Alkington *Salop*, 'ɔkɪŋtən, áwkingtŏn; 'ɔlkɪŋtən, áwlkingtŏn
Alkrington *Gtr. M'chester*, 'ɔlkrɪŋtən, áwlkringtŏn
Allaker, *f.n.*, 'æləkər, álăkĕr
Allam, *f.n.*, 'æləm, álăm
Allard, *f.n.*, 'ælɑrd, álaard

Allason, *f.n.*, 'æləsən, álǎssŏn
Allaun, *f.n.*, ə'lɔn, àláwn
Allbeury, *f.n.*, ɔl'bjʊərɪ, awl-
byōŏri
Allchin, *f.n.*, 'ɔltʃɪn, áwlchin
Allen, *f.n.*, 'ælɪn, álĕn
Allenby, Viscount, 'ælənbɪ,
álĕnbi
Aller *Devon*, 'ælər, álĕr
Aller *Somerset*, 'ɒlər, óllĕr; 'ɔlər,
áwlĕr
Allerton, Baron, 'ælərtən, álĕrtŏn
Allerton *Merseyside*, *Somerset*,
'ælərtən, álĕrtŏn
Allerton *W. Yorks.*, 'ɒlərtən,
óllĕrtŏn
Allerton, Chapel, *Leeds*, *Somer-
set*, 'tʃæpl 'ælərtən, cháppl
álĕrtŏn
Allerton Bywater *W. Yorks.*,
'ælərtən 'baɪwɔtər, álĕrtŏn
bí-wawtĕr
Allerton Mauleverer *N. Yorks.*,
'ɒlərtən mɔ'levərər, óllĕrtŏn
mawlévvĕrĕr
Alles, *f.n.*, 'ælɪz, álĕz
Allesley *W. Midlands*, 'ɔlzlɪ,
áwlzli
Allestree *Derby.*, 'ælɪstrɪ, álĕss-
tree
Allet *Cornwall*, 'ælɪt, álĕt
Alleyne, *f.n.*, æ'leɪn, aláyn; æ'lɪn,
aleĕn; 'ælən, álĕn
Alleynian, *one educated at Dul-
wich College*, ə'leɪnɪən,
ăláyniǎn
Alleyn Park *Dulwich*, 'ælɪn, áleen
Alleyn's School *Dulwich*, 'ælɪnz,
álĕnz
Alleyne's Grammar School
Stevenage, 'æleɪnz, álaynz
Allfrey, *f.n.*, 'ɔlfrɪ, áwlfri
Allhallows *Kent*, ɔl'hæloʊz, awl-
-hálōz
Allhusen, *f.n.*, ɔl'hjuːzən, awl-
-héwzĕn; æl'hjuːzən, al-héwzĕn
Allibone, *f.n.*, 'ælɪboʊn, álĭbōn
Allighan, *f.n.*, 'ælɪgən, álĭgǎn
Allingham, *f.n.*, 'ælɪŋəm, áling-ăm
Allington *Dorset*, *Kent*, *Wilts.*,
'ælɪŋtən, álingtŏn
Alliss, *f.n.*, 'ælɪs, áliss
Allitt, *f.n.*, 'ælɪt, álit
Allner, *f.n.*, 'ɒlnər, áwlnĕr
Alloa *Central*, 'æloʊə, álō-ǎ
Allott, *f.n.*, 'ælət, álŏt
Allsebrook, *f.n.*, 'ɔlsbrʊk, áwlss-
brŏŏk
Allsop, *f.n.*, 'ɔlsɒp, áwlssop
Allsopp, *f.n.*, 'ɔlsɒp, áwlssop
Allt, *f.n.*, ɔlt, awlt
Allt-Rhyd-y-Groes *Dyfed*, 'ælt rid
ə 'grɔɪs, áhlt-reed-ă-gróyss
Almack, *f.n.*, 'ɒlmæk, áwlmack

Alma-Tadema, *f.n.*, 'ælmə
'tædɪmə, álmă táddĕmă. *This is
also the pronunciation generally
associated with the Anglo-Dutch
painter.*
Almedingen, *f.n.*, ˌælmə'dɪŋgən,
alméding-gĕn
Almeley *H. & W.*, 'æmlɪ, ámli
Almer *Dorset*, 'ælmər, álmĕr
Almey, *f.n.*, 'ælmɪ, álmi
Almodington *W. Sussex*, æl'mɒd-
ɪŋtən, almóddingtŏn
Almond, *f.n.*, 'amənd, aámŏnd
Almondbank *Tayside*, 'amənd-
'bæŋk, aámŏndbánk
Almondbury *W. Yorks.*, 'eɪmbərɪ,
áymbŭri; 'ɔmbərɪ, áwmbŭri;
'ælməndbərɪ, ál-mŏndbŭri
Almondsbury *Avon*, 'amǝndzbərɪ,
aámŏndzbŭri; 'eɪmzbərɪ,
áymzbŭri
Almshoe, Little, *Herts.*, 'amʃu,
aám-shoo
Aln, River, *Northd.*, æln, aln
Alne *N. Yorks.*, ɔn, awn
Alne, Great *and* Little, *Warwicks.*,
ɔn, awn; ɔln, awln; æln, aln
Alness, Barony of, 'ɔlnes, áwl-
ness
Alness *H'land*, 'ɔlnɪs, áwlnĕss;
'ælnɪs, álnĕss
Alnham *Northd.*, 'ælnəm, álnăm
Alnmouth *Northd.*, 'ælnmaʊθ,
áln-mowth; 'eɪlnmaʊθ, áyl-
mowth
Alnwick, *f.n.*, 'ænɪk, ánnick
Alnwick *Northd.*, 'ænɪk, ánnick.
*Appropriate also for the Barony
of ~.*
Aloysius, *C.n.*, ˌæloʊ'ɪʃəs, alō-
-íshŭss
Alpass, *f.n.*, 'ɔlpəs, áwlpáss
Alperton *London*, 'ælpərtən,
álpĕrtŏn
Alphege, saint, 'ælfɪdʒ, álfĕj
Alpheton *Suffolk*, æl'fitən,
alféetŏn
Alpington *Norfolk*, 'ælpɪŋtən,
álpingtŏn
Alport, *f.n.*, 'ɔlpɔrt, áwlport.
Appropriate also for Baron ~.
Alresford, *f.n.*, 'ɔlzfərd, áwlzfŏrd
Alresford *Essex*, 'ɒlsfərd, aálss-
förd; 'eɪlsfərd, áylssförd
Alresford *Hants.*, 'ɒlzfərd, áwlz-
förd; 'ɑlzfərd, aálzförd
Alrewas *Staffs.*, 'ɔlrəs, áwlráss;
'ɔlrəwəs, áwlréwáss
Alsager *Ches.*, ɔl'seɪdʒər, awls-
sáyjĕr; 'ɔlsədʒər, áwlssájĕr
Alsatia, *old name for Whitefriars,
London*, æl'seɪʃə, alssáyshă
Alscott *Devon*, 'ɒlskət, áwlsskŏt.
But see pronunciation of

Alverdiscott, *which is the more usual form.*

Alsh, Loch, *H'land*, ælʃ, alsh

Alsop, *f.n.*, 'ɔlsɒp, áwlssop

Alston, *f.n.*, 'ɔlstən, álstŏn

Alston *Cumbria, Devon*, 'ɔlstən, áwlsstŏn

Alstone *Glos., Somerset, Staffs.*, 'ɔlstən, áwlsstŏn. *Appropriate for both places of the name in Gloucestershire.*

Alswyck Hall *Buntingford (Herts.)*, 'æsɪk, ássick

Alt, River, *Lancs.–Merseyside*, ɔlt, awlt

Altarnun *Cornwall*, ˌɔltər'nʌn, awltărnún

Altcar, Great, *Lancs.*, 'ɔltkɑr, áwltkaar

Altedesert *Co. Tyrone*, 'ɔltədezərt, áwltĕdezzĕrt

Altham, *f.n.*, 'ɔlθəm, áwl-thăm

Altham *Lancs.*, 'ɔlθəm, áwl-thăm; 'æltəm, áltăm; 'ɔltəm, áwltăm

Althaus, *f.n.*, 'ɔlthaʊs, áwlt-howss

Althorne *Essex*, 'ɔlθɔrn, áwl-thorn

Althorp, *f.n.*, 'ɔlθɔrp, áwl-thorp; 'ælθɔrp, ál-thorp

Althorp *Northants.*, 'ɔltrəp, áwltrŏp; 'ɔlθɔrp, áwl-thorp; 'ɔlθrəp, áwl-thrŏp. *The first pronunciation is that used by the family of the Earl Spencer, and is appropriate also for Viscount ~. The second is that used generally in the neighbourhood of the estate, and the third is now old-fashioned.*

Althorpe *Humberside*, 'ɔlθɔrp, áwl-thorp

Altimeg Hill, *S'clyde*, 'ɔltɪmeg, áwltimeg

Altnabreac *H'land*, ˌæltnə'brek, altnăbréck

Altnagelvin *Co. Derry*, ˌæltnə'gelvɪn, altnăgélvin

Altnamachin *Co. Armagh*, ˌæltnə'mækɪn, altnămáckin

Altnaveigh *Co. Armagh*, ˌæltnə'veɪ, altnăváy

Altofts *W. Yorks.*, 'ɔltɒfts, áwltŏfts; 'ɒltəs, óltŭss

Alton, *f.n.*, 'ɔltən, áwltŏn

Alton *Derby., Hants, Staffs.*, 'ɔltən, áwltŏn

Altries *Grampian*, 'æltrɪz, áltriz

Altrincham *Gtr. M'chester*, 'ɔltrɪŋəm, áwltring-ăm. *Appropriate also for the Barony of ~.*

Altsigh *H'land*, 'ælt'ʃi, ált-shée

Alty, *f.n.*, 'ɔltɪ, áwlti

Alun, *Welsh C.n.*, 'ælɪn, álin

Alva *Central*, 'ælvə, álvă

Alvar, *C.n.*, 'ælvɑr, álvaar; 'ælvər, álvăr

Alvarez, *f.n.*, æl'vɑrez, alváarez

Alvaston *Derby.*, 'ɔlvəstən, áwlvăstŏn; 'ɒlvəstən, ólvăstŏn

Alvechurch *H. & W.*, 'ɔlvtʃərtʃ, áwlv-church

Alvediston *Wilts.*, ˌælvɪ'dɪstən, alvĕdístŏn

Alveley *Salop*, 'ævlɪ, ávvli

Alverdiscott *Devon*, ˌælvər'dɪskət, alvĕr-dísskŏt. *A less usual form of this name is **Alscott**, q.v.*

Alverstoke *Hants*, 'ælvərstoʊk, álvĕrstoŏk

Alverthorpe *W. Yorks.*, 'ɔlvərθɔrp, áwlvĕr-thorp

Alves *Grampian*, 'ɑvɪs, áavĕss

Alvescot *Oxon.*, 'ɔlskət, áwlsskŏt; 'ælskət, álsskŏt; 'ælvɪskɒt, álvĕsskot

Alveston *Avon, Warwicks.*, 'ælvɪstən, álvĕstŏn

Alvie *H'land*, 'ælvɪ, álvi

Alvin, *C.n.*, 'ælvɪn, álvin

Alvingham *Lincs.*, 'ɔlvɪŋəm, áwlving-ăm; 'ælvɪŋəm, álving-ăm. *The first is appropriate also for Baron ~.*

Alvington *Glos.*, 'ælvɪŋtən, álvingtŏn

Alvington, West, *Devon*, 'ɔlvɪŋtən, áwlvingtŏn

Alwalton *Cambs.*, 'ɔlwɒltən, áwl-wawltŏn; 'ɔlwɒltən, áwl-woltŏn

Alway, *f.n.*, 'ɔlweɪ, áwl-way

Alwin Gallery *London*, 'ɔlwɪn, áwl-win

Alwinton *Northd.*, 'ælwɪntən, álwintŏn

Alwoodley *W. Yorks.*, 'ɔlwʊdlɪ, áwl-woŏdli; ɔl'wʊdlɪ, awl-woŏdli

Alwyn, Kenneth, *conductor*, 'ɔlwɪn, áwl-win

Alwyn, William, *composer*, 'ælwɪn, álwin

Alwyn House Rehabilitation Centre *Fife*, 'ɔlwɪn, áwl-win

Alyth *Tayside*, 'eɪlɪθ, áylith

Amadeus String Quartet, ˌæmə'deɪəs, ammădáy-ŭss

Amaury, *f.n.*, 'eɪmərɪ, áymări

Ambersham, South, *W. Sussex*, 'æmbərʃəm, ámbĕr-shăm

Ambion Hill, *Leics.*, 'æmbɪən, ámbi-ŏn

Am Bodach *H'land*, æm 'bɒtəx, am bóttŏx

Ambrosden *Oxon.*, 'æmbroʊzdən, ámbrōzdĕn

Amen Corner *City of London*, 'eɪmen, áymen

Amen House *City of London*, 'eɪmen, áymen

Amer, *f.n.*, 'eɪmər, áymĕr

Amersham *Bucks.*, 'æmərʃəm, ámmĕr-shăm

Amery, *f.n.*, 'eɪmərɪ, áymĕri

Ames, *f.n.*, eɪmz, aymz

Amey, *f.n.*, 'eɪmɪ, áymi

Amherst, *f.n.*, 'æmərst, ámmĕrst; 'æmhərst, ám-herst. *The first is the pronunciation of Earl ~ and of Baron ~ of Hackney.*

Amici String Quartet, ə'miːtʃɪ, ămeétchi

Amies, *f.n.*, 'eɪmɪz, áymiz

Amis, *f.n.*, 'eɪmɪs, áymiss

Amiss, *f.n.*, 'eɪmɪs, áymiss

Amlwch *Gwynedd*, 'æmlʊx, ámlōōch

Amman, River, *Dyfed*, 'æmən, ámmăn

Ammanford *Dyfed*, 'æmənfərd, ámmănfŏrd

Ammon, Barony of, 'æmən, ámmŏn

Ammonds, *f.n.*, 'æməndz, ámmŏndz

Amner, *f.n.*, 'æmnər, ámnĕr

Amoore, *f.n.*, 'eɪmʊər, áymōōr; 'eɪmɔr, áymor

Amor, *f.n.*, 'eɪmɔr, áymor

Amore, *f.n.*, 'eɪmɔr, áymor

Amory, *f.n.*, 'eɪmərɪ, áymŏri. *Appropriate also for the Viscountcy of ~.*

Amos, *f.n.*, 'eɪmɒs, áymoss

Amothe, *C.n.*, 'æməθɪ, ámmŏthee

Amphlett, *f.n.*, 'æmflɪt, ámflĕt

Ampleforth *N. Yorks.*, 'æmplfɔrθ, ámpl-forth

Ampney Crucis *Glos.*, 'æmpnɪ 'kruːsɪs, ámpni króossiss

Ampney St. Peter *Glos.*, 'æmpnɪ snt 'piːtər, ámpni sĭnt peétĕr

Ampthill *Beds.*, 'æmpθɪl, ámpt-hĭll. *Appropriate also for Baron ~.*

Amroth *Dyfed*, 'æmrɒθ, ámroth

Amulree *Tayside*, ,æml'ri, amml-reé. *Appropriate also for Baron ~.*

Amwell, Baron, 'æmwəl, ámwĕl

Amyes, *f.n.*, 'eɪmɪz, áymeez

an Athain, Loch *I. of Skye*, ən 'ɑn, ăn aán

Ancaster, Earl of, 'æŋkəstər, ánkăstĕr

Ancoats *Gtr. M'chester*, 'æŋkoʊts, ánkōts

An Comunn Gaidhealach *Highland Assoc.*, ən 'kɒmən 'gaɪləx, ăn kómmŭn gílăch

Ancram, Earl of, 'æŋkrəm, án-krăm

Ancram, *f.n.*, 'æŋkrəm, ánkrăm

Anderson, *f.n.*, 'ændərsən, ándĕrssŏn

Andover *Hants*, 'ændoʊvər, ándŏvĕr. *Appropriate also for Viscount ~.*

Andoversford *Glos.*, 'ændoʊvərzfərd, ándŏvĕrzfŏrd

Andrade, *f.n.*, 'ændreɪd, ándrayd

Andreas *I. of Man*, 'ændrəs, ándráss

André Deutsch *publishers*, 'ændreɪ 'dɔɪtʃ, ándray dóytch

Andreetti, *f.n.*, ,ændrɪ'etɪ, andri-étti

Andreoli, *f.n.*, ,ændrɪ'oʊlɪ, andri-óli

Aneurin, *Welsh C.n.*, ə'naɪrɪn, ănírin

Angarrick *Cornwall*, æŋ'gærɪk, ang-gárrick

Angas, *f.n.*, 'æŋgəs, áng-găss

Angelis, *f.n.*, 'ændʒəlɪs, ánjĕliss

Angell, *f.n.*, 'eɪndʒl, áynjl

Angers, *f.n.*, 'æŋgərz, áng-gĕrz

Angersleigh *Somerset*, 'eɪndʒərzlɪ, áynjĕrzlee

Angerstein, *f.n.*, 'æŋgərstɪn, áng-gĕrsteen; 'æŋgərstaɪn, áng-gĕrstīn. *The second is appropriate for John Julius ~, 18–19th-c. merchant and art collector.*

Angharad, *Welsh C.n.*, æŋ'hærəd, ang-hárrăd

Angier, *f.n.*, 'ændʒɪər, ánjeer

Angle *Dyfed*, 'æŋgl, áng-gl

Anglesey *Gwynedd*, 'æŋglsɪ, áng-gl-si. *Appropriate also for the Marquess of ~.*

Angmering *W. Sussex*, 'æŋmərɪŋ, áng-mĕring

Angove, *f.n.*, 'æŋgoʊv, áng-gōv

Angus, *C.n. and f.n.*, 'æŋgəs, áng-gŭss

Angus *Tayside*, 'æŋgəs, áng-gŭss. *Appropriate also for the Earl of ~.*

Anick *Northd.*, 'eɪnɪk, áynick

Anido, *f.n.*, ,ænɪdoʊ, ánnidŏ

Anketell, *f.n.*, 'æŋkətl, ánkĕtl

Anlaby *Humberside*, 'ænləbɪ, ánlăbi

Annacloy *Co. Down*, ,ænə'klɔɪ, annăklóy

Annaghmore *Co. Armagh*, ,ænəx'mɔr, annáchmór

Annahilt *Co. Down*, ,ænə'hɪlt, annă-hílt

Annakin, *f.n.*, 'ænəkɪn, ánnăkin

Annalong *Co. Down*, ,ænə'lɒŋ, annălóng

Annaly, *f.n.*, 'ænəlɪ, ánnăli. *Appropriate also for Baron ~.*

Annan, *f.n.*, 'ænən, ánnăn

Annear, *f.n.,* ə'nıər, ăne̊er
Annells, *f.n.,* 'ænlz, ánnlz
Annely Juda Fine Art *London,*
  'ænəlı 'dʒudə, ánnĕli jo͞odă
Annereau, *f.n.,* 'ænərou, ánnĕrō
Annesley, *f.n.,* 'ænzlı, ánzli.
  Appropriate also for Earl ~.
Annesley *Notts.,* 'ænızlı, ánnĕzli;
  'ænzlı, ánzli
Anness, *f.n.,* 'ænıs, ánnĕss
Annet *I. of Scilly,* 'ænıt, ánnĕt
Annett, *f.n.,* 'ænıt, ánnĕt
Annis, *f.n.,* 'ænıs, ánniss
Ansbacher, *f.n.,* 'ænzbækər,
  ánzbackĕr
Anscombe, *f.n.,* 'ænskəm,
  ánsskŏm
Ansell, *f.n.,* 'ænsl, ánssl
Ansley *Warwicks.,* 'ænzlı, ánzli
Anson, *f.n.,* 'ænsən, ánssŏn
Ansorge, *f.n.,* 'ænsɔrdʒ, ánssorj;
  'ænsɔrʒ, ánssorzh
Anstey *Devon, Dorset, Herts.,*
  Leics., 'ænstı, ánssti
Anstice, *f.n.,* 'ænstıs, ánstiss
Anstruther, *f.n.,* 'ænstrʌðər,
  ánstruthĕr
Anstruther *Fife,* 'ænstrʌðər,
  ánstruthĕr; 'eınstər, áynsstĕr
Ansty *Dorset, Warwicks., Wilts.,*
  'ænstı, ánssti
Ansty *W. Sussex,* æn'staı, ansstí
Anstye Cross *W. Sussex,* 'ænstaı
  'krɒs, ánssti króss
An Teallach *H'land,* æn 'tʃæləx,
  an chálach
Anthea, *C.n.,* 'ænθıə, ánthiă
Anthony, *C.n. and f.n.,* 'æntənı,
  ántŏni; 'ænθənı, ánthŏni
Antiquis, *f.n.,* æn'tıkwıs, antíck-
  wiss
Antony *Cornwall,* 'æntənı, ántŏni
Antrim *Co. name,* 'æntrım,
  ántrim. *Appropriate also for the
  Earl of* ~.
Antrobus, *f.n.,* 'æntrəbəs,
  ántrŏbŭss
Anwick, *f.n.,* 'ænık, ánnick
Anwoth *D. & G.,* 'ænwɒθ, án-
  woth
Anwyl, *f.n.,* 'ænwıl, ánwill
Apethorpe *Northants.,* 'æpθɔrp,
  áp-thorp; 'eıpθɔrp, áyp-thorp
Aplvor, Denis, *composer,* 'denıs
  æp'aıvər, dénniss ap-ívŏr
Appel, *f.n.,* ə'pel, ăpéll
Appelbe, *f.n.,* ə'pelbı, ăpélbi
Appleby, *f.n.,* 'æplbı, ápplbi
Appledram *see* **Apuldram**
Applegate, *f.n.,* 'æplgeıt, áppl-
  -gayt; 'æplgıt, áppl-git
Appletreewick *N. Yorks.,*
  'æpltri'wık, áppltree-wick
Aprahamian, Felix, *music critic,*

'fılıks ˌæprə'heımıən, fe̊eliks
  apprä-háymiăn
Apted, *f.n.,* 'æptıd, áptĕd
Apuldram, *also spelt* **Appledram,**
  W. Sussex, 'æpldrəm, áppl-
  dräm
Arabin, *f.n.,* ə'ræbın, ărábbin
Arbikie *Tayside,* ar'bıkı, aarbícki
Arbirlot *Tayside,* ar'bərlət,
  aarbírlŏt
Arblaster, *f.n.,* 'arblastər,
  áarblaastĕr
Arboe *Co. Tyrone,* ar'bou, aarbó
Arborfield *Berks.,* 'arbərfild,
  áarbŏrfeeld
Arbory *I. of Man,* 'arbərı,
  áarbŏri
Arbroath *Tayside,* ar'brouθ,
  aarbróth
Arbuthnot, *f.n.,* ar'bʌθnət, aar-
  búthnŏt
Arbuthnott, Viscount of,
  ar'bʌθnət, aarbúthnŏt
Arcedeckne, *f.n.,* artʃ'dikən,
  aartch-de̊ekĕn
Ardachie Lodge, *also spelt*
  Ardachy, *H'land,* 'ardəkı,
  áardăkee
Ardagh, *f.n.,* 'ardə, áardă
Ardcharnich *H'land,* ard'tʃarnıx,
  aard-cháarnich
Ardchattan *S'clyde,* ard'kætən,
  aardkáttăn
Ardd-lin *Powys,* 'arðlın, áarth-lin
Ardee, Baron of, ar'di, aarde̊e
Ardeer *S'clyde,* ar'dıər, aarde̊er
Ardeonaig *Central,* ar'dʒouneıg,
  aarjónayg; ar'dʒounıg, aarjónig
Ardersier *H'land,* ˌardər'sıər,
  aarde̊rsse̊er
Ardgay *H'land,* ard'gaı, aard-gí
Ardglass *Co. Down,* ard'glæs,
  aardgláss
Ardgour *H'land,* ard'gauər,
  aardgówr
Ardilaun, Barony of, ˌardı'lɔn,
  aardiláwn
Ardingly *W. Sussex,* ˌardıŋ'laı,
  aarding-lí
Ardivachar Point *W. Isles,* ˌardı-
  'væxər, aardiváchăr
Ardizzone, Edward, *painter and
  illustrator,* ˌardı'zouni,
  aardizóni
Ardkeen *Co. Down,* ard'kin,
  aardke̊en
Ardkenneth Chapel *W. Isles,*
  ard'kenıθ, aardkénnĕth
Ardlamont Point *S'clyde,* ard-
  'læmənt, aardlámmŏnt
Ardleigh *Essex,* 'ardlı, áardli
Ardmore *Grampian, H'land,
  S'clyde,* ard'mɔr, aardmór.

*This pronunciation is appropri-
ate for the names of headlands
on Islay (S'clyde), and Skye
(H'land), a harbour on the
Dornoch Firth (H'land), and
a distillery at Kennethmont
(Grampian).*

Ardnadam *S'clyde,* ard'nædəm,
aardnáddăm

Ardnamurchan *H'land,* ˌɑrdnə-
'mɜrxən, aardnämúrchăn

Ardoch *Tayside,* 'ɑrdɒx, áardoch

Ardovie *Tayside,* ar'dʌvɪ,
aardúvvi

Ardoyne *Co. Antrim,* ar'dɔɪn,
aardóyne

Ardrishaig *S'clyde,* ar'drɪʃɪg,
aardríshig; ar'drɪʃeɪg, aardrísh-
-ayg

Ardrossan *S'clyde,* ar'drɒsən,
aardróssăn. *Appropriate also
for Baron* ~.

Ards Peninsula *Co. Down,* ardz,
aardz

Ardtalnaig *Tayside,* ard'tælneɪg,
aardtálnayg

Ardvasar *I. of Skye,* ard'vazər,
aardvaazăr

Ardwick *Gtr. M'chester,* 'ardwɪk,
áardwick

Arenig *Gwynedd,* ə'renɪg, ărénnig

Arfon *Gwynedd,* 'arvɒn, áarvon

Argall, *f.n.,* 'argɒl, áargawl

Argent, *f.n.,* 'ardʒənt, áarjĕnt

Argoed *Gwent,* 'argɔɪd, áargoyd

Argoed *Salop,* ar'gouɪd, aargó-ĕd

Argyll, Duke of, ar'gaɪl, aargíl

Argyll and Bute *S'clyde,* ar'gaɪl
ənd 'bjut, aargíl ănd béwt

Arieli, Celia, *pianist,* 'sɪljə
ˌæri'eli, seeliă arri-élli

Arinagour *Coll (S'clyde),*
ˌærɪnəguər, árrinăgóōr

Aris, *f.n.,* 'ɛərɪs, áiriss; 'arɪs,
áariss

Arisaig *H'land,* 'ærɪseɪg, árrissayg

Ariss, *f.n.,* 'ɛərɪs, áiriss

Arkaig, Loch, *H'land,* 'arkeɪg,
áarkayg

Arkell, *f.n.,* 'arkl, áarkl; ar'kel,
aarkéll

Arkesden *Essex,* 'arksdən,
áarksdĕn

Arkholme *Lancs.,* 'arkhoum,
áark-hōm

Arlecdon *Cumbria,* 'arləkdən,
áarlĕkdŏn

Arlen, *f.n.,* 'arlən, áarlĕn

Arlesey *Beds.,* 'arlzɪ, áarlzi

Arleston *Salop,* 'arlstən, áarlsstŏn

Arlingham *Glos.,* 'arlɪŋəm,
áarling-ăm

Armadale *H'land, Lothian,*
'armədeɪl, áarmădayl.

*Appropriate for both places of
the name in Highland.*

Armagh, *f.n.,* ar'mɑ, aarmaá

Armagh *Co. name and town,*
ar'mɑ, aarmaá

Armathwaite *Cumbria,* 'arməθ-
weɪt, áarmăthwayt

Armley *W. Yorks.,* 'armlɪ, áarmli

Armoy *Co. Antrim,* ar'mɔɪ,
aarmóy

Arncroach *Fife,* arn'kroux, aarn-
-króch

Arndts, *f.n.,* arnts, aarnts

Arne, *f.n.,* arn, aarn

Arnell, *f.n.,* ar'nel, aarnéll

Arnesby *Leics.,* 'arnzbɪ, áarnzbi

Arnett, *f.n.,* 'arnɪt, áarnĕt

Arnolfini Gallery *Bristol,* arnəl-
'fini, aarnŏlfeéni

Arnott, *f.n.,* 'arnət, áarnŏt

Aronowitz, *f.n.,* ə'rɒnəwɪts,
ărónnŏ-wits. *Appropriate for
Cecil* ~, *viola player, and for
John* ~, *pianist.*

Aros *S'clyde,* 'arɒs, áaross

Arpinge *Kent,* 'arpɪndʒ, áarpinj

Arram, *f.n.,* 'ærəm, árrăm

Arran *S'clyde,* 'ærən, árrăn.
Appropriate also for the Earl of
~.

Arrantash, *f.n.,* 'ærəntæʃ, árränt-
ash

Arreton *I. of Wight,* 'ærətən,
árrĕtŏn

Arrochar *S'clyde,* 'ærəxər, árrŏ-
chăr

Artemiou, *f.n.,* ar'timju, aartée-
mew

Arthington, *f.n.,* 'arθɪŋtən,
áarthingtŏn

Arthog *Gwynedd,* 'arθɒg, áarthog

Arthurlie *S'clyde,* 'arθərlɪ,
áarthŭrli

Arthy, *f.n.,* 'arθɪ, áarthi

Articlave *Co. Derry,* artɪ'kleɪv,
aartikláyv

Arun, River, *W. Sussex,* 'ærən,
árrŭn. *Appropriate also for the
administrative district, which
takes its name from the river.*

Arundel *W. Sussex,* 'ærəndl,
árrŭndl. *Appropriate also for
the Earl of* ~.

Arundell of Wardour, Barony of,
'ærəndl əv 'wɔrdər, árrŭndl ŏv
wáwrdŭr

Arwel, *Welsh C.n.,* 'arwel, áarwel

Arwyn, Baron, 'arwɪn, áarwin

Asa, *C.n.,* 'eɪsə, áyssă

Ascham, Roger, *16th-c. scholar,*
'æskəm, ásskăm

Ascog *S'clyde,* 'æskɒg, ásskog

Ascoli, *f.n.,* 'æskəlɪ, ásskŏli

Ascot *Berks.,* 'æskət, ásskŏt

Asfordby *Leics.*, ˈæsfərdbɪ, ássfŏrdbi

Asgarby *Lincs.*, ˈæzgərbɪ, ázgărbi.
Appropriate for both places of the name in Lincolnshire.

Ashampstead *Berks.*, ˈæʃəmsted, áshămsted

Ashbee, *f.n.*, ˈæʃbɪ, áshbi

Ashbourne *Derby.*, ˈæʃbɔrn, áshborn

Ashburnham *E. Sussex*, æʃˈbərnəm, ashbúrnăm

Ashburton, Baron, ˈæʃbərtən, áshbŭrtŏn

Ashburton *Devon*, æʃˈbərtən, ashbúrtŏn

Ashby *Humberside, Norfolk*, ˈæʃbɪ, áshbi

Ashby-de-la-Launde *Lincs.*, ˈæʃbɪ də lə ˈlɔnd, áshbi dĕ lä láwnd

Ashby-de-la-Zouch *Leics.*, ˈæʃbɪ də lə ˈzuʃ, áshbi dĕ lä zoˈosh

Ashby St. Ledgers *Northants.*, ˈæʃbɪ snt ˈledʒərz, áshbi sĭnt léjjĕrz

Ashby Woulds *Leics.*, ˈæʃbɪ ˈwouldz, áshbi wōldz

Ashcombe, Baron, ˈæʃkəm, áshkŏm

Asher, *f.n.*, ˈæʃər, áshĕr

Asheridge *Bucks.*, ˈæʃrɪdʒ, áshrij

Ashill *Devon, Norfolk, Somerset*, ˈæʃɪl, ásh-hil

Ashkenazi, *f.n.*, ˌæʃkɪˈnɑzɪ, ashkĕnáazi

Ashleworth *Glos.*, ˈæʃlwɜrθ, áshlwurth

Ashmolean Museum *Oxford*, æʃˈmouliən, ashmŏˈliăn

Ashop Clough *Derby.*, ˈæʃəp ˈklʌf, áshŏp klúff

Ashorne *Warwicks.*, ˈæʃhɔrŋ, ásh-horn

Ashort, *f.n.*, ˈæʃərt, áshŏrt

Ashow *Warwicks.*, ˈæʃou, áshō

Ashplant, *f.n.*, ˈæʃplɑnt, ásh-plaant

Ashreigney *Devon*, æʃˈreɪnɪ, ashráyni

Ashton, *f.n.*, ˈæʃtən, áshtŏn

Ashton-in-Makerfield *Gtr. M'chester*, ˈæʃtən ɪn ˈmeɪkərfild, áshtŏn ĭn máykĕrfeeld

Ashton Keynes *Wilts.*, ˈæʃtən ˈkeɪnz, áshtŏn káynz

Ashurst *Kent, W. Sussex*, ˈæʃhɜrst, ásh-hurst

Ashwellthorpe *Norfolk*, ˈæʃwəlθɔrp, áshwĕl-thorp

Aske, *f.n.*, æsk, assk

Askern *S. Yorks.*, ˈæskərn, ásskĕrn

Askerswell *Dorset*, ˈæskərzwel, ásskĕrzwel

Askew, *f.n.*, ˈæskju, ásskew

Askham *Cumbria, Notts.*, ˈæskəm, ásskăm

Askwith, Barony of, ˈæskwɪθ, ásskwith

Aslackby *Lincs.*, ˈeɪzlbɪ, áyzlbi

Aslacton *Norfolk*, æzˈlæktən, azlácktŏn

Aslockton *Notts.*, ˈæzlɒktən, ázlocktŏn

Aspatria *Cumbria*, əsˈpeɪtrɪə, ăsspáytriă

Aspel, *f.n.*, ˈæspl, ásspl

Aspinall, *f.n.*, ˈæspɪnɒl, ásspinăl

Aspinwall, *f.n.*, ˈæspɪnwɔl, ásspinwawl

Aspland, *f.n.*, ˈæsplænd, ásspland

Aspley Guise *Beds.*, ˈæsplɪ ˈgaɪz, ásspli gíz

Asprey, *f.n.*, ˈæsprɪ, ásspri

Asquith, *f.n.*, ˈæskwɪθ, ásskwith. *Family name of the Earl of Oxford and* ∼.

Assersohn, *f.n.*, ˈæsərsən, ássĕrssŏn

Assheton, *f.n.*, ˈæʃtən, áshtŏn

Assinder, *f.n.*, ˈæsɪndər, ássindĕr

Assynt *H'land*, ˈæsɪnt, ássint

Astell, *f.n.*, æsˈtel, asstéll

Asterby *Lincs.*, ˈeɪstərbɪ, áysstĕrbi

Asthall Leigh *Oxon.*, ˈæstəl ˈli, ásstawl leˈe; ˈæstəl ˈleɪ, ásstawl láy

Astins, *f.n.*, ˈæstɪnz, ásstinz

Astle, *f.n.*, ˈæstl, ásstl

Astles, *f.n.*, ˈæstlz, ásstlz

Astman, *f.n.*, ˈæstmən, ásstmăn

Aston Ingham *Glos.*, ˈæstən ˈɪŋəm, ásstŏn ing-ăm

Aston Rowant *Oxon.*, ˈæstən ˈrouənt, ásstŏn rō-ănt

Astor, Viscount, ˈæstər, ásstŏr

Astor of Hever, Baron, ˈæstər əv ˈhivər, ásstŏr ŏv heˈevĕr

Atack, *f.n.*, ˈeɪtæk, áytack

Atchison, *f.n.*, ˈætʃɪsən, átchissŏn

Atha, *f.n.*, ˈæθə, áthă

Athawes, *f.n.*, ˈæθɔz, áth-awz; ˈæthɔz, át-hawz

Athelney *Somerset*, ˈæθəlnɪ, áthĕlni

Athelstaneford *Lothian*, ˈæθəlsteɪnfɔrd, áthĕlstaynford; ˈelʃənfərd, élshänfŏrd

Athenaeum Club *London*, ˌæθɪˈniəm, athĕneˈe-ŭm

Atherstone *Warwicks.*, ˈæθərstoun, áthĕrsstōn

Atherton, *f.n.*, ˈæθərtən, áthĕrtŏn; ˈæðərtən, áthĕrtŏn

Atherton *Gtr. M'chester*, ˈæðərtən, áthĕrtŏn

Athey, *f.n.,* 'æθɪ, áthi

Athill, *f.n.,* 'æðɪl, áthil; 'æthɪl, át-hil; 'æθɪl, áthil

Athlone, Earldom of, æθ'loun, athlón

Athlumney, Barony of, əθ'lʌmnɪ, äthlúmni

Atholl, Duke of, 'æθl, áthl

Atienza, *f.n.,* ˌætɪ'enzə, atti-énzä

Attenborough, *f.n.,* 'ætənbərə, áttěnbŏrŏ

Atter, *f.n.,* 'ætər, áttěr

Attercliffe *S. Yorks.,* 'ætərklɪf, áttěrkliff

Attewell, *f.n.,* 'ætwel, átwel

Attleborough *Norfolk,* 'ætlbərə, áttlbŭră

Attlee, *f.n.,* 'ætlɪ, áttli. *Appropriate also for Earl* ~.

Atwick *Humberside,* 'ætɪk, áttick

Aubertin, *f.n.,* 'oubərtɪn, óbĕrtin

Aubery, *f.n.,* 'ɔbərɪ, áwbĕri

Auchaber *Grampian,* ɒ'xɑbər, ocháabĕr

Auchendennan *S'clyde,* ˌɒxən-'denən, ochĕndénnăn

Auchengeich Colliery *Chryston (S'clyde),* ˌɒxən'gɪx, ochĕn-géech

Auchenlarie *D. & G.,* ˌɒxən'lɛərɪ, ochĕnláiri

Auchenlochan *S'clyde,* ˌɒxən-'lɒxən, ochĕnlóchăn

Auchernach Lodge *Grampian,* ɒ'xɛərnəx, ochairnăch

Auchinachie, *f.n.,* ɒ'xɪnəxɪ, ochínnăxi

Auchincruive *S'clyde,* ˌɒxɪn'kruv, ochin-króov

Auchindachie, *also spelt* **Auchindachy,** *Grampian,* ɒ'xɪnəxɪ, ochínnăchi

Auchindoir *Grampian,* ˌɒxɪn'dɔɪər, ochindóyr

Auchindrain *S'clyde,* 'ɒxɪndreɪn, óchindrayn

Auchinleck, Field Marshal Sir Claude, ˌɒxɪn'lek, ochinléck

Auchinleck *S'clyde,* ˌɒxɪn'lek, ochinléck

Auchinleck, Boswell of, 'bɒzwəl əv 'æflek, bózwĕl ŏv áffleck

Auchmore *Central see* **Achmore**

Auchmuty, *f.n.,* ɒk'mjutɪ, ockméwti

Auchnagatt *Grampian,* ˌɒxnə'gæt, ochnăgát

Auchterarder *Tayside,* ˌɒxtər-'ɑrdər, ochtĕraárdĕr

Auchterderran *Fife,* ˌɒxtər'derən, ochtĕrdérrăn

Auchterhouse *Tayside,* 'ɒxtər-haus, óchtĕr-howss

Auchterless *Grampian,* ˌɒxtər'les, ochtĕrléss

Auchterlonie, *f.n.,* ˌɒxtər'lounɪ, ochtĕrlóni

Auchtermuchty *Fife,* ˌɒxtər'mʌxtɪ, ochtĕrmúchti

Auchtertool *Fife,* ˌɒxtər'tul, ochtĕr-toól

Auckengill, *also spelt* **Auckingill,** *H'land,* 'ɒkɪŋgɪl, óckin-gil; 'aukɪŋgɪl, ówkin-gil

Auden, *f.n.,* 'ɔdən, áwdĕn

Audenshaw *Gtr. M'chester,* 'ɔdənʃɔ, áwdĕn-shaw

Audigier, *f.n.,* 'ɔdɪʒeɪ, áwdizhay

Audlem *Ches.,* 'ɔdləm, áwdlĕm

Audley, Baroness, 'ɔdlɪ, áwdli

Audley End *Essex,* 'ɔdlɪ 'end, áwdli énd

Audus, *f.n.,* 'ɔdəs, áwdüss

Auerbach, *f.n.,* 'ɔrbæk, órback

Augener, *f.n.,* 'ɔgənər, áwgĕnĕr

Auger, *f.n.,* 'ɔgər, áwgĕr

Augher *Co. Tyrone,* 'ɒxər, óchĕr

Aughertree *Cumbria* 'ɒfərtrɪ, óffĕrtree; 'æfərtrɪ, áffĕrtree

Aughnacloy *Co. Tyrone,* ˌɒxnə-'klɔɪ, ochnăklóy

Aughrim *Co. Down,* 'ɒxrɪm, óchrim

Aughton *Humberside, S. Yorks.,* 'ɔtən, áwtŏn

Aughton *nr. Lancaster (Lancs.),* 'æftən, áfftŏn

Aughton *nr. Ormskirk (Lancs.),* 'ɔtən, áwtŏn

Augill Castle *Cumbria,* 'ɔgɪl, áwgil

Augustine, *f.n.,* ɔ'gʌstɪn, awgústin

Aukin, *f.n.,* 'ɒkɪn, áwkin

Auld, *f.n.,* ɔld, awld

Auldearn *H'land,* ɔld'ɜrn, awldérn

Auldgirth *D. & G.,* 'ɔldgɑrθ, áwld-girth

Auliff, *f.n.,* 'ɔlɪf, áwlif

Aultguish, Stream, *H'land,* ɒlt-'guɪʃ, awltgoó-ish

Aultbea *H'land,* ɒlt'beɪ, awltbáy

Ault Hucknall *Derby.,* 'ɒlt 'hʌknɔl, áwlt húcknăl

Aumonier, Stacy, *author,* 'steɪsɪ ou'mounɪeɪ, stáyssi ōmóni-ay

Aunger, *f.n.,* 'ɔndʒər, áwnjĕr

Aust *Avon,* ɒst, awsst

Austen, *f.n.,* 'ɒstɪn, ósstĕn; 'ɔstɪn, áwsstĕn

Austick, *f.n.* 'ɒstɪk, áwstick

Austin, *f.n.,* 'ɒstɪn, ósstin; 'ɔstɪn, áwsstin

Austwick, *f.n.,* 'ɒstwɪk, ósstwick

Austwick *N. Yorks.,* 'ɒstwɪk, áwsstwick; 'ɒstɪk, ósstick

Authers, *f.n.,* 'ɔθərz, áwthĕrz

Auton, *f.n.,* 'ɒtən, áwtŏn

Auty, *f.n.,* 'ɔtɪ, áwti
Ava, Earl of, 'ɑvə, aávā
Ava, *C.n.,* 'ɑvə, aávā
Avann, *f.n.,* ə'væn, ăván
Avaulds *Grampian,* 'jævlz, yávvlz
Avebury *Wilts.,* 'eɪvbərɪ, áyvbūri; 'eɪbərɪ, áybūri. *The first is appropriate also for Baron* ∼.
Aveley *Essex,* 'eɪvlɪ, áyvli
Aveling, *f.n.,* 'eɪvəlɪŋ, áyvĕling; 'eɪvlɪŋ, áyvling
Ave Maria Lane *City of London,* 'ɑvɪ mə'riə, aávi mărée-ă
Aven, River, *see* **Aan**
Aven and Innerdale, Lord, 'eɪvən ənd 'ɪnərdeɪl, áyvĕn ănd ínnĕrdayl
Avendaño, *f.n.,* ˌævɪn'dɑnjoʊ, avvĕndaányō
Avenell, *f.n.,* 'eɪvənəl, áyvĕnĕl
Avening *Glos.,* 'eɪvnɪŋ, áyv-ning
Averham *Notts.,* 'ɛərəm, áirăm
Averill, *f.n.,* 'ævərɪl, ávvĕril
Avern, *f.n.,* 'ævərn, ávvĕrn; ə'vɜrn, ăvérn
Aves, *f.n.,* eɪvz, ayvz
Aveton Gifford *Devon,* 'ɔtən 'dʒɪfərd, áwtŏn jíffŏrd; 'ævɪtən 'gɪfərd, ávvĕtŏn gíffŏrd
Aviemore *H'land,* ˌævɪ'mɔr, avvimór
Avill, River, *Somerset,* 'ævɪl, ávvil
Avington *Berks., Hants,* 'ævɪŋtən, ávvingtŏn
Avishays, *also spelt* **Avishayes,** *Somerset,* 'ævɪʃeɪz, ávvis-hayz; 'ævɪʃeɪz, ávvi-shayz. *The spelling* **Avishays** *and the first pronunciation apply to the historic house and to the agricultural and sporting estate.* **Avishayes,** *pronounced either way, is appropriate for the modern housing site.*
Avison, *f.n.,* 'eɪvɪsən, áyvissŏn. *Appropriate for Charles* ∼, *18th-c. composer.*
Aviss, *f.n.,* 'eɪvɪs, áyviss
Avoch, *f.n.,* 'ævəx, ávvŏch
Avoch *H'land,* ɔx, awch
Avon, Earl of, 'eɪvən, áyvŏn
Avon, River, *Avon,* 'eɪvən, áyvŏn. *Appropriate also for the county name, which is taken from that for the river.*
Avon, River, *Central,* 'eɪvən, áyvŏn
Avon, River, *Devon,* 'ævən, ávvŏn
Avon, Loch *and* River, *Grampian,* ɑn, aan
Avon, River, *tributary of the Severn,* 'eɪvən, áyvŏn. *This is*

the river which flows through Stratford-upon-Avon and empties into the Severn at Tewkesbury, Glos.
Avon Carrow *Warwicks.,* 'eɪvən 'kæroʊ, áyvŏn kárrō
Avonmouth *Avon,* 'eɪvənmaʊθ, áyvŏnmowth
Avon Tyrell *Hants,* 'eɪvən 'tɪrəl, áyvŏn tírrĕl
Avonwick *Devon,* 'ævənwɪk, ávvŏn-wick
Avory, *f.n.,* 'eɪvərɪ, áyvŏri
Avoth, *f.n.,* 'eɪvɒθ, áyvoth
Awbery, *f.n.,* 'ɔbərɪ, áwbĕri
Awbridge *Hants,* 'eɪbrɪdʒ, áybrij
Awe, Loch, *S'clyde,* ɔ, aw
Awliscombe *Devon,* 'ɔlɪskəm, áwlisskŏm
Awre *Glos.,* ɔr, or
Awsworth *Notts.,* 'ɒzwərθ, ózwŭrth
Axholme *Humberside,* 'ækshoʊm, ácks-hōm
Axmouth *Devon,* 'æksmaʊθ, ácksmowth
Axon, *f.n.,* 'æksən, ácksŏn
Ayckbourn, *f.n.,* 'eɪkbɔrn, áykborn
Aycliffe *Durham,* 'eɪklɪf, áyklif
Ayer, *f.n.,* ɛər, air
Ayers, *f.n.,* ɛərz, airz; 'eɪərz, áy-ĕrz
Ayerst, *f.n.,* 'eɪərst, áy-ĕrst; 'aɪərst, í-ĕrst
Aykroyd, *f.n.,* 'eɪkrɔɪd, áykroyd
Aylburton *Glos.,* 'eɪlbərtən, áylburtŏn
Aylen, *f.n.,* 'eɪlən, áylĕn
Ayles, *f.n.,* eɪlz, aylz
Aylesbeare *Devon,* 'eɪlzbɪər, áylzbeer
Aylesbury *Bucks.,* 'eɪlzbərɪ, áylzbūri
Aylesford, Earl of, 'eɪlzfərd, áylzfŏrd
Aylesham *Kent,* 'eɪlʃəm, áyl-shăm
Aylestone *Leics.,* 'eɪlstən, áylsstŏn. *Appropriate also for Baron* ∼.
Aylett, *f.n.,* 'eɪlɪt, áylĕt
Ayliffe, *f.n.,* 'eɪlɪf, áyliff
Ayling, *f.n.,* 'eɪlɪŋ, áyling
Aylmer, *f.n.,* 'eɪlmər, áylmĕr
Aylmerton *Norfolk,* 'eɪlmərtən, áylmĕrtŏn
Aylsham *Norfolk,* 'eɪlʃəm, áyl-shăm; 'eɪlsəm, áylssăm; 'ɑlʃəm, aál-shăm
Aylward, *f.n.,* 'eɪlwərd, áylwărd; 'eɪlwɔrd, áylwawrd
Aylwen, *f.n.,* 'eɪlwɪn, áylwĕn
Aymestrey *H. & W.,* 'eɪmstrɪ, áymsstri

Aynho *Northants.*, 'eɪnhoʊ, áyn-hō
Ayot St. Lawrence *Herts.*, 'eɪət snt 'lɒrəns, áy-ŏt sĭnt lórrĕnss
Ayr *S'clyde*, ɛər, air
Ayris, *f.n.*, 'ɛərɪs, áiriss
Ayrst, *f.n.*, ɛərst, airst
Ayrton, *f.n.*, 'ɛərtən, áirtŏn
Ayscough, *f.n.*, 'eɪzkoʊ, áyzkō; 'eɪskoʊ, áysskō; 'æskoʊ, ásskō
Aysgarth *N. Yorks.*, 'eɪzgɑrθ, áyzgaarth
Ayshea, *C.n.*, 'eɪʃə, áyshă
Ayton, Great, *N. Yorks.*, 'eɪtən, áytŏn
Aytoun, William Edmonstoune, *Scottish poet*, 'edmənstən 'eɪtən, édmŏnstŏn áytŏn
Aza, *f.n.*, 'eɪzə, áyză

B

Babcock, *f.n.*, 'bæbkɒk, bábkock
Babell, William, *composer*, 'beɪbl, báybl
Babell *Clwyd*, 'bæbeɬ, bábbeḥl
Babergh *Suffolk*, 'beɪbər, báybĕr
Bablockhythe *Oxon.*, 'bæblək-haɪð, báblŏck-hīth
Babraham *Cambs.*, 'beɪbrəm, báybräm
Bach, *f.n.*, bɑk, baak
Bacharach, *f.n.*, 'bækəræk, báckärack
Bache, *f.n.*, beɪtʃ, baytch; beɪʃ, baysh
Bachell, *f.n.*, 'beɪtʃl, báytchl
Bachymbyd Bach *Clwyd*, bə'xʌmbɪd 'bɑx, bǎ̱ḥúmbid baᶜaḥ
Backhouse, *f.n.*, 'bækəs, báckŭss; 'bækhaʊs, báck-howss
Bacon, *f.n.*, 'beɪkən, báykŏn
Baconian, *pertaining to Francis Bacon*, beɪ'koʊnɪən, baykṓn-iän
Bacup *Lancs.*, 'beɪkəp, báykŭp
Bacuzzi, *f.n.*, bə'kʌzɪ, băkúzzi
Badcock, *f.n.*, 'bædkoʊ, bádkō
Baddeley, *f.n.*, 'bædəlɪ, báddĕli; 'bædlɪ, bádli
Baddeley, North, *Hants*, 'bædzlɪ, bádzli
Baddesley, South, *Hants*, 'bædɪzlɪ, báddĕzli; 'bædzlɪ, bádzli
Baddesley Clinton *Warwicks.*, 'bædzlɪ 'klɪntən, báddĕzli klíntŏn; 'bædzlɪ 'klɪntən, bádzli klíntŏn

Baddesley Ensor *Warwicks.*, 'bædɪzlɪ 'enzɔr, báddĕzli énzor; 'bædzlɪ 'enzɔr, bádzli énzor
Badel, *f.n.*, bə'del, bădéll. *Appropriate for Alan ~, actor, and Sarah ~, actress.*
Badeley, *f.n.*, 'bædlɪ, bádli. *Appropriate also for the Barony of ~.*
Badenoch, *f.n.*, 'beɪdnɒk, báyd-nock
Badenoch *H'land*, 'bædənɒx, báddĕnoc̱h
Baden-Powell, Baron, 'beɪdən 'poʊəl, báydŏn pṓ-ĕl
Bader, *f.n.*, 'bɑdər, ba´adĕr. *Appropriate for Group Captain Sir Douglas ~.*
Badgworthy Water, *also spelt* Bagworthy, *Devon*, 'bædʒərɪ 'wɒtər, bájjĕri wáwtĕr
Badham, *f.n.*, 'bædəm, báddăm
Badoney *Co. Tyrone*, bə'dʌnɪ, bădúnni
Baelz, *f.n.*, belts, belts
Baerlein, *f.n.*, 'bɛərlaɪn, báirlīn
Bage, *f.n.*, beɪdʒ, bayj
Bagehot, *f.n.*, 'bædʒət, bájjŏt; 'bægət, bággŏt. *The first was the pronunciation of Walter ~, economist and journalist.*
Bagenal, *f.n.*, 'bægnəl, bágnäl; 'bægənəl, bággĕnäl
Bager, *f.n.*, 'beɪdʒər, báyjĕr
Baggallay, *f.n.*, 'bægəlɪ, bággäli
Bagier, *f.n.*, 'beɪdʒər, báyjĕr
Bagillt *Clwyd*, 'bægɪɬt, bággiḥlt
Baginton *Warwicks.*, 'bægɪntən, bággintŏn
Baglan *W. Glam.*, 'bæglən, báglän
Bagley, *f.n.*, 'bæglɪ, bágli
Baglin, *f.n.*, 'bæglɪn, báglin
Bagnall *Staffs.*, 'bægnəl, bágnäl
Bagnari, *f.n.*, bæg'nɑrɪ, bag-naári
Bagnell, *f.n.*, 'bægnəl, bágnĕl
Bagnold, *f.n.*, 'bægnoʊld, bág-nōld
Bagot, Baron, 'bægət, bággŏt
Bagrie, *f.n.*, 'bægrɪ, bágri
Bagrit, *f.n.*, 'bægrɪt, bágrit
Baguley, *f.n.*, 'bægəlɪ, bággŭli; 'bæglɪ, bágli; 'bægjʊlɪ, bágg-yŏŏli
Baguley *Gtr. M'chester*, 'bæglɪ, bágli
Bagworthy Water *see* Badgworthy Water
Baharie, *f.n.*, bə'hɑrɪ, bă-haári
Baigent, *f.n.*, 'beɪdʒənt, báyjĕnt
Baildon *W. Yorks.*, 'beɪldən, báyldŏn
Bailey, *f.n.*, 'beɪlɪ, báyli

Bailhache, *f.n.*, 'beɪlhætʃ, báyl--hatch

Bailliere-Tindall, *publishers*, 'beɪlɪər 'tɪndl, báyli-ĕr tíndl

Baillieston *S'clyde*, 'beɪlɪstən, báylistŏn

Baillieu, *f.n.*, 'beɪlju, báylew. *Appropriate also for Baron ∼.*

Baillon, *f.n.*, 'beɪlən, báylŏn

Bain, River, *N. Yorks.*, beɪn, bayn

Baird, *f.n.*, beərd, baird

Bairstow, *f.n.*, 'beərstoʊ, báirsstō

Baiton, *f.n.*, 'beɪtən, báytŏn

Bakewell *Derby.*, 'beɪkwel, báykwel

Bakowski, *f.n.*, bə'kɒfskɪ, băkófski

Bala *Gwynedd*, 'bælə, bálă

Balado *Tayside*, bə'lædoʊ, băláddō

Balblair Forest, *H'land*, 'bælbleər, bálblair

Balby *S. Yorks.*, 'bɔlbɪ, báwlbi

Balch, *f.n.*, bɔlʃ, bawlsh

Balchen, *f.n.*, 'bæltʃɪn, báltchĕn. *This is the pronunciation associated with the 18th-c. Admiral of the name.*

Balchin, Nigel, *author*, 'bɔltʃɪn, báwltchin

Balcomb, *f.n.*, 'bɔlkəm, báwlkŏm

Balcombe *W. Sussex*, 'bɔlkəm, báwlkŏm

Balcon, *f.n.*, 'bɔlkən, báwlkŏn. *Appropriate for Sir Michael ∼, film producer, and Jill ∼, actress.*

Balden, *f.n.*, 'bɔldən, báwldĕn

Baldernock *S'clyde*, bɔl'dɜrnək, bawldérnŏk

Balderston, *f.n.*, 'bɔldərstən, báwldĕrstŏn

Baldhu *Cornwall*, bæl'dju, baldéw; bɔl'dju, bawldéw; bɔl'du, bawldoo

Baldick, *f.n.*, 'bɔldɪk, báwldick

Baldock, *f.n.*, 'bɔldɒk, báwldock

Baldock *Herts.*, 'bɔldɒk, báwldock

Baldovan *Tayside*, bæl'dɒvən, bal-dóvvăn

Baldovie *Tayside*, bæl'dʌvɪ, bal-dúvvi

Baldragon *Tayside*, bæl'drægən, bal-drággŏn

Baldry, *f.n.*, 'bɔldrɪ, báwldri

Baldslow *E. Sussex*, 'bɔldzloʊ, báwldz-lō

Baldwin, *f.n.*, 'bɔldwɪn, báwldwin. *Appropriate also for Earl ∼ of Bewdley.*

Balerno *Lothian*, bə'lɜrnoʊ, bălérnō. *Appropriate also for Baron ∼.*

Balfe, *f.n.*, bælf, balf

Balfour, *f.n.*, 'bælfər, bálfür; 'bælfɔr, bálfor. *The second is appropriate for the Earl of ∼ and for Baron ∼ of Inchrye.*

Balfour of Burleigh, Baron, 'bælfər əv 'bɜrlɪ, bálfür ŏv búrli

Balfron *Central*, bæl'frɒn, balfrón

Balgavies Loch *Tayside*, bæl-'gæviz, balgávviz

Balgay *Tayside*, bæl'geɪ, balgáy

Balgedie *Tayside*, bæl'gedɪ, balgéddi

Balgonie, *f.n.*, bæl'goʊnɪ, bal-gŏni

Balguy, *f.n.*, 'bɔlgɪ, báwlgi

Balham *London*, 'bæləm, bálăm

Balhatchet, *f.n.*, bæl'hætʃɪt, bal--hátchĕt

Balhousie Castle *Tayside*, bæl-'haʊzɪ, bal-hówzi

Baliol, *f.n.*, 'beɪlɪɔl, báyli-ŏl

Balivanich *Benbecula (W. Isles)*, ˌbælɪ'vænɪx, balivánnich

Ball, *f.n.*, bɔl, bawl

Ballabrooie *I. of Man*, ˌbælə'bruɪ, balăbroŏ-i

Ballachulish *H'land*, ˌbælə'hulɪʃ, balăhoŏlish

Ballacraine *I. of Man*, ˌbælə'kreɪn, balăkráyn

Ballagh *Co. Fermanagh, Co. Tyrone*, 'bælə, bálă

Ballagher, *f.n.*, 'bæləgər, báláğĕr

Ballam, Higher and Lower, *Lancs.* 'bæləm, bálăm

Ballantine, *f.n.*, 'bæləntaɪn, bálăntīn

Ballantrae *S'clyde*, ˌbælən'treɪ, balăn-tráy

Ballantyne, *f.n.*, 'bæləntaɪn, bálăntīn

Ballard, *f.n.*, 'bælɑrd, bálaard; 'bælərd, bálărd

Ballardie, *f.n.*, bə'lɑrdɪ, bălaárdi

Ballasalla *I. of Man*, ˌbælə'sælə, balássălă

Ballater *Grampian*, 'bælətər, bálătĕr

Ballaugh *I. of Man*, bə'lɑf, bălaaf

Ballechin *Tayside*, bə'lexɪn, băléchin

Balleine, *f.n.*, bæ'len, balén

Ballengeich *Central*, ˌbælən'gɪx, balén-géech

Ballham, *f.n.*, 'bɒləm, báwlăm

Ballinahatty *Co. Tyrone*, ˌbælɪnə-'hætɪ, balinăhátti

Ballinamallard *Co. Fermanagh*, ˌbælɪnə'mælərd, balinămálărd

Ballinaskeagh *Co. Down*, ˌbælɪnə'skeɪ, balinăskáy

Ballindalloch *Grampian*, ‚bælɪn-ˈdæləx, balindálŏch

Ballinderry *Co. Antrim*, ‚bælɪn-ˈderɪ, balindérri

Ballinger *Bucks.*, ˈbælɪndʒər, bálinjĕr

Ballingry *Fife*, bəˈlɪŋgrɪ, băling-gri

Ballinluig *Tayside*, ‚bælɪnˈluɪg, balinloo-ig

Ballintogher *Co. Down*, ‚bælɪn-ˈtɒxər, balintóchĕr

Ballintoy *Co. Antrim*, ‚bælɪnˈtɔɪ, balintóy

Balliol College, *Oxford Univ.*, ˈbeɪlɪəl, báyli-ŏl

Balloch *H'land*, bæˈlɒx, balóch

Balloch *S'clyde*, ˈbæləx, bálŏch

Balloch Buie *Grampian*, ˈbæləx ˈbuɪ, bálŏch boŏ-i

Ballochmyle *S'clyde*, ‚bæləxˈmaɪl, balŏchmíl

Balloo *Co. Down*, bəˈlu, băloŏ

Ballyards *Co. Armagh*, ‚bælɪˈɑrdz, bali-aárdz

Ballyaughlis *Co. Down*, ‚bælɪ-ˈɒxlɪs, bali-óchliss

Ballybannon *Co. Down*, ‚bælɪ-ˈbænən, balibánnŏn

Ballycairn *Co. Antrim*, ‚bælɪ-ˈkeərn, balikáirn

Ballycarry *Co. Antrim*, ‚bælɪˈkærɪ, balikárri

Ballycastle *Co. Antrim*, ‚bælɪˈkɑsl, balikaássl

Ballyclare *Co. Antrim*, ‚bælɪˈklɛər, balikláir

Ballycoan *Co. Down*, ‚bælɪˈkouən, balikŏ-än

Ballycopeland *Co. Down*, ‚bælɪ-ˈkouplənd, balikŏpländ

Ballycultra *Co. Down*, ‚bælɪkəlˈtrɔ, balikúltráw

Ballydavey *Co. Down*, ‚bælɪ-ˈdeɪvɪ, balidáyvi

Ballydivity *Co. Antrim*, ‚bælɪ-ˈdɪvɪtɪ, balidívviti

Ballydougan *Co. Down*, ‚bælɪ-ˈdugən, balidoŏgän

Ballydrain *Co. Down*, ‚bælɪˈdreɪn, balidráyn

Ballyeglish *Co. Derry*, ‚bælɪˈeɪglɪʃ, bali-áyglish

Ballyfinaghy *Co. Antrim*, ‚bælɪ-ˈfɪnəxɪ, balifínnăchi

Ballygally *Co. Antrim*, ‚bælɪˈgælɪ, baligáli

Ballygawley *Co. Tyrone*, ‚bælɪ-ˈgɔlɪ, baligáwli

Ballygilbert *Co. Down*, ‚bælɪ-ˈgɪlbərt, baligílbĕrt

Ballygomartin *Co. Antrim*, ‚bælɪgouˈmɑrtɪn, baligŏmaártin

Ballygowan *Co. Down*, ‚bælɪ-ˈgauən, baligówän

Ballygrainey *Co. Down*, ‚bælɪ-ˈgreɪnɪ, baligráyni

Ballyhackamore *Co. Down*, ‚bælɪˈhækəmɔr, baliháckămor

Ballyhalbert *Co. Down*, ‚bælɪ-ˈhælbərt, balihálbĕrt

Ballyhanwood *Co. Down*, ‚bælɪ-ˈhænwud, balihánwoŏd

Ballyholme *Co. Down*, ‚bælɪ-ˈhoum, balihŏm

Ballyhornan *Co. Down*, ‚bælɪ-ˈhɔrnən, balihórnän

Ballykelly *Co. Derry*, ‚bælɪˈkelɪ, balikélli

Ballykilbeg *Co. Down*, ‚bælɪkɪl-ˈbeg, balikilbég

Ballykinlar *Co. Down*, ‚bælɪˈkɪnlər, balikínlär

Ballylesson *Co. Down*, ‚bælɪˈlesən, baliléssŏn

Ballylumford *Co. Antrim*, ‚bælɪ-ˈlʌmfərd, balilúmförd

Ballymacarrett *Co. Down*, ‚bælɪməˈkærɪt, balimăkárrĕt

Ballymachan *Belfast*, ‚bælɪ-ˈmæxən, balimáchän

Ballymaconaghy *Co. Down*, ‚bælɪməˈkɒnəxɪ, balimăkónnăchi

Ballymaconnell *Co. Down*, ‚bælɪməˈkɒnl, balimăkónnl

Ballymacormick *Co. Down*, ‚bælɪməˈkɔrmɪk, balimăkórmick

Ballymagorry *Co. Tyrone*, ‚bælɪməˈgɒrɪ, balimăgórri

Ballymaguigan *Co. Derry*, bælɪməˈgwɪgən, balimăgwíggän

Ballymena *Co. Antrim*, ‚bælɪ-ˈminə, baliméená

Ballymenoch *Co. Down*, ‚bælɪ-ˈminəx, baliméenŏch

Ballymoney *Co. Antrim*, ‚bælɪ-ˈmʌnɪ, balimúnni

Ballynafeigh *Co. Down*, ‚bælɪnə-ˈfaɪ, balinaáfí

Ballynahinch *Co. Down*, ‚bælɪnəˈhɪnʃ, balinăhínsh

Ballynure *Co. Antrim*, ‚bælɪ-ˈnjuər, balinyŏŏr

Ballyquintin *Co. Down*, ‚bælɪ-ˈkwɪntɪn, balikwíntin

Ballyrashane *Co. Derry*, ‚bælɪrə-ˈʃeɪn, baliräsháyn

Ballyrobert *Co. Down*, ‚bælɪ-ˈrɒbərt, baliróbbĕrt

Ballyronan *Co. Derry*, ‚bælɪ-ˈrounən, balirŏnän

Ballyroney *Co. Down*, ‚bælɪ-ˈrounɪ, balirŏni

Ballysallagh *Co. Down*, ‚bælɪ-ˈsælə, balissálá

Ballysillan *Co. Antrim*, ‚bælɪˈsɪlən, balissíllän

Ballystockart Co. Down, ˌbælɪ-
'stɒkərt, balıstóckärt
Ballywalter Co. Down, ˌbælɪ-
'wɔltər, bali-wáwltĕr
Ballywillan Co. Down, ˌbælɪ'wɪlən,
bali-wíllăn
Balmacara H'land, ˌbælməˈkɑrə,
balmăkaˈärä
Balmaghie D. & G., ˌbælməˈgi,
balmăgeé
Balmaha Central, ˌbælməˈhɑ,
balmăhaˈa
Balmedie Grampian, bælˈmedɪ,
balméddi
Balmer, f.n., 'bɑmər, baˈamĕr
Balmerino, f.n., bælˈmɛərnɪ,
balmáirni
Balmerino Fife, ˌbælməˈrinoʊ,
balmĕreénô
Balmoral Grampian, Co. Antrim,
bælˈmɒrəl, balmórrăl
Balnacra H'land, ˌbælnəˈkrɑ,
balnăkraˈa
Balnaguard Tayside, ˌbælnəˈgɑrd,
balnăgaˈard
Balnain H'land, bælˈneɪn,
balnáyn
Balnave, f.n., bælˈneɪv, balnáyv
Balne S. Yorks., bɒn, bawn
Balniel, Lord, bælˈnil, balneˈel
Balogh, Baron, 'bælɒg, bálog
Balornock S'clyde, bəˈlɔrnək,
bălórnŏk
Balquharn Grampian, bælˈhwɑrn,
bal-whaˈarn
Balquhidder Central, bælˈhwɪdər,
bal-whíddĕr; bælˈkwɪdər,
bal-kwíddĕr
Balranald N. Uist (W. Isles),
bælˈrænəld, balránnäld
Balsall Heath W. Midlands,
'bɔlsl 'hiθ, báwlssl heéth
Balshagray S'clyde, bælˈʃægreɪ,
bal-shágray
Balsham Cambs., 'bɔlʃəm, báwl-
-shäm
Balston, f.n., 'bɒlstən, báwlsstŏn
Baltasound Shetland, 'bæltəsund,
báltăsoond
Baltonsborough Somerset,
'bɒltənzbərə, báwltŏnzbŭră;
'bɒlzbəri, báwlzbŭri
Balvenie Grampian, bælˈvenɪ,
balvénni
Bambaras Music hall, Newcastle-
upon-Tyne, 'bæmbrəz, bámbrăz
Bambridge, f.n., 'beɪmbrɪdʒ,
báymbrij
Bambrough, f.n., 'bæmbrə, bám-
bră
Bamburgh Northd., 'bæmbərə,
bámbŭră
Bamford, f.n., 'bæmfərd, bámfŏrd
Bamfyld, f.n., 'bæmfɪld, bámfeeld

Bamont, f.n., 'beɪmənt, báymŏnt
Bampfylde, f.n., 'bæmpfild,
bámpfeeld. Family name of
Lord Poltimore.
Bamrah, f.n., 'bæmrɑ, bámraa
Banbridge Co. Down, bæn'brɪdʒ,
banbrij; 'bænbrɪdʒ, bánbrij
Banagher Co. Derry, 'bænəxər,
bánnácħĕr
Banavie H'land, 'bænəvɪ, bánnävi
Banbury Oxon., 'bænbərɪ, bán-
bŭri; 'bæmbərɪ, bámbŭri
Banbury of Southam, Baron,
'bænbərɪ əv 'saʊðəm, bánbŭri
ŏv sówtħăm
Bance, f.n., bæns, banss
Banchory Grampian, 'bæŋkərɪ,
bánkŏri; 'bæŋxərɪ, bánxŏri
Banchory-Devenick Grampian,
'bæŋkərɪ 'devənɪk, bánkŏri
dévvĕnick; 'bæŋxərɪ 'devənɪk,
bánxŏri dévvĕnick
Banchory-Ternan Grampian,
'bæŋkərɪ 'tɛərnən, bánkŏri
táirnän; 'bæŋxərɪ 'tɛərnən,
bánxŏri táirnän
Banc-y-ffordd Dyfed ˌbæŋkəˈfɔrð,
bankăfórtħ
Bandey, f.n., 'bændɪ, bándi
Banff Grampian, bæmf, bamf;
bænf, banf
Bangor Clwyd, Gwynedd, Co.
Down, 'bæŋgər, báng-gŏr.
Appropriate also for Viscount ~.
Bangour Lothian, bæŋ'gaʊər,
bang-gówr
Banham, f.n., 'bænəm, bánnăm
Bank-Ffos-Felen Dyfed, ˌbæŋk
foʊs 'veln, bank fŏss véllĕn
Bankyfelin Dyfed, ˌbæŋkəˈvelɪn,
bankăvéllin
Bannard, f.n., 'bænɑrd, bánnaard
Bannatyne, f.n., 'bænətaɪn,
bánnătīn
Bannatyne, Port, S'clyde, pɔrt
'bænətaɪn, port bánnătīn
Bannell, f.n., 'bænl, bánnl
Banner Hey Merseyside, 'bænər
'heɪ, bánnĕr háy
Bannerman of Kildonan, Barony
of, 'bænərmən əv kɪl'dɒnən,
bánnĕrmăn ŏv kildónnăn
Bannockburn Central, 'bænək-
bərn, bánnŏkburn
Bannon, f.n., 'bænən, bánnŏn
Bantham Devon, 'bæntəm,
bántăm
Banwell Avon, 'bænwəl, bán-wĕl
Banyard, f.n., 'bænjɑrd, bán-
-yaard
Bapchild Kent, 'bæptʃaɪld, báp-
-child
Barachnie S'clyde, bəˈræxnɪ,
băráchni

Barassie *S'clyde*, bə'ræsɪ, bărássi

Barbirolli, Sir John, *conductor*, ˌbɑrbɪ'rɒlɪ, baarbirólli

Barbour, *f.n.*, 'bɑrbər, baárbŭr

Barcaldine *S'clyde*, bɑr'kældɪn, baarkáldin

Barclay, *f.n.*, 'bɑrklɪ, baárkli

Barcloy *D. & G.*, bər'klɔɪ, bărklóy

Barcombe *E. Sussex*, 'bɑrkəm, baárkŏm

Barcroft, *f.n.*, 'bɑrkrɒft, baárkroft

Bardgett, Herbert, *conductor*, 'bɑrdʒet, baárjet

Bardill, *f.n.*, 'bɑrdl, baárdl; 'bɑrdɪl, baárdil

Bardsey Island *Gwynedd*, 'bɑrdsɪ, baárdssi

Bareau, **Paul**, *economist*, 'pɒl 'bærou, páwl bárrō

Barfreston *Kent*, 'bɑrfrɪstən, baárfrĕstŏn

Bargany *S'clyde*, bɑr'genɪ, baar-génni

Bargeddie *S'clyde*, bɑr'gedɪ, baargéddi

Barger, *f.n.*, 'bɑrdʒər, baárjĕr

Bargery, *f.n.*, 'bɑrdʒərɪ, baárjĕri

Bargh, *f.n.*, bɑrdʒ, baarj; bɑrf, baarf; bɑrg, baarg

Bargoed *Mid Glam.*, 'bɑrgɔɪd, baárgoyd

Barham, *f.n.*, 'bærəm, bárrăm; 'bɑrəm, baárăm. *The second is appropriate for Baron* ~.

Barham *Cambs.*, 'bɑrəm, baárăm; 'bærəm, bárrăm

Barham *Kent*, 'bærəm, bárrăm

Barharrow *D. & G.*, bɑr'hærou, baar-hárrō

Barholm *Lincs.*, 'bærəm, bárrŏm

Baring, *f.n.*, 'beərɪŋ, báiring; 'bærɪŋ, bárring

Baring-Gould, The Revd. **Sabine**, *author and hymn-writer*, 'seɪbɪn 'beərɪŋ 'guld, sáybin báiring góold

Barkisland *W. Yorks.*, 'bɑrkɪslənd, baárkissländ; 'basländ, baássländ

Barklye *E. Sussex*, bɑrk'laɪ, baarklí

Barlanark *S'clyde*, bɑr'lænərk, baar-lánnärk

Barlas, *f.n.*, 'bɑrləs, baárlăss

Barlass, *f.n.*, 'bɑrləs, baárlăss

Barlaston *Staffs.*, 'bɑrləstən, baárlăstŏn

Barlavington *W. Sussex*, bɑr-'lævɪŋtən, baarlávvington

Barlborough *Derby.*, 'bɑrlbərə, baárlbŭră; 'bɑrbərə, baárbŭră

Barlestone *Leics.*, 'bɑrlstoun, baárlsstŏn

Barlinnie Prison *Glasgow*, bɑr'lɪnɪ, baarlínni

Barmouth *Gwynedd*, 'bɑrməθ, baármŭth

Barnabe, *f.n.*, 'bɑrnəbɪ, baárnăbi

Barnadier, *f.n.*, ˌbɑrnə'dɪər, baarnădeér

Barnard, *f.n.*, 'bɑrnərd, baár-naard; 'bɑrnərd, baárnărd

Barnard Castle *Durham*, 'bɑrnərd 'kɑsl, baárnărd kaássl

Barnard Gate *Oxon.*, 'bɑrnərd 'geɪt, baárnărd gáyt

Barnardiston, *f.n.*, ˌbɑrnər'dɪstən, baarnărdístŏn

Barnbow *W. Yorks.*, bɑrn'bou, baarnbṓ; 'bɑrnbou, baárnbō

Barneby, *f.n.*, 'bɑrnəbɪ, baárnĕbi

Barnehurst *London*, 'bɑrnhərst, baárn-hurst

Barnell, *f.n.*, bɑr'nel, baarnéll

Barnet, *f.n.*, 'bɑrnɪt, baárnĕt

Barnett, *f.n.*, 'bɑrnɪt, baárnĕt; bɑr'net, baarnétt

Barnoldswick *Lancs.*, bɑr'nouldz-wɪk, baarnṓldzwick; 'bɑrlɪk, baárlik

Barnstaple *Devon* 'bɑrnstəpl, baárnstăpl

Barou, *f.n.*, bə'ru, băróo

Barraclough, *f.n.*, 'bærəklʌf, bárrăkluff

Barrass, *f.n.*, 'bærəs, bárrăss

Barraud, *f.n.*, 'bærɒd, bárrawd

Barrell, *f.n.*, 'bærəl, baárrĕl

Barrington, *f.n.*, 'bærɪŋtən, bárringtŏn

Barripper *Cornwall*, bə'rɪpər, băríppĕr

Barritt, *f.n.*, 'bærət, bárrĕt

Barrogil Castle *H'land*, 'bærougɪl, bárrōgil. *Former name of the Castle of Mey, q.v.*

Barrow-in-Furness *Cumbria*, 'bærou ɪn 'fɜrnɪs, bárrō in fúrnĕss

Barry *S. Glam.*, 'bærɪ, bárri

Barsham, *f.n.*, 'bɑrʃəm, baár-shăm

Barsham *Suffolk*, 'bɑrʃəm, baár-shăm. *Appropriate also for East, West, and North* ~ *in Norfolk, and the historic East* ~ *Manor.*

Barsotti, *f.n.*, 'bɑr'zɒtɪ, baarzótti

Barstow, *f.n.*, 'bɑrstou, baársstō

Bartell, *f.n.*, bɑr'tel, baartéll

Bartelski, *f.n.*, bɑr'telskɪ, baar-télski

Bartestree *H. & W.*, 'bɑrtɪstrɪ, baártĕstree

Bartholomew, *f.n.*, bɑr'θɒləmju, baarthóllŏmew

Barthomley *Ches.*, 'bɑrθəmlɪ, baárthŏmli

Bartleet, *f.n.*, 'bɑrtlit, baártleet

Bartlett, *f.n.,* 'bɑrtlɪt, baártlĕt
Barton-in-Fabis, *Notts.,* 'bɑrtən ɪn 'feɪbɪs, baártŏn in fáybiss
Barton Seagrave *Northants.,* 'bɑrtən 'sigreɪv, baártŏn seé-grayv
Barttelot, *f.n.,* 'bɑrtəlɒt, baártĕlot
Baruck, *f.n.,* bə'rʊk, bărŏŏk
Barugh *f.n.,* bɑrf, baarf
Barugh *Cumbria,* bɑrf, baarf
Barugh, Great *and* Little, *N. Yorks.,* bɑrf, baarf
Barugh *S. Yorks.,* bɑrk, baark
Barwick, *f.n.,* 'bærɪk, bárrick; 'bɑrwɪk, baárwick
Barwick *Norfolk, Somerset,* 'bærɪk, bárrick
Barwick-in-Elmet *W. Yorks.,* 'bærɪk ɪn 'elmɪt, bárrick in élmĕt
Baschurch *Salop,* 'bæstʃɑrtʃ, báss-churtch
Basébé, *f.n.,* bə'seɪbɪ, băssáybi
Baseden, *f.n.,* 'beɪzdən, báyzdĕn
Baseley, *f.n.,* 'beɪzlɪ, báyzli
Basevi, George, *19th-c. architect,* bə'seɪvɪ, băssáyvi
Basford *Ches., Staffs.,* 'bæsfərd, bássfŏrd
Basford, *Notts.,* 'beɪsfərd, báyssfŏrd
Basildon *Berks., Essex,* 'bæzldən, bázzldŏn
Basing, Baron, 'beɪzɪŋ, báyzing
Basingstoke *Hants,* 'beɪzɪŋstoʊk, báyzingstōk
Baskind, *f.n.,* 'bæskɪnd, básskind
Baslow *Derby.,* 'bæzloʊ, bázlō
Basnett, *f.n.,* 'bæznet, báznett
Bason, *f.n.,* 'bæsən, bássŏn
Bassaleg *Gwent,* 'beɪzlɪɡ, báyzlig; bæ'sæleɡ, bassáleg
Bassenthwaite *Cumbria,* 'bæsənθweɪt, bássĕnthwait
Bassetlaw *Notts.,* 'bæsɪt'lɔ, bássĕtláw
Bassham, *f.n.,* 'bæsəm, bássăm
Bassingbourn *Cambs.,* 'bæsɪŋbɔrn, bássingborn
Bassingfield *Notts.,* 'bæsɪŋfɪld, bássingfeeld
Bassingthwaite, *f.n.,* 'bæsɪŋθweɪt, bássingthwayt
Bastedo, *f.n.,* bəs'tidoʊ, băsteédō
Baster, *f.n.,* 'bæstər, básstĕr
Basterfield, *f.n.,* 'bæstərfɪld, básstĕrfeeld
Bastie, *f.n.,* 'bæstɪ, bássti
Bastin, *f.n.,* 'bæstɪn, básstin
Baston *Lincs.,* 'bæstən, básstŏn
Bastonford *H. & W.,* 'bæstənfərd, básstŏnford
Baswich *Staffs.,* 'bæsɪdʒ, bássij; 'bæsɪtʃ, bássitch

Batchelor, *f.n.,* 'bætʃɪlər, bátchĕlŏr
Bate, *f.n.,* beɪt, bayt
Baterip, *f.n.,* 'bætərɪp, báttĕrip
Bates, *f.n.,* beɪts, bayts
Bateson, *f.n.,* 'beɪtsən, báytsŏn
Batham, *f.n.,* 'beɪθəm, báythăm
Bathavon *Avon,* 'bɑθeɪvən, baáth-ayvŏn
Bathealton *Somerset,* 'bætltən, báttltŏn
Batheaston *Avon,* bɑ'θistən, baatheéstŏn; 'bætɪstən, báttistŏn
Bather, *f.n.,* 'bæðər, báthĕr; 'bæθər, báthĕr
Bathford *Avon,* bɑθ'fɔrd, baath-fórd
Batho, *f.n.,* 'bæθoʊ, báthō; 'beɪθoʊ, báythō
Bathurst, *f.n.,* 'bæθərst, báthurst; 'bæθɑrst, báth-hurst. *The first is appropriate for Earl ∼ and for Viscount Bledisloe's family name.*
Batley *W. Yorks.,* 'bætlɪ, bátli
Batsford, *f.n.,* 'bætsfərd, bátsfŏrd
Battagel, *f.n.,* 'bætədʒl, báttăjl
Battersea *London,* 'bætərsɪ, báttĕrssi
Battershill, *f.n.,* 'bætərʃɪl, báttĕr-shil
Battes, *f.n.,* 'bætɪs, báttĕss
Battine, *f.n.,* 'bætin, bátteen
Battisford *Suffolk,* 'bætɪsfərd, báttissfŏrd
Battishill, *f.n.,* 'bætɪʃɪl, bátti-shil; 'bætɪʃl, báttishl
Battleby *Tayside,* 'bætlbɪ, báttlbi
Battlefield *Glasgow,* 'bætlfɪld, báttl-feeld
Battlesbridge *Essex,* 'bætlzbrɪdʒ, báttlz-brij
Battye, *f.n.,* 'bætɪ, bátti
Baty, *f.n.,* 'beɪtɪ, báyti
Baublys, *f.n.,* 'bɒblɪs, báwbliss
Baudains, *f.n.,* 'boʊdeɪnz, bŏdaynz
Baufield, *f.n.,* 'baʊfɪld, bówfeeld
Baugh, *f.n.,* bɔ, baw
Baughan, *f.n.,* bɒn, bawn; 'bɔən, báw-ăn; 'bɒfən, bóffăn
Baughen, *f.n.,* bɒn, bawn; 'bɔən, báw-ĕn; 'bɒfən, bóffĕn
Baughurst *Hants,* 'bɒɡhərst, báwg-hurst
Baulard, *f.n.,* 'boʊlɑrd, bŏlaard
Baulch, *f.n.,* bɒltʃ, bawltch
Baumber *Lincs.,* 'bɒmbər, báwmbĕr
Baumber *Lincs.,* 'bɒmbər, báwmbĕr
Baunton *Glos.,* 'bɒntən, báwntŏn
Baur, *f.n.,* 'baʊər, bowr
Baverstock, *f.n.,* 'bævərstɒk, bávvĕrsstock

Bavin, *f.n.*, 'bævɪn, bávvin; 'beɪvɪn, báyvin

Bawburgh *Norfolk*, 'beɪbər, báybĕr; 'bɔbərə, báwbŭră

Bawden, *f.n.*, 'bɔdən, báwdĕn

Bawdeswell *Norfolk*, 'bɔdzwəl, báwdzwĕl

Bawdsey *Suffolk*, 'bɔdzɪ, báwdzi

Bawor, *f.n.*, 'bauər, bówĕr

Bawtree, *f.n.*, 'bɔtrɪ, báwtri

Baxandall, *f.n.*, 'bæksəndɔl, bácksăndawl

Baxendale, *f.n.*, 'bæksəndeɪl, bácksĕndayl

Baxendine, *f.n.*, 'bæksəndaɪn, bácksĕndīn

Baxter, *f.n.*, 'bækstər, báckstĕr

Bayard, *f.n.*, 'beɪɑrd, báy-aard

Baylham *Suffolk*, 'beɪləm, báylăm

Baynard's Castle *see* Castle Baynard

Baynard's Green *Oxon.*, 'beɪnɑrdz 'grin, báynaardz gréen

Bazalgette, *f.n.*, 'bæzldʒɛt, bázzl-jet

Bazeley, *f.n.*, 'beɪzlɪ, báyzli

Bazell, *f.n.*, bə'zel, băzéll

Bazett, *f.n.*, 'bæzɪt, bázzĕt

Bazin, *f.n.*, 'beɪzɪn, báyzin

Beacham, *f.n.*, 'bitʃəm, beétchăm

Beachy Head *E. Sussex*, 'bitʃɪ 'hed, beétchi héd

Beacon Lough *Tyne & Wear*, 'bikən 'lɒf, beékŏn lóff

Beaconsfield *Bucks.*, 'bekənzfild, béckŏnzfeeld'; 'bikənzfild, beékŏnzfeeld. *The second is appropriate also for the Earldom of ~.*

Beaford *Devon*, 'bifərd, beéfŏrd

Beagh's Forest *Co. Antrim*, 'beɪəx, báy-ach

Beaglehole, *f.n.*, 'biglhoul, beégl-hōl

Beahan, *f.n.*, 'biən, bee-ăn

Beament, *f.n.*, 'bimənt, beémĕnt

Beaminster *Dorset*, 'bemɪnstər, bémminstĕr

Beamish, *f.n.*, 'bimɪʃ, beémish

Beamont, *f.n.*, 'bimənt, beémŏnt

Bean, *f.n.*, bin, been

Beanacharan, Loch, *H'land*, ˌbjænə'xærən, byannăchárrăn

Beanes, *f.n.*, beɪnz, baynz

Beaney, *f.n.*, 'binɪ, beéni

Beardsall, *f.n.*, 'bɪərdsl, beérdssl

Beardsell, *f.n.*, 'bɪərdsl, beérdssl

Beardsley, *f.n.*, 'bɪərdzlɪ, beérdzli. *Appropriate for Aubrey ~, 19th-c. artist.*

Beare *Devon*, bɪər, beer

Beare Green *Surrey*, 'beər 'grin, báir gréen

Bearley *Warwicks.*, 'bɪərlɪ, beérli

Bearpark *Durham*, 'bɪər'park, beer-páark

Bearsden *S'clyde*, beərz'den, bairzdén

Bearsted *Kent*, 'barsted, bérssted; 'beərsted, báirssted. *The first is appropriate for Viscount ~.*

Bearstone *Salop*, 'bɪərstən, beérstŏn

Bearwardcote *Derby.*, 'bærəkət, bárräkŏt

Beastall, *f.n.*, 'bistl, beéstl

Beaton, *f.n.*, 'bitən, beétŏn

Beattie, *f.n.*, 'bitɪ, beéti

Beattock *D. & G.*, 'bitək, beé-tŏk

Beatty, Earl, 'bitɪ, beéti

Beauchamp *Gwent*, 'bitʃəm, beétchăm. *Appropriate also for the Earldom of ~.*

Beauchamp of Powyke, Baron, 'bitʃəm əv 'pouɪk, beétchăm ŏv pṓ-ik

Beauchief *S. Yorks.*, 'bitʃɪf, beétchif

Beauclerk, *f.n.*, 'bouklɛər, bṓ-klair; bou'klɛər, bōkláir. *The first is appropriate for the Duke of St. Albans' family name.*

Beaudesert *Warwicks.*, bou-'dezərt, bōdézzĕrt; ˌboudɪ'zɛər, bōdĕzáir; 'belzər, bélzĕr

Beaufort, Duke of, 'boufərt, bṓfŏrt

Beaufoy, *f.n.*, 'boufɔɪ, bṓfoy

Beaulieu *Hants*, 'bjulɪ, béwli

Beauly *H'land*, 'bjulɪ, béwli

Beaumanor *Leics.*, bou'mænər, bōmánnŏr

Beaumaris *Gwynedd*, bou'mærɪs, bōmárriss

Beaumont, *f.n.*, 'boumənt, bṓmŏnt; 'boumɒnt, bṓmont. *The first is appropriate also for Baron ~ of Whitley.*

Beaumont *Cumbria*, 'bimənt, beémŏnt

Beausale *Warwicks.*, 'bjusl, béwssl

Beausire, *f.n.*, bou'sɪər, bōsseér

Beauvoir, *f.n.*, 'bouvwɑr, bṓvwaar

Beavan, *f.n.*, 'bevən, bévvăn

Beavis, *f.n.*, 'bivɪs, beéviss

Beavon, *f.n.*, 'bevən, bévvŏn

Beaworthy *Devon*, 'bɪwɜrðɪ, bee-wurthi; 'bauərɪ, bówĕri

Beba, *f.n.*, 'bibə, beébă

Bebe, *f.n.*, 'bibɪ, beébi

Bechely, *f.n.*, 'bitʃlɪ, beétchli

Becher's Brook *Aintree race-course, Liverpool*, 'bitʃərz 'bruk, beétchĕrz brŏŏk

Bechervaise, *f.n.,* 'betʃərveɪz, bétchĕrvayz; 'beʃərveɪz, béshĕrvayz

Bechhofer, *f.n.,* 'bekhoʊfər, béck-hōfĕr

Becke, *f.n.,* bek, beck

Beckermet *Cumbria,* be'kɜrmɪt, beckérmĕt

Beckinsale, *f.n.,* 'bekɪnseɪl, béckinssayl

Beckles, *f.n.,* 'beklz, bécklz

Bective, Earl of, 'bektɪv, bécktiv

Bedale *N. Yorks.,* 'bɪdl, beédl. *The local* ~ *Hunt, however, is pronounced* 'bɪdeɪl, beédayl.

Bedales School *Hants,* 'bɪdeɪlz, beédaylz

Beddall, *f.n.,* 'bedɔl, béddawl

Beddau *Mid Glam.,* 'beðaɪ, béthī

Beddgelert *Gwynedd,* beɪð-'gelərt, bayth-géllĕrt

Beddingham *E. Sussex,* ˌbedɪŋ-'hæm, bedding-hám

Beddoes, Thomas *Lovell, 19th-c. poet and dramatist,* 'lʌvl 'bedoʊz, lúvvl béddōz

Bedel, *f.n.,* 'bɪdl, beédl

Bedells, *f.n.,* bə'delz, bĕdéllz

Bedenham *Hants,* 'bedənəm, béddĕnăm

Bedford *Beds.,* 'bedfərd, bédfŏrd. *Appropriate also for the Duke of* ~.

Bedham *W. Sussex,* bed'hæm, bed-hám

Bedlinog *Mid Glam.,* bed'lɪnɒg, bedleénog

Bedruthan *Cornwall,* bɪ'drʌðən, bĕdrúthăn

Bedstone *Salop,* 'bedstən, béd-stŏn

Bedwas *Mid Glam.,* 'bedwæs, bédwass

Bedwell, *f.n.,* 'bedwel, bédwel

Bedwellty *Gwent,* bed'weltɪ, bed-wéhlti

Beebee, *f.n.,* 'bibi, beébee

Beech, *f.n.,* bitʃ, beetch

Beecham, *f.n.,* 'bitʃəm, beétchăm

Beeleigh *Essex,* 'bili, beélee; 'bɪlɪ, beéli

Beer, *f.n.,* bɪər, beer

Beerbohm, *f.n.,* 'bɪərboʊm, beér-bōm. *Appropriate for Sir Max* ~, *author and caricaturist, and Sir Herbert* ~*-Tree, actor.*

Beesands *Devon,* 'bisændz, beé-sandz

Beese, *f.n.,* biz, beez

Beeswing *D. & G.,* 'bizwɪŋ, beézwing

Beetham, *f.n.,* 'biθəm, beéthăm

Beetham *Cumbria,* 'biðəm, beéthăm

Beeton, *f.n.,* 'bitən, beétŏn

Begbroke *Oxon.,* 'begbrʊk, bégbrŏŏk

Begelly *Dyfed,* bɪ'gelɪ, bĕgélli

Begent, *f.n.,* 'bɪdʒənt, beéjĕnt

Beggearn Huish *Somerset,* 'begɜrn 'hjuɪʃ, béggern héw-ish

Beguildy *Powys,* bɪ'gaɪldɪ, bĕgíldi

Behague, *f.n.,* bɪ'heɪg, bĕ-háyg

Beharrell, *f.n.,* bɪ'hærəl, bĕ-hárrĕl

Behnes, William, *19th-c. sculptor,* 'beɪnɪz, báynĕz; beɪnz, báynz. *These pronunciations are based merely on usage, not on historical evidence. The sculptor was of German origin.*

Behrens, *f.n.,* 'beərənz, báirĕnz

Beighton, *f.n.,* 'beɪtən, báytŏn

Beighton *Norfolk,* 'baɪtən, bítŏn; 'beɪtən, báytŏn

Beighton *S. Yorks.,* 'beɪtən, báytŏn; 'baɪtən, bítŏn

Beilby, *f.n.,* 'bɪlbɪ, beélbi

Beinn a'Chaolais *S'clyde,* ˌben ə 'xɜɪlɪʃ, ben ă chō-ilish

Beinn-an-Oir *S'clyde,* ˌben ən 'ɔr, ben ăn ór

Beinn Eighe *see* **Ben Eay**

Beinn Laoigh *S'clyde–Central border,* ben 'lɜɪ, ben lŏ-i

Beinn Siantaidh *S'clyde,* ben 'ʃɪəntɪ, ben sheé-änti

Beint, *f.n.,* baɪnt, bīnt

Beit, *f.n.,* baɪt, bīt. *Appropriate for Alfred and Sir Otto* ~, *the financiers and philanthropists associated with the Rhodes foundation.*

Beith, *f.n.,* biθ, beeth

Beith *S'clyde,* bɪð, beeth

Bejda, *f.n.,* 'beɪdə, báydă

Bekesbourne *Kent,* 'bɪksbɔrn, beéksborn

Bekonscot *model village in Beaconsfield,* 'bekənzkɒt, béckŏnzkot

Belah, River, *Cumbria,* 'bɪlə, beélă

Belaugh *Norfolk,* 'bɪlə, beélaa; 'bɪlɔ, beélaw; 'bɪloʊ, beélō; 'bɪlu, beéloo

Belbroughton *H. & W.,* bel'brɒtən, belbráwtŏn

Belchamp Otten *Essex,* 'belʃəm 'ɒtən, bél-shăm óttĕn. *Appropriate also for Belchamp St. Paul, and Belchamp Walter.*

Belchem, *f.n.,* 'beltʃəm, béltchĕm

Belcher, *f.n.,* 'beltʃər, béltchĕr

Belchier, *f.n.,* 'belʃɪeɪ, bélshi-ay

Belcoo *Co. Fermanagh,* bel'ku, belkoó

Belfast *Co. Antrim–Co. Down*, bel'fʌst, belfáast; 'belfʌst, bélfaast

Belhaven and Stenton, Baron, bel'heivən, bel-háyvĕn

Belhelvie *Grampian*, bel'helvɪ, bel-hélvi

Belhus *Essex*, 'beləs, béllŭss

Belim, *f.n.*, 'belɪm, béllim

Belisha, *f.n.*, bə'liʃə, bĕléeshă

Bellaghy *Co. Derry*, be'læxɪ, belláchi

Bellairs, *f.n.*, be'lɛərz, belláirz

Bellak, *f.n.*, 'belæk, béllack

Bellamy, *f.n.*, 'beləmɪ, béllămi

Bellars, *f.n.*, 'belɑrz, béllaarz

Bellasis, *f.n.*, 'beləsɪs, béllässiss; be'leɪsɪs, belláyssiss

Bellasis *Cleveland*, 'beləsɪs, béllässiss

Bellasis *Northd.*, bɪ'læsɪs, bĕlássiss

Bell-Burnell, *f.n.*, ˌbel bər'nel, bell burnéll

Bellchambers, *f.n.*, 'beltʃeɪmbərz, béllchaymbĕrz

Belleau *Lincs.*, 'belou, béllō; 'belu, bélloo

Belleek *Co. Fermanagh*, bɪ'lik, bĕléek

Bellenger, *f.n.*, 'belɪndʒər, béllĕnjĕr

Belle Tout *site of old Beachy Head lighthouse*, 'bel 'tut, béll toót

Bellew, *f.n.*, 'belju, béllew. *Appropriate also for Baron ~.*

Bellinger, *f.n.*, 'belɪndʒər, béllinjĕr

Bellingham, *f.n.*, 'belɪŋhəm, bélling-hăm; 'belɪŋəm, bélling-ăm; 'belɪndʒəm, béllinjăm

Bellingham *London*, 'belɪŋəm, bélling-ăm

Bellingham *Northd.*, 'belɪndʒəm, béllinjăm

Belliver *Devon*, 'belɪvər, béllivĕr

Bellm, *f.n.*, 'beləm, béllĕm

Belloc, Hilaire, *author and poet*, 'hɪlɛər 'belɒk, híllair béllock

Bellshill *Lothian, S'clyde*, 'belzˈhɪl, béllz-hill

Bellue, *f.n.*, 'belju, béllew

Bellyse, *f.n.*, 'belɪs, bélliss

Belmore, Earl, 'belmɔr, bélmor

Belmore, *f.n.*, 'belmɔr, bélmor

Beloe, *f.n.*, 'bilou, beélō

Beloff, *f.n.*, 'belɒf, bélloff

Belsay *Northd.*, 'belsɪ, bélssi

Belthorn *Lancs.*, 'belθɔrn, bélthorn

Beltinge *Kent*, 'beltɪndʒ, béltinj

Beltingham *Northd.*, 'beltɪndʒəm, béltinjăm

Belvedere *Kent*, belvɪ'dɪər, belvĕdeér

Belvoir, *f.n.*, 'bivər, beévĕr

Belvoir *Leics.*, 'bivər, beévĕr

Belvoir Park, *Belfast*, 'bivər, beévĕr

Bembaron, *f.n.*, bem'bærən, bembárrŏn

Bemersyde *Borders*, 'bimərsaɪd, beémĕrssīd

Benacre *Suffolk*, 'beneɪkər, bénaykĕr

Benad, *f.n.*, bɪ'næd, bĕnádd

Ben Alder *Inverness*, ben 'ældər, ben áldĕr

Ben Attow *H'land*, ben 'ætou, ben áttō

Benbecula *W. Isles*, ben'bekjʊlə, benbéck-yōōlă

Ben Cruachan *S'clyde*, ben 'kruəxən, ben kroó-ăchăn

Bendelow, *f.n.*, 'bendɪlou, béndĕlō

Benderloch *S'clyde*, 'bendərlɒx, béndĕrloch

Ben Eay *H'land*, ben 'eɪ, ben áy

Benefield, Upper *and* Lower, *Northants.*, 'benɪfild, bénnifeeld

Benenden *Kent*, 'benəndən, bénnĕndĕn; ˌbenən'den, bennĕn-dén. *The latter is rarely heard now.*

Benenson, *f.n.*, 'benənsən, bénnĕnssŏn

Benest, *f.n.*, 'benest, bénnest; bɪ'nest, bĕnést

Benet, *f.n.*, 'benɪt, bénnĕt. *From the history of the name it seems probable that this was the pronunciation of the 16th-c. madrigal composer, J. Benet.*

Beneveian, Loch, *also spelt* **Benevean**, *H'land*, ˌbenɪ'vɪən, bennĕveé-ăn

Beney, *f.n.*, 'binɪ, beéni

Benfleet *Essex*, 'benflit, bénfleet

Bengeo *Herts.*, 'bendʒou, bénjō

Bengeyfield, *f.n.*, 'bendʒɪfild, bénjifeeld

Bengough, *f.n.*, 'bengɒf, bén-goff

Benhall *Suffolk*, 'benl, bénnl

Benhar *S'clyde*, ben'hɑr, ben-haár

Benholm *Grampian*, 'benhoum, bén-hōm

Benians, *f.n.*, 'benɪənz, bénni-ănz

Ben Ime *S'clyde*, ben 'imə, ben eémĕ

Beningfield, *f.n.*, 'benɪŋfild, bénningfeeld

Benke, *f.n.*, 'beŋkɪ, bénki

Ben Ledi *Central*, ben 'ledɪ, ben léddi

Ben Macdhui *Grampian*, ˌben mək'duɪ, ben măkdoó-i

Bennachie *Grampian*, ˌbenə'xi, bennăchée

Bennane Head S'clyde, 'benən
'hed, bénnän héd
Bennell, f.n., 'benl, bénnl
Bennellick, f.n., bɪ'nelɪk, bĕnéllick
Bennett, f.n., 'benɪt, bénnĕt
Ben Nevis H'land, ben 'nevɪs,
ben névviss
Benoliel, f.n., ˌbenoʊ'liəl,
bennŏlée-ĕl
Ben Rhydding W. Yorks., ben
'rɪdɪŋ, ben rídding
Ben Rinnes Grampian, ben 'rɪnɪs,
ben rínnĕss
Bensham Tyne & Wear, 'benʃəm,
bén-shäm
Benson, f.n., 'bensən, bénssŏn
Benson Oxon., 'bensən, bénssŏn
Benstead, f.n., 'bensted, bénsted
Bentall, f.n., 'bentɔl, béntawl
Benthall, f.n., 'bentɔl, béntawl;
'benθɔl, bén-thawl
Bentham, f.n., 'benθəm, bén-
-thäm; 'bentəm, béntäm. The
first is appropriate for Jeremy
~, 18–19th-c. author and
founder of University College
London.
Bentham Glos., 'benθəm, bén-
-thäm
Bentham, High and Lower, N.
Yorks., 'benθəm, bén-thäm
Bentilee Staffs., ˌbentɪ'li, bentilée
Bentinck, f.n., 'bentɪŋk, béntink.
A member of the family asserts
that 'bentɪk, béntick is simply a
popular misconception.
Bentine, f.n., ben'tin, bentéen
Bentwich, f.n., 'bentwɪtʃ, bént-
witch
Ben Venue Central, ˌben və'nju,
ben vĕnéw
Benwick Cambs., 'benɪk, bénnick
Benyon, f.n., 'benjən, bén-yŏn
Benzie, f.n., 'benzɪ, bénzi
Beoley H. & W., 'bɪlɪ, béeli
Beowulf, A.-S. epic hero,
'beɪoʊwʊlf, báy-ō-wŏŏlf;
'beɪəwʊlf, báy-ō-wŏŏlf
Beragh Co. Tyrone, 'beərə, báirä
Berain Clwyd, 'beraɪn, bérrīn
Bere Alston Devon, 'bɪər 'ɔlstən,
béer áwlsstŏn
Beregi, f.n., 'berəgɪ, bérrĕgi
Berenson, f.n., 'berənsən, bérrĕns-
sŏn
Bere Regis Dorset, 'bɪər 'ridʒɪs,
béer réejiss
Beresford, f.n., 'berɪsfərd,
bérrĕsfŏrd
Berger, f.n., 'bɜrdʒər, bérjĕr
Bergh Apton Norfolk, 'bɜr 'æptən,
bér áptŏn
Bergmann, f.n., 'bɜrgmən,
bérgmän

Bergonzi, f.n., bər'gɒnzɪ, bĕrgónzi
Beringer, f.n., 'berɪndʒər, bérrin-
jĕr
Beriosova, Svetlana, ballerina,
svet'lanə beər'jɒsəvə, svetlaánä
bair-yóssŏvä
Berkeley, f.n., 'bɑrklɪ, baárkli.
Appropriate also for Baroness ~.
Berkeley Glos., 'bɑrklɪ, baárkli
Berkhamsted Herts., 'bɜrkəmsted,
bérkämsted
Berkley Somerset, 'bɑrklɪ, baárkli
Berkoff, f.n., 'bɜrkɒf, bérkoff
Berkshire Co. name 'bɑrkʃər,
baárk-shĕr
Berkswell W. Midlands,
'bɑrkswel, baárkswel; 'bɜrkswel,
bérkswel
Berkswich Staffs., 'bɑrkswɪtʃ,
baárkswitch
Berkyngechirche, A.-S. name for
Barking-by-the-Tower, London,
'bɑrkɪŋtʃɑrtʃ, baárkingtchurtch
Bermange, f.n., bər'mɑʒ, bĕr-
maángzh
Bermel, f.n., bər'mel, bĕrméll
Bernal, f.n., bər'næl, bĕrnál;
'bɜrnəl, bérnäl
Bernard, C.n., 'bɜrnərd, bérnärd
Bernard, Anthony, composer and
conductor, 'æntənɪ bər'nɑrd,
ántŏni bĕrnaárd
Bernardin, f.n., 'bɜrnərdɪn,
bérnärdin
Bernays, f.n., bər'neɪz, bĕrnáyz
Bernelle, f.n., bər'nel, bĕrnéll
Bernera S'clyde, 'bɜrnərə, bér-
nĕrä. Appropriate also for the
name of two islands, Great ~
and Little ~, in the W. Isles.
Berners, Baroness, 'bɜrnərz,
bérnĕrz. Appropriate also for
Lord ~, the composer.
Bernhard, C.n., 'bɜrnhɑrd, bérnhärd
Bernhard, f.n., 'bɜrnhɑrd, bérn-
-haard; bɑrn'hɑrd, bern-haárd
Bernhardt, f.n., 'bɜrnhɑrt, bérn-
-haart
Bernice, C.n., 'bɜrnɪs, bérniss;
bər'nis, bĕrneéss
Bernicia part of anc. Northumbria,
bɜr'nɪʃə, bĕrníshä
Bernstein, f.n., 'bɜrnstaɪn, bérn-
stīn; 'bɜrnstin, bérnsteen. The
first is appropriate for Baron ~.
Berrick Salome Oxon., 'berɪk
'sæləm, bérrick sállŏm
Berriew Powys, 'berɪu, bérri-oo
Berrynarbor Devon, ˌberɪ'nɑrbər,
berrinaárbŏr
Bertalot, f.n., 'bɜrtəloʊ, bértälō
Bertera, f.n., beər'teərə, bairtáirä
Berthengam Clwyd, bər'θeŋgəm,
bérthéng-gäm

Berthon, *f.n.,* 'bɜrθən, bérthŏn
Berthoud, *f.n.,* 'bɜrtu, bértoo; bɛər'tu, bairtóo
Bertie, *f.n.,* 'bɑːtɪ, baˈarti. *Family name of the Earl of Lindsey and Abingdon.*
Bertie of Thame, Viscountcy of, 'bɑːtɪ əv 'teɪm, baˈarti ŏv táym
Bertin, *f.n.,* 'bɜrtɪn, bértin
Berwick *E. Sussex,* 'berɪk, bérrick. *Appropriate also for the Barony of* ~.
Berwick St. John *Wilts.,* 'berɪk snt 'dʒɒn, bérrick sînt jón
Berwick-upon-Tweed *Northd.,* 'berɪk əpɒn 'twid, bérrick ŭpon twéed
Berwyn Mountains *Clwyd* (mainly), 'bɜərwɪn, báirwin. *Although principally situated in Clwyd, the* ~ *Mountains are also partly in Powys and Gwynedd.*
Besant, *f.n.,* bɪ'zænt, bĕzánt; 'besənt, béssănt; 'bezənt, bézzănt. *The second was the pronunciation of Annie* ~, *social reformer.*
Bescoby, *f.n.,* 'beskoʊbɪ, béskōbi
Besier, *f.n.,* 'besjeɪ, béss-yay; 'bezjeɪ, béz-yay
Besley, *f.n.,* 'bezlɪ, bézli
Bessacarr, *S. Yorks.,* 'besəkər, béssăkăr
Bessant, *f.n.,* 'besənt, béssănt
Bessborough, Earl of, 'bezbərə, bézbŭră
Bessbrook *Co. Armagh,* 'besbrʊk, béssbrŏŏk
Bessell, *f.n.,* 'besl, béssl; bɪ'sel, bĕséll
Besselsleigh *Oxon.,* 'beslz'li, bésslz-lée
Bessone, *f.n.,* be'soʊn, bessőn
Bestharris, *f.n.,* 'best'hærɪs, bést-hárriss
Besthorpe *Norfolk, Notts.,* 'besθɔrp, béss-thorp
Beswick, *f.n.,* 'bezɪk, bézzick. *Appropriate also for Baron* ~.
Beswick *Gtr. M'chester,* 'besɪk, béssick
Beswick *Humberside,* 'bezɪk, bézzick
Betham *Somerset,* 'betəm, béttăm
Bethell, *f.n.,* 'beθl, béthl. *Appropriate also for Baron* ~.
Bethersden *Kent,* 'beθərzdən, béthĕrzdĕn
Bethesda *Dyfed, Gwynedd,* be'θezdə, bethézdă
Bethune, *f.n.,* 'bitn, béetn; bɪ'θjun, bĕthéwn

Betjeman, Sir John, *Poet Laureate,* 'betʃɪmən, bétchĕmăn
Betsham *Kent,* 'betsəm, bétsăm
Bettaney, *f.n.,* 'betənɪ, béttăni
Betteshanger *Kent* 'betshæŋər, béts-hang-ĕr
Bettice, *f.n.,* 'betɪs, béttiss
Bettws Bledrws *Dyfed,* 'betʊs 'bledrʊs, béttŏŏss blédrŏŏss
Bettws-y-Coed *Gwynedd,* 'betʊs ə 'kɔɪd, béttŏŏss ă kóyd
Bettws-yn-Rhos *Clwyd,* 'betʊs ən 'hroʊs, béttŏŏss ăn róss
Beuden, *f.n.,* 'bjudən, béwdĕn
Beult, River, *Kent,* belt, belt
Beuno, *Welsh saint,* 'baɪnɔ, bínaw
Beuttler, *f.n.,* 'bɔɪtlər, bóytlĕr
Bevan, Aneurin, *politician,* ə'naɪrɪn 'bevən, ănírin bévvăn
Bevercotes *Notts.,* 'bevərkoʊts, bévvĕrkŏts
Bevere *H. & W.,* 'bevərɪ, bévvĕri
Beveridge of Tuggal, Barony of, 'bevərɪdʒ əv 'tʌgl, bévvĕrij ŏv túggl
Beverley, Earl of, 'bevərlɪ, bévvĕrli
Beves, *f.n.,* 'bivɪs, béevĕss
Bevin, *f.n.,* 'bevɪn, bévvin
Bevins, *f.n.,* 'bevɪnz, bévvinz
Bevir, *f.n.,* 'bivər, béevĕr
Bevis, *f.n.,* 'bivɪs, béeviss; 'bevɪs, bévviss
Bevis Marks *St. in London,* 'bevɪs 'mɑrks, bévviss maˈarks
Bewaldeth *Cumbria,* bju'ældəθ, bew-áldĕth
Bewdley *H. & W.,* 'bjudlɪ, béwdli
Bewes, *f.n.,* bjuz, bewz
Bewhay, *f.n.,* 'bjuheɪ, béw-hay
Bewick, *f.n.,* 'bjuɪk, béw-ick. *Appropriate for Thomas* ~, *18–19th-c. wood engraver, and therefore also for* ~'s swan.
Bews, *f.n.,* bjuz, bewz
Bewsher, *f.n.,* 'bjuʃər, béwshĕr
Beyer, *f.n.,* bɛər, bair; 'baɪər, bí-ĕr
Beyfus, *f.n.,* 'beɪfəs, báyfŭss; 'baɪfəs, bífŭss
Beynon, *f.n.,* 'baɪnən, bínŏn; 'beɪnən, báynŏn
Beyton *Suffolk,* 'beɪtən, báytŏn
Beyts, *f.n.,* beɪts, bayts
Bezant, *f.n.,* bɪ'zænt, bĕzánt; 'bezənt, bézzănt
Bezer, *f.n.,* 'bizər, béezĕr
Beznosiuk, *f.n.,* ˌbeznoʊ'sjuk, bezznōssyŏŏk
Bezzant, *f.n.,* bɪ'zænt, bĕzánt
Bias, *f.n.,* 'baɪəs, bí-ăss
Bibby, *f.n.,* 'bɪbɪ, bíbbi
Bibury *Glos.* 'baɪbərɪ, bíbŭri
Bicât, *f.n.,* 'bikɑ, béekaa

Bicester *Oxon.*, 'bɪstər, bísstĕr.
Appropriate also for Baron ∼.
Bichard, *f.n.*, 'bɪʃɑrd, beé-shaard
Bickerdike, *f.n.*, 'bɪkərdaɪk,
bíckĕrdīk
Bickleigh *Devon*, 'bɪkli, bíck-lee
Bicort, *f.n.* 'baɪkɔrt, bí-kort
Biddell, *f.n.*, 'bɪdl, bíddl; bɪ'del,
bidéll
Biddenden *Kent*, 'bɪdəndən,
bíddĕndĕn
Biddestone *Wilts.*, 'bɪdɪstən,
bíddĕstŏn
Biddie, *f.n.*, 'bɪdɪ, bíddi
Biddle, *f.n.*, 'bɪdl, bíddl
Biddlesden *Bucks.*, 'bɪlzdən,
bílzdĕn
Biddulph, *f.n.*, 'bɪdʌlf, bíddulf.
Appropriate also for Baron ∼.
Biddulph *Staffs.*, 'bɪdʌlf, bíddulf
Bideford *Devon*, 'bɪdɪfərd,
bíddĕfŏrd
Biden, *f.n.*, 'baɪdən, bídĕn
Bidwell, *f.n.*, 'bɪdwel, bídwel
Bieber, *f.n.*, 'bibər, beébĕr
Biek, *f.n.*, bik, beek
Bielby, *f.n.*, 'bɪlbɪ, beélbi
Bierer, *f.n.*, 'bɪərər, beérĕr
Bierley *W. Yorks.*, 'baɪərlɪ, bírli
Bierton *Bucks.*, 'bɪərtən, beértŏn
Biffen, *f.n.*, 'bɪfɪn, bíffĕn
Bigelow, *f.n.*, 'bɪgɪloʊ, bíggĕlō
Bigge, *f.n.*, bɪg, big
Biggar *Cumbria, S'clyde*, 'bɪgər,
bíggăr
Bigham, *f.n.*, 'bɪgəm, bíggăm
Bignian *Co. Down*, 'bɪnjən, bín-
-yăn
Bilainkin, George, *author*,
bɪ'leɪŋkɪn, biláynkin
Bilbster *H'land*, 'bɪlpstər,
bílpstĕr
Bildeston *Suffolk*, 'bɪldɪstən,
bíldĕstŏn
Bilgora, *f.n.*, bɪl'gɒrə, bilgórră
Billenness, *f.n.*, 'bɪlɪnɪs, bíllĕnĕss
Billericay *Essex*, ˌbɪlə'rɪkɪ,
billĕrícki
Billesdon *Leics.*, 'bɪlzdən, bílz-
dŏn
Billett, *f.n.*, 'bɪlɪt, bíllĕt
Billinge *Merseyside*, 'bɪlɪndʒ,
bíllinj
Billingham *Cleveland*, 'bɪlɪŋhəm,
bílling-hăm
Billmeir, *f.n.*, 'bɪlmaɪər, bílmīr
Bilsington *Kent*, 'bɪlzɪŋtən,
bílzingtŏn
Bilyard, *f.n.*, 'bɪljɑrd, bíl-yaard
Binder, *f.n.*, 'baɪndər, bíndĕr.
Appropriate for Pearl ∼,
painter.
Binderton *W. Sussex*, 'bɪndərtən,
bíndĕrtŏn

Binge, Ronald, *composer*, bɪndʒ,
binj
Bingham, *f.n.*, 'bɪŋəm, bíng-ăm.
Appropriate also for Baron ∼.
Bingley *W. Yorks.*, 'bɪŋlɪ, bíng-li
Binks, *f.n.*, bɪŋks, binks
Binsey *Cumbria*, 'bɪnzɪ, bínzi
Binski, *f.n.*, 'bɪnskɪ, bínski
Binyon, Laurence, *poet and art
critic*, 'lɒrəns 'bɪnjən, lórrĕnss
bín-yŏn
Bion, *f.n.*, 'bíən, beé-ŏn
Birchall, *f.n.*, 'bɜrtʃl, bírtchl
Birchenough, *f.n.*, 'bɜrtʃɪnʌf,
bírchĕnuff
Birches Head *Staffs.*, ˌbɜrtʃɪz
'hed, birtchĕz hédd
Birchington *Kent*, 'bɜrtʃɪŋtən,
bírtchingtŏn
Birchmore, *f.n.*, 'bɜrtʃmɔr,
bírtchmor
Birdsall, *f.n.*, 'bɜrdsɔl, bírdssawl;
'bɜrdsl, bírdssl
Birkbeck, *f.n.*, 'bɜrbek, bírbeck;
'bɜrkbek, bírkbeck
Birkbeck College, *Univ. of
London*, 'bɜrkbek, bírkbeck
Birkenhead *Merseyside*, ˌbɜrkən-
'hed, birkĕn-héd; 'bɜrkənhed,
bírkĕn-hed. *The second is
appropriate for the Earl of* ∼.
Birkett, Baron, 'bɜrkɪt, bírkĕt
Birmingham *W. Midlands*,
'bɜrmɪŋəm, bírming-ăm
Birnam *Tayside*, 'bɜrnəm, bírnăm
Birnbryer, *f.n.*, 'bɜrnbraɪər,
bírnbrī-ĕr
Birnie, *f.n.*, 'bɜrnɪ, bírni
Birnstingl, *f.n.*, 'bɜrnstɪŋgl,
bírn-sting-gl
Birrane, *f.n.*, bɪ'reɪn, birráyn
Birrell, *f.n.*, 'bɪrəl, bírrĕl
Birsay *Orkney*, 'bɜrzeɪ, bírzay.
Appropriate also for Lord ∼.
Birss, *f.n.*, bɜrs, birss
Birstall *W. Yorks.*, 'bɜrstəl,
bírstawl
Birtles, *f.n.*, 'bɜrtlz, bírtlz
Biscombe, *f.n.*, 'bɪskəm, bíss-
kŏm
Biscovey *Cornwall*, 'bɪskəveɪ,
bískŏvay
Bisham *Berks.*, 'bɪsəm, bíssăm
Bishop Auckland *Durham*, 'bɪʃəp
'ɔklənd, bíshŏp áwkländ
Bishop's Frome *H. & W.*, 'bɪʃəps
'frum, bíshŏps froóm
Bishop's Lydeard *Somerset*,
'bɪʃəps 'lɪdɪərd, bíshŏps
líddi-ărd
Bishop's Nympton *Devon*, 'bɪʃəps
'nɪmptən, bíshŏps nímtŏn
Bishop's Stortford *Herts.*, 'bɪʃəps
'stɔrtfərd, bíshŏps stórtfŏrd;

'bɪʃəps 'stɔrfərd, bíshŏps stór-
fŏrd
Bishop's Tachbrook *Warwicks.*,
'bɪʃəps 'tætʃbrʊk, bíshŏps
tátchbrŏŏk
Bishopsteignton *Devon*,
'bɪʃəps'teɪntən, bíshŏpstáyntŏn
Bishopston *Avon, W. Glam.*,
'bɪʃəpstən, bíshŏpstŏn
Bishop's Waltham *Hants*, 'bɪʃəps
'wɔlθəm, bíshŏps wáwl-thăm;
'bɪʃəps 'wɔltəm, bíshŏps
wáwltăm
Bishopwearmouth *Tyne & Wear*,
'bɪʃəp'wɪərmaʊθ, bíshŏp-
-weermouth
Bispham, *f.n.*, 'bɪspəm, bíspăm;
'bɪsfəm, bísfăm
Bispham *Lancs.*, 'bɪspəm, bíspăm
Bissell, *f.n.*, 'bɪsl, bissl
Bisset, *f.n.*, 'bɪzɪt, bízzĕt; 'bɪsɪt,
bíssĕt
Bissoe *Cornwall*, 'bɪsoʊ, bíssō
Bistre *Clwyd*, 'bɪstər, bísstĕr
Bitham Hall *Warwicks.*, 'bɪθəm,
bíthăm
Bithell, *f.n.*, 'bɪθl, bíthl
Bitterley *Salop*, 'bɪtərlɪ, bíttĕrli
Bittesby *Leics.*, 'bɪtsbɪ, bítsbi
Bitteswell *Leics.*, 'bɪtɪzwel,
bíttĕzwel
Bizeray, *f.n.*, 'bɪzəreɪ, bízzĕray
Bizony, *f.n.*, bɪ'zoʊnɪ, bizŏni
Blabhein *see* **Blaven**
Blaby *Leics.*, 'bleɪbɪ, bláybi
Blackadder, River, *Borders*,
'blækədər, bláckădĕr
Blackawton *Devon*, blæk'ɔtən,
blackáwtŏn
Blackbird Leys *Oxford*,
'blækbərd 'liz, bláckbird leéz
Black Bourton *Oxon.*, 'blæk
'bɔrtən, bláck bórtŏn
Blackfenn *London*, blæk'fen,
black-fénn
Blackley *Gtr. M'chester*, 'bleɪklɪ,
bláykli
Blackness *Central*, blæk'nes,
black-néss
Blackwater *Cornwall, Dorset,
Hants, I. of Wight*, 'blækwɔtər,
bláckwawtĕr
Blackwatertown *Co. Armagh*,
blæk'wɔtərtaʊn, black-wáwtĕr-
-town
Blackwood *Gwent*, 'blæk'wʊd,
bláck-wŏŏd
Blackwood *S'clyde*, 'blækwʊd,
bláckwŏŏd
Blacon *Ches.*, 'bleɪkən, bláykŏn
Blacow, *f.n.*, 'bleɪkoʊ, bláykō
Bladon *Oxon.*, 'bleɪdən, bláydŏn
Blaenannerch *Dyfed*, blaɪn'ænɜrx,
blīnánnerch

Blaenau Ffestiniog *Gwynedd*,
'blaɪnaɪ fes'tɪnjɒg, blīnī
festín-yog
Blaenavon *Gwent*, blaɪn'ævən,
blīnávvŏn
Blaenclydach *Mid Glam.*, blaɪn-
'klɪdəx, blīn-klíddăch
Blaen-Cwm *Mid Glam.*, blaɪn-
'kʊm, blīn-kŏŏm
Blaengarw *Mid Glam.*, blaɪn-
'gæru, blīn-gárroo
Blaengwawr *Mid Glam.*, blaɪn-
'gwaʊər, blīn-gwówr
Blaengwrach *W. Glam.*, blaɪn-
'gwrɑx, blīn-gwráach; blaɪn-
'grɑx, blīn-gráach. *Welsh
speakers pronounce 'gwrach' as
one syllable by treating the 'w'
as a rounding of the lips to
accompany the 'r'.*
Blaenhirwaun Colliery *Dyfed*,
blaɪn'hɜrwaɪn, blīn-hírwīn
Blaenhonddan *W. Glam.*, blaɪn-
'hɒnðən, blīn-hónthăn
Blaenllecha *Mid Glam.*, blaɪn-
'ɬexə, blīn-ɬéchă. *Another
form*, Blaenllechau, *may be
pronounced* blaɪn'ɬexaɪ, blīn-
ɬéchī
Blaenllechau *Mid Glam.*, blaɪn-
'ɬexaɪ, blīn-ɬéchī. *Another form*,
Blaenllecha, *may be pronounced*
blaɪn'ɬexə, blīn-ɬéchă.
Blaen Llynfi *W. Glam.*, blaɪn
'ɬʌnvɪ, blīn hlúnvi; blaɪn 'ɬɪnvɪ,
blīn hlínvi.
Blaenpenal *Dyfed*, blaɪn'penæl,
blīn-pénnal
Blaen-Plwyf *Dyfed*, 'blaɪn 'plʊɪv,
blīn plŏŏi-iv
Blaenporth *Dyfed*, blaɪn'pɔrθ,
blīn-pórth
Blaenserchan Colliery *Gwent*,
blaɪn'sɛərxən, blīn-sáirchăn
Blaen-y-Cwm *Gwent, Mid Glam.*,
ˌblaɪn ə 'kʊm, blīn ă kŏŏm.
*Appropriate for both places of
the name in Mid Glam.*
Blagden, *f.n.*, 'blægdən, blágdĕn
Blagg, *f.n.*, blæg, blagg
Blagrave, *f.n.*, 'blægreɪv, blágrayv
Blagrove, *f.n.*, 'bleɪgroʊv,
bláygrŏv
Blaikie, *f.n.*, 'bleɪkɪ, bláyki
Blaina *Gwent*, 'blaɪnə, blínă
Blair Atholl *Tayside*, blɛər 'æθl,
blair áthl
Blairgowrie *Tayside*, blɛər'gaʊrɪ,
blairgówri
Blairquhan Castle *S'clyde*,
blɛər'hwæn, blair-whán
Blaisdon *Glos.*, 'bleɪzdən, bláyzdŏn
Blakenall *Staffs.*, 'bleɪknl,
bláyknăl

Blakeney, f.n., 'bleɪknɪ, bláykni
Blakeney Glos., Norfolk, 'bleɪknɪ, bláykni
Blakenhall Staffs., 'bleɪkənhɔl, bláykĕn-hawl
Blakenham, Great and Little, Suffolk, 'bleɪkənəm, bláykĕnăm. Appropriate also for Viscount ~.
Blaker, f.n., 'bleɪkər, bláykĕr
Blakesley Northants., 'bleɪkslɪ, bláykssli
Blakiston, f.n., 'bleɪkɪstən, bláykiston; 'blækɪstən, bláckiston
Blakstad, f.n., 'blækstæd, bláckstad
Blamey, f.n., 'bleɪmɪ, bláymi
Blamire, f.n., blə'maɪər, blămír
Blamires, f.n., blə'maɪərz, blămírz
Blanch, f.n., blɑnʃ, blaansh
Blanchard, f.n., 'blæntʃɑrd, blántchaard; 'blæntʃərd, blántchărd
Blanchett, f.n., 'blæntʃɪt, blántchĕt
Blanchland Northd., 'blænʃlənd, blánshländ
Blandford, Marquess of, 'blændfərd, blándfŏrd
Blans, f.n., blænz, blannz
Blanshard, f.n., 'blænʃɑrd, blán-shaard
Blantyre S'clyde, 'blæntaɪər, blántír
Blarmacfoldach H'land, ˌblɑrmək-'foultjɔx, blaarmăk-fŏlt-yăch
Blaston Leics., 'bleɪstən, bláystŏn
Blatherwycke Northants., 'blæðərwɪk, bláthĕrwick
Blathwayt, f.n., 'blæθweɪt, bláth-wayt
Blaven, also spelt Blabhein, I. of Skye, 'blavən, blaávĕn
Blawith Cumbria, blɑð, blaath. Appropriate for both places of the name in Cumbria.
Blaxhall Suffolk, 'blæksl, blácksl
Blaydon Haughs Tyne & Wear, 'bleɪdən 'hɒfs, bláydŏn hóffs
Bleach, f.n., blitʃ, bleetch
Bleackley, f.n., 'blɪklɪ, bleékli
Bleacrag Hill, Cumbria, 'bleɪ-'kræg, bláykrágg
Bleadon Avon, 'blidən, bleédŏn
Bleakley, f.n., 'bleɪklɪ, bláykli
Bleaklow Derby., 'blɪkloʊ, bleéklō
Blea Moor N. Yorks., 'bli 'mʊər, bleé mŏŏr
Blean Kent, blin, bleen
Blean N. Yorks., bleɪn, blayn
Bleaney, f.n., 'blinɪ, bleéni

Bleary Co. Armagh, 'blɪərɪ, bleéeri
Bleasby Lincs., Notts., 'blizbɪ, bleézbi
Bleasdale, f.n., 'blizdeɪl, bleézdayl
Blease, f.n., bliz, bleez; blis, bleess
Bleazard, f.n., 'blizɑrd, bleézaard; 'blezɑrd, blézzaard
Blech, f.n., blek, bleck. Appropriate also for the ~ String Quartet.
Bleddfa Powys, 'bleðvə, bléthvă
Bledisloe, Viscount, 'bledɪsloʊ, bléddisslō
Blemundsbury House Holborn (London), 'blemzbərɪ, blémz-búri
Blencathra Cumbria, blen'kæθrə, blen-káthră
Blencowe, f.n., 'blenkoʊ, blénkō
Blenheim Palace Oxon., 'blenɪm, blénnĕm
Blenkiron, f.n., blenk'aɪərn, blenkírn
Blennerhassett, f.n., 'blenər-hæsɪt, blénnĕr-hassĕt; ˌblenər-'hæsɪt, blennĕr-hássĕt
Bles, f.n., bles, bless. Appropriate also for Geoffrey ~, publishers.
Blessed, f.n., 'blesɪd, bléssĕd
Bletchingley Surrey, 'bletʃɪŋlɪ, blétching-li
Bletsoe Beds., 'bletsoʊ, blétsō
Blewbury Oxon., 'blubərɪ, bloóbúri
Blezard, f.n., 'blezɑrd, blézzaard
Blidworth Notts., 'blɪdwərθ, blídwurth
Bligh, f.n., blaɪ, blī
Blindell, f.n., 'blɪndl, blíndl
Blindley Heath Surrey, 'blaɪndlɪ 'hiθ, blíndli heéth
Blin-Stoyle, f.n., 'blɪn 'stɔɪl, blín stóyl
Blishen, f.n., 'blɪʃən, blíshĕn
Blisland Cornwall, 'blɪzlənd, blízländ
Blisworth Northants., 'blɪzwərθ, blízwurth
Blithfield Staffs., 'blɪfild, blíffeeld
Blizard, f.n., 'blɪzɑrd, blízzaard
Blofield Norfolk, 'bloʊfild, blófeeld
Blogue, f.n., bloʊg, blōg
Blohm, f.n., bloʊm, blōm
Blois, f.n., blɔɪs, bloyss
Blom, f.n., blɒm, blom
Blomefield, f.n., 'blumfild, bloómfeeld
Blomfield, f.n., 'blɒmfild, blóm-feeld; 'blʌmfild, blúmfeeld; 'blumfild, bloómfeeld; 'blumfild, bloómfeeld

Blomiley, *f.n.,* 'blɒmɪlɪ, blómmili
Blo' Norton *Norfolk,* 'bloʊ
  'nɔrtən, blṓ nórtŏn
Blonstein, *f.n.,* 'blɒnstɪn, blón-
  steen
Bloomstein, *f.n.,* 'blumstaɪn,
  blóom-stīn
Blorenge, Mt., *Gwent,* 'blɒrendʒ,
  blórrenj
Bloundelle, *f.n.,* 'blʌndl, blúndl
Blount, *f.n.,* blʌnt, blunt
Blower, *f.n.,* 'bloʊər, blṓ-ĕr;
  'blaʊər, blówĕr
Bloxham, *f.n.,* 'blɒksəm, blócksăm
Bloxwich *W. Midlands,* 'blɒks-
  wɪtʃ, blóckswitch
Blubberhouses *N. Yorks.,*
  'blʌbərhaʊzɪz, blúbbĕr-howzĕz
Blumer, *f.n.,* 'blumər, blóomĕr
Blundell, *f.n.,* 'blʌndl, blúndl
Blundellian, *one educated at
  Blundell's School,* blʌn'delɪən,
  blundélliăn
Blundeston *Suffolk,* 'blʌndɪstən,
  blúndĕstŏn
Blunsom, *f.n.,* 'blʌnsəm, blúnssŏm
Bluntisham *Cambs.,* 'blʌntɪʃəm,
  blúnti-shăm; 'blʌntɪsəm,
  blúntissăm
Blyth, *f.n.,* blaɪ, blī; blaɪð, blīth;
  blaɪθ, blīth. *The first is appro-
  priate for Baron ~.*
Blythborough, *f.n.,* 'blaɪbərə,
  blī́būră
Blythburgh *Suffolk,* 'blaɪbrə,
  blī́bră
Blytheman, William, *Tudor
  composer,* 'blaɪθmən, blī́thmăn
Blythswood *S'clyde,* 'blaɪðzwʊd,
  blī́thz-wŏŏd
Blyton, *f.n.,* 'blaɪtən, blī́tŏn
Boadicea, queen of the **Iceni**
  (*q.v.*), boʊədɪ'sɪə, bōădĭssée-ă.
  Another form is **Boudicca,** *q.v.*
Boady, *f.n.,* 'boʊdɪ, bódi
Boaks, *f.n.,* boʊks, bōks
Boal, *f.n.,* boʊl, bōl
Boarhunt *Hants,* 'bɔrhʌnt, bór-
  -hunt; 'brɒnt, bórrŭnt
Boase, *f.n.,* boʊz, bōz
Boateng, *f.n.,* 'bwateŋ, bwáateng
Boath, *f.n.,* boʊθ, bōth
Boat of Garten *H'land,* 'boʊt əv
  'gartən, bŏt ŏv gáartĕn
Boatte, *f.n.,* boʊt, bōt
Bobbingworth *Essex,* 'bɒbɪŋwɜrθ,
  bóbbing-wurth. *The post office
  is* **Bovinger,** *q.v.*
Bochaton, *f.n.,* 'bɒkətən, bóckătŏn
Bochmann, *f.n.,* 'bɒxmæn,
  bóchman
Boconnoc *Cornwall,* bə'kɒnək,
  bŏkónnŏk
Bocquet, *f.n.,* 'boʊkeɪ, bókay

Boddam-Whetham, *f.n.,* 'bɒdəm
  'wetəm, bóddăm wéttăm
Boddey, *f.n.,* 'bɒdɪ, bóddi
Boddice, *f.n.,* 'bɒdɪs, bóddiss
Boddis, *f.n.,* 'bɒdɪs, bóddiss
Bodedern *Gwynedd,* bɒd'edɛərn,
  boddéddairn
Bodelwyddan *Clwyd,* ˌbɒdl'wiðən,
  boddl-wéethăn
Bodenham *H. & W.,* 'bɒdənəm,
  bóddĕnăm
Bodfari *Clwyd,* bɒd'færɪ, bod-
  fárri
Bodfean *Gwynedd,* bɒd'veɪən,
  bodváy-ăn. *Also spelt* **Boduan,**
  q.v.
Bodffordd *Gwynedd,* 'bɒtfɔrð,
  bótforth
Bodiam *E. Sussex,* 'boʊdɪəm,
  bṓdiăm; 'bɒdɪəm, bóddiăm
Bodinnar, *f.n.,* 'bɒdɪnar, bóddi-
  naar
Bodist Colliery *Dyfed,* 'bɒdɪst,
  bóddist
Bodleian Library, *Oxford,*
  bɒd'liən, bodlée-ăn; 'bɒdlɪən,
  bódliăn
Bodley Head, *publishing house,*
  'bɒdlɪ 'hed, bóddli héd
Bodmer, *f.n.,* 'bɒdmər, bódmĕr
Bodnant *Gwynedd,* 'bɒdnænt,
  bód-nant
Bodorgan *Anglesey,* bɒ'dɔrgən,
  boddórgăn. *Appropriate for both
  places of the name on Anglesey.*
Bodriggy *Cornwall,* bə'drɪgɪ,
  bŏdréegi
Bodrugan's Leap, *Cornwall,*
  bə'drʌgən, bŏdrúggăn
Boduan *Gwynedd,* bə'diən,
  bŏdée-ăn. *Also spelt* **Bodfean,**
  q.v.
Body, *f.n.,* 'bɒdɪ, bóddi
Boe, *f.n.,* boʊ, bō
Boehm, *f.n.,* boʊm, bōm;
  'boʊəm, bṓ-ĕm
Boersma, *f.n.,* 'boʊərzmə,
  bṓórzmă
Boevey, *f.n.,* 'buvɪ, bóovi
Boex, *f.n.,* 'boʊeks, bṓ-ecks
Boffey, *f.n.,* 'bɒfɪ, bóffi
Bogany Point *I. of Bute,* 'bɒgənɪ,
  bóggăni
Bogdanov, *f.n.,* bɒg'danəv,
  boggdáanŏv
Boger, *f.n.,* 'boʊdʒər, bójĕr
Boggart Hole Clough *Gtr.
  M'chester,* 'bɒgart 'hoʊl 'klʌf,
  bóggărt hṓl klúff
Boggis, *f.n.,* 'bɒgɪs, bóggiss
Boghall Bridge *Lothian,* 'bɒghɒl,
  bóg-hawl
Bogue, *f.n.,* boʊg, bōg
Bohana, *f.n.,* boʊ'hanə, bō-haánă

Bohanna, *f.n.,* bou'hænə, bō-hánnä

Boharm *Grampian,* bou'harm, bō-haárm

Bohn, *f.n.,* boun, bōn

Bohun, *f.n.,* bun, boon. *Appropriate for the historical family name of the Earls of Hereford, Essex and Northampton.*

Bohunt Manor *Liphook (Hants),* 'bouhʌnt, bō-hunt

Boileau, *f.n.,* 'boilou, bóylō

Bois, *f.n.,* boiz, boyz

Boisdale *S. Uist (W. Isles),* 'boizdeil, bóyzdayl

Boisragon, *f.n.,* 'bprəgən, bórrăgŏn

Boissevain, *f.n.,* 'bwazivein, bwaázēvayn

Boissier, *f.n.,* 'boisjər, bóyss-yĕr

Boivie, *f.n.,* 'beivi, báyvi

Bojen, *f.n.,* 'boiən, bóy-ĕn

Bolam, *f.n.,* 'boulǝm, bőlăm

Bolam *Northd.,* 'boulǝm, bőlăm

Boland, *f.n.,* 'boulǝnd, bőlănd

Bolas Magna, *also called* **Great Bolas,** *Salop,* 'boulǝs 'mægnǝ, bőlăss mágnă

Boldon *Tyne & Wear,* 'bouldǝn, bőldŏn

Boldre, *f.n.,* 'bouldǝr, bőldĕr

Boldre *Hants,* 'bouldǝr, bőldĕr

Boleat, *f.n.,* 'bouliat, bŏli-ăt

Bolenowe *Cornwall,* bǝ'lenou, bŏlénnŏ

Boleskine *H'land,* bɒ'leskin, boléskin

Boleyn, *f.n.,* bǝ'lin, bōlín; 'bulin, bōolin; bu'lin, bōoleén. *The first two are most popularly associated with Anne ~.*

Bolger, *f.n.,* 'bɒldʒǝr, bóljĕr

Bolingbroke and St. John, Viscount, 'bulinbruk ǝnd 'sindʒǝn, bŏolingbrŏok ănd sínjŏn

Bolingey *Cornwall* bǝ'lindʒi, bŏlínji

Bolitho, *f.n.,* bǝ'laiθou, bŏlíthō

Bolitho *Cornwall,* bǝ'laiθou, bŏlíthō

Bollin, River, *Ches.,* 'bɒlin, bóllin

Bollinger, *f.n.,* 'bɒlindʒǝr, bóllinjĕr

Bollingham *H. & W.,* 'bɒlindʒǝm, bóllinjăm; 'bɒliŋǝm, bólling-ăm

Bolloten, *f.n.,* 'bɒlǝtǝn, bóllŏtĕn

Bolney *W. Sussex,* 'boulni, bőlni; 'bouni, bőni

Bolnhurst *Beds.,* 'bounhǝrst, bőn-hurst

Bols, *f.n.,* boulz, bōlz

Bolsover, *f.n.,* 'bɒlsouvǝr, bólssōvĕr

Bolsover *Derby.,* 'boulzouvǝr, bőlzōvĕr

Bolster, *f.n.,* 'boulstǝr, bőlsstĕr

Bolton by Bowland *Lancs.,* 'boultǝn bai 'bɒlǝnd, bőltŏn bī bólländ; 'boultǝn bai 'boulǝnd, bőltŏn bī bőländ

Boltz, *f.n.,* boults, bōlts

Bolventor *Cornwall,* bɒl'ventǝr, bolvéntŏr

Bomberg, *f.n.,* 'bɒmbǝrg, bómberg

Bomere Heath *Salop,* 'boumiǝr 'hiθ, bőmeer héeth

Bompas, *f.n.,* 'bʌmpǝs, búmpăss

Bonallack, *f.n.,* bǝ'nælǝk, bŏnálăk

Bonaly *Lothian,* bǝ'næli, bŏnáli

Bonar, *f.n.,* 'bɒnǝr, bónnăr; 'bounǝr, bőnăr. *The second is appropriate for the ~ Professorship of International Economics in the University of Glasgow.*

Bonar Bridge *H'land,* 'bounǝr 'bridʒ, bőnăr bríj; 'bɒnǝr 'bridʒ, bónnăr bríj

Bonarjee, *f.n.,* 'bɒnǝrdʒi, bónnărji

Bonavia, *f.n.,* ,bɒnǝ'viǝ, bonnăvée-ă

Bonawe *S'clyde,* bɒ'nɔ, bonnáw

Boncath *Dyfed,* 'bɒŋkæθ, bónkath

Bondi, *f.n.,* 'bɒndi, bóndi

Bonell, *f.n.,* bǝ'nel, bŏnéll

Bo'ness *Central,* bou'nes, bōnéss

Bonett, *f.n.,* 'bɒnit, bónnĕt

Boney, *f.n.,* 'bʌni, búnni

Bonifazi, *f.n.,* ,bɒni'fætsi, bonnifátsi

Boningale *Salop,* 'bɒniŋgeil, bónning-gayl

Bonkle *S'clyde,* 'bʌŋkl, búnkl

Bonkyl *Borders,* 'bɒŋkl, bónkl

Bonnamy, *f.n.,* 'bɒnǝmi, bónnămi

Bonnetard, *f.n.,* 'bɒnitard, bónnĕtaard

Bonnett, *f.n.,* 'bɒnit, bónnĕt

Bonney, *f.n.,* 'bɒni, bónni

Bonome, *f.n.,* 'bɒnǝm, bónnŏm

Bonong, *f.n.,* bǝ'nɒŋ, bŏnóng

Bonskeid *Tayside,* bɒn'skid, bonsskéed

Bonsor, *f.n.,* 'bɒnsǝr, bónssŏr

Bontddu *Gwynedd,* bɒnt'ði, bont-thée

Bontine, *f.n.,* bɒn'tin, bonteén; 'bɒntin, bóntin

Bont-newydd *Clwyd,* bɒnt'newið, bont-né-with

Bontnewydd *Dyfed, Gwynedd,* bɒnt'newið, bontné-with

Bonvilston *S. Glam.,* 'bɒnvilstǝn, bónvilstŏn; 'boulstǝn, bőlsstŏn

Bonwick, *f.n.*, 'bɒnwɪk, bónwick
Bonwit, *f.n.*, 'bɒnwɪt, bónwit
Bonymaen *W. Glam.*, ˌboʊnə-
  'maɪn, bōnămín
Bonynge, *f.n.*, 'bɒnɪŋ, bónning
Bonython, *f.n.*, bɒ'naɪðən,
  bonníthŏn
Boobbyer, *f.n.*, bu'baɪər, boobí-ĕr
Boobyer, *f.n.*, 'bubjər, boʻob-yĕr
Boodle, *f.n.*, 'budl, boʻodl
Boodle's Club *London*, 'budlz,
  boʻodlz
Bookham *Surrey*, 'bʊkəm,
  boʻokăm
Boord, *f.n.* bɔrd, bord
Boorde, *f.n.*, buərd, boʻord
Booroff, *f.n.*, 'buərɒf, boʻoroff
Boosbeck *Cleveland*, 'buzbek,
  boʻozbeck
Boosey, *f.n.*, 'buzɪ, boʻozi
Boost, *f.n.*, bust, boost
Booth, *f.n.*, buð, booth
Bootham *N. Yorks.*, 'buðəm,
  boʻothăm
Boothby, Baron, 'buðbɪ, boʻothbi
Boothman, *f.n.*, 'buðmən,
  boʻothmăn
Boothroyd, *f.n.*, 'buθrɔɪd,
  boʻothroyd; 'buðrɔɪd,
  boʻothroyd
Bootle *Cumbria, Merseyside*,
  'butl, boʻotl
Bootle-Wilbraham, *f.n.*, 'butl
  'wɪlbrəm, boʻotl wílbrăm.
  *Family name of Baron
  Skelmersdale.*
Booy, *f.n.*, bɔɪ, boy
Boquhanran *S'clyde*, boʊ-
  'hwænrən, bō-whánrăn;
  boʊ'hwɒnrən, bō-whónrăn;
  boʊ'hænrən, bō-hánrăn
Boreel, *f.n.*, bɒ'reɪl, borráyl
Boreham, *f.n.*, 'bɔrəm, báwrăm
Borenius, *f.n.*, bə'rɪnɪəs, bŏrée-
  niŭss
Boreray *Two islands in W. Isles*,
  'bɒrərə, bórrĕră
Borestone *Central*, bɔr'stoʊn,
  bór-stŏn
Borgue *D. & G.*, *H'land*, bɔrg,
  borg
Borlase, *f.n.*, 'bɔrleɪs, bórlayss
Borocourt Hospital *Berks.*,
  'bʌrəkɔrt, búrrŏkort
Borodale, Viscount, 'bɒrədeɪl,
  bórrŏdayl
Borrego, *f.n.*, bə'rigoʊ, bŏreégō
Borrell, *f.n.*, bə'rel, bŏréll
Borreraig *I. of Skye*, 'brəreɪg,
  bórrĕrayg
Borrett, *f.n.*, 'bɒrɪt, bórrĕt; bə'ret,
  bŏrétt
Borrowash *Derby.*, 'bɒroʊwɒʃ,
  bórrō-wosh

Borrowes, *f.n.*, 'bʌroʊz, búrrōz
Borrows, *f.n.*, 'bɒroʊz, bórrōz
Borth *Dyfed*, bɔrθ, borth
Borthwick, *f.n.*, 'bɔrθwɪk,
  bórthwick
Borth-y-gest *Gwynedd*, ˌbɔrθ ə
  'gest, borth ă gést
Borve *W. Isles*, bɔrv, borv
Borwick, *f.n.*, 'bɒrɪk, bórrick.
  Appropriate also for Baron ~.
Borwick *Lancs.*, 'bɒrɪk, bórrick
Bosahan *Cornwall*, bə'seɪn,
  bŏssáyn
Bosanquet, *f.n.*, 'boʊzənket,
  bŏ́zănket
Boscastle *Cornwall*, 'bɒskɑsl,
  bósskaassl; 'bɒskæsl, bósskassl
Boscaswell, Higher *and* Lower,
  Cornwall, bəs'kæzwəl, bŏss-
  kázwĕl
Boscawen, *f.n.*, bɒs'koʊən,
  boskó-ĕn; bəs'koʊən, boskó-ĕn;
  bɒs'kɔən, boskáw-ĕn. *The first
  is the pronunciation of Viscount
  Falmouth's family name.*
Boscobel *Salop*, 'bɒskəbel,
  bóskŏbel. *Appropriate also for*
  ~ *House, where Charles II hid
  after the Battle of Worcester.*
Bose, *f.n.*, boʊz, bōz
Bosfranken *Cornwall*, bəs'fræŋkən,
  bŏsfránkĕn
Bosham *W. Sussex*, 'bɒzəm,
  bózzăm
Boshell, *f.n.*, 'boʊʃl, bŏ́shl
Bosher, *f.n.*, 'boʊʃər, bŏ́shĕr
Boshier, *f.n.*, 'boʊʃər, bŏ́shĕr
Bosisto, *f.n.*, bə'sɪstoʊ, bŏsíssto
Bosistow *Cornwall*, bə'sɪstoʊ,
  bŏssístō
Boskenwin *Cornwall*, bəs'kenwɪn,
  bŏsskénwin
Bosleake *Cornwall*, bəs'lik,
  bŏssléek
Bosley, *f.n.*, 'bɒzlɪ, bózli; 'bɒslɪ,
  bóssli
Bossiney *Cornwall*, bə'sɪnɪ,
  bŏssínni
Bossom, *f.n.*, 'bɒsəm, bóssŏm.
  *Appropriate also for the
  Barony of* ~.
Boston *Lincs.*, 'bɒstən, bósstŏn
Bosullow *Cornwall*, bə'sʌloʊ,
  bŏssúllō
Boswall, *f.n.*, 'bɒzwəl, bózwăl
Boswell of Auchinleck, 'bɒzwəl
  əv 'æflek, bózwĕl ŏv ǎffleck
Bosworth *Leics.*, 'bɒzwərθ,
  bózwŭrth
Boteler, *f.n.*, 'boʊtlər, bŏ́tlĕr
Botetourt, Baron, 'bɒtɪtɔrt,
  bóttĕtort
Botham, *f.n.*, 'bɒθəm, bóthăm;
  'boʊθəm, bŏ́thăm

Bothamsall *Notts.*, 'bɒðəmsɔl, bóthămssawl

Bothel and Threapland *Cumbria*, 'bɒθl ənd 'θriplənd, bóthl ănd thréeplănd

Bothenhampton *Dorset*, ˌbɒθən-'hæmptən, bothĕn-hámptŏn

Bothnagowan *Grampian*, ˌbɒθnə-'gaʊən, bothnăgów-ăn. *Old name of* **Pitgaveny**, *q.v.*

Bothwell *S'clyde*, 'bɒθwəl, bóthwĕl; 'bɒðwəl, bóthwĕl. *Both are used for the Earl of ~, third husband of Mary, Queen of Scots.*

Bothwellhaugh *S'clyde*, 'bɒðwəl-'hɒx, bóthwĕlhóch

Botley *Hants*, 'bɒtlɪ, bóttli

Botolph, saint, 'bɒtɒlf, bóttolf

Botreaux, Barony of, bə'truː, bŏtró

Botriphnie *Grampian*, bou'trɪfnɪ, bōtrífni

Botterill, *f.n.*, 'bɒtərɪl, bóttĕril

Bottesford *Humberside*, *Leics.*, 'bɒtɪsfərd, bóttĕssfŏrd

Bottisham *Cambs.*, 'bɒtɪʃəm, bótti-shăm

Bottome, Phyllis, *author*, bə'toʊm, bŏtóm

Bottrall, *f.n.*, 'bɒtrəl, bótrăl

Bottwnnog, *Gwynedd*, *see* **Bottwnnog**

Bottwnog, *also spelt* **Bottwnnog**, **Botwnog**, *Gwynedd*, bɒ'tʊnɒg, bottŏŏnog

Botwnnog, *Gwynedd*, *see* **Bottwnog**

Boty, *f.n.*, 'boʊtɪ, bóti

Bouch, Sir Thomas, *19th-c. civil engineer*, baʊtʃ, bowtch

Boucher, *f.n.*, 'baʊtʃər, bówtchĕr

Bouchier, *f.n.*, 'baʊtʃər, bówtchĕr; 'buʃɪeɪ, bóoshi-ay. *The second is appropriate for Chili ~, film actress.*

Boucicault, **Dion**, *actor-manager*, 'daɪən 'busɪkoʊ, dí-ŏn bóossikō

Boucock, *f.n.*, 'boʊkɒk, bókock

Boud, *f.n.*, baʊd, bowd

Boudicca, queen of the **Iceni** (*q.v.*), 'budɪkə, bóodickă; boʊ'dɪkə, bōdickă. *Another form is* **Boadicea**, *q.v.*

Bough, *f.n.*, bɒf, boff

Boughey, *f.n.*, 'boʊɪ, bó-i

Boughrood *Powys*, 'bɒxrud, bóchrood

Boughton, *f.n.*, 'baʊtən, bówtŏn; 'bɒtən, báwtŏn. *The first is appropriate for Rutland ~, the composer.*

Boughton *Cambs.*, *Northants.*, 'baʊtən, bówtŏn

Boughton *Ches.*, *Kent*, 'bɒtən, báwtŏn

Boughton *Notts.*, 'butən, bóotŏn; 'baʊtən, bówtŏn

Boughton Aluph *Kent*, 'bɒtən 'æləf, báwtŏn álŭf

Boughton Malherbe *Kent*, 'bɒtən 'mælərbɪ, báwtŏn málĕrbi

Boughton Monchelsea *Kent*, 'bɒtən 'mʌntʃlsɪ, báwtŏn múntchlssi

Bould, *f.n.*, boʊld, bōld

Boulge *Suffolk*, buldʒ, boolj; bouldʒ, bŏlj

Boulmer *Northd.*, 'bumər, bóomĕr

Boult, *f.n.*, boʊlt, bōlt. *Appropriate for Sir Adrian ~, conductor.*

Boulter, *f.n.*, 'boʊltər, bṓltĕr

Boultham *Lincs.*, 'butəm, bóotăm

Boulton, *f.n.*, 'boʊltən, bóltŏn

Boulton *Derby.*, 'boʊltən, bóltŏn

Boumphrey, *f.n.*, 'bʌmfrɪ, búmfri

Boundstone *Surrey*, 'baʊndstoʊn, bówndstŏn

Bouquet, *f.n.*, bu'keɪ, bŏŏkáy

Bourchier, *f.n.*, 'baʊtʃər, bówtchĕr

Bourdeaux, *f.n.*, bɔr'doʊ, bordó

Bourdillon, *f.n.*, bɔr'dɪlən, bordíl-lŏn; bɔr'dɪljən, bordíl-yŏn; bɑr'dɪljən, bŭrdíl-yŏn. *The first is appropriate for Tom ~, mountaineer.*

Bourgeois, *f.n.*, 'buərʒwɑ, bŏŏrzhwaa

Bourke, *f.n.*, bɜrk, burk. *Appropriate for the family name of the Earl of Mayo.*

Bourlet, *f.n.*, 'buərleɪ, bŏŏrlay; 'buərlet, bŏŏrlet

Bourn *Cambs.*, bɔrn, born

Bourne, *f.n.*, bɔrn, born; buərn, bŏŏrn; bɜrn, burn

Bournville *W. Midlands*, 'bɔrnvɪl, bórnvil

Bourtie *Grampian*, 'buərtɪ, bŏŏrti

Bourton, *f.n.*, 'bɔrtən, bórtŏn

Bourton, *Avon*, *Bucks.*, *Dorset*, *Oxon.*, 'bɔrtən, bórtŏn

Bourton, Great *and* Little, *Oxon.*, 'bɔrtən, bórtŏn

Bourton-on-the-Water *Glos.*, 'bɔrtən ɒn ðə 'wɔtər, bórtŏn on thē wáwtĕr

Bourtree Bush *Grampian*, 'buərtrɪ 'buʃ, bŏŏrtri bŏŏsh

Bousfield, *f.n.*, 'baʊsfɪld, bówssfeeld

Bouskell, *f.n.*, 'baʊskl, bówsskl

Boustead, *f.n.*, 'baʊstɪd, bówsstĕd

Boutal, *f.n.*, 'baʊtl, bówtl

Boutall, *f.n.,* 'baʊtl, bówtl; bu'tæl, bootál

Boutell, *f.n.,* bu'tel, bōōtéll

Boutflower, *f.n.,* 'boʊflaʊər, bóflowĕr; 'buːflaʊər, bóoflowĕr

Boutle, *f.n.,* 'buːtl, bóotl

Bouton, *f.n.,* 'buːtən, bóotŏn

Bouttell, *f.n.,* bu'tel, bōōtéll

Boutwood, *f.n.,* 'baʊtwʊd, bówt-wŏod

Bouverie, *f.n.,* 'buːvərɪ, bóovĕri

Boveney *Bucks.,* 'bʌvnɪ, búvni; 'bɒvənɪ, bóvvĕni

Bovenschen, *f.n.,* 'boʊvənʃən, bóvĕn-shĕn; boʊ'vɒnʃən, bōvón-shĕn

Boverton *S. Glam.,* 'bɒvərtən, bóvvĕrtŏn

Bovey Tracey *Devon,* 'bʌvɪ 'treɪsɪ, búvvi tráyssi

Bovingdon *Herts.,* 'bɒvɪŋdən, bóvvingdŏn

Bovinger *Essex,* 'bɒvɪndʒər, bóvvinjĕr

Bovington *Dorset,* 'bɒvɪŋtən, bóvvingtŏn

Bovis, *f.n.,* 'boʊvɪs, bóviss

Bow *Cumbria, Devon, London,* boʊ, bō. *Appropriate for both places of the name in Devon.*

Bowater, *f.n.,* 'boʊwɔtər, bó-wawtĕr

Bowbeck *Suffolk,* 'boʊbek, bóbeck

Bowd *Devon,* baʊd, bowd

Bowden, *f.n.,* 'boʊdən, bódĕn; 'baʊdən, bówdĕn. *The first is appropriate for Baron ~, the second for the family name of Baron Aylestone.*

Bowden *Borders, Devon,* 'baʊdən, bówdĕn

Bowden, *Great and Little, Leics.,* 'baʊdən, bówdĕn

Bowder Stone *Cumbria,* 'baʊdər stoʊn, bówdĕr stōn

Bowditch, *f.n.,* 'baʊdɪtʃ, bówditch

Bowdon, *f.n.,* 'boʊdən, bódŏn

Bowdon *Gtr. M'chester,* 'boʊdən, bódŏn

Bowe, *f.n.,* boʊ, bō

Bowen, *f.n.,* 'boʊɪn, bó-ĕn

Bower, *f.n.,* 'baʊər, bówĕr

Bowerchalke *Wilts.,* 'baʊərtʃɔk, bówĕrtchawk

Bowerman, *f.n.,* 'baʊərmən, bówĕrmăn

Bowers, *f.n.,* 'baʊərz, bówĕrz

Bowers Gifford *Essex,* 'baʊərz 'gɪfərd, bówĕrz giffŏrd

Bowes, *f.n.,* boʊz, bōz

Bowes *Durham,* boʊz, bōz

Bowes-Lyon, *f.n.,* 'boʊz 'laɪən,

boz lī-ŏn. *Family name of the Earl of Strathmore.*

Bowes Park *London,* 'boʊz 'pɑrk, bōz paark

Bowett, *f.n.,* 'baʊɪt, bówĕt

Bow Fell *Cumbria,* 'boʊ 'fel, bó féll

Bowhill, *f.n.,* 'boʊhɪl, bó-hil

Bowie, *f.n.,* 'baʊɪ, bów-i; 'boʊɪ, bó-i. *The second is appropriate for David ~, singer.*

Bowker, *f.n.,* 'baʊkər, bówkĕr

Bowlby, *f.n.,* 'boʊlbɪ, bólbi

Bowlee *Gtr. M'chester,* boʊ'liː, bōléé

Bowles, *f.n.,* boʊlz, bōlz

Bowley, *f.n.,* 'boʊlɪ, bóli

Bowling *S'clyde, W. Yorks.,* 'boʊlɪŋ, bóling

Bowlly, *f.n.,* 'boʊlɪ, bóli

Bowman, *f.n.,* 'boʊmən, bómăn

Bowmore *S'clyde,* 'boʊ'mɔr, bó-mór

Bown, *f.n.,* baʊn, bown

Bownas, *f.n.,* 'boʊnəs, bónăss

Bowness, *f.n.,* boʊ'nes, bōnéss

Bowness *Cumbria,* boʊ'nes, bōnéss. *Appropriate for all localities of this name in Cumbria.*

Bow of Fife *Fife,* 'baʊ əv 'faɪf, bów ŏv fíf

Bowood *Wilts.,* 'boʊwʊd, bó-wŏod

Bowra, Sir Maurice, *scholar and author,* 'baʊrə, bówră

Bowring, *f.n.,* 'baʊərɪŋ, bówring. *Appropriate also for the ~ Group of Companies, and hence for the ~ Bowl, awarded to the winners of the 'Varsity Rugby match.*

Bowser, *f.n.,* 'baʊzər, bówzĕr

Bowsher, *f.n.,* 'baʊʃər, bówshĕr

Bowskill, *f.n.,* 'boʊskɪl, bó-skill

Bow Street *Dyfed,* 'boʊ strit, bó street

Bowtell, *f.n.,* boʊ'tel, bōtéll

Bowyer, *f.n.,* 'boʊjər, bó-yĕr

Bowyer Tower, *Tower of London,* 'boʊjər, bó-yĕr

Boyagis, *f.n.,* 'bɔɪədʒɪs, bóy-ăjiss

Boyars, *f.n.,* 'bɔɪərz, bóy-ărz

Boycott, *f.n.,* 'bɔɪkɒt, bóykott

Boydell, *f.n.,* bɔɪ'del, boydéll

Boyd-Orr, Barony of, 'bɔɪd 'ɔr, bóyd ór

Boyer, *f.n.,* 'bɔɪər, bóy-ĕr

Boyndlie *Grampian,* 'bɔɪndlɪ, bóyndli

Boys, *f.n.,* bɔɪz, boyz

Boyson, *f.n.,* 'bɔɪsən, bóyssŏn

Boz, *pen-name of Charles Dickens,* bɒz, bozz. *The English*

Pronouncing Dictionary *notes that* bouz, bōz, *the original pronunciation, is not often heard now.*
Bozeat *Northants.*, 'bouzɪæt, bōzi-at; 'bouʒət, bōʒhăt
Braaid *I. of Man*, breɪd, brayd
Braal *H'land*, brɔl, brawl
Brabant, *f.n.*, 'bræbənt, brábbănt; brə'bænt, brăbánt
Brabazon of Tara, Baron, 'bræbəzən əv 'tɑrə, brábbăzŏn ŏv taárə
Brabin, *f.n.*, 'breɪbɪn, bráybin
Brabourne *Kent*, 'breɪbɔrn, bráy-born; 'breɪbərn, bráybŭrn. *The second is appropriate for Baron* ~.
Brabrooke, *f.n.*, 'breɪbrok, bráybrŏŏk
Brabyn, *f.n.*, 'breɪbɪn, bráybin
Brabyn's Brow Canal, *Ches.*, 'bræbɪnz 'brau, brábbinz brów
Bracadale *I. of Skye*, 'brækədeɪl, bráckădayl
Bracher, *f.n.*, 'breɪtʃər, bráytchĕr
Braco *Tayside*, 'breɪkou, bráykŏ
Bracon Ash *Norfolk*, 'brækən æʃ, bráckŏn ash
Bracondale *Norfolk*, 'brækəndeɪl, bráckŏndayl
Braddell, *f.n.*, 'brædl, bráddl
Braddock, *f.n.*, 'brædək, bráddŏk
Braddock *Cornwall*, 'brædək, bráddŏk
Bradenham *Bucks.*, *Norfolk*, 'brædənəm, bráddĕnăm
Bradford, *f.n.*, 'brædfərd, brádfŏrd
Bradford *Cornwall*, *Derby.*, *Devon*, *Gtr. M'chester*, *W. Yorks.*, 'brædfərd, brádfŏrd
Bradish, *f.n.*, 'breɪdɪʃ, bráydish
Bradlaugh, *f.n.*, 'brædlɔ, brádlaw
Bradley *Ches.*, *Clwyd*, *Cumbria*, *Derby.*, *Hants*, *Humberside*, *H. & W.*, *W. Yorks.*, 'brædlɪ, brádli. *Appropriate also for* ~ *Green* (*H. & W.*), ~ *Mills* (*W. Yorks.*), *and* ~ *Mount* (*Ches.*).
Bradley *N. Yorks.*, *Staffs.*, *W. Midlands*, 'breɪdlɪ, bráydli
Bradley, **Great** *and* **Little**, *Suffolk*, 'brædlɪ, brádli
Bradley, **Great** *and* **West**, *Somerset*, 'brædlɪ, brádli
Bradley, **High** *and* **Low**, *N. Yorks.*, 'brædlɪ, brádli
Bradley, **North**, *Wilts.*, 'brædlɪ, brádli
Bradley Common *Ches.*, 'breɪdlɪ 'komən, bráydli kómmŏn
Bradley Fold *Gtr. M'chester*, 'brædlɪ 'fould, brádli fŏld

Bradley Green *H. & W.*, *Warwicks.*, 'brædlɪ 'grin, brádli gréen
Bradley in the Moors *Staffs.*, 'brædlɪ ɪn ðə 'muərz, brádli in thĕ mŏŏrz
Bradmore *W. Midlands*, 'brædmər, brádmor
Bradninch *Devon*, 'brædnɪntʃ, brádnintch
Bradsell, *f.n.*, 'brædzl, brádzl
Brady, *f.n.*, 'breɪdɪ, bráydi
Braefoot Bay *Fife*, 'breɪfot, bráyfŏŏt
Braemar *Grampian*, breɪ'mɑr, braymaár
Braeriach *Grampian-Highland border*, breɪ'rɪəx, bray-rée-ăch
Brafield *Northants.*, 'breɪfɪld, bráyfeeld
Braham, *f.n.*, 'breɪəm, bráy-ăm
Brahams, *f.n.*, 'breɪəmz, bráy-ămz
Brahan, *f.n.*, brɔn, brawn
Brahan Castle *H'land*, brɑn, braan. *Appropriate also for the* ~ *Seer, Scottish soothsayer: see* **Coinneach Odhar.**
Braich-y-Pwll *Gwynedd*, ˌbraɪx ə 'puɬ, brĭch ă póohl
Braid, *f.n.*, breɪd, brayd
Brainin, Norbert, *violinist*, 'nɔrbərt 'braɪnɪn, nórbĕrt brínin
Brainshaugh *Northd.*, 'breɪnzhɑf, bráynz-haaf
Braishfield *Hants*, 'breɪʃfɪld, bráysh-feeld
Braithwaite, *f.n.*, 'breɪθweɪt, bráythwayt
Braithwell *S. Yorks.*, 'breɪθwel, bráythwel
Bramah, Ernest, *19th–20th-c. author*, 'bramə, braámă
Bramah, Joseph, *18th–19th-c. inventor*, 'bræmə, brámmă; 'bramə, braámă
Bramall, *f.n.*, 'bræmɔl, brámawl
Brambletye *E. Sussex*, 'bræmbltaɪ, brámbltī
Bramcote *Notts.*, *Warwicks.*, 'bræmkət, brámkŏt
Bramerton *Norfolk*, 'bræmərtən, brámmĕrtŏn
Bramford *Suffolk*, 'bramfərd, braámförd
Bramhall *Gtr. M'chester*, 'bræmhɔl, brám-hawl
Bramham *W. Yorks.*, 'bræməm, brám-măm
Bramhope *W. Yorks.*, 'bræm-houp, brám-hŏp
Bramley *Derby.*, *S. Yorks.*, *W. Yorks.*, 'bræmlɪ, brámli
Brammall, *f.n.*, 'bræml, brámml

Brampton *Cambs.*, 'bræmptən, brámptŏn

Bramshill *Hants*, 'bræmzhıl, brámz-hil

Brancaster Staithe *Norfolk*, 'bræŋkəstər 'steıð, bránkăstĕr stáyth

Brancepeth *Durham*, 'brɑnspəθ, braánsspĕth. *Appropriate also for Baron* ~.

Brancker, *f.n.*, 'bræŋkər, bránkĕr

Brandane, *f.n.*, bræn'deın, brandáyn

Brander, *f.n.*, 'brændər, brándĕr

Brander, Pass of, *S'clyde*, 'brændər, brándĕr

Brandeston *Suffolk*, 'brændıstən, brándĕstŏn

Brandis Corner *Devon*, 'brændıs 'kərnər, brándiss kórnĕr

Brandiston *Norfolk*, 'brændıstən, brándistŏn

Brandlesholme *Gtr. M'chester*, 'brændlzhoum, brándlz-hōm

Branfil, *f.n.*, 'brænfıl, bránn-fil

Branfill, *f.n.*, 'brænfıl, bránn-fil

Brangwyn, *f.n.*, 'bræŋgwın, bráng-gwin

Brant-Broughton *Lincs.*, 'brænt 'brutən, bránt broótŏn

Brantham *Suffolk*, 'brænθəm, brán-thăm

Brashaw, *f.n.*, 'breıʃɔ, bráy-shaw

Brasher, *f.n.*, 'breıʃər, bráyshĕr

Brass, *f.n.*, brɑs, braass

Brassey, *f.n.*, 'bræsı, brássi. *Appropriate also for Baron* ~ *of* **Apethorpe**, 'æpθɔrp, áp-thorp

Brassington, *f.n.*, 'bræsıŋtən, brássingtŏn

Brasted *Kent*, 'breıstɛd, bráyssted

Bratoft *Lincs.*, 'breıtɒft, bráytoft

Brat Tor *Devon*, 'bræt 'tɔr, brát tór

Braughing *Herts.*, 'bræfıŋ, bráffing

Braun, *f.n.*, braun, brown

Braund, *f.n.*, brɔnd, brawnd

Braunholtz, *f.n.*, 'braunhoults, brówn-hōlts

Braunstone *Leics.*, 'brɒnstən, bráwnstŏn

Braunton *Devon*, 'brɒntən, bráwntŏn

Bravington, *f.n.*, 'brævıŋtən, brávvingtŏn

Brawdy *Dyfed*, 'brɔdı, bráwdi

Brazell, *f.n.*, brə'zel, brăzéll

Brazier, *f.n.*, 'breızıər, bráyziĕr

Brazil, *f.n.*, 'bræzl, brázzl; brə'zıl, brăzíll; 'bræzıl, brázzil. *The first is appropriate for Angela* ~, *writer.*

Brea *Cornwall*, breı, bray

Breadalbane *Central–Tayside*, brı'dælbın, brĕdálbin; brı'dɔlbın, brĕdáwlbin. *The second is appropriate for the Earl of* ~.

Breadsell, *f.n.*, bred'sel, bredsséll

Breage *Cornwall*, brig, breeg

Breakell, *f.n.*, 'breıkl, bráykl

Breakey, *f.n.*, 'breıkı, bráyki

Breaks, *f.n.*, breıks, brayks

Brealey, *f.n.*, 'brıəlı, breé-ăli

Breamore *Hants*, 'bremər, brémmŏr

Brean *Somerset*, brin, breen

Brearley, *f.n.*, 'brıərlı, breérli

Breaston *Derby.*, 'brıstən, breésstŏn

Breay, *f.n.*, breı, bray

Brech, *f.n.*, brek, breck

Brechfa *Dyfed*, 'brexvə, bréchvă

Brechin, *f.n.*, 'brixın, breéchin

Brechin *Tayside*, 'brixın, breéchin

Brecknock, *f.n.*, 'breknɒk, brécknock

Brecknock, *former alternative name for* **Brecon**, *Powys*, 'breknɒk, brécknock; 'breknək, brécknŏk

Breckon, *f.n.*, 'brekən, bréckŏn

Brecon *Powys*, 'brekən, bréckŏn. *Appropriate also for Baron* ~.

Bredenbury *H. & W.*, 'bridənbərı, breédĕnbŭri

Bredin, *f.n.*, 'bridın, breédin

Bredon *H. & W.*, 'bridən, breédŏn

Bredons Hardwick *H. & W.*, 'bridənz 'hɑrdwık, breédŏnz haárdwick

Bredwardine *H. & W.*, 'bredwər'daın, bredwárdín

Breggin, *f.n.*, 'bregın, bréggin

Brehony, *f.n.*, brı'hounı, brĕ-hóni

Breich *Lothian*, brix, breech

Breidden *Powys*, 'braıðən, brí̄thĕn

Breightmet *Gtr. M'chester*, 'breıtmıt, bráytmĕt; 'braıtmıt, brí̄tmĕt

Breighton *Humberside*, 'breıtən, bráytŏn

Breinton *H. & W.*, 'breıntən, bráyntŏn

Brenack, *f.n.*, 'brenək, brénnăk

Brenard, *f.n.*, 'brenɑrd, brénnaard

Brenchley *Kent*, 'brentʃlı, bréntchli

Brenel, *f.n.*, brı'nel, brĕnéll

Brent Eleigh *Suffolk*, 'brent 'ilı, brént eéli

Brenzett *Kent*, 'brenzıt, brénzĕt

Brereton, *f.n.*, 'brɛərtən, bráirtŏn; 'brıərtən, breértŏn

Brereton *Staffs.*, 'brıərtən, breértŏn

Bresler, *f.n.*, 'brezlər, brézlĕr

Bressay *Shetland*, 'bresei, bréssay

Bretforton *H. & W.*, 'brefərtən, bréffŏrtŏn; 'bretfərtən, brét-fŏrtŏn

Brettargh Holt *Cumbria*, 'bretər 'hoult, bréttär hŏlt

Brettell, *f.n.*, brɪ'tel, brĕtéll

Brettingham-Smith, *f.n.*, 'bretɪŋ-əm 'smɪθ, brétting-ăm smíth

Brewham, North *and* South, *Somerset*, 'bruəm, broo-ăm

Brewis, *f.n.*, 'bruɪs, broo-iss

Brewood *Staffs.*, brud, brood

Breydon Water *Norfolk*, 'breɪdən 'wɔtər, bráydŏn wáwtĕr

Brian, Havergal, *composer*, 'hævərgəl 'braɪən, hávvĕrgăl brí-ăn

Briault, *f.n.*, 'brioʊ, brée-ō

Bricett, Great *and* Little, *Suffolk*, 'braɪsɪt, brísset

Brickell, *f.n.*, brɪ'kel, brickéll

Bricusse, *f.n.*, 'brɪkəs, bríckŭss

Bridburg, *f.n.*, 'brɪdbərg, brídburg

Bridell *Dyfed*, 'brɪdeł, bríddehl

Bridestowe *Devon*, 'brɪdɪstoʊ, bríddĕstō; 'brɪstoʊ, brístō

Bridgend *Cornwall, S'clyde*, 'brɪdʒend, bríjjend

Bridgend *Cumbria, Dyfed, Mid Glam.*, brɪdʒ'end, brijjénd

Bridge of Earn *Tayside*, 'brɪdʒ əv 'ɜrn, bríj ŏv érn

Bridge of Feugh *Grampian*, 'brɪdʒ əv 'fjux, bríj ŏv féwch

Bridge of Gaur *Tayside*, 'brɪdʒ əv 'gɔr, bríj ŏv gór

Bridge of Orchy *S'clyde*, 'brɪdʒ əv 'ɔrxɪ, bríj ŏv órchi

Bridge of Weir *S'clyde*, 'brɪdʒ əv 'wɪər, bríj ŏv weér

Bridger, *f.n.*, 'brɪdʒər, bríjjĕr

Bridgette, *f.n.*, brɪ'dʒet, brijét

Bridgnorth *Salop*, 'brɪdʒnɔrθ, bríj-north

Bridgwater *Somerset*, 'brɪdʒ-wɔtər, bríj-wawtĕr

Bridie, James, *author*, 'braɪdɪ, brídi. *Pen name of Dr O. H. Mavor.*

Bridlington *Humberside*, 'brɪd-lɪŋtən, brídlingtŏn

Bridport *Dorset*, 'brɪdpɔrt, bríd-port

Bridson, *f.n.*, 'braɪdsən, brídssŏn

Bridstow *H. & W.*, 'brɪdstoʊ, brídstō

Briege, *Irish C.n.*, briʒ, breezh

Brien, *f.n.*, 'braɪən, brí-ĕn

Brierley, *f.n.*, 'braɪərlɪ, brí-ĕrli; 'brɪərlɪ, breérli

Brierley *S. Yorks.*, 'braɪərlɪ, brí-ĕrli; 'brɪərlɪ, breérli

Brierley Hill *W. Midlands*, 'braɪərlɪ 'hɪl, brí-ĕrli híll

Brierly, *f.n.*, 'braɪərlɪ, brí-ĕrli

Briers, *f.n.*, 'braɪərz, brí-ĕrz

Brigginshaw, *f.n.*, 'brɪgɪnʃɔ, bríggin-shaw

Brighouse *W. Yorks.*, 'brɪghaʊs, bríg-howss

Brighstone *I. of Wight*, 'braɪstən, brísstŏn

Brightholmlee *S. Yorks.*, 'braɪ-təmh, brítŏmli

Brightling *E. Sussex*, 'braɪtlɪŋ, brítling

Brightlingsea *Essex*, 'braɪtlɪŋsi, brítlingssee

Brighton *Cornwall, E. Sussex*, 'braɪtən, brítŏn

Briginshaw, *f.n.*, 'brɪgɪnʃɔ, bríggin-shaw

Brigstock *Northants.*, 'brɪgstɒk, brig-stock

Briley, *f.n.*, 'braɪlɪ, bríli

Brilles, *f.n.*, 'brɪlɪs, bríllĕss

Brimacombe, *f.n.*, 'brɪməkum, brímmăkoom

Brimblecombe, *f.n.*, 'brɪmbl-koum, brímblkōm

Brimelow, *f.n.*, 'brɪmɪloʊ, brímmēlō. *Appropriate also for Baron ~.*

Brimicombe, *f.n.*, 'brɪmɪkəm, brímmikŏm

Brimilow, *f.n.*, 'brɪmɪloʊ, brímmilō

Brind, *f.n.*, brɪnd, brind

Bringsty *H. & W.*, 'brɪŋstɪ, bringsti

Brinkheugh *Northd.*, 'brɪŋkhjuf, brínk-hewf

Brinscall *Lancs.*, 'brɪnskl, brínsskl

Brinsea *Avon*, 'brɪnzɪ, brínzi

Brio, *f.n.*, 'brioʊ, brée-ō

Briody, *f.n.*, 'braɪədɪ, brí-ŏdi

Brisby, *f.n.*, 'brɪzbɪ, brízbi

Brisco, *f.n.*, 'brɪskoʊ, brískō

Briscoe, *f.n.*, 'brɪskoʊ, brískō

Bristol *Avon*, 'brɪstl, brísstl

Bristolian, *native of Bristol*, brɪs-'toʊlɪən, bristṓli·ăn

Brithdir *Gwynedd, Mid Glam.*, 'brɪθdɪər, bríthdeer

Briton Ferry *W. Glam.*, 'brɪtən 'ferɪ, bríttŏn férri

Britten, *f.n.*, 'brɪtən, bríttĕn

Britwell Salome *Oxon.* 'brɪtwəl 'sæləm, brítwĕl sálóm

Brize Norton *Oxon.*, 'braɪz 'nɔrtən, bríz nórtŏn

Broadbridge, *f.n.*, 'brɔdbrɪdʒ, bráwdbrij

Broad Chalke *Wilts.* 'brɔd tʃɔk, bráwd chawk

Broadclyst *Devon* 'brɔdklıst, bráwdklist

Broad Halfpenny Down *Hambledon (Hants)*, 'brɔd 'hafpenı 'daʊn, bráwd haáfpenni dówn

Broadhembury *Devon*, brɔd-'hembərı, brawdhémbŭri

Broadis, *f.n.*, 'brɔdıs, bráwdiss

Broadmoor *Berks.*, 'brɔdmʊər, bráwd-mōōr

Broadstairs *Kent*, 'brɔdstɛərz, bráwd-stairz

Broadwas *H. & W.*, 'brɔdwəs, bráwd-wăss

Broadwoodwidger *Devon*, 'brɔdwʊd'wıdʒər, bráwdwŏŏd-wíjĕr

Broady, *f.n.*, 'broʊdı, brŏdi

Brocas, Viscount, 'brɒkəs, bróckăss

Brocklebank-Fowler, *f.n.*, 'brɒklbæŋk 'faʊlər, brócklbank fówlĕr

Broderick, *f.n.*, 'brɒdərık, bróddĕrik

Broderip, *f.n.*, 'brɒdrıp, bródrip

Brodgar, Ring of, *Orkney*, 'brɒdgər, bród-gär

Brodick *S'clyde*, 'brɒdık, bróddik

Brodie, *f.n.*, 'broʊdı, brŏdi

Brodrick, *f.n.*, 'brɒdrık, bródrik

Broe, *f.n.*, broʊ, brŏ

Brogan, *f.n.*, 'broʊgən, brŏgän

Brogyntyn *Salop* brɒ'gʌntın, broggúntin

Broke, *f.n.*, brʊk, brŏōk

Bromborough *Merseyside*, 'brɒmbərə, brómbŭră

Brome, *f.n.*, broʊm, brŏm

Brome *Suffolk*, brum, broom

Bromet, *f.n.*, 'brɒmıt, brómmĕt

Bromford *W. Midlands*, 'brɒmfərd, brómfŏrd

Bromham *Beds.*, 'brɒməm, brómmăm

Bromham *Wilts.*, 'brʌməm, brúmmăm

Bromhead, *f.n.*, 'brʌmhed, brúm-hed

Bromholm *Norfolk*, 'brʊmhoʊm, brŏōm-hōm

Bromley, *f.n.*, 'brʌmlı, brúmli; 'brɒmlı, brómli

Bromley *London*, 'brɒmlı, brómli. *The old pronunciation,* 'brʌmlı, *brúmli, seems to have succumbed completely to the spelling pronunciation.*

Bromley *S. Yorks., W. Midlands*, brɒmlı, brómli

Bromley, Great *and* Little, *Essex*, 'brɒmlı, brómli

Bromley Cross *Gtr. M'chester*, 'brɒmlı 'krɒs, brómli króss

Brompton *Kent*, 'brɒmptən, brómptŏn

Brompton Ralph *Somerset*, 'brɒmptən 'rælf, brómptŏn rálf

Bromsgrove *H. & W.*, 'brɒmzgroʊv, brómzgrŏv

Bromwich *see* **West Bromwich**

Bromyard *H. & W.*, 'brɒmjərd, bróm-yaard; 'brɒmjərd, bróm-yärd

Bronach, saint, 'broʊnəx, brŏnă**ch**

Bronant *Dyfed*, 'brɒnənt, brón-nänt

Brongwendraeth *Dyfed*, brɒn-'gwendraıθ, bron-gwéndrīth

Brongwyn *Dyfed*, 'brɒngwın, brón-gwin

Bronllys *Powys*, 'brɒnɬıs, brón--**h**leess

Brontë, *f.n.*, 'brɒntı, brónti. *Appropriate for authors Charlotte, Anne, and Emily ∼, and their brother Branwell ∼.*

Bronwen, *Welsh C.n.*, 'brɒnwen, brónwen

Bronydd *Powys*, 'brɒnıð, brón-ni**th**

Bron-y-Foel *Gwynedd*, ˌbrɒnə'vɔıl, bronnävóyl

Brooke of Ystradfellte, Baroness, 'brʊk əv ˌʌstrəd'veɪteɪ, brŏŏk ŏv ussträd-véhltay

Brookes, *f.n.*, brʊks, brŏŏks

Brookholding, *f.n.*, 'brʊkhoʊldıŋ, brŏŏkhŏlding

Broom, Loch, *H'land*, 'brum, brŏom

Broome, *f.n.*, brum, broom

Broomhead, *f.n.*, 'brumhed, brŏom-hed

Broomieknowe *Lothian*, ˌbrumı-'naʊ, broominów

Brophy, *f.n.*, 'broʊfı, brŏfi

Brora *H'land*, 'brɔrə, bráwră

Broseley *Salop*, 'broʊzlı, brŏzli

Brotchie, *f.n.*, 'brɒtʃı, brótchi

Brotherton, *f.n.*, 'brʌðərtən, brú**th**ĕrtŏn

Brough, *f.n.*, brʌf, bruff

Brough *Cumbria, Humberside*, brʌf, bruff

Brough *H'land*, brɒx, bro**ch**

Broughall, *f.n.*, 'braʊəl, brów-ăl

Broughall *Salop*, 'brɒfl, bróffl

Brougham, *f.n.*, brum, brŏōm; 'broʊəm, brŏ-ăm; 'bruəm, broo-ăm; broom, brŏm

Brougham *Cumbria*, brum, broom; brɒm, brawm

Brougham and Vaux, Baron, 'brum ənd 'vɒks, brŏŏm ănd váwks

Brougher Mountain *Co. Fermanagh*, 'brɔxər, bráwchĕr
Broughshane *Co. Antrim*, brə'ʃeɪn, brŏ-sháyn. *Appropriate also for Baron ~.*
Broughton, *f.n.*, 'brɔtən, bráwtŏn; 'braʊtən, brówtŏn. *The first is appropriate for Baron Fairhaven's family name.*
Broughton *Borders, Clwyd, Cumbria, Hants, Humberside, Lancs., Lincs., Oxon., Salop, Staffs.*, 'brɔtən, bráwtŏn
Broughton *Northants.*, 'braʊtən, brówtŏn
Broughton *Mid Glam.*, 'brʌftən, brúfftŏn
Broughton Bay *W. Glam.*, 'brʌftən, brúfftŏn
Broughton Gifford *Wilts.*, 'brɔtən 'gɪfərd, bráwtŏn gífförd; 'brɔtən 'dʒɪfərd, bráwtŏn jífförd
Broughty Ferry *Tayside*, 'brɔtɪ 'ferɪ, bráwti férri
Brough-under-Stainmore *Cumbria*, 'brʌf ʌndər 'steɪnmɔr, brúff úndĕr stáynmor. *More simply* **Brough.**
Browell, *f.n.*, 'braʊəl, brówĕl
Browett, *f.n.*, 'broʊɪt, brŏ-ĕt
Browitt, *f.n.*, 'broʊɪt, brŏ-it
Browne, Hablot K. 'hæbloʊ 'braʊn, háblŏ brówn. *Better known as 'Phiz', fiz, fizz, illustrator of* Pickwick Papers.
Brownjohn, *f.n.*, 'braʊndʒɒn, brównjon
Broxbourne *Herts.*, 'brɒksbɔrn, bróc̄ks-born
Broxis, *f.n.*, 'brɒksɪs, bróc̄ksiss
Bruan *H'land*, 'bruən, broŏ-än
Bruar *Tayside*, 'bruər, broŏ-är
Bruce-Chwatt, *f.n.*, 'brus 'kwɒt, broŏss kwótt
Bruce-Gardyne, *f.n.*, 'brus gar'daɪn, broŏss gaardín
Bruce Lockhart, *f.n.*, 'brus 'lɒkərt, broŏss lóckärt
Bruce of Melbourne, Viscountcy of, 'brus əv 'melbərn, broŏss ŏv mélbŭrn
Bruche *Ches.*, bruʃ, broosh
Bruck, *f.n.*, brʊk, brŏŏk
Bruckheimer, *f.n.*, 'brʊkhaɪmər, brŏŏk-hīmĕr
Brudenell, Baron, 'brudənəl, broŏdĕnĕl
Bruen, *f.n.*, 'bruən, broŏ-ĕn
Bruera *Ches.*, bru'ɛərə, broŏ-áirä
Bruford, *f.n.*, 'brufərd, broŏförd
Bruisyard *Suffolk*, 'bruʒard, broŏzhaard

Brummagem, *local form of* **Birmingham,** 'brʌmədʒəm, brúmmăjĕm
Brundall *Norfolk*, 'brʌndl, brúndl
Brundrett, *f.n.*, 'brʌndrɪt, brúndrĕt
Brunel, *f.n.*, bru'nel, broŏnéll. *Appropriate for Sir Marc Isambard ~, and Isambard Kingdom ~, 18th–19th-c. civil engineers. Isambard is pronounced* 'ɪzambard, ízzämbaard.
Bruning, *f.n.*, 'brunɪŋ, broŏning
Brunner, *f.n.*, 'brʌnər, brúnnĕr
Brunt, *f.n.*, brʌnt, brunt
Bruntisfield, Baron, 'brʌntsfɪld, brúntsfeeld
Bruxner, *f.n.*, 'brʊksnər, brŏŏksnĕr
Bryce, *f.n.*, braɪs, brīss
Brychan, *Welsh C.n.*, 'brʌxən, brúchän
Brydon, *f.n.*, 'braɪdən, brídŏn
Brydone, *f.n.*, 'braɪdən, brídŏn
Bryher *I. of Scilly*, 'braɪər, brī-ĕr
Brymbo *Clwyd*, 'brɪmboʊ, brímbō; 'brʌmboʊ, brúmbō
Brymer, *f.n.*, 'braɪmər, brímĕr
Brynamman *Dyfed*, brɪn'æmən, brinámmän
Bryncethin *Mid Glam.*, brɪn'keθɪn, brin-kéthin
Bryncoch *Mid Glam., W. Glam.*, brɪn'koʊx, brin-kóc̄h
Bryncroes *Gwynedd*, brɪn'krɔɪs, brin-króyss
Bryneglwys *Clwyd*, brɪn'egluɪs, brinégloŏ-iss
Bryn Euryn *Clwyd*, brɪn 'aɪrɪn, brin írin
Brynffynon *Gwynedd*, brɪn'fʌnən, brin-fúnnŏn
Brynglas *Gwent*, brɪn'glas, brin-glaáss
Bryngwyn *Gwent*, 'brɪŋgwɪn, bríng-gwin
Brynhyfryd *W. Glam.*, brɪn'hʌvrɪd, brin-húvvrid
Bryniau *Clwyd*, 'brʌnjaɪ, brún-yī
Bryning, *f.n.*, 'braɪnɪŋ, bríning
Brynkir *Gwynedd*, 'brɪŋkɪər, brínkeer
Brynmawr *Gwent*, brɪn'maʊər, brin-mówr
Brynmenyn *Mid Glam.*, brɪn'menɪn, brin-ménnin
Bryn Pydew *Gwynedd*, 'brɪn 'pʌdju, brín púddew
Brynrefail *Gwynedd*, brɪn'revaɪl, brin-révvīl. *Appropriate for both places of the name in Gwynedd.*
Brynsiencyn *Gwynedd*, brɪn'ʃeŋkɪn, brin-shénkin
Bryony, *C.n.*, 'braɪənɪ, brí-ŏni

Buachaille Etive Mór *S'clyde*, 'buǝxeɪl 'etɪv 'mɔr, boó-ăchayl éttiv mór

Buccleuch *Borders*, bǝ'klu, bŭklóo. *Appropriate also for the Duke of* ~.

Buchan, *f.n.*, 'bʌxǝn, búchăn; 'bʌkǝn, búckăn. *The first is appropriate for John* ~, *first Baron Tweedsmuir, author and statesman.*

Buchan *Grampian*, 'bʌxǝn, búchăn. *Appropriate also for the Earl of* ~.

Buchanan, *f.n.*, bǝ'kænǝn, bŭkánnăn; bju'kænǝn, bew-kánnăn. *The first is appropriate for Professor Sir Colin* ~, *author of the* ~ *Report* (Traffic in Towns). *It is also normal Scottish usage.*

Buchell, *f.n.*, bu'ʃel, boo-shéll

Bucher, *f.n.*, 'buʃǝr, boóshĕr

Buchinch *Central*, 'bʌk'ɪnʃ, búckínsh

Buchlyvie *Central*, bʌk'laɪvɪ, bucklívi

Buckden *Cambs.*, 'bʌkdǝn, búckdĕn

Bucke, *f.n.*, bjuk, bewk

Buckeridge, *f.n.*, 'bʌkǝrɪdʒ, búckĕrij

Buckfastleigh *Devon*, 'bʌkfǝst'li, búckfaast-leé

Buckie *Grampian*, 'bʌkɪ, búcki

Buckingham *Bucks.*, 'bʌkɪŋǝm, búcking-ăm

Buckinghamshire, Earl of, 'bʌkɪŋǝmʃǝr, búcking-ămshĕr

Buckland Filleigh *Devon*, 'bʌklǝnd 'fɪlɪ, búcklănd fílli

Buckland Tout Saints *Devon*, 'bʌklǝnd 'tu 'seɪnts, búcklănd toó saynts

Bucknall, *f.n.*, 'bʌknǝl, búcknăl

Bucknall *Staffs.*, 'bʌknǝl, búcknăl

Bucknell, *f.n.*, 'bʌknǝl, búcknĕl

Buckoke, *f.n.*, 'bʌkouk, búckōk

Buddig, *Welsh C.n.*, 'bɪðɪg, bíthig

Bude *Cornwall*, bjud, bewd

Budle *Northd.*, 'bjudl, béwdl

Budleigh Salterton *Devon*, 'bʌdlɪ 'sɔltǝrtǝn, búdli sáwltĕrtǝn; 'bʌdlɪ 'sɒltǝrtǝn, búdli sóltĕrtŏn

Budock *Cornwall*, 'bjudɒk, béwdock

Bueb, *f.n.*, 'bjueb, béw-eb

Buerk, *f.n.*, bɜrk, burk

Buerton *Ches.*, 'bjuǝrtǝn, béwĕrtŏn

Buesst, *f.n.*, bjust, bewsst

Buggé, *f.n.*, 'bugeɪ, boógay

Buggs, *f.n.*, bjugz, bewgz; bʌgz, buggz

Bught Park *Inverness*, bʌxt, bucht

Bugle *Cornwall*, 'bjugl, béwgl

Bugner, *f.n.*, 'bʌgnǝr, búgnĕr; 'bugnǝr, boógnĕr

Buick, *f.n.*, 'bjuɪk, béw-ick

Buildwas *Salop*, 'bɪldwǝs, bíld-wăss

Builth Wells *Powys*, 'bɪlθ 'welz, bílth wéllz

Buist, *f.n.*, 'bjuɪst, béw-ist; bjust, bewsst

Buittle *D. & G.*, 'bɪtl, bíttl; 'bjutl, béwtl

Bukatzsch, *f.n.*, 'bjukætʃ, béwkatch

Bukht, *f.n.*, bʌkt, buckt

Bulbarrow *Dorset*, 'bʊl'bærou, boólbárrō

Bulbrook, *f.n.*, 'bʊlbrʊk, boólbrōŏk

Bulcote *Notts.*, 'bʊlkǝt, boólkŏt

Buley, *f.n.*, 'bjulɪ, béwli

Bulkeley, *f.n.*, 'bʌlklɪ, búlkli

Bulkeley *Ches.*, 'bʌlklɪ, boókli

Bulkley, *f.n.*, 'bʌlklɪ, búlkli

Bullard, *f.n.*, 'bʊlǝrd, boólărd; 'bʊlard, boólaard

Bulleid, *f.n.*, 'bʊlid, boóleed; bu'lid, bōoleéd

Buller, *f.n.*, 'bʊlǝr, boólĕr

Bullimore, *f.n.*, 'bʊlɪmɔr, boólimor

Bullough, *f.n.*, 'bʊlǝ, boólă; 'bʊlou, boólō

Bullus, *f.n.*, 'bʊlǝs, boólŭss

Bulmer, *f.n.*, 'bʊlmǝr, boólmĕr

Bulphan *Essex*, 'bʊlvǝn, boólvăn

Bulteel, *f.n.*, 'bʊltɪl, boólteel

Bultitude, *f.n.*, 'bʌltɪtjud, búltitewd

Bulverhythe *E. Sussex*, ,bʊlvǝr-'haɪð, boólvĕr-híth

Bulwell *Notts.*, 'bʊlwǝl, boólwĕl

Bulwer, *f.n.*, 'bʊlwǝr, boólwĕr

Bulwick *Northants.*, 'bʊlɪk, boólick

Bumpus, *f.n.*, 'bʌmpǝs, búmpŭss

Bunchrew *H'land*, bʌŋ'kru, bunkróo; bǝŋ'kru, bŭnkróo

Bunessan *S'clyde*, bǝ'nesǝn, bŭnéssăn

Bungay *Suffolk*, 'bʌŋgɪ, búng-gi

Bunting, *f.n.*, 'bʌntɪŋ, búnting

Bunwell *Norfolk*, 'bʌnwǝl, búnwĕl

Buqué, *f.n.*, 'bju'keɪ, béwkáy

Burberry, *f.n.*, 'bɜrbǝrɪ, búrbĕri

Burbury, *f.n.*, 'bɜrbǝrɪ, búrbŭri

Burchard, *f.n.*, 'bɜrtʃard, búrtchaard

Burcher, *f.n.*, 'bɜrtʃǝr, búrtchĕr

Burder, *f.n.*, 'bɜrdǝr, búrdĕr

Burdett, f.n., 'bɜrdet, búrdet; bər'det, burdétt

Burdett-Coutts, Baroness, philanthropist, 'bɜrdet 'kuts, búrdet koóts

Bure, River, Norfolk, bjuǝr, byoor

Bures Essex–Suffolk border, bjuǝrz, byoorz

Burgate Suffolk, 'bɜrgeɪt, búrgayt

Burge, f.n., bɜrdʒ, burj

Burges, f.n., 'bɜrdʒɪz, búrjĕz

Burgess, f.n., 'bɜrdʒɪs, búrjĕss

Burgh, f.n., 'bʌrǝ, búrrǎ; bɜrg, burg; bǝr, bur. The first is appropriate for Baron ~.

Burgh Suffolk, bɜrg, burg

Burgh-by-Sands Cumbria, 'brʌf baɪ 'sændz, brúff bī sándz

Burgh Castle Norfolk, 'bʌrǝ 'kɑsl, búrrǎ kaássl

Burghclere Hants, 'bɜrkleǝr, búrklair. Appropriate also for the Barony of ~.

Burghead Grampian, bɜrg'hed, burg-héd

Burghersh, Baron, 'bɜrgɜrʃ, búrgersh

Burghfield Berks., 'bɜrfild, búrfeeld

Burgh Heath Surrey, 'bʌrǝ 'hiθ, búrrǎ heéth; 'bǝr 'hiθ, búr heéth

Burgh House Hampstead (London), bɜrg, burg

Burghill H. & W., bɜrg'hɪl, burg-híll

Burgh-le-Marsh Lincs., 'bʌrǝ lǝ 'mɑrʃ, búrrǎ lĕ maársh; 'bɜrlɪ 'mɑrʃ, búrli maársh

Burghley, Baron, 'bɜrlɪ, búrli

Burgh-on-Bain Lincs., 'bʌrǝ ɒn 'beɪn, búrrǎ on báyn; 'brʌf ɒn 'beɪn, brúff on báyn

Burgh St. Peter Norfolk, 'bʌrǝ snt 'pitǝr, búrrǎ sĭnt peétĕr

Burgin, f.n., 'bɜrgɪn, búrgin; 'bɜrdʒɪn, búrjin

Burgon, f.n., 'bɜrgǝn, búrgŏn

Burgoyne, f.n., 'bɜrgɔɪn, búrgoyn

Burham Kent, 'bʌrǝm, búrrǎm

Burhop, f.n., 'bʌrǝp, búrrŏp

Buriton Hants, 'berɪtǝn, bérritŏn

Burke, f.n., bɜrk, burk

Burke-Collis, f.n., 'bɜrklɪs, baárkliss; 'bɜrk 'kɒlɪs, búrk kólliss

Burkhard, f.n., 'bɜrkǝrd, búrkǎrd

Burkinshaw, f.n., 'bɜrkɪnʃɔ, búrkin-shaw

Burleigh Castle Tayside, 'bɜrlɪ, búrli

Burlingjobb Powys, ,bɜrlɪŋ'dʒɒb, burling-jóbb

Burlton, f.n., 'bɜrltǝn, búrltŏn

Burnaston Derby., 'bɜrnǝstǝn, búrnǎstŏn

Burnell, f.n., bɜr'nel, burnéll

Burneside Cumbria, 'bɜrnǝsaɪd, búrnĕssīd; 'bɜrnsaɪd, búrnssīd

Burness, f.n., bɜr'nes, burnéss

Burnet, f.n., 'bɜrnɪt, búrnĕt; bǝr'net, bŭrnétt

Burnett, f.n., 'bɜrnɪt, búrnĕt; bɜr'net, burnétt; bǝr'net, bŭrnétt

Burngullow Cornwall, bɜrn'gʌlou, burn-gúllō

Burnham Overy Staithe Norfolk, 'bɜrnǝm 'ouvǝrɪ 'steɪð, búrnǎm óvĕri stáyth

Burnhope Durham, 'bɜrnhoup, búrn-hōp

Burnish, f.n., 'bɜrnɪʃ, búrnish

Burntisland Fife, bɜrnt'aɪlǝnd, burnt-íland

Burpham Surrey, W. Sussex, 'bɜrfǝm, búrfăm

Burras, f.n., 'bʌrǝs, búrrǎss

Burrator Devon, 'bʌrǝ'tɔr, búrrǎ-tór

Burravoe Shetland, 'bʌrǝvou, búrrǎvō. Appropriate for both places of the name in Shetland.

Burray Island Orkney, 'bʌreɪ, búrray

Burrell, f.n., 'bʌrǝl, búrrĕl

Burringham Humberside, 'bʌrɪŋ-ǝm, búrring-ǎm

Burrough, f.n., 'bʌrou, búrrō; 'bʌrǝ, búrrǎ

Burroughes, f.n., 'bʌrouz, búrrōz

Burroughs, f.n., 'bʌrouz, búrrōz

Burry W. Glam., 'bʌrɪ, búrri

Burry Holmes W. Glam., 'bʌrɪ 'houmz, búrri hōmz

Burry Port Dyfed, 'bʌrɪ 'pɔrt, búrri pórt

Burscough Lancs., 'bɜrskou, búrsskō

Bursledon Hants, 'bɜrzldǝn, búrzldŏn

Burslem Staffs., 'bɜrzlǝm, búrzlĕm

Burstall, f.n., 'bɜrstɔl, búrsstawl

Burt, f.n., bɜrt, burt

Burtchaell, f.n., 'bɜrtʃl, búrtchl

Burton, f.n., 'bɜrtǝn, búrtŏn

Burton Lazars Leics., 'bɜrtǝn 'læzǝrz, búrtŏn lázzǎrz

Burton Pedwardine Lincs., 'bɜrtǝn 'pedwǝrdaɪn, búrtŏn pédwǎrdīn

Burton Pynsent Somerset, 'bɜrtǝn 'pɪnsǝnt, búrtŏn pínssĕnt

Burton upon Stather Humberside, 'bɜrtǝn ǝpɒn 'stæðǝr, búrtŏn ŭpon státhĕr

Burtonwood *Ches.*, 'bɜrtən'wʊd, búrtŏnwŏŏd
Burwardsley *Ches.*, 'bɜrwərdzlɪ, búrwărdzli
Burwarton *Salop*, 'bɜrwərtən, búrwărtŏn
Burwash *E. Sussex*, 'bɜrwɒʃ, búrwosh; 'bʌrəʃ, búrräsh
Burwasher, native of **Burwash**, 'bʌrəʃər, búrräshĕr
Burwell, *f.n.*, 'bɜrwel, búrwel; 'bɜrwəl, búrwĕl
Burwell *Cambs.*, *Lincs.*, 'bɜrwel, búrwĕl
Bury, *f.n.*, 'berɪ, bérri; 'bjʊərɪ, byŏŏri. *The first is appropriate for Viscount* ~.
Bury *Gtr. M'chester*, *W. Sussex*, 'berɪ, bérri
Bury Fen *Cambs.*, 'berɪ 'fen, bérri fén
Bury St. Edmunds *Suffolk*, 'berɪ snt 'edməndz, bérri sĭnt édmŭndz
Busby, *f.n.*, 'bʌzbɪ, búzzbi
Bushby, *f.n.*, 'bʊʃbɪ, bŏŏshbi
Bushelle, *f.n.*, bʊ'ʃel, bŏŏ-shéll
Bushnell, *f.n.*, 'bʊʃnəl, bŏŏshnĕl
Buskell, *f.n.*, 'bʌskl, bússkl
Busler, *f.n.*, 'bʌzlər, búzzlĕr
Bussell, *f.n.*, 'bʌsl, bússl
Buston, *f.n.*, 'bʌstən, bússtŏn
Busutilli, *f.n.*, ˌbʊsʊ'tɪlɪ, bŏŏssŏŏ-tílli
Busvine, *f.n.*, 'bʌzvaɪn, búzzvīn
Buszard, *f.n.*, 'bʌzərd, búzzărd
Butchart, *f.n.*, 'bʊtʃart, bŏŏ-tchaart; 'bʊtʃərt, bŏŏtchărt
Bute, *I. of*, bjut, bewt. *Appropriate also for the Marquess of* ~.
Buthlay, *f.n.*, 'bʌθleɪ, búthlay
Butler-Bowdon, *f.n.*, 'bʌtlər 'boʊdən, bútlĕr bŏdŏn. *Family name relating to the Barony of Grey de Ruthyn.*
Butley *Ches.*, *Suffolk*, 'bʌtlɪ, bútli
Butlin, *f.n.*, 'bʌtlɪn, bútlin
Buttar, *f.n.*, 'bʌtar, búttaar
Butter, *f.n.*, 'bʌtər, búttĕr
Butters, *f.n.*, 'bʌtərz, búttĕrz
Butterwick *Lincs.*, 'bʌtərwɪk, búttĕrwick
Buxhall *Suffolk*, 'bʌksɔl, búcksawl
Buzan, *f.n.*, bju'zæn, bewzán
Buzeman, *f.n.*, 'bjuzmən, béwzmän
Bwlch Gwyn *Clwyd*, bʊlx 'gwɪn, bŏŏlch gwín
Bwlchllan *Dyfed*, bʊlx'læn, bŏŏlch-hlán
Bwlch Newydd *Dyfed*, bʊlx 'newɪð, bŏŏlch né-wĭth

Bwlch-y-Cibau *Powys*, ˌbʊlxə-'kibaɪ, bŏŏlchăkéebī
Bwlchysarnau *Powys*, ˌbʊlxə-'sarnaɪ, bŏŏlchässaárnī
Bwllfa *W. Glam.*, 'bʊlvə, bŏŏhlvă
Byam, *f.n.*, 'baɪəm, bí-ăm
Byars, *f.n.*, 'baɪərz, bí-ärz
Byatt, *f.n.*, 'baɪət, bí-ăt
Bygott, *f.n.*, 'baɪɡɒt, bígott
Byham, *f.n.*, 'baɪəm, bí-ăm
Byker *Tyne & Wear*, 'baɪkər, bíkĕr
Bylaugh *Norfolk*, 'bɪlɑ, beélaa; 'bɪloʊ, beélŏ; 'baɪlɑ, bílaa; 'baɪloʊ, bílŏ; 'baɪlə, bílaw
Bylchau *Clwyd*, 'bʌlxaɪ, búlchī
Byles, *f.n.*, baɪlz, bilz
Byllam, *f.n.*, 'bɪləm, bíllăm
Bynea *Dyfed*, 'bɪnjə, bín-yă
Byng, *f.n.*, bɪŋ, bing
Byrne, *f.n.*, bɜrn, burn
Byron, *f.n.*, 'baɪərən, bírŏn
Byshottles *Durham*, 'baɪʃɒtlz, bíshottlz
Bysouth, *f.n.*, 'baɪsaʊθ, bíssowth
Bysshe, *f.n.*, bɪʃ, bish. *Appropriate also for Percy* ~ *Shelley, poet.*
Bythesea, *f.n.*, 'baɪθsi, bíth-see
Bytheway, *f.n.*, 'baɪðəweɪ, bíthĕway; 'baɪθweɪ, bíth-way
Byton *H. & W.*, 'baɪtən, bítŏn
Byward Tower *Tower of London*, 'baɪwərd, bí-wărd

C

Caban Coch *Powys*, 'kæbən 'koʊx, kábbăn kóch
Cabeldu, *f.n.*, kə'beldju, kăbéldew
Cabell, *f.n.*, 'kæbl, kábbl
Cabot, *f.n.*, 'kæbət, kábbŏt. *This is the pronunciation generally used for John and Sebastian* ~, *explorers.*
Cabourn, *also spelt* **Cabourne**, *Lincs.*, 'keɪbərn, káybŏrn
Cabrach *Grampian*, 'kæbrəx, kábrăch; 'kɑbrəx, ka'abrăch
Cabus *Lancs.*, 'keɪbəs, káybüss
Caccia, *f.n.*, 'kætʃə, kátchă. *Appropriate also for Baron* ~.
Cachemaille, *f.n.*, 'kæʃmaɪl, káshmīl; 'kæʃmeɪl, káshmayl
Cadbury, *f.n.*, 'kædbərɪ, kádbŭri
Cadby, *f.n.*, 'kædbɪ, kádbi
Caddonfoot *Borders*, ˌkædən'fʊt, kaddŏnfŏŏt
Caddoo, *f.n.*, kæ'du, kaddóo

Cadeby *Leics.*, *S. Yorks.*, 'keɪdbɪ, káydbi

Cadell, *f.n.*, 'kædl, kádd̦l; kəˈdel, kǎdéll. *The first is appropriate for Jean ~, actress, and the second for Selina ~, actress.*

Cader Idris *Gwynedd*, 'kædər 'ɪdrɪs, káddĕr ídriss

Cadgwith *Cornwall*, 'kædʒwɪð, kájwith; 'kædʒwɪθ, kájwith

Cadishead *Gtr. M'chester*, 'kædɪzhed, káddiz-hed

Cadle, *f.n.*, 'keɪdl, káydl

Cadle *W. Glam.*, 'kædleɪ, kádlay

Cadnant Brook *Anglesey*, 'kædnænt, kádnant

Cadogan, Earl, kəˈdʌgən, kădúggăn

Cadoux, *f.n.*, kəˈdu, kădóo

Cadoxton *S. Glam.*, 'kædɒkstən, káddŏkstŏn

Cadwaladr, Dilys, *Welsh poet*, 'dɪlɪs kæd'wælədər, dílliss kadwáládĕr

Cadwaladyr, *f.n.*, kæd'wælədər, kadwáládĕr

Cadwallader, *f.n.*, kæd'wɒlədər, kadwóládĕr

Cadwgan, *f.n.*, kəˈdʊgən, kădóogăn

Cady, *f.n.*, 'keɪdɪ, káydi

Cadzow, *f.n.*, 'kædzoʊ, kádzō

Cadzow *S'clyde*, 'kædzoʊ, kádzō

Caegarw *Mid Glam.*, kaɪˈgæru, kīgárroo; kiˈgæru, keegárroo

Caenby *Lincs.*, 'keɪnbɪ, káynbi

Caerau *Mid Glam.*, *Powys*, *S. Glam.*, 'kaɪraɪ, kīrī

Caerbwdi Bay, *Dyfed*, kaɪərˈbudɪ, kīrboódi

Caer Caradoc *Salop*, 'kaɪər kəˈrædɒk, kír kăráddock

Caerdeon *Gwynedd*, karˈdeɪən, kaardáy-ŏn; kaɪərˈdeɪən, kīrdáy-ŏn

Caerdydd, *Welsh name for Cardiff*, ˌkaɪərˈdið, kīrdéeth

Caergeiliog *Gwynedd*, kaɪərˈgaɪljɒg, kīrgíl-yog

Caergwrle *Clwyd*, kaɪərˈgʊərlɪ, kīrgoórli

Caergybi, *Welsh form of Holyhead*, *Anglesey*, kaɪərˈgʌbɪ, kīrgúbbi

Caerhays, *also spelt* **Carhays**, *Cornwall*, karˈheɪz, kaar-háyz; kəˈreɪz, kăráyz. *Historians prefer the spelling Carhays.*

Caerhays Castle *Cornwall*, karˈheɪz, kaar-háyz

Caerhun *Gwynedd*, kaɪərˈhɪn, kīr-héen. *Appropriate for both places of the name in Gwynedd.*

Caerlaverock *D. & G.*, kɛərˈlævərɒk, kairlávvĕrock

Caerleon *Gwent*, karˈliən, kaarleé--ŏn; kərˈliən, kărleé-ŏn; kaɪərˈliən, kīrleé-ŏn

Caernarvon *Gwynedd*, kərˈnarvən, kărnaárvŏn

Caerphilly *Mid Glam.*, kərˈfɪlɪ, kărfílli

Caersalem *W. Glam.*, kaɪərˈsæləm, kīr-sálĕm

Caersws *Powys*, kaɪərˈsus, kīr-soóss

Caerwent *Gwent*, kaɪərˈwent, kīrwént

Caerwys *Clwyd*, 'kaɪərwɪs, kírwiss

Caffarey, *f.n.*, 'kæfərɪ, káffári

Caffery, *f.n.*, 'kæfərɪ, káffĕri

Caffyn, *f.n.*, 'kæfɪn, káffin

Cahal, *f.n.*, kəˈhæl, kă-hál

Cahan, *f.n.*, kɑn, kaan

Cahill, *f.n.*, 'kɑhɪl, kaá-hil

Cahir, *Irish C.n.*, 'kæhər, ká-hŭr

Cahusac, *f.n.*, *also spelt* **Cahuzac**, kɑ'hjuzæk, kaa-héwzack

Cainey, *f.n.*, 'keɪnɪ, káyni

Caink, *f.n.*, keɪŋk, kaynk

Caie, *f.n.*, kaɪ, kī

Caird, *f.n.*, kɛərd, kaird

Cairnbulg *Grampian*, 'kɛərnˈbʌlg, káirn-búlg

Caiger, *f.n.*, 'keɪdʒər, káyjĕr

Caillard, *f.n.*, 'kaɪər, kí-aar

Cairncross, *f.n.*, kɛərnˈkrɒs, kairn-króss

Cairngorms *H'land–Grampian*, 'kɛərnˈgɔrmz, káirn-górmz

Cairntoul *Grampian*, kɛərnˈtul, kairntoól; kɛərnˈtaul, kairntówl

Caister *Norfolk*, 'keɪstər, káystĕr

Caistor *Lincs.*, 'keɪstər, káystŏr

Caithness, Earl of, 'keɪθnes, káythness

Caithness *H'land*, 'keɪθnɪs, káythnĕss

Caius, *f.n.*, kiz, keez

Caius College *see* **Gonville and Caius** College

Calbourne *I. of Wight*, 'kælbɔrn, kálborn

Calcot, *f.n.*, 'kɒlkət, káwlkŏt; 'kælkət, kálkŏt

Calcot Row *Berks.*, 'kælkət 'roʊ, kálkŏt rṓ

Calcott, *f.n.*, 'kɒlkət, káwlkŏt; 'kælkət, kálkŏt

Caldarvan *S'clyde*, kəlˈdarvən, kăldaárvăn

Caldbeck *Cumbria*, 'kɒldbek, káwldbeck; 'kɒdbek, káwdbeck

Caldcleugh, *f.n.*, 'kɒldklʌf, káwldkluff; 'kɑldklʌf, kaáldkluff

Caldecote, Viscount, 'kɔldɪkət, káwldĕkŏt

Caldecott Ches., Oxon., 'kɔldɪkət, káwldĕkŏt

Caldecott Leics., 'kɔldɪkɒt, káwldĕkott

Calder, f.n., 'kɔldər, káwldĕr

Calder, Rivers, 'kɔldər, káwldĕr. Appropriate for rivers of this name in Cumbria, Lancs. (two), and W. Yorks.

Calder and Boyars, publishers, 'kɔldər ənd 'bɔɪərz, káwldĕr ănd bóy-ărz

Caldercruix S'clyde, ‚kɔldər'kruks, kawldĕrkroóks

Calderon, f.n., 'kældərən, káldĕrŏn; 'kɔldərən, káwldĕrŏn

Calderstones Merseyside, 'kɔldərstounz, káwldĕrstōnz

Caldew, River, Cumbria, 'kɔldju, káwldew

Caldmore W. Midlands, 'kɑmər, kaámŏr

Caldons D. & G., 'kɔldənz, káwldŏnz

Caldow, f.n., 'kældou, káldō

Caldwell, f.n., 'kɔldwel, káwldwel

Caldy Merseyside, 'kɔldɪ, káwldi

Caldy Island Dyfed, 'kɔldɪ 'aɪlənd, káwldi íland

Caledon Co. Tyrone, 'kælɪdən, kálĕdŏn. Appropriate also for the Earl of ~.

Calenick Cornwall, kə'lenɪk, kălénnick

Caley, f.n., 'keɪlɪ, káyli

Calfe, f.n., kɑf, kaaf

Calgary I. of Mull, 'kælgərɪ, kálgări

Calke Derby., kɔk, kawk

Calkwell, also spelt Cawkwell, Lincs., 'kɔkwel, káwkwel

Calladine, f.n., 'kælədɪn, kálădeen

Callaghan, f.n., 'kæləhən, kálăhăn

Callaly Northd., 'kælətɪ, kálăli; kə'lælɪ, kăláli

Callander Central, 'kæləndər, kálăndĕr

Callanish, also spelt Callernish, I. of Lewis, 'kælənɪʃ, kálănish

Callard, f.n., 'kælɑrd, kálaard

Callear, f.n., 'kælɪər, káli-ĕr; kə'lɪər, kăléer

Callernish, see also Callanish, I. of Lewis, 'kælərnɪʃ, kálĕrnish

Callestick Cornwall, kə'lestɪk, kăléstick; 'klestɪk, kléstick

Callieu, f.n., kæl'ju, kal-yoó

Callil, f.n., kə'lɪl, kălíl

Callington Cornwall, 'kælɪŋtən, kálingtŏn

Callis Mill Hebden Bridge (W. Yorks.), 'kælɪs 'mɪl, káliss míll

Callus, f.n., 'kæləs, kálŭss

Calman, f.n., 'kælmən, kálmăn

Calne Wilts., kɑn, kaan

Calne and Calstone, Viscount, 'kɑn ənd 'kælstən, kaán ănd kálstŏn

Calow Derby., 'keɪlou, káylō

Calshot Hants, 'kælʃɒt, kál-shot

Calstock Cornwall, 'kælstɒk, kálstock

Calstone Wellington Wilts., 'kælstən 'welɪŋtən, kálstŏn wéllingtŏn

Calthorpe, f.n., 'kɔlθɔrp, káwl-thorp; 'kælθɔrp, kál-thorp. The first is appropriate for Baron ~.

Calthorpe Norfolk, 'kælθɔrp, kál-thorp

Calton S'clyde, 'kaltən, kaáltŏn

Calton Hill Edinburgh, 'kɔltən 'hɪl, káwltŏn híll

Calveley Ches., 'kɑvlɪ, kaávli; 'kɔvlɪ, káwvli

Calver, f.n., 'kælvər, kálvĕr; 'kɑvər, kaávĕr

Calverhall Salop, 'kælvərhɔl, kálvĕr-hawl

Calverley W. Yorks., 'kɑvərlɪ, kaávĕrli; 'kɔvlɪ, káwvli. The first is appropriate for Baron ~.

Calverley, Charles Stuart, 19th-c. poet, 'kɑvərlɪ, kaávĕrli; 'kælvərlɪ, kálvĕrli. The first is the pronunciation used by his direct descendants, hence probably his own. The second seems to be otherwise common usage, e.g. in the English departments of universities, etc.

Calver Sough Derby., 'kɑvər 'sʌf, kaávĕr súff

Calvert, f.n., 'kælvərt, kálvĕrt; 'kɔlvərt, káwlvĕrt

Calverton Notts., 'kælvərtən, kálvĕrtŏn; 'kɑvərtən, kaávĕrtŏn

Calvine Tayside, kæl'vin, kal-véen

Calvocoressi, f.n., ‚kælvəkə'resɪ, kalvŏkŏréssi

Calwell, f.n., 'kɔlwəl, káwlwĕl

Cam, River, mainly Cambs., kæm, kam

Camascross Skye, ‚kæməs'krɒs, kammáskróss

Camasunary Skye, ‚kæmə'sjunərɪ, kammásséwnări

Camberley Surrey, 'kæmbərlɪ, kámbĕrli

Camberwell London, 'kæmbər-wəl, kámbĕr-wĕl; 'kæmbərwel, kámbĕr-wel

Cambois Northd., 'kæməs, kámmŭs; 'kæmɪs, kámmiss

Camborne *Cornwall,* 'kæmbɔrn, kámborn
Cambrian, *pertaining to Wales,* 'kæmbrɪən, kámbriǎn
Cambridge *Cambs., Glos.,* 'keɪmbrɪdʒ, káymbrij
Cambusavie *H'land,* ˌkæmbəs-'ævɪ, kambŭssávvi
Cambusbarron *Central,* ˌkæmbəs-'bærən, kambŭssbárrŏn
Cambuslang *S'clyde,* ˌkæmbəs-'læŋ, kambŭsslàng
Cambusnethan *S'clyde,* ˌkæmbəs-'neθən, kambŭssnéthǎn
Camden, *f.n.,* 'kæmdən, kámdĕn
Cameley *Avon,* 'keɪmlɪ, káymli
Camelford *Cornwall,* 'kæmlfərd, kámmlfŏrd
Camelon *Central,* 'kæmələn, kámmĕlŏn
Camerer-Cuss, *f.n.,* 'kæmərər 'kʌs, kámmĕrĕr kúss
Cameron of Lochiel, *f.n.,* 'kæmə-rən əv lɒ'xɪl, kámmĕrŏn ŏv lochéel
Camerton *Avon, Cumbria,* 'kæmərtən, kámmĕrtŏn
Camidge, *f.n.,* 'kæmɪdʒ, kámmij
Camlachie *S'clyde,* kæm'læxɪ, kamláchi
Camlan *Gwynedd,* 'kæm'læn, kám-lán
Camlough *Co. Armagh,* 'kæmlɒx, kámloch
Cammaerts, *f.n.,* 'kæmərts, kámmĕrts
Camoys, *Baron,* 'kæmɔɪz, kám-moyz
Campagnac, *f.n.,* kæm'pænjæk, kampán-yack; kəm'pænjæk, kəmpán-yack
Campbell, *f.n.,* 'kæmbl, kámbl
Campbell and Cowal, *Earl of,* 'kæmbl ənd 'kaʊəl, kámbl ǎnd kówǎl
Campbell of Monzie, *f.n.,* 'kæmbl əv mə'ni, kámbl ŏv mŏneé
Campbell-Savours, *f.n.,* 'kæmbl 'seɪvərz, kámbl- sáyvŏrz
Campbeltown *S'clyde,* 'kæmbl-taʊn, kámbltown; 'kæmbltən, kámbltŏn
Campden, *f.n.,* 'kæmdən, kámdĕn. *Appropriate also for Viscount* ∼.
Campey, *f.n.,* 'kæmpɪ, kámpi
Campoli, Alfredo, *violinist,* æl'freɪdoʊ 'kæmpəlɪ, alfráydō kámpŏli
Campsall *S. Yorks.,* 'kæmpsl, kámpssl
Campsie *S'clyde,* 'kæmpsɪ, kámpsi
Camrose *Dyfed,* 'kæmroʊz, kámrōz

Camsey, *f.n.,* 'kæmzɪ, kámzi
Camulodunum, *Roman name for* **Colchester,** 'kæmjʊloʊ'djʊnəm, kám-yōōlŏdéwnŭm; 'kæmʊloʊ-'dʊnəm, kámōōlŏdoōnŭm
Camus, *f.n.,* 'kæməs, kámmŭss
Canavan, *f.n.,* 'kænəvən, kánnǎvǎn
Canaway, *f.n.,* 'kænəweɪ, kánnǎway
Candian, *f.n.,* 'kændɪən, kándi-ǎn
Candler, *f.n.,* 'kændlər, kándlĕr
Candlin, *f.n.,* 'kændlɪn, kándlin
Candlish, *f.n.,* 'kændlɪʃ, kándlish
Canel, *f.n.,* kə'nel, kǎnéll
Canelle, *f.n.,* kə'nel, kǎnéll
Canetti, Elias, *author,* eɪ'liæs kə'netɪ, aylee-ass kǎnétti
Canewdon *Essex,* kə'njʊdən, kǎnéwdŏn
Canna *H'land,* 'kænə, kánnǎ
Cannadine, *f.n.,* 'kænədaɪn, kánnǎdin
Cannel, *f.n.,* kə'nel, kǎnéll
Cannell, *f.n.,* 'kænl, kánnl
Cannetty, *f.n.,* 'kænɪtɪ, kánnĕti
Cannich *H'land,* 'kænɪx, kánnich
Canonbury *London* 'kænənbərɪ, kánnŏnbŭri
Canon Frome *H. & W.,* 'kænən 'frʌm, kánnŏn froóm
Canon Pyon *H. & W.,* 'kænən 'paɪən, kánnŏn pí-ŏn
Cant, *f.n.,* kænt, kant
Cantab., *abbreviation of* **Canta-brigian,** 'kæntæb, kántab
Cantabrigian, *pertaining to* **Cambridge** *or its University,* ˌkæntə'brɪdʒɪən, kantăbríjjiǎn
Cantamir, *f.n.,* 'kæntəmɪər, kántămeer
Cantelo, *f.n.,* 'kæntɪloʊ, kántĕlō
Cantelowes Gardens, *London park,* 'kæntɪloʊz, kántĕlōz
Canter, *f.n.,* 'kæntər, kántĕr
Canterbury *Kent,* 'kæntərbərɪ, kántĕrbŭri; 'kæntərberɪ, kántĕrberri
Cantuar, *Archbishop of* **Canter-bury***'s signature* 'kæntjʊɑr, kánt-yōō-aar
Canvey Island *Essex,* 'kænvɪ 'aɪlənd, kánvi íland
Canwick *Lincs.,* 'kænɪk, kánnick
Caol *H'land,* kɔl, köl
Capaldi, *f.n.,* kə'pældɪ, kăpáldi; kə'pɒldɪ, kăpáwldi
Cap Coch *Mid Glam.,* kæp 'kɒux, kap kóch
Cape Cornwall *Cornwall,* keɪp 'kɔrnwəl, kayp kórnwǎl
Capel, *f.n.,* 'keɪpl, káypl
Capel *Kent, Surrey,* 'keɪpl, káypl
Capel Curig *Gwynedd,* 'kæpl 'kɪrɪg, káppl kírrig

Capel-ed *Gwent*, 'kæpl 'ed, káppl édd

Capel-le-Ferne *Kent*, 'keɪpl lə 'fɑːn, káypl lě férn

Capell, *f.n.*, 'keɪpl, káypl

Capel Mair *Dyfed*, 'kæpl 'maɪər, káppl mír

Capel Mawr *Gwynedd*, 'kæpl 'mauər, káppl mówr

Capener, *f.n.*, 'keɪpənər, káypěněr

Capenerhurst, *f.n.*, kə'penərhɜrst, kǎpénněr-hurst

Capenhurst *Ches.*, 'keɪpənhɜrst, káypěnhurst

Capern, *f.n.*, 'keɪpərn, káypěrn

Capewell, *f.n.*, 'keɪpwel, káypwel

Cape Wrath *H'land*, keɪp 'rɑːθ, kayp ráath; keɪp 'rɒθ, kayp ráwth; keɪp 'ræθ, kayp ráth; keɪp 'rɒθ, kayp róth

Capheaton *Northd.*, kæp'hiːtən, kap-héetŏn

Caplan, *f.n.*, 'kæplən, káplăn

Capon, *f.n.*, 'keɪpən, káypŏn

Caporn, *f.n.*, 'keɪpɔrn, káypŏrn

Cappagh *Co. Tyrone*, 'kæpə, káppă

Cappercleuch *Borders*, 'kæpərklux, káppěrklooch

Capron, *f.n.*, 'keɪprən, káyprŏn

Caputh *Tayside*, 'keɪpəθ, káypŭth

Caradoc, *Welsh C.n., also spelt Caradog*, kə'rædɒk, kǎráddock

Caradon *Cornwall*, 'kærədən, kárrădŏn. *Appropriate also for Baron ~*.

Caravias, *f.n.*, ˌkærə'viəs, karrăvée-ăss

Carbery, Baron, 'kɑrbəri, kaárběri

Carbery, *f.n.*, 'kɑrbəri, kaárběri

Carbis Bay *Cornwall*, 'kɑrbɪs 'beɪ, kaárbiss báy

Carbost *Skye*, 'kɑrbɒst, kaárbosst. *Appropriate for both places of the name on Skye.*

Carburton *Notts.*, 'kɑrbərtən, kaárbŭrtŏn

Carcanet *Press, publishers*, 'kɑrkənet, kaárkǎnet

Cardenden *Fife*, ˌkɑrdən'den, kaárděnděn

Cardiff *S. Glam.*, 'kɑrdɪf, kaárdif

Cardigan *Dyfed*, 'kɑrdɪgən, kaárdigǎn. *Appropriate also for the Earl of ~.*

Cardinall, *f.n.*, 'kɑrdɪnl, kaárdinnl

Cardinham *Cornwall*, kɑr'dɪnəm, kaardínnăm

Cardnell, *f.n.*, 'kɑrdnel, kaárd-nel

Cardowan *S'clyde*, kɑr'dauən, kaardów-ăn

Cardus, Sir Neville, *writer*, 'nevl 'kɑrdəs, névvl kaárdŭss

Careglefn *Anglesey*, ˌkærɪg'levn, karrěglévvn

Careston *Tayside*, 'kɑrɪstən, kaárěstŏn

Carew, *f.n.*, kə'ruː, kǎroó; 'kɛəri, káiri. *The first is appropriate for Baron ~, and for Thomas ~, 17th-c. poet.*

Carew *Dyfed*, 'kɛəri, káiri; 'kɛəru, káiroo

Carew, Seaton, *Cleveland*, 'sitən kə'ruː, séetŏn kǎroó

Carewe, *f.n.*, kə'ruː, kǎroó

Carey, *f.n.*, 'kɛəri, káiri

Carfin *S'clyde*, kɑr'fɪn, kaar-fín

Carfraemill *Borders*, 'kɑrfreɪ'mɪl, kaárfraymill

Cargen *D. & G.*, 'kɑrgən, kaárgěn

Cargill, *f.n.*, kɑr'gɪl, kaargíll; 'kɑrgɪl, kaárgil

Carham *Northd.*, 'kærəm, kárrăm

Carharrack *Cornwall*, kɑr'hærək, kaar-hárrăk; kər'hærək, kǎr-hárräk

Carhart, *f.n.*, 'kɑrhɑrt, kaár-haart

Carhays *see* Caerhays

Carholme Racecourse *Lincoln*, 'kɑrhoum, kaár-hŏm

Caridia, *f.n.*, kə'rɪdɪə, kǎríddiǎ

Carie *Tayside*, 'kɑri, kaári

Carin, *f.n.*, 'kærɪn, kárrin

Carinish *N. Uist*, 'kɑrɪnɪʃ, kaárinish; 'kærɪnɪʃ, kárrinish

Carkeet-James, *f.n.*, 'kɑrkɪt 'dʒeɪmz, kaárkeet jáymz

Carland *Cornwall*, 'kɑrlænd, kaárland

Carleton, Baron, 'kɑrltən, kaárltŏn

Carleton, *f.n.*, 'kɑrltən, kaárltŏn

Carleton Forhoe *Norfolk*, 'kɑrltən 'fɔrhou, kaárltŏn fŏr-hṓ

Carleton Road, *London*, kɑr'litən, kaarléetŏn

Carlill, *f.n.*, 'kɑr'lɪl, kaar-líll

Carline, *f.n.*, 'kɑrlaɪn, kaárlīn

Carlinghow *W. Yorks.*, ˌkɑrlɪŋ'hau, kaarling-hów

Carlisle, *f.n.*, kɑr'laɪl, kaarlíl

Carlisle *Cumbria*, kɑr'laɪl, kaar-líl; 'kɑrlaɪl, kaárlīl. *The first is recognized national usage; the second is preferred locally. The first is also appropriate for the Earl of ~.*

Carlops *Borders*, 'kɑrlɒps, kaár-lops

Carlton Colville *Suffolk*, 'kɑrltən 'kɒlvɪl, kaárltŏn kólvil

Carluke *S'clyde*, kɑr'luk, kaar-loók

Carlyle, *f.n.*, kɑr'laɪl, kaarlíl; 'kɑrlaɪl, kaárlīl. *The first is appropriate for Thomas ~, essayist and historian.*

Carlyon, f.n., kɑr'laɪən, kaarlí--ōn

Carlyon Bay Cornwall, kɑr'laɪən 'beɪ, kaarlí-ōn báy

Carman, f.n., 'kɑrmən, káarmǎn

Carmarthen Dyfed, kər'mɑrðən, kărmaáarthĕn

Carmedy, f.n., 'kɑrmədɪ, káarmĕdi

Carmel Clwyd, Dyfed, Gwynedd, 'kɑrmel, káarmel

Carmichael, f.n., kɑr'maɪkl, kaarmíkl; kɑr'mɪxl, kaarmíchl

Carmyllie Tayside, kɑr'maɪlɪ, kaarmíli

Carnaby Street London, 'kɑrnəbɪ, káarnăbi

Carnac, f.n., 'kɑrnæk, káarnack

Carnalea Co. Down, ˌkɑrnə'li, kaarnăleé

Carnane I. of Man, kɑr'neɪn, kaarnáyn

Carnarvon, Earl of, kər'nɑrvən, kărnaáarvŏn

Carn Brea Cornwall, 'kɑrn 'breɪ, káarn bráy

Carnearney Co. Antrim, kɑr-'nɛərnɪ, kaarnáirni

Carnegie, f.n., kɑr'negɪ, kaar-néggi; kɑr'neɪgɪ, kaarnáygi. *The first is that of the Earl of Northesk's family name. Both pronunciations are current in Scotland, and usage for the ~ Trust consequently varies with individual speakers.*

Carnegy, f.n., kɑr'negɪ, kaarnéggi; kɑr'neɪgɪ, kaarnáygi

Carnell, f.n., kɑr'nel, kaarnéll

Carnkie Cornwall, kɑrn'kaɪ, kaarn-kí. *Appropriate for both places of this name in Cornwall.*

Carnlough Co. Antrim, 'kɑrnlɒx, káarnloch

Carnmenellis Cornwall, ˌkɑrnmɪ-'nelɪs, kaarn-mĕnélliss

Carnmoney Co. Antrim, kɑrn-'mʌnɪ, kaarn-múnni

Carno Powys, 'kɑrnoʊ, káarnō

Carnoustie Tayside, kɑr'nustɪ, kaarnoóosti

Carntyne S'clyde, kɑrn'taɪn, kaarntín

Carnwadric S'clyde, kɑrn'wɒdrɪk, kaarn-wóddrick

Carnwath S'clyde, kɑrn'wɒθ, kaarnwóth. *Appropriate also for the Earldom of ~.*

Carnyorth Cornwall, kɑrn'jɔrθ, kaarn-yórth

Caro, f.n., 'kɑroʊ, káarō

Caroe, f.n., 'kɛəroʊ, káirō; 'kæroʊ, kárrō

Carolan, f.n., 'kærələn, kárrŏlǎn

Caron, f.n., 'kærɒn, kárron; kə'rɒn, kărón

Carothers, f.n., kə'rʌðərz, kărúthĕrz

Carpmael, f.n., 'kɑrpmeɪl, káarpmayl

Carpmale, f.n., 'kɑrpmeɪl, káarpmayl

Carr, f.n., kɑr, kaar

Carra Beag Tayside, 'kærə 'beɪk, kárrá báyk

Carrad, f.n., 'kærəd, kárrăd

Carrawburgh Fort Northd., 'kærəbrʌf, kárrăbruff

Carrbridge H'land, 'kɑr'brɪdʒ, kaár-bríj

Carreghofa Powys, ˌkærɪg'hoʊvə, karrĕg-hóvă

Carrell, f.n., kə'rel, kăréll

Carreras, f.n., kə'rɪərəz, kăreéräz

Carrick-a-Rede, islet, Co. Antrim, ˌkærɪk ə 'rid, karrick ă reéd

Carrickfergus Co. Antrim, ˌkærɪk-'fɑrgəs, karrickférgüss

Carrick-Mannan Co. Down, ˌkærɪk'mænən, karrick-mánnăn

Carritt, f.n., 'kærɪt, kárrit

Carrivick, f.n., kə'rɪvɪk, kărívvick

Carrocher, f.n., 'kærəxər, kárrŏchĕr

Carrodus, f.n., 'kærədəs, kárrŏdüss

Carrothers, f.n., kə'rʌðərz, kărúthĕrz

Carrowdore Co. Down, 'kærədɔr, kárrădor

Carrowreagh Co. Antrim, ˌkæroʊ-'reɪə, karrō-ráy-ă

Carrowreagh Co. Down, ˌkæroʊ-'reɪ, karrō-ráy

Carruth, f.n., kə'ruθ, kăroóoth

Carruthers, f.n., kə'rʌðərz, kărúthĕrz

Carryduff Co. Down, ˌkærɪ'dʌf, karridúff

Carse, f.n., kɑrs, kaarss

Carse of Gowrie Tayside, 'kɑrs əv 'gaʊrɪ, kaárss ŏv gówri

Carsfad D. & G., kɑrs'fæd, kaarss-fád

Carshalton London, kɑr'ʃɔltən, kaar-sháwltŏn. *Although apparently no longer heard, there was previously a pronunciation* keɪs'hɒtən, *kayss-háwtŏn.*

Carsluith D. & G., kɑr'sluθ, kaar-slóoth

Carsphairn D. & G., kɑrs'fɛərn, kaarss-fáirn

Carstairs, f.n., kɑr'stɛərz, kaar--stáirz; 'kɑrstɛərz, káar-stairz

Carstairs S'clyde, kɑr'stɛərz, kaar-stáirz

Carteret, *f.n.*, 'kɑrtəret, kaʹartĕret; 'kɑrtərɪt, kaʹartĕrĕt. *The first is generally considered appropriate for John ~, Earl Granville, 18th-c. diplomatist and statesman.*

Carterhaugh *Borders*, 'kɑrtər'hɒx, kaʹartĕr-hóch

Carthew, *f.n.*, 'kɑrθju, kaʹarthew

Carthusian, *one educated at Charterhouse School*, kɑr-'θjuzɪən, kaar-théwziăn

Cartier, *firm*, 'kɑrtɪeɪ, kaʹarti-ay

Cartmel *Cumbria*, 'kɑrtməl, kaʹart-mĕl

Cartmel Fell *Cumbria*, 'kɑrtməl 'fel, kaʹartmĕl féll

Carton de Wiart, *f.n.*, 'kɑrtən də 'waɪərt, kaʹartŏn dĕ wí-ărt

Cartwright, *f.n.*, 'kɑrtraɪt, kaʹartrīt

Carus, *f.n.*, 'keərəs, káirŭss; 'kærəs, kárrŭss

Caruth, *f.n.*, kə'ruθ, kărooʹth

Caruthers, *f.n.*, kə'rʌðərz, kărúʹthĕrz

Carvell, *f.n.*, kɑr'vel, kaarvéll

Carwadine, *f.n.*, 'kɑrwədin, kaʹarwădeen

Carwardine, *f.n.*, 'kɑrwərdin, kaʹarwărdeen; karwər'din, kaarwărdeʹen

Carway *Dyfed*, 'kɑrweɪ, kaʹarway

Carwinnen *Cornwall*, kɑr'wɪnən, kaarwínnĕn

Carwithen, *f.n.*, kɑr'wɪðən, kaarwíthĕn

Cary, *f.n.*, 'keərɪ, káiri

Carysfort, *f.n.*, 'kærɪsfɔrt, kárrisfort

Casasola, *f.n.*, ˌkæsə'soʊlə, kassássōlá

Cascob *Powys*, 'kæskɒb, kásskob

Casdagli, *f.n.*, kæz'dæglɪ, kazdáglí

Casken, *f.n.*, 'kæskɪn, kásskĕn

Casley, *f.n.*, 'keɪzlɪ, káyzli

Caslon, *f.n.*, 'kæzlɒn, kázzlon

Casselden, *f.n.*, 'kæsldən, kássldĕn

Cassillis *S'clyde*, 'kæslz, kásslz. *Appropriate also for the Earl of ~.*

Cassini, *f.n.*, kə'sinɪ, kǎsseeni

Cassiobury Park *Herts.*, 'kæsɪoʊbərɪ 'pɑrk, kássiōbūri paʹark

Casson, *f.n.*, 'kæsən, kássŏn

Castagnola, *f.n.*, ˌkæstə'noʊlə, kasstänōlá

Castaldini, *f.n.*, ˌkæstəl'dinɪ, kasstáldeéni

Castell, *f.n.*, kæs'tel, kasstéll

Castellain, *f.n.*, 'kæstɪleɪn, kásstēlayn

Castellan, *f.n.*, 'kæstelən, kásstellän

Castell Coch *S. Glam.*, 'kæsteł 'koux, kásstehl kô̱ch

Castelnau *London thoroughfare*, 'kɑslnɔ, kaʹasslnaw; 'kɑslnoʊ, kaʹasslnō

Castle-an-Dinas *Cornwall*, 'kɑsl ən 'daɪnəs, kaʹassl än dínăss

Castlebay *Barra* (*W. Isles*), 'kɑslbeɪ, kaʹasslbay

Castle Baynard, *Ward of the City of London*, 'kɑsl 'beɪnɑrd, kaʹassl báynaard

Castle Bromwich *W. Midlands*, 'kɑsl 'brɒmɪtʃ, kaʹassl bróm-mitch

Castle Bytham *Lincs.*, 'kɑsl 'baɪðəm, kaʹassl bíthăm

Castle Cary *Somerset*, 'kɑsl 'keərɪ, kaʹassl káiri

Castlecaulfield *Co. Tyrone*, ˌkɑsl'kɔfild, kaasslkáwfeeld

Castle Combe *Wilts.*, 'kɑsl 'kum, kaʹassl koʹom

Castledawson *Co. Derry*, ˌkɑsl-'dɔsən, kaassldáwssŏn

Castlederg *Co. Tyrone*, ˌkɑsl-'dɜrg, kaassldérg

Castle Donington *Leics.*, 'kɑsl 'dɒnɪŋtən, kaʹassl dónningtŏn

Castledoor *Cornwall*, ˌkɑsl'dɔr, kaassldór

Castle Douglas *D. & G.*, 'kɑsl 'dʌgləs, kaʹassl dúglàss

Castleford *W. Yorks.*, 'kɑslfərd, kaʹasslfŏrd

Castle Leod *H'land*, 'kɒsl 'laʊd, kaʹassl lówd

Castle Malwood *Hants*, 'kɑsl 'mɒlwʊd, kaʹassl máwlwŏod

Castle of Mey *H'land*, 'kɑsl əv 'meɪ, kaʹassl ŏv máy

Castlereagh, *Viscount*, 'kɑslreɪ, kaʹassl-ray

Castlereagh *Co. Down*, ˌkɑsl'reɪ, kaassl-ráy

Castlerock *Co. Antrim*, ˌkɑsl'rɒk, kaassl-róck

Castlerosse, *Viscountcy of*, 'kɑslrɒs, kaʹassl-ross

Castletown *H'land*, 'kɑsltaʊn, kaʹassltown

Castletown *I. of Man*, 'kɑsl'taʊn, kaʹassltówn

Castleward *Co. Down*, ˌkɑsl'wɔrd, kaasslwáwrd

Castlewellan *Co. Down*, ˌkɑsl-'welən, kaasslwéllän

Castley, *f.n.*, 'kæstlɪ, kásstli

Caston *Norfolk*, 'kɑstən, kaʹastŏn; 'kæsən, kássŏn; 'kæstən, kásstŏn

Castor *Cambs.*, 'kæstər, kásstŏr

Caswall, *f.n.*, 'kæzwəl, kázwăl

Catch, *f.n.*, kætʃ, katch

Catchpole, *f.n.*, 'kætʃpoʊl, kátchpōl

Catcleugh *Northd.*, 'kætklʌf, kátkluff; 'kætklif, kátkleef

Catelinet, *f.n.*, 'kætlɪneɪ, kátlinay

Cater, *f.n.*, 'keɪtər, káytĕr

Caterham *Surrey*, 'keɪtərəm, káytĕrăm

Catesby, *f.n.*, 'keɪtsbɪ, káytsbi

Cathays *S. Glam.*, kə'teɪz, kătáyz

Cathcart, *f.n.*, 'kæθkɑrt, káthkaart. *Also appropriate for Earl* ~.

Cathcart *S'clyde*, kæθ'kɑrt, kathkaárt

Cathedine *Powys*, kə'θedɪn, kăthéddin

Catherwood, *f.n.*, 'kæθərwʊd, káthĕr-wōōd; 'kæðərwʊd, káthĕr-wōōd

Cathie, *f.n.*, 'keɪθɪ, káythi

Cathles, *f.n.*, 'kæθlz, káthlz

Cathro, *f.n.*, 'kæθroʊ, káthrō

Cation, *f.n.*, 'keɪʃən, káyshŏn

Catisfield *Hants*, 'kætɪsfɪld, káttissfeeld

Catmur, *f.n.*, 'kætmər, kátmŭr

Cato, *f.n.*, 'keɪtoʊ, káytō

Caton, *f.n.*, 'keɪtən, káytŏn

Caton *Lancs.*, 'keɪtən, káytŏn

Cator, *f.n.*, 'keɪtər, káytŏr

Catrine *S'clyde*, 'kætrɪn, kátrin

Catriona, *C.n.*, kə'triənə, kătree-ónă

Cattanach, *f.n.*, 'kætənəx, káttănăch

Cattell, *f.n.*, kə'tel, kătéll

Catterline *Grampian*, 'kætərlaɪn, káttĕrlīn

Cattewater *see* Catwater

Cattistock *Dorset*, 'kætɪstɒk, káttistock

Catto, Baron, 'kætoʊ, káttō

Catwater, The, *Devon*, 'kætwɒtər, kátwawtĕr. *The spelling* Cattewater *appears to be an older variation.*

Catwick *Humberside*, 'kætɪk, káttick

Caudle, *f.n.*, 'kɔdl, káwdl

Caughey, *f.n.*, 'kæxɪ, káchi

Caughley *Salop*, 'kɑflɪ, káafli. *Appropriate also for the 18-c.* ~ *porcelain ware.*

Caulcutt, *f.n.*, 'kɔlkət, káwlkŭt

Caulfeild, *f.n.*, 'kɒfɪld, káwfeeld

Caulfield, *f.n.*, 'kɒfɪld, káwfeeld; 'kɒlfɪld, káwlfeeld

Caunce, *f.n.*, kɒns, kawnss, kɒns, konss

Caunsall *H. & W.*, 'kɒnsl, káwnssl

Causer, *f.n.*, 'kɔzər, káwzĕr

Causley, *f.n.*, 'kɔzlɪ, káwzli; 'keɪzlɪ, káyzli

Causton, Thomas, *18th-c. composer*, 'kɒstən, káwstŏn. *Also sometimes spelt* Caustun *or* Cawston.

Caute, *f.n.*, koʊt, kōt

Cautley, *f.n.*, 'kɔtlɪ, káwtli

Cava Island *Orkney*, 'kɑvə, kaávă

Cavanagh, *f.n.*, 'kævənə, kávvănă; kə'vænə, kăvánnă

Cavander, *f.n.*, 'kævəndər, kávvăndĕr

Cavanna, *f.n.*, kə'vænə, kăvánnă

Cavell, *f.n.*, 'kævl, kávvl; kə'vel, kăvéll. *The first is appropriate for Nurse Edith* ~.

Cavenagh, *f.n.*, 'kævənə, kávvěnă

Cavendish, *f.n.*, 'kævəndɪʃ, kávvĕndish

Cavers, *f.n.*, 'keɪvərz, káyvĕrz

Cavers *Borders*, 'keɪvərz, káyvĕrz

Caversham *Berks.*, 'kævərʃəm, kávvĕr-shăm

Cavers Hill *Borders*, 'keɪvərz 'hɪl, káyvĕrz híl

Caverswall *Staffs.*, 'kævərzwɔl, kávvĕrz-wawl

Cavey, *f.n.*, 'keɪvɪ, káyvi

Cavin, *f.n.*, 'keɪvɪn, káyvin

Cawardine, *f.n.*, kə'wɔrdɪn, kaw-wáwrdin

Cawdell, *f.n.*, kə'del, kawdéll

Cawdor *H'land*, 'kɔdər, káwdŏr. *Appropriate also for Earl* ~.

Cawkwell *see* Calkwell

Cawley, *f.n.*, 'kɒlɪ, káwli

Cawood, *f.n.*, 'keɪwʊd, káy-wōōd

Cawood *Lancs.*, *N. Yorks.*, 'keɪwʊd, káy-wōōd

Cawsand *Cornwall*, 'kɒsænd, káwssand

Cawston, *f.n.*, 'kɒstən, káwstŏn. *See also* Thomas Causton.

Cawston *Norfolk*, 'kɒstən, káwsstŏn

Cawthra, *f.n.*, 'kɔθrə, káwthră

Caxton Gibbet *Cambs.*, 'kækstən 'dʒɪbɪt, káckstŏn jíbbĕt

Cayzer, *f.n.*, 'keɪzər, káyzĕr

Cazabon, *f.n.*, 'kæzəbɒn, kázzăbon

Cazalet, *f.n.*, 'kæzəlɪt, kázzălĕt

Cazalet-Keir, *f.n.*, 'kæzəlɪt 'kɪər, kázzălĕt keér

Cazenove, *f.n.*, 'kæzɪnoʊv, kázzĕnōv

Cearns, *f.n.*, kɛərnz, kairnz

Cearr, *f.n.*, kɑr, kaar

Cecil, *f.n.*, 'sesl, séssl; 'sɪsl, síssl. *The second is appropriate for the family name of the Marquess of*

Exeter and that of the Marquess of Salisbury; consequently also for Lord David ～ and for the late Viscount ～ of Chelwood.

Cedric, *C.n.,* 'sedrɪk, sédrick; 'sɪdrɪk, seédrick

Cefn *Clwyd,* 'kevn, kévvn

Cefn Caeau *Dyfed,* ˌkevn 'kaɪaɪ, kevvn kî-I

Cefn Coch *Powys,* 'kevn 'kɒx, kévvn kóch

Cefn Coed *Mid Glam.,* ˌkevn 'kɔɪd, kevvn kóyd

Cefneithyn *Dyfed,* ˌkevn'aɪθɪn, kevvn-îthin; ˌkevn'eɪθɪn, kevvn-áythin

Cefn Golau *Mid Glam.,* ˌkevn 'gɒlaɪ, kevvn gólī

Cefn Hirgoed *Mid Glam.,* ˌkevn 'haːgɔɪd, kevvn hírgoyd

Cefn Mably *Mid Glam.,* ˌkevn 'mæblɪ, kevvn mábbli

Cefn Mawr *Clwyd,* ˌkevn 'mauər, kevvn mówr

Cefnpennar *Mid Glam.,* ˌkevn-'penər, kevvnpénnăr

Cefn-y-Bedd *Clwyd,* ˌkevn ə 'beð, kevvn ă béth; ˌkevn ə 'beɪð, kevvn ă báyth. *This is also appropriate for the former name of* Cilmery, *Powys (q.v.).*

Ceinwen, *Welsh C.n.,* 'kaɪnwen, kínwen

Ceirchiog *Anglesey,* 'kaɪərxjɒg, kîrch-yog

Ceiriog, *River, Clwyd,* 'kaɪrɪɒg, kíri-og

Cellan, *f.n.,* 'keɬən, kéḥlän

Cellier, *f.n.,* 'seljeɪ, séll-yay

Celner, *f.n.,* 'selnər, sélněr

Celoria, *f.n.,* sɪ'lɔːrɪə, sĕláwriă

Celt, *member of Celtic race,* kelt, kelt; selt, selt. *In Scotland and Northern Ireland the second is the more popular, and the only pronunciation ever heard for the Glasgow Celtic and Belfast Celtic football teams is* 'seltɪk, séltick.

Cemaes Bay *Anglesey,* 'kemaɪs 'beɪ, kémmīss báy

Cemm, *f.n.,* kem, kemm

Cemmaes *Powys,* 'kemaɪs, kémmīss

Cemmes Road *Powys,* 'kemɪs, kémmiss

Cenarth *Dyfed,* 'kenaːθ, kénnaarth

Cennydd, *Welsh C.n.,* 'kenɪð, kénnith

Centlivre, Susannah, *17th–18th-c. playwright and actress,* sɪnt'liːvər, sintleévěr; sɪnt'lɪvər, sintlívvěr. *There appears to be*

no positive evidence about her own pronunciation, and today she is known by both.

Ceredig, *f.n.,* kə'redɪg, kĕréddig

Ceredigion *Dyfed,* ˌkerə'dɪgɪɒn, kerrĕdíggi-on

Cerely, *f.n.,* 'sɪərlɪ, seérli

Ceres *Fife,* 'sɪərɪz, seériz

Ceresole, *f.n.,* 'serɪsoul, sérrĕssōl

Ceri, *Welsh C.n.,* 'kerɪ, kérri

Ceridwen, *Welsh C.n.,* kə'rɪdwen, kĕrídwen

Cerig Gwynion *Powys,* 'kerɪg 'gwɪnɪən, kérrig gwínniŏn

Cerne Abbas *Dorset,* 'sɜːn 'æbəs, sérn ábbăss

Cerney, North *and* South, *Glos.,* 'sɜːnɪ, sérni

Cernioge *Clwyd,* kɛərn'jɒgeɪ, kairn-yóggay

Cerrig-y-Drudion *Clwyd,* 'kerɪg ə 'drɪdjɒn, kérrig ă dríd-yon

Cesarewitch, *horse race,* sɪ'zærəwɪtʃ, sĕzárrĕwitch

Ceserani, *f.n.,* ˌsizə'raːnɪ, seezĕraáni

Cestrian, *native of Chester,* 'sestrɪən, séstriăn

Chabot, *f.n.,* 'ʃæbou, shábbō

Chaceley *Glos.,* 'tʃeɪslɪ, cháyssli

Chacewater *Cornwall,* 'tʃeɪswɔːtər, cháysswawtěr

Chacombe *Northants.,* 'tʃeɪkəm, cháykŏm. *An older spelling is* **Chalcombe.**

Chadbon, *f.n.,* 'tʃædbɒn, chádbon

Chadderton *Lancs.,* 'tʃædərtən, chádděrtŏn

Chaddesden *Derby.,* 'tʃædəzdən, cháddězděn

Chaddlehanger *Devon,* 'tʃædlhæŋər, cháddl-hang-ěr; 'tʃælɪŋər, cháling-ěr

Chadshunt *Warwicks.,* 'tʃædzhʌnt, chádz-hunt; 'tʃædzʌnt, chádzunt

Chafer, *f.n.,* 'tʃeɪfər, cháyfěr; 'ʃeɪfər, sháyfěr

Chaffe, *f.n.,* tʃeɪf, chayf

Chaffey, *f.n.,* 'tʃeɪfɪ, cháyfi

Chagford *Devon,* 'tʃægfərd, chággfŏrd

Chagrin, Francis, *composer,* 'frɑːnsɪs 'ʃægræ, fraánssiss shágrang

Chailey *E. Sussex,* 'tʃeɪlɪ, cháyli

Chaillet, *f.n.,* 'ʃaɪjeɪ, shî-yay

Chain, *f.n.,* tʃeɪn, chayn

Chalcombe *see* **Chacombe**

Chaldon *Surrey,* 'tʃɔldən, cháwldŏn. *Appropriate also for East and West ～, both in Dorset. East ～ is alternatively known*

as ~ Herring, 'tʃɔldən 'herɪŋ, cháwlďön hérring.

Chale *I. of Wight*, tʃeɪl, chayl

Chalfield, Great *and* Little, *Wilts.*, 'tʃɑlfɪld, cha'alfeeld

Chalfont, Baron, 'tʃælfɒnt, chálfont

Chalfont St. Giles *Bucks.*, 'tʃælfənt snt 'dʒaɪlz, chálfŏnt sĭnt jīlz; 'tʃɑfənt snt 'dʒaɪlz, cha'afŏnt sĭnt jīlz

Chalfont St. Peters *Bucks.*, 'tʃælfənt snt 'piːtərz, chálfŏnt sĭnt peéterz; 'tʃɑfənt snt 'piːtərz, cha'afŏnt sĭnt peéterz

Chalford *Glos.*, 'tʃælfərd, chálfŏrd

Chalford *Wilts.*, 'tʃɑfərd, cha'afŏrd

Chalgrove *Oxon.*, 'tʃælɡrouv, chálgrŏv

Chalk, *f.n.*, tʃɔk, chawk

Chalker, *f.n.*, 'tʃɔkər, cháwkĕr

Chalkley, *f.n.*, 'tʃɔklɪ, cháwkli

Challacombe *Devon*, 'tʃæləkəm, chálăkŏm

Challands, *f.n.*, 'tʃæləndz, chálăndz

Challes, *f.n.*, 'tʃælɪs, chálĕss

Challis, *f.n.*, 'tʃælɪs, cháliss

Challock *Kent*, 'tʃɒlək, chóllŏk

Challoner, *f.n.*, 'tʃælənər, chálŏnĕr

Challow, East *and* West, *Oxon.*, 'tʃælou, chálŏ

Chalmers, *f.n.*, 'tʃɑmərz, cha'amĕrz; 'tʃælmərz, chálmĕrz. *The first is appropriate for the Barony of* ~.

Chaloner, *f.n.*, 'tʃælənər, chálŏnĕr

Chalvey *Berks.*, 'tʃɑvɪ, cha'avi; 'tʃɑlvɪ, cha'alvi

Chalvington *E. Sussex*, 'tʃælvɪŋtən, chálvingtŏn; 'tʃɑlvɪŋtən, cha'alvingtŏn

Chamberlain, *f.n.*, 'tʃeɪmbərlɪn, cháymbĕrlin; 'tʃeɪmbərleɪn, cháymbĕrlayn

Chamier, *f.n.*, 'ʃæmɪər, shámmi-ĕr

Champany *Lothian*, 'tʃæmpənɪ, chámpăni

Champelovier, *f.n.*, ˌtʃæmpə-'louvɪər, champĕlóvi-ĕr

Champernowne, *f.n.*, 'tʃæmpər-naun, chámpĕrnown

Champneys, *f.n.*, 'tʃæmpnɪz, chámpniz

Chanctonbury Ring *W. Sussex*, 'tʃæŋktənbərɪ 'rɪŋ, chánktŏnbŭri ríng

Chanderhill *Derby.*, 'tʃændər'hɪl, chándĕr-hill; 'tʃandər'hɪl, cha'andĕr-hill

Chandler, *f.n.*, 'tʃɑndlər, cha'andlĕr

Chandos, *title of nobility*, 'ʃændɒs, shándoss. *Appropriate for both the present Viscount* ~, *and the Duchy of* ~.

Chandos, *f.n.*, 'ʃændɒs, shándoss; 'tʃændɒs, chándoss

Chandos-Pole, *f.n.*, 'ʃændɒs 'pul, shándoss pool

Changue *S'clyde*, tʃæŋ, chang

Channon, *f.n.*, 'tʃænən, chánnŏn; 'ʃænən, shánnŏn

Chaorunn, Loch, *S'clyde*, 'xɜrən, chúr-ŭn

Chapel Allerton *Leeds, Somerset*, 'tʃæpl 'ælərtən, cháppl álĕrtŏn

Chapel-en-le-Frith *Derby.*, 'tʃæpl en lə 'frɪθ, cháppl en lĕ frith

Chapel of Garioch *Grampian*, 'tʃæpl əv 'ɡɪərɪ, cháppl ŏv geéri

Chapin, *f.n.*, 'tʃeɪpɪn, cháypin

Chaplin, *f.n.*, 'tʃæplɪn, cháplin

Chaplyn, *f.n.*, 'tʃæplɪn, cháplin

Chapman, *f.n.*, 'tʃæpmən, chápmăn

Chappell, *f.n.*, 'tʃæpl, cháppl

Chappory, *f.n.*, 'tʃæpərɪ, cháppŏri

Chaproniere, *f.n.*, ˌʃæprə'nɪər, shaprŏneér; ˌʃæprən'jeər, shaprŏn-yair

Chard, *f.n.*, tʃɑrd, chaard

Chardet, *f.n.*, 'ʃɑrdeɪ, sha'arday

Charig, *f.n.*, 'tʃærɪɡ, chárrig

Charing *Kent*, 'tʃærɪŋ, chárring; 'tʃeərɪŋ, cháiring

Charlbury *Oxon.*, 'tʃɑrlbərɪ, cha'arlbŭri

Charlecote Park *Warwicks.*, 'tʃɑrlkout 'pɑrk, cha'arlkŏt pa'ark

Charlemont *Co. Armagh*, 'tʃɑrlɪmənt, cha'arlĕmŏnt. *Appropriate also for Viscount* ~.

Charleton, *f.n.*, 'tʃɑrltən, cha'arltŏn

Charleton, East *and* West, *Devon*, 'tʃɑrltən, cha'arltŏn

Charlier, *f.n.*, 'tʃɑrlɪeɪ, cha'arli-ay

Charman, *f.n.*, 'tʃɑrmən, cha'armăn; 'ʃɑrmən, sha'armăn

Charmouth *Dorset*, 'tʃɑrmauθ, cha'armowth

Charoux, Siegfried, *sculptor*, 'siɡfrid ʃə'ru, seégfreed shároó

Charques, *f.n.*, 'tʃɑrkwɪz, cha'ar-kwĕz; 'ʃɑrkwɪz, sha'arkwĕz

Charrosin, Frederick, *composer*, 'tʃærousɪn, chárróssin

Charteris, *f.n.*, 'tʃɑrtərɪs, cha'artĕriss; 'tʃɑrtərz, cha'artĕrz. *The first is appropriate for the family name of the Earl of Wemyss, and for Leslie* ~, *writer.*

Chartres, *f.n.*, 'tʃɑrtərz, chaártĕrz

Charwelton *Northants.*, tʃɑr-'weltən, chaar-wéltŏn

Chastleton *Oxon.*, 'tʃæsltən, chássltŏn

Chaston, *f.n.*, 'tʃæstən, chásstŏn

Chater, *f.n.*, 'tʃeitər, cháytĕr

Chathill *Northd.*, 'tʃæt'hil, chát-hill

Chatteris *Cambs.*, 'tʃætəris, cháttĕriss

Chatto and Windus, *publishers*, 'tʃætou ənd 'windəs, cháttō ănd wíndŭss

Chaudoir, *f.n.*, 'ʃoudwɑr, shŏdwaar

Chaul End *Beds.*, 'tʃɔl 'end, cháwl énd

Chaundler, *f.n.*, 'tʃɔndlər, cháwndlĕr

Chavasse, *f.n.*, ʃə'væs, shăváss

Chave, *f.n.*, tʃeiv, chayv

Chawleigh *Devon*, 'tʃɔli, cháwli

Chaworth, Baron, 'tʃawərθ, chaá-wŭrth

Chawton *Hants.*, 'tʃɔtən, cháwtŏn

Chendle Hulme *Gtr. M'chester*, 'tʃidl 'hjum, chéedl héwm

Cheam *London*, tʃim, cheem

Chearsley *Bucks.*, 'tʃiərzli, chéerzli

Checker, *f.n.*, 'tʃekər, chéckĕr

Chedburgh *Suffolk*, 'tʃedbərə, chédbŭră

Chediston *Suffolk*, 'tʃedistən, chéddistŏn

Chedzoy *Somerset*, 'tʃedzɔi, chédzoy

Cheesman, *f.n.*, 'tʃizmən, chéez-măn

Cheetham, *f.n.*, 'tʃitəm, chéetăm

Cheetham Hill *Gtr. M'chester*, 'tʃitəm 'hil, chéetăm híll

Chegwin, *f.n.*, 'tʃegwin, chégwin

Cheke, *f.n.*, tʃik, cheek

Cheldon *Devon*, 'tʃeldən, chéldŏn

Chelfham *Devon*, 'tʃelfəm, chélfăm

Chelioti, *f.n.*, keli'outi, kelli-óti

Chell, *f.n.*, tʃel, chell

Chellaston *Derby.*, 'tʃeləstən, chéllăstŏn

Chelmer, River, *Essex*, 'tʃelmər, chélmĕr. *Appropriate also for Baron ~.*

Chelmondiston *Suffolk*, 'tʃelmstən, chélmsstŏn

Chelmsford *Essex*, 'tʃelmsfərd, chélmssfŏrd; 'tʃemsfərd, chémssfŏrd

Chelsea *London*, 'tʃelsi, chélssi. *Appropriate also for Viscount ~.*

Chelsham *Surrey*, 'tʃelʃəm, chél-shăm

Chelveston *Northants.*, tʃel-'vestən, chelvésstŏn; 'tʃelstən, chélsstŏn

Chenappa, *f.n.*, 'tʃenəpə, chénnăpă

Chenevix, *f.n.*, 'tʃenəviks, chénnĕvicks; 'ʃenəviks, shénnĕvicks

Chenevix-Trench, *f.n.*, 'ʃenəviks 'trentʃ, shénnĕvicks trénch

Cheney, *f.n.*, 'tʃeini, cháyni; 'tʃini, cheéni

Chenies, *f.n.*, 'tʃeiniz, cháyniz

Chenies *Bucks.*, 'tʃeiniz, cháyniz; 'tʃiniz, cheéniz

Chenil Galleries *London*, 'tʃenil, chénnil

Chepstow *Gwent*, 'tʃepstou, chépstō

Chequerbent *Gtr. M'chester*, 'tʃekərbent, chéckĕrbent

Chequers *Bucks.*, 'tʃekərz, chéckĕrz

Chere, *f.n.*, ʃiər, sheer

Cherhill *Wilts.*, 'tʃeril, chérril

Cherkley Court *Surrey*, 'tʃɑrkli 'kɔrt, chérkli kórt

Cherns, *f.n.*, tʃɜrnz, chernz

Cherrill, *f.n.*, 'tʃeril, chérril

Cherwell, Barony of, 'tʃɑrwel, chaárwell

Cherwell, River, *Northants.-Oxon.*, 'tʃɑrwəl, chaárwĕl. *Appropriate also for the admin. dist. of Oxon., which takes its name from the river.*

Chesham *Bucks.*, 'tʃeʃəm, chésh-ăm

Cheshire *Co. name*, 'tʃeʃər, chéshĕr

Cheshunt *Herts.*, 'tʃesənt, chéssŭnt

Chesil Beach *Dorset*, 'tʃezl 'bitʃ, chézzl beétch

Chesneau, *f.n.*, 'tʃesnou, chéssnō

Chesney, *f.n.*, 'tʃezni, chézni

Chesterfield *Derby.*, 'tʃestərfild, chéstĕrfeeld. *Appropriate also for the Earldom of ~.*

Chester-le-Street *Durham*, 'tʃestər li 'strit, chéstĕrli street

Chestle, *f.n.*, 'tʃesl, chéssl

Cheswardine *Salop*, 'tʃezwərdain, chézwărdin

Chesworth, *f.n.*, 'tʃezwɜrθ, chézwurth

Chetham's Hospital & College *Manchester*, 'tʃitəmz, cheétămz. *Named after Humphrey ~ (1580–1655), a Manchester merchant.*

Chetham-Strode, Warren, *author*, 'wɒrən 'tʃetəm 'stroud, wórrĕn chéttăm strŏd

Chettiscombe *Devon,* 'tʃetɪskəm, chéttiskŏm; 'tʃeskəm, chésskŏm

Chettle, *f.n.,* 'tʃetl, chéttl

Chetwode, *f.n.,* 'tʃetwʊd, chétwōōd. *Appropriate also for Baron* ~.

Chetwyn, *f.n.,* 'tʃetwɪn, chétwin

Chetwynd, *f.n.,* 'tʃetwɪnd, chétwind. *Appropriate also for Viscount* ~.

Chevalier, *f.n.,* ʃɪ'vælɪeɪ, shĕváli-ay. *Appropriate for Albert* ~, *music-hall artist.*

Chevallier, *f.n.,* ˌʃevə'lɪər, shevväléer

Cheveley Park *Cambs.,* 'tʃivlɪ 'pɑrk, chéevli paárk

Chevening *Kent,* 'tʃivnɪŋ, chéevning

Chevenix, *f.n.,* 'ʃevənɪks, shévvĕnicks

Chevet *W. Yorks.,* 'tʃevɪt, chévvĕt

Chevington *Suffolk, Northd.,* 'tʃevɪŋtən, chévvingtŏn. *In Northd., appropriate for* ~ *Drift, East* ~, *and West* ~.

Chevins, *f.n.,* 'tʃevɪnz, chévvinz

Cheviot Hills *Borders–Northd.,* 'tʃɪvɪət, cheéviŏt; 'tʃevɪət, chévvĭŏt. *A theory that the first pronunciation is used north of the Border, and the other on the English side, has been discredited by observation over a long period. The truth appears to be that the former is almost invariably used in the Border country, in both England and Scotland, and that it is speakers from further south who favour the second. A third pronunciation,* 'tʃɪvɪət, chívvĭŏt, *has been heard in Edinburgh for the cloth of the name.*

Chevreau, Cecile, *actress,* sɪ'sil 'ʃevrou, sĕsseel shévrō

Chewton, Viscount, 'tʃutən, choótŏn

Cheylesmore *W. Midlands,* 'tʃaɪlzmɔr, chílzmor. *Appropriate also for the Barony of* ~.

Cheyne, *f.n.,* 'tʃeɪnɪ, cháyni; tʃeɪn, chayn; tʃin, cheen. *The first is appropriate for* ~ *Walk and* ~ *Row, Chelsea (London).*

Chichele, Henry, *15th-c. benefactor and founder of All Souls College, Oxford,* 'tʃɪtʃɪlɪ, chítchĕli

Chicksands *Beds.,* 'tʃɪksændz, chícksandz

Chiddenton, *f.n.,* 'tʃɪdənʃən, chídděn-shŏn

Chiddingly *E. Sussex,* ˌtʃɪdɪŋ'laɪ, chidding-lí

Chidell, *f.n.,* tʃɪ'del, chidéll

Chideock *Dorset* 'tʃɪdək, chídŏck

Chidgey, *f.n.,* 'tʃɪdʒɪ, chijji

Chidlow *Ches.,* 'tʃɪdloʊ, chídlō

Chiedozie, *f.n.,* tʃɪ'doʊzi, chidózi

Chiene, *f.n.,* ʃin, sheen

Chieveley *Berks.,* 'tʃivlɪ, cheévli

Chigwell *Essex,* 'tʃɪgwəl, chígwĕl

Chilbolton *Hants,* tʃɪl'boʊltən, chilbóltŏn

Childe, *f.n.,* tʃaɪld, chīld

Childerditch *Essex,* 'tʃɪldərdɪtʃ, chílderditch

Childerhouse, *f.n.,* 'tʃɪldərhaʊs, chíldĕr-howss

Childers, Erskine, *author,* 'ɜrskɪn 'tʃɪldərz, érsskin chíldĕrz

Childerstone, *f.n.,* 'tʃɪldərstoʊn, chíldĕrstŏn

Childer Thornton *Ches.,* 'tʃɪldər 'θɔrntən, chíldĕr thórntŏn

Child Okeford *Dorset,* 'tʃaɪld 'oʊkfərd, chíld ókförd. *A local variation is* 'tʃɪlɪ 'ɒkfərd, chílli óckförd.

Child's Ercall *Salop,* 'tʃaɪldz 'ɑrkl, chíldz aárkl

Childwall *Merseyside,* 'tʃɪlwɒl, chíl-wawl

Childwickbury *Herts.,* 'tʃɪlɪkbəri, chíllickbŭri

Childwick Green *Herts.,* 'tʃɪlɪk 'grin, chíllick green

Chilham *Kent,* 'tʃɪləm, chíllăm

Chillesford *Suffolk,* 'tʃɪlzfərd, chílzförd

Chillingham *Northd.,* 'tʃɪlɪŋəm, chilling-ăm

Chiltern Hills *Oxon.–Bucks.–Beds.–Herts.,* 'tʃɪltərn, chíltĕrn

Chilthorne Domer *Somerset,* 'tʃɪlθɔrn 'doʊmər, chíll-thorn dómĕr

Chilton Foliat *Wilts.,* 'tʃɪltən 'foʊlɪət, chíltŏn fóliăt

Chilton Polden *Somerset,* 'tʃɪltən 'poʊldən, chíltŏn póldĕn

Chilver, *f.n.,* 'tʃɪlvər, chílvĕr

Chilvers Coton *Warwicks.,* 'tʃɪlvərz 'koʊtən, chílvĕrz kótŏn

Chineham *Hants,* 'tʃɪnəm, chínnăm

Chinnery, *f.n.,* 'tʃɪnəri, chínnĕri

Chipchase, *f.n.,* 'tʃɪptʃeɪs, chíptchayss

Chipping Campden *Glos.,* 'tʃɪpɪŋ 'kæmdən, chipping kámdĕn

Chipping Norton *Oxon.,* 'tʃɪpɪŋ 'nɔrtən, chipping nórtŏn

Chipping Sodbury *Avon,* 'tʃɪpɪŋ 'sɒdbəri, chípping sódbŭri

Chirbury *Salop*, 'tʃɜrbərı, chírbŭri
Chirk *Clwyd*, tʃɜrk, chirk
Chirol, *f.n.*, 'tʃırəl, chírrŏl
Chirton *Tyne & Wear, Wilts.*,
'tʃɜrtən, chírtŏn
Chishill, Great *and* Little, *Cambs.*,
'tʃızl, chízzl
Chisholm, *f.n.*, 'tʃızəm, chízzŏm
Chisledon *Wilts.*, 'tʃızldən,
chízzldŏn
Chissell, *f.n.*, tʃı'zel, chizéll;
'tʃızl, chízzl
Chiswell, *f.n.*, 'tʃızwel, chízwel;
'tʃızwəl, chízwĕl
Chiswick *London*, 'tʃızık, chíz-
zick
Chiswick Eyot *London*, 'tʃızık
'eıt, chízzick áyt
Chittlehamholt *Devon*, 'tʃıtləm-
hoolt, chíttl-ăm-hōlt
Chivas, *f.n.*, 'ʃıvæs, shívvass
Chivenor *Devon*, 'tʃıvnər, chívnŏr
Chivers, *f.n.*, 'tʃıvərz, chívvĕrz
Choat, *f.n.*, tʃoʊt, chōt
Choate, *f.n.*, tʃoʊt, chōt
Chobham *Surrey*, 'tʃɒbəm,
chóbbăm
Chobham Farm *London*, 'tʃɒbəm,
chóbbăm
Cholderton *Wilts.*, 'tʃoʊldərtən,
chṓldĕrtŏn
Cholmeley, *f.n.*, 'tʃʌmlı, chúmli
Cholmondeley, *f.n.*, 'tʃʌmlı,
chúmli. *Family name of Baron
Delamere.*
Cholmondeley *Ches.*, 'tʃʌmlı,
chúmli. *Appropriate also for the
Marquess of* ~.
Cholmondeston *Ches.*, 'tʃɒmsən,
chómssŏn
Cholsey *Oxon.*, 'tʃoʊlzı, chṓlzi
Chomley, *f.n.*, 'tʃʌmlı, chúmli
Chorley Wood *Herts.*, 'tʃɔrlı 'wʊd,
chórli wǒod
Chorlton, *f.n.*, 'tʃɔrltən, chórltŏn
Chorlton-cum-Hardy *Gtr.
M'chester*, 'tʃɔrltən kʌm 'hɑrdı,
chórltŏn kum haárdi
Chote, *f.n.*, tʃoʊt, chōt
Chouffot, *f.n.*, 'ʃufoʊ, shoófō
Choveaux, *f.n.*, ʃə'voʊ, shŏvó;
'tʃoʊvoʊ, chóvō
Chovil, *f.n.*, 'tʃoʊvıl, chóvil
Chown, *f.n.*, tʃaʊn, chown
Chowns, *f.n.*, tʃaʊnz, chownz
Chrimes, *f.n.*, kraımz, krīmz
Chrishall *Essex*, 'krıʃəl, kríss-
-hawl
Christ, *f.n.*, krıst, krisst
Christian Malford *Wilts.*, 'krıstjən
'mɒlfərd, kríst-yăn máwlfŏrd
Christie, *f.n.*, 'krıstı, kríssti
Christison, *f.n.*, 'krıstısən,
krístissŏn

Christleton *Ches.*, 'krısltən,
kríssltŏn
Christopherson, *f.n.*, krıs'tɒfərsən,
kristófférsŏn
Christou, *f.n.*, 'krıstu, krísstoo
Christow *Devon*, 'krıstoʊ,
krísstō
Chroisg, Loch, *H'land*, xrɔısk,
chroysk
Chronnell, *f.n.*, 'krɒnl, krónnl
Chruikhorn, *f.n.*, 'krʊkhɔrn,
krǒokhorn
Chrysostom, saint, 'krısəstəm,
kríssŏstŏm
Chryston *S'clyde*, 'kraıstən,
krísstŏn
Chulmleigh *Devon*, 'tʃʌmlı,
chúmli
Churchill, *f.n.*, 'tʃɜrtʃıl, chúrtchil
Churchman, *f.n.*, 'tʃɜrtʃmən,
chúrtchmăn
Church Stowe *Northants.*,
'tʃɜrtʃ 'stoʊ, chúrtch stṓ
Chute, *f.n.*, tʃut, choot
Chuter, *f.n.*, 'tʃutər, choótĕr
Chuter-Ede, *f.n.*, 'tʃutər 'id,
choótĕr eéd. *Pronunciation of
the late Baron* ~.
Chwilog *Gwynedd*, 'xwilɒg,
chweélog
Chyandour *Cornwall*, 'ʃaıəndaʊər,
shí-ăndowr; 'tʃaıəndaʊər,
chí-ăndowr
Chynoweth, *f.n.*, ʃı'noʊəθ,
shinnó-ĕth
Chysoyster *Cornwall*, tʃaı'sɔstər,
chīssáwstĕr
Ciaran, *Irish C.n.*, 'kıərən, keéerăn
Cieslewicz, *f.n.*, si'ezləvıtʃ,
see-ézzlĕvitch
Cigman, *f.n.*, 'sıgmən, sígmăn
Cilan *Gwynedd*, 'kılən, killăn
Cilcain *Clwyd*, 'kılken, kilken
Cilcarw *Dyfed*, kıl'kæru,
kilkárroo
Cilcennin *Dyfed*, kıl'kenın,
kilkénnin. *Appropriate also for
the Viscountcy of* ~.
Cilcewydd *Powys*, kıl'kewıð,
kilké-with
Cilfrew *W. Glam.*, ˌkılvrı'u,
kilvri-oó
Cilfynydd *Mid Glam.*, kıl'vʌnıð,
kilvúnnith
Cilgerran *Dyfed*, kıl'gerən,
kilgérrăn
Cilie Aeron *Dyfed*, 'kıljə 'aırɒn,
kíl-yĕ íron
Ciliene *Powys*, kıl'jenə, kil-
-yénnĕ
Cilmery, *also spelt* Cilmeri,
Powys, kıl'merı, kilmérri
Cilrhedyn *Dyfed*, kıl'hredın,
kilréddin

Cilshafe Uchaf *Dyfed*, kıl'ʃævə 'ıxəv, kil-sháv-vĕ íchăv

Cilybebyll *W. Glam.*, ˌkılə'bebıɬ, killăbébbihl

Cil-y-Cwm *Dyfed*, ˌkılə'kʊm, killăkóŏm

Cil-y-Maenllwyd *Dyfed*, ˌkılə-'mænɬʊıd, killămán-hlóŏid

Cimla *W. Glam.*, 'kımlə, kímlă

Cinque Ports *E. Sussex, Kent*, 'sıŋk pɔrts, sínk ports. *This is the collective name for the towns of Hastings, Romney, Hythe, Dover and Sandwich, which combined for defensive purposes. Other towns later joined, so that there are now more than the original five of the name.*

Cippenham *Berks.*, 'sıpənəm, sippĕnăm

Cipriani, *18th-c. Florentine-English painter*, ˌsıprı'ɑnı, sipri-áani

Cirencester *Glos.*, 'saıərənsestər, sírênssesstĕr; 'sısıtər, síssitĕr. *The latter, although no longer commonly heard, has not entirely disappeared from use. For some, it is particularly associated with one of the older spellings, Ciceter.*

Ciro's *London club and restaurant*, 'sıərou, seérŏ

Ciste Dubh, *also spelt* **Dhubh**, *H'land*, 'kıʃtə 'du, kíshtĕ doó

Citrine, *f.n.*, sı'trin, sitréen. *Appropriate also for Baron* ~.

Clachan *Skye*, 'klæxən, kláchăn

Clachtoll *H'land*, 'klæx'toʊl, klách-tól

Clackmannan *Central*, klæk-'mænən, klackmánnăn; klək'mænən, klăkmánnăn

Claddagh *Co. Fermanagh*, 'klædə, kláddă

Clady *Co. Tyrone*, 'klædı, kláddi

Clady Circuit *Belfast*, 'klædı, kláddi

Cladymore *Co. Armagh*, ˌklædı-'mɔr, kladdimór

Claerwen, *River, Dyfed–Powys*, 'klaıərwen, klír-wen

Clagh Ouyre *I. of Man*, 'klæk 'aʊər, kláck ówr

Clague, *f.n.*, kleıg, klayg; kleg, kleg

Clancarty, *Earl of*, klæn'kɑrtı, klan-kaárti

Clandeboye *Co. Down*, 'klændı-bɔı, klándĕboy. *Appropriate also for Viscount* ~.

Clanmorris, *Baron*, klæn'mɒrıs, klanmórriss

Clannaborough *Devon*, 'klænəbərə, klánnăbŭră

Clanricarde, *f.n.*, klæn'rıkərd, klanríckărd. *Appropriate also for the Earl of* ~.

Clanwilliam, *Earl of*, klæn'wıljəm, klanwíll-yăm

Clapham *London, N. Yorks.*, 'klæpəm, kláppăm

Clapshoe, *f.n.*, 'klæpʃu, kláp-shoo

Clapworthy *Devon*, 'klæpərı, kláppĕri

Clarabut, *f.n.*, 'klærəbʌt, klárră-but

Clarach *Dyfed*, 'klærəx, klárrăch

Clarbeston *Dyfed*, 'klɑrbəstən, klaárbĕstŏn

Clare, *f.n.*, klɛər, klair

Clarendon, *Earl of*, 'klærəndən, klárrĕndŏn

Clarina, *Barony of*, klə'raınə, klărínă

Claringbull, *f.n.*, 'klærıŋbʊl, klárringbŏŏl

Clarke, *f.n.*, klɑrk, klaark

Claro, *f.n.*, 'klɛəroʊ, kláırō

Claro Barracks *N. Yorks.*, 'klɛəroʊ, kláırō

Clatteringshaws *Loch D. & G.*, 'klætərıŋʃɔz, kláttĕring-shawz

Claudy *Co. Derry*, 'klɒdı, kláwdi

Claughton, *f.n.*, 'klɒtən, kláwtŏn

Claughton *Lancs.*, 'klæftən, kláfftŏn. *Appropriate for the name of the village in the Lune valley.*

Claughton *Merseyside*, 'klɒtən, kláwtŏn. *Appropriate also for Baron Evans of* ~.

Claughton-on-Brock *Lancs.*, 'klaıtən ɒn 'brɒk, klíttŏn on bróck

Clausen, *f.n.*, 'klaʊsən, klówssĕn; 'klɒsən, kláwssĕn. *The first is appropriate for Sir George* ~ (1852–1944), *landscape and figure painter.*

Clauson, *f.n.*, 'klɒsən, kláwssŏn

Claverdon *Warwicks.*, 'klævərdən, klávvĕrdŏn; 'klɑrdən, klaárdŏn

Claverham *Avon*, 'klævərəm, klávvĕrăm

Claverhouse, *f.n.*, kleıvərhaʊs, kláyvĕr-howss

Claverhouse *Tayside*, 'kleıvər-haʊs, kláyvĕr-howss. *Appropriate also for John Graham of* ~, *Scottish soldier.*

Clavering, *f.n.*, 'klævərıŋ, klávvĕring

Clavering *Essex*, 'kleıvərıŋ, kláyvĕring

Claverley *Salop*, 'klævərlı, klávvĕrli

Claverton *Avon*, 'klævərtən, klávvĕrtŏn. *Appropriate also for* ~ *Down.*

Clayhidon *Devon*, 'kleɪhaɪdən, kláy-hīdŏn

Cleadon *Tyne and Wear*, 'klidən kléedŏn

Cleal, *f.n.*, klil, kleel

Cleanthous, *f.n.*, klɪ'ænθəs, kli-ánthüss

Clearwell *Glos.*, 'klɪər'wel, kléerwéll; klɪər'wel, kleerwéll; 'klɪərwel, kléerwell

Cleary, *f.n.*, 'klɪərɪ, kléeri

Cleasby, *f.n.*, 'klɪzbɪ, kléezbi

Clease, *f.n.*, klis, kleess

Cleather, *f.n.*, 'kleðər, kléthĕr

Cleator *Cumbria*, 'klitər, kléetŏr

Cleckheaton *W. Yorks.*, klek-'hitən, kleck-héetŏn

Cleddau, River, *Dyfed*, 'kleðaɪ, kléthī

Cledwyn, *Welsh C.n.*, 'kledwɪn, klédwin. *Appropriate also for Baron* ~ *of Penrhos.*

Cleese, *f.n.*, kliz, kleez

Cleethorpes *Humberside*, 'kliθɔrps, klée-thorps

Clegyr *Dyfed*, 'klegər, kléggŭr

Clehonger *H. & W.*, 'klɒŋgər, klóng-gĕr

Cleland, *f.n.*, 'kleland, klélländ; 'klɪland, kléeländ

Cleland *S'clyde*, 'kleland, klélländ

Cleland House *London*, 'kliland, kléeländ

Clemak, *f.n.*, 'klimæk, kléemack

Clemenger, *f.n.*, 'klemɪndʒər, klémmĕnjĕr

Clemitson, *f.n.*, 'klemɪtsən, klémmitsŏn

Clemmow, *f.n.*, 'klemou, klémmō

Clemo, *f.n.*, 'klemou, klémmō

Clenchwarton *Norfolk*, 'klenʃwərtən, klénshwawrtŏn

Clennell, *f.n.*, klə'nel, klĕnéll

Cleobury, *f.n.*, 'kloubərɪ, klóbŭri; 'klɪbərɪ, kléebŭri

Cleobury Mortimer *Salop*, 'klɪbərɪ 'mɔrtɪmər, klíbbŭri mórtimĕr

Cleobury North *Salop*, 'klɪbərɪ 'nɔrθ, klíbbŭri nórth

Clerici, *f.n.*, 'klerɪsɪ, klérrissi

Clerk, *f.n.*, klɑrk, klaark

Clerke, *f.n.*, klɑrk, klaark

Clervaux *N. Yorks.*, 'klɪərvɒks, kláirvawks

Clery, *f.n.*, 'klɪərɪ, kléeri

Clettraval *N. Uist*, 'kletrəvæl, kléttrăval

Clevedon *Avon*, 'klivdən, kléevdŏn

Cleveleys *Lancs.*, 'klivlɪz, kléevliz

Cleverdon, *f.n.*, 'klevərdən, klévvĕrdŏn

Cleverley, *f.n.*, 'klevərlɪ, klévvĕrli

Cleverly, *f.n.*, 'klevərlɪ, klévvĕrli

Clewlow, *f.n.*, 'kluloʊ, klóolō

Cley *Norfolk*, klaɪ, klī; kleɪ, klay

Clibborn, *f.n.*, 'klɪbərn, klíbborn

Cliburn *Cumbria*, 'klaɪbərn, klíbŭrn

Clickhimin, Loch, *Shetland*, 'klɪkɪmɪn, klíckimin

Cliddesden *Hants*, 'klɪdɪzdən, klíddĕzdĕn

Clifford, *C.n. and f.n.*, 'klɪfərd, klíffŏrd

Cliffords Mesne *Glos.*, 'klɪfərdz 'min, klíffŏrdz méen

Clifton of Leighton Bromswold, Baron, 'klɪftən əv 'leɪtən 'brʌmzwould, klíftŏn ŏv láytŏn brúmzwōld

Clifton Reynes *Bucks.*, 'klɪftən 'reɪnz, klíftŏn ráynz

Clilverd, *f.n.*, 'klɪvərd, klívvĕrd

Climie, *f.n.*, 'klaɪmɪ, klími

Clipsham *Leics.*, 'klɪpʃəm, klíp-shăm; 'klɪpshəm, klíps-häm

Clipstone *Notts.*, 'klɪpstoun, klípstŏn

Clitheroe *Lancs.*, 'klɪðərou, klíthĕrō. *Appropriate also for Baron* ~.

Clitherow, *f.n.*, 'klɪðərou, klíthĕrō

Cliveden *Bucks.*, 'klɪvdən, klívdĕn

Cliviger *Lancs.*, 'klɪvɪdʒər, klívvijĕr

Cloan *Tayside*, kloun, klōn

Clocaenog *Clwyd*, klou'kaɪnɒg, klōkínog

Clode, *f.n.*, kloud, klōd

Cloete, *f.n.*, klou'iti, klō-éeti; 'kluti, klóoti

Cloford *Avon*, 'kloufərd, klófŏrd

Clogher, *f.n.*, 'klɒxər, klóchĕr

Clogher *Co. Tyrone*, 'klɒxər, klóchĕr

Clogwyn Du'r Arddu *Gwynedd*, klou'guɪn dɪər 'arðɪ, klōgoó-in deer aárthee

Clogwyn-y-Person *Gwynedd*, klou'guɪn ə 'pɛərsɒn, klōgoó-in ă páirsson

Clompus, *f.n.*, 'klɒmpəs, klómpüss

Clonaneese *Co. Tyrone*, ˌklɒnə-'nis, klonnănéess

Clonard *Co. Antrim*, 'klɒnərd, klónnärd

Clonbrock, *f.n.*, klɒn'brɒk, klonbróck

Cloncurry, *f.n.*, klɒn'kʌrɪ, klon-kúrri

Clonmacate Co. Armagh, ˌklɒnmə'keɪt, klon-măkáyt

Clonmell, f.n., klɒn'mel, klon-méll

Clonmore, f.n., klɒn'mɔr, klon-mór

Clontivrim Co. Fermanagh, klɒn'tɪvrɪm, klontívvrim

Clontoe Co. Tyrone, klʌn'toʊ, kluntő. Also spelt **Cluntoe**

Clopet, f.n., 'kloʊpeɪ, klópay

Clophill Beds., 'klɒphɪl, klóp-hill

Close, f.n., kloʊs, klōss

Clother, f.n., 'kloʊðər, klóthĕr

Clothier, f.n., 'kloʊðɪər, klóthiĕr

Clough, f.n., klʌf, kluff

Clough Co. Down, klɒx, kloch

Clough, River, Cumbria, klʌf, kluff

Clougha Pike Lancs., 'klɒfə 'paɪk, klóffă pík

Cloughenery Co. Tyrone, ˌklɒxə'neərɪ, klochĕnáiri

Cloughey Co. Down, 'klɒxɪ, klóchi

Clough Fold Lancs., 'klʌf 'foʊld, klúff főld

Cloughmills Co. Antrim, klɒx-'mɪlz, klochmíllz

Cloughogue Co. Armagh, klɒx-'oʊg, klochőg

Cloughton N. Yorks., 'klaʊtən, klówtŏn; 'kloʊtən, klőtŏn

Clousta Shetland, 'klustə, kloóstă

Clouston, f.n., 'klustən, kloósstŏn; 'klaʊstən, klówsstŏn

Clouston, J. Storer, author, 'stɔrər 'klustən, stáwrĕr kloósstŏn

Clovelly Devon, klə'velɪ, klŏvélli

Clovenfords Borders, ˌkloʊvən-'fɔrdz, klővĕnfórdz

Cloverley Salop, 'klɒvərlɪ, klóvvĕrli

Clow, f.n., kloʊ, klő

Clowes, f.n., klaʊz, klowz; kluz, klooz

Clowne Derby., klaʊn, klown

Cluanie, Loch, H'land, 'klunɪ, kloóni; 'kluənɪ, kloó-ăni

Clubbe, f.n., klʌb, klubb

Clucas, f.n., 'klukəs, kloókăss

Clulow, f.n., 'klulou, kloólő

Clumber Park Notts., 'klʌmbər 'pɑrk, klúmbĕr paárk. This gives its name to the Clumber spaniel.

Clun Salop, klʌn, klun. Appropriate also for Baron ~, and for the River ~ which flows through Shropshire and joins the River Teme.

Clunbury Salop, 'klʌnbərɪ, klúnbŭri

Clunes, H'land, klunz, kloonz

Clungunford Salop, klʌn'gʌnfərd, klun-gúnfŏrd

Clunie, f.n., 'klunɪ, kloóni

Clunie, Grampian, Tayside, 'klunɪ, kloóni

Clunies, f.n., 'klunɪz, kloóniz

Cluntoe Co. Tyrone, klʌn'toʊ, kluntő. Also spelt **Clontoe**

Clunton Salop, 'klʌntən, klúntŏn

Cluse, f.n., kluz, klooz

Clutsam, f.n., 'klʌtsəm, klútsăm

Clutton Avon, 'klʌtən, klúttŏn

Clwyd, River, Clwyd, 'kluɪd, kloo-id. Appropriate also for the county name, which is taken from that of the river, and for Baron ~.

Clwydian Range Clwyd, klu'ɪdɪən, kloo-íddiăn

Clydach Gwent, W. Glam., 'klɪdəx, klíddăch; 'klʌdəx, klúddăch. Appropriate also for the River ~ (Dyfed), ~ Terrace (Gwent), and ~ Vale (Mid Glam.).

Clyde, River, S'clyde, klaɪd, klīd

Clydesmuir, Baron, 'klaɪdzmjuər, klídzmyoŏr

Clyffe Pypard Wilts., 'klɪf 'paɪpərd, klíff pípărd

Clynder S'clyde, 'klɪndər, klíndĕr

Clynderwen, also spelt **Clunderwen,** Dyfed, klɪn'deərwən, klindáirwĕn

Clyne W. Glam., klaɪn, klīn

Clynnog Gwynedd, 'klʌnɒg, klúnnog

Clynnogfawr Gwynedd, 'klʌnɒg-'vauər, klúnnogvówr

Clypse Circuit I. of Man, klɪps, klips

Clyro Powys, 'klaɪrou, klírő

Clyst, River, Devon, klɪst, klisst

Clywedog Valley Dyfed, klɪ-'wedɒg, kliwéddog

Cnwch Coch Dyfed, 'knux 'koux, knoóch kőch. Initial -k is pronounced.

Coad, f.n., koʊd, kőd

Coade, f.n., koʊd, kőd. Appropriate also for the building-stone mixture known as ~ stone, associated in the 18th c. with Mrs Eleanor ~.

Coady, f.n., 'koʊdɪ, kődi

Coagh Co. Tyrone, koʊx, kōch

Coaker, f.n., 'koʊkər, kőkĕr

Coakley, f.n., 'koʊklɪ, kőkli

Coalbrookdale Salop, 'koʊlbruk-'deɪl, kőlbrŏok-dáyl

Coalisland Co. Tyrone, koʊl-'aɪlənd, kōlíländ

Coalsnaughton Central, koʊlz-'nɔtən, kőlznáwtŏn

Coase, f.n., koʊz, kőz

Coate *Wilts.,* koʊt, kōt. *Appro-priate for both places of this name in Wilts.*
Coatesgate *D. & G.,* 'koʊts'geɪt, kōts-gáyt
Coatham *Cleveland,* 'koʊtəm, kōtäm
Cobairdy *Grampian,* koʊ'bɛərdɪ, kōbáirdi
Cobban, *f.n.,* 'kɒbən, kóbbän
Cobbold, *f.n.,* 'kɒboʊld, kóbbōld. *Appropriate also for Baron ~.*
Coberley *Glos.,* 'kʌbərlɪ, kúbbĕrli
Coberman, *f.n.,* 'koʊbərmən, kóbĕrmän
Cobham, *f.n.,* 'kɒbəm, kóbbäm
Cobley, *f.n.,* 'kɒblɪ, kóbbli
Cobrin, *f.n.,* 'kɒbrɪn, kóbbrin
Cochran, *f.n.,* 'kɒxrən, kóchrăn; 'kɒkrən, kóckrăn
Cochrane, *f.n.,* 'kɒxrən, kóchrăn; 'kɒkrən, kóckrăn
Cockayne, *f.n.,* kɒ'keɪn, kockáyn
Cock Bridge *Grampian,* 'kɒk brɪdʒ, kóck brij
Cockburn, *f.n.,* 'koʊbərn, kóbūrn; 'koʊbərn, kóburn
Cockburnspath *Borders,* 'koʊbərnz'pɑθ, kóbūrnzpaáth
Cockcroft, *f.n.,* 'kɒkkrɒft, kóck--kroft; 'koʊkrɒft, kókroft. *The first is appropriate for Sir John ~, physicist.*
Cocke, *f.n.,* koʊk, kōk
Cockell, *f.n.,* 'kɒkl, kóckl
Cockenzie *Lothian,* kə'kenzɪ, kōkénzi
Cockerell, *f.n.,* 'kɒkərəl, kóckĕrĕl
Cockerham, *f.n.,* 'kɒkərəm, kóckĕräm
Cockerington *Lincs.,* 'kɒkərɪŋtən, kóckĕringtŏn
Cockerline, *f.n.,* 'kɒkərlaɪn, kóckĕrlīn
Cockermouth *Cumbria,* 'kɒkərmaʊθ, kóckĕr-mowth; 'kɒkərməθ, kóckĕr-mŭth
Cockernhoe Green *Herts.,* 'kɒkərnhoʊ, kóckĕrn-hō
Cockett *W. Glam.,* 'kɒkɪt, kóckĕt
Cockfield, *f.n.,* 'koʊfild, kó-feeld
Cockley Cley *Norfolk,* 'kɒklɪ 'klaɪ, kóckli klī
Cockram, *f.n.,* 'kɒkrəm, kóckräm
Cockroft, *f.n.,* 'kɒkrɒft, kóckroft; 'koʊkrɒft, kókroft
Cocks, *f.n.,* kɒks, kocks
Cockshott, *f.n.,* 'koʊʃɒt, kó-shot
Cockshut, *f.n.,* 'kɒkʃʌt, kóck--shut; 'koʊʃu, kó-shoo
Cockshutt *Salop,* 'kɒkʃʌt, kóck--shut
Codham Hall *Essex,* 'kɒdəm, kóddäm

Codicote *Herts.,* 'kɒdɪkət, kóddikŏt
Codsall *Staffs.,* 'kɒdsl, kódssl
Coe, *f.n.,* koʊ, kō
Coed Dolgarrog *Gwynedd,* ˌkɔɪd dɒl'gærɒg, koyd dolgárrog
Coed-ffranc *W. Glam.,* kɔɪd-'fræŋk, koydfránk
Coed Gorswen *Gwynedd,* ˌkɔɪd gɔrs'wen, koyd gorss-wén
Coedpenmaen *Mid Glam.,* ˌkɔɪdpen'maɪn, koyd-pen-mín
Coed Poeth *Clwyd,* kɔɪd 'pɔɪθ, koyd póyth
Coed Rheidol Nature Reserve *Dyfed,* kɔɪd 'hraɪdɒl, koyd rídol
Coed Tremadoc Nature Reserve *Gwynedd,* ˌkɔɪd trɪ'mædɒk, koyd trĕmáddock
Coed-y-Brenin Forest *Gwynedd,* ˌkɔɪdə'brenɪn, koyd-ă-brénnin
Coegnant Colliery *Mid Glam.,* 'kɔɪgnænt, kóyg-nant
Coetmore, *f.n.,* 'kɔɪtmɔr, kóytmor
Coffill, *f.n.,* 'kɒfɪl, kóffil
Cogan Pill *S. Glam.,* 'koʊgən 'pɪl, kōgăn pill
Cogenhoe, *f.n.,* 'kʊknoʊ, kŏŏknō
Cogenhoe *Northants.,* 'kʊknoʊ, kŏŏknō; 'koʊgənhoʊ, kōgĕn-hō
Cogers, The, *London inn,* 'kɒdʒərz, kójjĕrz
Coggeshall, *f.n.,* 'kɒgzɒl, kógzawl
Coggeshall *Essex,* 'kɒgɪʃl, kóggĕshl; 'kɒksl, kócksl
Coggle, *f.n.,* 'kɒgl, kóggl
Coghill, *f.n.,* 'kɒghɪl, kóg-hil
Coghlan, *f.n.,* 'koʊlən, kṓlăn
Cogill, *f.n.,* 'koʊgɪl, kōgil
Cogry *Co. Antrim,* 'kɒgrɪ, kógri
Cohen, *f.n.,* 'koʊɪn, kṓ-ĕn
Cohn, *f.n.,* koʊn, kōn
Coinneach Odhar, *the Brahan Seer,* 'kɒnjəx 'oʊər, kón-yăch ó-ĕr
Coity *Mid Glam.,* 'kɔɪtɪ, kóyti
Cokayne, *f.n.,* kɒ'keɪn, kockáyn
Coke, *f.n.,* kʊk, kŏŏk; koʊk, kōk. *The first is appropriate for the Earl of Leicester's family name.*
Colan *Cornwall,* 'kɒlən, kóllăn
Colaton Raleigh *Devon,* 'kɒlətən 'rɒlɪ, kóllătŏn ráwli
Colborn, *f.n.,* 'koʊbərn, kóbūrn
Colborne, *f.n.,* 'koʊlbərn, kōl-būrn; 'kɒlbərn, kólborn
Colbren *W. Glam.,* 'kɒlbren, kólbren
Colbrook *Powys,* 'koʊlbrʊk, kōlbrŏŏk
Colbury *Hants.,* 'koʊlbərɪ, kólbŭri
Colby, *f.n.,* 'kɒlbɪ, kólbi
Colchester *Essex,* 'koʊltʃəstər, kóltchĕstĕr

Colclough, *f.n.*, 'koʊlklʌf kól-
   kluff; 'koʊklı, kókli
Cold Hesledon *Durham*, 'koʊld
   'hesldən, kóld héssldŏn
Cold Hiendley *W. Yorks.*, 'koʊld
   'hindlı, kóld héendli
Coldingham *Borders*, 'koʊldıŋəm,
   kólding-ăm
Coldred *Kent*, 'koʊldrıd, kóldrĕd
Coldrick, *f.n.*, 'koʊldrık, kóldrick
Coldwaltham *W. Sussex*, 'koʊld-
   'wɒləm, kóldwáwl-thăm
Coleclough, *f.n.*, 'koʊlklaʊ,
   kólklow; 'koʊlklʌf, kólkluff
Coleford *Glos.*, 'koʊlfərd, kól-
   fŏrd
Colehan, *f.n.*, 'koʊləhən, kólĕhăn
Colehill *Dorset*, 'kɒlhıl, kól-hil;
   'koʊlhıl, kól-hil
Coleman, *f.n.*, 'koʊlmən, kólmăn
Coleorton *Leics.*, kɒl'ɔrtən,
   kolórtŏn
Coleraine *Co. Derry*, koʊl'reın,
   kólráyn. *Appropriate also for
   Baron ~.*
Coleridge, *f.n.*, 'koʊlrıdʒ, kólrij.
   Appropriate also for Baron ~.
Coleridge-Taylor, Avril, *com-
   poser*, 'ævrıl 'koʊlərıdʒ 'teılər,
   ávreel kólĕrij táylŏr
Colerne *Wilts.*, 'kɒlərn, kóllĕrn;
   'kʌlərn, kúllĕrn; kə'lərn,
   kólĕrn. *The third is the pro-
   nunciation used by RAF
   personnel for their airfield.*
Coleshill, *f.n.*, 'koʊlzhıl, kólz-hill
Coleshill *Oxon.*, 'koʊlzhıl, kólz-
   -hil
Colet, *f.n.*, 'kɒlıt, kóllĕt
Colfox, *f.n.*, 'koʊlfɒks, kólfocks
Colgan, *f.n.*, 'kɒlgən, kólgăn
Colgrain, Baron, 'kɒlgreın,
   kólgrayn
Colin, *C.n. and f.n.*, 'kɒlın, kóllin
Colinton *Edinburgh*, 'kɒlıntən,
   kóllintŏn
Colintraive *S'clyde*, ˌkɒlın'traıv,
   kollintrív
Coll Island *S'clyde*, kɒl, kol
Collard, *f.n.*, 'kɒlɑrd, kóllaard
Collaro, *f.n.*, kə'lɑroʊ, kŏláarō
Colleano, *f.n.*, kə'linoʊ, kŏléenō
Colleau, *f.n.*, 'kɒloʊ, kóllō
Collender, *f.n.*, 'kɒlındər,
   kóllĕndĕr
Colles, *f.n.*, 'kɒlıs, kólliss
Collessie *Fife*, kə'lesı, kŏléssi
Collet, *f.n.*, 'kɒlıt, kóllĕt
Colley, *f.n.*, 'kɒlı, kólli
Collier, *f.n.*, 'kɒlıər, kólli-ĕr
Collingbourne Ducis *Wilts.*,
   'kɒlıŋbərn 'djusıs, kólling-born
   déwsiss
Collinge, *f.n.*, 'kɒlındʒ, kóllinj

Collingham *W. Yorks.*, 'kɒlıŋəm,
   kólling-ăm
Collinson, *f.n.*, 'kɒlınsən, kóllinsŏn
Collison, *f.n.*, 'kɒlısən, kóllissŏn
Collopy, *f.n.*, 'kɒləpı, kóllŏpi
Collow, *f.n.*, 'kɒloʊ, kóllō
Colman, *f.n.*, 'kɒlmən, kólmăn;
   'koʊlmən, kólmăn
Colmanell, saint, ˌkɒlmə'nel,
   kolmănéll
Colmer, *f.n.*, 'kɒlmər, kól-mĕr
Colmonell *S'clyde*, ˌkɒlmɒ'nel,
   kolmonnéll
Colnaghi *London fine art dealers*,
   kɒl'nɑgı, kolnáagi
Colnbrook *Bucks.*, 'koʊnbrʊk,
   kŏnbrŏŏk; 'koʊlnbrʊk, kóln-
   brŏŏk
Colne, *f.n.*, koʊn, kōn
Colne, *Lancs.*, koʊn, kōn
Colne, River, *W. Yorks.*, koʊn,
   kōn. *Appropriate also for the ~
   Valley Parliamentary Division.*
Colne Engaine *Essex*, ˌkoʊn
   ən'geın, kōn ĕn-gáyn
Colney *Norfolk*, 'koʊnı, kóni
Colney Heath *Herts.*, 'koʊnı 'hiθ,
   kóni héeth
Coln St. Aldwyn *Glos.*, 'koʊn snt
   'ɔldwın, kōn sĭnt áwldwin
Colomb, *f.n.*, 'kɒləm, kóllŏm;
   'kɒlɒm, kóllom
Colonsay Island, *S'clyde*, 'kɒlən-
   zeı, kóllŏnzay
Colquhoun, *f.n.*, kə'hun, kŏ-hoŏn
Colsell, *f.n.*, 'koʊlsl, kólssl
Colsterworth *Lincs.*, 'koʊlstər-
   wərθ, kólsstĕrwúrth
Colston, *f.n.*, 'koʊlstən, kólsstŏn
Colston Basset, *Notts.*, 'koʊlstən
   'bæsıt, kólsstŏn bássĕt
Colston Hall, *Bristol*, 'koʊlstən,
   kólsstŏn
Coltart, *f.n.*, 'koʊltɑrt, kóltaart
Coltishall *Norfolk*, 'koʊltıʃəl,
   kólti-shawl; 'koʊltıshəl,
   kóltiss-hawl; 'koʊltıʃl, kóltiss-
   awl; 'koʊltıʃl, kóltishl; 'koʊlsl,
   kólssl. *The last of these is now
   considered old-fashioned.*
Colum, *f.n.*, 'kɒləm, kóllŭm
Columba, saint, kə'lʌmbə,
   kólúmbă
Colvend *D. & G.*, kɒlv'end,
   kolvénd
Colville, *f.n.*, 'kɒlvıl, kólvil
Colville of Culross, Viscount,
   'kɒlvıl ɒv 'kurɒs, kólvil ŏv
   koó-ross
Colvin, *f.n.*, 'kɒlvın, kólvin
Colwall *H. & W.*, 'kɒlwəl, kólwăl
Colwich *Staffs.*, 'kɒlwıtʃ, kól-
   witch
Colwick *Notts.*, 'kɒlık, kóllick

Colworth *W. Sussex*, 'kɒlwɜrθ, kólwurth

Colwyn, Baron, 'kɒlwɪn, kólwin

Colwyn Bay *Clwyd*, 'kɒlwɪn 'beɪ, kólwin báy

Colyford *Devon*, 'kɒlɪfərd, kólliförd

Colyton *Devon*, 'kɒlɪtən, kóllitön. *Appropriate also for Baron ~.*

Coman, *f.n.*, 'koʊmən, kốmăn

Combe, *f.n.*, kum, koom; koʊm, kōm

Combe Cross *Devon*, 'kum 'krɒs, koʹom króss

Combe in Teignhead, *also spelt* **Combeinteignhead**, *Devon*, 'kum ɪn 'tinhed, koʹom in téen-hed

Comben, *f.n.*, 'kɒmbən, kómbĕn

Combepyne, *see* **Combpyne**, *Devon*

Comber, *f.n.*, 'kɒmbər, kómbĕr

Comber *Co. Down*, 'kʌmbər, kúmbĕr

Comberbach *Ches.*, 'kʌmbər-bætʃ, kúmbĕrbatch

Combermere, Viscount, 'kʌmbərmɪər, kúmbĕrmeer. *Hence also for ~ Barracks, Windsor (Berks.).*

Comberti, *f.n.*, kɒm'beərtɪ, kom-báirti

Comberton *Cambs.*, 'kɒmbərtən, kómbĕrtŏn

Comboy, *f.n.*, 'kɒmbɔɪ, kómboy

Combpyne, *also spelt* **Combe-pyne**, *Devon*, 'kum'paɪn, koom-pín

Combrook *Warwicks.*, 'kɒmbrʊk, kómbrŏŏk

Combwich *Somerset*, 'kʌmɪdʒ, kúmmij; 'kʌmɪtʃ, kúmmitch; 'kʌmɪdʒ, koʹomij; 'kʌmɪtʃ, koʹomitch

Comby, *f.n.*, 'kɒmbɪ, kómbi

Comer, *f.n.*, 'koʊmər, kốmĕr

Comerford, *f.n.*, 'kɒmərfərd, kómmĕrförd

Comeskey, *f.n.*, kə'meskɪ, kŏméski

Comgall, saint, 'kɒmgəl, kómgăl

Comiston *Lothian*, 'kɒmɪstən, kómmistŏn

Compton, *f.n.*, 'kʌmptən, kúmp-tŏn; 'kɒmptən, kómptŏn. *The first is correct for the Marquess of Northampton's family name. It is also appropriate for Sir ~ Mackenzie, author, and for Fay ~, actress.*

Compton *Berks.*, 'kɒmptən, kómptŏn

Compton *Hants*, 'kʌmptən, kúmp-tŏn

Compton-Burnett, Ivy, *author*, 'kʌmptən 'bɜrnɪt, kúmptŏn búrnĕt

Compton Castle *Devon*, 'kɒmptən 'kɑsl, kómptŏn kaʹassl

Compton Chamberlayne *Wilts.*, 'kɒmptən 'tʃeɪmbərlɪn, kómptŏn cháymbĕrlin

Compton Down *Hants*, 'kɒmptən 'daʊn, kómptŏn dówn

Compton Pauncefoot *Somerset*, 'kɒmptən 'pɒnsfʊt, kómptŏn páwnssfŏŏt

Compton Valence *Dorset*, 'kɒmptən 'væləns, kómptŏn válĕnss

Compton Wynyates, *also spelt* **Wyniates, Winyates**, *War-wicks.*, 'kɒmptən 'wɪnjeɪts, kómptŏn wín-yayts; 'kʌmptən 'wɪnjeɪts, kúmptŏn wín-yayts. *The first is the local village pro-nunciation. The second is used, appropriately, by the Marquess of Northampton for his family seat.*

Comrie, *f.n.*, 'kɒmrɪ, kómri

Comrie *Fife, Tayside*, 'kɒmrɪ, kómri

Comyn, *f.n.*, 'kʌmɪn, kúmmin

Comyns, *f.n.*, 'kʌmɪnz, kúmminz

Conacher, *f.n.*, 'kɒnəxər, kón-năchĕr

Conan, *C.n. and f.n.*, 'kɒnən, kónnăn; 'koʊnən, kốnăn

Conan Doyle, Sir Arthur, *author*, 'koʊnən 'dɔɪl, kốnăn dóyl. *This is the family pronunciation, although he is also popularly known as* 'kɒnən, kónnăn.

Conant, *f.n.*, 'kɒnənt, kónnănt; 'koʊnənt, kốnănt

Conbeer, *f.n.*, 'kɒnbɪər, kónbeer

Concannon, *f.n.*, kɒn'kænən, kon-kánnŏn

Condell, *f.n.*, kɒn'del, kondéll

Condicote *Glos.*, 'kɒndɪkət, kóndikŏt

Condorrat *S'clyde*, kən'dɒrət, kŏndórrăt

Condover *Salop*, 'kʌndoʊvər, kúndŏvĕr

Condra, *f.n.*, 'kɒndrə, kóndră

Conesford, Barony of, 'kɒnɪsfərd, kónnĕsförd

Coneygarth *Northd.*, 'koʊnɪgɑrθ, kốni-gaarth

Coneysthorpe *N. Yorks.*, 'kʌnɪs-θɔrp, kúnniss-thorp; 'koʊnɪs-θɔrp, kốniss-thorp

Conger Hill *Beds.*, 'kɒŋɡər, kóng-gĕr

Congleton *Ches.*, 'kɒŋɡltən, kóng-gltŏn. *Appropriate also for Baron ~.*

Congresbury *Avon*, 'kɒŋzbrı,
kóngzbri; 'kumzbərı, koómz-
būri. *The first is the local
pronunciation; the other is said
to originate in Bristol.*

Conibear, *f.n.*, 'koʊnıbeər,
kónibair

Coningham, *f.n.*, 'kʌnıŋəm,
kúnning-ăm

Coningsby *Lincs.*, 'kɒnıŋzbı,
kónningzbi; 'kʌnıŋzbı, kún-
ningzbi

Conington *Cambs.*, 'kɒnıŋtən,
kónning-tŏn

Conisbee, *f.n.*, 'kɒnızbı, kónnizbi

Conisbrough, *also spelt* Conis-
borough, *S. Yorks.*, 'kɒnısbərə,
kónnissbūrå

Coniscliffe, High *and* Low, *Durham*, 'kɒnısklıf, kónniss-kliff

Conisholme *Lincs.*, 'kɒnıshoʊm,
kónniss-hōm; 'kɒnızhoʊm,
kónniz-hōm; 'kɒnıʃoʊm,
kónni-shōm

Coniston Water *Cumbria*, 'kɒnıs-
tən 'wɔːtər, kónnistŏn wáwtĕr

Conlig *Co. Down*, kən'lıg, kŏnlíg

Connah, *f.n.*, 'kɒnə, kónnå

Connah's Quay *Clwyd*, 'kɒnəz 'ki,
kónnåz kée

Connaught, Dukedom of, 'kɒnɔt,
kónnawt

Connaughton, *f.n.*, 'kɒnətən,
kónnătŏn

Connel Ferry *S'clyde*, 'kɒnl 'ferı,
kónnl férri

Connell, *f.n.*, 'kɒnl, kónnl; kə'nel,
kŏnéll

Connelly, *f.n.*, 'kɒnəlı, kónnĕli;
kə'nelı, kŏnélli

Connolly, *f.n.*, 'kɒnəlı, kónnŏli

Connor *Co. Antrim*, 'kɒnər,
kónnŏr

Connor Downs *Cornwall*, 'kɒnər
'daʊnz, kónnŏr dównz

Connswater *Co. Down*, 'kɒnz-
wɔːtər, kónz-wawtĕr

Conolly, *f.n.*, 'kɒnəlı, kónnŏli

Conon *H'land*, 'kɒnən, kónnŏn

Cononley *N. Yorks.*, 'kɒnənlı,
kónnŏnli

Consett *Durham*, 'kɒnsıt, kónssĕt;
'kɒnset, kónsset

Considine, *f.n.*, 'kɒnsıdaın,
kónssidin

Constable, *f.n.*, 'kʌnstəbl, kúnstăbl; 'kɒnstəbl, kónstăbl. *The
first is appropriate for John ~,
the painter and his family.*

Constable Burton *N. Yorks.*,
'kʌnstəbl 'bɜːtən, kúnstăbl
búrtŏn

Constantine, *f.n.*, 'kɒnstəntaın,
kónstăntin

Constantine *Cornwall*, 'kɒnstəntaın, kónstāntīn

Contin *H'land*, 'kɒntın, kóntin

Conway, *former spelling of*
Conwy *q.v.*, *Gwynedd*, 'kɒnweı,
kónway

Conwil Cayo *Dyfed*, 'kɒnwıl
'kaıoʊ, kónwil kí-ō

Conwy *Gwynedd*, 'kɒnwı, kónwi

Conybeare, *f.n.*, 'kɒnıbıər, kónni-
beer; 'kʌnıbıər, kúnnibeer

Conyer *Kent*, 'kʌnjər, kún-yĕr;
'kɒnjər, kón-yĕr

Conyers, *f.n.*, 'kɒnjərz, kón-yĕrz

Conyngham, Marquess, 'kʌnıŋəm,
kúnning-ăm

Cooden *E. Sussex*, 'kudən,
koódĕn; ku'den, koodén

Cookstown *Co. Tyrone*, 'kuks-
taʊn, koókstown

Coole Pilate *Ches.*, 'kul 'paılət,
koól pílăt

Coolin Hills *see* Cuillin

Coombe, *f.n..*, kum, koom

Coombs, *f.n.*, kumz, koomz

Coomes, *f.n.*, kumz, koomz

Coope, *f.n.*, kup, koop

Coopersale *Essex*, 'kupərseıl,
koópěrssayl

Copelin, *f.n.*, 'koʊplın, kóplin

Copestake, *f.n.*, 'koʊpsteık,
kŏpstayk

Copinsay *Orkney*, 'kɒpınseı,
kóppinssay

Copland, *f.n.*, 'koʊplənd, kóplănd

Copleston, *f.n.*, 'kɒplstən, kópplstŏn

Copley, *f.n.*, 'kɒplı, kópli

Coplin, *f.n.*, 'kɒplın, kóplin

Copped Hall *Essex*, 'kɒpt 'hɒl,
kópt háwl

Coppela, *f.n.*, 'kɒpələ, kóppĕlå

Coppell, *f.n.*, 'kɒpl, kóppl

Copperashouse *W. Yorks.*,
'kɒpərzhaʊs, kóppĕrzhowss

Coppinger, *f.n.*, 'kɒpındʒər,
kóppinjĕr

Coppins *Bucks.*, 'kɒpınz, kóppinz

Copplestone *Devon*, 'kɒplstən,
kópplstŏn

Coppull *Lancs.*, 'kɒpl, kóppl

Coquet *Northd.*, 'koʊkıt, kókĕt.
*Appropriate for both river and
island of this name.*

Coquetdale *Northd.*, 'koʊkıtdeıl,
kókitdayl

Coral, *f.n.*, 'kɒrəl, kórrăl

Corbally, *f.n.*, 'kɔːbəlı, kórbăli

Corbally *Co. Antrim*, kɔː'bælı,
korbáli

Corbet, *f.n.*, 'kɔːbıt, kórbĕt

Corbett, *f.n.*, 'kɔːbıt, kórbĕt

Corbishley, *f.n.*, 'kɔːbıʃlı, kór-
bishli

Corbould, f.n., 'kɔrbould, kór-bōld

Corbridge Northd., 'kɔrbrɪdʒ, kórbrij

Corcoran, f.n., 'kɔrkərən, kórkŏrăn

Cordeaux, f.n., 'kɔrdou, kórdō

Cordell, f.n., kɔr'del, kordéll

Cordiner, f.n., 'kɔrdɪnər, kórdinĕr

Cordingley industrial prison Surrey, 'kɔrdɪŋlɪ, kórding-li

Coren, f.n., 'kɔrən, kórrĕn

Corina, f.n., kə'rinə, kŏreĕnă

Cork and Orrery, Earl of, 'kɔrk ənd 'ɒrərɪ, kórk ănd órrĕri

Corken, f.n., 'kɔrkən, kórkĕn

Corkett, f.n., kɔr'ket, korkétt

Corkin, f.n., 'kɔrkɪn, kórkin

Corlett, f.n., 'kɔrlɪt, kórlĕt

Corley, f.n., 'kɔrlɪ, kórli

Cornelius, f.n., kɔr'niliəs, kornéeli-ŭss

Cornhill Grampian, kɔrn'hɪl, korn-híll

Cornillie, f.n., kɔr'nilɪ, kornéeli

Cornwall Co. name, 'kɔrnwəl, kórnwăl

Cornwallis, f.n., kɔrn'wɒlɪs, kornwólliss. Appropriate also for Baron ~.

Corpach H'land, 'kɔrpəx, kórpăch

Corpusty Norfolk, 'kɔrpəstɪ, kórpŭsti

Corrard Co. Fermanagh, kə'rɑrd, kŏraárd

Corregan Rocks I. of Scilly, kə'regən, kŏréggăn

Corrie S'clyde, 'kɒrɪ, kórri

Corriehalloch H'land, ˌkɒrɪ'hæləx, korri-hálŏch

Corriemulzie H'land, ˌkɒrɪ'mʌlzɪ, korri-múlzi

Corrievreckan, Strait of, S'clyde, ˌkɒrɪ'vrekən, korrivréckăn

Corrieyairack Pass H'land, ˌkɒrɪ'jærək, korri-yárrăck

Corrigan, f.n., 'kɒrɪgən, kórrigăn

Corringham Essex, 'kɒrɪŋəm, kórring-ăm

Corris Gwynedd, 'kɒrɪs, kórriss

Corrour Forest Tayside–H'land border, kɒ'ruər, korróŏr

Corsellis, f.n., kɔr'selɪs, korsélliss

Corsham Wilts., 'kɔrʃəm, kór-shăm

Corsley Wilts., 'kɔrslɪ, kórssli

Corslwyn, f.n., 'kɔrsluɪn, kórsslŏō-in

Corstorphine Edinburgh, kər'stɔrfɪn, kŏrsstórfin

Cors Tregaron Nature Reserve Dyfed, 'kɔrs trɪ'gærən, kórss trĕgárrŏn

Cortachy Tayside, 'kɔrtəxɪ, kórtáchi; kɔr'tæxɪ, kortáchi

Corteen, f.n., kɔr'tin, korteén

Coruisk, Loch, I. of Skye, kə'ruʃk, kŏróŏshk

Corvedale, Viscount, 'kɔrvdeɪl, kórvdayl

Corwen Clwyd, 'kɔrwən, kórwĕn

Cory, f.n., 'kɔrɪ, káwri

Coryat, Thomas, 16th–17th-c. traveller, 'kɒrɪət, kórri-ăt. The surname is sometimes spelt Coryate.

Coryton, f.n., 'kɒrɪtən, kórritŏn

Coryton Devon, 'kɒrɪtən, kórritŏn

Coryton Essex, 'kɒrɪtən, káwritŏn

Coseley W. Midlands, 'kouzlɪ, kŏzli

Cosen, Benjamin, 17th-c. composer, also spelt Cosin, Cosyn, 'kʌzən, kúzzĕn

Cosens, f.n., 'kʌzənz, kúzzĕnz

Cosford Suffolk, 'kɒsfərd, kóssfŏrd

Cosham Hants, 'kɒsəm, kóssăm

Cosin, Benjamin, see Cosen

Coslany Norwich, 'kɒzlənɪ, kózlăni

Cossall Notts., 'kɒsl, kóssl

Cossington Leics., 'kɒsɪŋtən, kóssingtŏn; 'kʌsɪŋtən, kússingtŏn

Cossins, f.n., 'kʌzɪnz, kúzzinz

Costain, f.n., 'kɒsteɪn, kóstayn; kɒs'teɪn, kostáyn

Coste, f.n., koust, kōst; kɒst, kosst

Costello, f.n., kə'stelou, kŏstéllō; 'kɒstɪlou, kóstĕlō

Costelloe, f.n., 'kɒstɪlou, kóstĕlō

Costessey Norfolk, 'kɒsɪ, kóssi

Costin, f.n., 'kɒstɪn, kóstin

Costock Notts., 'kɒstɒk, kóstock

Coston Leics., 'kousən, kóssŏn

Cosyn, Benjamin, see Cosen

Cotehele House Cornwall, kə'til, kōteél; kət'hil, kŏt-heél

Cotehill Cumbria, 'kouthɪl, kót-hil

Cotesbach Leics., 'koutsbætʃ, kótsbatch

Cotgrave Notts., 'kɒtgreɪv, kótgrayv

Cotham Avon, 'kɒtəm, kóttăm

Cothay, f.n., 'kouθeɪ, kŏ-thay

Cothelstone Somerset, 'kʌðlsstŏn, kúthlsstŏn; 'kɒtlstən, kóttlsstŏn

Cotheridge H. & W., 'kɒðərɪdʒ, kóthērij

Cotherstone Durham, 'kʌðərstən, kúthĕrstŏn

Cothi, River, Dyfed, 'kɒθɪ, kóthi

Cothill Oxon., 'kɒt'hɪl, kót-híll

Cotmanhay *Derby.*, 'kɒtmənheɪ, kótmăn-hay

Cotmaton *Devon*, kɒt'meɪtən, kotmáytŏn

Coton, *f.n.*, 'koutən, kótŏn

Coton *Cambs.*, 'koutən, kótŏn

Cotswolds, The, *Oxon.–Avon*, 'kɒtswouldz, kóttswŏldz

Cottell, *f.n.*, kə'til, kŏtéel

Cottenham, Earl of, 'kɒtnəm, kót-năm

Cottenham *Cambs.*, 'kɒtņəm, kóttn-ăm

Cottesbrooke *Northants.*, 'kɒtɪsbrʊk, kóttĕssbrŏŏk

Cottesloe, Baron, 'kɒtslou, kótslŏ

Cottesmore *Leics.*, 'kɒtsmɔr, kóttsmor

Cottle, *f.n.*, 'kɒtl, kóttl

Cottrell, *f.n.*, 'kɒtrəl, kóttrĕl; kə'trel, kŏtréll

Couch, *f.n.*, kutʃ, kootch

Coucher, *f.n.*, 'kautʃər, kówtchĕr

Couchman, *f.n.*, 'kuʃmən, kóosh-măn; 'kautʃmən, kówtchmăn

Coughlan, *f.n.*, 'kɒxlən, kóchlăn; 'kɒglən, kóglăn

Coughlin, *f.n.*, 'kɒxlɪn, kóchlin; 'kɒglɪn, kóglin

Coughton, *H. & W.*, 'koutən, kótŏn

Coughton *Warwicks.*, 'koutən, kótŏn; 'kautən, kówtŏn. *The first is usual for the National Trust property of ~ Court.*

Coughtrey, *f.n.*, 'kautrɪ, kówtri; 'kɒtrɪ, káwtri; 'kutrɪ, kootri; 'koutrɪ, kótri; 'kɒftrɪ, kófftri

Coughtrie, *f.n.*, 'kɒftrɪ, kófftri

Coul *H'land, Tayside*, kul, kool

Coulbeck, *f.n.*, 'kulbek, kóolbeck

Coulcher, *f.n.*, 'kultʃər, kóoltchĕr

Couldrey, *f.n.*, 'kuldrɪ, kóoldri; 'kuldreɪ, kóoldray; 'kouldrɪ, kóldri

Couldry, *f.n.*, 'kuldrɪ, kóoldri

Couldwell, *f.n.*, 'kouldwel, kóldwel

Coull, *f.n.*, kul, kool

Coull *Fife, Grampian*, kul, kool

Coulling, *f.n.*, 'kulɪŋ, kóoling

Coulman, *f.n.*, 'koulmən, kólmăn

Coulport *S'clyde*, 'kulpɔrt, kóolport

Coulsdon *London*, 'koulzdən, kólzdŏn; 'kulzdən, kóolzdŏn

Coulshaw, *f.n.*, 'kulʃɔ, kóol-shaw

Coulson, *f.n.*, 'koulsən, kólssŏn; 'kulsən, kóolssŏn

Coulston, *f.n.*, 'kulstən, kóolstŏn

Coult, *f.n.*, koult, kōlt; kult, koolt

Coultas, *f.n.*, 'kultæs, kóoltass

Coulter, *f.n.*, 'kultər, kóoltĕr; 'koultər, kóltĕr

Coulthard, *f.n.*, 'kultard, kóoltaard; 'koulθard, kól-thaard

Coulton, *f.n.*, 'koultən, kóltŏn

Councell, *f.n.*, 'kaunsl, kównssl

Coundon *W. Midlands*, 'kaundən, kówndŏn

Counihan, *f.n.*, 'kunɪhən, kóoni--hăn

Countess Wear *Devon*, 'kauntɪs 'wɪər, kówntĕss weér

Countesthorpe *Leics.*, 'kauntɪsθɔrp, kówntĕss-thorp

Countisbury *Devon*, 'kauntɪsbərɪ, kówntiss-búri

Coupar Angus *Tayside*, ˌkupər 'æŋgəs, koopăr áng-gŭss

Coupe, *f.n.*, kup, koop

Couper, *f.n.*, 'kupər, kóopĕr

Coupland, *f.n.*, 'kuplənd, kóopländ; 'koupländ, kŏpländ

Coupland *Cumbria*, 'kupländ, kóopländ

Coupland *Northd.*, 'koupländ, kŏpländ

Coupland Beck *Cumbria*, 'koupländ 'bek, kŏpländ béck

Cournane, *f.n.*, kuər'næn, kŏŏrnáne

Courtauld, *f.n.*, 'kɔrtou, kórtō; 'kɔrtould, kórtōld. *Although the first is the pronunciation of the late Samuel ~'s family, the latter is now invariably used for the ~ Institutes and for the firm of ~s Ltd.*

Courtenay, *f.n.*, 'kɔrtnɪ, kórtni

Courthope, *f.n.*, 'kɔrthoup, kórt-hōp; 'kɔrtoup, kórtōp. *The first is appropriate for the Barony of ~.*

Courtier, *f.n.*, 'kɔrtjər, kórt-yĕr

Courtneidge, *f.n.*, 'kɔrtnɪdʒ, kórtnij

Courtney, *f.n.*, 'kɔrtnɪ, kórtni

Courtown, Earl of, 'kɔrtaun, kórtown

Cousens, *f.n.*, 'kʌzənz, kúzzĕnz

Couser, *f.n.*, 'kauzər, kówzĕr

Cousins, *f.n.*, 'kʌzɪnz, kúzzĕnz

Cousland, *f.n.*, 'kauzlænd, kówzland

Cousland *Lothian*, 'kauzlənd, kówzländ

Coutts, *f.n.*, kuts, koots

Couzens, *f.n.*, 'kʌzənz, kúzzĕnz

Cove, *f.n.*, kouv, kōv

Covehithe *Suffolk*, 'kouv'haɪð, kŏv-hífh

Coveley, *f.n.*, 'kouvəlɪ, kŏvĕli

Covell, *f.n.*, kou'vel, kŏvéll; kə'vel, kŏvéll

Coven, *f.n.*, 'kouvən, kŏvĕn

Coven *Staffs.*, 'koʊvən, kṓvĕn
Coveney, *f.n.*, 'koʊvənɪ, kṓvĕni
Coveney *Cambs.*, 'koʊvnɪ, kṓv-ni
Covenham *Lincs.*, 'koʊvənəm,
  kṓvĕnăm
Covenhope *H. & W.*, 'kɒnəp,
  kónnŏp; 'koʊvənhoʊp,
  kṓvĕn-hōp
Covent Garden *London*, 'kɒvənt
  'gɑːdən, kóvvĕnt gaárdĕn;
  'kʌvənt 'gɑːdən, kúvvĕnt
  gaárdĕn
Coventry, *f.n.*, 'kɒvəntrɪ, kóvvĕn-
  tri; 'kʌvəntrɪ, kúvvĕntri
Coventry *W. Midlands*, 'kɒvəntrɪ,
  kóvvĕntri; 'kʌvəntrɪ, kúvvĕntri.
  *The first is appropriate for the
  Earl of* ∼.
Coverack *Cornwall*, 'kʌvəræk,
  kúvvĕrack; 'kɒvəræk, kóvvĕrack
Coverdale, *f.n.*, 'kʌvədeɪl,
  kúvvĕrdayl
Covesea *H'land*, koʊ'siː, kōsséé
Covey-Crump, *f.n.*, 'kʌvɪ 'krʌmp,
  kúvvi krúmp
Covington, *f.n.*, 'kɒvɪŋtən,
  kóvvingtŏn
Covington *Cambs.*, 'kɒvɪŋtən,
  kóvvingtŏn
Cowal *S'clyde*, 'kaʊəl, kówăl;
  kaʊl, kowl
Coward, *f.n.*, 'kaʊəd, kówărd
Cowbit *Lincs.*, 'kʌbɪt, kúbbit
Cowbridge *S. Glam.*, 'kaʊbrɪdʒ,
  kówbrij
Cowcher, *f.n.*, 'kaʊtʃər, kówtchĕr
Cowdell, *f.n.*, kaʊ'del, kowdéll
Cowden *Kent*, kaʊ'den, kowdén
Cowdenbeath *Fife*, ˌkaʊdən'biːθ,
  kowdĕn-béeth
Cowderoy, *f.n.*, 'kaʊdərɔɪ,
  kówdĕroy
Cowdray, Viscount, 'kaʊdrɪ,
  kówdri
Cowdrey, *f.n.*, 'kaʊdrɪ, kówdri
Cowell, *f.n.*, 'kaʊəl, kówĕl;
  'koʊəl, kṓ-ĕl
Cowen, *f.n.*, 'kaʊən, kówĕn;
  'koʊən, kṓ-ĕn
Cowes *I. of Wight*, kaʊz, kowz
Cowie, *f.n.*, 'kaʊɪ, kówi
Cowin, *f.n.*, 'kaʊɪn, kówin
Cowlairs *S'clyde*, 'kaʊ'lɛərz,
  ków-láirz
Cowles, *f.n.*, kaʊlz, kowlz; koʊlz,
  kōlz
Cowley, *f.n.*, 'kaʊlɪ, kówli.
  Appropriate also for Earl ∼.
Cowley, *Oxon.*, 'kaʊlɪ, kówli
Cowling, *Lancs.*, 'kaʊlɪŋ, kówling;
  'koʊlɪŋ, kṓling
Cowlinge *Suffolk*, 'kuːlɪndʒ,
  kóolinj
Cowpe *Lancs.*, kaʊp, kowp

Cowpen *Northd.*, 'kuːpən, kóopĕn;
  'kaʊpən, kówpĕn
Cowpen Bewley *Cleveland*,
  'kuːpən 'bjuːlɪ, kóopĕn béwli
Cowper, *f.n.*, 'kuːpər, kóopĕr;
  'kaʊpər, kówpĕr. *The first is
  appropriate for the 18th-c. poet,
  William* ∼.
Cowper Powys, John, *author*,
  'kuːpər 'poʊɪs, kóopĕr pṓ-iss
Cowplain *Hants*, 'kaʊpleɪn,
  kówplayn
Cowsill, *f.n.*, 'kaʊzɪl, kówzil
Cowtan, *f.n.*, 'kaʊtən, kówtăn
Coxe, *f.n.*, kɒks, kocks
Coxhoe *Durham*, 'kɒkshoʊ,
  kócks-hō
Coyne, *f.n.*, kɔɪn, koyn
Coytrahen *Mid Glam.*, ˌkɔɪtrə-
  'heɪn, koytrŭ-háyn
Cozens, *f.n.*, 'kʌzənz, kúzzĕnz
Cozens-Hardy, Barony of,
  'kʌzənz 'hɑːdɪ, kúzzĕnz haárdi
Crabbe, George, *poet (1784–
  1832)*, kræb, krabb
Crabtree, *f.n.*, 'kræbtrɪ, krábtree
Craddock, *f.n.*, 'krædək, krád-
  dŏck
Cradley *H. & W.*, 'krædlɪ, krádli
Cradley *W. Midlands*, 'kreɪdlɪ,
  kráydli
Cradley Heath *W. Midlands*,
  'kreɪdlɪ 'hiːθ, kráydli héeth
Cradock, *f.n.*, 'krædək, kráddŏck;
  'kreɪdɒk, kráydock
Craen, *f.n.*, kreɪn, krayn
Crafthole *Cornwall*, 'krɑːfthoʊl,
  kraáft-hōl
Crag Lough *Northd.*, 'kræg 'lɒf,
  krág lóff
Crago, *f.n.*, 'kreɪgoʊ, kráygō
Craigantlet *Co. Down*, kreɪg-
  'æntlət, kraygántlĕt
Craigavad *Co. Down*, ˌkreɪgə'væd,
  kraygăváđ
Craig Cerrig-Gleisiad Nature
  Reserve *Powys*, 'kraɪg 'kerɪg
  'glaɪsjæd, krī́g kérrig glíss-yad
Craigdhu *H'land*, 'kreɪg'du,
  kráyg doo
Craigellachie *Grampian*, kreɪg-
  'elʌxɪ, kraygéllăchi
Craigendoran *S'clyde*, ˌkreɪgən-
  'dɒrən, kraygĕndórrăn
Craigie, *f.n.*, 'kreɪgɪ, kráygi
Craigie *S'clyde*, *Tayside*, 'kreɪgɪ,
  kráygi
Craigievar *Grampian*, ˌkreɪgɪ'vɑr,
  kraygivaár
Craiglockhart *Lothian*, kreɪg-
  'lɒkərt, krayg-lóckărt
Craiglour-Achin *Grampian*, kreɪg-
  'laʊrəxɪn, krayglówră<u>ch</u>in; *also
  written* **Craig Lowrigan**, *and*

pronounced kreɪg 'lɑʊrɪgən, krayg lówrigăn
Craigmillar *Edinburgh*, kreɪg-'mɪlər, krayg-millăr
Craigmyle, Baron, kreɪg'maɪl, kraygmíl
Craigneuk *S'clyde*, kreɪg'njuk, krayg-néwk
Craignure *S'clyde*, kreɪg'njʊər, krayg-nyōŏr
Craig-ny-Baa, *also spelt* **Creg-ny-Baa**, *I. of Man*, 'kreɪg nɪ 'bɑ, kráyg-ni-baa
Craigowan *Grampian*, kreɪ'gaʊən, kraygów-än
Craig Willies Hill, *I. of Man*, kreɪg 'wɪlɪz, krayg wílliz
Craig-y-Deryn *Gwynedd*, ˌkraɪgə-'derɪn, krĭg-ă-dérrin
Craig-y-Llyn *Mid Glam.*, ˌkraɪgə-'łɪn, krĭg-ă-hlin
Craig-y-Nos *Powys*, ˌkraɪgə'nous, krĭgănóss
Crail *Fife*, kreɪl, krayl
Cramond *Lothian*, 'kræmənd, krámmŏnd; 'krɑmənd, kraamŏnd
Cranage *Ches.*, 'krænɪdʒ, kránnij
Cranagh *Co. Tyrone*, 'krænə, kránnă
Cranham, *f.n.*, 'krænəm, kránnăm
Crank ny Mona *I. of Man*, 'krænk nɪ 'moʊnə, kránk ni mónă
Cranleigh *Surrey*, 'krænlɪ, kránli
Cranleighan, *one educated at Cranleigh School*, kræn'liən, kranleé-än
Cranwich *Norfolk*, 'krænɪtʃ, kránnitch
Crayke *N. Yorks.*, kreɪk, krayk
Crarae *S'clyde*, 'krærɪ, krárri
Crashaw, Richard, *17th-c. poet*, 'kræʃo, krásh-aw
Crask of Aigas *H'land*, 'kræʃk əv 'eɪgəʃ, kráshk ŏv áygăsh
Craske, *f.n.*, krɑsk, kraask; kræsk, krassk
Craster, *f.n.*, 'krɑstər, kraástĕr
Crathes *Grampian*, 'kræθɪz, kráthĕz
Crathie *Grampian*, 'kræθɪ, kráthi
Crathorn, *f.n.*, 'kreɪθɔrn, kráy--thorn
Crathorne, Baron, 'kreɪθɔrn, kráy-thorn
Crauford, *f.n.*, 'krɔfərd, kráwfŏrd
Craven, *f.n.*, 'kreɪvən, kráyvĕn
Craven Arms *Salop*, 'kreɪvən 'ɑrmz, kráyvĕn aármz
Crawford and Balcarres, Earl of, 'krɔfərd ənd bæl'kærɪs, kráwfŏrd ănd balkárrĕss
Crawght, *f.n.*, krɔt, krawt

Crawhall, *f.n.*, krə'hɔl, kră-háwl
Crawley, *f.n.*, 'krɔlɪ, kráwli
Crawshaw, *f.n.*, 'krɔʃo, kráw-shaw
Crawshay, *f.n.*, 'krɔʃeɪ, kráw-shay
Crawt, *f.n.*, krɔt, krawt
Crayford *London*, 'kreɪfərd, kráyfŏrd
Creacombe *Devon*, 'krikəm, kreékŏm
Creagan *S'clyde*, 'krigən, kreégăn
Creagh, *f.n.*, kreɪ, kray
Creaghan, *f.n.*, 'krigən, kreégăn
Creag Meaghaidh Mt. *H'land*, 'kreɪg 'megɪ, kráyg méggi
Creak, *f.n.*, krik, kreek
Crean, *f.n.*, krin, kreen; 'kriən, kreé-än
Creaney, *f.n.*, 'krinɪ, kreéni
Creasy, *f.n.*, 'krisɪ, kreéssi
Creaton, Great *and* Little, *Northants.*, 'kritən, kreétŏn
Creber, *f.n.*, 'kribər, kreébĕr
Crebilly *Co. Antrim*, krə'bɪlɪ, krĕbílli
Credenhill *H. & W.*, 'kredənhɪl, krédděn-hil; 'krɪdənhɪl, kreedĕn-hil
Crediton *Devon*, 'kredɪtən, kréddĭtŏn
Cree, *f.n.*, krɪ, kree
Creegor, *f.n.*, 'krigər, kreégŏr
Crees, *f.n.*, kris, kreess; kriz, kreez
Creese, *f.n.*, kris, kreess
Creetown *D. & G.*, 'kritaʊn, kreétown
Creffield, *f.n.*, 'krefɪld, kréffeeld
Cregagh *Co. Down*, 'kreɪgə, kráygă
Cregan, *f.n.*, 'krigən, kreégăn
Cregeen, *f.n.*, krɪ'dʒin, krĭjeén
Cregneish *I. of Man*, kreg'niʃ, kreg-neésh
Creg-ny-Baa *see* **Craig-ny-Baa**
Crehan, *f.n.*, 'kriən, kreé-än
Creich *Fife, H'land, S'clyde*, krix, kreech
Creighton, *f.n.*, 'kraɪtən, krítŏn; 'kreɪtən, kráytŏn
Creigiau *Mid Glam.*, 'kraɪgjaɪ, krĭg-yī
Creme, *f.n.*, krim, kreem
Cremer, *f.n.*, 'krimər, kreémĕr
Cremyll *Cornwall*, 'kremɪl, krémmil; 'kreml, krémml
Creran, Loch *and* River, *S'clyde*, 'krɪərən, kreérăn
Crerand, *f.n.*, 'krɪərənd, kreérănd
Crerar, *f.n.*, 'kreərər, kráirăr; 'krɪərər, kreérăr
Cresselly *Dyfed*, krɪs'elɪ, krĕssélli
Creswell, *f.n.*, 'krezwəl, krézwĕl
Creswell *Derby.*, 'kreswel, krésswel; 'kreswəl, krésswĕl

Creswick, *f.n.,* 'krezɪk, krézzick
Creunant, *also spelt* **Crynant,** *W. Glam.,* 'kraɪnənt, krínänt
Crevenagh *Co. Tyrone,* 'krevnə, krévnä
Crewe *Ches.,* kru, kroo
Crewkerne *Somerset,* 'krukзrn, króokern
Crianlarich *Central,* ˌkriən'lærɪx, kree-änlárrich
Cribbett, *f.n.,* 'krɪbɪt, kríbbĕt
Crib-Goch *Gwynedd,* 'krib 'gɔux, kreéb góch
Crib-y-Ddysgl *Gwynedd,* ˌkrib ə 'ðɪskl, kreeb ă thískl
Cribyn *Dyfed,* 'krɪbɪn, kreébin; 'krɪbɪn, kríbbin
Criccieth *Gwynedd,* 'krɪkɪəθ, krícki-ĕth
Crich *Derby.,* kraɪtʃ, krītch
Crichel Down *Dorset,* 'krɪtʃl 'daʊn, krítchl dówn
Crichton, *f.n.,* 'kraɪtən, krítŏn
Crickadarn *Powys,* krɪk'ædзrn, krickáddärn
Cricket Malherbie *Somerset,* 'krɪkɪt 'mælзrbɪ, kríckĕt málĕrbi
Crickhowell *Powys,* krɪk'haʊəl, krick-hówĕl
Crieff *Tayside,* krif, kreef
Crier, *f.n.,* 'kraɪзr, krí-ĕr
Criggion *Powys,* 'krɪgjɒn, kríg-yon
Crighton, *f.n.,* 'kraɪtən, krítŏn
Crimond *Grampian,* 'krɪmənd, krímmŏnd
Crimplesham *Norfolk,* 'krɪmpl-ʃəm, krímpl-shăm
Crinan *S'clyde,* 'krɪnən, krínnăn
Cringleford *Norfolk,* 'krɪŋglfзrd, kring-glfórd
Cringletie *Borders,* krɪŋ'letɪ, kring-létti
Crisell, *f.n.,* krɪ'sel, krisséll
Crisp, *f.n.,* krɪsp, krisp
Critchley, *f.n.,* 'krɪtʃlɪ, krítchli
Critoph, *f.n.,* 'krɪtɒf, kríttoff
Crittall, *f.n.,* 'krɪtɔl, kríttawl
Croal, *River, Lancs.–Gtr. M'chester,* kroʊl, krōl
Croall, *f.n.,* kroʊl, krōl
Croan, *f.n.,* kroʊn, krōn
Croasdell, *f.n.,* 'kroʊzdel, krózdel
Crockernwell *Devon,* 'krɒkзrnwel, króckĕrn-wel
Crocketford *D. & G.,* 'krɒkɪtfзrd, króckĕtfŏrd
Crockford, *f.n.,* 'krɒkfзrd, króckfŏrd
Crockford's Club *London,* 'krɒkfзrdz, króckfŏrdz
Croeserw *W. Glam.,* krɔɪs'eru, kroyssérroo
Croesfaen *Mid Glam.,* krɔɪs'vaɪn, kroyss-vín

Croesor *Gwynedd,* 'krɔɪsзr, króyssor
Croesyceiliog *Gwent,* ˌkrɔɪsə-'kaɪljɒg, kroyssă-kíl-yog
Croftamie *S'clyde,* krɒft'æmɪ, kroftámmi
Croghan, *f.n.,* 'kroʊən, kró-än
Croham Hurst *London,* 'kroʊəm 'hзrst, kró-äm húrst
Croke, *f.n.,* kroʊk, krōōk
Croker, *f.n.,* 'kroʊkзr, krókĕr
Crom *Co. Fermanagh,* krʌm, krumm
Cromac *Co. Antrim,* 'krɒmək, krómmäk
Cromartie, *Earl of,* 'krɒmзrtɪ, krómmärti
Cromarty *H'land,* 'krɒmзrtɪ, krómmärti
Crombie, *f.n.,* 'krɒmbɪ, krómbi; 'krʌmbɪ, krúmbi
Crome, *f.n.,* kroʊm, krōm
Cromer *Herts., Norfolk,* 'kroʊmзr, krómĕr. *Appropriate also for the Earl of* ~.
Cromey, *f.n.,* 'krʌmɪ, krúmmi
Cromford *Derby.,* 'krɒmfзrd, krómfŏrd
Cromie, *f.n.,* 'kroʊmɪ, krómi
Cromlech *Co. Down,* 'krʌmləx, krúmlech
Crommelin, *f.n.,* 'krʌmlɪn, krúmlin
Crompton, *f.n.,* 'krɒmptən, krómptŏn. *Appropriate for Samuel* ~, *inventor of the weaving shuttle.*
Crondall *Hants,* 'krʌndl, krúndl; 'krɒndl, króndl
Croney, *f.n.,* 'kroʊnɪ, króni
Cronin, *f.n.,* 'kroʊnɪn, krónin
Cronk-ny-Mona *I. of Man,* 'krɒŋk nə 'moʊnə, krónk nĕ mónă
Crookating *Shetland,* 'krʊkətɪŋ, króokäting
Crook of Devon *Tayside,* 'krʊk əv 'devən, króok ŏv dévvŏn
Croome d'Abitot *H. & W.,* 'krum 'dæbɪtoʊ, króom dábbitō
Cropredy *Oxon.,* 'krɒprədɪ, króprĕdi
Crosby *Cumbria, Humberside, Merseyside,* 'krɒzbɪ, krózbi
Croser, *f.n.,* 'kroʊzзr, krózĕr
Crosier, *f.n.,* 'kroʊzзr, krózi-ĕr
Crosland, *f.n.,* 'krɒslənd, króssländ
Crossbychan *Mid Glam.,* krɒs-'bʌxən, kross-búchăn
Crossflatts *W. Yorks.,* 'krɒsflæts, króss-flats
Crossgar *Co. Down,* krɒs'gɑr, krossgaár
Crosshill *Fife, S'clyde,* 'krɒs'hɪl, króss-híll

Crossmaglen *Co. Armagh*, ˌkrɒsmə'glen, kross-măglén
Crossmyloof *S'clyde*, ˌkrɒsmɪ'luf, krossmiloof
Crossraguel Abbey *S'clyde*, krɒs-'reɪgl, krossráygl
Crosthwaite-Eyre, *f.n.*, 'krɒsθweɪt 'ɛər, króss-thwayt áir
Croston *Lancs.*, 'krɒstən, krósstŏn
Crostwick *Norfolk*, 'krɒstwɪk, króst-wick; 'krɒstɪk, króstick; 'krɒsɪk, króssick
Crothers, *f.n.*, 'krʌðərz, krúthĕrz
Crotty, *f.n.*, 'krɒtɪ, krótti
Crouch, *f.n.*, krautʃ, krowtch
Crouch *Kent*, krutʃ, krootch
Croucher, *f.n.*, 'krautʃər, krów-tchĕr
Croughton *Northants.*, 'krəʊtən, krṓtŏn
Crow, *f.n.*, krəʊ, krō
Crowan *Cornwall*, 'krauən, krówăn
Crowborough *E. Sussex*, 'krəʊ-bərə, krṓbŭră
Crowcombe *Somerset*, 'krəʊkəm, krṓkŏm
Crowcroft, *f.n.*, 'krəʊkrɒft, krṓkroft
Crowden, *f.n.*, 'kraudən, krówdĕn
Crowden *Derby.*, 'krəʊdən, krṓdĕn
Crowder, *f.n.*, 'kraudər, krówdĕr
Crowdy, *f.n.*, 'kraudɪ, krówdi
Crowe, *f.n.*, krəʊ, krō
Crowest, *f.n.*, 'krəʊɪst, krṓ-ĕst
Crowland, *also spelt* **Croyland**, *Lincs.*, 'krəʊlənd, krṓlănd
Crowlas *Cornwall*, 'kraʊləs, krówlăss
Crowle *H. & W.*, krəʊl, krōl; kraʊl, krowl
Crowle *Humberside*, krəʊl, krōl
Crowley, *f.n.*, 'krəʊlɪ, krṓli
Crows-an-Wra *Cornwall*, 'kraʊs-ən'reɪ, krówss ăn ráy
Crowson, *Lamar*, *pianist*, lə'mɑr 'krausən, lămáar krówssŏn
Crowther, *f.n.*, 'krauðər, krówthĕr. *Appropriate also for Baron* ∼.
Crowthorne *Berks.*, 'krəʊθɔrn, krṓ-thorn
Croxdale *Durham*, 'krɒksdəl, króckssdăl
Croxton *Humberside*, *Norfolk*, 'krɒkstən, króckstŏn
Croxton, South, *Leics.*, 'krəʊsən, krṓssŏn; 'krəʊstən, krṓsstŏn; 'krəʊzən, krṓzŏn
Croxton Kerrial *Leics.*, 'krəʊsən 'kerɪəl, krṓssŏn kérriăl
Croyland *see* **Crowland**
Crozier, *f.n.*, 'krəʊzɪər, krṓzi-ĕr; 'krəʊʒər, krṓzhĕr

Cruachan, Falls of, *S'clyde*, 'kruəxən, kroo-áchăn
Cruchley, *f.n.*, 'krʌtʃlɪ, krútchli
Cruddas, *f.n.*, 'krʌdəs, krúddăss
Cruden Bay *Grampian*, 'krudən 'beɪ, krooděn báy
Crudwell *Wilts.*, 'krʌdwel, krúd-wel
Crug-y-Bar *Dyfed*, ˌkrɪg ə 'bɑr, kreeg ă báar
Crug-y-Byddar *Powys*, ˌkrɪg ə 'bʌðər, kreeg ă búthăr
Cruickshank, *f.n.*, 'krʊkʃæŋk, krŏŏk-shank
Cruikshank, *f.n.*, 'krʊkʃæŋk, krŏŏk-shank
Crum, *f.n.*, krʌm, krum
Crumlin *Co. Antrim*, *Gwent*, 'krʌmlɪn, krúmlin
Crunwere *Dyfed*, 'krʌnwɛər, krúnwair
Crutchley, *f.n.*, 'krʌtʃlɪ, krútchli
Crutwell, *f.n.*, 'krʌtwəl, krútwĕl
Cruwys Morchard *Devon*, 'kruz 'mɔrtʃərd, krooz mórtchărd
Crwys *Welsh C.n.*, 'kruɪs, kroo-iss
Crwys *W. Glam.*, 'kruɪs, kroo-iss
Cryer, *f.n.*, 'kraɪər, krí-ĕr
Crymmych *Dyfed*, 'krʌmɪx, krúmmich
Crynant *see* **Creunant**
Crysell, *f.n.*, 'kraɪsl, kríssl
Cubbin, *f.n.*, 'kʌbɪn, kúbbin
Cubert *Cornwall*, 'kjubərt, kéw-bĕrt
Cubitt, *f.n.*, 'kjubɪt, kéwbit
Cublington, *Bucks.*, 'kʌblɪŋtən, kúblingtŏn
Cuchullin Hills *see* **Cuillin**
Cuckfield *W. Sussex*, 'kʊkfɪld, kŏŏkfeeld
Cuckmere, River, *E. Sussex*, 'kʊkmɪər, kŏŏkmeer
Cuckney, *f.n.*, 'kʌknɪ, kúckni
Cuckney *Notts.*, 'kʌknɪ, kúckni
Cucksey, *f.n.*, 'kʊksɪ, kŏŏksi
Cuckston, *f.n.*, 'kʊkstən, kŏŏkstŏn
Cuddeford, *f.n.*, 'kʌdɪfərd, kúddĕford
Cuddesdon *Oxon.*, 'kʌdzdən, kúdzdŏn
Cuddihay, *f.n.*, 'kʌdɪheɪ, kúddi-hay
Cude, *f.n.*, kjud, kewd
Cudworth *S. Yorks.*, 'kʌdwərθ, kúdwŏrth; 'kʌdərθ, kúddŏrth
Cuffe, *f.n.*, kʌf, kuff
Cuillin Hills, *also spelt* **Coolin**, **Cuchullin**, *Skye*, 'kulɪn, koólin
Culbone *Somerset*, 'kʌlbəʊn, kúlbōn
Culcavey *Co. Down*, kəl'keɪvɪ, kŭlkáyvi

Culcheth *Gtr. M'chester*, 'kʌltʃəθ, kúltchĕth

Culdrose *Cornwall*, kʌl'drouz, kuldróz

Culduthel *H'land*, kʌl'dʌθl, kuldúthl

Culf,*f.n.*, kʌlf, kulf

Culgaith *Cumbria*, kʌl'geiθ, kulgáyth; kʊl'geiθ, kōōlgáyth; 'kʊlgeiθ, kōōlgayth

Culham *Oxon.*, 'kʌləm, kúllăm

Culhane,*f.n.*, kʌl'hein, kul-háyn

Culkein *H'land*, 'kʊlkein, kōōlkayn

Cullamore *Co. Tyrone*, ˌkʌlə'mɔr, kullămór

Cullavoe *see* **Cullivoe**

Cullen,*f.n.*, 'kʌlən, kúllĕn

Cullen *Grampian*, 'kʌlən, kúllĕn

Cullercoats *Tyne & Wear*, 'kʌlərkouts, kúllĕrkōts

Cullinan,*f.n.*, 'kʌlinən, kúllinăn

Cullivoe, *also spelt* **Cullavoe**, *Shetland*, 'kʌlivou, kúllivō

Culloden *H'land*, kə'lodən, kŭlóddĕn; kə'loudən, kŭlóddĕn

Cullompton *Devon*, 'kʌləmptən, kúllŏmptŏn; kə'lʌmptən, kŭlúmptŏn

Cullybackey *Co. Antrim*, ˌkʌli-'bæki, kullibácki

Cullyhanna *Co. Armagh*, ˌkʌli-'hænə, kulli-hánnă

Culm, *River*, *Somerset–Devon*, kʌlm, kulm

Culme-Seymour,*f.n.*, 'kʌlm 'simər, kúlm séemor

Culmstock *Devon*, 'kʌlmstɒk, kúlm-stock

Culnady *Co. Derry*, kəl'nædi, kŭlnáddi

Culpeper,*f.n.*, 'kʌlpepər, kúll- -peppĕr

Culrain *H'land*, kʌl'rein, kulráyn

Culross,*f.n.*, 'kʌlrɒs, kúlross

Culross *Fife*, 'kʊrəs, kōō-rŏss

Culsalmond *Grampian*, kʌl-'sæmənd, kul-sámmŏnd

Culter *Grampian*, *S'clyde*, 'kutər, kōōtĕr

Cultoquhey *Tayside*, ˌkʌltə'hwai, kultŏ-whí

Cultra *Co. Down*, kəl'trɒ, kŭltráw

Cults *Fife*, *Grampian*, kʌlts, kults

Culzean *Castle S'clyde*, kə'lein, kŭláyn

Cumberbeach,*f.n.*, 'kʌmbərbitʃ, kúmbĕrbeetch

Cumberland *former Co. name*, 'kʌmbərlənd, kúmbĕr-lănd

Cumberlege,*f.n.*, 'kʌmbərlidʒ, kúmbĕrlĕj

Cumbernauld *S'clyde*, ˌkʌmbər-'nɔld, kumbĕrnáwld

Cumbes,*f.n.*, kumz, koomz

Cumbrae, *Great and Little*, *S'clyde*, 'kʌmbrei, kúmbray

Cumbrian, *pertaining to Cumberland or Cumbria*, 'kʌmbriən, kúmbriăn

Cumdivock *Cumbria*, kʌm'divək, kumdívvŏk

Cumine,*f.n.*, 'kʌmin, kúmmin

Cuminestown *Grampian*, 'kʌminztaun, kúmminz-town

Cuming *Museum London*, 'kʌmiŋ, kúmming

Cummertrees *D. & G.*, 'kʌmər-triz, kúmmĕr-treéz

Cumnock *S'clyde*, 'kʌmnək, kúmnŏk

Cumnor *Oxon.*, 'kʌmnər, kúm-nŏr

Cumrew *Cumbria*, kʌm'ru, kumroó; kʌmri'u, kumri-oó

Cumwhinton *Cumbria*, kʌm-'hwintən, kum-whíntŏn; kʊm-'hwintən, kōōm-whíntŏn

Cunard,*f.n.*, kju'nard, kewnaárd

Cundell,*f.n.*, 'kʌndl, kúndl

Cuneo, *Terence*, *painter*, 'kjuniou, kéwniō

Cuningham,*f.n.*, 'kʌniŋəm, kúnning-ăm

Cuninghame,*f.n.*, 'kʌniŋəm, kúnning-ăm

Cunliffe,*f.n.*, 'kʌnlif, kúnlif

Cunningham of Hyndhope, Viscountcy of, 'kʌniŋəm əv 'haindhoup, kúnning-ăm ŏv hínd-hōp

Cunobelin, *ancient king, also spelt* **Cunobeline**, kʊ'nɒbəlin, kōōnóbbĕlin

Cunyngham,*f.n.*, 'kʌniŋəm, kúnning-ăm

Cupar *Fife*, 'kupər, kōōpăr

Cupit,*f.n.*, 'kjupit, kéwpit

Cupitt,*f.n.*, 'kjupit, kéwpit

Curgenven,*f.n.*, kər'genvən, kŭrgénvĕn; kər'ginvən, kŭr-gínvĕn

Curigwen, *Welsh C.n.*, kə'rigwen, kŭrígwen

Curle,*f.n.*, kɜrl, kurl

Curphey,*f.n.*, 'kɜrfi, kúrfi

Curraghmore *Co. Fermanagh*, ˌkʌrə'mɔr, kurrămór

Curran,*f.n.*, 'kʌrən, kúrrăn

Currell,*f.n.*, 'kʌrəl, kúrrĕl

Currie *Lothian*, 'kʌri, kúrri

Curry Rivel *Somerset*, 'kʌri 'raivl, kúrri rívl

Cursiter,*f.n.*, 'kɜrsitər, kúrssi-tĕr

Cursley,*f.n.*, 'kɜrzli, kúrzli

Cursue,*f.n.*, kɜr'sju, kursséw

Curteis,*f.n.*, 'kɜrtis, kúrtiss

Curthoys, *f.n.,* kər'tɔɪz, kurtóyz; kərˈθɔɪz, kur-thóyz; ˈkərθɔɪz, kúr-thoyz; ˈkərtɔɪz, kúrtoyz

Curtois, *f.n.,* ˈkərtɔɪz, kúrtoyz; ˈkərtɪs, kúrtiss

Cury *Cornwall,* ˈkjʊəri, kyŏŏri

Cury Cross *Cornwall,* ˈkjʊəri ˈkrɒs, kyŏŏri króss

Curzon, Viscount, ˈkərzən, kúrzŏn

Cusack, *f.n.,* ˈkjuːsæk, kéwssack

Cusgarne *Cornwall,* kəzˈgɑrn, kŭzgaárn

Cush, *f.n.,* kʊʃ, kŏŏsh

Cushendall *Co. Antrim,* ˌkʊʃənˈdɔl, kŏŏshĕndáwl

Cushendun, Barony of, ˌkʌʃənˈdʌn, kushĕndún

Cushendun *Co. Antrim,* ˌkʊʃənˈdʌn, kŏŏshĕndún

Cushine, *f.n.,* ˈkʊʃaɪn, kŏŏshín

Cushing, *f.n.,* ˈkʊʃɪŋ, kŏŏshing

Cushuish *Somerset,* kəsˈhjuːʃ, küss-héwish

Cusick, *f.n.,* ˈkjuːsɪk, kéwssick

Cutforth, *f.n.,* ˈkʌtfɔrθ, kútforth

Cuthbe, *f.n.,* ˈkʌθbɪ, kúthbi

Cuthbert, *C.n. and f.n.,* ˈkʌθbərt, kúthbért

Cuthill, *f.n.,* ˈkʌθɪl, kúth-il; ˈkʌθɪl, kút-hil

Cutner, *f.n.,* ˈkʌtnər, kútnĕr

Cuttell, *f.n.,* kəˈtel, kŭtéll

Cuttress, *f.n.,* ˈkʌtrɪs, kúttrĕss

Cuxham *Oxon.,* ˈkʊksəm, kŏŏksăm; ˈkʌksəm, kúcksăm

Cuxton *Kent,* ˈkʌkstən, kúckstŏn

Cuxwold *Lincs.,* ˈkʌkswoʊld, kúckswōld

Cuyler, *f.n.,* ˈkaɪlər, kílĕr

Cwm *Clwyd, Gwent,* kʊm, kŏŏm. *Appropriate also for the River* ~ *(Powys).*

Cwmcarn *Gwent,* kʊmˈkarn, kŏŏmkaárn

Cwmaman *Mid Glam.,* kʊmˈæmən, kŏŏmámmăn

Cwmamman *Dyfed,* kʊmˈæmən, kŏŏmámmăn

Cwmann *Dyfed* kʊmˈæn, kŏŏmán

Cwmannogisaf *Clwyd,* kʊmˈænɒgˈɪsæv, kŏŏm-ánnog-íssav

Cwm Avon *Gwent, W. Glam.,* kʊm ˈævən, kŏŏm ávvŏn

Cwmbach *Dyfed, Mid Glam., Powys,* kʊmˈbax, kŏŏmbaách

Cwmbran *Gwent,* kʊmˈbran, kŏŏmbraán

Cwmbwrla *W. Glam.,* kʊmˈbʊərlə, kŏŏmbŏŏrlă

Cwmcarn *Gwent,* kʊmˈkarn, kŏŏmkaárn

Cwmcelyn *Gwent,* kʊmˈkelɪn, kŏŏmkéllin

Cwmclydach *W. Glam.,* kʊmˈklɪdəx, kŏŏm-klíddăch; kʊmˈklʌdəx, kŏŏm-klúddăch

Cwmcothi *Dyfed,* kʊmˈkɒθɪ, kŏŏmkóthi

Cwmdare *Mid Glam.,* kʊmˈdɛər, kŏŏmdáir

Cwmdu *Dyfed, Powys, W. Glam.,* kʊmˈdi, kŏŏm-déé

Cwmfelin *Mid Glam.,* kʊmˈvelɪn, kŏŏmvéllin

Cwmfelinfach *Gwent,* kʊmˌvelɪnˈvax, kŏŏmvellinvaách

Cwm Ffrwd *Dyfed,* kʊm ˈfrud, kŏŏm froód

Cwmffrwdoer *Gwent,* ˌkʊmfrudˈɔɪər, kŏŏmfroodóyr

Cwmgiedd *Powys,* kʊmˈgiəð, kŏŏmgeé-ĕth

Cwmgors *W. Glam.,* kʊmˈgɔrs, kŏŏmgórss

Cwmgwrach *W. Glam.,* kʊmˈgwrax, kŏŏmgwraách; kʊmˈgrax, kŏŏmgraách. *Welsh speakers pronounce 'gwrach' as one syllable by treating the 'w' as a rounding of the lips to accompany the 'r'.*

Cwm Idwal Nature Reserve *Gwynedd,* kʊm ˈɪdwəl, kŏŏm ídwăl

Cwmllinfell *see* **Cwmllynfell**

Cwmllynfell, *also spelt* **Cwmllinfell,** *W. Glam.,* kʊmˈɬʌnveɬ, kŏŏm-hlún-vehl

Cwmmawr *Dyfed,* kʊmˈmaʊər, kŏŏm-mówr

Cwmparc *Mid Glam.,* kʊmˈpark, kŏŏmpaárk

Cwmpennar *Mid Glam.,* kʊmˈpenər, kŏŏmpénnăr

Cwm Prysor *Gwynedd,* kʊm ˈprʌsɔr, kŏŏm prússor

Cwmrheidol *Dyfed,* kʊmˈhraɪdɒl, kŏŏmrídol

Cwm Silyn *Gwynedd,* kʊm ˈsɪlɪn, kŏŏm sillin

Cwmstradllyn *Gwynedd,* kʊmˈstrædɬɪn, kŏŏmstrádhlin

Cwmsyfiog *Mid Glam.,* kʊmˈsɪvjɒg, kŏŏmssív-yog

Cwmtillery *Gwent,* ˌkʊmtɪˈlɛəri, kŏŏmtiláiri

Cwm Tryweryn *Gwynedd,* kʊm ˈtrɪˈwerɪn, kŏŏm tri-wérrin; ˌkʊm trʌˈwerɪn, kŏŏm tru-wérrin

Cwmtwrch *W. Glam.,* kʊmˈtʊərx, kŏŏmtŏŏrch

Cwmyglo *Dyfed, Gwynedd,* ˌkʊməˈglou, kŏŏmăglṓ

Cwmyoy *Gwent,* kʊmˈjɔɪ, kŏŏm-yóy

Cwm-yr-Eglwys *Dyfed,* ˌkʊm ər ˈeglʊɪs, kŏŏm-ŭr-églŏŏiss

Cwmystwyth *Dyfed*, kʊm'ʌstwɪθ, kōōmústwith

Cydweli, *Welsh form of* **Kidwelly**, *q.v.*, *Dyfed*, kɪd'welɪ, kidwélli

Cyfarthfa *Mid Glam.*, kə'vɑrθvə, küvaárth-vä

Cyfeiliog *Powys*, kə'vaɪljɒg, küvíl-yog

Cyfoeth-y-Brenin *Dyfed*, 'kʌvɔɪθ ə 'brenɪn, kúvvoyth ä brénnin

Cyfronydd *Powys*, kə'vrɒnɪð, küvrónnith

Cylwik, *f.n.*, 'sɪlwɪk, síll-wick

Cymau *Clwyd*, 'kʌmaɪ, kúmmī

Cymmer *Mid Glam.*, 'kʌmər, kúmmer

Cymmrodorion Society, *London Welsh society*, ˌkʌmrə'dɒrɪən, kumrōdórri-ŏn

Cymric party, *Welsh political party*, 'kʌmrɪk, kúmrick

Cynan, *Welsh C.n.*, 'kʌnən, kúnnăn

Cyncoed *S. Glam.*, kɪn'kɔɪd, kin-kóyd

Cynddylan, *Welsh C.n.*, kʌn-'ðʌlən, kunthúllän

Cynghordy *Dyfed*, kʌŋ'hɒrdɪ, kung-hórdi

Cynheidre Colliery *Dyfed*, kʌn-'haɪdreɪ, kun-hídray

Cynlais *Powys*, 'kʌnlaɪs, kúnlīss

Cynog *Powys*, 'kʌnɒg, kúnnog

Cynon, River, *Mid Glam.*, 'kʌnən, kúnnŏn

Cynric, *Welsh C.n.*, 'kʌnrɪk, kúnrick

Cyntwell *S. Glam.*, 'sɪntwel, síntwel

Cynull Mawr *Dyfed*, 'kʌnɫ 'mauər, kúnnihl mówr

Cynwyd *Clwyd*, 'kʌnʊɪd, kúnnōō-id

Cyriax, *f.n.*, 'sɪrɪæks, sírri-acks

Cyster, *f.n.*, 'sɪstər, sísstĕr

Cysyllte *Clwyd*, kə'sʌɫteɪ, küs-súhltay

Czerkawska, *f.n.*, tʃər'kæfskə, chĕrkáfskä

D

D'Abbes, *f.n.*, dæbz, dabz

D'Abernon, Viscountcy of, 'dæbərnən, dábbĕrnŏn

d'Abo, *f.n.*, 'dɑbou, daábō

Daborn, *f.n.*, 'deɪbɔrn, dáyborn

D'Abreu, *f.n.*, 'dæbru, dábroo

Dacombe, *f.n.*, 'deɪkəm, dáykŏm

Dacorum *Herts.*, də'kɔrəm, dăkáwrŭm

Dacre, Baroness, 'deɪkər, dáykĕr

Dacre of Gillesland, Baron, 'deɪkər əv 'gɪlzlənd, dáykĕr ŏv gílzländ

Dacre of Glanton, Baron, 'deɪkər əv 'glæntən, dáykĕr ŏv glántŏn

Dacres, *f.n.*, 'deɪkərz, dáykĕrz

Dadd, *f.n.*, dæd, dadd

Daer and Shortcleuch, Baron, 'deər ənd 'ʃɔrtklu, dáir ănd shórtkloo

Daer Water, River, *S'clyde*, 'dɑr 'wɒtər, daár wáwtĕr

D'Aeth, *f.n.*, deθ, deth; deɪθ, dayth; dɪθ, deeth

Dafen *Dyfed*, 'dævən, dávvĕn

Dafydd, *Welsh C.n.*, 'dævɪð, dávvith

Dagenham *London*, 'dægənəm, dággĕnăm

Dagg, *f.n.*, dæg, dag

Daggar, *f.n.*, 'dægər, dággăr

Daglish, *f.n.*, 'dæglɪʃ, dáglish

D'Aguiar, *f.n.*, 'dægjʊɑr, dág-yōō-aar

D'Aguilar, *f.n.*, 'dægwɪlər, dágwillăr

Dagul, *f.n.*, 'deɪgl, dáygl

Daiches, *f.n.*, 'deɪʃɪs, dáyshĕss; 'daɪxɪs, díchĕss

Dailly *S'clyde*, 'deɪlɪ, dáyli

Daimpré, *f.n.*, 'dæmpreɪ, dámpray

Daine, *f.n.*, deɪn, dayn

Dakeyne, *f.n.*, də'keɪn, dăkáyn

Dakin, *f.n.*, 'deɪkɪn, dáykin

Dalbeattie *D. & G.*, dəl'bitɪ, dălbéeti

Dalberg, *f.n.*, 'dælbərg, dálberg

D'Albiac, *f.n.*, 'dɒlbiæk, dáwlbi--ack

Dalbury Lees *Derby.*, 'dɒlbərɪ 'liz, dáwlbŭri léez

Dalby, *f.n.*, 'dɒlbɪ, dáwlbi; 'dælbɪ, dálbi

Dalby *Leics.*, 'dɒlbɪ, dáwlbi; 'dɒlbɪ, dólbi

Dalby *Lincs.*, 'dɒlbɪ, dáwlbi

Daldy, *f.n.*, 'dældɪ, dáldi

Dalgetty, *f.n.*, dæl'getɪ, dalgétti; dəl'getɪ, dălgétti

Dalgety, *f.n.*, dæl'getɪ, dalgétti; dəl'getɪ, dălgétti

Dalgety Bay *Fife*, dəl'getɪ, dălgétti

Dalgleish, *f.n.*, dæl'gliʃ, dalgléesh

Dalhousie, Earl of, dæl'hauzɪ, dalhówzi. *Appropriate also for* ∼ *Castle*.

Daliburgh *W. Isles*, 'dælɪbərə, dálibŭră

Daligan, *f.n.*, 'dælɪgən, dáligăn

Dalkeith *Lothian*, dæl'kiθ, dal-kéeth. *Appropriate also for the Earl of* ∼.

Dall, *f.n.*, dæl, dal; dɒl, dawl

Dallas *Grampian,* 'dæləs, dáláss
Dalley, *f.n.,* 'dælɪ, dáli
Dalling, *f.n.,* 'dælɪŋ, dáling
Dallinghoo *Suffolk,* ˌdælɪŋ'huː, daling-hoó
Dallington *Northants.,* 'dælɪŋtən, dálingtŏn
Dallington *E. Sussex,* 'dælɪŋtən, dálingtŏn; 'dɒlɪŋtən, dóllingtŏn
Dally, *f.n.,* 'dælɪ, dáli
Dalmahoy *Lothian,* ˌdælmə'hɔɪ, dalmahóy
Dalmeny *Lothian,* dæl'menɪ, dalménni; dəl'menɪ, dălménni. *The first is appropriate for Baron* ~.
Dalmore *W. Isles,* dæl'mɔr, dalmór. *Appropriate also for* ~ *Distillery.*
Dalnacardoch *Tayside,* ˌdælnə-'kɑːrdəx, dalnăkaárdŏ<u>ch</u>
Dalnaspidal *Tayside,* ˌdælnə'spɪdl, dalnă-spíddl
Dalness *S'clyde,* dæl'nes, dal-néss
Daloni, *C.n.,* 'dælənɪ, dálŏni
Dalriada *Co. Antrim,* ˌdælrɪ'ædə, dalri-áddă
Dalry *Edinburgh,* dəl'raɪ, dălrí
Dalrymple, *f.n.,* dəl'rɪmpl, dăl-rímpl; dæl'rɪmpl, dalrímpl; 'dælrɪmpl, dálrimpl. *The first is appropriate for the family name of the Earl of Stair and thus also for Viscount* ~.
Dalrymple *S'clyde,* dəl'rɪmpl, dălrímpl
Dalserf *S'clyde,* dəl'sɜrf, dăl-sérf
D'Alton, *f.n.,* 'dɔltən, dáwltŏn
Dalton, *f.n.,* 'dɔltən, dáwltŏn
Daltry, *f.n.,* 'dɔltrɪ, dáwltri
Dalway, *f.n.,* 'dɔlweɪ, dáwlway
Dalwhinnie *H'land,* dəl'hwɪnɪ, dăl-whínni
Dalwood, *f.n.,* 'dælwʊd, dálwŏŏd
Dalwood *Devon,* 'dɒlwʊd, dáwl-wŏŏd; 'dælwʊd, dálwŏŏd
Daly, *f.n.,* 'deɪlɪ, dáyli
Dalyell of the Binns, *f.n.,* di'el əv ðə 'bɪnz, dee-éll ŏv th<u>ē</u> bínz
Dalzell, *f.n.,* di'el, dee-éll; 'dælzel, dálzel. *The first is appropriate for Baron Hamilton of* ~.
Dalzell-Payne, *f.n.,* di'el 'peɪn, dee-éll páyn
Dalziel, *f.n.,* di'el, dee-éll; 'dælzɪl, dálzeel
Dalziel *S'clyde,* di'el, dee-éll
Dalziel of Kirkcaldy, Barony of, di'el əv kɜr'kɒdɪ, dee-éll ŏv kŭrkóddi
Dalziel of Wooler, Barony of, 'dælzɪl əv 'wʊlər, dálzeel ŏv wŏŏlĕr

Daman, William, *Elizabethan composer,* 'deɪmən, dáymăn
Damant, *f.n.,* də'mænt, dămánt
D'Ambrumenil, *f.n.,* dæm-'brʌmənəl, dambrúmmĕnĕl; dɒm'brumənəl, dombroómĕnĕl
Damer, *f.n.,* 'deɪmər, dáymĕr
Damerell, *f.n.,* 'dæmərəl, dámmĕrĕl
Damerham *Hants.,* 'dæmərəm, dámmĕrăm
Damiano, *f.n.,* ˌdæmɪ'ɑnoʊ, dammi-aánō
Dammarell, *f.n.,* 'dæmərəl, dámmărĕl
Dampier, *f.n.,* 'dæmpɪər, dámpi-ĕr
Danaher, *f.n.,* 'dænəhər, dánnă-hĕr
Danby Wiske *N. Yorks.,* 'dænbɪ 'wɪsk, dánbi wísk
Danckwerts, *f.n.,* 'dæŋkwərts, dánkwĕrts
Dancy, *f.n.,* 'dænsɪ, dánssi
Dancyger, *f.n.,* 'dænsɪgər, dánssigĕr
Daneman, *f.n.,* 'deɪnmən, dáyn-măn
Dangan, Viscount, 'dæŋgən, dáng-găn
Daniell, *f.n.,* 'dænjəl, dán-yĕl
Dankworth, *f.n.,* 'dæŋkwɜrθ, dánkwurth; 'dæŋkwərθ, dánkwŭrth
Dannreuther, *f.n.,* 'dænrɔɪtər, dánroytĕr
Danos, *f.n.,* 'deɪnɒs, dáynoss
d'Antal, *f.n.,* 'dæntl, dántl
Danvers, *f.n.,* 'dænvərz, dánvĕrz
Danyel, *f.n.,* 'dænjəl, dán-yĕl
Danygraig *Gwent,* ˌdænə'graɪg, dannăgríg
Dan yr Ogof Caves *Powys,* ˌdæn ər 'ɒgɒv, dan ăr óggov
Danziger, *f.n.,* 'dæntsɪgər, dántsiggĕr
D'Arcy de Knayth, Baroness, 'dɑrsɪ də 'neɪθ, daárssi dĕ náyth
Darent, River, *Kent,* 'dærənt, dárrĕnt
Darenth *Kent,* 'dærənθ, dárrĕnth
Daresbury *Ches.,* 'dɑrzbərɪ, daárzbŭri. *Appropriate also for Baron* ~.
Darewski, *f.n.,* də'ruskɪ, dăroóski
Dargavel, *f.n.,* 'dɑrgəvəl, daár-găvel
Darite *Cornwall,* də'raɪt, dărít
Darke, *f.n.,* dɑrk, daark
Darlaston *W. Midlands,* 'dɑrlə-stən, daárlăstŏn
Darlingscott *Warwicks.,* 'dɑrskət, daársskŏt
Darlington *Durham,* 'dɑrlɪŋtən, daárlingtŏn

Darlow, *f.n.*, 'dɑːrlou, daárlō
Darnac, *f.n.*, 'dɑːrnæk, daárnack
Darnall *S. Yorks.*, 'dɑːrnl, daárnl
Darowen *Powys*, də'rouən, dărŏ-ĕn
Darragh, *f.n.*, 'dærə, dárră; 'dærəx, dárrăᴄh
Darsham *Suffolk*, 'dɑːrʃəm, daár-shăm
Dartmouth *Devon*, 'dɑːrtməθ, daártmŭth. *Appropriate also for the Earl of ~.*
Darvall, *f.n.*, 'dɑːrvl, daárvl
Darvel *S'clyde*, 'dɑːrvl, daárvl
Darvell, *f.n.*, 'dɑːrvl, daárvl
Darwen *Lancs.*, 'dɑːrwɪn, daárwĕn; 'dærən, dárrĕn
Darwin, *f.n.*, 'dɑːrwɪn, daárwin
Daryll, *f.n.*, 'dærɪl, dárril
Daryush, *f.n.*, 'dærɪʊʃ, dárri-ōōsh
Dasent, *f.n.*, 'deɪsənt, dáyssĕnt
Dashper, *f.n.*, 'dæʃpər, dáshpĕr
Dassells *Herts.*, 'dæslz, dásslz
Dassie, *f.n.*, 'dæsɪ, dássi
Dastor, *f.n.*, 'dæstər, dástor
Daszak, *f.n.*, 'dæʃæk, dáshack
Datson, *f.n.*, 'dætsən, dátssŏn
Datyner, *f.n.*, 'dætɪnər, dáttinĕr
Daube, *f.n.*, dɔb, dawb; 'daubə, dówbĕ
Daubeney, *f.n.*, 'dɔbnɪ, dáwb-ni
Dauncey, *f.n.*, 'dɔnsɪ, dáwnssi
Dauntsey, *f.n.*, 'dɔntsɪ, dáwntssi
Dauthieu, *f.n.*, 'doutʒə, dŏt-yŏ
Davaar *S'clyde*, də'vɑr, dăvaár
Davan-Wetton, *f.n.*, 'deɪvən 'wetən, dáyvăn wéttŏn
Davenham *Ches.*, 'deɪvənəm, dáyvĕnăm; 'deɪnəm, dáynăm
Davenport, *f.n.*, 'dævənpɔrt, dávvĕnport
Daventry *Northants.*, 'dævəntrɪ, dávvĕntri; 'deɪntrɪ, dáyntri. *The first is appropriate for Viscount ~.*
Davern, *f.n.*, 'dævərn, dávvĕrn
Davey, *f.n.*, 'deɪvɪ, dáyvi
Davidge, *f.n.*, 'dævɪdʒ, dávvij
Davidson, *f.n.*, 'deɪvɪdsən, dáyvidssŏn
Davidstow *Cornwall*, 'deɪvɪdstou, dáyvidsstō
Davie, *f.n.*, 'deɪvɪ, dáyvi. *See also* **Thorpe Davie.**
Davier, *f.n.*, 'dævɪeɪ, dávvi-ay
Davies, *f.n.*, 'deɪvɪs, dáyviss
d'Avigdor-Goldsmid, *f.n.*, 'dævɪgdər 'gouldsmɪd, dávvigdor góldsmid
Davin, *f.n.*, 'dævɪn, dávvin
Davinson, *f.n.*, 'dævɪnsən, dávvinssŏn
Davion, *f.n.*, 'dævɪən, dávvi-ŏn

Daviot, Gordon, *author*, 'dævɪət, dávvi-ŏt. *Although Elizabeth McIntosh derived this pen-name from the Inverness-shire village of Daviot, she chose to pronounce it differently.*
Daviot, *Grampian*, *H'land*, 'deɪvɪət, dáyvi-ŏt
Davis, *f.n.*, 'deɪvɪs, dáyviss
Davison, *f.n.*, 'deɪvɪsən, dáyvissŏn
Davson, *f.n.*, 'dævsən, dávssŏn
Davyhulme *Gtr. M'chester*, 'deɪvɪhjum, dáyvi-hewm
Dawbarn, *f.n.*, 'dɔbərn, dáwbărn
Dawick, Viscount, 'dɔ-ɪk, dáw--ick
Dawley Magna *Salop*, 'dɔlɪ 'mægnə, dáwli mágná
Dawlish *Devon*, 'dɔlɪʃ, dáwlish
Dawnay, *f.n.*, 'dɔnɪ, dáwni. *Appropriate also for Baron ~.*
Dawsholm *Glasgow*, 'dɔzhəlm, dáwz-hōlm
Dawson, *f.n.*, 'dɔsən, dáwssŏn
Daymond, *f.n.*, 'deɪmənd, dáymŏnd
Ddôl *Clwyd*, ðoul, ᴛhōl
Dduallt *Gwynedd*, 'ðiælt, thée-ahlt
Deacy, *f.n.*, 'disɪ, deéssi
Deakin, *f.n.*, 'dikɪn, deékin
Dealtry, *f.n.*, 'dɔltrɪ, dáwltri
Deamer, *f.n.*, 'dimər, deémĕr
Dearden, *f.n.*, 'dɪərdən, deérdĕn
Dearling, *f.n.*, 'dɪərlɪŋ, deérling
Dearmer, *f.n.*, 'dɪərmər, deérmĕr
Dearne, River, *W. & S. Yorks.*, dɜrn, dern
Dearnley, *f.n.*, 'dɜrnlɪ, dérnli
Dearsley, *f.n.*, 'dɪərzlɪ, deérzli
Dearth, *f.n.*, dɜrθ, derth
Deas, *f.n.*, diz, deez
Dease, *f.n.*, dis, deess
Deason, *f.n.*, 'disən, deéssŏn
De'ath, *f.n.*, di'eθ, dee-áth
Debach *Suffolk*, 'debɪdʒ, débbij
De Banzie, *f.n.*, də 'bænzɪ, dĕ bánzi
De Bartolome, *f.n.*, də bɑr-'tɒləmeɪ, dĕ baartóllŏmay
De Bathe, *f.n.*, də 'bɑθ, dĕ baáth
Debbane, *f.n.*, dɪ'bæn, débánn
De Beer, *f.n.*, də 'bɪər, dĕ beér
de Bellaigue, *f.n.*, də bel'eɪg, dĕ belláyg
Deben, River, *Suffolk*, 'dibən, deébĕn
Debeney, *f.n.*, 'debənɪ, débbĕni
Debenham, *f.n.*, 'debənəm, débbĕnăm
Debenham *Suffolk*, 'debənəm, débbĕnăm
Debens, *f.n.*, 'debɪnz, débbĕnz
Debes, *f.n.*, dɪ'bez, débézz

de Bettoyne, *f.n.*, də bə'tɔɪn, dĕ bĕtóyn

De Blank, The Rt. Revd Joost, 'jɔʊst də 'blæŋk, yŏst dĕ blánk

De Blaquiere, Barony of, də 'blækjər, dĕ bláck-yĕr

De Blieck, *f.n.*, də 'blik, dĕ bleék

De Bono, *f.n.*, də 'boʊnoʊ, dĕ bṓnō

De Bounevialle, *f.n.*, də 'bunvɪæl, dĕ boónvi-al

Debrett, *f.n.*, də'bret, dĕbrétt

De Broke, *f.n.*, də 'brʊk, dĕ broŏk

De Bruyne, *f.n.*, də 'brunɪ, dĕ broónay

De Buf, *f.n.*, də 'bʌf, dĕ búff

De Bunsen, *f.n.*, də 'bʌnsən, dĕ búnssĕn

De Burgh, *f.n.*, də 'bɜrg, dĕ búrg

De Buriatte, *f.n.*, də 'bjʊərɪæt, dĕ byoóri-at

Deby, *f.n.*, 'dibɪ, deébi

De Candole, *f.n.*, də 'kændoʊl, dĕ kándōl

De Carteret, *f.n.*, də 'kɑrtrət, dĕ kaártrĕt

De Casembroot, *f.n.*, də 'kæsəmbrut, dĕ kássĕmbroot

De Chair, *f.n.*, də'tʃɛər, dĕ cháir; də 'ʃɛər, dĕ sháir

Decies, Baron, 'diʃiz, deésheez

Decimus, *f.n.*, 'desɪməs, déssimŭss

De Comarmond, *f.n.*, də kə-'mɑrmənd, dĕ kŏmaármŏnd

De Coucey, *f.n.*, də 'kusɪ, dĕ koóssi

De Courcey, *f.n.*, də 'kɔrsɪ, dĕ kórssi

De Courcy, *f.n.*, də 'kɔrsɪ, dĕ kórssi; də 'kʊərsɪ, dĕ koŏrssi; də 'kɜrsɪ, dĕ kúrssi. *The first is appropriate for Baron Kingsdale's family name.*

De Crespigny, *f.n.*, də 'krepɪnɪ, dĕ kréppini

de Csilléry, *f.n.*, də 'tʃɪlɛərɪ, dĕ chíll-airi

De Cusance, *f.n.*, də 'kuzɑns, dĕ koózaanss

Dederich, *f.n.*, 'dedərɪtʃ, déddĕritch

Dedow, *f.n.*, 'didoʊ, deédō

De Eresby, *f.n.*, 'dɪərzbɪ, deérzbi

De Felice, *f.n.*, di fɪ'lis, dee fĕleéss

De Ferranti, *f.n.*, də fə'rænti, dĕ fĕránti

Deffee, *f.n.*, də'fi, dĕfeé

Defferary, *f.n.*, ,defə'rɛərɪ, deffĕráiri

Defoe, Daniel, *18th-c. author*, dɪ'foʊ, dĕfṓ

De Francia, *f.n.*, də 'frɑnsɪə, dĕ fraánsiă

De Francquen, *f.n.*, də 'fræŋkwɪn, dĕ fránkwĕn

Defrates, *f.n.*, dɪ'freɪts, dĕfráyts

De Frece, *f.n.*, də 'fris, dĕ freéss

De Freitas, *f.n.*, də 'freɪtəs, dĕ fráytăss

Defries, *f.n.*, də'fris, dĕfreéss

Deganwy *Gwynedd*, dɪ'gænʊɪ, dĕgánoō-i

De Garis, *f.n.*, də 'gærɪs, dĕ gárriss

De Gaury, *f.n.*, də 'gɔrɪ, dĕ gáwri

De Gernier, *f.n.*, də 'dʒɜrnɪər, dĕ jérniĕr

De Glehn, *f.n.*, də 'glen, dĕ glén

de Grunwald, Anatole, *film producer*, 'ænətɒl də 'grunvæld, ánnătol dĕ groónvald

De Guingand, *f.n.*, də 'gægɑ̃, dĕ gáng-gaang

D'Egville, *f.n.*, 'degvɪl, dégvil

De Haes, *f.n.*, də 'heɪz, dĕ háyz

Dehaney, *f.n.*, də'heɪnɪ, dĕ-háyni

Deheubarth, *ancient Welsh kingdom*, de'haɪbɑrθ, de-híbaarth

Dehn, *f.n.*, deɪn, dayn

de Hoghton, *f.n.*, də 'hɒtən, dĕ háwtŏn

Deighton, *f.n.*, 'daɪtən, dítŏn; 'deɪtən, dáytŏn. *The second is appropriate for Len ~, author.*

Deighton *W. Yorks.*, 'ditən, deétŏn

Deildre Isaf *Gwynedd*, 'daɪldrɪ 'ɪsæv, díldri íssav

Deiniolen *Gwynedd*, daɪn'jɒlən, dīn-yóllĕn

Deirdre, *C.n.*, 'dɪərdrɪ, deérdri

De Jonge, *f.n.*, də 'jʌŋ, dĕ yúng

De Jongh, *f.n.*, də 'jɒŋ, dĕ yóng

de Keyser, *f.n.*, də 'kaɪzər, dĕ kízĕr

Dekker, *f.n.*, 'dekər, déckĕr

De Krassel, *f.n.*, də 'kræsl, dĕ krássl

de la Bedoyère, *f.n.*, də lɑ ,bedwə'jɛər, dĕ laa bedwă-yáir

De la Bère, *f.n.*, ,delə'bɪər, dĕllăbéer

De Labilliere, *f.n.*, də lɑ'bɪljər, dĕ laabíl-yĕr

Delaboie *Cornwall*, 'deləboʊl, déllăbōl; ,delə'boʊl, dellăbṓl

Delacombe, *f.n.*, 'deləkum, déllăkoom

Delacour, *f.n.*, 'deləkʊər, délläkoŏr

Delacourt-Smith, Baron, 'deləkɔrt 'smɪθ, délläkort smíth

de la Ferté, *f.n.*, də lɑ 'fɛərteɪ, dĕ laa fáirtay

Delafons, *f.n.*, 'deləfɒnz, délläfonz

de la Fuente, *f.n.,* də lə fʊ'entɪ, dĕ lä fōō-énti

Delahaye, *f.n.,* 'deləheɪ, délla-hay

De la Haye, *f.n.,* də la 'heɪ, dĕ laa háy

de la Mahotiere, *f.n.,* də la ˌmaoʊ'tjeər, dĕ laa maa-ō-tyáir

Delamain, *f.n.,* 'deləmeɪn, déllämayn

de la Mare, *f.n.,* ˌdelə'meər, dellă-máir; 'deləmeər, déllămair. *The first is appropriate for the poet, Walter ~.*

De la Marr, *f.n.,* də lə 'mar, dĕ lä maár

Delamere, Baron, ˌdelə'mɪər, dellăméer

Delamere *Ches.,* 'deləmɪər, déllă-meer

De la Motte, *f.n.,* də la 'mɒt, dĕ laa mótt

Delane, *f.n.,* də'leɪn, dĕláyn

Delaney, *f.n.,* dɪ'leɪnɪ, dĕláyni

De Lange, *f.n.,* də 'lãʒ, dĕ laángzh

De-la-Noy, *f.n.,* 'delənɔɪ, déllănoy

Delap, *f.n.,* də'læp, dĕláp

De la Pasture, *f.n.,* də 'læpətʃər, dĕ láppătchĕr

de la Poer Beresford, *f.n.,* də la 'pʊər 'berɪsfərd, dĕ laa pṓōr bérrĕsfŏrd. *Family name of the Marquess of Waterford and of Baron* **Decies.**

de la Pole, *f.n.,* də la 'pʊl, dĕ laa pṓōl

Delapré Abbey *Northants.,* 'deləpreɪ, déllápray

Delargy, *f.n.,* də'largɪ, dĕlaárgi

De Larrinaga, *f.n.,* də ˌlærɪ'nagə, dĕ larrináagă

De La Rue, *f.n.,* ˌdelə'ru, dellărōó

De La Salle, *f.n.,* də la 'sal, dĕ laa saál

De la Torre, *f.n.,* də la 'tɔr, dĕ laa tór

De Laubenque, *f.n.,* də 'loʊbeŋk, dĕ lóbenk

De La Warr, Earl, 'deləweər, déllăwair

Delbanco, *f.n.,* del'bæŋkoʊ, delbánkō

Delderfield, *f.n.,* 'deldərfild, déldĕrfeeld

Delephine, *f.n.,* 'deləpin, déllĕpeen

De Lestang, *f.n.,* də 'leɪtã, dĕ láytaang

Delevingne, *f.n.,* 'deləvin, déllĕveen

Delfont, *f.n.,* 'delfɒnt, délfont. *Appropriate also for Baron ~.*

Delgaty Castle, *also spelt* **Delgatie,** *Grampian,* 'delgətɪ, délgăti

De Lingen, *f.n.,* də 'lɪŋən, dĕ líng-ĕn

De Lisle, *f.n.,* də 'laɪl, dĕ líl

De L'Isle, Viscount, də 'laɪl, dĕ líl

Delith, *C.n.,* 'delɪθ, déllith

Delius, Frederick, *composer,* 'dilɪəs, déeliŭss

Deller, *f.n.,* 'delər, déllĕr

Dellow, *f.n.,* 'deloʊ, déllō

Del Mar, *f.n.,* del 'mar, del maár

Deloitte, *f.n.,* də'lɔɪt, dĕlóyt

Delomosne, *f.n.,* 'deləmoʊn, déllōmōn

De Lotbinière, *f.n.,* də 'loʊbɪnjeər, dĕ lóbin-yair

Del Renzio, *f.n.,* del 'renzɪoʊ, del rénziō

Delrez, *f.n.,* 'delreɪ, déllray

Del Riego, Teresa, *composer,* tə'reɪzə del rɪ'eɪgoʊ, tĕráyză del ri-áygō

Del Strother, *f.n.,* del 'strʌðər, del strúthĕr

del Tufo, *f.n.,* del 'tufoʊ, del tóofō

de Lukacz-Leisner, *f.n.,* də 'lukætʃ 'leznər, dĕ lóokatch lézznĕr

Delury, *f.n.,* də'lʊərɪ, dĕlṓōri

Delval, *f.n.,* del'væl, delvál

Delves *W. Midlands,* delvz, delvz

Demaid, *f.n.,* də'meɪd, dĕmáyd

de Manio, *f.n.,* də 'mænɪoʊ, dĕ mánniō

Demant, *f.n.,* dɪ'mænt, dĕmánt

Demarco, *f.n.,* də'markoʊ, dĕmaárkō

De Mauley, Baron, də 'mɔlɪ, dĕ máwli

Demel, *f.n.,* 'deml, démml

De Minvielle, *f.n.,* də 'menvəl, ménvĕl

De Moleyns, *f.n.,* də 'mʌlɪnz, dĕ múllĕnz; 'deməlinz, démmō-leenz. *The first is also appropriate for Baron ~. See* **Eveleigh-de-Moleyns.**

De Montalt, Baron, ˌdemənt'ælt, demmŏntált

De Montmorency, *f.n.,* də ˌmɒntmə'rensɪ, dĕ montmŏr-énssi; də ˌmõmə'rãsɪ, dĕ mõngmŏraángssi. *The second was the pronunciation of the late Viscount of Mountmorres.*

Demoulpied, *f.n.,* də'moʊlpɪed, dĕmṓlpi-edd

Dempster, *f.n.,* 'dempstər, démp-stĕr

De Muralt, *f.n.,* də 'mjʊərælt, dĕ myṓōralt

Demuth, *f.n.,* də'mjuθ, dĕméwth; 'demət, démmŭt; də'muθ, dĕ-mṓōth; də'muθ, dĕmóōth

Denaby *S. Yorks.*, 'denəbɪ, dénnăbi. *Appropriate also for Denaby Main near by.*

Denbigh *Clwyd*, 'denbɪ, dénbi. *Appropriate also for the Earl of ~.*

Dench, *f.n.*, dentʃ, dentch

Deneke, *f.n.*, 'denɪkɪ, dénnĕki. *Appropriate for the Clara Sophie ~ scholarship at Oxford University.*

De Nevers, *f.n.*, də 'nevərz, dĕ névvĕrz

Dengie *Essex*, 'dendʒɪ, dénji

Denholm *Borders*, 'denəm, dénnŏm

Denholme *W. Yorks.*, 'denhɒlm, dén-hollm

Dening, *f.n.*, 'denɪŋ, dénning

Denne, *f.n.*, den, den

Dennehy, *f.n.*, 'denəhɪ, dénnĕ-hi

Denney, *f.n.*, 'denɪ, dénni

Dennistoun *S'clyde*, 'denɪstən, dénnistŏn

Denny, *f.n.*, 'denɪ, dénni

Denselow, *f.n.*, 'denzɪloʊ, dénzĕlō

Dent, *f.n.*, dent, dent

Dent-de-Lion *Kent*, 'dændɪlaɪən, dándili-ŏn

Denton *Cambs.*, *Norfolk*, *Oxon.*, 'dentən, déntŏn

Denwick *Northd.*, 'denɪk, dénnick

Denys, *C.n.*, 'denɪs, dénniss

de Nys, *f.n.*, də 'nis, dĕ neéss

Denzil, *C.n.*, 'denzɪl, dénzil

Deopham *Norfolk*, 'dipəm, deépăm ; 'difəm, deéfăm

Depden *Suffolk*, 'depdən, dépdĕn

de Peyer, *f.n.*, də 'paɪər, dĕ pí-ĕr

Deptford *London*, 'detfərd, déttfŏrd

De Piro, *f.n.*, də 'pɪəroʊ, dĕ peérō

Depledge, *f.n.*, dɪ'pledʒ, dĕpléjj

Deplidge, *f.n.*, 'deplɪdʒ, déplij

De Polnay, *f.n.*, də 'poʊlneɪ, dĕ pólnay; də 'pɒlneɪ, dĕ pólnay

Depport, *f.n.*, 'depɔrt, dépport

De Quesne, *f.n.*, də 'keɪn, dĕ káyn

Derby *Derby.*, 'dɑrbɪ, daárbi. *Appropriate also for the Earl of ~.*

Derbyshire, *f.n.*, 'dɑrbɪʃər, daárbishĕr

Dereham *Norfolk*, 'dɪərəm, deérăm

De Reyghère, *f.n.*, də 'reɪgər, dĕ ráygĕr

Derges, *f.n.*, 'dɜrdʒɪs, dérjĕss

Deri, *f.n.*, 'deərɪ, dáiri

Deri *Mid Glam.*, 'derɪ, dérri

Dering, *f.n.*, 'dɪərɪŋ, deéring

Deritend *W. Midlands*, ˌderɪt'end, derrit-énd

d'Erlanger, *f.n.*, 'deərlɑʒeɪ, dáirlaang-zhay

Dernawilt *Co. Fermanagh*, ˌdɜrnə-'wɪlt, dernăwílt

Derner, *f.n.*, 'dɜrnər, dérnĕr

De Roet, *f.n.*, də 'roʊɪt, dĕ rṓ-ĕt

de Rohan, *f.n.*, də 'roʊən, dĕ rṓ-ăn

de Ros, Baroness, də 'rus, dĕ roóss

Derriaghy, *also spelt* **Derryaghy**, *Co. Antrim*, ˌderɪ'æxɪ, derri-áchi

Derry *Co. name.* 'derɪ, dérri

Derryaghy *see* **Derriaghy**

Derrygonnelly *Co. Fermanagh*, ˌderɪ'gɒnəlɪ, derrigónnĕli

Derrylin *Co. Fermanagh*, ˌderɪ'lɪn, derrilín

Dersingham *Norfolk*, 'dɜrzɪŋəm, dérzing-ăm

Derville, *f.n.*, 'dɜrvɪl, dérvil

Dervock *Co. Antrim*, 'dɜrvɒk, dérvock

Derwen *Clwyd*, *Mid Glam.*, 'deərwɪn, dáirwĕn

Derwenlas *Powys*, ˌdeərwɪn'las, dairwĕnlaáss

Derwent, Baron, 'dɑrwənt, daárwĕnt

Derwenthaugh *Tyne & Wear*, 'deərwənthɑf, dáirwĕnt-haaf; 'dɜrwənthɒf, dérwĕnt-hoff

Derwentwater *Cumbria*, 'dɜrwənt-wɒtər, dérwĕnt-wawtĕr. *Appropriate also for the Earldom of ~, attainted after the Jacobite rebellion of 1715.*

Deryck, *C.n.*, 'derɪk, dérrick

de St. Croix, *f.n.*, də snt 'krwɑ, dĕ sınt krwaá; də snt 'krɔɪ, dĕ sınt króy

de Ste. Croix, *f.n.*, də snt 'krwɑ, dĕ sınt krwaá; də snt 'krɔɪ, dĕ sınt króy

De Sales, *f.n.*, də 'salz, dĕ saálz

De Salis, *f.n.*, də 'sælɪs, dĕ sáliss; də 'salz, dĕ saálz; də 'seɪlɪs, dĕ sáyliss

De Saram, *f.n.*, də 'sɛərəm, saírăm

Desart, Earldom of, 'dezərt, dézzărt

de Satgé, *f.n.*, də 'sætdʒeɪ, dĕ sátjay

De Saubergue, *f.n.*, də 'soʊbɜrg, dĕ sṓberg

De Saumarez, *f.n.*, də 'sɒmərɪz, dĕ sómmărĕz; də 'sɒmərez, dĕ sómmărezz. *The first is appropriate for Baron ~.*

De Sausmarez, *f.n.*, də 'sɒmərɪz, dĕ sómmărĕz; də 'sɒmərez, dĕ sómmărezz

de Saxe, *f.n.*, də 'sæks, dĕ sácks
Desbois, *f.n.*, deɪ'bwɑ, daybwáa
Desborough, *f.n.*, 'dezbərə,
  dézbŭrå. *Appropriate also for
  the Barony of ~.*
Desch, *f.n.*, deʃ, desh
Deschamps, *f.n.*, 'deʃən, déshăn;
  'deɪʃɑ̃, dáy-shaang
Des Champs, *f.n.*, 'deʃən, déshăn;
  'deɪ ʃɑ̃, dáy shaang
De Selincourt, *f.n.*, də 'selɪnkɔrt,
  dĕ séllin-kort
Desertmartin *Co. Derry*, ˌdezərt-
  'mɑrtɪn, dezzĕrtmaártin
De Sevin, *f.n.*, də sɪ'vɪn, dĕ
  sĕvéen
Desford *Leics.*, 'desfərd, déssfŏrd
Desforges, *f.n.*, deɪ'fɔrdʒ, dayfórj
Des Graz, *f.n.*, deɪ 'grɑ, day graá
Deslandes, *f.n.*, deɪ'lɑ̃d, day-
  laángd
de Soissons, *f.n.*, də 'swɑsɔ̃, dĕ
  swaássong
Desoutter, *f.n.*, dɪ'sutər, dĕssoó-
  tĕr
De Souza, *f.n.*, də 'suzə, dĕ soózå
De Stein, *f.n.*, də 'staɪn, dĕ stín
De Stroumillo, *f.n.*, də 'strumɪloʊ,
  dĕ stroómilŏ
Desvaux, *f.n.*, dɪ'voʊ, dĕvó;
  deɪ'voʊ, dayvó
Des Voeux, *f.n.*, deɪ 'vɜ, day võ
Dethick, *Derby.*, 'deθɪk, déthick
De Thuillier, *f.n.*, də 'twɪlɪər, dĕ
  twilliĕr
Dettmer, *f.n.*, 'detmər, déttmĕr
Deuchar, *f.n.*, 'djuxər, déwchăr
Deuchrie Dod, *Lothian*, 'djuxrɪ
  'dɒd, déwchri dód
Deugh, *Water of, D. & G.*, djux,
  dewch
De Valence, *f.n.*, də væ'lɑ̃s, dĕ
  valaángss
De Valera, *f.n.*, də və'lɛərə, dĕ
  văláirå
Devall, *f.n.*, də'væl, dĕvál
Devally, *f.n.*, dɪ'væli, dĕváli
Devaney, *f.n.*, dɪ'veɪnɪ, dĕváyni
Devas, *f.n.*, dɪ'væs, dĕváss
Develin, *f.n.*, dɪ'velɪn, dĕvéllin
Deveney, *f.n.*, 'divnɪ, deévni
Devenish, *f.n.*, 'devənɪʃ, dév-
  vĕnish; 'dɪvənɪʃ, deévĕnish
Deverell, *f.n.*, 'devərəl, dévvĕrĕl
Devereux, *f.n.*, 'devəruks, dév-
  vĕrooks; 'devəreks, dévvĕrecks;
  'devərə, dévvĕrå; 'devəru,
  dévvĕroo; 'devəroʊ, dévvĕrŏ.
  *The first is that of the family
  name of Viscount Hereford,
  although the second is said to be
  usual in the former counties of
  Hereford and Montgomery. A
  descendant of the Elizabethan*

*Robert ~, Earl of Essex, also
  favours the first.*
Deveron, *River, Grampian,*
  'devərən, dévvĕrŏn
Devers, *f.n.*, 'divərz, deévĕrz;
  'devərz, dévvĕrz
De Vesci, *Viscount*, də 'vesɪ, dĕ
  véssi
Deveson, *f.n.*, 'divɪsən, deévĕssŏn
de Veulle, *f.n.*, də 'vɛl, dĕ võl
Devey, *f.n.*, dɪ'vi, dĕvée; 'dɪvɪ,
  deévi
De Villiers, *f.n.*, də 'vɪlərz, dĕ
  villĕrz; də 'vɪljərz, dĕ víl-yĕrz.
  *The first is appropriate for
  Baron ~.*
Devine, *f.n.*, dɪ'vin, dĕvéen;
  dɪ'vaɪn, dĕvín
de Vitré, *f.n.*, də 'vitrɪ, dĕ véetri
Devizes *Wilts.*, dɪ'vaɪzɪz, dĕvízĕz
Devlin, *f.n.*, 'devlɪn, dévlin
Devoke Water *Cumbria*, 'devək
  'wɒtər, dévvŏk wáwtĕr
Devol, *f.n.*, də'voʊl, dĕvól
Devon *Co. name*, 'devən, dévvŏn
Devon, *River, Notts.*, 'dɪvən,
  deévŏn
Devon, *River, Tayside–Central,*
  'devən, dévvŏn
Devonald, *f.n.*, 'devənəld,
  dévvŏnăld
Devons, *f.n.*, 'devənz, dévvŏnz
Devoran *Cornwall*, 'devərən,
  dévvŏrăn; 'devrən, dévrŏn
de Waal, *f.n.*, də 'vɑl, dĕ vaál
Dewar, *f.n.*, 'djuər, dyŏ̄-ăr
De Warfaz, *f.n.*, də 'wɔrfæz, dĕ
  wáwrfaz
De Warrenne, *f.n.*, də 'wɒrən, dĕ
  wórrĕn
Dewes, *f.n.*, djuz, dewz
Dewi, *Welsh C.n.*, 'dewi, dé-wi
De Wolff, *f.n.*, də 'wʊlf, dĕ woólf
Dewrance, *f.n.*, 'djuərəns,
  dyŏ̄ránss
Dey, *f.n.*, deɪ, day
de Yevele, *f.n.*, də 'jivəlɪ, dĕ
  yéevĕli. *Appropriate for Henry
  ~, 14th-c. master-mason and
  architect.*
D'Eyncourt, *f.n.*, 'deɪŋkɔrt, dáynk-
  ort; 'deɪŋkərt, dáynkŭrt
De Zoete, *f.n.*, də 'zut, dĕ zoót;
  də 'zutə, dĕ zoótĕ
De Zouche, *f.n.*, də 'zuʃ, dĕ zoósh
de Zulueta, *f.n.*, də ˌzulu'etə, dĕ
  zooloo-éttă
Dhenin, *f.n.*, 'denɪn, dénnin
Dhooge, *f.n.*, doʊg, dōg
Dhu Varren *Co. Antrim*, 'du
  'værən, doō várrĕn
Diack, *f.n.*, 'daɪək, dí-ăk
Diane, *C.n.*, daɪ'æn, dī-ánn;
  dɪ'æn, di-ánn

Diaper

Diaper, *f.n.,* 'daɪəpər, dí-ăpĕr
Dibden, *f.n.,* 'dɪbdən, díbdĕn
Dibden Purlieu *Hants,* 'dɪbdən 'pɜrlju; díbdĕn púrlew
Dibdin, *f.n.,* 'dɪbdɪn, díbdin
Dibnah, *f.n.,* 'dɪbnə, díbnă
Dichmont, *f.n.,* 'dɪtʃmɒnt, dítchmont
Dickens, *f.n.,* 'dɪkɪnz, díckĕnz
Dickenson, *f.n.,* 'dɪkɪnsən, díckĕnssŏn
Dicker, *f.n.,* 'dɪkər, díckĕr
Dickins, *f.n.,* 'dɪkɪnz, díckinz; 'dɪkənz, díckĕnz
Dickinson, *f.n.,* 'dɪkɪnsən, díckinssŏn; 'dɪkənsən, díckĕnssŏn
Dicksee, *f.n.,* 'dɪksɪ, dícksi
Didion, *f.n.,* 'dɪdɪən, díddi-ŏn
Dielhenn, *f.n.,* 'dɪlən, deelĕn
Dienes, *f.n.,* dinz, deenz
Digbeth Institute *Birmingham,* 'dɪgbəθ, dígbĕth
Digges, *f.n.,* dɪgz, digz
Diggins, *f.n.,* 'dɪgɪnz, dígginz
Dighty Water *Tayside,* 'dɪxtɪ 'wɔtər, díchti wáwtĕr
Diglis *H. & W.,* 'dɪglɪs, dígliss
Dihewid, *also spelt* **Dihewyd,** *Dyfed,* di'hewɪd, dee-hé-wid
Dilger, *f.n.,* 'dɪldʒər, díljĕr
Dilhorne, Viscount, 'dɪlən, díllŏn
Dilhorne *Staffs.,* 'dɪlɔrn, díllŏrn; 'dɪlɔrn, dillorn
Dilke, *f.n.,* dɪlk, dilk
Dillwyn *see* **Dilwyn**
Dilly, *f.n.,* 'dɪlɪ, dílli
Dilworth, *f.n.,* 'dɪlwɜrθ, dílwurth
Dilwyn *Welsh C.n., also spelt* **Dillwyn,** 'dɪlwɪn, dílwin
Dilwyn, *f.n.,* 'dɪlwɪn, dílwin
Dilys, *Welsh C.n.,* 'dɪlɪs, dilliss
Dimbleby, *f.n.,* 'dɪmblbɪ, dímblbi
Dimelow, *f.n.,* 'dɪmɪloʊ, dímmĕlō
Diment, *f.n.,* 'daɪmənt, dímĕnt
Dimmock, *f.n.,* 'dɪmək, dímmŏk
Dimoline, *f.n.,* 'dɪməlin, dímmŏleen
Dimont, *f.n.,* 'daɪmənt, dímŏnt
Dimuantes, *f.n.,* ˌdɪmju'æntɪz, dimmew-ánteez
Dinas, *Dyfed, Gwynedd, Mid Glam.,* 'dɪnæs, deénass. *Appropriate for both places of the name in Dyfed, and also for both in Gwynedd.*
Dinas Mawddwy *Gwynedd,* 'dɪnæs 'maʊðʊɪ, deénass mówthoo-i
Dinas Oleu *Gwynedd,* 'dɪnæs 'oʊlaɪ, deénass ṓli
Dinas Powis *S. Glam.,* 'dɪnæs 'paʊɪs, dínnass pów-iss
Dinchope *Salop,* 'dɪntʃəp, díntchŏp

Dinedor *H. & W.,* 'daɪn'dɔr, dín-dór
Dineen, *f.n.,* dɪ'nin, dineén
Dinefwr Castle *Dyfed,* dɪ'nevʊər, dinévvōōr. *Welsh form of* **Dynevor,** *q.v.*
Dinenage, *f.n.,* 'daɪnɪdʒ, dínij
Dines, *f.n.,* daɪnz, dīnz
Dingestow *Gwent,* 'dɪndʒɪstoʊ, dínjĕstō
Dinglay, *f.n.,* 'dɪŋgleɪ, díng-glay
Dingley, *f.n.,* 'dɪŋlɪ, díng-li; 'dɪŋglɪ, díng-gli
Dingwall *H'land,* 'dɪŋwəl, díng-wawl; 'dɪŋwəl, díng-wăl
Dinnie, *f.n.,* 'dɪnɪ, dínni
Dinorwic *Gwynedd,* dɪ'nɔrwɪk, dinórwick
Diosgydd Uchaf *Gwynedd,* di'ɒsgɪð 'ɪxav, dee-óssgith íchăv
Diosy, *f.n.,* di'oʊzɪ, dee-ózi
Diplock, *f.n.,* 'dɪplɒk, díplock
Diptford *Devon,* 'dɪpfərd, dípförd
Dirac, *f.n.,* dɪ'ræk, diráck
Dirleton *Lothian,* 'dɜrltən, dírltŏn
Discoed *Powys,* 'dɪskɔɪd, dísskoyd
Diseworth *Leics.,* 'daɪzwɜrθ, dízwurth
Dishforth *N. Yorks.,* 'dɪʃfərθ, dísh-förth
Disley, *f.n.,* 'dɪzlɪ, dízzli
Dispain, *f.n.,* 'dɪspeɪn, dísspayn
Disraeli, *f.n.,* dɪz'reɪlɪ, dizráyli
Diss *Norfolk,* dɪs, diss
Disserth *Powys,* 'dɪsərθ, díssĕrth
Ditcheat *Somerset,* 'dɪtʃɪt, dítchĕt
Dittisham *Devon,* 'dɪtɪsəm, díttisăm; 'dɪtɪʃəm, ditti-shăm; 'dɪtsəm, dítsăm
Divell, *f.n.,* 'daɪvl, dívl
Divin, *f.n.,* 'dɪvɪn, dívvin
Divine, *f.n.,* dɪ'vaɪn, divín
Divis *Co. Antrim,* 'dɪvɪs, dívviss
Dixey, *f.n.,* 'dɪksɪ, dícksi
Doagh *Co. Antrim,* doʊx, dōch
Dobell, *f.n.,* doʊ'bel, dōbéll
Dobie, *f.n.,* 'doʊbɪ, dṓbi
Dobing, *f.n.,* 'doʊbɪŋ, dṓbing
Dobrée, *f.n.,* 'doʊbreɪ, dṓbray. *Appropriate for Bonamy,* 'bɒnəmɪ, bónnămi ~, *scholar and writer, and Georgina* ~, *clarinettist.*
Dobry, *f.n.,* 'dɒbrɪ, dóbri
Dochart, River, *Central,* 'dɒxərt, dóchărt
Docherty, *f.n.,* 'dɒxərtɪ, dóchĕrti
Dochfour, Loch, *H'land,* dɒx'fʊər, dochfóōr
Docwra, *f.n.,* 'dɒkrə, dóckră

Dodgson, *f.n.*, 'dɒdʒsən, dójssŏn; 'dɒdsən, dódssŏn. *The first is appropriate for Stephen ~, composer, the second for Charles ~, mathematician and author of 'Alice in Wonderland'.*

Dodington, *f.n.*, 'dɒdɪŋtən, dóddingtŏn

Dodkin, *f.n.*, 'dɒdkɪn, dódkin

Dodman Point *Cornwall*, 'dɒdmən, dódmän

Dodwell, *f.n.*, 'dɒdwəl, dódwĕl; 'dɒdwel, dódwel

Doel, *f.n.*, 'dəʊəl, dó-ĕl

Doepel, *f.n.*, dəʊ'pel, dōpéll

D'Offay, *f.n.*, 'dɒfeɪ, dóffay

Doggart, *f.n.*, 'dɒgərt, dóggărt

Doggett, *f.n.*, 'dɒgɪt, dóggĕt

Doghan, *f.n.*, 'dəʊgən, dógăn

Doherty, *f.n.*, 'dɒxərtɪ, dóchĕrti; 'dɒhərtɪ, dó-hĕrti; 'dəʊhərtɪ, dó-hĕrti; 'dəʊərtɪ, dó-ĕrti

Doig, *f.n.*, dɔɪg, doyg; 'dəʊɪg, dó-ɪg

Dolan, *f.n.*, 'dəʊlən, dólän

Dolau *Mid Glam.*, *Powys*, 'dəʊlaɪ, dólī

Dolaucothi *Dyfed*, ˌdɒlaɪ'kɒθɪ, dollī-kóthi

Dolbadarn Castle *Gwynedd*, dɒl'bædərn, dolbáddărn

Dolbenmaen *Gwynedd*, ˌdɒlben-'maɪn, dolbenmín

Dolcoath *Cornwall*, dəl'kəʊθ, dŏlkóth

Doldowlod *Powys*, dɒl'daʊlɒd, doldówlod

Dolemore, *f.n.*, 'dɒlɪmər, dóllĕmor

Dolerw Park *Mid Glam.*, 'dɒl'ɛəru, dól-áiroo

Doley, *f.n.*, 'dəʊlɪ, dóli

Dolforwyn *Powys*, dɒl'vɔrwɪn, dolvórwin

Dolgarrog *Gwynedd*, dɒl'gærɒg, dolgárrog

Dolgellau *Gwynedd*, dɒl'geɬaɪ, dolgéhlī. Dolgellau *has superseded* **Dolgelley** (*q.v.*) *as the official spelling.*

Dolgelley, *former spelling for* **Dolgellau**, *q.v.*, *Gwynedd*, dɒl'geɬɪ, dolgéhli. *Since the change in spelling in August 1958, this pronunciation is no longer appropriate.*

Dolgoch *Gwynedd*, dɒl'gəʊx, dolgóch

Dolhendre *Gwynedd*, dɒl'hendrɪ, dol-héndri

D'Olier, *f.n.*, dɒ'lɪər, dolleér; 'dəʊljeɪ, dól-yay

Dolin, **Anton**, *British ballet dancer*, 'æntɒn 'dɒlɪn; ánton dóllin

Dollan, *f.n.*, 'dəʊlən, dólän

Dollar *Central*, 'dɒlər, dóllăr

Dollimore, *f.n.*, 'dɒlɪmər, dóllimor

Dolmetsch, *f.n.*, 'dɒlmetʃ, dólmetch

Dolobran *Powys*, də'lɒbræn, dŏlóbran

Dolton, *f.n.*, 'dɒltən, dólltŏn

Dolton *Devon*, 'dəʊltən, dóltŏn

Dolwyddelan *Gwynedd*, ˌdɒlwɪ-'ðelən, dolwithéllän

Dol-y-Gaer *Powys*, ˌdɒlə'gɛər, dollăgáir

Dominey, *f.n.*, 'dɒmɪnɪ, dómmini

Dominy, *f.n.*, 'dɒmɪnɪ, dómmini

Domleo, *f.n.*, 'dɒmlɪəʊ, dómliō

Donagh *Co. Fermanagh*, 'dəʊnə, dónă

Donaghadee *Co. Down*, ˌdɒnəxə'di, donnăchădeé

Donaghcloney *Co. Down*, ˌdɒnə-'kləʊnɪ, donnăklóni

Donaghey, *f.n.*, 'dɒnəxɪ, dónnăchi

Donaghmore *Co. Tyrone*, ˌdɒnəx-'mɔr, donnăchmór

Donaghy, *f.n.*, 'dɒnəxɪ, dónnăchi; 'dɒnəhɪ, dónnă-hi

Donald, *C.n. and f.n.*, 'dɒnld, dónnld

Donaldson, *f.n.*, 'dɒnldsən, dónnldssŏn

Donard, *saint*, 'dɒnərd, dónnărd

Donat, **Robert**, *actor*, 'dəʊnæt, dónat

Donati, *f.n.*, də'nɑtɪ, dōnáati

Doncaster *S. Yorks.*, 'dɒŋkəstər, dónkăstĕr. *Appropriate also for the Earl of ~.*

Done, *f.n.*, dəʊn, dōn

Donegall, Marquess of, 'dɒnɪgɔl, dónnĕgawl

Donelly, *f.n.*, 'dɒnəlɪ, dónnĕli

Doneraile, Viscount, 'dʌnəreɪl, dúnnĕrayl

Donert, *f.n.*, 'dɒnərt, dónnĕrt

Dongray, *f.n.*, 'dɒŋgreɪ, dóng-gray

Doniach, *f.n.*, 'dɒnjæk, dón-yack

Donibristle *Fife*, ˌdɒnɪ'brɪsl, donnibríssl

Donington, Barony of, 'dʌnɪŋtən, dúnnĭngtŏn

Donington *Lincs.*, *Salop*, 'dɒnɪŋtən, dónningtŏn

Donington-on-Bain *Lincs.*, 'dɒnɪŋtən ɒn 'beɪn, dónningtŏn on báyn; 'dʌnɪŋtən ɒn 'beɪn, dúnningtŏn on báyn

Donlevy, *f.n.*, dɒn'livɪ, donleévi

Donmall, *f.n.*, 'dɒnməl, dónmäl

Donnachie, *f.n.*, 'dɒnəxɪ, dónnăchi

Donne, *f.n.*, dɒn, donn; dʌn, dun. *Although usage varies for the 17th-c. poet and divine, John ~,* *there is some evidence that he used the second.*

Donnegan, *f.n.,* 'dɒnɪgən, dónnĕgăn

Donnellan, *f.n.,* 'dɒnələn, dónnĕllăn

Donnelly, *f.n.,* 'dɒnəlɪ, dónnĕli

Donnet, *f.n.,* 'dɒnɪt, dónnĕt

Donnett, *f.n.,* 'dʌnɪt, dúnnĕt

Donohoe, *f.n.,* 'dʌnəhu, dúnnŏhoo; 'dɒnəhu, dónnŏhoo; 'dɒnəhou, dónnŏhō

Donoughmore, Earl of, 'dʌnəmɔr, dúnnŏmor

Donovan, *f.n.,* 'dʌnəvən, dúnnŏvăn; 'dɒnəvən, dónnŏvăn. *The second is appropriate for the Barony of ~.*

Donyatt *Somerset,* 'dɒnjət, dón-yăt

Doran, *f.n.,* 'dɔrən, dáwrăn

Dore, *f.n.,* dɔr, dor

Dormand, *f.n.,* 'dɔrmænd, dór-mand

Dornoch *H'land,* 'dɔrnəx, dórnŏ<u>ch</u>

Dorow, *f.n.,* 'dɒrou, dórrō

Dorrell, *f.n.,* 'dɒrəl, dórrĕl

Dorset *Co. name,* 'dɔrsɪt, dórssĕt

Dorté, *f.n.,* 'dɔrtɪ, dórti

Dotrice, *f.n.,* də'tris, dŏtreéss

Douai College, *also spelt* **Douay,** *Berks.,* 'dauɛɪ, dów-ay. *The ~ Bible is pronounced both* 'duɛɪ, doó-ay *and* 'dauɛɪ, dów-ay.

Doublebois *Cornwall,* 'dʌblbɔɪz, dúbbl-boyz

Douch, *f.n.,* dautʃ, dowtch; dutʃ, dootch

Doudney, *f.n.,* 'daudnɪ, dówdni; 'dudnɪ, doódni

Douet, *f.n.,* 'duɛɪ, doó-ay

Dougall, *f.n.,* dugl, doógl

Dougan, *f.n.,* 'dugən, doógăn

Dougherty, *f.n.,* 'dɒxərtɪ, dóchĕrti; 'douərtɪ, dŏ-érti; 'dauərtɪ, dów-érti

Doughton *Glos.,* 'dʌftən, dúfftŏn

Doughty, *f.n.,* 'dautɪ, dówti. *Appropriate also for* ~ *St., London.*

Douglas, *C.n. and f.n.,* 'dʌgləs, dúgláss

Douglas-Home, *f.n.,* 'dʌgləs 'hjum, dúgláss héwm. *This is the family name of the Earls of Home. The pronunciation is thus appropriate for Sir Alec ~* (*Baron* **Home** *of the Hirsel, q.v.*), *politician, Henry* ~, *ornithologist, and William* ~, *playwright.*

Douglas and Clydesdale, Marquess of, 'dʌgləs ənd 'klaɪdzdeɪl, dúgláss ănd klídzdayl

Douglass, *f.n.,* 'dʌgləs, dúgláss

Douie, *f.n.,* 'djuɪ, déw-i; 'duɪ, doó-i; 'dauɪ, dów-i

Doulting *Somerset,* 'doultɪŋ, dólting; 'daultɪŋ, dówlting

Doulton, *f.n.,* 'doultən, dóltŏn

Dounby *Orkney,* 'dunbɪ, doónbi

Doune, Lord, dun, doon

Doune *Central, S'clyde,* dun, doon

Dounreay *H'land,* 'dunreɪ, doónray. *There is an older form* **Downreay,** *pronounced* 'daunreɪ, dównray

Douro, Marquess, 'duərou, doŏrō

Dousland *Devon,* 'dauzlənd, dówzländ

Douthwaite, *f.n.,* 'dauθweɪt, dówthwayt

Dovaston, *f.n.,* 'dʌvəstən, dúvvăstŏn

Dove, River, *Derby.–Staffs. border,* dʌv, duvv

Dovedale, *stretch of R. Dove Valley on Derby.–Staffs. border,* 'dʌvdeɪl, dúvdayl

Dovenby *Cumbria,* 'dʌvənbɪ, dúvvĕnbi

Dovendale *Lincs.,* 'dʌvəndeɪl, dúvvĕndayl

Dover, *f.n.,* 'douvər, dóvĕr

Dover *Kent,* 'douvər, dóvĕr

Doverdale, Barony of, 'dʌvərdeɪl, dúvvĕrdayl

Doveridge *Derby.,* 'dʌvərɪdʒ, dúvvĕrij

Doveton, *f.n.,* 'dʌvtən, dúvvtŏn

Dovey, *f.n.,* 'douvɪ, dóvi; 'dʌvɪ, dúvvi

Dovey, River, *Gwynedd–Powys,* 'dʌvɪ, dúvvi. *The Welsh spelling is* **Dyfi,** *q.v.*

Dow, *f.n.,* dau, dow

Dowally *Tayside,* 'dauəlɪ, dów-ăli

Dowanhill *S'clyde,* 'dauənhɪl, dówăn-hil

Dowd, *f.n.,* daud, dowd

Dowdall, *f.n.,* 'daudl, dówdl

Dowden, *f.n.,* 'daudən, dówdĕn

Dowdeswell *Glos.,* 'daudzwəl, dówdzwĕl

Dowding, *f.n.,* 'daudɪŋ, dówding

Dowell, *f.n.,* 'dauəl, dów-ĕl

Dower, *f.n.,* 'dauər, dówĕr

Dowie, *f.n.,* 'dauɪ, dów-i

Dowlais *Mid Glam.,* 'daulaɪs, dówlíss

Dowland, John, *16th–17th-c. lutenist and composer,* 'daulənd, dówländ

Dowland *Devon,* 'daulənd, dówländ

Dowle, *f.n.,* daul, dowl

Dowler, *f.n.,* 'daulər, dówlĕr

Dowling, *f.n.*, 'daʊlɪŋ, dówling
Dowlish Wake *Somerset*, 'daʊlɪʃ, dówlish
Down *Co. name*, daʊn, down
Downend *Avon, I. of Wight*, daʊn'end, down-énd
Downes, *f.n.*, daʊnz, downz
Downham *Kent*, 'daʊnəm, dówn-ăm
Downpatrick *Co. Down*, daʊn-'pætrɪk, downpátrick
Downreay *see* **Dounreay**
Dowsby *Lincs.*, 'daʊzbɪ, dówzbi
Dowse, *f.n.*, daʊs, dowss
Dowsing, Inner *and* Outer, *shoals, off Lincs. coast*, 'daʊzɪŋ, dówzing
Dowson, *f.n.*, 'daʊsən, dówssŏn
Doyle, *f.n.*, dɔɪl, doyl
Dozmary Pool *Cornwall*, 'dɒzmrɪ 'puːl, dóz-mri poól
Draffen, *f.n.*, 'dræfən, dráffĕn
Draffin, *f.n.*, 'dræfɪn, dráffin
Drage, *f.n.*, dreɪdʒ, drayj
Draisey, *f.n.*, 'dreɪzɪ, dráyzi
Drakelow *Derby.*, 'dreɪkloʊ, dráyklō
Drake's Broughton *H. & W.*, 'dreɪks 'brɔtən, dráyks bráwtŏn
Draughton *Northants.*, 'drɔtən, dráwtŏn
Draughton *N. Yorks.*, 'dræftən, dráfftŏn
Dravers, *f.n.*, 'dreɪvərz, dráyvĕrz
Dreaper, *f.n.*, 'dreɪpər, dráypĕr
Drefach *Dyfed*, dre'vɑx, drev-váàch
Drellingore *Kent*, 'drelɪŋgər, drélling-gor
Drever, *f.n.*, 'drɪvər, dreévĕr
Drewe, *f.n.*, dru, droo
Drewsteignton *Devon*, 'druz-'teɪntən, droóztáyntŏn
Dreyer, *f.n.*, 'dreɪər, drí-ĕr
Drian Gallery, *London art gallery*, 'drɪən, dreé-ăn
Dribbell, *f.n.*, drɪ'bel, dribéll
Driberg, *f.n.*, 'draɪbɜrg, dríberg
Driby *Lincs.*, 'draɪbɪ, dríbi
Driffield *Glos., Humberside*, 'drɪfɪld, driffeeld
Drighlington *W. Yorks.*, 'drɪglɪŋtən, dríglingtŏn; 'drɪlɪntən, dríllingtŏn
Drimnin *H'land*, 'drɪmnɪn, drímnin
Droeshout, Martin, *17th-c. Anglo-Flemish engraver, also spelt* Maerten, mɑrtɪn 'drushaʊt, maártin droóss-howt
Drogheda, Earl of, 'drɔɪɪdə, dróy-ĕ-dă
Drogo Castle *Devon*, 'droʊgoʊ, drŏgō

Droitwich *H. & W.*, 'drɔɪtwɪtʃ, dróyt-witch
Dromantine *see* **Drumantine**
Dromara *Co. Down*, drə'mærə, drōmárrä
Dromgoole, *f.n.*, drɒm'gul, dromgoól
Dromore, *Co. Down, Co. Tyrone*, drə'mɔr, drōmór
Dronfield *Derby.*, 'drɒnfild, drónfeeld
Drower, *f.n.*, 'draʊər, drówĕr
Drown, *f.n.*, draʊn, drown
Droylsden *Gtr. M'chester*, 'drɔɪlzdən, dróylzdĕn
Drucker, *f.n.*, 'drʊkər, droókĕr
Drughorn, *f.n.*, 'drʌghɔrn, drúg--horn
Druiff, *f.n.*, 'druɪf, droó-iff
Druimuachdar *see* **Drumochter**
Drumachose *Co. Derry*, ˌdrʌmə'koʊz, drummäkóz
Drumalbyn, Baron, drʌm'ælbɪn, drumálbin
Drumaness *Co. Down*, ˌdrʌmə-'nes, drummănéss
Drumantine, *also spelt* **Dromantine,** *Co. Down*, 'drʌməntaɪn, drúmmăntin
Drumaroad *Co. Down*, ˌdrʌmə-'roʊd, drummărṓd
Drumbeg *H'land*, drəm'beg, drŭmbég
Drumbo *Co. Down*, drəm'boʊ, drŭmbṓ
Drumbuie *H'land*, drʌm'buɪ, drumboó-i
Drumelzier *Borders*, drʌ'mɪljər, drummeél-yĕr
Drumhain *Skye*, 'drʊmɪn, droómin
Drumlanrig and Sanquhar, Earl of, drʌm'lænrɪg ənd 'sæŋkər, drum-lánrig ănd sánkăr
Drumlithie *Grampian*, drʌm'lɪθɪ, drumlíthi
Drumloughar *Co. Armagh*, drʌm-'loʊər, drum-lṓ-ĕr
Drumm, *f.n.*, drʌm, drum
Drummond, *f.n.*, drʌmənd, drúmmŏnd
Drummore *D. & G.*, drə'mɔr, drŭmór
Drummossie Moor *H'land*, drʌ'mɒsɪ, drumáwssi
Drumnadrochit *H'land*, ˌdrʌmnə-'drɒxɪt, drumnădróchit
Drumoak *Grampian*, drʌ'moʊk, drummók
Drumochter, Pass of, *H'land–Tayside*, drə'mɒxtər, drŭm-óchtĕr. *The Gaelic spelling is* **Druimuachdar.**
Drumquhassle *Central*, drʌm-'hwæsl, drumwhássl

Drumry *S'clyde*, drʌm'raɪ, drum-rí

Drumsheugh *Edinburgh*, drʌm-'ʃux, drum-shooch

Drury, *f.n.*, 'drʊərɪ, droŏri

Drws-y-Nant *Gwynedd*, ,drusə-'næt, droossănánt

Dryburgh, *f.n.*, 'draɪbərə, dríbŭră

Dryburgh Abbey *Borders*, 'draɪbərə, dríbŭră

Dryden, *f.n.*, 'draɪdən, drídĕn

Drygrange *Borders*, 'draɪgreɪndʒ, drígraynj

Drymen *Central*, 'drɪmən, drímmĕn

Drysdale, *f.n.*, 'draɪzdeɪl, drízdayl

Duan, *f.n.*, 'djʊən, dyoŏ-ăn

Duane, *f.n.*, du'eɪn, doo-áyn

Duarte, *f.n.*, 'djuɑrt, déw-aart

Dubbey, *f.n.*, 'dʌbɪ, dúbbi

Dubell, *f.n.*, dju'bel, dewbéll

Dubens, *f.n.*, 'djubənz, déwbĕnz

Dubh Artach Rocks *off S'clyde coast*, 'du 'ɑrtəx, doō aártăch

Du Boulay, *f.n.*, du 'buleɪ, doō boolay; dju 'buleɪ, dew boōlay

Du Buisson, *f.n.*, 'djubɪsən, déwbissŏn

Du Cane, *f.n.*, dju 'keɪn, dew káyn

Du Cann, *f.n.*, dju 'kæn, dew kánn

Duce, *f.n.*, djus, dewss

Ducharme, *f.n.*, du'ʃɑrm, doo--shaarm

Duchemin, *f.n.*, 'duʃəmɪn, dooshĕmin

Duchesne, *f.n.*, du'ʃeɪn, doo--sháyn; dju'ʃeɪn, dew-sháyn

Duchin, *f.n.*, 'dutʃɪn, doŏtchin

Ducie, Earl of, 'djusɪ, déwssi

Duckinfield *Ches.*, 'dʌkɪnfild, dúckinfeeld

Du Cros, *f.n.*, dju 'krou, dew krŏ

Ducrow, *f.n.*, dju'krou, dewkrŏ

Du Croz, *f.n.*, dju 'krou, dew krŏ

Duddeston *W. Midlands*, 'dʌdɪstən, dúddĕstŏn

Duddleswell *E. Sussex*, 'dʌdlzwel, dúddlzwel

Dudeney, *f.n.*, 'djudnɪ, déwd-ni; 'djudn̩i, déwdn-i; 'djudnɛi, déwdn-ay; 'dudnɪ, doŏd-ni

Du Deney, *f.n.*, dju 'denɪ, dew dénni

Dudhope, Viscount, 'dʌdəp, dúddŏp

Duerden, *f.n.*, 'djuərdən, dyoŏr-dĕn

Duff, *f.n.*, dʌf, duff

Duffell, *f.n.*, 'dʌfl, dúffl

Dufferin and Ava, Marquess of, 'dʌfərɪn ənd 'avə, dúfferin ănd aavă

Duffes, *f.n.*, 'dʌfɪs, dúffĕss

Duffield, *f.n.*, 'dʌfild, dúffeeld

Dufftown *Grampian*, 'dʌftaʊn, dúfftown; 'dʌftən, dúfftŏn

Duffus, *f.n.*, 'dʌfəs, dúffŭss

Dufour, *f.n.*, du'fʊər, doōfoŏr

Dufton, *f.n.*, 'dʌftən, dúfftŏn

Dugan, *f.n.*, 'dugən, doŏgăn. *Appropriate also for the Barony of ~ of Victoria.*

Duggan, *f.n.*, 'dʌgən, dúggăn

Duggin, *f.n.*, 'dʌgɪn, dúggin

Duggleby, *f.n.*, 'dʌglbɪ, dúgglbi

Duguid, *f.n.*, 'djugɪd, déwgid

Duignan, *f.n.*, 'daɪgnən, dígnăn

Dukesfield *Northd.*, 'dʌksfild, dúcksfeeld

Dukinfield *Gtr. M'chester*, 'dʌkɪnfild, dúckinfeeld

Dulais, River, *Dyfed*, 'dɪlaɪs, dillíss; 'dɪləs, dilláss

Dulake, *f.n.*, 'djuleɪk, déwlayk

Dulas Valley *Powys*, 'djuləs, déwlăss

Duley, *f.n.*, 'djulɪ, déwli

Dulieu, *f.n.*, də'lju, dĕléw

Dull *Tayside*, dʌl, dull

Dullatur *S'clyde*, 'dʌlətər, dúllătŭr

Dullea, *f.n.*, dju'leɪ, dewláy; dʌ'leɪ, dulláy

Dullingham *Cambs.*, 'dʌlɪŋəm, dúlling-ăm

Dulnain, River, *H'land*, 'dʌlnən, dúlnăn

Dulnain Bridge *H'land*, 'dʌlnən 'brɪdʒ, dúlnăn bríj

Duloe *Cornwall*, 'djulou, déwlŏ

Dulson, *f.n.*, 'dʌlsən, dúlssŏn

Dulverton *Devon*, 'dʌlvərtən, dúlvĕrtŏn. *Appropriate also for Baron ~.*

Dulwich *London*, 'dʌlɪdʒ, dúllij; 'dʌlɪtʃ, dúllitch

Duly, *f.n.*, 'djulɪ, déwli

Dumaresq, *f.n.*, dʊ'merɪk, doōmérrik; dju'merɪk, dew-mérrik

Dumas, *f.n.*, dju'mɑ, dewmaá

du Maurier, *f.n.*, du 'mɒrɪeɪ, doo mórri-ay. *This is the family pronunciation of Sir Gerald ~, actor-manager, and of Daphne ~, author.*

Dumbarton *S'clyde*, dəm'bɑrtən, dŭmbaártŏn

Dumbuck *S'clyde*, dʌm'bʌk, dumbúck

Dumfries *D. & G.*, dəm'fris, dŭmfréess. *Appropriate also for the Earl of ~.*

Dummer *Hants*, 'dʌmər, dúmmĕr

Dumont, *f.n.*, dju'mɒnt, dewmónt; dy'mõ, dümőng

Dùn *St. Kilda (W. Isles)*, dun, doon

Dunadry *Co. Antrim*, dʌn'ædrɪ, dunádri

Dunalastair *Tayside*, dʌn'ælɪstər, dunálistär

Dunalley, *Baron*, dʌn'ælɪ, dunáli

Dunamanagh *Co. Tyrone*, ˌdʌnə'mænə, dunnämánnä

Dunant, *f.n.*, dʊ'nænt, dōōnánt

Dunball *Somerset*, 'dʌnbɔl, dúnbawl

Dunbar, *f.n.*, dʌn'bɑr, dunbaʼar

Dunbar *Lothian*, dʌn'bɑr, dun-baʼar

Dunbartonshire *former Co. name*, dʌn'bɑrtənʃaɪər, dunbaʼártōn-shĩr. *Dunbartonshire is now part of Strathclyde Region.*

Dunblane *Central*, dʌn'bleɪn, dunbláyn

Duncalfe, *f.n.*, dʌn'kɑf, dun-kaʼaf

Duncan, *C.n. and f.n.*, 'dʌŋkən, dúnkän

Duncannon, *Viscount*, dʌn'kænən, dunkánnŏn

Duncansby Head *H'land*, 'dʌŋ-kənzbɪ, dúnkänzbi

Dunchideock *Devon*, 'dʌntʃɪdək, dúntchiddŏk

Duncombe, *f.n.*, 'dʌŋkəm, dúnkŏm

Dundarave *Co. Antrim*, ˌdʌndə-'reɪv, dundáráyv

Dundas, *f.n.*, dʌn'dæs, dundáss

Dundee *Tayside*, dʌn'di, dundeé. *Appropriate also for the Earl of ~.*

Dundela, *Belfast*, dʌn'dilə, dundeélä. *But the football team is pronounced* dʌn'delə, dun-déllä.

Dundonald *S'clyde*, dʌn'dɒnld, dundónnld. *Appropriate also for the Earl of ~.*

Dundonian *native of Dundee*, dʌn'doʊnɪən, dundōniän

Dundrod *Co. Antrim*, dʌn'drɒd, dundród

Dundrum *Co. Armagh, Co. Down*, dʌn'drʌm, dundrúm

Dundry *Avon*, 'dʌndrɪ, dúndri

Dunedin, *Viscountcy of*, dʌn'idɪn, dunneédin

Dunfermline *Fife*, dʌn'fɜrmlɪn, dunférmlin

Dungannon *Co. Tyrone*, dʌn-'gænən, dun-gánnŏn

Dungarvan, *Viscount*, dʌn'gɑrvən, dun-gaʼárvän

Dungate, *f.n.*, 'dʌngeɪt, dún-gayt

Dungavel *S'clyde*, dʌn'geɪvl, dun-gáyvl; dʌn'gævl, dun-gávvl

Dungeness *Kent*, ˌdʌndʒə'nes, dunjénéss

Dungiven *Co. Derry*, dʌn'gɪvən, dun-gívvĕn

Dunglass, *Barony of*, dʌn'glɑs, dun-glaʼass

Dunhill, *f.n.*, 'dʌnhɪl, dún-hil

Dunholme *Lincs.*, 'dʌnəm, dúnnŏm

Dunino *Fife*, dʌn'inoʊ, duneénō

Dunipace, *f.n.*, 'dʌnɪpeɪs, dúnni-payss

Dunipace *Central*, 'dʌnɪpeɪs, dúnnipayss

Dunira *Tayside*, dʌn'ɪərə, duneérä

Dunkeld *Tayside*, dʌn'keld, dun-kéld

Dunkerley, *f.n.*, 'dʌŋkərlɪ, dúnkĕrli

Dunkeswell *Devon*, 'dʌŋkɪzwel, dúnkĕzwel

Dunkley, *f.n.*, 'dʌŋklɪ, dúnkli

Dunlop, *f.n.*, dʌn'lɒp, dunlóp; 'dʌnlɒp, dúnlop. *The second is appropriate for the tyre and sports goods group of companies.*

Dunlop *S'clyde*, dʌn'lɒp, dunlóp

Dunloy *Co. Antrim*, dʌn'lɔɪ, dun-lóy

Dunluce *Co. Antrim*, dʌn'lus, dunloʼoss. *Appropriate also for Viscount ~.*

Dunmail Raise *Cumbria*, 'dʌnmeɪl 'reɪz, dúnmayl ráyz

Dunmore *Co. Down*, dʌn'mɔr, dun-mór. *Appropriate also for the Earl of ~.*

Dunmow, *Great & Little, Essex*, 'dʌnmoʊ, dún-mō

Dunmurry *Co. Antrim*, dʌn'mʌrɪ, dun-múrri

Dunnet *H'land*, 'dʌnɪt, dúnnĕt

Dunnett, *f.n.*, 'dʌnɪt, dúnnĕt

Dunnichen *Tayside*, dʌn'ɪxən, duníchĕn

Dunnico, *f.n.*, 'dʌnɪkoʊ, dúnnikō

Dunnose *I. of Wight*, dʌ'noʊz, dunnŏ́z

Dunnottar Castle *Grampian*, dʌn-'ɒtər, dunóttär

Dunoon *S'clyde*, dʌn'un, dunoʼon

Dunphail *Grampian*, dʌn'feɪl, dunfáyl

Dunphie, *f.n.*, 'dʌnfɪ, dúnfi

Dunraven and Mountearl, *Earl of*, dʌn'reɪvən ənd maʊnt'ɜrl, dunráyvĕn ănd mowntérl

Dunrich, *f.n.*, dʌn'rɪtʃ, dunrítch

Dunrobin Castle *H'land*, dʌn-'rɒbɪn, dunróbbin

Dunrossil of Vallaquie, *Viscount*, dʌn'rɒsɪl əv 'væləkwɪ, dunróssil ŏv válăkwi

Duns *Borders*, dʌnz, dunz

Dunsany, *Baron of*, dʌn'seɪnɪ, dunsáyni

Dunseverick *Co. Antrim*, dʌn-'sevərik, dunsĕvvĕrik

Dunsfold *Surrey*, 'dʌnzfoᵘld, dúnz-fōld

Dunsheath, *f.n.*, dʌn'ʃiθ, dun-shéeth; dʌnz'hiθ, dunz-héeth

Dunsinane Hill *Tayside*, dʌn-'sɪnən, dun-sínnăn. *The pro-nunciation called for in Shakespeare's 'Macbeth' is* ˌdʌnsɪ'neɪn, dunsináyn *or* 'dʌnsɪneɪn, dúnssinayn

Dunstaffnage Castle *S'clyde*, dʌn'stæfnɪdʒ, dunstáffnij

Dunstan, *f.n.*, 'dʌnstən, dún-stăn

Dunstanburgh *Northd.*, 'dʌnstən-bərə, dúnstănbŭră

Duntelchaig, Loch, *H'land*, ˌdʌntl'xeɪg, duntlcháyg

Duntisbourne Rouse *Glos.*, 'dʌntɪsbərn 'raᵘs, dúntissborn rówss

Duntocher *S'clyde*, dʌn'tɒxər, duntóchĕr

Duntze, *f.n.*, dʌnts, dunts

Dunure *S'clyde*, dʌn'jᵘər, dun-yŏŏr

Dunvant *W. Glam.*, 'dʌnvənt, dúnvănt

Dunvegan *Skye*, dʌn'vegən, dunvéggăn; dʌn'veɪgən, dunváygăn

Dunwear *Somerset*, dʌn'weər, dunwáir; dʌn'wɪər, dunwéer

Dunwich *Suffolk*, 'dʌnɪtʃ, dún-nitch

Dunwood *Staffs.*, 'dʌnwᵘd, dúnwŏŏd

Dunwoody, *f.n.*, dʌn'wᵘdɪ, dun-wŏŏdi

Du Plat, *f.n.*, dju 'plɑ, dew plaá

Duployen, *f.n.*, duploɪ'en, dooploy-énn

Dupont, *f.n.*, dju'pɒnt, dewpónt; 'djupɒnt, déwpont

Dupplin, Viscount, 'dʌplɪn, dúpplin

Dupplin Castle *Tayside*, 'dʌplɪn, dúpplin

Dupré, *f.n.*, du'preɪ, doopráy

Duprée, *f.n.*, du'preɪ, doopráy; dju'pri, dewprée

Duprez, *f.n.*, du'preɪ, doopráy; dju'preɪ, dewpráy; dju'pri, dewprée

Duquenoy, *f.n.*, djᵘ'kenwɑ, dyŏŏkénwaa

Durance, *f.n.*, dju'rɑns, dew-raánss; dju'ræns, dewránss

Durand, *f.n.*, djᵘə'rænd, dyŏŏr-ánd; dju'rænd, dewránd

Durant, *f.n.*, djᵘə'rænt, dyŏŏránt

Durbin, *f.n.*, 'dərbɪn, dúrbin

Durden, *f.n.*, 'dərdən, dúrdĕn

Durell, *f.n.*, djᵘə'rel, dyŏŏréll

Dures, *f.n.*, djᵘə'reɪ, dyŏŏráy

Duret, *f.n.*, 'djᵘəreɪ, dyŏŏray

d'Urfey, Thomas, *17th-c. poet, song-writer, and dramatist*, 'dərfɪ, dúrfi. *Also known as Tom Durfey.*

Durgnat, *f.n.*, 'dərgnæt, dúrg-nat

Durham *Co. name*, 'dʌrəm, dúr-răm. *Appropriate also for the Earldom of* ~.

Durie, *f.n.*, 'djᵘərɪ, dyŏŏri

Durisdeer *D. & G.*, 'dʌrɪzdɪər, dúrrizdeer

Durkar *W. Yorks.*, 'dərkər, dúrkăr

Durlacher, *f.n.*, 'dərlækər, dúr-lackĕr

Durness *H'land*, 'dərnɪs, dúr-nĕss

Duror, River, *S'clyde*, 'dᵘərər, dŏŏrŏr

Durrad, *f.n.*, 'dʌrəd, dúrrăd

Durrant, *f.n.*, 'dʌrənt, dúrrănt

Durrell, *f.n.*, 'dʌrəl, dúrrĕl. *Appropriate for Lawrence* ~, *author and poet, and for Gerald* ~, *author and zoologist.*

Dursley *Glos.*, 'dərzlɪ, dúrzli

Durweston *Dorset*, 'dʌrəstən, dúrrĕstŏn

Du Sautoy, *f.n.*, du 'soᵘtɔɪ, dōō sŏtoy

Du Seautois, *f.n.*, 'djusətɔɪ, déwssĕtoy

Duthie, *f.n.*, 'dʌθɪ, dúthi

Duthil *H'land*, 'dʌθɪl, dúth-il

Duthoit, *f.n.*, du'θɔɪt, doo-thóyt

Dutoit, *f.n.*, dju'twɑ, dewtwaá

Du Toit, *f.n.*, dju 'twɑ, dew twaá; du 'twɑ, doo twaá

Dutot, *f.n.*, dy'toᵘ, dütó

Duttine, *f.n.*, dʌ'tin, duttéen

Dutton, *f.n.*, 'dʌtən, dúttŏn

Duval, *f.n.*, dju'væl, dewvál

Du Vivier, *f.n.*, du 'vɪvɪeɪ, dōō vívvi-ay

Duxford *Cambs.*, 'dʌksfərd, dúcksfŏrd

Dwan, *f.n.*, dwɒn, dwon

Dwight, *f.n.*, dwaɪt, dwīt

Dwygyfylchi *Gwynedd*, ˌdᵘɪgə-'vʌlxɪ, dōō-i-gávúlchi

Dwynwen, *Welsh C.n.*, 'dᵘɪnwen, dŏŏ-in-wen

The form dʌn, dun used to indicate the unstressed prefix Dun- in Celtic names is that used in careful speech. Its occurrence as dən, dŭn is equally frequent and acceptable.

Dwyran *Gwynedd*, 'dʊɪræn, dŏŏ-i-ran

Dwyryd, *f.n.*, 'dʊɪrɪd, dŏŏ-i-rid

Dwyryd, River, *Gwynedd*, 'dʊɪrɪd, dŏŏ-i-rid

Dyas, *f.n.*, 'daɪəs, dí-ăss

Dyball, *f.n.*, 'daɪbɔl, díbawl

Dyce, *Grampian*, daɪs, dïss

Dyche, *f.n.*, daɪtʃ, dïtch

Dyde, *f.n.*, daɪd, dïd

Dyer, *f.n.*, 'daɪər, dí-ĕr

Dyfatty *Dyfed*, dʌ'vætɪ, duvvátti

Dyfed *Co. name*, 'dʌvɪd, dúvvĕd

Dyffryn *Gwynedd, Mid Glam., S. Glam.*, 'dʌfrɪn, dúffrin

Dyffryn Ardudwy *Gwynedd*, 'dʌfrɪn ɑr'dɪdʊɪ, dúffrin aardeédŏŏ-i

Dyffryn Maelor *Clwyd*, 'dʌfrɪn 'maɪlər, dúffrin mílor

Dyfi, River, *Gwynedd, Powys*, 'dʌvɪ, dúvvi. *The English spelling is* **Dovey**, *q.v.*

Dyfnallt, *Welsh Bardic or C.n.*, 'dʌvnælt, dúvnahlt

Dyfrig *Welsh C.n.*, 'dʌvrɪg, dúvv-rig

Dykes, *f.n.*, daɪks, dïks

Dylan, *C.n.*, 'dʌlən, dúllăn; 'dɪlən, dillăn. *See* **Dylan Thomas** *under his surname.*

Dylife *Powys*, dʌ'liːvə, dulleévə

Dymchurch *Kent*, 'dɪmtʃɑrtʃ, dímtchurch

Dyment, *f.n.*, 'daɪmənt, dímĕnt

Dymock, *f.n.*, 'dɪmək, dímmŏk

Dymock *Glos.*, 'dɪmək, dímmŏk

Dymoke, *f.n.*, 'dɪmək, dímmŏk

Dymond, *f.n.*, 'daɪmənd, dímŏnd

Dyneley, *f.n.*, 'daɪnlɪ, dínli

Dynevor, *f.n.*, 'dɪnɪvər, dínnĕvŏr. *Appropriate also for Baron ~.*

Dynevor Castle *Dyfed*, 'dɪnɪvər, dínnĕvŏr. *This is the English form and pronunciation used outside and, to some extent, inside Wales. ~ Grammar School in Swansea, however, is pronounced* dɪ'nevər, dinévvŏr. *The Welsh language spelling is* **Dinefwr**, *q.v.*

Dyrham *Avon*, 'dɪrəm, dírrăm

Dysart, Countess of, 'daɪsərt, díssárt

Dysart *Fife*, 'daɪzərt, dízărt

Dyscarr *Notts.*, 'daɪskɑr, dísskaar

Dyserth *Clwyd*, 'dɪsərθ, díssĕrth

Dyson, *f.n.*, 'daɪsən, díssŏn

Dysyny, River, *Gwynedd*, də'sʌnɪ, dŭssúnni

Dytham, *f.n.*, 'daɪθəm, díthăm

Dzvonkus, *f.n.*, dɪ'vɒŋkəs, divónküss

E

Eaborn, *f.n.*, 'ɪbɔrn, eéborn

Eadie, *f.n.*, 'idɪ, eédi

Eadon, *f.n.*, 'idən, eédŏn

Eadweard, *C.n.*, 'edwərd, édwărd

Eady, *f.n.*, 'idɪ, eédi

Eager, *f.n.*, 'igər, eégĕr

Eagger, *f.n.*, 'igər, eégĕr

Eaglescarnie *Lothian*, ˌiglz-'keɑrnɪ, eeglzkáirni

Eaglesham *S'clyde*, 'iglsəm, eéglssăm

Eakring *Notts.*, 'ikrɪŋ, eékring

Eales, *f.n.*, ilz, eelz

Ealing *London*, 'ilɪŋ, eéling

Eames, *f.n.*, imz, eemz; eɪmz, aymz

Eamonn, *C.n.*, 'eɪmən, áymŏn

Eamont, River, *Cumbria*, 'imənt, eémŏnt; 'jæmənt, yámmŏnt

Eanswythe, saint, 'iənswɪθ, eé--ănsswith

Earby *Lancs.*, 'ɪərbɪ, eérbi

Eardisland *H. & W.*, 'ɜrdzlənd, érdzländ

Eardisley *H. & W.*, 'ɜrdzlɪ, érdzli

Eardly, *f.n.*, 'ɜrdlɪ, érdli

Earengey, *f.n.*, 'ɛərɪndʒeɪ, áirĕnjay

Earith *Cambs.*, 'ɪərɪθ, eérith

Earle, *f.n.*, ɜrl, erl

Earley, *f.n.*, 'ɜrlɪ, érli

Earley *Berks.*, 'ɜrlɪ, érli

Earls, *f.n.*, ɜrlz, erlz

Earls Colne *Essex*, 'ɜrlz 'koʊn, érlz kŏn

EarlStonham *Suffolk*, 'ɜrl 'stɒnəm, érl stónnăm

Earlstoun, Loch, *D. & G.*, 'ɜrlztən, érlztŏn

Earn, Loch *and* River, *Tayside*, ɜrn, ern

Earp, *f.n.*, ɜrp, erp

Earsdon *Tyne & Wear*, 'ɜrzdən, érzdŏn

Earsham *Norfolk*, 'ɜrʃəm, ér-shăm

Earsman, *f.n.*, 'ɪərzmən, eérzmăn

Earswick *N. Yorks.*, 'ɪərzwɪk, eérzwick

Earwaker, *f.n.*, 'ɜrəkər, ér-ăkĕr; 'erəkər, érrăkĕr; 'ɪərweɪkər, eérwaykĕr

Earwicker, *f.n.*, 'erɪkər, érrickĕr

Eashing *Surrey*, 'iʃɪŋ, eéshing

Easington *Durham, Northd.*, 'izɪŋtən, eézingtŏn

Eason, *f.n.*, 'isən, eéssŏn

Eassie *Tayside*, 'isɪ, eéssi

Eastaugh, *f.n.*, 'istɔ, eéstaw

East Bergholt *Suffolk*, 'ist 'bɜrghoʊlt, eést bérg-hŏlt

East Bierley *W. Yorks.*, 'ist 'baɪərlɪ, eest bírli

Eastbourne *E. Sussex*, 'istbɔrn, eestborn

East Challow *Oxon.*, 'ist 'tʃælou, eest chálō

East Cowick *Humberside*, 'ist 'kauɪk, eest ków-ick

East Donyland *Essex*, 'ist 'dɒnɪlənd, eest dónniländ

Easterbrook, *f.n.*, 'istərbrʊk, eestĕrbrŏŏk

East Freugh *D. & G.*, 'ist 'frux, eest froóch

East Goscote *Leics.*, 'ist 'gɒskout, eest gósskōt

East Grinstead *W. Sussex*, 'ist 'grɪnstɪd, eest grínsstĕd

East Guldeford *E. Sussex*, 'ist 'gɪlfərd, eest gílförd

Easthampstead *Berks.*, 'ist-'hæmpstɪd, eest-hámpstĕd; 'istəmstɪd, eestămsted

East Hartlepool *Cleveland*, 'ist 'hɑrtlɪpul, eest haártlipool

East Heslerton *N. Yorks.*, 'ist 'heslərtən, eest hésslĕrtŏn

Eastham *Merseyside*, 'istəm, eestăm

East Hoathly *E. Sussex*, 'ist houθ'laɪ, eest hōth-líf

East Horsley *Surrey*, 'ist 'hɔrzlɪ, eest hórzli

Eastleigh *Hants*, 'ist'li, eest-leé

East Lockinge *Oxon.*, 'ist 'lɒkɪndʒ, eest lóckinj

East Malling *Kent*, 'ist 'mɔlɪŋ, eest máwling

East Marden *W. Sussex*, 'ist 'mɑrdən, eest maárdĕn

East Meon *Hants*, 'ist 'miən, eest meé-ŏn

East Mersea *Essex*, 'ist 'mɜrzɪ, eest mérzi

East Molesey *Surrey*, 'ist 'moulzɪ, eest mólzi

Eastnor *H. & W.*, 'istnɔr, eest-nor. *Appropriate also for* ~ *Castle.*

Easton Mauduit *Northants.*, 'istən 'mɔdɪt, eestŏn máwdit

East Ravendale *Humberside*, 'ist 'reɪvəndeɪl, eest ráyvĕndayl

Eastry *Kent*, 'istrɪ, eestri

East Somerton *Norfolk*, 'ist 'sʌmərtən, eest súmmĕrtŏn

Eastwood, *f.n.*, 'istwʊd, eestwŏŏd

East Yelland *Devon*, 'ist 'jelənd, eest yélănd

Eathie *see* **Ethie**

Eathorne, *f.n.*, 'iθɔrn, eé-thorn

Eaton, *f.n.*, 'itən, eétŏn

Eaton Socon *Cambs.*, 'itən 'soukən, eétŏn sókŏn

Eaudyke *Lincs.*, 'judaɪk, yéwdīk; 'udaɪk, oódīk

Eayrs, *f.n.*, ɛərz, airz

Ebbe, saint, eb, ebb

Ebbesbourne Wake *Wilts.*, 'ebzbɔrn 'weɪk, ébzborn wáyk

Ebbisham, Baron, 'ebɪʃəm, ébbi-shăm

Ebbrell, *f.n.*, 'ebrəl, ébbrĕl

Ebbutt, *f.n.*, 'ebət, ébbŭt

Ebbw Vale *Gwent*, 'ebu 'veɪl, ébboo váyl

Eberle, *f.n.*, 'ebərlɪ, ébbĕrli

Ebernoe House *W. Sussex*, 'ebərnou, ébbĕrnō

Ebers, *f.n.*, 'ebərz, ébbĕrz

Ebery, *f.n.*, 'ibərɪ, eebĕri

Ebor, *Archbishop of York's signature*, 'ibɔr, eebor

Eboracum, *Roman name for York*, i'bɒrəkəm, eebórrăkŭm

Ebor Handicap, *horse-race*, 'ibɔr, eebor

Ebrahim, *f.n.*, 'ibrəhɪm, eébră-him

Ebrington *Glos.*, 'ebrɪŋtən, ébbringtŏn; 'ʌbərtən, yúbbĕrtŏn. *The first is appropriate for Viscount* ~. *The other, strictly local and used largely by older residents, is a legacy of an earlier form of the name.*

Ebury, Baron, 'ibərɪ, eébŭri

Ecchinswell *Hants*, 'etʃɪnzwel, étchinzwel

Ecclefechan *D. & G.*, ,ekl'fexən, eckl-féchăn

Eccles, *f.n.*, 'eklz, écklz. *Appropriate also for Viscount* ~.

Eccles Gtr. M'chester, 'eklz, écklz

Ecclesall *S. Yorks.*, 'eklzɔl, écklzawl

Eccleshall *Staffs.*, 'eklʃl, éckl-shl; 'eklʃɔl, éckl-shawl

Ecclesmachan *Lothian*, ,eklz-'mæxən, ecklzmáchăn

Echlin, *f.n.*, 'exlɪn, échlin; 'eklɪn, écklin

Eckersall, *f.n.*, 'ekərsl, éckĕrssl

Eckersley, *f.n.*, 'ekərzlɪ, éckĕrzli

Eckhard, *f.n.*, 'ekhɑrd, éck-haard

Edale *Derby.*, 'ideɪl, eédayl

Eday *Orkney*, 'ideɪ, eéday

Eddrachillis Bay *H'land*, ,edrə-'kɪlɪs, edrăkilliss

Ede, *f.n.*, id, eed

Edeirnion, Vale of, *also spelt* **Edeyrnion,** *Gwynedd–Clwyd*, ə'daɪərnjɒn, ĕdírn-yon

Edelman, *f.n.*, 'edlmən, éddlmăn; 'eɪdlmən, áydlmăn

Edelsten, *f.n.*, 'edlstən, éddlstĕn

Eden, *f.n.*, 'idən, eédĕn

Edenbridge *Kent*, 'idənbrıdʒ, eédĕn-brij

Edenderry *Co. Down*, 'idən'derı, eédĕndérri

Edenfield *Lancs.*, 'idənfild, eédĕnfeeld

Edensor *Derby.*, 'enzər, énzŏr; 'ensər, énssŏr

Edern, *also spelt* **Edeyrn**, *Gwynedd*, 'edɛərn, éddairn

Ederney *Co. Fermanagh*, 'edərnı, éddĕrni

Edeyrn *see* **Edern**

Edeyrnion *see* **Edeirnion**

Edgbaston *W. Midlands*, 'edʒbəstən, éj-bǎstŏn

Edgcumbe, Baron, 'edʒkəm, éjkūm

Edgebolton *Salop*, edʒ'boultən, ej-bóltŏn

Edgecombe, *f.n.*, 'edʒkəm, éj-kŏm

Edgell, *f.n.*, 'edʒəl, éjjĕl

Edgoose, *f.n.*, ed'gus, ed-goóss

Edholm, *f.n.*, 'edhoum, éd-hōm

Edial *Staffs.*, 'edıəl, éddiäl

Edinburgh *Lothian*, 'edınbərə, éddinbŭrǎ; 'ednbərə, éddnbŭrǎ

Edinger, *f.n.*, 'edındʒər, éddinjĕr

Edington *Borders*, 'idıŋtən, eédingtŏn

Edington *Somerset*, *Wilts.*, 'edıŋtən, éddingtŏn

Edington Burtle *Somerset*, 'edıŋtən 'bərtl, éddingtŏn búrtl

Edisbury, *f.n.*, 'edısbərı, éddiss-būri

Edkins, *f.n.*, 'edkınz, édkinz

Edlingham *Northd.*, 'edlındʒəm, éddlinjäm

Edmead, *f.n.*, 'edmid, édmeed

Edmond, *f.n.*, 'edmənd, édmŏnd

Edmondbyers *see* **Edmundbyers**

Edmonds, *f.n.*, 'edməndz, édmŏndz

Edmondstone, *f.n.*, 'edmənstoun, édmŏnstōn

Edmundbyers, *also spelt* **Edmondbyers**, *Durham*, 'edməndbaıərz, édmŭndbī-ĕrz

Edmunds, *f.n.*, 'edməndz, édmŭndz

Edney, *f.n.*, 'edni, édni

Ednyfed, *C.n.*, ed'nʌvıd, ednúv-vĕd

Edolls, *f.n.*, 'edəlz, éddŏlz

Edradour Distillery *Tayside*, ,edrə-'dauər, edrǎdówr

Edradynate *Tayside*, ,edrə-'dainıt, edrǎdínit

Edrich, *f.n.*, 'edrıtʃ, édritch

Edridge, *f.n.*, 'edrıdʒ, édrij

Edstaston *Salop*, 'edstæstən, édstasstŏn

Edwalton *Notts.*, ed'wɔltən, edwáwltŏn

Edward, *C.n.*, 'edwərd, édwărd

Edwardes, *f.n.*, 'edwərdz, édwărdz

Edwardian, *pertaining to the era of King Edward VII*, ed-'wɔrdıən, edwáwrdiän; ed'wardıən, edwaárdiän

Edwards, *f.n.*, 'edwərdz, édwărdz

Edyvean, *f.n.*, 'edıvın, éddiveen

Edzell *Tayside*, 'edzl, éddzl

Eele, *f.n.*, il, eel

Efail Isaf *Mid Glam.*, 'evaıl 'ısæv, évvīl íssav

Efemey, *f.n.*, 'efımı, éffĕmi

Egan, *f.n.*, 'igən, eégän

Egerton, *f.n.*, 'edʒərtən, éjjĕrtŏn

Egerton *Gtr. M'chester*, 'edʒərtən, éjjĕrtŏn

Eggesford *Devon*, 'egzfərd, éggzfŏrd

Eggington *Beds.*, 'egıŋtən, éggingtŏn

Egginton, *f.n.*, 'egıntən, éggintŏn

Egginton *Derby.*, 'egıntən, éggintŏn

Egilsay *Orkney*, 'egılseı, éggilssay

Eglingham *Northd.*, 'eglındʒəm, égglinjäm

Eglinton and Winton, Earl of, 'eglıntən ənd 'wıntən, égglintŏn ănd wintŏn

Eglish *Co. Armagh*, *Co. Tyrone*, 'eglıʃ, égglish

Eglon, *f.n.*, 'eglɒn, égglon

Egloshayle *Cornwall*, ,egləs'heıl, eglóss-háyl

Egloskerry *Cornwall*, ,egləs'kerı, eglósskérri

Eglwyseg *Clwyd*, e'gluıseg, egloó-isseg

Eglwysfach *Dyfed*, ,egluıs'vax, egloó-issvaach

Eglwyswrw *Dyfed*, ,egluıs'uəru, egloó-issŏóroo

Egmanton *Notts.*, 'egməntən, éggmäntŏn

Egmere *Norfolk*, 'egmıər, éggmeer

Egmont, Earl of, 'egmɒnt, égmont

Egremont, *Cumbria*, *Merseyside*, 'egrımənt, éggrĕmŏnt

Egremont and Leconfield, Baron, 'egrımɒnt ənd 'lekənfild, éggrĕmont ănd léckŏnfeeld

Ehen, River, *Cumbria*, 'iən, eé-ĕn

Ehrmann, *f.n.*, 'eərmən, áirmän

Eidda *Gwynedd*, 'aıðə, íthǎ

Eiddwen, *Welsh C.n.*, 'aıðwen, íth-wen

Eidinow, *f.n.*, 'aıdınau, ídinow

Eifion, *Welsh C.n.*, 'aıvıɒn, ívi-on

Eigg *H'land*, eg, egg
Eighton Banks *Tyne & Wear*,
  'eɪtən 'bæŋks, áytŏn bánks;
  'aɪtən 'bæŋks, ítŏn bánks
Eigra *Welsh C.n.*, 'aɪgrə, ígră
Eil, Loch, *H'land*, il, eel
Eildon Hills *Borders*, 'ɪldən,
  éeldŏn
Eilean Donan *H'land*, 'elən
  'dɒnən, éllăn dónnăn
Eilean More, *name of several islets
  in Scotland*, 'elən 'mɔr, éllăn
  mór
Eilian *Welsh Bardic and C.n.*,
  'aɪlɪən, íliăn
Eiloart, *f.n.*, 'aɪlouɑrt, ílō-aart
Eils, *f.n.*, ilz, eelz
Eiluned *Welsh C.n.*, aɪ'lɪnəd,
  íleenĕd
Einion *Welsh C.n.*, 'aɪnɪɒn, íni-on
Einzig, *f.n.*, 'aɪnzɪg, ínzig
Eira, *Welsh C.n.*, 'aɪrə, íră
Eirene, *C.n.*, aɪ'rinɪ, ʌreeni
Eirlys, *Welsh C.n.*, 'aɪərlɪs, írliss
Eirwyn, *Welsh C.n.*, 'aɪərwɪn,
  írwin
Eisteddfa Gurig *Powys*, aɪs'teðvə
  'gɪrɪg, ʌstéthvă gírrig
Eisteddfod, *pl.* Eisteddfodau,
  Welsh Bardic festival,
  aɪ'steðvɒd, ʌstéthvod;
  ,aɪsteð'vɒdaɪ, ʌstethvóddí
Eite, *f.n.*, aɪt, ít
Eitshal *I. of Lewis*, 'eɪtʃəl, áytch-
  ăl
Ekserdjian, *f.n.*, ɪk'sɜrdʒən,
  ĕksérjăn
Elan Valley Reservoir *Powys*,
  'ɪlən, éelăn
Eland House *London*, 'ilənd,
  éelănd
Elboz, *f.n.*, 'elbɒz, élbozz
Elburton *Devon*, 'elbərtən, élbŭr-
  tŏn
Elchies Forest *Grampian*, 'elxɪz,
  élchiz
Elcho, Lord, 'elkou, élkō
Elder, *f.n.*, 'eldər, éldĕr
Elderslie, *Kilmarnock & Loudoun
  (S'clyde)*, 'eldərzlɪ, éldĕrzli
Elderslie, *Renfrew (S'clyde)*,
  ,eldərz'li, eldĕrzleé; 'eldərzlɪ,
  éldĕrzli
Eldred, *f.n.*, 'eldrɪd, éldrĕd;
  'eldred, éldred
Eldridge, *f.n.*, 'eldrɪdʒ, éldrij
Eleazar, *f.n.*, ,elɪ'zar, ellēzaár
Element, *f.n.*, 'elɪmənt, éllĕmĕnt
Elerch *Dyfed*, 'eleərx, éllairch
Elers, *f.n.*, 'elərz, éllĕrz
Eley, *f.n.*, 'ilɪ, éeli
Elfed, *Welsh C.n.*, 'elved, élved
Elford, *f.n.*, 'elfərd, élfŏrd
Elfyn, *Welsh C.n.*, 'elvɪn, élvin

Elgar, Sir Edward, *composer*,
  'elgɑr, élgaar. *Although this is
  the pronunciation by which the
  composer is usually known, there
  is a suggestion that he may have
  called himself* 'elgər, élgăr.
Elger, *f.n.*, 'elgər, élgĕr
Elgin *Grampian*, 'elgɪn, élgin.
  Appropriate also for the Earl of
  ~ and Kincardine, *q.v., and for
  the* ~ Marbles.
Elgin and Kincardine, Earl of,
  'elgɪn ənd kɪn'kɑrdɪn, élgin ănd
  kin-kaárdin
Elgoll *Skye*, 'elgɒl, élgol
Elgy, *f.n.*, 'eldʒɪ, élji
Elham *Kent*, 'iləm, éelăm
Elia, *pen-name of Charles Lamb*,
  'ilɪə, éeliă
Eliades, *f.n.*, ɪ'laɪədiz, ĕlí-ădeez
Elias, *f.n.*, ɪ'laɪəs, ĕlí-ăss
Elibank, Baron, 'elɪbæŋk, éllibank
Elidyr-Fawr *Gwynedd*, e'lɪdər
  'vauər, elíddĕr vówr
Elie *Fife*, 'ilɪ, éeli
Elien, *Bishop of Ely's signature*,
  'eɪlɪən, áyliĕn
Eling *Hants*, 'ilɪŋ, éeling
Eliot, *f.n.*, 'elɪət, élliŏt
Eliott, *f.n.*, 'elɪət, élliŏt
Elizabeth, *C.n.*, ɪ'lɪzəbəθ,
  ĕlízzăbĕth
Elizabethan, *pertaining to
  Elizabeth*, ɪ,lɪzə'biθən, ĕliză-
  béethăn
Elkan, *f.n.*, 'elkən, élkăn; 'elkɑn,
  élkaan. *The second is appro-
  priate for Benno* ~, *sculptor*.
Elkesley *Notts.*, 'elkslɪ, élksli
Elkind, *f.n.*, 'elkaɪnd, élkīnd
Elkins, *f.n.*, 'elkɪnz, élkinz
Ell, *f.n.*, el, ell
Ellenbogen, *f.n.*, 'elənbougən,
  éllĕnbōgĕn
Ellerdine *Salop*, 'elərdaɪn, éllĕrdīn
Ellerman, *f.n.*, 'elərmən, éllĕrmăn
Ellerton, *f.n.*, 'elərtən, éllĕrtŏn
Elles, *f.n.*, 'elɪs, éllĕss
Ellesborough *Bucks.*, 'elzbərə,
  élzbŭră
Ellesmere, Earl of, 'elzmɪər,
  élzmeer
Ellesmere Port *Ches.*, 'elzmɪər
  'pɔrt, élzmeer pórt
Ellice, *f.n.*, 'elɪs, élliss
Ellicock, *f.n.*, 'elɪkɒk, éllikock
Ellinger, *f.n.*, 'elɪndʒər, éllinjĕr
Ellingham *Hants, Norfolk*,
  'elɪŋəm, élling-ăm
Ellingham *Northd.*, 'elɪndʒəm,
  éllinjăm
Elliot, *f.n.*, 'elɪət, élliŏt
Elliott, *f.n.*, 'elɪət, élliŏt
Ellis, *f.n.*, 'elɪs, élliss

Ellough *Suffolk*, 'elou, éllō
Elloughton *Humberside*, 'elətən, éllótŏn
Elmet Hall *W. Yorks.*, 'elmet, élmett
Elmham, North *and* South, *Norfolk*, 'elməm, élmăm
Elmsall, North *and* South, *W. Yorks.*, 'emsl, émssl
Elphick, *f.n.*, 'elfik, élfick
Elphinstone, *f.n.*, 'elfinstən, élfinstŏn; 'elfinstoun, élfinstōn. *The first is appropriate for Baron ~.*
Elrig *D. & G.*, 'elrig, élrig
Else, *f.n.*, els, els, elss
Elsecar *S. Yorks.*, 'elsikər, élssĕkăr
Elsham *Humberside*, 'elʃəm, él-shăm
Elsing *Norfolk*, 'elziŋ, élzing
Elslack *N. Yorks.*, el'slæk, elsslǎck
Elsom, *f.n.*, 'elsəm, élssŏm
Elsternwick *Humberside*, 'elstərnwik, élstērnwick. *This is the ecclesiastical name. The postal name is* **Elstronwick**, *q.v.*
Elston, *f.n.*, 'elstən, élstŏn
Elstow *Beds.*, 'elstou, élsstō
Elstronwick *Humberside*, 'elstrənwik, élstrónwick. *This is the postal name. The ecclesiastical name is* **Elsternwick**, *q.v.*
Elswick *Tyne & Wear*, 'elzik, élzick
Elswood, *f.n.*, 'elzwʊd, élzwŏod
Elsynge Hall *Enfield* (*London*), 'elsiŋ, élssing
Elt, *f.n.*, elt, elt
Eltham *London*, 'eltəm, éltăm
Eltisley *Cambs.*, 'eltizli, éltizli
Eltringham *Northd.*, 'eltrindʒəm, éltrinjăm
Eluned, *Welsh C.n.*, el'ined, eléened; el'ined, elínned
Elveden *Suffolk*, 'elvdən, élvdĕn; 'eldən, éldĕn. *The second is appropriate for Viscount ~.*
Elvetham *Hants*, 'elviθəm, élvéthăm
Elwell, *f.n.*, 'elwəl, élwĕl; 'elwel, élwel
Elwes, *f.n.*, 'elwiz, élwĕz
Elwick *Durham*, 'elwik, élwick
Elwick *Northd.*, 'elik, éllick
Elwy, River, *Clwyd*, 'elʊi, éllŏo-i
Ely, *f.n.*, 'ili, éeli
Ely *Cambs.*, *S. Glam.*, 'ili, éeli. *Appropriate also for the Marquess of ~.*
Ely, River, *Mid Glam.–S. Glam.*, 'ili, éeli

Elyhaugh *Northd.*, 'ilihaf, éeli-haaf; 'ilihɒf, éeli-hoff
Embery, *f.n.*, 'embəri, émbĕri
Embsay *N. Yorks.*, 'empsei, émpsay
Emburey, *f.n.*, 'embəri, émbŭri
Emeleus, *f.n.*, ˌemi'liəs, emmĕlée-ŭss
Emeney, *f.n.*, 'eməni, émmĕni
Emeny, *f.n.*, 'eməni, émmĕni
Emere, *f.n.*, e'miər, emméer
Emlyn, *C.n. and f.n.*, 'emlin, émlin
Emmens, *f.n.*, 'emənz, émmĕnz
Emmet, *f.n.*, 'emit, émmĕt. *Appropriate also for the Barony of ~.*
Empringham, *f.n.*, 'empriŋəm, émpring-ăm
Emptage, *f.n.*, 'emptidʒ, émptij
Emrys, *Welsh C.n.*, 'emris, émriss
Emyr, *Welsh C.n.*, 'emiər, émmeer
Endellion *Cornwall*, ən'deliən, ĕndélliŏn
Energlyn *Mid Glam.*, 'enərglin, énnérglin. *Appropriate also for Baron ~.*
Engelbach, *f.n.*, 'eŋglbæk, éng-gl-back
Englefield, *f.n.*, 'eŋglfild, éng-gl-feeld
Enham Alamein *Hants*, 'enəm 'æləmein, énnăm álămayn
Enid, *C.n.*, 'inid, éenid; 'enid, énnid. *The second is the Welsh pronunciation.*
Ennals, *f.n.*, 'enlz, énnlz
Ennisdale, Barony of, 'enisdeil, énnisdayl
Enniskillen *Co. Fermanagh*, ˌenis'kilən, enniskíllĕn. *Appropriate also for the Earl of ~.*
Enochdhu *Tayside*, 'inəx'du, éenŏ<u>ch</u>-doo
Enraght, *f.n.*, 'enrit, énrit
Enright, *f.n.*, 'enrait, énrīt
Ensor, *f.n.*, 'ensɔr, énssor
Enterkin, Stream, *D. & G.*, 'entərkin, éntĕrkin
Enterkinfoot *D. & G.*, ˌentərkin'fʊt, entĕrkinfŏot
Enthoven, *f.n.*, 'enthouvən, ént-hōvĕn; en'touvən, entóvĕn
Enticknap, *f.n.*, 'entiknæp, énticknap; ˌentik'næp, enticknáp
Enticknapp, *f.n.*, 'entiknæp, énticknap
Entract, *f.n.*, 'ɒntrækt, óntrackt
Entwistle, *f.n.*, 'entwisl, éntwissl
Enyd, *C.n.*, 'enid, énnid
Enys, *f.n.*, 'eniz, énniz
Enzie *Grampian*, 'eŋi, éng-i

Eochar *S. Uist*, 'ɪəxər, ee-ŏchăr. *The Gaelic spelling is* **Iochdar**, *q.v.*

Eothen School *Surrey*, 'iouθen, ee-ōthen

Eport, Loch, *N. Uist*, 'ipɔrt, eeport

Eppstein, *f.n.*, 'epstain, épstīn

Eppynt *Powys*, 'epɪnt, éppint

Epsom *Surrey*, 'epsəm, épssŏm

Epstein, Sir Jacob, *sculptor*, 'epstain, épstīn

Ercall, High *and* Child's, *Salop*, 'ɑrkl, áarkl

Erchless Castle *H'land*, 'ɛərklɪs, áirklĕss

Ercolani, *f.n.*, ɜrkə'lɑnɪ, erkŏláani

Erddig, *also spelt* **Erthig**, *Clwyd*, 'ɛərðɪg, áírthig

Ereira, *f.n.*, ɪ'rɛərə, ĕráiră

Eresby *Lincs.*, 'ɪərzbɪ, éerzbi

Erewash, River, *Derby.–Notts. boundary*, 'erɪwɒʃ, érrĕ-wosh

Eriboll, Loch, *H'land*, 'erɪbɒl, érribol

Ericht, Loch *and* River, *Tayside*, 'erɪxt, érricht

Ericsson, *f.n.*, 'erɪksən, érriksŏn

Eridge Green *E. Sussex*, 'erɪdʒ érrij

Eridge Green *E. Sussex*, 'erɪdʒ 'grin, érrij gréen

Eriska *S'clyde*, 'erɪskə, érriskă

Eriskay *W. Isles*, 'erɪskeɪ, érriskay; 'erɪskɪ, érriski

Erisort, Loch, *W. Isles*, 'erɪsɔrt, érrissort

Eriswell *Suffolk*, 'erɪswəl, érrisswĕl

Erith *London*, 'ɪərɪθ, éerith

Erlanger, *f.n.*, ɛər'læŋər, airláng-ĕr

Erlbeck, *f.n.*, 'ɜrlbek, érlbeck

Erlestoke *Wilts.*, 'ɜrlstouk, érl-stōk

Erlich, *f.n.*, 'ɛərlɪx, áirlich

Erne, Earl of, ɜrn, ern

Ernesettle *Devon*, 'ɜrnɪsetl, érnissettl

Ernle, Barony of, 'ɜrnlɪ, érnli

Erraid *S'clyde*, 'ɛərɪdʒ, áirij

Errigal, Co. *Tyrone*, 'erɪgəl, érrigăl. *In the title of Viscount Alexander of Tunis and of ~, derived from ~ in Co. Donegal in the Republic of Ireland, the pronunciation is* 'erɪgəl, érrigawl.

Errington, *f.n.*, 'erɪŋtən, érringtŏn

Eritt, *f.n.*, 'erɪt, érrit

Errochty Water, River, *Tayside*, 'erəxtɪ 'wɔtər, érrŏchti wáwtĕr

Erroll, Earl of, 'erəl, érrŏl

Erskine, *f.n.*, 'ɜrskɪn, érsskin

Erskine of Rerrick, Baron, 'ɜrskɪn əv 'rerɪk, érsskin ŏv rérrick

Erskine *S'clyde*, 'ɜrskɪn, érsskin

Erthig *see* **Erddig**

Ervine, *f.n.*, 'ɜrvɪn, érvin

Ervine, St. John, *author and dramatist*, 'sɪndʒən 'ɜrvɪn, sinjŏn érvin

Erw *Dyfed*, 'eru, érroo

Erwood *Powys*, 'erud, érrŏŏd

Erwyd, *C.n.*, 'eruɪd, érrŏŏ-id

Eryri, *name sometimes given to* Mount Snowdon, ə'rɑrɪ, ĕrúrri. *The name means 'eagle top'.*

Escley Brook, River, *H. & W.*, 'esklɪ 'bruk, éskli brŏŏk

Esclusham *Clwyd*, es'kluʃəm, eskloó-sham

Escoffey, *f.n.*, ɪs'kɒfɪ, ĕskóffi

Escott, *f.n.*, 'eskət, éssköt

Esdaile, *f.n.*, 'ezdeɪl, ézdayl

Esgairgeiliog *Powys*, ,esgaɪər-'gaɪljɒg, essgīrgíl-yog

Esh *Durham*, eʃ, esh

Esha Ness *Shetland*, 'eʃə nes, éshă ness

Esher *Surrey*, 'iʃər, eeshĕr. *Appropriate also for Viscount ~.*

Esholt *W. Yorks.*, 'eʃɒlt, ésholt

Eskdaill, Lord, 'eskdeɪl, éskdayl

Eskdalemuir *D. & G.*, 'eskdeɪl-'mjuər, éskdaylmyoŏr

Eskew, *f.n.*, 'eskju, ésskew

Esk Hause *Cumbria*, 'esk 'hɔz, ésk háwz

Eskmeals *Cumbria*, 'eskmilz, éskmeelz

Esler, *f.n.*, 'eslər, ésslĕr

Esmond, *C.n. and f.n.*, 'ezmənd, ézmönd

Esmonde, *f.n.*, 'ezmənd, ézmŏnd

Espinasse, *f.n.*, 'espɪnæs, éspinass

Essame, *f.n.*, 'eseɪm, éssaym

Essendine *Leics.*, 'esəndaɪn, éssĕndīn

Essendon, Barony of, 'esəndən, éssĕndŏn

Essenhigh, *f.n.*, 'esənhaɪ, éssĕn-hī

Essinger, *f.n.*, 'esɪndʒər, éssinjĕr

Essex *Co. name*, 'esɪks, éssĕks

Esslemont, *f.n.*, 'eslmənt, éssl-mŏnt

Esswood, *f.n.*, 'eswud, ésswŏŏd

Estcourt, *f.n.*, 'eskɔrt, éskort

Esthwaite Water *Cumbria*, 'esθweɪt 'wɔtər, éssthwayt wáwtĕr

Estorick, *f.n.*, 'estərɪk, ésstŏrick

Etal *Northd.*, 'itl, eetl; 'etl, éttl

Etall, *f.n.*, 'etɔl, éttawl

Etches, *f.n.*, 'etʃɪz, étchĕz

Etchingham *E. Sussex*, ,etʃɪŋ-'hæm, etching-hám

Etheldreda, saint, 'eθldridə, éthldreedă

Etheredge, *f.n.*, 'eθərɪdʒ, étherĕj

Etherege, *f.n.*, 'eθərɪdʒ, étherĕj

Etheridge, *f.n.*, 'eθərɪdʒ, étherij

Etherton, *f.n.*, 'eðərtən, éthertŏn

Ethie, *also spelt* **Eathie**, H'land, 'iθɪ, éethi

Etive, Loch *and* River, S'clyde, 'etɪv, éttiv

Eton College *Berks.*, 'itən, eétŏn

Etonian, *one educated at* **Eton** *College*, i'tounɪən, eetṓniăn

Ettershank, *f.n.*, 'etərʃæŋk, étter-shank

Ettlinger, *f.n.*, 'etlɪŋər, étling-ĕr

Ettrick *Borders*, 'etrɪk, étrick

Etty, *f.n.*, 'etɪ, étti

Etwall *Derby.*, 'etwɔl, étwawl

Eugene, *C.n.*, ju'ʒeɪn, yoozháyn; 'judʒin, yoójeen; ju'dʒin, yoojeén

Euler, *f.n.*, 'julər, yoólĕr; 'ɔɪlər, óylĕr

Eunson, *f.n.*, 'junsən, yoónssŏn

Eurfryn, *Welsh C.n.*, 'aɪərvrɪn, írvrin

Eurich, *f.n.*, 'juərɪk, yoórick

Eurig, *Welsh C.n.*, 'aɪərɪg, írig

Eustelle, *C.n.*, jus'tel, yoostéll

Euston *Suffolk*, 'justən, yoós-tŏn

Euxton *Lancs.*, 'ekstən, éckstŏn

Evand, *f.n.*, 'evənd, évvănd

Evans, Beriah Gwynfe, *Welsh divine*, bə'raɪə 'gwɪnvə 'evənz, bĕríă gwínvĕ évvănz

Evanton H'land, 'evəntən, évvăn-tŏn

Evedon *Lincs.*, 'ivdən, eévdŏn

Eveleigh, *f.n.*, 'ivlɪ, eévli

Eveleigh-de-Moleyns, *f.n.*, 'ivlɪ 'deməlɪnz, eévli démmŏleenz. *Family name of Baron Ventry.*

Eveline, *C.n.*, 'ivlɪn, eévlin

Eveling, *f.n.*, 'ivlɪŋ, eévling

Evely, *f.n.*, 'ivlɪ, eévli

Evelyn, *C.n.*, 'ivlɪn, eévlin; 'evlɪn, évlin

Evelyn, John, *English diarist (1620–1706)*, 'ivlɪn, eévlin

Evemy, *f.n.*, 'evɪmɪ, évvĕmi

Evenjobb *Powys*, ˌevən'dʒɒb, evvĕnjób

Evenley *Northants.*, 'evənlɪ, eévĕnli

Evenlode *Glos.*, 'ivənloud, eévĕnlōd

Evennett, *f.n.*, 'evɪnet, évvĕnet

Everest, *f.n.*, 'evərɪst, évvĕrĕst

Everett, *f.n.*, 'evərɪt, évvĕrĕt

Everill, *f.n.*, 'evərɪl, évvĕril

Everingham, *f.n.*, 'evərɪŋəm, évvĕring-ăm

Evers, *f.n.*, 'evərz, évvĕrz; 'ivərz, eévĕrz

Evershed, *f.n.*, 'evərʃed, évvĕr-shed. *Appropriate also for the Barony of* ~.

Eversholt *Beds.*, 'evərʃɒlt, évvĕr-sholt

Every, *f.n.*, 'evrɪ, évvri; 'evərɪ, évvĕri

Evesham *H. & W.*, 'ivʃəm, eév-shăm; 'ɪvʃəm, eévĕ-shăm; 'isəm, eéssăm. *Appropriate also for the Vale of* ~.

Evetts, *f.n.*, 'evits, évvĕts

Evie *Orkney*, 'ivɪ, eévi

Evill, *f.n.*, 'evɪl, évvil

Evington *Glos.*, *Leics.*, 'evɪŋtən, évvingtŏn

Evington Place *Kent*, 'ivɪŋtən, eévingtŏn

Ewart, *f.n.*, 'juərt, yoó-ărt

Ewart *Northd.*, 'juərt, yoó-ärt

Ewe, Loch, H'land, ju, yoo

Ewell *Surrey*, 'juəl, yoó-ĕl

Ewelme *Oxon.*, 'juelm, yoó-elm

Ewen, *f.n.*, 'juən, yoó-ĕn

Ewenny *Mid Glam.*, ɪ'wenɪ, ĕ-wénni

Ewing, *f.n.*, 'juɪŋ, yoó-ing

Ewins, *f.n.*, 'juɪnz, yoó-inz; 'juɪnz, yoó-inz

Ewloe *Clwyd*, 'julou, yoólō

Ewood Bridge *Lancs.*, 'iwud 'brɪdʒ, ee-wŏŏd bríj

Ewyas Harold *H. & W.*, 'juəs 'hærəld, yoó-ăss hárrŏld

Exceat *E. Sussex*, 'eksit, éckseet

Excell, *f.n.*, ek'sel, eckséll

Exe, River, *Somerset–Devon*, eks, ecks

Exelby, *f.n.*, 'ekslbɪ, écksslbi

Exeter *Devon*, 'eksɪtər, écksĕtĕr. *Appropriate also for the Marquess of* ~.

Exford *Somerset*, 'eksfərd, écksford

Exmouth *Devon*, 'eksməθ, écksmũth. *Appropriate also for Viscount* ~.

Exon, *f.n.*, 'eksən, écksŏn

Exstance, *f.n.*, 'ekstəns, éckstănss

Exwick *Devon*, 'ekswɪk, éckswick

Ey, River, *Grampian*, eɪ, ay

Eyam, *f.n.*, im, eem

Eyam *Derby.*, im, eem

Eyck, *f.n.*, aɪk, īk

Eyden, *f.n.*, 'eɪdən, áydĕn

Eydon *Northants.*, 'idən, eédŏn

Eye *Cambs.*, *H. & W.*, *Northants.*, aɪ, ī

Eyemouth *Borders*, 'aɪmauθ, ímowth

Eyers, *f.n.*, ɛərz, airz

Eyet, *f.n.*, 'aɪət, í̄-ĕt
Eyke *Suffolk*, aɪk, īk
Eykyn, *f.n.*, 'ɪkɪn, ée̓kin
Eyles, *f.n.*, aɪlz, īlz
Eynesbury *Cambs.*, 'eɪnzbərɪ, áynzbŭri
Eynhallow Island *Orkney*, aɪn-'hælou, īn-hálō
Eynon *f.n. and Welsh C.n.*, 'aɪnən, ínŏn
Eynsford *Kent*, 'eɪnzfərd, áynzfŏrd
Eynsham *Oxon.*, 'enʃəm, én-shăm; 'eɪnʃəm, áyn-shăm
Eype *Dorset*, ip, eep
Eyre, *f.n.*, ɛər, air
Eyre and Spottiswoode, *publishers*, 'ɛər ənd 'spɒtɪswʊd, áir ănd spóttiswōod
Eyre Methuen, *publishers*, 'ɛər 'meθjuən, áir méth-yoo-ĕn
Eyres, *f.n.*, ɛərz, airz
Eysenck, *f.n.*, 'aɪzeŋk, ízenk
Eyston, *f.n.*, 'istən, ée̓stŏn
Eythorne *Kent*, 'eɪθɔrn, áy-thorn
Eytle, *f.n.*, 'aɪtl, ítl
Eyton, *f.n.*, 'aɪtən, ítŏn; 'itən, ée̓tŏn
Eyton *Clwyd*, 'itən, ée̓tŏn. *Appropriate for both places of this name in Clwyd.*
Eyton *H. & W.*, 'eɪtən, áytŏn
Eyton-on-the-Weald Moors *Salop*, 'aɪtən ɒn ðə 'wild 'mʊərz, ítŏn on thē wée̓ld mōorz
Eywood *H. & W.*, 'eɪwʊd, áywōod
Ezard, *f.n.*, 'izɑrd, ée̓zaard
Ezra, *f.n.*, 'ezrə, ézzră

F

Faber, *f.n.*, 'feɪbər, fáybĕr. *Appropriate also for ~ and ~, publishers.*
Fabian, *f.n.*, 'feɪbɪən, fáybi-ăn
Fâche, *f.n.*, faʃ, faash
Facit *Lancs.*, 'feɪsɪt, fáyssit
Faed, *f.n.*, feɪd, fayd
Fagan, *f.n.*, 'feɪgən, fáygăn
Fage, *f.n.*, feɪdʒ, fayj
Fageant, *f.n.*, 'feɪdʒənt, fáyjănt
Fagence, *f.n.*, 'feɪdʒəns, fáyjĕnss
Fahey, *f.n.*, feɪ, fay
Fahie, *f.n.*, feɪ, fáy-i; faɪ, fáa-i
Fahy, *f.n.*, 'fɑhɪ, fáa-hi
Faichney, *f.n.*, 'feɪxnɪ, fáychni
Faiers, *f.n.*, 'feɪərz, fáy-ĕrz
Faifley *S'clyde*, 'feɪflɪ, fáyfli
Fairbairn, *f.n.*, 'fɛərbɛərn, fáirbairn

Fairbank, *f.n.*, 'fɛərbæŋk, fáirbank
Fairbanks, *f.n.*, 'fɛərbæŋks, fáirbanks
Fairbotham, *f.n.*, 'fɛərbɒθəm, fáirboth-ăm
Fairclough, *f.n.*, 'fɛərklʌf, fáirkluff; 'fɛərklou, fáirklō
Fairfoull, *f.n.*, 'fɛərfaʊl, fáirfowl
Fairgrieve, *f.n.*, 'fɛərgriv, fáirgreev
Fairhall, *f.n.*, 'fɛərhɔl, fáir-hawl
Fairhaven, Baron, 'fɛərheɪvən, fáir-hayvĕn
Fairley, *f.n.*, 'fɛərlɪ, fáirli
Fairman, *f.n.*, 'fɛərmən, fáirmăn
Fairmaner, *f.n.*, 'fɛərmænər, fáirmannĕr; fɛər'mænər, fair-mánnĕr
Fairminer, *f.n.*, 'fɛərmɪnər, fáirminnĕr
Fairservice, *f.n.*, 'fɛərsɜrvɪs, fáir-serviss
Fairwarp *E. Sussex*, 'fɛərwɔrp, fáirwawrp
Fakenham *Norfolk*, 'feɪkənəm, fáykĕnăm
Fala *Lothian*, 'fælə, fálă
Falco, *f.n.*, 'fælkou, fálkō
Falcon, *f.n.*, 'fɔkən, fáwkŏn; 'fɒlkən, fáwlkŏn
Falconbridge, *f.n.*, 'fɔkənbrɪdʒ, fáwkŏnbrij
Falconer, *f.n.*, 'fɔlkənər, fáwlkŏnĕr; 'fɔknər, fáwknĕr; 'fɒlkənər, fólkŏnĕr
Faldingworth *Lincs.*, 'fɔldɪŋwərθ, fáwlding-wŭrth
Falfield *Avon*, 'fælfild, fálfeeld
Falk, *f.n.*, fɔlk, fawlk; fɔk, fawk
Falkender, *f.n.*, 'fɔlkəndər, fáwlkĕndĕr. *Appropriate also for Baroness ~.*
Falkiner, *f.n.*, 'fɔknər, fáwknĕr
Falkirk *Central*, 'fɔlkərk, fáwlkŭrk
Falkland, Viscount, 'fɔklənd, fáwkländ
Falkland *Fife*, 'fɔlklənd, fáwlkländ
Falkus, *f.n.*, 'fɔlkəs, fáwlküss
Falla, *f.n.*, 'fælə, fálă
Fallapit *Devon*, 'fæləpɪt, fáläpit
Fallas, *f.n.*, 'fæləs, fálass
Falle, *f.n.*, fɔl, fawl
Faller, *f.n.*, 'fælər, fálĕr
Fallin *Central*, fə'lɪn, fălín
Falloon, *f.n.*, fə'lun, fălóon
Falmer *E. Sussex*, 'fælmər, fál-mĕr
Falmouth *Cornwall*, 'fælməθ, fálmŭth. *Appropriate also for Viscount ~.*
Falstone *Northd.*, 'fælstoun, fálstōn

Fan Frynych *Powys*, væn 'vrʌnɪx, van vrúnnich

Fannich, Mountains, River *and* Loch, *H'land*, 'fænɪx, fánnich

Fanning, *f.n.*, 'fænɪŋ, fánning

Fanshawe, *f.n.*, 'fænʃɔ, fán-shaw

Fant, *f.n.*, fænt, fant

Fantham, *f.n.*, 'fænθəm, fán-thäm

Fanthorpe, *f.n.*, 'fænθɔrp, fán--thorp

Fanum House, *Basingstoke (Hants)*, 'feɪnəm, fáynŭm. *Headquarters of the Automobile Association. Many other offices of the AA throughout the United Kingdom bear the same name.*

Fara, Island, *also spelt* **Faray, Pharay**, *Orkney*, 'færə, fárrä

Faragher, *f.n.*, 'færəgər, fárrăgĕr

Farago, *f.n.*, 'færəgou, fárrăgö

Faray, Island, *also spelt* **Fara, Pharay**, *Orkney*, 'færə, fárrä

Farcet *Cambs.*, 'farsɪt, faárssĕt

Far Cotton *Northants.*, 'far 'kɒtən, faár kóttŏn

Fareham *Hants*, 'feərəm, fáir-äm

Farey, *f.n.*, 'feərɪ, fáiri

Fargie, *f.n.*, 'fargɪ, faárgi

Faringdon, *Berks.*, 'færɪŋdən, fárringdŏn. *Appropriate also for Baron ~.*

Faris, *f.n.*, 'færɪs, fárriss

Farjeon, *f.n.* 'fardʒən, faárjŏn

Farmbrough, *f.n.*, 'farmbrə, faármbră

Farnaby, *f.n.*, 'farnəbɪ, faárnäbi

Farncombe, *f.n.*, 'farŋkəm, faárnkŏm

Farne Islands, *Northd.*, farn, faarn

Farnell *Tayside*, 'farnl, faárnl

Farquhar, *f.n.*, 'farkər, faárkär; 'farkwər, faárkwär. *Both are used for George ~, the 17th-c. Irish dramatist.*

Farquharson, *f.n.*, 'farkərsən, faár-kärssŏn; 'farkwərsən, faárkwär-ssŏn

Farr *H'land*, far, faar

Farragon Hill *Tayside*, 'færəgən, fárrăgŏn

Farrar, *f.n.*, 'færər, fárrăr

Farrington Gurney *Avon*, 'færɪŋtən 'gərnɪ, fárrington gúrni

Farsley *W. Yorks.*, 'farzlɪ, faárzli

Farvis, *f.n.*, 'farvɪs, faárviss

Fashanu, *f.n.*, 'fæʃənu, fáshänoo

Faskally, Loch, *Tayside*, 'faskəlɪ, faáskäli; 'fasklɪ, faáskli

Faslane Bay *S'clyde*, fæz'leɪn, fazláyn; fəs'leɪn, fässláyn

Fasnakyle *H'land*, ˌfæsnə'kaɪl, fassnäkíl

Faucett, *f.n.*, 'fɔsɪt, fáwssĕt

Faucitt, *f.n.*, 'fɔsɪt, fáwssit

Faugh *Cumbria*, fæf, faff; fɑf, faaf

Faughan, River, *Co. Derry*, 'fɒxən, fóchän

Faul, *f.n.*, fɔl, fawl

Faulconbridge, *f.n.*, 'fɔlkənbrɪdʒ, fáwlkŏnbrij

Fauldhouse *Lothian*, 'fɔldhaʊs, fáwld-howss

Faulds, *f.n.*, foʊldz, földz; fɔldz, fawldz. *The first is appropriate for Andrew ~, actor and politician.*

Faulkbourne *Essex*, 'fɔbərn, fáwburn; 'fɔbərn, fáwborn

Faulkes, *f.n.*, 'fɔlks, fawlks

Faulkner, *f.n.*, 'fɔknər, fáwknĕr

Faulks, *f.n.*, foʊks, föks

Faupel, *f.n.*, foʊ'pel, föpéll

Faure, *f.n.*, fɔr, for

Fausset, *f.n.*, 'fɔsɪt, fáwssĕt; 'fɒsɪt, fóssĕt

Faust, *f.n.*, faʊst, fowst

Fauvel, *f.n.*, foʊ'vel, fövéll

Faux, *f.n.*, fɒks, fawks; foʊ, fö

Favarger, *f.n.*, fə'varʒər, fävaár-zhĕr

Favell, *f.n.*, 'feɪvl, fáyvl

Faversham *Kent*, 'fævərʃəm, fávvĕr-shäm

Faville, *f.n.*, 'fævɪl, fávvil; 'feɪvɪl, fáyvil

Favor Royal *Co. Tyrone*, 'feɪvər 'rɔɪəl, fáyvŏr róyäl

Fawcett, *f.n.*, 'fɔsɪt, fáwssĕt; 'fɒsɪt, fóssĕt

Fawdry, *f.n.*, 'fɔdrɪ, fáwdri

Fawks, *f.n.*, fɒks, fawks

Fawssett, *f.n.*, 'fɔsɪt, fáwssĕt

Fayer, *f.n.*, feər, fair; 'feɪər, fáy-ĕr

Fayerman, *f.n.*, 'feɪərmən, fáy-ĕrmän

Fayers, *f.n.*, feərz, fairz; 'feɪərz, fáy-ĕrz

Fayrer, *f.n.*, 'feərər, fáirĕr

Fazackerley, *f.n.*, fə'zækərlɪ, fäzáckĕrli

Fazakerley, *f.n.*, fə'zækərlɪ, fäzáckĕrli

Fazakerley *Merseyside*, fə'zækərlɪ, fäzáckĕrli

Fazan, *f.n.*, fə'zæn, fäzánn

Fazekas, *f.n.*, fə'zeɪkəs, fäzáykäss

Fazeley *Staffs.*, 'feɪzlɪ, fáyzli

Fearenside, *f.n.*, 'farnsaɪd, fárn-síd

Fearn, *f.n.*, fərn, fern; feərn, fairn

Fearn *H'land*, farn, fern

Fearnan *Tayside*, 'farnən, férnän

Fearne, *f.n.*, fərn, fern; feərn, fairn

Fearon, *f.n.*, 'fɪərən, feerŏn

Featherstone, *f.n.*, 'feðərstən, féthĕrsstŏn; 'fərstən, férsstŏn

Featherstonehaugh, *f.n.*, *also spelt* Featherstonhaugh, Fetherstonhaugh, 'feðərstənhɔ, féthërstön-haw'; 'fænʃə, fán--shaw'; 'festənhɔ, féstön-haw'; 'fisənhei, féessön-hay'; 'fiərstənhɔ, féerstön-haw

Feavearyear, *f.n.*, 'fevjər, fév-yĕr

Feaver, *f.n.*, 'fivər, féevĕr

Fecher, *f.n.*, 'fetʃər, fétchĕr

Fechlie, *f.n.*, 'fexli, féchli

Feckenham *H. & W.*, 'fekənəm, féckĕnăm; 'feknəm, fécknăm

Feenan, *f.n.*, 'finən, féenăn

Feeny *Co. Derry*, 'fini, féeni

Fehily, *f.n.*, 'fili, féeli

Feighan, *f.n.*, 'fiən, fée-ăn

Feilden, *f.n.*, 'fildən, féeldĕn

Feilding, *f.n.*, 'fildiŋ, féelding

Feiling, *f.n.*, 'failiŋ, fíling

Feist, *f.n.*, fist, feest

Felindre *Powys*, ve'lindrə, velíndrĕ. *Cf.* **Velindre.** *There are many places of this name throughout Wales.*

Felin-foel *Dyfed*, ˌvelin'vɔil, vellinvóyl; ˌvelin'voul, vellinvól

Felin-hen *Gwynedd*, ˌvelin'heiən, vellin-háy-ĕn

Fellgett, *f.n.*, 'felgit, féllgĕt

Fellowes, *f.n.*, 'felouz, féllōz

Felmersham *Beds.*, 'felmərʃəm, félmĕr-shăm

Felmingham, *f.n.*, 'felmiŋəm, félming-ăm

Felpham *W. Sussex*, 'felphəm, félp-hăm; 'felpəm, félpăm; 'felfəm, félfăm

Felsted *Essex*, 'felstid, félstĕd

Feltham *London*, 'feltəm, féltăm

Feltwell *Norfolk*, 'feltwel, féltwel

Fenay Bridge *W. Yorks.*, 'feni 'bridʒ, fénni brij

Fen Ditton *Cambs.*, 'fen 'ditən, fén díttön

Fendrich, *f.n.*, 'fendritʃ, féndritch

Fenemore, *f.n.*, 'fenimɔr, fénnĕmor

Feniscowles *Lancs.*, 'feniskoulz, fénnisskölz

Fennah, *f.n.*, 'fenə, fénnă

Fennell, *f.n.*, 'fenl, fénnl

Fennelly, *f.n.*, 'fenəli, fénnĕli

Fennessy, *f.n.*, 'fenisi, fénnĕssi

Fenoulhet, *f.n.*, 'fenəlei, fénnŏlay

Fenstanton *Cambs.*, fen'stæntən, fenstántön

Fentiman, *f.n.*, 'fentimən, féntimăn

Fentum, *f.n.*, 'fentəm, féntŭm

Fenwick, *f.n.*, 'fenik, fénnick; 'fenwik, fén-wick

Fenwick *Northd.*, 'fenik, fénnick

Feock *Cornwall*, 'fiɒk, fée-ock

Feoffees Town Hall, The, *Colyton (Devon)*, 'fifiz, féefeez

Feord, *f.n.*, 'fiɔrd, fée-ord

Ferbrache, *f.n.*, 'fərbræʃ, férbrash

Fereday, *f.n.*, 'feridei, férrĕday

Ferens, *f.n.*, 'ferənz, férrĕnz

Ferensway *Hull (Humberside)*, 'ferinzwei, férrĕnz-way

Fergus, *C.n.*, 'fərgəs, férgüss

Ferguslie *S'clyde*, ˌfərgəs'li, fergüsslée

Ferguson, *f.n.*, 'fərgəsən, férgüssön

Fergusson, *f.n.*, 'fərgəsən, férgüssön

Ferintosh *H'land*, ˌferin'tɒʃ, ferintósh

Ferman, *f.n.*, 'fərmən, férmăn

Fermanagh *Co. name and town*, fər'mænə, fērmánnă. *Appropriate also for Baron ~.*

Fermont, *f.n.*, 'fərmɒnt, férmont

Fermoy, Baron, fər'mɔi, fĕrmóy

Fermoy *Centre King's Lynn*, fər'mɔi, fĕrmóy

Fernald, *f.n.*, 'fərnəld, férnăld

Fernau, *f.n.*, 'fərnou, férnō

Ferneyhough, *f.n.*, 'fərnihou, férni-hō

Fernie, *f.n.*, 'fərni, férni

Fernihough, *f.n.*, 'fərnihou, férni--hō; 'fərnihʌf, férni-huff

Fernyhalgh *Lancs.*, 'fərnihaf, férni-huff; 'fərnihælʃ, férni--halsh

Fernyhough, *f.n.*, 'fərnihou, férni-hō; 'fərnihʌf, férni-huff

Ferrand, *f.n.*, 'ferənd, férrănd

Ferrar, *f.n.*, 'ferər, férrăr

Ferrier, *f.n.*, 'feriər, férri-ĕr

Ferriggi, *f.n.*, fə'ridʒi, fĕréeji

Ferryside *Dyfed*, ˌferi'said, ferri-síd

Fertel, *f.n.*, 'fərtl, fértĕl

Feshie, River, *H'land*, 'feʃi, féshi

Feshie Bridge *H'land*, 'feʃi 'bridʒ, féshi brij

Fethaland Point *Shetland*, 'feidəlænd, fáydăland

Fetherstonhaugh, *f.n.*, *see* Featherstonehaugh

Fetlar *Shetland*, 'fetlər, fétlăr

Fetterangus *Grampian*, ˌfetər'æŋgəs, fettĕráng-güss

Fettes, *f.n.*, 'fetiz, féttĕz; 'fetis, féttĕss

Fettes College *Lothian*, 'fetis, féttĕss

Fettesian, *one educated at* Fettes *College*, fə'tiziən, fĕtéeziăn

Feugh, Bridge of, *Grampian*, fjux, fewch

Feugh, Water of, *Grampian*, fjux, fewch

Feversham, Baron, 'fevərʃəm, févvĕr-shăm

Fewings, *f.n.*, 'fjuːŋz, féw-ingz

Fewkes, *f.n.*, fjuks, fewks

Fewston *N. Yorks.*, 'fjustən, féwsstŏn

Fewtrell, *f.n.*, 'fjutrəl, féwtrĕl

Ffairfach *Dyfed*, ˌfaɪərˈvax, fīrváach

Ffaldau *W. Glam.*, 'fældaɪ, fáldī

Ffestiniog *Gwynedd*, fes'tɪnjɒg, festín-yog

Ffion, *Welsh C.n.*, 'fɪɒn, fée-on

Ffolkes, *f.n.*, fouks, fōks

Fforest-fach *W. Glam.*, ˌfɒrɪstˈvax, forrĕst-váách

Fforest Fawr *Powys*, ˌfɒrɪstˈvaʊər, forrĕst vówr

Ffoulkes, *f.n.*, fouks, fōks; fuks, fooks

Ffrangcon, *f.n.*, 'fræŋkən, fránk-ŏn

Ffrangcon-Davies, Gwen, *actress*, ˌgwen ˈfræŋkən ˈdeɪvɪs, gwén fránkŏn dáyviss

ffrench-Beytagh, *f.n.*, 'frenʃ ˈbitə, frénsh bĕétă

Ffynnongroyw, *also spelt* **Ffynnon Groew,** *Clwyd*, ˌfʌnənˈgrɔɪu, funnŏn-gróy-oo

Fiander, *f.n.*, faɪˈændər, fī-ándĕr

Fiddes *Grampian*, 'fɪdɪs, fiddĕss

Fidelis, *C.n.*, fɪˈdeɪlɪs, fidáyliss

Fidelo, *f.n.*, fɪˈdeloʊ, fidéllŏ

Fidler, *f.n.*, 'fɪdlər, fídlĕr; 'fidlər, feédlĕr

Fidra, Isle of, *Lothian*, 'fɪdrə, feédră

Field Dalling *Norfolk*, 'fild 'dɔlɪŋ, feéld dáwling

Fielding, *f.n.*, 'fildɪŋ, feélding. *Appropriate for Henry ∼, 18th-c. author.*

Fienburgh, *f.n.*, 'fɪnbərə, feénbŭră

Fiennes, *f.n.*, faɪnz, fīnz

Fife *Scotland*, faɪf, fīf

Fifield Bavant *Wilts.*, 'faɪfild 'bævənt, fīfeeld bávvănt

Figgis, *f.n.*, 'fɪgɪs, figgiss

Figgures, *f.n.*, 'fɪgərz, fíggŭrz

Figheldean *Wilts.*, 'faɪldɪn, fīldeen

Figueroa, *f.n.*, ˌfɪgəˈroʊə, figgĕrő-ă

Figures, *f.n.*, 'fɪgərz, fíggŭrz

Filby, *f.n.*, 'fɪlbɪ, fílbi

Filcher, *f.n.*, 'fɪltʃər, fíltchĕr

Fildes, *f.n.*, faɪldz, fīldz

Filey *N. Yorks.*, 'faɪlɪ, fíli

Filleigh *Devon*, 'fɪlɪ, filli

Fillongley *Warwicks.*, 'fɪlɒŋlɪ, fillong-li

Filmer, *f.n.*, 'fɪlmər, fílmĕr

Finaghy *Co. Antrim*, 'fɪnaxɪ, fínnáchi

Finavon *Forfar*, fɪn'eɪvən, fináyvŏn

Finborough Parva *Suffolk*, ˈfɪnbərə ˈpɑrvə, fínbŭră páarvă

Fincastle *Tayside*, fɪn'kɑsl, fin-káassl. *Appropriate also for Viscount ∼.*

Finchale *Durham*, 'fɪŋkl, fínkl. *Appropriate also for ∼ Abbey.*

Fincham, *f.n.*, 'fɪntʃəm, fíntchăm

Finchampstead *Berks.*, 'fɪnʃəmsted, fínshămsted

Finchingfield *Essex*, 'fɪnʃɪŋfild, fínshingfeeld

Finchley *London*, 'fɪntʃlɪ, fíntchli; 'fɪnʃlɪ, fínshli

Findern *Derby.*, 'fɪndərn, fíndĕrn

Findhorn *Grampian*, 'fɪndhɔrn, fínd-horn

Findlater, *f.n.*, 'fɪnlətər, fínlătĕr; 'fɪndlətər, fíndlătĕr

Findlater *Grampian*, 'fɪndlətər, fíndlătĕr

Findlay, *f.n.*, 'fɪnlɪ, fínli; 'fɪndlɪ, fíndli

Findley, *f.n.*, 'fɪndlɪ, fíndli

Findochty *Grampian*, fɪn'dɒxtɪ, findóchti; fɪ'nextɪ, finnéchti

Finedon *Northants.*, 'faɪndən, fíndŏn

Finer, *f.n.*, 'faɪnər, fínĕr

Fingal, *Norse hero*, 'fɪŋgl, fíng-gl

Fingal's Cave *Staffa*, 'fɪŋglz 'keɪv, fíng-glz káyv

Fingalian, *pertaining to* **Fingal**, fɪŋˈgeɪlɪən, fing-gáyliăn

Fingall, Earl of, fɪŋ'gɔl, fing-gáwl

Fingest *Bucks.*, 'fɪndʒɪst, finjĕst

Fingland, *f.n.*, 'fɪŋlənd, fíng-lánd

Fingringhoe *Essex*, 'fɪŋrɪŋhoʊ, fíng-ring-hō

Finis, *f.n.*, 'fɪnɪs, fínniss

Finkelstein, *f.n.*, 'fɪŋkəlstaɪn, fínkĕl-stīn

Finlay, *f.n.*, 'fɪnlɪ, finli

Finlayson, *f.n.*, 'fɪnlɪsən, fínlissŏn

Finnart *S'clyde*, 'fɪnɑrt, fínnărt

Finnerty, *f.n.*, 'fɪnərtɪ, fínnĕrti

Finney, *f.n.*, 'fɪnɪ, fínni

Finnie, *f.n.*, 'fɪnɪ, fínni

Finnieston *S'clyde*, 'fɪnɪstən, fínnistŏn

Finnissy, *f.n.*, 'fɪnɪsɪ, fínnissi

Finnucane, *f.n.*, fɪ'nukən, finoo-kăn; fɪ'njukən, finéwkăn

Finsberg, *f.n.*, 'fɪnzbərg, fínzberg

Finsbury Park *London*, 'fɪnzbərɪ ˈpɑrk, fínzbŭri páark

Finstown *Orkney*, 'fɪnstən, fínsstŏn

Fintona *Co. Tyrone*, 'fɪntənə, fíntŏnă

Finucane, f.n., fı'nukən, finoókän; fı'njukən, finéwkayn; fı'njukən, finéwkän

Finvoy Co. Antrim, 'fınvɔı, fínvoy

Finzean Grampian, 'fıŋən, fing-än

Finzi, Gerald, composer, 'fınzı, fínzi

Fionda, f.n., fı'ɒndə, fi-óndä

Fior, f.n., 'fiɔr, fée-or

Firle, West, E. Sussex, fərl, firl

Firmager, f.n., 'fərmədʒər, fírmäjĕr

Firman, f.n., 'fərmən, fírmän

Firminger, f.n., 'fərmındʒər, fírminjĕr

Firth, f.n., fərθ, firth

Firth of Forth separates Lothian and Fife regions, 'fərθ əv 'fɔrθ, fírth ŏv fórth

Firth of Lorn S'clyde, 'fərθ əv 'lɔrn, fírth ŏv lórn

Fisch, f.n., fıʃ, fish

Fisherie Grampian, 'fıʃərı, físhĕri

Fishguard Dyfed, 'fıʃgɑrd, físhgaard

Fishwick, f.n., 'fıʃwık, físh-wick

Fison, f.n., 'faısən, físsŏn

Fitchew, f.n., 'fıtʃu, fítchoo

Fitzailwyn, f.n., fıts'eılwın, fits-áylwin

Fitzgerald, f.n., fıts'dʒerəld, fits-jérräld

Fitzgibbon, f.n., fıts'gıbən, fits-gíbbŏn

Fitzhardinge, f.n., fıts'hɑrdıŋ, fits-haárding

Fitzpatrick, f.n., fıts'pætrık, fits-pátrick

Fitzrandolph, f.n., fıts'rændɒlf, fits-rándolf

Fitzroy, f.n., 'fıtsrɔı, fítsroy

Fitzsimons, f.n., fıts'saımənz, fits-símŏnz

Fitzwalter, Baron, fıts'wɔltər, fits-wáwltĕr

Flach, f.n., flæk, flack

Flackes, f.n., flæks, flacks

Flaherty, f.n., 'flɑhərtı, flaá-hĕrti; 'flɑərtı, flaá-ĕrti

Flamsteed, f.n., 'flæmstid, flám-steed

Flannan Isles W. Isles, 'flænən, flánnän

Flat Holm Island S. Glam., 'flæt houm, flát hōm

Flavell, f.n., 'fleıvl, fláyvl; flə'vel, flävéll

Flavin, f.n., 'fleıvın, fláyvin

Flawith N. Yorks., 'flɔ-ıθ, fláw--ith; flɔıθ, floyth

Flax Bourton Avon, 'flæks 'bɔrtən, flácks bórtŏn

Fleggburgh Norfolk, 'flegbərə, flégbŭrä

Fleggon, f.n., 'flegɒn, fléggon

Fleischman, f.n., 'flaıʃmən, flíshmän

Flekier, f.n., 'flekıər, fléckeer

Fleming, f.n., 'flemıŋ, flémming

Flemons, f.n., 'flemənz, flémmŏnz

Flessati, f.n., flə'satı, flĕssaáti

Fletcher, f.n., 'fletʃər, flétchĕr

Flett, f.n., flet, flett

Fleur de Lis Gwent, ,flər də 'li, flur dĕ lée

Fleure, f.n., flər, flur

Flewin, f.n., 'fluın, floó-in

Flint Clwyd, flınt, flint

Flintham Notts., 'flıntəm, flíntäm

Flitwick Beds., 'flıtık, flíttick

Floate, f.n., flout, flōt

Flood, f.n., flʌd, fludd

Floore see Flore

Flore, also spelt Floore, Northants., flɔr, flor

Florey, f.n., 'flɔrı, fláwri. Appropriate also for the Barony of ~.

Floris, f.n., 'flɒrıs, flórriss

Flotta Island Orkney, 'flɒtə, flóttä

Floud, f.n., flʌd, fludd

Flower, f.n., 'flavər, flówĕr

Flury, f.n., 'fluərı, floóri

Flux, f.n., flʌks, flucks

Fochabers Grampian, 'fɒxəbərz, fóchäbĕrz

Fochriw Mid Glam., 'vɒxrıu, vóchri-oo

Foco Novo, theatre company, 'foukou 'nouvou, fókō nóvō

Foden, f.n., 'foudən, fódĕn

Foel Powys, vɔıl, voyl

Fogarty, f.n., 'fougərtı, fógärti

Fogerty, f.n., 'fougərtı, fógĕrti

Foges, f.n., 'fougıs, fógĕss

Foggin, f.n., 'fɒgın, fóggin

Fogou Caves Cornwall, 'fugu, foógoo

Folan, f.n., 'foulən, fólän

Folger, f.n., 'fɒlgər, fólgĕr

Foljambe, f.n., 'fuldʒəm, foóljäm. Family name of the Earl of Liverpool.

Folkard, f.n., 'foukərd, fókärd; 'foulkɑrd, fól-kaard; 'fɒlkɑrd, fól-kaard

Folke Dorset, fouk, fōk

Folkes, f.n., fouks, fōks

Folkestone Kent, 'foukstən, fókstŏn. Appropriate also for Viscount ~.

Folking W. Sussex, 'fɒlkıŋ, fól--king

Folkingham Lincs., 'fɒkıŋəm, fócking-äm

Folkington E. Sussex, 'fouıŋtən, fó-ingtŏn

Folwell, f.n., 'fɒlwəl, fól-wĕl

Fomison, *f.n.,* 'fɒmɪsən, fómmis-sŏn

Fontaine, *f.n.,* 'fɒnteɪn, fóntayn

Fonteyn, Dame **Margot,** *ballerina,* 'mɑrgoʊ 'fɒnteɪn, maárgō fóntayn; fon'teɪn, fontáyn. *Dame Margot herself finds that the stress varies according to the context.*

Fookes, *f.n.,* fuks, fooks

Foord, *f.n.,* fɔrd, ford

Foort, *f.n.,* fɔrt, fort

Foot, *f.n.,* fʊt, fŏŏt

Footdee *Grampian,* fʊt'di, fŏŏt-dée; 'fɪtɪ, fítti

Footler, *f.n.,* 'fʊtlər, fŏŏtlĕr

Forbes, *f.n.,* 'fɔrbɪs, fórbĕss; fɔrbz, forbz. *The first, which is appropriate for Baron ~ and for the Master of ~, is more usual in what used to be Aberdeenshire, the home county of the Clan Forbes.*

Forbes-Sempill, *f.n.,* 'fɔrbɪs 'sempl, fórbĕss sémpl. *Family name of the Barons of Sempill.*

Ford, Ford Madox, *author,* 'fɔrd 'mædəks 'fɔrd, fórd máddŏcks fórd. *Formerly* **Ford Madox Hueffer,** *q.v.*

Forde, *f.n.,* fɔrd, ford

Fordell *Fife,* fɔr'del, fordéll

Fordham *Cambs.,* 'fɔrdəm, fórdăm

Fordoun *Grampian,* fɔr'dun, fordóon

Fordred, *f.n.,* 'fɔrdrɪd, fórdrĕd

Fordwich *Kent,* 'fɔrdwɪtʃ, fórdwitch; 'fɔrdɪtʃ, fórditch

Fordyce, *f.n.,* fɔr'daɪs, fordíss

Fordyce *Grampian,* fɔr'daɪs, fordíss

Foren, *f.n.,* 'fɔrən, fáwrĕn

Fores, *f.n.,* fɔrz, forz

Forestier, *f.n.,* 'fɒrɪstjər, fórrĕst-yĕr

Forfar *Tayside,* 'fɔrfər, fórfăr

Forgan, *f.n.,* 'fɔrgən, fórgăn

Forgandenny *Tayside,* ,fɔrgən-'denɪ, forgăndénni

Forkhill, *also spelt* **Forkill,** *Co. Armagh,* 'fɔrkɪl, fórkill

Formatine, Viscount, fər'matɪn, fŏrmaátin

Forncett St. Mary *Norfolk,* 'fɔrnsɪt snt 'meərɪ, fórnssĕt sĭnt maíri

Forncett St. Peter *Norfolk,* 'fɔrnsɪt snt 'pitər, fórnssĕt sĭnt péetĕr

Fornsete, John of, *13th-c. composer,* 'fɔrnset, fórnsett

Forrabury *Cornwall,* 'fɒrəbərɪ, fórrăbŭri

Forran, *f.n.,* fɔ'ræn, fawránn

Forres *Grampian,* 'fɒrɪs, fórrĕss. *Appropriate also for Baron ~.*

Forster, *f.n.,* 'fɔrstər, fórstĕr; 'fɒstər, fósstĕr. *The first is appropriate for E. M. ~, author, the second for the late Baron ~ of Harraby.*

Forsyth, *f.n.,* fər'saɪθ, forssíth

Forsythe, *f.n.,* fər'saɪθ, forssíth; fər'saɪð, forssíth; 'fərsaɪθ, fórssíth

Fortbreda *Co. Down,* fɔrt'brɪdə, fortbreédă

Forte, *f.n.,* 'fɔrtɪ, fórti

Forter *Castle Tayside,* 'fɔrtər, fórtĕr

Fortescue, Earl, 'fɔrtɪskju, fórtĕskew

Forteviot *Tayside,* fɔr'tɪvɪət, fortéeviŏt. *Appropriate also for Baron ~.*

Forth, River, *Central,* fɔrθ, forth

Fortingall *Tayside,* 'fɔrtɪŋgl, fórting-gl

Fortrose *H'land,* 'fɔrtroʊz, fórtrōz

Fortuin, *f.n.,* 'fɔrtjʊɪn, fórt-yŏŏ-in; fər'taɪn, fortín

Foryd, Stream, *Gwynedd,* 'vɒrɪd, vórrid

Fosdyke *Lincs.,* 'fɒzdaɪk, fózdík

Foster, *f.n.,* 'fɒstər, fósstĕr

Fotheringhay *Northants.,* 'fɒðər-ɪŋheɪ, fóthering-hay; 'fɒðərɪŋgeɪ, fótheringgay. *The first is the village pronunciation today. The other is more usual for historic ~ Castle.*

Foubert *Place London,* 'fubərt, foóbĕrt

Foudland *Grampian,* 'faʊdlənd, fówdländ

Foula *Shetland,* 'fulə, foólă

Foulden *Borders,* 'fuldən, foólděn

Foulds, *f.n.,* fouldz, fōldz. *Appropriate for John ~, composer.*

Foulger, *f.n.,* 'fuldʒər, foóljĕr; 'fuldʒər, foóljĕr; 'fouldʒər, fōljĕr; 'fɒldʒər, fóljĕr; 'fulgər, foólgĕr

Foulis, *f.n.,* faʊlz, fowlz

Foulis *H'land,* faʊlz, fowlz. *Appropriate also for ~ Castle.*

Foulis Ferry *H'land,* 'faʊlz 'ferɪ, fówlz férri

Foulkes, *f.n.,* foʊks, fōks; faʊks, fowks

Foulness *Essex, Humberside,* 'faʊl'nes, fówl-néss. *In Essex this is an island; in Humberside, a river.*

Foulridge *Lancs.*, 'fʊʊlrɪdʒ, fṓlrij

Foulsham, *f.n.*, 'fʊlʃəm, fṓol--shăm

Foulsham *Norfolk*, 'fʊʊlʃəm, fṓl-shăm; 'fʊlʃəm, fṓol-shăm; 'fʊʊlsəm, fṓolssăm

Foulshiels *Borders*, 'faʊl'ʃilz, fṓwl-sheélz

Fountaine, *f.n.*, 'faʊntɪn, fówntin

Fourcin, *f.n.*, 'fɔrsɪn, fórssin

Four Gotes *Cambs.*, 'fɔr goʊts, fór gṓts

Foux, *f.n.*, fuks, fooks

Fovant *Wilts.*, 'fɒvənt, fóvvănt

Foweraker, *f.n.*, 'faʊəreɪkər, fówĕraykĕr

Fowey *Cornwall*, 'fɔɪ, foy

Fowke, *f.n.*, foʊk, fōk; faʊk, fowk

Fowkes, *f.n.*, foʊks, fōks; faʊks, fowks

Fowlds, *f.n.*, foʊldz, fōldz

Fowles, *f.n.*, faʊlz, fowlz

Fowlis Easter *Tayside*, 'faʊlz 'istər, fówlz eéstĕr

Fowlis Wester *Tayside*, 'faʊlz 'westər, fówlz wéstĕr

Fowlmere *Cambs.*, 'faʊlmɪər, fówlmeer

Fownhope *H. & W.*, 'faʊnhoʊp, fówn-hōp

Fox, Uffa, *yacht designer*, 'ʌfə 'fɒks, úffá fócks

Foxell, *f.n.*, 'fɒksl, fócksl

Foxen, *f.n.*, 'fɒksən, fócksĕn

Foxhole *W. Glam.*, 'fɒkshoʊl, fócks-hōl

Foxt *Staffs.*, fɒkst, fockst

Foy, *f.n.*, fɔɪ, foy

Foyle, *f.n.*, fɔɪl, foyl

Fozzard, *f.n.*, 'fɒzard, fózzaard

Fradin, *f.n.*, 'freɪdɪn, fráydin

Fraenkel, *f.n.*, 'fræŋkl, fránkl

Frahill, *f.n.*, frɑl, fraal

Framingham *Norfolk*, 'fræmɪŋəm, frámming-ăm

Franche *H. & W.*, frɒnʃ, fraansh

Francillon, *f.n.*, fræn'sɪlən, fran--síllŏn

Francke, *f.n.*, 'fræŋkɪ, fránki

Francome, *f.n.*, 'fræŋkəm, fránkŏm

Franey, *f.n.*, 'freɪnɪ, fráyni

Frankau, *f.n.*, 'fræŋkoʊ, fránkō; 'fræŋkaʊ, fránkow. *The first is appropriate for* Gilbert ∼, *author, and for* Pamela ∼, *author.*

Frankel, *f.n.*, 'fræŋkl, fránkl

Frankell, *f.n.*, 'fræŋkl, fránkl

Frankenburgh, *f.n.*, 'fræŋkənbərg, fránkĕnburg

Franklin, *f.n.*, 'fræŋklɪn, fránklin

Franklyn, *f.n.*, 'fræŋklɪn, fránklin

Frant *E. Sussex*, frænt, frant

Fraser, *f.n.*, 'freɪzər, fráyzĕr

Fraser of Allander, Barony of, 'freɪzər əv 'æləndər, fráyzĕr ŏv áländĕr

Fraser of Dineiddwg, Baronetcy of, 'freɪzər əv dɪ'naɪðʊg, fráyzĕr ŏv diníthŏŏg

Fraserburgh *Grampian*, 'freɪzərbərə, fráyzĕrbŭră

Frater, *f.n.*, 'freɪtər, fráytĕr

Frating *Essex*, 'freɪtɪŋ, fráyting

Frazer, *f.n.*, 'freɪzər, fráyzĕr

Freake, *f.n.*, frik, freek

Freakes, *f.n.*, friks, freeks

Frears, *f.n.*, frɛərz, frairz; frɪərz, freerz

Frecheville *S. Yorks.*, 'fretʃvɪl, frétchvil

Fredman, *f.n.*, 'fredmən, frédmän

Freegard, *f.n.*, 'frigɑrd, freégaard

Freeson, *f.n.*, 'frisən, freéssŏn

Freethy, *f.n.*, 'friθɪ, freéthi

Freiston *Lincs.*, 'fristən, freésstŏn

Freke, *f.n.*, frik, freek

Fremantle, *f.n.*, 'frimæntl, free-mantl; frɪ'mæntl, freemántl

Fremington *Devon*, 'fremɪŋtən, frémmingtŏn

French, *f.n.*, frenʃ, frensh

Frenchay *Avon*, 'frenʃeɪ, frén-shay

Frere, *f.n.*, frɪər, freer; frɛər, frair

Fressanges, *f.n.*, 'fresɑʒ, frés-saangzh

Freswick *H'land*, 'frezwɪk, fréz-wick; 'frezɪk, frézzick

Freuchie *Fife*, 'fruxɪ, froóchi

Freud, *f.n.*, frɔɪd, froyd

Freugh, East *and* West, *D. & G.*, frux, frooch

Freyberg, *f.n.*, 'fraɪbərg, fríberg. *Appropriate also for Baron* ∼.

Freyer, *f.n.*, 'frɪər, freé-ĕr; 'fraɪər, frí-ĕr

Freyhan, *f.n.*, 'fraɪhən, frí-hän

Fricker, *f.n.*, 'frɪkər, frickĕr

Frideswide, *8th-c. abbess*, 'frɪdɪswɪdə, fríddĕssweedĕ

Fridge, *f.n.*, frɪdʒ, frij

Fried, *f.n.*, frid, freed

Friedman, *f.n.*, 'fridmən, freéd-män

Frieght, *f.n.*, freɪt, frayt; fraɪt, frīt

Friel, *f.n.*, fril, freel

Friend, *f.n.*, frend, frend

Friern Barnet *London*, 'fraɪərn 'bɑrnɪt, frí-ĕrn baárnĕt; 'frɪərn 'bɑrnɪt, freérn baárnĕt

Friesden *see* **Frithsden**

Friese-Greene, William, *motion-picture pioneer*, 'friz 'grin, freéz greén

Frieth *Bucks.*, friθ, freeth
Frindsbury *Kent*, 'frındzbərı, fríndzbŭri
Frinton-on-Sea *Essex*, 'frıntən ɒn 'si, fríntön on seé
Friockheim *Tayside*, 'frikım, freékim
Frisch, *f.n.*, frıʃ, frish
Frise, *f.n.*, friz, freez
Friskney *Lincs.*, 'frısknı, frískni
Friters, *f.n.*, 'fritərz, freétērz
Fritham *Hants*, 'friðəm, fríthăm
Frithelstock *Devon*, 'friθlstɒk, fríthl-stock
Frithsden, *also spelt* Friesden, *Herts.*, 'frizdən, freézdĕn; 'frızdən, frízdĕn
Frizelle, *f.n.*, frı'zel, frizéll
Frizinghall *W. Yorks.*, 'fraızıŋhɔl, frízing-hawl
Frizington *Cumbria*, 'frızıŋtən, frízzingtön
Frocester *Glos.*, 'frɒstər, frósstēr
Frodin, *f.n.*, 'froudın, fródin
Frodingham *Humberside*, 'frɒdıŋəm, fródding-ăm
Frodsham *Ches.*, 'frɒdʃəm, fród-shăm
Froest, *f.n.*, 'frouıst, frô-ĕst
Fromanteel, *f.n.*, 'froumәntil, frômänteel
Frome *Somerset*, frum, froom
Frome, *Rivers, Dorset, Somerset*, frum, froom
Frome Vauchurch *Dorset*, 'frum 'voutʃartʃ, froôm vôchurtch
Fron *Clwyd, Gwynedd, Powys*, vrɒn, vron
Fronallt *Gwynedd*, 'vrɒnəlt, vrónnählt
Froncysyllte, *also spelt* Fronsysylltau, Vroncysyllte, *Clwyd*, ˌvrɒnkə'sʌltei, vron-kässúhltay
Frongoch *Gwynedd*, vrɒn'goux, vron-góch
Frood, *f.n.*, frud, frood
Frossard, *f.n.*, 'frɒsard, fróssaard
Frostenden *Suffolk*, 'frɒsəndən, fróssĕndĕn
Froswick *Cumbria*, 'frɒsık, fróssick
Froud, *f.n.*, fraud, frowd
Froude, *f.n.*, frud, frood. *Appropriate for James Anthony ~, 19th-c. historian.*
Frow, *f.n.*, frau, frow
Frowde, *f.n.*, fraud, frowd
Fryd, *f.n.*, frid, frid
Fryirs, *f.n.*, 'fraıərz, frí-ĕrz
Fryston *N. Yorks.*, 'fraıstən, frísstön
Fuchs, *f.n.*, fuks, foóks; fuks, fooks. *The first is appropriate*

for Sir Vivian ~, geologist and explorer.
Fuest, *f.n.*, fjust, fewst
Fugaccia, *f.n.*, fu'gætʃıә, foôgátch-iă
Fuge, *f.n.*, fjudʒ, fewj
Fuinary *S'clyde*, 'fjunәrı, féwnări
Fujino, *f.n.*, 'fjudʒınou, féwjinō
Fuke, *f.n.*, fjuk, fewk
Fulbourn *Cambs.*, 'fulbɔrn, foól-born
Fulham *London*, 'fuləm, foólăm
Fulke, *C.n. and f.n.*, fulk, foólk
Fulker, *f.n.*, 'fulkər, foólkĕr
Fulkes, *f.n.*, fulks, foólks
Fulking *W. Sussex*, 'fulkıŋ, foólking
Fullom, *f.n.*, 'fuləm, foólŏm
Fulmodestone *Norfolk*, 'fulməs-tən, foólmĕstŏn
Fulstow *Lincs.*, 'fulstou, foóls-stō
Fulwell *London*, 'fulwel, foól-wel
Fundenhall *Norfolk*, 'fʌndənhɔl, fúndĕn-hawl
Furlonge, *f.n.*, 'fɜrlɒŋ, fúrlong
Furnace *Dyfed, S'clyde*, 'fɜrnıs, fúrniss
Furnas, *f.n.*, 'fɜrnıs, fúrniss
Furneaux, Viscount, 'fɜrnou, fúrnō
Furnell, *f.n.*, fɜr'nel, furnéll
Furness, *f.n.*, 'fɜrnıs, fúrnĕss; fɜr'nes, furnéss. *The first is appropriate for Viscount ~.*
Furneux Pelham *Herts.*, 'fɜrnıks 'peləm, fúrnicks péllăm; 'fɜrnou 'peləm, fúrnō péllăm
Furnivall, Barony of, 'fɜrnıvl, fúrnivl
Furth, *f.n.*, fɜrθ, furth
Fuseli, Henry, *18th–19th-c. painter and author*, 'fjuzəlı, féwzĕli; fju'zelı, fewzélli. *Perhaps the most commonly accepted of a variety of pronunciations. He was originally Johann Heinrich Füssli, a native of Zurich.*
Fushiebridge *Lothian*, 'fuʃıbrıdʒ, foóshibrij
Fussell, *f.n.*, 'fʌsl, fússl
Fussey, *f.n.*, 'fʌsı, fússi
Futrille, *f.n.*, fjutrıl, féwtril
Fyfield, *f.n.*, 'faıfild, fífeeld
Fylde *Lancs.*, faıld, fild
Fyleman, *f.n.*, 'faılmən, fílmăn
Fylingdales *N. Yorks.*, 'faılıŋdeılz, fíling-daylz
Fyne, Loch, *S'clyde*, faın, fín
Fysh, *f.n.*, faıʃ, fish
Fyson, *f.n.*, 'faısən, físsŏn
Fyvel, *f.n.*, 'faıvl, fívl
Fyvie *Grampian*, 'faıvı, fívi

G

Gabain, *f.n.*, 'gə'beɪn, găbáyn
Gabalfa *S. Glam.*, gə'bælvə, găbálvă
Gabbitas, *f.n.*, 'gæbɪtæs, găbbitass
Gaber, *f.n.*, 'geɪbər, gáybĕr
Gabor, *f.n.*, 'gabɔr, gaábor
Gabriel, *C.n. and f.n.*, 'geɪbrɪəl, gáybri-ĕl
Gadbury, *f.n.*, 'gædbərɪ, gádbŭri
Gaddarn, *f.n.*, gə'darn, gădáarn
Gaddesby *Leics.*, 'gædzbɪ, gádzbi
Gaddesden, Great *and* Little, *Herts.*, 'gædzdən, gádzdĕn
Gadfan, *Welsh C.n.*, 'gædvən, gádvăn
Gadie Burn *Grampian*, 'gadɪ 'bərn, gaádi búrn
Gadlys *Mid Glam.*, *S. Glam.*, 'gædlɪs, gádliss
Gaenor, *Welsh C.n.*, 'geɪnər, gáynŏr; 'gaɪnər, gínor
Gaenor, *f.n.*, 'geɪnər, gáynŏr
Gaerwen *Gwynedd*, 'gaɪərwən, gírwĕn
Gaetjens, *f.n.*, 'geɪtjənz, gáyt-yĕnz
Gaffin, *f.n.*, 'gæfɪn, gáffin
Gagan, *f.n.*, 'geɪgən, gáygăn
Gage, *f.n.*, geɪdʒ, gayj
Gahan, *f.n.*, 'geɪən, gáy-ăn; gan, gaan
Gaick Forest *H'land*, 'gaɪk, gaá-ick; gaɪk, gík
Gaiger, *f.n.*, 'geɪdʒər, gáyjĕr
Gaillard, *f.n.*, 'geɪlɑrd, gáylaard; 'gaɪɑrd, gí-aard
Gainford, Baron, 'geɪnfərd, gáynfŏrd
Gainsborough *Lincs.*, 'geɪnzbərə, gáynzbŭră. *Appropriate also for the Earl of ~.*
Gair, *f.n.*, geər, gair
Gairdner, *f.n.*, 'gardnər, gaárdnĕr; 'geərdnər, gáirdnĕr
Gaire, *f.n.*, geər, gair
Gairloch *H'land*, 'geərlɒx, gáirloch
Gaisgill *Cumbria*, 'geɪzgɪl, gáyzgil
Gaitens, *f.n.*, 'geɪtənz, gáytĕnz
Gaitskell, *f.n.*, 'geɪtskəl, gáytskĕl. *Appropriate also for Baroness ~.*
Galashiels *Borders*, ˌgælə'ʃɪlz, gală-shéelz
Galbally *Co. Tyrone*, 'gælbəlɪ, gálbăli
Galbraith, *f.n.*, gæl'breɪθ, galbráyth

Galby *Leics.*, 'gɔlbɪ, gáwlbi
Gale, *C.n. and f.n.*, geɪl, gayl
Galena, *f.n.*, gə'linə, găleená
Galgate *Lancs.*, 'gɔlgeɪt, gáwlgayt
Galgorm *Co. Antrim*, gæl'gɔrm, galgórm
Galica, *f.n.*, gə'lɪtsə, gălítsă
Galitzine, *f.n.*, gæ'lɪtsɪn, galítseen
Gall, *f.n.*, gɔl, gawl
Gallacher, *f.n.*, 'gæləxər, gáláchĕr; 'gæləhər, gálă-hĕr
Gallagher, *f.n.*, 'gæləxər, gáláchĕr
Gallannaugh, *f.n.*, 'gælənɔ, gálănaw
Gallati, *f.n.*, gə'lætɪ, gălátti
Galleozzie, *f.n.*, ˌgælɪ'ɒtsɪ, gali-ótsi
Gallovidian, native of **Galloway**, ˌgæloʊ'vɪdɪən, galōvíddiăn
Galloway *D. & G.*, 'gæləweɪ, gálŏ-way. *Appropriate also for the Earl of ~.*
Gallwey, *f.n.*, 'gɔlweɪ, gáwlway
Galmpton *Devon*, 'gæmptən, gámptŏn
Galpern, *f.n.*, 'gælpərn, gálpĕrn
Galpin, *f.n.*, 'gælpɪn, gálpin
Galston *S'clyde*, 'gɔlstən, gáwlstŏn
Galsworthy, *f.n.*, 'gɔlzwɜrðɪ, gáwlzwurthi; 'gælzwərðɪ, gálzwurthi. *Although the first was the pronunciation of John ~, author, some members of the family prefer to use the second.*
Galwally *Co. Antrim*, gæl'wælɪ, galwáli
Galway, Viscount, 'gɔlweɪ, gáwlway
Gaman, *f.n.*, 'geɪmən, gáymăn
Gambier, *f.n.*, 'gæmbɪər, gámbi-ĕr
Gamblin, *f.n.*, 'gæmblɪn, gámblin
Gambold, *f.n.*, 'gæmboʊld, gámbōld
Gambon, *f.n.*, 'gæmbɒn, gámbon
Gamesley *Derby.*, 'geɪmzlɪ, gáymzli
Gamjee, *f.n.*, 'gæmdʒɪ, gámjee
Gamlen, *f.n.*, 'gæmlɪn, gámlĕn
Gamlin, *f.n.*, 'gæmlɪn, gámlin
Gamlingay *Cambs.*, 'gæmlɪŋeɪ, gámling-gay
Gammans, *f.n.*, 'gæmənz, gámmănz
Gammell, *f.n.*, 'gæml, gámml
Gammie, *f.n.*, 'gæmɪ, gámmi
Gamon, *f.n.*, 'geɪmən, gáymŏn
Gampell, *f.n.*, 'gæmpl, gámpl
Gandar, *f.n.*, 'gændər, gándăr
Gandee, *f.n.*, 'gændɪ, gándi
Gandy, *f.n.*, 'gændɪ, gándi
Gangel, *f.n.*, 'gæŋgl, gáng-gl
Gannaway *Co. Down*, 'gænəweɪ, gánnă-way

Gannon, *f.n.,* 'gænən, gánnŏn

Gaping Gill Hole, *also spelt* **Ghyll,** *N. Yorks.,* 'geɪpɪŋ 'gɪl, gáyping gill

Garard, *f.n.,* 'gærərd, gárraard

Garboldisham *Norfolk,* 'garblʃəm, ga'arbl-shăm

Garcia, *f.n.,* 'garsɪə, ga'arssiă; 'garʃɪə, ga'arshiă

Garcke, *f.n.,* 'garkɪ, ga'arki

Gard, *f.n.,* gard, gaard

Gardiner, *f.n.,* 'gardnər, ga'ardnĕr. *Appropriate also for Baron* ∼.

Gardy Loo Gully *Ben Nevis,* 'gardɪ 'lu, ga'ardi loó

Gardyne, *f.n.,* gar'daɪn, gaardín

Garel-Jones, *f.n.,* 'gærəl 'dʒoʊnz, gárrĕl-jónz

Gare Loch, The, *S'clyde,* 'gɛər lɒx, gáir loch

Garendon *Leics.,* 'gærəndən, gárrĕndŏn

Garfield, Leon, *author,* 'liən 'garfild, leé-ŏn gaarfeeld

Garforth *W. Yorks.,* 'garfərθ, ga'ar-fŏrth

Garigue, *f.n.,* 'gærɪgju, gárrigew

Garin, *f.n.,* 'gærɪn, gárrin

Garioch, *f.n.,* 'gærɪəx, gárriŏch

Garioch *Grampian,* 'gɪərɪ, geéri

Garlieston *D. & G.,* 'garlɪstən, ga'arlistŏn

Garlinge Green *Kent,* 'garlɪndʒ 'grin, ga'arlinj greén

Garmonsway, *f.n.,* 'garmənzweɪ, ga'armŏnzway

Garmoyle, Viscount, gar'mɔɪl, gaarmóyl

Garnant *Dyfed,* 'garnænt, ga'ar-nant

Garndiffaith *Gwent,* garn'dɪfaɪθ, gaarndiffíth

Garnedd-wen *Clwyd,* ‚garnəð-'wen, gaarnĕth-wén

Garneddwen *Gwynedd,* gar-'neðwən, gaarnéth-wĕn

Garnet, *f.n.,* 'garnɪt, ga'arnĕt

Garnethill *Glasgow,* ‚garnɪt'hɪl, gaarnĕt-híll

Garnett, *f.n.,* 'garnɪt, ga'arnĕt

Garn-fach *Gwent,* garn'vax, gaarnva'ach

Garngoch Common *W. Glam.,* garn'gɒx, gaarn-góch

Garnsworthy, *f.n.,* 'garnzwɜrðɪ, ga'arnzwurthi. *Appropriate also for the Barony of* ∼.

Garrard, *f.n.,* 'gærard, gárraard

Garrett, *f.n.,* 'gærɪt, gárrĕt

Garron Point *Co. Antrim,* 'gærən, gárrŏn

Garry, River, *Tayside,* 'gærɪ, gárri

Garryduff *Co. Antrim,* ‚gærɪ'dʌf, garridúff

Garscadden *Glasgow,* gars-'kædən, gaarsskáddĕn

Garside, *f.n.,* 'garsaɪd, ga'arssíd

Garsven *Skye,* 'garʃven, ga'arsh--ven

Gartcosh *S'clyde,* gart'kɒʃ, gaart-kósh

Garten, Loch, *H'land,* 'gartən, ga'artĕn

Garthbeibio *Powys,* garθ-'baɪbjou, gaarthbíb-yō

Garthbrengy *Powys,* garθ'breŋgɪ, gaarthbréng-gi

Gartheli *Dyfed,* gar'θelɪ, gaar--thélli

Garthmyl *Powys,* garθ'mil, gaarth-meél

Gartnavel Hospital *Glasgow,* gart'neɪvəl, gaart-náyvĕl

Gartocharn *S'clyde,* ‚gartə'xarn, gaartŏcha'arn

Gartsherrie *S'clyde,* gart'ʃerɪ, gaart-shérri

Garvagh, *f.n.,* 'garvə, ga'arvă

Garvagh *Co. Derry,* 'garvə, ga'arvă. *Appropriate also for Baron* ∼.

Garvald *Lothian,* 'garvəld, ga'arvăld

Garve *H'land,* garv, gaarv

Garvellach Isles, *also spelt* **Garvelloch,** *S'clyde,* gar'veləx, gaarvéllăch

Garvestone *Norfolk,* 'garvɪstən, ga'arvĕstŏn

Garvice, *f.n.,* 'garvɪs, ga'arviss

Garw *Mid Glam.,* 'gæru, gárroo

Garwell, *f.n.,* 'garwel, ga'arwel

Gary, *f.n.,* 'gɛərɪ, gáiri

Gascoigne, *f.n.,* 'gæskɔɪn, gásskoyn

Gascoin, *f.n.,* 'gæskɔɪn, gásskoyn

Gascoine, *f.n.,* 'gæskɔɪn, gásskoyn

Gascoyne, *f.n.,* 'gæskɔɪn, gásskoyn

Gaselee, *f.n.,* 'geɪzlɪ, gáyzli

Gash, *f.n.,* gæʃ, gash

Gaskell, *f.n.,* 'gæskl, gásskl

Gaskil, *f.n.,* 'gæskɪl, gásskil; 'gæskl, gásskl

Gassiot, *f.n.,* 'gæsɪət, gássiŏt

Gastrell, *f.n.,* 'gæstrəl, gástrĕl

Gatacre, *f.n.,* 'gætəkər, gáttăckĕr

Gateacre *Merseyside,* 'gætəkər, gáttăkĕr

Gatehouse of Fleet *D. & G.,* 'geɪthaʊs əv 'flit, gáyt-howss ŏv fleét

Gater, *f.n.,* 'geɪtər, gáytĕr

Gateshead *Tyne & Wear,* 'geɪtshed, gáyts-hed

Gathercole, *f.n.,* 'gæðərkoʊl, gáthĕr-kōl

Gathorne, *f.n.,* 'geɪθɔrn, gáy-thorn

Gathurst *Gtr. M'chester*, 'gæθərst, gáth-ŭrst

Gatlish, *f.n.*, 'gætlɪʃ, gátlish

Gatrell, *f.n.*, 'gætrəl, gátrĕl

Gatt, *f.n.*, gæt, gat

Gatward, *f.n.*, 'gætwɔrd, gátwawrd

Gatwick Airport *W. Sussex*, 'gætwɪk, gátwick

Gau, *f.n.*, gaʊ, gow

Gaubert, *f.n.*, 'goʊbɛər, góbair

Gauci, *f.n.*, 'gaʊtʃɪ, gówtchi

Gaudin, *f.n.*, 'gɔdɪn, gáwdin

Gaughan, *f.n.*, 'gɒhən, gó-hăn

Gauhan, *f.n.*, 'gɒhən, gó-hăn

Gauld, *f.n.*, gɔld, gawld

Gault, *f.n.*, gɔlt, gawlt; gɒlt, golt

Gauna, *f.n.*, 'gɒnə, gáwnă

Gauntlett, *f.n.*, 'gɒntlɪt, gáwntlĕt

Gausden, *f.n.*, 'gɔzdən, gáwzdĕn

Gaussen, *f.n.*, 'goʊsən, góssĕn

Gavall, *f.n.*, gə'væl, găvál

Gaved, *f.n.*, gævɪd, gávvĕd

Gavegan, *f.n.*, 'gævɪgən, gávvēgăn; gə'vegən, găvéggăn

Gaveston, *f.n.*, 'gævɪstən, gávvĕstŏn

Gavey, *f.n.*, 'geɪvɪ, gáyvi

Gavin, *C.n.*, 'gævɪn, gávvin

Gavinton *Borders*, 'gævɪntən, gávvintŏn

Gawith, *f.n.*, 'gaʊɪθ, gów-ith; 'geɪwɪθ, gáy-with

Gaymer, *f.n.*, 'geɪmər, gáymĕr

Gayton *Norfolk*, 'geɪtən, gáytŏn

Geake, *f.n.*, gik, geek

Geanies *H'land*, 'gɪnɪs, géeniss

Geard, *f.n.*, gɪərd, geerd

Geary, *f.n.*, 'gɪərɪ, géeri

Geaussent, *f.n.*, 'ʒoʊsɒŋ, zhóssong

Gebbie, *f.n.*, 'gebɪ, gébbi

Gebhard, *f.n.*, 'gebhard, gébhaard

Geddes, *f.n.*, 'gedɪs, géddĕss. *Appropriate also for Baron* ~.

Geddinge *Kent*, 'gedɪndʒ, géddinj

Geddington *Northants.*, 'gedɪŋtən, géddingtŏn

Geduld, *f.n.*, 'gedəld, géddŭld

Gedye, *f.n.*, 'gedɪ, géddi

Gee, *f.n.*, dʒɪ, jee

Geen, *f.n.*, gin, geen

Geesin, *f.n.*, 'gɪsɪn, géessin

Geeson, *f.n.*, 'dʒɪsən, jéessŏn

Geeston *Leics.*, 'gɪstən, géesstŏn

Geevor *Cornwall*, 'gɪvər, géevŏr

Geffen, *f.n.*, 'gefən, géffĕn

Geffrye Museum *London*, 'dʒefrɪ, jéffri

Gegan, *f.n.*, 'gɪgən, géegăn

Gegg, *f.n.*, geg, geg

Geiger, *f.n.*, 'gaɪgər, gígĕr

Geikie, *f.n.*, 'gɪkɪ, géeki

Geldeston *Norfolk*, 'geldstən, géldsstŏn; 'geldestən, géldesstŏn; 'gelstən, gélsstŏn

Geliot, *f.n.*, 'dʒelɪɒt, jélliŏt

Gell, *f.n.*, gel, gell; dʒel, jell

Gellan, *f.n.*, 'gelən, géllăn

Gellatly, *f.n.*, 'gelɒtlɪ, géllătli; gə'lætlɪ, gĕlátli

Gellender, *f.n.*, 'geləndər, géllĕndĕr

Geller, *f.n.*, 'gelər, géllĕr

Gelli *Mid Glam.*, 'gelɪ, géḥli

Gelli Aur, *Carmarthen County Agricultural College*, 'gelɪ 'aɪər, géḥli 'aïŏr

Gelli-gaer *Mid Glam.*, ˌgelɪ'gaɪər, geḥli-gír

Gelli Uchaf *Dyfed*, ˌgelɪ 'ɪxæv, geḥli íchavv; ˌgelɪ 'ɪxav, geḥli íxav, geḥli eechaav

Gelliceidrim *Colliery Dyfed*, ˌgelɪ'keɪdrɪm, geḥlikáydrim; ˌgelɪ'kaɪdrɪm, geḥlikídrim

Gellilydan *Gwynedd*, ˌgelɪ'lʌdən, geḥli-lúddăn

Gelling, *f.n.*, 'gelɪŋ, gélling

Gemmell, *f.n.*, 'geml, gémml

Gemmill, *f.n.*, 'geml, gémml

Gendros *W. Glam.*, 'gendrɒs, géndross

Genese, *f.n.*, dʒə'nis, jĕnéess

Genn, *f.n.*, gen, gen

Gent, *f.n.*, dʒent, jent

Gentry, *f.n.*, 'dʒentrɪ, jéntri

Geoffrey, *C.n.*, 'dʒefrɪ, jéffri

Geoghegan, *f.n.*, 'geɪgən, gáygăn

George-Brown, *Baron*, 'dʒɔrdʒ 'braʊn, jórj brówn

Georgeham *Devon*, 'dʒɔrdʒhæm, jórj-ham

Georgiadis, *f.n.*, ˌdʒɔrdʒɪ'adɪs, jorji-aádiss

Geraghty, *f.n.*, 'gerətɪ, gérrăti

Geraint, *Welsh C.n.*, 'geraɪnt, gérrint

Gerald, *C.n. and f.n.*, 'dʒerəld, jérrăld

Gerber, *f.n.*, 'dʒɜrbər, jérbĕr

Gercken, *f.n.*, 'gɜrkɪn, gérkĕn

Gerdes, *f.n.*, gɜr'diz, gerdéez

Gerhard, Roberto, *composer*, rə'bɜrtoʊ 'dʒerard, rŏbértō jérraard

Gerhardi, *f.n.*, dʒɜr'hardɪ, jĕr-haárdi

Gerhardie, William, *author*, dʒɜr'hardɪ, jĕr-haárdi

Gerhold, *f.n.*, 'gɜrhoʊld, gér-hōld

Gérin, *f.n.*, 'ʒeræ̃, zhérrang

Germain, *f.n.*, 'dʒɜrmeɪn, jérmayn

Germoe *Cornwall*, 'gɜrmoʊ, gérmō

Gerngross, *f.n.*, 'gɜrŋgrɒs, gérn-gross

Gerrans *Cornwall*, 'gerənz, gérránz

Gerrish, *f.n.*, 'gerɪʃ, gérrish

Gershon, *f.n.*, 'gɜrʃən, gér-shŏn

Gershuny, *f.n.*, gər'ʃunɪ, gĕr-shŏŏni

Gerson, *f.n.*, 'gɛərsən, gáirssŏn

Gertler, *f.n.*, 'gɜrtlər, gértlĕr

Gerty, *f.n.*, 'gɜrtɪ, gérti

Gervase, *C.n.*, 'dʒɜrveɪz, jérvayz; 'dʒɜrvɪz, jérviz

Gervis, *f.n.*, 'dʒɑrvɪs, jaárviss

Getgood, *f.n.*, 'getgʊd, gét-gŏŏd

Gethin, *f.n.*, 'geθɪn, géth-in

Gething, *f.n.*, 'geθɪŋ, géth-ing

Gharbaoui, *f.n.*, gɑr'baʊɪ, gaarbów-i

Ghey, *f.n.*, dʒaɪ, jī

Ghika, *f.n.*, 'gikə, geékă

Giarchi, *f.n.*, 'dʒɑrkɪ, jaárki

Gibberd, *f.n.*, 'gɪbərd, gíbbĕrd

Gibbes, *f.n.*, gɪbz, gibz

Gibbon, *f.n.*, 'gɪbən, gíbbŏn

Gibbons, *f.n.*, 'gɪbənz, gíbbŏnz

Gibbons, Grinling, *17th–18th-c. woodcarver and sculptor*, 'grɪnlɪŋ 'gɪbənz, grínling gíbbŏnz

Gibbs, *f.n.*, gɪbz, gibz

Gibson, *f.n.*, 'gɪbsən, gíbssŏn

Gick, *f.n.*, dʒɪk, jick

Gidal, *f.n.*, gɪ'dæl, gidál

Giddens, *f.n.*, 'gɪdənz, gíddĕnz

Gidding, Great *and* Little, *Cambs.*, 'gɪdɪŋ, gídding

Gidea Park *Essex*, 'gɪdɪə 'pɑrk, gíddiă paárk

Gidman, *f.n.*, 'gɪdmən, gídmăn

Gielgud, Sir John, *actor*, 'gilgʊd, geélgŏŏd

Gieve, *f.n.*, giv, geev

Giffard, *f.n.*, 'dʒɪfərd, jiffárd; 'gɪfərd, giffaard. *The first is appropriate for the family name of the Earl of Halsbury.*

Giffnock *S'clyde*, 'gɪfnək, giffnŏk

Gifford, *f.n.*, 'dʒɪfərd, jiffŏrd; 'gɪfərd, giffŏrd. *The first is appropriate for Baron ~, the second for the ~ Lectureships at the University of St. Andrews.*

Gifford *Lothian*, 'gɪfərd, giffŏrd. *Appropriate also for the Earl of ~.*

Gifford, Aveton, *Devon*, 'ɒtən 'dʒɪfərd, áwtŏn jiffŏrd; 'ævɪtən 'gɪfərd, ávvĕtŏn giffŏrd

Gifford, Bowers, *Essex*, 'baʊərz 'gɪfərd, bówĕrz giffŏrd

Gifford, Broughton, *Wilts.*, 'brɒtən 'gɪfərd, bráwtŏn giffŏrd; 'brɒtən 'dʒɪfərd, bráwtŏn jiffŏrd

Gifford, Stoke, *Avon*, 'stoʊk 'gɪfərd, stŏk giffŏrd

Gifford Water *Lothian*, 'gɪfərd, giffŏrd

Giggleswick *N. Yorks.*, 'gɪglzwɪk, gígglz-wick

Gigha *S'clyde*, 'giə, geé-ă

Gight Castle *Grampian*, gɪxt, gicht

Gil, *f.n.*, gɪl, gill

Gilberdyke, *also spelt* Gilberdike, *Humberside*, 'gɪlbərdaɪk, gílbĕrdīk

Gilbert, *C.n. and f.n.*, 'gɪlbərt, gílbĕrt

Gilbey, *f.n.*, 'gɪlbɪ, gílbi

Gilbreath, *f.n.*, gɪl'breɪθ, gil-bráyth

Gilcomston *Aberdeen*, 'gɪlkəmstən, gilkŏmsstŏn

Gilcrux *Cumbria*, 'gɪlkruz, gilkrooz

Gildea, *f.n.*, 'gɪldeɪ, gilday; gɪl'deɪ, gildáy

Gilder, *f.n.*, 'gɪldər, gildĕr

Gilderoy, *f.n.*, 'gɪldərɔɪ, gíldĕroy

Gildersome *W. Yorks.*, 'gɪldərsəm, gíldĕrssŏm

Giles, *f.n.*, 'dʒaɪlz, jīlz

Gileston *S. Glam.*, 'dʒaɪlztən, jílztŏn

Gilfach Fargoed *S. Glam.*, 'gɪlvax 'vɑrgɔɪd, gilvaach vaárgoyd

Gilfach Goch *Mid Glam.*, 'gɪlvax 'goʊx, gilvaach gŏch

Gilford *Co. Down*, 'gɪlfərd, gilfŏrd

Gilham, *f.n.*, 'gɪləm, gillăm

Gilhooley, *f.n.*, gɪl'hulɪ, gil-hoóli

Gilkes, *f.n.*, dʒɪlks, jilks

Gilks, *f.n.*, dʒɪlks, jilks

Gill, *f.n.*, gɪl, gill

Gillam, *f.n.*, 'gɪləm, gillăm

Gillan Creek *Cornwall*, 'gɪlən 'krik, gíllăn kreék

Gillard, *f.n.*, 'gɪlɑrd, gíllaard; gɪ'lɑrd, gilaárd; gɪl'gɑrd, gillárd

Gilleney, *f.n.*, dʒɪ'linɪ, jileéni

Giller, *f.n.*, 'gɪlər, gíllĕr

Gilles, *f.n.*, 'gɪlɪs, gíllĕss

Gillesland *see* Dacre of Gillesland, Baron

Gillespie, *f.n.*, gɪ'lespɪ, gilésspi

Gillet, *f.n.*, 'gɪlɪt, gíllĕt; dʒɪ'let, jilétt

Gillett, *f.n.*, 'gɪlɪt, gíllĕt; dʒɪ'let, jilétt

Gilletts Crossing *Lancs.*, 'dʒɪlets 'krɒsɪŋ, jíllets króssing

Gilley, *f.n.*, 'gɪlɪ, gilli

Gilliam, *f.n.*, 'gɪlɪəm, gilliăm

Gilliat, *f.n.*, 'gɪlɪət, gilliăt

Gillick, *f.n.*, 'gɪlɪk, gíllick

Gillie, *f.n.*, 'gılı, gílli
Gillies, *f.n.*, 'gılıs, gilliss
Gilligan, *f.n.*, 'gılıgən, gílligăn
Gilling, *f.n.*, 'gılıŋ, gilling
Gilling *N. Yorks.*, 'gılıŋ, gilling
Gillingham, *f.n.*, 'gılıŋəm, gilling-ăm; 'dʒılıŋəm, jilling-ăm
Gillingham *Dorset, Norfolk*, 'gılıŋəm, gilling-ăm
Gillingham *Kent*, 'dʒılıŋəm, jilling-ăm
Gillingwater, *f.n.*, 'gılıŋwɔtər, gílling-wawtĕr
Gillinson, *f.n.*, 'gılınsən, gillins-sŏn
Gillis, *f.n.*, 'gılıs, gilliss
Gillott, *f.n.*, 'dʒılət, jillŏt; 'gılət, gillŏt
Gilman, *f.n.*, 'gılmən, gílmăn
Gilmorehill *Glasgow*, 'gılmɔr'hıl, gilmŏr-híll
Gilmorton *Leics.*, gıl'mɔrtən, gilmórtŏn
Gilmour, *f.n.*, 'gılmər, gílmŭr; 'gılmɔr, gílmor
Gilnahirk *Co. Down*, ‚gılnə'hɜrk, gilnă-hírk
Gilpin, *f.n.*, 'gılpın, gilpin
Gilroy, *f.n.*, 'gılrɔı, gílroy
Gilsland *Northd.*, 'gılzlənd, gílzländ
Gilwell Park *Essex*, 'gılwəl 'pɑrk, gílwĕl paárk
Gilwern *Gwent*, 'gılwɛərn, gíl-wairn
Gilwhite, *f.n.*, 'gılhwaıt, gil-whít
Gilzean, *f.n.*, gı'lin, gileén; gıl'zin, gilzeén
Gimbert, *f.n.*, 'gımbərt, gímbĕrt
Gimingham *Norfolk*, 'gımıŋəm, gímming-ăm
Gimson, *f.n.*, 'gımsən, gímssŏn; 'dʒımsən, jímssŏn
Ginclough *Ches.*, 'dʒınklʌf, jín-kluff
Ginever, *f.n.*, 'dʒınıvər, jínnĕvĕr
Gingell, *f.n.*, 'gındʒl, gínjl; 'dʒındʒel, jínjel
Ginley, *f.n.*, 'gınlı, gínli
Ginn, *f.n.*, gın, gin
Ginner, *f.n.*, 'dʒınər, jínnĕr
Ginsburg, *f.n.*, 'gınzbɜrg, ginzburg
Ginsbury, *f.n.*, 'gınzbərı, ginzbūri
Giordan, *f.n.*, 'dʒɔrdən, jórdăn
Giovene, *f.n.*, dʒı'ouvənı, ji-ŏvéni
Gipping, *River, Suffolk*, 'gıpıŋ, gipping
Gipps, *f.n.*, gıps, gips
Gipson, *f.n.*, 'gıpsən, gípssŏn
Girouard, *f.n.*, 'dʒıruɑrd, jírrōō--aard
Girthon *D. & G.*, 'gɜrθən, gírthŏn
Girvan *S'clyde*, 'gɜrvən, gírvăn
Girvin, *f.n.*, 'gɜrvın, gírvin

Gisborough, Baron, 'gızbərə, gízbŭră
Gisburn *Lancs.*, 'gısbɜrn, gíssburn
Gisleham *Suffolk*, 'gızləm, gíz-lăm; 'gısləm, gísslăm
Gislingham *Suffolk*, 'gızlıŋəm, gízling-ăm
Gissane, *f.n.*, gı'seın, gissáyn
Gissing *Norfolk*, 'gısıŋ, gissing
Gitsham, *f.n.*, 'gıt-ʃəm, gít-shăm
Gittins, *f.n.*, 'gıtınz, gíttinz
Gittisham *Devon*, 'gıtısəm, gittissăm; 'gıtıʃəm, gítti-shăm; 'gıtsəm, gitsăm
Gittoes, *f.n.*, 'gıtouz, gíttōz
Gittus, *f.n.*, 'gıtəs, gíttŭss
Givens, *f.n.*, 'gıvənz, givvĕnz
Givons Grove *Surrey*, 'dʒıvənz 'grouv, jívvŏnz grōv
Gladestry *Powys*, 'gleıdstrı, gláyd-stri
Gladstone, *f.n.*, 'glædstən, gládstŏn
Gladstone of Hawarden, Barony of, 'glædstən əv 'hɑrdən, gládstŏn ŏv haárdĕn
Gladwell, *f.n.*, 'glædwəl, gládwĕl
Glais *W. Glam.*, glaıs, glíss
Glaisdale *N. Yorks.*, 'gleızdeıl, gláyzdayl
Glaisher, *f.n.*, 'gleıʃər, gláyshĕr
Glaister, *f.n.*, 'gleıstər, gláysstĕr
Glamis *Tayside*, glamz, glaamz. *Appropriate also for Baron ~.*
Glamorgan, *Mid, South, West, Co. names*, glə'mɔrgən, glămórgăn
Glancy, *f.n.*, 'glænsı, glánssi
Glanely, Barony of, glæn'ilı, glaneéli
Glanffrwd, *Welsh C.n.*, 'glænfrud, glánfrood
Glangrwyney *Powys*, glæn'grʊını, glan-grōō-inni
Glangwili *Dyfed*, glæn'gwılı, glan-gwíli
Glan Llugwy *Gwynedd*, glæn 'ɬıgʊı, glan ɬligōō-i
Glan-llyn *Mid Glam., Gwynedd*, glæn'ɬın, glan-ɬlín
Glan-rhyd *Powys*, glæn'hrid, glanreéd
Glanusk, Baron, glæn'ʌsk, glanúsk. *Appropriate also for Glan Usk Park (Powys).*
Glanville, *f.n.*, 'glænvıl, glánvil
Glanwydden *Gwynedd*, glæn-'wıðən, glanwíthĕn
Glanyllin *Gwynedd*, ‚glænə'ɬın, glannă-ɬlín
Glanyrafon, *also spelt* Glan-yr-afon, *Gwynedd*, ‚glænər'ævən, glannĕrávvŏn

Glapthorn *Northants.*, 'glæpθɔrn, gláp-thorn

Glaramara *Cumbria*, 'glærə'mɑrə, glárrämaárä

Glarryford *Co. Antrim*, 'glærɪfərd, glárrïförd

Glas Island *H'land*, glas, glaass

Glasbury *Powys*, 'gleɪzbərɪ, gláyzbŭri

Glasby, *f.n.*, 'glæzbɪ, glázbi

Glascodine, *f.n.*, 'glæskoʊdaɪn, glásskōdīn

Glascoed, *also spelt* **Glasgoed**, *Clwyd, Gwent*, 'glæskɔɪd, glásskoyd. *Appropriate for both places of this name in Clwyd.*

Glascwm, *also spelt* **Glasgwm**, *Powys*, 'glæskʊm, glásskŏom. *Appropriate for both places of this name in Powys.*

Glasfryn *Clwyd*, 'glæsvrɪn, glássvrin

Glasgoed *see* **Glascoed**

Glasgow *S'clyde*, 'glasgoʊ, glaásgō; 'glaskoʊ, glaásskō; 'glazgoʊ, glaázgō. *For ~* **Celtic** *(football club) see* **Celt.**

Glasgwm *see* **Glascwm**

Glaslyn, River, *Gwynedd*, 'glæslɪn, glásslin

Glassalt Shiel Lodge *Grampian*, 'glæsəlt 'ʃil, glássält shéel

Glasscock, *f.n.*, 'glaskɒk, gláasskock; 'glaskoʊ, glaásskō

Glasser, *f.n.*, 'glæsər, glássër

Glass Houghton *W. Yorks.*, 'glas 'haʊtən, glaáss hówtŏn

Glaston *Leics.*, 'gleɪstən, gláysstŏn

Glastonbury *Somerset*, 'glastənbərɪ, glaástŏnbŭri; 'glæstənbərɪ, glásstŏnbŭri

Glaswegian, *native of* **Glasgow**, glas'widʒən, glaass-wéejän; glaz'widʒən, glaaz-wéejän

Glatton, *Cambs.*, 'glætən, gláttŏn

Glatz, *f.n.*, glæts, glatts

Glavin, *f.n.*, 'glævɪn, glávvin

Glazebury *Ches.*, 'gleɪzbərɪ, gláyzbŭri

Glazer, *f.n.*, 'gleɪzər, gláyzër

Glazier, *f.n.*, 'gleɪzɪər, gláyzi-ër

Gleadless *S. Yorks.*, 'glidlɪs, gléedléss

Gleadow, *f.n.*, 'gledoʊ, gléddō

Gleadowe, *f.n.*, 'gledoʊ, gléddō

Gleadthorpe Grange *Notts.*, 'glidθɔrp 'greɪndʒ, gléed-thorp gráynj

Gleichen, *f.n.*, 'glaɪxən, glíchěn

Glenalmond *Tayside*, glen'amənd, glenaámŏnd

Glenamara of Glenridding, Baron, ˌglenə'mɑrə əv glen'rɪdɪŋ, glennämaárä ŏv glenrídding

Glenanne *Co. Armagh*, glen'æn, glenán

Glenapp, Viscount, glen'æp, glenáp

Glenariff *Co. Antrim*, glen'ærɪf, glenárrif

Glenarm *Co. Antrim*, glen'ɑrm, glenaárm

Glenartney *Tayside*, glen'ɑrtnɪ, glenaártni

Glen Avon *Grampian*, glen 'ɑn, glen aán

Glenavy *Co. Antrim*, glen'eɪvɪ, glenáyvi. *Appropriate also for Baron ~.*

Glenbervie *Grampian*, glen'bɜrvɪ, glenbérvi

Glenboig *S'clyde*, glen'boʊɪg, glenbō-ig

Glenbruar *Tayside*, glen'bruər, glenbroó-är

Glenbuchat *Grampian*, glen-'bʌkət, glenbúckät

Glencaple *D. & G.*, glen'keɪpl, glen-káypl

Glencarse *Tayside*, glen'kɑrs, glen-kaárss

Glen Chas *I. of Man*, glen 'tʃæs, glen cháss

Glencoe *H'land*, glen'koʊ, glen-kō

Glenconner, *f.n.*, glen'kɒnər, glen-kónnër. *Appropriate also for Baron ~.*

Glencross, *f.n.*, glen'krɒs, glen-króss

Glendaruel *S'clyde*, ˌglendə'ruəl, glendäroó-ël

Glenday, *f.n.*, 'glendeɪ, glénday

Glendenning, *f.n.*, glen'denɪŋ, glendénning

Glendevon *Central–Tayside border*, glen'devən, glendévvŏn. *Appropriate also for Baron ~.*

Glendinning, *f.n.*, glen'dɪnɪŋ, glendínning

Glendochart *D. & G.*, glen'dɒxərt, glendóchärt

Glen Dochart *Central*, glen 'dɒxərt, glen dóchärt

Glendower, Owen, *14th–15th-c. Welsh chieftain*, 'oʊɪn glen-'daʊər, ō-ën glendówr. *The Welsh form is* **Owain Glyndwr**, *q.v.*

Glendronach Distillery *Grampian*, glen'drɒnəx, glendrónnǎch

Glendyne, Baron, glen'daɪn, glendín

Gleneagles *Tayside*, glen'iglz, glenéeglz

Glenegedale Airport *S'clyde*, glen'egideɪl, glenéggědayl

Glenelg *H'land*, glen'elg, glenélg

Glen Errochty *Tayside*, glen 'erəxtɪ, glen érróchti

Glen Etive *S'clyde*, glen 'etɪv, glen éttiv

Glenfarclas Distillery *Grampian*, glen'fɑrkləs, glenfáarkläss

Glenfarg *Tayside*, glen'fɑrg, glenfáarg

Glen Fernait *Tayside*, glen 'fərnɪt, glen férnit

Glenfernate *Tayside*, glen'fərnɪt, glenférnit

Glenfeshie *H'land*, glen'feʃɪ, glenféshi

Glenfiddich Distillery *Grampian*, glen'fɪdɪx, glenfíddich

Glen Finglass *Central*, glen 'fɪŋləs, glen fíng-läss; glen 'fɪŋgləs, glen fíng-gläss

Glenfinnan *H'land*, glen'fɪnən, glenfínnăn

Glengarnock *S'clyde*, glen'gɑrnək, glen-gáarnŏk

Glen Girnaig *Tayside*, glen 'gərnɪg, glen gírnig

Glengormley *Co. Antrim*, glen-'gɔrmlɪ, glen-górmli

Glenguin *see* **Tedder of ∼**, Baron.

Glenholm *Borders*, glen'houm, glen-hōm

Glenisla *Tayside*, glen'aɪlə, glenílä

Glenkinchie Distillery *Lothian*, glen'kɪnʃɪ, glen-kínshi

Glenkinglas of Cairndow, Baron, glen'kɪnləs əv kɛərn'du, glen--kínläss ŏv kairndoo

Glenlee *D. & G.*, glen'li, glen-leé

Glen Lee *Tayside*, glen 'li, glen leé

Glenlivet *Grampian*, glen'lɪvɪt, glen-lívvĕt

Glenlochar *D. & G.*, glen'lɒxər, glen-lóchăr

Glenmanus *Co. Derry*, glen-'mænəs, glen-mánnŭss

Glenmorangie Distillery *H'land*, ,glenmə'rændʒɪ, glen-mŏránji

Glenochil *Central*, glen'ouxl, glenóchl

Glen Ogle *Central*, glen 'ougl, glen ŏgl

Glenorchy *S'clyde*, glen'ɔrxɪ, glenórchi. *Appropriate also for Lord ∼.*

Glenrinnes *Grampian*, glen'rɪnɪs, glenrínnĕss

Glenrothes *Fife*, glen'rɒθɪs, glen-róthĕss

Glenrothes Distillery *Grampian*, glen'rɒθɪs, glenróthĕss

Glenshane Pass *Co. Derry*, glen-'ʃeɪn, glen-sháyn

Glenshee *Tayside*, glen'ʃi, glen--sheé

Glenshesk, River, *Co. Antrim*, glen'ʃesk, glen-shésk

Glen Shira *S'clyde*, glen 'ʃɪərə, glen sheérä

Glentanar, Barony of, glen'tænər, glen-tánnär

Glentham *Lincs.*, 'glenθəm, glén-thäm

Glentoran, Baron, glen'tɔrən, glen-táwrän

Glen Truim *H'land*, glen 'truɪm, glen troó-im

Glenwherry *Co. Antrim*, glen-'hwerɪ, glen-whérri

Glerawly, Viscount, glə'rɔlɪ, glĕráwli

Glevum, *Roman name for* **Gloucester**, 'glivəm, gleévŭm

Gliksten, *f.n.*, 'glɪkstən, glíck-stĕn

Glimps Holm *Orkney*, 'glɪmps houm, glímps hōm

Gloag, *f.n.*, gloug, glōg

Gloddaeth *Gwynedd*, 'glɒðaɪθ, glóthīth

Glogue *Dyfed*, gloug, glōg

Glomach, Falls of, *H'land*, 'gloumax, glōmăch

Glooston *Leics.*, 'glustən, gloóosstŏn

Glossop, *f.n.*, 'glɒsəp, glóssŏp

Gloucester *Glos.*, 'glɒstər, glós-stĕr. *Appropriate also for HRH the Duke of ∼.*

Glover, *f.n.*, 'glʌvər, glúvvĕr

Glubb, *f.n.*, glʌb, glub

Gluckman, *f.n.*, 'glʌkmən, glúckmăn

Gluckstein, *f.n.*, 'glʌkstaɪn, glúcks-teen

Glusburn *N. Yorks.*, 'glʌzbərn, glúzzbŭrn

Glyders, The, *Gwynedd*, 'glɪdərz, glíddĕrz. *Twin peaks, known individually as ∼* **Fach**, 'glɪdər 'vɑx, glíddĕr vaách, *and ∼* **Fawr**, 'glɪdər 'vauər, glíddĕr vówr.

Glyme, River, *Oxon.*, glaɪm, glīm

Glympton *Oxon.*, 'glɪmptən, glímptŏn

Glyn, *f.n.*, glɪn, glin

Glyncorrwg *W. Glam.*, glɪn'kɒrug, glin-kórroŏg

Glynde *E. Sussex*, glaɪnd, glīnd

Glyndebourne *E. Sussex*, 'glaɪnd-bɔrn, glíndborn. *Home of the ∼ Opera.*

Glyndwr, Owain, *14th–15th-c. Welsh chieftain*, 'ouaɪn glɪn-'duər, ó-īn glindoŏr; 'ouɪn glɪn'duər, ó-ĕn glindoŏr. *The*

English form is **Owen Glen-dower**, *q.v.*

Glyndyfrdwy *Clwyd*, glɪn-'dʌvərdʊɪ, glindúvvĕrdōō-i

Glynn, *f.n.*, glɪn, glin

Glynn *Cornwall, Dyfed, Gwynedd, Co. Antrim*, glɪn, glin. *Appropriate for both places of the name in Dyfed.*

Glynne, *f.n.*, glɪn, glin

Glynogwr *Mid Glam.*, gli'nɒgʊər, glinóggōōr

Glyntawe *Powys*, glɪn'taʊɪ, glintów-i

Glyn Traian *Clwyd*, glɪn 'traɪən, glin trí-ăn

Glyn-y-Groes *Clwyd*, ˌglɪnə'grɔɪs, glin-ă-gróyss

Gnoll, The, *Neath* (*W. Glam.*), ðə 'nɒl, thĕ nóll

Gnosall *Staffs.*, 'nɒʊsl, nŏssl

Goacher, *f.n.*, 'goʊʃər, gṓshĕr

Goalen, *f.n.*, 'goʊlən, gṓlĕn

Goatcher, *f.n.*, 'goʊtʃər, gŏ́tchĕr

Goater, *f.n.*, 'goʊtər, gŏ́tĕr

Goathland *N. Yorks.*, 'goʊθlənd, gṓthlănd

Goathurst *Somerset*, 'goʊθɜrst, gŏ-thurst

Gobernuisgach Lodge *H'land*, ˌgoʊbər'nɪsgəx, gōbĕrníss-găch

Gobey, *f.n.*, 'goʊbɪ, gṓbi

Gobion *Gwent*, 'goʊbjɒn, gŏ́b-yon

Goble, *f.n.*, 'goʊbl, gṓbl

Gobowen *Salop*, gɒ'boʊɪn, gobbṓ-ĕn

Godalming *Surrey*, 'gɒdlmɪŋ, góddl-ming

Godber, *f.n.*, 'gɒdbər, gódbĕr

Godbold, *f.n.*, 'gɒdboʊld, gód-bōld

Goddard, *f.n.*, 'gɒdərd, góddărd; 'gɒdard, góddaard. *The first is appropriate for the Barony of* ∼.

Godde, *f.n.*, goʊd, gŏd

Godden, *f.n.*, 'gɒdən, góddĕn

Godding, *f.n.*, 'gɒdɪŋ, gódding

Godefroy, *f.n.*, 'gɒdɪfrɔɪ, góddĕ-froy

Goderich, Viscountcy of, 'gʊdrɪtʃ, gŏ́odritch

Godin, *f.n.*, 'goʊdɪn, gṓdin

Godiva, Lady, *Saxon heroine*, gə'daɪvə, gŏdívă

Godmanchester *Cambs.*, 'gɒdmən'tʃestər, gódmăn-chéstér

Godmanstone *Dorset*, 'gɒdmən-stən, gódmănstŏn

Godmersham *Kent*, 'gɒdmərʃəm, gódmĕr-shăm

Godolphin *Cornwall*, gə'dɒlfɪn, gŏdólfin. *Appropriate also for the Barony of* ∼.

Godreaman *Mid Glam.*, ˌgɒdrɪ-'æmən, goddri-ámmăn

Godre'r-graig *W. Glam.*, ˌgɒdrər'graig, godrĕrgrḗg

Godrevy *Cornwall*, gə'drivɪ, gŏdrḗevi

Godshill *Hants.*, 'gɒdzhɪl, gódz-hil

Goehr, *f.n.*, gɜr, gur. *Appropriate for Alexander* ∼, *composer, and Walter* ∼, *conductor.*

Gogar Bank *Lothian*, 'goʊgər 'bæŋk, gṓgăr bánk

Gogay, *f.n.*, gə'geɪ, gōgáy

Gogerddan *Dyfed*, goʊ'gɛərðən, gōgáirthăn

Gohorry, *f.n.*, gə'hɒrɪ, gŏ-hórri

Golant *Cornwall*, gə'lænt, gōlánt; goʊ'lænt, gōlánt

Golborne *Gtr. M'chester*, 'goʊl-bɔrn, gṓlborn

Golcar *W. Yorks.*, 'goʊkər, gṓkăr

Goldesgeyme, *f.n.*, 'goʊldəzgeɪm, gṓldĕzgaym

Golding, *f.n.*, 'goʊldɪŋ, gṓlding

Goldington *Beds.*, 'goʊldɪŋtən, gṓldingtŏn

Goldrei, *f.n.*, 'goʊldrɪ, gṓldri

Goldschmidt, *f.n.*, 'goʊldʃmɪt, gṓld-shmitt

Goldsithney *Cornwall*, 'goʊld-'sɪðnɪ, gṓld-síthni

Goldsmid, *f.n.*, 'goʊldsmɪd, gṓld-smid

Goldsmith, *f.n.*, 'goʊldsmɪθ, gṓld-smith

Goldstein, *f.n.*, 'gɒldstaɪn, góldd-stīn

Goldstone, *f.n.*, 'goʊldstoʊn, gṓld-stōn

Goldsworthy, *f.n.*, 'goʊldzwɜrðɪ, gṓldz-wurthi

Golfa *Powys*, 'gɒlvə, gólvă

Golightly, *f.n.*, gə'laɪtlɪ, gōlítli

Gollancz, Sir Victor, *author and publisher*, gə'lænts, gōlánts

Golombek, *f.n.*, gə'lɒmbek, gōlómbek

Golspie *H'land*, 'gɒlspɪ, gólsspi

Gomeldon *Wilts.*, 'gɒməldən, gómmĕldŏn

Gomersal, *W. Yorks.*, 'gɒmərsl, gómmĕrssl

Gomersall, *f.n.*, 'gɒmərsl, góm-mĕrssl

Gomez, *f.n.*, 'goʊmez, gṓmezz

Gomme, *f.n.*, gɒm, gomm

Gomperts, *f.n.*, 'gɒmpərts, góm-pĕrts

Gompertz, *f.n.*, 'gɒmpərts, góm-pĕrts

Gomshall *Surrey*, 'gɒmʃl, góm-shl; 'gamʃl, gúm-shl

Gonalston *Notts.*, 'gɒnlstən, gónnlstŏn

Gonella, *f.n.*, gə'nelə, gŏnéllă
Gonley, *f.n.*, 'gɒnlɪ, gónli
Gonne, *f.n.*, gɒn, gonn
Gonvena *Cornwall*, 'gɒnvɪnə, gónveenă
Gonville and Caius College, *Univ. of Cambridge*, 'gɒnvɪl ənd 'kiz, gónvil ănd keez
Gooch, *f.n.*, gutʃ, gootch
Goodale, *f.n.*, 'gudeɪl, gŏŏdayl
Goodameavy *Devon*, ,gudə'mivɪ, gŏŏdăméevi
Goodden, *f.n.*, 'gudən, gŏŏdĕn
Goode, *f.n.*, gud, gŏŏd
Goodenough, *f.n.*, 'gudɪnʌf, gŏŏdĕnuff
Gooderham, *f.n.*, 'gudərəm, gŏŏdĕrăm
Goodeve, *f.n.*, 'gudiv, gŏŏdeev
Goodfellow, *f.n.*, 'gudfeloʊ, gŏŏdfellŏ
Goodhand-Tait, *f.n.*, 'gudhænd 'teɪt, gŏŏd-hand táyt
Goodhart, *f.n.*, 'gudhɑrt, gŏŏd--haart
Goodhew, *f.n.*, 'gudhju, gŏŏd-hew
Gooding, *f.n.*, 'gudɪŋ, gŏŏding
Goodlad, *f.n.*, 'gudlæd, gŏŏd-lad
Goodnestone *Kent*, 'gudnestən, gŏŏdnesstŏn; 'gʌnstən, gúnsstŏn
Goodrham, *f.n.*, 'gudrəm, gŏŏdrăm
Goodrick, *f.n.*, 'gudrɪk, gŏŏdrick
Goodwick *Dyfed*, 'gudɪk, gŏŏdick
Goodyear, *f.n.*, 'gudjər, gŏŏd-yĕr
Googe, *f.n.*, gudʒ, gooj
Goolden, *f.n.*, 'guldən, gŏŏldĕn
Goonbell *Cornwall*, gun'bel, goonbéll
Goonhavern *Cornwall*, gun-'hævərn, goon-hávvĕrn; gə'nævərn, gŏnávvĕrn
Goonhilly Downs *Cornwall*, gun-'hɪlɪ, gŏŏn-hílli
Goonvrea *Cornwall*, gun'vreɪ, goonvráy
Goorney, *f.n.*, 'guərnɪ, gŏŏrni
Goosey *Berks.*, 'guzɪ, gŏŏzi
Goosnargh *Lancs.*, 'gusnər, gŏŏssnăr
Goossens, *f.n.*, 'gusənz, gŏŏssĕnz. *Appropriate for Sir Eugene* ~, ju'ʒeɪn, yoozháyn, *composer and conductor; Léon* ~, 'leɪɒn, láy--on, *oboist; and Sidonie* ~, sɪ'doʊnɪ, sidóni, *harpist.*
Goraghwood *Co. Armagh*, 'gɔrəwʊd, gáwră-wŏŏd
Goran Haven *see* **Gorran Haven**
Gordeno, *f.n.*, gɔr'dinoʊ, gor-déenŏ
Gordon, *C.n. and f.n.*, 'gɔrdən, górdŏn

Gordonstoun School *Grampian*, 'gɔrdənztən, górdŏnztŏn
Gore, *f.n.*, gɔr, gor
Gorell, *f.n.*, 'gɒrəl, górrĕl. *Appropriate also for Baron* ~.
Goren, *f.n.*, 'gɔrən, gáwrĕn
Gorgie *Edinburgh*, 'gɔrgɪ, górgi
Gorham, *f.n.*, 'gɔrəm, gáwrăm
Gorhambury *Herts.*, 'gɒrəmbərɪ, górrămbŭri
Goring, *f.n.*, 'gɔrɪŋ, gáwring
Goring *Oxon.*, 'gɔrɪŋ, gáwring
Gorleston *Norfolk*, 'gɔrlstən, górlsstŏn
Gorman, *f.n.*, 'gɔrmən, górmăn
Gormanston, Viscount, 'gɔrmənstən, górmănstŏn
Gornall, *f.n.*, 'gɔrnl, górnl
Goronwy, *Welsh C.n.*, gɒ'rɒnwɪ, gorrónwi
Gorran Haven *Cornwall*, 'gɒrən 'heɪvən, górrăn háyvĕn
Gorsedd *Clwyd*, 'gɔrseð, górsseth
Gorseinon *W. Glam.*, gɔr'saɪnən, gorssínŏn
Gors-las *Dyfed*, gɔrs'lɑs, gorsslaáss
Gortin *Co. Tyrone*, 'gɔrtjɪn, górt-yin
Gosberton Clough *Lincs.*, 'gɒzbərtən 'klaʊ, gózbĕrtŏn klów; 'gɒzbərtən 'klʌf, gózbĕrtŏn klúff
Goschen, Viscount, 'goʊʃən, gó--shĕn
Goscote *W. Midlands*, 'gɒskoʊt, gósskŏt
Goscote, East, *Leics.*, 'gɒskoʊt, gósskŏt
Gosforth *Northd.*, 'gɒsfərθ, góssfŏrth
Gosnell, *f.n.*, 'gɒznəl, gózznĕl
Gosney, *f.n.*, 'gɒznɪ, gózzni
Gosport *Hants*, 'gɒspɔrt, góssport
Goss, *f.n.*, gɒs, goss
Gossage, *f.n.*, 'gɒsɪdʒ, góssij
Gostelow, *f.n.*, 'gɒstɪloʊ, gósstĕlŏ
Goswick *Northd.*, 'gɒzɪk, gózzick
Gotell, *f.n.*, gə'tel, gŏtéll
Gotham *Notts.*, 'goʊtəm, gótăm
Gothard, *f.n.*, 'gɒθɑrd, góth-aard
Gotla, *f.n.*, 'gɒtlə, góttlă
Gotobed, *f.n.*, 'gɒtəbed, góttŏbed; 'goʊtəbed, gótŏbed
Gottwaltz, *f.n.*, 'gɒtwɒlts, gót-wawlts
Goudge, *f.n.*, gudʒ, gooj. *Appropriate for Elizabeth* ~, *author.*
Goudhurst *Kent*, 'gaʊdhərst, gówd-hurst
Goudie, *f.n.*, 'gaʊdɪ, gówdi
Goudy, *f.n.*, 'gaʊdɪ, gówdi

Gouge, _f.n._, gaʊdʒ, gowj
Gough, _f.n._, gɒf, goff. _Appropriate also for Viscount_ ~.
Goulburn, _f.n._, 'gʊlbɜrn, góolburn
Goulceby _Lincs._, 'goʊlsbɪ, góolssbi
Gould, _f.n._, guːld, goold; goʊld, gōld
Gouldborn, _f.n._, 'goʊldbɔrn, góldborn
Goulden, _f.n._, 'guːldən, góoldĕn; 'goʊldən, góldĕn
Goulding, _f.n._, 'guːldɪŋ, góolding
Gouldsmith, _f.n._, 'goʊldsmɪθ, góldsmith
Goulik, _f.n._, 'guːlɪk, góolick
Goullart, _f.n._, 'guːlɑrt, góolaart
Goullet, _f.n._, gu'let, goolétt
Gourgey, _f.n._, 'gʊədʒɪ, góorji
Gourlay, _f.n._, 'gʊərlɪ, góorli
Gourley, _f.n._, 'gʊərlɪ, góorli
Gourlie, _f.n._, 'gʊərlɪ, góorli
Gourock _S'clyde_, 'gʊərək, góorŏk
Goutthrappel _S'clyde_, gaʊt'θræpl, gowt-thráppl
Govan, _f.n._, 'gʌvən, gúvván
Govan _S'clyde_, 'gʌvən, gúvván
Gove, _f.n._, goʊv, gōv
Gover, _f.n._, 'goʊvər, góvĕr
Goveton _Devon_, 'gʌvɪtən, gúvvĕtŏn
Govett, _f.n._, 'gʌvɪt, gúvvĕt
Gow, _f.n._, gaʊ, gow
Gowdridge, _f.n._, 'gaʊdrɪdʒ, gówdrij
Gower, _f.n._, 'gaʊər, gówĕr; gɔr, gor. _See also_ Leveson-Gower.
Gowerton _W. Glam._, 'gaʊərtən, gówĕrtŏn
Gowing, _f.n._, 'gaʊɪŋ, gówing
Gowling, _f.n._, 'gaʊlɪŋ, gówling
Gowrie _Tayside_, 'gaʊərɪ, gówri. _Appropriate also for the Earl of_ ~.
Goyt, River, _Derby._–Gtr. _M'chester_, gɔɪt, goyt
Grabham, _f.n._, 'græbəm, grábbăm
Gracie, _f.n._, 'greɪsɪ, gráyssi
Grade, Baron, greɪd, grayd
Gradon, _f.n._, 'greɪdən, gráydŏn
Gradwell, _f.n._, 'grædwel, grádwel
Graebner, _f.n._, 'greɪbnər, gráybnĕr
Graef, _f.n._, greɪf, grayf
Graeme, _f.n._, 'greɪəm, gráy-ĕm; greɪm, graym
Graffham _W. Sussex_, 'græfəm, gráffăm
Grafftey, _f.n._, 'grɑftɪ, graáfti
Grafham _Cambs._, 'grɑfəm, graáfăm
Grafham _Surrey_, 'græfəm, gráffăm
Graham, _C.n. and f.n._, 'greɪəm, gráy-ăm

Graham of Claverhouse, John, _Scottish soldier_, 'greɪəm əv 'kleɪvərhaʊs, gráy-ăm ŏv kláyvĕr-howss
Grahamston _Central_, 'greɪəmstən, gráy-ămsstŏn
Graig _Clwyd, Gwynedd_, graɪg, grīg
Graig Goch _Powys_, graɪg 'goʊx, grīg gṓch
Graig Wen _Gwent, Mid Glam._, graɪg 'wen, grīg wén
Graigwen Gold Mine _Gwynedd_, graɪg'wen, grīg-wén
Grainger, _f.n._, 'greɪndʒər, gráynjĕr
Gralak, _f.n._, 'grælæk, grálack
Grampians, The, _Scottish mountain system_, 'græmpɪənz, grámpiănz
Grampound _Cornwall_, 'græmpaʊnd, grámpownd
Grandison, _f.n._, 'grændɪsən, grándissŏn
Grandtully _Tayside_, 'grɑntlɪ, graántli; 'græntlɪ, grántli
Grangemouth _Central_, 'greɪndʒmaʊθ, gráynj-mowth
Gransha _Co. Down_, 'grænʃə, grán-shă
Grant, _f.n._, grɑnt, graant; grænt, grant
Granta, River, _Cambs._, 'græntə, grántă; 'grɑntə, graántă. _Alternative name for some stretches of the_ Cam.
Grantchester _Cambs._, 'grɑntʃɪstər, graántchĕstĕr; 'græntʃɪstər, grántchĕstĕr. _The first is appropriate for Baron_ ~.
Grantham, _f.n._, 'grænθəm, grán-thăm
Grantham _Lincs._, 'grænθəm, grán-thăm
Granthier, _f.n._, 'grænθɪər, gránthi-ĕr
Granton _Lothian_, 'græntən, grántŏn
Grantown-on-Spey _H'land_, 'græntaʊn ɒn 'speɪ, grántown on spáy; 'græntən ɒn 'speɪ, grántŏn on spáy
Grantshouse _Borders_, 'grants-haʊs, graánts-howss
Granville, _f.n._, 'grænvɪl, gránvil. _Appropriate also for Earl_ ~.
Granville of Eye, Baron, 'grænvɪl əv 'aɪ, gránvil ŏv í
Grasmere _Cumbria_, 'grɑsmɪər, graássmeer
Grassington _N. Yorks._, 'grɑsɪŋtən, graássingtŏn
Grasso, _f.n._, 'grɑsoʊ, graássō
Grateley _Hants_, 'greɪtlɪ, gráytli
Gratiaen, _f.n._, 'greɪʃən, gráy-shĕn

Gration, *f.n.,* 'greɪʃən, gráy-shŏn
Grattan, *f.n.,* 'grætən, gráttăn
Gratton *Staffs.,* 'grætən, gráttŏn
Graveley, *f.n.,* 'greɪvlɪ, gráyv-li
Graveley *Cambs., Herts.,* 'greɪvlɪ, gráyv-li
Gravelly Hill *W. Midlands,* 'grævlɪ 'hɪl, grávvl-i híll
Gravesham *Kent,* 'greɪvʃəm, gráyvshăm
Graveson, *f.n.,* 'greɪvsən, gráyvssŏn
Gravett, *f.n.,* 'grævɪt, grávvĕt
Gravina, *f.n.,* grə'viːnə, grăveénă
Gray, *f.n.,* greɪ, gray
Greager, *f.n.,* 'gregər, gréggĕr
Greasbrough, *S. Yorks.,* 'grizbrə, greézbrŏ
Greasby *Merseyside,* 'grizbɪ, greézbi
Greasley *Notts.,* 'grizlɪ, greézli
Great Alne *Warwicks.,* 'greɪt 'ɔn, gráyt áwn; 'greɪt 'ɔln, gráyt áwln
Great Bolas, *also called* **Bolas Magna,** *Salop,* 'greɪt 'boʊləs, gráyt bólăss
Great Bourton *Oxon.,* 'greɪt 'bɔrtən, gráyt bórtŏn
Great Bowden *Leics.,* 'greɪt 'baʊdən, gráyt bówdĕn
Great Bradley *Somerset, Suffolk,* 'greɪt 'brædlɪ, gráyt brádli
Great Bromley *Essex,* 'greɪt 'brɒmlɪ, gráyt brómli
Great Creaton *Northants.,* 'greɪt 'kritən, gráyt kreétŏn
Great Cumbrae *S'clyde,* 'greɪt 'kʌmbreɪ, gráyt kúmbray
Great Gaddesden *Herts.,* 'greɪt 'gædzdən, gráyt gádzdĕn
Greatham *Cleveland,* 'gritəm, greétăm
Great Harrowden *Northants.,* 'greɪt 'hæroʊdən, gráyt hárrōdĕn
Great Hautbois *Norfolk,* 'greɪt 'hɒbɪs, gráyt hóbbiss
Greathead, *f.n.,* 'greɪthed, gráyt-hed
Great Houghton *Northants.,* 'greɪt 'hoʊtən, gráyt hótŏn
Great Houghton *S. Yorks.,* 'greɪt 'haʊtən, gráyt hówtŏn
Greatorex, *f.n.,* 'greɪtəreks, gráytŏrecks
Great Ponton *Lincs.,* 'greɪt 'pɒntən, gráyt póntŏn
Great Saughall *Ches.,* 'greɪt 'sɒkl, gráyt sáwkl
Great Shelford *Cambs.,* 'greɪt 'ʃelfərd, gráyt shélfŏrd
Great Staughton *Cambs.,* 'greɪt 'stɔtən, gráyt stáwtŏn
Great Stukeley *Cambs.,* 'greɪt 'stjuklɪ, gráyt stéwkli
Great Thorness *I. of Wight,* 'greɪt θɔr'nes, gráyt thornéss
Great Totham *Essex,* 'greɪt 'tɒtəm, gráyt tóttăm
Great Wakering *Essex,* 'greɪt 'weɪkərɪŋ, gráyt wáykĕring
Great Walsingham *Norfolk,* 'greɪt 'wɒlzɪŋəm, gráyt wáwlzing-ăm
Great Waltham *Essex,* 'greɪt 'wɒltəm, gráyt wáwltăm
Great Warley *Essex,* 'greɪt 'wɔrlɪ, gráyt wáwrli
Great Wilbraham *Cambs.,* 'greɪt 'wɪlbrəm, gráyt wílbrăm; 'greɪt 'wɪlbrəhæm, gráyt wílbrăham
Great Wymondley *Herts.,* 'greɪt 'waɪməndlɪ, gráyt wímŏndli
Great Wyrley *Staffs.,* 'greɪt 'wɔrlɪ, gráyt wúrli
Great Yarmouth *Norfolk,* 'greɪt 'jɑrməθ, gráyt yaármūth
Greaves, *f.n.,* greɪvz, grayvz; grivz, greevz. *The first is appropriate for the Countess of* **Dysart**'s *family name.*
Grech, *f.n.,* gretʃ, gretch
Greenall, *f.n.,* 'grinɔl, greénawl
Greenaway, *f.n.,* 'grinəweɪ, greénă-way
Greenbaum, Kyla, *pianist,* 'kaɪlə 'grinbaʊm, kílă greénbowm
Greene, *f.n.,* grin, green
Greengrass, *f.n.,* 'gringrɑs, green-graass
Greengross, *f.n.,* 'gringrɒs, green-gross
Greenhalgh, *f.n.,* 'grinhælʃ, green-halsh; 'grinhɒlʃ, green-holsh; 'grinhældʒ, green-halj; 'grinhɔl, green-hawl
Greenhalgh *Lancs.,* 'grinhælʃ, green-halsh; 'grinhɔlʃ, green-hawlsh
Greenhaugh *Norfolk,* 'greɪt 'grinɒf, green-off
Greenhough, *f.n.,* 'grinɒf, green-off; 'grinhɒf, green-hoff; 'grinhoʊ, green-hō; 'grinhaʊ, green-how; 'grinhʌf, green-huff; 'grinʌf, greenuff
Greenhow, *f.n.,* 'grinoʊ, greénō; 'grinhaʊ, green-how
Greenisland *Co. Antrim,* grin'aɪlənd, greeníländ
Greenlaw *Borders,* 'grinlə, green-law
Greenock *S'clyde,* 'grinək, greénŏk
Greenough, *f.n.,* 'grinoʊ, greénō
Greenslade, *f.n.,* 'grinsleɪd, green-slayd

Greenwich *London*, 'grɪnɪdʒ, grínnij; 'grɪnɪtʃ, grínnitch; 'grenɪtʃ, grénnitch

Greenwood of Holbourne, Viscount, 'grinwʊd əv 'hɒlbʊərn, gréenwŏŏd ŏv hólbŏŏrn

Gregg, *f.n.*, greg, greg

Grego, *f.n.*, 'grigoʊ, gréegō

Gregoire, *f.n.*, 'gregwɑr, grégwaar

Gregor, *C.n.*, 'gregər, gréggŏr

Gregorowski, *f.n.*, ˌgregə'rɒskɪ, greggŏrósski

Gregory, *C.n. and f.n.*, 'gregərɪ, gréggŏri

Gregynog Hall *Powys*, grɪ'gʌnɒg, grĕgúnnog

Greig, *f.n.*, greg, greg

Greim, *f.n.*, grim, greem

Grein, *f.n.*, graɪn, grīn

Grenfell, *f.n.*, 'grenfəl, grénfĕl. *Appropriate also for Baron ∼.*

Grenofen *Devon*, 'grenəfən, grénnŏfĕn

Grenoside *S. Yorks.*, 'grenoʊsaɪd, grénnōssīd

Gresham, *f.n.*, 'greʃəm, gréshăm; 'gresəm, gréssăm

Gresham *Norfolk*, 'greʃəm, gréshăm

Gresley, *f.n.*, 'grezlɪ, grézli

Gressingham *Lancs.*, 'gresɪŋəm, gréssing-ăm

Gretabridge *Durham*, 'gritəbrɪdʒ, gréetăbrij

Greta Hall *Cumbria*, 'gritə 'hɔl, gréetă háwl

Greville, Baron, 'grevɪl, grévvil

Grey de Ruthyn, Barony of, 'greɪ də 'ruθɪn, gráy dĕ róothin

Greyn, *f.n.*, greɪn, grayn

Greysouthen *Cumbria*, 'greɪsun, gráyssoon

Greystoke *Cumbria*, 'greɪstoʊk, gráysstōk

Greywell *Hants*, 'greɪ'wel, gráy-wéll; 'gruəl, grōo-ĕl

Grianan *W. Isles*, 'grinən, gréen-ăn

Gribbin Head *Cornwall*, 'grɪbɪn 'hed, gríbbin héd

Grice, *f.n.*, graɪs, grīss

Gridley, *f.n.*, 'grɪdlɪ, grídli

Grier, *f.n.*, grɪər, greer

Grierson, *f.n.*, 'grɪərsən, gréerssŏn

Grieve, *f.n.*, griv, greev

Griew, *f.n.*, gru, groo

Griffith, *f.n.*, 'grɪfɪθ, gríffith

Griffiths, *f.n.*, 'grɪfɪθs, gríffiths

Grimethorpe *S. Yorks.*, 'graɪmθɔrp, grím-thorp

Grimond, *f.n.*, 'grɪmənd, grímmŏnd

Grimsargh *Lancs.*, 'grɪmzər, grímzăr

Grimscar *W. Yorks.*, 'graɪmzkɑr, grímzkaar

Grimsetter *Orkney*, 'grɪmstər, grímstĕr

Grimshaw, *f.n.*, 'grɪmʃɔ, grím-shaw

Grindale *Humberside*, 'grɪndl, gríndl

Grindrod, *f.n.*, 'grɪndrɒd, gríndrod

Grinke, *f.n.*, 'grɪŋkɪ, grínki

Grinstead, East and West, *W. Sussex*, 'grɪnstɪd, grínsstĕd. *Appropriate also for Baron ∼.*

Grisdale, *f.n.*, 'grɪzdeɪl, grízdayl

Grisdale *Cumbria*, 'graɪzdeɪl, grízdayl

Grisewood, *f.n.*, 'graɪzwʊd, grízwŏŏd

Grist, *f.n.*, grɪst, grisst

Gristhorpe *N. Yorks.*, 'grɪsθɔrp, gríss-thorp

Griswold, *f.n.*, 'grɪzwoʊld, grízwōld

Grives, *f.n.*, grɪvz, greevz

Grizedale *Cumbria*, 'graɪzdeɪl, grízdayl

Groby *Leics.*, 'grubɪ, gróobi

Grocott, *f.n.*, 'groʊkɒt, grókott

Grocyn, William, *15th–16th-c. priest and scholar*, 'groʊsɪn, gróssin

Groeslon *Gwynedd*, 'grɔɪslɒn, gróysslon

Groeswen *Mid Glam.*, grɔɪs'wen, groyss-wén

Grogan, *f.n.*, 'groʊgən, grógăn

Grogarry *S. Uist*, 'grɒgərɪ, gróggări

Gronow, Rees Howell, *19th-c. Welsh author*, 'ris 'haʊəl 'grɒnoʊ, reéss hówĕl grónnō

Groombridge *E. Sussex–Kent*, 'grum'brɪdʒ, gróom-bríj

Groomsport *Co. Down*, 'grumzpɔrt, gróomzport

Grose, *f.n.*, groʊs, grōss

Groser, *f.n.*, 'groʊsər, gróssĕr; 'grɒsər, gróssĕr

Grosmont *Gwent*, 'grɒsmənt, gróssmŏnt

Grosmont *N. Yorks.*, 'groʊmənt, grómŏnt; 'groʊsmənt, gróssmŏnt

Gross, *f.n.*, grɒs, gross; groʊs, grōss

Grosseteste, Robert, *also spelt* **Grossetete, Grossetête,** *13th-c. Bishop of Lincoln*, 'groʊsteɪt, gróustayt; 'groʊstest, gróustest. *The first pronunciation is appropriate for all three spellings.*

Grosvenor, *f.n.*, 'groʊvnər, gróv--nŏr; 'groʊvənər, gróvĕnŏr. *The first is appropriate for the family name of the Duke of Westminster.*

Grote, *f.n.*, groʊt, grōt

Groton *Suffolk*, 'grɒtən, gráwtŏn; 'groʊtən, grótŏn

Grotton *Gtr. M'chester*, 'grɒtən, gróttŏn

Groucott, *f.n.*, 'groʊkət, grókŏt

Groucutt, *f.n.*, 'groʊkət, grókŭt

Grouse, *f.n.*, graʊs, growss

Grout, *f.n.*, graʊt, growt

Groves, *f.n.*, groʊvz, grōvz

Growbart, *f.n.*, 'graʊbart, grów-baart

Gruenberg, *f.n.*, 'grunbɜrg, groónberg

Gruffydd, *f.n.*, 'grɪfɪð, gríffĭth

Grugeon, *f.n.*, 'gruʒən, groózhon

Gruinard, Bay, Island, River, *and* Forest, *H'land*, 'grɪnjərd, grín--yărd

Grundisburgh *Suffolk*, 'grʌndz-bərə, grúndzbŭră

Grunert, *f.n.*, 'grunərt, groónĕrt

Grunhut, *f.n.*, 'grunhʊt, groón--hŏŏt

Grunwell, *f.n.*, 'grʌnwel, grúnwel

Grupe, *f.n.*, grup, groop

Gryfe Water, *also spelt* **Gryffe**, *S'clyde*, graɪf 'wɔtər, grīf wáwtĕr

Grygar, *f.n.*, 'graɪgar, grígaar

Guare, *f.n.*, gwɛər, gwair

Guaspari, *f.n.*, gwəs'parɪ, gwáss-paári

Guay *Tayside*, gaɪ, gī

Gubba, *f.n.*, 'gʌbə, gúbbă

Gubbay, *f.n.*, 'gʌbɪ, gúbbi

Guckian, *f.n.*, 'gʊkɪən, goókiăn

Gudgin, *f.n.*, 'gʌdʒɪn, gújjin

Guedalla, *f.n.*, gwɪ'dælə, gwĕdálă

Gueritz, *f.n.*, 'gerɪts, gérrits

Gueroult, *f.n.*, 'geroʊ, gérrō

Guerrier, *f.n.*, 'gerɪər, gérri-ĕr

Guest, *f.n.*, gest, gest

Guggisberg, *f.n.*, 'gʌgɪsbɜrg, gúggisberg

Guignard, *f.n.*, 'ginjar, geén-yaar

Guihard, *f.n.*, 'gihard, gee-haard

Guilden Morden *Cambs.*, 'gɪldən 'mɔrdən, gíldĕn mórdĕn

Guildford *Surrey*, 'gɪlfərd, gíl-fŏrd

Guilding, *f.n.*, 'gɪldɪŋ, gilding

Guilford, Earl of, 'gɪlfərd, gílfŏrd

Guilford, *f.n.*, 'gɪlfərd, gílfŏrd

Guillamore, Viscountcy of, 'gɪlə-mər, gíllămor

Guillaume, *f.n.*, 'gioʊm, gee-ōm

Guillebaud, *f.n.*, 'gɪlboʊ, geélbō; 'gɪlɪboʊ, gíllibō. *The first is*

appropriate for Claude ~, economist.

Guillemard, *f.n.*, 'gɪlmar, gílmaar

Guillermin, *f.n.*, 'gɪlərmɪn, gíllĕrmin

Guillery, *f.n.*, 'gɪlərɪ, gílleri

Guilmant, *f.n.*, 'gɪlmɒnt, gilmont

Guilsborough *Northants.*, 'gɪlz-bərə, gílzbŭră

Guilsfield *Powys*, 'gɪlzfild, gílz-feeld

Guinan, *f.n.*, gɪ'næn, ginán

Guinane, *f.n.*, gɪ'næn, ginán

Guinee, *f.n.*, 'gɪnɪ, gínni

Guiney, *f.n.*, 'gaɪnɪ, gíni

Guinnane, *f.n.*, gɪ'næn, ginán

Guinness, *f.n.*, 'gɪnɪs, gínnĕss

Guion, *f.n.*, 'gaɪən, gí-ŏn

Guisachan *H'land*, 'uʃəxən, oóshăchăn

Guisborough *Cleveland*, 'gɪzbərə, gízbŭră

Guise, *f.n.*, gaɪz, gīz

Guiseley *W. Yorks.*, 'gaɪzlɪ, gízli

Guist *Norfolk*, gaɪst, gisst

Guiting Power *Glos.*, 'gaɪtɪŋ 'paʊər, gíting pówĕr

Guiver, *f.n.*, 'gaɪvər, gívĕr

Gulbenkian Foundation, gʊl-'beŋkɪən, goólbénkiăn

Gulland, *f.n.*, 'gʌlənd, gúllănd

Gullane *Lothian*, 'gɪlən, gíllăn; 'gʌlən, gúllăn

Gulleford, *f.n.*, 'gʌlɪfərd, gúlli-fŏrd

Gulvain *H'land*, 'gulvɪn, goólvin

Gulval *Cornwall*, 'gʌlvəl, gúlvăl

Gumbs, *f.n.*, gʌmz, gummz

Gummer, *f.n.*, 'gʌmər, gúmmĕr

Gummery, *f.n.*, 'gʌmərɪ, gúmmĕri

Gunderson, *f.n.*, 'gʌndərsən, gúndĕrssŏn

Gunnell, *f.n.*, 'gʌnl, gúnnl

Gunness *Lincs.*, 'gʌnɪs, gúnnĕss

Gunningham, *f.n.*, 'gʌnɪŋəm, gúnning-ăm

Gunnislake *Cornwall*, 'gʌnɪzleɪk, gúnnizlayk

Gunson, *f.n.*, 'gʌnsən, gúnssŏn

Gunter, *f.n.*, 'gʌntər, gúntĕr

Gunwalloe *Cornwall*, gʌn'wɒloʊ, gun-wóllō

Gunwalloe Towans *Cornwall*, gʌn'wɒloʊ 'taʊənz, gun-wóllō tówănz

Gunyon, *f.n.*, 'gʌnjən, gún-yŏn

Gurnards Head *Cornwall*, 'gɜrnardz 'hed, gúrnărdz héd

Gurnos *Mid Glam.*, *Powys*, 'gɜr-nɒs, gúrnoss

Gurr, *f.n.*, gɜr, gur

Gurteen, *f.n.*, 'gɜrtin, gúrteen

Gustard, *f.n.*, 'gʌstərd, gústărd

Gutch, *f.n.*, gʌtʃ, gutch

Guthrie, Sir Tyrone, *theatrical producer,* tɪ'rovn 'gʌθrɪ, tirrṓn gúthri

Gutteridge, *f.n.,* 'gʌtərɪdʒ, gúttĕrij

Guy, *C.n.,* gaɪ, gī

Guyan, *f.n.,* 'gaɪən, gí-ăn

Guyatt, *f.n.,* 'gaɪət, gí-ăt

Guyer, *f.n.,* 'gaɪər, gí-ĕr

Guyhirn *Cambs.,* 'gaɪhɜːn, gí-hirn

Guyler, *f.n.,* 'gaɪlər, gílĕr

Guyon, *f.n.,* 'gaɪən, gí-ŏn

Guyot, *f.n.,* 'gaɪət, gí-ŏt

Guyott, *f.n.,* 'gaɪət, gí-ŏt

Gwaelod-y-Garth *Mid Glam.,* 'gwaɪlɒd ə 'gɑːθ, gwílod ă gaárth

Gwaen-cae-Gurwen *see* **Gwaun--cae-Gurwen**

Gwaenysgor *see* **Gwaunysgor**

Gwalchmai *Gwynedd,* 'gwælxmaɪ, gwálchmī

Gwanwyn, *C.n.,* gwæn'wɪn, gwann-wínn

Gwastaden *Powys,* gwəs'tædən, gwăstáddĕn

Gwatkin, *f.n.,* 'gwɒtkɪn, gwótkin

Gwaun-cae-Gurwen, *also spelt* **Gwaen-cae-Gurwen,** *W. Glam.,* 'gwaɪn kə 'gɜːwən, gwín kă gúrwĕn

Gwaunysgor, *also spelt* **Gwaenysgor,** *Clwyd,* gwaɪn'ʌsgər, gwīnússgor

Gwbert *Dyfed,* 'gʊbərt, gŏobĕrt

Gweek *Cornwall,* gwik, gweek

Gwenddwr *Powys,* 'gwenduər, gwéndoor; 'gwenðuər, gwén--thŏor

Gwendraeth Fach, *River, Dyfed,* 'gwendraɪθ 'vax, gwéndrīth vaách

Gwendraeth Fawr, *River, Dyfed,* 'gwendraɪθ 'vauər, gwéndrīth vówr

Gwen-ffrwd, *Stream, Dyfed,* gwen'frud, gwen-frŏod

Gwennap *Cornwall,* 'gwenəp, gwénnăp

Gwernaffield *Clwyd,* 'gwɛərnə'fild, gwáirnăféeld

Gwernymynydd *Clwyd,* ˌgwɛərnə'mʌnɪð, gwairnĕmúnnith

Gwersyllt *Clwyd,* 'gwɛərsɪɫt, gwáirssihlt

Gwespyr *Clwyd,* 'gwespər, gwésspĕr

Gwilym, *f.n.,* 'gwɪlɪm, gwíllim

Gwinear *Cornwall,* 'gwɪnɪər, gwínneer

Gwineas Rock, *also called* **Gwinges** Rock, *Cornwall,* 'gwɪnɪəs, gwínniăss

Gwinfryn, *Welsh C.n.,* 'gwɪnvrɪn, gwínvrin

Gwinges Rock, *also called* **Gwineas** Rock, *Cornwall,* 'gwɪndʒɪz, gwínjĕz

Gwion, *Welsh C.n.,* 'gwɪɒn, gwée-on

Gwithian *Cornwall,* 'gwɪðɪən, gwíthiăn

Gwnnws *Mid Glam.,* 'gʊnʊs, gŏonŏoss

Gwrych Castle *Clwyd,* gwrix, gwreech; grix, greech. *In order to pronounce the first of these as one syllable, Welsh speakers treat the 'w' as a rounding of the lips to accompany the 'r'.*

Gwy, River, *Gwynedd,* 'gʊɪ, gŏo-i. *This is the Welsh name of the* **Wye,** *q.v.*

Gwyddelwern *Clwyd,* gwɪð-'elwɜːn, gwithélwern

Gwydion, *Welsh C.n.,* 'gwɪdɪən, gwíddiŏn

Gwynant, Lake, *Gwynedd,* 'gwɪnænt, gwínnant

Gwyndâf, *Welsh Bardic name,* 'gwɪndæv, gwíndav

Gwynedd *Co. name,* 'gwɪnəð, gwínnĕth. *Appropriate also for Viscount ~.*

Gwynedd, Hywel ab Owain, *12th-c. Welsh prince,* 'hauəl æb 'ouɪn 'gwɪnəð, hówĕl ab ṓ-in gwínnĕth

Gwynfe *Dyfed,* 'gwɪnvə, gwínvă

Gwynfil *Dyfed,* 'gwɪnvɪl, gwínvil

Gwynfor, *Welsh C.n.,* 'gwɪnvər, gwínvor

Gwynfynydd *Powys,* gwɪn'vʌnɪð, gwin-vúnnith

Gwynn, *f.n.,* gwɪn, gwin

Gwyther, *f.n.,* 'gwaɪðər, gwíthĕr; 'gwɪðər, gwíthĕr

Gwytherin *Clwyd,* gwɪθ'erɪn, gwithérrin

Gyde, *f.n.,* gaɪd, gīd

Gye, *f.n.,* dʒaɪ, jī

Gyffylliog *Clwyd,* gə'fʌɬjɒg, gŭfúhl-yog

Gyle, *f.n.,* gaɪl, gīl

Gymer, *f.n.,* 'gaɪmər, gímĕr

Gyngell, *f.n.,* 'gɪndʒl, gínjl

Gyppeswyke Plate, *sheep-farming trophy,* 'gɪpswɪk, gípswick

H

Haacke, *f.n.,* 'hækɪ, hácki

Habermehl, *f.n.,* 'habərmeɪl, haábĕrmayl

Habershon, *f.n.,* 'hæbərʃən, hábbĕr-shŏn

Haceby *Lincs.*, 'heɪsbɪ, háyssbi

Hackett, *f.n.*, 'hækɪt, háckĕt

Hackshaw, *f.n.*, 'hækʃɔ, háck--shaw

Hadath, Gunby, *author*, 'gʌnbɪ 'hædəθ, gúnbi háddăth

Hadaway, *f.n.*, 'hædəweɪ, háddă-way

Haddenham *Cambs.*, 'hædnəm, háddn-ăm

Haddiscoe *Norfolk*, 'hædɪskoʊ, háddisskō

Haddo, Methlic, Tarves and Kellie, Lord, 'hædoʊ 'meθlɪk 'tɑrvɪs ənd 'kelɪ, háddo méthlick ta'arvĕss ănd kélli

Haddon, *f.n.*, 'hædən, háddŏn

Haddow, *f.n.*, 'hædoʊ, háddō

Haddrill, *f.n.*, 'hædrɪl, hádril

Haden, *f.n.*, 'heɪdən, háydĕn

Haden-Guest, Baron, 'heɪdən 'gest, háydĕn gést

Hadnall *Salop*, 'hædnəl, hád-năl

Hadow, *f.n.*, 'hædoʊ, háddō

Hadrian's Wall *Cumbria–Northd.–Tyne & Wear*, 'heɪdrɪənz 'wɔl, háydriănz wáwl

Hadzor *H. & W.*, 'hædzər, hádzŏr

Haeems, *f.n.*, 'haɪəmz, hí-ămz

Hafner, *f.n.*, 'hæfnər, háfnĕr

Hafod, *Clwyd, Dyfed, Mid Glam., W. Glam.*, 'hævɒd, hávvod. *Appropriate for both places of the name in Dyfed.*

Hafodyrynys *Gwent*, 'hævɒdər-'ʌnɪs, hávvodărúnniss

Hagan, *f.n.*, 'heɪgən, háygăn

Hagen, *f.n.*, 'heɪgən, háygĕn

Haggar, *f.n.*, 'hægɑr, hággaar; 'hægər, hággăr

Hagnaby Priory *Lincs.*, 'hægnəbɪ, hágnăbi

Hague, *f.n.*, heɪg, hayg

Hahessy, *f.n.*, 'heɪəsɪ, háy-ĕssi

Haig, *f.n.*, heɪg, hayg. *Appropriate also for Earl* ~.

Haigh, *f.n.*, heɪg, hayg

Haigh *Gtr. M'chester*, heɪ, hay

Haight, *f.n.*, haɪt, hīt

Haighton *Lancs.*, 'haɪtən, hítŏn

Hailes, Barony of, heɪlz, haylz

Hailes Castle *Lothian*, heɪlz, haylz

Haileyburian, *one educated at* **Haileybury** *College*, ,heɪlɪ-'bjʊərɪən, haylibyŏŏriăn

Haileybury *Herts.*, 'heɪlɪbərɪ, háylibŭri

Hailsham *E. Sussex*, 'heɪlʃəm, háyl-shăm. *Appropriate also for the Viscountcy of* ~.

Hailsham of Saint Marylebone, Baron, 'heɪlʃəm əv snt 'mærɪ-

boʊn, háyl-shăm ŏv sɪnt márribōn

Hain, *f.n.*, heɪn, hayn

Hainault *London*, 'heɪnɔt, háynawt

Haire, *f.n.*, hɛər, hair. *Appropriate also for the Barony of* ~.

Hairmyres *S'clyde*, hɛər'maɪərz, hairmírz

Hakin *Dyfed*, 'heɪkɪn, háykin

Hakluyt, Richard, *16th-c. historian and geographer*, 'hæklut, háck-loot; 'hæklwɪt, háckl-wit. *The former is much the more usual traditional pronunciation, but there is some evidence that the second was current in his own day.*

Halahan, *f.n.*, 'hæləhən, hálăhăn

Halam *Notts.*, 'heɪləm, háylăm

Halas, *f.n.*, 'hæləs, hálăss

Halbeath *Fife*, 'hɒlbɪθ, háwl-beeth

Halcrow, *f.n.*, 'hælkroʊ, hálkrō

Haldane, *f.n.*, 'hɒldən, háwldăn; 'hɒldeɪn, háwldayn

Haldon, Great *and* **Little,** *Devon*, 'hɒldən, háwldŏn. *Appropriate also for the Barony of* ~.

Halebarns *Gtr. M'chester*, heɪl-'bɑrnz, haylba'arnz

Haler, *f.n.*, 'heɪlər, háylĕr

Halesowen *W. Midlands*, heɪlz-'oʊɪn, haylzō-ĕn

Halewood *Merseyside*, 'heɪl'wʊd, háylwŏŏd

Haley, *f.n.*, 'heɪlɪ, háyli

Halford, *f.n.*, 'hælfərd, hálfŏrd; 'hɒlfərd, háwlfŏrd

Halford *Salop*, 'hɒlfərd, háwlfŏrd

Halford *Warwicks.*, 'hælfərd, hálfŏrd; 'hɑfərd, há'afŏrd

Halfpenny, *f.n.*, 'hɒfpənɪ, haáf-pĕni

Halket, *f.n.*, 'hælkɪt, hálkĕt

Halkett, *f.n.*, 'hælkɪt, hálkĕt; 'hɒlkɪt, háwlkĕt; 'hækɪt, háckĕt

Halkirk *H'land*, 'hɒlkərk, háwl-kirk

Halkyn *Clwyd*, 'hælkɪn, hálkin

Hallam, *f.n.*, 'hæləm, hálăm

Hallam *parliamentary division of Sheffield*, 'hæləm, hálăm

Hallamshire Hospital *Sheffield*, 'hæləmʃər, hálăm-shĕr

Halland *E. Sussex*, 'hælɒnd, hálănd

Hallas, *f.n.*, 'hæləs, hálăss

Hallaton *Leics.*, 'hælətən, hálătŏn

Hallatrow *Avon*, 'hælətroʊ, hálătrō

Hallé, *f.n.*, 'hæleɪ, hálay. *Appropriate also for the* ~ *Orchestra.*

Hallen *Avon*, 'hælən, hálĕn

Hallesy, *f.n.*, 'hælɪsɪ, hálĕssi

Hallett, *f.n.*, 'hælɪt, hálĕt
Hallewell, *f.n.*, 'hælɪwel, háli-wel
Halley, Edmond, *astronomer and mathematician*, 'hælɪ, háli
Halliday, *f.n.*, 'hælɪdeɪ, háliday
Hallin *Skye*, 'hælɪn, hálin
Hallinan, *f.n.*, 'hælɪnən, hálinän
Halling *Kent*, 'hɒlɪŋ, háwling
Hallingbury, Great *and* Little, *Essex*, 'hɒlɪŋbərɪ, hóllingbüri; 'hɒlɪŋbərɪ, háwlingbüri
Hallisey, *f.n.*, 'hælɪsɪ, hálissi
Hall i' th' Wood *Gtr. M'chester*, 'hɒlɪt 'wʊd, háwlit wood
Halliwell, *f.n.*, 'hælɪwel, háli-wel
Hallmark, *f.n.*, 'hɒlmɑrk, háwl-maark
Halloughton *Notts.*, hæ'lɒtən, haláwtŏn
Halmore *Glos.*, 'hælmɔr, hálmor
Halnaker *W. Sussex*, 'hænəkər, hánnăkĕr
Halpern, *f.n.*, 'hælpərn, hálpĕrn
Halpin, *f.n.*, 'hælpɪn, hálpin
Halsall, *f.n.*, 'hælsl, hálssl; 'hɒlsl, háwlssl
Halsall *Lancs.*, 'hɒlsl, háwlssl
Halsbury, Earl of, 'hɒlzbərɪ, háwlzbüri
Halse, *f.n.*, hæls, halss; hɒls, hawlss
Halse *Northants.*, hæls, halss; hɒs, hawss
Halse *Somerset*, hɒls, hawlss
Halsetown *Cornwall*, 'hɒlztaʊn, háwlztown
Halsey, *f.n.*, 'hælsɪ, hálssi; 'hɒlzɪ, háwlzi; 'hɒlsɪ, háwlssi
Halstan, *f.n.*, 'hɒlstən, háwlstän
Halstead, *f.n.*, 'hælsted, hálstĕd; 'hælstɪd, hálstĭd
Halstock *Dorset*, 'hɒlstɒk, háwlstock
Halstow, Lower, *Kent*, 'lovər 'hælstoʊ, lṓ-ĕr hálsstṓ
Halswell, *f.n.*, 'hælzwel, hálzwel
Haltemprice *Humberside*, 'hɒltəmpraɪs, háwltĕmpriss
Halton Holgate, *also spelt* Halton Holegate, *Lincs.*, 'hɒltən 'hɒlgeɪt, háwltŏn hólgayt
Halward, *f.n.*, 'hælwərd, hálwărd
Halwell *Devon*, 'hælwel, hálwel; 'hɒlwel, háwlwel
Halwill *Devon*, 'hælwɪl, hálwil; 'hɒlwɪl, háwlwil
Hambley, *f.n.*, 'hæmblɪ, hámbli
Hambloch, *f.n.*, 'hæmblɒk, hámblock
Hambourg, *f.n.*, 'hæmbɜrg, hámburg
Hambro, *f.n.*, 'hæmbroʊ, hámbrō; 'hæmbrə, hámbră

Hambrook, *f.n.*, 'hæmbrʊk, hámbrook
Hamburger, *f.n.*, 'hæmbɜrgər, hámburgĕr
Hamer, *f.n.*, 'heɪmər, háymĕr
Hameringham *Lincs.*, 'hæmərɪŋəm, hámmĕring-äm
Hamerton *Cambs.*, 'hæmərtən, hámmĕrtŏn
Hamey, *f.n.*, 'heɪmɪ, háymi
Hamfallow *Glos.*, hæm'fæloʊ, hamfálō
Hamilton, *f.n.*, 'hæmltən, hámml-tŏn
Hamilton *S'clyde*, 'hæmltən, hámmltŏn
Hamilton of Dalzell, Baron, 'hæmltən əv di'el, hámmltŏn ŏv dee-éll
Hamiltonsbawn *Co. Armagh*, ˌhæmltənz'bɔn, hammltŏnz-báwn
Hamish, *C.n.*, 'heɪmɪʃ, háymish
Hammant, *f.n.*, 'hæmənt, hámmänt
Hammill, *f.n.*, 'hæmɪl, hámmil
Hammond, *f.n.*, 'hæmənd, hámmŏnd
Hammonds, *f.n.*, 'hæməndz, hámmŏndz
Hamnett, *f.n.*, 'hæmnɪt, hám-nĕt
Hamoaze *R. Tamar estuary*, *Cornwall–Devon*, 'hæmoʊz, hámmōz
Hamond, *f.n.*, 'hæmənd, hámmŏnd
Hampden, Viscount, 'hæmdən, hámdĕn
Hampden, *f.n.*, 'hæmdən, hámdĕn
Hampden Park *S'clyde*, *E. Sussex*, 'hæmdən 'pɑrk, hámdĕn páark
Hampshire *Co. name*, 'hæmpʃər, hámp-shĕr
Hampson, *f.n.*, 'hæmsən, hámssŏn
Hampstead *London*, 'hæmpstɪd, hámpstĕd; 'hæmpsted, hámpsted
Hamsey *E. Sussex*, 'hæmzɪ, hámzi
Hamsterley *Durham*, 'hæmstərlɪ, hámstĕrli
Hanak, *f.n.*, 'hænək, hánnăk
Hanbury, *f.n.*, 'hænbərɪ, hánbüri
Hanchant, *f.n.*, 'hænʃənt, hán-shänt
Hancock, *f.n.*, 'hæŋkɒk, hánk-ock
Handcock, *f.n.*, 'hændkɒk, hánd-kock
Handel, George Frideric, *composer*, 'hændl, hándl. *The original German was* Händel, *pronounced* 'hendl, héndl.

Handelian, *pertaining to* **Handel,** hæn'diliən, handeéliăn
Hankin, *f.n.,* 'hæŋkın, hánkin
Hannahstown *Co. Antrim,* 'hænəztaυn, hánnăztown
Hanrahan, *f.n.,* 'hænrəhən, hánră-hăn
Hanratty, *f.n.,* hæn'rætɪ, hanrátti
Hansard, *f.n.,* 'hænsard, hánssaard
Hanslope *Bucks.,* 'hænsloυp, hánsslōp
Happisburgh *Norfolk,* 'heızbərə, háyzbŭră
Harberton *Devon,* 'harbərtən, haárbĕrtŏn. *Appropriate also for Viscount* ~.
Harbertonford *Devon,* 'harbərtən-fərd, haárbĕrtŏnford
Harborne *W. Midlands,* 'harbɔrn, haárborn
Harcourt, *f.n.,* 'harkɔrt, haárkort; 'harkərt, haárkŭrt. *The second is appropriate for the Viscountcy of* ~.
Hardaker, *f.n.,* 'hardeıkər, haárdaykĕr
Harden, *f.n.,* 'hardən, haárdĕn
Hardenhuish *Wilts.,* 'harnıʃ, haárnish; ,hardən'hjuıʃ, haardĕn-héwish
Harding, *f.n.,* 'hardıŋ, haárding
Hardinge, *f.n.,* 'hardıŋ, haárding; 'hardındʒ, haárdinj. *The first is appropriate for Viscount* ~.
Hardinge of Penshurst, Baron, 'hardıŋ əv 'penzhərst, haárding ŏv pénz-hurst
Hardres, *f.n.,* hardz, haardz
Hardres, Lower *and* Upper, *Kent,* hardz, haardz
Hardress, *f.n.,* 'hardres, haárdress
Hardwicke, Earl of, 'hardwık, haárdwick
Hardwicke, Sir Cedric, *actor,* 'sidrık 'hardwık, seédrick haárdwick
Hardy, *f.n.,* 'hardı, haárdi
Harefield *London, Hants,* 'heər-fild, háirfeeld
Harehaugh *Northd.,* 'heərhaf, háir-haaf
Harenc, *f.n.,* 'hærɒŋ, hárrong
Haresceugh *Cumbria,* 'heərskjuf, háirskewf
Harewood, *f.n.,* 'heərwυd, háir-wŏod
Harewood *W. Yorks.,* 'harwυd, haárwŏod; 'heərwυd, háirwŏod. *The first is appropriate for the Earl of* ~ *and for* ~ *House. The second is usual in the village.*

Harford, *f.n.,* 'harfərd, haárfŏrd
Hargan, *f.n.,* 'hargən, haárgăn
Harger, *f.n.,* 'hardʒər, haárjĕr
Hargham *Norfolk,* 'harfəm, haárfăm
Hargreaves, *f.n.,* 'hargrivz, haár-greevz; 'hargreıvz, haárgrayvz. *In its native North of England, the first is appropriate. The second was that of Mrs Alice* ~, *the original Alice in Wonderland.*
Haringey *London,* 'hærıŋgeı, hárring-gay
Harington, *f.n.,* 'hærıŋtən, hárringtŏn
Harkness, *f.n.,* 'harknıs, haárk-nĕss
Harkouk, *f.n.,* har'kuk, haarkoók
Harlaxton *Lincs.,* 'harləkstən, haárlăkstŏn
Harle, *f.n.,* harl, haarl
Harlech *Gwynedd,* 'harləx, haár-lĕch. *Appropriate also for Baron* ~.
Harlesden *London,* 'harlzdən, haárlzdĕn
Harlestone *Northants.,* 'harlstən, haárlstŏn
Harlow *Essex,* 'harloυ, haárlō
Harmes, *f.n.,* harmz, haarmz
Harmondsworth *London,* 'harməndzwərθ, haármŏndzwurth
Harneis, *f.n.,* 'harnıs, haárniss
Haroldswick *Shetland,* 'hærəldz-wık, hárrŏldzwick
Harpenden *Herts.,* 'harpəndən, haárpĕndĕn
Harpham, *f.n.,* 'harpəm, haárpăm
Harpole *Northants.,* 'harpoυl, haárpōl
Harpwood, *f.n.,* 'harpwυd, haárp-wŏod
Harraby *Cumbria,* 'hærəbı, hár-răbi
Harragin, *f.n.,* 'hærəgın, hárrăgin
Harrap, *f.n.,* 'hærəp, hárrăp
Harray *Orkney,* 'hærı, hárri
Harré, *f.n.,* hə'reı, háráy
Harrhy, *f.n.,* 'hærı, hárri
Harries, *f.n.,* 'hærıs, hárriss
Harrietsham *Kent,* 'hærıət-ʃəm, hárriĕt-shăm
Harris, *f.n.,* 'hærıs, hárriss
Harriseahead *Staffs.,* 'hærisi'hed, hárrissee-héd
Harrod, *f.n.,* 'hærəd, hárrŏd
Harrogate *N. Yorks.,* 'hærəgıt, hárrŏgit
Harrold *Beds.,* 'hærəld, hárrŏld
Harrop, *f.n.,* 'hærəp, hárröp
Harrovian, *one educated at* **Harrow School,** hə'roυvıən, hărróvian
Harrow, *f.n.,* 'hæroυ, hárrō

Harrow *London*, 'hærou, hárrō
Harrowden, Great *and* Little, *Northants.*, 'hæroudən, hárrōděn
Harrup, *f.n.*, 'hærəp, hárrŭp
Hart, *f.n.*, hart, haart
Hartcup, *f.n.*, 'hartkʌp, haárt-kup
Hartford *Cambs.*, 'hartfərd, haártförd
Hartham *Herts.*, 'hartəm, haártăm
Harthan, *f.n.*, 'harðən, haárthăn
Hartismere, Baron, 'hartızmɪər, haártizmeer
Hartlebury *H. & W.*, 'hartlbərı, haártlbŭri
Hartlepool *Cleveland*, 'hartlıpul, haártlipool
Hartley Wespall *Hants*, 'hartlı 'wespɔl, haártli wéspawl
Hartley Wintney *Hants*, 'hartlı 'wıntnı, haártli wíntni
Hartoch, *f.n.*, 'hartɒk, haártock
Hartopp, *f.n.*, 'hartɒp, haártop
Hartpury *Glos.*, 'hartpərı, haártpŭri
Hartshorn, *f.n.*, 'hartshɔrn, haárts-horn
Hartshorne, *f.n.*, 'hartshɔrn, haárts-horn
Hartsilver, *f.n.*, 'hartsılvər, haártsilvĕr
Hartung, *f.n.*, 'hartʌŋ, haártung
Harvey of Tasburgh, Baron, 'harvı əv 'teızbərə, haárvi ŏv táyzbŭrǎ
Harwell *Berks.*, 'harwəl, haárwĕl
Harwich *Essex*, 'hærıdʒ, hárrij; 'hærıtʃ, hárritch
Harwood, *f.n.*, 'harwud, haárwŏŏd
Hasbury *W. Midlands*, 'hæzbərı, házbŭri
Haselbech, *f.n.*, 'heızlbıtʃ, háyzlbeetch
Haseldine, *f.n.*, 'hæzldaın, házzldīn
Haseler, *f.n.*, 'heızlər, háyzlĕr
Haseley *Warwicks.*, 'heızlı, háyzli
Haseley, Great *and* Little, *Oxon.*, 'heızlı, háyzli
Haselor *Warwicks.*, 'heızlɔr, háyzlor
Hashagen, *f.n.*, 'hæʃəgən, hásh-ăgĕn
Haskeir *W. Isles*, hə'skıər, hă-skéer
Hasketon *Suffolk*, 'hæskıtən, hásskĕtŏn
Haslam, *f.n.*, 'hæzləm, házlăm
Haslemere *Surrey*, 'heızlmıər, háyzlmeer
Hasler, *f.n.*, 'hæzlər, házlĕr

Haslett, *f.n.*, 'heızlıt, háyzlĕt; 'hæzlıt, házlĕt
Haslingden *Lancs.*, 'hæzlıŋdən, házlingdĕn
Haslingfield *Cambs.*, 'heızlıŋfıld, háyzlingfeeld; 'hæzlıŋfıld, házlingfeeld
Hassall, *f.n.*, 'hæsl, hássl
Hassard, *f.n.*, 'hæsard, hássaard
Haster *H'land*, 'hæstər, hásstĕr
Hastie, *f.n.*, 'heıstı, háyssti
Hastings, *f.n.*, 'heıstıŋz, háysstingz
Hastings *E. Sussex*, 'heıstıŋz, háysstingz
Haston, *f.n.*, 'hæstən, hásstŏn
Haswell, *f.n.*, 'hæzwel, házwel
Hatch Beauchamp *Somerset*, 'hætʃ 'bitʃəm, hátch béetchăm
Hatfield Peverel *Essex*, 'hætfıld 'pevərəl, hátfeeld pévvĕrĕl
Hathaway, *f.n.*, 'hæθəweı, háthă-way
Hathern *Leics.*, 'hæðərn, háthĕrn
Hathersage *Derby.*, 'hæðərseıdʒ, háthĕr-sayj
Hatherton, Baron, 'hæðərtən, háthĕrtŏn
Hathorn, *f.n.*, 'hɔθərn, háwthorn; 'heıθərn, háythorn; 'hæθərn, háthorn
Hathorne, *f.n.*, 'hɔθərn, háwthŏrn
Hattersley, *f.n.*, 'hætərzlı, háttĕrzli
Hatton, *f.n.*, 'hætən, háttŏn
Hauger, *f.n.*, 'hɔgər, háwgĕr
Haugh, Nether *and* Upper, *S. Yorks.*, hɔf, hawf
Haugham *Kent*, 'hʌfəm, húffăm
Haugham *Lincs.*, 'hæfəm, háffăm
Haughley *Suffolk*, 'hɔlı, háwli
Haughmond Hill *Salop*, 'hɔmənd 'hıl, háwmŏnd hill; 'heımənd 'hıl, háymŏnd hill
Haughney, *f.n.*, 'hɒxnı, hóchni
Haugh of Urr *D. & G.*, hax əv '3r, haách ŏv úr
Haughton, *f.n.*, 'hɔtən, háwtŏn
Haughton *Gtr. M'chester*, *Notts.*, *Powys*, 'hɔtən, háwtŏn
Haughton-le-Skerne *Durham*, 'hɔtən lə 'skərn, háwtŏn lĕ skérn
Haulbowline Rock *Co. Down*, hɔl'boulın, hawlbólin
Haulgh *Gtr. M'chester*, hɒf, hoff
Hauser, *f.n.*, 'hɔzər, háwzer
Hautbois, Great *and* Little, *Norfolk*, 'hɒbıs, hóbbiss
Hauxton *Cambs.*, 'hɔkstən, háwkstŏn
Hauxwell *N. Yorks.*, 'hɔkswel, háwkswel
Havant *Hants*, 'hævənt, hávvănt

Havard, f.n., 'hævərd, hávvărd
Havell, f.n., 'hævl, hávvl. Appro-
    priate for E. B. ~, Indian-art
    historian.
Havely, f.n., 'hævəlɪ, hávvĕli
Havenhand, f.n., 'heɪvənhænd,
    háyvĕn-hand
Haverah Park N. Yorks., 'hævərə
    'park, hávvĕră páark
Haverfordwest Dyfed, ,hævər-
    fərd'west, havvĕrförd-wést;
    ,harfərd'west, haarförd-wést
Havergate Island Suffolk, 'hævər-
    geɪt, hávvĕrgayt
Haverhill Suffolk, 'heɪvrɪl,
    háyvril
Haverigg Cumbria, 'hævərɪg,
    hávvĕrig
Havering-atte-Bower London,
    'heɪvərɪŋ ætɪ 'bauər, háyvĕring
    atti bówĕr
Haveringland Norfolk, 'heɪvərɪŋ-
    lənd, háyvĕring-lănd
Havers, f.n., 'heɪvərz, háyvĕrz
Haverton Hill Cleveland, 'hævər-
    tən 'hɪl, hávvĕrtŏn híll
Haviland, f.n., 'hævɪlənd, hávvi-
    lănd
Haward, f.n., 'heɪwərd, háywărd;
    'hɔːrd, háw-ărd; hard, haard;
    hɔrd, hord
Hawarden, Viscount, 'heɪwɔrdən,
    háy-wawrdĕn
Hawarden, f.n., 'hardən, haárdĕn
Hawarden, Clwyd, 'hardən, haár-
    dĕn. Appropriate also for the
    Barony of Gladstone of ~.
Haweis, f.n., 'hɔ-ɪs, háw-iss
Hawes N. Yorks., hɔz, hawz
Hawes Water, Lake, Cumbria,
    'hɔzwɔtər, háwz-wawtĕr
Hawick Borders, 'hɔ-ɪk, háw-ick
Hawkes, f.n., hɔks, hawks
Hawkinge Kent, 'hɔkɪndʒ, háw-
    kinj
Haworth, f.n., 'hauərθ, hów-ŭrth
Haworth W. Yorks., 'hauərθ,
    hów-ŭrth; 'hɔərθ, háw-ŭrth
Hawridge Bucks., 'hærɪdʒ, hárrij
Haws, f.n., hɔz, hawz
Hawtrey, f.n., 'hɔtrɪ, háwtri
Haxell, f.n., 'hæksl, hácksl
Haxey Humberside, 'hæksɪ,
    hácksi
Hayball, f.n., 'heɪbɔl, háybawl
Haycock, f.n., 'heɪkɒk, háykock
Hayden, f.n., 'heɪdən, háydĕn
Haydn, C.n., 'heɪdn, háydn
Haydock, f.n., 'heɪdɒk, háydock
Haydock Merseyside, 'heɪdɒk,
    háydock
Haydon, f.n., 'heɪdən, háydŏn.
    Appropriate for Benjamin ~,
    19th-c. historical painter.

Hayes, f.n., heɪz, hayz
Hayhow, f.n., 'heɪhou, háy-hō
Hayhurst, f.n., 'heɪhərst, háy-
    -hŭrst
Hayland, f.n., 'heɪlənd, háylănd
Hayle Cornwall, heɪl, hayl.
    Appropriate also for the river of
    this name.
Hayman, f.n., 'heɪmən, háymăn
Hays, f.n., heɪz, hayz
Haysom, f.n., 'heɪsəm, háyssŏm
Hayter, f.n., 'heɪtər, háytĕr
Haytor Devon, 'heɪ'tɔr, háy-tór
Hayward, f.n., 'heɪwərd, háywărd
Hazan, f.n., hə'zæn, hăzánn
Hazard, f.n., 'hæzərd, házzaard
Hazeldine, f.n., 'heɪzldaɪn, háyzl-
    dīn; 'heɪzldɪn, háyzldeen
Hazell, f.n., 'heɪzl, háyzl
Hazlerigg, f.n., 'heɪzlrɪg, háyzlrig.
    Appropriate also for Baron ~.
Hazlitt, f.n., 'heɪzlɪt, háyzlĕt;
    'hæzlɪt, házlĕt. Although the
    second is now usual, the first was
    that of William ~, essayist and
    critic, and is still used by his
    descendants.
Hazlitt Gallery London, 'hæzlɪt,
    házlit
Hazzard, f.n., 'hæzərd, házzărd
Heacham Norfolk, 'hetʃəm,
    hétchăm; 'hitʃəm, héetchăm
Headfort, Marquess of, 'hedfərt,
    hédfŏrt
Headingley W. Yorks., 'hedɪŋlɪ,
    hédding-li
Headlam, f.n., 'hedləm, hédlăm
Heaf, f.n., hif, heef
Heage Derby., hidʒ, heej
Heaks, f.n., hiks, heeks
Heal, f.n., hil, heel
Healaugh N. Yorks., 'hilə, héelă
Heald, f.n., hild, heeld
Healy, f.n., 'hilɪ, héeli
Heamoor Cornwall, 'heɪmɔr, háy-
    mor
Heanen, f.n., 'hinən, héenĕn
Heaney, f.n., 'hinɪ, héeni
Heanor Derby., 'hinər, héenŏr;
    'heɪnər, háynŏr
Heanton Punchardon Devon,
    'hentən 'pʌnʃərdən, héntŏn
    pún-shărdŏn; 'hentən 'pʌnʃər-
    dən, háyntŏn pún-shărdŏn
Heape, f.n., hip, heep
Hearn, f.n., hɜrn, hern
Heaslip, f.n., 'heɪslɪp, háysslip
Heath, f.n., hiθ, heeth
Heathcoat, f.n., 'heθkət, héthkŏt
Heathcoat Amory, f.n., 'heθkət
    'eɪmərɪ, héthkŏt áymŏri
Heathcock, f.n., 'hiθkɒk, héeth-
    kock
Heathcote, C.n., 'heθkət, héthkŏt

Heathcote, *f.n.*, 'heθkət, héthkŏt; 'hiθkout, héethkōt
Heathcote *Derby.*, 'heθkət, héthkŏt
Heathcote-Drummond-Willoughby, *f.n.*, 'heθkət 'drʌmənd 'wıləbı, héthkŏt drúmmŏnd willŏbi. *Family name of the Earl of Ancaster.*
Heather *Leics.*, 'hiðər, héethĕr
Heathery Cleugh *Durham*, 'heðərı 'klʌf, héthĕri klúff
Heathfield *Devon*, *Dyfed*, *Cumbria*, 'hiθfild, héethfeeld
Heathorn, *f.n.*, 'hiθɔrn, hée-thorn
Heathrow *London*, 'hiθ'rou héeth-rő
Heatlie, *f.n.*, 'hitlı, héetli
Heaver, *f.n.*, 'hivər, héevĕr
Heaviside, *f.n.*, 'hevısaıd, hévvissíd
Heawood, *f.n.*, 'heıwud, háywōōd
Heaword, *f.n.*, 'heıwərd, háywürd
Hebburn *Tyne & Wear*, 'hebərn, hébburn
Hebditch, *f.n.*, 'hebdıtʃ, hébditch
Hebel, *f.n.*, 'hebl, hébbl
Heber, *f.n.*, 'hibər, héebĕr
Hebers *Gtr. M'chester*, 'hibərz, héebĕrz
Hebert, *f.n.*, 'hibərt, héebĕrt
Hebron *Dyfed*, *Gwynedd*, 'hebrɒn, hébbron
Heckmondwike *W. Yorks.*, 'hekməndwaık, héckmŏndwīk
Hedgecock, *f.n.*, 'hedʒkɒk, héjkock
Hedgehope *Northd.*, 'hedʒəp, héjjŏp
Hedleyhope *Durham*, 'hedlı-'houp, hédli-hōp
Hednesford *Staffs.*, 'hensfərd, hénssförd; 'hedʒfərd, héjförd
Hedon *Humberside*, 'hedən, héddön
Heelas, *f.n.*, 'hiləs, héeláss
Heffernan, *f.n.*, 'hefərnən, héffĕrnän
Hegarty, *f.n.*, 'hegərtı, héggärti
Heggie, *f.n.*, 'hegı, héggi
Heigham *Norfolk*, 'heıəm, háy-ăm
Heighington *Durham*, 'heıŋtən, háy-ingtŏn; 'haıŋtən, hí-ingtŏn; 'haıntən, híntŏn
Heighington *Lincs.*, 'heıŋtən, háy-ingtŏn; 'hiıŋtən, hée-ingtŏn
Heighton, *f.n.*, 'heıtən, háytŏn
Heighway, *f.n.*, 'heıweı, háy-way; 'haıweı, hí-way
Heilbron, *f.n.*, 'haılbrɒn, hílbron
Heilgers, *f.n.*, 'haılgərz, hílgĕrz
Heilpern, *f.n.*, 'haılpərn, hílpĕrn
Heim Gallery *London*, haım, hīm
Heinekey, *f.n.*, 'haınıkı, hínĕki

Heinemann, *f.n.*, 'haınəmən, hínĕmän
Heiney, *f.n.*, 'haını, híni
Heisker *W. Isles*, 'haıskər, hísskĕr
Hele, *f.n.*, hil, heel; 'hilı, héeli
Hele *Devon*, hil, heel
Hele Stone *Stonehenge (Wilts.)*, 'hil stoun, héel stŏn
Helena, *C.n.*, 'helınə, héllĕnä; hə'linə, hĕléenä
Helensburgh *S'clyde*, 'helənzbərə, héllĕnzbŭră
Helenus, *C.n.*, 'helınəs, héllĕnüss
Helhoughton *Norfolk*, hel'houtən, hel-hótŏn; hel'hautən, hel--hówtŏn
Helier, saint, 'heliər, hélli-ĕr
Helions Bumpstead *Essex*, 'hiliənz 'bʌmpsted, héeli-ŏnz búmpsted
Hellewell, *f.n.*, 'helıwel, hélli--wel
Hellicar, *f.n.*, 'helıkɑr, héllikaar
Hellingly *E. Sussex*, ˌhelıŋ'laı, helling-lí
Helliwell, *f.n.*, 'helıwel, hélliwel
Hellowell, *f.n.*, 'heləwel, héllŏ--wel
Hellyar, *f.n.*, 'heljər, hél-yär
Helme, *f.n.*, helm, helm
Helmingham *Suffolk*, 'helmıŋəm, hélming-ăm
Helmore, *f.n.*, 'helmɔr, hélmor
Helmsley *N. Yorks.*, 'helmzlı, hélmzli; 'hemzlı, hémzli
Helston *Cornwall*, 'helstən, hélsstŏn
Helvellyn *Cumbria*, hel'velın, helvéllin
Helwick Shoals *and* lightship, *off W. Glam.*, 'helık, héllick
Hely, *f.n.*, 'hilı, héeli
Helyer, *f.n.*, 'heliər, hélli-ĕr
Heman, *f.n.*, 'himən, héemän
Hemans, *f.n.*, 'hemənz, hémmänz
Hemerdon *Devon*, 'hemərdən, hémmĕrdŏn
Hemery, *f.n.*, 'hemərı, hémmĕri
Heming, *f.n.*, 'hemıŋ, hémming
Hemingbrough *N. Yorks.*, 'hemıŋbrʌf, hémming-bruff
Hemingford Abbots *Cambs.*, 'hemıŋfərd 'æbəts, hémmingförd ábbŏts
Hemingford Grey *Cambs.*, 'hemıŋfərd 'greı, hémmingförd gráy
Hemmerde, *f.n.*, 'hemərdı, hémmĕrdi
Hempel, *f.n.*, 'hempl, hémpl
Hemswell *Lincs.*, 'hemzwel, hémzwel
Hemy, *f.n.*, 'hemı, hémmi

Hemyock *Devon*, 'hemjɒk, hém-yock; 'hemiɒk, hémmi-ock

Henbrow, *f.n.*, 'henbrou, hénbrō

Henderskelfe Castle, *N. Yorks.*, 'hendərskelf, héndĕr-skelf. *Castle Howard was built on the site of this former castle.*

Henderson, *f.n.*, 'hendərsən, héndĕrssŏn

Hendreforgan *Mid Glam.*, ˌhendrı'vɔrgən, hendrivórgăn

Hendri *Powys*, 'hendrı, héndri

Hendy, *f.n.*, 'hendı, héndi

Hene, *f.n.*, 'hinı, héeni

Heneage, *f.n.*, 'henıdʒ, hénnij. *Appropriate also for the Barony of* ~.

Henebery, *f.n.*, 'henıbərı, hénnĕbĕri

Heneghan, *f.n.*, 'henıgən, hénnĕgăn

Heneglwys *Gwynedd*, hen'egluıs, henéglŏŏ-iss

Heneker, *f.n.*, 'henıkər, hénnĕkĕr

Hengoed *Mid Glam.*, 'heŋgɔıd, héng-goyd

Heniarth *Powys*, 'henjarθ, hén-yaarth; 'henıarθ, hénni-aarth

Henig, *f.n.*, 'henıg, hénnig

Henlere, *f.n.*, 'henlıər, hénleer

Henley-in-Arden *Warwicks.*, 'henlı ın 'ardən, hénli in aárdĕn

Henley-on-Thames *Oxon.*, 'henlı ɒn 'temz, hénli on témz

Henllan *Clwyd, Dyfed, Gwent*, 'henłæn, hén-hlan

Henllan Amgoed *Dyfed*, 'henłæn 'æmgɔıd, hén-hlan ámgoyd

Henlow *Beds.*, 'henlou, hénlō

Hennebry, *f.n.*, 'henıbrı, hénnĕbri

Hennessey, *f.n.*, 'henısı, hénnéssi

Hennessy, *f.n.*, 'henısı, hénnéssi

Henniker, Baron, 'henıkər, hénnikĕr

Henocq, *f.n.*, 'henɒk, hénnock

Henri, *f.n.*, 'henrı, hénri

Henriques, *f.n.*, hen'rikız, hen-réékĕz

Henschel, Sir George, *composer*, 'henʃl, hénshl

Henshall, *f.n.*, 'henʃl, hénshl; 'henʃɔl, hén-shawl

Hensher, *f.n.*, 'henʃər, hén-shĕr

Henshilwood, *f.n.*, 'henʃlwud, hénshl-wŏŏd

Henstead *Suffolk*, 'henstıd, hén-stĕd

Henwick *H. & W.*, 'henwık, hénwick

Heolgerrig *Mid Glam.*, heıəl-'gerıg, hay-ŏl-gérrig

Heol-y-cyw *Mid Glam.*, ˌheıəl ə 'kju, hay-ŏl ă kéw

Hepburn, *f.n.*, 'hebərn, hébburn; 'hebərn, hébbŭrn

Hepburn *Northd.*, 'hebərn, héb-burn

Hepburne, *f.n.*, 'hebərn, hébbŭrn

Heppell, *f.n.*, 'hepl, héppl

Heppenstall, *f.n.*, 'hepənstɔl, héppĕn-stawl

Hepplewhite, *f.n.*, 'heplʍaıt, hépplwhīt

Heptonstall *W. Yorks.*, 'heptən-stɔl, héptŏn-stawl

Hepworth, *f.n.*, 'hepwɜrθ, hép-wurth

Herapath, *f.n.*, 'herəpaθ, hérrá-paath

Herbecq, *f.n.*, 'hɜrbek, hérbeck

Herbison, *f.n.*, 'hɜrbısən, hérbis-sŏn

Herdwick, *breed of sheep*, 'hɜrd-wık, hérdwick

Hereford *H. & W.*, 'herıfərd, hérrĕfŏrd. *Appropriate also for Viscount* ~.

Heren, *f.n.*, 'herən, hérrĕn

Herford, *f.n.*, 'hɜrfərd, hérfŏrd

Hergest Ridge, *hill range, H. & W.*, 'hargıst, haárgĕst

Herincx, Raimund, *opera singer*, 'reımənd 'herıŋks, ráymŭnd hérrinks

Heriot *Borders*, 'herıət, hérriŏt

Herklots, *f.n.*, 'harklɒts, hérklots

Herkness, *f.n.*, 'harknıs, haárk-nĕss

Herkomer, *f.n.*, 'hɜrkəmər, hér-kŏmĕr

Herlihy, *f.n.*, 'hɜrlıhı, hérli-hi

Hermaness *Shetland*, 'hɜrmənes, hérmăness

Hermes, *f.n.*, 'hɜrmiz, hérmeez. *Appropriate for Gertrude* ~, *sculptor.*

Hermges, *f.n.*, 'hɜrmdʒiz, hérm-jeez

Herner, *f.n.*, 'hɜrnər, hérnĕr

Heron, *f.n.*, 'herən, hérrŏn

Herriard *Hants*, 'herıərd, hérriărd

Herries, Baroness, 'herıs, hérriss

Herrin, *f.n.*, 'herın, hérrin

Herringshaw, *f.n.*, 'herıŋʃɔ, hérring-shaw

Herriot, *f.n.*, 'herıət, hérriŏt

Herschell, *f.n.*, 'hɜrʃl, hérshl. *Appropriate also for Baron* ~.

Herstmonceux, *also spelt* **Hurstmonceaux, Hurstmonceux**, *E. Sussex*, ˌhɜrstmən'sju, herstmŏn-séw; ˌhɜrstmən'su, herstmŏn-soó

Hertford *Herts.*, 'harfərd, haár-fŏrd; 'hartfərd, haártfŏrd. *The first is appropriate for the Marquess of* ~.

Hertford College *Univ. of Oxford*, 'hɑːfərd, haárford
Hertingfordbury *Herts.*, 'hɑːtɪŋfərdberɪ, haártingfördberri
Hervey, *f.n.*, 'hɑːvɪ, haárvi
Herwald, *f.n.*, 'hɜːwəld, hérwáld
Heseltine, *f.n.*, 'hesltaɪn, héssltīn. *Appropriate for Philip ~, whose pseudonym as composer is Peter Warlock.*
Heselton, *f.n.*, 'hesltən, héssltŏn
Heshel, *f.n.*, 'heʃl, héshl
Hesilrige, *f.n.*, 'hezɪlrɪdʒ, hézzilrij
Hesketh, *f.n.*, 'heskəθ, héskěth. *Appropriate also for Baron ~.*
Heslerton, East *and* West, *N. Yorks.*, 'heslərtən, hésslěrtŏn
Hesmondhalgh, *f.n.*, 'hezməndhɔː, hézmŏnd-haw; 'hezməndhælʃ, hézmŏnd-halsh; 'hezməndhɒltʃ, hézmŏnd-hawltch
Hespe, *f.n.*, hesp, hessp
Hessary Tor *Devon*, 'hesərɪ 'tɔr, héssári tór
Hessé, *f.n.*, 'hesɪ, héssi
Hessenford *Cornwall*, 'hesənfərd, héssénfŏrd
Hessett *Suffolk*, 'hesɪt, héssĕt
Hession, *f.n.*, 'hesɪən, héssiŏn; 'heʃən, héshŏn
Hessle *Humberside*, 'hezl, hézzl
Heston *London*, 'hestən, hésstŏn
Heswall *Merseyside*, 'hezwəl, hézwǎl
Hethel *Norfolk*, 'heθl, héthl
Hetley, *f.n.*, 'hetlɪ, hétli
Hetton-le-Hole *Tyne & Wear*, 'hetən lə 'hoʊl, héttŏn lĕ hól
Heugh, *f.n.*, hju, hew
Heugh *Northd.*, hjuf, hewf
Heughan, *f.n.*, 'hjuən, héw-ăn
Heulwen, *Welsh C.n.*, 'haɪlwen, híIwen
Heulyn, *f.n.*, 'heɪlɪn, háylin
Heuston, *f.n.*, 'hjustən, héwstŏn
Heveningham Hall, *Suffolk*, 'henɪŋəm, hénning-ăm
Hever *Kent*, 'hivər, héevĕr
Heversham *Cumbria*, 'hevərʃəm, hévvĕr-shăm
Hevingham, *f.n.*, 'hevɪŋəm, hévving-ăm
Hewardine, *f.n.*, 'hjuərdin, héw-ărdeen
Hewart, Viscountcy of, 'hjuərt, héw-ărt
Hewaswater *Cornwall*, 'hjuəswɒtər, héw-ăss-wawtĕr
Hewelsfield *Glos.*, 'hjuəlzfild, héw-ĕlzfeeld
Hewett, *f.n.*, 'hjuɪt, héw-ĕt
Hewish, *f.n.*, 'hjuɪʃ, héw-ish

Hewitson, *f.n.*, 'hjuɪtsən, héw-itsŏn
Hewitt, *f.n.*, 'hjuɪt, héw-it
Hewlett, *f.n.*, 'hjulɪt, héwlĕt
Heworth *N. Yorks.*, 'hjuərθ, héw-ŭrth
Hext, *f.n.*, hekst, hekst
Hey, *f.n.*, heɪ, hay
Heycock, *f.n.*, 'heɪkɒk, háykock
Heyes, *f.n.*, heɪz, hayz
Heyford, Lower *and* Upper, *Northants., Oxon.*, 'heɪfərd, háyfŏrd
Heyford, Nether, *Northants.*, 'neðər 'heɪfərd, néthĕr háyfŏrd
Heyford at Bridge, *also called* **Lower Heyford**, *Oxon.*, 'heɪfərd ət 'brɪdʒ, háyfŏrd ăt brij
Heyford Warren, *also called* **Upper Heyford**, *Oxon.*, 'heɪfərd 'wɒrən, háyfŏrd wórrĕn
Heygate, *f.n.*, 'heɪgeɪt, háygayt; 'heɪgɪt, háygit
Heygen, *f.n.*, 'heɪgən, háygĕn
Heyhoe, *f.n.*, 'heɪhoʊ, háyhō
Heyner, *f.n.*, 'heɪnər, háynĕr
Heyno, *f.n.*, 'heɪnoʊ, háynō
Heyop *Powys*, 'heɪɒp, háy-ŏp
Heyrod *Gtr. M'chester*, 'herəd, hérrŏd
Heys, *f.n.*, heɪz, hayz
Heysham *Lancs.*, 'hiʃəm, hée-shăm
Heyshott *W. Sussex*, 'heɪʃɒt, háy-shot
Heytesbury, Baron, 'hetsbərɪ, hétsbŭri
Heytesbury *Wilts.*, 'heɪtsbərɪ, háytsbŭri
Heyther, *f.n.*, 'heðər, héthĕr. *Appropriate for William ~, founder of the Chair of Music at Oxford Univ., 1622.*
Heythrop *Oxon.*, 'hiθrəp, héethrŏp. *Appropriate also for the ~ Hunt.*
Heyting, *f.n.*, 'heɪtɪŋ, háyting
Heywood *Gtr. M'chester, Wilts.*, 'heɪwʊd, háywōod
Hibaldstow *Humberside*, 'hɪbldstoʊ, híbblstō
Hibberd, *f.n.*, 'hɪbərd, híbbĕrd
Hibbert, *f.n.*, 'hɪbərt, híbbĕrt
Hibbitt, *f.n.*, 'hɪbɪt, híbbit
Hickin, *f.n.*, 'hɪkɪn, híckin
Hickinbotham, *f.n.*, 'hɪkɪnbɒθəm, híckinbothăm
Hidcote *Glos.*, 'hɪdkət, hídkŏt
Hider, *f.n.*, 'haɪdər, hídĕr
Hiendley, South, *W. Yorks.*, 'hɪndlɪ, héendli
Higgens, *f.n.*, 'hɪgɪnz, híggĕnz
Higgins, *f.n.*, 'hɪgɪnz, hígginz

Higham, *f.n.,* 'haɪəm, hí-ăm
Higham *Kent,* 'haɪəm, hí-ăm
Higham *S. Yorks.,* 'haɪəm, hí-ăm;
  'hɪkəm, híckăm
Higham Ferrers *Northants.,*
  'haɪəm 'ferərz, hí-ăm férrĕrz
Higham Gobion *Beds.,* 'haɪəm
  'goubɪən, hí-ăm góbiŏn
Higham's Park *London,* 'haɪəmz
  'pɑːrk, hí-ămz paárk
High Bradley *N. Yorks.,* 'haɪ
  'brædlɪ, hí brádli
Highbury *London,* 'haɪbərɪ,
  híbŭri
Highclere *Hants,* 'haɪklɪər,
  híkleer
High Coniscliffe *Durham,* 'haɪ
  'kɒnɪsklɪf, hí kónniss-kliff
High Ercall *Salop,* 'haɪ 'ɑːrkl, hí
  aárkl
Highgate, *f.n.,* 'haɪgeɪt, hígayt
High Halden *Kent,* 'haɪ 'hɔːldən,
  hí háwldĕn
High Legh *Ches.,* 'haɪ 'liː, hí lée
Highley *Salop,* 'haɪlɪ, híli
Highnam *Glos.,* 'haɪnəm, hínăm
High Wych *Herts.,* 'haɪ 'waɪtʃ,
  hí wítch
High Wycombe *Bucks.,* 'haɪ
  'wɪkəm, hí wíckŏm
Hilaire, *f.n.,* hɪ'leər, hiláir
Hilbre *Island* *Merseyside,* 'hɪlbrɪ,
  hílbri
Hildenborough *Kent,* 'hɪldənbʌrə,
  híldĕn-burră
Hildersham *Cambs.,* 'hɪldərʃəm,
  híldĕr-shăm
Hilderstone *Staffs.,* 'hɪldərstən,
  híldĕrsstŏn
Hildreth, *f.n.,* 'hɪldrɪθ, híldrĕth
Hiley, *f.n.,* 'haɪlɪ, híli
Hilgay *Norfolk,* 'hɪlgeɪ, hílgay
Hillcoat, *f.n.,* 'hɪlkoʊt, hílkōt
Hilleary, *f.n.,* 'hɪlərɪ, hillĕri
Hiller, *f.n.,* 'hɪlər, híllĕr
Hillery, *f.n.,* 'hɪlərɪ, hillĕri
Hillhead *Devon, S'clyde,* 'hɪl'hed,
  híll-héd
Hillier, *f.n.,* 'hɪlɪər, hílli-ĕr
Hillsborough *S. Yorks.,* 'hɪlzbərə,
  hílzbŭră
Hillswick *Shetland,* 'hɪlzwɪk,
  hílzwick
Hinchcliffe, *f.n.,* 'hɪnʃklɪf, hínsh-
  -kliff
Hinchingbrooke, *Viscountcy of,*
  'hɪnʃɪŋbrʊk, hínshing-brŏōk;
  'hɪntʃɪŋbrʊk, híntching-brŏōk
Hind, *f.n.,* haɪnd, hínd; hɪnd,
  hinnd
Hindell, *f.n.,* 'hɪndl, híndl
Hinden, *f.n.,* 'hɪndən, híndĕn
Hinderclay *Suffolk,* 'hɪndərkleɪ,
  híndĕrklay

Hinderwell *N. Yorks.,* 'hɪndərwel,
  híndĕrwel
Hindle, *f.n.,* 'hɪndl, híndl
Hindley, *f.n.,* 'hɪndlɪ, híndli;
  'haɪndlɪ, híndli
Hindley *Gtr. M'chester,* 'hɪndlɪ,
  híndli
Hindlip *H. & W.,* 'hɪndlɪp, hínd-
  lip. *Appropriate also for Baron*
  ~.
Hindmarsh, *f.n.,* 'haɪndmɑːrʃ,
  híndmaarsh
Hindolveston, *also spelt* **Hindol-**
  vestone, *Norfolk,* 'hɪndl'vestən,
  híndlvéstŏn; 'hɪlvɪstən, hílvĕs-
  tŏn
Hindsford *Gtr. M'chester,*
  'haɪndzfərd, híndzfŏrd
Hindshaw, *f.n.,* 'haɪndʃə, hínd-
  -shaw
Hindsley, *f.n.,* 'haɪndzlɪ, híndzli
Hindson, *f.n.,* 'haɪndsən, híndssŏn
Hinks, *f.n.,* hɪŋks, hinks
Hints *Staffs.,* hɪnts, hints
Hinwick *Beds.,* 'hɪnɪk, hínnick
Hiorns, *f.n.,* 'haɪərnz, hí-ŏrnz
Hiort *St. Kilda (W. Isles),* hɜrt,
  hurt
Hipkin, *f.n.,* 'hɪpkɪn, hípkin
Hippisley, *f.n.,* 'hɪpslɪ, hípsli
Hirnant *Powys,* 'hɜrnænt, hírnant
Hirnant, *River, Dyfed,* 'hɜrnænt,
  hírnant
Hiron, *f.n.,* 'haɪərɒn, híron
Hirons, *f.n.,* 'haɪərɒnz, híronz
Hirsh, *f.n.,* hɜrʃ, hirsh
Hirwaun, *also spelt* **Hirwain,** *Mid*
  Glam., 'hɜrwaɪn, heérwin;
  'hɜrwɪn, hírwin
Hirwaun, *also spelt* **Hirwain,**
  River, Dyfed, 'hɪərwaɪn, heér-
  win; 'hɜrwɪn, hírwin
Hiscock, *f.n.,* 'hɪskoʊ, hískō;
  'hɪskɒk, hískock
Hiscox, *f.n.,* 'hɪskoʊ, hískō
Hiseman, *f.n.,* 'haɪzmən, hízmăn
Hitchcock, *f.n.,* 'hɪtʃkɒk, hítch-
  -kock
Hitchens, *f.n.,* 'hɪtʃənz, hítchĕnz
Hoar, *f.n.,* hɔr, hor
Hoare, *f.n.,* hɔr, hor
Hoathly, *East and West, Sussex,*
  hoʊθ'laɪ, hōth-lí
Hoban, *f.n.,* 'hoʊbən, hóbăn
Hobart, *f.n.,* 'hoʊbɑrt, hóbaart;
  'hʌbərt, húbbărt. *The second is*
  thought by some to be appro-
  priate for the name of the 17th-c.
  Sir Henry ~, *judge, and founder*
  of Blickling Hall in Norfolk.
Hobart-Hampden, *f.n.,* 'hʌbərt
  'hæmdən, húbbărt hámdĕn.
  Family name of the Earl of
  Buckinghamshire.

Hobbins, *f.n.*, 'hɒbınz, hóbbinz
Hobday, *f.n.*, 'hɒbdeı, hóbday
Hobley, *f.n.*, 'hoʊblı, hóbli
Hobourn, *f.n.*, 'hoʊbərn, hóburn
Hobsbaum, *f.n.*, 'hɒbzbaʊm, hóbzbowm
Hobsbawm, *f.n.*, 'hɒbzbɔm, hóbzbawm
Hoby, *f.n.*, 'hoʊbı, hóbi
Hockney, *f.n.*, 'hɒknı, hóckni
Hockwold *Norfolk*, 'hɒkwoʊld, hóckwōld
Hodder & Stoughton, *publishers*, 'hɒdər ənd 'stoʊtən, hódděr ǎnd stótŏn
Hoddesdon *Herts.*, 'hɒdzdən, hódzdŏn
Hoddinott, *f.n.*, 'hɒdınɒt, hóddinot
Hoddle, *f.n.*, 'hɒdl, hóddl
Hodgart, *f.n.*, 'hɒdʒərt, hójjärt
Hodgens, *f.n.*, 'hɒdʒənz, hójjĕnz
Hodghton, *f.n.*, 'hɒdʒtən, hójtŏn
Hodgson, *f.n.*, 'hɒdʒsən, hójssŏn
Hodsoll, *f.n.*, 'hɒdsl, hódssl
Hoenes, *f.n.*, 'hoʊnes, hóness
Hoey, *f.n.*, 'hoʊı, hó-i; hɔı, hoy
Hoffe, *f.n.*, hɒf, hoff
Hogan, *f.n.*, 'hoʊgən, hógǎn
Hogarth, *f.n.*, 'hoʊgɑrθ, hógaarth; 'hɒgərt, hóggärt. *The first is traditional for William ~, painter and engraver. The second is usual in Cumbria.*
Hoggan, *f.n.*, 'hɒgən, hóggǎn
Hoggard, *f.n.*, 'hɒgɑrd, hóggaard
Hoggart, *f.n.*, 'hɒgərt, hóggärt
Hoggarth, *f.n.*, 'hɒgərt, hóggärt
Hoggeston *Bucks.*, 'hɒgstən, hógstŏn
Hogh, *f.n.*, hoʊ, hō
Hoghton, *f.n.*, 'hɒtən, háwtŏn
Hoghton *Lancs.*, 'hɒtən, háwtŏn
Hoghton Towers *Lancs.*, 'hɒtən 'taʊərz, háwtŏn tówěrz; 'hoʊtən 'taʊərz, hōtŏn tówěrz
Hogsflesh, *f.n.*, 'hoʊfleı, hóflay; 'hɒgzfleʃ, hógzflesh
Hogwood, *f.n.*, 'hɒgwʊd, hóg-wōōd
Holbeach *Lincs.*, 'hɒlbıtʃ, hólbeetch
Holbech, *f.n.*, 'hɒlbıtʃ, hólbeetch
Holbeche House *Staffs.*, 'hɒlbıtʃ, hólbeetch
Holbeck *Notts.*, *W. Yorks.*, 'hɒlbek, hólbeck
Holbeton *Devon*, 'hoʊlbıtən, hólbětŏn
Holborn, *f.n.*, 'hɒlbərn, hólbůrn
Holborn *London*, 'hoʊbərn, hóbůrn; 'hoʊlbərn, hólbůrn

Holborn *H'land*, hoʊl'bɔrn, hōl-bórn
Holborne, *f.n.*, 'hoʊbərn, hóbůrn
Holbourne *see* **Greenwood of ~, Viscount**
Holbrook *Suffolk*, 'hoʊlbrʊk, hólbrŏŏk
Holbrooke, Joseph (*also spelt* Josef), *composer*, 'hoʊlbrʊk, hólbrŏŏk
Holburn *district of Aberdeen*, 'hoʊbərn, hóburn
Holburne of Menstrie Museum *Bath*, 'hoʊbərn əv 'menstrı, hóbůrn ŏv ménstri
Holcombe, *f.n.*, 'hoʊlkəm, hól-kŏm
Holcombe *Gtr. M'chester*, 'hɒlkəm, hóllkŏm
Holcombe Burnell *Devon*, 'hoʊkəm 'bɜrnəl, hókům búrnĕl
Holcombe Rogus *Devon*, 'hoʊkəm 'roʊgəs, hókŏm rōgůss
Holden, *f.n.*, 'hoʊldən, hóldĕn
Holdenby *Northants.*; 'hoʊldənbı, hóldĕnbi. *Formerly* **Holmby**, *q.v.*
Holderness, *f.n.*, 'hoʊldərnıs, hóldĕrnĕss
Holderness *Humberside*, 'hoʊldərnıs, hóldĕrnĕss
Holdsworth, *f.n.*, 'hoʊldzwərθ, hóldzwůrth
Holdtum, *f.n.*, 'hoʊltəm, hóltūm
Hole of Murroes *Tayside*, 'hoʊl əv 'mʌroʊz, hól ŏv múrrōz; 'hoʊl əv 'mɒrıs, hól ŏv mórriss. *Also called* **Kellas**, *q.v.*
Holford, *f.n.*, 'hɒlfərd, hóllfŏrd
Holford *Somerset*, 'hoʊlfərd, hólfŏrd
Holgate, *f.n.*, 'hoʊlgeıt, hólgayt
Holinshed, Raphael, *16th-c. chronicler*, 'hɒlınʃed, hóllin--shed. *Traditional pronunciation.*
Holker *Cumbria*, 'hʊkər, hŏŏkěr; 'hɒlkər, hóllkěr
Holkham *Norfolk*, 'hɒlkəm, hóllkäm; 'hoʊlkəm, hólkäm. *The second is used by the family of the Earl of Leicester and is therefore appropriate for ~ Hall. The first is usual in the village.*
Hollabon, *f.n.*, 'hɒləbən, hóllă-bŏn
Hollabone, *f.n.*, 'hɒləboʊn, hóllă-bŏn
Holland, *f.n.*, 'hɒlənd, hólländ
Hollenden, Baron, 'hɒləndən, hóllĕndĕn
Holles, *f.n.*, 'hɒlıs, hóllĕss
Hollesley *Suffolk*, 'hoʊzlı, hózli
Hollies *Staffs.*, 'hɒlız, hólliz

Hollingshead, *f.n.*, 'hɒlɪŋzhed, hóllingz-hed
Hollingsworth, *f.n.*, 'hɒlɪŋzwɜrθ, hóllingzwurth
Hollingworth, *f.n.*, 'hɒlɪŋwɜrθ, hólling-wurth
Hollins, *f.n.*, 'hɒlɪnz, hóllinz
Hollinshead, *f.n.*, 'hɒlɪnzhed, hóllinz-hed
Hollinwell *Notts.*, 'hɒlɪnwel, hóllinwel
Holm Cultram Abbey *Cumbria*, 'hoʊm 'kʌltrəm, hóm kúltrăm
Holme *Cambs.*, hoʊm, hōm
Holmesdale *Surrey–Kent*, 'hoʊmzdeɪl, hómzdayl. *Appropriate also for Viscount ~.*
Holm Patrick, Baron, 'hoʊm 'pætrɪk, hóm pátrick
Holman, *f.n.*, 'hoʊlmən, hólmăn
Holmbury St. Mary *Surrey*, 'hoʊmbəri snt 'mɛəri, hómbŭri sĭnt máiri
Holmby *Northants.*, 'hoʊmbɪ, hómbi. *Older name of* **Holdenby**, *q.v.*
Holme, *f.n.*, hoʊm, hōm
Holme *Norfolk*, hoʊm, hōm
Holme Moss *moor on borders of Derby. and W. Yorks.*, 'hoʊm 'mɒs, hóm móss
Holme Pierrepont *Notts.*, 'hoʊm 'pɪərpɒnt, hóm péerpont
Holmer Green *Bucks.*, 'hoʊmər 'grin, hómĕr gréen
Holmes, *f.n.*, hoʊmz, hōmz
Holmes à Court, *f.n.*, 'hoʊmz ə 'kɔrt, hómz ă kórt. *Family name of Baron Heytesbury.*
Holmfirth *W. Yorks.*, 'hoʊm'fɜrθ, hóm-firth
Holmpton *Humberside*, 'hoʊmtən, hómtŏn
Holmstrom, *f.n.*, 'hoʊmstrəm, hómström
Holne *Devon*, hoʊn, hōn
Holness, *f.n.*, 'hoʊlnɪs, hólnĕss
Holnest *Dorset*, 'hɒlnest, hólnest
Holnicote *Somerset*, 'hʌnɪkət, húnnikŏt
Holroyd, *f.n.*, 'hɒlrɔɪd, hólroyd
Holst, Gustav, *composer*, 'gʊstav 'hoʊlst, gŏostaav hólst
Holsworthy *Devon*, 'hoʊlzwɜrðɪ, hólzwurthi
Holt *Clwyd*, *Norfolk*, hoʊlt, hōlt
Holtby, *f.n.*, 'hoʊltbɪ, hóltbi
Holter, *f.n.*, 'hoʊltər, hóltĕr
Holtham, *f.n.*, 'hoʊlθəm, hól-thăm; 'hoʊðəm, hó-thăm; 'hɒlθəm, hól-thăm
Holton-cum-Beckering *Lincs.*, 'hoʊltən kʌm 'bekərɪŋ, hóltŏn kum béckĕring

Holton Heath *Dorset*, 'hɒltən 'hiθ, hólltŏn héeth
Holtum, *f.n.*, 'hoʊltəm, hóltŭm
Holtye *E. Sussex*, hoʊl'taɪ, hōltí
Holverston *Norfolk*, 'hɒlvərstən, hólvĕrstŏn
Holwell *Dorset*, 'hɒlwəl, hólwĕl
Holwick *Durham*, 'hɒlwɪk, hólwick
Holwill, *f.n.*, 'hɒlwɪl, hólwil
Holybourne *Hants.*, 'hɒlɪbərn, hólliborn
Holyhead *Gwynedd*, 'hɒlɪ'hed, hólli-héd; 'hɒlɪhed, hólli-hed
Holyport *Berks.*, 'hɒlɪpɔrt, hólliport
Holyroodhouse, Palace of, *Edinburgh*, 'hɒlɪrud'haʊs, hóllirood-hówss
Holystone *Northd.*, 'hoʊlɪstoʊn, hólistōn
Holytown *S'clyde*, 'hɒlɪtaʊn, hóllitown
Holywell Row *Suffolk*, 'hɒlɪwel 'roʊ, hólliwel rố
Holywood *Belfast*, *D. & G.*, 'hɒlɪwʊd, hólliwŏod
Homa, *f.n.*, 'hoʊmə, hómă
Homan, *f.n.*, 'hoʊmən, hómăn
Homard, *f.n.*, 'hoʊmɑrd, hómaard
Home, *f.n.*, hjum, hewm; hoʊm, hōm. *The first is appropriate for the Earldom of ~.*
Home of the Hirsel, Baron, 'hjum əv ðə 'hɜrsl, héwm ŏv thē hírssl
Homer Green *Merseyside*, 'hoʊmər 'grin, hómĕr gréen
Homersfield *Suffolk*, 'hɒmərzfild, hómmĕrzfeeld; 'hʌmərzfild, húmmĕrzfeeld
Homerton *London*, 'hɒmərtən, hómmĕrtŏn. *Appropriate also for ~ College, Cambridge.*
Homfray, *f.n.*, 'hɒmfrɪ, hómfri
Honddu, River, *Powys*, 'hɒnðɪ, hónthi
Hone, *f.n.*, hoʊn, hōn
Honer, *f.n.*, 'hoʊnər, hónĕr
Honess, *f.n.*, 'hoʊnes, hóness
Honey, *f.n.*, 'hʌnɪ, húnni
Honeycombe, *f.n.*, 'hʌnɪkoʊm, húnnikōm
Honicknowle *Devon*, 'hɒnɪknoʊl, hónnick-nōl
Honiley *Warwicks.*, 'hɒnɪlɪ, hónnili
Honing *Norfolk*, 'hoʊnɪŋ, hón-ing
Honingham *Norfolk*, 'hʌnɪŋəm, húnning-ăm
Honington *Lincs.*, 'hɒnɪŋtən, hónningtŏn

Honington *Suffolk*, 'hɒnɪŋtən, hónningtŏn; 'hʌnɪŋtən, húnningtŏn
Honiton *Devon*, 'hʌnɪtən, húnnitŏn; 'hɒnɪtən, hónnitŏn
Honley *W. Yorks.*, 'hɒnlɪ, hónli
Honney, *f.n.*, 'hʌnɪ, húnni
Honri, *f.n.*, 'hɒnrɪ, hónri
Honywood, *f.n.*, 'hʌnɪwʊd, húnniwŏŏd
Hoo *Kent*, hu, hoo
Hoodless, *f.n.*, 'hʊdlɪs, hŏŏdlĕss
Hooe *E. Sussex*, hu, hoo
Hooke, *f.n.*, hʊk, hŏŏk
Hookway, *f.n.*, 'hʊkweɪ, hŏŏkway
Hooley, *f.n.*, 'hʊlɪ, hŏŏli
Hoo St. Werburgh *Kent*, 'hu snt 'wɜːbərg, hoo sĭnt wérburg
Hooson, *f.n.*, 'husən, hŏŏssŏn
Hooton Pagnell *S. Yorks.*, 'hutən 'pægnəl, hŏŏtŏn págnĕl; 'hʌtən 'pænl, húttŏn pánl
Hope & Lyne, *theatrical agents*, 'hoʊp ənd 'laɪn, hṓp ănd lín
Hopetoun House *Lothian*, 'hoʊptən, hṓptŏn. *Appropriate also for the Earl of* ~.
Hopkins, *f.n.*, 'hɒpkɪnz, hópkinz
Hoptrough, *f.n.*, 'hɒptroʊ, hóptrō
Hopwas *Staffs.*, 'hɒpwəs, hópwăss; 'hɒpəs, hóppăss
Horabin, *f.n.*, 'hɒrəbɪn, hórrăbin
Horam, *f.n.*, 'hɒrəm, háwräm
Horan, *f.n.*, 'hɒrən, háwrăn
Horbury, *f.n.*, 'hɔːbərɪ, hórbŭri
Hore-Belisha, Barony of, 'hɔː bə'liːʃə, hór bĕleésha
Hore-Ruthven, *f.n.*, 'hɔː 'rɪvən, hór rívvĕn
Horham *Suffolk*, 'hɒrəm, hórrăm
Horkstow *Humberside*, 'hɔːkstoʊ, hórkstṓ
Horlick, *f.n.*, 'hɔːlɪk, hórlick
Horndean *Hants*, hɔːn'diːn, horndéen
Horninglow *Staffs.*, 'hɔːnɪŋloʊ, hórning-lō
Horningsea *Cambs.*, 'hɔːnɪŋsɪ, hórning-see
Hornsea *Humberside*, 'hɔːnsɪ, hórnssee
Hornsey *London*, 'hɔːnzɪ, hórnzi
Hornstein, *f.n.*, 'hɔːnstɪn, hórnsteen
Horrell, *f.n.*, 'hɒrəl, hórrĕl
Horrigan, *f.n.*, 'hɒrɪgən, hórrigăn
Horringer *Suffolk*, 'hɒrɪndʒər, hórrinjĕr
Horrocks, *f.n.*, 'hɒrəks, hórrŏks
Horsbrugh, *f.n.*, 'hɔːsbrə, hórssbră; 'hɔːzbrə, hórzbră
Horseheath *Cambs.*, 'hɔːshiːθ, hórss-heeth
Horsell *Surrey*, 'hɔːsl, hórssl

Horsey, *f.n.*, 'hɔːsɪ, hórssi
Horsey *Norfolk*, 'hɔːsɪ, hórssi
Horsfall, *f.n.*, 'hɔːsfəl, hórssfawl
Horsfield, *f.n.*, 'hɔːsfiːld, hórssfeeld
Horsforth *W. Yorks.*, 'hɔːsfərθ, hórss-förth
Horsham *W. Sussex*, 'hɔːʃəm, hór-shăm
Horsham-St.-Faith *Norfolk*, 'hɔːʃəm snt 'feɪθ, hór-shăm sĭnt fáyth
Horsley, East *and* West, *Surrey*, 'hɔːzlɪ, hórzli
Horsley Woodhouse *Derby.*, 'hɔːzlɪ 'wʊdhaʊs, hórzli wŏŏd-howss
Horsmonden *Kent*, ˌhɔːzmən'den, horzmŏndén
Horsted Keynes *W. Sussex*, 'hɔːstɪd 'keɪnz, hórsstĕd káynz
Horwich *Gtr. M'chester*, 'hɒrɪtʃ, hórritch
Horwood, *f.n.*, 'hɔːwʊd, hórwŏŏd
Hose, *f.n.*, hoʊz, hōz
Hose, *Leics.*, hoʊz, hōz
Hoseason, *f.n.*, hoʊ'siːzən, hōsséézŏn; ˌhoʊsɪ'eɪsən, hōssi-áyssŏn; ˌhoʊsɪ'æsən, hōssi-ássŏn
Hosey, *f.n.*, 'hoʊzɪ, hṓzi
Hosford, *f.n.*, 'hɒsfərd, hóssförd
Hosier, *f.n.*, 'hoʊzɪər, hṓzi-ĕr
Hoste, *f.n.*, hoʊst, hōst
Hotham, *f.n.*, 'hʌðəm, húthăm. *Appropriate also for Baron* ~.
Hotham *Humberside*, 'hʌðəm, húthăm
Hothfield *Kent*, 'hɒθfɪld, hóthfeeld. *Appropriate also for Baron* ~.
Hotine, *f.n.*, 'hoʊtiːn, hṓteen
Hoton *Leics.*, 'hoʊtən, hṓtŏn
Hotwells *Avon*, 'hɒtwelz, hótwelz
Houblon, *f.n.*, 'hublɒ̃, hŏŏblŏ̃ng
Houchen, *f.n.*, 'haʊtʃɪn, hówtchĕn
Houchin, *f.n.*, 'haʊtʃɪn, hówtchin
Hough, *f.n.*, hʌf, huff; hɒf, hoff; haʊ, how
Hough *Ches.*, hʌf, huff
Houghall *Durham*, 'hɒfl, hóffl
Hougham, *f.n.*, 'hʌfəm, húffăm
Hougham *Lincs.*, 'hʌfəm, húffăm
Hough Green *Ches.*, 'hʌf 'griːn, húff gréen
Hough-on-the-Hill *Lincs.*, 'hʌf ɒn ðə 'hɪl, húff on thē hill; 'hɒf ɒn ðə 'hɪl, hóff on thē hill
Houghton, *f.n.*, 'hɒtən, háwtŏn; 'haʊtən, hówtŏn; 'hoʊtən, hṓtŏn. *The second is appropriate for Douglas* ~, *politician and broadcaster, later Baron* ~ **of Sowerby**, *q.v.*

Houghton *Cambs.*, 'houtən, hŏ́tŏn
Houghton *Hants.*, 'houtən, hŏ́tŏn;
 'hautən, hów̆tŏn
Houghton *Lancs.*, 'hɔtən, háwtŏn;
 'hautən, hów̆tŏn
Houghton *Norfolk*, 'hautən, hów-
 tŏn; 'houtən, hŏ́tŏn
Houghton, Glass, *W. Yorks.*,
 'glɑs 'hautən, glɑ́ass hów̆tŏn
Houghton, Great *and* **Little**,
 Northants., 'houtən, hŏ́tŏn
Houghton, Great *and* **Little**, *W.
 Yorks.*, 'hautən, hów̆tŏn
Houghton Bridge *W. Sussex*,
 'houtən 'brɪdʒ, hŏ́tŏn brij;
 'hautən 'brɪdʒ, hów̆tŏn brij
Houghton Conquest *Beds.*,
 'hautən 'kɒŋkwest, hów̆tŏn
 kónkwest
Houghton-le-Side *Durham*,
 'hautən lə 'said, hów̆tŏn lĕ síd;
 'hautənli 'said, hów̆tŏnli síd
Houghton-le-Spring *Tyne & Wear*,
 'houtən lə 'sprɪŋ, hŏ́tŏn lĕ
 spring; 'houtənlɪ 'sprɪŋ, hŏ́tŏnli
 spring
Houghton of Sowerby, Baron,
 'hautən əv 'souərbɪ, hów̆tŏn ŏv
 só-ĕrbi. *See also* **Houghton**, *f.n.*
Houghton-on-the-Hill *Leics.*,
 'houtən ɒn ðə 'hɪl, hŏ́tŏn on the͟
 hill
Houghton Regis *Beds.*, 'hautən
 'rɪdʒɪs, hów̆tŏn réejiss
Houlden, *f.n.*, 'houldən, hŏ́ldĕn;
 'huldən, hoóldĕn
Houlder, *f.n.*, 'houldər, hŏ́ldĕr
Houldsworth, *f.n.*, 'houldzwərθ,
 hŏ́ldzwurth
Houlgate, *f.n.*, 'houlgeɪt, hŏ́lgayt
Hoult, *f.n.*, hoult, hōlt
Houlton, *f.n.*, 'houltən, hŏ́ltŏn
Houndstone *Somerset*, 'haund-
 stən, hów̆ndstŏn
Hounsfield, *f.n.*, 'haunzfild,
 hów̆nzfeeld
Hourd, *f.n.*, huərd, hoórd
Hourigan, *f.n.*, 'huərɪgən, hoóri-
 găn
Hourn, Loch, *H'land*, huərn,
 hoórn
Housden, *f.n.*, 'hauzdən, hów̆zdĕn
House, *f.n.*, haus, howss
House of Gight *Grampian*, 'haus
 əv 'gɪxt, hów̆ss ŏv gicht
Housego, *f.n.*, 'hausgou, hów̆ss-
 gō
Househillwood *Glasgow*, 'hauzl-
 wud, hów̆zl-wo͞od
Housley, *f.n.*, 'hauzlɪ, hów̆zli
Housman, *f.n.*, 'hausmən, hów̆ss-
 măn. *This is appropriate for
 A. E.* ∼, *poet, and for his
 brother Laurence, artist and*

playwright. *The latter particu-
 larly confirmed that they
 pronounced it with -s, not -z.*
Houson, *f.n.*, 'hausən, hów̆ssŏn
Houston, *f.n.*, 'hustən, hoóstŏn;
 'hjustən, héwsstŏn; 'haustən,
 hów̆sstŏn
Houston *Lothian, S'clyde*, 'hustən,
 hoóstŏn
Houstoun, *f.n.*, 'hustən, hoóstŏn
Houthuesen, *f.n.*, 'hautʃɪsən,
 hów̆tchĕssŏn; 'hauthjuzən,
 hów̆t-hewzĕn. *The second is
 appropriate for the painter
 Albert* ∼.
Houton *Orkney*, 'hautən, hów̆tŏn.
 Appropriate also for ∼ *Bay.*
Hove *E. Sussex*, houv, hōv
Hovell, *f.n.*, 'hɒvl, hóvvl; 'houvl,
 hŏ́vl
Hoveringham *Notts.*, 'hɒvərɪŋəm,
 hóvvĕring-ăm
Hovers, *f.n.*, 'houvərz, hŏ́vĕrz
Hoveton *Norfolk*, 'hɒftən, hóff-
 tŏn; 'hʌftən, húfftŏn; 'hɒvɪtən,
 hóvvĕtŏn
Hovey, *f.n.*, 'houvɪ, hŏ́vi
Hovingham *N. Yorks.*, 'hɒvɪŋəm,
 hóvving-ăm
Howard, *C.n. and f.n.*, 'hauərd,
 hów̆ărd
Howard de Walden, Baron,
 'hauərd də 'wɔldən, hów̆ărd dĕ
 wáwldĕn
Howard of Glossop, Baron,
 'hauərd əv 'glɒsəp, hów̆ărd ŏv
 glóssŏp
Howard of Penrith, Baron,
 'hauərd əv 'penrɪθ, hów̆ărd ŏv
 pénrith
Howarth, *f.n.*, 'hauərθ, hów̆ărth
Howatch, *f.n.*, 'hautʃ, hów̆ătch
Howden, *f.n.*, 'haudən, hów̆dĕn
Howden *Humberside, Lothian*,
 'haudən, hów̆dĕn
Howden-le-Wear *Durham*,
 'haudən lə 'wɪər, hów̆dĕn lĕ
 weer
Howdon-on-Tyne *Tyne & Wear*,
 'haudən ɒn 'taɪn, hów̆dŏn on
 tín
Howe, Earl, hau, how
Howe, *f.n.*, hau, how
Howell, *f.n.*, 'hauəl, hów̆ĕl
Howells, *f.n.*, 'hauəlz, hów̆ĕlz
Howe of Corrichie *Grampian*,
 'hau əv 'kɒrɪxɪ, hów̆ ŏv kór-
 richi
Howes, *f.n.*, hauz, howz
Howgill, *f.n.*, 'haugɪl, hów̆gil
Howick *Northd.*, 'houɪk, hŏ́-ick
Howick of Glendale, Baron,
 'houɪk əv glen'deɪl, hŏ́-ick ŏv
 glendáyl

Howie, *f.n.*, 'haʊɪ, hów-i
Howitt, *f.n.*, 'haʊɪt, hów-it
Howlett, *f.n.*, 'haʊlɪt, hówlĕt
Howley *Somerset*, 'hoʊlɪ, hóli
Howorth, *f.n.*, 'haʊərθ, hówŭrth
Howse, *f.n.*, haʊz, howz; haʊs, howss
Howson, *f.n.*, 'haʊsən, hówssŏn
Hoxne *Suffolk*, 'hɒksən, hócksĕn
Hoy Island *Orkney*, hɔɪ, hoy
Hoyer, *f.n.*, 'hɔɪər, hóyĕr
Hozier, *f.n.*, 'hoʊzɪər, hózi-ĕr
Huband, *f.n.*, 'hjubænd, héwband
Hubback, *f.n.*, 'hʌbək, húbbăk
Hubbard, *f.n.*, 'hʌbərd, húbbărd
Hubbart, *f.n.*, 'hʌbərt, húbbărt
Huby *N. Yorks.*, 'hjubɪ, héwbi
Huccaby *Devon*, 'hʌkəbɪ, húckăbi
Hucclecote *Glos.*, 'hʌklkoʊt, húcklkŏt
Hudard, *f.n.*, 'hʌdərd, húddărd
Hudis, *f.n.*, 'hjudɪs, héwdiss
Hudson, *f.n.*, 'hʌdsən, húdssŏn
Hudspith, *f.n.*, 'hʌdspɪθ, húdss-pith
Hueffer, Ford Madox, *author*, 'fɔrd 'mædəks 'hwefər, ford máddŏcks whéffĕr. *Original name of* Ford Madox Ford, *q.v.*
Huehns, *f.n.*, 'hjuɪnz, héw-ēnz
Huelin, *f.n.*, 'hjulɪn, héwlin
Huff, *f.n.*, hʌf, huff
Hugessen, *f.n.*, 'hjugɪsən, héw-gĕssĕn
Huggate *Humberside*, 'hʌgɪt, húggit
Hugh, *C.n.*, hju, hew
Hughes, *f.n.*, hjuz, hewz
Hughes, Arwel, *composer*, 'arwel 'hjuz, áarwel héwz
Hughes, Owain Arwel, *conductor*, 'oʊaɪn 'arwel 'hjuz, ó-īn aárwel héwz
Hughesdon, *f.n.*, 'hjuzdən, héwz-dŏn
Hughson, *f.n.*, 'hjusən, héwssŏn
Hugill, *f.n.*, 'hjugɪl, héwgil
Hugill *Cumbria*, 'hjugɪl, héwgil
Huguenin, *f.n.*, 'hjugənɪn, héw-gĕnin
Huhne, *f.n.*, hjun, hewn
Huish, *f.n.*, 'hjuɪʃ, héw-ish; hʌʃ, hush
Huish Champflower *Somerset*, 'hjuɪʃ 'tʃæmpflaʊər, héwish chámpflowĕr
Huish Episcopi *Somerset*, 'hjuɪʃ ə'pɪskəpɪ, héwish ĕpísskŏpi
Hulbert, *f.n.*, 'hʌlbərt, húlbĕrt
Hulke, *f.n.*, hʌlk, hulk
Hullah, *f.n.*, 'hʌlə, húllă
Hullavington *Wilts.*, hə'lævɪŋtən, hŭlávvingtŏn; 'hʌlɪŋtən, húllingtŏn

Hulme, *f.n.*, hjum, hewm
Hulme, *Staffs.*, hjum, hewm
Hulse, *f.n.*, hʌls, hulss
Humber, River, *Humberside*, 'hʌmbər, húmbĕr
Hume, *f.n.*, hjum, hewm
Hummel, *f.n.*, 'hʌml, húmml
Hummerston, *f.n.*, 'hʌmərstən, húmmĕrstŏn
Humpherston, *f.n.*, 'hʌmfərstən, húmfĕrstŏn
Humphrey, *C.n. and f.n.*, 'hʌmfrɪ, húmfri
Humphreys, *f.n.*, 'hʌmfrɪz, húm-friz
Humphries, *f.n.*, 'hʌmfrɪz, húm-friz
Humpoletz, *f.n.*, 'hʌmpəlɪts, húmpŏlĕts
Humshaugh *Northd.*, 'hʌmzhɑf, húmz-haaf
Huna *H'land*, 'hunə, hoónă
Huncote *Leics.*, 'hʌŋkət, húnkŏt
Hungarton, Barony of, 'hʌŋgərtən, húng-gärtŏn
Hungarton, *also spelt* Hungerton, *Leics.*, 'hʌŋgərtən, húng-gärtŏn
Hungerford *Berks.*, 'hʌŋgərfərd, húng-gĕrford; 'hʌŋgərfərd, húng-gĕrfŏrd. *The second is also appropriate for Baron* ~.
Hungerford Bridge *London*, 'hʌŋgərfərd, húng-gĕrfŏrd
Hungerford Newtown *Berks.*, 'hʌŋgərfərd 'njutaʊn, húng-gĕrfŏrd néwtown
Hungerton *see* Hungarton
Hunmanby *N. Yorks.*, 'hʌnmənbɪ, húnmănbi
Hunslet *W. Yorks.*, 'hʌnslɪt, húnslĕt
Hunstanton *Norfolk*, hʌn'stæntən, hunsstántŏn; 'hʌnstən, húnsstŏn
Hunter, *f.n.*, 'hʌntər, húntĕr
Hunterian, *pertaining to John Hunter, 18th-c. Scottish surgeon*, hʌn'tɪərɪən, hunteériăn
Huntingdon *Cambs.*, 'hʌntɪŋdən, húntingdŏn. *Appropriate also for the Earl of* ~.
Huntly *Grampian*, 'hʌntlɪ, húntli
Huntshaw *Devon*, 'hʌnʃə, hún-shaw
Huntspill *Somerset*, 'hʌntspɪl, húntspil
Hunwick *Durham*, 'hʌnwɪk, húnwick
Hurcomb, *f.n.*, 'hɜrkəm, húrkŏm
Hurdis, *f.n.*, 'hɜrdɪs, húrdiss
Hurll, *f.n.*, hɜrl, hurl
Hurndall, *f.n.*, 'hɜrndl, húrndl
Hurrell, *f.n.*, 'hʌrəl, húrrĕl; 'hʊərəl, hoórĕl

Hurren, *f.n.*, 'hʌrən, húrrĕn
Hursley *Hants*, 'hɜrzlɪ, húrzli
Hurstmonceaux *or* **Hurstmonceux** *see* **Herstmonceux**
Hurstpierpoint *W. Sussex*, 'hɜrstpɪər'pɔɪnt, húrstpeer-póynt
Hush, *f.n.*, hʌʃ, hush
Huskinson, *f.n.*, 'hʌskɪnsən, hússkinssŏn
Huskisson, *f.n.*, 'hʌskɪsən, hússkissŏn
Hussein, *f.n.*, hʊ'seɪn, hōōssáyn
Hussey, *f.n.*, 'hʌsɪ, hússi
Hutber, *f.n.*, 'hʌtbər, hútbĕr
Hutchens, *f.n.*, 'hʌtʃɪnz, hútchĕnz
Hutcheon, *f.n.*, 'hʌtʃən, hútchĕn
Hutcheson, *f.n.*, 'hʌtʃɪsən, hútchĕssŏn
Hutchings, *f.n.*, 'hʌtʃɪŋz, hútchingz
Hutchinson, *f.n.*, 'hʌtʃɪnsən, hútchinssŏn
Huth, *f.n.*, huθ, hooth
Hutton Buscel, *also spelt* **Hutton Bushel** *N. Yorks.*, 'hʌtən 'bʊʃl, húttŏn bŏŏshl
Hutton-le-Hole *N. Yorks.*, 'hʌtən lɪ 'hoʊl, húttŏn-li-hōl
Huw, *Welsh C.n.*, hju, hew
Huxley, Aldous, *author*, 'oldəs 'hʌkslɪ, áwldŭss húcksli
Huyton *Merseyside*, 'haɪtən, hítŏn
Huyton with Roby *Merseyside*, 'haɪtən wɪð 'roʊbɪ, hítŏn with rŏbi
Huzzard, *f.n.*, 'hʌzərd, húzzaard
Hyacinth, saint, 'haɪəsɪnθ, hí-ássinth
Hyde, *f.n.*, haɪd, hīd
Hydleman, *f.n.*, 'haɪdlmən, hídlmăn
Hykeham, North *and* South, *Lincs.*, 'haɪkəm, híkăm
Hylton, *f.n.*, 'hɪltən, hiltŏn
Hyman, *f.n.*, 'haɪmən, hímăn
Hymans, *f.n.*, 'haɪmənz, hímănz
Hynd, *f.n.*, haɪnd, hīnd
Hyndburn *Lancs.*, 'haɪndbərn, hínd-burn
Hyndhope *Borders*, 'haɪndhoʊp, hínd-hōp
Hyndland *Glasgow*, 'haɪndlənd, híndlănd
Hyndley, Viscountcy of, 'haɪndlɪ, híndli
Hyndman, *f.n.*, 'haɪndmən, híndmăn
Hyslop, *f.n.*, 'hɪzləp, hízlŏp
Hytch, *f.n.*, haɪtʃ, hītch
Hytner, *f.n.*, 'haɪtnər, hítnĕr
Hywel, *Welsh C.n.*, 'haʊəl, hówĕl

I

Ia, saint, 'ɪə, ée-ă
Iago, *Welsh C.n.*, 'jɑgoʊ, yaágō
Iain, *C.n.*, *also spelt* **Ian**, 'ɪən, ée-ăn
I'Anson, *f.n.*, aɪ'ænsən, ī-ánssŏn
Ianthe, *C.n.*, aɪ'ænθɪ, ī-ánthi
Iball, *f.n.*, 'aɪbɔl, íbawl
Ibbs, *f.n.*, ɪbz, ibbz
Ibrox Park *Glasgow*, 'aɪbrɒks 'pɑrk, íbrocks paárk
Ibstone *Bucks.*, 'ɪbstən, íbbstŏn
Iceni, *ancient British tribe*, aɪ'saɪnaɪ, īsséenī
Iceton, *f.n.*, 'aɪstən, ísstŏn
Icke, *f.n.*, aɪk, īk; ɪk, ick
Ickes, *f.n.*, 'ɪkɪs, ickĕss
Icklesham *E. Sussex*, 'ɪklʃəm, íckl-shăm
Icomb *Glos.*, 'ɪkəm, íckŏm
Iddesleigh *Devon*, 'ɪdzlɪ, ídzli. *Appropriate also for the Earl of* ~.
Iddon, *f.n.*, 'ɪdən, íddŏn
Ide *Devon*, ɪd, eed
Ideford *Devon*, 'ɪdfərd, ídfŏrd
Iden, *f.n.*, 'aɪdən, ídĕn
Iden *E. Sussex*, 'aɪdən, ídĕn
Idiens, *f.n.*, 'ɪdɪənz, íddiĕnz
Idle *W.Yorks.*, 'aɪdl, ídl
Idle, River, *Notts.*, 'aɪdl, ídl
Idless *Cornwall*, 'ɪdlɪs, éedlĕss
Idloes, *Welsh C.n.*, 'ɪdlɔɪs, ídloyss
Idmiston *Wilts.*, 'ɪdmɪstən, ídmisstŏn
Idridgehay *Derby.*, 'aɪdrɪdʒheɪ, ídrij-hay; 'ɪðəseɪ, íthĕssay
Idris, *C.n.*, 'ɪdrɪs, ídriss
Idwal, *Welsh C.n.*, 'ɪdwəl, ídwăl
Iestyn, *Welsh C.n.*, 'jestɪn, yéstin
Ieuan, *Welsh C.n.*, 'jaɪjən, yí-yän
Ievers, *f.n.*, 'aɪvərz, ívĕrz
Ife, *f.n.*, aɪf, īf
Ifield, *f.n.*, 'aɪfild, ífeeld
Ifold *W. Sussex*, 'aɪfoʊld, í-fōld
Ifor, *Welsh C.n.*, 'ivər, éevor; 'aɪvər, ívŏr
Ightham, *f.n.*, 'aɪtəm, ítăm
Ightham *Kent*, 'aɪtəm, ítăm
Igoe, *f.n.*, 'aɪgoʊ, ígō
Iken *Suffolk*, 'aɪkən, íkĕn
Ikerrin, Viscount, 'aɪkerɪn, í-kerrin
Ikin, *f.n.*, 'aɪkɪn, íkin
Ilam *Staffs.*, 'aɪləm, ílăm
Ilbert, *f.n.*, 'ɪlbərt, ílbĕrt
Ilchester *Somerset*, 'ɪltʃɪstər, íltchĕstĕr. *Appropriate also for the Earl of* ~.
Iles, *f.n.*, aɪlz, īlz

Ilett, *f.n.*, 'aɪlɪt, ílĕt
Ilford *London*, 'ɪlfərd, ilförd
Iliffe, *f.n.*, 'aɪlɪf, ílíff. *Appropriate also for Baron* ~.
Iline, *f.n.*, 'aɪlaɪn, ílín
Ilkeston *Derby.*, 'ɪlkɪstən, ílkĕstŏn. *Appropriate also for the Barony of* ~.
Ilketshall *Suffolk*, 'ɪlkɪʃəl, ílkĕ-shawl. *Appropriate for the villages of* ~ *St. Andrew,* ~ *St. John,* ~ *St. Lawrence, and* ~ *St. Margaret.*
Ilkley *W. Yorks.*, 'ɪlklɪ, ílkli
Illingworth, *f.n.*, 'ɪlɪŋwərθ, illing-wurth; 'ɪlɪŋwərθ, illing-würth
Illogan *Cornwall*, ɪ'lʌgən, illúggăn
Illtud, *Welsh C.n.*, 'ɪɬtɪd, iḥltid
Illtyd, *saint*, 'ɪɬtɪd, iḥltid
Ilmer *Bucks.*, 'ɪlmər, ílmĕr
Ilott, *f.n.*, 'aɪlɒt, ílot
Ilsley, East *and* West, *Berks.*, 'ɪlzlɪ, ílzli
Ilsley Down *Berks.*, 'ɪlzlɪ, ílzli
Imbusch, *f.n.*, 'ɪmbʊʃ, ím-bōōsh
Imeson, *f.n.*, 'aɪmɪsən, ímĕssŏn; 'aɪmsən, ímssŏn
Imhof, *f.n.*, 'ɪmhoʊf, ím-hōf
Imi, *f.n.*, 'ɪmɪ, eémi
Imison, *f.n.*, 'aɪmɪsən, ímissŏn
Imisson, *f.n.*, 'ɪmɪsən, ímmissŏn
Imlach, *f.n.*, 'ɪmləx, ímlách
Immingham *Humberside*, 'ɪmɪŋəm, imming-ăm
Imogen, *C.n.*, 'ɪmədʒən, ímmŏjĕn
Imray, *f.n.*, 'ɪmreɪ, ímray
Ince, *f.n.*, ɪns, inss
Inchcape, Earl of, ɪnʃ'keɪp, insh-káyp
Inchcruin *Central*, ɪnʃ'kruɪn, insh-kroó-in
Inchinnan *S'clyde*, ɪnʃ'ɪnən, insh-ínnăn
Inchiquin, Baron of, 'ɪntʃɪkwɪn, íntchikwin
Inchmahome *Central*, 'ɪnʃmə'hoʊm, ínshmă-hŏm
Inchnadamph *H'land*, ɪnʃnə'dæmf, inshnădámf
Inchrye Abbey *Fife*, ɪnʃ'raɪ, insh-rí
Inchture *Tayside*, ɪnʃ'tjʊər, insh-tyŏŏr
Inchtuthil *Tayside*, ɪnʃ'tjuθɪl, insh-téw-thil
Inchyra *Tayside*, ɪnʃ'aɪərə, inshíră. *Appropriate also for Baron* ~.
Ind Coope, *brewers*, 'ɪnd 'kup, ind koóp
Ingatestone *Essex*, 'ɪŋgətstoʊn, íng-găt-stŏn
Inge, *f.n.*, ɪŋ, ing
Ingelow, *f.n.*, 'ɪndʒɪloʊ, ínjĕlō

Ingestre, Viscount, 'ɪŋgɪstrɪ, íng-gĕstri
Ingham, *f.n.*, 'ɪŋəm, ing-ăm
Ingleton *N. Yorks.*, 'ɪŋgltən, íng-gltŏn
Inglis, *f.n.*, 'ɪŋglz, ing-glz; 'ɪŋglɪs, ing-gliss. *The first is Scottish, the second Northern Irish and southern English.*
Ingold, *f.n.*, 'ɪŋgoʊld, ing-gōld
Ingoldisthorpe *Norfolk*, 'ɪŋglzθɔrp, ing-glz-thorp
Ingliston *Lothian*, 'ɪŋglztən, íng-glz-tŏn; 'ɪŋglstən, ing-glsstŏn
Ingoldmells *Lincs.*, 'ɪŋgəmelz, ing-gŏmelz
Ingpen, *f.n.*, 'ɪŋpen, ing-pen
Ingram, *f.n.*, 'ɪŋgrəm, ing-grăm
Ingrams, *f.n.*, 'ɪŋgrəmz, ing-grămz
Ingrebourne, River, *Essex*, 'ɪŋgrɪbɔrn, ing-grĕborn
Ingress, *f.n.*, 'ɪŋgrɪs, ing-grĕss
Ingrey, *f.n.*, 'ɪŋgrɪ, ing-gri
Ings, *f.n.*, ɪŋz, ingz
Ingwersen, *f.n.*, 'ɪŋwərsən, ing-wérssĕn
Inishanier *Co. Down*, ˌɪnɪʃ'ænɪər, innish-ánni-ĕr
Inishargie *Co. Down*, ˌɪnɪʃ'argɪ, innish-aárgi
Inisharoan *Co. Down*, ˌɪnɪʃə'roʊn, innish-ărōn
Inkpen *Berks.*, 'ɪŋkpen, ínkpen
Inman, *f.n.*, 'ɪnmən, ínmăn
Innellan *S'clyde*, ɪn'elən, inéllăn
Innerleithen *Borders*, ˌɪnər'liðən, innĕrleethĕn
Innes, *f.n.*, 'ɪnɪs, ínnĕss; 'ɪnɪz, ínnĕz
Innes of Edingight, *f.n.*, 'ɪnɪs əv 'idɪn'gɪxt, ínnĕss ŏv eédin-gícht
Innes of Learney, Sir Thomas, *late Lord Lyon King of Arms*, 'ɪnɪs əv 'lɛrnɪ, ínnĕss ŏv láirni
Innes-Ker, *f.n.*, 'ɪnɪs 'kar, ínnĕss kaár; 'ɪnɪs 'kɛər, ínnĕss káir. *The first is appropriate for the Duke of Roxburghe's family name.*
Inns, *f.n.*, ɪnz, innz
Insch *Grampian*, ɪntʃ, intch
Instone, *f.n.*, 'ɪnstoʊn, ínstŏn
Instow *Devon*, 'ɪnstoʊ, ínstŏ
Intake *S. Yorks.*, 'ɪnteɪk, íntayk. *Appropriate for the districts of this name in both Doncaster and Sheffield.*
Inver *H'land*, 'ɪnvər, ínvĕr. *Appropriate also for the Loch and River of this name.*
Inverallochy *Grampian*, ˌɪnvər-'æləxɪ, invĕrálochi

Inveraray S'clyde, ,ınvər'ɛərı, invĕráiri; ,ınvər'ɛərə, invĕráirä

Inverarity Tayside, ,ınvər'ærıtı, invĕrárriti

Inverbervie Grampian, ,ınvər-'bɜrvı, invĕrbĕrvi

Invereighty Tayside, ,ınvər'aıtı, invĕriti

Inverewe House H'land, ,ınvər'ju, invĕr-yoo

Inverey Grampian, ,ınvər'eı, invĕráy

Inverinate H'land, ,ınvər'ınıt, invĕrĕenit

Inverkeilor Tayside, ,ınvər'kilər, invĕrkĕilŏr

Inverkeithing Fife, ,ınvər'kiðıŋ, invĕrkĕething

Inverlochy H'land, ,ınvər'lɒxı, invĕrlóchi

Invermoriston H'land, ,ınvər-'mɒrıstən, invĕrmórristŏn

Inverness H'land, ,ınvər'nes, invĕrnéss

Invernessian, native of Inverness, ,ınvər'nızıən, invĕrnĕezïän

Inverquharity Tayside, ,ınvər-'hwɒrıtı, invĕrwháwriti; ,ınvər-'hwɒrıtı, invĕrwháariti

Inversnaid Central, ,ınvər'sneıd, invĕr-snáyd

Inveruglas S'clyde, ,ınvər'ugləs, invĕróoglãss

Inverurie Grampian, ,ınvər'uərı, invĕróŏri

Ioan, Welsh C.n., 'jouən, yó-än

Iochdor S. Uist, 'iəxkər, ĕe-ŏchkär. See also Eochar.

Iolo, Welsh C.n., 'joulou, yólō

Iona S'clyde, aı'ounə, ī-ónä

Ionides, f.n., aı'ɒnıdiz, ī-ónnideez

Ions, f.n., 'ıənz, ĕe-ŏnz

Iorns, f.n., 'aıərnz, í-ürnz

Iorwerth, Welsh C.n., 'jɔrwɛərθ, yór-wairth

Iping W. Sussex, 'aıpıŋ, íping

Ipplepen Devon, 'ıplpen, ípplpen

Ipswich Suffolk, 'ıpswıtʃ, ípswitch

Iredell, f.n., 'aıərdel, írdel

Iremonger, f.n., 'aıərmʌŋgər, írmung-gĕr

Ireby, Low, Cumbria, 'aıərbı, írbi

Irens, f.n., 'aıərɒnz, frĕnz

Ireshopeburn Durham, 'aıʃəp-bɜrn, íss-hŏp-burn

Ireson, f.n., 'aıərsən, frssŏn

Irfonwy, Welsh C.n., ɜr'vɒnuı, irvónnŏŏ-i

Irlam Gtr. M'chester, 'ɜrləm, írläm

Irlam o' the Height Gtr. M'chester, 'ɜrləm ə 'ðaıt, írläm ŏ thít

Irnham Lincs,. 'ɜrnəm, írnäm

Irongray D. & G., 'aıərəngreı, frŏn-gray

Irthlingborough Northants., 'ɜrθ-lıŋbərə, írthling-bŭrä

Irvine, f.n., 'ɜrvın, írvin

Irvine S'clyde, 'ɜrvın, írvin

Irvinestown Co. Fermanagh, 'ɜrvınztaun, írvinztown

Irving, f.n., 'ɜrvıŋ, írving

Irwell, River, Lancs., 'ɜrwel, írwel

Isacke, f.n., 'aızək, ízäk

Isador, f.n., 'ızədɔr, ízzädor

Isard, f.n., 'ızard, ízzaard

Isbister, f.n., 'aızbıstər, ízbisstĕr; 'ızbıstər, ízzbisstĕr

Ise Brook Northants., 'aızə bruk, íz brōok

Isel Cumbria, 'aızl, ízl

Isepp, f.n., 'ızep, ĕezepp

Isfield E. Sussex, 'ısfıld, íssfeeld

Isham, f.n., 'aıʃəm, í-shäm

Isham Northants., 'aıʃəm, í-shäm

Isherwood, f.n., 'ıʃərwud, ishĕr-wŏŏd

Isington Hants, 'ızıŋtən, ízzingtŏn

Isis, River, Oxon., 'aısıs, íssiss

Islandmagee Co. Antrim, ,aıländ-mə'gi, īländmägĕe

Islay S'clyde, 'aılə, ílä; 'aıleı, ílay

Isleham Cambs., 'aızləm, ízl-äm

Isle of Thanet Kent, 'aıl əv 'θænıt, íl ŏv thännĕt

Isle of Wight 'aıl əv 'waıt, íl ŏv wít

Isleworth London, 'aızlwɜrθ, ízl--wurth; 'aızlwɜrθ, ízl-wŭrth

Isley Walton Leics., 'ızlı 'wɒltən, ízzli wáwltŏn

Islington London, 'ızlıŋtən, ízzling-tŏn

Islip, f.n., 'ızlıp, ízlip. Appropriate also for the ~ Chapel in Westminster Abbey.

Islip Northants., Oxon., 'aıslıp, ísslip

Islwyn, Welsh C.n., 'ısluın, ísslŏŏ-in

Ismay, f.n., 'ızmeı, izmay. Appropriate also for the Barony of ~.

Ison, f.n., 'aısən, íssŏn

Issigonis, Sir Alec, car designer, ,ısı'gounıs, issigóniss

Istance, f.n., 'aıstəns, ístänss

Isted, f.n., 'aısted, ístedd

Itchen Hants, 'ıtʃən, ítchĕn

Itchenor W. Sussex, 'ıtʃınər, ítchĕnor

Ithell, f.n., 'aıθl, íthl

Ithon, River, Powys, 'aıθɒn, íthon

Ivay, f.n., 'aıveı, ívay

Iveagh, Earl of, 'aıvə, ívä

Iveagh Co. Down, 'aıveı, ívay

Ivelaw, f.n., 'aıvılɒ, ívĕlaw

Iver *Bucks.*, 'aıvər, ívĕr

Iver Heath *Bucks.*, 'aıvər 'hiθ, ívĕr héeth

Ives, *f.n.*, aıvz, īvz

Iveson, *f.n.*, 'aıvsən, ív-sŏn

Ivimey, *f.n.*, 'aıvımı, ívimi

Ivin, *f.n.*, 'aıvın, ívin

Ivington *H. & W.*, 'ıvıŋtən, ívvingtŏn

Iwade *Kent*, 'aı'weıd, í-wáyd

Iwan, *Welsh C.n. and f.n.*, 'juən, yoó-ăn

Iwerne, River, *Dorset*, 'juərn, yoó-ern

Iwerne Courtney *Dorset*, 'juərn 'kɔrtnı, yoó-ern kórtni

Ixer, *f.n.*, 'ıksər, ícksĕr

Izard, *f.n.*, 'aızərd, ízaard; 'aızərd, ízărd; 'ızərd, ízzărd

Izatt, *f.n.*, 'aızət, ízăt

Izbicki, *f.n.*, 'ızbıkı, ízbicki

Izen, *f.n.*, 'aızən, ízĕn

Izod, *f.n.*, 'ızəd, ízzŏd

Izzard, *f.n.*, 'ızɑrd, ízzaard; 'ızərd, ízzărd

Izzett, *f.n.*, 'aızıt, ízĕt

J

Jackett, *f.n.*, 'dʒækıt, jáckĕt

Jackson, *f.n.*, 'dʒæksən, jácksŏn

Jacobi, *f.n.*, 'dʒækəbı, jáckŏbi

Jacobs, *f.n.*, 'dʒeıkəbz, jáykŏbz

Jacobstow *Cornwall*, 'dʒeıkəb-stou, jáykŏb-stō

Jacoby, *f.n.*, dʒə'koubı, jăkóbi; 'dʒækəbı, jáckŏbi

Jacot, *f.n.*, 'dʒækou, jáckō

Jacottet, *f.n.*, 'dʒækəteı, jáckŏtay

Jacques, *f.n.*, dʒeıks, jayks; dʒæks, jacks. *The first is appropriate for Baron* ~.

Jaeger, *f.n.*, 'jeıgər, yáygĕr

Jaekel, *f.n.*, 'dʒeıkl, jáykl

Jaffe, *f.n.*, 'dʒæfı, jáffi

Jaffé, *f.n.*, 'dʒæfeı, jáffay

Jaffray, *f.n.*, 'dʒæfrı, jáffri

Jago, *f.n.*, 'dʒeıgou, jáygō

Jagoe, *f.n.*, 'dʒeıgou, jáygō

Jaguer, *f.n.*, 'dʒægjuər, jág-yōŏr

Jakins, *f.n.*, 'dʒeıkınz, jáykinz

Jakobi, *f.n.*, 'dʒækəbı, jáckŏbi

Jalland, *f.n.*, 'dʒælənd, jáländ

Jamblin, *f.n.*, 'dʒæmblın, jám-blin

James, *C.n. and f.n.*, dʒeımz, jaymz

Jameson, *f.n.*, 'dʒemısən, jémmis-sŏn; 'dʒımısən, jímmissŏn; 'dʒeımsən, jáymssŏn; 'dʒæmı-sən, jámmissŏn; 'dʒeımısən, jáymissŏn

Jamieson, *f.n.*, 'dʒımısən, jímmis-sŏn; 'dʒemısən, jémmissŏn; 'dʒeımısən, jáymissŏn; 'dʒæmı-sən, jámmissŏn

Janis, *f.n.*, 'dʒænıs, jánniss

Janisch, *f.n.*, 'jeınıʃ, yáynish

Janson, *f.n.*, 'dʒænsən, jánssŏn

Japhet, *f.n.*, 'dʒæfıt, jáffĕt

Jaque, *f.n.*, dʒeık, jayk

Jaques, *f.n.*, dʒeıks, jayks; dʒæks, jacks

Jaquest, *f.n.*, 'dʒeıkwıst, jáyk-wĕst

Jaray, *f.n.*, 'dʒæreı, járray

Jarché, *f.n.*, 'dʒɑrʃeı, jaár-shay

Jardine, *f.n.*, 'dʒɑrdin, jaárdeen

Jarlshof *Shetland*, 'jɑrlzhɒf, yaárlz-hoff

Jarman, *f.n.*, 'dʒɑrmən, jaármăn

Jarred, *f.n.*, 'dʒærəd, járrĕd

Jarrett, *f.n.*, 'dʒærıt, járrĕt

Jarvis, *f.n.*, 'dʒɑrvıs, jaárviss

Jasper, *C.n. and f.n.*, 'dʒæspər, jásspĕr

Jast, *f.n.*, dʒæst, jasst

Jay, *f.n.*, dʒeı, jay

Jaywick *Essex*, 'dʒeıwık, jáy-wick

Jeacock, *f.n.*, 'dʒikɒk, jéekock

Jeacocke, *f.n.*, 'dʒeıkou, jáykō

Jeaffreson, *f.n.*, 'dʒefərsən, jéffĕrssŏn; 'dʒefrısən, jéfrĕssŏn

Jeal, *f.n.*, dʒil, jeel

Jeans, *f.n.*, dʒinz, jeenz

Jeater, *f.n.*, 'dʒitər, jéetĕr

Jeavons, *f.n.*, 'dʒevənz, jévvŏnz

Jeayes, *f.n.*, dʒeız, jayz

Jedburgh *Borders*, 'dʒedbərə, jédbŭră. *Appropriate also for Baron* ~.

Jedrzejczak, *f.n.*, jen'dʒeıtʃæk, yen-jáytchack

Jeffares, *f.n.*, 'dʒefərz, jéffärz

Jeffcock, *f.n.*, 'dʒefkɒk, jéfkock

Jefferies, *f.n.*, 'dʒefrız, jéffriz

Jefferis, *f.n.*, 'dʒefərıs, jéffĕriss

Jefferson, *f.n.*, 'dʒefərsən, jéffĕr-sŏn

Jeffes, *f.n.*, dʒefs, jeffs

Jeffress, *f.n.*, 'dʒefrıs, jéffrĕss

Jeffries, *f.n.*, 'dʒefrız, jéffriz

Jeffroy, *f.n.*, 'dʒefrɔı, jéffroy

Jeger, *f.n.*, 'dʒeıgər, jáygĕr. *Appropriate also for Baroness* ~.

Jekyll, *f.n.*, 'dʒikl, jéekl; 'dʒıkıl, jéekil; 'dʒekl, jéckl. *The first is appropriate for Gertrude* ~, *horticulturalist and author. There is some evidence that R. L. Stevenson intended the first for his character in 'Dr* ~

and Mr Hyde', but the pronunciation in popular use is the third.
Jellicoe, Earl, 'dʒelɪkoʊ, jéllikō
Jenks, *f.n.,* dʒeŋks, jenks
Jennens, *f.n.,* 'dʒenɪnz, jénnĕnz
Jenner, *f.n.,* 'dʒenər, jénnĕr
Jennings, *f.n.,* 'dʒenɪŋz, jénningz
Jenyns, *f.n.,* 'dʒenɪnz, jénninz
Jenyth, *C.n.,* 'dʒenɪθ, jénnith
Jeonney, *f.n.,* dʒɪ'oʊnɪ, ji-ōni
Jephcott, *f.n.,* 'dʒefkɒt, jéffkot
Jeram, *f.n.,* 'dʒerəm, jérrăm
Jerdein, *f.n.,* dʒər'din, jĕrdéen
Jerningham, *f.n.,* 'dʒɜrnɪŋəm, jérning-ăm
Jerrom, *f.n.,* 'dʒerəm, jérrŏm
Jersey, Earl of, 'dʒɜrzɪ, jérzi
Jervaulx *N. Yorks.,* 'dʒɜrvoʊ, jérvō. *Appropriate also for ~ Abbey. It appears that an old pronunciation,* 'dʒɑrvɪs, jaárviss, *is still used by some local speakers.*
Jervis, *f.n.,* 'dʒɑrvɪs, jaárviss; 'dʒɑrvɪs, jaárviss. *The first is appropriate for the family name of the 18th-c. admiral, the Earl of St. Vincent.*
Jervois, *f.n.,* 'dʒɑrvɪs, jaárviss
Jervoise, *f.n.,* 'dʒɜrvɪs, jérviss
Jesse, *f.n.,* 'dʒesɪ, jéssi
Jessel, *f.n.,* 'dʒesl, jéssl
Jesson, *f.n.,* 'dʒesən, jéssŏn
Jessup, *f.n.,* 'dʒesəp, jéssŭp
Jeuda, *f.n.,* 'dʒudə, joodă
Jeudwine, *f.n.,* 'dʒudwaɪn, joodwīn; 'dʒudwɪn, joodwin
Jeune, *f.n.,* ʒ3n, zhön; ʒun, zhoon
Jevington *E. Sussex,* 'dʒevɪŋtən, jévvingtŏn
Jeyes, *f.n.,* dʒeɪz, jayz
Jeynes, *f.n.,* dʒeɪnz, jaynz
Joad, *f.n.,* dʒoʊd, jōd
Job, *f.n.,* dʒoʊb, jōb
Jobar, *f.nt,* 'dʒoʊbɑr, jōbaar
Jobling, *f.n.,* 'dʒɒblɪŋ, jóbbling
Jocelyn, *C.n. and f.n.,* 'dʒɒslɪn, jósslin. *Appropriate also for Viscount ~.*
Jockel, *f.n.,* 'dʒɒkl, jóckl
Jodrell, *f.n.,* 'dʒɒdrəl, jódrĕl. *Appropriate also for the ~ Chair of Zoology and Comparative Anatomy in the University of London.*
Jodrell Bank *experimental station Ches.,* 'dʒɒdrəl 'bæŋk, jódrĕl bánk
Joekes, *f.n.,* 'jukɪs, yóokĕss
Joffe, *f.n.,* 'dʒɒfeɪ, jóffay
Johnes, *f.n.,* dʒoʊnz, jōnz
Johnian Society *St John's Coll., Cambridge,* 'dʒoʊnɪən, jóniăn

Johnsey, *f.n.,* 'dʒɒnzɪ, jónzi
Johnson, *f.n.,* 'dʒɒnsən, jónssŏn
Johnston, *f.n.,* 'dʒɒnstən, jónstŏn; 'dʒɒnsən, jónssŏn
Johnstone, *f.n.,* 'dʒɒnstən, jónstŏn; 'dʒɒnsən, jónssŏn; 'dʒɒnstoʊn, jónstōn
Johnstone *Devon,* 'dʒɒnstən, jónsstŏn
Johnstown *Clwyd, Dyfed,* 'dʒɒnztaʊn, jónztown
Joldwynds *Surrey,* 'dʒoʊldwɪndz, jŏldwindz
Joll, *f.n.,* dʒɒl, joll
Jolliff, *f.n.,* 'dʒɒlɪf, jóllif
Jolliffe, *f.n.,* 'dʒɒlɪf, jóllif
Jonasson, *f.n.,* 'dʒɒnəsən, jónnässŏn
Jones, *f.n.,* dʒoʊnz, jōnz
Jonesborough *Co. Armagh,* 'dʒoʊnzbərə, jónzbŭră
Jonker, *f.n.,* 'dʒɒŋkər, jónkĕr
Jonson, Ben, *16th–17th-c. dramatist,* 'ben 'dʒɒnsən, bén jónssŏn
Jope, *f.n.,* dʒoʊp, jōp
Jopling, *f.n.,* 'dʒɒplɪŋ, jóppling
Jordanhill *S'clyde,* 'dʒɔrdən'hɪl, jórdăn-hil
Jory, *f.n.,* 'dʒɔrɪ, jáwri
Joshi, *f.n.,* 'dʒoʊʃɪ, jóshi
Josipovici, *f.n.,* dʒoʊzɪpə'vitʃɪ, jōzipōvéetchi
Joss, *f.n.,* dʒɒs, joss
Joubert de la Ferté, *f.n.,* 'ʒubɛər də lɑ 'fɛərteɪ, zhóobair dĕ laa fáirtay
Joughin, *f.n.,* 'dʒoʊɪn, jō-in; 'dʒoʊkɪn, jóckin
Joule, *f.n.,* dʒul, jool; dʒoʊl, jōl; dʒaʊl, jowl. *Information obtained for the BBC in 1933 by the late Professor Arthur Lloyd James and evidence submitted by scientists to 'Nature' in Sept.–Nov. 1943 show that the first is correct for James Prescott ~, the 19th-c. scientist, after whom the unit of energy was named.*
Joules, *f.n.,* dʒulz, joolz
Jourdain, *f.n.,* ʒʊər'deɪn, zhŏordáyn
Journeaux, *f.n.,* 'ʒʊərnoʊ, zhŏornō
Jousiffe, *f.n.,* 'ʒoʊzɪf, zhóʒif
Jowell, *f.n.,* 'dʒoʊəl, jów-ĕl; 'dʒoʊəl, jó-ĕl
Jowers, *f.n.,* 'dʒoʊərz, jówĕrz
Jowett, *f.n.,* 'dʒaʊɪt, jów-ĕt; 'dʒoʊɪt, jó-ĕt
Jowitt, *f.n.,* 'dʒaʊɪt, jów-it; 'dʒoʊɪt, jó-it. *The second is appropriate for the Earldom of ~.*
Jowle, *f.n.,* dʒaʊl, jowl; dʒul, jool; dʒoʊl, jōl

Joynson, *f.n.*, 'dʒɔɪnsən, jóynssŏn
Jubb, *f.n.*, dʒʌb, jubb
Juchau, *f.n.*, 'dʒuʃou, joÓoshō
Juckes, *f.n.*, dʒuks, jooks
Juett, *f.n.*, 'dʒuɪt, joÓ-ĕt
Jukes, *f.n.*, dʒuks, jooks
Juler, *f.n.*, 'dʒulər, joÓlĕr
Julnes, *f.n.*, dʒulnz, joÓlnz
Julyan, *f.n.*, 'dʒuljən, joÓl-yăn
June, *f.n.*, dʒun, joon
Junor, *f.n.*, 'dʒunər, joÓonŏr
Jura *S'clyde*, 'dʒuərə, joÓŏrǎ
Jurby *I. of Man*, 'dʒɜrbɪ, júrbi
Justham, *f.n.*, 'dʒʌstəm, jústăm
Justicz, *f.n.*, 'dʒʌstɪs, jústiss
Juta, *f.n.*, 'dʒutə, joÓtǎ

K

Kaberry, *f.n.*, 'keɪbərɪ, káybĕri
Kadisch, *f.n.*, 'kɑdɪʃ, kaádish
Kadleigh, *f.n.*, 'kædlɪ, kádli
Kagan, *f.n.*, 'keɪgən, káygǎn. *Appropriate also for Baron* ~.
Kahan, *f.n.*, kɑ'hɑn, kă-haán
Kahn, *f.n.*, kɑn, kaan. *Appropriate also for Baron* ~.
Kalamuniak, *f.n.*, ˌkælə'munɪæk, kalǎmoÓni-ack
Kaldor, Baron, 'kældɔr, káldor
Kalindjian, *f.n.*, kə'lɪndʒən, kǎlínjǎn
Kames Bay *S'clyde*, keɪmz, kaymz
Kanareck, *f.n.*, 'kænərek, kánnǎreck
Kanocz, *f.n.*, 'kɒnɒts, kónnawts
Kapica, *f.n.*, kə'pikə, kǎpéekǎ
Kaplan, *f.n.*, 'kæplən, káplǎn
Karen, *C.n.*, 'kærən, kárrĕn; 'kɑrən, kaárĕn
Karen, *f.n.*, 'kærən, kárrĕn
Karmel, *f.n.*, 'kɑrməl, kaármĕl
Karpeles, *f.n.*, 'kɑrpɪlɪz, kaárpĕleez
Kasia, *C.n.*, 'kæʃə, káshǎ
Kassell, *f.n.*, 'kæsl, kássl
Kassimatis, *f.n.*, ˌkæsɪ'mɑtɪs, kassimaátiss
Katin, *f.n.*, 'keɪtɪn, káytin
Katrine, Loch, *Central*, 'kætrɪn, kátrin
Katz, *f.n.*, kæts, kats
Kaufman, *f.n.*, 'kɔfmən, káwfmăn
Kavanagh, *f.n.*, 'kævənə, kávvănă; kə'vænə, kăvánnă
Kawerau, *f.n.*, 'kɑvrɑʊ, kaávrow
Kay, *f.n.*, keɪ, kay
Kazantzis, *f.n.*, kə'zæntsɪs, kăzántsiss

Kaznowski, *f.n.*, kæz'nɒfskɪ, kaznófski
Kea *Cornwall*, ki, kee
Keadby *Humberside*, 'kɪdbɪ, kéedbi
Keady *Co. Armagh, Co. Derry*, 'kɪdɪ, kéedi
Kealey, *f.n.*, 'kilɪ, kéeli
Keane, *f.n.*, kin, keen; keɪn, kayn
Keaney, *f.n.*, 'kinɪ, kéeni
Kear, *f.n.*, kɪər, keer
Kearey, *f.n.*, 'kɪərɪ, kéeri
Kearley, *f.n.*, 'kɪərlɪ, kéerli
Kearney, *f.n.*, 'kɜrnɪ, kérni; 'kɑrnɪ, kaárni
Kearney *Co. Down*, 'kɜrnɪ, kérni
Kearsey, *f.n.*, 'kɜrzɪ, kérzi
Kearsley, *f.n.*, 'kɪərzlɪ, kéerzli
Kearsley *Gtr. M'chester*, 'kɜrzlɪ, kérzli
Kearsney *Kent*, 'kɜrznɪ, kérzni
Kearton, *f.n.*, 'kɪərtən, kéertŏn; 'kɜrtən, kértŏn. *The first is appropriate for Baron* ~.
Keates, *f.n.*, kits, keets
Keating, *f.n.*, 'kitɪŋ, kéeting
Keatinge, *f.n.*, 'kitɪŋ, kéeting
Keatley, *f.n.*, 'kitlɪ, kéetli
Keats, *f.n.*, kits, keets
Keay, *f.n.*, keɪ, kay
Keble, *f.n.*, 'kibl, kéebl. *Appropriate for John* ~, *19th-c. divine and poet.*
Kedington, *also spelt* Ketton, *Suffolk*, 'kedɪŋtən, kéddingtŏn; 'ketən, kéttŏn. *Older residents use only the second pronunciation.*
Kedleston *Derby.*, 'kedlstən, kédlstŏn
Kedourie, *f.n.*, kə'duərɪ, kĕdŏóri
Keeble, *f.n.*, 'kibl, kéebl
Keeffe, *f.n.*, kif, keef
Keele *Staffs.*, kil, keel
Keeler, *f.n.*, 'kilər, kéelĕr
Keeling, *f.n.*, 'kilŋ, kéeling
Keene, *f.n.*, kin, keen
Keenlyside, *f.n.*, 'kinlɪsaɪd, kéenlissīd
Kegan, *f.n.*, 'kigən, kéegăn
Kegie, *f.n.*, 'kigɪ, kéegi
Kehelland *Cornwall*, kɪ'helənd, kĕhélländ
Kehoe, *f.n.*, kjou, kyō; 'kihou, kée-hō
Keig, *f.n.*, kig, keeg
Keig *Grampian*, kig, keeg
Keighley, *f.n.*, 'kiθlɪ, kéethli; 'kilɪ, keéli
Keighley *W. Yorks.*, 'kiθlɪ, kéethli
Keighlian, *one educated at* Keighley *Grammar School*, 'kilɪən, kéeliăn

Keightley, f.n., 'kıtlı, kéetli
Keigwin, f.n., 'kegwın, kégwin
Keill, f.n., kil, keel
Keiller, f.n., 'kılər, kéelēr
Keinton Mandeville Somerset,
  'kentən 'mændıvıl, kéntŏn
  mándēvil
Keir, f.n., kıər, keer
Keisby Lincs., 'keızbı, káyzbi;
  'keısbı, káyssbi
Keiss H'land, kis, keess
Keith, C.n. and f.n., kiθ, keeth
Keith Grampian, kiθ, keeth
Keith of Kinkel, Baron, 'kiθ əv
  kın'kel, keeth ŏv kin-kéll
Kekewich, f.n., 'kekıwıtʃ, kéckĕ-
  witch; 'kekwıtʃ, kéckwitch;
  'kekwıdʒ, kéckwij
Kelburn, Viscount of, 'kelbərn,
  kélbŭrn
Kelcey, f.n., 'kelsı, kélssi
Kelk, f.n., kelk, kelk
Kell, f.n., kel, kell
Kelland, f.n., 'kelənd, kéllănd
Kellas Grampian, Tayside, 'keləs,
  kélläss
Kellaway, f.n., 'keləweı, kéllă-
  -way
Kelleher, f.n., 'keləhər, kéllĕ-hĕr
Kellett, f.n., 'kelıt, kéllĕt
Kellett-Bowman, f.n., 'kelıt 'bou-
  mən, kéllĕt-bówmăn
Kelleway, f.n., 'keləweı, kéllĕway
Kelley, f.n., 'kelı, kélli
Kellingley N. Yorks., 'kelıŋlı,
  kélling-li
Kellock, f.n., 'kelɒk, kéllock
Kellogg, f.n., 'kelɒg, kéllogg
Kelmscot Oxon., 'kemskət, kéms-
  skŏt
Kelsale Suffolk, 'kelseıl, kélsayl
Kelsall, f.n., 'kelsl, kélssl
Kelsey, f.n., 'kelsı, kélssi; 'kelzı,
  kélzi
Kelso Borders, 'kelsou, kélssō
Kelvedon Essex, 'kelvıdən,
  kélvēdŏn
Kelvinhaugh S'clyde, 'kelvınhɔ,
  kélvin-haw; 'kelvınhɒx,
  kélvin-hoch
Kelvinside Glasgow, ,kelvın'saıd,
  kelvinssíd
Kelynack Cornwall, ke'laınək,
  kelínăk; 'klaınək, klínăk
Kemback Fife, 'kembæk, kém-
  back
Kemeys-Tynte, f.n., 'kemıs 'tınt,
  kémmiss tínt
Kempinski, f.n., kem'pınskı,
  kempínski
Kempsey H. & W., 'kemsı,
  kémssi; 'kemzı, kémzi
Kempshall, f.n., 'kempʃəl, kémp-
  -shăl

Kemptown E. Sussex, 'kemp-
  taun, kémptown
Kemsley, Viscount, 'kemzlı,
  kémzli
Kenardington Kent, kə'nardıŋtən,
  kēnáardingtŏn
Kendal Cumbria, 'kendl, kéndl
Kendall, f.n., 'kendl, kéndl
Kendoon, Loch, D. & G., 'ken-
  'dun, kén-doón
Kendrick, f.n., 'kendrık, kéndrick
Kenfig Hill Mid Glam., 'kenfıg
  'hıl, kénfig híll
Kenidjack Cornwall, kın'ıdʒæk,
  kēníjjack
Kenlis, Baron, ken'lıs, kenlíss
Kenmare, Earldom of, ken'mɛər,
  kenmáir
Kenmore H'land, 'kenmɔr, kén-
  mor
Kennair, f.n., ken'ɛər, kennáir
Kennaird, f.n., ken'ɛərd, ken-
  náird
Kennard, f.n., kenard, kénnaard;
  kı'nard, kēnáard
Kennerleigh Devon, 'kenərlı,
  kénnĕrli
Kennet, Baron, 'kenıt, kénnĕt
Kennethmont Grampian, ke-
  'neθmənt, kennéthmŏnt
Kennett, f.n., 'kenıt, kénnĕt
Kennoway, f.n., 'kenəweı,
  kénnŏ-way
Kennoway Fife, 'kenəweı,
  kénnŏ-way
Kenshole, f.n., 'kenzhoul, kénz-
  -hōl; 'kenʃoul, kén-shōl
Kent, f.n., kent, kent
Kent Co. name, kent, kent.
  Appropriate also for HRH the
  Duke of ~.
Kentigern, saint, 'kentıgərn,
  kéntigĕrn
Kenward, f.n., 'kenwərd, kén-
  wărd
Kenwick Salop, 'kenık, kénnick
Kenwyn Cornwall, 'kenwın, kén-
  win
Kenyon, f.n., 'kenjən, kén-yŏn
Keogh, f.n., 'kiou, kee-ō; kjou,
  kyō
Keohane, f.n., ki'oun, kee-ón;
  ki'eın, kee-áyn; ki'æn, kee-án
Keough, f.n., 'kiou, kee-ō; kjou,
  kyō
Keown, f.n., kjoun, kyōn; ki'oun,
  kee-ón; 'kioun, kee-ōn
Keppel, f.n., 'kepl, képpl
Keppochhill Glasgow, 'kepəx'hıl,
  képpŏch-híll
Ker, f.n., kar, ker; kɛər, kair; kɑr.
  kaar. The third is appropriate
  for Baron ~.
Kerby, f.n., 'karbı, kérbi

Keren, Viscountcy of, 'kerən, kérrĕn

Keresley *W. Midlands,* 'kɜrzlɪ, kérzli; 'kɑrzlɪ, káarzli

Kerfoot, *f.n.,* 'kɜrfut, kérfŏŏt

Kerman, *f.n.,* 'kɜrmən, kérmăn

Kermeen, *f.n.,* kər'min, kĕrmeen

Kermode, *f.n.,* 'kɜrmoʊd, kérmōd

Kernaghan, *f.n.,* 'kɜrnəhən, kérnähän

Kernahan, *f.n.,* 'kɜrnəhən, kérnähän

Kernick, *f.n.,* 'kɜrnɪk, kérnick

Kernoghan, *f.n.,* 'kɜrnəhən, kérnŏ-hän

Kernohan, *f.n.,* 'kɜrnəhən, kérnŏhän

Kernot, *f.n.,* 'kɜrnət, kérnŏt; 'kɜrnoʊ, kérnō

Kerr, *f.n.,* kɜr, ker; kɛər, kair; kɑr, kaar

Kerrera *S'clyde,* 'kerərə, kérrĕră

Kerrier *Cornwall,* 'kerɪər, kérri-ĕr

Kerrigan, *f.n.,* 'kerɪgən, kérrigăn

Kerruish, *f.n.,* kə'ruʃ, kĕroŏsh

Kersal *Gtr. M'chester,* 'kɜrzl, kérzl

Kersey *Suffolk,* 'kɜrzɪ, kérzi

Kershaw, *f.n.,* 'kɜrʃɔ, kér-shaw. *Appropriate also for Baron* ~.

Kershope, Burn, *Scotland–England border,* 'kɜrsəp, kérssŏp

Kerslake, *f.n.,* 'kɑrzleɪk, káarzlayk

Kersner, *f.n.,* 'kɜrznər, kérznĕr

Kesgrave *Suffolk,* 'kezgreɪv, kézgrayv

Kestelman, *f.n.,* 'kestəlmən, késtĕlmän

Kesteven, Barony of, 'kestɪvən, késtĕvĕn

Kesteven *Lincs.,* kes'tivən, kesteevĕn. *Appropriate for the administrative districts of North and South* ~.

Keswick *S'clyde,* 'kezɪk, kézzick; 'kezwɪk, kéz-wick

Keswick *Cumbria,* 'kezɪk, kézzick

Ketelbey, Alfred, *composer,* kə'telbɪ, kĕtélbi

Kettel, *f.n.,* kɪ'tel, kĕtéll

Kettering *Northants.,* 'ketərɪŋ, kéttĕring

Kettle, *f.n.,* 'ketl, kéttl

Ketton *see* **Kedington**

Kettyle, *f.n.,* 'ketl, kéttl

Kevill, *f.n.,* 'kevɪl, kévvil

Keville, *f.n.,* 'kevɪl, kévvil

Kewley, *f.n.,* 'kjulɪ, kéwli

Key, *f.n.,* kɪ, kee

Keyes, Baron, kiz, keez

Keyham *Leics.,* 'kiəm, kée-ăm

Keyingham *Humberside,* 'keɪŋ-həm, káy-ing-hăm; 'keɪnɪnhəm, kénnin-hăm; 'kenɪŋhəm, kénning-hăm

Keymer, *f.n.,* 'kimər, keémĕr

Keymer *W. Sussex,* 'kimər, keémĕr; 'kaɪmər, kímĕr

Keynes, *f.n.,* keɪnz, kaynz. *Appropriate for John Maynard* ~ *(later Baron* ~ *), economist, 1883–1946.*

Keynes, Ashton, *Wilts.,* 'æʃtən 'keɪnz, áshtŏn káynz

Keynes, Horsted, *W. Sussex,* 'hɔrstɪd 'keɪnz, hórsstĕd káynz

Keynes, Milton, *Bucks.,* 'mɪltən 'kɪnz, míltŏn keénz

Keynsham *Avon,* 'keɪnʃəm, káyn-shăm

Keyser, *f.n.,* 'kizər, keézĕr; 'kaɪzər, kízĕr

Keyseɪ Ullmann, *merchant bankers,* 'kizər 'ʊlmən, keézĕr ōŏlmän

Keysoe *Beds.,* 'kisoʊ, keéssō

Keyston *Cambs.,* 'kistən, keéstŏn

Keyte, *f.n.,* kaɪt, kīt; kit, keet

Keyworth *Notts.,* 'kiwɜrθ, keéwurth

Khambatta, *f.n.,* kæm'bɑtə, kambáátä

Kibworth Beauchamp *Leics.,* 'kɪbwɜrθ 'bitʃəm, kíbwurth beétchăm

Kibworth Harcourt *Leics.,* 'kɪbwɜrθ 'hɑrkɔrt, kíbwurth háarkort

Kidderminster *H. & W.,* 'kɪdərmɪnstər, kiddĕrminstĕr

Kidel, *f.n.,* kɪ'del, kidéll

Kidman, *f.n.,* 'kɪdmən, kídmăn

Kidsgrove *Staffs.,* 'kɪdzgroʊv, kidz-grōv

Kidwelly *Dyfed,* kɪd'welɪ, kidwélli. *See also* **Cydweli.**

Kielder *Northd.,* 'kɪldər, keéldĕr

Kielty, *f.n.,* 'kɪltɪ, keélti

Kiely, *f.n.,* 'kɪlɪ, keéli; 'kaɪlɪ, kíli

Kiessimal Castle *see* **Kishmul** Castle

Kiggell, *f.n.,* 'kɪgl, kíggl

Kighley, *f.n.,* 'kɪlɪ, keéli

Kightly, *f.n.,* 'kaɪtlɪ, kítli

Kilbarchan *S'clyde,* kɪl'bɑrxən, kilbáarchăn

Kilbirnie *S'clyde,* kɪl'bɜrnɪ, kilbírni

Kilbowie *S'clyde,* kɪl'baʊɪ, kilbów-i

Kilbracken, Baron, kɪl'brækən, kilbráckĕn

Kilbride *S'clyde,* kɪl'braɪd, kilbríd

Kilbroney *Co. Down,* kɪl'broʊnɪ, kilbróni

Kilbucho *Borders*, kıl'bʊxoʊ, kil-boŏchŏ

Kilburn, *f.n.*, 'kılbərn, kílburn

Kilburn *London*, 'kılbərn, kílbŭrn; 'kılbərn, kílburn

Kilcalmonell *S'clyde*, kıl'kælmə-'nel, kilkálmŏnéll

Kilchattan *S'clyde*, kıl'xætən, kilcháttän

Kilchattan Bay *S'clyde*, kıl'kætən 'beı, kilkáttän báy

Kilchoan *H'land*, kıl'xoʊən, kilchŏ́-än; ,kılə'xoʊən, killáchŏ́-än

Kilchrenan *S'clyde*, kıl'krenən, kilkrénnän

Kilchrist *H'land*, 'kılkrıst, kílkrist

Kilchurn, *f.n.*, kıl'xɜrn, kilchúrn

Kilchurn Castle *S'clyde*, kıl'tʃɜrn, kiltchúrn

Kilclief *Co. Down*, kıl'klif, kil-kléef

Kilcoan *Co. Antrim*, kıl'koʊn, kil-kŏn

Kilconquhar *Fife*, kıl'kɒŋkər, kil-kónkär; kı'nʌxər, kinúchär

Kilcoursie, Viscount, kıl'kɔrsı, kilkórssi

Kilcreggan *S'clyde*, kıl'kregən, kilkréggän

Kildalton *S'clyde*, kıl'dæltən, kil-dáltŏn

Kildare, Marquess of, kıl'dɛər, kildáir

Kildonan *H'land*, *S'clyde*, kıl-'dɒnən, kildónnän

Kildwick *N. and W. Yorks. border*, 'kıldwık, kíldwick

Kilfedder, *f.n.*, kıl'fedər, kilféddĕr

Kilgarriff, *f.n.*, kıl'gærıf, kilgárriff

Kilgetty *Dyfed*, kıl'getı, kilgétti

Kilgour, *f.n.*, kıl'gaʊər, kilgówr

Kilgraston *Tayside*, kıl'græstən, kilgrásstŏn

Kilham, *f.n.*, 'kıləm, kíllăm

Kilian, *f.n.*, 'kılıən, killi-än

Kilkeel *Co. Down*, kıl'kil, kilkéel

Kilkewydd *Powys*, kıl'kewıð, kilké-with. *English spelling of* Cilcewydd, *q.v.*

Kilkhampton *Cornwall*, kılk-'hæmptən, kilk-hámptŏn

Killadeas *Co. Fermanagh*, ,kılə-'dıs, killádéess

Killagan *Co. Antrim*, kı'lægən, kilággän

Killamarsh *Derby.*, 'kıləmarʃ, killámaarsh

Killanin, Baron, kı'lænın, kilánnin

Killar, *f.n.*, 'kılɑr, killaar

Killay *W. Glam.*, kı'leı, kiláy

Killea *Co. Derry*, kı'leı, kiláy

Killead *Co. Antrim*, kı'lid, kiléed

Killearn, Baron, kı'lɜrn, kilérn

Killelagh *Co. Derry*, kı'leılı, kiláyli

Killermont *Glasgow*, 'kılərmənt, kíllĕrmŏnt. *The pronunciation of* ~ *Golf Course is* kı'lɛərmənt, kiláirmŏnt.

Killeter *Co. Tyrone*, kı'litər, killéetĕr

Killichronan *S'clyde*, ,kılı'xroʊnən, killichrŏ́nän

Killick, *f.n.*, 'kılık, kíllick

Killiechassie *Tayside*, ,kılı'hæsı, killi-hássi

Killiecrankie *Tayside*, ,kılı'kræŋkı, killikránki

Killin *Central*, kı'lın, kilín

Killinchy *Co. Down*, kı'lınʃı, kilínshi

Killingholme *Humberside*, 'kılıŋhoʊm, killing-hōm

Killisport *S'clyde*, 'kılıspɔrt, kíllisport

Killough *Co. Down*, kı'lɒx, kilóch

Killowen *Co. Derry*, *Co. Down*, kıl'oʊın, kilŏ́-ĕn

Killwick, *f.n.*, 'kılwık, kílwick

Killylea *Co. Armagh*, ,kılı'leı, killiláy

Killyleagh *Co. Down*, ,kılı'leı, killiláy

Killywhan *D. & G.*, ,kılı'hwɒn, killi-whón

Kilmacolm *S'clyde*, ,kılmə'koʊm, kilmăkŏm

Kilmaine, Baron, kıl'meın, kilmáyn

Kilmany *Fife*, kıl'menı, kilménni. *Appropriate also for Baron* ~.

Kilmarnock *S'clyde*, kıl'mɑrnək, kilmáarnŏk. *Appropriate also for Baron* ~.

Kilmaronock *S'clyde*, ,kılmə'rɒnək, kilmărónnŏk

Kilmersdon *Somerset*, 'kılmərzdən, kílmĕrzdŏn

Kilmister, *f.n.*, 'kılmıstər, kílmisstĕr

Kilmorack *H'land*, kıl'mɒrək, kilmáwrăk

Kilmorey, Earl of, kıl'mʌrı, kilmúrri

Kilmuir, Earldom of, kıl'mjʊər, kilmyŏ̄r

Kilmun *S'clyde*, kıl'mʌn, kilmún

Kilnasaggart Bridge *Co. Armagh*, ,kılnə'sægərt, kilnăsággärt

Kilndown *Kent*, 'kılndaʊn, kílndown

Kilninver *S'clyde*, kıl'nınvər, kilnínvĕr

Kilnwick *Humberside*, 'kılık, kíllick

Kiloh, *f.n.*, 'kaıloʊ, kílō

Kilpheder *W. Isles*, kıl'fedər, kilféddĕr

Kilraughts *Co. Antrim*, kɪl'ræts, kilráts

Kilravock Castle *H'land*, kɪl'rɒk, kill-róck

Kilrea *Co. Derry*, kɪl'reɪ, kilráy

Kilroot *Co. Antrim*, kɪl'rut, kil-roót

Kilroy-Silk,*f.n.*, 'kɪlrɔɪ 'sɪlk, kílroy-sílk

Kilry *Tayside*, 'kɪlrɪ, kílri

Kilsyth *S'clyde*, kɪl'saɪθ, kil-síth

Kiltarlity *H'land*, kɪl'tɑrlɪtɪ, kil--taárliti

Kilve *Somerset*, kɪlv, kilv

Kilwaughter *Co. Antrim*, kɪl-'wɔtər, kilwáwtĕr

Kilwinning *S'clyde*, kɪl'wɪnɪŋ, kilwínning

Kimball,*f.n.*, 'kɪmbl, kímbl

Kimberley,*f.n.*, 'kɪmbərlɪ, kímbĕrli

Kimbolton *H. & W.*, *Cambs.*, kɪm'boʊltən, kimbóltŏn

Kimche,*f.n.*, 'kɪmtʃɪ, kímtchi

Kimmance,*f.n.*, 'kɪməns, kímmănss

Kinahan, *f.n.*, 'kɪnəhən, kínnăhăn

Kinally,*f.n.*, kɪ'nælɪ, kináli

Kinawley *Co. Fermanagh*, kɪ'nɒlɪ, kináwli

Kinbane *Co. Antrim*, kɪn'bɒn, kinbáwn

Kincaid,*f.n.*, kɪn'keɪd, kin-káyd

Kincairney,*f.n.*, kɪn'kɛərnɪ, kin--káirni

Kincardine *H'land*, kɪn'kɑrdɪn, kin-kaárdin. *Appropriate also for* ~ *and Deeside, administrative district of Grampian region, and* ~ *Castles, Grampian and Tayside.*

Kincardine O'Neil *Grampian*, kɪn-'kɑrdɪn oʊ'nil, kin-kaárdin ōnéel

Kincardine-on-Forth *Fife*, kɪn-'kɑrdɪn ɒn 'fɔrθ, kin-kaárdin on fórth

Kinclaven *Tayside*, kɪn'kleɪvən, kin-kláyvĕn

Kincraig *H'land*, kɪn'kreɪg, kin--kráyg

Kinder Scout *Derby.*, 'kɪndər skaʊt, kínndĕr skowt

Kindersley, *Baron*, 'kɪndərzlɪ, kínndĕrzli

Kindregan,*f.n.*, kɪn'drɪgən, kin-dréegăn

Kine,*f.n.*, kaɪn, kīn

Kinellar *Grampian*, kɪ'nelər, kinéllăr

Kineton *Warwicks.*, 'kaɪntən, kíntŏn

Kinfauns *Tayside*, kɪn'fɔnz, kin-fáwnz

Kingdon,*f.n.*, 'kɪŋdən, kíngdŏn

Kingennie *Tayside*, kɪn'genɪ, kin--génni

Kingham,*f.n.*, 'kɪŋəm, kíng-ăm

Kinglake,*f.n.*, 'kɪŋleɪk, kíng-layk

Kinglassie *Fife*, kɪŋ'læsɪ, king--lássi

Kingoldrum *Tayside*, kɪn'goʊld-rəm, kin-góldrŭm

Kingsale, *Baron*, kɪn'seɪl, kin-sáyl

Kingsbury,*f.n.*, 'kɪŋzbərɪ, kíngz-bŭri

King's Caple *H. & W.*, 'kɪŋz 'keɪpl, kíngz káypl

Kingscavil *Lothian*, kɪŋz'keɪvɪl, kingz-káyvil

Kingscote,*f.n.*, 'kɪŋzkət, kíngzkŏt

Kingscott,*f.n.*, 'kɪŋzkɒt, kíngzkot

Kingsford,*f.n.*, 'kɪŋzfərd, kíngz-fŏrd

Kingskerswell *Devon*, kɪŋz-'kɜrzwəl, kingzkérzwĕl

Kingsley,*f.n.*, 'kɪŋzlɪ, kíngzli

Kingsnympton *Devon*, 'kɪŋz-'nɪmtən, kingzními̇́mtŏn

King's Somborne *Hants*, 'kɪŋz 'sɒmbɔrn, kíngz sómborn

Kings Tamerton *Devon*, 'kɪŋz 'tæmərtən, kíngz támmĕrtŏn

Kingsteignton *Devon*, 'kɪŋz-'teɪntən, kingz-táyntŏn

Kingsterndale *Derby.*, kɪŋ'stɜrn-deɪl, king-stérndayl

Kingston Bagpuize, *also spelt* **Bagpuze**, *Oxon.*, 'kɪŋstən 'bægpjuz, kíngstŏn bágpewz

Kingston Blount *Oxon.*, 'kɪŋstən 'blʌnt, kíngstŏn blúnt

Kingston Buci *W. Sussex*, 'kɪŋstən 'bjusɪ, kíngstŏn béwssi

Kingston Matravers *Dorset*, 'kɪŋstən mə'trævərz, kíngstŏn mátrávvĕrz

Kingston-upon-Hull *Humberside*, 'kɪŋstən əpɒn 'hʌl, kíngstŏn ŭpon húll

Kingswear *Devon*, 'kɪŋzwɪər, kingzweer

Kingswinford *W. Midlands*, kɪŋ-'swɪnfərd, king-swínfŏrd

Kingussie *H'land*, kɪŋ'jusɪ, king--yoóssi

Kininmonth,*f.n.*, kɪ'nɪnmənθ, kinnínmŏnth; 'kɪnɪnmənθ, kínninmŏnth

Kininmonth *Grampian*, kɪ'nɪn-mənθ, kinnínmŏnth

Kinloch,*f.n.*, kɪn'lɒx, kinlóch

Kinlochbervie *H'land*, 'kɪnlɒx-'bɜrvɪ, kinloch-bérvi

Kinlocheil *H'land*, 'kɪnlɒx'il, kín-lochéel

Kinlochewe *H'land*, 'kɪnlɒx'ju, kínloch-yoó

Kinlochleven *H'land*, 'kınlɒx-'livən, kínlochleévĕn

Kinlochmoidart *H'land*, 'kınlɒx-'mɔɪdərt, kínlochmóydärt

Kinlochourn *H'land*, 'kınlɒx-'hʊərn, kínloch-hŏ́orn

Kinloch Rannoch *Tayside*, 'kınlɒx 'rænəx, kínloch ránnŏch

Kinloss *Grampian*, kın'lɒs, kin-lóss. *Appropriate also for Baroness* ~.

Kinmel Park *Clwyd*, 'kınməl 'park, kínmĕl paárk; 'kıml 'park, kímml paárk

Kinmond, *f.n.*, 'kınmənd, kín-mŏnd

Kinnaber Junction *Tayside*, kı-'neıbər, kináybĕr

Kinnaird *Tayside*, kı'neərd, kin-áird. *Appropriate also for Baron* ~.

Kinne, *f.n.*, 'kını, kínni

Kinnear, *f.n.*, kı'nıər, kineér; kı'neər, kináir

Kinnegar *Co. Down*, ,kınə'gar, kinnĕgaár

Kinneil *Central*, kı'nil, kineél

Kinnesswood *Tayside*, kı'neswʊd, kinéss-wŏ́od

Kinniburgh, *f.n.*, 'kınıbərə, kínni-bŭră

Kinninmonth, *f.n.*, kı'nınmənt, kinnínmŏnt; kı'nınmənθ, kinnínmŏnth

Kinnock, *f.n.*, 'kınək, kínnŏk

Kinnon, *f.n.*, 'kınən, kínnŏn

Kinnoull *Tayside*, kı'nul, kinóol. *Appropriate also for the Earl of* ~.

Kinoulton *Notts.*, kı'nultən, kinóoltŏn

Kinrade, *f.n.*, 'kınreıd, kínrayd

Kinross *Tayside*, kın'rɒs, kinróss. *Appropriate also for Baron* ~.

Kinsella, *f.n.*, 'kınsələ, kínssĕlă; kın'selə, kinssélá

Kinsey, *f.n.*, 'kınzı, kínzi

Kintore *Grampian*, kın'tɔr, kintór. *Appropriate also for the Earl of* ~.

Kintyre *S'clyde*, kın'taıər, kintír

Kintyre and Lorne, Marquess of, kın'taıər ənd 'lɔrn, kintír ănd lórn

Kinvig, *f.n.*, kın'vıg, kinvíg

Kinwarton *Warwicks.*, 'kınərtən, kínnärtŏn; 'kınwərtən, kínwär-tŏn

Kipling, Rudyard, *author*, 'rʌdjərd 'kıplıŋ, rúd-yärd kípling

Kipling Cotes *Humberside*, 'kıplıŋ koʊts, kípling kŏts

Kippax *W. Yorks.*, 'kıpæks, kíp-packs

Kirby, *f.n.*, 'kɜrbı, kírbi

Kirby Bedon *Norfolk*, 'kɜrbı 'bidən, kírbi beédŏn

Kirbye, *f.n.*, 'kɜrbı, kírbi

Kirby Wiske *N. Yorks.*, 'kɜrbı 'wısk, kírbi wísk

Kirch, *f.n.*, kɜrtʃ, kirtch

Kirkaldie, Viscount, kər'kɒdı, kŭrkáwdi

Kirkbean *D. & G.*, kɜrk'bin, kirk-beén

Kirkbride, *f.n.*, kɜrk'braıd, kirk-bríd

Kirkbride *Cumbria*, kɜrk'braıd, kirkbríd

Kirkburton *W. Yorks.*, kɜrk'bɜrtən, kirkbúrtŏn

Kirkby, *f.n.*, 'kɜrbı, kírbi; 'kɜrkbı, kírkbi

Kirkby *Merseyside*, 'kɜrbı, kírbi

Kirkby-in-Ashfield *Notts.*, 'kɜrkbı ın 'æʃfild, kírkbi in áshfeeld

Kirkby-in-Malhamdale *N. Yorks.*, 'kɜrbı ın 'mæləmdeıl, kírbi in málămdayl

Kirkby Lonsdale *Cumbria*, 'kɜrbı 'lɒnzdeıl, kírbi lónzdayl

Kirkby Malham *N. Yorks.*, 'kɜrbı 'mæləm, kírbi málăm

Kirkby Mallory *Leics.*, 'kɜrkbı 'mælərı, kírkbi málŏri

Kirkby Malzeard *N. Yorks.*, 'kɜrbı 'mælzərd, kírbi málzărd

Kirkby Moorside *N. Yorks.*, 'kɜrbı 'mʊərsaıd, kírbi mŏor-síd

Kirkby Stephen *Cumbria*, 'kɜrbı 'stivən, kírbi steévĕn

Kirkby Thore *Cumbria*, 'kɜrbı 'θɔr, kírbi thór; 'kɜrbı 'fjʊər, kírbi féw-ĕr

Kirkcaldy *Fife*, kər'kɒdı, kŭr-kóddi; kər'kɒdı, kŭrkáwdi

Kirkcubbin *Co. Down*, kər'kʌbın, kirkúbbin

Kirkcudbright *D. & G.*, kər'kubrı, kŭrkoóbri

Kirk Deighton *N. Yorks.*, kɜrk 'ditən, kirk deétŏn

Kirkden *Tayside*, kɜrk'den, kŭrkdén

Kirkgate *Bradford, Leeds* (both *W. Yorks.*), 'kɜrgeıt, kírgayt

Kirkgate *Edinburgh*, 'kɜrgıt, kírgit

Kirkgunzeon *D. & G.*, kər'gʌnjən, kŭrgún-yŏn

Kirkhaugh *Northd.*, 'kɜrkhɑf, kírk-haaf; 'kɜrkhɔ, kírk-haw

Kirkheaton *W. Yorks.*, kɜrk'hitən, kirk-heétŏn

Kirkhill *H'land*, kɜrk'hıl, kírk-hill

Kirkhope *Borders*, 'kɜrkhoʊp, kírkhŏp

Kirkleatham *Cleveland*, kɜrk-'liðəm, kirk-leéthăm

Kirk Leavington *Cleveland*, kɜrk
'levɪŋtən, kirk lévvington.
Another spelling is **Levington.**

Kirklees *W. Yorks.*, kɜrk'liz,
kirkléez

Kirkley Foggo, *f.n.*, 'kɜrklɪ 'foʊ-
goʊ, kírkli fốgō

Kirkliston *Lothian*, kɜrk'lɪstən,
kürklístŏn

Kirkmichael *S'clyde*, kɜrk'maɪkl,
kürkmíkl

Kirkoswald *Cumbria, S'clyde*,
kɜrk'ɒzwɔld, kirk-ózwáld

Kirkpatrick, *f.n.*, kɜrk'pætrɪk,
kirkpátrick

Kirkstall Abbey *W. Yorks.*, 'kɜrk-
stɔl, kírkstawl

Kirkstone Pass *Cumbria*, 'kɜrk-
stən, kírkstŏn

Kirkup, *f.n.*, 'kɜrkəp, kírkŭp

Kirkwall *Orkney*, 'kɜrkwɔl, kírk-
wawl. *Appropriate also for*
Viscount ∼.

Kirk Yetholm *Borders*, kɜrk
'jetəm, kirk yéttŏm

Kirriemarian, *native of* **Kirriemuir**,
,kɪrɪ'meərɪən, kirrimáiriăn

Kirriemuir *Tayside*, ,kɪrɪ'mjuər,
kirri-myóŏr

Kirtomy *H'land*, kɜr'tɒmɪ, kir-
tómmi

Kirwan, *f.n.*, 'kɜrwən, kírwăn

Kishmul Castle, *also spelt* **Kismull, Kiessimal**, *W. Isles*,
'kɪʃməl, kíshmŭl

Kishorn *H'land*, 'kɪʃɔrn, kísh-orn

Kislingbury *Northants.*, 'kɪzlɪŋ-
bərɪ, kízling-bŭri

Kismeldon Bridge *Cornwall*, kɪz-
'meldən, kizméldŏn

Kismull Castle *see* **Kishmul**
Castle

Kissane, *f.n.*, kɪ'sæn, kissán

Kitcat, *f.n.*, 'kɪtkæt, kítkat

Kitcatt, *f.n.*, 'kɪtkæt, kítkat

Kitchell, *f.n.*, 'kɪtʃl, kítchl

Kitchen, *f.n.*, 'kɪtʃɪn, kítchĕn

Kitchener, *f.n.*, 'kɪtʃɪnər, kítchĕnĕr

Kitchener of Khartoum, Earl,
'kɪtʃɪnər əv kɑr'tum, kítchĕnĕr
ŏv kaartoóm

Kitchin, *f.n.*, 'kɪtʃɪn, kítchin

Kitshowe Bridge *Cumbria*, 'kɪts-
haʊ, kíts-how

Kitson, *f.n.*, 'kɪtsən, kítsŏn

Kiver, *f.n.*, 'kaɪvər, kívĕr

Kiveton Park *S. Yorks.*, 'kɪvɪtən
kívvĕtŏn

Klasicki, *f.n.*, klæ'ʃɪtskɪ, klashéet-
ski

Kleinwort, *f.n.*, 'klaɪnwɔrt, klín-
-wawrt

Klimcke, *f.n.*, 'klɪmkɪ, klímki

Klug, *f.n.*, klʌg, klug

Klugg, *f.n.*, klʌg, klug

Klugh, *f.n.*, klu, kloo

Klugman, *f.n.*, 'klugmən, kloóg-
män

Kluth, *f.n.*, klʌθ, kluth

Kmiecik, *f.n.*, k'mjetʃɪk, k-myé-
tchick

Knaith *Lincs.*, neɪð, nay<u>th</u>; neɪθ,
nayth

Knapp, *f.n.*, næp, napp

Knapwell *Cambs.*, 'næpwel, náp-
wel

Knaresborough *N. Yorks.*, 'nɛərz-
bərə, náirzbŭră. *Appropriate*
also for the Barony of ∼.

Knatchbull, *f.n.*, 'nætʃbʊl, nátch-
bŏŏl

Knavesmire Race Course *N.*
Yorks., 'neɪvzmaɪər, náyvz-mír

Kneale, *f.n.*, nil, neel

Knebworth *Herts.*, 'nebwərθ,
nébwŭrth

Kneebone, *f.n.*, 'niboʊn, neébōn

Kneen, *f.n.*, nin, neen

Kneesworth *Cambs.*, 'nizwərθ,
neézwŭrth

Kneeton *Notts.*, 'nitən, neétŏn

Kneller, *f.n.*, 'nelər, néllĕr.
Appropriate also for ∼ **Hall**,
London.

Knevett, *f.n.*, 'nevɪt, névvĕt

Knibs, *f.n.*, nɪbz, nibz

Knight, *f.n.*, naɪt, nīt

Knighton, *f.n.*, 'naɪtən, nítŏn

Knighton *Powys, I. of Wight*,
'naɪtən, nítŏn

Knights Enham *Hants*, 'naɪts
'enəm, nīts énnăm

Knightshayes Court *Devon*,
'naɪtsheɪz, nítz-hayz

Knipe, *f.n.*, naɪp, nīp

Kniveton *Derby.*, 'naɪvtən, nívtŏn;
'nɪftən, níftŏn

Knock *Cumbria*, nɒk, nock

Knockagh *Co. Antrim*, 'nɒkə,
nóckă

Knockando *Grampian*, nɒ'kændoʊ,
nockándō

Knockbracken *Co. Down*, nɒk-
'brækən, nockbráckĕn

Knockbreda *Co. Down*, nɒk-
'breɪdə, nockbráydă

Knockcloghrim *Co. Derry*, nɒk-
'lɒkrɪm, nock-lóckrim

Knockdow, *f.n.*, nɒk'du, nockdoó

Knockholt *Kent*, 'nɒkhoʊlt, nóck-
-hōlt

Knocklayd *Co. Antrim*, nɒk'leɪd,
nockláyd

Knocknacarry *Co. Antrim*,
,nɒknə'kærɪ, nocknăkárri

Knodishall *Suffolk*, 'nɒdɪʃl,
nóddi-shl

Knokin *see* **Strange of Knokin**
Knole *Kent*, noʊl, nōl
Knollys, Viscount, noʊlz, nōlz
Knook *Wilts.*, nʊk, nŏŏk
Knott, *f.n.*, nɒt, nott
Knowle *W. Midlands*, noʊl, nōl
Knowler, *f.n.*, 'noʊlər, nṓlĕr
Knowles, *f.n.*, noʊlz, nōlz
Knowsley *Merseyside*, 'noʊzlɪ, nṓzli
Knox-Johnston, *f.n.*, 'nɒks 'dʒɒnstən, nócks jónn-stŏn
Knox-Mawer, *f.n.*, 'nɒks 'mɔr, nócks mór
Knoydart *H'land*, 'nɔɪdərt, nóy-därt; 'nɔɪdɑrt, nóydaart
Knucklas *Powys*, 'nʌkləs, núck-läss
Knussen, *f.n.*, 'nʌsən, nússĕn. *Appropriate for Oliver ~, composer.*
Knuston *Northants.*, 'nʌstən, nús-stŏn
Knutsford *Ches.*, 'nʌtsfərd, núts-fŏrd
Knypersley *Staffs.*, 'naɪpərzlɪ, nípĕrzli
Knyvett, *f.n.*, 'nɪvɪt, nívvĕt
Knyvette, *f.n.*, nɪ'vet, nivétt
Knyvet-Wilson, *f.n.*, 'nɪvɪt 'wɪlsən nívvĕt wilssŏn
Kobziak, *f.n.*, 'kɒbziæk, kóbzi-ack
Kohler, *f.n.*, 'koʊlər, kṓlĕr
Kolankiewicz, *f.n.*, ˌkɒlæŋ'kjevɪtʃ, kolankyévvitch
Koltai, *f.n.*, 'koʊltaɪ, kṓltī
Kops, *f.n.*, kɒps, kopss
Koralek, *f.n.*, 'kɒrələk, kórrăleck
Kornberg, *f.n.*, 'kɔrnbɜrg, kórn--berg
Kortright, *f.n.*, 'kɔrtraɪt, kórtrīt
Kossoff, *f.n.*, 'kɒsɒf, kóssoff
Kough, *f.n.*, kjoʊ, kyō
Kraay, *f.n.*, kreɪ, kray
Kraemer, *f.n.*, 'kreɪmər, kráymĕr
Krailsheimer, *f.n.*, 'kreɪlzhaɪmər, kráylz-hīmĕr
Kreeger, *f.n.*, 'krigər, kreégĕr
Kreiman, *f.n.*, 'kraɪmən, krímän
Krein, *f.n.*, kraɪn, krīn
Kremer, *f.n.*, 'krimər, kreémĕr
Krichefski, *f.n.*, krɪ'tʃefskɪ, kritchéfski
Kris, *f.n.*, krɪs, kriss
Krishnamurti, *f.n.*, ˌkrɪʃnə'mʊərtɪ, krishnămŏŏrti
Krumb, *f.n.*, krʌm, krum
Kruse, *f.n.*, kruz, krooz
Kuggar *Cornwall*, 'kʌgər, kúggăr; 'kɪgər, kíggăr
Kuipers, *f.n.*, 'kaɪpərz, kípĕrz
Kumm, *f.n.*, kʊm, kŏŏm
Kupfermann, *f.n.*, 'kʊpfərmæn, kŏŏpfĕr-man

Kurakin, *f.n.*, kjʊ'rɑkɪn, kyŏŏ-raákin
Kureishi, *f.n.*, kʊ'reɪʃɪ, kŏŏráyshi
Kutscherauer, *f.n.*, 'kʊtʃeraʊər, kŏŏtchĕrowĕr
Kwella, *f.n.*, 'kwelə, kwéllă
Kyffin, *f.n.*, 'kʌfɪn, kúffin; 'kɪfɪn, kiffin
Kyleakin *Skye*, kaɪl'ækɪn, kīl-áckin
Kyle of Durness *H'land*, 'kaɪl əv 'dɜrnɪs, kīl ŏv dúrnĕss
Kyle of Lochalsh *H'land*, 'kaɪl əv lɒx'ælʃ, kīl ŏv lochálsh
Kyle Rhea *H'land*, 'kaɪl 'reɪ, kīl ráy
Kyle Sku *H'land*, 'kaɪl 'skju, kīl skéw
Kyles Morar *H'land*, 'kaɪlz 'mɔrər, kīlz máwrăr
Kyles of Bute *S'clyde*, 'kaɪlz əv 'bjut, kīlz ŏv béwt
Kyllachy, *f.n.*, 'kaɪlɒxɪ, kílăchi
Kyllo, *f.n.*, 'kaɪloʊ, kílŏ
Kylsant, Barony of, kɪl'sænt, kilssánt
Kynance Cove *Cornwall*, 'kaɪnæns, kínanss
Kynaston, *f.n.*, 'kɪnəstən, kínnäs-tŏn
Kynnersley, *f.n.*, 'kɪnərzlɪ, kín-nĕrzli
Kynoch, *f.n.*, 'kaɪnɒx, kínoch
Kynsey, *f.n.*, 'kɪnzɪ, kínzi
Kynynmound, *f.n.*, kɪ'nɪnmənd, kinnínmünd
Kysow, *f.n.*, 'kaɪsoʊ, kíssō

L

Labbett, *f.n.*, 'læbɪt, lábbĕt
La Belle Sauvage Yard *London*, lɑ 'bel soʊ'vɑʒ, laa béll sōvaázh
Labone, *f.n.*, lə'boʊn, lăbṓn
Labouchere, *f.n.*, ˌlæbu'ʃɛər, lab-boosháir; 'læbuʃɛər, lábboo--shair
Labovitch, *f.n.*, 'læbəvɪtʃ, lábbŏ-vitch
La Brooy, *f.n.*, lɑ 'broʊɪ, laa brṓ-i
Lacaille, *f.n.*, lə'keɪ, lăkáy
Lacey, *f.n.*, 'leɪsɪ, láyssi
La Chard, *f.n.*, lɑ 'tʃɑrd, laa chaárd
Lache *Ches.*, leɪtʃ, laytch
Lachmann, *f.n.*, 'lɑkmən, laák-män
Lackenby *Cleveland*, 'lækənbɪ, láckĕnbi
Lacock *Wilts.*, 'leɪkɒk, láykock. *Appropriate also for ~ Abbey.*

Lacon, *f.n.,* 'leɪkən, láykŏn
Ladbroke, *f.n.,* 'lædbrʊk, ládbrŏŏk
Ladbrook, *f.n.,* 'lædbrʊk, ládbrŏŏk
Laddow Rocks *Gtr. M'chester,* 'lædoʊ, láddō
Ladefoged, *f.n.,* 'lædɪfoʊgɪd, láddĕfŏgĕd
Ladell, *f.n.,* læ'del, laddéll
Lader, *f.n.,* 'leɪdər, láydĕr
Ladhar Bheinn *H'land,* lɑ 'veɪn, laa váyn
Ladhope *Borders,* 'lædəp, láddŏp
Ladock *Cornwall,* 'lædək, láddŏck
Lafcadio, *f.n.,* læf'kɑdioʊ, lafkaádiō
Laffan, *f.n.,* lə'fæn, láfán
Laffeaty, *f.n.,* 'læfɪtɪ, láffĕti
Lafford, *f.n.,* 'læfərd, láffŏrd
Lafontaine, *f.n.,* lə'fɒnteɪn, láfóntayn
La Fontaine, *f.n.,* lə 'fɒnteɪn, lä fóntayn
Lagan, River, *Co. Down,* 'lægən, lággăn
Laggan, Loch, *Central,* 'lægən, lággăn
Lahee, *f.n.,* lə'hi, lähée
Laid *H'land,* leɪd, layd
Laidlaw, *f.n.,* 'leɪdlɔ, láyd-law
Laidler, *f.n.,* 'leɪdlər, láydlĕr
Laidlow, *f.n.,* 'leɪdloʊ, láydlō
Laighwood *Tayside,* 'leɪxwʊd, láychwŏŏd
Laindon *Essex,* 'leɪndən, láyndŏn
Laindon Hills, *also called* **Langdon Hills** *q.v., Essex,* 'leɪndən 'hɪlz, láyndŏn híllz
Laing, *f.n.,* leɪŋ, layng; læŋ, lang
Laing Art Gallery *Newcastle upon Tyne,* leɪŋ, layng
Laira *Devon,* 'leərə, láirä
Laird, *f.n.,* leərd, laird
Lairg *H'land,* leərg, lairg
Laister Dyke *W. Yorks.,* 'leɪstər daɪk, láysstĕr dīk
Laithwaite, *f.n.,* 'leɪθweɪt, láythwayt
Lakenham *Norfolk,* 'leɪkənəm, láykĕnăm
Lakenheath *Suffolk,* 'leɪkənhiθ, láykĕn-heeth
Laker, *f.n.,* 'leɪkər, láykĕr
Lalage, *C.n.,* 'læləgɪ, lálăgi; 'lælədʒɪ, lálăji
Laleham *Surrey,* 'leɪləm, láylăm
Laleston *Mid Glam.,* 'læləstən, lálĕstŏn
Lam, *f.n.,* læm, laem, lam
Lamancha *Borders,* lə'mæŋkə, lämánkă
Lamarsh *Essex,* 'læmɑrʃ, lámmaarsh

Lamas, *also spelt* **Lammas,** *Norfolk,* 'læməs, lámmăss
Lamb, *f.n.,* læm, laem, lam
Lambeg *Co. Antrim,* læm'beg, lambég
Lambelet, *f.n.,* 'læmbəlɪt, lámbĕlĕt
Lambert, *f.n.,* 'læmbərt, lámbĕrt
Lamberton, *f.n.,* 'læmbərtən, lámbĕrtŏn
Lambeth *London,* 'læmbəθ, lámbĕth
Lambethan, *pertaining to* **Lambeth,** læm'biθən, lambéethăn
Lambhill *S'clyde,* 'læm'hɪl, lám-híll
Lamb Holm *Orkney,* 'læm hoʊm, lám hōm
Lambie, *f.n.,* 'læmbɪ, lámbi
Lambley, *f.n.,* 'læmlɪ, lámli
Lamborn, *f.n.,* 'læmbɔrn, lám-born
Lamerton *Borders,* 'læmərtən, lámmĕrtŏn
Lamesley *Tyne & Wear,* 'leɪmzlɪ, láymzli
Laming, *f.n.,* 'leɪmɪŋ, láyming; 'læmɪŋ, lámming
Lamington *S'clyde,* 'læmɪŋtən, lámmingtŏn. *Appropriate also for the Barony of* ~.
Lamlash *S'clyde,* ləm'læʃ, lám-lásh; læm'læʃ, lam-lásh
Lammas *see* **Lamas**
Lamond, *f.n.,* 'læmənd, lámmŏnd
Lamont, *f.n.,* 'læmənt, lámmŏnt; lə'mɒnt, lämónt. *The first is the usual Scottish pronunciation, the second the Northern Irish.*
Lamorbey *London,* 'læmərbɪ, lámmŏrbi
Lamorna *Cornwall,* lə'mɔrnə, lämórnä
Lamorran *Cornwall,* lə'mɒrən, lämórrăn
Lamotte, *f.n.,* lə'mɒt, lämótt
Lampe, *f.n.,* læmp, lamp; 'læmpɪ, lámpi
Lampeter *Dyfed,* 'læmpɪtər, lámpĕtĕr
Lamphey *Dyfed,* 'læmfɪ, lámfi. *Appropriate also for* ~ *Palace.*
Lamplugh, *f.n.,* 'læmplu, lám-ploo
Lamplugh *Cumbria,* 'læmplu, lám-ploo; 'læmplə, lám-plä
Lampson, *f.n.,* 'læmpsən, lámpssŏn
Lanark *S'clyde,* 'lænərk, lánnärk
La Nauze, *f.n.,* lə 'nɒz, lä náwz
Lancashire *Co. name,* 'læŋkəʃər, lánkäsher
Lancaster, *f.n.,* 'læŋkəstər, lánkästĕr
Lancaster *Lancs.,* 'læŋkəstər, lánkästĕr

Lancastrian, *pertaining to* **Lancaster** *or* **Lancashire**, læŋ-'kæstrɪən, lankásstri-ăn
Lancaut *Glos.*, læn'koʊt, lankôt
Lance, *C.n. and f.n.*, lɑns, laanss
Lancefield, *f.n.*, 'lɑnsfild, laánssfeeld
Lancelot, *C.n.*, 'lɑnsɪlɒt, laánssĕlot; 'lɑnslɒt, laánsslot
Lancelot, *f.n.*, 'lɑnsɪlɒt, laánssĕlot
Lanchbery, *f.n.*, 'lɑnʃbərɪ, laánshbĕri
Lancing *W. Sussex*, 'lɑnsɪŋ, laánssing
Landamare, *f.n.*, 'lændəmɑr, lándămaar
Landau, *f.n.*, 'lændoʊ, lándō; 'lændaʊ, lándow
Lander, *f.n.*, 'lændər, lándĕr
Landeryou, *f.n.*, 'lændərju, lándĕr-yoo
Landewednack *Cornwall*, ˌlændɪ-'wednək, landĕwédnăk
Landoger Trow, The, *historic Bristol inn*, 'lændɒgər 'traʊ, lándoggĕr trów
Landone, *f.n.*, 'lændən, lándŏn
Landore *W. Glam.*, læn'dɔr, landór
Landrake *Cornwall*, læn'dreɪk, landráyk
Landulph *Cornwall*, læn'dʌlf, landúlf
Lanercost *Cumbria*, 'lænərkɒst, lánnĕrkost
Lanesborough, Earl of, 'leɪnzbərə, láynzbŭră
Lanfear, *f.n.*, 'lænfɪər, lánfeer
Lanfine House, *S'clyde*, læn'fin, lanfeén
Langar *Notts.*, 'læŋgər, láng-găr
Langdon Hills, *also called* **Laindon Hills** *q.v.*, *Essex*, 'lændən 'hɪlz, lángdŏn hillz
Lange, *f.n.*, lændʒ, lanj
Langenhoe *Essex*, 'læŋgənhoʊ, láng-gĕn-hō
Langer, *f.n.*, 'læŋər, láng-ĕr
Langford, *f.n.*, 'læŋfərd, lángförd
Langham, *f.n.*, 'læŋəm, láng-ăm
Langho *Lancs.*, 'læŋoʊ, láng-ō
Langholm *D. & G.*, 'læŋəm, láng-ŏm
Langley, *f.n.*, 'læŋlɪ, láng-li
Langloan *S'clyde*, 'læŋloʊn, láng-lōn
Langold *Notts.*, 'læŋgoʊld, láng-gōld
Langridge, *f.n.*, 'læŋgrɪdʒ, láng-grij
Langrishe, *f.n.*, læŋ'griʃ, lang-gréesh
Langstaff, *f.n.*, 'læŋstɑf, lángstaaf

Langstone, *parliamentary div. of Portsmouth*, 'læŋstən, lángstŏn
Langstrothdale *N. Yorks.*, læŋ-'strɒθdeɪl, lang-stróth-dayl
Langton Matravers *Dorset*, 'læŋtən mə'trævərz, lángtŏn mătrávvĕrz
Langwathby *Cumbria*, læŋ'wɒθbɪ, lang-wóthbi
Langwith, Nether, *Notts.*, 'læŋwɪθ, láng-with
Langwith, Upper, *Derby.*, 'læŋgwɪθ, láng-gwith
Lanherne *Cornwall*, læn'hɜrn, lan-hérn
Lanhydrock *Cornwall*, læn'haɪdrək, lan-hídrŏk
Lanier, *f.n.*, 'lænjər, lán-yĕr
Lanivet *Cornwall*, læn'ɪvɪt, lannívvĕt
Lanjeth *Cornwall*, læn'dʒeθ, lanjéth
Lankester, *f.n.*, 'læŋkɪstər, lánkĕstĕr
Lanlivery *Cornwall*, læn'lɪvərɪ, lan-lívvĕri
Lanreath *Cornwall*, læn'reθ, lanréth
Lansdown, *f.n.*, 'lænzdaʊn, lánzdown
Lanteglos *Cornwall*, læn'teglɒs, lantéglōss; læn'teɪglɒs, lantáygloss
Lanyon Cromlech *Cornwall*, 'lænjən 'krɒmlek, lán-yŏn krómleck
Lapage, *f.n.*, lə'peɪdʒ, lăpáyj
Lapal *W. Midlands*, 'læpl, láppl
Laphroaig Distillery *S'clyde*, lə'frɔɪg, lăfróyg
Lapotaire, *f.n.*, ˌlæpɒ'tɛər, lappottáir
Lappage, *f.n.*, lə'peɪdʒ, laapáyj
Laraine, *C.n.*, lə'reɪn, lăráyn
Largo *Fife*, 'lɑrgoʊ, laárgō
Larkby, *f.n.*, 'lɑrkbɪ, laárkbi
Larkhill *Wilts.*, 'lɑrk'hɪl, laárk-híll
Larkins, *f.n.*, 'lɑrkɪnz, laárkinz
Larmor, *f.n.*, 'lɑrmər, laármör
Larmour, *f.n.*, 'lɑrmər, laármŭr
La Roche, *f.n.*, lɑ 'rɒʃ, laa rósh
Laryea, *f.n.*, laɪ, lī
Lascelles, *f.n.*, 'læslz, lásslz. *Appropriate also for Viscount ~.*
Lasdun, *f.n.*, 'læzdən, lázdŭn
Lash, *f.n.*, læʃ, lash
Lasham *Hants*, 'læsəm, lássăm; 'læʃəm, láshăm. *The first is the traditional village pronunciation. The second is familiar to those using the Gliding Centre.*
Lashmar, *f.n.*, 'læʃmɑr, láshmaar

Laslett, *f.n.*, 'læzlɪt, lázlĕt
Lassodie *Fife*, læ'soʊdɪ, lassódi
Lasswade *Lothian*, læs'weɪd, lasswáyd
Latchem, *f.n.*, 'lætʃəm, látchĕm
Lategan, *f.n.*, 'lætɪgən, láttĕgăn
La Terriere, *f.n.*, lɑ 'terɪeər, laa térri-air
Latey, *f.n.*, 'leɪtɪ, láyti
Latham, *f.n.*, 'leɪθəm, láythăm; 'leɪðəm, láythăm. *The first is appropriate for Baron ~.*
Latham-Koenig, *f.n.*, 'leɪθəm 'kɜnɪg, láythăm kö́nig
Lathan, *f.n.*, 'leɪθən, láythăn
Lathbury, *f.n.*, 'læθbərɪ, láthbŭri
Latheron *H'land*, 'læðərən, láthĕrŏn
Lathey, *f.n.*, 'leɪθɪ, láythi
Lathom, *f.n.*, 'leɪθəm, láythŏm; 'leɪðəm, láythŏm
Lathom *Lancs.*, 'leɪðəm, láythŏm
Latimer, *f.n.*, 'lætɪmər, láttimĕr
La Touche, *f.n.*, lɑ 'tuʃ, laa toósh
Latreille, *f.n.*, lə'treɪl, làtráyl; lə'trɪl, làtréel; lɑ'treɪ, laatráy
Latymer, Baron, 'lætɪmər, láttimĕr
Lauder, *f.n.*, 'lɔdər, láwdĕr
Lauder *Borders*, 'lɔdər, láwdĕr
Lauderdale *Borders*, 'lɔdərdeɪl, láwdĕrdayl. *Appropriate also for the Earl of ~.*
Laugharne, *f.n.*, lɑrn, laarn
Laugharne *Dyfed*, lɑrn, laarn
Laugherne House *H. & W.*, lɔrn, lorn
Laughlan, *f.n.*, 'lɒxlən, lóchlăn
Laughland, *f.n.*, 'lɒxlənd, lóchlănd
Laughton, *f.n.*, 'lɔtən, láwtŏn
Laughton *E. Sussex*, 'lɔtən, láwtŏn
Launcells *Cornwall*, 'lɑnslz, laánsslz; 'lænslz, lánsslz
Launceston *Cornwall*, 'lɑnsən, laánssŏn; 'lɑnstən, laánsstŏn; 'lɔnsən, láwnssŏn; 'lɔnstən, láwnsstŏn
Laureen, *C.n.*, lɔ'rin, lawreén
Laurence, *C.n.*, 'lɒrəns, lórrĕnss
Laurie, *f.n.*, 'lɒrɪ, lórri
Laurier, *f.n.*, 'lɒrɪər, lórri-ĕr
Lauriston, *f.n.*, 'lɒrɪstən, lórristŏn
Lauriston Castle *Edinburgh*, 'lɒrɪstən, lórristŏn
Lauwers, *f.n.*, 'laʊərz, lów-ĕrz
Lauwerys, *f.n.*, 'laʊraɪz, lów-rīz
Lavant *W. Sussex*, 'lævənt, lávvănt
Lavarack, *f.n.*, 'lævəræk, lávvărack
Lavecock, *f.n.*, 'lævɪkɒk, lávvĕkock

Lavell, *f.n.*, 'lævl, lávvl; lə'vel, lăvéll
Lavendon *Bucks.*, 'lævəndən, lávvĕndŏn
Lavenham *Suffolk*, 'lævənəm, lávvĕnăm
Laver, *f.n.*, 'leɪvər, láyvĕr
Laver, River, *N. Yorks.*, 'lɑvər, laávĕr
Laverick, *f.n.*, 'lævərɪk, lávvĕrick
Lavernock Point *S. Glam.*, 'lævərnək, lávvĕrnŏk
Lavers, *f.n.*, 'leɪvərz, láyvĕrz
Laverstock *Wilts.*, 'lævərstɒk, lávvĕrstock
Laverstoke *Hants.*, 'lævərstoʊk, lávvĕrstōk
Laverton *Glos.*, 'lævərtən, lávvĕrtŏn
Laville, *f.n.*, lə'vil, lăvéel
Lavin, *f.n.*, 'lævɪn, lávvin
Lavington, West, *W. Sussex*, *Wilts.*, 'lævɪŋtən, lávvingtŏn
Lawday, *f.n.*, 'lɔdeɪ, láwday
Lawhitton *Cornwall*, lɔ'hwɪtən, law-whíttŏn; lɑ'hwɪtən, laa-whíttŏn
Lawler, *f.n.*, 'lɔlər, láwlĕr
Lawless, *f.n.*, 'lɔles, láwless
Lawley, *f.n.*, 'lɔlɪ, láwli
Lawrence, *C.n. and f.n.*, 'lɒrəns, lórrĕnss
Lawrie, *f.n.*, 'lɒrɪ, lórri
Lawshall *Suffolk*, 'lɔʃl, láwshl
Lawson, *f.n.*, 'lɔsən, láwssŏn
Lawther, *f.n.*, 'lɔðər, láwthĕr
Laxey, *I. of Man*, 'læksɪ, lácksi
Layard, *f.n.*, 'leɪɑrd, láy-aard; 'leɪərd, láy-ärd
Laycock, *f.n.*, 'leɪkɒk, láykock
Layer Breton *Essex*, 'leɪər 'bretən, láy-ĕr bréttŏn
Layer de la Haye *Essex*, 'leɪər də lɑ 'heɪ, láy-ĕr dĕ laa háy
Layham *Suffolk*, 'leɪəm, láy-ăm
Layton, *f.n.*, 'leɪtən, láytŏn
Lazar, *f.n.*, lə'zɑr, lăzaár
Lazard, *f.n.*, 'læzərd, lázzaard
Lazarenko, *f.n.*, ˌlæzə'reŋkoʊ, lazzăr-énkō
Lazell, *f.n.*, lə'zel, lăzéll
Lazenby, *f.n.*, 'leɪzənbɪ, láyzĕnbi
Lazonby, *f.n.*, 'leɪzənbɪ, láyzŏnbi
Lazonby *Cumbria*, 'leɪzənbɪ, láyzŏnbi
Lea, *f.n.*, li, lee
Leach, *f.n.*, litʃ, leetch
Leacock, *f.n.*, 'likɒk, leékock; 'leɪkɒk, láykock
Leadbeater, *f.n.*, 'ledbɪtər, lédbeetĕr; 'ledbɪtər, lédbittĕr; 'lidbɪtər, leédbeetĕr; 'lebɪtər, lébbitĕr

Leadbetter, *f.n.,* 'ledbetər, léd-
bettĕr; led'betər, ledbéttĕr
Leadbitter, *f.n.,* 'ledbıtər, léd-
bittĕr
Leaden, River, *H. & W.,* 'ledən,
léddĕn. *Also spelt* **Leddon.**
Leadenhall Street London, 'ledən-
hɔl, léddĕnhawl
Leadenham *Lincs.,* 'ledənəm,
léddĕnăm
Leadgate *Cumbria,* 'ledgıt, léd-git
Leadlay, *f.n.,* 'ledleı, léd-lay
Leah, *f.n.,* 'liə, lée-ă
Leahy, *f.n.,* 'lihı, lée-hi
Leakey, Louis Seymour Bazett,
*anthropologist and archaeologist
(1903–72),* 'luıs 'sımɔr 'bæzıt
'likı, loó-iss seémor bázzĕt leéki
Leal, *f.n.,* lil, leel
Leamington *Warwicks.,* 'lemıŋtən,
lémmingtŏn
Lean, *f.n.,* lin, leen
Leaning, *f.n.,* 'linıŋ, leéning
Leaper, *f.n.,* 'lipər, leépĕr
Leaphard, *f.n.,* 'lepərd, léppărd
Learmonth, *f.n.,* 'lɑrmənθ, lér-
mŏnth; 'lɛərmənθ, láirmŏnth;
'lıərmənθ, leérmŏnth; 'lɑrmənt,
lérmŏnt
Learmouth, *f.n.,* 'lıərmauθ, leér-
mowth
Learney *Grampian,* 'lɛərnı, láirni
Learoyd, *f.n.,* 'lıərɔıd, leér-oyd
Learthart, *f.n.,* 'lıərθɑrt, leér-
-thaart
Leasingthorne *Durham,* 'lizıŋθɔrn,
leézingthorn
Leask, *f.n.,* lisk, leesk
Leasowe *Merseyside,* 'lisou,
leéssō
Leatham, *f.n.,* 'liθəm, lée-thăm;
'liðəm, leéthăm
Leathart, *f.n.,* 'liθɑrt, lée-thaart
Leather, *f.n.,* 'leðər, léthĕr
Leatherland, *f.n.,* 'leðərlənd,
léthĕrlănd. *Appropriate also for
Baron ~.*
Leathers, Viscount, 'leðərz,
léthĕrz
Leathes, *f.n.,* liðz, leethz
Leavenheath *Suffolk,* 'levənhiθ,
lévvĕn-heeth
Leavening *N. Yorks.,* 'livnıŋ,
leév-ning
Leaver, *f.n.,* 'livər, leévĕr
Leavesden Green *Herts.,* 'livz-
dən, leévzdĕn
Leavey, *f.n.,* 'livı, leévi
Leavins, *f.n.,* 'levınz, lévvinz
Leavis, *f.n.,* 'livıs, leéviss
Leay, *f.n.,* leı, lay
Le Bars, *f.n.,* lə 'bɑrz, lĕ baárz
Lebon, *f.n.,* 'lıbɒn, leébon
Lebor, *f.n.,* lə'bɔr, lĕbór

Le Breton, *f.n.,* lə 'bretɒn, lĕ brét-
ton
Leburn, *f.n.,* 'lıbɜrn, leéburn
Lebus, *f.n.,* 'lıbəs, leébüss
Le Cain, *f.n.,* lə 'keın, lĕ káyn
Le Carré, *f.n.,* lə 'kæreı, lĕ kárray
Leche, *f.n.,* leʃ, lesh
Lechlade *Glos.,* 'letʃleıd, létch-
-layd
Lechmere, *f.n.,* 'letʃmıər, létch-
meer; 'leʃmıər, léshmeer
Leconfield *Humberside,* 'lekən-
fild, léckönfeeld. *Appropriate
also for Baron ~.*
Le Court *Hants.,* 'li 'kɔrt, lee kórt
Le Cren, *f.n.,* lə 'kren, lĕ krén
Lecropt *Central,* 'lekrɒpt, léck-
ropt
Lecumpher *Co. Derry,* lə'kʌmfər,
lĕkúmfĕr
Ledbury *H. & W.,* 'ledbərı, léd-
bŭri
Leddon, River, *see* **Leaden**
Ledeboer, *f.n.,* 'ledəbuər, léddĕ-
bōōr
Le Despencer, Baron, lə dı'spen-
sər, lĕ dĕspénssĕr
Ledgard, *f.n.,* 'ledʒɑrd, léjjaard
Ledigo, *f.n.,* 'ledıgou, léddigō
Ledingham, *f.n.,* 'ledıŋəm,
lédding-ăm
Ledoux, *f.n.,* lə'du, lĕdoó
Leech, *f.n.,* litʃ, leetch
Leedell, *f.n.,* li'del, leedéll
Leeds *Kent, W. Yorks.,* lidz,
leedz
Leedstown *Cornwall,* 'lidztaun,
leédztown
Leeming, *f.n.,* 'limıŋ, leéming
Leese, *f.n.,* lis, leess; liz, leez
Lefanu, *f.n.,* 'lefənju, léffănew;
lə'fɑnu, lĕfaánoo
Le Fanu, *f.n.,* 'lefənu, léffănoo;
'lefənju, léffănew
Lefeaux, *f.n.,* lə'fou, lĕfó
Lefebure, *f.n.,* 'lefəbjuər, léffĕ-
byōōr
Lefebvre, *f.n.,* lə'fivər, lĕféevĕr
Le Feuvre, *f.n.,* lə 'fivər, lĕ féevĕr
Lefeuvre, *f.n.,* lə'favr, lĕfóvr
Le Fevre, *f.n.,* lə 'feıvr, lĕ fáyvr
Lefevre, *f.n.,* lə'fivər, lĕféevĕr;
lə'fevr, lĕfévvr
Lefevre Galleries *London,*
lə'fɛːvr, lĕfévvr
Le Fleming, *f.n.,* lə 'flemıŋ, lĕ
flémming
Lefroy, *f.n.,* lə'frɔı, lĕfróy
Legacurry *Co. Down,* ˌlegə'kʌrı,
leggăkúrri
Legacy *Clwyd,* 'legəsı, légăssi
Le Gallienne, *f.n.,* lə 'gæljen, lĕ
gál-yen
Legard, *f.n.,* 'ledʒɑrd, léjjărd

Legat, *f.n.*, lə'gæt, lĕgát
Legburthwaite *Cumbria*, 'leg-bərθweıt, légbŭrthwayt
Leger Galleries *London*, 'ledʒər, léjĕr
Legerton, *f.n.*, 'ledʒərtən, léjĕrtŏn
Legerwood *Borders*, 'ledʒərwʊd, léjĕrwŏod
Leggate, *f.n.*, 'legeıt, léggayt; 'legət, léggăt
Leggatt, *f.n.*, 'legət, léggăt
Legge, *f.n.*, leg, leg
Leggett, *f.n.*, 'legət, léggĕt
Legh, *f.n.*, li, lee
Le Grice, *f.n.*, lə 'graıs, lĕ gríss
Le Gros, *f.n.*, lə 'groʊ, lĕ grṓ
Lehane, *f.n.*, lə'hɑn, lĕ-haán
Leheup, *f.n.*, 'liəp, lee-ŭp
Lehmann, *f.n.*, 'leımən, láymăn
Le Huray, *f.n.*, lə 'hjʊəreı, lĕ hyŏŏray
Leicester *Leics.*, 'lestər, lésstĕr. *Appropriate also for the Earl of* ~.
Leifer, *f.n.*, 'lifər, leéfĕr
Leigh, *f.n.*, li, lee. *Appropriate also for Baron* ~.
Leigh Delamere *Wilts.*, 'li 'deləmıər, leé déllămeer
Leigh-on-Mendip *Somerset*, 'laı ɒn 'mendıp, lī on méndip; 'li ɒn 'mendıp, leé on méndip
Leigh-on-Sea *Essex*, 'li ɒn 'si, leé on seé
Leigh Sinton *H. & W.*, 'laı 'sıntən, lī sínton
Leighterton *Glos.*, 'leıtərtən, láytĕrtŏn
Leighton, *f.n.*, 'leıtən, láytŏn
Leighton *Powys*, 'leıtən, láytŏn
Leighton Bromswold *Cambs.*, 'leıtən 'brɒmzwoʊld, láytŏn brómzwōld
Leighton Buzzard *Beds.*, 'leıtən 'bʌzərd, láytŏn búzzărd
Leinster, Duke of, 'lınstər, línsstĕr
Leinthall Earls *H. & W.*, 'lentl 'ɜrlz, léntl érlz
Leinthall Starkes *H. & W.*, 'lentl 'stɑrks, léntl staárks
Leintwardine *H. & W.*, 'lentwərdaın, léntwărdïn; 'lentwərdin, léntwărdeen; 'læntərdin, lántĕrdeen
Leire *Leics.*, lıər, leer; lɛər, lair
Leishman, *f.n.*, 'liʃmən, leéshmăn; 'lıʃmən, líshmăn
Leisten, *f.n.*, 'listən, leésstĕn
Leister, *f.n.*, 'lestər, lésstĕr
Leiston *Suffolk*, 'leıstən, láysstŏn
Leitch, *f.n.*, litʃ, leetch

Leith, *f.n.*, liθ, leeth
Leith *Lothian*, liθ, leeth
Leith, River, *Cumbria*, liθ, leeth
Leithen *Borders*, 'liðən, leéthĕn
Leither, *f.n.*, 'litər, leétĕr
Leitholm *Borders*, 'litəm, leétŏm
Leitrim *Co. Down*, 'litrım, leétrim. *Appropriate also for the Earldom of* ~.
Le Lacheyr, *f.n.*, lə 'læʃər, lĕ láshĕr
Leland, *f.n.*, 'lilənd, leélănd
Lelant *Cornwall*, le'lænt, lellánt; lı'lænt, lĕlánt
Lelean, *f.n.*, lə'lin, lĕleén
Leleu, *f.n.*, lə'lu, lĕlṓo
Lely, Sir Peter, *17th-c. painter*, 'lılı, leéli
Le Maitre, *f.n.*, lə 'meıtr, lĕ máytr
Leman, *f.n.*, 'lemən, lémmăn; 'limən, leémăn
Leman Sands *off the coast of Norfolk*, lı'mæn, lĕmán
Le Marchant, *f.n.*, lə 'mɑrtʃənt, lĕ maártchánt; lə 'marʃənt, lĕ maárshănt
Lemare, *f.n.*, lə'mɛər, lĕmáir
Le Mare, *f.n.*, lə 'mɛər, lĕ máir
Le Masurier, *f.n.*, lə mə'zjʊərıər, lĕ măzyŏŏri-ĕr
Le Mauviel, *f.n.*, lə 'moʊvjəl, lĕ mṓv-yĕl
Le Mesurier, *f.n.*, lə 'meʒərər, lĕ méżhĕrĕr; lə mə'zuərıeı, lĕ mĕzŏŏri-ay
Lemin, *f.n.*, lə'mın, lĕmínn
Lemoine, *f.n.*, lə'mɔın, lĕmóyn
Lemon, *f.n.*, 'lemən, lémmŏn
Lempfert, *f.n.*, 'lempfərt, lémp-fĕrt
Lempriere, *f.n.*, 'lemprıɛər, lémpri-air
Lenaderg *Co. Down*, ˌlenə'dɑrg, lennădérg
Lenadoon *Belfast*, ˌlenə'dun, lennădoón
Lenanton, *f.n.*, lə'næntən, lĕnántŏn
Lench, *f.n.*, lenʃ, lensh
Lenderyou, *f.n.*, 'lendərju, léndĕr-yoo
Lenehan, *f.n.*, 'lenəhən, lénnĕ-hăn
Le Neve, *f.n.*, lə 'niv, lĕ neév
Leney, *f.n.*, 'lini, leéni
Lennon, *f.n.*, 'lenən, lénnŏn
Lentaigne, *f.n.*, len'teın, lentáyn
Lenthall, *f.n.*, 'lentəl, léntawl; 'lentl, léntl
Lenton, *f.n.*, 'lentən, léntŏn
Lenwade *Norfolk*, 'lenweıd, lén-wayd
Leny, Pass *and* Falls of, *Central*, 'leni, lénni
Lenzie *S'clyde*, 'lenzı, lénzi

Leochel-Cushnie *Grampian*, 'lɒxl 'kʌʃnɪ, lóchl kúshni

Leod *see* **Castle Leod**

Leode *Co. Down*, led, led

Leodegar, saint, leɪ'ɒdɪgɑr, lay--óddĕgaar

Leofric, *C.n.*, 'lefrɪk, léffrick. *The pronunciation* 'leɪəfrɪk, láy-ŏ--frick *is appropriate for the Saxon lord of Coventry, husband of Lady* **Godiva**,, *q.v.*

Leominster *H. & W.*, 'lemstər, lémsstĕr

Leon, *C.n. and f.n.*, 'liən, leé-ŏn

Leonard, *C.n. and f.n.*, 'lenərd, lénnărd

Leonard Stanley *Glos.*, 'lenərd 'stænlɪ, lénnărd stánli

Leonardslee *W. Sussex*, ˌlenərdz-'li, lennárdzleé

Leonowens, *f.n.*, 'liənoʊɪnz, leé--ŏnŏ-ĕnz

Le Patourel, *f.n.*, lə 'pætʊərel, lĕ páttŏŏrel

Lephard, *f.n.*, 'lepɑrd, léppaard

Lepine, *f.n.*, lə'pin, lĕpeén

Le Poer, *f.n.*, lə 'pʊər, lĕ pŏŏr

Le Poer Trench, *f.n.*, lə 'pʊər 'trenʃ, lĕ pŏŏr trénsh

Leppard, *f.n.*, 'lepɑrd, léppaard

Le Prevost, *f.n.*, lə 'preɪvoʊ, lĕ práyvŏ

Le Quesne, *f.n.*, lə 'keɪn, lĕ káyn

Le Queux, *f.n.*, lə 'kju, lĕ kéw

Le Riche, *f.n.*, lə 'riʃ, lĕ reésh

Le Rougetel, *f.n.*, lə 'ruʒtel, lĕ roózhtel

Leroy, *f.n.*, lə'rɔɪ, lĕróy

Lerwegian, *native of* **Lerwick**, lɜr'wɪdʒən, lerweéjăn

Lerwick *Shetland*, 'lɜrwɪk, lérwick

Le Sage, *f.n.*, lə 'sɑʒ, lĕ saázh

Lescudjack *Cornwall*, lɪs'kʌdʒæk, lĕskújjack

Lesirge, *f.n.*, lə'sɜrʒ, lĕssírzh

Lesmahagow *S'clyde*, ˌlesmə-'heɪgoʊ, lessmă-háygŏ

Lesnes *see* **Lessness**

Lesnewth *Devon*, lez'njuθ, lez--néwth

Lesney *toy-manufacturing company*, 'lesnɪ, léssni

Lessells, *f.n.*, 'lesls, lésslss

Lesser, *f.n.*, 'lesər, léssĕr

Lessness, *formerly spelt* **Lesnes**, *London*, 'lesnɪs, léssnĕss

Lessore, *f.n.*, lə'sɔr, lĕssór

Lessudden *House Borders*, lə-'sʌdən, lĕssúddĕn

Lestocq, *f.n.*, 'lestɒk, lésstock

Lestor, *f.n.*, 'lestər, lésstŏr

L'Estrange, *f.n.*, lɪ'streɪndʒ, lĕstráynj

Le Sueur, *f.n.*, lə 'swɜr, lĕ swúr

Le Surf, *f.n.*, lə 'sɜrf, lĕ súrf

Leswalt *D. & G.*, les'wɒlt, less-wáwlt

Letham, *f.n.*, 'leθəm, léthăm

Lethbridge, *f.n.*, 'leθbrɪdʒ, léth-brij

Lethem, *f.n.*, 'leθəm, léthĕm

Lethendy *Tayside*, 'leθəndɪ, léthĕndi

Lethnot *Tayside*, 'leθnət, léthnŏt

Leuchars, *f.n.*, 'lukəs, loókăss

Leuchars *Fife*, 'luxərz, loóchărz

Leueen, *C.n.*, lu'in, loo-eén

Leutscher, *f.n.*, 'lutʃər, loótchĕr

Levack, *f.n.*, lə'væk, lĕváck

Levander, *f.n.*, lɪ'vændər, lĕván-dĕr

Levarne, *f.n.*, lə'vɑrn, lĕvaárn

Levatt, *f.n.*, lɪ'væt, lĕvát

Leven, *f.n.*, 'livən, leévĕn; 'levən, lévvĕn

Leven, *River, Cumbria*, 'levən, lévvĕn

Leven, *Rivers, Fife, H'land, S'clyde, N. Yorks.*, 'livən, leévĕn

Leven and Melville, Earl of, 'livən ənd 'melvɪl, leévĕn ănd mélvil

Levens, *f.n.*, 'levənz, lévvĕnz

Levens *Cumbria*, 'levənz, lévvĕnz

Levenshulme *Gtr. M'chester*, 'levənzhjum, lévvĕnz-hewm

Leventon, *f.n.*, 'levəntən, lévvĕn-tŏn

Lever, *f.n.*, 'livər, leévĕr

Leverhulme, Viscount, 'livərhjum, leévĕr-hewm

Leverington *Cambs.*, 'levərɪŋtən, lévvĕringtŏn

Leverstock Green *Herts.*, 'levər-stɒk 'grin, lévvĕrstock green

Leverton, *f.n.*, 'levərtən, lévvĕrtŏn

Leverton, North *and* South, *Notts.*, 'levərtən, lévvĕrtŏn

Levesley, *f.n.*, 'livzlɪ, leévzli; 'levəzlɪ, lévvĕzli

Leveson, *C.n.*, 'lusən, loóssŏn

Leveson-Gower, *f.n.*, 'lusən 'gɔr, loóssŏn gór. *Family name of Earl Granville.*

L'Evesque, *f.n.*, lə'vesk, lĕvésk

Levey, *f.n.*, 'livɪ, leévi; 'levɪ, lévvi

Levi, *f.n.*, 'levɪ, lévvi; 'livɪ, leévi

Levic, *f.n.*, 'levɪk, lévvick

Levick, *f.n.*, 'levɪk, lévvick

Levien, *f.n.*, lə'vin, lĕveén

Levin, *f.n.*, 'levɪn, lévvin

Levine, *f.n.*, lə'vin, lĕveén

Levinge, *f.n.*, 'levɪŋ, lévving

Levita, *f.n.*, lə'vitə, lĕveétă

Levy, *f.n.*, 'livɪ, leévi; 'levɪ, lévvi

Lewannick *Cornwall*, lɪ'wɒnɪk, lĕ-wónnick

Lewarne, *f.n.*, lə'wɔrn, lĕ-wáwrn
Lewarne *Cornwall*, lə'wɔrn, lĕ-wáwrn
Lewdown, *also spelt* Lew Down, *Devon*, 'luːdaʊn, loo-dówn
Lewell, *f.n.*, 'luəl, loo-ĕl
Lewenstein, *f.n.*, 'luənstin, loo-ĕnsteen
Lewes *E. Sussex*, 'luːs, loo-ĕss
Lewey, *f.n.*, 'luː, loo-i
Lewin, *f.n.*, 'luːn, loo-in
Lewinski, *f.n.*, lu'ɪnskɪ, loo-ínski
Lewis, *f.n.*, 'luːs, loo-iss
Lewitter, *f.n.*, lə'wɪtər, lĕ-wíttĕr
Lewknor *Oxon.*, 'luknər, loóknor
Lewry, *f.n.*, 'luərɪ, loóri
Lews *Castle I. of Lewis*, luz, looz
Lewsen, *f.n.*, 'luːsən, loóssĕn
Lewsey, *f.n.*, 'ljuːsɪ, léwssi
Lewthwaite, *f.n.*, 'luːθweɪt, loóthwayt
Lewtrenchard, *also spelt* Lew Trenchard, *Devon*, 'luːtrenʃərd, loó-trén-shărd
Ley, *f.n.*, leɪ, lay; li, lee
Leybourne *Kent*, 'leɪbərn, láyborn
Leyburn *N. Yorks.*, 'leɪbɜrn, láyburn
Leycester, *f.n.*, 'lestər, lésstĕr
Leycett *Staffs.*, 'lɪsɪt, léessĕt
Leyhill *Bucks.*, 'leɪhɪl, láy-hil
Leyland, *f.n.*, 'leɪlənd, láylănd
Leyland *Lancs.*, 'leɪlənd, láylănd
Leys, *f.n.*, liz, leez
Leysdown *Kent*, 'leɪzdaʊn, láyzdown
Leyshon, *f.n.*, 'laɪʃən, lí-shŏn; 'leɪʃən, láy-shŏn. *The first is usual in Wales.*
Leyton *London*, 'leɪtən, láytŏn
Leytonstone *London*, 'leɪtənstoʊn, léytŏn-stōn
Lezant *Cornwall*, le'zænt, lezzánt
Leziate *Norfolk*, 'lezɪət, lézziăt; 'ledʒɪt, léjjĕt
Liardet, *f.n.*, li'ardet, lee-aárdet
Lias, *f.n.*, 'laɪəs, lí-áss
Libanus *Powys*, 'lɪbənəs, líbbănŭss
Liberton *Edinburgh*, 'lɪbərtən, líbbĕrtŏn
Lickess, *f.n.*, 'lɪkɪs, líckĕss
Lickis, *f.n.*, 'lɪkɪs, líckiss
Lickiss, *f.n.*, 'lɪkɪs, líckiss
Licswm *see* Lixwm
Liddell, *f.n.*, 'lɪdl, líddl; lɪ'del, lidéll. *The first, which is still much the more usual for this spelling, is appropriate for Henry George ~, joint editor of Liddell and Scott's Greek-English lexicon, and for his daughter Alice ~, the heroine of 'Alice in Wonderland'.*
Liddle, *f.n.*, 'lɪdl, líddl

Lidell, *f.n.*, 'lɪdl, líddl; lɪ'del, lidéll
Lidgate *Suffolk*, 'lɪdgeɪt, líd-gayt
Lidgett, *f.n.*, 'lɪdʒɪt, líjjĕt
Lidstone, *f.n.*, 'lɪdstən, lídstŏn
Liebert, *f.n.*, 'lɪbərt, leébĕrt
Lienhardt, *f.n.*, 'liənhɑrt, leé-ĕn-haart
Liesching, *f.n.*, 'liʃɪŋ, leéshing
Lieven, *f.n.*, 'livən, leévĕn
Lightbown, *f.n.*, 'laɪtbaʊn, líftbown
Lightburn, *f.n.*, 'laɪtbɜrn, líftburn
Lightoller, *f.n.*, 'laɪtɒlər, líftollĕr
Ligoniel *Co. Antrim*, ˌlɪgə'niːl, liggŏneél
Ligonier, *f.n.*, ˌlɪgə'nɪər, liggŏneér
Lijertwood, *f.n.*, 'laɪdʒərtwʊd, líjĕrt-wōōd
Likeman, *f.n.*, 'laɪkmən, líkmăn
Lilburn, *f.n.*, 'lɪlbɜrn, lílburn
Lilleshall *Salop*, 'lɪlɪʃəl, lilli-shăl
Lilley, *f.n.*, 'lɪlɪ, lílli
Lilliput *Dorset*, 'lɪlɪpʊt, líllipŏŏt
Lillistone, *f.n.*, 'lɪlɪstən, lílistŏn
Lillywhite, *f.n.*, 'lɪlɪhwaɪt, lílli-whīt
Limavady *Co. Derry*, ˌlɪmə'vædɪ, limmăváddi
Limerick, *Earl of*, 'lɪmərɪk, límmĕrick
Limpenhoe *Norfolk*, 'lɪmpənhoʊ, límpĕn-hō
Limpkin, *f.n.*, 'lɪmpkɪn, límpkin
Linacre, *f.n.*, 'lɪnəkər, línnăkĕr
Lincoln, *f.n.*, 'lɪŋkən, línkŏn
Lincoln *Lincs.*, 'lɪŋkən, línkŏn
Lind, *f.n.*, lɪnd, lind
Lindesay, *f.n.*, 'lɪndzɪ, líndzi
Lindesay-Bethune, *f.n.*, 'lɪndzɪ 'biːtən, líndzi beétŏn. *Family name of the Earl of Lindsay.*
Lindgren, *f.n.*, 'lɪngrən, lín-grĕn
Lindisfarne *Northd.*, 'lɪndɪsfarn, líndiss-faarn
Lindley *Leics.*, *W. Yorks.*, 'lɪndlɪ, líndli
Lindop, *f.n.*, 'lɪndɒp, líndop
Lindores *Fife*, lɪn'dɔrz, lindórz
Lindridge, *f.n.*, 'lɪndrɪdʒ, líndrij
Lindsay, *Earl of*, 'lɪndzɪ, líndzi
Lindsay, *C.n. and f.n.*, 'lɪndzɪ, líndzi
Lindsell, *f.n.*, 'lɪndzl, líndzl
Linehan, *f.n.*, 'lɪnəhən, línnĕhăn
Ling, *f.n.*, lɪŋ, ling
Lingane, *f.n.*, 'lɪŋgeɪn, líng-gayn
Lingard, *f.n.*, 'lɪŋgard, líng-gaard
Lingay, *f.n.*, 'lɪŋgɪ, líng-gi
Lingen, *f.n.*, 'lɪŋgən, líng-ĕn
Lings, *f.n.*, lɪŋz, lingz
Lingstrom, *f.n.*, 'lɪŋstrəm, líng-strŏm
Linhope *Northd.*, 'lɪnəp, línnŏp

Linkie, *f.n.*, ˈlɪŋkɪ, línki
Linkinhorne *Cornwall*, ˈlɪŋkɪn-hɔːn, línkin-horn
Linklater, Eric, *author*, ˈlɪŋklətər, línklătĕr. *The author has confirmed this as his family pronunciation, although others frequently call him* ˈlɪŋkleɪtər, línklaytĕr.
Linlathen *Tayside*, lɪnˈlæθən, lin-láthĕn
Linley, Viscount, ˈlɪnlɪ, línli
Linlithgow *Lothian*, lɪnˈlɪθɡoʊ, linlíthgō. *Appropriate also for the Marquess of* ~.
Linnell, *f.n.*, ˈlɪnl, línnl
Linnhe, Loch, *H'land–S'clyde*, ˈlɪnɪ, línni
Linos, *f.n.*, ˈlɪnɒs, léenoss
Linsidemore *H'land*, ˈlɪnsaɪdˈmɔːr, línssīdmór
Linslade *Beds.*, ˈlɪnzleɪd, línz-layd
Linstead, *f.n.*, ˈlɪnstɛd, línsted
Linstrum, *f.n.*, ˈlɪnstrəm, línstrŭm
Linthwaite, *f.n.*, ˈlɪnθweɪt, línth-wayt
Lintott, *f.n.*, ˈlɪntɒt, líntot
Lintrathen *Tayside*, lɪnˈtreɪðən, lintráythĕn
Linwood *Lincs.*, *S'clyde*, ˈlɪnwʊd, línwŏŏd
Linzell, *f.n.*, lɪnˈzɛl, linzéll
Lipkin, *f.n.*, ˈlɪpkɪn, lípkin
Lippiatt, *f.n.*, ˈlɪpɪət, líppi-ăt
Lippiett, *f.n.*, ˈlɪpɪət, líppi-ĕt
Lipscomb, *f.n.*, ˈlɪpskəm, lípskŏm
Lipsidge, *f.n.*, ˈlɪpsɪdʒ, lípssij
Liptrot, *f.n.*, ˈlɪptrɒt, líptrot
Lipyeat, *f.n.*, ˈlɪpɪət, líppi-ăt
Lisahally *Co. Derry*, ˌlɪsəˈhælɪ, lissáháli
Lisam, *f.n.*, ˈlaɪsəm, líssăm
Lisbane *Co. Down*, lɪsˈbæn, liss-bán
Lisbellaw *Co. Fermanagh*, ˌlɪsbɪˈlɔ, lissbĕláw
Lisbuoy *Co. Tyrone*, lɪsˈbɔɪ, liss-bóy
Lisburn *Cos. Antrim–Down*, ˈlɪzbərn, lízburn
Lisburne, Earl of, ˈlɪzbərn, lízbŭrn
Lisdoonan *Co. Down*, lɪsˈdunən, lissdoónăn
Lisemore, *f.n.*, ˈlɪzmɔːr, lízmor
Lisk, *f.n.*, lɪsk, lissk
Liskeard *Cornwall*, lɪsˈkɑːd, liss-kaárd
Lisle, *f.n.*, laɪl, líl. *Appropriate also for Baron* ~.
Lismoyne *Co. Antrim*, lɪsˈmɔɪn, lissmóyn
Lisnadill *Co. Armagh*, ˌlɪsnəˈdɪl, lissnădíll

Lisnagarvey *Co. Antrim*, ˌlɪsnəˈɡɑːrvɪ, lissnăgaárvi
Lisnalinchy *Co. Antrim*, ˌlɪsnəˈlɪnʃɪ, lissnálínshi
Lisnamallard *Co. Tyrone*, ˌlɪsnəˈmælərd, lissnămálărd
Lisnaskea *Co. Fermanagh*, ˌlɪsnəˈskiː, lissnä-skée
Lisney, *f.n.*, ˈlɪznɪ, lízni
Lissan *Cos. Derry–Tyrone*, ˈlɪsən, líssăn
Lister, *f.n.*, ˈlɪstər, lísstĕr. *Appropriate for Joseph Jackson* ~, *microscopist, and for his son Joseph, later Baron* ~, *surgeon*.
Listooder *Co. Down*, lɪsˈtudər, lisstoódĕr
Listowel, Earl of, lɪsˈtoʊəl, lisstō-ĕl
Lisvane *S. Glam.*, lɪzˈveɪn, lizváyn. *The Welsh name is* **Llys-faen**, *q.v.*
Litheby, *f.n.*, ˈlɪðəbɪ, líthĕbi
Litherland, *f.n.*, ˈlɪðərlænd, líthĕrland
Lithgow, *f.n.*, ˈlɪθɡoʊ, líthgō
Littell, *f.n.*, lɪˈtɛl, litéll
Litterick, *f.n.*, ˈlɪtərɪk, líttĕrick
Little Almshoe *Herts.*, ˈlɪtl ˈɑːmʃu, líttl aámshoo
Little Alne *Warwicks.*, ˈlɪtl ˈɒn, líttl áwn; ˈlɪtl ˈɔln, líttl áwln
Little Bourton *Oxon.*, ˈlɪtl ˈbɔːrtən, líttl bórtŏn
Little Bowden *Leics.*, ˈlɪtl ˈbaʊdən, líttl bówdĕn
Little Bradley *Suffolk*, ˈlɪtl ˈbrædlɪ, líttl brádli
Little Bromley *Essex*, ˈlɪtl ˈbrɒmlɪ, líttl brómli
Littlebury Green *Essex*, ˈlɪtlbərɪ ˈɡriːn, líttlbŭri gréen
Little Compton *Warwicks.*, ˈlɪtl ˈkɒmptən, líttl kómptŏn
Little Creaton *Northants.*, ˈlɪtl ˈkriːtən, líttl kréetŏn
Little Cumbrae *S'clyde*, ˈlɪtl ˈkʌmbreɪ, líttl kúmbray
Little Fransham *Norfolk*, ˈlɪtl ˈfrænʃəm, líttl fránshăm
Little Gaddesden *Herts.*, ˈlɪtl ˈɡædzdən, líttl gádzdĕn
Little Harrowden *Northants.*, ˈlɪtl ˈhæroʊdən, líttl hárrōdĕn
Little Hautbois *Norfolk*, ˈlɪtl ˈhɒbɪs, líttl hóbbiss
Little Houghton *Northants.*, ˈlɪtl ˈhoʊtən, líttl hótŏn
Little Houghton *S. Yorks.*, ˈlɪtl ˈhɒtən, líttl háwtŏn
Little Ponton *Lincs.*, ˈlɪtl ˈpɒntən, líttl póntŏn
Littler, *f.n.*, ˈlɪtlər, líttlĕr

Little Saughall *Ches.*, 'lɪtl 'sɔkl, líttl sáwkl
Little Shelford *Cambs.*, 'lɪtl 'ʃelfərd, líttl shélfŏrd
Little Staughton *Beds.*, 'lɪtl 'stɔtən, líttl stáwtŏn
Littlestone-on-Sea *Kent*, 'lɪtlstən ɒn 'siː, líttlstŏn on seé
Little Stonham *Suffolk*, 'lɪtl 'stɒnəm, líttl stónnăm
Little Stukeley *Cambs.*, 'lɪtl 'stjuklɪ, líttl stéwkli
Little Totham *Essex*, 'lɪtl 'tɒtəm, líttl tóttăm
Little Wakering *Essex*, 'lɪtl 'weɪkərɪŋ, líttl wáykĕring
Little Walsingham *Norfolk*, 'lɪtl 'wɒlzɪŋəm, líttl wáwlzing-ăm
Little Waltham *Essex*, 'lɪtl 'wɒltəm, líttl wáwltăm
Little Warley *Essex*, 'lɪtl 'wɔrlɪ, líttl wáwrli
Little Wilbraham *Cambs.*, 'lɪtl 'wɪlbrəm, líttl wílbrăm; 'lɪtl 'wɪlbrəhæm, líttl wílbrăham
Little Wymondley *Herts.*, 'lɪtl 'waɪməndlɪ, líttl wímŏndli
Little Wyrley *Staffs.*, 'lɪtl 'wɜrlɪ, líttl wúrli
Litton Cheney *Dorset*, 'lɪtən 'tʃeɪnɪ, líttŏn cháyni
Lium, *f.n.*, 'liəm, leé-ŭm
Liveing, *f.n.*, 'lɪvɪŋ, lívving
Lively, *f.n.*, 'laɪvlɪ, lívli
Livens, *f.n.*, 'lɪvənz, lívvěnz
Liver Building *Liverpool*, 'laɪvər, lívěr
Livermore, *f.n.*, 'lɪvərmɔr, lívvěr-mor
Liverpool *Merseyside*, 'lɪvərpul, lívvěrpool
Liverpudlian, *native of* **Liverpool**, ˌlɪvər'pʌdlɪən, livvěrpúdlian
Liversedge *W. Yorks.*, 'lɪvərsedʒ, lívvěr-sej
Liversuch, *f.n.*, 'lɪvərsʌtʃ, lívver-sutch
Livesey, *f.n.*, 'lɪvsɪ, lívssi; 'lɪvzɪ, lívzi
Livingstone, *f.n.*, 'lɪvɪŋstən, lívving-stŏn; 'lɪvɪŋstoun, lívving-stōn
Lixwm, *also spelt* **Licswm**, *Clwyd*, 'lɪksum, lícksŏom
Lizard *Cornwall*, 'lɪzərd, lízzărd
Lizars, *f.n.*, lɪ'zarz, lizzaárz
Llai, *also spelt* **Llay**, *Clwyd*, ɬaɪ, hlī
Llain-goch *Gwynedd*, ɬaɪn'goux, hlīn-góch
Llanaelhaiarn *Gwynedd*, ˌɬænaɪl-'haɪərn, hlanīl-hí-ărn
Llanafan *Dyfed*, ɬæn'ævən, hlanávvăn

Llanafan Fawr *Powys*, ɬæn'ævən 'vauər, hlanávvăn vówr
Llanallgo *Gwynedd*, ɬæn'æɬgou, hlanáhlgō
Llanarmon *Clwyd, Gwynedd*, ɬæn'armɒn, hlanaármon
Llanarmon Dyffryn Ceiriog *Clwyd*, ɬæn'armɒn 'dʌfrɪn 'kaɪərjɒg, hlanaármon dúffrin kír-yog
Llanarmon-yn-ial *Clwyd*, ɬæn'armɒn ən 'jal, hlanaármon-ăn-yaál
Llanarth *Dyfed, Gwent*, 'ɬænarθ, hlánaarth
Llan-arth Fawr *Dyfed*, ɬæn'arθ 'vauər, hlanaárth vówr
Llanarthney *Dyfed*, ɬæn'arθnɪ, hlanaárthni
Llanasa *Clwyd*, ɬæn'æsə, hlanássă
Llanbadarn Fawr *Dyfed*, ɬæn-'bædərn 'vauər, hlanbáddărn vówr
Llanbadarn-y-Creuddyn *Dyfed*, ɬæn'bædərn ə 'kraɪðɪn, hlanbáddărn ă kríthin
Llanbadoc *Gwent*, ɬæn'bædɒk, hlanbáddock
Llanbadrig *Gwynedd*, ɬæn'bædrɪg, hlanbádrig
Llanbeblig *Gwynedd*, ɬæn'beblɪg, hlan-béblig
Llanbedr *Gwynedd, Powys*, 'ɬæn-bedər, hlánbeddĕr
Llan-bedr *Gwent*, ɬæn'bedər, hlanbéddĕr
Llanbedr-goch *Gwynedd*, 'ɬæn-bedər 'goux, hlánbeddĕr-góch
Llanbedrog *Gwynedd*, ɬæn'bedrɒg, hlanbédrog
Llanbedrycennin *Gwynedd*, 'ɬæn-bedərə'kenɪn, hlánbeddĕr-ă--kénnin
Llanberis *Gwynedd*, ɬæn'berɪs, hlanbérriss
Llanbister *Powys*, ɬæn'bɪstər, hlanbísstĕr
Llanblethian *S. Glam.*, ɬæn-'bleðɪən, hlanbléthi-ăn
Llanboidy *Dyfed*, ɬæn'bɔɪdɪ, hlanbóydi
Llan-borth *Dyfed*, ɬæn'bɔrθ, hlan-bórth
Llanbradach *Mid Glam.*, ɬæn-'brædəx, hlanbráddăch
Llanbrynmair *Powys*, ˌɬænbrɪn-'maɪər, hlanbrin-mír
Llancaiach, *also spelt* **Llancaeach**, *Mid Glam.*, ɬæn'kaɪəx, hlan-kí--ăch
Llancynfelin *Dyfed*, ˌɬænkɪn'velɪn, hlan-kin-véllin
Llandaff *S. Glam.*, 'ɬændəf, lándăf; 'ɬændæf, hlándaff.
Although the first is widespread

local usage, the second is pre-ferred by the clergy of ~ Cathedral and by the BBC in Cardiff. The Welsh language form is Llandaf, pronounced ɬænˈdɑv, ˌhlandaˈav.

Llandarcy *W. Glam.*, ɬænˈdɑrsɪ, ˌhlandaˈarssi

Llanddaniel *Gwynedd*, ɬænˈðænjəl, ˌhlanˈthán-yĕl

Llanddarog *Dyfed*, ɬænˈðærɒg, ˌhlanˈthárrog

Llanddeiniol *Dyfed*, ɬænˈðaɪnjɒl, ˌhlanˈthĭn-yol

Llanddeiniolen *Gwynedd*, ˌɬænðaɪnˈjɒlən, ˌhlanthĭn-yóllĕn

Llandderfel *Gwynedd*, ɬænˈðɛərvel, ˌhlanˈtháirvel

Llanddetty *Powys*, ɬænˈðetɪ, ˌhlanˈthétti

Llanddeusant *Dyfed*, *Gwynedd*, ɬænˈðaɪsænt, ˌhlanˈthĭssant

Llanddew *Powys*, 'ɬændoʊ, lándō; ɬænˈðju, ˌhlan-théw

Llanddewi Aberarth *Dyfed*, ɬænˈðewɪ ˌæbərˈɑrθ, ˌhlanˈthé-wi abbĕraˈarth; ɬænˈðjuɪ ˌæbərˈɑrθ, ˌhlanthéw-i abbĕraarth

Llanddewi Brefi *Dyfed*, ɬænˈðewɪ ˈbreɪvɪ, ˌhlanthé-wi bráyvi; ɬænˈðjuɪ ˈbreɪvɪ, ˌhlanthéw-i bráyvi

Llanddewi'r Cwm *Powys*, ɬænˈðewɪər ˈkʊm, ˌhlanthé-weer kóŏm; ɬænˈðjuər ˈkʊm, ˌhlanthéw-ĕr kŏŏm

Llanddewi Velfrey *Dyfed*, ɬænˈðewɪ ˈvelfreɪ, ˌhlanthé-wi vélfray

Llanddoget *Gwynedd*, ɬænˈðɒgɪt, ˌhlanthóggĕt

Llanddona *Gwynedd*, ɬænˈðɒnə, ˌhlanthónna

Llanddowror *Dyfed*, ɬænˈðaʊrɔr, ˌhlanthówror

Llanddulas *Clwyd*, ɬænˈðɪləs, ˌhlanthíllăss

Llanddyfnan *Gwynedd*, ɬænˈðʌvnən, ˌhlanthúvnăn

Llandebie *Dyfed*, ˌɬændəˈbieɪ, ˌhlandĕbeé-ay

Llandecwyn *Gwynedd*, ɬænˈdekwɪn, ˌhlandéckwin

Llandefailog *Powys*, ˌɬændəˈvaɪlɒg, ˌhlandĕvílog

Llandefailog-fach *Powys*, ˌɬændəˈvaɪlɒg ˈvɑx, ˌhlandĕvílog vaˈach

Llandefalle *Powys*, ˌɬændəˈvæɬeɪ, ˌhlandĕváhlay

Llandefeilog *Dyfed*, ˌɬændəˈvaɪlɒg ˌhlandĕvílog

Llandegai *Gwynedd*, ˌɬændəˈgaɪ, ˌhlandĕgí

Llandegfan *Gwynedd*, ɬænˈdegvæn, ˌhlandégvan

Llandegla *Clwyd*, ɬænˈdeglə, ˌhlandéglă

Llandegley *Powys*, ɬænˈdegleɪ, ˌhlandéglay

Llandeilo, *also spelt* **Llandilo**, *Dyfed*, ɬænˈdaɪloʊ, ˌhlandílō

Llandeilo Bertholau *Gwent*, ɬænˈdaɪloʊ bɛərˈθɒlaɪ, ˌhlandílō bair-thóllī

Llandeilo Graban *Powys*, ɬænˈdaɪloʊ ˈgræbən, ˌhlandílō grábbăn

Llandeilo'r-fân *Dyfed*, ɬænˈdaɪlɔrˈvɑn, ˌhlandílor-vaˈan

Llandeloy *Dyfed*, ˌɬændəˈlɔɪ, ˌhlandĕlóy

Llandenny *Gwent*, ɬænˈdenɪ, ˌhlandénni

Llandevaud *Gwent*, ˌɬændəˈvɒd, ˌhlandĕváwd

Llandewi Ystradenny *Gwent*, ɬænˈdewɪ ˌʌstrədˈenɪ, ˌhlandé-wi usstrádenni; ɬænˈdewɪ ˌʌstrədˈenɪ, ˌhlandéw-i usstrádenni

Llandilo *see* **Llandeilo**

Llandinabo *H. & W.*, ˌɬændɪˈneɪboʊ, landinaýbō

Llandinam *Powys*, ɬænˈdinæm, ˌhlandéenam

Llandinorwig *Gwynedd*, ˌɬændɪˈnɔrwɪg, ˌhlandinórwig

Llandogo *Gwent*, ɬænˈdoʊgoʊ, ˌhlandōgō

Llandough *S. Glam.*, lænˈdɒk, landóck

Llandovery *Dyfed*, ɬænˈdʌvrɪ, ˌhlandúvvri

Llandow *S. Glam.*, lænˈdaʊ, landów

Llandre *Dyfed*, 'ɬændreɪ, ˌhlándray

Llandrillo *Clwyd*, ɬænˈdrɪɬoʊ, ˌhlandríhlō

Llandrindod Wells *Powys*, ɬænˈdrɪndɒd ˈwelz, ˌhlandríndod wéllz

Llandrinio *Powys*, ɬænˈdrɪnjoʊ, ˌhlandrín-yō

Llandudno *Gwynedd*, ɬænˈdɪdnoʊ, ˌhlandídnō

Llandulas *Powys*, ɬænˈdɪləs, ˌhlandíllăss

Llandwrog *Gwynedd*, ɬænˈduərɒg, ˌhlandŏŏrog

Llandyfodwg *Mid Glam.*, ˌɬændəˌvoʊdʊg, ˌhlandăvódōŏg

Llandyfriog *Dyfed*, ˌɬændəˈvrɪɒg, ˌhlandăvrée-og

Llandyfrydog *Gwynedd*, ˌɬændəˈvrʌdɒg, ˌhlandăvrúddog

Llandygwydd *Dyfed*, ɬænˈdʌgwɪð, ˌhlandúgwith

Llandyrnog *Clwyd*, ɬænˈdərnɒg, ˌhlandúrnog

Llandysilio *Powys*,,ˌɬændə'sɪljou, ɬlandŭssíl-yō

Llandysiliogogo *Dyfed*, ˌɬændə-'sɪljou'gougou, ɬlandŭssíl-yō-gōgō

Llandysul *Dyfed*, *Powys*, ɬæn'dɪsɪl, ɬlandíssil; ɬæn'dʌsɪl, ɬlandússil

Llanedeyrn *S. Glam.*, ɬæn'edɛərn, ɬlan-éddairn. *The Welsh form is* Llanedern.

Llanedwen *Gwynedd*, ɬæn'edwɪn, ɬlanédwën

Llanedy *Dyfed*, ɬæn'eɪdɪ, ɬlanáydi

Llanegryn *Gwynedd*, ɬæn'egrɪn, ɬlanégrin

Llanegwad *Dyfed*, ɬæn'egwəd, ɬlanégwäd

Llaneilian *Gwynedd*, ɬæn'aɪljən, ɬlaníl-yän

Llanelian *Gwynedd*, ɬæn'eljən, ɬlanél-yän

Llanelidan *Clwyd*,,ɬænɪ'lidən, ɬlannĕléedän

Llanelieu *Powys*, ɬæn'ilju, ɬlanée-lew; ɬæn'ilju, laneélew

Llanellen *Gwent*, ɬæn'elɪn, ɬlanéllën

Llanelli, *formerly spelt* Llanelly, *Dyfed*, *Powys*, ɬæn'eɬɪ, ɬlanéhli

Llanelltyd *Gwynedd*, ɬæn'eɬtɪd, ɬlanéhltid

Llanelly *see* Llanelli

Llanelwedd *Powys*, ɬæn'elwɪð, ɬlanélwĕth

Llanenddwyn *Gwynedd*, ɬæn-'enðuɪn, ɬlanénthōō-in

Llanengan *Gwynedd*, ɬæn'eŋən, ɬlanéng-än

Llanerchymedd *Gwynedd*, ,ɬænɛərxə'meɪð, ɬlanairchämáyth

Llanerfyl *Powys*, ɬæn'ɛərvɪl, ɬlanáirvil

Llaneugrad *Gwynedd*, ɬæn'aɪgræd, ɬlanígrad

Llanfabon *Mid Glam.*, ɬæn'væbən, ɬlanvábbön

Llanfachraeth, *also spelt* Llanfachreth, *Gwynedd*, ɬæn'væxrəθ, ɬlanváchrĕth. *Appropriate for both places of the name in Gwynedd.*

Llanfaelog *Gwynedd*, ɬæn'vaɪlɒg, ɬlanvílog

Llan-faes, *Powys*, ɬæn'vaɪs, ɬlanvíss

Llanfaethlu *Gwynedd*, ɬæn'vaɪθlɪ, ɬlanvíthli

Llanfair *Gwynedd*, 'ɬænvaɪər, ɬlánvīr

Llanfair-ar-y-bryn *Dyfed*, 'ɬænvaɪər ær ə 'brɪn, ɬlánvīr-arrä-brín

Llanfair Caereinion *Powys*, 'ɬænvaɪər kɑr'aɪnjən, ɬlánvīr kaarín-yon

Llanfair Clydogau *Dyfed*, 'ɬænvaɪər klɪ'dougaɪ, ɬlánvīr klídōgī

Llanfairfechan *Gwynedd*, ,ɬæn-vaɪər'vexən, ɬlanvīr-véchän

Llanfair-is-gaer *Gwynedd*, 'ɬænvaɪər'isgaɪər, ɬlánvīr-eéss-gīr

Llanfair Kilgeddin *Gwent*, 'ɬænvaɪər kɪl'gedɪn, ɬlánvīr kilgéddin

Llanfair Mathafarn Eithaf *Gwynedd*, 'ɬænvaɪər məθ'æfərn 'aɪθæv, ɬlánvīr mätháffaarn íthav

Llanfair Nant-y-gof *Dyfed*, 'ɬænvaɪər ,næntə'gouv, ɬlánvīr nant-ä-góv

Llanfair Pwllgwyngyll *Gwynedd*, 'ɬænvaɪər puɬ'gwɪngɪɬ, ɬlánvīr poohl-gwin-gihl. *The accepted abbreviation is* Llanfair P.G. *At the other end of the scale, however, it is traditionally the longest Welsh place name, and, as such, it appears at the bottom of this page.*

Llanfair Talhaiarn *Clwyd*, 'ɬænvaɪər tæl'haɪərn, ɬlánvīr tal-hí-ärn

Llanfair Waterdine, Baron Hunt of, 'ɬænvaɪər 'wɒtərdaɪn, ɬlánvīr wáwtérdīn

Llanfairynghornwy *Gwynedd*, ,ɬænvaɪərəŋ'hɔrnuɪ, ɬlanvīr-ŭng-hórnōō-i

Llanfallteg *Dyfed*, ɬæn'væɬteg, ɬlanváɬteg

Llan-fawr *Gwynedd*, ɬæn'vauər, ɬlanvówr

Llanfechain *Powys*, ɬæn'vexaɪn, ɬlanvéchīn

Llanfechan *Powys*, ɬæn'vexən, ɬlanvéchän

Llanfechell *Gwynedd*, ɬæn'vexeɬ, ɬlanvéchehl

Llanfeigan *Powys*, ɬæn'vaɪgən, ɬlan-vígän

Llanferres *Clwyd*, ɬæn'veres, ɬlanvérress

Llan-ffwyst, *also known as* Llanfoist *q.v.*, *Gwent*, ɬæn'fuɪst, ɬlanfōō-ist

Llanfigael, *also spelt* Llanfigel *q.v.*, *Gwynedd*, ɬæn'vigaɪl, ɬlanveégïl

Llanfair-pwllgwyngyll-gogerychwyrndrobwll-llandysilio-gogogoch *Gwyn* 'ɬænvaɪərpuɬ'gwɪngɪɬgou'gerə'xwərn'droubuɬɬændə'sɪliougougou'goux, ɬlánvīr-poohl-gwin-gihl-gō-gérrä-chwírn-dróboohl-ɬlandŭssílli-ō-gōgōgóç *See* Llanfair Pwllgwyngyll *above*.

Llanfigel, *also spelt* **Llanfigael** *q.v.,* *Gwynedd,* ˌɬæn'vɪgel, hlanvíggel

Llanfihangel *Powys,* ˌɬænvɪ'hæŋəl, hlanvi-háng-ĕl

Llanfihangel Abercywyn *Dyfed,* ˌɬænvɪ'hæŋəl ˌæbər'kauɪn, hlanvi-háng-ĕl abbĕrkáuwín

Llanfihangel-ar-arth *Dyfed,* ˌɬænvɪ'hæŋəl ɑr 'ɑrθ, hlanvi--háng-ĕl-aar-áarth

Llanfihangel Cwm Du *Powys,* ˌɬænvɪ'hæŋəl kʊm 'di, hlanvi--háng-ĕl kōŏm deé

Llanfihangel Esceifiog *Gwynedd,* ˌɬænvɪ'hæŋəl es'kaɪvjɒg, hlanvi--háng-ĕl eskív-yog

Llanfihangel Fechan *Powys,* ˌɬænvɪ'hæŋəl 'vexən, hlanvi--háng-ĕl véchăn

Llanfihangel Glyn Myfyr *Clwyd,* ˌɬænvɪ'hæŋəl glin 'mʌvər, hlanvi-háng-ĕl glin múvvĕr

Llanfihangel Nant Brân *Powys,* ˌɬænvɪ'hæŋəl nænt 'brɑn, hlanvi-háng-ĕl nant brá'an

Llanfihangel Tal-y-llyn *Powys,* ˌɬænvɪ'hæŋəl ˌtælə'ɬɪn, hlanvi--háng-ĕl tal-ă-hlín

Llanfihangel-y-fedw *Gwent,* ˌɬænvɪ'hæŋəl ə 'vedu, hlanvi--háng-ĕl ă véddoo. *Welsh name for* **Michaelston-y-Vedw,** *q.v.*

Llanfihangel Ystrad *Dyfed,* ˌɬænvɪ'hæŋəl ˌʌstrad, hlanvi--háng-ĕl ústrăd

Llanfilo *Powys,* ɬæn'vɪloʊ, hlan-villō

Llanfoist, *also known as* **Llan--ffwyst** *q.v.,* *Gwent,* ɬæn'vɔɪst, hlanvóysst

Llanfrechfa *Gwent,* ɬæn'vrexvə, hlanvréchvǎ

Llanfrothen *Gwynedd,* ɬæn'vrɒθən, hlanvróthĕn

Llanfrynach *Powys,* ɬæn'vrʌnəx, hlanvrúnnǎch

Llanfwrog *Clwyd, Gwynedd,* ɬæn-'vʊərɒg, hlanvōŏrog

Llanfyllin *Powys,* ɬæn'vʌɬɪn, hlan-vúhlin

Llanfynydd *Clwyd, Dyfed,* ɬæn-'vʌnɪð, hlanvúnnith

Llanfyrnach *Powys,* ɬæn'vɜrnəx, hlanvúrnǎch

Llangadfan *Powys,* ɬæn'gædvən, hlan-gádvǎn

Llangadog *Dyfed,* ɬæn'gædɒg, hlan-gáddog

Llangadwaladr *Clwyd, Gwynedd,* ˌɬængæd'wælədər, hlan-gadwá-lădĕr

Llangaffo *Gwynedd,* ɬæn'gæfoʊ, hlan-gáffō

Llangammarch Wells *Powys,* ɬæn'gæmɑrx 'welz, hlan-gám-maarch wéllz

Llanganten *Powys,* ɬæn'gæntən, hlan-gántĕn

Llangar *Clwyd,* 'ɬæŋgər, hláng--găr

Llangathen *Dyfed,* ɬæn'gæθən, hlan-gáthĕn

Llangattock, *Barony of,* ɬæŋ-'gætək, lang-gáttŏk

Llangattock *Powys,* ɬæn'gætɒk, hlan-gáttock

Llangedwyn *Clwyd,* ɬæn'gedwin, hlan-gédwin

Llangefni *Gwynedd,* ɬæn'gevnɪ, hlan-gévni

Llangeinor *Mid Glam.,* ɬæn'gaɪnɔr, hlan-gínor

Llangeinwen *Gwynedd,* ɬæn'gaɪn-wen, hlan-gín-wen

Llangeitho *Dyfed,* ɬæn'gaɪθoʊ, hlan-gíthō

Llangeler *Dyfed,* ɬæn'gelər, hlan--géllĕr

Llangelynin *Gwynedd,* ˌɬæŋgɪ-'lʌnɪn, hlan-gĕlúnnin. *Appro--priate for both places of the name in Gwynedd.*

Llangendeirne, *also spelt* **Llangen-deyrn,** *Dyfed,* ˌɬæŋgən'daɪərn, hlan-gĕndírn

Llangennech *Dyfed,* ɬæn'genəx, hlan-génnĕch

Llangenny *Powys,* ɬæn'genɪ, hlan-génni

Llangernyw *Clwyd,* ɬæn'gɜərnju, hlan-gäirnew

Llangian *Gwynedd,* ɬæn'gɪən, hlan-gee-ăn

Llangibby *Gwent,* ɬæn'gɪbɪ, hlan--gíbbi

Llanginning, *now* **Llangynin** *q.v.,* *Dyfed,* ɬæn'gɪnɪŋ, hlan-gínning

Llangiwg *W. Glam.,* ɬæn'gjuk, hlan-géwk

Llanglydwen *Dyfed,* ɬæn'glɪdwen, hlan-glíd-wen

Llangoed *Gwynedd,* 'ɬæŋgɔɪd, hláng-goyd

Llangoedmor *Dyfed,* ɬæn'gɔɪdmɔr, hlan-góydmor; ɬæn'gɔɪtmɔr, hlan-góytmor

Llangollen *Clwyd,* ɬæn'gɒɬən, hlan-góhlĕn

Llangorse *Powys,* ɬæn'gɔrs, hlan--górss

Llangower, *also spelt* **Llangywer, Llangywair,** *Gwynedd,* ɬæn-'gauər, hlan-gówĕr

Llangranog *Dyfed,* ɬæn'grænɒg, hlan-gránnog

Llangristiolus *Gwynedd,* ˌɬæn-grɪstɪ'ɒlɪs, hlan-grissti-ólliss

Llangrwyn, *also spelt* **Llangrwyney** *q.v., Powys,* ɫæn'gruɪn, hlan-
-groo-in

Llangrwyney *also spelt* **Llangrwyn,** *q.v., Powys,* ɫæn'gruɪneɪ, hlan-groo'-inay

Llangua *Gwent,* ɫæn'giə, hlan-gée-ä

Llangunllo *Powys,* ɫæn'gʌnɫou, hlan-gún-hlō

Llangunnock *Dyfed,* ɫæn'gʌnɒk, hlan-gúnnock

Llangunnor *Dyfed,* ɫæn'gʌnɔr, hlan-gúnnor

Llangurig *Powys,* ɫæn'gɪrɪg, hlan-gírrig

Llangwm *Clwyd, Dyfed,* 'ɫæŋgʊm, hláng-gōōm

Llan-gwm *Gwent,* ɫæn'gʊm, hlan-gōōm

Llangwnnadl *Gwynedd,* ɫæn-'gʊnædl, hlan-gōōn-addl

Llangwstenin *Gwynedd,* ˌɫæŋgʊst-'enɪn, hlan-gōōsténnin

Llangwyfan *Clwyd,* ɫæn'guɪvən, hlan-goo-ivän

Llangwyllog *Gwynedd,* ɫæn-'guɪɫɒg, hlan-gwíhlog

Llangwyryfon *Dyfed,* ˌɫæŋgwɪər-'ʌvən, hlan-gweerúvvŏn

Llangybi *Dyfed, Gwent, Gwynedd,* ɫæn'gʌbɪ, hlan-gúbbi

Llangyfelach *W. Glam.,* ˌɫæŋgə-'veləx, hlan-gǔ-vélläch

Llangynhafal *Clwyd,* ˌɫæŋgʌn-'hævəl, hlan-gun-hávväl

Llangynidr *Powys,* ɫæn'gʌnɪdər, hlan-gúnnidĕr

Llangyniew *Powys,* ɫæn'gʌnju, hlan-gúnnew

Llangynin, *formerly* **Llanginning** *q.v., Dyfed,* ɫæn'gʌnɪn, hlan--gúnnin

Llangynog *Dyfed, Powys,* ɫæn-'gʌnɒg, hlan-gúnnog

Llangynwyd *Mid Glam.,* ɫæn-'gʌnʊɪd, hlan-gúnnōō-id

Llangywair *see* **Llangower**

Llangywer *see* **Llangower**

Llanhamlach *Powys,* ɫæn'hæmlæx, hlan-hám-lach

Llanharan *Mid Glam.,* ɫæn'hærən, hlan-hárrän

Llanharry *Mid Glam.,* ɫæn'hærɪ, hlan-hárri

Llanhilleth *Gwent,* ɫæn'hɪləθ, hlan-hílléth

Llanhowell *Dyfed,* ɫæn'haʊəl, hlan-hówĕl

Llanidan *Gwynedd,* ɫæn'idən, hlaneédän

Llanidloes *Powys,* ɫæn'ɪdlɔɪs, hlanídloyss

Llaniestyn *Gwynedd,* ɫæn'jestɪn, hlan-yésstin

Llanigon *Powys,* ɫæn'aɪgən, hlanígŏn

Llanilar *Dyfed,* ɫæn'ilɑr, hlaneé-laar

Llanion *Dyfed,* 'ɫænjən, lán-yŏn

Llanishen *Gwent, S. Glam.,* ɫæn'ɪʃən, lanishĕn

Llanllawddog *Dyfed,* ɫæn'ɫaʊðɒg, hlan-hlów-thog

Llanllechid *Gwynedd,* ɫæn'ɫexɪd, hlan-hléchid

Llanlleonfel *Powys,* ˌɫænɫeɪ'ɒnvel, hlan-hlay-ónvel

Llanllowel *Gwent,* ɫæn'ɫaʊəl, hlan-hlówĕl

Llanllugan *Powys,* ɫæn'ɫɪgən, hlan-hlíggän

Llanllwchaiarn *Powys,* ˌɫænɫux-'haɪərn, hlan-hlooch-hí-ärn

Llanllwni *Dyfed,* ɫæn'ɫʊnɪ, hlan-hlōōni

Llanllyfni *Gwynedd,* ɫæn'ɫʌvnɪ, hlan-hlúvni

Llanmerewig *Powys,* ˌɫænme-'rewɪg, hlanmerré-wig

Llanmorlais *W. Glam.,* ɫæn'mɔr-laɪs, hlan-mórliss

Llannefydd *Clwyd,* ɫæn'evɪð, hlanévvith

Llan-non *Dyfed,* ɫæn'ɒn, hlanón

Llannor *Gwynedd,* 'ɫænɔr, hlánnor

Llanon *Dyfed,* ɫæn'ɒn, hlanón

Llanover *Gwent,* ɫæn'oʊvər, hlanóvĕr

Llanpumsaint, *formerly spelt* **Llanpumpsaint,** *Dyfed,* ɫæn-'pɪmsaɪnt, hlan-pímssīnt

Llanrhaeadr ym Mochnant *Clwyd,* ɫæn'hraɪədər ʌm 'mɒxnənt, hlanrí-ädĕr um móchnänt

Llanrhaeadr yng Nghinmerch, *formerly spelt* **Llanrhaiadr yn Cinmerch** *q.v., Clwyd,* ɫæn-'hraɪədər ʌŋ 'hɪnmeɪərx, hlanrí-ädĕr ung hínmay-ĕrch

Llanrhaiadr yn Cinmerch, *former spelling of* **Llanrhaeadr yng Nghinmerch** *q.v., Clwyd,* ɫæn'hraɪədər ʌŋ 'kʌmərx, hlanrí-ädĕr ung kúmmĕrch

Llanrhidian *W. Glam.,* ɫæn-'hrɪdjən, hlan-ríd-yän

Llanrhychwyn *Gwynedd,* ɫæn-'hrʌxwɪn, hlanrúchwin

Llanrhyddlad *Gwynedd,* ɫæn-'hrɪðlæd, hlanríthlad

Llanrhystyd, *also spelt* **Llanrhy-stud,** *Dyfed,* ɫæn'hrʌstɪd, hlanrússtid

Llanrug *Gwynedd,* ɫæn'rɪg, hlanreég

Llanrwst *Gwynedd,* ɫæn'rust, hlanro'ost

Llansadwrn *Dyfed, Gwynedd,* ɫæn'sæduərn, hlan-sáddōōrn

Llansaint *Dyfed*, ˈɬænˈsaɪnt, <u>hlán</u>-sɪ́nt

Llansamlet *W. Glam.*, ɬænˈsæmlɪt, <u>hl</u>an-sámlĕt

Llansantffraid *Powys*, ɬænsæntˈfraɪd, <u>hl</u>an-santfrı́d

Llansantffraid-ym-Mechain *Powys*, ɬænsæntˈfraɪd ʌm ˈmexaɪn, <u>hl</u>an-santfrı́d um méch<u>ī</u>n

Llansawel *Dyfed*, ɬænˈsaʊəl, <u>hl</u>an-sówĕl

Llansilin *Clwyd*, ɬænˈsɪlɪn, <u>hl</u>an-síllin

Llanspyddid *Powys*, ɬænˈspʌdɪd, <u>hl</u>an-spúthid

Llanstadwell *Dyfed*, ɬænˈstædwel, <u>hl</u>an-stád-wel

Llanstephan *Powys*, ɬænˈstefən, <u>hl</u>an-stéffán

Llantarnam *Gwent*, ɬænˈtɑrnəm, <u>hl</u>antaárnăm

Llanthony *Gwent*, ɬænˈtoʊnɪ, <u>hl</u>antŏ́nī

Llantilio Crossenny *Gwent*, ɬænˈtɪljoʊ krɒˈsenɪ, <u>hl</u>antíl-yŏ krossénni

Llantood *Dyfed*, ˈlæntʊd, lántood

Llantrisaint Fawr, *also spelt* **Llantrissent Fawr**, *Gwent*, ɬænˈtrɪsənt ˈvaʊər, <u>hl</u>antríssănt vówr

Llantrisant *Gwent, Gwynedd, Mid Glam.*, ɬænˈtrɪsənt, <u>hl</u>antríssănt

Llantrissent Fawr *see* **Llantrisaint Fawr**

Llantrithyd *S. Glam.*, ɬænˈtrɪθɪd, <u>hl</u>antríthid

Llantwit Fardre *Mid Glam.*, ˈɬæntwɪt ˈvɑrdreɪ, <u>hl</u>ántwit vaárdray

Llantwit Major *S. Glam.*, ˈlæntwɪt ˈmeɪdʒər, lántwit máyjŏr

Llantysilio *Clwyd*, ɬæntəˈsɪljoʊ, <u>hl</u>antŭssíl-yŏ

Llanuwchllyn *Gwynedd*, ɬænˈjuxlɪn, <u>hl</u>anéwchlin

Llanvaches *Gwent*, ɬænˈvæxɪs, <u>hl</u>anváchĕss

Llanvair Discoed *Gwent*, ˈɬænvaɪər ˈdɪskɔɪd, <u>hl</u>ánvīr dísskoyd

Llanvetherine *Gwent*, ɬænˈveθrɪn, <u>hl</u>anvéthrin. *The Welsh form is* **Llanwytherin**, *q.v.*

Llanvihangel Crucorney *Gwent*, ˌɬænvɪˈhæŋəl krʊˈkɔrnɪ, <u>hl</u>anvi-háng-ĕl krŏŏkórni

Llanwarne *H. & W.*, ɬænˈwɔrn, <u>hl</u>an-wáwrn

Llanwddyn *Powys*, ɬænˈʊðɪn, <u>hl</u>anŏŏthin

Llanwenarth *Gwent*, ɬænˈwenɑrθ, <u>hl</u>anwénnaarth

Llanwenllwyfo *Gwynedd*, ɬænwɪnˈɬʊɪvoʊ, <u>hl</u>anwĕn-<u>hl</u>ŏŏ-ivŏ

Llanwenog *Dyfed*, ɬænˈwenɒg, <u>hl</u>an-wénnog

Llanwern *Gwent*, ɬænˈwɛərn, <u>hl</u>an-waírn

Llanwinio *Dyfed*, ɬænˈwɪnjoʊ, <u>hl</u>an-wín-yŏ

Llanwnda *Dyfed, Gwynedd*, ɬænˈʊndə, <u>hl</u>anŏŏndá

Llanwnen *Dyfed*, ɬænˈʊnən, <u>hl</u>anŏŏnĕn

Llanwnog *Powys*, ɬænˈʊnɒg, <u>hl</u>anŏŏnog

Llanwonno *Mid Glam.*, ɬænˈwʌnoʊ, <u>hl</u>an-wúnnŏ

Llanwrda *Dyfed*, ɬænˈʊərdə, <u>hl</u>anŏŏrdá

Llanwrin *Powys*, ɬænˈʊərɪn, <u>hl</u>anŏŏrin

Llanwrthwl *Powys*, ɬænˈʊərθʊl, <u>hl</u>anŏŏrthŏŏl

Llanwrtyd *Powys*, ɬænˈʊərtɪd, <u>hl</u>anŏŏrtid

Llanwyddelan *Powys*, ɬænwɪˈðelən, <u>hl</u>anwi-ˈðelan

Llanwytherin *Gwent*, ɬænwɪˈθerɪn, <u>hl</u>anwithérrin. *The English form is* **Llanvetherine**, *q.v.*

Llanyblodwell *Salop*, ɬænəˈblɒdwəl, <u>hl</u>anăblódwĕl

Llanybri *Dyfed*, ɬænəˈbri, <u>hl</u>annăbrée

Llanybyther *Dyfed*, ɬænəˈbʌðər, <u>hl</u>anăbúthĕr

Llan-y-cefn *Dyfed*, ɬænəˈkevn, <u>hl</u>anăkévvn

Llanychâr *Dyfed*, ɬænəˈxɑr, <u>hl</u>anăchaár

Llanychllwydog *Dyfed*, ɬænəxˈɬʊɪdɒg, <u>hl</u>an<u>ch</u>-<u>hl</u>ŏŏ-idog

Llanycil *Gwynedd*, ɬænˈʌkɪl, <u>hl</u>anúckil

Llan-y-crwys *Dyfed*, ɬænəˈkrʊɪs, <u>hl</u>anăkrŏŏ-iss

Llanymawddwy *Gwynedd*, ɬænəˈmaʊðʊɪ, <u>hl</u>anămówth<u>oo</u>-i

Llanymynech *Powys*, ɬænəˈmʌnɪx, <u>hl</u>anămúnn<u>ĕch</u>; , ɬænəˈmʌnex, <u>hl</u>anămúnnech

Llanynghenedl *Gwynedd*, ɬænəŋˈhenɪdl, <u>hl</u>anŭng-hénnĕdl

Llanynis *Clwyd*, ɬænˈʌnɪs, <u>hl</u>anúnniss

Llanynys Rhewl *Clwyd*, ɬænˈʌnɪs hreˈul, <u>hl</u>anúnniss re-oól

Llanyrafon *Gwent*, ɬænərˈævən, <u>hl</u>anărávvŏn

Llanyre *Powys*, ɬænˈɪər, <u>hl</u>anéer; ɬænˈaɪər, <u>hl</u>anír

Llanystumdwy *Gwynedd*, ɬænəˈstɪmdʊɪ, <u>hl</u>anăstímdŏŏ-i

Llawhaden *Dyfed*, ɬaʊˈhædən, <u>hl</u>ow-háddĕn

Llawryglyn *Powys*, ɬaʊərəˈglɪn, <u>hl</u>owr-áglín

Llay see **Llai**

Llechryd *Mid Glam.*,'ɬexrɪd, hléchrid

Llechylched *Gwynedd*,ɬeɪ'xʌlxɪd, hlaychúlchĕd

Lletty Brongu *Mid Glam.*,'ɬetɪ 'brɒŋgɪ, hlétti bróng-gi

Llewellin, Barony of, lə'welɪn, lĕ-wéllin

Llewellyn,*f.n.*,ɬə'welɪn, hlĕ-wéllin; lə'welɪn, lĕ-wéllin; lʊ'elɪn, lōō-éllin

Llewelyn,*f.n.*,ɬə'welɪn, hlĕ-wéllin; lə'welɪn, lĕ-wéllin; lʊ'elɪn, lōō-éllin

Llewelyn-Davies of Hastoe, Baroness, lʊ'elɪn 'deɪvɪs əv 'hæstoʊ, lōō-éllin dáyviss ŏv hásstō

Lleyn Peninsula *Gwynedd*,ɬin, hleen

Llidiart-y-Waun *Powys*,'ɬɪdjɑrtə-'waɪn, hlídyaart-ă-wín

Lligwy see **Llugwy**

Llinos, *Welsh C.n.*,'ɬɪnɒs, hléenoss

Lliswerry *Gwent*,ɬis'werɪ, hleess-wérri

Llithfaen *Gwynedd*,'ɬiθvaɪn, hlíth-vīn

Lliwedd *Gwynedd*, 'ɬiweð, hlée-weth;'ɬuɪð, hlōō-ĕth

Llowes *Powys*,'ɬoʊɪs, hlṓ-ĕss

Lloyd,*f.n.*, lɔɪd, loyd. *Appropriate also for Baron* ~.

Lloyd George of Dwyfor, Earl, 'lɔɪd 'dʒɔrdʒ əv 'dʊɪvər, lóyd jórj ŏv dōō-i-vor

Lluest Wen *Mid Glam.*,'ɬiest 'wen, hlée-est wén

Llugwy, *also spelt* **Lligwy**, River, *Gwynedd*,'ɬigʊɪ, hléegōō-i

Llwchwr *W. Glam.*,'ɬuxʊər, hlóochōōr

Llwydcoed *Mid Glam.*,'ɬuɪdkɒd, hlṓō-idkod;'ɬuɪdkɔɪd, hlṓō-idkoyd

Llwydiarth *Powys*,'ɬuɪdjɑrθ, hlṓō-id-yaarth

Llwyncelyn *Dyfed*,,ɬuɪn'kelɪn, hlṓō-in-kéllin

Llwyngwril *Gwynedd*,,ɬuɪn'gʊərɪl, hlṓō-in-gōōril

Llwynhendy *Dyfed*,,ɬuɪn'hendɪ, hlṓō-in-héndi

Llwyn Madoc *Gwynedd*,,ɬuɪn 'mædɒk, hlṓō-in máddock

Llwyn-on Reservoir *Mid Glam.*, 'ɬuɪn'ɒn, hlṓō-in-ón

Llwynypia *Mid Glam.*,,ɬuɪnə'piə, hlṓō-in-ăpée-ă

Llyn Brianne *Dyfed–Powys*,ɬin brɪ'æneɪ, hlin bri-ánnay

Llyn Cau *Gwynedd*,ɬin 'kaɪ, hlin kí

Llyn Celyn *Gwynedd*,ɬin 'kelɪn, hlin kéllin

Llynclys *Salop*, 'lʌŋklɪs, lúnkliss;'ɬʌŋklɪs, hlúnkliss

Llyn Cwellyn *Gwynedd*,ɬin 'kwelɪn, hlin kwéhlin

Llyn Mymbyr *Gwynedd*,ɬin 'mʌmbər, hlin múmbĕr

Llyn Ogwen *Gwynedd*,ɬin 'ɒgwen, hlin ógwen

Llyn Padarn *Gwynedd*,ɬin 'pædərn, hlin páddărn

Llyn Safaddan *Powys*,,ɬin sə-'væðən, hlin săváthăn

Llyn Tegid *Gwynedd*,ɬin 'tegɪd, hlin téggid. *This is the Welsh name for* **Bala** *Lake*.

Llysfaen *Clwyd*,'ɬisvain, hlíssvīn

Llysfaen *Gwynedd*,ɬis'vain, hleessvīn

Llys-faen *S. Glam.*,ɬis'vain, hleess-vīn. *The English name is* **Lisvane**, *q.v.*

Llys-wen *Dyfed, Powys*,ɬis'wen, hleesswén

Llysworney *S. Glam.*, lɪz'wɜrnɪ, lizwúrni

Llys-y-frân *Dyfed*,,ɬisə'vran, hleessăvraan

Llywelyn,*f.n.*,ɬə'welɪn, hlĕ-wéllin

Llywelyn ap Gruffydd, *13th-c. Prince of Wales*,ɬə'welɪn æp 'grɪfið, hlĕ-wéllin ap gríffith

Loach,*f.n.*, loʊtʃ, lôtch

Loader,*f.n.*, 'loʊdər, lṓdĕr

Loads,*f.n.*, loʊdz, lṓdz

Loanhead *Lothian*, 'loʊn'hed, lón-héd

Loasby,*f.n.*, 'loʊzbɪ, lṓzbi

Lobjoit,*f.n.*, 'lɒbdʒɔɪt, lóbjoyt

Lobscombe Corner *Wilts.*, 'lɒbzkəm 'kɔrnər, lóbzkŏm kórnĕr

Loch, Baron, lɒx, loch

Lochaber *H'land*, lɒ'xabər, loch-aábĕr

Lochailort *H'land*, lɒ'xaɪlərt, lochílŏrt

Lochaline *H'land*, lɒ'xælɪn, lochá-lin

Lochalsh *H'land*, lɒ'xælʃ, lochálsh

Loch an Athain *Skye*, 'lɒx ən 'an, lóch ăn aán

Loch an Eilean *H'land*, 'lɒx ən 'ilan, lóch ăn eelăn

Lochboisdale *W. Isles*, lɒx-'bɔɪzdeɪl, lochbóyzdayl

Lochbuie *S'clyde*, lɒx'buɪ, lochbōō-i

Lochearnhead *Central*, lɒx'ɜrn-'hed, lochérn-héd

Lochee *Tayside*, lɒ'xi, lochée

Locheilside *H'land*, lɒ'xil'saɪd, locheél-síd

Locheport *W. Isles*, lɒx'ipɔrt, lochéeport
Lochgelly *Fife*, lɒx'gelɪ, lochgélli
Lochgilphead *S'clyde*, lɒx'gɪlphed, lochgilp-hed
Lochiel, *f.n.*, lɒ'xil, locheél
Lochinvar *D. & G.*, ˌlɒxɪn'vɑr, lochinvaár
Lochinver *H'land*, lɒ'xɪnvər, lochínvĕr
Lochlea *S'clyde*, 'lɒxlɪ, lóchli
Lochlee *Tayside*, lɒx'li, lochleé
Lochluichart *H'land*, lɒx'luɪxərt, lochloo-ichárt; lɒx'luxərt, lochloochárt
Lochmaben *D. & G.*, lɒx'meɪbən, lochmáybĕn
Lochmaddy *W. Isles*, lɒx'mædɪ, lochmáddi
Loch na Creitheach *Skye*, 'lɒx nə 'krihəx, lóch nǎ kreé-hǎch
Lochnagar *Grampian*, ˌlɒxnə'gɑr, lochnǎgaár
Loch nan Uamh *H'land*, 'lɒx nən 'uəv, lóch nǎn oó-ǎv
Loch of Lintrathen *Tayside*, 'lɒx əv lɪn'treɪðən, lóch ŏv lintráy-thĕn
Loch of the Lowes *Tayside*, 'lɒx əv ðə 'lauz, lóch ŏv thĕ lówz
Lochrane, *f.n.*, 'lɒxrən, lóchrăn; 'lɒkrən, lóckrăn
Lochranza *S'clyde*, lɒx'rænzə, loch-ránzǎ
Lochrutton *D. & G.*, lɒx'rʌtən, lochrúttŏn
Lochtreighead *H'land*, lɒx'trighed, lochtreég-hed
Lochwinnoch *S'clyde*, lɒx'wɪnəx, lochwinnŏch
Lochy, *Loch, H'land*, 'lɒxɪ, lóchi
Lockerbie *D. & G.*, 'lɒkərbɪ, lóckĕrbi
Lockhart, *f.n.*, 'lɒkərt, lóckărt; 'lɒkhɑrt, lóck-haart. *The first is appropriate for the family name*, **Bruce** ~.
Lockie, *f.n.*, 'lɒkɪ, lócki
Lockinge, *East and West, Oxon.*, 'lɒkɪndʒ, lóckinj
Lockspeiser, *f.n.*, 'lɒkspaɪzər, lóckspīzĕr
Lockyer, *f.n.*, 'lɒkjər, lóck-yĕr
Locock, *f.n.*, 'loukɒk, lókock
Loddiswell *Devon*, 'lɒdɪzwel, lóddizwel
Loddon, *River, Hants.*, 'lɒdən, lóddŏn
Lode *Cambs.*, loud, lōd
Loder, *f.n.*, 'loudər, lódĕr
Loe Bar, *also spelt* **Loo Bar**, *Cornwall*, 'lu 'bɑr, loó baár
Loeber, *f.n.*, 'loubər, lóbĕr
Loelia, *C.n.*, 'liliə, leéliă

Loewe, *f.n.*, lou, lō; 'louɪ, ló-i
Loewen, *f.n.*, 'louən, ló-ĕn
Lofthouse, *f.n.*, 'lɒfthaus, lóft-howss; 'lɒftəs, lóftüss
Loftus, *f.n.*, 'lɒftəs, lóftüss
Logan, *f.n.*, 'lougən, lógăn
Logie, *f.n.*, 'lougɪ, lógi
Logiealmond *Tayside*, ˌlougɪ-'amənd, lōgi-aámŏnd
Logie Coldstone *Grampian*, ˌlougɪ 'koulstən, lōgi kóllstŏn
Logierait *Tayside*, ˌlougə'reɪt, lōgĕráyt; ˌlougɪ'reɪt, lōgiráyt
Logue, *f.n.*, loug, lōg
Lohan, *f.n.*, lɒn, lawn
Lois, *C.n.*, 'louɪs, ló-iss
Loiseau, *f.n.*, 'lwazou, lwaázō
Loman, *f.n.*, 'loumən, lómăn
Lomas, *f.n.*, 'loumas, lómăss
Lombe, *f.n.*, loum, lōm
Lomond, *Loch, Central–S'clyde*, 'loumənd, lómŏnd
Londesborough, *Baron*, 'lɒndzbərə, lóndzbŭră
London, 'lʌndən, lúndŏn
London Colney *Herts.*, 'lʌndən 'kounɪ, lúndŏn kóni
Londonderry *Co. Derry*, ˌlʌndən-'derɪ, lundŏndérri; 'lʌndəndərɪ, lúndŏndĕri. *The second is appropriate for the Marquess of* ~.
Lonergan, *f.n.*, 'lɒnərgən, lónnĕrgăn
Longannet *Point Fife*, lɒŋ'ænɪt, long-ánnĕt
Longay *Skye*, 'lɒŋgeɪ, lóng-gay
Long Compton *Warwicks.*, 'lɒŋ 'kɒmptən, lóng kómptŏn
Longforgan *Tayside*, lɒŋ'fɔrgən, longfórgăn
Longformacus *Borders*, ˌlɒŋfər-'meɪkəs, long-fŏrmáyküss
Longhorsley *Northd.*, 'lɒŋ'hɔrslɪ, lóng-hórssli
Longhoughton *Northd.*, 'lɒŋ-'hautən, lóng-hówtŏn; 'lɒŋ-'houtən, lóng-hótŏn
Longleat *Wilts.*, 'lɒŋlit, lóng-leet
Longlevens *Glos.*, 'lɒŋ'levənz, lóng-lévvĕnz
Long Mynd *Salop*, 'lɒŋ mɪnd, lóng minnd
Longney *Glos.*, 'lɒŋnɪ, lóng-ni
Longnor *Staffs.*, 'lɒŋnər, lóng-nŏr
Longriggend *S'clyde*, 'lɒŋrɪg'end, lóng-rig-énd
Longsight *Gtr. M'chester*, 'lɒŋ-'saɪt, lóng-sīt
Longsleddale *Cumbria*, lɒŋ'slɪdl, long-slíddl
Longsowerby *Cumbria*, lɒŋ-'sauərbɪ, long-sówĕrbi
Longtown *Cumbria, H. & W.*, 'lɒŋtaun, lóngtown

Longuet, *f.n.*, 'lɒŋgɪt, lóng-gĕt

Lonie, *f.n.*, 'loʊnɪ, lṓni

Lonmay *Grampian*, lɒn'meɪ, lon-máy

Lon-y-Glyder *Gwynedd*, 'loʊn ə 'glɪdər, lón ă glíddĕr

Loo Bar *see* **Loe Bar**

Looe *Cornwall*, lu, loo

Loose *Kent*, luz, looz

Loosley Row *Bucks.*, 'luzlɪ 'roʊ, lóozli rṓ

Lopes, *f.n.*, 'loʊpəz, lṓpĕz

Loppert, *f.n.*, 'lɒpərt, lóppĕrt

Lorenz, *f.n.*, 'lɒrənz, lórrĕnz

Loretto School *Lothian*, lə'retoʊ, lŏréttṓ

Lorettonian, *one educated at* **Loretto** School, ˌlɒrɪ'toʊnɪən, lorrĕtṓniăn

Lorie, *f.n.*, 'lɒrɪ, lórri

Lorimer, *f.n.*, 'lɒrɪmər, lórrimĕr

Lorne, *C.n. and f.n.*, lɔrn, lorn

Lorne *S'clyde*, lɔrn, lorn. *Appropriate also for the Marquess of ~ and for the Firth of ~.*

Lorrimer, *f.n.*, 'lɒrɪmər, lórrimĕr

Loseley Park *Surrey*, 'loʊzlɪ 'park, lózli paárk

Losey, *f.n.*, 'loʊzɪ, lózi

Loshak, *f.n.*, 'loʊʃæk, ló-shack

Losinska, *f.n.*, lɒ'sɪnskə, lossínskă

Lossiemouth *Grampian*, ˌlɒsɪ-'maʊθ, lossimówth

Lostock Hall *Lancs.*, 'lɒstɒk 'hɔl, lósstock háwl

Lostwithiel *Cornwall*, lɒs'wɪθɪəl, losswithi-ĕl; lɒst'wɪθɪəl, losst-wíthi-ĕl

Lotery, *f.n.*, 'loʊtərɪ, lṓtĕri

Lothbury *City of London*, 'loʊθ-bərɪ, lṓthbŭri; 'lɒθbərɪ, lóthbŭri

Lothersdale *N. Yorks.*, 'lɒðərz-deɪl, lóthĕrzdayl

Lothian *Scottish region*, 'loʊðɪən, lṓthiăn. *Appropriate also for the Marquess of ~.*

Lothingland *Suffolk*, 'loʊðɪŋlænd, lṓthing-land

Lotterby, *f.n.*, 'lɒtərbɪ, lóttĕrbi

Louarch, *f.n.*, 'loʊərk, ló-ărk

Louch, *f.n.*, laʊtʃ, lowtch

Loudan, *f.n.*, 'laʊdən, lówdăn

Loudon, *f.n.*, 'laʊdən, lówdŏn

Loudoun, *f.n.*, 'laʊdən, lówdŏn

Loudoun Hill *S'clyde*, 'laʊdən, lówdŏn. *Appropriate also for the Countess of ~.*

Lough, *f.n.*, lʌf, luff; loʊ, lō; lɒx, loch

Loughans, *f.n.*, 'lʌfənz, lúffănz

Loughborough *Leics.*, 'lʌfbərə, lúffbŭră

Lough Bradan Forest *Co. Armagh*, lɒx 'brædən, loch bráddăn

Loughbrickland *Co. Down*, lɒx-'brɪklənd, loch-bríckländ

Lough Foyle *Cos. Donegal–Londonderry*, lɒx 'fɔɪl, loch fóyl

Loughgall *Co. Armagh*, lɒx'gɔl, lochgáwl

Loughgiel *Co. Antrim*, lɒx'gil, lochgéel

Loughlin, *f.n.*, 'lɒxlɪn, lóchlin; 'lɒklɪn, lócklin

Loughmuck *Co. Tyrone*, lɒx'mʌk, lochmúck

Lough Neagh *N. Ireland*, lɒx 'neɪ, loch náy

Loughor *W.Glam.*, 'lʌxər, lúchŏr

Loughor, River, *Dyfed*, 'lʌxər, lúchŏr

Loughran, *f.n.*, 'lɒxrən, lóchrăn

Loughrey, *f.n.*, 'lɒxrɪ, lóchri

Loughrigg *Cumbria*, 'lʌfrɪg, lúffrig

Loukes, *f.n.*, laʊks, lowks

Lound Hall *Notts.*, laʊnd, lownd

Lourie, *f.n.*, 'laʊərɪ, lówri

Lousada, *f.n.*, lu'sɑdə, loossaádă; lu'zɑdə, loozaádă

Lousley, *f.n.*, 'laʊzlɪ, lówzli

Louth, Baron, laʊð, lowth

Louth *Lincs.*, laʊθ, lowth

Loutit, *f.n.*, 'lutɪt, loótit

Louttit, *f.n.*, 'lutɪt, loótit

Lovat, Baron, 'lʌvət, lúvvăt

Lovejoy, *f.n.*, 'lʌvdʒɔɪ, lúvjoy

Lovelace, Earl of, 'lʌvleɪs, lúv-layss

Lovel and Holland, Baron, 'lʌvl ənd 'hɒlənd, lúvvl ănd hólländ

Lovell, *f.n.*, 'lʌvl, lúvvl

Lover, *Wilts.*, 'loʊvər, lóvĕr

Loveridge, *f.n.*, 'lʌvrɪdʒ, lúvrij

Lovett, *f.n.*, 'lʌvɪt, lúvvĕt

Loveys, *f.n.*, 'lʌvɪz, lúvviz

Lovibond, *f.n.*, 'lʌvɪbɒnd, lúvvibond

Lovill, *f.n.*, 'lʌvɪl, lúvvil

Low, *f.n.*, loʊ, lō

Lowater, *f.n.*, 'loʊətər, ló-ătĕr

Low Bradley *N. Yorks.*, 'loʊ 'brædlɪ, ló brádli

Lowbridge, *f.n.*, 'loʊbrɪdʒ, lóbrij

Lowbury, *f.n.*, 'loʊbərɪ, lóbŭri

Lowca *Cumbria*, 'laʊkə, lówkă

Low Coniscliffe *Durham*, 'loʊ 'kɒnɪsklɪf, ló kónniss-kliff

Lowdell, *f.n.*, laʊ'del, lowdéll

Lowden, *f.n.*, 'laʊdən, lówdĕn

Lowder, *f.n.*, 'laʊdər, lówdĕr

Lowdham *Notts., Suffolk*, 'laʊd-əm, lówdăm

Lowe, *f.n.*, loʊ, lō

Lowell, *f.n.*, 'loʊəl, ló-ĕl

Lowenthal, *f.n.*, 'loʊəntæl, ló-ĕntal

Lower, *f.n.*, 'loʊər, ló-ĕr

Lower Benefield *Northants.*, 'loʊər 'benıfild, lṓ-ĕr bénnifeeld
Lower Halstow *Kent*, 'loʊər 'hælstoʊ, lṓ-ĕr hálsstō
Lower Heyford, *also sometimes called* **Heyford at Bridge**, *Oxon.*, 'loʊər 'heıfərd, lṓ-ĕr háyförd
Lower Shuckburgh *Warwicks.*, 'loʊər 'ʃʌkbərə, lṓ-ĕr shúck-bŭrā
Lower Slaughter *Glos.*, 'loʊər 'slɔtər, lṓ-ĕr sláwtĕr
Lower Wyche *H. & W.*, 'loʊər 'wıtʃ, lṓ-ĕr wítch
Lowes, *f.n.*, loʊz, lōz
Lowesby *Leics.*, 'loʊzbı, lṓzbi
Lowestoft *Suffolk*, 'loʊstɒft, lṓsstoft; 'loʊstaıft, lṓsstöft; 'loʊstəf, lṓsstöf
Loweswater *Cumbria*, 'loʊzwɔtər, lṓzwawtĕr
Lowick *Cumbria*, 'loʊık, lṓ-ick
Lowick *Northd.*, 'loʊık, lṓ-ick; 'laʊık, lówick
Low Ireby *Cumbria*, 'loʊ 'aıərbı, lṓ írbi
Lowis, *f.n.*, 'loʊıs, lṓ-iss; 'laʊıs, lówiss
Lowke, *f.n.*, loʊk, lōk
Lowles, *f.n.*, loʊlz, lṓlz; laʊlz, lowlz
Lown, *f.n.*, laʊn, lown
Lownie, *f.n.*, 'laʊnı, lówni
Lowry, *f.n.*, 'laʊərı, lówri
Lowson, *f.n.*, 'loʊsən, lṓssŏn
Lowther, *f.n.*, 'laʊðər, lówthĕr; 'loʊðər, lṓthĕr
Lowther *Cumbria*, 'laʊðər, lówthĕr
Lowthers, The, *D. & G.–S'clyde*, 'laʊðərz, lówthĕrz
Lowthian, *f.n.*, 'loʊðıən, lṓthiăn
Lowton *Gtr. M'chester*, 'loʊtən, lṓtŏn
Loydall, *f.n.*, 'lɔıdl, lóydl
Lozells *W. Midlands*, loʊ'zelz, lōzéllz
Luard, *f.n.*, 'luɑrd, lṓo-aard
Lubbock, *f.n.*, 'lʌbək, lúbbŏk
Lubenham *Leics.*, 'lʌbənəm, lúbbĕnăm
Lubnaig, Loch, *Central*, 'lubneıg, lṓob-nayg; 'lubnıg, lṓob-nig
Lucan, Earl of, 'lukən, lṓo-kăn
Lucas, *f.n.*, 'lukəs, lṓo-kăss
Lucasian, *pertaining to* **Lucas**, lu'keızıən, loo-káyziăn. *Appropriate for the* ~ *Chair of Mathematics, Univ. of Cambridge.*
Luccombe *Somerset*, 'lʌkəm, lúckŏm
Luce, *f.n.*, lus, looss

Luce Bay *D. & G.*, lus, looss
Luchford, *f.n.*, 'lʌtʃfərd, lútchförd
Lucie, *f.n.*, 'lusı, lṓossi
Lucken, *f.n.*, 'lʌkən, lúckĕn
Luckes, *f.n.*, 'lʌkıs, lúckĕss
Lucock, *f.n.*, 'lukɒk, lṓo-kock
Lucraft, *f.n.*, 'lukrɑft, lṓo-kraaft
Luddesdown *Kent*, 'lʌdzdaʊn, lúdzdown
Luder, *f.n.*, 'ludər, lṓodĕr
Ludgershall *Bucks.*, *Wilts.*, 'lʌdgərʃl, lúd-gĕr-shl; 'lʌgərʃl, lúggĕr-shl
Ludgvan *Cornwall*, 'lʌdʒən, lújjăn
Ludlow *Salop*, 'lʌdloʊ, lúdlō
Ludovic, *C.n.*, 'ludəvık, lṓodŏvick
Luetchford, *f.n.*, 'letʃfərd, létchförd
Luffness *Lothian*, lʌf'nes, luff-néss
Luffrum, *f.n.*, 'lʌfrəm, lúffrŭm
Lugar *S'clyde*, 'lugər, lṓogăr
Lugard, Barony of, lu'gɑrd, loo-gaárd
Lugard, *f.n.*, 'lugɑrd, lṓogaard
Luget, *f.n.*, lu'ʒeı, loozháy
Lugg, *f.n.*, lʌg, lug
Lugwardine *H. & W.*, 'lʌgwərdin, lúgwärdeen
Luing *S'clyde*, lıŋ, ling. *Appropriate also for the* ~ *breed of cattle.*
Luker, *f.n.*, 'lukər, lṓo-kĕr
Lulsgate *Avon*, 'lʌlzgeıt, lúllzgayt
Lumbis, *f.n.*, lʌmz, lummz
Lumley, *f.n.*, 'lʌmlı, lúmli
Lummis, *f.n.*, 'lʌmıs, lúmmiss
Lumphanan *Grampian*, ləm'fænən, lŭmfánnăn
Lumsden, *f.n.*, 'lʌmzdən, lúmzdĕn
Lunan, *f.n.*, 'lunən, lṓonăn
Lunan *Tayside*, 'lunən, lṓonăn
Luncarty *Tayside*, 'lʌŋkərtı, lúnkărti
Lund, *f.n.*, lʌnd, lund
Lundie, *f.n.*, 'lʌndı, lúndi
Lundy Island *Devon*, 'lʌndı, lúndi
Lune, *f.n.*, lun, loon
Lune, River, *Cumbria*, lun, loon
Lunghi, *f.n.*, 'lʌŋgı, lúng-gi
Lungley, *f.n.*, 'lʌŋlı, lúng-li
Lunnes, *f.n.*, 'lʌnıs, lúnnĕss
Lunt, *f.n.*, lʌnt, lunt
Lupino, *f.n.*, lu'pinoʊ, lṓopéenō
Lupton, *f.n.*, 'lʌptən, lúptŏn
Lurgan *Co. Armagh*, 'lɜrgən, lúrgăn. *Appropriate also for Baron* ~.

Lurgashall *W. Sussex*, 'lɜrgəʃl, lúrgă-shl

Lurie, *f.n.*, 'ljʊərɪ, lyŏŏri

Lurigethan *Co. Antrim*, ˌlʌrɪ'giən, lurrigée-ăn

Luscombe, *f.n.*, 'lʌskəm, lússkŏm

Lush, *f.n.*, lʌʃ, lush

Lusher, *f.n.*, 'lʌʃər, lúshĕr

Luskentyre *W. Isles*, 'lʌskəntaɪər, lúskĕntīr

Luss *S'clyde*, lʌs, luss

Lussa *S'clyde*, 'lʌsə, lússă

Lustgarten, *f.n.*, 'lʌstgɑrtən, lústgaartĕn

Lustleigh *Devon*, 'lʌstlɪ, lústlee

Lutener, *f.n.*, 'lʊtənər, lŏŏtĕnĕr

Luthrie *Fife*, 'lʌθrɪ, lúthri

Luton *Beds.*, 'lʌtən, lóotŏn

Lutterworth *Leics.*, 'lʌtərwərθ, lúttĕrwŏrth

Luttrell, *f.n.*, 'lʌtrəl, lúttrĕl

Lutwyche, *f.n.*, 'lʌtwɪtʃ, lútwitch

Luty, *f.n.*, 'lʌtɪ, lŏŏti

Lutyens, *f.n.*, 'lʌtjənz, lút-yĕnz. *Appropriate for Sir Edward ~, architect, and Elizabeth ~, composer.*

Luxon, *f.n.*, 'lʌksən, lúcksŏn

Luxulyan *Cornwall*, lʌk'sɪljən, lucksíl-yăn

Luya, *f.n.*, 'lujə, lŏŏ-yă

Lyall, *f.n.*, 'laɪəl, lí-ăl; laɪl, líl

Lybster *H'land*, 'laɪbstər, líbstĕr

Lyburn, *f.n.*, 'laɪbərn, líburn

Lycett, *f.n.*, 'laɪsɪt, líssĕt

Lydart *Gwent*, 'laɪdɑrt, lídărt

Lydd *Kent*, lɪd, lid

Lydden *Kent*, 'lɪdən, líddĕn

Lydekker, *f.n.*, lɪ'dekər, liddéckĕr; laɪ'dekər, līdéckĕr; 'laɪdekər, lídeckĕr

Lyden, *f.n.*, 'laɪdən, lídĕn

Lydford, *f.n.*, 'lɪdfərd, lídfŏrd

Lydgate *Gtr. M'chester*, 'lɪdgeɪt, lídgayt; 'lɪdgɪt, líd-git

Lydgate *W. Yorks.*, 'lɪdgɪt, líd-git; 'lɪgɪt, líggit

Lydiard Millicent *Wilts.*, 'lɪdɪərd 'mɪlɪsənt, líddi-ărd míllissĕnt

Lydiard Park *Wilts.*, 'lɪdɪərd 'pɑrk, líddiărd paárk

Lydiard Tregoze, *also spelt* **Tregoz**, *Wilts.*, 'lɪdɪərd trɪ'guːz, líddi-ărd trĕgóoz; 'lɪdɪərd trɪ'gouz, líddi-ărd trĕgóz. *But see* **St. John of ~**, *Baron.*

Lydiate *Lancs.*, 'lɪdɪət, líddiăt

Lydney *Glos.*, 'lɪdnɪ, líd-ni

Lydway *Wilts.*, 'laɪdweɪ, lídway

Lyell, *f.n.*, 'laɪəl, lí-ĕl. *Appropriate also for Baron ~.*

Lyford, *f.n.*, 'laɪfərd, lífŏrd

Lyford *Oxon.*, 'laɪfərd, lífŏrd

Lygoe, *f.n.*, 'laɪgou, lígō

Lygon, *f.n.*, 'lɪgən, líggŏn

Lyle, *f.n.*, laɪl, līl

Lyly, *f.n.*, 'lɪlɪ, lílli. *Usually associated also with John ~, 16th-c. dramatist and novelist.*

Lymbery, *f.n.*, 'lɪmbərɪ, límbĕri

Lyme Regis *Dorset*, 'laɪm 'riːdʒɪs, līm réejiss

Lyminge *Kent*, 'lɪmɪndʒ, límminj; 'laɪmɪndʒ, líminj

Lymington *Hants*, 'lɪmɪŋtən, límmingtŏn. *Appropriate also for Viscount ~.*

Lyminster *W. Sussex*, 'lɪmɪnstər, límminstĕr

Lymm *Ches.*, lɪm, lim

Lympany, Moura, *pianist*, 'lɪmpənɪ, mŏŏră límpăni

Lympne *Kent*, lɪm, lim

Lympstone *Devon*, 'lɪmpstən, límpstŏn

Lynas, *f.n.*, 'laɪnəs, línăss

Lynch, *f.n.*, lɪnʃ, linsh

Lynch-Blosse, *f.n.*, 'lɪntʃ 'blɒs, líntch blóss

Lyndon, *f.n.*, 'lɪndən, líndŏn

Lyne, *f.n.*, laɪn, līn

Lyneham *Wilts.*, 'laɪnəm, línăm

Lynemouth *Northd.*, 'laɪnmaʊθ, línmowth

Lynher, *River*, *Cornwall*, 'laɪnər, línĕr

Lynmouth *Devon*, 'lɪnməθ, lín-mŭth

Lynott, *f.n.*, 'laɪnət, línŏt

Lynturk *Grampian*, lɪn'tɜrk, lintúrk

Lyons, *f.n.*, 'laɪənz, lí-ŏnz

Lyonshall *H. & W.*, 'laɪənz'hɒl, lí-ŏnz-háwl

Lysaght, *f.n.*, 'laɪsət, líssăt; 'laɪsɑt, líssaat. *The first is appropriate for Baron Lisle's family name.*

Lysons, *f.n.*, 'laɪsənz, líssŏnz

Lyster, *f.n.*, 'lɪstər, lísstĕr

Lytchett Matravers *Dorset*, 'lɪtʃɪt mə'trævərz, lítchĕt mătrávvĕrz

Lyte, *f.n.*, laɪt, līt

Lyth, *f.n.*, laɪθ, līth

Lyth *H'land*, laɪθ, līth

Lythall, *f.n.*, 'laɪθl, líth-l

Lytham St. Annes *Lancs.*, 'lɪðəm snt 'ænz, líthăm sĭnt ánz

Lyttelton, *f.n.*, 'lɪtltən, líttltŏn

Lyttle, *f.n.*, 'lɪtl, líttl

Lyttleton, *f.n.*, 'lɪtltən, líttltŏn

Lytton, *Earl of*, 'lɪtən, líttŏn

Lyulph, *C.n.*, 'laɪʊlf, lí-ŭlf

Lyveden *Northants.*, 'lɪvdən, lívdĕn. *Appropriate also for Baron ~.*

Lywood, *f.n.*, 'laɪwʊd, lí-wŏŏd

M

Maas, *f.n.*, mɑz, maaz
Maaz, *f.n.*, mɑz, maaz
Mabane, *f.n.*, mə'beɪn, măbáyn
Mabayn, *f.n.*, mə'beɪn, măbáyn
Mabe *Cornwall*, meɪb, mayb
Mabel, *C.n.*, 'meɪbl, máybl
Maberly, *f.n.*, 'mæbərlɪ, mábběrli
Mabey, *f.n.*, 'meɪbɪ, máybi
Mably, *f.n.*, 'mæblɪ, mábli
Mabon, *f.n.*, 'mæbɒn, mábbon;
  'meɪbən, máybŏn. *The first is
  the Welsh pronunciation, the
  second the Scottish.*
Maby, *f.n.*, 'meɪbɪ, máybi
McAdam, *f.n.*, mə'kædəm, mă-
  káddăm
McAdden, *f.n.*, mə'kædən, mă-
  káddĕn
Macadie, *f.n.*, mə'kædɪ, măkáddi
Macafee, *f.n.*, 'mækəfɪ, máckăfee
McAleese, *f.n.*, ˌmækə'lis, mack-
  ăléess
McAlery, *f.n.*, ˌmækə'lɪərɪ, mack-
  ăléeri
McAlister, *f.n.*, mə'kælɪstər,
  măkálistĕr
McAllister, *f.n.*, mə'kælɪstər, mă-
  kálistĕr
McAloon, *f.n.*, ˌmækə'lun, mack-
  ăloón
Macalpine, *f.n.*, mə'kælpɪn,
  măkálpin; mə'kælpaɪn, mă-
  kálpīn
McAlpine, *f.n.*, mə'kælpɪn, mă-
  kálpin; mə'kælpaɪn, măkálpīn
Macan, *f.n.*, mə'kæn, măkán
McAnally, *f.n.*, ˌmækə'nælɪ,
  mackănáli
Macanaspie, *f.n.*, ˌmækə'næspɪ,
  mackănásspi
Macara, *f.n.*, mə'kɑrə, măka'ară;
  mə'kærə, măkárrä
McArdle, *f.n.*, mə'kɑrdl, măka'ardl
MacArthur, *f.n.*, mə'kɑrθər, mă-
  ka'arthŭr
McAslin, *f.n.*, mə'kɒzlɪn, măkáwz-
  lin
McAteer, *f.n.*, 'mækətɪər, máck-
  ăteer
McAuliffe, *f.n.*, mə'kɒlɪf, mă-
  káwliff
McAvoy, *f.n.*, 'mækəvɔɪ, máck-
  ăvoy
MacBain, *f.n.*, mək'beɪn, măkbáyn
McBean, *f.n.*, mək'beɪn, măk-
  báyn; mək'bin, măkbéen
MacBeath, *f.n.*, mək'beθ, măkbéth
MacBeth, *f.n.*, mək'beθ, măkbéth
McBirney, *f.n.*, mək'bɜrnɪ, măk-
  bírni

McBrain, *f.n.*, mək'breɪn, măk-
  bráyn
McBratney, *f.n.*, mək'brætnɪ,
  măkbrátni
MacBrayne, *f.n.*, mək'breɪn, măk-
  bráyn
McBrien, *f.n.*, mək'braɪən, măk-
  brí-ĕn
McBrinn, *f.n.*, mək'brɪn, măkbrín
McCabe, *f.n.*, mə'keɪb, măkáyb
McCahearty, *f.n.*, ˌmækə'hɑrtɪ,
  mackă-ha'arti
MacCaig, *f.n.*, mə'keɪg, măkáyg
McCaig, *f.n.*, mə'keɪg, măkáyg
McCaldin, *f.n.*, mə'kɒldɪn, mă-
  káwldin
McCall, *f.n.*, mə'kɒl, măkáwl
McCallin, *f.n.*, mə'kælɪn, măkálin
MacCallum, *f.n.*, mə'kæləm,
  măkálŭm
McCalmont, *f.n.*, mə'kælmənt,
  măkálmŏnt
McCammon, *f.n.*, mə'kæmən,
  măkámmŏn
McCance, *f.n.*, mə'kæns, măkánss
MacCandless, *f.n.*, mə'kændlɪs,
  măkándlĕss
McCann, *f.n.*, mə'kæn, măkán
McCarthy, *f.n.*, mə'kɑrθɪ, mă-
  ka'arthi
McCartney, *f.n.*, mə'kɑrtnɪ, mă-
  ka'artni
McCaughan, *f.n.*, mə'kæxən,
  măka̱chăn; mə'kɒn, măkáwn
McCaughey, *f.n.*, mə'kæxɪ, măka̱-
  chi; mə'kæhɪ, măkă-hi; mə-
  'kɒfɪ, măkóffi
McCheane, *f.n.*, mək't∫in, măk-
  -tchéen; mək't∫eɪn, măk-tcháyn
MacCheyne, *f.n.*, mək'∫eɪn, măk-
  -sháyn
McChlery, *f.n.*, mə'klɪərɪ, măk-
  léeri
McClatchie, *f.n.*, mə'klæt∫ɪ,
  măklátchi
MacClean, *f.n.*, mə'kleɪn, măkláyn; mə'klin, măkléen
McClenaghan, *f.n.*, mə'klenəxən,
  măklénă̱chăn
McClenahan, *f.n.*, mə'klenəhən,
  măklénăhăn
McClenaughan, *f.n.*, mə'klenəxən,
  măklénă̱chăn
Macclesfield *Ches.*, 'mæklzfɪld,
  mácklzfeeld
McClintock, *f.n.*, mə'klɪntɒk,
  măklíntock
McCloskey, *f.n.*, mə'klɒskɪ,
  măklóski
McCloughin, *f.n.*, mə'klʊɪn,
  măklŏŏ-in
McCloughry, *f.n.*, mə'klɒrɪ,
  măklórri
McCloy, *f.n.*, mə'klɔɪ, măklóy

Maccoby, *f.n.*, 'mækəbɪ, máckŏbi
MacColl, *f.n.*, mə'kɒl, mäkól
McComb, *f.n.*, mə'koʊm, mäkốm
McCombe, *f.n.*, mə'koʊm, mäkốm
McCombie, *f.n.*, mə'kɒmbɪ, mäkómbi
MacConachie, *f.n.*, mə'kɒnəxɪ, mäkónnăchi
McConachy, *f.n.*, mə'kɒnəxɪ, mäkónnăchi
McConaghy, *f.n.*, mə'kɒnəxɪ, mäkónnăchi
McConalogue, *f.n.*, mə'koʊnəloʊg, mäkốnălōg
McConnach, *f.n.*, mə'kɒnəx, mäkónnăch
McCormack, *f.n.*, mə'kɔrmək, mäkórmäk
McCorquodale, *f.n.*, mə'kɔrkədeɪl, mäkórkŏdayl
McCoubrey, *f.n.*, mə'kubrɪ, mäkoóbri
McCowen, *f.n.*, mə'kaʊən, mäkówĕn
McCracken, *f.n.*, mə'krækən, mäkráckĕn
McCrae, *f.n.*, mə'kreɪ, mäkráy
McCraw, *f.n.*, mə'krɔ, mäkráw
McCrea, *f.n.*, mə'kreɪ, mäkráy
McCreadie, *f.n.*, mə'kridɪ, mäkreédi; me'kredɪ, mäkréddi
McCready, *f.n.*, me'kridɪ, mäkreédi; me'kredɪ, mäkréddi
McCreechan, *f.n.*, mə'krixən, mäkreéchăn
McCrindle, *f.n.*, mə'krɪndl, mäkríndl
McCrirrick, *f.n.*, mə'krɪrɪk, mäkrírrik
McCrudden, *f.n.*, mə'krʌdən, mäkrúddĕn
MacCue, *f.n.*, mə'kju, mäkéw
McCue, *f.n.*, mə'kju, mäkéw
McCullagh, *f.n.*, mə'kʌlə, mäkúllä
McCulloch, *f.n.*, mə'kʌləx, mäkúllŏch; mə'kʌlək, mäkúllŏk
McCullough, *f.n.*, mə'kʌləx, mäkúllŏch
MacCunn, *f.n.*, mə'kʌn, mäkúnn
McCusker, *f.n.*, mə'kʌskər, mäkúskĕr
McCutcheon, *f.n.*, mə'kʌtʃən, mäkútchĕn
McDermid, *f.n.*, mək'dɜrmɪd, mäkdérmid
MacDermot, *f.n.*, mək'dɜrmət, mäkdérmŏt
McDiarmid, *f.n.*, mək'dɜrmɪd, mäkdérmid
McDona, *f.n.*, mək'dʌnə, mäkdúnnä; mək'dɒnə, mäkdónnä
McDonagh, *f.n.*, mək'dʌnə, mäkdúnnä; mək'dɒnə, mäkdónnä

Macdonald, *f.n.*, mək'dɒnld, mäkdónnld
Macdonald of Gwaenysgor, Baron, mək'dɒnld əv gwain-'ʌsgɔr, mäkdónnld ŏv gwīnússgor
Macdonell, *f.n.*, mək'dɒnl, mäkdónnl; ,mækdə'nel, macdŏnéll. *The second is appropriate for the author, A. G.* ~.
McDonell, *f.n.*, mək'dɒnl, mäkdónnl; ,mækdə'nel, mackdŏnéll
McDonnell, *f.n.*, mək'dɒnl, mäkdónnl; ,mækdə'nel, mackdŏnéll
McDonogh, *f.n.*, mək'dʌnə, mäkdúnnä; mək'dɒnə, mäkdónnä
McDonough, *f.n.*, mək'dʌnə, mäkdúnnä; mək'dɒnə, mäkdónnä
McDouall, *f.n.*, mək'duəl, mäkdoó-äl
McDougall, *f.n.*, mək'dugl, mäkdoógl
McDowall, *f.n.*, mək'daʊəl, mäkdówäl
McDowell, *f.n.*, mək'daʊəl, mäkdówĕl; mək'doʊəl, mäkdố-ĕl
MacDuff, *f.n.*, mək'dʌf, mäkdúff
Mace, *f.n.*, meɪs, mayss
McEacharn, *f.n.*, mə'kexərn, mäkéchärn; mə'kexrən, mäkéchrän; mə'kekrən, mäkéckrän
McEachern, *f.n.*, mə'kexərn, mäkéchĕrn; mə'kexrən, mäkéchrĕn; mə'kekrən, mäkéckrĕn
McEachran, *f.n.*, mə'kexrən, mäkéchrän
McEchern, *f.n.*, mə'kexərn, mäkéchĕrn; mə'kexrən, mäkéchrĕn
Macedo, *f.n.*, mə'sidoʊ, mässeédō
MacElderry, *f.n.*, 'mæklderɪ, mácklderri
McEldowney, *f.n.*, ,mækl'daʊnɪ, mackldównɪ; 'mækldaʊnɪ, máckldowni
McElhone, *f.n.*, 'mæklhoʊn, mácklhon
McElligott, *f.n.*, mə'kelɪgət, mäkélligŏt
McElroy, *f.n.*, 'mæklrɔɪ, mácklroy
McElveny, *f.n.*, mə'kelvənɪ, mäkéllvĕni
McEnaney, *f.n.*, ,mækə'nenɪ, mackĕnénni
McEneaney, *f.n.*, ,mækə'ninɪ, mackĕneéni
McEnery, *f.n.*, mə'kenərɪ, mäkénnĕri
McEnroe, *f.n.*, 'mækɪnroʊ, máckĕnrō
MacEntagart, *f.n.*, ,mækən'tægərt, mackĕntággärt
McEntee, *f.n.*, ,mækən'ti, mackĕntee; mə'kentɪ, mäkénti

MacEntegart, *f.n.*, ˌmækənˈtegərt, mackĕntéggärt; məˈkentəgɑrt, mäkéntĕgaart

MacEntegart, *f.n.*, ˌmækənˈtegərt, mackĕntéggärt

McEvedy, *f.n.*, məˈkevədɪ, mäkévvĕdi

McEvoy, *f.n.*, ˈmækɪvɔɪ, máckĕvoy

McEwen, *f.n.*, məˈkjuən, măkéwĕn

M'Ewen, *f.n.*, məˈkjuən, măkéwĕn

McFadyean, *f.n.*, məkˈfædjən, măkfád-yĕn

Macfadyen, *f.n.*, məkˈfædjən, măkfád-yĕn

McFadzean, *f.n.*, məkˈfædjən, măkfád-yĕn. *Appropriate also for Baron* ~.

MacFarlane, *f.n.*, məkˈfɑrlən, măkfaárlän

MacFarquhar, *f.n.*, məkˈfɑrkər, măkfaárkär

McFie, *f.n.*, məkˈfi, măkfée

Macfin *Co. Antrim*, mækˈfɪn, mackfín

McFinn, *f.n.*, məkˈfɪn, măkfín

McGahern, *f.n.*, məˈgæxərn, măgáchĕrn

McGahey, *f.n.*, məˈgæxɪ, măgáchi

McGaughey, *f.n.*, məˈgɔɪ, măgóy

MacGeach, *f.n.*, məˈgeɪ, măgáy

McGeagh, *f.n.*, məˈgeɪ, măgáy

MacGee, *f.n.*, məˈgi, măgeé

McGee, *f.n.*, məˈgi, măgeé

McGeechan, *f.n.*, məˈgixən, măgeéchän

McGeoch, *f.n.*, məˈgiəx, măgeé-ŏch

McGeough, *f.n.*, məˈgou, măgó

McGeown, *f.n.*, məˈgjoun, măgyón

MacGhee, *f.n.*, məˈgi, măgeé

McGhee, *f.n.*, məˈgi, măgeé

McGhie, *f.n.*, məˈgi, măgeé

MacGill, *f.n.*, məˈgɪl, măgíll

MacGillesheatheanaich, *f.n.*, mɑxˌgɪləˈhehənɪx, măch-gillĕ-hé-hăneech

McGillewie, *f.n.*, məˈgɪləwɪ, măgíllĕ-wi

McGillicuddy, *f.n.*, ˈmæglɪkʌdɪ, máglikuddi

McGilligan, *f.n.*, məˈgɪlɪgən, măgílligän

MacGillivray, Pittendrigh, *19th-c. poet*, ˈpɪtənˈdrɪx məˈgɪlɪvreɪ, píttĕndrích măgíllivray

McGillivray, *f.n.*, məˈgɪlɪvrɪ, măgíllivri; məˈgɪlvrɪ, măgílvri; məˈgɪlɪvreɪ, măgíllivray

McGimpsey, *f.n.*, məˈdʒɪmpsɪ, măjímpsi

McGinn, *f.n.*, məˈgɪn, măgínn

MacGladdery, *f.n.*, məˈglædərɪ, măgláddĕri

McGladdery, *f.n.*, məˈglædərɪ, măgláddĕri

MacGladery, *f.n.*, məˈglædərɪ, măgláddĕri

McGladery, *f.n.*, məˈglædərɪ, măgláddĕri

McGlashan, *f.n.*, məˈglæʃən, măgláshän

M'Glashan, *f.n.*, məˈglæʃən, măgláshän

McGlone, *f.n.*, məˈgloun, măglón

McGoffen, *f.n.*, məˈgɒfən, măgóffĕn

McGonagall, *f.n.*, məˈgɒnəgl, măgónnägl. *Appropriate for William* ~, *Scottish doggerel poet.*

McGonagle, *f.n.*, məˈgɒnəgl, măgónnägl

MacGonnigle, *f.n.*, məˈgɒnɪgl, măgónnigl

MacGoohan, *f.n.*, məˈguən, măgoó-än

McGoohan, *f.n.*, məˈguən, măgoó-än

McGougan, *f.n.*, məˈgugən, măgoögän

McGough, *f.n.*, məˈgɒf, măgóff

McGovern, *f.n.*, məˈgʌvərn, măgúvvĕrn

McGowan, *f.n.*, məˈgauən, măgówän

McGrady, *f.n.*, məˈgrædɪ, măgráddi

McGrath, *f.n.*, məˈgrɑ, măgraá; məˈgræθ, măgráth; məˈgrɑθ, măgraáth

McGredy, *f.n.*, məˈgridɪ, măgreédi

Macgregor, *f.n.*, məˈgregər, măgréggŏr

MacGregor, *f.n.*, məˈgregər, măgréggŏr

McGregor, *f.n.*, məˈgregər, măgréggŏr

M'Gregor, *f.n.*, məˈgregər, măgréggŏr

McGrigor, *f.n.*, məˈgregər, măgréggŏr; məˈgrɪgər, măgríggŏr. *The first is appropriate for the late Admiral Sir Rhoderick* ~.

McGroarty, *f.n.*, məˈgrɔrtɪ, măgrórti

McGrogan, *f.n.*, məˈgrougən, măgrógän

McGugan, *f.n.*, məˈgugən, măgoógän

McGuigan, *f.n.*, məˈgwɪgən, măgweégän; məˈgwɪgən, măgwiggän

McGuinness, *f.n.*, məˈgɪnɪs, măgínnĕss

McGuire, *f.n.*, məˈgwaɪər, măgwír

McHale, *f.n.*, məkˈheɪl, măk-háyl

Machansire and Polmont, Lord, 'mæxənʃaɪər ənd 'poʊlmɒnt, máchăn-shīr ănd pṓlmont

Machell, f.n., 'meɪtʃl, máytchl

Machen, f.n., 'meɪtʃɪn, máytchĕn; 'mæxɪn, máckĕn; 'mæxən, máchĕn. *The third is the Welsh pronunciation.*

Machen *Mid Glam.*, 'mæxən, máchĕn

Machent, f.n., 'meɪtʃənt, máytchĕnt

Machin, f.n., 'meɪtʃɪn, máytchin

Machlis, f.n., 'mæklɪs, máckliss

Machphelah *N. Yorks.*, mæk'pilə, mackpéelă

Machray, f.n., mə'kreɪ, măkráy

Machrihanish *S'clyde*, ˌmæxrɪ-'hænɪʃ, ma͟chri-hánnish

Machynlleth *Powys*, mə'xʌnɬəθ, má͟chún-hḻĕth

McIldowie, f.n., ˌmækɪl'duɪ, mackildoo-i; ˌmækɪl'daʊɪ, mackildów-i

MacIlhatton, f.n., ˌmækɪl'hætən, mackilháttŏn

McIlroy, f.n., 'mækɪlrɔɪ, máckil-roy; ˌmækɪl'rɔɪ, mackilróy

MacIlvenna, f.n., ˌmækɪl'venə, mackilvénnă

McIlwee, f.n., ˌmækl'wi, mackl-wée

MacIlwham, f.n., 'mækɪlʍwæm, máckil-wham

Macilwraith, f.n., 'mækɪlreɪθ, máckilrayth

McIlwraith, f.n., 'mækɪlreɪθ, máckilrayth

McInally, f.n., ˌmækɪ'næli, macki-náli

MacInerney, f.n., ˌmækɪ'nɜrnɪ, mackinérni

McInerny, f.n., ˌmækɪ'nɜrnɪ, mackinérni

MacInnes, f.n., mə'kɪnɪs, măkín-nĕss

McInroy, f.n., 'mækɪnrɔɪ, máckin-roy

McIntosh, f.n., 'mækɪntɒʃ, máck-intosh

Macintyre, f.n., 'mækɪntaɪər, máckintīr

MacIntyre, f.n., 'mækɪntaɪər, máckintīr

McIntyre, f.n., 'mækɪntaɪər, máckintīr

McInulty, f.n., ˌmækɪ'nʌltɪ, mackinúlti

McIver, f.n., mə'kaɪvər, măkívĕr; mə'kivər, măkéevĕr

McIvor, f.n., mə'kaɪvər, măkívŏr; mə'kivər, măkéevŏr

McKail, f.n., mə'keɪl, măkáyl

Mackarness, f.n., 'mækərnes, máckărness

McKarness, f.n., 'mækərnes, máckărness

Mackay, f.n., mə'kaɪ, măkí

McKay, f.n., mə'kaɪ, măkí; mə'keɪ, măkáy

McKeag, f.n., mə'kig, măkéeg; mə'keɪg, măkáyg

McKeague, f.n., mə'keɪg, măkáyg

M'Keague, f.n., mə'keɪg, măkáyg

McKean, f.n., mə'kin, măkéen

McKeand, f.n., mə'kind, mă-kéend; mə'kiənd, măkée-ănd

McKee, f.n., mə'ki, măkée

McKellar, f.n., mə'kelər, măkéllăr

McKelvey, f.n., mə'kelvɪ, măkélvi

Macken, f.n., 'mækɪn, máckĕn

Mackendrick, f.n., mə'kendrɪk, măkéndrick

MacKendrick, f.n., mə'kendrɪk, măkéndrick

McKenna, f.n., mə'kenə, măkénnă

Mackenzie, f.n., mə'kenzɪ, mă-kénzi

McKenzie, f.n., mə'kenzɪ, măkén-zi

Mackeown, f.n., mə'kjoʊn, mă-kyṓn

McKeown, f.n., mə'kjoʊn, mă-kyṓn

Mackereth, f.n., mə'kerəθ, mă-kérrĕth

McKernan, f.n., mə'kɜrnən, măkérnăn

McKerness, f.n., mə'kɜrnɪs, mă-kérnĕss

Mackeson, f.n., 'mækɪsən, máck-ĕssŏn

Mackesy, f.n., 'mækəsɪ, máckĕssi

Mackey, f.n., 'mækɪ, mácki

McKey, f.n., mə'ki, măkée

McKibbin, f.n., mə'kɪbɪn, măkíb-bin

Mackichan, f.n., mə'kixən, măkeechă̱n

Mackie, f.n., 'mækɪ, mácki

Mackie of Benshie, Baron, 'mækɪ əv 'benʃɪ, mácki ŏv bénshi

MacKie, f.n., mə'ki, măkée

McKie, f.n., mə'ki, măkée; mə'kaɪ, măkí. *The second is appropriate for Sir William ~, organist and one time Master of the Choristers at Westminster Abbey.*

McKinlay, f.n., mə'kɪnlɪ, măkínli

McKinnon, f.n., mə'kɪnən, măkín-nŏn

McKnight, f.n., mək'naɪt, măknít

Mackrell, f.n., mə'krel, măkréll

Mackrill, f.n., mə'krɪl, măkríll

Mackworth *Derby.*, 'mækwɜrθ, máckwurth

McLachlan, *f.n.*, mə'klɒxlən, măklŏchlăn; mə'klɒklən, măklŏcklăn
McLafferty, *f.n.*, mə'klæfərtɪ, măklắffĕrti
McLagan, *f.n.*, mə'klægən, măklăggăn
McLaine, *f.n.*, mə'kleɪn, măkláyn
Maclaren, *f.n.*, mə'klærən, măklárrĕn
MacLaren, *f.n.*, mə'klærən, măklárrĕn
McLarnon, *f.n.*, mə'klɑrnən, măklaárnŏn
McLauchlan, *f.n.*, mə'klɒxlən, măklŏchlăn; mə'klɒklən, măklŏcklăn
McLauchlin, *f.n.*, mə'klɒxlɪn, măklŏchlin; mə'klɒklɪn, măklŏcklin
McLaughlin, *f.n.*, mə'klɒxlɪn, măklŏchlin; mə'glɒxlɪn, măglŏchlin; mə'klɒklɪn, măklŏcklin
McLaurin, *f.n.*, mə'klɔrɪn, măkláwrin; mə'klɒrɪn, măklŏrrin
McLaverty, *f.n.*, mə'klævərtɪ, măklávvĕrti
Maclay, *f.n.*, mə'kleɪ, măkláy. *Appropriate also for Baron ~.*
McLay, *f.n.*, mə'kleɪ, măkláy
McLea, *f.n.*, mə'kleɪ, măkláy
Maclean, *f.n.*, mə'kleɪn, măkláyn; mə'klin, măkleén
McLean, *f.n.*, mə'kleɪn, măkláyn
McLear, *f.n.*, mə'kliər, măkleér
McLeavy, *f.n.*, mə'klivɪ, măkleévi
McLeay, *f.n.*, mə'kleɪ, măkláy
MacLehose, *f.n.*, 'mæklɪhoʊz, mácklĕhōz; 'mæklhoʊz, máckl-hōz
McLeish, *f.n.*, mə'kliʃ, măkleésh
McLelland, *f.n.*, mə'klelənd, măklélländ
Maclennan, *f.n.*, mə'klenən, măklénnăn
Macleod, *f.n.*, mə'klaʊd, măklówd
MacLeod, *f.n.*, mə'klaʊd, măklówd
Macleod of Borve, Baroness, mə'klaʊd əv 'bɔrv, măklówd ŏv bórv
MacLeod of Fuinary, Baron, mə'klaʊd əv 'fjunərɪ, măklówd ŏv féwnări
McLeod, *f.n.*, mə'klaʊd, măklówd
McLernon, *f.n.*, mə'klɑrnən, măklaárnŏn
McLevy, *f.n.*, mə'klivɪ, măkleévi
Maclise, *f.n.*, mə'klis, măkleéss
McLoughlin, *f.n.*, mə'klɒxlɪn, măklŏchlin
MacLucas, *f.n.*, mə'klukəs, măklóokăss

McLucas, *f.n.*, mə'klukəs, măklóokăss
MacLurg, *f.n.*, mə'klɜrg, măklúrg
McMahon, *f.n.*, mək'mɑn, măkmaán
Macmanaway, *f.n.*, mək'mænəweɪ, măkmánnăway
McManus, *f.n.*, mək'mænəs, măkmánnŭss; mək'mɑnəs, măkmaánŭss; mək'meɪnəs, măkmáynŭss
MacMath, *f.n.*, mək'mɑθ, măkmaáth
McMenemey, *f.n.*, mək'menəmɪ, măkménnĕmi
McMenemy, *f.n.*, mək'menəmɪ, măkménnĕmi
MacMillan, *f.n.*, mək'mɪlən, măkmíllăn
McMorrough, *f.n.*, mək'mɒroʊ, măkmórrō
McMullen, *f.n.*, mək'mʌlən, măkmúllĕn
MacMurdie, *f.n.*, mək'mɜrdɪ, măkmúrdi
McMynn, *f.n.*, mək'mɪn, măkmín
MacNab, *f.n.*, mək'næb, măk-náb
Macnaghten, Barony of, mək'nɒtən, măk-náwtĕn
McNaghton, *f.n.*, mək'nɒtən, măk-náwtŏn
McNall, *f.n.*, mək'nɒl, măk-náwl
Macnalty, *f.n.*, mək'nɒltɪ, măk-náwlti
Macnamara, *f.n.*, ˌmæknə'mɑrə, mack-nămaáră
McNamee, *f.n.*, ˌmæknə'mi, mack-námeé
McNaught, *f.n.*, mək'nɒt, măk-náwt
McNaughton, *f.n.*, mək'nɒtən, măk-náwtŏn
McNearney, *f.n.*, mək'nɜrnɪ, măk-nérni
MacNeice, *f.n.*, mək'nis, măk-neéss
McNeil, *f.n.*, mək'nil, măk-neél
MacNeilage, *f.n.*, mək'nilɪdʒ, măk-neélij
McNeill, *f.n.*, mək'nil, măk-neél
McNeillie, *f.n.*, mək'nilɪ, măk-neéli
McNichol, *f.n.*, mək'nɪkl, măk-níckl
McNiff, *f.n.*, mək'nɪf, măk-niff
MacNiven, *f.n.*, mək'nɪvən, măk-nívvĕn
Maconachie, *f.n.*, mə'kɒnəxɪ, măkónnăchi; mə'kɒnəkɪ, măkónnăki
Maconchy, Elizabeth, *composer*, mə'kɒŋkɪ, măkónki
Maconochie, *f.n.*, mə'kɒnəxɪ, măkónnŏchi; mə'kɒnəkɪ, măkónnŏki

Macosquin *Co. Derry*, məˈkɒskɪn, măkósskin
McOstrich, *f.n.*, məˈkɒstrɪtʃ, măkóstritch
McOuat, *f.n.*, məˈkauət, măkówăt
MacOwan, *f.n.*, məˈkouən, măkó-ăn
McPhail, *f.n.*, məkˈfeɪl, măkfáyl
MacPhee, *f.n.*, məkˈfi, măkfeé
McPherson, *f.n.*, məkˈfɜrsən, măkférssŏn
Macpherson of Drumochter, Baron, məkˈfɑrsən əv drəˈmɒxtər, măkférssŏn ŏv drŭmóchtĕr
McQuade, *f.n.*, məˈkweɪd, măkwáyd
McQuarrie, *f.n.*, məˈkwɒrɪ, măkwórri
McQuisten, *f.n.*, məˈkwɪstən, măkwísstĕn
McQuoid, *f.n.*, məˈkwɔɪd, măkwóyd
McQuown, *f.n.*, məˈkjuən, măkéwŏn
Macready, *f.n.*, məˈkriːdɪ, măkreédi. *Appropriate for William Charles ~, 19th-c. actor-manager.*
McReady, *f.n.*, məˈkriːdɪ, măkreédi; məˈkredɪ, măkréddi
McReay, *f.n.*, məˈkreɪ, măkráy
MacRobb, *f.n.*, məˈkrɒb, măkróbb
McRorie, *f.n.*, məˈkrɔrɪ, măkráwri
McRory, *f.n.*, məˈkrɔrɪ, măkráwri
McShane, *f.n.*, məkˈʃeɪn, măk-sháyn
McSwiney, *f.n.*, məkˈswɪnɪ, măksweéni; məkˈswɪnɪ, măkswínni
McTaggart, *f.n.*, məkˈtægərt, măktággărt
McVay, *f.n.*, məkˈveɪ, măkváy
MacVeagh, *f.n.*, məkˈveɪ, măkváy
McVean, *f.n.*, məkˈveɪn, măkváyn; məkˈvin, măkveén
McVeigh, *f.n.*, məkˈveɪ, măkváy
McVey, *f.n.*, məkˈveɪ, măkváy
McVicar, *f.n.*, məkˈvɪkər, măkvíckăr
McVie, *f.n.*, məkˈvi, măkveé
McVitie, *f.n.*, məkˈvɪtɪ, măkvítti
McVittie, *f.n.*, məkˈvɪtɪ, măkvítti
McWatters, *f.n.*, məkˈwɒtərz, măkwáwtĕrz
McWhirter, *f.n.*, məkˈhwɜrtər, măkwhírtĕr
MacWilliam, *f.n.*, məkˈwɪljəm, măkwíl-yăm
Madan, *f.n.*, ˈmædən, máddăn
Madden, *f.n.*, ˈmædən, máddĕn
Madderty *Tayside*, ˈmædərtɪ, máddĕrti
Madel, *f.n.*, məˈdel, mădéll
Madeley *Staffs.*, ˈmeɪdlɪ, máydli

Maden, *f.n.*, ˈmeɪdən, máydĕn
Madian, *f.n.*, ˈmeɪdɪən, máydi-ăn
Madin, *f.n.*, ˈmeɪdɪn, máydin
Madingley *Cambs.*, ˈmædɪŋlɪ, mádding-li
Madley *H. & W.*, ˈmædlɪ, mádli
Madoc, *f.n.*, ˈmædək, máddŏk
Madresfield *H. & W.*, ˈmædərz-fild, máddĕrzfeeld
Madron *Cornwall*, ˈmædrən, máddrŏn
Maeckelberghe, *f.n.*, məˈkelbɜrg, măkéllberg
Maegraith, *f.n.*, məˈgreɪθ, mă-gráyth
Maelor, Baron, ˈmaɪlɔr, mílor
Maenan *Gwynedd*, ˈmaɪnən, mínăn. *Appropriate also for the Barony of ~.*
Maenclochog *Dyfed*, maɪnˈklɒxɒg, mín-klóchog
Maendy *S. Glam.*, ˈmaɪndɪ, míndi
Maentwrog *Gwynedd*, maɪnˈtuərɒg, míntoórog
Maer *Cornwall, Staffs.*, mɛər, mair
Maer Rocks *Devon*, mɛər, mair
Maerdy *Clwyd*, ˈmɑrdɪ, maárdi; ˈmeɪər'dɪ, máyĕr-deé
Maerdy *Dyfed, Gwent*, ˈmɑrdɪ, maárdi
Maerdy *Mid Glam.*, ˈmɑrdɪ, maárdi; ˈmaɪərdɪ, mírdi
Maes-car *Powys*, maɪsˈkɑr, míss-kaár
Maesgeirchen *Gwynedd*, maɪs-ˈgaɪərxən, míssgírchĕn; maɪs-ˈgɛərxən, míssgaírchĕn
Maes-glas *Clwyd, Gwent*, maɪs-ˈglɑs, míssglaáss
Maesglasau *Powys*, maɪsˈglæsaɪ, míssglássi
Maeshowe Tumulus *Orkney*, meɪzˈhau, mayz-hów
Maes-llwch Castle *Powys*, maɪs-ˈɬux, míss-hloóch
Maesmynis *Powys*, maɪsˈmʌnɪs, míssmúnniss
Maesteg *Mid Glam.*, maɪsˈteɪg, místáyg
Maes-y-coed *Clwyd, Mid Glam.*, ˌmaɪsəˈkɔɪd, míss-ă-kóyd
Maesycrugiau *Dyfed*, ˌmaɪsə-ˈkrɪgaɪ, míssăkríg-yī
Maesycwmmer *Gwent*, ˌmaɪsə-ˈkumər, míssăkoómĕr
Maes-y-dderwen *W. Glam.*, ˌmaɪsəˈðɛərwen, míss-ă-tháirwen
Maes-y-dre *Clwyd*, ˌmaɪsəˈdreɪ, míss-ă-dráy
Magarshack, *f.n.*, ˈmægərʃæk, mággărshack
Magauran, *f.n.*, məˈgɔrən, mă-gáwrăn

Magdalen *Norfolk*, 'mægdələn, mágdälën
Magdalen College *Univ. of Oxford*, 'mɔdlɪn, máwdlën
Magdalene College *Univ. of Cambridge*, 'mɔdlɪn, máwdlën
Magee, *f.n.*, məˈgi, mágeé
Magennis, *f.n.*, məˈgenɪs, mǎgénniss
Mager, *f.n.*, 'meɪdʒər, máyjër; 'meɪgər, máygër
Maggs, *f.n.*, mægz, maggz
Maghaberry *Co. Antrim*, məˈgæbərɪ, mǎgábbëri
Maghera *Co. Derry, Co. Down*, ˌmæxəˈrɑ, machérȧa
Magherafelt *Co. Derry*, 'mæxərə-ˈfelt, machërȧfélt
Magheragall *Co. Antrim*, ˌmæxərəˈgɔl, machërȧgáwl
Magherahamlet *Co. Down*, ˌmæxərəˈhæmlɪt, machërȧ-hámlët
Magheralin *Co. Armagh–Co. Down*, ˌmæxərəˈlɪn, machërȧlín; ˌmærəˈlɪn, marrȧlín
Magherally *Co. Down*, ˌmæxəˈrælɪ, machërȧli
Magheramorne, Barony of, ˌmɑrəˈmɔrn, maarȧmórn
Magheramorne *Co. Antrim*, ˌmæxərəˈmɔrn, machërȧmórn
Magheraveely *Co. Fermanagh*, ˌmæxərəˈvilɪ, machërȧvéeli
Maghery *Co. Armagh*, 'mæxərɪ, máchëri
Maghull *Merseyside*, məˈgʌl, mǎgúll
Magill, *f.n.*, məˈgɪl, mǎgíll
Magilligan *Co. Derry*, məˈgɪlɪgən, mǎgílligȧn. *Appropriate also for ~ Strand.*
Maginess, *f.n.*, məˈgɪnɪs, mǎgínnëss
Maginnis, *f.n.*, məˈgɪnɪs, mǎgínniss
Magnac, *f.n.*, 'mænjæk, mán-yack
Magnay, *f.n.*, 'mægneɪ, mágnay; 'mægnɪ, mágni; mæg'neɪ, magnáy
Magniac, *f.n.*, 'mænjæk, mán-yack
Magnus, *C.n.*, 'mægnəs, mágnüss
Magnusson, *f.n.*, 'mægnəsən, mágnüssön
Magonet, *f.n.*, 'mægənet, mággönet
Magor *Gwent*, 'meɪgər, máygör
Magrath, *f.n.*, məˈgrɑ, mȧgráa
Magri, *f.n.*, 'mægrɪ, mággri
Maguire, *f.n.*, məˈgwaɪər, mȧgwír
Maguiresbridge *Co. Fermanagh*, məˈgwaɪərzˈbrɪdʒ, mȧgwírzbríj
Magwood, *f.n.*, 'mægwʊd, mágwŏŏd

Mahaddie, *f.n.*, məˈhædɪ, mȧháddi
Mahan, *f.n.*, mɑn, maan
Mahany, *f.n.*, 'mɑnɪ, maáni
Mahee Island *Co. Down*, məˈhi, mȧheé
Maher, *f.n.*, mɑr, maar; 'meɪər, máy-ër
Mahir, *f.n.*, 'meɪhər, máy-hër
Mahlowe, *f.n.*, 'mɑloʊ, maálō
Mahon, *f.n.*, mɑn, maan; 'mæhən, má-hŏn
Mahoney, *f.n.*, 'mɑənɪ, maá-ŏni; məˈhoʊnɪ, mȧhóni
Mahony, *f.n.*, 'mɑnɪ, maáni
Mahood, *f.n.*, məˈhʊd, mǎ-hŏŏd
Maia, *f.n.*, 'maɪə, mí-ȧ
Maidenmoor (Maiden Moor) Hill *Cumbria*, 'meɪdənˈmʊər, máydën mŏŏr
Maidstone *Kent*, 'meɪdstoʊn, máydstōn; 'meɪdstən, máydstŏn
Mailer, *f.n.*, 'meɪlər, máylër
Maillard, *f.n.*, 'meɪlɑrd, máylaard
Maina, *C.n.*, 'meɪnə, máynȧ
Maindee *Gwent*, 'meɪndɪ, máyndi
Maindy *S. Glam.*, 'meɪndɪ, máyndi; 'maɪndɪ, míndi
Maingot, *f.n.*, 'mængoʊ, máng-gō
Mainland Island *Shetland*, 'meɪnlænd, máynland
Mainwaring, *f.n.*, 'mænərɪŋ, mánnȧring; 'meɪnwɛərɪŋ, máynwairing. *The second is usual in Wales.*
Mair, *Welsh C.n.*, 'maɪər, mír
Mair, *f.n.*, mɛər, mair
Mairants, *f.n.*, 'mɛərənts, máirȧnts; məˈrænts, mërȧnts
Maire, *f.n.*, mɛər, mair
Mairet, *f.n.*, 'mɛərɪ, máiri
Mairhi, *C.n.*, 'mɑrɪ, maári
Mais, *f.n.*, meɪz, mayz. *Appropriate also for Baron ~.*
Maisel, *f.n.*, 'maɪzl, mízl; 'meɪzl, máyzl
Maisemore *Glos.*, 'meɪzmɔr, máyzmor
Maison, *f.n.*, 'meɪsən, máyssŏn
Maison Dieu Hall *Dover*, 'meɪzõ 'dju, máyzõngdéw; 'meɪzən 'dju, máyzŏn déw
Maitland, *f.n.*, 'meɪtlənd, máytländ
Majdalany, *f.n.*, ˌmædʒdəˈleɪnɪ, majdäláyni
Majendie, *f.n.*, 'mædʒəndɪ, májjëndi
Major, *f.n.*, 'meɪdʒər, máyjör
Makerstoun *Borders*, 'mækərstən, máckërstön
Makgill, *f.n.*, məˈgɪl, mǎgíll
Makins, *f.n.*, 'meɪkɪnz, máykinz
Makower, *f.n.*, məˈkaʊər, mǎkówër

Malahide, *f.n.,* 'mæləhaɪd, málă-
-hïd

Malan, *f.n.,* 'mælən, málăn;
məˈlɑn, măláan; məˈlæn,
mălán

Malbon, *f.n.,* 'mælbən, málbŏn

Malborough *Devon,* 'mɔlbərə,
máwlbŭră

Malcolm, *C.n. and f.n.,* 'mælkəm,
málkŏm; 'mɔlkəm, máwlkŏm

Malden, *f.n.,* 'mɔldən, máwldĕn

Malden *Surrey,* 'mɔldən, máwldĕn

Maldon *Essex,* 'mɔldən, máwldŏn

Maldwyn, *C.n.,* 'mældwɪn, máld-
win; 'mɔldwɪn, máwldwin. *The
first is the Welsh pronunciation.*

Malempre, *f.n.,* məˈlempreɪ,
mălémpray

Malet, *f.n.,* 'mælət, málĕt

Maley, *f.n.,* 'meɪlɪ, máyli

Malgwyn Castle *Dyfed,* 'mælgwɪn,
málgwin

Malikyan, *f.n.,* ˌmælɪkˈjɑn, malik-
-yáan

Malim, *f.n.,* 'meɪlɪm, máylim

Malindine, *f.n.,* 'mælɪndaɪn,
málindïn

Malins, *f.n.,* 'mælɪnz, málinz;
'meɪlɪnz, máylinz

Malkin, *f.n.,* 'mælkɪn, málkin

Mall, The, *London,* ðə 'mæl, thĕ
mál

Mallabar, *f.n.,* 'mæləbɑr, máläbaar

Mallaby, *f.n.,* 'mælətɪ, máläbi

Mallaig *H'land,* 'mæleɪg, málayg

Mallalieu, *f.n.,* 'mæləlju, málălew;
'mæləljə, málăl-yö

Mallandaine, *f.n.,* 'mæləndeɪn,
máländayn

Mallet, *f.n.,* 'mælət, málĕt

Malletsheugh *S'clyde,* 'mælət-ʃux,
málĕt-shoo**ch**

Malling, East *and* West, *Kent,*
'mɔlɪŋ, máwling

Malloch, *f.n.,* 'mæləx, málŏ**ch**

Mallone, *f.n.,* məˈloʊnɪ, mălóni

Mallowan, *f.n.,* 'mæloʊən, málō-ăn

Malltraeth Bay *Anglesey,* 'mæl-
traɪθ, máhl**dr**ïth

Mallusk *Co. Antrim,* məˈlʌsk,
mălúsk

Mallwyd *Gwynedd,* 'mæloɪd,
máhl**oo**-id

Malmesbury *Wilts.,* 'mɑmzbərɪ,
máamzbŭri. *Appropriate also
for the Earl of ~.*

Malone, *f.n.,* məˈloʊn, mălóne

Malpas, *f.n.,* 'mælpəs, málpăss

Malpas *Ches.,* 'mɔlpəs, máwlpăss;
'mælpəs, málpăss; 'mɔpəs,
máwpăss. *The first is appropriate for Viscount ~.*

Malpas *Cornwall,* 'moʊpəs,
mópăss

Malpas *Gwent,* 'mælpəs, málpăss

Malpass, *f.n.,* 'mælpæs, málpass

Malsbury, *f.n.,* 'mɔlzbərɪ, máwlz-
bŭri

Maltby, *f.n.,* 'mɔltbɪ, máwltbi

Malthus, Thomas, *18th–19th-c.
economist,* 'mælθəs, málthŭss

Malthusian, *pertaining to* **Malthus,**
mælˈθjuziən, mal-théwziăn

Malton *N. Yorks.,* 'mɔltən, máwl-
tŏn

Maltravers, Baron, mælˈtrævərz,
maltrávvĕrz

Malvern *H. & W.,* 'mɔlvərn,
máwlvĕrn; 'mɒvərn, máwvĕrn.
*The first is appropriate for
Viscount ~.*

Malycha, *f.n.,* 'mælɪkɪ, máliki

Malyon, *f.n.,* 'mæljən, mál-yŏn

Mamhilad *Gwent,* mæmˈhaɪləd,
mam-hílăd

Mamore deer forest *H'land,*
məˈmɔr, mămór

Manaccan *Cornwall,* məˈnækən,
mănáckăn

Manadon *Devon,* 'mænədən, mán-
nădŏn

Manafon *Powys,* mænˈævən, man-
návvŏn

Manaton *Devon,* 'mænətən, mán-
nătŏn

Manbré, *f.n.,* 'mænbreɪ, mánbray

Mance, *f.n.,* mæns, manss

Manchée, *f.n.,* mænˈʃi, man-shée;
mɒnˈʃeɪ, mon-sháy

Manchester *Gtr. M'chester,*
'mæntʃɪstər, mántchĕstĕr;
'mæntʃestər, mántchestĕr

Manchip, *f.n.,* 'mæntʃɪp, mán-ship

Mancunian, *native of* **Manchester,**
mænˈkjuniən, mankéwniăn

Mandel, *f.n.,* mænˈdel, mandéll

Mandelstam, *f.n.,* 'mændlstəm,
mándlstăm

Mander, *f.n.,* 'mændər, mándĕr;
'mɑndər, máandĕr. *The first is
usual in Staffs.*

Manders, *f.n.,* 'mændərz, mándĕrz

Manderson, *f.n.,* 'mændərsən,
mánderssŏn

Mandeville, Viscount, 'mændɪvɪl,
mándĕvil

Manduell, *f.n.,* 'mændjuəl,
mándyŏo-ĕl

Manea *Cambs.,* 'meɪnɪ, máyni

Maney, *f.n.,* 'meɪnɪ, máyni

Mangan, *f.n.,* 'mæŋən, máng-ăn

Mangin, *f.n.,* 'mæŋgɪn, máng-gin

Mangold, *f.n.,* 'mæŋgoʊld, máng-
-gŏld

Mangotsfield *Avon,* 'mæŋgətsfild,
máng-gŏtsfeeld

Manhood, *f.n.,* 'mænhʊd, mán-
-hŏod

Mankowitz, Wolf, *author,* 'wʊlf 'mæŋkəvɪtʃ, woŏlf mánkŏvitch
Manktelow, *f.n.,* 'mæŋktɪlou, mánktĕlō
Manley, *f.n.,* 'mænlɪ, mánli
Mann, *f.n.,* mæn, man
Manners, *f.n.,* 'mænərz, mánnĕrz
Manning, *f.n.,* 'mænɪŋ, mánning
Manningham, *f.n.,* 'mænɪŋəm, mánning-ăm
Mannion, *f.n.,* 'mænjən, mán-yŏn
Manod *Gwynedd,* 'mænɒd, mán-nod
Manorbier *Dyfed,* ˌmænər'bɪər, mannŏrbéer
Manordeifi *Dyfed,* ˌmænər'daɪvɪ, mannŏrdívi
Manordilo *Dyfed,* ˌmænər'daɪlou, mannŏrdílō
Manordougherty *Co. Armagh,* ˌmænər'dɒxərtɪ, mannŏrdóchĕrti
Mansel, *f.n.,* 'mænsl, mánssl
Mansell, *f.n.,* 'mænsl, mánssl
Mansergh, *f.n.,* 'mænzər, mánzĕr; 'mænsər, mánssĕr; 'mænsərdʒ, mánsserj
Mansergh *Cumbria,* 'mænzər, mánzĕr
Mansey, *f.n.,* 'mænsɪ, mánssi
Mansfield, *f.n.,* 'mænsfɪld, mánssfeeld
Mansfield *Notts.,* 'mænsfɪld, mánssfeeld. *Appropriate also for the Earl of* ~.
Manson, *f.n.,* 'mænsən, mánssŏn
Manston *Kent,* 'mænstən, mánstŏn
Mantas, *f.n.,* 'mæntæs, mántass
Manton, *f.n.,* 'mæntən, mántŏn
Mantovani, *f.n.,* ˌmæntə'vɑnɪ, mantŏváani
Manuden *Essex,* 'mænjʊdən, mán-yoŏdĕn
Manuel, *f.n.,* 'mænjʊəl, mán-yoŏ-ĕl
Manus, *f.n.,* 'meɪnəs, máynŭss
Manwaring, *f.n.,* 'mænərɪŋ, mánnăring
Manx *pertaining to the I. of Man,* mæŋks, manks
Manydown *Hants,* 'mænɪdaʊn, mánnidown
Manzoni, *f.n.,* mæn'zoʊnɪ, manzóni
Maple, *f.n.,* 'meɪpl, máypl
Mapledurwell *Hants,* ˌmeɪpl-'dɜːwel, maypldúrwel
Mapleton *Derby.,* 'meɪpltən, máypltŏn; 'mæpltən, máppltŏn
Maplin Sands *off Essex coast,* 'mæplɪn 'sændz, máplin sándz
Maquarie, *f.n.,* mə'kwɒrɪ, mǎkwórri
Maralin *Co. Down,* ˌmærə'lɪn, marrálin

Marazion *Cornwall,* ˌmærə'zaɪən, marrází-ŏn
March *Cambs.,* mɑrtʃ, maartch
Marchesi, *f.n.,* mɑr'kisɪ, maarkéessi
Marchwiel *Clwyd,* mɑrx'wiəl, maarchwée-ĕl
Marcousé, *f.n.,* mɑr'kuzeɪ, maarkoózay
Mardall, *f.n.,* 'mɑrdl, maárdl
Marden *Kent,* 'mɑrdən, maárdĕn; mɑr'den, maardén
Marden *H. & W., Wilts.,* 'mɑrdən, maárdĕn
Marden, East, West *and* North, *W. Sussex,* 'mɑrdən, maárdĕn
Maree, Loch, *H'land,* mə'ri, mărée
Mareham le Fen *Lincs.,* 'mɛərəm lə 'fen, máirăm lĕ fén
Mareham on the Hill *Lincs.,* 'mɛərəm ɒn ðə 'hɪl, máirăm on thĕ híll
Marett, *f.n.,* 'mærɪt, márrĕt
Margach, *f.n.,* 'mɑrgə, maárgă
Margadale, Baron, 'mɑrgədeɪl, maárgădayl
Margadale of Islay, Baron, 'mɑrgədeɪl əv 'aɪlə, múrgădayl ŏv ílă
Margam *W. Glam.,* 'mɑrgəm, maárgăm
Margaretting *Essex,* ˌmɑrgə'retɪŋ, maargărétting
Margary, *f.n.,* 'mɑrgərɪ, maárgări
Margate *Kent,* 'mɑrgeɪt, maárgayt
Margerison, *f.n.,* mɑr'dʒerɪsən, maarjérrissŏn; 'mɑrdʒərɪsən, maárjĕrissŏn
Margesson, *f.n.,* 'mɑrdʒɪsən, maárjĕssŏn. *Appropriate also for Viscount* ~.
Margetson, *f.n.,* 'mɑrgɪtsən, maárgĕtsŏn
Margetts, *f.n.,* 'mɑrgɪts, maárgĕts
Margochis, *f.n.,* mɑr'goʊʃɪ, maargóshi
Margolin, *f.n.,* mɑr'goʊlɪn, maargólin
Margoliouth, *f.n.,* mɑr'goʊlɪəθ, maargóli-ūth. *Appropriate for D. S.* ~, *classical scholar and orientalist.*
Margolis, *f.n.,* mɑr'goʊlɪs, maargóliss
Margolyes, *f.n.,* 'mɑrgəlɪz, maárgŏleez
Margulies, *f.n.,* 'mɑrgʊlɪs, maárgooliss; 'mɑrgʊlɪs, maárgōoleess; mɑr'gʊlɪz, maargooliz
Marham *Norfolk,* 'mærəm, márrăm; 'mɑrəm, maárăm. *The first is the traditional local pronunciation. The second is used*

for the Royal Air Force station by RAF personnel.

Marhamchurch *Cornwall*, 'mærəm-tʃɑrtʃ, márrămchurtch

Marholm *Cambs.*, 'mærəm, márrŏm

Marian-glas *Gwynedd*, ˌmæriən-'glas, marriăn-glaáss

Marillier, *f.n.*, mə'rɪljər, măríl-yĕr

Marindin, *f.n.*, mə'rɪndɪn, mărín-din

Mariner, *f.n.*, 'mærɪnər, márrinĕr

Marino *Co. Down*, mə'rinou, măréenō

Marischal, *f.n.*, 'mɑrʃl, maárshl

Marischal College *Univ. of Aberdeen*, 'mɑrʃl, maárshl

Marjoram, *f.n.*, 'mɑrdʒərəm, maárjŏrăm

Marjoribanks, *f.n.*, 'mɑrtʃbæŋks, maártch-banks

Market Bosworth *Leics.*, 'mɑrkɪt 'bɒzwərθ, maárkĕt bózwŭrth

Market Rasen *Lincs.*, 'mɑrkɪt 'reɪzən, maárkĕt ráyzĕn

Market Weighton *Humberside*, 'mɑrkɪt 'wɪtən, maárkĕt weetŏn

Markham, *f.n.*, 'mɑrkəm, maárkăm

Markillie, *f.n.*, mɑr'kɪlɪ, maar-kílli

Markinch *Fife*, 'mɑrk'ɪnʃ, maárk-ínsh

Marklew, *f.n.*, 'mɑrklu, maárkloo

Marklye *E. Sussex*, mɑrk'laɪ, maárklí

Markova, Alicia, *ballerina*, ə'lisiə mɑr'kouvə, ăléessiă maarkóvă

Markshall *Essex*, 'mɑrkʃɔl, maárks-hawl; 'mɑrksl, maárkssl

Marks of Broughton, Baron, 'mɑrks əv 'brɔtən, maárks ŏv bráwtŏn

Marks Tey *Essex*, 'mɑrks 'teɪ, maárks táy

Markwick, *f.n.*, 'mɑrkwɪk, maárk-wick

Markyate Street *Herts.*, 'mɑrkjeɪt strit, maárk-yayt street

Marlais, *Welsh C.n.*, 'mɑrlaɪs, maárlíss

Marlborough, Duke of, 'mɔlbrə, máwlbră

Marlborough *Wilts.*, 'mɔlbrə, máwlbră; 'mɔlbərə, máwlbŭră

Marlborough House *London*, 'mɔlbrə, máwlbră; 'mɔlbərə, máwlbŭră

Marlburian, *one educated at Marlborough College*, mɔl-'bjʊərɪən, mawlbyóoriăn

Marler, *f.n.*, 'mɑrlər, maárlĕr

Marloes *Dyfed*, 'mɑrlouz, maárlōz

Marlow *Bucks.*, 'mɑrlou, maárlō

Marlowe, *f.n.*, 'mɑrlou, maárlō

Marnham, *f.n.*, 'mɑrnəm, maárnăm

Marnhull *Dorset*, 'mɑrnəl, maárnŭl

Marochan, *f.n.*, 'mærəkən, márrŏkăn

Marown *I. of Man*, mə'raun, marówn

Marquand, *f.n.*, 'mɑrkwənd, maárkwŏnd

Marques, *f.n.*, mɑrks, maarks

Marquis, *f.n.*, 'mɑrkwɪs, maárkwiss; 'mɑrki, maárkee

Marre, *f.n.*, mɑr, maar

Marreco, *f.n.*, mə'rekou, măréckō

Marriott, *f.n.*, 'mærɪət, márriŏt

Marris, *f.n.*, 'mærɪs, márriss

Marsden, *f.n.*, 'mɑrzdən, maárzdĕn

Marshall, *f.n.*, 'mɑrʃl, maárshl

Marshalsea Prison *Southwark (London)*, 'mɑrʃlsɪ, maárshlsi

Marsham *Norfolk*, 'mɑrʃəm, maár-shăm

Marsh Baldon *Oxon.*, 'mɑrʃ 'bɒldən, maársh báwldŏn

Marsingall, *f.n.*, 'mɑrsɪŋgl, maár-ssing-gl

Marson, *f.n.*, 'mɑrsən, maárssŏn

Marston Moor *N. Yorks.*, 'mɑrstən, maárstŏn

Martel, *f.n.*, mɑr'tel, maartéll

Martell, *f.n.*, mɑr'tel, maartéll

Martens, *f.n.*, 'mɑrtɪnz, maártĕnz mɑr'tenz, maarténz

Martensson, *f.n.*, 'mɑrtənsən, maártĕnssŏn

Martham *Norfolk*, 'mɑrθəm, maár-thăm

Martin, *C.n. and f.n.*, 'mɑrtɪn, maártin

Martineau, *f.n.*, 'mɑrtɪnou, maártinō

Martlesham *Suffolk*, 'mɑrtlʃəm, maártl-shăm

Martletwy *Dyfed*, ˌmɑrtl'twaɪ, maartl-twí

Martonmere, Baron, 'mɑrtənmɪər, maártŏnmeer

Martyr, *f.n.*, 'mɑrtər, maártĕr

Martyr Worthy *Hants.*, 'mɑrtər 'wərðɪ, maártĕr wŭr<u>th</u>i

Marvell, *f.n.*, 'mɑrvl, maárvl. *Appropriate for Andrew ~, 17th-c. poet and satirist.*

Marvin, *f.n.*, 'mɑrvɪn, maárvin

Marwenne, saint, 'mɑrwɪn, maár-win

Marwick, *f.n.*, 'mɑrwɪk, maár-wick

Marwick Head *Orkney*, 'mɑrwɪk, maár-wick

Maryculter *Grampian*, ˌmɛərɪ-
'kutər, mairi-kóŏtĕr
Maryhill *S'clyde*, 'mɛərɪ'hɪl,
máiri-híll
Marylebone *London*, 'mærɪləbən,
márrĭlĕbŏn; 'mærələbən,
márrĕlĕbŏn; 'mærɪbən, márri-
bŏn; 'marlɪbən, maárlibŏn.
*The first two are appropriate for
the Parish Church of St.* ~.
Maryon-Davies, *f.n.*, 'mærɪən
'deɪvɪs, márri-ŏn dáyviss
Mary Tavy *Devon*, 'mɛərɪ 'teɪvɪ,
máiri táyvi
Masbrough *S. Yorks.*, 'mæzbərə,
mázbŭrǎ
Mascherpa, *f.n.*, mə'ʃɜrpə,
mǎshérpǎ
Maschwitz, *f.n.*, 'mæʃwɪts, mǎsh-
wits
Mase, *f.n.*, meɪs, mayss
Masham, *f.n.*, 'mæsəm, mássǎm;
'mæʃəm, máshǎm
Masham *N. Yorks.*, 'mæsəm,
ˌmássǎm. *Appropriate also for
Baron* ~.
Masham, *breed of sheep*, 'mæsəm,
mássǎm; 'mæʃəm, máshǎm.
*Those acquainted with the place
in N. Yorks. generally use the
first pronunciation.*
Masheder, *f.n.*, 'mæʃɪdər, másh-
ĕdĕr
Maskell, *f.n.*, 'mæskl, másskl
Maskelyne, *f.n.*, 'mæskəlɪn,
másskĕlin
Maskery, *f.n.*, 'mæskərɪ, másskĕri
Maskrey, *f.n.*, 'mæskrɪ, másskri
Maslen, *f.n.*, 'mæzlən, mázlĕn
Mason, *f.n.*, 'meɪsən, máyssŏn
Massee, *f.n.*, 'mæsi, mássee
Massereene *Co. Antrim*, 'mæsə-
rin, mássĕreen
Massereene and Ferrard, Vis-
count, 'mæsərin ənd 'ferard,
mássĕreen and férraard
Massey, *f.n.*, 'mæsɪ, mássi
Massie, *f.n.*, 'mæsɪ, mássi
Massinger, *f.n.*, 'mæsɪndʒər,
mássinjĕr. *Considered appro-
priate also for Philip* ~, *16th–
17th-c. dramatist.*
Massocchi, *f.n.*, mæ'sɒkɪ, mas-
sócki
Masson, *f.n.*, 'mæsən, mássŏn
Massow, *f.n.*, 'mæsoʊ, mássō
Masters, *f.n.*, 'mastərz, maáss-
tĕrz
Masterton, *f.n.*, 'mastərtən,
maásstĕrtŏn
Mastrick *Grampian*, 'mæstrɪk,
mástrick
Matalon, *f.n.*, 'mætəlɒn, máttălon
Matanle, *f.n.*, mə'tænlɪ, mǎtánli

Matchan, *f.n.*, 'mætʃən, mátchǎn
Mateer, *f.n.*, mə'tɪər, mǎteér
Mater Hospital *Belfast*, 'matər,
maátĕr
Mates, *f.n.*, meɪts, mayts
Mathafarn *Powys*, mæ'θævərn,
mathávvǎrn
Mathen, *f.n.*, 'maθən, maáthĕn
Mather, *f.n.*, 'mæðər, máthĕr;
'meɪðər, máythĕr; 'meɪθər,
máythĕr
Mathers, *f.n.*, 'meɪðərz, máythĕrz.
*Appropriate also for the Barony
of* ~.
Mathers, E. Powys, *author and
scholar*, 'poʊɪs 'meɪðərz, pó-iss
máythĕrz
Matheson, *f.n.*, 'mæθɪsən,
máthĕssŏn
Mathias, *f.n.*, mə'θaɪəs, mǎthí-ǎss
Mathie, *f.n.*, 'mæθɪ, máthi
Mathon *H. & W.*, 'meɪðɒn,
máython
Mathrafal, *also spelt* **Mathraval,**
Powys, mæθ'rævəl, mathrávvǎl
Mathry *Dyfed*, 'mæθrɪ, máthri
Matier, *f.n.*, mə'tɪər, mǎteér
Matlaske *Norfolk*, 'mætlæsk,
mátlassk
Maton, *f.n.*, 'meɪtən, máytŏn
Matravers *Dorset*, mə'trævərz,
mǎtrávvĕrz
Mattacks, *f.n.*, 'mætəks, máttǎcks
Mattam, *f.n.*, 'mætəm, máttǎm
Mattersey *Notts.*, 'mætərsɪ, mát-
tĕrssi
Matthay, *f.n.*, 'mæteɪ, máttay
Matthes, *f.n.*, 'mæθɪz, máthĕz
Matthias, *f.n.*, mə'θaɪəs, máthí-
-áss
Mattishall *Norfolk*, 'mætɪʃl,
máttishl
Maturin, *f.n.*, 'mætjʊərɪn, mát-
-yōōrin
Mauchline *S'clyde*, 'mɒxlɪn,
móchlin
Maude, *f.n.*, mɔd, mawd
Maudling, *f.n.*, 'mɔdlɪŋ, máwdling
Mauduit, *f.n.*, 'moʊdwɪ, mŏdwee
Maufe, Sir Edward, *architect*,
mɔf, mawf
Mauger, *f.n.*, 'meɪdʒər, máyjĕr
Maugersbury *Glos.*, 'mɔzbərɪ,
máwzbŭri
Maugham, *f.n.*, mɔm, mawm;
'mɒfəm, móffǎm. *The first is
appropriate for the Viscountcy
of* ~.
Maugham, W. Somerset, *author*,
'sʌmərsɪt 'mɔm, súmmĕrssĕt
máwm
Maughan, *f.n.*, mɔn, mawn
Maughenby *Cumbria*, 'mæfənbɪ,
máffĕnbi

Maughold *I. of Man*, 'mækəld, máckŏld

Maule, *f.n.*, mɔl, mawl

Mauleverer, *f.n.*, mə'levərər, mŏlévvĕrĕr; mɔ'levərər, maw-lévvĕrĕr

Maumbury Rings *Dorset*, 'mɔmbəri, máwmbŭri

Maund, *f.n.*, mɔnd, mawnd

Maunder, *f.n.*, 'mɔndər, máwndĕr

Maunsell, *f.n.*, 'mænsl, mánssl

Maurice, *f.n.*, 'mɒrɪs, mórriss; mə'ris, mŏréess

Mautby *Norfolk*, 'mɔbɪ, máwbi

Mavius, *f.n.*, 'meɪvɪəs, máyviúss

Mavor, *f.n.*, 'meɪvər, máyvŏr. *Appropriate for Dr O. H.* ~, *whose pen name was* **James Bridie**, *q.v.*

Mavrogordato, *f.n.*, ˌmævrɔʊɡər-'dɑtɔʊ, mavrōgordaátō

Maw, *f.n.*, mɔ, maw

Mawddach, River, *Gwynedd*, 'maʊðəx, mówthăch

Mawdesley, *f.n.*, 'mɔdzlɪ, máwdzli

Mawhinney, *f.n.*, mə'hwɪnɪ, mă-whínni

Mawnan *Cornwall*, 'mɔnən, máwnăn

Maxen, *f.n.*, 'mæksən, mácksĕn

Maxey *Cambs.*, 'mæksɪ, mácksi

Maxim, *f.n.*, 'mæksɪm, mácksim

Maxse, *f.n.*, 'mæksɪ, mácksi

Maxwell, *f.n.*, 'mækswəl, mácks-wĕl; 'mækswel, máckswel

Maxwelltown *D. & G.*, 'mækswəl-taʊn, máckswĕltown; 'mæks-wəltən, máckswĕltŏn

Maxwelton *S'clyde*, 'mækswəltən, máckswĕltŏn

May, *f.n.*, meɪ, may

Mayall, *f.n.*, 'meɪəl, máy-ăl; 'meɪɔl, máy-awl

Maybole *S'clyde*, meɪ'bɔʊl, may-bṓl

Maydon, *f.n.*, 'meɪdən, máydŏn

Mayer, *f.n.*, 'meɪər, máy-ĕr; mɛər, mair

Mayger, *f.n.*, 'meɪdʒər, máyjĕr; 'meɪɡər, máygĕr

Mayhew, *f.n.*, 'meɪhju, máy-hew

Maynard, *f.n.*, 'meɪnərd, máy-nărd; 'meɪnɑrd, máynaard

Mayne, *f.n.*, meɪn, mayn

Mayneard, *f.n.*, 'meɪnɪɑrd, máyni-aard

Mayo, Earl of, 'meɪɔʊ, máy-ō

Mayobridge *Co. Down*, ˌmeɪɔʊ-'brɪdʒ, may-ō-bríj

Mayon, *also spelt* **Mean**, *Cornwall*, meɪn, mayn

Mays, *f.n.*, meɪz, mayz

Mayson, *f.n.*, 'meɪsən, máyssŏn

Mayvor, *f.n.*, 'meɪvər, máyvŏr

Meachem, *f.n.*, 'mitʃəm, mée-tchĕm

Meacher, *f.n.*, 'mitʃər, méetchĕr

Meade, *f.n.*, mid, meed

Meaden, *f.n.*, 'midən, méedĕn

Meaford *Staffs.*, 'mefərd, méffŏrd; 'mifərd, méefŏrd

Meagher, *f.n.*, mɑr, maar

Meaker, *f.n.*, 'mikər, méekĕr

Meakin, *f.n.*, 'mikɪn, méekin

Mean *see* **Mayon**

Mearles, *f.n.*, mɜrlz, merlz

Mearne, *f.n.*, mɜrn, mern

Mearns, The, *Grampian*, ðə 'mɛərnz, thĕ máirnz. *Ancient name of Kincardineshire* (*now part of Grampian Region*).

Mears, *f.n.*, mɜrz, meerz

Measach, Falls of, *H'land*, 'mesəx, méssăch

Measham *Leics.*, 'miʃəm, mée-shăm

Meath, Earl of, miθ, meeth

Meathop *Cumbria*, 'miθəp, mée-thŏp

Meaux *Humberside*, mjus, mewss

Meavy *Devon*, 'mivɪ, méevi

Meazey, *f.n.*, 'meɪzɪ, máyzi

Mebyon Kernow, *Cornish political party*, 'mebɪən 'kɜrnɔʊ, méb-biŏn kérnō

Meczies, *f.n.*, 'mekzɪz, méck-zizz

Medak, *f.n.*, 'meɪdæk, máydack

Medawar, *f.n.*, 'medəwər, méddă-wăr

Medcraft, *f.n.*, 'medkrɑft, méd-kraaft

Meddings, *f.n.*, 'medɪŋz, méd-dingz

Medhurst, *f.n.*, 'medhɜrst, méd-hurst

Medlicott, *f.n.*, 'medlɪkɒt, médli-kot

Medmenham *Bucks.*, 'mednəm, méd-năm

Medomsley *Durham*, 'medəmzlɪ, méddŏmzli

Medstead *Hants*, 'medsted, médsted

Medus, *f.n.*, 'midəs, méedŭss

Meehan, *f.n.*, 'miən, mée-ăn

Meekums, *f.n.*, 'mikəmz, mée-kŭmz

Meert, *f.n.*, mɪərt, meert

Meeth *Devon*, miθ, meeth

Meetham, *f.n.*, 'miðəm, mée-thăm

Megahey, *f.n.*, mɪ'gæhɪ, mĕgá-hi; mɪ'gæxɪ, mĕgáchi

Megan, *Welsh C.n.*, 'megən, méggăn

Megarry, *f.n.*, mɪ'gærɪ, mĕgárri

Megaw, *f.n.*, mɪ'gɔ, mĕgáw

Meggison, *f.n.*, 'megɪsən, méggis-sŏn

Mehan, *f.n.*, 'miən, mée-ăn

Meharg, *f.n.*, mɪ'hɑrg, mĕha'arg

Meheux, *f.n.*, 'meɪhju, máyhew

Mehew, *f.n.*, 'mihju, mée-hew; 'miu, mée-oo

Mehmedagi, *f.n.*, ˌmeməˈdɑdʒɪ, memmĕda'aji

Meier, *f.n.*, 'maɪər, mí-ĕr

Meifod *Powys*, 'maɪvɒd, mívod

Meiggs, *f.n.*, megz, meggz

Meigh, *f.n.*, mi, mee; meɪ, may

Meigle *Tayside*, 'migl, meégl

Meikle, *f.n.*, 'mikl, meékl

Meiklejohn, *f.n.*, 'mɪkldʒɒn, míckljon; 'mikldʒɒn, meékljon

Meikleour *Tayside*, mɪ'kluər, mĕklŏŏr

Meilen, *f.n.*, 'maɪlən, mílĕn

Mein, *f.n.*, min, meen

Meinardi, *f.n.*, meɪ'nɑrdɪ, may-naárdi

Meinciau *Dyfed*, 'maɪŋkjaɪ, mínk-yī

Meinertzhagen, *f.n.*, 'maɪnərts-hagən, mínĕrts-haagĕn

Meir *Staffs.*, mɪər, meer

Meirion, *Welsh C.n.*, 'maɪrɪɒn, mírı-on

Mekie, *f.n.*, 'mikɪ, meéki

Melachrino, *f.n.*, ˌmeləˈkrinoʊ, mellákreénŏ

Melbourn *Cambs.*, 'melbɔrn, mélborn

Melbourne *Derby.*, 'melbɔrn, mélborn

Melbury Abbas *Dorset*, 'melbərɪ 'æbəs, mélbŭri ábbăss

Melchett, Baron, 'meltʃɪt, méltchĕt

Melcio, *f.n.*, 'melsɪoʊ, mélssi-ō

Meldreth *Cambs.*, 'meldrəθ, méldrĕth

Meldrum *Grampian*, 'meldrəm, méldrŭm

Melgund, Viscount, 'melgʌnd, mélgund

Melhuish, *f.n.*, 'melhjuɪʃ, mél-hewish; mel'hjuɪʃ, mel-héwish; me'ljuɪʃ, melléwish; 'melɪʃ, méllish; 'melʊɪʃ, méllŏŏ-ish

Melia, *f.n.*, 'milɪə, meéliă

Meliden, *Clwyd*, 'melɪdən, méllidĕn

Melincryddan *W. Glam.*, ˌmelɪn-ˈkrɪðən, mellin-kríthăn; ˌmelɪn-ˈkrʌðən, mellin-krúthăn

Melindwr *Dyfed*, me'lɪnduər, mellíndŏŏr

Melin Ifan Ddu *Mid Glam.*, 'melɪn 'ɪvən 'ðɪ, méllin ívvăn <u>th</u>eé

Melksham *Wilts.*, 'melkʃəm, mélk-shăm

Mellaart, *f.n.*, 'melɑrt, méllaart

Mellett, *f.n.*, 'melɪt, méllĕt

Mellinger, *f.n.*, 'melɪndʒər, mél-linjĕr

Mellingey *Cornwall*, me'lɪndʒɪ, mellínji

Mellis *Suffolk*, 'melɪs, mélliss

Mellor, *f.n.*, 'melər, méllŏr

Mellors, *f.n.*, 'melərz, méllŏrz

Melluish, *f.n.*, 'meljuɪʃ, méllew-ish

Melly, *f.n.*, 'melɪ, mélli

Melmerby *N. Yorks.*, 'melmərbɪ, mélmĕrbi; 'melərbɪ, méllĕrbi

Meloy, *f.n.*, mɪ'lɔɪ, mĕlóy

Melrose *Borders*, 'melroʊz, mélrōz

Meltham *W. Yorks.*, 'melθəm, mél-thăm

Melton Constable *Norfolk*, 'meltən 'kʌnstəbl, méltŏn kúnstăbl

Melton Mowbray *Leics.*, 'meltən 'moʊbreɪ, méltŏn mŏbray

Melvaig *H'land*, mel'veɪg, mel-váyg

Melvich *H'land*, 'melvɪx, mélvi<u>ch</u>

Melville, *f.n.*, 'melvɪl, mélvil

Memus *Tayside*, 'miməs, mée-mŭss

Menabilly *Cornwall*, ˌmenəˈbɪlɪ, mennábilli

Menage, *f.n.*, mɪ'nɑʒ, mĕna'a<u>zh</u>

Menai *Gwynedd*, 'menaɪ, ménnī. *Appropriate for both the ~ Bridge and the ~ Strait.*

Menary, *f.n.*, 'menərɪ, ménnări

Menaul, *f.n.*, me'nɔl, mennáwl

Mendel, *f.n.*, 'mendl, méndl

Mendelssohn, *f.n.*, 'mendlsən, méndlssŏn

Meneely, *f.n.*, mɪ'nilɪ, mĕneéli

Menell, *f.n.*, 'menl, ménnl

Menevia, *Welsh bishopric*, mɪ-'nivɪə, mĕneéviă

Menges, *f.n.*, 'meŋgɪz, méng-giz; 'menɪs, méng-ĕss. *The first is appropriate for Herbert ~, conductor and composer.*

Menheniot *Cornwall*, mən'henɪət, mĕn-hénniŏt

Menmuir, *f.n.*, 'menmjʊər, mén-myŏŏr

Menneer, *f.n.*, mə'nɪər, mĕneér

Mennell, *f.n.*, mɪ'nel, mĕnéll

Mennich, *f.n.*, 'menɪʃ, ménnish

Mennie, *f.n.*, 'menɪ, ménni

Menpes, *f.n.*, 'menpes, ménpess; 'menpɪz, ménpiz

Menston *W. Yorks.*, 'menstən, ménstŏn

Menstrie *Central*, 'menstrɪ, ménsstri

Menteith, Lake of, *Central*, mən-'tiθ, mĕnteéth

Menteth, *f.n.*, mən'tiθ, mĕnteéth

Menuhin, Yehudi, *violinist*, jə'hudi
'menjuɪn, yĕ-hoódi mén-yōō-in.
*Mr Menuhin himself accepts the
above popular English pronunciation. The Russian and
Hebrew version is* mə'nuxɪn,
mĕnoochin

Menzies, *f.n.*, 'mɪŋɪs, míng-iss;
'mɪŋɪz, ming-iz; 'menzɪz, menz-
iz. *The first two are indigenous
Scottish pronunciations.*

Meo, *f.n.*, 'meɪoʊ, máy-ō

Meole Brace *Salop*, 'mil 'breɪs,
meél bráyss

Meols *Lancs.*, milz, meelz

Meon, River, *Hants*, 'mɪən, mée-
-ŏn

Meon, East *and* West, *Hants*,
'mɪən, mée-ŏn

Meopham *Kent*, 'mepəm, méppăm

Mepal *Cambs.*, 'mipl, meépl

Meppershall *Beds.*, 'mepərʃl,
méppĕrshl

Merbecke, John, *16th-c. musician
and composer*, 'mɑrbek, maár-
beck

Merchant, *f.n.*, 'mɜrtʃənt, mér-
tchănt

Merchiston *Lothian*, 'mɜrkɪstən,
mérkistŏn

Merchistoun Hall *Hants*, 'mɜrtʃɪs-
tən, mértchistŏn

Mercy, *f.n.*, 'mɜrsɪ, mérssi

Meredith, *C.n. and f.n.*, mə'redɪθ,
mĕréddith; 'merədɪθ, mérrĕdith.
*The first is the Welsh pronuncia-
tion.*

Meredydd, *Welsh C.n. and f.n.*,
mə'redɪð, mĕréddith; mə'redɪθ,
mĕréddith

Merevale *Warwicks.*, 'merɪveɪl,
mérrĕvayl

Mereweather, *f.n.*, 'merɪweðər,
mérrĭwethĕr

Merewether, *f.n.*, 'merɪweðər,
mérrĭwethĕr

Mereworth, Baron, 'merɪwərθ,
mérrĕwŭrth

Mereworth *Kent*, 'merɪwɜrθ,
mérrĕwurth

Merfyn, *Welsh C.n.*, 'mɜrvɪn, mér-
vin

Meriden *W. Midlands*, 'merɪdən,
mérridĕn

Merioneth *former Co. name*,
ˌmerɪ'ɒnəθ, merri-ónnĕth.
*Appropriate also for the Earl of
~.*

Merkelis, *f.n.*, mər'keɪlɪs, mĕrkáy-
liss

Mermagen, *f.n.*, 'mɜrməgən, mér-
măgĕn

Merrell, *f.n.*, 'merəl, mérrĕl

Merrion, *f.n.*, 'merɪən, mérriŏn

Merryweather, *f.n.*, 'merɪweðər,
mérriwethĕr

Merse, The, *Borders*, mɜrs, merss

Mersea, East *and* West, *Essex*,
'mɜrzɪ, mérzi

Mersey, River, *Gtr. M'chester–
Merseyside*, 'mɜrzɪ, mérzi.
Appropriate also for Viscount ~.

Mersham *Kent*, 'mɜrzəm, mérzăm

Mersham-le-Hatch *Kent*, 'mɜrzəm
lə 'hætʃ, mérzăm lĕ hátch

Merstham *Surrey*, 'mɜrstəm, mérstăm

Merthyr *Dyfed*, 'mɜrθər, mérthĕr.
Appropriate also for Baron ~.

Merthyr Tydfil *Mid Glam.*, 'mɜrθər 'tɪdvɪl, mérthĕr tídvil

Meryweather, *f.n.*, 'merɪweðər,
mérriwethĕr

Mescall, *f.n.*, 'meskl, mésskl

Meshaw *Devon*, 'meʃɔ, mésh-aw

Messel, *f.n.*, 'mesl, méssl

Messenger, *f.n.*, 'mesɪndʒər,
méssĕnjĕr

Messent, *f.n.*, 'mesənt, méssĕnt

Messer, *f.n.*, 'mesər, méssĕr

Messervy, *f.n.*, mɪ'sɜrvɪ, mĕssérvi

Messina, *f.n.*, mɪ'sinə, mĕsseénă

Mestel, *f.n.*, mes'tel, mestéll

Meszaros, *f.n.*, mɪ'zɑrɒs, mĕzaá-
ross

Metcalfe, *f.n.*, 'metkɑf, métkaaf;
'metkəf, métkăf

Meteyard, *f.n.*, 'metjɑrd, mét-
-yaard

Metherall, *f.n.*, 'meðərəl, méthĕr-
awl

Methil *Fife*, 'meθɪl, méth-il

Methley *W. Yorks.*, 'meθlɪ,
méthli

Methold, *f.n.*, 'meθoʊld, méth-ōld

Methuen, Baron, 'meθuɪn,
méthōō-ĕn

Methuen, *f.n.*, 'meθjuɪn, méth-
yōō-ĕn. *Appropriate also for ~
& Co., publishers.*

Methven, *f.n.*, 'meθvən, méthvĕn

Methven *Tayside*, 'meθvən,
méthvĕn

Metrebian, *f.n.*, ˌmetrɪ'bjɑn,
metrĕbyaán

Meurant, *f.n.*, mjuə'rænt, myōō-
ránt

Meurig, *Welsh C.n.*, 'maɪrɪg, mí-
-rig

Meurwyn, *Welsh C.n.*, 'maɪərwɪn,
mír-win

Meux, *f.n.*, mjuks, mewks; mjuz,
mewz; mju, mew. *The first is
appropriate for the firm of
brewers.*

Mevagissey *Cornwall*, ˌmevə'gɪsɪ,
mevvăgíssi; ˌmevə'gɪzɪ, mevvă-
gízzi

Mewes, *f.n.,* 'mevis, mévvĕss. *This is appropriate for the architectural firm of ~ and Davis, builders of the London Ritz Hotel.*

Mewett, *f.n.,* 'mjuit, méw-ĕt

Mexborough, Earl of, 'meksbərə, mécksbŭră

Mey *H'land,* mei, may. *Appropriate also for the Castle of ~.*

Meyer, *f.n.,* 'maiər, mí-ĕr; meər, mair; 'meiər, máy-ĕr; miər, meer

Meyerstein, *f.n.,* 'maiərstain, mí--ĕrsstīn

Meyjes, *f.n.,* meiz, mayz

Meyllteyrn *Gwynedd,* meł'taiərn, mehłtírn

Meynell, *f.n.,* 'menl, ménnl

Meyrick, *f.n.,* 'merik, mérrick

Meysey, *f.n.,* 'meizi, máyzi

Mhachair, Loch, *W. Isles,* 'væxər, váchăr

Miall, *f.n.,* 'maiəl, mí-ăl

Micallef, *f.n.,* mi'kælif, mikálĕf

Michael, *C.n. and f.n.,* 'maikl, míkl

Michaelchurch Escley *H. & W.,* 'maikltʃərtʃ 'eskli, míkltchurtch éskli

Michaelhouse College *Univ. of Cambridge,* 'maiklhaus, míkl--howss. *In 1546 this college merged with King's Hall to form Trinity College.*

Michaelis, *f.n.,* mi'keilis, mickáy-liss; mi'kailis, mickíliss

Michaelson, *f.n.,* 'maiklsən, míklssŏn

Michaelston-y-Vedw *Gwent,* 'maiklstən ə 'vedu, míklsstŏn ă véddoo

Michaelstow *Cornwall,* 'maiklstoʊ, míklsstō

Micheldever *Hants,* 'mitʃldevər, mítchldevvĕr

Michelham, Baron, 'mitʃələm, mítchĕlăm

Michell, *f.n.,* mi'ʃel, mishéll

Michelli, *f.n.,* mi'keli, mikélli

Michelmore, *f.n.,* 'mitʃlmər, mítchlmor

Michelson, *f.n.,* 'mitʃlsən, mítchlssŏn

Michie, *f.n.,* 'mixi, míchi; 'mixi, meéchi; 'miki, mícki

Mickel, *f.n.,* 'mikl, míckl

Micklebring *S. Yorks.,* 'miklbriŋ, mícklbring

Mickleover *Derby.,* 'mikloʊvər, míckl-ōvĕr

Midanbury *Hants,* 'midənbəri, míddănbŭri

Middleham *N. Yorks.,* 'midləm, míddl-ăm

Middlemiss, *f.n.,* 'midlmis, míddl-miss

Middlesbrough *Cleveland,* 'midlzbrə, míddlzbră

Middlesceugh *Cumbria,* 'midlz-koʊ, míddlzkō

Middle Stoughton *Somerset,* 'midl 'stɔtən, míddl stáwtŏn

Middleton, *f.n.,* 'midltən, míddl-tŏn

Middleton Tyas *N. Yorks.,* 'midltən 'taiəs, míddltŏn tí-ăss

Middle Wallop *Hants,* 'midl 'wɒləp, míddl wóllŏp

Middleweek, *f.n.,* 'midlwik, míddlweek

Middlewich *Ches.,* 'midlwitʃ, míddlwitch

Mides, *f.n.,* 'maidiz, mídeez

Midgley, *f.n.,* 'midʒli, míjjli

Midleton, Earldom of, 'midltən, míddltŏn

Midlothian *Lothian,* mid'loʊðiən, midlṓthiăn. *Appropriate also for the Earl of ~.*

Midsomer Norton *Avon,* 'mid-sʌmər 'nɔrtən, mídsummĕr nórtŏn

Miers, *f.n.,* 'maiərz, mí-ĕrz

Miesch, *f.n.,* miʃ, meesh

Miéville, *f.n.,* 'mjeivil, myáyvil

Mighall, *f.n.,* 'maiəl, mí-ăl

Mighell, *f.n.,* 'maiəl, mí-ĕl

Mikardo, *f.n.,* mi'kardoʊ, mika'ar-dō

Mikellatos, *f.n.,* ˌmikə'lɑtɒs, mickĕlaátoss

Mikes, George, *author,* 'mikeʃ, meékesh

Mikhial, *f.n.,* 'mikl, meékl

Milan, *f.n.,* mi'læn, milánn

Milbourne, *f.n.,* 'milbɔrn, mílborn

Milburn, *f.n.,* 'milbərn, mílburn

Milburne, *f.n.,* 'milbərn, mílburn

Mildenhall *Suffolk,* 'mildənhɔl, míldĕnhawl

Mildenhall *Wilts.,* 'mildənhɔl, míldĕnhawl. *Sometimes spelt* **Minal** *and pronounced* 'mainɒl, mínawl

Mildmay, *f.n.,* 'maildmei, míldmay

Mildmay of Flete, Barony of, 'maildmei əv 'flit, míldmay ŏv fleét

Mildwater, *f.n.,* 'maildwɒtər, míld-wawtĕr

Miles, *C.n. and f.n.,* mailz, mīlz

Milford Haven *Dyfed,* 'milfərd 'heivən, mílfŏrd háyvĕn

Milkina, Nina, *pianist,* 'ninə 'milkinə, neénă mílkeenă

Millais, Sir John, *painter,* 'milei, míllay

Millan, *f.n.*, 'mɪlən, míllăn

Millar, *f.n.*, 'mɪlər, míllăr

Millard, *f.n.*, 'mɪlɑrd, míllaard

Millbay *Devon*, mɪl'beɪ, milbáy

Miller, *f.n.*, 'mɪlər, míllĕr

Milles, *f.n.*, mɪlz, millz

Milliband, *f.n.*, 'mɪlɪbænd, mílliband

Millichap, *f.n.*, 'mɪlɪtʃæp, míllitchap

Millichope, *f.n.*, 'mɪlɪtʃoup, míllitchōp

Milligan, *f.n.*, 'mɪlɪgən, mílligăn

Milliken, *f.n.*, 'mɪlɪkən, míllikĕn

Millings, *f.n.*, 'mɪlɪŋz, míllingz

Millington, *f.n.*, 'mɪlɪŋtən, míllingtŏn

Millisle *D. & G.*, mɪl'aɪl, millíl

Millwall *London*, 'mɪl'wɔl, míll--wáwl; 'mɪlwəl, mílwăl

Millward, *f.n.*, 'mɪlwɔrd, milwawrd

Milmo, *f.n.*, 'mɪlmou, mílmō

Milnathort *Tayside*, ˌmɪlnə'θɔrt, milnăthórt

Milne, *f.n.*, mɪln, miln; mɪl, mill

Milner, *f.n.*, 'mɪlnər, mílnĕr

Milnes, *f.n.*, mɪlnz, milnz; mɪlz, millz

Milngavie *S'clyde*, mʌl'gaɪ, mulgí; mɪl'gaɪ, milgí

Milton, *f.n.*, 'mɪltən, míltŏn

Milton Keynes *Bucks.*, 'mɪltən 'kinz; miltŏn kéenz

Milward, *f.n.*, 'mɪlwərd, mílwărd

Milwich *Staffs.*, 'mɪlɪtʃ, míllitch

Mimram, River, *Herts.*, 'mɪmræm, mímram

Minack *Cornwall*, 'mɪnək, mínnăk

Minal *see* Mildenhall *Wilts.*

Minay, *f.n.*, 'maɪneɪ, mínay

Minchinton, *f.n.*, 'mɪntʃɪntən, míntchintŏn

Minear, *f.n.*, mɪ'nɪər, mineér

Minell, *f.n.*, mɪ'nel, minéll

Minera *Clwyd*, mɪ'nerə, minérră

Mines, *f.n.*, maɪnz, mīnz

Mineter, *f.n.*, 'mɪnɪtər, mínnĕtĕr

Minety *Wilts.*, 'maɪntɪ, mínti

Minffordd *Gwynedd*, 'mɪnfɔrð, mínforth

Mingary, Loch, *S'clyde*, 'mɪŋgərɪ, ming-gări

Mingay Island *H'land*, 'mɪŋgeɪ, ming-gay

Mingulay *W. Isles*, 'mɪŋgʊleɪ, ming-gŏolay

Miningsby *Lincs.*, 'mɪnɪŋzbɪ, mínningzbi

Minns, *f.n.*, mɪnz, minnz

Minogue, *f.n.*, mɪ'noug, minóg

Minoprio, *f.n.*, mɪ'noupriou, minóprió

Minshull, *f.n.*, 'mɪnʃl, mínshl

Minshull Vernon *Ches.*, 'mɪnʃl 'vərnən, mínshl vérnŏn

Minsmere *Suffolk*, 'mɪnzmɪər, mínzmeer

Minster Lovell *Oxon.*, 'mɪnstər 'lʌvl, mínsstĕr lúvvl

Minter, *f.n.*, 'mɪntər, míntĕr

Mintlaw *Grampian*, 'mɪnt'lɔ, míntláw

Minto *Borders*, 'mɪntou, míntō. *Appropriate also for the Earl of* ~.

Mirfield *W. Yorks.*, 'mərfild, mírfeeld

Mirfin, *f.n.*, 'mərfɪn, mírfin

Mirzoeff, *f.n.*, 'mərtsɒf, mírtsoff

Miscampbell, *f.n.*, mɪs'kæmbl, miskámbl

Miserden *Glos.*, 'mɪzərdən, mízzĕrdĕn

Mishcon, *f.n.*, 'mɪʃkɒn, míshkon

Mishnish *S'clyde*, 'mɪʃnɪʃ, míshnish

Miskin, *f.n.*, 'mɪskɪn, mísskin

Miskin *Mid Glam.*, 'mɪskɪn, mísskin

Miskiw, *f.n.*, 'mɪskju, mískew

Misterton *Dorset*, 'mɪstərtən, místĕrtŏn

Mita, *C.n.*, 'mitə, méetă

Mitcham *London*, 'mɪtʃəm, mítchăm

Mitchamian, *native of* Mitcham, mɪ'tʃeɪmɪən, mitcháymiăn

Mitchard, *f.n.*, 'mɪtʃɑrd, mítchaard

Mitchell, *f.n.*, 'mɪtʃl, mítchl

Mitchenere, *f.n.*, ˌmɪtʃɪ'neər, mitchĕnáir

Mitford, *f.n.*, 'mɪtfərd, mítförd

Mithian *Cornwall*, 'mɪðɪən, míthiăn

Mitrany, *f.n.*, mɪ'trænɪ, mitránni

Mivart, *f.n.*, 'maɪvərt, mívărt

Mizen, *f.n.*, 'maɪzən, mízĕn

Mizler, *f.n.*, 'mɪzlər, mízzlĕr

Mizzi, *f.n.*, 'mɪtsɪ, mítsi

Moate, *f.n.*, mout, mōt

Mobberley *Ches.*, 'mɒbərlɪ, móbbĕrli

Moberly, *f.n.*, 'moubərlɪ, móbĕrli

Mobsby, *f.n.*, 'mɒbzbɪ, móbzbi

Mocatta, *f.n.*, mou'kætə, mōkáttă

Mochan, *f.n.*, 'mɒkən, móckăn

Mochdre *Clwyd, Powys*, 'mɒxdreɪ, móchdray

Mochrum *D. & G.*, 'mɒxrəm, móchrŭm

Modbury *Devon*, 'mɒdbərɪ, módbŭri

Moelfre *Clwyd, Gwynedd*, 'mɔɪlvreɪ, móylvray

Moelwyn, *Welsh C.n.*, 'mɔɪlwɪn, móylwin

Moelyci *Gwynedd*, mɔɪ'lʌkɪ, moylúcki

Moeran, *f.n.*, 'mɔrən, máwrăn

Moffat, *f.n.*, 'mɒfət, móffăt

Moffat *D. & G.*, 'mɒfət, móffăt

Moger, *f.n.*, 'moʊdʒər, mōjĕr

Mogey, *f.n.*, 'moʊgɪ, mōgi

Moggach, *f.n.*, 'mɒgəx, móggă<u>ch</u>

Mohan, *f.n.*, 'moʊhæn, mō-han

Moidart *H'land*, 'mɔɪdərt, móydărt

Moignard, *f.n.*, 'mɔɪnjɑrd, móyn--yaard

Moilliet, *f.n.*, 'mɔɪlɪet, móyli-et

Moin, The, *H'land*, mɔɪn, moyn

Moir, *f.n.*, 'mɔɪər, moyr

Moira *Leics.*, 'mɔɪrə, móyră

Moiseiwitsch, Benno, *pianist*, 'benoʊ mɔɪ'zeɪɪvɪtʃ, bénnō moyzáy-ivitch

Moiseiwitsch, Tanya, *stage designer*, 'tænjə mɔɪ'zeɪɪvɪtʃ, tányă moyzáy-ivitch

Moiser, *f.n.*, 'mɔɪzər, móyzĕr

Molash *Kent*, 'moʊlæʃ, mōlash

Mold *Clwyd*, moʊld, mōld

Molenan *Co. Derry*, mə'lenən, mōlénnăn

Molendinar, Burn, *Glasgow*, ˌmoʊlən'daɪnər, mōlĕndínăr

Molesey, East *and* West, *Surrey*, 'moʊlzɪ, mōlzi

Molesworth *Cambs.*, 'moʊlzwərθ, mōlzwŏrth

Moline, *f.n.*, moʊ'lin, mōleén

Molineux football stadium *Wolverhampton*, 'mɒlɪnju, móllinew

Molland-Botreaux *Devon*, 'mɒlənd 'bɒtrɪks, móllănd bóttricks

Mollard, *f.n.*, 'mɒlɑrd, móllaard

Molle, *f.n.*, mɒl, moll

Mollo, *f.n.*, 'mɒloʊ, móllō

Molloy, *f.n.*, mə'lɔɪ, mŏlóy

Molony, *f.n.*, mə'loʊnɪ, mōlóni

Molseed, *f.n.*, 'moʊlsɪd, mōlseed

Molson, *f.n.*, 'moʊlsən, mōlssŏn. *Appropriate also for Baron* ∼.

Molteno, *f.n.*, mɒl'tinoʊ, mol-teénō

Molyneaux, *f.n.*, 'mɒlɪnoʊ, móllinō

Molyneux, *f.n.*, 'mɒlɪnju, móllinew; 'mælɪnjuks, múllinewks; 'mɒlɪnjuks, móllinewks; 'mælɪnju, múllinew. *The first is appropriate for the Earl of Sefton's family name and therefore for Viscount* ∼.

Momerie, *f.n.*, 'mʌmərɪ, múmmĕri

Monadhliadh Mountains *H'land*, 'moʊnə'liə, mōnălee'-ă

Monaghan, *f.n.*, 'mɒnəhən, mónnă-hăn

Monahan, *f.n.*, 'mɒnəhən, mónnă-hăn

Monair, *f.n.*, mɒ'nɛər, monnáir

Monar, Loch, *H'land*, 'moʊnər, mōnăr

Moncaster, *f.n.*, 'mʌŋkəstər, múnkăstĕr

Monck, *f.n.*, mʌŋk, munk. *Appropriate also for Viscount* ∼.

Monckton, *f.n.*, 'mʌŋktən, múnktŏn

Monckton of Brenchley, Viscount, 'mʌŋktən əv 'brentʃlɪ, múnktŏn ŏv bréntchli

Moncreiff, *f.n.*, mən'krif, mŏn-kreéf. *Appropriate also for Baron* ∼.

Moncreiffe, *f.n.*, mən'krif, mŏn-kreéf. *Appropriate also for Sir Iain* ∼ *of that Ilk.*

Moncrieff, *f.n.*, mən'krif, mŏn-kreéf; mɒn'krif, mon-kreéf

Moncrieffe, *f.n.*, mən'krif, mŏn-kreéf

Moncur, *f.n.*, mɒn'kɜr, mon-kúr

Mondynes *Grampian*, mɒn'daɪnz, mondínz

Monea *Co. Fermanagh*, mʌ'neɪ, munnáy

Money, *f.n.*, 'mʌnɪ, múnni

Moneydie *Tayside*, mɒ'nidɪ, monneédi; mɒ'naɪdɪ, monnídi

Moneyglass *Co. Antrim*, ˌmʌnɪ'glas, munniglaáss

Moneymore *Co. Derry*, ˌmʌnɪ-'mɔr, munnimór

Moneypenny, *f.n.*, 'mʌnɪpenɪ, múnnipenni; 'mɒnɪpenɪ, mónnipenni

Moneyreagh *Co. Tyrone*, ˌmʌnɪ-'reɪ, munniráy

Mongeham, Great *and* Little, *Kent*, 'mʌndʒəm, múnjăm

Monger, *f.n.*, 'mʌŋgər, múng-gĕr

Mongewell *Oxon.*, 'mʌndʒwel, múnjwel

Moniaive *D. & G.*, ˌmɒnɪ'aɪv, monni-ív

Monifieth *Tayside*, ˌmʌnɪ'fiθ, munnifeéth

Monikie *Tayside*, mə'nikɪ, mōneéki

Monkhouse, *f.n.*, 'mʌŋkhaʊs, múnk-howss

Monkman, *f.n.*, 'mʌŋkmən, múnkmăn

Monks Eleigh *Suffolk*, mʌnks 'ilɪ, munks eéli

Monkton *Dyfed, Mid & S. Glam.*, 'mʌŋktən, múnktŏn

Monkwearmouth *Tyne & Wear*, mʌŋk'wɪərmaʊθ, munk--weérmowth

Monlough *Co. Down*, 'mɒnlɒx, mónlo<u>ch</u>

Monmouth *Gwent*, 'mʌnməθ, múnmŭth; 'mɒnməθ, mónmŭth

Monnet, *f.n.*, 'mɒneɪ, mónnay

Monnow, River, *Gwent*, 'mʌnoʊ, múnnō; 'mɒnoʊ, mónnō

Monquhitter *Grampian*, mɒn-'hwɪtər, monwhíttĕr

Monro, *f.n.*, 'mʌn'roʊ, mŏnrō; mʌn'roʊ, munrō; mɒn'roʊ, monrō

Monsarrat, *f.n.*, 'mɒnsəræt, mónssărat; ˌmɒnsə'ræt, monssărát

Monsell, *f.n.*, 'mʌnsl, múnssl. *Appropriate also for Viscount* ~.

Monsey, *f.n.*, 'mɒnsɪ, mónssi

Monslow, *f.n.*, 'mɒnzloʊ, mónzlō

Monson, *f.n.*, 'mʌnsən, múnssŏn; 'mɒnsən, mónssŏn. *The first is appropriate for Baron* ~.

Montacute *Somerset*, 'mɒntəkjut, móntăkewt

Montagnon, *f.n.*, mɒn'tænjɒ, montán-yŏng; mɒ'tænjɒ, mŏng-tán-yŏng

Montagu of Beaulieu, Baron, 'mɒntəgju əv 'bjulɪ, móntăgew ŏv béwli

Monté, *f.n.*, 'mɒnteɪ, móntay

Monteagle, Baron, mən'tigl, mŏnteégl

Montefiore, *f.n.*, ˌmɒntɪ'fjɔrɪ, montĕfyáwri

Monteith, *f.n.*, mɒn'tiθ, monteéth

Montgomerie, *f.n.*, mənt'gʌmərɪ, mŏntgúmmĕri; mən'gʌmərɪ, mŏn-gúmmĕri; mənt'gɒmərɪ, mŏntgómmĕri

Montgomery, *f.n.*, mənt'gʌmərɪ, mŏntgúmmĕri; mən'gʌmərɪ, mŏn-gúmmĕri; mənt'gɒmərɪ, mŏntgómmĕri

Montgomery *Powys*, mənt'gʌmrɪ, mŏntgúmri; mənt'gɒmərɪ, mŏntgómmĕri

Montgomery of Alamein, Viscount, mənt'gʌmərɪ əv 'æləmeɪn, mŏntgúmmĕri ŏv álămayn

Montpelier *Bristol* mɒnt'pelɪər, montpélli-ĕr

Montresor, *f.n.*, 'mɒntrezər, móntrezzŏr

Montrose *Tayside*, mɒn'troʊz, montrṓz; mən'troʊz, mŏntrṓz. *The first is appropriate for the Duke of* ~.

Monyash *Derby.*, 'mʌnɪæʃ, múnni-ash

Monymusk *Grampian*, ˌmɒnɪ-'mʌsk, monnimússk

Monzie *Tayside*, mɒ'ni, monneé; mə'ni, mŏneé

Monzievaird *Tayside*, ˌmɒnɪ'vɛərd, monniváird

Mooney, *f.n.*, 'munɪ, moóni

Moonie, *f.n.*, 'munɪ, moóni

Moonzie *Fife*, 'munzɪ, moónzi

Moorat, *f.n.*, 'mʊəræt, moőrat

Moore, *f.n.*, mʊər, moŏr

Moorfea *Hoy (Orkney)*, mʊər'feɪ, moŏr-fáy

Moorfoot, *f.n.*, 'mʊərfʊt, moŏr-foŏt

Moorhead, *f.n.*, 'mʊərhed, moŏr-hed

Moortown *W. Yorks.*, 'mʊərtaʊn, moŏrtown

Moos, *f.n.*, mus, mooss

Morahan, *f.n.*, 'mɒrəhən, mórră-hăn

Moran, *f.n.*, 'mɒrən, máwrən; 'mɒrən, mórrăn; mə'ræn, mŏrán; *The first is appropriate for Baron* ~.

Morant, *f.n.*, mə'rænt, mŏránt

Morar *H'land*, 'mɒrər, máwrăr

Moray *Grampian*, 'mʌrɪ, múrri. *Appropriate also for the Earl of* ~ *and the* ~ *Firth*.

Morcom, *f.n.*, 'mɔrkəm, mórkŏm

Mordaunt, *f.n.*, 'mɔrdənt, mór-dănt; 'mɔrdɒnt, mórdawnt

Mordecai, *f.n.*, 'mɔrdɪkaɪ, mór-dĕkī

Mordiford *H. & W.*, 'mɔrdɪfərd, mórdifŏrd

Mordue, *f.n.*, 'mɔrdju, mórdew

More, *f.n.*, mɔr, mor

Morebath *Devon*, 'mɔrbəθ, mór-baath

Morecambe, *f.n.*, 'mɔrkəm, mórkăm

Morecambe *Lancs.*, 'mɔrkəm, mórkăm

Morehen, *f.n.*, 'mɔrhen, mór-hen

Moreing, *f.n.*, 'mɔrɪŋ, máwring

Morel, *f.n.*, mə'rel, mawréll; mə'rel, mŏréll

Moreland, *f.n.*, 'mɔrlənd, mórländ

Moreleigh *Devon*, 'mɔrlɪ, mórli

Morell, *f.n.*, mɒ'rel, morréll; mə'rel, mŏréll

Morelle, *f.n.*, mə'rel, mŏréll

Morena, *f.n.*, mɒ'rinə, morreénă

Moresby, *f.n.*, 'mɔrzbɪ, mórzbi

Moresby *Cumbria*, 'mɒrɪsbɪ, mórrĕssbi

Moreton, *f.n.*, 'mɔrtən, mórtŏn

Moreton Morrell *Warwicks.*, 'mɔrtən 'mɒrəl, mórtŏn mórrĕl

Morey, *f.n.*, 'mɒrɪ, máwri

Morfa Rhuddlan *Clwyd*, 'mɔrvə 'hrɪðlæn, mórvă ríthlan

Morfudd, *Welsh C.n.*, 'mɔrvɪð, mórvith

Morgan, *f.n.*, 'mɔrgən, mórgăn

Morgenstern, *f.n.*, 'mɔrgənstɜrn, mórgĕnsstern

Moriarty, *f.n.,* ˌmɒrɪˈɑːrtɪ, morri-
-aárti

Morice, *f.n.,* ˈmɒrɪs, mórriss

Morin, *f.n.,* ˈmɔːrɪn, máwrin

Morison, *f.n.,* ˈmɒrɪsən, mórrissŏn

Morissy, *f.n.,* ˈmɒrɪsɪ, mórrissi

Morland, *f.n.,* ˈmɔːlənd, mórlănd

Morley, *f.n.,* ˈmɔːlɪ, mórli

Moro, *f.n.,* ˈmɒrou, mórrō

Morpeth *Northd.,* ˈmɔːrpəθ, mór-
pĕth

Morpurgo, *f.n.,* mɔːrˈpɜːrgou, mor-
púrgō

Morrah, *f.n.,* ˈmɒrə, mórră

Morrell, *f.n.,* məˈrel, mŏréll;
mɒˈrel, morréll; ˈmʌrəl, múrrĕl.
*The third is appropriate for
Lady Ottoline ~.*

Morrell, Moreton, *Warwicks.,*
ˈmɔːrtən ˈmɒrəl, mórtŏn mórrĕl

Morrick, *f.n.,* ˈmɒrɪk, mórrick

Morris, *f.n.,* ˈmɒrɪs, mórriss

Morrison, *f.n.,* ˈmɒrɪsən, mórrissŏn

Morrissey, *f.n.,* ˈmɒrɪsɪ, mórrissi

Morrow, *f.n.,* ˈmɒrou, mórrō

Morse, *f.n.,* mɔːrs, morss

Morshead, *f.n.,* ˈmɔːrzhed, mórz-
-hed

Mortehoe *Devon,* ˈmɔːrthou, mórt-
-hō

Morteshed, *f.n.,* ˈmɔːrtɪʃed,
mórtĕ-shed

Mortimer, *f.n.,* ˈmɔːrtɪmər, mórtimĕr

Mortlach *Grampian,* ˈmɔːrtləx,
mórtlă<u>ch</u>

Mortlake *London,* ˈmɔːrtleɪk, mórt-
-layk

Morton, *f.n.,* ˈmɔːrtən, mórtŏn

Morvah *Cornwall,* ˈmɔːrvə, mórvă

Morwena, *Welsh C.n.,* mɔːrˈwenə,
morwénnă

Morwenstow *Cornwall,* ˈmɔːrwɪn-
stou, mórwĕnsstō

Mosborough *S. Yorks.,* ˈmɒzbrə,
mózbră; ˈmɒzbərə, mózbŭră

Moscow *S'clyde,* ˈmɒskou,
mósskō

Moseley, *f.n.,* ˈmouzlɪ, mózli

Moser, *Prof. Sir* **Claus,** ˈklaus
ˈmouzər, klówss mózĕr

Mosley, *f.n.,* ˈmouzlɪ, mózli;
ˈmɒzlɪ, mózzli

Mosley Common *Gtr. M'chester,*
ˈmɒslɪ ˈkɒmən, móssli kómmŏn

Mossley *Co. Antrim,* ˈmɒslɪ,
móssli

Moss Side *Gtr. M'chester,* ˈmɒs
ˈsaɪd, móss síd

Mosterton *Dorset,* ˈmɒstərtən,
mósstĕrtŏn

Mostyn *Clwyd,* ˈmɒstɪn, mósstin.
Appropriate also for Baron ~.

Mothecombe *Devon,* ˈmʌðəkəm,
mú<u>th</u>ĕkŭm

Motley, *f.n.,* ˈmɒtlɪ, móttli

Mottershead, *f.n.,* ˈmɒtərzhed,
móttĕrz-hed

Motteux, Peter Anthony, *17th–
18th-c. translator and dramatist,*
ˈmɒtɜː, móttö

Mottistone, Baron, ˈmɒtɪstən,
móttistŏn

Motyer, *f.n.,* məˈtɪər, mŏtéer

Mouat, *f.n.,* ˈmouət, mó-ăt

Moubray, *f.n.,* ˈmoubreɪ, mớbray

Moughtin, *f.n.,* ˈmɒtɪn, máwtin

Moughton, *f.n.,* ˈmoutən, mótŏn

Mouillot, *f.n.,* ˈmujou, moo-yō

Mouland, *f.n.,* ˈmulənd, móoländ;
muˈlænd, mooländ

Mouldsworth *Ches.,* ˈmouldz-
wɜːrθ, mớldzwurth

Moule, *f.n.,* moul, mōl; mul, mool

Moulin *Tayside,* ˈmulɪn, móolin

Moulinearn *Tayside,* ˌmulɪnˈɑːrn,
moolinaárn

Moulsecoomb, *also spelt* **Moulse-
coombe, Moulsecombe,**
E. Sussex, ˈmoulskum, mớls-
skoom

Moulsford *Oxon.,* ˈmoulzfərd,
mớlzfŏrd

Moulsham *Chelmsford (Essex),*
ˈmoulʃəm, mớl-shăm

Moulsoe *Bucks.,* ˈmoulsou,
mớlssō

Moulson, *f.n.,* ˈmoulsən, mớlssŏn

Moulton *Ches., Northants.,* ˈmoultən, mớltŏn

Moulton Eaugate *Lincs.,* ˈmoultən
ˈɪgeɪt, mớltŏn éegayt; ˈmoultən
ˈɪgət, mớltŏn éegăt

Moultrie, *f.n.,* ˈmutrɪ, móotri

Mouncer, *f.n.,* ˈmaunsər, mównssĕr

Mounsey, *f.n.,* ˈmaunsɪ, mównssi

Mountain Ash *Mid Glam.,* ˈmaun-
tɪn ˈæʃ, mówntin ásh

Mountbatten of Burma, Countess,
maunt ˈbætən əv ˈbɜːrmə, mownt-
báttĕn ŏv búrmă

Mount Edgcumbe, Earl of,
maunt ˈedʒkəm, mownt éjkŭm

Mount Edgcumbe and Valletort,
Viscount, maunt ˈedʒkəm *and*
ˈvælɪtɔːrt, mownt éjkŭm ănd
válitort

Mountevans, Baron, maunt ˈevənz,
mowntévvănz

Mountfort, *f.n.,* ˈmauntfɔːrt,
mówntfort; ˈmauntfərt, mównt-
fŏrt

Mountgarret, Viscount, maunt-
ˈgærɪt, mowntgárrĕt

Mountjoy, *f.n.,* maunt ˈdʒɔɪ,
mownt-jóy; ˈmauntdʒɔɪ,
mównt-joy

Mount Kedar *D. & G.*, maʊnt 'kidər, mownt keedăr

Mountpottinger *Co. Down*, maʊnt'pɒtɪndʒər, mownt- -póttinjĕr

Mount Sorrel *Wilts.*, maʊnt 'sɒrəl, mownt sórrĕl

Mourby, *f.n.*, 'mɔrbɪ, mórbi

Mourne Mountains *Co. Down*, mɔrn, morn

Mousa *Shetland*, 'muzə, mo′oză

Mousehold *Norfolk*, 'maʊshoʊld, mówss-hōld. *Appropriate also for* ~ *Heath.*

Mousehole *Cornwall*, 'maʊzl, mówzl

Mousley, *f.n.*, 'maʊslɪ, mówssli

Mouswald *D. & G.*, 'musl, moóssl

Moutell, *f.n.*, moʊ'tel, mōtéll

Moverley, *f.n.*, 'moʊvərlɪ, móvĕrli

Movilla *Co. Down*, moʊ'vɪlə, mōvíllă

Mowat, *f.n.*, 'moʊət, mó-ăt; 'maʊət, mów-ăt

Mowbray, Segrave and Stourton, Baron, 'moʊbrɪ 'sɪgreɪv ənd 'stɜrtən, móbri seégrayv ănd stŭrtŏn

Mow Cop *Ches.–Staffs.*, 'maʊ 'kɒp, mów kóp

Mowden Hall *Darlington*, 'maʊdən, mówdĕn

Mower, *f.n.*, 'moʊər, mó-ĕr

Mowhan *Co. Armagh*, 'moʊən, mó-ăn

Mowlem, *f.n.*, 'moʊləm, mólĕm

Mowling, *f.n.*, 'moʊlɪŋ, móling

Mowll, *f.n.*, moʊl, mōl

Mowsley *Leics.*, 'maʊzlɪ, mówzli; 'moʊzlɪ, mózli

Moya, *f.n.*, 'mɔɪə, móy-ă

Moyallon *Co. Down*, mɔɪ'ælən, moy-állŏn

Moyarget *Co. Antrim*, mɔɪ'ɑrgɪt, moy-a′argĕt

Moyers, *f.n.*, 'mɔɪərz, móyĕrz

Moyes, *f.n.*, mɔɪz, moyz

Moygashel *Co. Tyrone*, mɔɪ'gæʃl, moygáshl

Moyise, *f.n.*, 'mɔɪɪz, móy-iz

Moylena *Co. Antrim*, mɔɪ'linə, moyleénă

Moynahan, *f.n.*, 'mɔɪnəhən, móynă-hăn

Moynihan, Baron, 'mɔɪnɪən, móyni-ăn

Moyola *Co. Derry*, mɔɪ'oʊlə, moy-ōlă. *Appropriate also for Baron* ~.

Moys, *f.n.*, mɔɪz, moyz

Moyse, *f.n.*, mɔɪz, moyz

Moyses, *f.n.*, 'mɔɪzɪs, móyzĕss

Mozley, *f.n.*, 'moʊzlɪ, mózli

Muchalls *Grampian*, 'mʌxlz, múchlz

Muchelney *Somerset*, 'mʌtʃəlnɪ, mútchĕlni

Muck *H'land*, mʌk, muck

Muckamore *Co. Antrim*, ˌmʌkə-'mɔr, muckămór

Muckle Flugga *Shetland*, 'mʌkl 'flʌgə, múckl flúggă

Muddiman, *f.n.*, 'mʌdɪmən, múddimăn

Mudeford *Dorset*, 'mʌdɪfərd, múddĕfŏrd

Mudell, *f.n.*, mə'del, mŭdéll

Mudie, *f.n.*, 'mjudɪ, méwdi

Mugdock Castle *S'clyde*, 'mʌgdɒk, múgdock

Muggerhanger *Beds.*, 'mʊər-hæŋər, moór-hang-ĕr

Muggeridge, *f.n.*, 'mʌgərɪdʒ, múggĕrij

Mugginton *Derby.*, 'mʌgɪntən, múggintŏn

Muggleswick *Durham*, 'mʌglzwɪk, múgglzwick

Muggoch, *f.n.*, 'mʌgəx, múggŏch

Mughan, *f.n.*, 'mjuhən, méw-hăn

Mugiemoss *Grampian*, 'mʌgɪmɒs, múggimoss

Mugliston, *f.n.*, 'mʌglɪstən, múgglistŏn

Mugridge, *f.n.*, 'mʌgrɪdʒ, múgrij

Muick, Loch *and* River, *Grampian*, mɪk, mick

Muil, *f.n.*, mjul, mewl

Muill, *f.n.*, mjul, mewl

Muille, *f.n.*, mjul, mewl

Muinzer, *f.n.*, 'mʊnzər, moónzĕr

Muir, *f.n.*, mjʊər, myoór

Muirden, *f.n.*, mjʊər'den, myoŏr-dén

Muirhead, *f.n.*, 'mjʊərhed, myoŏr- -hed

Muirhouses *Central*, 'mʌrɪz, múrriz

Muir of Ord *H'land*, 'mjʊər əv 'ɔrd, myoŏr ŏv órd

Muirshiel, Viscount, 'mjʊərʃil, myoŏr-sheel

Mukle, *f.n.*, 'mjuklɪ, méwkli

Mulbarton *Norfolk*, mʌl'bɑrtən, mulbaártŏn

Mulben *Grampian*, mʌl'ben, mul- bén

Mulcaghey, *f.n.*, mʌl'kæxɪ, mul- káchi

Mulcahy, *f.n.*, mʌl'kæhɪ, mulká-hi

Mulchrone, *f.n.*, mʌl'kroʊn, mulkrón

Mulcock, *f.n.*, 'mʌlkɒk, múlkock

Mulder, *f.n.*, 'mʌldər, múldĕr

Muldoon, *f.n.*, mʌl'dun, muldoón

Muldowney, *f.n.*, mʌl'daʊnɪ, muldówni

Mule, *f.n.*, mjul, mewl
Mulgrew, *f.n.*, mʌl'gru, mulgroo
Mulhall, *f.n.*, məl'hɒl, mŭl-háwl
Mulhare, *f.n.*, mʌl'hɛər, mul-háir
Mulhern, *f.n.*, mʌl'hɜrn, mul-hérn
Mulholland, *f.n.*, mʌl'hɒlənd, mul--hólländ
Mull *S'clyde*, mʌl, mull. *Appropriate also for the Sound of ~.*
Mullaghbane *Co. Armagh*, ˌmʌlə'glɑs, mullăglaáss
Mullagh Ouyre *I. of Man*, 'mulək 'auər, moolǎck ówr
Mullally, *f.n.*, mʌ'læli, mulláli
Mullaly, *f.n.*, mʌ'leɪli, mulláyli
Mullan, *f.n.*, 'mʌlən, múllǎn
Mullans, *f.n.*, 'mʌlənz, múllǎnz
Mullardoch, Loch, *H'land*, mʌ'lɑrdɒx, mullaárdo<u>ch</u>
Mullen, *f.n.*, 'mʌlən, múllěn
Muller, *f.n.*, 'mʌlər, múllěr
Mulley, *f.n.*, 'mʌli, múlli
Mulligan, *f.n.*, 'mʌligən, múlligǎn
Mullinar, *f.n.*, 'mʌlinər, múllinǎr
Mulliner, *f.n.*, 'mʌlinər, múlliněr
Mullineux, *f.n.*, 'mʌlinə, múllinǎ
Mullins, *f.n.*, 'mʌlinz, múllinz
Mullion *Cornwall*, 'mʌliən, múllión
Mullo, *f.n.*, 'mʌlou, múllō
Mull of Kintyre *S'clyde*, 'mʌl əv kɪn'taɪər, múll ǒv kintír
Mull of Oa *S'clyde*, 'mʌl əv 'ou, múll ǒv ō
Mullyard *Co. Antrim*, ˌmʌli'ɑrd, mulli-aárd
Mulock, *f.n.*, 'mjulɒk, méwlock
Mulot, *f.n.*, 'mjulou, méwlō
Mulrine, *f.n.*, mʌl'raɪn, mulrín
Mulso, *f.n.*, 'mʌlsou, múlssō
Muncaster, *f.n.*, 'mʌŋkəstər, múnkǎstěr
Munda, saint, 'mʌndə, múndǎ
Munday, *f.n.*, 'mʌndeɪ, múnday
Mundesley *Norfolk*, 'mʌnzli, múnzli
Mundford *Norfolk*, 'mʌndfərd, múndförd
Mungean, *f.n.*, 'mʌndʒən, múnjǎn
Mungo, *C.n.*, 'mʌŋgou, múng-gō
Mungrisdale *Cumbria*, mʌŋ-'graɪzdeɪl, mung-grízdayl
Munnelly, *f.n.*, 'mʌnəli, múnněli
Munns, *f.n.*, mʌnz, munnz
Munro, *f.n.*, mən'rou, mŭnró; mʌn'rou, munró
Munroe, *f.n.*, mən'rou, mŭnró; mʌn'rou, munró
Munrow, *f.n.*, 'mʌnrou, múnrō
Muntham Woods *W. Sussex*, 'mʌnθəm, múnthǎm
Munthe, *f.n.*, 'mʌnti, múnti
Muraille, *f.n.*, mjuə'reɪl, myooráyl
Murdin, *f.n.*, 'mɜrdɪn, múrdin

Murdoch, *f.n.*, 'mɜrdəx, múrdŏ<u>ch</u>; 'mɜrdɒk, múrdock
Mure, *f.n.*, mjuər, myoōr
Murgett, *f.n.*, 'mɜrgɪt, múrgět
Murie, *f.n.*, 'mjuəri, myoōri
Murless, *f.n.*, 'mɜrlɪs, múrlěss
Murlough *Co. Down*, 'mɜrlɒx, múrlo<u>ch</u>
Murnaghan, *f.n.*, 'mɜrnəhən, múrnǎhǎn
Murphy, *f.n.*, 'mɜrfɪ, múrfi
Murrant, *f.n.*, 'mʌrənt, múrrǎnt
Murray, *f.n.*, 'mʌri, múrri
Murrell, *f.n.*, 'mʌrəl, múrrěl; mʌ'rel, murréll
Murricane, *f.n.*, 'mʌrɪkeɪn, múrrikayn
Murrill, *f.n.*, 'mʌrɪl, múrril
Murroes *Tayside*, 'mʌrouz, múrrōz; 'mɒrɪs, mórriss
Murrow *Cambs.*, 'mʌrə, múrrǎ
Murtagh, *f.n.*, 'mɜrtə, múrtǎ
Murthly *Tayside*, 'mɜrθli, múrthli
Murtle *Grampian*, 'mɜrtl, múrtl
Muschamp, *f.n.*, 'mʌskəm, músskäm
Musgrave, *f.n.*, 'mʌzgreɪv, múzzgrayv
Musidora Stakes, *horse-race*, ˌmjusɪ'dɒrə, mewssidáwrǎ
Musselburgh *Lothian*, 'mʌslbərə, músslbŭrǎ
Mussett, *f.n.*, 'mʌsɪt, mússět
Must, *f.n.*, mʌst, musst
Mustill, *f.n.*, 'mʌstɪl, músstil
Muthill *Tayside*, 'mjuθɪl, méw-thil
Mutley *Devon*, 'mʌtli, múttli
Mutter, *f.n.*, 'mʌtər, múttěr
Muybridge, Eadweard, *photographic pioneer*, 'edwərd 'maɪbrɪdʒ, édwǎrd míbrij
Myatt, *f.n.*, 'maɪət, mí-ǎt
Mycock, *f.n.*, 'maɪkɒk, míkock; 'maɪkou, míkō
Myddfai *Dyfed*, 'mʌðvaɪ, múthvī; 'mɪðvaɪ, míthvī
Myddleton, *f.n.*, 'mɪdltən, míddltŏn
Mydrim *Dyfed*, 'maɪdrɪm, mídrim
Myers, *f.n.*, 'maɪərz, mí-ěrz
Myerscough, *f.n.*, 'maɪərskou, mí-ěrsskō; 'maɪərskɒf, mí-ěrsskoff
Myerscough *Lancs.*, 'maɪərskou, mí-ěrsskō
Myfanwy, *Welsh C.n.*, mə'vænwɪ, mŭvánwi
Mylechreest, *f.n.*, 'mɪlkrist, mílkreest
Myles, *f.n.*, maɪlz, mīlz
Mylne, *f.n.*, mɪln, miln
Mylod, *f.n.*, 'maɪlɒd, mílod
Mylor *Cornwall*, 'maɪlər, mílŏr
Mylrea, *f.n.*, mɪl'reɪ, milráy

Mynachdy *Cardiff*, məˈnækdɪ, mŭnákdi
Mynett, *f.n.*, ˈmaɪnɪt, mínĕt; maɪˈnet, mīnétt
Mynors, *f.n.*, ˈmaɪnərz, mínŏrz
Mynott, *f.n.*, ˈmaɪnət, mínŏt
Mynyddcerrig *Dyfed*, ˌmʌnɪð-ˈkerɪg, munnithkérrig
Mynyddislwyn *Gwent*, ˌmʌnɪð-ˈɪslʊɪn, munnithíssloŏ-in
Myrddin-Evans, Sir **Guildhaume** *international labour expert*, ˈgɪldoʊm ˈmərðɪn ˈevənz, gíldōm múrthin évvănz
Myroe *Co. Derry*, maɪˈroʊ, mīró
Mysliwiec, *f.n.*, mɪʃˈlivies, mishleévi-ess
Mytchett *Surrey*, ˈmɪtʃɪt, mítchĕt
Mytholm *W. Yorks.*, ˈmaɪðəm, míthŏm
Mytholmroyd *W. Yorks.*, ˌmaɪðəmˈrɔɪd, míthōmróyd
Mythop *Lancs.*, ˈmaɪθɒp, míth-op
Myton *Warwicks.*, ˈmaɪtən, mítŏn
Myton upon Swale *N. Yorks.*, ˈmaɪtən əpɒn ˈsweɪl, mítŏn ŭpon swáyl
Mytton, *f.n.*, ˈmɪtən, míttŏn

N

Naan, *f.n.* nɑn, naan
Naar, *f.n.*, nɑr, naar
Naas, Baron, neɪs, nayss
Nabarro, *f.n.*, nəˈbɑroʊ, năbaárō
Naburn *N. Yorks.*, ˈneɪbərn, náybŭrn
Naden, *f.n.*, ˈneɪdən, náydĕn
Naesmith, *f.n.*, ˈneɪsmɪθ, náyssmith
Nagel, *f.n.*, ˈneɪgl, náygl; ˈnɑgl, naágl
Nagele, *f.n.*, nəˈgelɪ, năgélli
Nagington, *f.n.*, ˈnægɪŋtən, nággingtŏn
Nahum, *C.n.*, ˈneɪhəm, náy-hŭm
Naidoo, *f.n.*, ˈnaɪdu, nídoo
Nairac, *f.n.*, ˈneəræk, náirack
Nairn *H'land*, neərn, nairn
Nairne, Baroness, neərn, nairn
Naish, *f.n.*, neɪʃ, naysh; næʃ, nash
Nalder, *f.n.*, ˈnɔldər, náwldĕr
Nall, *f.n.*, nɒl, nawl
Nallen, *f.n.*, ˈnælən, nálĕn
Nally, *f.n.*, ˈnælɪ, náli
Nalty, *f.n.*, ˈnæltɪ, nálti
Namier, *f.n.*, ˈneɪˌmɪər, náy-meer
Nancegollan *Cornwall*, ˌnænsɪ-ˈgɒlən, nanssĕgóllän

Nancekivell, *f.n.*, næns'kɪvl, nansskívvl; ˈnænskɪvl, nánss-kivvl; ˌnænskɪˈvel, nansski-véll
Nancekuke *Cornwall*, næns'kjuk, nansskéwk
Nancledra *Cornwall*, næn'kledrə, nan-klédrä
Nanjizal Bay *Cornwall*, næn'dʒɪzl, nanjízzl
Nankeville, *f.n.*, ˈnæŋkɪvɪl, nánkĕvil
Nanmor, River, *Gwynedd*, ˈnæn-mɔr, nán-mor
Nannerch *Clwyd*, ˈnænɛərx, nánnairch
Nantbwlch-yr-Haiarn *Gwynedd*, nænt'bʊlx ər ˈhaɪərn, nant-boŏlch ŭr hí-ärn
Nantclwyd *Clwyd*, nænt'klʊɪd, nantkloŏ-id
Nantcwnlle *Dyfed*, nænt'kʊnɬeɪ, nantkoŏnlhay
Nant Eos *Dyfed*, nænt 'eɪɒs, nant áy-oss
Nantffrancon *Gwynedd*, nænt-ˈfræŋkən, nantfránkŏn
Nantgaredig *Dyfed*, ˌnæntgə-ˈredɪg, nantgəréddig
Nantgarw *Mid Glam.*, nænt'gæru, nantgárroo
Nantgwynant *Dyfed*, nænt-ˈgwɪnænt, nantgwinnant
Nantlle *Gwynedd*, ˈnæntɬeɪ, nánt-hlay
Nantmel *Powys*, ˈnæntmel, nánt-mel; ˈnænt'meɪl, nántmáyl
Nant Peris *Gwynedd*, nænt 'perɪs, nant pérriss
Nantwich *Ches.*, ˈnæntwɪtʃ, nánt-witch; ˈnæntwaɪtʃ, nántwítch
Nant-y-bwch *Gwent*, ˌnæntə'bux, nantăboŏch
Nant-y-Bwch, River, *Powys*, ˌnæntə'bux, nantăboŏch
Nant-y-caws *Dyfed*, ˌnæntə'kaʊs, nantăkówss
Nantyffyllon *Mid Glam.*, ˌnæntə-ˈfʌɪɒn, nantăfúhlon
Nant-y-glo *Gwent*, ˌnæntə'gloʊ, nantăglÓ
Nant-y-groes *Gwent*, ˌnæntə'grɔɪs, nantăgróyss
Nant-y-moel *Mid Glam.*, ˌnæntə-ˈmɔɪl, nantămóyl
Nantyronen *Dyfed*, ˌnæntə-ˈroʊnən, nantărónĕn
Napier, *f.n.*, ˈneɪpɪər, náyp-yĕr; nə'pɪər, năpéer. *The first is appropriate for John ~, inventor of logarithms.*
Napier and Ettrick, Baron, ˈneɪpjər ənd 'etrɪk, náyp-yĕr ănd éttrick

Napier of Magdala, Baron, 'neɪpjər əv mæg'dalə, náyp-yĕr ŏv magdáală
Napley, *f.n.*, 'næplɪ, nápli
Narberth *Dyfed*, 'nɑrbərθ, naár-bĕrth
Nares, *f.n.*, nɛərz, nairz
Naser, *f.n.*, 'neɪzər, náyzĕr
Nasmith, *f.n.*, 'neɪsmɪθ, náyssmith
Nason, *f.n.*, 'neɪsən, náyssŏn
Nasse, *f.n.*, 'næsɪ, nássi
Nassim, *f.n.*, nə'sim, năsseém
Nateley Scures *Hants*, 'neɪtlɪ 'skjʊərz, náytli skéw-ĕrz
Nathan, *f.n.*, 'neɪθən, náythăn. *Appropriate also for Baron* ~.
Natt, *f.n.*, næt, nat
Nattrass, *f.n.*, 'nætrəs, nátrăss
Naulls *f.n.*, nɔlz, nawlz
Navan *Co. Armagh*, 'nævən, návvăn
Navar *Tayside*, 'neɪvər, náyvăr
Navenby *Lincs.*, 'neɪvənbɪ, náy-vĕnbi; 'nævənbɪ, návvĕnbi
Navin, *f.n.*, 'nævɪn, návvin
Navratil, *f.n.*, 'nævrətɪl, návrátil
Naworth *Cumbria*, 'naʊərθ, nów-ürth; 'nɑwərθ, naá-würth
Naworth Castle *Cumbria*, 'nɑərθ, naá-ĕrth; nɑrθ, naarth
Naylor, *f.n.*, 'neɪlər, náylŏr
Nazeing *Essex*, 'neɪzɪŋ, náyzing
Neagh, Lough, *N. Ireland*, lɒx 'neɪ, loch náy
Neagle, *f.n.*, 'nigl, néegl
Neal, *C.n. and .fn.*, nil, neel
Neale, *f.n.*, nil, neel
Neaman, Yfrah, *violinist*, 'ifrə 'nimən, éefră néemăn
Nears, *f.n.*, nɪərz, neerz
Neary, *f.n.*, 'nɪərɪ, neéri
Neath *W. Glam.*, niθ, neeth
Neath, River, *Powys–W. Glam.*, niθ, neeth
Neatishead *Norfolk*, 'nitshed, neéts-hed; 'nitished, neétiss-hed; 'nitsted, neétsted. *The second is used by Service personnel for the local RAF Station. The third is the traditional local pronunciation, rarely heard nowadays.*
Neave, *f.n.*, niv, neev
Neaverson, *f.n.*, 'nevərsən, névvĕrssŏn; 'nivərsən, neévĕrssŏn
Nebo *Dyfed, Gwynedd*, 'nebʊ, nébbŏ
Nechells *W. Midlands*, 'nitʃlz, neétchlz
Neden, *f.n.*, 'nidən, neédĕn
Needham, *f.n.*, 'nidəm, neédăm
Needingworth *Cambs.*, 'nidɪŋwərθ, neéding-wŏrth
Needle, *f.n.*, 'nidl, neédl

Neesham, *f.n.*, 'niʃəm, neé-shăm
Negus, *f.n.*, 'nigəs, neégŭss
Neidpath Castle *Borders*, 'nidpaθ, neédpaath
Neild, *f.n.*, nild, neeld
Neilgrove, *f.n.*, 'nilgroʊv, neél-grŏv
Neill, *f.n.*, nil, neel
Neilson, *f.n.*, 'nilsən, neélssŏn
Neivens, *f.n.*, 'nɪvənz, neévĕnz
Nelligan, *f.n.*, 'nelɪgən, nélligăn
Nelmes, *f.n.*, nelmz, nelmz
Nelson *Lancs., Mid Glam.*, 'nelsən, nélssŏn
Nemeer, *f.n.*, 'nemɪər, némmeer
Nendrum Abbey *Co. Down*, 'nendrʌm, néndrum
Nene, River, *Northants.–Norfolk–Lincs.*, nen, nen; nin, neen. *The first of these is used in the neighbourhood of Northampton; the second in the neighbourhood of Peterborough and in Norfolk–Lincs.*
Nepean, *f.n.*, nɪ'pin, nĕpéen
Nercwys, *also spelt* **Nerquis**, *Clwyd*, 'nɛərkwɪs, náirkwiss; 'nɜrkwɪs, nérkwiss
Nesbitt, *f.n.*, 'nezbɪt, nézbit
Neslen, *f.n.*, 'nezlɪn, nézlĕn
Ness, Loch *and* River, *H'land*, nes, ness
Nessler, *f.n.*, 'neslər, nésslĕr
Nethan, River, *S'clyde*, 'neθən, néthăn
Nether Alderley *Ches.*, 'neðər 'ɔldərlɪ, néthĕr áwldĕrli
Netheravon *Wilts.*, 'neðəreɪvən, néthĕrayvŏn
Nether Broughton *Leics.*, 'neðər 'brɔtən, néthĕr bráwtŏn
Nethercote *Warwicks.*, 'neðərkət, néthĕrkŏt
Nether Haugh *S. Yorks.*, 'neðər 'hɔf, néthĕr háwf
Nether Heage *Derby.*, 'neðər 'hidʒ, néthĕr heéj
Nether Heyford *Northants.*, 'neðər 'heɪfərd, néthĕr háyfŏrd
Nether Langwith *Notts.*, 'neðər 'læŋwɪθ, néthĕr láng-with
Nether Lypiatt *Glos.*, 'neðər 'lɪpɪət, néthĕr líppi-ăt
Netherne *Surrey*, 'neðərn, néthĕrn
Netherthorpe, Baron, 'neðərθɔrp, néthĕr-thorp
Nether Wallop *Hants*, 'neðər 'wɒləp, néthĕr wóllŏp
Nether Wasdale, *also spelt* **Netherwastdale**, *Cumbria*, 'neðər 'wɒsdl, néthĕr wóssdl. **Netherwastdale** *is the ecclesiastical spelling.*

Nethy Bridge *H'land,* 'neθɪ 'brɪdʒ, néthi bríj
Nettel, *f.n.,* nə'tel, nĕtéll
Netteswell *Essex,* 'netswel, nétswel
Nettheim, *f.n.,* 'nethaɪm, nét-hīm
Nettlecombe *Somerset,* 'netlkum, néttlkoom
Nettleham *Lincs.,* 'netləm, néttl-ăm
Nettleingham, *f.n.,* 'netlɪŋhəm, néttling-hăm
Neubert, *f.n.,* 'njubərt, néwbĕrt
Neuss, *f.n.,* nɔɪs, noyss
Neustatter, *f.n.,* 'njustætər, néwstattĕr
Neve, *f.n.,* niv, neev
Neven, *f.n.,* 'nevən, névvĕn
Nevendon *Essex,* 'nevəndən, névvĕndŏn
Nevern, *f.n.,* 'nevərn, névvĕrn
Neves, *f.n.,* nivz, neevz
Nevile, *C.n.,* and *f.n.,* 'nevɪl, névvil; 'nevl, névvl
Nevill, *C.n. and f.n.,* 'nevɪl, névvil; 'nevl, névvl
Neville, *C.n. and f.n.,* 'nevɪl, névvil; 'nevl, névvl
Nevin *Gwynedd,* 'nevɪn, névvin
Nevis, Loch, *H'land,* 'nevɪs, névviss
Nevisburgh *H'land,* 'nevɪsbərə, névvissbŭră
Newark *Cambs.,* 'njuərk, néwărk
Neway, *f.n.,* 'njuweɪ, néw-way
Newbegin, *f.n.,* 'njubɪgɪn, néwbiggin
Newberry, *f.n.,* 'njubərɪ, néwbĕri
Newbert, *f.n.,* 'njubərt, néwbĕrt
Newbery, *f.n.,* 'njubərɪ, néwbĕri
Newbiggin-by-the-Sea *Northd.,* 'njubɪgɪn, néwbiggin
Newbigging, *f.n.,* 'njubɪgɪn, néwbigging; nju'bɪgɪn, newbígging
Newbigin, *f.n.,* 'njubɪgɪn, néwbiggin
Newbold, *f.n.,* 'njubould, néwbōld
Newbolt, *f.n.,* 'njuboult, néwbōlt
Newborough *Cambs., Gwynedd,* 'njubərə, néwbŭră
Newbould, *f.n.,* 'njubould, néwbōld
Newboult, *f.n.,* 'njuboult, néwbōlt
Newbrough *Northd.,* 'njubrʌf, néwbruff
Newbury, *f.n.,* 'njubərɪ, néwbŭri
Newby, *f.n.,* 'njubɪ, néwbi
New Byth *Grampian,* 'nju 'baɪθ, néw bíth
Newcastle *Co. Down, Gwent, Mid Glam.,* 'njukɑsl, néwkaassl
Newcastle Emlyn *Dyfed,* 'njukɑsl 'emlɪn, néwkaassl émlin

Newcastleton *Borders,* nju-'kɑsltən, newkáasslton
Newcastle-under-Lyme *Staffs.,* 'njukɑsl ʌndər 'laɪm, néwkaassl undĕr līm
Newcastle upon Tyne *Tyne & Wear,* 'njukɑsl əpɒn 'taɪn, néwkaassl ŭpon tín; nju'kæsl əpɒn 'taɪn, newkássl ŭpon tín. *The second, being the local pronunciation, should normally take precedence over the other. Here, however, is a case where the first is firmly established national usage.*
New Clipstone *Notts.,* 'nju 'klɪpstoʊn, néw klípstōn
Newcomen, Thomas, *inventor (1663–1729),* 'njukʌmən, néwkummĕn
Newcraighall *Lothian,* 'njukreɪg-'hɔl, néw-krayg-háwl
New Cumnock *S'clyde,* 'nju 'kʌmnək, néw kúmnŏk
Newdigate, Sir Roger, *18th-c. antiquary,* 'njudɪgeɪt, néwdigayt; 'njudɪgɪt, néwdigit. *Hence also for the ~ Prize for English verse.*
Newell, *f.n.,* 'njuəl, néwĕl
Newens, *f.n.,* 'njuənz, néwĕnz
Newent *Glos.,* 'njuənt, néw-ĕnt
Newfound *Hants,* 'njufaʊnd, néwfownd
New Galloway *D. & G.,* nju 'gæləweɪ, new gálŏ-way
Newham *London,* 'njuəm, néw-ăm; 'nju'hæm, néw-hám
Newham *Northd.,* 'njuəm, néw-ăm. *Appropriate for both places of the name in Northumberland.*
Newhaven *E. Sussex, Lothian,* 'njuheɪvən, néw-hayvĕn
New Houghton *Derby.,* 'nju 'hʌftən, néw húftŏn
Newill, *f.n.,* 'njuɪl, néw-il
Newington *Edinburgh,* 'njuɪŋtən, néwingtŏn
New Kyo *Durham,* 'nju 'kaɪoʊ, néw kí-ō
Newlove, *f.n.,* 'njulʌv, néwluv
Newlyn *Cornwall,* 'njulɪn, néwlin
Newman, *f.n.,* 'njumən, néwmăn
Newmark, *f.n.,* 'njumɑrk, néwmaark
Newmarket *Suffolk,* 'njumɑrkɪt, néwmaarkĕt
Newmills *Gwent,* nju'mɪlz, new-míllz
Newmilns *S'clyde,* nju'mɪlz, newmíllz
Newnes, *f.n.,* njunz, newnz

New Pitsligo *Grampian*, 'nju pɪt'slaɪgou, néw pitslígŏ

Newport Pagnell *Bucks.*, 'njupɔrt 'pægnəl, néwport págnĕl

Newquay *Cornwall*, 'njuki, néw-kee

New Quay *Dyfed* 'nju 'ki, néw kée

Newrick, *f.n.*, 'njurɪk, néw-rick

New Romney *Kent*, 'nju 'rɒmnɪ, néw rómni; 'nju 'rʌmnɪ, néw rúmni

Newry *Co. Down*, 'njʊərɪ, nyŏŏri

Newsham, *f.n.*, 'njuzəm, néwzăm

Newsome, *f.n.*, 'njusəm, néws-sŏm

Newsome *W. Yorks.*, 'njuzəm, néwzŏm

Newson, *f.n.*, 'njusən, néwssŏn

Newstone, *f.n.*, 'njustən, néws-stŏn

Newth, *f.n.*, njuθ, newth

Newtimber *W. Sussex*, 'njutɪmbər, néwtĭmbĕr

Newton, *f.n.*, 'njutən, néwtŏn

Newton Flotman *Norfolk*, 'njutən 'flɒtmən, néwtŏn flóttmăn

Newton Kyme *N. Yorks.*, 'njutən 'kaɪm, néwtŏn kím

Newton Mearns *S'clyde*, 'njutən 'mɛərnz, néwtŏn máirnz

Newtonmore *H'land*, 'njutən'mɔr, néwtŏnmór

Newton Morrell *N. Yorks.*, *Oxon.*, 'njutən 'mɒrəl, néwtŏn mórrĕl

Newton Purcell *Oxon.*, 'njutən 'pɜrsl, néwtŏn púrssl

Newton Reigny *Cumbria*, 'njutən 'reɪnɪ, néwtŏn ráyni

Newton St. Cyres *Devon*, 'njutən snt 'saɪərz, néwtŏn sĭnt sírz

Newton St. Loe *Avon*, 'njutən snt 'lou, néwtŏn sĭnt lṓ

Newtonstewart *D. & G.*, 'njutən'stjʊərt, néwtŏn-styŏŏ-ärt

Newtownabbey *Co. Antrim*, 'njutən'æbɪ, néwtŏnábbi

Newtownards *Co. Down*, 'njutən-'ɑrdz, néwtŏnaardz

Newtownbreda *Co. Down*, 'njutən-'bridə, néwtŏnbréedă; 'njutən-'breɪdə, néwtŏnbráydă

Newtownbutler *Co. Fermanagh*, 'njutən'bʌtlər, néwtŏnbúttlĕr

Newtown Crommelin *Co. Antrim*, 'njutən 'krʌmlɪn, néwtŏn krúmlin

Newtownhamilton *Co. Armagh*, 'njutən'hæmɪltən, néwtŏn-hámmiltŏn

Newtown St. Boswells *Borders*, 'njutən snt 'bɒzwəlz, néwtŏn sĭnt bózwĕlz

Newydd *Powys*, 'newɪð, né-wiᵭ

Neylan, *f.n.*, 'neɪlən, náylăn

Neyland *Dyfed*, 'neɪlənd, náy-länd

Neyroud, *f.n.*, 'neɪrud, náy-rood

Niall, *C.n. and f.n.*, nil, neel; 'naɪəl, ní-äl

Nian, *f.n.*, 'nɪən, née-ăn

Nias, *f.n.*, 'naɪəs, ní-ăss

Niblo, *f.n.*, 'nɪblou, níbblō

Nice, *f.n.*, nis, neess

Nicholls, *f.n.*, 'nɪklz, nícklz

Nicholson, *f.n.*, 'nɪklsən, níckls-sŏn

Nickalls, *f.n.*, 'nɪklz, nícklz

Nickels, *f.n.*, 'nɪklz, nícklz

Nicklin, *f.n.*, 'nɪklɪn, níck-lin

Nickolls, *f.n.*, 'nɪklz, nícklz

Nicol, *C.n. and f.n.*, 'nɪkl, níckl

Nicoll, *f.n.*, 'nɪkl, níckl

Nicolson, *f.n.*, 'nɪklsən, níckls-sŏn

Niddrie *Lothian*, 'nɪdrɪ, níddri

Niddry *Lothian*, 'nɪdrɪ, níddri

Nidon *Somerset*, 'naɪdən, nídŏn

Nield, *f.n.*, nild, neeld

Nieman, *f.n.*, 'naɪmən, nímăn; 'nimən, néemăn

Nieman, Alfred, *composer*, 'naɪmən, nímăn

Niemeyer, *f.n.*, 'nimaɪər, neemí-ĕr

Nifosi, *f.n.*, nɪ'fouzɪ, nifózi

Nigel, *C.n. and f.n.*, 'naɪdʒl, níjl

Nighy, *f.n.*, naɪ, ní

Nihill, *f.n.*, 'naɪhɪl, níhil

Niklaus, *f.n.*, 'nɪklou, nícklō

Nilsson, *f.n.*, 'nɪlsən, nílssŏn

Nimmie, *f.n.*, 'nɪmɪ, nímmi

Nimmo, *f.n.*, 'nɪmou, nímmō

Nimmy, *f.n.*, 'nɪmɪ, nímmi

Nind, *f.n.*, nɪnd, ninnd; naɪnd, nínd

Nineham, *f.n.*, 'naɪnəm, nínăm

Niner, *f.n.*, 'naɪnər, nínĕr

Nisbet, *f.n.*, 'nɪzbɪt, nízbĕt

Nisbett, *f.n.*, 'nɪzbɪt, nízbĕt

Nissel, *f.n.*, 'nɪsl, níssl

Nith, River, *S'clyde–D. & G.*, nɪθ, nith

Nith, Thorthorwald and Ross, Viscount, 'nɪθ tər'θɒrəld ənd 'rɒs, níth tŏr-thórrăld ănd róss

Niton *I. of Wight*, 'naɪtən, nítŏn

Nitshill *Glasgow*, 'nɪts'hɪl, níts-híll

Niven, *f.n.*, 'nɪvən, nívvĕn

Nivison, *f.n.*, 'nɪvɪsən, nívvissŏn

Nixon, *f.n.*, 'nɪksən, nickssŏn

Noakes, *f.n.*, nouks, nŏks

Nobel School, The, *Stevenage (Herts.)*, nou'bel, nōbéll

Nobes, *f.n.*, noubz, nŏbz

Noblet, *f.n.*, 'nɒblɪt, nóbblĕt

Nolan, *f.n.,* 'noʊlən, nṓlăn
Nollekens, Joseph, *18th–19th-c. sculptor,* 'nɒlɪkənz, nŏllĕkĕnz
Nolloth, *f.n.,* 'nɒləθ, nŏllŏth. *Appropriate also for the ~ professorship and scholarships at the Univ. of Oxford.*
Nonely *Salop,* 'nʌnəlɪ, nŭnnĕli
Nonington *Kent,* 'nɒnɪŋtən, nŏnningtŏn; 'nʌnɪŋtən, nŭnnington
Nonsuch Palace *Surrey,* 'nʌnsʌtʃ, nŭn-sutch; 'nɒnsʌtʃ, nŏn-sutch. *The first is usual among scholars. Locally, however, at* **Nonsuch** Park, *the site of the original Tudor palace, the second is current today.*
Nonsuch Park *Surrey,* 'nɒnsʌtʃ, nŏn-sutch
Nont Sarah's *W. Yorks.,* 'nɒnt 'sɛərəz, nŏnt sáirăz
Nonweiler, *f.n.,* 'nɒnwilər, nŏn-weelĕr
Noormohammed, *f.n.,* ˌnʊərmə-'hæmɪd, nṓŏrmŏ-hámmĕd
Norbury, *f.n.,* 'nɔrbərɪ, nórbŭri
Nordelph *Norfolk,* 'nɔrdelf, nórdelf
Nore, The, *Thames Estuary,* nɔr, nor
Norfolk *Co. name,* 'nɔrfək, nórfŏk. *Appropriate also for the Duke of ~.*
Norglen *Belfast,* 'nɔr'glen, nór-glénn
Norham *Northd.,* 'nɒrəm, nórr-ăm
Norie, *f.n.,* 'nɒrɪ, nórri
Norledge, *f.n.,* 'nɔrlɪdʒ, nórlĕj
Normanbrook, Barony of, 'nɔrmənbrʊk, nórmănbrṓŏk
Normansell, *f.n.,* 'nɔrmənsl, nórmănssl
Normanton, *f.n.,* 'nɔrməntən, nórmăntŏn
Norquoy, *f.n.,* 'nɔrkɪ, nórki
Norreys, Baron, 'nɒrɪs, nórriss
Norris, *f.n.,* 'nɒrɪs, nórriss
Northall, *f.n.,* 'nɔrθɔl, nórthawl
Northam, *f.n.,* 'nɔrðəm, nórthăm
Northampton *Northants.,* nɔr-'θæmptən, northámptŏn; nɔr'hæmptən, north-hámptŏn. *The first is appropriate for the Marquess of ~.*
North Baddesley *Hants,* 'nɔrθ 'bædzlɪ, north bádzli
Northbourne, Baron, 'nɔrθbərn, nórthbŭrn
North Bradley *Wilts.,* 'nɔrθ 'brædlɪ, north brádli
Northcliffe, *f.n.,* 'nɔrθklɪf, north-kliff

Northcote, *f.n.,* 'nɔrθkət, nórth-kŏt; 'nɔrθkɒt, nórth-kott
North Elmham *Norfolk,* 'nɔrθ 'elməm, north élmăm
Northenden *Gtr. M'chester,* 'nɔrðəndən, nórthĕndĕn
Northesk, Earl of, nɔrθ'esk, northésk
North Holmwood *Surrey,* 'nɔrθ 'hoʊmwʊd, north hṓm-wṓŏd
North Hykeham *Lincs.,* 'nɔrθ 'haɪkəm, north híkăm
Northiam *E. Sussex,* 'nɔrðɪəm, nórthiăm
Northill *Beds.,* 'nɔrθhɪl, north-hil
Northleigh *nr. Colyton (Devon),* 'nɔrθli, nórthlee
Northleigh *nr. Goodleigh (Devon),* 'nɔrθli, nórthlee; 'nɔrli, nórlee
North Leigh *Oxon.,* 'nɔrθ 'li north lée
North Leverton *Notts.,* 'nɔrθ 'levərtən, north lévvĕrtŏn
North Marden *W. Sussex,* 'nɔrθ 'mardən, north maárdĕn
Northmaven *Shetland,* nɔrθ-'meɪvən, northmáyvĕn
Northolme *Lincs.,* 'nɔrθoʊm, nór-thōm
Northowram *W. Yorks.,* nər-'θaʊərəm, nŏr-thówrăm
Northrepps *Norfolk,* 'nɔrθreps, nórthreps
North Ronaldsay *Orkney,* 'nɔrθ 'rɒnldseɪ, north rónnld-say; 'nɔrθ 'rɒnldʃeɪ, north rónnld--shay
Northsceugh *Cumbria,* 'nɔrθ-skjuf, north-skewf
North Shields *Tyne & Wear,* 'nɔrθ 'ʃildz, north sheéldz
North Tawton *Devon,* 'nɔrθ 'tɔtən, north táwtŏn
Northumberland *Co. name,* nɔr'θʌmbərlənd, northúmbĕr-lănd
Northumbrian, *pertaining to* **Northumberland,** nɔr'θʌmbrɪən, northúmbriăn
North Walsham *Norfolk,* 'nɔrθ 'wɒlʃəm, north wáwl-shăm
North Waltham *Hants,* 'nɔrθ 'wɒlθəm, north wáwl-thăm
Northwich *Ches.,* 'nɔrθwɪtʃ, nórth-witch
Norton Hawkfield *Avon,* 'nɔrtən 'hɒkfild, nórtŏn háwkfeeld
Norwell *Notts.,* 'nɒrəl, nórrĕl
Norwell Woodhouse *Notts.,* 'nɒrəl 'wʊdhaʊs, nórrĕl wṓŏd--howss
Norwich *Norfolk,* 'nɒrɪdʒ, nórrij; 'nɒrɪtʃ, nórritch. *The first is appropriate for Viscount ~.*

Norwick *Shetland*, 'nɔrwɪk, nór-wick

Norwood, *f.n.*, 'nɔrwʊd, nór-wōŏd

Nostell Priory *W. Yorks.*, 'nɒstl, nóstl

Nosworthy,*f.n.*, 'nɒzwɜrðɪ, nózwurthi

Notariello,*f.n.*, ,noʊtɑrɪ'eloʊ, nōtaari-éllō

Nothe Promontory, The, *Dorset*, noʊð, nōth

Notley,*f.n.*, 'nɒtlɪ, nóttli

Nott, *f.n.*, nɒt, nott

Nottingham *Notts.*, 'nɒtɪŋəm, nótting-ăm

Noup Head *Orkney*, 'nup 'hed, noóp hédd

Novar *H'land*, noʊ'vɑr, nōváar

Novar Toll *H'land*, noʊ'vɑr 'toʊl, nōváar tōl

Nove,*f.n.*, noʊv, nōv

Novello,*f.n.*, nə'veloʊ, nŏvéllō

Novis,*f.n.*, 'noʊvɪs, nóviss

Novocastrian, *native of New-castle upon Tyne*, ,noʊvoʊ-'kæstrɪən, nōvōkásstriăn

Nowell,*f.n.*, 'noʊəl, nō-ĕl

Nowlin,*f.n.*, 'noʊlɪn, nólin

Nowton *Suffolk*, 'noʊtən, nótŏn

Nudd,*f.n.*, nʌd, nudd

Nugee,*f.n.*, 'nudʒɪ, noójee

Nugent,*f.n.*, 'njudʒənt, néwjĕnt. *Appropriate also for Baron ~ of Guildford.*

Nunan,*f.n.*, 'njunən, néwnăn

Nunburnholme, Baron, nʌn-'bɜrnəm, nunbúrnŏm

Nuneaton *Warwicks.*, nʌn'itən, nunéetŏn

Nuneham Courtenay *Oxon.*, 'njunəm 'kɔrtnɪ, néwnăm kórtni

Nunney *Avon*, 'nʌnɪ, núnni

Nunns,*f.n.*, nʌnz, nunnz

Nunwick *N. Yorks.*, 'nʌnɪk, núnnick

Nupen,*f.n.*, 'njupən, néwpĕn

Nuthall,*f.n.*, 'nʌtəl, núttawl

Nuthall *Notts.*, 'nʌtl, núttl

Nuthampstead *Herts.*, 'nʌtəmsted, núttămsted

Nuttall,*f.n.*, 'nʌtəl, núttawl

Nuttgens,*f.n.*, 'nʌtdʒənz, nútjĕnz; 'nʌtʃənz, nútchĕnz

Nygaard,*f.n.*, 'naɪgɑrd, nígaard

Nyholm,*f.n.*, 'naɪhoʊm, ní-hōm

Nymans *W. Sussex*, 'naɪmənz, nímănz

Nymet Rowland *Devon*, 'nɪmɪt 'roʊland, nímmĕt rṓlănd

Nymet Tracey *Devon*, 'nɪmɪt 'treɪsɪ, nímmĕt tráyssi

O

Oa *S'clyde*, oʊ, ō

Oadby *Leics.*, 'oʊdbɪ, ódbi

Oakenclough *Lancs.*, 'oʊkənklju, ókĕn-klew; 'oʊkənklaʊ, ókĕn--klow; 'oʊkənklʌf, ókĕn-kluff

Oaksey, Baron, 'oʊksɪ, óksi

Oaten,*f.n.*, 'oʊtən, ótĕn

Oates,*f.n.*, oʊts, ōts

Oath *Somerset*, oʊð, ōth

Oaze Deep *Thames Estuary*, 'oʊz 'dip, ōz deép

Oban *S'clyde*, 'oʊbən, óbăn

Obbard,*f.n.*, 'oʊbard, óbaard

O'Brien,*f.n.*, oʊ'braɪən, ōbrí-ĕn

Oby *Norfolk*, 'oʊbɪ, óbi

O'Callaghan,*f.n.*, oʊ'kæləhən, ōkálă-hăn; oʊ'kæləgən, ōkálăgăn

O'Cathain,*f.n.*, ,oʊkə'hɔɪn, ō-kă--hóyn

Ochil Hills *Central–Tayside*, 'oʊxl, óchl

Ochiltree *S'clyde*, 'ɒxɪltrɪ, óchiltree; 'ɒxɪltrɪ, óchiltree. *Appropriate also for ~ Castle.*

Ochs,*f.n.*, ɒks, ocks

Ochterlony,*f.n.*, ,ɒxtər'loʊnɪ, ochtĕrlóni

Ocklynge *E. Sussex*, 'ɒklɪndʒ, ócklinj

Ockrent,*f.n.*, 'ɒkrənt, óckrĕnt

O'Clarey,*f.n.*, oʊ'klɛərɪ, ōkláiri

O'Clee,*f.n.*, oʊ'klɪ, ōkleé

Ocle Pychard *H. & W.*, 'oʊkl 'pɪtʃərd, ókl pítchărd

O'Connor,*f.n.*, oʊ'kɒnər, ōkónnŏr

Odam,*f.n.*, 'oʊdəm, ódăm

O'Dea,*f.n.*, oʊ'di, ōdeé; oʊ'deɪ, ōdáy

Odell *Beds.*, 'oʊdl, ódl

Odey,*f.n.*, 'oʊdɪ, ódi

Odham,*f.n.*, 'ɒdəm, óddăm

Odhams Press *publishers*, 'ɒdəmz, óddămz

Odiham *Hants.*, 'oʊdɪəm, ódi-ăm

Odlum,*f.n.*, 'ɒdləm, óddlŭm

O'Doherty,*f.n.*, oʊ'dɒxərtɪ, ōdóchĕrti

Odom,*f.n.*, 'oʊdɒm, ódom

O'Donell,*f.n.*, oʊ'dɒnl, ōdónnl

O'Donovan,*f.n.*, oʊ'dʌnəvən, ōdúnnŏvăn

O'Dowda,*f.n.*, oʊ'daʊdə, ōdówdă

Odsal *W. Yorks.*, 'ɒdzl, óddzl

Oertling,*f.n.*, 'ɜrtlɪŋ, értling

Oettle,*f.n.*, 'oʊtl, ótl

Oetzmann,*f.n.*, 'oʊtsmən, ótsmăn

O'Ferrall,*f.n.*, oʊ'færal, ōfárrĕl

Offaly, Earl of, 'ɒfəlɪ, óffăli

Offenbach 184 **Onions**

Offenbach, *f.n.*, 'ɒfənbak, óffĕn-
baak
Offord Cluny *Cambs.*, 'ɒfərd
'kluni, óffŏrd klóoni
Offord D'Arcy, *also spelt* Offord
Darcy, *Cambs.*, 'ɒfərd 'dɑrsi,
óffŏrd daárssi
O'Flaherty, *f.n.*, ou'flɑhərtı,
ōflaá-hĕrti; ou'flɑərtı, ōflaá-ĕrti
O'Gara, *f.n.*, ou'gɑrə, ōgaáră
Ogg, *f.n.*, ɒg, ogg
Oghill *Co. Derry*, 'ɒxɪl, óchil
Ogilvie, *f.n.*, 'ouglvı, óglvi
Ogilvy, *f.n.*, 'ouglvı, óglvi
Ogley, *f.n.*, 'ɒglı, óggli
Ogley Locks *Staffs.*, 'ɒglı, óggli
Ogmore *Mid Glam.*, 'ɒgmɔr,
ógmor
Ogof Ffynnonddu *W. Glam.*,
'ougɒv ˌfʌnən'ði, ógov funnŏn-
-thée
O'Grady, *f.n.*, ou'greɪdı, ōgráydi
Ogwell *Devon*, 'ougwel, ógwel
Ogwen, Lake *and* River,
Gwynedd, 'ɒgwen, ógwen
O'Hagan, *f.n.*, ou'heɪgən, ō-
-háygăn
O'Halloran, *f.n.*, ou'hæIərən,
ō-hálŏrăn
O'Hana, *f.n.*, ou'hænə, ō-hánnă
O'Hare, *f.n.*, ou'heər, ō-háir
O'Hear, *f.n.*, ou'heər, ō-háir
O'Herlihi, *f.n.*, ou'hərlıhı, ō-
-hérli-hi
O'Keefe, *f.n.*, ou'kif, ōkéef
O'Keeffe, *f.n.*, ou'kif, ōkéef
Okeford Fitzpaine *Dorset*, 'ouk-
fərd fɪts'peɪn, ókfŏrd fitspáyn.
A local version is 'fɪpənı 'ɒkfərd,
fíppĕni óckfŏrd.
Okehampton *Devon*, ouk'hæmp-
tən, ōk-hámptŏn
Okell, *f.n.*, 'oukl, ókl
Okeover, *f.n.*, 'oukouvər, ókōvĕr
Olantigh Towers *Kent*, 'ɒləntı
'tauərz, óllănti tówĕrz
Olave, *C.n.*, 'ɒlɪv, óllıv
Olchfa *Swansea*, ɒlx'vɑ, olch-vaá
Oldbury-on-Severn *Glos.*,
'ouldbərı ɒn 'sevərn, óldbŭri on
sévvĕrn
Olderfleet *Co. Antrim*, 'ouldər-
flit, óldĕrfleet
Oldhamstocks *Lothian*, ould-
'hæmstɒks, ōld-hámstocks
Olding, *f.n.*, 'ouldıŋ, ólding
Old Man of Storr *Skye*, 'ould
'mæn əv 'stɔr, óld mán ŏv
stór
Old Meldrum *Grampian*, 'ould
'meldrəm, óld méldrŭm
Oldpark *Salop*, 'ouldpɑrk, óld-
paark
Old Romney *Kent*, 'ould 'rɒmnı,

óld rómni; 'ould 'rʌmnı, óld
rúmni
Old Steine, The, *Brighton*, 'ould
'stin, óld stéen
Old Swinford, *also spelt* Old-
swinford, *W. Midlands*, 'ould
'swɪnfərd, óld swínfŏrd
Oldys, William, *17th-c. antiquar-
ian & bibliographer*, ouldz, óldz
O'Leary, *f.n.*, ou'lıərı, ōléeri
Olender, *f.n.*, ə'lerdər, ōléndĕr
Olerenshaw, *f.n.*, ˌɒlə'renʃɔ,
ollĕrénshaw
Olivere, *f.n.*, ɒlı'vɪər, ollivéer
Olivier, *f.n.*, ə'lıvıeı, ólívvi-ay;
ɒ'lıvıər, ollívvi-ĕr. *The first is
appropriate for Baron* ~, *other-
wise Sir Laurence* ~, *actor.*
Ollerenshaw, *f.n.*, ˌɒlə'renʃɔ,
ollĕrénshaw; 'ɒlərənʃɔ, óllĕrĕn-
-shaw
Olliffe, *f.n.*, 'ɒlıf, ólliff
Ollivant, *f.n.*, 'ɒlıvənt, óllivănt
Olliver Duchet watch tower
Richmond (N. Yorks.), 'ɒlıvər
'dʌkɪt, óllivĕr dúckĕt
O'Loghlen, *f.n.*, ou'lɒxlən,
ōlóchlĕn
O'Loughlin, *f.n.*, ou'lɒxlın,
ōlóchlin
Olrig *H'land*, 'ɒlrıg, ólrig
Olsen, *f.n.*, 'oulsən, ólssĕn
Olsson, *f.n.*, 'oulsən, ólssŏn
Olton *W. Midlands*, 'oultən, óltŏn
Olumide, *C.n.*, ɒ'lumıdeı,
olóomidday
Olver, *f.n.*, 'ɒlvər, ólvĕr
Olveston *Avon*, 'oulvıstən,
ólvĕsstŏn; 'oulstən, ólsstŏn
Omagh *Co. Tyrone*, 'oumə, ōmă
O'Malley, *f.n.*, ou'mælı, ōmáli;
ou'meılı, ōmáyli
Oman, *f.n.*, 'oumən, ómăn
Omand, *f.n.*, 'oumənd, ómănd
O'Mara, *f.n.*, ou'mɑrə, ōmaáră
Ombersley *H. & W.*, 'ɒmbərzlı,
ómbĕrzli
O'Meara, *f.n.*, ou'mɑrə, ōmaáră;
ou'meərə, ōmáiră
Ommanney, *f.n.*, 'ɒmənı, ómmăni
Omoa *S'clyde*, ou'mouə, ōmō-ă
Onchan *I. of Man*, 'ɒŋkən, ónkăn
Onecote *Staffs.*, 'ɒnkət, ón-kŏt
O'Neill, *f.n.*, ou'nil, ōnéel
Ongar *Essex*, 'ɒŋgər, óng-găr
Onibury *Salop*, 'ɒnıbərı, ónnibŭri
Onich *H'land*, 'ounıx, ónich
Onions, *f.n.*, 'ʌnjənz, ún-yŏnz;
ou'naıənz, ōnī-ŏnz; ə'naıənz,
ŏnī-ŏnz. *The first is appropriate
for C. T.* ~, *philologist, gram-
marian and an editor of the
Oxford English Dictionary; also
for Oliver* ~, *author.*

Onllwyn *W. Glam.*, 'ɒnɫʊɪn, ónhlōo-in

Onny, River, *Salop*, 'ɒnɪ, ónni

Onslow, *f.n.*, 'ɒnzloʊ, ónzlō. *Appropriate also for the Earl of ~.*

Oonagh, *C.n.*, 'uːnə, óonă

Oosterhuis, *f.n.*, 'oʊstərhaʊs, óstĕr-howss

Openshaw, *f.n.*, 'oʊpənʃɔ, ópĕn-shaw

Openshaw *Gtr. M'chester*, 'oʊpənʃɔ, ópĕn-shaw

Opie, *f.n.*, 'oʊpɪ, ópi

Oppenheim, *f.n.*, 'ɒpənhaɪm, óppĕn-hīm

Orage, *f.n.*, ɔ'rɑʒ, awráa<u>zh</u>

Oram, *f.n.*, 'ɔːrəm, áwrăm

Oranmore and Browne, Baron, 'ɒrənmɔr ənd 'braʊn, órrănmor ănd brówn

Orbach, *f.n.*, 'ɔrbæk, órback

Orcadian, *native of the* **Orkney Islands**, ɔr'keɪdɪən, orkáydiăn

Orchy *see* **Bridge of Orchy**

Orczy, Baroness, *author*, 'ɔrtsɪ, órtsi

Orda, *f.n.*, 'ɔrdə, órdă

Orde-Powlett, *f.n.*, 'ɔrd 'pɒlɪt, órd páwlĕt. *Family name of Baron Bolton.*

Ordiquhill *Grampian*, ˌɔrdɪ'hwɪl, ordi-whíll

O'Reilly, *f.n.*, oʊ'raɪlɪ, ō-ríli

Oreston *Devon*, ə'restən, ōrésstŏn

Orfordness *Suffolk*, 'ɔrfərd'nes, órfŏrdnéss

Organe, *f.n.*, ɔr'geɪn, orgáyn

Orgel, *f.n.*, 'ɔrgl, órgl

Orgelist, *f.n.*, 'ɔrdʒəlɪst, órjĕlist

Orgreave *S. Yorks.*, 'ɔrgriv, órgreev

Oriel, *f.n.*, 'ɔrɪəl, áwri-ĕl

Oriel, Baron, 'ɔrɪəl, áwri-ĕl

Oritor *Co. Tyrone*, 'ɒrɪtər, órritŏr

Orkney Islands, 'ɔrknɪ, órkni. *Appropriate also for the Earl of ~.*

Orlebar, *f.n.*, 'ɔrlɪbɑr, órlĕbaar

Orlestone *Kent*, 'ɔrlstən, órlsstŏn

Orleton *H. & W.*, 'ɔrltən, órltŏn

Orlock *Co. Down*, 'ɔrlɒk, órlock

Ormathwaite, Baron, 'ɔrməθweɪt, órmăthwayt

Ormeau *Belfast*, ɔr'moʊ, ormṓ

Ormelie, *f.n.*, 'ɔrməlɪ, órmĕli

Ormerod, *f.n.*, 'ɔrmrɒd, órmrod; 'ɔrmərɒd, órmĕrod

Ormiston, *f.n.*, 'ɔrmɪstən, órmis-stŏn

Ormiston *Lothian*, 'ɔrmɪstən, órmisstŏn

Ormonde, Marquess of, 'ɔrmənd, órmŏnd

Ormonde, *f.n.*, 'ɔrmənd, órmŏnd

Ormrod, *f.n.*, 'ɔrmrɒd, órmrod

Ormsby-Gore, *f.n.*, 'ɔrmzbɪ 'gɔr, órmzbi gór

Ornadel, *f.n.*, 'ɔrnədel, órnădel

Ornbo, *f.n.*, 'ɔrnboʊ, órnbō

O'Rorke, *f.n.*, oʊ'rɔrk, ō-rórk

O'Rourke, *f.n.*, oʊ'rɔrk, ō-rórk

Orpin, *f.n.*, 'ɔrpɪn, órpin

Orpington *London*, 'ɔrpɪŋtən, órpington

Orr, *f.n.*, ɔr, or

Orrick, *f.n.*, 'ɒrɪk, órrick

Orridge, *f.n.*, 'ɒrɪdʒ, órrij

Orton Longueville *Cambs.*, 'ɔrtən 'lɒŋvɪl, órtŏn lóng-vil

Ortzen, *f.n.*, 'ɔrtsən, órtsĕn

Osbaldeston *Lancs.*, ˌɒzbəl'destən, ozbăldésstŏn

Osborn, *f.n.*, 'ɒzbɔrn, ózborn; 'ɒzbərn, ózbŭrn

Osborne, *f.n.*, 'ɒzbɔrn, ózborn; 'ɒzbərn, ózbŭrn

Osbourne, *f.n.*, 'ɒzbɔrn, ózborn; 'ɒzbərn, ózbŭrn

Osea Island *Essex*, 'oʊzɪ, ózi; 'oʊsɪ, óssi

Osers, *f.n.*, 'oʊzərz, ózĕrz

Osgerby, *f.n.*, 'ɒzgərbɪ, ózgĕrbi

O'Shagar, *f.n.*, oʊ'ʃɑgər, ō-shaágăr

O'Shaughnessy, *f.n.*, oʊ'ʃɔnəsɪ, ō-sháwnĕssi

O'Shea, *f.n.*, oʊ'ʃeɪ, ō-sháy; oʊ'ʃi, ō-shee

Osland, *f.n.*, 'ɒzlənd, ózzländ

Osler, *f.n.*, 'oʊslər, óssler; 'ɒslər, óssler; 'ɒzlər, ózzler

Osmaston *Derby.*, 'ɒzməstən, ózmăsstŏn

Osney *Oxon.*, 'oʊznɪ, ózni

Osoba, *f.n.*, oʊ'soʊbə, ōssóbă

Ospringe *Kent*, 'ɒsprɪndʒ, óssprinj

Ossett *W. Yorks.*, 'ɒsɪt, óssĕt

Ostle, *f.n.*, 'ɒstl, óstl

Ostler, *f.n.*, 'oʊstlər, óstlĕr

Oswaldestre, Baron, 'ɒzwəldestər, ózwáldesstĕr

Oswaldtwistle *Lancs.*, 'ɒzwəldtwɪsl, ózwáld-twissl; 'ɒzltwɪsl, ózzl-twissl

Oswestry *Salop*, 'ɒzwəstrɪ, ózwĕstri

Otham *Kent*, 'ɒtəm, óttăm

Othery *Somerset*, 'oʊðərɪ, ṓthĕri

Othick, *f.n.*, 'θɪk, óthick

Otley, *f.n.*, 'ɒtlɪ, óttli

Otley *W. Yorks.*, 'ɒtlɪ, óttli

Otterham *Cornwall*, 'ɒtərəm, óttĕrăm

Ottery St. Mary *Devon*, 'ɒtərɪ snt 'meərɪ, óttĕri sĭnt máiri

Ottinge *Kent*, 'ɒtɪndʒ, óttinj

Ottolangui, *f.n.,* ˌɒtoʊ'læŋgwɪ, ottŏláng-gwi

Ottoline, *C.n.,* 'ɒtəlin, óttŏleen

Ottoway, *f.n.,* 'ɒtweɪ, óttŏ-way

Otway, *f.n.,* 'ɒtweɪ, óttway

Oudot, *f.n.,* 'udoʊ, oódŏ

Ough, *f.n.,* oʊ, ō

Ougham, *f.n.,* 'əm, áw-ăm

Oughtershaw *N. Yorks.,* 'aʊtərʃɔ, ówtĕr-shaw

Oughterside *Cumbria,* 'aʊtərsaɪd, ówtĕrssīd

Oughtibridge *S. Yorks.,* 'utɪbrɪdʒ, oótibrij; 'aʊtɪbrɪdʒ, ówtibrij; 'ɔːtɪbrɪdʒ, áwtibrij; 'oʊtɪbrɪdʒ, ótibrij

Oughton, *f.n.,* 'aʊtən, ówtŏn; 'ɔːtən, áwtŏn

Oughton, River, *Herts.,* 'ɔːtən, áwtŏn

Oughtrington *Ches.,* 'utrɪŋtən, oótrington

Ouin, *f.n.,* 'oʊɪn, ó-in

Ould, *f.n.,* oʊld, ōld; uld, oold

Ouless, *f.n.,* 'ulɪs, oóless

Oulton, *f.n.,* 'oʊltən, ṓltŏn

Oulton *Staffs., Suffolk, W. Yorks.,* 'oʊltən, ṓltŏn

Oulton Broad *Suffolk,* 'oʊltən 'brɔd, ṓltŏn bráwd

Oulton Park *Ches.,* 'oʊltən 'pɑrk, ṓltŏn paárk

Oundle *Northants.,* 'aʊndl, ówndl

Oury, *f.n.,* 'urɪ, oó-ri; 'ʊərɪ, oŏri

Ousby *Cumbria,* 'uzbɪ, oózbi

Ousdale *H'land,* 'aʊzdeɪl, ówzdayl

Ousden, *also spelt* **Owsden,** *Suffolk,* 'aʊzdən, ówzdĕn

Ouseley, *f.n.,* 'uzlɪ, oózli

Ousey, *f.n.,* 'uzɪ, oózi

Ousley, *f.n.,* 'uzlɪ, oózli

Ousman, *f.n.,* 'uzmən, oózmăn

Ouston, *f.n.,* 'aʊstən, ówsstŏn

Ouston *Durham,* 'aʊstən, ówsstŏn

Outen, *f.n.,* 'aʊtən, ówtĕn

Outhwaite, *f.n.,* 'aʊθweɪt, ówthwayt; 'oʊθweɪt, ṓthwayt; 'uθweɪt, oóthwayt

Outlane *W. Yorks.,* 'aʊtleɪn, ówtlayn

Outram, *f.n.,* 'utrəm, oótrăm; 'aʊtrəm, ówtrăm. *The first is appropriate for George ~ & Co., newspaper publishers, the second for Benjamin ~, canal designer (1764–1805).*

Outred, *f.n.,* 'utred, oótred; 'aʊtred, ówtred

Outstack, The, *Shetland,* 'aʊtstæk, ówt-stack

Ouvry, *f.n.,* 'uvrɪ, oóvri

Oved, *f.n.,* oʊ'ved, ōvéd

Ovenden, *f.n.,* 'ɒvəndən, óvvĕn-dĕn; 'oʊvəndən, ṓvĕndĕn

Ovenden *W. Yorks.,* 'ɒvəndən, óvvĕndĕn

Ovens, *f.n.,* 'ʌvənz, úvvĕnz

Over *Cambs., Ches.,* 'oʊvər, óvĕr

Over *Glos.,* 'ʌvər, óvvĕr

Over Alderley *Ches.,* 'oʊvər 'ɔːldərlɪ, óvĕr áwldĕrli

Overcombe *Dorset,* 'oʊvərkum, óvĕrkoom

Overend, *f.n.,* 'oʊvərend, óvĕrend

Overstone *Northants.,* 'oʊvərstən, óvĕrstŏn

Overton, *f.n.,* 'oʊvərtən, óvĕrtŏn

Overton *Ches., Clwyd, Hants, W. Glam.,* 'oʊvərtən, óvĕrtŏn

Over Wallop *Hants,* 'oʊvər 'wɒləp, óvĕr wóllŏp

Over Whitacre *Warwicks.,* 'oʊvər hwɪtəkər, óvĕr whíttăkĕr

Ovett, *f.n.,* 'oʊvet, óvett

Oving *Bucks., W. Sussex,* 'oʊvɪŋ, óving

Ovingdean *E. Sussex,* 'oʊvɪŋdin, óving-deen; 'ɒvɪŋdin, óvving--deen

Ovingham *Northd.,* 'ɒvɪndʒəm, óvvinjăm

Ovington *Norfolk,* 'oʊvɪŋtən, óvingtŏn

Ovington *Northd.,* 'ɒvɪŋtən, óvvingtŏn

Owain, *Welsh C.n.,* 'oʊaɪn, ó-īn

Owen, *C.n. and f.n.,* 'oʊɪn, ó-ĕn

Ower, *f.n.,* 'aʊər, ów-ĕr

Ower *Hants,* 'aʊər, ów-ĕr

Owermoigne *Dorset,* 'oʊərmɔɪn, ṓ-ĕrmoyn

Owers, *f.n.,* 'oʊərz, ṓ-ĕrz; 'aʊərz, ów-ĕrz

Owers *light-vessel, off Hants coast,* 'aʊərz, ów-ĕrz

Owersby *Lincs.,* 'aʊərzbɪ, ów-ĕrzbi; 'oʊərzbɪ, ṓ-ĕrzbi

Owler Bar *Derby.,* 'aʊlər 'bɑr, ówlĕr baár

Owlerton *S. Yorks.,* 'oʊlərtən, ṓlĕrtŏn

Owles, *f.n.,* oʊlz, ōlz; aʊlz, owlz; ulz, oolz

Owmby *Lincs.,* 'oʊmbɪ, ómbi. *Appropriate for both places of the name in Lincolnshire.*

Owsden *see* **Ousden**

Owslebury *Hants,* 'ʌslbərɪ, ússlbŭri; 'ʌzlbərɪ, úzzlbŭri

Owst, *f.n.,* oʊst, ōsst

Owthorpe *Notts.,* 'aʊθɔrp, ówthorp

Owtram, *f.n.,* 'aʊtrəm, ówtrăm

Oxford *Oxon.,* 'ɒksfərd, ócksfŏrd

Oxford and Asquith, Earl of, 'ɒksfəd ənd 'æskwıθ, ócksförd ănd ásskwith
Oxfuird, Viscount of, 'ɒksfuərd, ócksfóord
Oxhey Herts., 'ɒksı, ócksi
Oxley, f.n., 'ɒkslı, ócksli
Oxnard, f.n., 'ɒksnərd, ócksnärd
Oxonian, member of **Oxford** Univ., ɒk'soʊnıən, ocksóniăn
Oxtoby, f.n., 'ɒkstəbı, óckstöbi
Oxwich W. Glam., 'ɒkswıtʃ, óckswitch
Oyne Grampian, ɔın, oyn
Oystermouth W. Glam., 'ɔıstərmaʊθ, óystĕrmowth
Ozell, f.n., oʊ'zel, özéll
Ozengell Grange Kent, 'oʊzəngel 'greındʒ, ŏzĕn-gel gráynj
Ozols, f.n., 'ɒzlz, ózzlz

P

Pabo Gwynedd, 'pæboʊ, pábbō
Pace, f.n., peıs, payss
Pachesham Surrey, 'pætʃısəm, pátchĕssăm
Packer, f.n., 'pækər, páckĕr
Packham, f.n., 'pækəm, páckăm
Padarn, Lake, Gwynedd, 'pædərn, páddärn
Paddick, f.n., 'pædık, páddick
Paddock, f.n., 'pædək, páddŏk
Padel, f.n., 'pɒdl, paádl
Padell, f.n., pɑ'del, paadéll
Padgham, f.n., 'pædʒəm, pájjăm
Padiham Lancs., 'pædıəm, páddi-ăm
Padmore, f.n., 'pædmɔr, pádmor
Padog Gwynedd, 'pædɒg, páddog
Padstow Cornwall, 'pædstoʊ, pádsstō
Padwick, f.n., 'pædwık, pád-wick
Paget, f.n., 'pædʒıt, pájjĕt
Paget of Beaudesert, Baron, 'pædʒıt əv 'boʊdızeər, pájjĕt ŏv bŏdézair
Pagham W. Sussex, 'pægəm, pággăm
Pagin, f.n., 'peıgın, páygin
Paglesham Essex, 'pæglʃəm, pággl-shăm
Paice, f.n., peıs, payss
Paignton Devon, 'peıntən, páyntŏn
Pailin, f.n., 'peılın, páylin
Pain, f.n., peın, payn
Painscastle Powys, 'peınzkɑsl, páynz-kaassl
Painswick Glos., 'peınzwık, páynzwick

Paish, f.n., peıʃ, paysh
Paisible, f.n., 'peızıbl, páyzibl
Paisley S'clyde, 'peızlı, páyzli
Pakenham, f.n., 'pækənəm, páckĕnăm. Appropriate for the Earl of Longford's family name and for Baron ~.
Pakenham Suffolk, 'peıkənəm, páykĕnăm
Pakington, f.n., 'pækıŋtən, páckingtŏn
Palairet, f.n., 'pæləret, páläret
Paley, f.n., 'peılı, páyli
Palfery, f.n., 'pɒlfrı, páwlfri
Palfrey, f.n., 'pɒlfrı, páwlfri
Palfry, f.n., 'pɒlfrı, páwlfri
Palgrave, f.n., 'pælgreıv, pálgrayv; 'pɒlgreıv, páwlgrayv. The first is appropriate for Francis ~, 19th-c. Professor of Poetry at the Univ. of Oxford and compiler of 'The Golden Treasury'.
Palgrave Suffolk, 'pælgreıv, pálgrayv
Palin, f.n., 'peılın, páylin
Paling, f.n., 'peılıŋ, páyling
Palk, f.n., pɒk, pawk; pɒlk, pawlk
Pallant, f.n., 'pælənt, pálänt
Palles, f.n., 'pælıs, páléss
Pallion Tyne & Wear, 'pælıən, páli-ŏn
Palliser, f.n., 'pælısər, pálissĕr
Pall Mall London, 'pæl 'mæl, pál mál; 'pel 'mel, péll méll
Pallot, f.n., 'pæloʊ, pálō
Palm, f.n., pɑm, paam
Palmer, f.n., 'pɑmər, paámĕr
Palmes, f.n., pɑmz, paamz
Palnackie D. & G., pæl'nækı, palnácki
Palsgrave, f.n., 'pælzgreıv, pálzgrayv
Pampisford Cambs., 'pæmpısfərd, pámpissförd
Panchen, f.n., 'pæntʃın, pántchĕn
Paneth, f.n., 'pænıθ, pánnĕth
Pankhurst, f.n., 'pæŋkhərst, pánkhurst
Panmure Castle Tayside, pæn-'mjuər, pan-myóor
Pannal N. Yorks., 'pænl, pánnl
Pannell, f.n., 'pænl, pánnl
Panteg Gwent, pæn'teıg, pantáyg
Pant-Glas Gwynedd, pænt'glas, pant-gláass
Pantlin, f.n., 'pæntlın, pántlin
Pantony, f.n., 'pæntənı, pántŏni
Pantperthog Gwynedd, pænt-'peərθɒg, pantpáirth-og
Pantycelyn Dyfed, ˌpæntə'kelın, pantăkéllin
Pant-y-dŵr Powys, ˌpæntə'duər, pantădóor

Pantyffynnon *Dyfed*, ‚pæntə'fʌnən, pantăfúnnŏn

Pantygasseg *Gwent*, ‚pæntə-'gæseg, pantăgásseg

Pantygraig-wen *Mid Glam.*, ‚pæntəgraɪg'wen, pantăgrīg--wén

Pant-y-mwyn *Clwyd*, ‚pæntə-'mʊɪn, pantămoo-in

Pantyscallog *Mid Glam.*, ‚pæntə-'skælɒg, pantăskáhlog

Pant-y-waun *Mid Glam.*, ‚pæntə-'waɪn, pantă-wín

Papa Stour *Shetland*, 'papə 'stoər, paápă stoŏr

Papa Westray *Orkney* 'papə 'westreɪ, paápă wéstray

Papillon, *f.n.*, pə'pɪlən, păpíllŏn

Papworth, *f.n.*, 'pæpwərθ, páp-wurth

Papworth Everard *Cambs.*, 'pæpwərθ 'evəraːd, pápwŏrth évvĕraard

Papworth St. Agnes *Cambs.*, 'pæpwərθ snt 'ægnɪs, pápwŏrth sĭnt ágnĕss

Paradwys *Gwynedd*, pæ'ræduɪs, parráddoo-iss

Paravicini, *f.n.*, ‚pærəvɪ'tʃiːni, parrăvitchéeni

Parbroath, *Lord*, paːr'brouθ, paarbróth

Parcell, *f.n.*, paːr'sel, paarsséll

Pardoe, *f.n.*, 'paːrdou, paárdō

Pardovan *Lothian*, paːr'dʌvən, paardúvvăn

Pares, *f.n.*, peərz, pairz

Pargiter, *f.n.*, 'paːrdʒɪtər, paárjitĕr. *Appropriate also for Baron* ∼.

Parham, *f.n.*, 'pærəm, párrăm

Parham *Suffolk, W. Sussex*, 'pærəm, párrăm

Parham Park *W. Sussex*, 'pærəm 'paːrk, párrăm paárk

Paris, *f.n.*, 'pærɪs, párriss

Parish, *f.n.*, 'pærɪʃ, párrish

Parker, *f.n.*, 'paːrkər, paárkĕr

Parkeston *Essex*, 'paːrkstən, paárkstŏn

Parkeston Quay *Essex*, 'paːrkstən 'kiː, paárkstŏn kée

Parkgate *Co. Antrim*, 'paːrkgeɪt, paárk-gayt

Parkin, *f.n.*, 'paːrkɪn, paárkin

Parkinson, *f.n.*, 'paːrkɪnsən, paárkinssŏn

Parkmore *Co. Antrim*, paːrk'mɔr, paarkmór

Parkstone *Dorset*, 'paːrkstən, paárkstŏn

Parlane, *f.n.*, 'paːrleɪn, paárlayn; paːr'leɪn, paarláyn

Parlour, *f.n.*, 'paːrlər, paárlŭr

Parmée, *f.n.*, 'paːrmeɪ, paármay

Parmenter, *f.n.*, 'paːrmɪntər, paár-mĕntĕr

Parminter, *f.n.*, 'paːrmɪntər, paár-mintĕr

Parmiter, *f.n.*, 'paːrmɪtər, paár-mitĕr

Parmley, *f.n.*, 'paːrmlɪ, paármli

Parnell, *f.n.*, paːr'nel, paarnéll; 'paːrnl, paárnl

Parnwell, *f.n.*, 'paːrnwəl, paárnwĕl

Parotte, *f.n.*, pə'rɒt, părótt

Parracombe *Devon*, 'pærəkum, párrăkoom

Parrett, *f.n.*, 'pærɪt, párrĕt

Parrett, *River, Dorset–Somerset*, 'pærɪt, párrĕt

Parrott, *f.n.*, 'pærət, párrŏt

Parry, *f.n.*, 'pærɪ, párri

Parsley, *f.n.*, 'paːrzlɪ, paárzli

Parslow, *f.n.*, 'paːrzlou, paárzlō

Partick *S'clyde*, 'paːrtɪk, paártick

Partickhill *S'clyde*, 'paːrtɪk'hɪl, paártick-hill

Partridge, *f.n.*, 'paːrtrɪdʒ, paártrij

Pasco, *f.n.*, 'pæskou, pásskō

Pascoe, *f.n.*, 'pæskou, pásskō

Pashley, *f.n.*, 'pæʃlɪ, páshli

Pask, *f.n.*, pæsk, passk

Pasley, *f.n.*, 'peɪzlɪ, páyzli

Pasmore, *f.n.*, 'pasmor, paássmor

Passant, *f.n.*, 'pæsənt, pássănt

Passenham *Northants.*, 'pasənəm, paássĕnăm

Paston, *f.n.*, 'pæstən, pásstŏn

Patchett, *f.n.*, 'pætʃɪt, pátchĕt

Patel, *f.n.*, pə'tel, pătéll

Pater, *f.n.*, 'peɪtər, páytĕr

Paterson, *f.n.*, 'pætərsən, páttĕrs-sŏn

Patey, *f.n.*, 'peɪtɪ, páyti

Path of Condie *Tayside*, 'paθ əv 'kɒndɪ, paáth ŏv kóndi

Patmore, *f.n.*, 'pætmor, pátmor

Patney *Wilts.*, 'pætnɪ, pát-ni

Paton, *f.n.*, 'peɪtən, páytŏn

Patrick, *C.n. and f.n.*, 'pætrɪk, pátrick

Patrington *Humberside*, 'pætrɪŋ-tən, pátringtŏn

Patriss, *f.n.*, 'pætrɪs, pátriss

Patrixbourne *Kent*, 'pætrɪksbɔrn, pátricksborn

Patterson, *f.n.*, 'pætərsən, páttĕrs-sŏn

Pattie, *f.n.*, 'pætɪ, pátti

Pattishall *Northants.*, 'pætɪʃl, páttishl

Pattison, *f.n.*, 'pætɪsən, páttissŏn

Pattreiouex, *f.n.*, 'pætrɪou, pátri-ō

Pauer, *f.n.*, 'pauər, pówĕr

Paulerspury *Northants.*, 'pɒlərz-pəri, páwlĕrzpŭri

Paulin, *f.n.*, 'pɒlɪn, páwlin

Paulina, *one educated at St. Paul's Girls' School,* pɔ'laɪnə, pawlína

Pauline, *one educated at St. Paul's School,* 'pɔlaɪn, páwlīn

Paulton, *f.n.,* 'poʊltən, póltŏn

Pauncefort, *f.n.,* 'pɔnsfərt, páwnssfört

Pauncefote, *f.n.,* 'pɔnsfət, páwnssfŏt. *Appropriate also for the Barony of ∼.*

Pauperhaugh *Northd.,* 'pɔpərhɑf, páwpĕr-haaf

Pavely, *f.n.,* 'peɪvlɪ, páyvli

Pavenham *Beds.,* 'peɪvənəm, páyvĕnăm

Paver, *f.n.,* 'peɪvər, páyvĕr

Pavey, *f.n.,* 'peɪvɪ, páyvi

Pavey Arc *Cumbria,* 'peɪvɪ 'ɑrk, páyvi aárk

Paviere, *f.n.,* 'pævjɛər, páv-yair

Paviour, *f.n.,* 'peɪvjər, páyv-yŭr

Pavitt, *f.n.,* 'pævɪt, pávvit

Pavlow, *f.n.,* 'pævloʊ, pávlō

Pavy, *f.n.,* 'peɪvɪ, páyvi

Pawley, *f.n.,* 'pɔlɪ, páwli

Pawlyk, *f.n.,* 'pɔlɪk, páwlick

Pawsey, *f.n.,* 'pɔzɪ, páwzi; 'pɔsɪ, páwssi

Paxton, *f.n.,* 'pækstən, páckstŏn

Payan, *f.n.,* 'peɪən, páy-än

Paylor, *f.n.,* 'peɪlər, páylŏr

Paynter, *f.n.,* 'peɪntər, páyntĕr

Paynting, *f.n.,* 'peɪntɪŋ, páynting

Peabody, *f.n.,* 'pibədɪ, peébŏdi; 'pibɒdɪ, peéboddi; 'peɪbɒdɪ, páyboddi

Peacey, *f.n.,* 'pisɪ, peéssi

Peachell, *f.n.,* 'pitʃl, peétchl

Peachey, *f.n.,* 'pitʃɪ, peétchi

Peacock, *f.n.,* 'pikɒk, peékock

Peaker, *f.n.,* 'pikər, peékĕr

Peakirk *Cambs.,* 'pikərk, peékirk

Pear, *f.n.,* pɪər, peer

Pearce, *f.n.,* pɪərs, peerss

Pearcey, *f.n.,* 'pɪərsɪ, peérssi

Pearmain, *f.n.,* 'pɛərmeɪn, páirmayn

Pearn, *f.n.,* pərn, pern

Pears, *f.n.,* pɪərz, peerz; pɛərz, pairz. *The first is appropriate for Sir Peter ∼, singer.*

Pearsall, *f.n.,* 'pɪərsl, peérssl

Pearson, *f.n.,* 'pɪərsən, peérssŏn

Peart, *f.n.,* pɪərt, peert

Pease, *f.n.,* piz, peez

Peasgood, *f.n.,* 'pizgʊd, peézgŏŏd

Peasholm *N. Yorks.,* 'pizhoʊm, peéz-hōm

Peaston *Lothian,* 'peɪstən, páysstŏn

Peate, *f.n.,* pit, peet

Peay, *f.n.,* peɪ, pay

Pebardy, *f.n.,* 'pebərdɪ, pébbărdi

Peberdy, *f.n.,* 'pebərdɪ, pébbĕrdi

Pechell, *f.n.,* 'pitʃl, peétchl

Peckham *London,* 'pekəm, péckăm

Pecorini, *f.n.,* ˌpekə'rinɪ, peckŏréeni

Pecry, *f.n.,* 'pekrɪ, péckri

Pedair Ffordd *Powys,* 'pedaɪər 'fɔrð, péddīr fórth

Peddelty, *f.n.,* 'pedltɪ, péddlti

Peden, *f.n.,* 'pidən, peédĕn

Peden *S'clyde,* 'pidən, peédĕn

Pedlow, *f.n.,* 'pedloʊ, pédlō

Pedraza, *f.n.,* pɪ'drɑzə, pĕdráază

Pedwardine *H. & W.,* 'pedwərdaɪn, pédwărdīn

Peebles *Borders,* 'piblz, peéblz

Peggie, *f.n.,* 'pegɪ, péggi

Pegna, *f.n.,* 'penjə, pén-yă

Pegnall, *f.n.,* 'pegnəl, pégnăl

Pegram, *f.n.,* 'pigrəm, peégrăm

Peierls, *f.n.,* 'paɪərlz, pí-ĕrlz

Peile, *f.n.,* pil, peel

Peill, *f.n.,* pil, peel

Peirce, *f.n.,* pɪərs, peerss

Peirse, *f.n.,* pɪərz, peerz

Peirson, *f.n.,* 'pɪərsən, peérssŏn

Peiser, *f.n.,* 'paɪzər, pízĕr

Peisley, *f.n.,* 'pizlɪ, peézli

Pejic, *f.n.,* 'pedʒɪk, péjjik

Pelaw *Tyne & Wear,* 'pilə, peélă; 'pilɔ, peélaw

Pelham, *f.n.,* 'peləm, péllăm

Pelletier, *f.n.,* 'peltɪeɪ, pélti-ay

Pellew, *f.n.,* pə'lju, pĕléw

Pelloe, *f.n.,* 'peloʊ, péllō

Pellsyeat *Cumbria,* 'pelzjɪt, péllz-yeet

Pelynt *Cornwall,* pə'lɪnt, pĕlínt; plɪnt, plint

Pembrey *Dyfed,* pem'breɪ, pembráy

Pembroke, *f.n.,* 'pembrʊk, pémbrŏŏk

Pembroke *Dyfed,* 'pembrʊk, pémbrŏŏk'; 'pembrək, pémbrŏk

Pembroke College *Univs. of Cambridge and Oxford,* 'pembrʊk, pémbrŏŏk

Pen-allt *Gwent,* pen'ælt, pennáhlt

Penally *Dyfed,* pən'ælɪ, pĕnáli; pen'ælɪ, pennáli

Penally Point *Cornwall,* pen'ælɪ, pennáli

Penarth *S. Glam.,* pə'nɑrθ, pĕnaárth

Penberthy, *f.n.,* pen'bərðɪ, penbérthi; 'penbərðɪ, pénbĕrthi; pen'bərθɪ, penbérthi; 'penbərθɪ, pénbĕrthi

Penboyr *Dyfed,* pen'bɔɪər, penbóyr

Penbuallt *Powys,* pen'biælt, penbeé-ahlt

Pencader *Dyfed*, pen'kædər, pen--káddĕr

Pencaitland *Lothian*, pen'keitlənd, pen-káyt-länd

Pencalenick *Cornwall*, ˌpenkə-'lenik, pen-kälénnik

Pencarnisiog *Gwynedd*, ˌpenkɑr-'niʃɒg, pen-kaarníss-yog; ˌpenkɑr'niʃɒg, pen-kaarnishog

Pencarreg *Dyfed*, pen'kæreg, pen-kárreg

Pencerig *Powys*, pen'kerig, pen-kérrig

Pen-clawdd *W. Glam.*, pen'klauð, pen-klówth

Pencoed *Mid Glam.*, pen'kɔid, pen-kóyd

Pencoys *Cornwall*, pen'kɔiz, pen-kóyz

Pencraig *H. & W.*, 'pen'kreig, pén-kráyg

Pencraig *Powys*, 'penkraig, pén--krīg; 'peŋkraig, pénkrig

Pendarves *Point Cornwall*, pen'dɑrvis, pendaárvĕss

Pendeen *Cornwall*, pen'din, pendeén

Pendell Court *Surrey*, 'pendl 'kɔrt, péndl kórt

Pendennis *Point Cornwall*, pen-'denis, pendénniss

Penderyn *Mid Glam.*, pen'derin, pendérrin

Pendeulwyn *Mid Glam.*, pen-'dailwin, pendílwin. *The English form is* **Pendoylan**, *q.v.*

Pendine *Dyfed*, pen'dain, pendín

Pendlebury, *f.n.*, 'pendlbəri, péndlbŭri

Pendomer *Somerset*, pen'doumər, pendṓmĕr

Pendoylan *Mid Glam.*, pen-'dɔilən, pendóylän. *The Welsh form is* **Pendeulwyn**, *q.v.*

Pendoylan *S. Glam.*, pen'dɔilən, pendóylän

Pendrous, *f.n.*, 'pendrəs, péndrŭss

Pendry, *f.n.*. 'pendri, péndri

Pendse, *f.n.*, 'pendzi, péndzi

Penegoes *Powys*, pen'egɔis, penéggoyss

Penfold, *f.n.*, 'penfould, pénfōld

Penfound House *Cornwall*, pən'faund 'haus, pĕnfównd hówss

Pengam *Gwent, S. Glam.*, 'peŋgəm, péng-găm

Pengegon *Cornwall*, pen'gegən, pen-géggŏn

Pengelly, *f.n.*, peŋ'geli, peng-gélli

Pengersick *Cornwall*, pen'gɜrsik, pen-gérssick

Pengwern *Clwyd*, 'pengwɜrn, pén--gwern

Penhaligon, *f.n.*, pen'hæligən, pen-háligŏn

Peniarth *Gwynedd*, 'penjɑrθ, pén--yaarth

Penicuik *Lothian*, 'penikuk, pénnikŏok

Peniel *Clwyd, Dyfed*, 'penjəl, pén--yĕl

Penifiler *Skye*, ˌpeni'filər, penni-feélĕr

Penisarwaen, *also spelt* **Penisa'r--waun**, *Gwynedd*, pen'isɑr'wain, peníssár-wín

Penistone *S. Yorks.*, 'penistən, pénnistŏn

Penkhull *Staffs.*, 'peŋkl, pénkl

Pen-lan *W. Glam.*, pen'læn, penlán

Penlee *Cornwall*, pen'li, penleé

Penlle'r-gaer *W. Glam.*, ˌpenlər-'gɑr, penhlĕr-gaár

Pen-llin *S. Glam.*, pen'ɬin, pen--hleén. *But see also* **Penllyne.**

Penlline *see* **Penllyne**

Penllwyn-gwent *Gwent*, pen'ɬuin 'gwent, pen-hlŏó-in gwént

Pen Llŷn *Gwynedd*, pen 'ɬin, pen hleén

Penllyn *Gwynedd*, 'penɬin, pén--hlin

Penllyne, *also spelt* **Penlline**, *S. Glam.*, pen'ɬain, pen-hlín. *These are locally accepted semi-anglicized forms. The Welsh-language form is* **Pen-llin**, *q.v.*

Penmachno *Gwynedd*, pen-'mæxnou, penmáchnō

Penmaen-mawr *Gwynedd*, ˌpenmain'mauər, penmīn-mówr

Penmon *Gwynedd*, 'penmɒn, pénmon

Penmynydd *Gwynedd*, pen'mʌnið, penmúnnith

Pennal *Gwynedd*, 'penæl, pénnal

Pennan *Grampian*, 'penən, pénnän

Pennant *Dyfed, Powys*, 'penænt, pénnant

Pennefather, *f.n.*, 'penifeðər, pénnifethĕr; 'penifɑðər, pénni-faathĕr

Pennell, *f.n.*, 'penl, pénnl

Pennells, *f.n.*, 'penlz, pénnlz

Pennethorne, *f.n.*, 'peniθɔrn, pénni-thorn

Pennines, The, *mountain chain, Derby.–Cheviot Hills*, 'penainz, pénninz

Penninghame *D. & G.*, 'peniŋhəm, pénning-hăm

Penning-Rowsell, *f.n.*, 'peniŋ 'rausl, pénning rówssl

Pennington, *f.n.*, 'peniŋtən, pén--ningtŏn

Pennycuick, *f.n.*, 'penɪkʊk, pénnikōōk; 'penɪkwɪk, pénni--kwick; 'penɪkjuk, pénnikewk

Pennyfather, *f.n.*, 'penɪfeðər, pénnifethĕr; 'penɪfaðər, pénni-faathĕr

Pennyman, *f.n.*, 'penɪmən, pénni-măn

Penparcau *Dyfed*, pen'pɑrkaɪ, penpaárkī

Penpedairheol *Gwent*, pen-'pedaɪər'heɪɒl, penpéddĭr-háy-ol

Penpedairhoel *Mid Glam.*, pen-'pedaɪər'hɔɪl, penpéddĭr-hóyl

Penpergwm *Gwent*, pen'pɛərgʊm, penpáirgōōm

Penponds *Cornwall*, pen'pɒndz, penpóndz

Penrhiw-ceiber *Mid Glam.*, ‚penhrɪu'kaɪbər, penri-oo-kíbĕr

Penrhiwlas *Gwynedd*, ‚penhrɪ'uləs, penri-oólăss

Penrhiwtyn *W. Glam.*, ‚penhrɪ-'utɪn, penri-oótin

Pen-rhos *Gwent, Powys*, pen-'hrous, penróss

Pen-rhos *Gwynedd*, 'pen'hrous, pén-róss

Penrhos *Gwynedd*, 'penhrɒs, pénross; 'penhrous, pénróss

Penrhos Lligwy *Anglesey*, pen-'hrous 'ɬigʊi, penróss ɬíggōō-i

Penrhyn, *Baron*, 'penrɪn, pénrín

Penrhyn-coch *Dyfed*, ‚penhrɪn-'koux, penrin-kóch

Penrhyndeudraeth *Gwynedd*, ‚penhrɪn'daɪdraɪθ, penrin--dídrīth

Penrice *Cornwall, W. Glam.*, pen'raɪs, penríss

Penrith *Cumbria*, 'penrɪθ, pénrith; 'pɪərɪθ, peérith

Penrose, *f.n.*, 'penrouz, pénróz; pen'rouz, penróz

Penryn *Cornwall*, pen'rɪn, penrín

Pen-sarn *Clwyd, Gwynedd*, pen-'sɑrn, penssaárn

Pensarn *Dyfed*, 'pensɑrn, péns-saarn

Penselwood *Somerset*, pen-'selwʊd, penssélwŏŏd

Penshaw *Tyne & Wear*, 'penʃə, pén-shä; 'penʃɔ, pén-shaw

Pentewan *Cornwall*, pen'tjuən, pentéw-än

Pentir *Gwynedd*, 'pentɪər, pénteer

Pentire Head *Cornwall*, pen'taɪər, pentír

Pentland Firth *sea area between Orkney and Scottish mainland*, 'pentlənd, péntländ

Pentland Hills *S'clyde–Lothian*, 'pentlənd, péntländ

Penton *Cumbria*, pen'tɒn, pentón

Pentonville *London*, 'pentənvɪl, péntŏnvil

Pentraeth *Gwynedd*, 'pentraɪθ, péntrith

Pentre *Clwyd, Powys*, 'pentrə, péntră

Pentre *Mid Glam., W. Glam.*, 'pentreɪ, péntray

Pentreath, *f.n.*, pen'triθ, pen-treéth

Pentre-bach *Powys*, ‚pentrə'bax, pentrăbaách

Pentrebach *Dyfed, Mid Glam.*, ‚pentrə'bax, pentrăbaách

Pentre Celyn *Clwyd*, ‚pentrə 'kelɪn, pentră kéllin

Pentrefelin *Dyfed, Gwynedd*, ‚pentrə'velɪn, pentrăvéllin

Pentrefoelas *Clwyd*, ‚pentrə-'vɔɪləs, pentrăvóyläss

Pentre-llyn-cymmer *Clwyd*, ‚pentrəlɪn'kʌmər, pentrăhlin--kúmmĕr

Pentre-poeth *Gwent*, ‚pentrə'pɔɪθ, pentrăpóyth

Pentre Poeth *W. Glam.*, ‚pentrə 'pɔɪθ, pentră póyth

Pentre Uchaf *Clwyd*, ‚pentrə 'ɪxæv, pentră íchav

Pentrich *Derby.*, 'pentrɪtʃ, pén-tritch

Pentwyn *Dyfed, Gwent, Mid Glam.*, pen'tuɪn, pentōō-in. *Appropriate for both places of the name in Gwent, and both in Mid Glam.*

Pen-twyn *Gwent*, pen'tuɪn, pentōō-in

Pentwyn-mawr *Gwent*, pen‚tuɪn-'mauər, pentōō-in-mówr

Pentyla *Mid Glam.*, pen'tʌlə, pen-túllä; pen'tɪlə, pentíllä

Pentyrch *Mid Glam.*, pen'tɜrx, pentírch; pen'tɜrk, pentírk

Pentyrch *Powys*, 'pentɜrx, pén-tirch

Penwarden, *f.n.*, pen'wɔrdən, penwáwrdĕn

Pen-waun *Mid Glam.*, pen'waɪn, penwín

Penwill, *f.n.*, 'penwɪl, pénwil

Penwith *Cornwall*, pen'wɪθ, pen-with

Penwortham *Lancs.*, 'penwərðəm, pénwŭrthăm

Pen-y-banc *Dyfed*, ‚penə'bæŋk, pennăbánk

Penyberth *Gwynedd*, pe'nʌbərθ, pennúbberth; pe'nʌbərθ, pen-núbbĕrth

Pen-y-bont *Clwyd, Dyfed, Gwent*, ‚penə'bɒnt, pennăbónt. *Appropriate for all three places of the name in Clwyd.*

Penybont *Dyfed, Powys*, ˌpenə-'bɒnt, pennăbónt

Pen-y-cae *Powys*, ˌpenə'kaɪ, pennăkí

Penydarren *Mid Glam.*, ˌpenə-'dærən, pennădárrĕn

Pen-y-fai *Mid Glam.*, ˌpenə'vaɪ, pennăví

Pen-y-fan *Powys*, ˌpenə'væn, pennăvăn

Pen-y-ffordd *Clwyd*, ˌpenə'fɔrð, pennăfórth

Penygelli *Gwynedd*, ˌpenə'geɫi, pennăgéhli

Penygenffordd *Powys*, ˌpenə-'genfɔrð, pennăgénforth

Penyghent *N. Yorks.*, ˌpenɪgent, pénnigent

Pen-y-gors *Mid Glam.*, ˌpenə'gɔrs, pennăgórss

Pen-y-graig *Mid Glam.*, ˌpenə-'graɪg, pennăgríg

Pen-y-groes *S. Glam.*, ˌpenə'grɔɪs, pennăgróyss

Penygwryd *Gwynedd*, ˌpenə-'guərɪd, pennăgŏŏrid

Pen-y-lan *S. Glam.*, ˌpenə'læn, pennălán

Penyrheolgerrig *Mid Glam.*, ˌpenrɪul'gerɪg, pénri-ool-gérrig

Pen-y-waun *Mid Glam.*, ˌpenə-'waɪn, pennă-wín

Penzance *Cornwall*, pen'zæns, penzánss

Peock, *f.n.*, 'piək, pée-ŏk

Peover *Ches.*, 'pivər, péevĕr

Peowrie, *f.n.*, 'pauərɪ, pówri

Peper Harow *Surrey*, 'pepər 'hærou, péppĕr hárrō

Peppard Common *Oxon.*, 'pepɑrd 'kɒmən, péppaard kómmŏn

Peppiatt, *f.n.*, 'pepɪət, péppi-ăt

Pepys, *f.n.*, 'pepɪs, péppiss; pips, peeps; peps, pepps. *The first is appropriate for the family name of the Earl of Cottenham. The second was apparently that of the diarist, Samuel ~, and this is the pronunciation used today by the ~ Cockerell family, lineal descendants of the diarist's sister Paulina.*

Pepys Cockerell, *f.n.*, 'pips 'kɒkərəl, péeps kóckĕrĕl

Perceval, *f.n.*, 'pɑrsɪvəl, pérssĕvăl

Percuil Ferry *Cornwall*, 'pɑrkjul, pérkewl. *An older form is* **Porthcuel**, *q.v.*

Percy, *C.n. and f.n.*, 'pɑrsɪ, pérssi

Perdiswell Park *H. & W.*, 'pɑr-dɪswəl, pérdisswĕl

Perdita, *C.n.*, 'pɑrdɪtə, pérdită

Perebourne, *f.n.*, 'perɪbɔrn, pérrĕborn

Perelman, *f.n.*, 'perəlmən, pérrĕl-măn

Peress, *f.n.*, 'peres, pérress

Pergamon Press, *publishers*, 'pɑr-gəmən, pérgămŏn

Perham, *f.n.*, 'perəm, pérrăm

Periton, *f.n.*, 'perɪtən, pérritŏn

Perkins, *f.n.*, 'pɑrkɪnz, pérkinz

Perks, *f.n.*, pɑrks, perks

Perne, *f.n.*, pɑrn, pern

Pernel, *f.n.*, pɑr'nel, pernéll

Perott, *f.n.*, 'perət, pérrŏt

Perou, *f.n.*, pə'ru, pĕróo

Perowne, *f.n.*, pə'roun, pĕrón

Perranarworthal *Cornwall*, ˌperənər'wɜrðl, perrănărwúrthl

Perranporth *Cornwall*, ˌperən-'pɔrθ, perránpórth

Perranuthnoe *Cornwall*, ˌperə-'njuθnou, perrănéwthnō; ˌperə'nʌθnou, perrănúthnō. *Although the second is used extensively in the West Country, the first is the local pronunciation.*

Perranwell *Cornwall*, ˌperən'wel, perránwéll

Perranzabuloe *Cornwall*, ˌperən-'zæbjulou, perrănzáb-yŏŏlō

Perren, *f.n.*, 'perɪn, pérrĕn

Perret, *f.n.*, 'pereɪ, pérray

Perrett, *f.n.*, 'perɪt, pérrĕt

Perrin, *f.n.*, 'perɪn, pérrin

Perring, *f.n.*, 'perɪŋ, pérring

Perrins, *f.n.*, 'perɪnz, pérrinz

Perris, *f.n.*, 'perɪs, pérriss

Perry, *f.n.*, 'perɪ, pérri

Pershouse, *f.n.*, 'pɑrshaus, pérss-howss

Persse, *f.n.*, pɑrs, perss

Perth *Tayside*, pɑrθ, perth

Pertwee, *f.n.*, 'pɑrtwi, pértwee

Perutz, *f.n.*, pə'ruts, pĕróots

Pery, *f.n.*, 'pɛərɪ, páiri; 'pɪərɪ, péeri; 'perɪ, pérri. *The first is appropriate for the Earl of Limerick's family name.*

Peschek, *f.n.*, 'peʃek, pésheck

Pestel, *f.n.*, 'pestl, pésstl

Pestell, *f.n.*, pes'tel, pesstéll

Pestridge, *f.n.*, 'pestrɪdʒ, pésstrij

Petch, *f.n.*, petʃ, petch

Peterborough *Cambs.*, 'pitərbərə, péetĕrbŭră

Peterculter *Grampian*, ˌpitər-'kutər, peetĕrkóotĕr

Peterhead *Grampian*, ˌpitər'hed, peetĕr-héd

Peterkin, *f.n.*, 'pitərkɪn, péetĕrkin

Peterlee *Durham*, ˌpitər'li, peetĕr-lée

Peters, *f.n.*, 'pitərz, péetĕrz

Petersen, *f.n.*, 'pitərsən, péetĕrs-sĕn

Petersfinger *Wilts.*, 'pitərzfiŋgər, péetĕrz-fíng-gĕr

Petersham *London*, 'pitərʃəm, péetĕr-shăm

Peterstone super Ely *S. Glam.*, 'pitərstən ,supər 'ili, péetĕrsstŏn soopĕr éeli

Peter Tavy *Devon*, 'pitər 'teɪvi, péetĕr táyvi

Petham *Kent*, 'petəm, péttăm

Pethen, *f.n.*, 'peθən, péthĕn

Petheram, *f.n.*, 'peðərəm, péthĕrăm

Petherbridge, *f.n.*, 'peðərbrɪdʒ, péthĕrbrij

Petherick, *f.n.*, 'peθərɪk, péthĕrick

Pethick-Lawrence, Barony of, 'peθɪk 'lɒrəns, péthick lórrĕnss

Petit, *f.n.*, 'petɪt, péttit

Peto, *f.n.*, 'pitoʊ, péetō

Petre, *f.n.*, 'pitər, péetĕr. *Appropriate also for Baron* ~.

Petrides, *f.n.*, pɪ'tridɪz, pĕtréedĕz

Petrie, Sir Flinders, *Egyptologist*, 'flɪndərz 'pitrɪ, flíndĕrz péetri

Petrie, *f.n.*, 'pitrɪ, péetri

Petrockstow *Devon*, 'petrɒkstoʊ, pétrocksstō

Petrox, saint, 'petrɒks, péttrocks

Pettener, *f.n.*, 'petənər, péttĕnĕr

Petteril, River, *Cumbria*, 'petrɪl, péttril

Pettican, *f.n.*, 'petɪkən, péttikăn

Pettifer, *f.n.*, 'petɪfər, péttifĕr

Pettigo *Co. Fermanagh*, 'petɪgoʊ, péttigō

Pettigrew, *f.n.*, 'petɪgru, péttigroo

Pettingell, *f.n.*, 'petɪŋgl, pétting-gl

Pettinger, *f.n.*, 'petɪndʒər, péttinjĕr

Pettistree *Suffolk*, 'petɪstri, péttisstree

Pettit, *f.n.*, 'petɪt, péttit

Pevensey *E. Sussex*, 'pevənzi, pévvĕnzi

Pevsner, Sir Nikolaus, *art historian*, 'nɪkələs 'pevznər, níckŏláss pévznĕr

Pewsey *Wilts.*, 'pjuzɪ, péwzi

Pewsham *Wilts.*, 'pjuʃəm, péw-shăm

Peyre, *f.n.*, 'peər, pair

Peyton, *f.n.*, 'peɪtən, páytŏn

Pfammatter, *f.n.*, 'fæmətər, fámmătĕr

Phaidon Press, *publishers*, 'faɪdən, fídŏn

Phairkettle, *f.n.*, 'feərketl, fáirkettl

Pharay, *also spelt* **Fara**, *Orkney*, 'feərə, fárrå

Phayre, *f.n.*, feər, fair

Phelan, *f.n.*, 'filən, féelăn; 'feɪlən, fáylăn. *The first is normal in England, the second is the Northern Irish pronunciation.*

Phelops, *f.n.*, 'felɒps, féllops

Phelps, *f.n.*, felps, felps

Phemister, *f.n.*, 'femɪstər, fémmisstĕr

Philbin, *f.n.*, 'fɪlbɪn, fílbin

Philie, *f.n.*, 'fɪli, fílli

Philiphaugh *Borders*, 'fɪlɪp'hɒx, fíllip-hóch

Philipson, *f.n.*, 'fɪlɪpsən, fíllipsŏn

Phillack *Cornwall*, 'fɪlək, fílläk

Philleigh *Cornwall*, 'fɪli, filli; 'fɪli, fillee

Philorth *Grampian*, fɪ'lɔrθ, filórth

Philp, *f.n.*, fɪlp, filp

Phipps, *f.n.*, fɪps, fipps

Phizacklea, *f.n.*, fɪ'zæklɪə, fizzácklià

Phoebe, *C.n.*, 'fibɪ, féebi

Phyllida, *C.n.*, 'fɪlɪdə, fíllidä

Phythian-Adams, *f.n.*, 'fɪθɪən 'ædəmz, fíthiän áddămz

Piachaud, *f.n.*, 'pɪaʃoʊ, pée-áshō

Picard, *f.n.*, 'pɪkɑrd, píckaard

Picarda, *f.n.*, pɪ'kɑrdə, pikaárdä

Piccadilly *London*, ,pɪkə'dɪlɪ, pickădílli

Piché, *f.n.*, 'pɪʃeɪ, péeshay

Pichard, *f.n.*, 'pɪkɑrd, píckaard

Pickavance, *f.n.*, 'pɪkəvæns, píckăvanss

Pickaver, *f.n.*, pɪ'keɪvər, pikáyvĕr

Pickerell, *f.n.*, 'pɪkərəl, píckĕrĕl

Pickering, *f.n.*, 'pɪkərɪŋ, píckĕring

Pickett, *f.n.*, 'pɪkɪt, pickĕt

Pickford, *f.n.*, 'pɪkfərd, píckfŏrd

Pickles, *f.n.*, 'pɪklz, pícklz

Pickstock, *f.n.*, 'pɪkstɒk, píckstock

Pickthorne, *f.n.*, 'pɪkθɔrn, píck-thorn

Pickvance, *f.n.*, 'pɪkvæns, píckvanss

Pidding, *f.n.*, 'pɪdɪŋ, pídding

Piddinghoe *E. Sussex*, ,pɪdɪŋ'hu, pidding-hóo

Piddletrenthide *Dorset*, ,pɪdl'trentaɪd, piddltréntid

Pidduck, *f.n.*, 'pɪdək, píddŭck

Pidley *Cambs.*, 'pɪdlɪ, pídli

Pidsley, *f.n.*, 'pɪdzlɪ, pídzli

Piears, *f.n.*, pɪərz, peerz

Piegza, *f.n.*, pɪ'egzə, pi-égzä

Pielou, *f.n.*, pi'lu, peelóo

Pierce, *f.n.*, pɪərs, peerss

Piercebridge *Durham*, 'pɪərsbrɪdʒ, péerss-brij

Piercy, *f.n.*, 'pɪərsɪ, péerssi. *Appropriate also for Baron* ~.

Pierpont, *f.n.*, 'pɪərpənt, péerpŏnt

Pierrepoint, *f.n.*, 'pɪərpɔɪnt, péerpoynt

Pierrepont, *f.n.*, 'pɪərpənt, péerpŏnt

Piers, *C.n.*, pɪərz, peerz

Pierssené, *f.n.*, 'pɪərsneɪ, péerss- nay
Piggott, *f.n.*, 'pɪgət, píggŏt
Pignéguy, *f.n.*, pɪn'jeɪgɪ, pin-yáygi
Pignon, *f.n.*, 'pɪnjõ, péen-yõng
Pigot, *f.n.*, 'pɪgət, píggŏt
Pigou, *f.n.*, 'pɪgu, píggoo
Pika, *f.n.*, 'pɪkə, peeká
Pike, *f.n.*, paɪk, pík
Pikett, *f.n.*, 'paɪkɪt, píkĕt
Pilbeam, *f.n.*, 'pɪlbim, pílbeem
Pilbrow, *f.n.*, 'pɪlbrou, pílbrō
Pilch, *f.n.*, pɪltʃ, piltch
Pilcher, *f.n.*, 'pɪltʃər, píltchĕr
Pilger, *f.n.*, 'pɪldʒər, píljĕr
Pilley, *f.n.*, 'pɪlɪ, pílli
Pillgwenlly *Gwent*, pɪɬ'gwenɬɪ, piḻ̱l-gwénḻ̱li
Pilling, *f.n.*, 'pɪlɪŋ, pílling
Pillinger, *f.n.*, 'pɪlɪndʒər, píllinjĕr
Pillow, *f.n.*, 'pɪlou, pílló
Pimperne *Dorset*, 'pɪmpərn, pímpĕrn
Pinchbeck, *f.n.*, 'pɪnʃbek, pínsh- -beck; 'pɪntʃbek, píntch-beck
Pinchen, *f.n.*, 'pɪnʃən, pínshĕn
Pinches, *f.n.*, 'pɪnʃɪz, pínshĕz
Pincus, *f.n.*, 'pɪŋkəs, pínküss
Pinel, *f.n.*, pɪ'nel, pinéll
Pinero, *f.n.*, pɪ'nɪərou, pinéerō; pɪ'nɛərou, pináirō. *The first is appropriate for Sir Arthur Wing ~, playwright.*
Pinfield, *f.n.*, 'pɪnfild, pínfeeld
Pinged *Dyfed*, 'pɪŋed, píng-ged
Pinhoe *Devon*, pɪn'hou, pin-hó
Pinkerton, *f.n.*, 'pɪŋkərtən, pínkĕr- tŏn
Pinmachar *S'clyde*, pɪn'mæxər, pin-máchăr
Pinmill *Suffolk*, 'pɪnmɪl, pínmill
Pinnegar, *f.n.*, 'pɪnɪgər, pínnĕgăr
Pinnell, *f.n.*, pɪ'nel, pinéll
Pinniger, *f.n.*, 'pɪnɪdʒər, pínnijĕr
Pinter, *f.n.*, 'pɪntər, pínter. *Appropriate for Harold ~, playwright.*
Pinwhattle *S'clyde*, pɪn'hwætl, pin-wháttl
Pinwherry *S'clyde*, pɪn'hwerɪ, pin- -whérri
Pinyoun, *f.n.*, pɪn'jaun, pin-yówn; pɪn'joun, pin-yón
Piper, *f.n.*, 'paɪpər, pípĕr
Pipewell *Northants.*, 'pɪpwel, pípwel
Pipon, *f.n.*, 'pɪpon, péepon
Pirant, *f.n.*, 'pɪrənt, pírrănt
Piratin, *f.n.*, pɪ'rætɪn, piráttin
Pirbright *Surrey*, 'pɜrbraɪt, pírbrīt
Pirie, *f.n.*, 'pɪrɪ, pírri
Pirnie, *f.n.*, 'pɜrnɪ, pírni
Pisciottani, *f.n.*, ˌpɪskɪə'tɑnɪ, pisskiŏtaani

Pishill *Oxon.*, 'pɪʃɪl, písh-il
Pistyll *Gwynedd*, 'pɪstɪɬ, písstiḻ̱l
Pitblado, *f.n.*, pɪt'bleɪdou, pit- bláydō
Pitcairn, *f.n.*, pɪt'kɛərn, pitkáirn
Pitcalzean House *H'land*, pɪt- 'kæljən, pitkál-yĕn
Pitcruvie *Fife*, pɪt'kruvɪ, pit- -króovi
Pitfichie Castle *Grampian*, pɪt- 'fɪxɪ, pitfíchi
Pitfirrane Park *Fife*, pɪt'fɪrən, pitfírrăn
Pitfodels *Grampian*, pɪt'fɒdlz, pitfóddlz
Pitgaveny *Grampian*, pɪt'geɪvənɪ, pitgáyvĕni
Pithey, *f.n.*, 'pɪθɪ, píthi; 'pɪðɪ, píthi
Pitlochry *Tayside*, pɪt'lɒxrɪ, pit- lóchri
Pitreavie *Fife*, pɪ'trivɪ, pitréevi
Pitscottie *Fife*, pɪt'skɒtɪ, pitskótti
Pitsea *Essex*, 'pɪtsɪ, pítsee
Pitsligo *Grampian*, pɪt'slaɪgou, pitslígō
Pittenweem *Fife*, ˌpɪtən'wim, pittĕnweém
Pitteuchar *Fife*, pɪt'juxər, pit- -yóochăr
Pittodrie *Grampian*, pɪ'tɒdrɪ, pitóddri
Pittondrigh, *f.n.*, 'pɪtəndraɪ, pít- tŏndrī
Pizey, *f.n.*, 'paɪzɪ, pízi
Pizzey, *f.n.*, 'pɪzɪ, pízzi; 'pɪtsɪ, pítsi
Pladdies *Co. Down*, 'plædɪz, pláddiz
Plaid Cymru, *Welsh National Party*, 'plaɪd 'kamrɪ, plíd kúmri
Plainmoor *Devon*, 'pleɪnmuər, pláynmŏor
Plaisted, *f.n.*, 'pleɪstɪd, pláysstĕd
Plaistow, *f.n.*, 'pleɪstou, pláysstō
Plaistow *Derby., H. & W.*, 'pleɪstou, pláysstō
Plaistow *London*, 'plɑstou, plaàss- stō; 'plæstou, plásstō. *Appropriate for the ~ parliamentary division.*
Plaistow *Kent*, 'plɑstou, plaàsstō; 'pleɪstou, pláysstō
Plaistow *W. Sussex*, 'plæstou, plásstō
Plaitford *Hants*, 'pleɪtfərd, pláyt- fŏrd
Plamenatz, *f.n.*, 'plæmɪnæts, plámmĕnats
Planterose, *f.n.*, 'plæntərouz, plaántĕrōz
Plaskow, *f.n.*, 'plæskou, plásskō
Plasnewydd *S. Glam.*, plæs- 'njuɪð, plass-néw-iṯh

Plastow, *f.n.*, 'plæstou, plásstō
Plas-y-Brenin *Gwynedd*, 'plas ə
  'brenɪn, pláass ă brénnin
Plater, *f.n.*, 'pleɪtər, pláytĕr
Plath, *f.n.*, plæθ, plath
Platt, *f.n.*, plæt, platt
Platting *Gtr. M'chester*, 'plætɪŋ,
  plátting
Platts, *f.n.*, plæts, platts
Plaxtol *Kent*, 'plækstəl, pláckstŏl
Playle, *f.n.*, pleɪl, playl
Pleasance, *f.n.*, 'plezəns, plézz-
  änss
Pleasington *Lancs.*, 'plezɪŋtən,
  plézzingtŏn
Pleasley *Derby.*, 'plezlɪ, plézzli
Pleass, *f.n.*, plis, pleess; ples,
  pless
Pleshey *Essex*, 'pleʃɪ, pléshi
Pleydell, *f.n.*, 'pledl, pléddl;
  pleɪ'del, playdéll
Pleydell-Bouverie, *f.n.*, 'pledl
  'buvərɪ, pléddl boovĕri. *Family
  name of the Earl of Radnor.*
Pliatzky, *f.n.*, plɪ'ætskɪ, pli-átski
Plimmer, *f.n.*, 'plɪmər, plímmĕr
Plinlimmon, *also spelt* Plynlimon,
  Dyfed, plɪn'lɪmən, plinlímmŏn.
  The Welsh form of the name is
  Pumlumon, *q.v.*
Plomer, *f.n.*, 'plumər, ploomĕr.
  Appropriate for William ~,
  author.
Plomley, *f.n.*, 'plʌmlɪ, plúmli
Plouviez, *f.n.*, 'pluvɪeɪ, ploovi-ay
Plowden, *f.n.*, 'plaudən, plówdĕn.
  Appropriate also for Baron ~.
Plowman, *f.n.*, 'plaumən, plów-
  män
Plowright, *f.n.*, 'plauraɪt, plów-
  rīt
Plugge, *f.n.*, plʌg, plug
Plumbe, *f.n.*, plʌm, plum
Plumbridge *Co. Tyrone*, plʌm-
  'brɪdʒ, plum-bríj
Plume, *f.n.*, plum, ploom
Plumer, Viscountcy of, 'plumər,
  ploomĕr
Plummer, *f.n.*, 'plʌmər, plúmmĕr
Plumptre, *f.n.*, 'plʌmtrɪ, plúmtree
Plumtre, *f.n.*, 'plʌmtrɪ, plúmtree
Plungar *Leics.*, 'plʌŋgɑr, plúng-
  -gaar
Plunkett, *f.n.*, 'plʌŋkɪt, plúnkĕt
Pluscarden Priory *Grampian*,
  'plʌskərdən, plússkärdĕn
Plymen, *f.n.*, 'plaɪmən, plímĕn
Plymouth *Devon*, 'plɪməθ, plím-
  mŭth
Plymtree *Devon*, 'plɪmtrɪ, plím-
  tree
Plynlimon *see* Plinlimmon

Pochin, *f.n.*, 'poutʃɪn, pótchin;
  'pʌtʃɪn, pútchin
Pocock, *f.n.*, 'poukɒk, pókock
Podds, *f.n.*, pɒdz, podz
Poderis, *f.n.*, pə'dɛərɪs, pŏdáiriss
Podevin, *f.n.*, 'poudəvɪn, pódĕvin
Podington *Beds.*, 'pɒdɪŋtən, pód-
  dingtŏn
Poel, *f.n.*, 'pouel, pó-el
Poeton, *f.n.*, 'pouɪtən, pó-ĕtŏn
Poett, *f.n.*, 'pouɪt, pó-ĕt
Pogson, *f.n.*, 'pɒgsən, póggssŏn
Point Lynas *Anglesey*, pɔɪnt
  'laɪnəs, poynt línäss
Pointon, *f.n.*, 'pɔɪntən, póyntŏn
Poirier, *f.n.*, 'pɒrɪər, pórri-ĕr
Polak, *f.n.*, 'poulək, pólăk;
  'poulæk, pólack
Polan, *f.n.*, 'poulən, pólăn
Polapit *Cornwall*, 'pɒləpɪt, póllä-
  pit
Polbathic *Cornwall*, pɒl'bæθɪk,
  polbáthick
Polden Hills *Somerset*, 'poulдən
  'hɪlz, póldĕn hillz
Poldhu *Cornwall*, pɒl'dju, poldéw
Pole, *f.n.*, poul, pōl; pul, pool
Polegate *E. Sussex*, 'poulgeɪt,
  pólgayt
Polesden Lacey *Surrey*, 'poulz-
  dən 'leɪsɪ, pólzdĕn láyssi
Polgigga *see* Poljigga
Pol Hill *Kent*, 'pɒl 'hɪl, pól hill
Poliakov, *f.n.*, 'pɒljəkɒf, pól-
  -yăkoff
Poling *W. Sussex*, 'poulɪŋ, póling
Poljigga, *also spelt* Polgigga,
  Cornwall, pɒl'dʒɪgə, poljíggă
Polkemmet *Lothian*, pɒl'kemɪt,
  polkémmĕt
Polkerris *Cornwall*, pɒl'kerɪs,
  polkérriss
Pollak, *f.n.*, 'pɒlək, póllăk
Pollard, *f.n.*, 'pɒlɑrd, póllaard
Pollock, *f.n.*, 'pɒlək, póllŏk
Pollokshields *S'clyde*, 'pɒlək-
  'ʃildz, póllŏk-shéeldz
Pollphail *S'clyde*, 'pɒlfeɪl, pólfayl
Polmadie *S'clyde*, ,pɒlmə'di,
  polmädée
Polmont *Central*, 'poulmənt, pól-
  mŏnt
Polperro *Cornwall*, pɒl'perou,
  polpérrō
Polruan *Cornwall*, pɒl'ruən,
  polroo-än
Polson, *f.n.*, 'poulsən, pólssŏn
Polstead *Suffolk*, 'poulsted,
  pólssted
Poltalloch *S'clyde*, pɒl'tæləx,
  poltálŏch
Poltimore *Devon*, 'poultɪmər, pól-
  timor. *Appropriate also for
  Baron* ~.

Polton *Lothian*, 'poultən, pṓltŏn

Polwarth, *f.n.*, 'pɒlwərθ, pṓlwärth

Polwarth *Lothian*, 'poulwərθ, pṓlwärth

Polwhele, *f.n.*, pɒl'wil, polweel

Polwhele *Cornwall*, pɒl'wil, polweel

Polygon *Southampton*, 'pɒlɪgən, pṓlĭgŏn

Polzeath *Cornwall*, pɒl'zeθ, polzéth

Pomeroy, *f.n.*, 'poumrɔɪ, pṓmroy; 'pɒmərɔɪ, pómmĕroy. *The first is appropriate for the family name of Viscount Harberton.*

Pomeroy *Co. Tyrone*, 'pɒmərɔɪ, pómmĕroy

Pomfret, *f.n.*, 'pʌmfrɪt, púmfrĕt

Pompey, *popular name for Portsmouth*, 'pɒmpɪ, pómpi

Pomphrey, *f.n.*, 'pɒmfrɪ, pómfri

Ponfeigh *S'clyde*, pɒn'feɪ, ponfáy

Ponsanooth *Cornwall*, pɒnz'nuθ, ponz-noóth

Ponsford, *f.n.*, 'pɒnsfərd, pónssförd

Ponsonby, *f.n.*, 'pʌnsənbɪ, púnssŏnbi; 'pɒnsənbɪ, pónssŏnbi

Ponsonby *Cumbria*, 'pʌnsənbɪ, púnssŏnbi; 'pɒnsənbɪ, pónssŏnbi

Ponsonby of Shulbrede, Baron, 'pʌnsənbɪ əv 'ʃulbrɪd, púnssŏnbi ŏv shoólbreed

Ponsonby of Sysonby, Baron, 'pʌnsənbɪ əv 'saɪzənbɪ, púnssŏnbi ŏv sízŏnbi

Pontardawe *W. Glam.*, ,pɒntər'daʊeɪ, pontárdów-ay

Pontarddulais *W. Glam.*, ,pɒntər'ðɪlaɪs, pontaarthilliss. *The English form is* **Pontardulais**, *q.v.*

Pontardulais *W. Glam.*, ,pɒntər'dɪlaɪs, pontárdílliss; ,pɒntər'dɪləs, pontárdílläss; ,pɒntər'dʌləs, pontárdúlläss. *The Welsh form is* **Pontarddulais**, *q.v.*

Pontcysyllte *Clwyd*, ,pɒntkə'sʌlteɪ, pontküssúhltay

Pont-dôl-goch *Powys*, ,pɒntdoʊl'goʊx, pont-dṓlgóch

Pontefract *W. Yorks.*, 'pɒntɪfrækt, póntĕfrackt. *An old local form, which survives in the name of the liquorice sweets known as 'Pomfret cakes', is pronounced* 'pʌmfrɪt, púmfrĕt *or* 'pɒmfrɪt, pómfrĕt

Ponteland *Northd.*, pɒnt'iland, ponteéländ

Ponterwyd *Dyfed*, pɒnt'ɛərwɪd, pontáirwid

Pontesbury *Salop*, 'pɒntɪzbərɪ, póntĕzbŭri

Pontet, *f.n.*, 'pɒntɪt, póntĕt; 'pɒnteɪ, póntay

Pontfadog *Clwyd*, pɒnt'vædɒg, pontváddog

Pont-faen *Dyfed, Powys*, pɒnt'vaɪn, pontvín

Pontfaen *Dyfed*, pɒnt'vaɪn, pont-vín

Pontfenny *Dyfed*, pɒnt'venɪ, pontvénni

Ponthenry, *also spelt* **Pont Henry**, *Dyfed*, pɒnt'henrɪ, pont-hénri

Pontlase, Pontlasse *see* **Pontlassau**

Pontlassau, *also spelt* **Pontlase**, **Pontlasse**, *Mid Glam.*, pɒnt'læseɪ, pontlássay

Pontllan-fraith *Gwent*, ,pɒntɬæn'vraɪθ, pont-hlanvríth

Pont-lliw *W. Glam.*, pɒnt'ɬju, pont-hléw

Pontlottyn *Mid Glam.*, pɒnt'lɒtɪn, pontlóttin

Pontlyfni *Gwynedd*, pɒnt'lʌvnɪ, pont-lúvni

Pontneathvaughan *Powys*, ,pɒntniθ'vɒn, pont-neethváwn. *The Welsh form is* **Pontneddfechan**, *q.v.*

Pontneddfechan *Powys*, ,pɒntneð'vexən, pont-nethvéchän. *The English form is* **Pontneathvaughan**, *q.v.*

Pontnewydd *Gwent*, pɒnt'newɪð, pontné-with

Pontnewynydd *Gwent*, ,pɒntnə'wanɪð, pontnĕwúnnith

Ponton, Great *and* Little, *Lincs.*, 'pɒntən, póntŏn

Pontop *Durham*, 'pɒntɒp, póntop

Pontop Pike *Durham*, 'pɒntɒp 'paɪk, póntop pík

Pontrhydfendigaid *Dyfed*, ,pɒnt-hridven'dɪgaɪd, pontreed-vendéegíd

Pont-rhyd-y-fen *W. Glam.*, ,pɒnt-hridə'ven, pontreedävén; ,pɒnt-hridə'ven, pontridävén

Pontrilas *H. & W.*, pɒnt'raɪləs, pontríläss

Pontrobert *Powys*, pɒnt'rɒbərt, pont-róbbĕrt

Pontsticill *Mid Glam.*, pɒnt'stɪkɪɬ, pontstíckihl

Pontyates *Dyfed*, pɒnt'jeɪts, pont-yáyts

Pontyberem *Dyfed*, ,pɒntə'berəm, pontäbérrĕm

Pontybodkin *Clwyd*, ,pɒntə'bɒdkɪn, pontäbódkin

Pont-y-clun *Mid Glam.*, ,pɒntə'klɪn, pontäkleén

Pontycymmer, *also spelt* **Ponty-cymer,** *Mid Glam.,* ˌpɒntə-ˈkʌmər, pontăkúmmĕr
Pont-y-gwaith *Mid Glam.,* ˌpɒntəˈgwaiθ, pontăgwíth
Pontymister *Gwent,* ˌpɒntəˈmistər, pontămísstĕr
Pontymoile *Gwent,* ˌpɒntəˈmɔil, pontămóyl
Pontypool *Gwent,* ˌpɒntəˈpuːl, pontăpoõl
Pontypridd *Mid Glam.,* ˌpɒntə-ˈpriːð, pontăpreéth
Pontyrhyl *Mid Glam.,* ˌpɒntəˈril, pontărill
Poock, *f.n.,* puk, pook
Pook, *f.n.,* puk, pook
Poole, *f.n.,* puːl, pool
Poolewe *H'land,* puːlˈjuː, poõléw
Popham, *f.n.,* ˈpɒpəm, póppăm
Popkin, *f.n.,* ˈpɒpkin, pópkin
Pople, *f.n.,* ˈpoupl, pópl
Poplett, *f.n.,* ˈpɒplit, póplĕt
Porchester, Baron, ˈpɔːtʃistər, pórtchĕsstĕr
Porges, *f.n.,* ˈpɔːdʒiz, pórjĕz
Poringland *Norfolk,* ˈpɔːriŋlænd, páwring-land; ˈpɔːrlænd, pórland
Porkellis *Cornwall,* pɔːˈkelis, porkélliss
Portadown *Co. Armagh,* ˌpɔːtəˈdaun, portădówn
Portaferry *Co. Down,* ˌpɔːtəˈferi, portăférri
Portal, *f.n.,* ˈpɔːtl, pórtl
Portal of Hungerford, Viscount, ˈpɔːtl əv ˈhʌŋgərfərd, pórtl ŏv húng-gĕrförd
Portarlington, Earl of, pɔːtˈɑːliŋtən, portaárlingtŏn
Portaskaig *S'clyde,* pɔːtˈæskeig, portásskayg
Portavadie, *also spelt* **Porta-vaidue,** *S'clyde,* ˌpɔːtəˈvædi, portăváddi
Portavoe *Co. Down,* ˌpɔːtəˈvou, portăvố
Portavogie *Co. Down,* ˌpɔːtə-ˈvougi, portăvốgi
Portballintrae *Co. Antrim,* pɔːtˌbælinˈtrei, port-balintráy
Port Bannatyne *S'clyde,* port ˈbænətain, port bánnătĭn
Portbraddon *Co. Antrim,* pɔːtˈbrædən, port-bráddŏn
Portbury *Avon,* ˈpɔːtbəri, pórt-bŭri
Porteinon *see* **Port Eynon**
Porteous, *f.n.,* ˈpɔːtjəs, pórt-yŭss; ˈpɔːtiəs, pórti-ŭss
Portesham *Dorset,* ˈpɔːtiʃəm, pórtĕ-shăm

Port Eynon, *also spelt* **Porteynon, Porteinon,** *W. Glam.,* pɔːt ˈainən, port ínŏn
Portglenone *Co. Antrim,* ˌpɔːtglə-ˈnoun, portglĕnốn
Porth, *f.n.,* pɔːθ, porth
Porthallow *Cornwall,* pɔːθˈælou, porth-álố
Porthcawl *Mid Glam.,* pɔːθˈkɔːl, porthkáwl; pɔːθˈkaul, porthkówl
Porthcuel Ferry *Cornwall,* ˈpɔːθ-kjuːl, pórthkewl. *The modern name is* **Percuil,** *q.v.*
Porthcurno *Cornwall,* pɔːθˈkɜːnou, porthkúrnố
Porth Dinllaen *Gwynedd,* ˌpɔːθ dinˈɬain, porth din-hlín. *Another form is* **Portin-llaen,** *q.v.*
Porthleven *Cornwall,* pɔːθˈlevən, porthlévvĕn
Porthmadog *Gwynedd,* pɔːθ-ˈmædɒg, porth-máddog
Porthoustock *Cornwall,* pɔːθ-ˈaustɒk, porth-ówsstock; ˈpraustɒk, prówsstock
Porthpean *Cornwall,* pɔːθˈpiən, porthpeé-ăn
Porthtowan *Cornwall,* pɔːθˈtauən, porthtów-ăn
Porth yr Aur *Gwynedd,* ˈpɔːθ ər ˈaiər, pórth ŭr ír
Porth-y-rhyd *Dyfed,* ˌpɔːθəˈhrid, porth-ă-reéd
Portincaple *S'clyde,* ˈpɔːtinkæpl, pórtin-kappl
Portin-llaen *Gwynedd,* ˌpɔːtinˈɬain, portin-hlín. *Another form is* **Porth Dinllaen,** *q.v.*
Portishead *Avon,* ˈpɔːtished, pórtiss-hed
Portland, Duke of, ˈpɔːtlənd, pórtlănd
Portlethen *Grampian,* pɔːtˈleθən, portléthĕn
Portloe *Cornwall,* pɔːtˈlou, portlố
Portmadoc *Gwynedd,* pɔːtˈmædək, portmáddŏk. *Former name of* **Porthmadog,** *q.v.*
Portmahomack *H'land,* ˌpɔːtmə-ˈhɒmək, portmă-hómmăk
Portman, *f.n.,* ˈpɔːtmən, pórtmăn
Portmeirion *Gwynedd,* pɔːt-ˈmeriən, port-mérri-ŏn
Portnahaven *S'clyde,* ˌpɔːtnə-ˈhævən, portnă-hávvĕn
Portnoid, *f.n.,* ˈpɔːtnɔid, pórt-noyd
Portobello *Edinburgh,* ˌpɔːtə-ˈbelou, portŏbéllố
Portquin *Cornwall,* pɔːtˈkwin, portkwín

Portreath *Cornwall*, pɔr'triθ, portréeth

Portree *H'land*, pɔr'tri, portrée

Portrush *Co. Antrim*, pɔrt'rʌʃ, portrúsh

Portscatho *Cornwall*, pɔrt'skæθoʊ, portskáthō

Port Seton *Lothian*, pɔrt 'sitən, port séetŏn

Portskewett *Gwent*, pɔrt'skjuɪt, portskéw-ĕt

Portslade-by-Sea *E. Sussex*, 'pɔrtsleɪd baɪ 'si, pórtslayd bī sée

Portsmouth *Hants*, 'pɔrtsməθ, pórtsmŭth

Portsoy *Grampian*, pɔrt'sɔɪ, port-sóy

Portstewart *Co. Derry*, pɔrt-'stjʊərt, port-styōō-ărt

Port Talbot *W. Glam.*, pɔrt 'tɔlbət, port táwlbŏt; pɔrt 'tælbət, port tálbŏt; pɔr'tɔlbət, portáwlbŏt; pɔr'tælbət, portálbŏt

Portugheis, *f.n.*, pɔrtjʊ'geɪz, portyōōgáyz

Possell, *f.n.*, pə'sel, pŏsséll

Posta, *f.n.*, 'pɒstə, pósstă

Postcombe *Oxon.*, 'poʊstkəm, pōstkŏm

Poster, *f.n.*, 'pɒstər, pósstĕr

Postgate, *f.n.*, 'poʊstgeɪt, pōst-gayt

Postles, *f.n.*, 'pɒslz, pósslz

Postlethwaite, *f.n.*, 'pɒslθweɪt, póssl-thwayt

Postling *Kent*, 'poʊstlɪŋ, pōstling

Poston, *f.n.*, 'pɒstən, pósstŏn

Postwick *Norfolk*, 'pɒzɪk, pózzick

Poton, *f.n.*, 'pɒtən, póttŏn

Potter Heigham *Norfolk*, 'pɒtər 'heɪəm, póttĕr háy-ăm; 'pɒtər 'haɪəm, póttĕr hí-ăm; 'pɒtər 'hæm, póttĕr hám

Potterspury *Northants.*, 'pɒtərzpəri, póttĕrzpŭri

Pottinger, *f.n.*, 'pɒtɪndʒər, póttinjĕr

Pougher, *f.n.*, 'paʊər, pówĕr; 'pʌfər, púffĕr

Poughill *Cornwall*, 'pɒfɪl, póffil; 'pʌfɪl, púffil

Poughill *Devon*, 'paʊɪl, pów-il

Poulett, Earl, 'pɒlɪt, páwlĕt

Poulner *Hants*, 'paʊnər, pównĕr; 'paʊlnər, pówlnĕr

Poulsen, *f.n.*, 'poʊlsən, pōlssén

Poulshot *Wilts.*, 'poʊlʃɒt, pōl-shot

Poulson, *f.n.*, 'poʊlsən, pōlssŏn

Poulter, *f.n.*, 'poʊltər, pōltĕr

Poultney *Leics.*, 'poʊltnɪ, pōltni

Poulton, *f.n.*, 'poʊltən, pōltŏn

Poulton-le-Fylde *Lancs.*, 'pultən lə 'faɪld, pōōltŏn lĕ fíld

Pounder, *f.n.*, 'paʊndər, pówndĕr

Poundstock *Cornwall*, 'paʊndstɒk, pówndstock

Pounteney, *f.n.*, 'paʊntnɪ, pówntni

Pountney, *f.n.*, 'paʊntnɪ, pówntni

Poupart, *f.n.*, 'pupart, pōōpaart; 'poʊpart, pŏpaart

Pouparts Junction *London*, 'puparts, pōōpaarts

Povall, *f.n.*, 'poʊvl, póvl

Pover, *f.n.*, 'poʊvər, póvĕr

Povey, *f.n.*, 'poʊvɪ, póvi; pə'veɪ, pŏváy

Povey's Cross *Surrey*, 'poʊvɪz 'krɒs, póviz króss

Pow, *f.n.*, paʊ, pow

Powburn *Northd.*, 'paʊbɜrn, pówburn

Powe, *f.n.*, paʊ, pow

Powell, *f.n.*, 'paʊəl, pówĕl; 'poʊəl, pó-ĕl. *The first is appropriate for Dilys ~, film critic and broadcaster; the second for Anthony ~, author.*

Powerscourt, Viscount, 'pɔrzkɔrt, pórz-kort

Powerstock *Dorset*, 'paʊərstɒk, pówĕrstock

Powick *H. & W.*, 'poʊɪk, pó-ick

Powis, Earl of, 'poʊɪs, pó-iss

Powis, *f.n.*, 'paʊɪs, pówiss

Powis Castle *Powys*, 'poʊɪs, pó-iss

Powlett, *f.n.*, 'pɒlɪt, páwlĕt

Powley, *f.n.*, 'poʊlɪ, póli; 'paʊlɪ, pówli

Pownall, *f.n.*, 'paʊnl, pównl

Powrie, *f.n.*, 'paʊərɪ, pówri

Powyke *see* **Beauchamp of Powyke**, Baron

Powys, *f.n.*, 'poʊɪs, pó-iss; 'paʊɪs, pówiss. *The first is appropriate for the family name of Baron Lilford; also for A. R. ~, church architect, John Cowper ~, poet and author, Llewelyn ~, author, Theodore Francis ~, author, and* **E.** ~ **Mathers**, *author and scholar.*

Powys *Co. name*, 'paʊɪs, pówiss

Poyntzpass *Co. Armagh*, pɔɪnts-'pas, poyntspáass

Praa Sands, Praah Sands *see* **Prah Sands**

Prador, *f.n.*, 'pradər, praádor

Praed, *f.n.*, preɪd, prayd

Pragnell, *f.n.*, 'prægnəl, prágnĕl

Prah Sands, *also spelt* **Praa, Praah**, *Cornwall*, 'preɪ 'sændz, práy sándz

Prangnell, *f.n.*, 'præŋnəl, práng-nĕl

Prashar, *f.n.*, prə'ʃɑr, prǎ-sháar
Prater, *f.n.*, 'preɪtər, práytěr
Pratley, *f.n.*, 'prætlɪ, prátli
Prawer, *f.n.*, 'prɑvər, praávěr
Praze *Cornwall*, preɪz, prayz
Predannack *Cornwall*, 'predənæk, préddǎnack; 'prednæk, préd-
-nack
Preece, *f.n.*, pris, preess
Preedy, *f.n.*, 'pridɪ, preédi
Preesall *Lancs.*, 'prizl, preézl
Preger, *f.n.*, 'preɪgər, práygěr
Prehen *Co. Derry*, prɪ'hen, prěhén
Preidel, *f.n.*, 'praɪdel, prídel
Prem, *f.n.*, prem, prem
Premru, *f.n.*, 'premru, prémroo
Prendergast, *f.n.*, 'prendərgæst, prénděrgasst
Prendwick *Northd.*, 'prendɪk, préndick
Prentice, *f.n.*, 'prentɪs, préntiss
Prentis, *f.n.*, 'prentɪs, préntiss
Prentiss, *f.n.*, 'prentɪs, préntiss
Prescelly Mountains, *also spelt* Prescely, *Dyfed*, pre'selɪ, pre-ssélli
Preshaw *Hants*, 'preʃɔ, préshaw
Pressey, *f.n.*, 'presɪ, préssi
Prestatyn *Clwyd*, pres'tætɪn, presstáttin
Presteigne *Powys*, pres'tin, pressteén
Prestige, *f.n.*, 'prestɪdʒ, préstij
Preston *Herts., Lancs.*, 'prestən, préstŏn
Prestonpans *Lothian*, 'prestən-'pænz, préstŏnpánz
Prestwick *Northd.*, 'prestɪk, préstick
Prestwick *S'clyde*, 'prestwɪk, préstwick. *Appropriate also for* ~ *Airport.*
Pretius, *f.n.*, 'preʃəs, préshūss
Pretty, *f.n.*, 'prɪtɪ, pritti; 'pretɪ, prétti
Pretyman, *f.n.*, 'prɪtɪmən, príttimǎn
Prevatt, *f.n.*, 'prɪvət, prívvăt
Prevezer, *f.n.*, prɪ'vizər, prěvéezěr
Previté, *f.n.*, prɪ'vitɪ, prěvéeti; 'prevɪtɪ, prévviti
Prevost, *f.n.*, prɪ'vou, prěvó; 'prevəst, prévvŏst; 'prevou, prévvō
Prewer, *f.n.*, 'pruər, próo-ěr
Preye, *f.n.*, preɪ, pray
Price, *f.n.*, praɪs, príss
Priday, *f.n.*, 'praɪdeɪ, príday
Prideaux, *f.n.*, 'prɪdou, príddō
Prideaux *Cornwall*, 'prɪdəks, príddūks
Prideaux-Brune, *f.n.*, 'prɪdou 'brun, príddō broón
Pridham, *f.n.*, 'prɪdəm, príddăm

Priechenfried, *f.n.*, 'prikənfrid, preékěnfreed
Priestland, *f.n.*, 'pristlənd, preést-länd
Priestley, *f.n.*, 'pristlɪ, preéstli
Princes Risborough *Bucks.*, 'prɪnsɪz 'rɪzbərə, prínssěz rízbŏrŏ
Princetown *Devon, Mid Glam.*, 'prɪnstaun, prínsstown
Pringle, *f.n.*, 'prɪŋgl, príng-gl
Prinknash Abbey *Glos.*, 'prɪnɪdʒ, prínnij
Prins, *f.n.*, prɪns, prinss
Prinsep, *f.n.*, 'prɪnsep, prínssep
Prioleau, *f.n.*, 'prɪəlou, prée-ōlō
Prion *Powys*, 'prɪɒn, prée-on
Prior, *f.n.*, 'praɪər, prí-ŏr
Priske, *f.n.*, prɪsk, prissk
Pritchard, *f.n.*, 'prɪtʃərd, prítchǎrd; 'prɪtʃard, pritchaard
Pritlove, *f.n.*, 'prɪtlʌv, prítluv
Privett, *Hants*, 'prɪvɪt, prívvět
Probert, *f.n.*, 'prɒbərt, próbběrt; 'proubərt, próběrt
Probus *Cornwall*, 'proubəs, próbūss
Probyn, *f.n.*, 'proubɪn, próbin
Prochazka, *f.n.*, prɒ'xæskə, prochásskǎ
Procope, *f.n.*, 'prɒkəpeɪ, próckŏpay
Procter, *f.n.*, 'prɒktər, prócktěr
Prodrick, *f.n.*, 'prɒdrɪk, pródrick
Profumo, *f.n.*, prə'fjumou, prŏféwmō
Progin, *f.n.*, 'proudʒɪn, prójin
Prolze, *f.n.*, proults, prólts
Proniewicz, *f.n.*, 'prɒnəvɪtʃ, prónnŏvitch
Prosen, *f.n.*, 'prouzən, prózěn
Prosser, *f.n.*, 'prɒsər, próssěr
Protasus, saint, prə'teɪzəs, prŏtáyzūss
Prothero, *f.n.*, 'prɒðərou, prŏthěrō; 'prʌðərou, prúthěrō
Protheroe, *f.n.*, 'prɒðərou, prŏthěrō; 'prʌðərou, prúthěrō
Protus, saint, 'proutəs, prótūss
Prout, *f.n.*, praut, prowt
Provan, *f.n.*, 'prɒvən, próvvăn; 'prouvən, próvăn
Provan *Glasgow*, 'prɒvən, próvvăn
Provis, *f.n.*, 'prouvɪs, próviss
Prowse, *f.n.*, praus, prowss; prauz, prowz
Prudhoe *Northd.*, 'prʌdou, prúd-dō; 'prʌdhou, prúd-hō
Prue, *f.n.*, pru, proo
Pruslin, *f.n.*, 'prʌslɪn, prússlin
Prusmann, *f.n.*, 'prʌsmən, prússmăn
Pryce, *f.n.*, praɪs, príss
Prynne, *f.n.*, prɪn, prinn

Prys, *f.n.,* pris, preess
Prytherch, *f.n.,* 'prʌðərx, prú-thĕrch; 'prʌðərk, prúthĕrk; 'priðɪk, príthick. *The first is the Welsh pronunciation.*
Puckey, *f.n.,* 'pʌkɪ, púcki
Puddefoot, *f.n.,* 'pʌdɪfʊt, púddĕ-foŏt; 'pʊdɪfʊt, poŏdĕfoŏt
Puddephat, *f.n.,* 'pʌdɪfæt, púddĕ-fat
Puddephatt, *f.n.,* 'pʌdɪfæt, púddĕfat; 'pʊdɪfæt, poŏdĕfat
Puddletown *Dorset,* 'pʌdltaʊn, púddltown
Puddy, *f.n.,* 'pʌdɪ, púddi
Pudney, *f.n.,* 'pʌdnɪ, púdni
Pudsey *W. Yorks.,* 'pʌdsɪ, púdssi
Puffett, *f.n.,* 'pʌfɪt, púffĕt
Puffin Island, *also* **St. Seiriol Island** *q.v., Gwynedd,* 'pʌfɪn, púffin
Pugh, *f.n.,* pju, pew
Pughe, *f.n.,* pju, pew
Pugin, *f.n.,* 'pjudʒɪn, péwjin
Pugmire, *f.n.,* 'pʌgmaɪər, púgmīr
Pulay, *f.n.,* 'puleɪ, poŏlay
Puleston, *f.n.,* 'pulstən, poŏlsstŏn
Pulfer, *f.n.,* 'pʊlfər, poŏlfĕr
Pullein, *f.n.,* 'pʊlɪn, poŏlĕn
Pullen, *f.n.,* 'pʊlɪn, poŏlĕn
Pulling, *f.n.,* 'pʊlɪŋ, poŏling
Pullinger, *f.n.,* 'pʊlɪndʒər, poŏlinjĕr
Pulloxhill *Beds.,* 'pʊləkshɪl, poŏlŏks-hil
Pulman, *f.n.,* 'pʊlmən, poŏlmän
Pulteney, *f.n.,* 'pʌltnɪ, púltni; 'pʊltnɪ, poŏltni
Pulteney Bridge *Bath,* 'pʌltənɪ, púltĕni
Pulvertaft, *f.n.,* 'pʌlvərtæft, púlvĕrtafft
Pumlumon *Dyfed,* pɪm'lɪmən, pimlímmŏn. *See also* **Plinlimmon.**
Pumpherston *Lothian,* 'pʌmfər-stən, púmfĕrstŏn
Pumphrey, *f.n.,* 'pʌmfrɪ, púmfri
Pumpsaint *Dyfed,* 'pɪmpsaɪnt, pímpsīnt
Puncheston *Dyfed,* 'pʌnʃɪstən, púnshĕsstŏn
Puncknowle *Dorset,* 'pʌnl, púnnl
Punshon, *f.n.,* 'pʌnʃən, púnshŏn
Purbrick, *f.n.,* 'pɜrbrɪk, púrbrick
Purcell, *f.n.,* 'pɜrsl, púrssl; pɜr'sel, púrsséll. *The first is appropriate for the 17th-c. composer, Henry ~.*
Purchese, *f.n.,* pɜr'tʃiz, purtchéez
Purdie, *f.n.,* 'pɜrdɪ, púrdi
Purdom, *f.n.,* 'pɜrdəm, púrdŏm
Purdon, *f.n.,* 'pɜrdən, púrdŏn

Purdue, *f.n.,* 'pɜrdju, púrdew
Purdy, *f.n.,* 'pɜrdɪ, púrdi
Purdysburn *Co. Down,* 'pɜrdɪz-bərn, púrdizburn
Purefoy, *f.n.,* 'pjʊərfɔɪ, pyoŏrfoy
Purfleet *Essex,* 'pɜrflɪt, púrfleet
Purgavie, *f.n.,* pɜr'geɪvɪ, purgáyvi
Puriton *Somerset,* 'pjʊərɪtən, pyoŏritŏn
Purleigh *Essex,* 'pɜrlɪ, púrli
Purnell, *f.n.,* pɜr'nel, purnéll
Pursey, *f.n.,* 'pɜrzɪ, púrzi
Purves, *f.n.,* 'pɜrvɪs, púrvĕss; pɜrvz, purvz
Purvey, *f.n.,* 'pɜrvɪ, púrvi
Pusey, *f.n.,* 'pjuzɪ, péwzi
Putnam, *f.n.,* 'pʌtnəm, pútt-näm
Putney *London,* 'pʌtnɪ, púttni
Putson *H. & W.,* 'pʌtsən, púttsŏn
Putt, *f.n.,* pʌt, putt
Putteridge Bury *Herts.,* 'pʌtərɪdʒ 'berɪ, púttĕrij bérri
Pwll *Dyfed,* puɬ, poohl
Pwllcrochan *Dyfed,* puɬ'krɒxən, poohlkróchän
Pwll-gwaun *Mid Glam.,* puɬ-'gwaɪn, poohl-gwín
Pwllheli *Gwynedd,* puɬ'helɪ, poohl-hélli; pu'ɬelɪ, poohlélli
Pwll-Meyric *Gwent,* puɬ'maɪrɪk, poohl-mírick
Pyburn, *f.n.,* 'paɪbərn, píburn
Pybus, *f.n.,* 'paɪbəs, píbüss
Pyecombe *W. Sussex,* 'paɪkum, píkoom
Pyer, *f.n.,* 'paɪər, pí-ĕr
Pyke, *f.n.,* paɪk, pík
Pyle *Mid Glam.,* paɪl, pīl
Pylle *Somerset,* pɪl, pill; paɪl, pīl
Pym, *f.n.,* pɪm, pim
Pyman, *f.n.,* 'paɪmən, pímän
Pymore *Cambs.,* 'paɪmɔr, pímor
Pyper, *f.n.,* 'paɪpər, pípĕr
Pyrah, *f.n.,* 'paɪərə, pírə
Pyrford *Surrey,* 'pɜrfərd, púrfŏrd
Pyrgo Park *Essex,* 'pɜrgoʊ, púrgō
Pytchley *Northants.,* 'paɪtʃlɪ, pítchli

Q

Quaddell, *f.n.,* kwə'del, kwŏdéll
Quaddy, *f.n.,* 'kwɒdɪ, kwóddi
Quadring *Lincs.,* 'kweɪdrɪŋ, kwáydring
Quaglino's Hotel & Restaurant *London,* kwæg'linuz, kwag-léenŏz
Quaid, *f.n.,* kweɪd, kwayd
Quaife, *f.n.,* kweɪf, kwayf

Quain, *f.n.*, kweɪn, kwayn. *Appropriate also for the ~ professorship of English in the University of London.*

Quant, *f.n.*, kwɒnt, kwont

Quantock Hills *Somerset*, 'kwɒntɒk, kwóntock

Quantrill, *f.n.*, 'kwɒntrɪl, kwóntril

Quarendon, *f.n.*, 'kwɒrəndən, kwórrĕndŏn

Quarff *Shetland*, kwɑrf, kwaarf

Quarles, *f.n.*, kwɔrlz, kwawrlz. *Appropriate for Francis ~, 16th-c. poet.*

Quarles *Norfolk*, kwɔrlz, kwawrlz

Quarley *Hants*, 'kwɔrlɪ, kwáwrli

Quarmby, *f.n.*, 'kwɔrmbɪ, kwáwrmbi

Quarndon *Derby.*, 'kwɔrndən, kwáwrndŏn

Quarr Abbey *I. of Wight*, kwɔr, kwawr

Quarrell, *f.n.*, 'kwɒrəl, kwórrĕl

Quartermaine, *f.n.*, 'kwɔrtərmeɪn, kwáwrtĕrmayn

Quartley, *f.n.*, 'kwɔrtlɪ, kwáwrtli

Quass, *f.n.*, kwɒs, kwoss

Quastel, *f.n.*, 'kwɒstel, kwósstel

Quatermain, *f.n.*, 'kwɒtərmeɪn, kwátĕrmayn

Quatermass, *f.n.*, 'kweɪtərmæs, kwáytĕrmass

Quatt *Salop*, kwɒt, kwott

Quay, *f.n.*, kweɪ, kway

Quaye, *f.n.*, kweɪ, kway

Quayle, *f.n.*, kweɪl, kwayl

Quealy, *f.n.*, 'kwilɪ, kwéeli

Quedgeley *Glos.*, 'kwedʒlɪ, kwéjjli

Queenborough *Kent*, 'kwinbərə, kwéenbŭră. *Appropriate also for the Barony of ~.*

Queenslie *S'clyde*, 'kwinz'li, kwéenz-lée

Quelch, *f.n.*, kwelʃ, kwelsh

Quemerford *Wilts.*, 'kʌmərfərd, kúmmĕrfŏrd

Queniborough *Leics.*, 'kwenɪbərə, kwénnibŭră

Quenington *Glos.*, 'kwenɪŋtən, kwénningtŏn. *Appropriate also for Viscount ~.*

Quennell, *f.n.*, kwɪ'nel, kwĕnéll

Quentin, *C.n. and f.n.*, 'kwentɪn, kwéntin

Querée, *f.n.*, 'kerɪ, kérri

Queripel, *f.n.*, 'kwerɪpel, kwérripel

Quernmore *Lancs.*, 'kwɔrmər, kwáwrmĕr; 'kwɑrmər, kwaarmĕr

Quertier, *f.n.*, 'kɜrtɪeɪ, kérti-ay

Quesnel, *f.n.*, kwɪ'nel, kwĕnéll; 'keɪnl, káynl

Quested, *f.n.*, 'kwestɪd, kwésstĕd

Quethiock *Cornwall*, 'kweðɪk, kwéθɪk, kwéthick; 'kwɪðɪk, kwíthick

Quibell, *f.n.*, kwɪ'bel, kwibéll; 'kwɪbl, kwíbbl; 'kwaɪbl, kwáibl; kwaɪ'bel, kwibéll. *The third is appropriate for the Barony of ~ of Scunthorpe.*

Quicke, *f.n.*, kwɪk, kwick

Quigley, *f.n.*, 'kwɪglɪ, kwígli

Quiller-Couch, Sir Arthur, *author*, 'kwɪlər 'kutʃ, kwíllĕr kóotch

Quilliam, *f.n.*, 'kwɪljəm, kwíl-yăm

Quilter, *f.n.*, 'kwɪltər, kwíltĕr

Quin, *f.n.*, kwɪn, kwin

Quinain, *f.n.*, kwɪ'neɪn, kwináyn

Quinan, *f.n.*, 'kwaɪnən, kwínăn

Quinault, *f.n.*, 'kwɪnəlt, kwinnŭlt

Quincey, *f.n.*, 'kwɪnsɪ, kwínssi

Quincy, *f.n.*, 'kwɪnsɪ, kwínssi

Quinion, *f.n.*, 'kwɪnɪən, kwínni-ŏn

Quinlan, *f.n.*, 'kwɪnlən, kwínlăn

Quinnell, *f.n.*, kwɪ'nel, kwinéll

Quintana, *f.n.*, kwɪn'tɑnə, kwin-taánă

Quinton, *f.n.*, 'kwɪntən, kwíntŏn

Quinton *Co. Down*, 'kwɪntən, kwíntŏn

Quirk, *f.n.*, kwɜrk, kwirk

Quirke, *f.n.*, kwɜrk, kwirk

Quitak, *f.n.*, 'kwɪtæk, kwíttack

Quixall, *f.n.*, 'kwɪksɔl, kwícksawl

Quoich, Loch *and* River, *H'land*, kɔɪx, koych

Quoile, River, *Co. Down*, kɔɪl, koyl

Quorn *Leics.*, kwɔrn, kwawrn. *Appropriate also for the ~ Hunt.*

Quothquan *S'clyde*, 'kwɒθ'kwɒn, kwóth-kwón

Quoyburray *Orkney*, 'kwaɪbʌrɪ, kwíburri

Quoyloo *Orkney*, 'kwaɪlu, kwíloo

Quy, *f.n.*, kwaɪ, kwī

Quy *Cambs.*, kwaɪ, kwī

R

Raad, *f.n.*, rɑd, raad

Raans Manor *Bucks.*, 'reɪnz, raynz

Raasay *Skye*, 'rɑseɪ, raássay

Raban, *f.n.*, 'reɪbən, ráybăn

Rabbetts, *f.n.*, rə'bets, răbétts

Rabin, *f.n.*, 'reɪbɪn, ráybin

Rabinovitch, *f.n.*, rə'bɪnəvɪtʃ, răbínnŏvitch

Rabinowitz, *f.n.*, rə'bɪnəwɪts, răbínnŏwits

Rachman, *f.n.*, 'rækmən, ráck-
mǎn

Racionzer, *f.n.*, ˌræsɪ'ɒnzər, rassi-
-ónzĕr

Radcliffe, *f.n.*, 'rædklɪf, rádkliff

Rademon *Co. Down,* rə'demən,
rǎdémmŏn

Radernie *Fife,* rə'dɜrnɪ, rǎdérni

Radford, *f.n.*, 'rædfərd, rádfŏrd

Radford Semele *Warwicks.,*
'rædfərd 'semɪlɪ, rádfŏrd
sémmĕli

Radice, *f.n.*, rə'diːtʃɪ, rǎdéetchi;
rə'diːtʃeɪ, rǎdéetchay

Radin, *f.n.*, 'reɪdɪn, ráydin

Radleian, *one educated at Radley
College,* ræd'liːən, radleé-ǎn

Radley, *f.n.*, 'rædlɪ, rádli

Radnor *Powys,* 'rædnər, rádnŏr.
*Appropriate also for the Earl
of ~.*

Rado, *f.n.*, 'reɪdoʊ, ráydō

Radyr *S. Glam.,* 'rædər, ráddĕr

Rae, *f.n.*, reɪ, ray

Rael, *f.n.*, reɪl, rayl

Raffan, *f.n.*, 'ræfən, ráffän

Raffell, *f.n.*, ræ'fel, raféll

Rafford *Grampian,* 'ræfərd,
ráffŏrd

Raffrey *Co. Down,* 'ræfrɪ, ráffri

Ragan, *f.n.*, 'reɪgən, ráygǎn

Ragg, *f.n.*, ræg, rag

Raggett, *f.n.*, 'rægɪt, rággĕt

Raghan, *f.n.*, 'reɪgən, ráygǎn

Raglan *Gwent,* 'rægglən, rágglǎn.
Appropriate also for Baron ~.

Ragosin, *f.n.*, 'rægəzɪn, rággŏzin

Rahere, *founder of St. Bartholomew the Great and of St.
Bartholomew's Hospital,*
'reɪhɪər, ráy-heer; rə'hɪər,
rǎ-héer; 'rɑhɪər, raá-heer

Rahilly, *f.n.*, 'rɑɪlɪ, raá-illi

Raholp *Co. Down,* rə'hɒlp, rǎ-
-hólp

Raikes, *f.n.*, reɪks, rayks

Rainbow, *f.n.*, 'reɪnboʊ, ráynbō

Raine, *f.n.*, reɪn, rayn

Rainger, *f.n.*, 'reɪndʒər, ráynjĕr

Rainier, *f.n.*, 'reɪnɪeɪ, ráyni-ay;
'reɪnɪər, ráyn-yĕr

Rainow *Ches.,* 'reɪnoʊ, ráynō

Rainsberry, *f.n.*, 'reɪnzbərɪ,
ráynzbĕri

Rainsford, *f.n.*, 'reɪnzfərd, ráynz-
fŏrd

Rainworth *Notts.,* 'reɪnwɜrθ,
ráynwurth

Rais, *f.n.*, reɪs, rayss

Raishbrook, *f.n.*, 'reɪʃbrʊk, ráysh-
brŏok

Raisman, *f.n.*, 'reɪzmən, ráyzmǎn

Raison, *f.n.*, 'reɪzən, ráyzŏn

Raistrick, *f.n.*, 'reɪstrɪk, ráysstrick

Raitt, *f.n.*, reɪt, rayt

Raitz, *f.n.*, raɪts, ríts

Ralegh, *f.n.*, *also spelt* **Raleigh,**
'rɔlɪ, ráwli; 'rɑlɪ, raáli; 'rælɪ,
ráli. *Sir Walter ~, 16th-c.
adventurer, although his name is
usually spelt* **Raleigh** *today,
never used this spelling himself,
and the indications are that his
own pronunciation was the first.
His treatment today, even
among scholars, seems to vary
according to taste. The third is
appropriate for the* **Raleigh**
bicycle.

Ralli, *f.n.*, 'rælɪ, ráli

Ralling, *f.n.*, 'rælɪŋ, ráling

Ralls, *f.n.*, rɒlz, rawlz

Raloo *Co. Antrim,* rə'lu, rǎlóo

Ralph, *C.n.*, rælf, ralf; reɪf, rayf;
ræf, raff. *The first is appropriate
for Sir ~ Richardson, actor, the
second for Dr ~ Vaughan
Williams, composer.*

Ralph, *f.n.*, rælf, ralf

Ralph Gore *yachting trophy,* 'reɪf
'gɔr, ráyf gór

Ralphs, *f.n.*, rælfs, ralfs

Ralston, *f.n.*, 'rɒlstən, ráwlsstŏn;
'rælstən, rálsstŏn

Ralston *S'clyde,* 'rɒlstən, ráwlsstŏn

Ramage, *f.n.*, 'ræmɪdʒ, rámmij

Rambaut, *f.n.*, 'rɒmboʊ, rómbō;
'rɑmboʊ, raámbō

Rambert, *Dame* **Marie,** *ballet
director,* 'mɑrɪ 'rɑ̃bɛər, maáree
raáng-bair. *This is Dame
Marie's pronunciation. The
Ballet Rambert is often called*
'rɒmbɛər, rómbair *in popular
usage.*

Rame *Cornwall,* reɪm, raym.
Appropriate also for ~ Head.

Ramelson, *f.n.*, 'ræmlsən, rámls-
sŏn

Ramore *Head Co. Antrim,* rə'mɔr,
rǎmór

Rampisham *Dorset,* 'ræmpɪʃəm,
rámpi-shäm

Rampton *Cambs.,* 'ræmptən,
rámptŏn

Ramsay, *f.n.*, 'ræmzɪ, rámzi.
Appropriate also for Baron ~.

Ramsbotham, *f.n.*, 'ræmzbɒθəm,
rámzboth-äm; 'ræmzbɒtəm,
rámzbóttäm. *The first is appropriate for Viscount Soulbury's
family name.*

Ramseyer, *f.n.*, 'ræmseɪər,
rámssay-ĕr

Ramsgate *Kent,* 'ræmzgeɪt, rámz-
gayt

Ramshaw, *f.n.*, 'ræmʃɔ, rám-shaw

Ramus, *f.n.,* 'reıməs, ráymŭss
Ramuz, *f.n.,* 'reımʌz, ráymuz
Ranalow, *f.n.,* 'rænəloʊ, ránnālō
Rance, *f.n.,* ræns, ranss
Ranchev, *f.n.,* 'ræntʃev, rántchev
Randall, *f.n.,* 'rændl, rándl
Randalstown *Co. Antrim,* 'rændlztaʊn, rándlztown
Randel, *f.n.,* 'rændl, rándl
Randles, *f.n.,* 'rændlz, rándlz
Randolph, *C.n. and f.n.,* 'rændɒlf, rándolf
Rands, *f.n.,* rændz, randz
Ranelagh, *f.n.,* rænılə, ránnélă
Ranelagh Gardens *London,* 'rænılə, ránnélă
Ranfurly, Earl of, 'rænfərlı, ránfûrli
Rangag, Loch, *H'land,* 'ræŋgæg, rán-gag
Ranger, *f.n.,* 'reındʒər, ráynjěr
Rankeillour, Nether *and* Over, *Fife,* ræŋ'kilər, rankéelŭr. *Appropriate also for Baron* ~.
Rankin, *f.n.,* 'ræŋkın, ránkin
Rankine, *f.n.,* 'ræŋkın, ránkin
Rankov, *f.n.,* 'ræŋkɒf, ránkoff
Rannoch *H'land,* 'rænəx, ránnŏch
Ransome, *f.n.,* 'rænsəm, ránssŏm
Ranulph, *C.n.,* 'rænʌlf, ránnulf
Raper, *f.n.,* 'reıpər, ráypěr
Raphael, *f.n.,* 'reıfl, ráyfl; 'ræfeıl, ráffayl; 'ræfeıəl, ráffay-ěl; 'ræfıəl, ráffi-ěl; 'reıfjəl, ráyf-yěl. *The third is appropriate for Frederic* ~, *author.*
Raphael Park *Essex,* 'reıfl, ráyfl
Rapoport, *f.n.,* 'ræpoʊpɔrt, ráppōport
Rapp, *f.n.,* ræp, rap
Rappitt, *f.n.,* 'ræpıt, ráppit
Rasharkin *Co. Antrim,* rə'ʃarkın, ră-shaárkin
Rashee *Co. Antrim,* rə'ʃi, ră-shée
Rashleigh, *f.n.,* 'ræʃli, ráshlee
Rasmussen, *f.n.,* ræs'musən, rassmoóssěn
Rassal Ashwood *H'land,* 'ræsl 'æʃwʊd, rássl áshwoŏd
Ratcheugh *Northd.,* 'rætʃəf, rátchŭf
Ratcliff, *f.n.,* 'rætklıf, rátkliff
Ratcliffe, *f.n.,* 'rætklıf, rátkliff
Ratendone, Viscount, 'rætəndʌn, ráttěndun
Rath, *f.n.,* ræθ, rath
Rathbone, *f.n.,* 'ræθboʊn, ráthbōn; 'ræθbən, ráthbŏn
Rathcavan, Baron, ræθ'kævən, rathkávvăn
Rathcreedan, Baron, ræθ'kridən, rathkréedăn
Rathdonnel, Baron, ræθ'dɒnl, rathdónnl

Rathe, *f.n.,* reıθ, rayth
Rathen *Grampian,* 'reıθən, ráythěn
Rathfriland *Co. Down,* ræθ'fraılənd, rathfríländ
Rathlin *Co. Antrim,* 'ræθlın, ráthlin
Rathmore, *f.n.,* ræθ'mɔr, rathmór
Ratho *Lothian,* 'raθoʊ, raáthō
Rathven *Grampian,* 'ræθvən, ráthvěn
Ratigan, *f.n.,* 'rætıgən, ráttigăn
Ratlinghope *Salop,* 'rætʃəp, rátchŏp
Rattale, *f.n.,* 'rætl, ráttl
Rattenbury, *f.n.,* 'rætənbərı, ráttěnbŭri
Rattigan, *f.n.,* 'rætıgən, ráttigăn
Rattle, *f.n.,* 'rætl, ráttl
Rattray, *f.n.,* 'rætrı, ráttri
Rattray *Tayside,* 'rætrı, ráttri
Raughton Head *Cumbria,* 'rɑftən 'hed, raáftŏn héd; 'rɒftən 'hed, rófftŏn héd
Raunds *Northants.,* rɔndz, rawndz
Ravelston *Lothian,* 'rævlstən, rávvlstŏn
Ravendale, East, *Humberside,* 'reıvəndeıl, ráyvěndayl
Ravenglass *Cumbria,* 'reıvənglɑs, ráyvěn-glaass
Raveningham *Norfolk,* 'rævənıŋəm, rávvěning-ăm; 'rævıŋəm, rávving-ăm; 'ræŋıŋəm, ránning-ăm. *The third is particularly associated with* ~ **Hall.**
Ravensbourne, River, *Kent,* 'reıvənzbɔrn, ráyvěnz-born
Ravensdale, Baron, 'reıvənzdeıl, ráyvěnzdayl
Ravenstruther *S'clyde,* 'reıvənstrɑðər, ráyvěn-struthěr
Raverat, *f.n.,* 'rɑvərɑ, raávěraa
Ravetta, *f.n.,* rə'vetə, răvéttă
Ravetz, *f.n.,* 'rævıts, rávvěts
Ravillious, *f.n.,* rə'vılıəs, răvílli-ŭss
Raw, *f.n.,* rɔ, raw
Rawlings, *f.n.,* 'rɔlıŋz, ráwlingz
Rawlins, *f.n.,* 'rɔlınz, ráwlinz
Raworth, *f.n.,* 'reıwərθ, ráy-wŭrth
Rawreth *Essex,* 'rɔrəθ, ráwrěth
Rawson, *f.n.,* 'rɔsən, ráwssŏn
Rawsthorne, *f.n.,* 'rɔsθɔrn, ráwss-thorn
Rawtenstall *Lancs.,* 'rɔtənstɔl, ráwtěnstawl; 'rɒtənstɔl, róttěnstawl
Rawthey, River, *Cumbria,* 'rɔðı, ráwthi
Raybould, *f.n.,* 'reıboʊld, ráybōld
Rayel, *f.n.,* 'reıəl, ráy-ěl

Rayleigh *Essex*, 'reɪlɪ, ráyli.
Appropriate also for Baron ~.
Raymont, *f.n.*, 'reɪmɒnt, ráymont
Rayner, *f.n.*, 'reɪnər, ráynĕr
Raynham, *f.n.*, 'reɪnəm, ráynăm
Raynsford, *f.n.*, 'reɪnzfərd, ráynz-förd
Rayson, *f.n.*, 'reɪsən, ráyssŏn
Razzall, *f.n.*, 'ræzl, rázzl
Rea, *f.n.*, reɪ, ray; rɪ, ree. *The second is appropriate for Baron* ~.
Read, *f.n.*, rid, reed
Reade, *f.n.*, rid, reed
Reader, *f.n.*, 'ridər, reédĕr
Readhead, *f.n.*, 'redhed, réd-hed
Reading *Berks.*, 'redɪŋ, rédding.
Appropriate also for the Mar-quess of ~.
Readman, *f.n.*, 'redmən, rédmăn
Reagh, Island, *Co. Down*, reɪ, ray
Reakes, *f.n.*, riks, reeks
Reaney, *f.n.*, 'reɪnɪ, ráyni; 'rinɪ, reéni. *The first is appropriate for P. H.* ~, *author of 'A Diction-ary of British Surnames'.*
Rearden, *f.n.*, 'rɪərdən, reérdĕn
Reason, *f.n.*, 'rizən, reézŏn
Reavell, *f.n.*, 'revl, révvl
Reavey, *f.n.*, 'rivɪ, reévi
Reavgli, *f.n.*, 'rivglɪ, reévgli
Reay, *f.n.*, reɪ, ray
Reay *H'land*, reɪ, ray. *Appropriate also for Baron* ~.
Rebak, *f.n.*, 'ribæk, reéback
Rebbeck, *f.n.*, 'rebek, rébbeck
Rebel, *f.n.*, rɪ'bel, rĕbéll
Recknell, *f.n.*, 'reknəl, récknĕl
Reculver *Kent*, rɪ'kʌlvər, rĕkúl-vĕr
Redadder, River, *Borders*, 'redadər, réddădĕr
Redcliffe-Maud, Barony of, 'redklɪf 'mɔd, rédkliff máwd
Reddick, *f.n.*, 'redɪk, réddick
Rede *Suffolk*, rid, reed
Redelinghuyes, *f.n.*, 'redlɪŋhjuz, rédling-hewz
Redenhall *Norfolk*, 'redənhɔl, réddĕn-hawl
Redesdale, Baron, 'ridzdeɪl, reédzdayl
Redfern, *f.n.*, 'redfərn, rédfern
Redgorton *Tayside*, 'red'gɔrtən, réd-górtŏn
Redhead, *f.n.*, 'redhed, réd-hed
Redheugh *Tyne & Wear*, 'red-hjuf, réd-hewf; 'redjuf, réddewf
Redman, *f.n.*, 'redmən, rédmăn
Redmond, *f.n.*, 'redmənd, réd-mönd
Redmoss *Grampian*, 'red'mɒs, réd-móss
Redrup, *f.n.*, 'redrʊp, rédrŏŏp

Redruth *Cornwall*, red'ruθ, red-roóth
Rée, *f.n.*, reɪ, ray
Reed, *f.n.*, rid, reed
Reekie, *f.n.*, 'rikɪ, reéki
Reepham, *Lincs., Norfolk*, 'rifəm, reéfăm
Rees, *f.n.*, ris, reess
Reese, *f.n.*, ris, reess
Reeves, *f.n.*, rivz, reevz
Reffell, *f.n.*, 'refl, réffl
Regen, *f.n.*, 'rigən, reégĕn
Reibbit, *f.n.*, 'raɪbɪt, ríbit
Reibel, *f.n.*, 'raɪbl, ríbl
Reich, *f.n.*, raɪk, rík
Reichel, *f.n.*, 'raɪxl, ríchl
Reid, *f.n.*, rid, reed
Reigate *Surrey*, 'raɪgɪt, rígit; 'raɪgeɪt, rígayt
Reighton *N. Yorks.*, 'raɪtən, reétŏn
Reilly, *f.n.*, 'raɪlɪ, ríli
Reinagle, G. P., *painter (1802–35)*, 'raɪnəgl, rínaagl
Reindorp, *f.n.*, 'raɪndɔrp, ríndorp
Reiner, *f.n.*, 'raɪnər, ráynĕr; 'raɪnər, rínĕr
Reinold, *f.n.*, 'raɪnould, rínöld
Reiss, *f.n.*, raɪs, ríss
Reiss *H'land*, ris, reess
Reiter, *f.n.*, 'raɪtər, rítĕr
Reith, *f.n.*, riθ, reeth. *Appropriate also for Baron* ~.
Reizenstein, Franz, *pianist and composer*, 'fræns 'raɪzənstaɪn, fránz rízĕnstin
Rejerrah *Cornwall*, rɪ'dʒerə, rĕjérrá
Relubbas *Cornwall*, rɪ'lʌbəs, rĕlúbbáss
Relugas *Grampian*, rɪ'lugəs, rĕloógáss
Remedios, *f.n.*, rə'meɪdɪɒs, rĕmáydi-oss
Remer, *f.n.*, 'rimər, reémĕr
Remes, *f.n.*, rimz, reemz
Remfry, *f.n.*, 'remfrɪ, rémfri
Renals, *f.n.*, 'renlz, rénnlz
Renault, *f.n.*, 'renoʊ, rénnō.
Appropriate for Mary ~, *author.*
Rencher, *f.n.*, 'rentʃər, réntchĕr
Rendall, *f.n.*, 'rendl, réndl
Rendcomb *Glos.*, 'rendkəm, réndkŏm
Rendell, *f.n.*, 'rendl, réndl; ren-'del, rendéll
René, *C.n.*, 'reneɪ, rénnay; 'rənɪ, rĕnáy; rə'neɪ, rĕnáy
Renée, *C.n.*, 'reneɪ, rénnay; 'rənɪ, rĕnáy; rə'neɪ, rĕnáy; 'rinɪ, reéni
Reney, *f.n.*, 'reneɪ, rénnay
Renfrew *S'clyde*, 'renfru, rénfroo
Renhold *Beds.*, 'renld, rénnld

Renier, *f.n.*, rə'nıər, rĕnéer
Renishaw *Derby.*, 'renıʃə, rénni-
-shaw. *Appropriate also for* ~
Hall.
Renish Point *W. Isles*, 'renıʃ,
rénnish
Rennell, *f.n.*, 'renl, rénnl. *Appro-
priate also for Baron* ~.
Renney, *f.n.*, 'renı, rénni
Rennie, *f.n.*, 'renı, rénni
Renold, *f.n.*, 'renld, rénnld
Renshaw, *f.n.*, 'renʃə, rén-shaw
Renton, *f.n.*, 'rentən, réntŏn
Rentoul, *f.n.*, ren'tul, rentóol;
'rentʊl, réntŏōl
Renwick, *f.n.*, 'renık, rénnick.
Appropriate also for Baron ~.
Renwick *Cumbria*, 'renık, rén-
nick; 'renwık, rénwick
Reoch, *f.n.*, 'rıɒx, rée-och
Rescobie *Tayside*, rı'skoʊbı,
rĕsskóbi
Reside, *f.n.*, rı'zaıd, rĕzíd
Resolis *H'land*, rı'soʊlıs, rĕssó-
liss
Resolven *W. Glam.*, rı'zɒlvən,
rĕzólvĕn
Restalrig *Edinburgh*, 'reslrıg,
résslrig
Restieaux, *f.n.*, 'restıoʊ, résti-ō
Restormel *Castle Cornwall*,
rıs'tɔːmǝl, rĕstórmĕl
Restronguet *Cornwall*, rıs'trɒŋgıt,
rĕstróng-gĕt
Retallick, *f.n.*, rı'tælık, rĕtálick
Reuel, *f.n.*, rʊǝl, rōō-ĕl
Reuter, *f.n.*, 'rɔıtər, róytĕr
Revans, *f.n.*, 'revənz, révvänz
Revell, *f.n.*, 'revl, révvl
Revelstoke *Devon*, 'revlstoʊk,
révvl-stōk. *Appropriate also for
Baron* ~.
Revesby *Lincs.*, 'rivzbı, réevzbi
Revie, *f.n.*, 'rivı, reévi
Revill, *f.n.*, 'revıl, révvil; 'revl,
révvl
Revis, *f.n.*, 'revıs, révviss
Rew, *f.n.*, ru, roo
Rewe *Devon*, ru, roo
Rey, *f.n.*, reı, ray. *Appropriate for
Margaret* ~, *sculptor.*
Reydon *Suffolk*, 'reıdən, ráydŏn
Reymerston *Norfolk*, 'remərstən,
rémmĕrsstŏn
Reynard, *f.n.*, 'renərd, rénnärd;
'renɑːd, rénnaard; 'reınɑːd,
ráynaard
Reynders, *f.n.*, 'raındərz, ríndĕrz
Reyner, *f.n.*, 'renər, rénnĕr;
'reınər, ráynĕr
Reynish, *f.n.*, 'reınıʃ, ráynish
Reynolds, *f.n.*, 'renldz, rénnldz
Reynoldston *W.Glam.*, 'renldstən,
rénnldstŏn

Reyntiens, *f.n.*, 'rentjənz, rént-
-yĕnz. *Appropriate for Patrick*
~, *stained-glass artist.*
Reyrolle, *f.n.*, 'reıroʊl, ráy-rōl
Rezler, *f.n.*, 'rezlər, rézlĕr
Rhae, *f.n.*, reı, ray
Rhandir-mwyn *Dyfed*, 'hrændıər-
'mʊın, rándeer-mōō-in
Rhayader *Powys*, 'hraıədər, rí-
-ădĕr. *Appropriate also for the
Barony of* ~.
Rhee, *f.n.*, ri, ree
Rhees, *f.n.*, ris, reess
Rheidol, *River, Dyfed*, 'hraıdɒl,
rídol
Rhenigidale *W. Isles*, 'renıgıdeıl,
rénnigidayl
Rhenish *Tower Lynmouth
(Devon)*, 'renıʃ, rénnish
Rhewl *Clwyd*, 'reʊl, ré-ōōl
Rhian, *Welsh C.n.*, 'hriən, reé-
-ăn
Rhiannon, *Welsh C.n.*, hri'ænən,
ree-ánnŏn
Rhianydd, *Welsh C.n.*, hri'ænıð,
ree-ánnith
Rhiconich *H'land*, ri'koʊnıx,
reekŏnich
Rhigos *Mid Glam.*, 'hrigɒs, rée-
goss; 'rıkɒs, ríckoss. *The second
is confined to local use.*
Rhind, *f.n.*, raınd, rīnd; rınd,
rinnd
Rhinns of Galloway, *also spelt*
Rinns, *D. & G.*, 'rınz əv 'gælə-
weı, rínnz ŏv gálŏ-way
Rhinns of Islay, *also spelt* Rinns,
S'clyde, 'rınz əv 'aılə, rínnz ŏv
ílǎ
Rhinns of Kells, *also spelt* Rinns,
D. & G., 'rınz əv 'kelz, rínnz ŏv
kéllz
Rhinog Fach *Gwynedd*, 'hrinɒg
'vax, réenog vaách
Rhinog Fawr *Gwynedd*, 'hrinɒg
'vaʊər, réenog vówr
Rhiwbina *S. Glam.*, ru'baınə,
roobínǎ; ‚hriu'baınə, ree-
-oobínǎ
Rhiwderyn *Gwent*, ‚hriu'derın,
ree-oodérrin
Rhiwlas *Clwyd, Gwynedd*, rı'ulǝs,
ri-óoláss
Rhodes, *f.n.*, roʊdz, rōdz
Rhondda *Mid Glam.*, 'hrɒndǝ,
rónthǎ
Rhoose *S. Glam.*, rus, rooss
Rhoscolyn *Gwynedd*, hroʊs'kɒlın,
rōsskóllin
Rhoscrowther, *also spelt* Rhos-
crowdder, *Dyfed*, rɒs'kraʊðər,
ross-krówthĕr
Rhos-ddu *Clwyd*, hroʊs'ði, rōss-
-theé

Rhosesmor *Clwyd*, hrous'esmɔr, rōsséssmor
Rhosgadfan *Gwynedd*, hrous-'gædvən, rōssgádvăn
Rhosier, *f.n.*, 'hrɒsjeər, róss-yair
Rhosllanerchrugog *Clwyd*, 'hrous-'łænərx'rigɒg, rōss-<u>hl</u>ánnĕrch-reégog
Rhos-maen *Dyfed*, hrous'maɪn, rōssmín
Rhos-meirch *Gwynedd*, hrous-'maɪərx, rōssmírch
Rhosneigr *Gwynedd*, hrous'naɪgər, rōssnígĕr
Rhossili *W. Glam.*, hrɒ'sɪlɪ, ros-sílli
Rhostryfan *Gwynedd*, hrous-'trʌvən, rōsstrúvvăn
Rhostyllen *Clwyd*, hrous'tʌɬɪn, rōsstú<u>hl</u>ĕn
Rhowniar, Outward Bound school, *Gwynedd*, 'raʊnɪər, równi-ăr
Rhos-y-bol *Gwynedd*, ˌhrousə'bɒl, rōssăbóll
Rhosymedre *Clwyd*, ˌhrousə-'medreɪ, rōssămédray
Rhu *S'clyde*, ru, roo
Rhuallt *Clwyd*, 'riæɬt, reé-a<u>hl</u>t
Rhudde, *f.n.*, rʌd, rudd
Rhuddlan *Clwyd*, 'hrɪðlæn, ríthlan
Rhum, *also spelt* **Rum**, *H'land*, rʌm, rum
Rhuthun *Clwyd*, 'hrɪθɪn, ríthun. *The English form is* **Ruthin**, *q.v.*
Rhyd-ddu *Gwynedd*, hrid'ði, reed-thee
Rhydderch, *f.n.*, 'hrʌðərx, rú<u>th</u>ĕrch
Rhydding *W. Glam.*, 'rɪdɪŋ, rídding
Rhydfelen *Mid Glam.*, hrid'velɪn, reedvéllĕn
Rhydlafar Hospital *S. Glam.*, hrid'lævər, reedlávvăr
Rhydlewis, *also spelt* **Rhyd Lewis**, *Dyfed*, hrid'luɪs, reed-lóo-iss
Rhydowen *Dyfed*, hrid'ouɪn, reedó-ĕn
Rhydwen, River, *Gwynedd*, 'hridwɛn, reédwen
Rhyd-y-felin *Dyfed*, ˌhridə'velɪn, reedăvéllin
Rhyd-y-fro *W. Glam.*, ˌhridə'vrou, reedávrŏ
Rhyd-y-main *Gwynedd*, ˌhridə-'maɪn, reedămín
Rhyd-y-mwyn *Clwyd*, ˌhridə-'muɪn, reedămŏŏ-in
Rhyl *Clwyd*, hrɪl, rill
Rhymney *Mid Glam.*, 'rʌmnɪ, rúmni

Rhynd *Tayside*, rɪnd, rinnd
Rhys, *f.n.*, ris, rees; raɪs, rīss. *Although the first is usual in Wales, the second is appropriate for Baron Dynevor's family name.*
Riach, *f.n.*, 'riəx, reé-ă<u>ch</u>
Riall, *f.n.*, 'raɪəl, rī-ăl
Ribbesford *H. & W.*, 'rɪbzfərd, ríbzfŏrd
Riccall *N. Yorks.*, 'rɪkɔl, ríckawl
Riccarton *S'clyde*, 'rɪkərtən, ríckărtŏn
Rice, *f.n.*, raɪs, rīss
Richard, *C.n. and f.n.*, 'rɪtʃərd, rítchărd
Richards, *f.n.*, 'rɪtʃərdz, rítchărdz
Richardson, *f.n.*, 'rɪtʃərdsən, rítchărdssŏn
Riche, *f.n.*, rɪtʃ, ritch
Richens, *f.n.*, 'rɪtʃənz, rítchĕnz
Richer, *f.n.*, 'rɪtʃər, rítchĕr
Richhill *Co. Armagh*, rɪtʃ'hɪl, ritch-híll
Richmond *London, N. Yorks., S. Yorks.*, 'rɪtʃmənd, rítchmŏnd
Rickard, *f.n.*, 'rɪkɑrd, ríckaard
Rickards, *f.n.*, 'rɪkɑrdz, ríckaardz
Rickarton *Grampian*, 'rɪkərtən, rickártŏn
Rickett, *f.n.*, 'rɪkɪt, ríckĕt
Ricketts, *f.n.*, 'rɪkɪts, rickĕts
Rickmansworth *Herts.*, 'rɪkmənzwərθ, rickmănzwurth
Ricôt, *f.n.*, 'rɪkou, rickŏ; 'rikou, reékŏ
Riddell, *f.n.*, 'rɪdl, riddl; rɪ'del, ridéll
Riddiough, *f.n.*, 'rɪdjou, ríd-yŏ
Riddoch, *f.n.*, 'rɪdɒx, ríddo<u>ch</u>
Rideal, *f.n.*, rɪ'dil, rideél
Ridealgh, *f.n.*, 'rɪdɪælʃ, ríddi-alsh; 'raɪdæld3, rídalj
Rideau, Baron, 'rɪdou, reédŏ
Ridehalgh, *f.n.*, 'raɪdhælʃ, ríd-halsh; 'rɪdɪhælʃ, ríddi-halsh
Rideout, *f.n.*, 'raɪdaut, rídowt
Rider, *f.n.*, 'raɪdər, rídĕr
Ridgeway, *f.n.*, 'rɪdʒweɪ, ríj-way
Ridgway, *f.n.*, 'rɪdʒweɪ, ríj-way
Riding, *f.n.*, 'raɪdɪŋ, ríding
Ridout, *f.n.*, 'rɪdaut, riddowt; 'raɪdaut, rídowt
Ridsdale, *f.n.*, 'rɪdzdeɪl, ridzdayl
Ridsdel, *f.n.*, 'rɪdzdəl, rídzdĕl
Ridz, *f.n.*, rɪdz, riddz
Riera, *f.n.*, ri'eərə, ree-áiră
Riesco, *f.n.*, rɪ'eskou, ri-ésskŏ
Rietty, *f.n.*, rɪ'etɪ, ri-étti
Rieu, *f.n.*, rɪ'u, ri-óo; 'riu, reé-oo. *The first is appropriate for Dr Emile Victor ~, former Editor of the Penguin Classics.*

Rievaulx, *f.n.,* 'rɪvəz, rívvăz
Rievaulx *N. Yorks.,* 'rɪvoʊ, réevō;
'rɪvəz, rívvăz. *Both are appropriate for ~ Abbey.*
Rifkind, *f.n.,* 'rɪfkɪnd, ríffkinnd
Rigal, *f.n.,* 'rɪgl, réegl
Rigby, *f.n.,* 'rɪgbɪ, rígbi
Rigg, *f.n.,* rɪg, rigg
Riggs, *f.n.,* rɪgz, riggz
Rigler, *f.n.,* 'rɪglər, rígglěr
Rignold, *f.n.,* 'rɪgnoʊld, ríg-nōld
Rimbault, *f.n.,* 'rɪmboʊlt, rím-bōlt
Rimell, *f.n.,* 'raɪml, ríml
Rimer, *f.n.,* 'raɪmər, rímĕr
Rimington *Lancs.,* 'rɪmɪntən, rímmingtŏn
Ringdufferin *Co. Down,* rɪŋ-'dʌfərɪn, ringdúfférin
Ringhaddy *Co. Down,* rɪŋ'hædɪ, ring-háddi
Ring's End *Cambs.,* rɪŋz 'end, ringz énd
Rinsey Head *Cornwall,* 'rɪnzɪ, rínzi
Rintoul, *f.n.,* rɪn'tul, rintoól; 'rɪntul, ríntool. *The first is the normal Scottish pronunciation.*
Riou, *f.n.,* 'riu, rée-oo
Ripon *N. Yorks.,* 'rɪpən, ríppŏn
Rippon, *f.n.,* 'rɪpən, ríppŏn
Risbridger, *f.n.,* 'rɪsbrɪdʒər, ríssbrijĕr
Risca *Gwent,* 'rɪskə, rísskă
Riseley *Beds.,* 'raɪzlɪ, rízli
Risman, *f.n.,* 'rɪzmən, rízzmăn
Rison, *f.n.,* 'raɪsən, ríssŏn
Ritchford, *f.n.,* 'rɪtʃfərd, rítchfŏrd
Ritchie, *f.n.,* 'rɪtʃɪ, rítchi
Ritchie-Calder, Barony of, 'rɪtʃɪ 'kɔldər, ritchi káwldĕr
Rittener, *f.n.,* 'rɪtnər, rítt-nĕr
Rittermann, *f.n.,* 'rɪtərmən, ríttĕr-măn
Ritzema, *f.n.,* 'rɪtsɪmə, rítsĕmă; rɪd'zimə, ridzéemă; rɪt'sɪmə, ritséemă
Rive, *f.n.,* raɪv, rīv; rɪv, reev
Rivelin *S. Yorks.,* 'rɪvəlɪn, rívvĕlin
Rivers, *f.n.,* 'rɪvərz, rívvĕrz
Rivet, *f.n.,* 'rɪveɪ, réevay
Rivett, *f.n.,* rɪ'vet, rivétt
Riviere, *f.n.,* 'rɪvɪɛər, rívvi-air; rɪv'jɛər, riv-yáir; rɪ'vɪər, rivvéer
Rivière, *f.n.,* 'rɪvɪɛər, rívvi-air; rɪv'jɛər, riv-yáir; rɪ'vɪər, rivvéer
Rivis, *f.n.,* 'rɪvɪs, rívviss
Rivvett, *f.n.,* 'rɪvɪt, rívvĕtt
Rizden, *f.n.,* 'rɪzdən, rízdĕn
Roach, *f.n.,* roʊtʃ, rōtch
Roaf, *f.n.,* roʊf, rōf
Roag, Loch, *W. Isles,* 'roʊæg, rō-ag

Roanhead *Grampian,* 'rɒnhed, rónn-hed; 'roʊnhed, rṓn-hed
Roast, *f.n.,* roʊst, rōst
Roath *Cardiff,* roʊθ, rōth
Robartes, *f.n.,* rə'bɑrts, rŏbaárts
Robarts, *f.n.,* rə'bɑrts, rŏbaárts
Robathan, *f.n.,* 'roʊbəθən, rōbáthăn
Robay, *f.n.,* 'roʊbeɪ, rṓbay
Robb Caledon Shipbuilders Ltd., 'rɒb 'kælɪdən, róbb kálédŏn
Robbie, *f.n.,* 'rɒbɪ, róbbi
Robbins, *f.n.,* 'rɒbɪnz, róbbinz
Robens, *f.n.,* 'roʊbənz, rṓbĕnz. *Appropriate also for Baron ~.*
Roberton, *f.n.,* 'rɒbərtən, róbbĕrtŏn
Roberts, *f.n.,* 'rɒbərts, róbbĕrts
Robertson, *f.n.,* 'rɒbərtsən, róbbĕrtsŏn
Robeston Wathen *Dyfed,* 'rɒbɪstən 'wɒðən, róbbĕstŏn wóthĕn
Robey, *f.n.,* 'roʊbɪ, rṓbi
Robieson, *f.n.,* 'rɒbɪsən, róbbissŏn
Robin, *C.n.,* 'rɒbɪn, róbbin
Robins, *f.n.,* 'rɒbɪnz, róbbinz; 'roʊbɪnz, rṓbinz
Robinson, *f.n.,* 'rɒbɪnsən, róbbinssŏn
Roblou, *f.n.,* 'rɒbloʊ, róbblō
Roborough *Devon,* 'roʊbərə, rṓbŭră. *Appropriate also for Baron ~.*
Robotham, *f.n.,* rə'boʊθəm, rŏbṓthăm
Robsart, *f.n.,* 'rɒbsɑrt, róbsaart. *Appropriate for Amy ~, wife of Robert Dudley, Earl of Leicester.*
Robson, *f.n.,* 'rɒbsən, róbssŏn; 'roʊbsən, rṓbssŏn. *The first is appropriate for Dame Flora ~, actress.*
Roby *Merseyside,* 'roʊbɪ, rṓbi
Rocester *Staffs.,* 'roʊstər, rṓstĕr
Roch, *f.n.,* roʊtʃ, rōtch; rɒtʃ, rotch
Roch *Dyfed,* roʊtʃ, rōtch. *Appropriate also for ~ Castle.*
Rochdale *Gtr. M'chester,* 'rɒtʃdeɪl, rótchdayl
Roche, *f.n.,* roʊtʃ, rōtch; rɒʃ, rōsh; rɒʃ, rosh. *The first is appropriate for the Barony of ~.*
Roche *Cornwall,* roʊtʃ, rōtch
Rochester *Kent,* 'rɒtʃɪstər, rótchĕstĕr
Rochford *Essex,* 'rɒtʃfərd, rótchfŏrd
Rochfort, *f.n.,* 'rɒtʃfərt, rótchfŏrt
Rockbeare *Devon,* 'rɒkbɪər, róckbeer; 'rɒkbər, róckbĕr
Rodbaston *Staffs.,* 'rɒdbəstən, ródbăstŏn

Roddam, *f.n.,* 'rɒdəm, róddăm
Roddis, *f.n.,* 'rɒdɪs, róddiss
Rodel *W. Isles,* 'roʊdl, ródl
Rodger, *f.n.,* 'rɒdʒər, rójjĕr
Rodgers, *f.n.,* 'rɒdʒərz, rójjĕrz
Rodick, *f.n.,* 'rɒdɪk, róddick
Roding *Essex,* 'roʊdɪŋ, róding;
  'ruðɪŋ, roóthing. *The second,
  the historical pronunciation, has
  gradually given way, although
  not entirely succumbed, to the
  former. The group of villages
  known as The Rodings includes
  Abbess ~, Aythorpe ~, Beau-
  champ ~, Berners ~, High ~,
  Leaden ~, Margaret ~, and
  White ~ or Roothing. Except
  in the last case, where Roothing
  has been retained in the name of
  the civil parish, it appears that
  Roding is now accepted as the
  standard spelling.*
Rodmersham *Kent,* 'rɒdmərʃəm,
  ródmĕr-shăm
Rodnight, *f.n.,* 'rɒdnaɪt, ródnīt
Rodon, *f.n.,* 'roʊdən, ródōn
Roe, *f.n.,* roʊ, rō
Roedean School *E. Sussex,*
  'roʊdin, ródeen
Roeg, *f.n.,* roʊg, rōg
Roehampton *London,* roʊ'hæmp-
  tən, rō-hámptŏn
Roemmele, *f.n.,* 'rɒmɪlɪ, rómmĕli
Roetter, *f.n.,* 'roʊtər, rṓtĕr
Rofe, *f.n.,* roʊf, rōf
Roffe, *f.n.,* rɒf, roff
Roffey, *f.n.,* 'rɒfɪ, róffi
Rogaly, *f.n.,* roʊ'geɪlɪ, rōgáyli
Rogart *H'land,* 'roʊgərt, rógărt
Roger, *C.n. and f.n.,* 'rɒdʒər,
  rójjĕr
Rogers, *f.n.,* 'rɒdʒərz, rójjĕrz
Rogerstone *Gwent,* 'rɒdʒərstən,
  rójjĕrstŏn
Roget, *f.n.,* 'roʊʒeɪ, rṓzhay
Rohan, *f.n.,* 'roʊən, rṓ-ăn
Rohrer, *f.n.,* 'rɔrər, ráwrĕr
Roissetter, *f.n.,* 'rɒsɪtər, róssitĕr
Rokeby *Durham,* 'roʊkbɪ, rókbi
Rokison, *f.n.,* 'roʊkɪsən, rókissŏn
Roland, *C.n. and f.n.,* 'roʊlənd,
  rṓlănd
Rolfe, *f.n.,* roʊf, rōf; rɒlf, rolf.
  *The first is appropriate for John
  ~, 16th–17th-c. colonist and
  husband of Pocahontas, and for
  Frederick ~, Baron Corvo,
  19th-c. author.*
Roll, *f.n.,* roʊl, rōl; rɒl, rol
Rollason, *f.n.,* 'rɒləsən, róllăssŏn
Rolle, Richard, *14th-c. hermit and
  author,* roʊl, rōl
Rollesby *Norfolk,* 'roʊlzbɪ,
  rólzbi

Rolleston, *f.n.,* 'roʊlstən, rólsstŏn
Rolleston *Notts.,* 'roʊlstən,
  rólsstŏn
Rollestone *Wilts.,* 'roʊlstən,
  rólsstŏn
Rollins, *f.n.,* 'rɒlɪnz, róllinz
Rollo, *f.n.,* 'rɒloʊ, róllō. *Appro-
  priate also for Baron ~.*
Rolls, *f.n.,* roʊlz, rōlz
Rolston, *f.n.,* 'roʊlstən, rólsstŏn
Rolt, *f.n.,* roʊlt, rōlt
Rolvenden *Kent,* 'rɒlvəndən,
  rólvĕndĕn
Romanby *N. Yorks.,* 'roʊmənbɪ,
  rṓmănbi
Romanes, *f.n.,* roʊ'mɑnɪz,
  rōmáanĕz; roʊ'mænɪs, rōmán-
  nĕss. *The first is appropriate for
  the ~ Lectureship, Univ. of
  Oxford.*
Rombaut, *f.n.,* 'rɒmboʊ, rómbō
Romeike, *f.n.,* roʊ'mɪkɪ, rōmeéki
Romer, *f.n.,* 'roʊmər, rṓmĕr
Romford, *f.n.,* 'rʌmfərd, rúmfŏrd;
  'rɒmfərd, rómfŏrd
Romford *London,* 'rɒmfərd, róm-
  fŏrd; 'rʌmfərd, rúmfŏrd
Romilly, *f.n.,* 'rɒmɪlɪ, rómmili.
  Appropriate also for Baron ~.
Romney, Earl of, 'rʌmnɪ, rúmni
Romney, *f.n.,* 'rʌmnɪ, rúmni;
  'rɒmnɪ, rómni
Romney, New *and* Old, *Kent,*
  'rɒmnɪ, rómni; 'rʌmnɪ, rúmni
Romney Marsh *Kent,* 'rɒmnɪ
  'mɑrʃ, rómni maársh
Romsey *Hants,* 'rʌmzɪ, rúmzi.
  Appropriate also for Baron ~.
Romsley *H. & W.,* 'rɒmzlɪ,
  rómzli
Rona *W. Isles,* 'roʊnə, rṓnă
Ronald, *C.n. and f.n.,* 'rɒnld,
  rónnld
Ronaldsay, North *and* South,
  Orkney, 'rɒnldseɪ, rónnld-say;
  'rɒnldʃeɪ, rónnld-shay
Ronaldshay, Earl of, 'rɒnldʃeɪ,
  rónnld-shay
Ronaldsway Airport, *I. of Man,*
  'rɒnldzweɪ, rónnldzway
Ronan, saint, 'roʊnən, rṓnăn
Ronane, *f.n.,* rɒ'neɪn, ronnáyn
Ronas Voe *Shetland,* 'roʊnəs
  'voʊ, rṓnăss vṓ
Ronay, *f.n.,* 'rɒneɪ, rónnay
Ronayne, *f.n.,* roʊ'neɪn, rōnáyn
Roney, *f.n.,* 'roʊnɪ, rṓni
Ronson, *f.n.,* 'rɒnsən, rónssŏn
Rook, *f.n.,* rʊk, roŏk
Rooley, *f.n.,* 'rʊlɪ, roóli
Room, *f.n.,* rum, room
Roome, *f.n.,* rum, room
Rooney, *f.n.,* 'runɪ, roóni
Roope, *f.n.,* rup, roop

Rooper, *f.n.*, 'ruːpər, róopĕr
Roos *Humberside*, ruːs, rooss
Roose, *f.n.*, ruːs, rooss
RoosmaleCocq, *f.n.*, 'ruːzmələ-'koʊk, róozmă-lĕkók
Rooss, *f.n.*, ruːs, rooss
Root, *f.n.*, ruːt, root
Rootes, *f.n.*, ruːts, roots
Rootham, *f.n.*, 'ruːtəm, róotăm
Roper, *f.n.*, 'roʊpər, rópĕr
Ropley *Hants*, 'rɒplɪ, róppli
Ropner, *f.n.*, 'rɒpnər, rópnĕr
Roques, *f.n.*, roʊks, rōks
Rosalie, *C.n.*, 'roʊzəlɪ, rózăli; 'rɒzəlɪ, rózzăli
Rosbotham, *f.n.*, 'rɒsbɒtəm, róssbottăm
Roscroggan *Cornwall*, rɒs'krɒgən, rosskróggăn
Rose, *f.n.*, roʊz, rōz
Rosebery, Earl of, 'roʊzbərɪ, rózbĕri
Rosehearty *Grampian*, roʊz-'hɑːrtɪ, rōz-haárti
Roseingrave, *f.n.*, 'roʊzɪŋgreɪv, rózin-grayv. *Specifically the 17th–18th-c. family of musicians.*
Rosemarkie *H'land*, roʊz'mɑːrkɪ, rōzmaárki
Rosen, *f.n.*, 'roʊzən, rózĕn
Rosenberg, *f.n.*, 'roʊzənbɜrg, rózĕnberg
Rosenthal, *f.n.*, 'roʊzəntɑːl, rózĕntaal; 'roʊzənθɔːl, rózĕn-thawl
Rosetta *Co. Down*, rə'zetə, rözéttă
Roseveare, *f.n.*, 'roʊzvɪər, rózveer
Roseworthy *Cornwall*, roʊz-'wɜrðɪ, rōzwúrthi
Rosherville *Kent*, 'roʊʃərvɪl, róshĕrvil; 'rɒzərvɪl, rózzĕrvil
Rosier, *f.n.*, 'roʊzɪər, rózi-ĕr
Roskell, *f.n.*, 'rɒskl, rósskl
Roskestal *Cornwall*, rɒs'kestl, rosskéstl
Roslea *Co. Fermanagh*, rɒs'leɪ, rossláy
Roslin *Lothian*, 'rɒzlɪn, rózzlin
Rosneath *S'clyde*, 'roʊz'niːθ, róz-néeth
Ross, *f.n.*, rɒs, ross
Ross and Cromarty *H'land*, 'rɒs ənd 'krɒmərtɪ, róss ănd krómmärti
Rossall, *f.n.*, 'rɒsl, róssl
Rossall School *Fleetwood* (*Lancs.*), 'rɒsl, róssl
Rossallian, *one educated at* **Rossall** *School*, rɒ'seɪlɪən, rossáyliăn
Rossendale *Lancs.*, 'rɒsəndeɪl, róssĕndayl

Rosser, *f.n.*, 'rɒsər, róssĕr
Rossetti, *f.n.*, rə'zetɪ, rözétti; rə'setɪ, rössétti. *Both are accepted usage for the family of Dante Gabriel ~, 19th-c. poet and painter.*
Rossiter, *f.n.*, 'rɒsɪtər, róssitĕr
Rosslyn, Earl of, 'rɒslɪn, rósslin
Rosslyn Chapel *Lothian*, 'rɒzlɪn, rózzlin
Rost, *f.n.*, rɒst, rosst
Rostal, *f.n.*, 'rɒstæl, rósstal
Rostrevor, *f.n.*, rɒs'trevər, rosstrévvŏr
Rostrevor *Co. Down*, rɒs'trevər, rosstrévvŏr
Rosudgeon *Cornwall*, rə'sʌdʒən, rössújjŏn
Rosyth *Fife*, rə'saɪθ, rössíth
Rotblat, *f.n.*, 'rɒtblæt, rótblat
Rotdon *Merseyside*, 'rɒtdɒn, rótdon
Roth, *f.n.*, rɒθ, roth; roʊθ, rōth
Rotha, *f.n.*, 'roʊðə, róthă
Rothamsted *Herts.*, 'rɒθəmsted, róthămsted
Rothay, River, *Cumbria*, 'rɒθeɪ, róthay
Rothbury *Northd.*, 'rɒθbərɪ, róthbŭri
Rothe, *f.n.*, roʊθ, rōth
Rothenstein, *f.n.*, 'roʊθənstaɪn, róthĕnstīn. *Appropriate for Sir William ~, portrait painter, Sir John ~, erstwhile Director of the Tate Gallery, and Michael ~, painter and print-maker.*
Rother, Rivers, 'rɒðər, róthĕr. *Appropriate for the following rivers: Derby.–S. Yorks.; Hants–W. Sussex; E. Sussex–Kent. Also for the ~ Valley parliamentary division, and the administrative division of E. Sussex.*
Rothera, *f.n.*, 'rɒðərə, róthĕră
Rotherfield *E. Sussex*, 'rɒðərfild, róthĕrfeeld
Rotherfield Peppard *Oxon.*, 'rɒðərfild 'pepɑrd, róthĕrfeeld péppaard
Rotherhithe *London*, 'rɒðərhaɪð, róthĕr-hīth
Rotherham, *f.n.*, 'rɒðərəm, róthĕrăm
Rotherham *S. Yorks.*, 'rɒðərəm, róthĕrăm
Rothermere, Viscount, 'rɒðər-mɪər, róthĕrmeer
Rotherwick, Baron, 'rɒðərwɪk, róthĕrwick
Rothes *Fife*, 'rɒθɪs, róthĕss; 'rɒθɪz, róthĕz. *The second is appropriate for the Earl of ~.*

Rothes *Grampian*, 'rɒθɪs, róthěss
Rothesay *S'clyde*, 'rɒθsɪ, róthssi
Rothholz, *f.n.*, 'rɒθhoʊlts, róth-hōlts
Rothiemay *Grampian*, ˌrɒθɪ'meɪ, rothimáy
Rothiemurchus *H'land*, ˌrɒθɪ'mɜrkəs, rothimúrkŭss
Rothienorman *Grampian*, ˌrɒθɪ-'nɔrmən, rothinórmăn
Rothley *Leics.*, 'roʊθlɪ, róthli
Rothney, *f.n.*, 'rɒθnɪ, róthni
Rothschild, Baron, 'rɒθstʃaɪld, róths-chïld
Rothwell, *f.n.*, 'rɒθwəl, róthwěl
Rothwell *Lincs., W. Yorks.*, 'rɒθwel, róthwell
Rothwell *Northants.*, 'rɒθwel, róthwell; 'roʊəl, rō-ěl
Rottingdean *E. Sussex*, 'rɒtɪndɪn, rótting-deen
Roubicek, *f.n.*, 'rubɪtʃek, roóbi-tcheck
Roucan *D. & G.*, 'rukən, roókăn
Roud, *f.n.*, raʊd, rowd
Roudham *Norfolk*, 'raʊdəm, rów-dăm
Roudsea Wood *Lancs.*, 'raʊdzɪ, rówdzi
Rough, *f.n.*, rʌf, ruff
Rougham *Norfolk, Suffolk*, 'rʌfəm, rúffăm
Roughan, *f.n.*, 'roʊən, rō-ăn
Roughdown *Hants*, 'raʊdaʊn, rówdown
Roughlee *Lancs.*, 'rʌf'li, rúff-lée
Rought, *f.n.*, rɔt, rawt; raʊt, rowt
Roughton, *f.n.*, 'raʊtən, rówtŏn
Roughton *Lincs.*, 'rutən, roótŏn
Roughton *Salop*, 'raʊtən, rówtŏn
Rough Tor *Cornwall*, 'raʊ 'tɔr, rów tór
Rouken Glen *S'clyde*, 'rukən 'glen, roókěn glén
Roulston, *f.n.*, 'roʊlstən, rólsstŏn
Roundhay Park *W. Yorks.*, 'raʊndeɪ, równday
Rountree, *f.n.*, 'raʊntrɪ, równtree
Rous, *f.n.*, raʊs, rowss. *Appropriate also for Baron ~.*
Rousay *Orkney*, 'raʊzeɪ, rówzay
Rousdon *Devon*, 'ruzdən, roózdŏn; 'raʊzdən, rówzdŏn
Rouse, *f.n.*, raʊs, rowss
Rousham *Oxon.*, 'raʊʃəm, rów-shăm; 'raʊsəm, rówssăm
Rousky *Co. Tyrone*, 'ruskɪ, roósski
Rous Lench *H. & W.*, 'raʊs 'lenʃ, rówss lénsh
Rouson, *f.n.*, 'raʊsən, rówssŏn
Roussak, *f.n.*, 'rusæk, roóssack
Roussel, *f.n.*, ru'sel, roōsséll
Rout, *f.n.*, raʊt, rowt

Routh, *f.n.*, raʊθ, rowth
Routier, *f.n.*, 'rutɪeɪ, roóti-ay
Routledge, *f.n.*, 'raʊtlɪdʒ, rówt-lěj; 'rʌtlɪdʒ, rútlěj
Routledge and Kegan Paul, *publishers*, 'raʊtlɪdʒ ənd 'kigən 'pɔl, rówtlěj ănd keégăn páwl
Routley, *f.n.*, 'raʊtlɪ, rówtli
Rowallan, Baron, roʊ'ælən, rō-álăn
Rowan, *f.n.*, 'roʊən, rō-ăn; 'raʊən, rówăn. *The second is usual in Scotland.*
Rowan Gallery *London*, 'roʊən, rō-ăn
Rowardennan *Central*, ˌraʊər-'denən, rowărdénnăn
Rowarth *Derby.*, 'raʊərθ, rówărth
Rowbotham, *f.n.*, 'roʊbɒtəm, rō-bottăm
Rowde *Wilts.*, raʊd, rowd
Rowden, *f.n.*, 'raʊdən, rówděn
Rowdon, *f.n.*, 'roʊdən, ródŏn
Rowe, *f.n.*, roʊ, rō
Rowell, *f.n.*, 'raʊəl, rówěl
Rowena, *C.n.*, roʊ'inə, rō-eénă
Rowett Research Institute *Bucksburn (Grampian)*, 'raʊɪt, rówět
Rowhedge *Essex*, 'roʊhedʒ, rō-hej; 'raʊhedʒ, rów-hej
Rowland, *f.n.*, 'roʊlənd, rólănd
Rowlatts Hill *Leics.*, 'raʊləts 'hɪl, rówlăts hill
Rowledge, *f.n.*, 'roʊlɪdʒ, rólěj
Rowledge *Surrey*, 'raʊlɪdʒ, rówlěj
Rowlett, *f.n.*, 'raʊlɪt, rówlět
Rowlette, *f.n.*, roʊ'let, rōlétt
Rowley, Barony of, 'roʊlɪ, róli
Rowley, *f.n.*, 'roʊlɪ, róli
Rowley Mile *Newmarket (Suffolk)*, 'roʊlɪ, róli
Rowley Regis *W. Midlands*, 'raʊlɪ 'ridʒɪs, rówli reéjiss
Rowling, *f.n.*, 'roʊlɪŋ, róling
Rowlinson, *f.n.*, 'roʊlɪnsən, rólinssŏn
Rowner *Hants*, 'raʊnər, równěr
Rowney, *f.n.*, 'raʊnɪ, równi; 'roʊnɪ, róni
Rowntree, *f.n.*, 'raʊntrɪ, równtree
Rowridge *I. of Wight*, 'raʊrɪdʒ, rów-rij
Rowse, *f.n.*, raʊs, rowss
Rowsell, *f.n.*, 'raʊsl, rówssl
Rowsley *Derby.*, 'roʊzlɪ, rózli
Rowson, *f.n.*, 'raʊsən, rówssŏn; 'roʊsən, róssŏn
Rowston *Lincs.*, 'raʊstən, rówsstŏn
Rowton, *f.n.*, 'raʊtən, rówtŏn
Rowton *Salop*, 'raʊtən, rówtŏn. *Appropriate also for ~ Castle in Shropshire.*

Roxburgh, *f.n.*, 'rɒksbərə, rócksbŭrǎ

Roxburgh *Borders*, 'rɒksbərə, rócksbŭrǎ

Roxburghe, Duke of, 'rɒksbərə, rócksbŭrǎ

Roxwell *Essex*, 'rɒkswel, róckswel

Royall, *f.n.*, 'rɔɪəl, róy-ăl

Royce, *f.n.*, rɔɪs, royss

Royle, *f.n.*, rɔɪl, royl

Royse, *f.n.*, rɔɪs, royss

Royston, *f.n.*, 'rɔɪstən, róysstŏn

Royston *Herts.*, *Somerset*, *S. Yorks.*, 'rɔɪstən, róysstŏn

Royton *Gtr. M'chester*, 'rɔɪtən, róytŏn

Rozentals, *f.n.*, rou'zentlz, rōzéntlz

Ruabon *Clwyd*, ru'æbən, roo--ábbŏn

Ruane, *f.n.*, ru'eɪn, rōō-áyn

Ruanlanihorne *Cornwall*, ‚ruən-'læniːhɔːn, roo-ănlánnihorn

Ruanne, *f.n.*, ru'æn, roo-ánn

Ruardean *Glos.*, 'ruərdin, rŏŏrdeen

Rubach, *f.n.*, 'rubax, róobaa<u>ch</u>

Rubbra, Edmund, *composer*, 'rʌbrə, rúbbrǎ

Rubery *H. & W.*, 'rubərɪ, róobĕri

Rubidge, *f.n.*, 'rubɪdʒ, róobij

Rubin, *f.n.*, 'rubɪn, roobin

Rubislaw *Grampian*, 'rubslɔ, róobsslaw; 'rubɪslɔ, róobisslaw

Rubra, *f.n.*, 'rubrə, róobrǎ

Ruchazie *S'clyde*, rʌx'heɪzɪ, ruch-háyzi

Ruchill *S'clyde*, 'rʌxɪl, rúchil

Ruchlaw *Lothian*, 'rʌxlɔ, rúchlaw

Rucker, *f.n.*, 'rukər, róokĕr

Ruckinge *Kent*, 'rʌkɪndʒ, rúckinj

Rudd, *f.n.*, rʌd, rudd

Ruddell, *f.n.*, 'rʌdl, rúddl

Rudgard, *f.n.*, 'rʌdgard, rúd-gaard

Rudge, *f.n.*, rʌdʒ, rujj

Rudgwick *W. Sussex*, 'rʌdʒwɪk, rújwick; 'rʌdʒɪk, rújjick

Rudhall *H. & W.*, 'rʌdɔl, rúdd-awl

Rudham, *f.n.*, 'rʌdəm, rúddăm

Rudkin, *f.n.*, 'rʌdkɪn, rúdkin

Rudolphi, *f.n.*, ru'dɒlfɪ, roŏdólfi

Rudry *Mid Glam.*, 'rʌdrɪ, rúddri

Rudyard *Staffs.*, 'rʌdʒərd, rújjărd

Ruff, *f.n.*, rʌf, ruff

Ruffe, *f.n.*, rʌf, ruff

Rufforth *N. Yorks.*, 'rʌfərθ, rúfförth

Rugbeian, *one educated at Rugby School*, rʌg'biən, rugbeé-ăn

Rugby *Warwicks.*, 'rʌgbɪ, rúgbi

Rugeley *Staffs.*, 'rudʒlɪ, roójli

Ruggles-Brise, *f.n.*, 'rʌglz 'braɪz, rúgglz bríz

Ruhrmund, *f.n.*, 'ruərmənd, roŏrmŭnd

Ruishton *Somerset*, 'ruɪʃtən, roŏ--ishtŏn

Rum *see* Rhum

Rumbelow, *f.n.*, 'rʌmbəlou, rúmbělō

Rumbold, *f.n.*, 'rʌmbould, rúmbōld

Rumens, Viscount, 'rumənz, róoměnz

Rumney, *f.n.*, 'rʌmnɪ, rúmni

Rumney *S. Glam.*, 'rʌmnɪ, rúmni

Rumsam, *f.n.*, 'rʌmsəm, rúmssăm

Rumsey, *f.n.*, 'rʌmzɪ, rúmzi

Runacre, *f.n.*, 'rʌnəkər, rúnnăkĕr

Runacres, *f.n.*, 'rʌnəkərz, rúnnăkĕrz

Runcie, *f.n.*, 'rʌnsɪ, rúnssi

Runciman, Viscount, 'rʌnsɪmən, rúnssimăn

Rundall, *f.n.*, 'rʌndl, rúndl

Runge, *f.n.*, rʌndʒ, runj

Runkerry *Co. Antrim*, rʌn'kerɪ, run-kérri

Runnalls, *f.n.*, 'rʌnlz, rúnnlz

Runtz, *f.n.*, rʌnts, runts

Rupp, *f.n.*, rʌp, rupp

Ruse, *f.n.*, rus, rooss

Rushall *H. & W.*, *W. Midlands*, 'rʌʃɔl, rúshawl

Rushall *Norfolk*, 'rʌʃhɔl, rúsh-hawl

Rushall *Wilts.*, 'rʌʃəl, rúshăl

Rushdie, **Salman**, *author*, sæl'man 'ruʃdɪ, salmaán róoshdi

Rushen *I. of Man*, 'rʌʃən, rúshĕn

Rusholme *Gtr. M'chester*, 'rʌʃhoum, rúsh-hōm. *Appropriate also for the Barony of* ~.

Rushyford *Durham*, 'rʌʃɪ'fərd, rúshi-fórd

Ruskin, *f.n.*, 'rʌskɪn, rússkin

Rusland *Cumbria*, 'rʌslənd, rússlănd

Russell, *f.n.*, 'rʌsl, rússl

Russell of Killowen, Baron, 'rʌsl əv kɪ'louɪn, rússl ŏv kiló-ĕn

Rusthall *Kent*, 'rʌsthɔl, rúst-hawl

Ruswarp *N. Yorks.*, 'rʌsərp, rússărp

Rutherford, *f.n.*, 'rʌðərfərd, rútḥĕrförd

Rutherglen *S'clyde*, 'rʌðərglən, rútḥĕrglĕn

Ruthin *Clwyd*, *S. Glam.*, 'rɪθɪn, ríthin

Ruthrieston *Grampian*, 'rʌðərstən, rútḥĕrstŏn

Ruthven, Baron, 'rɪvən, rívvĕn

Ruthven, *f.n.*, 'rɪvən, rívvĕn; 'ruθvən, roóthvĕn

Ruthven, Loch, *H'land*, 'rʌθvən, rúthvĕn

Ruthven of Canberra, Viscount, 'rɪvən əv 'kænbərə, rívvĕn ŏv kánbĕră

Ruthwaite *Cumbria*, 'rʌθweɪt, rúthwayt; 'rʌθət, rúth-ăt

Ruthwell *D. & G.*, 'rʌθwəl, rúthwĕl; 'rʌðwəl, rúthwĕl; 'rɪðl, ríthl

Rutland, *f.n.*, 'rʌtlənd, rútlănd

Rutland *Leics.*, 'rʌtlənd, rútlănd

Ruyton-Eleven-Towns *Salop*, 'raɪtən ɪ'levəntaʊnz, rítŏn--élévvĕntownz

Ryall, *f.n.*, 'raɪəl, rí-ăl

Ryan, *f.n.*, 'raɪən, rí-ăn

Ryarsh *Kent*, 'raɪɑːʃ, rí-aarsh

Rydal *Cumbria*, 'raɪdl, rídl. *Appropriate also for* ~ *Water.*

Rydz, *f.n.*, rɪdz, ridz

Ryhope *Tyne & Wear*, 'raɪəp, rí-ŏp

Rykwert, *f.n.*, 'rɪkwərt, ríckwĕrt

Ryland, *f.n.*, 'raɪlənd, ríländ

Rylands, *f.n.*, 'raɪləndz, ríländz

Rylett, *f.n.*, 'raɪlɪt, rílĕt

Ryme Intrinseca *Dorset*, 'raɪm ɪn'trɪnsɪkə, rím intrínssĕkă

Rynd, *f.n.*, rɪnd, rinnd

Ryrie, *f.n.*, 'raɪərɪ, ríri

Rysanek, *f.n.*, 'raɪsənɛk, ríssăneck

Ryton, *f.n.*, 'raɪtən, rítŏn

Ryton *Durham*, 'raɪtən, rítŏn

Ryton-on-Dunsmore *Warwicks.*, 'raɪtən ɒn 'dʌnzmər, rítŏn on dúnzmor

Ryves, *f.n.*, raɪvz, rívz

S

Saatchi, *f.n.*, 'sɑtʃɪ, saátchi

Sabbagh, *f.n.*, 'sæbə, sábbaa

Sabel, *f.n.*, 'seɪbl, sáybl

Sabelli, *f.n.*, sə'belɪ, săbélli

Sabeston, *f.n.*, 'sæbɪstən, sábbĕstŏn

Sabin, *f.n.*, 'seɪbɪn, sáybin; 'sæbɪn, sábbin

Sabina, *C.n.*, sə'biːnə, săbeénă

Sabine, *f.n.*, 'sæbaɪn, sábbīn

Sabit, *f.n.*, 'sæbɪt, sábbit

Sach, *f.n.*, seɪtʃ, saytch; seɪʃ, saysh

Sacher, *f.n.*, 'sækər, sáckĕr

Sachs, *f.n.*, sæks, sacks

Sackley, *f.n.*, 'sæklɪ, sáckli

Sackur, *f.n.*, 'sækər, sáckŭr

Sackville-West, Vita, *poet and novelist (1892–1962),* 'viːtə 'sækvɪl 'west, veétă sáckvil wést

Sacombe *Herts.*, 'seɪkəm, sáykŏm

Sacriston Heugh *Durham*, 'sækrɪstən 'hjuf, sáckristŏn héwf

Sadberge *Durham*, 'sædbɜːdʒ, sádberj

Saddell Abbey *S'clyde*, 'sædl, sáddl

Sadie, *f.n.*, 'seɪdɪ, sáydi

Sadleir, *f.n.*, 'sædlər, sádlĕr

Saffell, *f.n.*, 'sæfl, sáffl; sə'fel, săféll

Saffron Walden *Essex*, 'sæfrən 'wɔldən, sáffrŏn wáwldĕn

Sagar, *f.n.*, 'seɪɡər, sáygăr

Sager, *f.n.*, 'seɪɡər, sáygĕr

Saggar, *f.n.*, 'sægər, sággaar

Saham Toney *Norfolk*, 'seɪəm 'toʊnɪ, sáy-ăm tŏni

Saich, *f.n.*, seɪʃ, saysh

Saighton *Ches.*, 'seɪtən, sáytŏn

Sainsbury, *f.n.*, 'seɪnzbərɪ, sáynzbŭri. *Appropriate also for Baron* ~.

Saint, *f.n.*, seɪnt, saynt

St. Albans *Herts.*, sɪnt 'ɔlbənz, sīnt áwlbănz. *Appropriate also for the Duke of* ~.

St. Aldate's *Oxford*, snt 'ɔldɪts, sīnt áwldits; snt 'oʊldz, sīnt óldz

St. Aldwyn, Earl, snt 'ɔldwɪn, sīnt áwldwin

St. Andrews *Fife*, snt 'ændruz, sīnt ándrooz. *Appropriate also for the Earl of* ~.

St. Anthony in Menaege *Cornwall*, snt 'æntənɪ ɪn mɪ'niːg, sīnt ántŏni in mĕneég; snt 'æntənɪ ɪn mɪ'neɪg, sīnt ántŏni in mĕnáyg

St. Asaph *Clwyd*, snt 'æsəf, sīnt ássăf

St. Athan *S. Glam.*, snt 'æθən, sīnt áthăn

St. Aubyn, *f.n.*, snt 'ɔbɪn, sīnt áwbin

St. Audries *Somerset*, snt 'ɔdrɪz, sīnt áwdriz

St. Austell *Cornwall*, snt 'ɔstl, sīnt áwsstl; snt 'ɔsl, sīnt áwssl

St. Bathans Abbey *Borders*, snt 'bæθənz, sīnt báthănz

St. Benet's Abbey *Norfolk*, snt 'benɪts, sīnt bénnĕts

St. Breock *Cornwall*, snt 'briək, sīnt breé-ŏk

St. Breward *Cornwall*, snt 'bruərd, sīnt broó-ărd

St. Briavels *Glos.*, snt 'brevlz, sīnt brévvlz

St. Budeaux *Devon*, snt 'bjudoʊ, sīnt béwdō

St. Chloe *Glos.*, snt 'kloʊɪ, sīnt klό-i

St. Clair, *f.n.,* snt 'klɛər, sĭnt kláir; 'sɪŋklɛər, sínklair

St. Clair-Erskine, *f.n.,* snt 'klɛər 'ɜrskɪn, sĭnt kláir érsskin. *The first is the Welsh pronunciation. The Family name of the Earl of Rosslyn.*

St. Clare, *f.n.,* 'sɪŋklər, sínklăr

St. Clears *Dyfed,* snt 'klɛərz, sĭnt kláirz

St. Clement Danes *London,* snt 'klemənt 'deɪnz, sĭnt klémmĕnt dáynz

St. Clements *Cornwall,* snt 'klemənts, sĭnt klémmĕnts

St. Clether *Cornwall,* snt 'kleðər, sĭnt kléthĕr

St. Cloud *H. & W.,* snt 'klu, sĭnt klóo

St. Columb *Major and Minor Cornwall,* snt 'kʌləm, sĭnt kúllŭm; snt 'kɒləm, sĭnt kóllŭm

St. Cyres, *Viscount,* snt 'saɪərz, sĭnt sírz

St. Dennis *Cornwall,* snt 'denɪs, sĭnt dénniss

St. Dogmaels *Dyfed,* snt 'dɒgməlz, sĭnt dógmĕlz

St. Dogwells *Dyfed,* snt 'dɒgwəlz, sĭnt dógwĕlz

St. Dominick *Cornwall,* snt 'dɒmɪnɪk, sĭnt dómminick

St. Donat's *S. Glam.,* snt 'dɒnəts, sĭnt dónnăts. *Appropriate also for ~ Castle.*

St. Endellion *Cornwall,* snt en'delɪən, sĭnt endélliŏn

St. Enoder *Cornwall,* snt 'enədər, sĭnt énnŏdĕr

St. Enodoc *Cornwall,* snt 'enədɒk, sĭnt énnŏdock

St. Erth *Cornwall,* snt 'ɜrθ, sĭnt érth

St. Eval *Cornwall,* snt 'evl, sĭnt évvl

St. Ewe *Cornwall,* snt 'ju, sĭnt yóo

St. Fagan's *S. Glam.,* snt 'fægənz, sĭnt fággänz

Saintfield *Co. Down,* 'seɪntfild, sáyntfeeld

St. Fillan's *Tayside,* snt 'fɪlənz, sĭnt fillänz

St. Gennys *Cornwall,* snt 'genɪs, sĭnt génniss

St. Germans, *Earl of,* snt 'dʒɜrmənz, sĭnt jérmänz

St. Giles' *Cathedral Edinburgh,* snt 'dʒaɪlz, sĭnt jílz. *Traditionally, no optional possessive -s is used in the spelling, nor ɪz, -ĕz in the pronunciation.*

St. Gorran, *also spelt* **St. Goran,** *Cornwall,* snt 'gɒrən, sĭnt górrăn

St. Govan's *Head Dyfed,* snt 'gɒvənz, sĭnt góvvänz; snt 'gʌvənz, sĭnt gúvvänz. *The first is the Welsh pronunciation. The second tends to be heard on the English side of the Bristol Channel.*

St. Helier *London,* snt 'heljər, sĭnt héll-yĕr

St. Hilary *Cornwall, S. Glam.,* snt 'hɪləri, sĭnt hílläri

St. Ippolyts, *also spelt* **St. Ippollitts,** *Herts.,* snt 'ɪpəlɪts, sĭnt íppŏlits

St. Issey *Cornwall,* snt 'ɪzi, sĭnt ízzi

St. Ive *Cornwall,* snt 'iv, sĭnt éev

St. Ives *Cambs., Cornwall,* snt 'aɪvz, sĭnt ívz

St. James's, *Court of,* snt 'dʒeɪmzɪz, sĭnt jáymziz

St. John, *f.n.,* 'sɪndʒən, sínjŏn; snt 'dʒɒn, sĭnt jón. *The first is appropriate for Viscount Bolingbroke's family name.*

St. John of Bletso, *Baron,* 'sɪndʒən əv 'bletsoʊ, sínjŏn ŏv blétsō

St. John of Lydiard Tregoze, *Baron,* 'sɪndʒən əv 'lɪdiərd trə'gɒz, sínjŏn ŏv líddi-ärd trĕgózz

St. John's Point *H'land,* 'dʒɒnz 'pɔɪnt, sĭnt jónz póynt

St. Juliot *Cornwall,* snt 'dʒuliət, sĭnt jóoli-ŏt; snt 'dʒɪlt, sĭnt jílt

St. Just, *Baron,* snt 'dʒʌst, sĭnt júst

St. Just in Penwith *Cornwall,* snt 'dʒʌst ɪn pen'wɪθ, sĭnt júst in penwíth

St. Keverne *Cornwall,* snt 'kevərn, sĭnt kévvĕrn

St. Keyne *Cornwall,* snt 'keɪn, sĭnt káyn; snt 'kin, sĭnt kéen

St. Kilda *W. Isles,* snt 'kɪldə, sĭnt kíldă

St. Leger, *f.n.,* snt 'ledʒər, sĭnt léjjĕr; 'selɪndʒər, séllinjĕr. *The first is appropriate for Viscount Doneraile's family name, the second for the Yorkshire branch of the family.*

St. Levan *Cornwall,* snt 'levən, sĭnt lévvăn. *Appropriate also for Baron ~.*

St. Loyes *Devon,* snt 'lɔɪz, sĭnt lóyz

St. Lythan's *S. Glam.,* snt 'lɪðənz, sĭnt líthänz

St. Mabyn *Cornwall,* snt 'meɪbɪn, sĭnt máybin

St. Machar's *Cathedral Aberdeen,* snt 'mæxərz, sĭnt máchărz

St. MacNissi's College *Co. Antrim*, 'seɪnt mək'nɪsɪz, sáynt măk-néessiz

St. Martin in Meneage *Cornwall*, snt 'martɪn ɪn mɪ'nig, sɪnt maártin in mĕnéeg; snt 'martɪn ɪn mɪ'neɪg, sɪnt maártin in mĕnáyg

St. Martin's le Grand *London*, snt 'martɪnz lə 'grænd, sɪnt maártinz lĕ gránd

St. Mary Axe *City of London*, snt 'meərɪ 'æks, sɪnt máiri ácks; 'sɪmərɪ 'æks, símmări ácks

St. Marylebone *see* **Marylebone**

St. Mary-le-Strand *London*, snt 'meərɪ lə 'strænd, sɪnt máiri lĕ stránd

St. Mary Woolnooth *City of London Guild Church*, snt 'meərɪ 'wʊlnʊθ, sɪnt máiri wŏólnooth

St. Maur, *f.n.*, 'sɪmɔr, seémor

St. Mawes *Cornwall*, snt 'mɔz, sɪnt máwz

St. Mawgan in Meneage *Cornwall*, snt 'mɔgən ɪn mɪ'nig, sɪnt máwgăn in mĕnéeg; snt 'mɔgən ɪn mɪ'neɪg, sɪnt máwgăn in mĕnáyg

St. Mawgan-in-Pydar *Cornwall*, snt 'mɔgən ɪn 'paɪdar, sɪnt máwgăn in pídaar

St. Merryn *Cornwall*, snt 'merɪn, sɪnt mérrin

St. Mewan *Cornwall*, snt 'mjuən, sɪnt méw-ăn

St. Michael Penkevil *Cornwall*, snt 'maɪkl peŋ'kɪvl, sɪnt míkl penkívvl

St. Monance *Fife*, snt 'mʊnəns, sɪnt mŏnánss

St. Neot *Cornwall*, snt 'niət, sɪnt née-ŏt

St. Neots *Cambs.*, snt 'niəts, sɪnt née-ŏts

St. Ninian's Cathedral *Perth*, snt 'nɪnɪənz, sɪnt nínni-ănz

St. Olaves *Norfolk*, snt 'ɒlɪvz, sɪnt óllivz

Sainton, *f.n.*, 'seɪntən, sáyntŏn

St. Oswald, Baron, snt 'ɒzwəld, sɪnt ózwăld

St. Osyth *Essex*, snt 'ouzɪθ, sɪnt ózith; snt 'ousɪθ, sɪnt óssith

St. Pancras *London*, snt 'pæŋkrəs, sɪnt pánkrăss

St. Paul's Walden Bury *Herts.*, snt 'pɔlz 'wɔldən 'berɪ, sɪnt páwlz wáwldĕn bérri

St. Peter-at-Gowts *Lincoln church*, snt 'pitər ət 'gauts, sɪnt péetĕr ăt gówts

St. Pierre *Gwent*, snt pɪ'eər, sɪnt pi-áir. *Appropriate also for the*

~ *Golf Course, nr. Chepstow, Gwent.*

St. Pinnock *Cornwall*, snt 'pɪnək, sɪnt pínnŏk

St. Rollox *Glasgow*, snt 'rɒləks, sɪnt róllŏks

St. Romaine, *f.n.*, snt rə'meɪn, sɪnt rōmáyn

St. Salvator's College *Univ. of St. Andrews*, snt sæl'veɪtərz, sɪnt salváytŏrz

St. Seiriol Island, *also* **Puffin Island** *q.v., Gwynedd*, snt 'saɪərɪɒl, sɪnt sĩri-oll

St. Teath *Cornwall*, snt 'teθ, sɪnt téth

St. Teilo Priory *Cardiff*, snt 'taɪlou, sɪnt tílō

St. Tudy *Cornwall*, snt 'tjudɪ, sɪnt téwdi

St. Vigeans *Tayside*, snt 'vɪdʒənz, sɪnt víjjănz

St. Weonards *H. & W.*, snt 'wenərdz, sɪnt wénnărdz

St. Werburgh *Bristol*, snt 'wɜrbərg, sɪnt wérburg

St. Wynifred's Well *Clwyd*, snt 'wɪnɪfrədz, sɪnt wínnifrĕdz

Sala, George Augustus Henry, *19th-c. journalist and author*, 'salə, saálă

Salaman, *f.n.*, 'sæləmæn, sálăman; 'sæləmən, sálămăn

Salamé, *f.n.*, 'sæləmeɪ, sálămay

Salant, *f.n.*, 'seɪlənt, sáylănt

Salberg, *f.n.*, 'sɔlbɜrg, sáwlberg

Salcey Forest *Northants.*, 'sɔlsɪ, sáwlssi

Salcombe *Devon*, 'sɔlkəm, sáwlkŏm; 'sɒlkəm, sólkŏm

Sale *Gtr. M'chester*, seɪl, sayl

Sales, *f.n.*, seɪlz, saylz

Salew, *f.n.*, sə'lu, sălóo

Salford *Beds.*, 'sæfərd, sáffŏrd

Salford *Gtr. M'chester*, 'sɒlfərd, sólfŏrd; 'sɔlfərd, sáwlfŏrd

Salfords *Surrey*, 'sælfərdz, sálfŏrdz

Salhouse *Norfolk*, 'sæləs, sálŭss; 'sælhaus, sál-howss

Saline *Fife*, 'sælɪn, sálin

Salisbury *Wilts.*, 'sɔlzbərɪ, sáwlzbŭri; 'sɔlzbrɪ, sáwlzbri. *The first is appropriate for the Marquess of* ~.

Salisse, *f.n.*, sə'lis, săléess

Salkeld, *f.n.*, 'sɔlkeld, sáwlkeld

Salkeld *Cumbria*, 'sɔlkeld, sáwlkeld; 'sæfəld, sáffĕld

Salkield, *f.n.*, 'sɔlkild, sáwlkeeld

Sall, *also spelt* **Salle**, *Norfolk*, sɒl, sawl

Sallagh *Co. Antrim*, 'sælə, sálă

Salle *see* **Sall**

Sallis, *f.n.*, 'sælɪs, sáliss
Salmon, *f.n.*, 'sæmən, sámmŏn
Salmonby *Lincs.*, 'sæmənbɪ, sámmŏnbi; 'sælmənbɪ, sál-mŏnbi
Salmond, *f.n.*, 'sæmənd, sámmŏnd
Salop, *alternative name and abbrev. for Shropshire*, 'sæləp, sálŏp
Salopian, *one educated at* **Shrewsbury** *School*, sə'loupɪən, sălópiăn
Saloway, *f.n.*, 'sæləweɪ, sálŏ-way
Salpeter, *f.n.*, 'sælpɪtər, sálpeetĕr
Salsburgh *S'clyde*, 'sɔlzbərə, sáwlzbŭră
Salt, *f.n.*, sɔlt, sawlt; sɒlt, sollt
Saltaire *W. Yorks.*, sɔl'teər, sawltáir
Salter, *f.n.*, 'sɔltər, sáwltĕr; 'sɒltər, sólltĕr
Saltersford *Ches.*, 'sɔltərzfərd, sáwltĕrzfŏrd. *Appropriate also for Baron ~.*
Saltfleetby *Lincs.*, 'sɔltflitbɪ, sáwltfleetbi; 'sɒləbɪ, sólläbi
Salthouse *Norfolk*, 'sɔlthaʊs, sáwlt-howss
Saltley *W. Midlands*, 'sɔltlɪ, sáwltli
Saltoun, *f.n.*, 'sɔltən, sáwltŏn; 'sæltən, sáltŏn. *The first is appropriate for Baroness ~.*
Saltoun, *East and West, Lothian*, 'sɒltən, sáwltŏn
Salusbury, *f.n.*, 'sɔlzbərɪ, sáwlzbŭri
Salvesen, *f.n.*, 'sælvɪsən, sálvéssĕn
Salveson, *f.n.*, 'sælvɪsən, sálvéssŏn
Salway, *f.n.*, 'sɒlweɪ, sáwlway
Salwick *Lancs.*, 'sælɪk, sálick; 'sælwɪk, sálwick
Salzedo, *f.n.*, sæl'zeɪdoʊ, salzáydō
Samares, *f.n.*, 'sæməreɪ, sámmăray
Sambles, *f.n.*, 'sæmblz, sámblz
Samett, *f.n.*, 'sæmɪt, sámmĕt
Samlesbury *Lancs.*, 'sæmzbərɪ, sámzbŭri; 'samzbərɪ, saámzbŭri
Sammes, *f.n.*, sæmz, samz
Sampford Courtenay *Devon*, 'sæmpfərd 'kɔrtnɪ, sámpfŏrd kórtni
Sampford Spiney *Devon*, 'sæmpfərd 'spaɪnɪ, sámpfŏrd spíni
Sampson, *f.n.*, 'sæmpsən, sámpssŏn
Samson Island *I. of Scilly*, 'sæmsən, sámssŏn
Samuels, *f.n.*, 'sæmjʊəlz, sám-yōō-ĕlz
Samuely, *f.n.*, ˌsæmjʊ'elɪ, sam-yōō-élli

Sancreed *Cornwall*, sæŋ'krid, sankréed
Sandaig *S'clyde*, 'sændeɪg, sándayg
Sandars, *f.n.*, 'sændərz, sándărz
Sanday *Orkney*, 'sændeɪ, sánday
Sandbach, *f.n.*, 'sændbætʃ, sándbatch
Sandbach *Ches.*, 'sændbætʃ, sándbatch
Sandell, *f.n.*, 'sændl, sándl
Sandelson, *f.n.*, 'sændlsən, sándlssŏn
Sander, *f.n.*, 'sændər, sándĕr
Sanders, *f.n.*, 'sandərz, saándĕrz; 'sændərz, sándĕrz; 'sɒndərz, sáwndĕrz
Sanderson, *f.n.*, 'sandərsən, saándĕrssŏn; 'sændərsən, sándĕrssŏn
Sanderson of Ayot, Barony of, 'sændərsən əv 'eɪət, sándĕrssŏn ŏv áy-ŏt
Sandes, *f.n.*, sændz, sandz
Sandford, *f.n.*, 'sændfərd, sándfŏrd; 'sændfərd, sánd-ford; 'sænərd, sánnŏrd
Sandhaven *Grampian*, 'sændheɪvən, sánd-hayvĕn
Sandhurst Royal Military Academy *Berks.*, 'sændhɜrst, sándhurst
Sandiacre *Derby.*, 'sændɪeɪkər, sándi-aykĕr
Sandilands, *f.n.*, 'sændɪləndz, sándilăndz
Sandness *Shetland*, 'sændnes, sándness
Sandow, *f.n.*, 'sændoʊ, sándō
Sandridge *Herts.*, 'sandrɪdʒ, saándrij
Sandringham *Norfolk*, 'sændrɪŋəm, sándring-ăm
Sandry, *f.n.*, 'sændrɪ, sándri
Sands, *f.n.*, sændz, sandz
Sandwich *Kent*, 'sændwɪtʃ, sándwitch
Sandy, *f.n.*, 'sændɪ, sándi
Sandy *Beds.*, 'sændɪ, sándi
Sandyknowe Crags *Borders*, 'sændɪnaʊ, sándinów
Sandys, *f.n.*, sændz, sandz. *Appropriate also for Baron ~.*
Sanford, *f.n.*, 'sænfərd, sánfŏrd
Sanger, *f.n.*, 'sæŋər, sáng-ĕr
Sangster, *f.n.*, 'sæŋstər, sángstĕr
Sanquhar *D. & G.*, 'sæŋkər, sánkăr. *Appropriate also for the Earl of ~.*
Sansom, *f.n.*, 'sænsəm, sánssŏm
Sapcote *Leics.*, 'sæpkoʊt, sápkōt
Saphier, *f.n.*, 'sæfɪər, sáffeer
Sapiston *Suffolk*, 'sæpɪstən, sáppistŏn

Sapley *Cambs.*, 'sæplɪ, sáppli
Sapte, *f.n.*, sæpt, sapt
Sarell, *f.n.*, 'særəl, sárrĕl
Sargant, *f.n.*, 'sardʒənt, saárjănt
Sargeaunt, *f.n.*, 'sardʒənt, saár-
  jĕnt
Sargent, *f.n.*, 'sardʒənt, saárjĕnt
Sargisson, *f.n.*, 'sardʒɪsən, saár-
  jissŏn
Sarisbury *Hants*, 'sarzbərɪ, saárz-
  bŭri; 'seərzbərɪ, sáirzbŭri
Sarnau *Dyfed, Gwynedd, Powys*,
  'sarnaɪ, saárnī
Sarony, *f.n.*, sə'rounɪ, sărṓni
Sarratt *Herts.*, 'særət, sárrăt
Sarre *Kent*, sar, saar
Sarson, *f.n.*, 'sarsən, saársson
Sarstedt, *f.n.*, 'sarsted, saárssted
Sartoris, *f.n.*, 'sartərɪs, saártŏriss
Sartorius, *f.n.*, 'sartərɪs, saártŏriss
Sarum *Roman name for* **Salisbury**,
  'seərəm, sáirŭm
Sasse, *f.n.*, sæs, sass
Sassoon, *f.n.*, sə'sun, sássoón
Satchwell, *f.n.*, 'sætʃwel, sátchwel
Satow, *f.n.*, 'satou, saátō
Satterleigh *Devon*, 'sætərlɪ, sát-
  tĕrli
Sauchiehall Street *Glasgow*,
  ˌsɒxɪ'hɔl, sochiháwl
Sauer, *f.n.*, sɔr, sor
Saughall, Great *and* Little, *Ches.*,
  'sɒkl, sáwkl
Saughton *Lothian*, 'sɒxtən,
  sóchtŏn
Saughtree *Borders*, 'sɒxtrɪ,
  sóchtree
Saul *Co. Down, Glos.*, sɔl, sawl
Saulez, *f.n.*, 'sɒlɪ, sáwli; 'soulɪ,
  sṓli
Saumarez, *f.n.*, 'sɒmərɪz, sóm-
  mărĕz; 'soumərɪ, sṓmäri
Saundby, *f.n.*, 'sɒndbɪ, sáwndbi
Saunders, *f.n.*, 'sɒndərz, sáwn-
  dĕrz; 'sandərz, saándĕrz
Saundersfoot *Dyfed*, 'sɒndərzfut,
  sáwndĕrzfŏŏt
Saunderson, *f.n.*, 'sɒndərsən,
  sáwndĕrssŏn; 'sandərsən,
  saándĕrssŏn
Sauter, *f.n.*, 'soutər, sṓtĕr
Sauvage, *f.n.*, 'sævɪdʒ, sávvij;
  sou'vaʒ, sōvaázh
Sava, *f.n.*, 'savə, saávă
Savage, *f.n.*, 'sævɪdʒ, sávvij
Savernake *Wilts.*, 'sævərnæk,
  sávvĕrnack. *Appropriate also
  for* Viscount ~.
Savidge, *f.n.*, 'sævɪdʒ, sávvij
Savigear, *f.n.*, 'sævɪgɪər, sávvigeer
Savile, *f.n.*, 'sævɪl, sávvil; 'sævl,
  sávvl
Savile Club *London*, 'sævɪl,
  sávvil; 'sævl, sávvl

Savile Row *London*, 'sævɪl 'rou,
  sávvil rṓ; 'sævl 'rou, sávvl rṓ
Savins, *f.n.*, 'sævɪnz, sávvinz
Savory, *f.n.*, 'seɪvərɪ, sáyvŏri
Saward, *f.n.*, 'seɪwərd, sáywărd
Sawbridgeworth *Herts.*, 'sɒbrɪdʒ-
  wərθ, sáwbrijwŭrth. *An old
  pronunciation was* 'sæpswərθ,
  sápswŭrth.
Saweard, *f.n.*, 'seɪwərd, sáywărd
Sawel *Co. Derry–Co. Tyrone*,
  'sɒəl, sáw-ĕl
Sawrey, *f.n.*, 'sɔrɪ, sáwri
Sawston *Cambs.*, 'sɒstən, sáwstŏn
Sawtry *Cambs.*, 'sɒtrɪ, sáwtri
Sawyer, *f.n.*, 'sɔjər, sáw-yĕr
Saxavord *Shetland*, 'sæksə'vord,
  sácksăvórd
Saxilby *Lincs.*, 'sækslbɪ, sáckslbi
Saxmundham *Suffolk*, sæks-
  'mʌndəm, sacksmúndăm
Saxon, *f.n.*, 'sæksən, sácksŏn
Saxthorpe *Norfolk*, 'sæksθɔrp,
  sácks-thorp
Saxton, *f.n.*, 'sækstən, sáckstŏn
Saxty, *f.n.*, 'sækstɪ, sácksti
Sayce, *f.n.*, seɪs, sayss
Saye and Sele, Baron, 'seɪ ənd
  'sil, sáy ănd séel
Sayer, *f.n.*, seər, sair; 'seɪər,
  sáy-ĕr
Sayers, *f.n.*, seərz, sairz; 'seɪərz,
  sáy-ĕrz
Sayles, *f.n.*, seɪlz, saylz
Saynor, *f.n.*, 'seɪnər, sáynŏr
Sayres, *f.n.*, seərz, sairz
Saywell, *f.n.*, 'seɪwel, sáywel
Scadding, *f.n.*, 'skædɪŋ, skádding
Scadgell, *f.n.*, 'skædʒl, skájjl
Scafell *Cumbria*, 'skɔ'fel, skáw-
  féll
Scalasaig *S'clyde*, 'skæləseɪg,
  skálăssayg
Scalford *Leics.*, 'skɔlfərd, skáwl-
  fŏrd; 'skɒfərd, skáwfŏrd
Scalloway *Shetland*, 'skæləwə,
  skálŏ-wă
Scalpay *H'land, W. Isles*, 'skælpeɪ,
  skálpay
Scammell, *f.n.*, 'skæml, skámml
Scannell, *f.n.*, 'skænl, skánnl
Scapa Flow *Orkney*, 'skapə 'flou,
  skaápă flṓ
Scarba *S'clyde*, 'skarbə, skaárbă
Scarborough *N. Yorks.*, 'skar-
  bərə, skaárbŭră
Scarbrough, Earl of, 'skarbrə,
  skaárbră
Scardifield, *f.n.*, 'skardɪfild,
  skaárdifeeld
Scargill, *f.n.*, 'skargɪl, skaár-gill
Scarinish *S'clyde*, 'skærɪnɪʃ,
  skárrinish; skæ'rɪnɪʃ, skarrín-
  nish

Scarisbrick, *f.n.*, 'skɛərzbrɪk, skáïrzbrick
Scarisbrick *Lancs.*, 'skɛərzbrɪk, skáïrzbrick
Scarlett, *f.n.*, 'skɑrlət, skaárlĕt
Scartho, *also spelt* **Scarthoe**, *Humberside*, 'skɑrθoʊ, skaár--thō
Scarva *Co. Down*, 'skɑrvə, skaárvă
Scase, *f.n.*, skeɪs, skayss
Scaur, The, *Grampian*, skɔr, skor
Scavaig, Loch, *Skye*, 'skæveɪg, skávvayg
Scawen, *f.n.*, 'skɔən, skáw-ĕn
Sceales, *f.n.*, skilz, skeelz
Scears, *f.n.*, sɪərz, seerz
Sceats, *f.n.*, skits, skeets
Sceberras, *f.n.*, ˌʃebə'rɑs, shebbĕraáss
Scerri, *f.n.*, 'ʃerɪ, shérri
Scerry, *f.n.*, 'ʃerɪ, shérri
Schaffer, *f.n.*, 'ʃæfər, sháffĕr
Schapiro, *f.n.*, ʃə'pɪəroʊ, shăpéerō
Scharrer, *f.n.*, 'ʃɑrər, shaárĕr
Scharf, *f.n.*, ʃɑrf, shaarf
Schaschke, *f.n.*, 'ʃæskɪ, shásski
Schellenberg, *f.n.*, 'ʃelənbɜrg, shéllĕnberg
Scher, *f.n.*, ʃɜr, sher. *Appropriate for the Anna ~ Children's Theatre, Islington, London.*
Scherer, *f.n.*, 'ʃɛərər, sháïrĕr; 'ʃerər, shérrĕr
Schidlof, *f.n.*, 'ʃɪdlɒf, shídloff
Schiehallion *Tayside*, ʃɪ'hæljən, shĕ-hál-yŏn
Schild, *f.n.* ʃild, sheeld
Schilizzi, *f.n.*, skɪ'lɪtsɪ, skilítsi
Schiller, *f.n.*, 'ʃɪlər, shíllĕr
Schjelderup, *f.n.*, 'ʃeldrəp, shéldrŭp
Schlaen, *f.n.*, ʃleɪn, shlayn
Schlapp, *f.n.*, ʃlæp, shlapp
Schlazinger, *f.n.*, 'ʃlæzɪndʒər, shlázzinjĕr
Schlesinger, *f.n.*, 'ʃlesɪndʒər, shléssinjĕr
Schlie, *f.n.* sli, slee
Schmidt, *f.n.*, ʃmɪt, shmitt
Schofield, *f.n.*, 'skoʊfild, skófeeld
Scholefield, *f.n.*, 'skoʊlfild, skólfeeld
Scholes, *f.n.*, skoʊlz, skōlz. *Appropriate for Percy ~, musicologist.*
Scholey, *f.n.*, 'skoʊlɪ, skóli
Scholfield, *f.n.*, 'skoʊfild, skófeeld; 'skoʊlfild, skólfeeld
Schon, *f.n.*, ʃɒn, shonn
Schonell, *f.n.*, ʃɒ'nel, shonnéll
Schonfield, *f.n.*, 'skɒnfild, skónnfeeld

Schooling, *f.n.*, 'skulɪŋ, skóoling
Schoutze, *f.n.*, 'ʃʊtseɪ, shóotsay
Schouvaloff, *f.n.*, ʃu'valɒf, shoo-vaáloff
Schreiber, *f.n.*, 'ʃraɪbər, shríbĕr
Schroder, *f.n.*, 'ʃroʊdər, shródĕr
Schulcz-Paull, *f.n.*, 'ʃʊlts 'pɒl, shóolts páwl
Schulten, *f.n.*, 'skʊltən, skóoltĕn
Schuster, *f.n.*, 'ʃʊstər, shóostĕr
Schwabe, *f.n.*, 'ʃwɑbə, shwaábĕ
Schwartz, *f.n.*, ʃwɔrts, shwawrts
Sciama, *f.n.*, 'ʃɑmə, shaámă
Sciberras, *f.n.*, ˌʃɪbə'rɑs, shibbĕraáss
Sciennes, *f.n.*, ʃinz, sheenz
Scillonian, *native of the Isles of Scilly*, sɪ'loʊnɪən, silóniăn
Scilly, Isles of, 'sɪlɪ, sílli
Scissett *W. Yorks.*, sɪ'set, sissétt
Sclanders, *f.n.*, 'sklandərz, sklaándĕrz
Sclater, *f.n.*, 'sleɪtər, sláytĕr
Scobell, *f.n.*, skoʊ'bel, skōbéll
Scofield, *f.n.*, 'skoʊfild, skófeeld
Scole *Norfolk*, skoʊl, skōl
Scollan, *f.n.*, 'skɒlən, skóllăn
Scolt Head *Norfolk*, skɒlt, skollt
Scone *Tayside*, skun, skoon. *Appropriate also for Baron ~ and for the Stone of ~.*
Scoones, *f.n.*, skunz, skoonz
Scopes, *f.n.*, skoʊpz, skōps
Scopwick *Lincs.*, 'skɒpwɪk, skópwick
Scorer, *f.n.*, 'skɔrər, skáwrĕr
Scorgie, *f.n.*, 'skɔrdʒɪ, skórji
Scorrier *Cornwall*, 'skɒrɪər, skórri-ĕr
Scotby *Cumbria*, 'skɒtbɪ, skótbi
Scothern, *f.n.*, 'skɒθɜrn, skóthern; 'skɒðərn, skóthĕrn
Scothern *Lincs.*, 'skɒθɜrn, skóthern
Scotstoun *S'clyde*, 'skɒtstən, skótstŏn
Scott, *f.n.*, skɒt, skott
Scottow *Norfolk*, 'skɒtoʊ, skóttō
Scougal, *f.n.*, 'skugl, skóogl
Scougall, *f.n.*, 'skugl, skóogl
Scoular, *f.n.*, 'skulər, skóolăr
Scoullar, *f.n.*, 'skulər, skóolăr
Scouller, *f.n.*, 'skulər, skóolĕr
Scouloudi, *f.n.*, skʊ'lʊdɪ, skōō-lóŏdi
Scourfield, *f.n.*, 'skaʊərfild, skówrfeeld
Scourie *H'land*, 'skaʊərɪ, skówri
Scovell, *f.n.*, skoʊ'vel, skōvéll
Scowcroft, *f.n.*, 'skoʊkrɒft, skó--kroft
Scowen, *f.n.*, 'skoʊɪn, skó-ĕn
Scrabo *Co. Down*, 'skræboʊ, skrábbō

Scrafield *Lincs.*, 'skreɪfɪld, skráyfeeld

Scresort, Loch, *H'land*, 'skrɪzərt, skréezŏrt

Screveton *Notts.*, 'skrɪtən, skréetŏn

Scridain, Loch, *S'clyde*, 'skrɪdən, skréedän

Scrimgeour, *f.n.*, 'skrɪmdʒər, skrímjĕr

Scrivelsby *Lincs.*, 'skrɪvlzbɪ, skrívvlzbɪ; 'skrɪlzbɪ, skréelzbi

Scrivener, *f.n.*, 'skrɪvənər, skrívvĕnĕr

Scroggie, *f.n.*, 'skrɒgɪ, skróggi

Scroggs, *f.n.*, 'skrɒgz, skroggz

Scrooby *Notts.*, 'skrubɪ, skróobi

Scrope, *f.n.*, skrup, skroop

Scrubey, *f.n.*, 'skrubɪ, skróobi

Scruby, *f.n.*, 'skrubɪ, skróobi

Scruton, *f.n.*, 'skrutən, skróotŏn

Scrymgeour, *f.n.*, 'skrɪmdʒər, skrímjĕr

Scudamore, *f.n.*, 'skjudəmɔr, skéwdămor

Scull, *f.n.*, skʌl, skull

Scullion, *f.n.*, 'skʌljən, skúll-yŏn

Sculpher, *f.n.*, 'skʌlfər, skúllfĕr

Scunthorpe *Lincs.*, 'skʌnθɔrp, skúnthorp

Scupham, *f.n.*, 'skʌfəm, skúffăm

Scuse, *f.n.*, skjus, skewss

Scutt, *f.n.*, skʌt, skutt

Seabright, *f.n.*, 'sɪbraɪt, seé-brīt

Seacy, *f.n.*, 'sɪsɪ, seéssi

Seaford *E. Sussex*, si'fɔrd, seefórd

Seaforde *Co. Down*, 'sifɔrd, seéford

Seager, *f.n.*, 'sigər, seégĕr

Seago, *f.n.*, 'sigoʊ, seégō

Seagoe *Co. Armagh*, 'sigoʊ, seégō

Seagrave, *f.n.*, 'sigreɪv, seé-grayv

Seaham *Durham*, 'siəm, seé-ăm

Seahouses *Northd.*, 'sihaʊzɪz, seé-howzĕz

Seaman, *f.n.*, 'simən, seémän

Sea Palling *Norfolk*, si 'pɒlɪŋ, see páwling

Searchfield, *f.n.*, 'sɜrtʃfɪld, sértchfeeld

Searcy, *f.n.*, 'sɪərsɪ, seérssi

Searell, *f.n.*, 'serəl, sérrĕl

Searight, *f.n.*, 'sɪraɪt, seé-rīt

Searle, *f.n.*, sɜrl, serl

Sears, *f.n.*, sɪərz, seerz

Seasalter *Kent*, 'sisɔltər, seé-sawltĕr

Seascale *Cumbria*, 'sɪskeɪl, seé-skayl

Seathwaite *Cumbria*, 'sɪθweɪt, seé-thwayt

Seaton, *f.n.*, 'sɪtən, seétŏn

Seaton Carew *Cleveland*, 'sɪtən kə'ru, seétŏn kărόo

Seaton Delaval *Northd.*, 'sɪtən 'deləvəl, seétŏn déllăväl

Seaville *Cumbria*, 'sevɪl, sévvil

Seavington *Somerset*, 'sevɪŋtən, sévvingtŏn

Sebergham *Cumbria*, 'sebərəm, sébbĕräm

Secchie, *f.n.*, 'sekɪ, sécki

Secombe, *f.n.*, 'sikəm, seékŏm

Secondé, *f.n.*, sɪ'kɒndɪ, sĕkóndi

Secord, *f.n.*, 'sikɔrd, seékord

Secretan, *f.n.*, 'sekrɪtən, séckrĕtän

Secrett, *f.n.*, 'sikrɪt, seékrĕt

Sedbergh *Cumbria*, 'sedbər, sédbĕr; 'sedbərg, sédberg. *The first is appropriate for ∼ School.*

Sedberghian, *one educated at Sedbergh School*, sed'bɜrgɪən, sedbérgiän

Seddon, *f.n.*, 'sedən, séddŏn

Sedgehill *Wilts.*, 'sedʒhɪl, séj-hil; 'sedʒl, séjjl

Sedgwick, *f.n.*, 'sedʒwɪk, séjwick

Sedlescombe *E. Sussex*, 'sedlzkəm, séddlzkŏm

Seear, *f.n.*, 'sɪər, seé-ăr. *Appropriate also for Baroness ∼.*

Seend *Wilts.*, sind, seend

Segal, *f.n.*, 'sɪgl, seégl. *Appropriate also for Baron ∼.*

Segar, *f.n.*, 'sɪgər, seégär

Seghill *Northd.*, 'segɪl, ség-hil

Segontium, *Roman site at Caernarvon*, sɪ'gɒntɪəm, sĕgónti-ūm

Segrave, *f.n.*, 'sigreɪv, seégrayv. *See also Baron Mowbray, ∼ and Stourton.*

Segrue, *f.n.*, 'sigru, seégroo

Seif, *f.n.*, sif, seef

Seifert, *f.n.*, 'sifərt, seéfĕrt

Seigal, *f.n.*, 'sigl, seégl

Seighford *Staffs.*, 'sifərd, seéfórd; 'saɪfərd, sífórd

Seignior, *f.n.*, 'sinjər, seén-yŏr

Seil *S'clyde*, sil, seel

Seilebost *W. Isles*, 'ʃeɪlɪbɒst, sháylibosst

Seilern, *f.n.*, 'saɪlɜrn, sílern

Seiont, River, *Gwynedd*, 'saɪɒnt, sí-ont

Seiriol, *Welsh C.n.*, 'saɪərɪɒl, síri-ol

Seisdon *Staffs.*, 'sizdən, seézdŏn

Seivad, *f.n.*, 'sivæd, seévad

Seivwright, *f.n.*, 'sɪvraɪt, sívvrīt

Sekers, *f.n.*, 'sekərz, séckĕrz

Selham *W. Sussex*, 'sɪləm, seélăm; 'seləm, séllăm

Seligman, *f.n.*, 'selɪgmən, sélligmän

Seligmann, *f.n.*, 'selɪgmən, sélligmän

Selkirk *Borders*, 'selkərk, sélkirk
Sellack *H. & W.*, 'selək, séllăk
Sellar, *f.n.*, 'selər, séllăr
Sellars, *f.n.*, 'selərz, séllărz
Sellas, *f.n.*, 'seləs, séllăss
Sellers, *f.n.*, 'selərz, séllĕrz
Selley, *f.n.*, 'selı, sélli
Sellick, *f.n.*, 'selık, séllick
Sellindge *Kent*, 'selındʒ, séllinj
Selly Oak *W. Midlands*, 'selı
 'oʊk, sélli ṓk
Selmeston *E. Sussex*, 'selmztən,
 sélmztŏn
Selous, *f.n.*, sə'lu, sĕloó
Selsey *Glos.*, *W. Sussex*, 'selzı,
 sélzi
Selsey Bill *W. Sussex*, 'selzı 'bıl,
 sélzi bíll; 'selsı 'bıl, sélssi bíll
Selwick *Orkney*, 'selwık, sélwick
Selwyn, *f.n.*, 'selwın, sélwin
Semer *Suffolk*, 'simər, seémĕr
Semer Water, *also spelt* **Semmer
 Water**, *N. Yorks.*, 'semər
 'wɒtər, sémmĕr wáwtĕr
Semington *Wilts.*, 'semıŋtən,
 sémmingtŏn
Semmer Water *see* **Semer Water**
Sempill, Baroness, 'sempl, sémpl
Sendall, *f.n.*, 'sendɒl, séndawl
Senghenydd *Mid Glam.*, seŋ-
 'henıð, seng-hénnith
Sennen *Cornwall*, 'senən, sénnĕn
Sensier, *f.n.*, 'sensıər, sénsseer;
 'sɑsıeı, saángssi-ay
Serena, *C.n.*, sı'rinə, sĕreénă
Sereny, *f.n.*, sı'rinı, sĕreéni
Sergison, *f.n.*, 'sɑrdʒısən, saárjis-
 sŏn
Serota, *f.n.*, sə'roʊtə, sĕrótă.
 Appropriate also for Baroness
 ~.
Serpell, *f.n.*, 'sɜrpl, sérpl
Servaes, *f.n.*, sər'veız, sĕrváyz
Seskinore *Co. Tyrone*, ˌseskı'nɔr,
 sesskinór
Seton, *f.n.*, 'sitən, seétŏn
Setoun, *f.n.*, 'sitən, seétŏn
Sever, *f.n.*, 'sevər, sévvĕr
Severn, River, *Powys–Salop–
 H. & W.–Glos.*, 'sevərn, sévvĕrn
Severs, *f.n.*, 'sevərz, sévvĕrz
Sevier, *f.n.*, 'sevjər, sév-yĕr;
 sı'vıər, sĕveér
Seville, *f.n.*, 'sevıl, sévvil; 'sevl,
 sévvl
Seward, *f.n.*, 'sjuərd, syōō-ărd;
 'siwərd, seé-wărd
Sewell, *f.n.*, 'sjuəl, séw-ĕl
Sewerby *Humberside*, 'suərbı,
 soó-ĕrbi
Sewing, *f.n.*, 'siwıŋ, seé-wing
Sexton, *f.n.*, 'sekstən, séckstŏn
Seyd, *f.n.*, saıd, sīd
Seyers, *f.n.*, seərz, sairz

Seyler, Athene, *actress*, ə'θını
 'saılər, ătheéni sílĕr
Seymour, *f.n.*, 'simər, seémər;
 'simər, seémor; 'seımər, sáy-
 mūr. *The first is appropriate for
 the family name of the Duke of
 Somerset and of the Marquess
 of Hertford.*
Seys, *f.n.*, seıs, sayss; seız, sayz
Sezincote *Glos.*, 'sizənkət,
 seézĕn-kŏt; 'sizınkət, seézin-
 -kŏt; 'sezınkət, sézzin-kŏt
Sgiwen *see* **Skewen**
Sgurr Alasdair *Skye*, 'skuər
 'ælıstər, skoŏr álistăr
Sgurr Biorach *Skye*, 'skuər 'bırəx,
 skoŏr bírrăch
Sgurr Dearg *Skye*, 'skuər 'derıg,
 skoŏr dérrĕg
Sgurr na Banachdich *Skye*,
 'skuər nə 'bænəxdıx, skoŏr nă
 bánnăchdich
Sgurr nan Eag *Skye*, 'skuər nən
 'eık, skoŏr nän áyk
Sgurr nan Gillean *Skye*, 'skuər
 nən 'giljən, skoŏr nän geél-yăn
Sgurr na Stri *Skye*, 'skuər nə 'stri,
 skoŏr nă streé
Shackell, *f.n.*, 'ʃækl, sháckl
Shacklady, *f.n.*, 'ʃækleıdı, sháck-
 -laydi
Shackleton, *f.n.*, 'ʃækltən, sháckl-
 tŏn. *Appropriate also for Baron*
 ~.
Shackman, *f.n.*, 'ʃækmən, sháck-
 măn
Shaen, *f.n.*, ʃeın, shayn
Shaer, *f.n.*, ʃeər, shair
Shaffer, *f.n.*, 'ʃæfər, sháffĕr
Shafir, Shulamith, *pianist*, 'ʃulə-
 mıθ ʃæ'fıər, shoolámith shafféer
Shaftesbury *Dorset*, 'ʃaftsbərı,
 sháaftsbŭri. *Appropriate also
 for the Earl of* ~.
Shairp, *f.n.*, ʃɑrp, shaarp
Shakerley, *f.n.*, 'ʃækərlı, sháck-
 ĕrli
Shakerley *Gtr. M'chester*, 'ʃækər-
 lı, sháckĕrli
Shakerly, *f.n.*, 'ʃækərlı, sháckĕrli
Shakeshaft, *f.n.*, 'ʃeıkʃaft, sháyk-
 -shaaft
Shakespeare, *f.n.*, 'ʃeıkspıər,
 sháykspeer
Shalden *Hants*, 'ʃɒldən, sháwldĕn;
 'ʃɒldən, shólldĕn
Shaldon *Devon*, 'ʃɒldən, sháwldŏn;
 'ʃɒldən, shólldŏn
Shalfleet *I. of Wight*, 'ʃælflıt,
 shál-fleet
Shalford *Essex*, *Surrey*, 'ʃælfərd,
 shálfŏrd
Shallcross, *f.n.*, 'ʃælkrɒs, shál-
 kross

Shalmsford Street *Kent*, 'ʃælmz-fərd strit, shálmzförd street
Shanbally *Co. Down*, 'ʃænbælɪ, shánbali
Shankill *Co. Antrim*, 'ʃænkɪl, shánkil
Shanklin, *f.n.*, 'ʃæŋklɪn, shánklin
Shanklin *I. of Wight*, 'ʃæŋklɪn, shánklin
Shankly, *f.n.*, 'ʃæŋklɪ, shánkli
Shanley, *f.n.*, 'ʃænlɪ, shánli
Shannagh *Co. Down*, 'ʃænə, shánnă
Shannon, *f.n.*, 'ʃænən, shánnŏn
Shantallow *Co. Derry*, ʃæn'tælou, shantálŏ
Shap *Cumbria*, ʃæp, shap
Shapinsay *Orkney*, 'ʃæpɪnseɪ, sháppinssay
Shapiro, *f.n.*, ʃə'pɪərou, shăpéerŏ
Shapland, *f.n.*, 'ʃæplənd, shápländ
Shapley, *f.n.*, 'ʃæplɪ, shápli
Sharman, *f.n.*, 'ʃɑrmən, shaármăn
Sharp, *f.n.*, ʃɑrp, shaarp
Sharpe, *f.n.*, ʃɑrp, shaarp
Sharpenhoe *Beds.*, 'ʃɑrpənou, shaárpenŏ
Sharples, *f.n.*, 'ʃɑrplz, shaárplz
Sharpley, *f.n.*, 'ʃɑrplɪ, shaárpli
Sharpness *Glos.*, ʃɑrp'nes, shaárpnéss
Shasby, *f.n.*, 'ʃæzbɪ, sházbi
Shaughnessy, *f.n.*, 'ʃɔnəsɪ, sháwnĕssi. *Appropriate also for Baron* ~.
Shaugh Prior *Devon*, 'ʃɔ 'praɪər, sháw prí-ŏr
Shavington *Ches.*, 'ʃævɪŋtən, shávvington
Shaw, *f.n.*, ʃɔ, shaw
Shawcross, *f.n.*, 'ʃɔkrɒs, sháwkross. *Appropriate also for Baron* ~.
Shawell *Leics.*, 'ʃɑwəl, shaá-wěl
Shea, *f.n.*, ʃeɪ, shay
Shead, *f.n.*, ʃed, shed; ʃid, sheed
Sheaf, River, *Derby.–S. Yorks.*, ʃif, sheef
Sheaff, *f.n.*, ʃif, sheef
Sheard, *f.n.*, ʃɛərd, shaird; ʃɪərd, sheerd; ʃɜrd, sherd
Shearer, *f.n.*, 'ʃɪərər, sheérĕr
Shearlock, *f.n.*, 'ʃɪərlɒk, sheérlock
Shearman, *f.n.*, 'ʃɪərmən, sheérmăn; 'ʃɜrmən, shérmăn
Shearn, *f.n.*, ʃɜrn, shern
Shears, *f.n.*, ʃɪərz, sheerz
Shearsby *Leics.*, 'ʃɪərzbɪ, sheérzbi
Shebbear *Devon*, 'ʃebɪər, shéb-beer
Shebbeare, *f.n.*, 'ʃebɪər, shébbeer
Sheehy, *f.n.*, 'ʃihɪ, sheéhi
Sheen, *f.n.*, ʃin, sheen
Sheene, *f.n.*, ʃin, sheen

Sheepscombe *Glos.*, 'ʃepskəm, shépskŏm
Sheffield, *f.n.*, 'ʃefild, shéffeeld
Sheffield *S. Yorks.*, 'ʃefild, shéffeeld. *Appropriate also for Baron* ~.
Sheiham, *f.n.*, 'ʃaɪəm, shí-ăm
Shelburne, Earldom of, 'ʃelbərn, shélbŭrn
Sheldon, *f.n.*, 'ʃeldən, shéldŏn
Shelfanger *Norfolk*, 'ʃelfæŋgər, shélfang-gĕr
Shelford, Great *and* Little, *Cambs.*, 'ʃelfərd, shélförd
Shelland *Suffolk*, 'ʃelənd, shél-länd
Shelley, *f.n.*, 'ʃelɪ, shélli
Shelmerdine, *f.n.*, 'ʃelmərdin, shélmĕrdeen
Shelock, *f.n.*, 'ʃilɒk, sheélock; 'ʃelɒk, shéllock
Shelton, *f.n.*, 'ʃeltən, shéltŏn
Shelvey, *f.n.*, 'ʃelvɪ, shélvi
Shemming, *f.n.*, 'ʃemɪŋ, shémming
Shephalbury *Herts.*, 'ʃeplbəri, shépplbŭri
Shephall *Herts.*, 'ʃepl, shéppl
Shepheard, *f.n.*, 'ʃepərd, shéppĕrd
Shepherd, *f.n.*, 'ʃepərd, shéppĕrd
Shepherdine *Avon*, 'ʃepərdaɪn, shéppĕrdīn
Sheppard, *f.n.*, 'ʃepərd, shéppărd
Shepreth *Cambs.*, 'ʃeprəθ, shép-rĕth
Shepshed *Leics.*, 'ʃepʃed, shép-shed
Shepton Beauchamp *Somerset*, 'ʃeptən 'bitʃəm, shéptŏn bée-tchăm
Shepton Mallet *Somerset*, 'ʃeptən 'mælɪt, shéptŏn málĕt
Sher, *f.n.*, ʃɜr, sher
Shera, *f.n.*, 'ʃɪərə, sheéră
Sheraton, *f.n.*, 'ʃerətən, shérrătŏn. *Appropriate for Thomas* ~, *18th-c. cabinet-maker and furniture designer.*
Sherborne *Dorset*, 'ʃɜrbərn, shérbŭrn. *Appropriate also for Baron* ~.
Shere *Surrey*, ʃɪər, sheer
Sheret, *f.n.*, 'ʃerɪt, shérrĕt
Sherfield, Baron, 'ʃɜrfild, shérfeeld
Sherfield-on-Loddon *Hants*, 'ʃɜrfild ɒn 'lɒdən, shérfeeld on lóddŏn
Shergold, *f.n.*, 'ʃɜrgould, shér-gōld
Sheridan, *f.n.*, 'ʃerɪdən, shérridăn
Sheridan, Richard Brinsley, *18-c. dramatist*, 'rɪtʃərd 'brɪnzlɪ 'ʃerɪdən, rítchărd brínzli shérridăn

Sheriffmuir *Central*, 'ʃerɪf'mjʊər, shérriff-myóŏr
Sheringham *Norfolk*, 'ʃerɪŋəm, shérring-äm
Sherlaw, *C.n.*, 'ʃɜrlɔ, shérlaw
Sherlock, *f.n.*, 'ʃɜrlɒk, shérlock
Shermanbury *W. Sussex*, 'ʃɜrmənbərɪ, shérmänbŭri
Sherrin, *f.n.*, 'ʃerɪn, shérrin
Shetland Islands, 'ʃetlənd, shét-länd
Shettleston *S'clyde*, 'ʃetlstən, shéttlstŏn
Sheviock *Cornwall*, 'ʃevɪək, shévvi-ŏk
Shew, *f.n.*, ʃu, shoo
Shewell-Cooper, *f.n.*, 'ʃuəl 'kupər, shoo-ĕl kóopĕr
Shewen, *f.n.*, 'ʃuɪn, shóo-ĕn
Shewey, *f.n.*, 'ʃuɪ, shó-i
Shiant Isles *W. Isles*, 'ʃiənt, shée--änt
Shide *I. of Wight*, ʃaɪd, shīd
Shields, *f.n.*, ʃildz, sheeldz
Shields, North *and* South, *Tyne & Wear*, ʃildz, sheeldz
Shihwarg, *f.n.*, ʃɪ'varg, shivaárg
Shillaker, *f.n.*, 'ʃɪleɪkər, shíllaykĕr
Shillidy, *f.n.*, 'ʃɪldɪ, shíllidi
Shilling, *f.n.*, 'ʃɪlɪŋ, shílling
Shillingford *Devon*, 'ʃɪlɪŋfərd, shílling-fŏrd
Shillinglaw, *f.n.*, 'ʃɪlɪŋlɔ, shílling--law
Shimell, *f.n.*, 'ʃɪml, shímml
Shimna, River, *Co. Down*, 'ʃɪmnə, shímnă
Shincliffe *Durham*, 'ʃɪŋklɪf, shínk-liff
Shinebourne, *f.n.*, 'ʃaɪnbɔrn, shínborn
Shinkwin, *f.n.*, 'ʃɪŋkwɪn, shínkwin
Shinwell, *f.n.*, 'ʃɪnwəl, shínwĕl; 'ʃɪnwel, shínwell
Shipbourne *Kent*, 'ʃɪbərn, shíbbŭrn
Shipdham *Norfolk*, 'ʃɪpdəm, shípdäm; 'ʃɪpəm, shíppäm
Shiplake *Oxon.*, 'ʃɪpleɪk, shíplayk
Shipley, *f.n.*, 'ʃɪplɪ, shípli
Shipp, *f.n.*, ʃɪp, ship
Shippea Hill *Suffolk*, 'ʃɪpɪ 'hɪl, shíppi híll
Shipston-on-Stour *Warwicks.*, 'ʃɪpstən ɒn 'staʊər, shípstŏn on stówr
Shipton Bellinger *Hants.*, 'ʃɪptən 'belɪndʒər, shíptŏn béllinjĕr
Shipton Oliffe *Glos.*, 'ʃɪptən 'ɒlɪf, shíptŏn óliff
Shiremoor *Tyne & Wear*, 'ʃaɪərmʊər, shír-moor
Shirley, *C.n. and f.n.*, 'ʃɜrlɪ, shírli
Shirreff, *f.n.*, 'ʃɪrɪf, shírrĕf; 'ʃerɪf, shérrĕf

Shiskine *S'clyde*, 'ʃɪskɪn, shísskin
Shivas, *f.n.*, 'ʃɪvəs, shéevăss
Shlaen, *f.n.*, ʃleɪn, shlayn
Shobbrook, *f.n.*, 'ʃɒbrʊk, shób-broŏk
Shobrooke *Devon*, 'ʃoʊbrʊk, shóbroŏk
Shockett, *f.n.*, 'ʃɒkɪt, shóckĕt
Shocklach *Ches.*, 'ʃɒklɪtʃ, shóck-litch
Shoeburyness *Essex*, 'ʃubərɪ'nes, shoóbŭrinéss
Shoemake, *f.n.*, 'ʃumeɪk, shoó-mayk
Sholden *Kent*, 'ʃoʊldən, shóldĕn
Sholing *Hants*, 'ʃoʊlɪŋ, shóling
Sholto, *f.n.*, 'ʃɒltoʊ, shóltō
Shone, *f.n.*, ʃoʊn, shōn
Shonfield, *f.n.*, 'ʃɒnfɪld, shónn-feeld
Shooter, *f.n.*, 'ʃutər, shoótĕr
Shoreham *Kent*, 'ʃɔrəm, sháwräm
Shoreham-by-Sea *W. Sussex*, 'ʃɔrəm baɪ 'si, sháwräm bī sée
Short, *f.n.*, ʃɔrt, short
Shortlanesend *Cornwall*, ʃɔrtleɪnz'end, short-laynzénd
Shorto, *f.n.*, 'ʃɔrtoʊ, shórtō
Shorwell *I. of Wight*, 'ʃɔrwel, shórwel
Shotesham All Saints *Norfolk*, 'ʃɒtsəm ɔl 'seɪnts, shóttsăm awl sáynts
Shotesham St. Mary *Norfolk*, 'ʃɒtsəm snt 'meərɪ, shóttsăm sɪnt máiri
Shottisham *Suffolk*, 'ʃɒtsəm, shóttsăm
Shotwick *Ches.*, 'ʃɒtwɪk, shótwick
Shouksmith, *f.n.*, 'ʃʊksmɪθ, shoók-smith
Shouldham *Norfolk*, 'ʃoʊldəm, shóldăm
Shouldham Thorpe *Norfolk*, 'ʃoʊldəm 'θɔrp, shóldăm thórp
Shouler, *f.n.*, 'ʃulər, shoólĕr
Shoults, *f.n.*, ʃoʊlts, shōlts
Shove, Fredegond, *poet and author*, 'fredɪgɒnd 'ʃoʊv, fréddĕgond shóv
Showell, *f.n.*, 'ʃoʊəl, shó-ĕl
Shrawardine *Salop*, 'ʃreɪwərdaɪn, shráy-wär-dīn
Shrewsbury *Salop*, 'ʃroʊzbərɪ, shrózbŭri; 'ʃruzbərɪ, shroózbŭri. *The first is appropriate for the Earl of ~ and for the public school, but both are used in the town.*
Shrewton *Wilts.*, 'ʃrutən, shroótŏn
Shrimpton, *f.n.*, 'ʃrɪmptən, shrímp-tŏn
Shrivenham *Oxon.*, 'ʃrɪvənəm, shrívvĕnăm

Shrodells Wing *Watford General Hospital, Herts.*, ʃroʊ'delz, shrōdéllz

Shroton *Dorset*, 'ʃroʊtən, shrṓtŏn

Shryane, *f.n.*, 'ʃraɪən, shrí-ăn

Shuard, *f.n.*, 'ʃuɑrd, shoo-aard

Shube, *f.n.*, ʃub, shoob

Shuckburgh, *f.n.*, 'ʃʌkbərə, shúckbŭră

Shuckburgh, Lower *and* Upper, *Warwicks.*, 'ʃʌkbərə, shúckbŭră

Shudy Camps *Cambs.*, 'ʃudɪ 'kæmps, shoódi kámps

Shukman, *f.n.*, 'ʃʊkmən, shoók-măn

Shuldham, *f.n.*, 'ʃuldəm, shoóldăm

Shulman, *f.n.*, 'ʃulmən, shoólmăn

Shults, *f.n.*, ʃʌlts, shullts

Shurey, *f.n.*, 'ʃʊərɪ, shoóri

Shurmer, *f.n.*, 'ʃɜrmər, shúrmĕr

Shurrery *H'land*, 'ʃʌrərɪ, shúrrĕri

Shute, Baron, ʃut, shoot

Sian, *Welsh C.n.*, ʃan, shaan

Sibbett, *f.n.*, 'sɪbɪt, síbbĕt

Sibdon Carwood *Salop*, 'sɪbdən 'kɑrwʊd, síbdŏn kaárwŏŏd

Sible Hedingham *Essex*, 'sɪbl 'hedɪŋəm, síbbl hédding-ăm

Sibley, *f.n.*, 'sɪblɪ, síbbli

Sibree Hall *Coventry*, 'saɪbrɪ, síbri

Sibson, *f.n.*, 'sɪbsən, síbssŏn

Sibun, *f.n.*, 'saɪbən, síbŭn

Sich, *f.n.*, sɪtʃ, sitch

Sichell, *f.n.*, 'sɪtʃl, sitchl; 'sɪʃl, síshl

Sickert, *f.n.*, 'sɪkərt, síckĕrt. *Appropriate for Walter ~, painter and author.*

Sicklesmere *Suffolk*, 'sɪklzmɪər, sícklzmeer

Sicklinghall *N. Yorks.*, 'sɪklɪŋhɔl, síckling-hawl

Sidaway, *f.n.*, 'sɪdəweɪ, síddă-way

Sidcup *London*, 'sɪdkʌp, sídkup; 'sɪdkəp, sídkŭp

Siddall, *f.n.*, 'sɪdɔl, síddawl

Sidebotham, *f.n.*, 'saɪdbɒtəm, sídbottăm

Sidebottom, *f.n.*, 'sɪdbɒtəm, seédbottŏm; ‚sɪdɪbə'toʊm, siddibǒ'toúm; 'saɪdbɒtəm, sídbottŏm

Sidestrand *Norfolk*, 'saɪdstrænd, sídstrand; 'saɪdɪstrænd, sídĕsstrand

Sidey, *f.n.*, 'saɪdɪ, sídi

Sidford *Devon*, sɪd'fɔrd, sidfórd; 'sɪdfərd, sídford

Sidgreaves, *f.n.*, 'sɪdgrivz, sídgreevz

Sidlesham *W. Sussex*, 'sɪdlsəm, síddlssăm

Sidmouth *Devon*, 'sɪdməθ, sídmŭth

Sidor, *f.n.*, 'saɪdər, sídor

Siebert, *f.n.*, 'sibərt, seébĕrt

Sieff, *f.n.*, sif, seef. *Appropriate also for Baron ~.*

Sieman, *f.n.*, 'simən, seéman

Siemons, *f.n.*, 'simənz, seémŏnz

Sier, *f.n.*, sɪər, seer; 'saɪər, sír

Sieve, *f.n.*, sɪv, seev

Sieveking, *f.n.*, 'sivkɪŋ, seévking

Sievewright, *f.n.*, 'sɪvraɪt, sívv-rīt

Sievier, *f.n.*, 'sɪvjər, seév-yĕr

Sievwright, *f.n.*, 'sɪvraɪt, seévrīt

Sigal, *f.n.*, 'sɪgl, seégl

Siggins, *f.n.*, 'sɪgɪnz, sígginz

Sigsworth, *f.n.*, 'sɪgzwɜrθ, síggzwurth

Silchester *Hants*, 'sɪltʃɪstər, síltchĕstĕr

Sileby *Leics.*, 'saɪlbɪ, sílbi

Silhillian, *native of* Solihull, sɪl'hɪlɪən, silhílli-ăn

Silkin, *f.n.*, 'sɪlkɪn, sílkin. *Appropriate also for the Barony of ~.*

Silkstone *S. Yorks.*, 'sɪlkstoʊn, sílksstōn

Sill, *f.n.*, sɪl, sill

Sillars, *f.n.*, 'sɪlərz, síllărz

Sillence, *f.n.*, sɪ'lens, sillénss; 'saɪləns, sílĕnss

Sillita, *f.n.*, 'sɪlɪtə, síllită

Sillito, *f.n.*, 'sɪlɪtoʊ, síllitō

Sillitoe, *f.n.*, 'sɪlɪtoʊ, síllitō

Sillitto, *f.n.*, 'sɪlɪtoʊ, síllitō

Silloth *Cumbria*, 'sɪləθ, síllŏth

Sillyearn *Grampian*, ‚sɪlɪ'ɜrn, silli-érn

Silsoe *Beds.*, 'sɪlsoʊ, sílssō. *Appropriate also for Baron ~.*

Silver, *f.n.*, 'sɪlvər, sílvĕr

Silverman, *f.n.*, 'sɪlvərmən, sílvĕrmăn

Silverstone, *f.n.*, 'sɪlvərstoʊn, sílvĕrsstōn

Silverstone *Northants.*, 'sɪlvərstoʊn, sílvĕrsstōn

Silvertown *London*, 'sɪlvərtaʊn, sílvĕrtown

Silvester, *f.n.*, sɪl'vestər, silvéstĕr

Silvey, *f.n.*, 'sɪlvɪ, sílvi

Simak, *f.n.*, 'simæk, seémack

Simche, *f.n.*, 'sɪmtʃɪ, símtchi

Simeons, *f.n.*, 'sɪmɪənz, símmi-ŏnz

Simey, *f.n.*, 'saɪmɪ, sími

Simister, *f.n.*, 'sɪmɪstər, símmistĕr

Simmonds, *f.n.*, 'sɪməndz, símmŏndz; 'sɪmənz, símmŏnz

Simmons, *f.n.*, 'sɪmənz, símmŏnz

Simms, *f.n.*, sɪmz, simmz

Simon, *C.n. and f.n.*, 'saɪmən, símŏn. *Appropriate also for Viscount ~.*

Simond, *f.n.*, 'saɪmənd, sī́mŏnd
Simonds, *f.n.*, 'sɪməndz, sím-mŏndz; 'saɪməndz, sī́mŏndz.
The first is appropriate for the Viscountcy of ~.
Simonis, *f.n.*, sɪ'mounɪs, sim-mṓniss
Simon of Glaisdale, Baron, 'saɪmən əv 'gleɪzdeɪl, sī́mŏn ŏv gláyzdayl
Simon of Wythenshawe, Baron, 'saɪmən əv 'wɪðənʃɔ, sī́mŏn ŏv wíthĕnshaw
Simons, *f.n.*, 'saɪmənz, sī́mŏnz
Simonsbath *Somerset,* 'sɪmənz-bɑθ, símmŏnzbaath
Simonstone *Lancs.,* 'sɪmənstoun, símmŏnsstōn
Simpson, *f.n.*, 'sɪmpsən, símpsŏn
Sims, *f.n.*, sɪmz, simmz
Sinclair, *f.n.*, 'sɪŋkleər, sínklair; 'sɪŋklər, sínklăr. *The first is appropriate for Baron ~. The second is usual in Scotland.*
Sinclair of Cleeve, Baron, 'sɪŋklər əv 'kliv, sínklĕr ŏv kleév
Sindlesham *Berks.,* 'sɪndlʃəm, síndl-shăm
Sinead, *Irish C.n.*, ʃɪ'neəd, shinné-ăd
Singer, *f.n.*, 'sɪŋər, síng-ĕr
Singleton, *f.n.*, 'sɪŋgltən, síng-gltŏn
Siniawski, *f.n.*, ,sɪnɪ'æfskɪ, sinni-áfski
Sinnatt, *f.n.*, 'sɪnət, sínnăt
Sinodun Hill *Oxon.,* 'sɪnədən, sínnŏdŭn
Sinstadt, *f.n.*, 'sɪnstæt, sínstat
Sion Mills *Co. Tyrone,* 'saɪən 'mɪlz, sī́-ŏn míllz
Sired, *f.n.*, 'saɪərɪd, sī́rĕd
Sirett, *f.n.*, 'sɪrɪt, sírrĕt
Sirhowy *Gwent,* sər'haʊɪ, sir-hówi
Siriol, *Welsh C.n.*, 'sɪrɪɒl, sírri-ol
Sirrell, *f.n.*, 'sɪrəl, sírrĕl
Sisam, *f.n.*, 'saɪsəm, sī́ssăm
Sisland *Norfolk,* 'saɪzlənd, sī́z-lănd
Sisley, *f.n.*, 'sɪzlɪ, sízzli. *Appropriate also in English usage for the Anglo-French painter, Alfred ~.*
Sissinghurst *Kent,* 'sɪsɪŋhərst, síssing-hurst. *Appropriate also for ~ Castle.*
Siston *Avon,* 'saɪstən, sī́sstŏn; 'saɪsən, sī́ssŏn
Sisum, *f.n.*, 'saɪsəm, sī́ssŭm
Sitch, *f.n.*, sɪtʃ, sitch
Sithney *Cornwall,* 'sɪθnɪ, síthni
Sitwell, Sir Sacheverell, *author,* sə'ʃevərəl 'sɪtwəl, săshévvĕrĕl sítwĕl

Sizer, *f.n.*, 'saɪzər, sī́zĕr
Sizergh Castle *Cumbria,* 'saɪzər, sī́zĕr
Sizewell *Suffolk,* 'saɪzwəl, sī́zwĕl
Skakle, *f.n.*, 'skekl, skéckl ‣
Skamacre, *f.n.*, 'skæmeɪkər, skámmaykĕr
Skara Brae *Orkney,* 'skærə 'breɪ, skárrä bráy
Skea, *f.n.*, skɪ, skee
Skeabost *Skye,* 'skeɪbɒst, skáy-bosst
Skeaping, *f.n.*, 'skipɪŋ, skeéping
Skeat, *f.n.*, skit, skeet
Skeats, *f.n.*, skits, skeets
Skeavington, *f.n.*, 'skevɪŋtən, skévvington
Skegoniel *Co. Antrim,* ,skegə'nil, skeggŏneél
Skelhorn, *f.n.*, 'skelhɔrn, skélhorn
Skell, River, *N. Yorks.,* skel, skell
Skellern, *f.n.*, 'skelərn, skéllĕrn
Skelmersdale *Lancs.,* 'skelmərz-deɪl, skélmĕrzdayl. *Appropriate also for Baron ~.*
Skelmorlie *S'clyde,* 'skelmərlɪ, skélmŏrli
Skelsey, *f.n.*, 'skelsɪ, skélssi
Skelton, *f.n.*, 'skeltən, skéltŏn
Skelton *Cumbria,* 'skeltən, skéltŏn
Skelwith *Cumbria,* 'skelɪθ, skél-lith
Skemp, *f.n.*, skemp, skemp
Skempton, *f.n.*, 'skemptən, skémp-tŏn
Skene, *f.n.*, skin, skeen
Skernaghan Point *Co. Antrim,* 'skərnəxən, skérnăch̬ăn
Sker Point *Mid Glam.,* skeər, skair
Skerritt, *f.n.*, 'skerɪt, skérrit
Skerrow, Loch, *D. & G.,* 'skeroʊ, skérrō
Skerryvore *W. Isles,* ,skerɪ'vɔr, skerrivór
Sketch, *f.n.*, sketʃ, sketch
Skewen, *also spelt* **Sgiwen,** *W. Glam.,* 'skjuɪn, skéw-ĕn
Skeyton *Norfolk,* 'skaɪtən, skī́tŏn
Skidelsky, *f.n.*, skɪ'delskɪ, skidélski
Skidmore, *f.n.*, 'skɪdmɔr, skídmor
Skilbeck, *f.n.*, 'skɪlbek, skílbeck
Skinburness *Cumbria,* ,skɪnbər-'nes, skinbŭrnéss
Skinnard, *f.n.*, 'skɪnɑrd, skinnaard
Skinner, *f.n.*, 'skɪnər, skínnĕr
Skiport, Loch, *W. Isles,* 'skɪpərt, skíppŏrt
Skirlaugh, North *and* South, *Humberside,* 'skərloʊ, skírlō
Skirling *Borders,* 'skərlɪŋ, skírling
Skirrow, *f.n.*, 'skɪroʊ, skírrō
Skirsa *H'land,* 'skərzə, skírză

Skliros, *f.n.,* 'skliərɒs, skleéross
Skokholm, *also spelt* **Skokham,** *Dyfed,* 'skɒkhoum, skóck-hōm; 'skoukəm, skókăm
Skomer Island *Dyfed,* 'skoumər, skómĕr
Skone, *f.n.,* skoun, skōn
Skrimgeour, *f.n.,* 'skrɪmdʒər, skrímjŭr
Skrimshire, *f.n.,* 'skrɪmʃaɪər, skrímshīr
Skrine, *f.n.,* skrin, skreen; skraɪn, skrīn
Skues, *f.n.,* skjuz, skewz
Skye *H'land,* skaɪ, skī
Skyrme, *f.n.,* skɜrm, skirm
Slaap, *f.n.,* slɑp, slaap
Sladden, *f.n.,* 'slædən, sláddĕn
Slade, *f.n.,* sleɪd, slayd
Sladen, *f.n.,* 'sleɪdən, sláydĕn
Slaithwaite *W. Yorks.,* 'slæθweɪt, sláthwayt; 'slauɪt, slów-it
Slamannan *Central,* slə'mænən, slămánnăn
Slamin, *f.n.,* 'slæmɪn, slámmin
Slapin, Loch, *Skye,* 'slapɪn, slaápin
Slater, *f.n.,* 'sleɪtər, sláytĕr
Slatter, *f.n.,* 'slætər, sláttĕr
Slattery, *f.n.,* 'slætərɪ, sláttĕri
Slaugham *W. Sussex,* 'slæfəm, sláffăm; 'slɑfəm, slaáfăm
Slaughdon *Suffolk,* 'slɔdən, sláwdŏn
Slaughter, *f.n.,* 'slɔtər, sláwtĕr
Slaughter, Lower *and* Upper, *Glos.,* 'slɔtər, sláwtĕr
Slawith *N. Yorks.,* 'slauɪθ, slów-ith
Sleaford *Lincs.,* 'slifərd, sleéfŏrd
Sleat *Skye,* sleɪt, slayt
Sleath, *f.n.,* sliθ, sleeth
Slebech *Dyfed,* 'slebetʃ, slébbetch
Sledmere *Humberside,* 'sledmɪər, slédmeer
Sleeman, *f.n.,* 'slimən, sleémăn
Sleigh, *f.n.,* sleɪ, slay; sli, slee
Sleights *N. Yorks.,* slaɪts, slīts
Slemish *Co. Antrim,* 'slemɪʃ, slémmish
Slessenger, *f.n.,* 'slesɪndʒər, sléssĕnjĕr
Slessor, *f.n.,* 'slesər, sléssŏr
Slevin, *f.n.,* 'slevɪn, slévvin
Slieu Lhean *I. of Man,* 'slju 'len, sléw lén
Slievebane *Co. Antrim,* sliv'bæn, sleevbán
Slieve Bearnagh *Co. Down,* sliv 'bɛərnə, sleev báirnă
Slieve Donard *Co. Down,* sliv 'dɒnərd, sleev dónnărd
Slieve-na-Man *Co. Down,* ,slivnə'mæn, sleevnămán

Sligachan *Skye,* 'sligəxən, sleé-gǎchǎn
Sligo, Marquess of, 'slaɪgou, slígō
Slimon, *f.n.,* 'slɪmən, slímmŏn
Sloan, *f.n.,* sloun, slōn
Sloane, *f.n.,* sloun, slōn
Slochd *H'land,* slɒx, sloch
Slocombe, *f.n.,* 'sloukəm, slókŏm
Sloman, *f.n.,* 'sloumən, slómăn
Sloperton Cottage *Wilts.,* 'slou-pərtən 'kɒtɪdʒ, slópĕrtŏn kóttij. *Home of the poet Thomas Moore (1779–1852) for some years.*
Slough *Berks,* slau, slow
Slowey, *f.n.,* 'slouɪ, slō-i
Sloy, Loch, *S'clyde,* slɔɪ, sloy
Slydell, *f.n.,* slaɪ'del, slīdéll
Slynn, *f.n.,* slɪn, slin
Smaje, *f.n.,* smeɪdʒ, smayj
Smale, *f.n.,* smeɪl, smayl
Smalley, *f.n.,* 'smɔlɪ, smáwli
Smalley *Derby.,* 'smɔlɪ, smáwli
Smallpeice, *f.n.,* 'smɒlpɪs, smáwl-peess
Smarden *Kent,* 'smɑrdən, smaár-dĕn; 'smɑrdən, smaárden
Smart, *f.n.,* smɑrt, smaart
Smeaton, *f.n.,* 'smitən, smeétŏn
Smedley, *f.n.,* 'smedlɪ, smédli
Smeeth *Kent,* smið, smeeth
Smeeton, *f.n.,* 'smitən, smeétŏn
Smellie, *f.n.,* 'smelɪ, smélli
Smeterlin, *f.n.,* 'smetərlɪn, smét-tĕrlin
Smethurst, *f.n.,* 'smeθərst, sméth-urst; 'smeθhərst, sméth-hurst
Smethwick *W. Midlands,* 'smeðɪk, sméthick
Smibert, *f.n.,* 'smaɪbərt, smíbĕrt
Smieton, *f.n.,* 'smitən, smeétŏn
Smillie, *f.n.,* 'smaɪlɪ, smíli
Smily, *f.n.,* 'smaɪlɪ, smíli
Smirke, *f.n.,* smɜrk, smirk
Smith, *f.n.,* smɪθ, smith
Smithaleigh *Devon,* 'smɪðəlɪ, smíthălee
Smithells, *f.n.,* 'smɪðlz, smíthlz
Smithers, *f.n.,* 'smɪðərz, smíthĕrz
Smithfield *Cumbria,* 'smɪθfɪld, smíthfeeld
Smitton, *f.n.,* 'smɪtən, smíttŏn
Smolen, *f.n.,* 'smɒlen, smóllen
Smollett, *f.n.,* 'smɒlɪt, smóllĕt
Smurthwaite, *f.n.,* 'smɜrθweɪt, smúrthwayt
Smyrl, *f.n.,* smɜrl, smurl
Smyth, *f.n.,* smaɪθ, smīth; smith; smaɪð, smīth. *The second is appropriate for Dame Ethel ~, composer and conductor. The first is the usual Irish pronunciation.*

Smythe, *f.n.*, smaɪð, smĭth; smaɪθ, smĭth

Smythson, *f.n.*, 'smaɪðsən, smĭthssŏn

Snabdough *Northd.*, 'snæbdʌf, snábduff

Snaefell *I. of Man*, 'sneɪ'fel, snáy-féll

Snagge, *f.n.*, snæg, snag

Snailum, *f.n.*, 'sneɪləm, snáylŭm

Snaith, *f.n.*, sneɪθ, snayth

Snashall, *f.n.*, 'snæʃl, snáshl

Snatchwood *Gwent*, 'snætʃwʊd, snátchwŏŏd

Snaveley, *f.n.*, 'sneɪvlɪ, snáyvli

Snead, *f.n.*, snid, sneed

Sneezum, *f.n.*, 'snizəm, snéezŭm

Sneinton *Notts.*, 'snentən, snéntŏn

Snelling, *f.n.*, 'snelɪŋ, snélling

Snettisham *Norfolk*, 'snetɪʃəm, snétti-shăm; 'snetsəm, snétsăm; 'snetɪsəm, snéttissăm; snet-ʃəm, snét-shăm

Snewin, *f.n.*, 'snjuɪn, snéw-in

Snewing, *f.n.*, 'snjuɪŋ, snéw-ing

Sneyd, *f.n.*, snid, sneed

Sneyd *Staffs.*, snid, sneed

Snizort *H'land*, 'snaɪzərt, snízŏrt

Snizort, Loch, *H'land*, 'snaɪzərt, snízŏrt

Snoad, *f.n.*, snoʊd, snōd

Snodgrass, *f.n.*, 'snɒdgrɑs, snódgraass

Snodin, *f.n.*, 'snoʊdɪn, snódin

Snodland *Kent*, 'snɒdlənd, snódländ

Snoswell, *f.n.*, 'snɒzwəl, snózzwĕl

Snow, *f.n.*, snoʊ, snō

Snowdon *Gwynedd*, 'snoʊdən, snódŏn. *Appropriate also for the Earl of* ~.

Snowdonia *Gwynedd*, snoʊ'doʊnɪə, snōdṓniă

Snowdown Colliery *Kent*, 'snoʊdaʊn, snódown

Snoxall, *f.n.*, 'snɒksɔl, snóckssawl

Snoxell, *f.n.*, 'snɒksl, snóckssl

Soal, *f.n.*, soʊl, sōl

Soames, *f.n.*, soʊmz, sōmz. *Appropriate also for Baron* ~.

Soane, *f.n.*, soʊn, sōn

Soar *Mid Glam.*, *Powys*, 'soʊɑr, sṓ-aar

Soar, River, *Warwicks.–Leics.*, sɔr, sor

Soay *H'land*, *W. Isles*, 'soʊeɪ, sṓ-ay; 'soʊə, sṓ-ă

Sobas, *f.n.*, 'soʊbæs, sṓbass

Sobell, *f.n.*, 'soʊbel, sṓbell

Sobiotto, *f.n.*, soʊ'bjɒtoʊ, sōbyóttō

Sodor and Man, bishopric, 'soʊdər ənd 'mæn, sṓdŏr ănd mán

Sofaer, *f.n.*, soʊ'feər, sōfáir

Sofer, *f.n.*, 'soʊfər, sṓfĕr

Soham *Cambs.*, 'soʊəm, sṓ-ăm

Sohier, *f.n.*, 'soʊjər, sṓ-yĕr

Soke of Peterborough *Cambs.*, 'soʊk əv 'pitərbərə, sṓk ŏv péetĕrbŭră

Soley, *f.n.*, 'soʊlɪ, sṓli

Solent sea channel, 'soʊlənt, sṓlĕnt

Solihull *W. Midlands*, ,soʊlɪ'hʌl, sṓli-húll

Sollars, *f.n.*, 'sɒlərz, sóllărz

Sollas, *f.n.*, 'sɒləs, sóllăss

Sollas *W. Isles*, 'sɒləs, sóllăss

Solon, *f.n.*, 'soʊlɒn, sṓlon; 'soʊlən, sṓlŏn

Solsgirth *Tayside*, 'sɒlzgərθ, sólz-girth

Solti, Sir Georg, *conductor*, 'dʒɔrdʒ 'ʃɒltɪ, jórj shólti

Solva *Dyfed*, 'sɒlvə, sólvă

Solway Firth *part of Irish Sea*, 'sɒlweɪ, sólway

Somerby *Lincs.*, 'sʌmərbɪ, súmmĕrbi

Somercotes *Derby.*, 'sʌmərkoʊts, súmmĕrkōts

Somerfield, *f.n.*, 'sʌmərfild, súmmĕrfeeld

Somerhough, *f.n.*, 'sʌmərhɒf, súmmĕrhoff

Somerleyton *Suffolk*, 'sʌmərleɪtən, súmmĕrlaytŏn. *Appropriate also for Baron* ~.

Somers, *f.n.*, 'sʌmərz, súmmĕrz. *Appropriate also for Baron* ~.

Somersby *Lincs.*, 'sʌmərzbɪ, súmmĕrzbi

Somerset, *f.n.*, 'sʌmərsɪt, súmmĕrssĕt

Somerset *Co. name.* 'sʌmərsɪt, súmmĕrssĕt; 'sʌmərset, súmmĕrsset. *The first is appropriate for the Duke of* ~.

Somersham *Cambs.*, 'sʌmərʃəm, súmmĕr-shăm

Somerton, *f.n.*, 'sʌmərtən, súmmĕrtŏn. *Appropriate also for Viscount* ~.

Somerton *Somerset*, 'sʌmərtən, súmmĕrtŏn

Somerton, East *and* West, *Norfolk*, 'sʌmərtən, súmmĕrtŏn

Somervell, *f.n.*, 'sʌmərvəl, súmmĕrvĕl

Somerville, *f.n.*, 'sʌmərvɪl, súmmĕrvil

Sompting *W. Sussex*, 'sʌmptɪŋ, súmpting; 'sɒmptɪŋ, sómpting

Sondes, Earl, sɒndz, sondz

Sonnex, *f.n.*, 'sɒneks, sónnecks

Sonning *Berks.*, 'sʌnɪŋ, súnning; 'sɒnɪŋ, sónning

Soper, _f.n._, 'soʊpər, sṓpĕr. _Appropriate also for Baron ~._

Sopley _Hants_, 'sɒplɪ, sóppli

Soref, _f.n._, 'sɒrɪf, sórrĕf

Sorensen, _f.n._, 'sɒrənsən, sórrĕnssĕn

Sorley, _f.n._, 'sɔːlɪ, sórli

Sorrell, _f.n._, 'sɒrəl, sórrĕl; sə'rel, sŏréll

Soskice, _f.n._, 'sɒskɪs, sósskiss

Sotham, _f.n._, 'sʌðəm, súthăm

Sothcott, _f.n._, 'sɒθkɒt, sóthkott

Sotheby's, _auctioneers_, 'sʌðəbɪz, súthĕbiz

Sothers, _f.n._, 'sʌðərz, súthĕrz

Sotterley _Suffolk_, 'sɒtərlɪ, sóttĕrli

Soudley _Glos._, 'sudlɪ, sóodli

Souez, _f.n._, 'suɪz, sóo-ĕz

Soughton _Clwyd_, 'sɒtən, sáwtŏn. _The Welsh form of this name is_ **Sychdyn,** _q.v._

Soul, _f.n._, sul, sool

Soulbury _Bucks._, 'soʊlbərɪ, sṓlbŭri. _Appropriate also for Viscount ~._

Soulby, _f.n._, 'soʊlbɪ, sṓlbi

Soulby _Cumbria_, 'soʊlbɪ, sṓlbi

Souldern _Oxon._, 'soʊldərn, sṓldĕrn

Souldrop _Beds._, 'soʊldrɒp, sṓldrop

Soulsby, _f.n._, 'soʊlzbɪ, sṓlzbi

Sound of Mull, _sea passage_, 'saʊnd əv 'mʌl, sównd ŏv múll

Souness, _f.n._, 'sunɪs, sóonĕss

Sourin _Orkney_, 'saʊərɪn, sówrin

Sourton _Devon_, 'sɔːtən, sórtŏn

Souster, _f.n._, 'sustər, sóostĕr

Soutar, _f.n._, 'sutər, sóotăr

Souter, _f.n._, 'sutər, sóotĕr

Souter Point _Tyne & Wear_, 'sutər 'pɔɪnt, sóotĕr póynt

Southall, _f.n._, 'sʌðɔːl, súthawl; 'sʌðl, súthl

Southall _London_, 'saʊðɔːl, sówth-awl

Southam, _f.n._, 'saʊðəm, sówthăm

Southam _Warwicks._, 'saʊðəm, sówthăm

Southampton _Hants_, saʊθ'hæmptən, sowth-hámptŏn; saʊ-'θæmptən, sowthámptŏn

South Baddesley _Hants_, 'saʊθ 'bædɪzlɪ, sówth báddĕzli; 'saʊθ 'bædzlɪ, sówth bádzli

Southborough _Kent_, 'saʊθbərə, sówthbŭră. _Appropriate also for Baron ~._

Southby, _f.n._, 'saʊθbɪ, sówthbi

South Cerney _Glos._, 'saʊθ 'sɜːnɪ, sówth sérni

Southcombe, _f.n._, 'saʊθkəm, sówthkŏm

South Croxton _Leics._, 'saʊθ 'kroʊsən, sówth króssŏn; 'saʊθ 'kroʊstən, sówth króss-tŏn; 'saʊθ 'kroʊzən, sówth krózŏn

Southerndown _Mid Glam._, 'sʌðərndaʊn, súthĕrndown

Southerness _D. & G._, ˌsʌðər'nes, sŭthĕrnéss

Southers, _f.n._, 'sʌðərz, súthĕrz

Southerwood, _f.n._, 'sʌðərwʊd, súthĕrwŏod

Southery _Norfolk_, 'sʌðərɪ, súthĕri

Southesk, Earl of, saʊθ'esk, sowthésk

Southey, _f.n._, 'saʊðɪ, sówthi; 'sʌðɪ, súthi. _The first is appropriate for Robert ~, Poet Laureate._

Southey _S. Yorks._, 'saʊðɪ, sówthi

Southgate, _f.n._, 'saʊθgeɪt, sówthgayt; 'saʊθgɪt, sówthgit

South Heighton _E. Sussex_, 'saʊθ 'heɪtən, sówth háytŏn

South Hiendley _W. Yorks._, 'saʊθ 'hindlɪ, sówth heéndli

South Hykeham _Lincs._, 'saʊθ 'haɪkəm, sówth híkăm

South Kirby _W. Yorks._, 'saʊθ 'kɜːbɪ, sówth kírbi

Southleigh _Devon_, 'saʊθ'li, sówth-leé; 'saʊlɪ, sówlee

South Leverton _Notts._, 'saʊθ 'levərtən, sówth lévvĕrtŏn

South Malling _E. Sussex_, 'saʊθ 'mɒlɪŋ, sówth máwling

South Merstham _Surrey_, 'saʊθ 'mɜːstəm, sówth mérstăm

Southminster _Essex_, 'saʊθ-'mɪnstər, sowthmínstĕr

Southoe _Cambs._, 'saʊðoʊ, sówthō; 'saʊðoʊ, sówthō

Southorn, _f.n._, 'sʌðɔːrn, súthorn

Southowram _W. Yorks._, saʊθ-'aʊərəm, sowth-ówrăm

Southrepps _Norfolk_, 'saʊθreps, sówthrepps

Southrey _Lincs._, 'sʌðrɪ, súthri

Southron, _f.n._, 'sʌðrən, súthrŏn

South Ronaldsay _Orkney_, 'saʊθ 'rɒnldseɪ, sówth rónnld-say; 'saʊθ 'rɒnldʃeɪ, sówth rónnld-shay

Southrop _Glos._, 'sʌðərəp, súthĕrŏp

South Shields _Tyne & Wear_, 'saʊθ 'ʃildz, sówth sheéldz

South Walsham _Norfolk_, 'saʊθ 'wɒlʃəm, sówth wáwl-shăm

Southwark, _f.n._, 'sʌðərk, súthărk

Southwark _London_, 'sʌðərk, súthărk. _Appropriate also for ~ Cathedral._

Southwell,*f.n.*, 'sʌðl, súthl; 'saʊθwəl, sówthwĕl. *The first is appropriate for Viscount* ~.
Southwell *Dorset*, 'sʌðl, súthl
Southwell *Notts.*, 'sʌðl, súthl; 'saʊθwəl, sówthwĕl. *Hence also for the Lord Bishop of* ~.
Southwick *Hants*, 'sʌðɪk, súthick; 'saʊθwɪk, sówthwick
Southwick *Northants.*, 'sʌðɪk, súthick
Southwick *W. Sussex*, 'saʊθwɪk, sówthwick
Southwold *Suffolk*, 'saʊθwoʊld, sówth-wōld
Soutra *Lothian*, 'sutrə, sóotră
Souttar,*f.n.*, 'sutər, sóotăr
Soward,*f.n.*, 'saʊərd, sówărd
Sowden,*f.n.*, 'saʊdən, sődĕn
Sowe, River, *Coventry*, saʊ, sow
Sowels,*f.n.*, 'saʊəlz, ső-ĕlz
Sowerbucks,*f.n.*, 'saʊərbʌks, ső-ĕrbucks
Sowerbutts,*f.n.*, 'saʊərbʌts, sówĕrbutts
Sowerby,*f.n.*, 'saʊərbɪ, ső-ĕrbi; 'saʊərbɪ, sówĕrbi
Sowerby *N. Yorks.*, 'saʊərbɪ, sówĕrbi
Sowerby Bridge *W. Yorks.*, 'saʊərbɪ 'brɪdʒ, ső-ĕrbi bríj; 'saʊərbɪ 'brɪdʒ, sówĕrbi bríj
Sowerby parliamentary division *W. Yorks.*, 'saʊərbɪ, ső-ĕrbi; 'saʊərbɪ, sówĕrbi
Sowle,*f.n.*, saʊl, sōl
Sowler,*f.n.*, 'saʊlər, sówlĕr
Sowood,*f.n.*, 'saʊwʊd, sów-wŏod
Sowrey,*f.n.*, 'saʊərɪ, sówri
Sowry,*f.n.*, 'saʊərɪ, sówri
Sowton *Devon*, 'saʊtən, sówtŏn
Spadeadam Waste *Cumbria*, speɪd'ædəm, spaydáddăm
Spalding *Lincs.*, 'spɔldɪŋ, spáwlding
Spaldwick *Cambs.*, 'spɔldwɪk, spáwldwick
Spalford *Notts.*, 'spɔlfərd, spáwl-fŏrd; 'spɒlfərd, spólfŏrd
Spamount *Co. Tyrone*, 'spamaʊnt, spaámownt
Spanier,*f.n.*, 'spænjeɪ, spán-yay
Spanoghe,*f.n.*, 'spænoʊg, spán-nōg
Spanswick,*f.n.*, 'spænzwɪk, spánz-wick
Sparey,*f.n.*, 'spɛərɪ, spáiri
Sparham,*f.n.*, 'sparəm, spa-áräm
Sparham *Norfolk*, 'spærəm, spárräm
Spark,*f.n.*, spark, spaark
Sparrar,*f.n.*, 'spɛərər, spárrăr
Sparsholt *Hants*, 'sparʃoʊlt, spaár-shōlt

Spaull,*f.n.*, spɔl, spawl
Speaight,*f.n.*, speɪt, spayt
Spean, River, *H'land*, 'spiən, speé-ăn
Spean Bridge *H'land*, 'spiən 'brɪdʒ, speé-ăn bríj
Spearing,*f.n.*, 'spɪərɪŋ, speéring
Spearman,*f.n.*, 'spɪərmən, speér-măn
Spears,*f.n.*, spɪərz, speerz
Speight,*f.n.*, speɪt, spayt
Speir,*f.n.*, spɪər, speer
Speirs,*f.n.*, spɪərz, speerz
Speke *Merseyside*, spik, speek
Spence,*f.n.*, spens, spenss
Spenceley,*f.n.*, 'spenslɪ, spénssli
Spencer,*f.n.*, 'spensər, spénssĕr. *Appropriate also for Earl* ~.
Spender,*f.n.*, 'spendər, spéndĕr
Spens,*f.n.*, spenz, spenz. *Appropriate also for Baron* ~.
Spenser,*f.n.*, 'spensər, spénssĕr
Sperrin Mountains *Co. Derry–Co. Tyrone*, 'sperɪn, spérrin
Spetisbury *Dorset*, 'spetsbərɪ, spétsbúri
Spey, Loch *and* River, *H'land*, speɪ, spay
Speybridge *H'land*, 'speɪ'brɪdʒ, spáy-brij
Speyer,*f.n.*, spɛər, spair
Speymouth *Grampian*, 'speɪmaʊθ, spáymowth
Spice,*f.n.*, spaɪs, spīss
Spicer,*f.n.*, 'spaɪsər, spíssĕr
Spiegl,*f.n.*, 'spigl, speégl
Spier,*f.n.*, spɪər, speer
Spiers,*f.n.*, spaɪərz, spīrz
Spillane,*f.n.*, spɪ'leɪn, spilláyn
Spiller,*f.n.*, 'spɪlər, spíllĕr
Spilsbury,*f.n.*, 'spɪlzbərɪ, spíllz-búri
Spiridion,*f.n.*, spɪ'rɪdɪən, spiríddi-ŏn
Spiritus,*f.n.*, 'spɪrɪtəs, spírrĭtüss
Spitalfields *London*, 'spɪtlfɪldz, spíttlfeeldz
Spital Tongues *Tyne & Wear*, 'spɪtl 'taŋz, spíttl túngz
Spithead *Portsmouth Harbour*, 'spɪt'hed, spít-héd
Spittal,*f.n.*, 'spɪtl, spíttl
Spittal of Glenshee *Tayside*, 'spɪtl əv glen'ʃi, spíttl ŏv glen-shée
Spivey,*f.n.*, 'spaɪvɪ, spívi
Splott *Cardiff*, 'splɒt, splótt
Spofforth,*f.n.*, 'spɒfərθ, spófförth
Spofforth *N. Yorks.*, 'spɒfərθ, spófförth
Spon,*f.n.*, spɒn, sponn
Spondon *Derby.*, 'spɒndən, spón-dŏn
Spooner,*f.n.*, 'spunər, spóonĕr

Sporle *Norfolk*, spɔrl, sporl
Spottiswoode, *f.n.*, 'spɒtɪswʊd, spóttiswood; 'spɒtswʊd, spótswood. *The first is appropriate for the publishers Eyre and* ~.
Spouse, *f.n.*, spaʊz, spowz
Sprague, *f.n.*, spreɪg, sprayg
Spread, *f.n.*, spred, spred
Spreadborough, *f.n.*, 'spredbərə, sprédbŭră
Spriggs, *f.n.*, sprɪgz, spriggz
Springall, *f.n.*, 'sprɪŋɒl, spríng-awl
Springburn *S'clyde*, 'sprɪŋbərn, springburn
Springett, *f.n.*, 'sprɪŋɪt, spríng-ĕt
Springfield *Co. Antrim*, 'sprɪŋfiːld, springfeeld
Sproson, *f.n.*, 'sproʊsən, sprósson
Sproughton *Suffolk*, 'sprɔːtən, spráwtŏn
Sproul-Cran, *f.n.*, 'spraʊl 'kræn, sprówl kránn
Sproule, *f.n.*, sproʊl, spról; sprul, sprool
Sprouston *Borders*, 'spraʊstən, sprówsstŏn
Sprowston *Norfolk*, 'sproʊstən, sprósstŏn
Sproxton, *f.n.*, 'sprɒkstən, spróckstŏn
Spungin, *f.n.*, 'spʌŋgɪn, spúng-gin
Spurling, *f.n.*, 'spɜːlɪŋ, spúrling
Spurrell, *f.n.*, 'spʌrəl, spúrrĕl
Spurrier, *f.n.*, 'spʌrɪər, spúrri-ĕr
Squier, *f.n.*, 'skwaɪər, skwīr
Squire, *f.n.*, 'skwaɪər, skwīr
Squires, *f.n.*, 'skwaɪərz, skwīrz
Stacey, *f.n.*, 'steɪsɪ, stáyssi
Stadlen, *f.n.*, 'stædlən, stádlĕn
Staffa *S'clyde*, 'stæfə, stáffă
Stafford *Staffs.*, 'stæfərd, stáfförd
Stagg, *f.n.*, stæg, stag
Staiman, *f.n.*, 'steɪmən, stáymăn
Stainby *Lincs.*, 'steɪnbɪ, stáynbi
Stainer, *f.n.*, 'steɪnər, stáynĕr
Staines *Surrey*, steɪnz, staynz
Stainthorpe, *f.n.*, 'steɪnθɔrp, stáyn-thorp
Staithes *N. Yorks.*, steɪðz, stay<u>th</u>z
Stakehill *Gtr. M'chester*, 'steɪk-'hɪl, stáyk-hill
Stalbridge *Dorset*, 'stɔlbrɪdʒ, stáwlbrij
Stalham *Norfolk*, 'stæləm, stálăm
Stalisfield *Kent*, 'stælɪsfɪld, stálissfeeld
Stalker, *f.n.*, 'stɔkər, stáwkĕr; 'stælkər, stál-kĕr
Stallard, *f.n.*, 'stælərd, stálaard
Stallingborough *Humberside*, 'stalɪŋbərə, staálingbŭră
Stallworthy, *f.n.*, 'stɔlwɜrðɪ, stáwlwur<u>th</u>i

Stallybrass, *f.n.*, 'stælɪbrɑs, stáli-braass
Stalman, *f.n.*, 'stælmən, stálmăn
Stalybridge *Gtr. M'chester*, 'steɪlɪbrɪdʒ, stáylibrij
Stamfordham *Northd.*, 'stæmfərd-əm, stámfördăm; 'stænərtən, stánnĕrtŏn
Stamp, *f.n.*, stæmp, stamp
Stancliffe, *f.n.*, 'stænklɪf, stán--kliff
Standaloft, *f.n.*, 'stændəlɒft, stándăloft
Standedge *W. Yorks.*, 'stæned3, stánnej
Standeven, *f.n.*, 'stændivən, stándeevĕn
Standing, *f.n.*, 'stændɪŋ, stánding
Stanford, *f.n.*, 'stænfərd, stánförd
Stanford-le-Hope *Essex*, 'stæn-fərdlɪ'hoʊp, stánfördli-hóp
Stangar, *f.n.*, 'stæŋər, stáng-ăr
Stangboom, *f.n.*, 'stæŋbum, stángboom
Stangroom, *f.n.*, 'stæŋrum, stáng--rōōm; stæn'grum, stan-gróom
Stanhill *Lancs.*, 'stænhɪl, stánhil
Stanhoe *Norfolk*, 'stænoʊ, stánnō
Stanhope, *f.n.*, 'stænəp, stánnŏp. *Appropriate also for the Earldom of* ~.
Stanhope *Durham*, 'stænəp, stánnŏp
Stanier, *f.n.*, 'stænɪər, stánni-ĕr
Staniland, *f.n.*, 'stænɪlənd, stánni-lănd
Stanion *Northants.*, 'stænjən, stán-yŏn
Stanks *W. Yorks.*, stæŋks, stanks
Stanley, *C.n. and f.n.*, 'stænlɪ, stánli
Stanley of Alderley, Baron, 'stænlɪ əv 'ɔldərlɪ, stánli ŏv áwldĕrli
Stannard, *f.n.*, 'stænɑrd, stán-naard; 'stænərd, stánnărd
Stansfield, *f.n.*, 'stænzfɪld, stánzfeeld
Stansgate, Viscountcy of, 'stænz-geɪt, stánzgayt
Stansted Airport *Essex*, 'stæn-sted, stánssted
Stansted Mountfitchet *Essex*, 'stænsted maʊnt'fɪtʃɪt, stánssted mowntfítchĕt
Stanton, *f.n.*, 'stæntən, stántŏn; 'stɑntən, staántŏn
Stanton *Glos.*, 'stɑntən, staántŏn
Stanton-by-Bridge *Derby.*, 'stæn-tən baɪ 'brɪdʒ, stántŏn bī bríj
Stanwick, *f.n.*, 'stænɪk, stánnick
Stanwick *Northants.*, 'stænɪk, stánnick

Stanwick St. John *N. Yorks.*, 'stænɪk snt 'dʒɒn, stánnick sĭnt jón

Stanwix *Cumbria*, 'stænɪks, stánnicks

Stapleford *Cambs., Herts., Notts.*, 'steɪplfərd, stáyplfŏrd

Stapleford *Leics.*, 'stæplfərd, stápplfŏrd

Stapley, *f.n.*, 'stæplɪ, stápli; 'steɪplɪ, stáypli

Staploe *Beds.*, 'steɪploʊ, stáyp-lō

Stareton *Warwicks.*, 'stɑrtən, staártŏn

Stark, *f.n.*, stɑrk, staark

Starkey, *f.n.*, 'stɑrkɪ, staárki

Starlaw *Lothian*, 'stɑr'lɔ, staár-láw

Startin, *f.n.*, 'stɑrtɪn, staártin

Statham, *f.n.*, 'steɪθəm, stáythăm; 'steɪðəm, stáythăm

Stathe *Somerset*, steɪð, stay<u>th</u>

Stathern *Leics.*, 'stæθərn, stát-hern

Staton, *f.n.*, 'steɪtən, stáytŏn

Staub, *f.n.*, stɒb, stawb

Staudinger, *f.n.*, 'staʊdɪŋər, stówding-ĕr

Staughton, Great, *Cambs.*, 'stɒtən, stáwtŏn

Staughton, Little, *Beds.*, 'stɒtən, stáwtŏn

Staughton Green *Cambs.*, 'stɒtən 'grin, stáwtŏn gréen

Staughton Highway *Cambs.*, 'stɒtən 'haɪweɪ, stáwtŏn hí-way

Staughton Moor *Cambs.*, 'stɒtən 'mʊər, stáwtŏn mŏŏr

Staunton, *f.n.*, 'stɒntən, stáwntŏn

Stave, *f.n.*, steɪv, stayv

Staveacre, *f.n.*, 'steɪveɪkər, stáyvaykĕr

Staveley *Cumbria, Derby., N. Yorks.*, 'steɪvlɪ, stáyvli. *Appropriate for both places of the name in Cumbria.*

Staverton *Glos., Northants.*, 'stævərtən, stávvĕrtŏn

Stavordale Priory *Somerset*, 'stævərdeɪl, stávvŏrdayl

Staward *Northd.*, 'stɑwərd, staáwård

Stawell *Somerset*, stɔl, stawl

Staxigoe *H'land*, 'stæksɪgjoʊ, stácksig-yō

Stayt, *f.n.*, steɪt, stayt

Staythorpe *Notts.*, 'steɪθɔrp, stáy-thorp

Stead, *f.n.*, sted, sted; stɪd, steed

Steadman, *f.n.*, 'stedmən, stédmăn

Steart *Somerset*, 'stɪərt, stée-ărt

Stechford *W. Midlands*, 'stetʃfərd, stétchfŏrd

Steck, *f.n.*, stek, steck

Steddall, *f.n.*, 'stedɔl, stéddawl

Stedeford, *f.n.*, 'stedɪfərd, stéddĕford

Stedman, *f.n.*, 'stedmən, stédmän

Steed, *f.n.*, stid, steed

Steegman, *f.n.*, 'stidʒmən, stéejmän

Steele, *f.n.*, stil, steel

Steen, *f.n.*, stin, steen

Steep Holme Island *Avon*, 'stip hoʊm, stéep hōm

Steer, *f.n.*, stɪər, steer

Stein, *f.n.*, staɪn, stīn; stin, steen

Steinberg, *f.n.*, 'staɪnbɜrg, stín-berg

Steine, The Old, *Brighton*, stin, steen

Steinitz, *f.n.*, 'staɪnɪts, stínits

Steley, *f.n.*, 'stelɪ, stélli

Stelling Minnis *Kent*, 'stelɪŋ 'mɪnɪz, stélling mínniz

Stenalees *Cornwall*, ˌstenə'liz, stennăléez

Stenhousemuir *Central*, 'stenhaʊs'mjʊər, sténhowss-myóŏr

Stenigot *Lincs.*, 'stenɪgɒt, sténnigot

Stenning, *f.n.*, 'stenɪŋ, sténning

Stentiford, *f.n.*, 'stentɪfərd, sténtifŏrd

Stepaside *Dyfed, Powys*, ˌstepə'saɪd, steppăssíd; 'stepəsaɪd, stéppăssid

Stephen, *C.n.*, 'stivən, stéevĕn

Stephens, *f.n.*, 'stivənz, stéevĕnz

Stephenson, *f.n.*, 'stivənsən, stéevĕnssŏn

Steptoe, *f.n.*, 'steptoʊ, stéptō

Sterke, *f.n.*, stɑrk, staark

Sterling, *f.n.*, 'stɜrlɪŋ, stérling

Stern, *f.n.*, stɜrn, stern

Sterndale-Bennett, *f.n.*, 'stɜrndeɪl 'benɪt, stérndayl bénnĕt. *Appropriate also for the composer Sir William Sterndale Bennett (1816–75).*

Sterner, *f.n.*, 'stɜrnər, stérnĕr

Sternfeld, *f.n.*, 'stɜrnfeld, stérnfeld

Steuart, *f.n.*, 'stjʊərt, stéw-ärt; 'stjʊərt, styóŏ-ärt

Stevas, *f.n.*, 'stivæs, stéevass; 'stivəs, stéevăss

Stevens, *f.n.*, 'stivənz, stéevĕnz

Stevenson, *f.n.*, 'stivənsən, stéevĕnssŏn

Stevenston *S'clyde*, 'stivənztən, stéevĕnztŏn

Steventon *Berks., Hants.*, 'stivəntən, stéevĕntŏn

Stevington *Beds.*, 'stevɪŋtən, stévvingtŏn

Steward, *f.n.*, 'stjʊərd, stéw-ärd; 'stjʊərd, styóŏ-ärd

Stewart, *f.n.*, 'stjuərt, stéw-ărt;
'stjuərt, styōō-ärt
Steyn, *f.n.*, stain, stīn
Steyne *I. of Wight*, stin, steen
Steyne, The, *Worthing (W. Sussex)* ðə 'stin, <u>th</u>ē steen
Steyning *W. Sussex*, 'steniŋ, sténning
Steynor, *f.n.*, 'stinər, steenŏr
Stickells, *f.n.*, 'stiklz, stícklz
Sticklepath *Devon*, 'stiklpɑθ, stícklpaath
Stiebel, *f.n.*, 'stibl, steébl
Stiffkey *Norfolk*, 'stifki, stiffki; 'stuki, stóoki; 'stjuki, stéwki. *The two latter are rarely heard today.*
Stillwell, *f.n.*, 'stilwel, stillwel
Stilton *Cambs.*, 'stiltən, stíltŏn
Stinchar, River, *S'clyde*, 'stinʃər, stínshăr
Stiperstones *Salop*, 'staipərstoonz, stípərsstŏnz
Stirling, *f.n.*, 'stɜrliŋ, stírling
Stirling *Central, Grampian*, 'stɜrliŋ, stírling
Stirtloe *Cambs.*, 'stɜrtloo, stírt-lō
Stirton, *f.n.*, 'stɜrtən, stírtŏn
Stisted *Essex*, 'staistɪd, stí-sted
Stithians *Cornwall*, 'stiðiənz, stí<u>th</u>i-ănz
Stiven, *f.n.*, 'stivən, stívvĕn
Stivichall, *also spelt* **Styvechale**, *W. Midlands*, 'staitʃl, stítchl; 'staitʃəl, stítchawl
Stobart, *f.n.*, 'stoobɑrt, stóbaart
Stobo *Borders*, 'stooboo, stóbō
Stoborough *Dorset*, 'stoobərə, stóbŭră
Stock, *f.n.*, stɒk, stock
Stocking, *f.n.*, 'stɒkiŋ, stócking
Stockins, *f.n.*, 'stɒkinz, stóckinz
Stockleigh Pomeroy *Devon*, 'stɒkli 'pɒmərɔi, stóckli pómměroy
Stockley, *f.n.*, 'stɒkli, stóckli
Stockport *Ches.*, 'stɒkpɔrt, stóckport
Stocks, *f.n.*, stɒks, stocks
Stocksbridge *S. Yorks.*, 'stɒksbridʒ, stócks-brij
Stockton-on-Tees *Durham*, 'stɒktən ɒn 'tiz, stócktŏn-on-teéz
Stockwell, *f.n.*, 'stɒkwel, stóckwell; 'stɒkwəl, stóckwĕl
Stodart, *f.n.*, 'stɒdərt, stóddărt; 'stoodɑrt, stódaart; stoo'dɑrt, stōdáart
Stoddart, *f.n.*, 'stɒdərt, stóddărt; 'stɒdɑrt, stóddaart
Stody *Norfolk*, 'stʌdi, stúddi
Stoer, *f.n.*, stɔr, stor
Stoer *H'land*, 'stooər, stó-ĕr

Stoessiger, *f.n.*, 'stesidʒər, stéssijĕr
Stogdon, *f.n.*, 'stɒgdən, stógdŏn
Stogumber *Somerset*, stoo'gambər, stōgúmbĕr; 'stɒgəmbər, stóggŭmbĕr
Stogursey *Somerset*, stoo'gɜrzi, stōgúrzi
Stohl, *f.n.*, stool, stōl
Stoic, *one educated at Stowe School*, 'stooik, stó-ick
Stoke Bruern *Northants.*, 'stook 'bruərn, stŏk broó-ĕrn
Stoke d'Abernon *Surrey*, 'stook 'dæbərnən, stŏk dábbĕrnŏn
Stoke Damerel *Devon*, 'stook 'dæmərəl, stŏk dámmĕrĕl
Stoke Gifford *Avon*, 'stook 'gifərd, stŏk gíffŏrd
Stoke-in-Teignhead, *also spelt* **Stokeinteignhead,** *Devon*, 'stook in 'tinhed, stŏk in teénhed
Stoke Mandeville *Bucks.*, 'stook 'mændivil, stŏk mándĕvil
Stokenham *Devon*, ,stookən'hæm, stŏkĕnhám; 'stookənəm, stókĕnăm
Stoke-on-Trent *Staffs.*, 'stook ɒn 'trent, stŏk on trént
Stoke Pero *Somerset*, 'stook 'piəroo, stŏk peérō
Stoker, *f.n.*, 'stookər, stókĕr
Stokes, *f.n.*, stooks, stōks
Stokoe, *f.n.*, 'stookoo, stókō
Stoll, *f.n.*, stɒl, stoll
Stoller, *f.n.*, 'stɒlər, stóllĕr
Stollery, *f.n.*, 'stɒləri, stólléri
Stolz, *f.n.*, stɒlts, stollts
Stonar *Kent*, 'stɒnər, stónnăr
Stonards Brow *Surrey*, 'stɒnərdz 'brɑo, stónnărdz brów
Stonborough, *f.n.*, 'stoonbərə, stónbŭră
Stone, *f.n.*, stoon, stōn
Stonea *Cambs.*, 'stooni, stóni
Ston Easton *Somerset*, stɒn 'istən, ston eésstŏn
Stonebridge, *f.n.*, 'stoonbridʒ, stónbrij
Stonebyres *S'clyde*, 'stoonbaiərz, stónbīrz
Stoneclough *Gtr. M'chester*, 'stoonklʌf, stónkluff
Stonedge *Derby.*, 'stoonedʒ, stónej; 'stænedʒ, stánnej
Stonehaven *Grampian*, stoon-'heivn, stōn-háyvĕn; stein'hai, stayn-hí. *The first is appropriate also for Viscount* ~.
Stonehenge *Wilts.*, 'stoon'hendʒ, stón-hénj
Stoneleigh *Surrey*, 'stoon'li, stón-leé

Stoneleigh *Warwicks.*, 'stoʊnlɪ, stōnli. *Appropriate also for ~ Abbey.*

Stonely *Cambs.*, 'stoʊnlɪ, stōnli

Stoner, *f.n.*, 'stoʊnər, stōnĕr

Stoney, *f.n.*, 'stoʊnɪ, stōni

Stoney Houghton, *also spelt* **Stony Houghton,** *Derby.*, 'stoʊnɪ 'hʌftən, stōni húftŏn

Stonham *Suffolk*, 'stɒnəm, stónnăm

Stonham Aspal *Suffolk*, 'stɒnəm 'æspəl, stónnăm ásspawl

Stonier, *f.n.*, 'stoʊnɪər, stōni-ĕr

Stonnall *Staffs.*, 'stɒnl, stónnl

Stonor, *f.n.*, 'stoʊnər, stōnor; 'stɒnər, stónnŏr. *The first is appropriate for the family name of Baron Camoys.*

Stonor *Oxon.*, 'stoʊnər, stōnŏr

Stooke, *f.n.*, stʊk, stŏŏk

Stopham *W. Sussex*, 'stɒpəm, stóppăm

Stopher, *f.n.*, 'stoʊfər, stōfĕr

Stoppard, *f.n.*, 'stɒpɑrd, stóppaard

Storace, *f.n.*, 'stɒrɪs, stórrăss

Stordy, *f.n.*, 'stɔrdɪ, stórdi

Storey, *f.n.*, 'stɔrɪ, stáwri

Storm, *f.n.*, stɔrm, storm

Stormont, *f.n.*, 'stɔrmənt, stórmŏnt

Stormont *Tayside*, 'stɔrmənt, stórmŏnt. *Appropriate also for Viscount ~.*

Stormont Castle *Co. Down*, 'stɔrmənt, stórmŏnt

Stormontfield *Tayside*, 'stɔrməntfild, stórmŏntfeeld

Stormonth, *f.n.*, 'stɔrmənt, stórmŏnt

Stornoway *W. Isles*, 'stɔrnəweɪ, stórnŏ-way

Storr, *f.n.*, stɔr, stor

Storr, The, *Skye*, stɔr, stor

Storrier, *f.n.*, 'stɒrɪər, stórri-ĕr

Storrs, *f.n.*, stɔrz, storz

Stothard, *f.n.*, 'stɒðard, stóthaard; 'stɒðərd, stóthărd

Stothert, *f.n.*, 'stɒðərt, stóthĕrt

Stott, *f.n.*, stɒt, stott

Stottesdon *Salop*, 'stɒtɪzdən, stóttĕzdŏn

Stoughton, *f.n.*, 'stɒtən, stáwtŏn; 'staʊtən, stówtŏn; 'stoʊtən, stōtŏn. *The third is appropriate for the publisher Hodder & ~.*

Stoughton *Leics., W. Sussex*, 'stoʊtən, stōtŏn

Stoughton *Surrey*, 'staʊtən, stówtŏn. *Appropriate also for ~ Barracks.*

Stoughton, *Middle and West, Somerset*, 'stɒtən, stáwtŏn

Stoughton Cross *Somerset*, 'stɒtən 'krɒs, stáwtŏn króss

Stoulton *H. & W.*, 'stoʊltən, stōltŏn

Stour, *Rivers, H. & W., Oxon.-Warwicks.*, 'staʊər, stowr; 'stoʊər, stó-ĕr

Stour, *River, Kent*, stʊər, stŏŏr; 'staʊər, stowr. *Although the first is much more usual for the name of the river, see treatment of neighbouring* **Stourmouth.**

Stour, *River, Suffolk–Essex*, stʊər, stŏŏr. *This is the river associated with Constable.*

Stourbridge *W. Midlands*, 'staʊərbrɪdʒ, stówrbrij; 'stoʊərbrɪdʒ, stó-ĕrbrij

Stourbridge Common *Cambs.*, 'staʊərbrɪdʒ 'kɒmən, stówrbrij kómmŏn

Stourhead House *Wilts.*, 'stɔrhed, stór-hed; 'staʊərhed, stówr-hed

Stourmouth *Kent*, 'staʊərmaʊθ, stówrmowth; 'stʊərmaʊθ, stŏŏrmowth. *Although the first of these is more usual locally for the place name, it is interesting that the neighbouring River Stour is more often pronounced* stʊər, stŏŏr.

Stourport-on-Severn *H. & W.*, 'staʊərpɔrt ɒn 'sevərn, stówr-port on sévvĕrn; 'stʊərpɔrt ɒn 'sevərn, stŏŏrport on sévvĕrn

Stour Provost *Dorset*, 'staʊər 'prɒvəst, stówr próvvŏst

Stour Row *see* **Stower Row**

Stourton, *f.n.*, 'stɜrtən, stúrtŏn. *See also Baron* **Mowbray, Segrave and ~.**

Stourton *H. & W.*, 'stɔrtən, stórtŏn

Stourton *Wilts.*, 'stɜrtən, stúrtŏn; 'stɔrtən, stórtŏn

Stourton Caundle *Dorset*, 'stɔrtən 'kɒndl, stórtŏn káwndl; 'stɜrtən 'kɒndl, stúrtŏn káwndl

Stout, *f.n.*, staʊt, stowt

Stoute, *f.n.*, staʊt, stowt

Stovell, *f.n.*, stə'vel, stŏvéll; stoʊ-'vel, stōvéll; 'stoʊvl, stóvl

Stoven *Suffolk*, 'stʌvən, stúvvĕn

Stovold, *f.n.*, 'stoʊvɒld, stóvold; 'stoʊvoʊld, stóvvōld

Stow, *f.n.*, stoʊ, stō

Stow Bedon *Norfolk*, stoʊ 'bidən, stō béedŏn

Stowell, *f.n.*, 'stoʊəl, stó-ĕl

Stowell *Somerset*, 'stoʊəl, stó-ĕl; stoʊl, stōl

Stower Row, *also spelt* **Stour Row,** *Dorset*, 'staʊər 'roʊ, stówr rō

Stowey *Avon*, 'stoʊɪ, stó-i

Stowford *Devon*, 'stoʊfərd, stő-fŏrd

Stow Longa *Cambs.*, 'stoʊ 'lɒŋgə, stő lóng-gă

Stow Maries *Essex*, stoʊ 'mɑrɪz, stő maáriz

Stowmarket *Suffolk*, 'stoʊmɑrkɪt, stőmaarkĕt

Stow-on-the-Wold *Glos.*, 'stoʊ ɒn ðə 'woʊld, stő on <u>th</u>ē wőld

Stowting *Kent*, 'staʊtɪŋ, stówting

Strabane *Co. Tyrone*, strə'bæn, străbán. *Appropriate also for Viscount* ~.

Strabolgi, Baron, strə'boʊgɪ, străbőgi

Stracathro *Tayside*, strə'kæθroʊ, străkáthrő

Strachan, *f.n.*, 'stræxən, strá<u>ch</u>ăn; strɒn, strawn

Strachan *Grampian*, strɒn, strawn

Strachey, *f.n.*, 'streɪtʃɪ, stráytchi; 'stræxɪ, strá<u>ch</u>i

Strachie, *f.n.*, 'streɪtʃɪ, stráytchi. *Appropriate also for the Barony of* ~.

Strachur *S'clyde*, strə'xər, strá<u>ch</u>úr

Stradbroke *Suffolk*, 'strædbroʊk, strádbrŏŏk. *Appropriate also for the Earl of* ~.

Stradey Park rugby ground *Llanelli (Dyfed)*, 'strædɪ 'pɑrk, stráddi paárk

Stradishall *Suffolk*, 'strædɪʃɒl, stráddi-shawl

Stradling, *f.n.*, 'strædlɪŋ, strádling

Stradwick, *f.n.*, 'strædwɪk, strádwick

Strahan, *f.n.*, strɒn, strawn

Straiton *S'clyde*, 'streɪtən, stráytŏn

Straker, *f.n.*, 'streɪkər, stráykĕr

Strakosch, *f.n.*, 'strækɒʃ, stráckosh

Straloch *Tayside*, strə'lɒx, strálo<u>ch</u>

Strange, *f.n.*, streɪndʒ, straynj

Strange of Knokin, Baron, 'streɪndʒ əv 'nɒkɪn, stráynj ŏv nóckin

Stranger, *f.n.*, 'streɪndʒər, stráynjĕr

Strangeways *Gtr. M'chester*, 'streɪndʒweɪz, stráynjwayz

Strangford *H. & W.*, 'stræŋfərd, stráng-fŏrd

Strangways, *f.n.*, 'stræŋweɪz, stráng-wayz

Stranmillis *Co. Antrim*, stræn-'mɪlɪs, stranmílliss

Stranocum *Co. Antrim*, stræn'oʊkəm, stranőkŭm

Stranraer, *f.n.*, stræn'rɑr, stran-raár

Stranraer *D. & G.*, strən'rɑr, străn-raár

Strata Florida *Dyfed*, 'strætə 'flɒrɪdə, stráttá flórridă. *The Welsh form is* **Ystrad Fflur**, *q.v.*

Stratfieldsaye House *Hants*, 'strætfɪldseɪ, strátfeeldssay

Stratford-atte-Bowe *London*, 'strætfərd ætɪ 'boʊ, strátfŏrd atti bő; 'strætfərd ætɪ 'boʊɪ, strátfŏrd atti bő-i; 'strætfərd ætə 'boʊə, strátfŏrd attĕ bő-ĕ. *The first is a modern pronunciation of the historic name. The others are perhaps more familiar to students of Chaucer.*

Stratford-upon-Avon *Warwicks.*, 'strætfərd əpɒn 'eɪvən, strátfŏrd ŭpon áyvŏn

Strath, *f.n.*, strɑθ, straath

Strathalmond, Baron, stræθ-'amənd, strath-aámond

Strathardle *Tayside*, stræθ'ɑrdl, strathaárdl

Strathaven *S'clyde*, 'streɪvən, stráyvĕn

Strathblane *Central*, stræθ'bleɪn, strathbláyn

Strathclyde *admin. region of Scotland*, stræθ'klaɪd, strath-klíd. *Appropriate also for Baron* ~ *and for the University of* ~.

Strathcona, Baron, stræθ'koʊnə, strathkőnă

Strathdee, *f.n.*, stræθ'di, strathdeé

Strathearn *Tayside*, stræθ'ɜrn, strathérn

Stratheden, Baron, stræθ'idən, stratheédĕn

Stratherrick *H'land*, stræθ'erɪk, stratherríck

Strathfillan *Central*, stræθ'fɪlən, strathfíllăn

Strathkinness *Fife*, stræθ'kɪnɪs, strathkínnĕss

Strathleven *S'clyde*, stræθ'livən, strathleévĕn

Strathmiglo *Fife*, stræθ'mɪgloʊ, strathmíglō

Strathmore *H'land–Central*, stræθ'mɔr, strathmór

Strathmore and Kinghorne, Earl of, stræθ'mɔr ənd 'kɪŋhɔrn, strathmór ănd kíng-horn

Strathnaver *H'land*, stræθ'neɪvər, strathnáyvĕr

Strathpeffer *H'land*, stræθ'pefər, strathpéffĕr

The form stræθ-, strath-, *used to indicate the unstressed prefix* **Strath**-, *is that used in careful speech. Its occurrence as* strəθ-, străth- *is equally frequent and acceptable.*

Strathspey *H'land–Grampian*, stræθ'speɪ, strath-spáy. *Appropriate also for Baron* ~.
Strathtay *Tayside*, stræθ'teɪ, strathtáy
Straton, *f.n.*, 'strætən, stráttŏn
Straughan, *f.n.*, strɔn, strawn
Strauli, *f.n.*, 'strɔlɪ, stráwli
Strauss, *f.n.*, straʊs, strowss
Strauther, *f.n.*, 'strɔðər, stráwthĕr
Streat, *f.n.*, strit, street
Streatfeild, *f.n.*, 'stretfild, strétfeeld
Streatham *London*, 'stretəm, stréttăm
Streather, *f.n.*, 'streðər, stréthĕr
Streatlam *Durham*, 'stritləm, streétlăm
Streatley *Beds.*, 'stretlɪ, stréttli
Streatley *Berks.*, 'stritlɪ, streétli
Stredwick, *f.n.*, 'stredwɪk, strédwick
Street, *f.n.*, strit, street
Streethay *Staffs.*, 'strithei, streét-hay
Strensall *N. Yorks.*, 'strensl, strénssl
Strethall *Essex*, 'strethɔl, stréthawl
Stretham *Cambs.*, 'stretəm, stréttăm
Stretton Sugwas *H. & W.*, 'stretən 'sʌgəs, strét' tŏn súggăss
Strevens, *f.n.*, 'strevənz, strévvĕnz
Strichen *Grampian*, 'strɪxən, stríchĕn
Stride, *f.n.*, straɪd, strīd
Striguil *Castle Gwent*, 'strɪgɪl, stríggil
Stringer, *f.n.*, 'strɪŋər, stríng-ĕr
Striven, Loch, *S'clyde*, 'strɪvən, strívvĕn
Strode, *f.n.*, stroʊd, strōd
Strollamus *H'land*, 'strɒləməs, stróllămŭss
Stroma *H'land*, 'stroʊmə, strṓmă
Stromeferry *H'land*, stroʊm'ferɪ, strōm-férri
Stromness *Orkney*, 'strɒmnes, strómness; 'strʌmnes, strúmness
Stronachlachar *Central*, 'strɒnəx-'læxər, strónnăch-láchăr
Strong, *f.n.*, strɒŋ, strong
Stronge, *f.n.*, strɒŋ, strong
Strongitharm, *f.n.*, 'strɒŋɪθɑrm, stróng-ithaarm
Stronsay *Orkney*, 'strɒnzeɪ, strónzay
Strontian *H'land*, strɒn'tiən, strontee-ăn
Strood *Kent*, strud, strood
Stross, *f.n.*, strɒs, stross
Strother, *f.n.*, 'strʌðər, strúthĕr

Stroud, *f.n.*, straʊd, strowd
Stroud *Glos., Hants*, straʊd, strowd
Stroud Green *London*, 'straʊd 'grin, strówd greén
Stroudley, *f.n.*, 'straʊdlɪ, strówdli
Strouthous, *f.n.*, 'strʌðəz, strúthŏz
Strowan, *f.n.*, 'stroʊən, strṓ-ăn
Strowan *Tayside*, 'strauən, strów-ăn; 'struən, stroʻo-ăn
Stroxton *Lincs.*, 'strɒsən, stráwssŏn; 'strousən, stróssŏn
Stroyan, *f.n.*, 'strɔɪən, stróyăn
Struan *Tayside*, 'struən, stroʻo-ăn
Strube, *cartoonist*, 'strubɪ, stroʻobi
Strule, River, *Co. Tyrone*, strul, strool
Strumpshaw *Norfolk*, 'strʌmpʃə, strúmp-shă
Struve, *f.n.*, 'struvɪ, stroʻovi
Stuart, *f.n.*, 'stjuərt, stéw-ărt; 'stjuərt, styoʻo-ärt
Stuart of Findhorn, Viscount, 'stjuərt əv 'fɪndhɔrn, styoʻo-ärt ŏv fíndhorn
Stubbs, *f.n.*, stʌbz, stubbz
Stuchbury, *f.n.*, 'stʌtʃbrɪ, stútchbri
Stuchell, *f.n.*, 'stʊtʃl, stoʻotchl
Stuck, *f.n.*, stʌk, stuck
Stucke, *f.n.*, stjuk, stewk
Stucley, *f.n.*, 'stjuklɪ, stéwkli
Studd, *f.n.*, stʌd, studd
Studdal *Kent*, 'stʌdl, stúddl
Studdert, *f.n.*, 'stʌdərt, stúddĕrt
Studholme, *f.n.*, 'stʌdhoʊm, stúd-hōm
Studley *Warwicks.*, 'stʌdlɪ, stúdli
Studt, *f.n.*, stʌt, stutt
Stukeley, Great *and* Little, *Cambs.*, 'stjuklɪ, stéwkli
Stunell, *f.n.*, stə'nel, stŭnéll
Stunt, *f.n.*, stʌnt, stunt
Stuntney *Cambs.*, 'stʌntnɪ, stúnt-ni
Sturdee, *f.n.*, 'stərdɪ, stúrdi
Sturdy, *f.n.*, 'stərdɪ, stúrdi
Sturgate *Lincs.*, 'stərgeɪt, stúrgayt
Sturge, *f.n.*, 'stərdʒ, sturj
Sturley, *f.n.*, 'stərlɪ, stúrli
Sturmer, *f.n.*, 'stərmər, stúrmĕr
Sturminster Marshall *Dorset*, 'stərmɪnstər 'mɑrʃl, stúrminstĕr maárshl
Sturminster Newton *Dorset*, 'stərmɪnstər 'njutən, stúrminstĕr néwtŏn
Sturridge, *f.n.*, 'stʌrɪdʒ, stúrrij
Sturrock, *f.n.*, 'stʌrək, stúrrŏk
Sturry *Kent*, 'stʌrɪ, stúrri
Sturt, *f.n.*, stərt, sturt
Sturtevant, *f.n.*, 'stərtɪvənt, stúrtĕvănt

Sturtivant, *f.n.,* 'stɜrtɪvənt, stúrtivänt
Sturton *Humberside,* 'stɜrtən, stúrtŏn
Stuttaford, *f.n.,* 'stʌtəfərd, stúttăförd
Styal *Ches.,* 'staɪəl, stí-äl
Styche, *f.n.,* staɪtʃ, stítch
Styche Hall *Salop,* staɪtʃ, stítch
Styles, *f.n.,* staɪlz, stīlz
Styvechale *see* **Stivichall**
Suart, *f.n.,* 'sjuərt, séw-ärt
Suchet, *f.n.,* 'sujeɪ, sóoshay
Sudbourne *Suffolk,* 'sʌdbɔrn, súdborn
Sudbury, *f.n.,* 'sʌdbəri, súdbŭri
Suddaby, *f.n.,* 'sʌdəbi, súddăbi
Suddes, *f.n.,* 'sʌdɪs, súddĕss
Sudeley, Baron, 'sjudlɪ, séwdli
Sudley, Baron, 'sʌdlɪ, súdli
Suenson, *f.n.,* 'suənsən, sóo-ĕnssŏn
Sueter, *f.n.,* 'sjutər, séwtĕr; 'sutər, sóotĕr
Suffield, *f.n.,* 'sʌfild, súffeeld
Suffolk *Co. name,* 'sʌfək, súffŏk
Sugden, *f.n.,* 'sʌgdən, súgg-dĕn
Suggate, *f.n.,* 'sʌgeɪt, súggayt
Suggett, *f.n.,* 'sʌgɪt, súggĕt
Sugrew, *f.n.,* 'sugru, sóogroo
Sugrue, *f.n.,* sugru, sóogroo
Sugwas Pool *H. & W.,* 'sʌgəs 'pul, súggäss póol
Suilven *H'land,* 'sulvən, sóolvĕn
Suirdale, Viscount, 'ʃərdl, shúrdl
Suitters, *f.n.,* 'sutərz, sóotĕrz
Sulby *I. of Man,* 'sʌlbɪ, súllbi
Suleiman, *f.n.,* 'suleɪmæn, sóolayman
Sule Skerry *Orkney,* 'sul 'skerɪ, sóol skérri
Sulham *Berks.,* 'sʌləm, súllăm
Sulhamstead, *also spelt* **Sulhampstead,** *Berks.,* sʌl'hæmpstɪd, sullhámpstĕd
Sullivan, *f.n.,* 'sʌlɪvən, súllivăn
Sullom Voe *Shetland,* 'suləm 'vou, sóolŏm vṓ
Sully *S. Glam.,* 'sʌlɪ, súlli
Sulwen *Welsh C.n.,* 'silwən, séelwĕn
Sumbler, *f.n.,* 'sʌmblər, súmblĕr
Sumburgh Head *Shetland,* 'sʌmbərə, súmbŭră
Summerfield, *f.n.,* 'sʌmərfild, súmmĕrfeeld
Summers, *f.n.,* 'sʌmərz, súmmĕrz
Sumption, *f.n.,* 'sʌmpʃən, súmpshŏn
Sumsion, *f.n.,* 'sʌmʃən, súm-shŏn
Sunart, Loch, *H'land,* 'sunərt, sóonärt
Sunderland *Tyne & Wear,* 'sʌndərlənd, súndĕrländ

Sundquist, *f.n.,* 'sʌndkwɪst, súndkwist
Surbiton *London,* 'sɜrbɪtən, súrbitŏn
Surfleet, *f.n.,* 'sɜrflit, súrfleet
Surgenor, *f.n.,* 'sɜrdʒɪnɔr, súrjēnor; 'sɜrdʒɪnər, súrjēnŏr
Surguy, *f.n.,* 'sɜrgaɪ, súrgī
Surlingham *Norfolk,* 'sɜrlɪŋəm, súrling-ăm
Surplice, *f.n.,* 'sɜrplɪs, súrpliss
Surrey, *f.n.,* 'sʌrɪ, súrri
Surrey *Co. name,* 'sʌrɪ, súrri
Surridge, *f.n.,* 'sʌrɪdʒ, súrrij
Survaes, *f.n.,* 'sɜrveɪz, súrvayz
Suss, *f.n.,* sʌs, suss
Sussams, *f.n.,* 'sʌsəmz, sússämz
Susser, *f.n.,* 'sʌsər, sússĕr
Sussex, East *and* West, *Co. names,* 'sʌsɪks, sússĕks
Susskind, *f.n.,* 'suskɪnd, sóosskinnd. *Appropriate for Walter* ~ *and Peter* ~, *conductors.*
Sutcliffe, *f.n.,* 'sʌtklɪf, sútkliff
Suter, *f.n.,* 'sutər, sóotĕr
Sutherland, *f.n.,* 'sʌðərlənd, sútherländ
Sutherland *H'land,* 'sʌðərlənd, sútherländ. *Appropriate also for the Duke of* ~ *and the Countess of* ~.
Sutlieff, *f.n.,* 'sʌtlif, sútleef
Sutro, *f.n.,* 'sutrou, sóotrō
Sutter, *f.n.,* 'sʌtər, súttĕr
Suttie, *f.n.,* 'sʌtɪ, sútti
Suttle, *f.n.,* 'sʌtl, súttl
Sutton, *f.n.,* 'sʌtən, súttŏn
Sutton Coldfield *W. Midlands,* 'sʌtən 'kouldfild, súttŏn kṓldfeeld
Sutton Courtenay *Oxon.,* 'sʌtən 'kɔrtnɪ, súttŏn kórtni
Sutton Poyntz *Dorset,* 'sʌtən 'pɔɪnts, súttŏn póynts
Sutton Scotney *Hants,* 'sʌtən 'skɒtnɪ, súttŏn skótni
Sutton Veny *Wilts.,* 'sʌtən 'vɪnɪ, súttŏn véeni
Suzman, *f.n.,* 'suzmən, sóozmän
Swaby *Lincs.,* 'sweɪbɪ, swáybi
Swadlincote *Derby.,* 'swɒdlɪŋkout, swódlinkōt
Swaebe, *f.n.,* 'sweɪbɪ, swáybi
Swaffer, Hannen, *journalist ar.d dramatic critic,* 'hænən 'swɒfər, hánnĕn swóffĕr
Swaffham *Norfolk,* 'swɒfəm, swóffăm
Swaffham Bulbeck *Cambs.,* 'swɒfəm 'bulbek, swóffăm bŏŏlbeck
Swaffham Prior *Cambs.,* 'swɒfəm 'praɪər, swóffăm prí-ŏr

Swafield *Norfolk*, 'sweɪfild, swáyfeeld
Swalcliffe *Oxon.*, 'sweɪklɪf, swáykliff
Swales, *f.n.*, sweɪlz, swaylz
Swalwell *Tyne & Wear*, 'swɒlwel, swólwel
Swan, *f.n.*, swɒn, swonn
Swanage *Dorset*, 'swɒnɪdʒ, swónnij
Swanborough *E. Sussex*, 'swɒnbərə, swónnbŭră
Swanbourne *Bucks.*, 'swɒnbɔːn, swónnborn
Swanley *Kent*, 'swɒnlɪ, swónli
Swann, *f.n.*, swɒn, swonn
Swannell, *f.n.*, 'swɒnl, swónnl
Swanscombe *Kent*, 'swɒnzkəm, swónzkŏm
Swansea *W. Glam.*, 'swɒnzɪ, swónzi. *Appropriate also for Baron* ~.
Swanson, *f.n.*, 'swɒnsən, swónssŏn
Swanton Novers *Norfolk*, 'swɒntən 'nouvərz, swónntŏn nóvĕrz
Swanwick, *f.n.*, 'swɒnɪk, swónnick
Swanwick *Derby.*, 'swɒnɪk, swónnick
Swanzy, *f.n.*, 'swɒnzɪ, swónzi
Swardeston *Norfolk*, 'swɔːstən, swáwrsstŏn
Swarkestone, *also spelt* **Swarkeston**, *Derby.*, 'swɔːkstən, swáwrkstŏn
Swarland *Northd.*, 'swɔːlənd, swáwrländ
Swatman, *f.n.*, 'swɒtmən, swótmăn
Swaton *Lincs.*, 'sweɪtən, swáytŏn
Swatragh *Co. Derry*, 'swɒtrə, swótră
Swavesey *Cambs.*, 'sweɪvzɪ, swáyvzi; 'sweɪvəzɪ, swáyvĕzi
Sweatman, *f.n.*, 'swetmən, swétmăn
Sweet, *f.n.*, swit, sweet
Sweetland, *f.n.*, 'switlənd, sweétländ
Sweetman, *f.n.*, 'switmən, sweétmăn
Swefling *Suffolk*, 'sweflɪŋ, swéffling
Swenarton, *f.n.*, 'swenərtən, swénnărtŏn
Swenerton, *f.n.*, 'swenərtən, swénnĕrtŏn
Swetman, *f.n.*, 'swetmən, swétmăn
Swillies Channel *Gwynedd*, 'swɪlɪz, swilliz
Swillington *W. Yorks.*, 'swɪlɪŋtən, swilling-tŏn

Swimbridge, *also spelt* **Swymbridge**, *Devon*, 'swɪmbrɪdʒ, swímbrij
Swimer, *f.n.*, 'swaɪmər, swímĕr
Swinburne, *f.n.*, 'swɪnbərn, swínburn
Swindall, *f.n.*, 'swɪndɔl, swíndawl
Swindell, *f.n.*, 'swɪndel, swíndell
Swindells, *f.n.*, swɪn'delz, swindéllz; 'swɪndlz, swíndlz
Swinderby *Lincs.*, 'swɪndərbɪ, swíndĕrbi
Swindon *Wilts.*, 'swɪndən, swíndŏn
Swine *Humberside*, swaɪn, swīn
Swiney, *f.n.*, 'swaɪnɪ, swíni; 'swɪnɪ, swinni
Swiney *H'land*, 'swɪnɪ, sweéni
Swingler, *f.n.*, 'swɪŋglər, swíng-glĕr
Swinnerton, *f.n.*, 'swɪnərtən, swínnĕrtŏn
Swinnow *W. Yorks.*, 'swɪnou, swínnō
Swire, *f.n.*, 'swaɪər, swīr
Swithin, saint, 'swɪθɪn, swíthin; 'swɪðɪn, swithin
Swithland *Leics.*, 'swɪðlənd, swíthländ
Switzer, *f.n.*, 'swɪtsər, swítsĕr
Swona, island, *Pentland Firth*, 'swounə, swónă
Sword, *f.n.*, sɔːd, sord
Swordale *W. Isles*, 'sɔːdeɪl, sórdayl
Sworder, *f.n.*, 'sɔːdər, sórdĕr
Swymbridge *see* **Swimbridge**
Swyre *Dorset*, 'swaɪər, swīr
Sycharth *Clwyd*, 'sʌxɑrθ, súchaarth
Sychdyn *Clwyd*, 'sʌxdɪn, súchdin. *The English form of this name is* **Soughton**, *q.v.*
Sychnant Pass, *Gwynedd*, 'sʌxnənt, súchnănt
Sydee, *f.n.*, 'saɪdɪ, sídee
Sydenham *London, Co. Down.*, 'sɪdənəm, síddĕnăm
Syderstone *Norfolk*, 'saɪdərstoun, sídĕrsstŏn
Sydie, *f.n.*, 'saɪdɪ, sídi
Sydling St. Nicholas *Dorset*, 'sɪdlɪŋ snt 'nɪkələs, síddling sĭnt nícklăss
Syers, *f.n.*, 'saɪərz, sí-ĕrz
Syerston *Notts.*, 'saɪərstən, sí-ĕrsstŏn
Syfret, *f.n.*, 'saɪfrɪt, sífrĕt
Sygrove, *f.n.*, 'saɪgrouv, sígrōv
Sykes, *f.n.*, saɪks, sīks
Sylvester, *f.n.*, sɪl'vestər, silvéstĕr
Symbister *Shetland*, 'sɪmbɪstər, símbisstĕr

Syme, *f.n.,* saɪm, sīm
Symene, River, *Dorset,* saɪ'miːnɪ, sīméeni
Symes, *f.n.,* saɪmz, sīmz
Symington, *f.n.,* 'saɪmɪŋtən, símington
Symington *S'clyde,* 'saɪmɪŋtən, símington
Symon, *f.n.,* 'saɪmən, símŏn
Symonds, *f.n.,* 'sɪməndz, símmŏndz; 'saɪməndz, símŏndz. *The first is appropriate for John Addington* ∼, *19th-c. author and translator.*
Symondsbury *Dorset,* 'sɪmənzbərɪ, símmŏnzbŭri
Symond's Yat *H. & W.,* 'sɪməndz 'jæt, símmŏndz yát
Symons, *f.n.,* 'sɪmənz, símmŏnz; 'saɪmənz, símŏnz. *The first is that of the authors A. J. A.* ∼ *and Julian* ∼, *and of Arthur* ∼, *poet and critic.*
Synge, *f.n.,* sɪŋ, sing
Syon House *London,* 'saɪən, sí-ŏn
Syrad, *f.n.,* 'saɪəræd, sírad
Syrett, *f.n.,* 'saɪərɪt, sírĕt
Syrus, *f.n.,* 'saɪərʊs, sírŏŏss
Sysonby, Baron, 'saɪzənbɪ, sízŏnbi
Syston *Leics.,* 'saɪstən, sísstŏn
Sytchampton *H. & W.,* 'sɪtʃhæmptən, sítch-hamptŏn
Sywell *Northants.,* 'saɪwel, sí-wel
Szasz, *f.n.,* sæz, sazz
Szemerey, *f.n.,* 'zemərɪ, zémmĕri
Szerelmey, *f.n.,* sə'relmɪ, sĕrélmi
Szudek, *f.n.,* 'ʃudek, shoŏdeck

T

Taaffe, *f.n.,* tæf, taff
Tabberer, *f.n.,* 'tæbərər, tábbĕrĕr
Tabern, *f.n.,* 'tæbərn, tábbĕrn
Taberner, *f.n.,* 'tæbərnər, tábbĕrnĕr; tə'bərnər, tăbérnĕr
Tabley *Ches.,* 'tæblɪ, tábbli
Tabor, *f.n.,* 'teɪbər, táybor
Tabori, *f.n.,* tə'bɔrɪ, tăbáwri
Tachbrook Mallory *Warwicks.,* 'tætʃbrʊk 'mælərɪ, tátchbrŏŏk málŏri
Tack, *f.n.,* tæk, tack
Tacolneston *Norfolk,* 'tæklstən, tácklstŏn
Tadcaster *N. Yorks.,* 'tædkæstər, tádkasstĕr
Taf, River, *Dyfed,* tav, taav. *The English form is* **Taff,** *q.v.*
Tafarnau Bach *Gwent,* tə'varnaɪ 'bax, tăvaárnī baách

Taff, River, *Dyfed,* tæf, taff. *The Welsh form is* **Taf,** *q.v.*
Taff, River, *Powys–Mid Glam.– S. Glam.,* tæf, taff
Taffinder, *f.n.,* 'tæfɪndər, táffindĕr
Tagliaferro, *f.n.,* ,talɪə'feroʊ, taaliăférrō
Tahourdin, *f.n.,* 'tavərdɪn, tówĕrdin
Tailyour, *f.n.,* 'teɪljər, táyl-yor
Tain *H'land,* teɪn, tayn
Tainsh, *f.n.,* teɪnʃ, taynsh
Tainton, *f.n.,* 'teɪntən, táyntŏn
Tait, *f.n.,* teɪt, tayt
Takeley *Essex,* 'teɪklɪ, táykli
Talachddu *Powys,* tə'læxðɪ, tălách-thi
Talacre *Clwyd,* tæl'ækreɪ, taláckray. *Also appropriate for the Mostyns of* ∼.
Talaton *Devon,* 'tælətən, tálătŏn
Talbot, *f.n.,* 'tɔlbət, táwlbŏt; 'tɒlbət, tóllbŏt
Talbut, *f.n.,* 'tɔlbət, táwlbŭt; 'tɒlbət, tóllbŏt
Talerddig *Powys,* tæl'eərðɪg, taláirthig
Talfan, *Welsh C.n.,* 'tælvən, tálvăn
Talfourd, *f.n.,* 'tælfərd, tálfŏrd
Talfryn, *f.n.,* 'tælvrɪn, tálvrin
Talgarth *Powys,* 'tælgarθ, tálgaarth
Taliesin, *Welsh bardic name,* tæl'jesɪn, tal-yéssin
Talisker *Skye,* 'tælɪskər, táliskĕr
Talkin *Cumbria,* 'tɔkɪn, táwkin
Talland Bay *Cornwall,* 'tælənd, tálănd
Tallantire *Cumbria,* 'tæləntaɪər, tálăntīr
Talley *Dyfed,* 'tælɪ, táli
Tallington *Lincs.,* 'tælɪŋtən, tálingtŏn
Tallis, Thomas, *16th-c. composer,* 'tælɪs, táliss
Tallon, *f.n.,* 'tælən, tálŏn
Talog, *f.n.,* 'tælɒg, tálog
Talsarnau *Gwynedd,* tæl'sarnaɪ, tal-saárnī
Talwrn *Clwyd, Gwynedd,* 'tæluərn, tálŏŏrn. *Appropriate for both places of the name in Clwyd.*
Talybont *Dyfed, Powys,* ,tælə'bɒnt, talăbónt
Tal-y-bont *Gwynedd,* ,tælə'bɒnt, talăbónt. *Appropriate for all three places of the name in Gwynedd.*
Tal-y-llyn *Gwynedd,* ,tælə'ɬɪn, tală-hlín
Tal-y-sarn *Gwynedd,* ,tælə'sarn, tală-saárn
Talywaun *Gwent,* ,tælə'waɪn, tală-wín

Tamar, River, *Devon–Cornwall*, 'teɪmɑr, táymär

Tamerton Foliott *Devon,* 'tæmərtən 'foʊlɪət, támmértön fóliöt

Tames, *f.n.,* teɪmz, taymz

Tameside *Gtr. M'chester,* 'teɪmsaɪd, táymssïd

Tamsin, *C.n.,* 'tæmzɪn, támzin

Tamsyn, *C.n.,* 'tæmzɪn, támzin

Tamworth *Staffs.,* 'tæmwərθ, támwurth; 'tæmərθ, támmürth

Tanat, River, *Gwynedd–Powys,* 'tænət, tánnät

Tancred, *f.n.,* 'tæŋkrɪd, tánkréd

Tandragee, *also spelt* **Tanderagee,** *Co. Armagh,* ˌtændrə'giː, tandrăgeé

Tanerdy *Dyfed,* tæn'ɜrdɪ, tannérdi

Tangley *Hants,* 'tæŋlɪ, táng-li

Tangmere *W. Sussex,* 'tæŋmɪər, tángmeer

Tangye, *f.n.,* 'tæŋgɪ, táng-gi

Tanner, *f.n.,* 'tænər, tánner

Tanqueray, *f.n.,* 'tæŋkərɪ, tánkéri; 'tæŋkəreɪ, tánkéray

Tansor *Northants.,* 'tænsɔr, tánssor

Tantallon Castle *Lothian,* tæn'tælən, tantálön

Tantobie *Durham,* tæn'toʊbɪ, tantóbi

Tan-y-bwlch *Gwynedd,* ˌtænə'bulx, tannăboolch

Tanygrisiau *Gwynedd,* ˌtænə'grɪsjaɪ, tannăgríssyï

Tan-y-maes *Gwynedd,* ˌtænə'maɪs, tannămíss

Tan-yr-allt *Clwyd,* ˌtænər'ælt, tannáráhlt

Tappenden, *f.n.,* 'tæpəndən, táppénděn

Tapply, *f.n.,* 'tæplɪ, tápli

Tapscott, *f.n.,* 'tæpskɒt, tápskott

Tapsell, *f.n.,* 'tæpsl, tápssl

Tapsfield, *f.n.,* 'tæpsfɪld, tápsfeeld

Tarbat *H'land,* 'tɑrbət, taárbăt. *Appropriate also for Viscount ∼.*

Tarbatness *H'land,* 'tɑrbət'nes, taárbătnéss

Tarbolton *S'clyde,* tɑr'boʊltən, taarbóltön

Tarbrax *S'clyde,* tɑr'bræks, taarbrácks

Tardebigge *H. & W.,* 'tɑrdəbɪg, taárdébig

Tarenig, River, *Powys,* tə'renɪg, tărénnig

Target, *f.n.,* 'tɑrdʒɪt, taárjét

Tarkowski, *f.n.,* tɑr'kɒfskɪ, taarkófski

Tarner, *f.n.,* 'tɑrnər, taárnér

Tarporley *Ches.,* 'tɑrpərlɪ, taárpörli; 'tɑrplɪ, taárpli

Tarradale *H'land,* 'tærədeɪl, tárrădayl

Tarran, *f.n.,* 'tærən, tárrän

Tarrant Keynston *Dorset,* 'tærənt 'keɪnstən, tárränt káynsstön

Tarring *W. Sussex,* 'tærɪŋ, tárring

Tarrinzean and Mauchline, Lady, tə'rɪŋən ənd 'mɒxlɪn, tăríng-än ănd máwchlin

Tarskavaig *Skye,* 'tɑrskævɪg, taárskăvig

Tartaraghan *Co. Armagh,* tɑr'tærəhən, taartárrăhăn

Tarves *Grampian,* 'tɑrvɪs, taárvĕss

Tasburgh *Norfolk,* 'teɪzbərə, táyzbŭră

Tasker, *f.n.,* 'tæskər, tásskĕr

Tassagh *Co. Armagh,* 'tæsə, tássă

Tate, *f.n.,* teɪt, tayt. *Appropriate also for the ∼ Gallery, London.*

Tatem, *f.n.,* 'teɪtəm, táytĕm

Tatenhill *Staffs.,* 'teɪtənhɪl, táytĕnhil

Tatham, *f.n.,* 'teɪθəm, táy-thăm; 'teɪðəm, táy-thăm; 'tætəm, táttăm

Tatham *Lancs.,* 'teɪtəm, táytăm

Tatt, *f.n.,* tæt, tatt

Tattersall, *f.n.,* 'tætərsɔl, táttĕrsawl; 'tætərsl, táttĕrssl

Tattershall *Lincs.,* 'tætərʃl, táttĕr-shl

Tattingstone *Suffolk,* 'tætɪŋstən, táttingstön

Taubman, *f.n.,* 'tɔbmən, táwbmän

Taunton *Somerset,* 'tɔntən, táwntön; 'tɑntən, taántön

Taupin, *f.n.,* 'tɔpɪn, táwpin

Tausky, Vilem, *conductor,* 'vɪləm 'taʊskɪ, víllém tówski

Tavaré, *f.n.,* 'tævəreɪ, távvăray

Tavener, *f.n.,* 'tævənər, távvĕnĕr

Taverham *Norfolk,* 'teɪvərəm, táyvĕräm

Taverne, *f.n.,* tə'vɜrn, tăvérn

Tavy, River, *Devon,* 'teɪvɪ, táyvi

Tawe, River, *Powys–W. Glam.,* 'taʊeɪ, tów-ay

Tawell, *f.n.,* tɔl, tawl; 'tɔəl, táw-ĕl

Tay, Loch *and* River, *Tayside,* teɪ, tay

Tayar, *f.n.,* 'taɪər, tī-är

Taylor, *f.n.,* 'teɪlər, táylör

Taylor of Gryfe, Baron, 'teɪlər əv 'graɪf, táylör öv gríf

Taylour, *f.n.,* 'teɪlər, táylör

Taynuilt *S'clyde,* teɪ'nʊlt, taynoólt

Tayport *Fife,* 'teɪpɔrt, táyport

Tayside, Baron, 'teɪsaɪd, táy-sïd

Teaffe, *f.n.,* tɑf, taaf
Teague, *f.n.,* tig, teeg
Tealby *Lincs.,* 'tɪlbɪ, téelbi
Tean, River, *Staffs.,* tin, teen. *Appropriate also for Upper ~ and Lower ~, Staffs.*
Teape, *f.n.,* tip, teep
Tear, *f.n.,* tɪər, teer
Teare, *f.n.,* tɪər, teer
Tearlath, *Gaelic C.n.,* 'tʃɛərləx, cháirlǎch
Tearle, *f.n.,* tɜrl, terl
Teasdale, *f.n.,* 'tɪzdeɪl, teézdayl
Teastler, *f.n.,* 'tistlər, teéstlěr
Tebay, *f.n.,* tɪ'beɪ, tĕbáy
Tebay *Cumbria,* 'tibɪ, teébi
Tebbit, *f.n.,* 'tebɪt, tébbit
Tebbs, *f.n.,* tebz, tebbz
Tebbutt, *f.n.,* 'tebət, tébbŭt
Tebby, *f.n.,* 'tebɪ, tébbi
Tebworth *Beds.,* 'tebwərθ, tébwŭrth
Tecwyn, *Welsh C.n.,* 'tekwɪn, téckwin
Tedburn St. Mary *Devon,* 'tedbɜrn snt 'mɛərɪ, tédburn sĭnt máiri
Tedder of Glenguin, Baron, 'tedər əv glen'gwɪn, téddĕr ŏv glen-gwín
Teear, *f.n.,* 'tɪər, teé-ǎr
Teed, *f.n.,* tid, teed
Teetgen, *f.n.,* 'tidʒən, teéjĕn
Teevan, *f.n.,* 'tivən, teévǎn
Tegel, *f.n.,* 'tigl, teégl
Tegetmeier, *f.n.,* 'tegɪtmaɪər, téggĕtmīr
Teggin, *f.n.,* 'tegɪn, téggin
Tei, *f.n.,* teɪ, tay
Teich, *f.n.,* taɪk, tīk
Teichman, *f.n.,* 'taɪʃmən, tíshmän
Teifi, River, *also spelt* **Teivy,** *Dyfed,* 'taɪvɪ, tívi
Teifion, *Welsh C.n.,* 'taɪvɪən, tívi-ŏn
Teigh *Leics.,* ti, tee
Teign, River, *Devon,* tin, teen; tɪn, tin
Teigngrace *Devon,* 'tingreɪs, teéngrayss
Teignmouth *Devon,* 'tɪnməθ, tinmŭth; 'tinməθ, teénmŭth. *The first is appropriate for Baron ~.*
Teise, River, *Kent,* tiz, teez
Teivy, River, *see* **Teifi**
Teleri, *Welsh C.n.,* tɪ'lerɪ, tĕlérri
Telfer, *f.n.,* 'telfər, télfĕr
Telscombe *E. Sussex,* 'telskəm, télsskŏm
Temair *see* **Aberdeen and ~,** Marquess of
Temme, *f.n.,* 'temɪ, témmi

Temperton, *f.n.,* 'tempərtən, témpĕrtŏn
Temple, *f.n.,* 'templ, témpl
Temple Guiting *Glos.,* 'templ 'gaɪtɪŋ, témpl gíting
Templepatrick *Co. Antrim,* 'templ'pætrɪk, témpl-pátrick
Temple Sowerby *Cumbria,* 'templ 'saʊərbɪ, témpl sówĕrbi; 'templ 'sɔrbɪ, témpl sórbi
Tenby *Dyfed,* 'tenbɪ, ténbi
Tendeter, *f.n.,* ten'detər, tendéttĕr
Ten Kate, *f.n.,* ten 'kɑtə, ten káatĕ
Tenniel, Sir John, *cartoonist,* 'tenjəl, tén-yĕl
Tennyson, *f.n.,* 'tenɪsən, ténnissŏn
Tennyson Jesse, Fryn, *novelist,* 'frɪn 'tenɪsən 'dʒes, frín ténnissŏn jéss
Tenterden *Kent,* 'tentərdən, téntĕrdĕn
Ter, River, *Essex,* tɑr, taar
Terally *D. & G.,* tɪ'rælɪ, tĕráli
Tereshchuk, *f.n.,* 'terəʃʊk, térrĕshōōk
Terling *Essex,* 'tɑrlɪŋ, táarling; 'tɑrlɪŋ, térling
Terraine, *f.n.,* tɪ'reɪn, tĕráyn
Terregles *D. & G.,* tɪ'reglz, tĕrégglz
Terrell, *f.n.,* 'terəl, térrĕl
Terrington, *f.n.,* 'terɪŋtən, térringtŏn
Terrot, *f.n.,* 'terət, térrŏt
Terson, *f.n.,* 'tɜrsən, térssŏn
Terry, *f.n.,* 'terɪ, térri
Tertis, *f.n.,* 'tɜrtɪs, tértiss
Terwick *W. Sussex,* 'terɪk, térrick
Tester, *f.n.,* 'testər, tésstĕr
Teston *Kent,* 'tisən, teéssŏn
Tettenhall *W. Midlands,* 'tetənhɔl, téttĕnhawl
Tetzner, *f.n.,* 'tetsnər, tétsnĕr
Teulon, *f.n.,* 'tjulən, téwlŏn
Teversal *Notts.,* 'tevərsl, tévvĕrssl
Teversham *Cambs.,* 'tevərʃəm, tévvĕr-shäm
Teviot, Baron, 'tevɪət, tévvi-ŏt
Teviot, River, *Borders,* 'tivɪət, teévi-ŏt
Teviotdale *Borders,* 'tivɪətdeɪl, teévi-ŏtdayl
Tewkesbury *Glos.,* 'tjuksbərɪ, téwksbŭri
Teynham *Kent,* 'teɪnəm, táynăm; 'tenəm, ténnăm. *The second is appropriate for Baron ~.*
Teyte, Dame **Maggie,** *soprano (1888–1976),* 'mægɪ 'teɪt, mággi táyt
Thaarup, *f.n.,* 'tɑrʊp, taárōōp
Thacker, *f.n.,* 'θækər, tháckĕr

Thackeray, *f.n.,* 'θækərɪ, tháckĕri
Thackley *W. Yorks.,* 'θæklɪ, tháckli
Thackrah, *f.n.,* 'θækrə, tháckră
Thackwray, *f.n.,* 'θækreɪ, tháckray
Thain, *f.n.,* θeɪn, thayn
Thakeham *W. Sussex,* 'θeɪkəm, tháykăm
Thalben-Ball, George, *organist,* 'θælbən 'bɔl, thálbĕn báwl
Thame *Oxon.,* teɪm, taym
Thames, River, *London,* temz, temz
Thanet, Isle of, *Kent,* 'θænɪt, thánnĕt
Thankerton *S'clyde,* 'θæŋkərtən, thánkĕrtŏn
Thatcher, *f.n.,* 'θætʃər, thátchĕr
Thavenot, *f.n.,* 'tævənou, távvĕnō; 'tævənɒt, távvĕnot
Theakstone, *f.n.,* 'θɪkstoun, theékstŏn
Theale *Berks.,* θil, theel
Theiler, *f.n.,* 'taɪlər, tílĕr
Thellusson, *f.n.,* 'teləsən, téllŭssŏn
Thelnetham *Suffolk,* θel'niθəm, thelneéthăm; 'θelnəθəm, thélnĕthăm
Thelwall *Ches.,* 'θelwɔl, thél-wawl
Themerson, *f.n.,* 'temərsən, témmĕrssŏn
Theobald, *f.n.,* 'θɪəbold, theé-ŏbawld; 'tɪbəld, tíbbăld. *The second is appropriate for Lewis ~, 17th–18th-c. Shakespearian critic.*
Theobalds Park *Herts.,* 'θɪəbɔldz, theé-ŏbawldz
Theobald's Road *London,* 'θɪəbɔldz, theé-ŏbawldz; 'tɪbəldz, tíbbăldz
Thesiger, *f.n.,* 'θesɪdʒər, théssijĕr
Theunissen, *f.n.,* 'tenɪsən, ténnissĕn
Thevenard, *f.n.,* 'tevənɑrd, tévvĕnaard
Thew, *f.n.,* θju, thew
Thewes, *f.n.,* θjuz, thewz
Theydon Bois *Essex,* 'θeɪdən 'bɔɪz, tháydŏn bóyz
Thick, *f.n.,* θɪk, thick
Thicke, *f.n.,* θɪk, thick
Thicknesse, *f.n.,* 'θɪknɪs, thícknĕss
Thiebault, *f.n.,* 'θɪəbɒlt, theé-ĕbawlt
Thiman, *f.n.,* 'tɪmən, teémăn
Thirde, *f.n.,* θɜrd, third
Thirer, *f.n.,* 'θaɪrər, thírĕr
Thirkell, *f.n.,* 'θɜrkl, thírkl
Thirkettle, *f.n.,* 'θɜrketl, thírkettl
Thirsk *N. Yorks.,* θɜrsk, thirsk
Thoday, *f.n.,* 'θoudeɪ, thóday
Thody, *f.n.,* 'θoudɪ, thódi

Tholthorpe *N. Yorks.,* 'θɒlθɔrp, tháwlthorp; 'tɒlθɔrp, tólthorp
Thom, *f.n.,* tɒm, tom
Thomae, *f.n.,* 'toumeɪ, tṓmay
Thomas, *C.n. and f.n.,* 'tɒməs, tómmăss
Thomas, Dylan, *poet,* 'dɪlən 'tɒməs, díllăn tómmăss. *Although the Welsh pronunciation is more nearly 'dʌlən, dúllăn, the poet himself recommended the anglicized pronunciation of his Christian name.*
Thomason, *f.n.,* 'tɒməsən, tómmăssŏn
Thompson, *f.n.,* 'tɒmsən, tómssŏn; 'tɒmpsən, tómpssŏn
Thomson, *f.n.,* 'tɒmsən, tómssŏn
Thomson of Monifieth, Baron, 'tɒmsən əv ˌmʌnɪ'fiθ, tómssŏn ŏv munnifeéth
Thonger, *f.n.,* 'θɒŋər, thóng-ĕr; 'θɒŋgər, thóng-gĕr
Thonock *Lincs.,* 'θɒnək, thónnŏk
Thorburn, *f.n.,* 'θɔrbɜrn, thórburn
Thorby, *f.n.,* 'θɔrbɪ, thórbi
Thoresby *Notts.,* 'θɔrzbɪ, thórzbi
Thorley, *f.n.,* 'θɔrlɪ, thórli
Thorn, *f.n.,* θɔrn, thorn
Thornaby-on-Tees *N. Yorks.,* 'θɔrnəbɪ ɒn 'tiz, thórnăbi-on-teéz
Thorndike, *f.n.,* 'θɔrndaɪk, thórndīk
Thorne, *f.n.,* θɔrn, thorn
Thorne *S. Yorks.,* θɔrn, thorn
Thorne Gyme *S. Yorks.,* 'θɔrn 'gaɪm, thórn gím
Thorneloe, *f.n.,* 'θɔrnɪlou, thórnĕlō
Thorness *I. of Wight,* θɔr'nes, thornéss
Thorngumbald *Humberside,* 'θɔrŋgəmbold, thórng-gŭmbawld
Thornham *Norfolk,* 'θɔrnəm, thórnăm
Thornham Magna *Suffolk,* 'θɔrnəm 'mægnə, thórnăm mágnă
Thornham Parva *Suffolk,* 'θɔrnəm 'parvə, thórnăm paárvă
Thornhaugh *Cambs.,* 'θɔrnhɔ, thórn-haw
Thornhill, *f.n.,* 'θɔrnhɪl, thórn-hil
Thorning, *f.n.,* 'θɔrnɪŋ, thórning
Thornley, *f.n.,* 'θɔrnlɪ, thórnli
Thornliebank *S'clyde,* 'θɔrnlɪ'bæŋk, thórnlibánk
Thornton, *f.n.,* 'θɔrntən, thórntŏn
Thornton Heath *London,* 'θɔrntən 'hiθ, thórntŏn heéth
Thornton Hough *Merseyside,* 'θɔrntən 'hʌf, thórntŏn húff

Thorogood, *f.n.*, 'θʌrəgʊd, thúrrŏ-
good
Thorold, *C.n. and f.n.*, 'θɒrəld,
thórröld; 'θʌrəld, thúrröld;
'θɒrəʊld,thórröld. *The first is
appropriate for* ~ *Dickinson,
film director.*
Thorp, *f.n.*, θɔrp, thorp
Thorpe Davie, Cedric, *composer*,
'sedrık 'θɔrp 'deıvı, sédrick
thórp dáyvi
Thorpe-le-Soken *Essex*, 'θɔrp lə
'soʊkən, thórp lě sṓkěn
Thorpe Morieux *Suffolk*, 'θɔrp
mə'ru, thórp mŏróo
Thorrington *Essex*, 'θɒrıŋtən,
thórrington
Thouless, *f.n.*, 'θaʊles, thówless
Thousell, *f.n.*, 'θaʊsl, thówssl
Thovez, *f.n.*, 'θoʊvız, thóvěz
Thow, *f.n.*, θaʊ, thow
Threapland *Cumbria*, 'θrıpländ,
threepländ
Threave Castle *D. & G.*, θriv,
threev
Threekingham *Lincs.*, 'θrekıŋəm,
thrécking-ăm
Threlfall, *f.n.*, 'θrelfɔl, thrélfawl
Threlkeld *Cumbria*, 'θrelkeld,
thrélkeld
Thriplow, *also spelt* **Triplow**,
Cambs., 'trıploʊ, tríplō. **Triplow**
is the ecclesiastical spelling.
Thripp, *f.n.*, θrıp, thripp
Throapham *S. Yorks.*, 'θroʊpəm,
thrṓpăm
Througham *Glos.*, 'θrʌfəm, thrúf-
făm
Throwley *Kent*, 'θraʊlı, thrówli
Thrupp, *f.n.*, θrʌp, thrupp
Thrybergh *S. Yorks.*, 'θraıbər,
thríběr; 'θraıbərə, thríběră
Thubron, *f.n.*, 'θjubrən, théwbrŏn
Thuillier, *f.n.*, 'twıljər, twíll-yěr
Thurgarton *Norfolk, Notts.*,
'θɜrgərtən, thúrgărtŏn
Thurgoland *S. Yorks.*, 'θɜrgoʊ-
lænd, thúrgōland
Thurgood, *f.n.*, 'θɜrgʊd, thúrgood
Thurleigh *Beds.*, θɜr'laı, thur-lí
Thurley, *f.n.*, 'θɜrlı, thúrli
Thurling, *f.n.*, 'θɜrlıŋ, thúrling
Thurloxton *Somerset*, θɜr'lɒkstən,
thurlóckstŏn
Thurmaston *Leics.*, 'θɜrməstən,
thúrmăsstŏn
Thurne *Norfolk*, θɜrn, thurn
Thurnham *Kent*, 'θɜrnəm, thúrn-
ăm
Thurnscoe *S. Yorks.*, 'θɜrnzkoʊ,
thúrnzkō
Thurso *H'land*, 'θɜrsoʊ, thúrssō.
Appropriate also for Viscount
~.

Thurston, *f.n.*, 'θɜrstən, thúrsstŏn
Thurstonfield *Cumbria*, 'θrʌstən-
fild, thrússtŏnfeeld
Thwing *Humberside*, twıŋ, twing;
θwıŋ, thwing
Thynne, *f.n.*, θın, thin
Tiarks, *f.n.*, 'tiarks, tée-aarks
Tibbermore *Tayside*, ,tıbər'mɔr,
tibběrmór
Tibenham *Norfolk*, 'tıbənəm,
tíbběnăm
Ticciati, *f.n.*, tı'tʃatı, titcha'ati
Tice, *f.n.*, taıs, tíss
Ticehurst, *f.n.*, 'taıshɜrst, tíss-
-hurst
Tichborne *Hants*, 'tıtʃbɔrn,
títchborn
Tichelar, *f.n.*, 'tıtʃəlar, títchělaar
Ticher, *f.n.*, 'tıtʃər, títchěr
Tickell, *f.n.*, tı'kel, tickéll
Tickhill *S. Yorks.*, 'tıkhıl, tíckhil
Tickle, *f.n.*, 'tıkl, tíckl
Ticknall *Derby.*, 'tıknəl, tícknăl
Ticktum, *f.n.*, 'tıktəm, tícktŭm
Tidball, *f.n.*, 'tıdbɔl, tídbawl
Tideford *Cornwall*, 'tıdıfərd,
tídděfőrd
Tidenham *Glos.*, 'tıdənəm,
tíddĕnăm
Tideswell *Derby.*, 'taıdzwel,
tídzwel; 'tıdzl, tíddzl
Tidmarsh, *f.n.*, 'tıdmarʃ, tíd-
maarsh
Tiernan, *f.n.*, 'tıərnən, teérnăn
Tierney, *f.n.*, 'tıərnı, teérni
Tietjen, *f.n.*, 'titʃən, teétchĕn
Tievebulliagh *Co. Antrim*, tıv-
'bʊljə, teev-bŏŏl-yă
Tievenagh *Co. Tyrone*, 'tıvənə,
teévĕnă
Tiffin, *f.n.*, 'tıfın, tíffin
Tigar, *f.n.*, 'taıgər, tígăr
Tighe, *f.n.*, taı, tí
Tighnabruaich *S'clyde*, ,taınə-
'bruəx, tīnăbróo-á_ch_;, tınə-
'bruəx, tinnăbróo-á_ch_
Tilbe, *f.n.*, 'tılbı, tílbi
Tilbury, *f.n.*, 'tılbərı, tílbüri
Tilbury *Essex*, 'tılbərı, tílbüri
Tiley, *f.n.*, 'taılı, tíli
Tiller, *f.n.*, 'tılər, tíllĕr
Tillett, *f.n.*, 'tılıt, tíllĕt
Tilley, *f.n.*, 'tılı, tílli
Tillicoultry *Central*, ,tılı'kutrı,
tillikóotri
Tilling, *f.n.*, 'tılıŋ, tílling
Tillyard, *f.n.*, 'tıljard, till-yaard
Tillysburn *Co. Antrim*, ,tılız'bɜrn,
tillizbúrn
Tilmanstone *Kent*, 'tılmənstoʊn,
tílmănsstŏn
Tilshead *Wilts.*, 'tılzhed, tíllz-hed
Timberscombe *Somerset*, 'tım-
bərzkum, tímběrzkoom

Timewell, *f.n.*, 'taɪmwəl, tímwĕl
Timmins, *f.n.*, 'tɪmɪnz, tímminz
Timpson, *f.n.*, 'tɪmpsən, tímpssŏn
Tinbergen, *f.n.*, 'tɪnbɜːgən, tín-bergĕn
Tindall, *f.n.*, 'tɪndl, tínndl; 'tɪndɔl, tíndawl
Tindell, *f.n.*, 'tɪndel, tíndel; 'tɪndl, tínndl
Tinegate, *f.n.*, 'taɪngeɪt, tín-gayt
Tingay, *f.n.*, 'tɪŋgeɪ, tíng-gay
Tingewick *Bucks.*, 'tɪndʒwɪk, tínjwick
Tingey, *f.n.*, 'tɪŋgɪ, tíng-gi
Tingrith *Beds.*, 'tɪŋgrɪθ, tíng-grith
Tingwall *Shetland*, 'tɪŋwəl, tíng-wăl
Tinhay *Devon*, 'tɪnheɪ, tín-hay
Tink, *f.n.*, tɪŋk, tink
Tinne, *f.n.*, 'tɪnɪ, tínni
Tintagel *Cornwall*, tɪn'tædʒl, tintájjl
Tintern Abbey *Gwent*, 'tɪntərn, tíntĕrn
Tintern Parva *Gwent*, 'tɪntərn 'pɑːvə, tíntĕrn pa'arvă
Tinwald *D. & G.*, 'tɪnl, tínnl
Tiplady, *f.n.*, 'tɪpleɪdɪ, típlaydi
Tippett, *f.n.*, 'tɪpɪt, típpĕt. *Appropriate for Sir Michael* ~, *composer*.
Tipping, *f.n.*, 'tɪpɪŋ, típping
Tipton St. John *Devon*, 'tɪptən snt 'dʒɒn, típtŏn sĭnt jón
Tirabad *Powys*, tɪə'ræbæd, teerábbad
Tirbutt, *f.n.*, 'tɜːbət, tírbŭt
Tirebuck, *f.n.*, 'taɪəbʌk, tírbuck
Tiree, *also spelt* **Tyree**, *S'clyde*, taɪ'riː, tī-rée
Tirpentwys *Gwent*, tɪə'pentuɪs, teerpéntŏo-iss
Tir-phil *Mid Glam.*, tɪə'fɪl, teer-fíll
Tir-y-berth *Mid Glam.*, ,tɪə-'bɛəθ, tirrăbáirth
Tir-y-dail *Dyfed*, ,tɪərə'daɪl, teerădíl
Tisi, *f.n.*, 'tɪzɪ, téezi
Tissot, James, *Anglo-French painter, 1836–1902*, 'tiːsou, téessō
Tithby, *also spelt* **Tythby**, *Notts.*, 'tɪðbɪ, títhbi
Titheradge, *f.n.*, 'tɪðərɪdʒ, títhĕrij
Titley *H. & W.*, 'tɪtlɪ, titli
Titmus, *f.n.*, 'tɪtməs, títmŭss
Titshall, *f.n.*, 'tɪtsl, títtsl
Tittensor *Staffs.*, 'tɪtənsər, títtĕnssŏr
Tittleshall *Norfolk*, 'tɪtlʃəl, títtl-shawl
Titus, *f.n.*, 'taɪtəs, títŭss

Tiumpan Head *W. Isles*, 'tjumpən, tyŏompăn
Tiverton *Devon*, 'tɪvərtən, tívvĕr-tŏn
Tivetshall *Norfolk*, 'tɪvɪtʃəl, tívvĕts-hawl
Tividale *W. Midlands*, 'tɪvɪdeɪl, tívvidayl
Tixall *Staffs.*, 'tɪksɔl, tícksawl
Tizard, *f.n.*, 'tɪzɑːd, tízzaard; 'tɪzəd, tízzărd
Tjaden, *f.n.*, 'tʃɑdən, cha'adĕn
Tobermore *Co. Derry*, ,tʌbər'mɔr, tubbĕrmór
Tobermory *S'clyde*, ,toubər'mɔrɪ, tōbĕrmáwri
Tobias, *f.n.*, tə'baɪəs, tŏbí-ăss
Tobin, *f.n.*, 'toubɪn, tōbin
Toch, *f.n.*, tɒk, tock; tɒʃ, tosh
Tocher, *f.n.*, 'tɒxər, tóchĕr
Tockholes *Lancs.*, 'tɒkhoulz, tóckhōlz
Tockwith *N. Yorks.*, 'tɒkwɪθ, tóckwith
Todd, *f.n.*, tɒd, todd
Todds, *f.n.*, tɒdz, toddz
Todmorden *W. Yorks.*, 'tɒdmərdən, tódmŏrdĕn; 'tɒdmɔrdən, tódmorden
Toghill, *f.n.*, 'tɒghɪl, tóg-hil
Toker, *f.n.*, 'toukər, tōkĕr
Tokyngton *London*, 'toukɪŋtən, tōkingtŏn
Tolcarne *Cornwall*, tɒl'kɑrn, tol-ka'arn
Tolgullow *Cornwall*, tɒl'gʌlou, tolgúllō
Tolkien, J. R. R., *author and scholar*, 'tɒlkin, tólkeen
Toll, *f.n.*, tɒl, tol
Tolladay, *f.n.*, 'tɒlədeɪ, tólláday
Tollady, *f.n.*, 'tɒlədɪ, tóllădi
Tollemache, *f.n.*, 'tɒlmæʃ, tól-mash; 'tɒlmɑʃ, tólmaash. *The first is appropriate for Baron* ~.
Tollerton, *f.n.*, 'tɒlərtən, tóllĕrtŏn
Tollerton *Notts., N. Yorks.*, 'tɒlərtən, tóllĕrtŏn
Tollesbury *Essex*, 'toulzbərɪ, tōlz-bŭri
Tollesby *Cleveland*, 'toulzbɪ, tōlzbi
Tolleshunt d'Arcy *Essex*, 'toulz-hʌnt 'dɑːsɪ, tōlz-hunt da'arssi
Tolleshunt Knights *Essex*, 'toulz-hʌnt 'naɪts, tōlz-hunt níts
Tolleshunt Major *Essex*, 'toulz-hʌnt 'meɪdʒər, tōlz-hunt máyjŏr
Tol-Pedn-Penwith *Cornwall*, tɒl'pednpen'wɪθ, tolpéddn-penwith
Tolpuddle *Dorset*, 'tɒlpʌdl, tól-puddl; 'tɒlpɪdl, tólpíddl

Tolskithy *Cornwall*, tɒl'skɪθɪ, tolskíthi

Tolt Hill *I. of Wight*, tɔt, tawt

Tolworth *London*, 'tɒlwərθ, tólwürth; 'toulwərθ, tólwürth

Tomalin, *f.n.*, 'tɒməlɪn, tómmälin

Toman, *f.n.*, 'toumən, tŏmăn

Tomatin *H'land*, tə'mætɪn, tŏmáttin

Tombs, *f.n.*, tumz, toomz

Tombstone, *f.n.*, 'tumstoun, toŏmstōn

Tomelty, *f.n.*, 'tɒmltɪ, tómmlti

Tomes, *f.n.*, toumz, tōmz

Tomich *H'land*, 'tɒmɪx, tómmich

Tominey, *f.n.*, 'tɒmɪnɪ, tómmini

Tomintoul *Grampian*, ˌtɒmɪn'taul, tommintówl

Tomlinson, *f.n.*, 'tɒmlɪnsən, tómlinssön

Tomnahurich *H'land*, ˌtɒmnə-'huərɪx, tomnă-hoŏrich

Tomnavoulin *Grampian*, ˌtɒmnə-'vulɪn, tomnăvoolin

Tomney, *f.n.*, 'tɒmnɪ, tómni

Tompion, Thomas, *17th-c. clock-maker*, 'tɒmpɪən, tómpi-ŏn

Toms, *f.n.*, 'tɒmz, tommz

Tonbridge *Kent*, 'tʌnbrɪdʒ, túnbrij

Ton-du *Mid Glam.*, tɒn'di, tondée

Tone, River, *Somerset*, toun, tōn

Toner, *f.n.*, 'tounər, tŏnĕr

Tonfanau *Gwynedd*, tɒn'vænaɪ, tonvánnī

Tong, *f.n.*, tɒŋ, tong

Tonge, *f.n.*, tɒŋ, tong; tɒndʒ, tonj; tʌŋ, tung

Tonge *Kent*, Gtr. *M'chester*, tɒŋ, tong

Tonge-cum-Breightmet *Gtr. M'chester*, 'tɒŋ kʌm 'breɪtmət, tóng kum bráytmĕt; 'tɒŋ kʌm 'braɪtmət, tóng kum brítmĕt

Tonge Fold *Gtr. M'chester*, 'tɒŋ 'fould, tóng fóld

Tongland, *also spelt* **Tongueland**, *D. & G.*, 'tʌŋlənd, túng-länd

Tongue, *f.n.*, tʌŋ, tung

Tongue *H'land*, tʌŋ, tung

Tongueland *see* **Tongland**

Tongwynlais *S. Glam.*, tɒn'gwɪnlaɪs, ton-gwín-līss

Tonmawr *W. Glam.*, 'tɒnmauər, tónmowr

Tonna *W. Glam.*, 'tɒnə, tónnă

Tonpentre *Mid Glam.*, tɒn'pentreɪ, tonpéntray

Tonwell *Herts.*, 'tʌnl, túnnl

Tonypandy *Mid Glam.*, ˌtɒnə-'pændɪ, tonnăpándi

Tonyrefail *Mid Glam.*, ˌtɒnə-'revaɪl, tonnărévvīl

Tonysguboriau *Mid Glam.*, ˌtɒnəskɪ'bɒrɪaɪ, tonnŭskibórri-ī

Toobe, *f.n.*, 'tubɪ, toŏbee

Tooher, *f.n.*, 'tuər, toŏ-ĕr

Toombs, *f.n.*, tumz, toomz

Toomebridge *Co. Antrim*, tum-'brɪdʒ, toom-bríj

Toop, *f.n.*, tup, toop

Toot Baldon *Oxon.*, 'tut 'bɔldən, toŏt báwldŏn

Tooth, *f.n.*, tuθ, tooth

Toothill, *f.n.*, 'tuthɪl, toŏt-hil

Tooting Graveney *London*, 'tutɪŋ 'greɪvnɪ, toŏting gráyv-ni

Toovey, *f.n.*, 'tuvɪ, toŏvi

Topliss, *f.n.*, 'tɒplɪs, tópliss

Topolski, *f.n.*, tə'pɒlskɪ, tŏpólski

Toppesfield *Essex*, 'tɒpɪsfɪld, tóppĕssfeeld; 'tɒpsfɪld, tópsfeeld

Topping, *f.n.*, 'tɒpɪŋ, tópping

Topsham *Devon*, 'tɒpsəm, tópssäm; 'tɒpʃəm, tóp-shäm

Tor Achilty *H'land*, 'tɒr 'æxɪltɪ, tór áchilti

Tordoff, *f.n.*, 'tɔrdɒf, tórdoff

Torell, *f.n.*, 'tɒrəl, tórrĕl

Torksey *Lincs.*, 'tɔrksɪ, tórksi

Torlesse, *f.n.*, 'tɔrləs, tórlĕss

Torley, *f.n.*, 'tɔrlɪ, tórli

Tormarton *Avon*, 'tɔrmɑrtən, tórmaartŏn

Tormore *S'clyde*, tɔr'mɔr, tormór

Torness *Lothian*, tɔr'nes, tornéss

Torney, *f.n.*, 'tɔrnɪ, tórni

Torosay *Mull*, 'tɒrəseɪ, tórrŏssay

Torpantau *Powys*, tɔr'pæntaɪ, torpántī

Torpenhow *Cumbria*, trɪ'penə, tripénnă; 'tɔrpənhau, tórpĕn-how

Torphichen *Lothian*, tɔr'fɪxən, torfíchĕn. *Appropriate also for* Baron ~.

Torphins *Grampian*, tɔr'fɪnz, torfínz

Torpoint *Cornwall*, tɔr'pɔɪnt, torpóynt

Torquay *Devon*, tɔr'ki, torkée

Torquil, *C.n.*, 'tɔrkwɪl, tórkwil

Torrance, *f.n.*, 'tɒrəns, tórränss

Torrens, *f.n.*, 'tɒrənz, tórrĕnz

Torrie, *f.n.*, 'tɒrɪ, tórri

Torthorwald *D. & G.*, tɔr'θɒrəld, tŏr-thórräld; tər'θɒrwəld, tŏr--thórwäld

Torvill, *f.n.*, 'tɔrvɪl, tórvil

Torwoodlee *Borders*, ˌtɔrwud'li, torwoŏdlée

Tory, *f.n.*, 'tɒrɪ, táwri

Toseland, *f.n.*, 'touzɪlənd, tŏzĕländ

Toseland *Cambs.*, 'touzlənd, tŏzländ

Tosh, *f.n.*, tɒʃ, tosh

Tossell, *f.n.*, 'tɒsl, tóssl

Tosside Lancs.–N. Yorks. border, 'tɒsaɪd, tóssīd; 'tɒsɪd, tóssid; 'tɒsɪt, tóssit

Totham, Great and Little, Essex, 'tɒtəm, tóttăm

Tothill, f.n., 'tɒthɪl, tótt-hil; 'tɒtɪl, tóttil

Totley S. Yorks., 'tɒtlɪ, tóttli

Totnes Devon, 'tɒtnɪs, tótnĕss

Toton Notts., 'toʊtən, tóꞌtŏn

Tottenham London, 'tɒtənəm, tóttĕnăm

Totternhoe Beds., 'tɒtərnhoʊ, tóttĕrnhō

Tottman, f.n., 'tɒtmən, tóttmăn

Totton Hants, 'tɒtən, tóttŏn

Touch, f.n., taʊtʃ, towtch

Touch Fife, tux, tooch

Touche, f.n., tuʃ, toosh

Touchet, f.n., 'tʌtʃɪt, tútchĕt

Tough, f.n., tux, tooch; tʌf, tuff

Tough Grampian, tux, tooch

Touhey, f.n., 'tuɪ, tóo-i

Toulmin, f.n., 'tulmɪn, toolmin

Toulson, f.n., 'tulsən, tóolssŏn

Toulston N. Yorks., 'toʊlstən, tólsstŏn

Tourle, f.n., tɜrl, turl; tʊərl, tóŏrl

Tourneur, Turnour or **Turner**, Cyril, 16th–17th-c. dramatist, 'tɜrnər, túrnĕr

Tours, f.n., tʊərz, tóŏrz

Tourtel, f.n., tɔr'tel, tortéll

Tovell, f.n., 'toʊvl, tóvl

Tovey, f.n., 'toʊvɪ, tóvi; 'tʌvɪ, túvvi. The first is appropriate for Sir Donald Francis ∼, writer on music; the second for Baron ∼, Admiral of the Fleet.

Tovil Kent, 'tɒvɪl, tóvvil; 'tɒvl, tóvvl

Toward Point S'clyde, 'taʊərd, tów-ărd

Towb, f.n., taʊb, towb

Towcester Northants., 'toʊstər, tósstĕr

Towednack Cornwall, tə'wednək, tŏ-wédnăk

Towell, f.n., 'taʊəl, tówĕl

Towers, f.n., 'taʊərz, tówĕrz

Towgood, f.n., 'toʊgʊd, tógŏōd

Tow Law Durham, taʊ 'lɔ, tów láw

Towle, f.n., toʊl, tōl

Towler, f.n., 'taʊlər, tówlĕr

Towndrow, f.n., 'taʊndroʊ, tówndrō

Townend, f.n., 'taʊnend, tównend

Townsend, f.n., 'taʊnzend, tównzend

Townsend Thoresen Car Ferries Ltd. G.B., 'taʊnzend 'tɒrəsən, tównzend tórrĕssĕn

Townshend, f.n., 'taʊnzend, tównzend. Appropriate also for Marquess ∼.

Townshend Cornwall, 'taʊnz'end, tównz-énd

Townson, f.n., 'taʊnsən, tównssŏn

Towse, f.n., taʊz, towz

Towy, River, Dyfed, 'taʊɪ, tówi

Towyn, C.n., 'toʊɪn, tó-in

Towyn Clwyd, 'taʊɪn, tów-in

Toxteth Merseyside, 'tɒkstəθ, tóckstĕth

Toynbee, f.n., 'tɔɪnbɪ, tóynbi

Toyne, f.n., tɔɪn, toyn

Trabichoff, f.n., 'træbɪtʃɒf, trábbi-tchoff

Tracey, f.n., 'treɪsɪ, tráyssi

Tradescant, f.n., trə'deskənt, trădésskănt. Appropriate for John ∼, naturalist (1608–62), and hence for ∼ Gardens, Lambeth.

Trafalgar, Viscount, trə'fælgər, trăfálgăr. The sixth Earl Nelson advocated this pronunciation although mentioning that previous holders of the title had preferred ,træfl'gɑr, trafflgaár

Trafalgar House nr. Salisbury, ,træfl'gɑr, trafflgaár; trə'fælgər, trăfálgăr

Traherne, f.n., trə'hɜrn, tră-hérn

Trallong Powys, 'træɬɒŋ, tráɬlong

Trampleasure, f.n., 'træmpleʒər, trám-plezḥĕr

Train, f.n., treɪn, trayn

Tranchell, f.n., 'træŋkl, tránkl; 'træntʃel, trántchel

Tranent Lothian, trə'nent, trănént

Tranmire of Upsall, Baron, 'trænmaɪər əv 'ʌpsl, tránmīr ŏv úpssl

Trant, f.n., trænt, trannt

Tranter, f.n., 'træntər, trántĕr

Traprain, Viscount, trə'preɪn, trăpráyn

Traquair, f.n., trə'kweər, trăkwáir

Traquair Borders, trə'kweər, trăkwáir

Trathen, f.n., 'treɪθən, tráythĕn

Travers, f.n., 'trævərz, trávvĕrz

Traverse, f.n., 'trævərs, trávvĕrss

Traversi, f.n., trə'vɑrsɪ, trăvérssi

Travess, f.n., trə'ves, trăvéss

Travis, f.n., 'trævɪs, trávviss

Trawscoed Dyfed, 'traʊskɔɪd, trówsskoyd

Trawsfynydd Gwynedd, traʊs-'vʌnɪð, trowssvúnnith

Traynor, f.n., 'treɪnər, tráynŏr

Treacher, f.n., 'tritʃər, trétchĕr

Treacy, f.n., 'treɪsɪ, tráyssi

Treadwell, f.n., 'tredwəl, trédwĕl

Trealaw Mid Glam., trɪ'ælaʊ, tri-álow

Treales *Lancs.*, treɪlz, traylz
Trearddur Bay *Gwynedd*, treɪ-
 'arðɪər 'beɪ, tray-aártheer báy
Trease, *f.n.*, triz, treez
Trebanos *W. Glam.*, trɪ'bænɒs,
 trĕbánnoss
Trebarwith *Cornwall*, trɪ'bɑrwɪθ,
 trĕbaárwith
Trebble, *f.n.*, 'trebl, trébbl
Trebehor *Cornwall*, trɪ'bɪər, trĕ-
 beér
Trebey, *f.n.*, 'trɪbɪ, tréebi
Trebilcock, *f.n.*, trɪ'bɪlkoʊ, trĕ-
 bílkō; trɪ'bɪlkɒk, trĕbílkock
Trebullet *Cornwall*, trɪ'bʊlɪt,
 trĕbŏŏlĕt
Trebursye *Cornwall*, trɪ'bɜrzɪ,
 trĕbúrzi
Trecastle *Powys*, trɪ'kæsl, trĕ-
 kássl
Tredegar *Gwent*, trɪ'dɪgər, trĕ-
 deégär
Tredell, *f.n.*, trɪ'del, trĕdéll
Tredennick, *f.n.*, trɪ'denɪk, trĕ-
 dénnick
Tredree, *f.n.*, 'tredrɪ, trédree
Tree, *f.n.*, trɪ, tri, tree
Trefdraeth, *also spelt* Trevdraeth,
 Dyfed, 'trevdraɪθ, trévdrīth
Trefeglwys *Powys*, trɪv'egluɪs,
 trĕvéglŏŏ-iss
Trefgarne, *Baron*, 'trefgɑrn,
 tréffgaarn
Trefilan *Dyfed*, trɪv'ilæn, trĕvée-
 lan
Tre-fin *see* Trevine
Trefnant *Clwyd*, 'trevnænt, trév-
 nant
Trefonen *Salop*, trɪ'vɒnɪn, trĕ-
 vónnĕn
Trefor, *Welsh C.n.*, 'trevər, trévvŏr
Treforest *Mid Glam.*, trɪ'fɒrɪst,
 trĕfórrĕst
Trefriw *Gwynedd*, 'trevrɪu, trév-
 vri-oo
Trefusis, *f.n.*, trɪ'fjusɪs, trĕféwssiss
Tregadillett *Cornwall*, ˌtregə'dɪlɪt,
 treggädíllĕt
Tregaminian *Cornwall*, ˌtregə-
 'mɪnɪən, treggämínni-än
Treganthe *Cornwall*, trɪ'gænθɪ,
 trĕgánthi
Tregare *Gwent*, trɪ'gɛər, trĕgáir
Tregaron *Dyfed*, trɪ'gærən, trĕ-
 gárrŏn
Tregavethan *Cornwall*, ˌtregə-
 'veθən, treggävéthän
Tregear, *f.n.*, trɪ'gɪər, trĕgéer
Tregellas, *f.n.*, trɪ'geləs, trĕgéllãss
Tregelles, *f.n.*, trɪ'gelɪs, trĕgélliss
Tregenza, *f.n.*, trɪ'genzə, trĕgénzä
Tregeseal *Cornwall*, ˌtregə'siəl,
 treggĕsseé-äl; ˌtregə'sil, treggĕs-
 seél

Treglown, *f.n.*, trɪ'gloʊn, trĕglón;
 trɪ'gloʊn, treeglón
Tregolls *Cornwall*, trɪ'gɒlz, trĕ-
 góllz
Tregonetha *Cornwall*, ˌtregə'neθə,
 treggŏnéthã
Tregoning, *f.n.*, trɪ'gɒnɪŋ, trĕgón-
 ning
Tregony *Cornwall*, 'tregənɪ, trég-
 gŏni
Tregrehan *Cornwall*, tre'greɪn,
 tregráyn
Tregurrian *Cornwall*, trɪ'gʌrɪən,
 trĕgúrri-än
Tregynon *Powys*, trɪ'gʌnən, trĕ-
 gúnnŏn
Trehafod *Mid Glam.*, trɪ'hævəd,
 trĕ-hávvŏd
Trehane, *f.n.*, trɪ'heɪn, trĕháyn
Treharris *Mid Glam.*, trɪ'hærɪs,
 trĕ-hárriss
Trehearne, *f.n.*, trɪ'hɜrn, trĕ-hérn
Treherbert *Mid Glam.*, trɪ'hɜrbərt,
 trĕ-hérbĕrt
Treig, *Loch and River*, *H'land*,
 trig, treeg
Treitel, *f.n.*, 'traɪtl, trítl
Trekenner *Cornwall*, trɪ'kenər,
 trĕkénnĕr
Trelawney, *f.n.*, trɪ'lɒnɪ, trĕláwni
Trelawny, *f.n.*, trɪ'lɒnɪ, trĕláwni
Trelawnyd *Clwyd*, trɪ'laʊnɪd,
 trĕlównid
Trelease, *f.n.*, trɪ'lis, trĕleéss
Treleaven, *f.n.*, trɪ'levən, trĕ-
 lévvĕn
Tre-lech a'r Betws *Dyfed*, trɪ'leɪx
 ɑr 'betʊs, trĕláých aar béttŏŏss
Treleigh *Cornwall*, trɪ'leɪ, trĕláy
Trelewis *Mid Glam.*, trɪ'luɪs,
 trĕlŏŏ-iss; trɪ'ljuɪs, trĕléw-iss
Treligga *Cornwall*, trɪ'lɪgə, trĕ-
 líggä
Treliving, *f.n.*, trɪ'lɪvɪŋ, trĕlívving
Trelleck *Gwent*, 'trelek, trélleck
Treloar, *f.n.*, trɪ'lɔr, trĕlór
Treluggan *Cornwall*, trɪ'lʌgən,
 trĕlúggän
Tremain, *f.n.*, trɪ'meɪn, trĕmáyn
Trematon *Cornwall*, 'tremətən,
 trémmätŏn
Tremeer, *f.n.*, trɪ'mɪər, trĕmeér
Tremeirchion *Clwyd*, trɪ-
 'maɪərxɪɒn, trĕmírchi-on
Tremenheere, *f.n.*, 'tremənhɪər,
 trémmĕnheer
Tremethick, *f.n.*, trə'meθɪk,
 trĕméthick
Tremills, *f.n.*, 'tremlz, trémmlz
Tremlett, *f.n.*, 'tremlɪt, trémlĕt
Trenaman, *f.n.*, trɪ'nɑmən, trĕ-
 na´ämän
Trenance *Cornwall*, trɪ'næns,
 trĕnánss

Trenant *Cornwall*, trɪ'nænt, trĕ-nánt

Trenchard, Viscount, 'trenʃərd, trén-shård

Trencrom Hill *Cornwall*, tren-'krɒm, tren-krómm

Treneglos *Cornwall*, trɪ'neglɒs, trĕnégloss

Trengrouse, *f.n.*, 'treŋgrouz, tréng-gröz

Trengwainton *Cornwall*, trən-'gweɪntən, trĕn-gwáyntŏn

Trenowth *Cornwall*, trɪ'nauθ, trĕnówth

Trent, River, *Staffs.–Derby.– –Notts.–Humberside*, trent, trent

Trentham *Staffs.*, 'trentəm, tréntăm

Trentishoe *Devon*, 'trentɪʃou, tréntiss-hō

Treorchy *Mid Glam.*, trɪ'ɔrkɪ, tri-órki

Treppass, *f.n.*, trɪ'pæs, trĕpáss

Trepte, *f.n.*, 'treptɪ, tréptí

Trerice Manor *Cornwall*, trɪ'raɪs, trĕríss

Trerise, *f.n.*, trɪ'raɪz, trĕríz

Trerule Foot *Cornwall*, trɪ'rul 'fʊt, trĕroʻol fŏŏt

Tresardern, *f.n.*, 'tresərdərn, tréssärdern

Tresco *I. of Scilly*, 'treskou, trésskō

Tresham, *f.n.*, 'treʃəm, trésshăm

Tresham *Avon*, 'treʃəm, trésshăm

Treshnish Isles *S'clyde*, 'treʃnɪʃ, tréshnish

Tresillian *Cornwall*, trɪ'sɪlɪən, tréssílli-ăn

Tresman, *f.n.*, 'trezmən, trézmăn

Tresmeer *Cornwall*, trez'mɪər, trezmeér

Treswithian *Cornwall*, trɪ'swɪðɪən, trĕ-swíthi-ăn

Tretchikoff, *f.n.*, 'tretʃɪkɒf, trétchikoff

Trethewey, *f.n.*, trɪ'θjuɪ, trĕthéw-i

Trethewy, *f.n.* trɪ'θjuɪ, trĕthéw-i

Trethowan, *f.n.*, trɪ'θaʊən, trĕthówăn; trɪ'θoʊən, trĕthô-ăn

Treuddyn *Clwyd*, 'traɪðɪn, trɪ́thin

Trevan, *f.n.*, trɪ'væn, trĕván

Trevarrack *Cornwall*, trɪ'værək, trĕvárräk

Trevaskis, *f.n.*, trɪ'væskɪs, trĕvásskiss

Trevdraeth *see* **Trefdraeth**

Trevella *Cornwall*, trɪ'velə, trĕvéllă

Trevelyan, *f.n.*, trɪ'vɪljən, trĕvíl--yăn; trɪ'veljən, trĕvél-yăn. *The first is the usual Cornish*

pronunciation, the second the Northumbrian. The first is appropriate for George Macaulay ~, historian, and for Baron ~, diplomatist.

Trevena *Cornwall*, trɪ'vinə, trĕveénă

Treverbyn *Cornwall*, trɪ'vɜrbɪn, trĕvérbin

Treves, *f.n.*, trivz, treevz

Trevethick, *f.n.*, trɪ've θɪk, trĕvéthick

Trevethin, Baron, trɪ've θɪn, trĕvéthin

Trevett, *f.n.*, 'trevɪt, trévvĕt

Trevine, *also spelt* **Tre-fin**, *Dyfed*, trɪ'vin, trĕveén

Trevivian, *f.n.*, trɪ'vɪvɪən, trĕvívvi-ăn

Trevor, *C.n. and f.n.*, 'trevər, trévvŏr

Trevose Head *Cornwall*, trɪ'vouz, trĕvōz

Trew *Co. Tyrone*, tru, troo

Trewavas, *f.n.*, trɪ'wævəs, trĕ-wávváss

Treweek, *f.n.*, trɪ'wik, trĕ-weék

Trewellard *Cornwall*, trɪ'welərd, trĕ-wéllärd

Trewhela, *f.n.*, trɪ'hwelə, trĕ--whéllă

Trewidland *Cornwall*, trɪ'wɪdlənd, trĕ-wídländ

Trewin, *f.n.*, trɪ'wɪn, trĕ-win

Trewoon *Cornwall*, 'truən, troʻo-ŏn

Trewyddfa *W. Glam.*, trɪ'wɪðvə, trĕ-with-vă

Treyarnon Bay *Cornwall*, trɪ-'jɑrnən, trĕ-yaárnŏn

Trickett, *f.n.*, 'trɪkɪt, tríckĕt

Trier, *f.n.*, trɪər, treer

Trillick *Co. Tyrone*, 'trɪlɪk, tríllick

Trillo, *Welsh saint*, 'trɪlou, tríhlō

Trillo, *f.n.*, 'trɪlou, tríllō

Trimingham *Norfolk*, 'trɪmɪŋəm, trímming-ăm

Trimlestown, Baron, 'trɪmlztən, trímmlztŏn

Trimsaran *Dyfed*, trɪm'særən, trim-sárrăn

Trinafour *Tayside*, ,trɪnə'fʊər, trinnăfoŏr

Trinaman, *f.n.*, 'trɪnəmən, trínnă-măn; trɪ'nɒmən, trinaámăn

Trinant *Gwent*, 'trɪnænt, trínnănt

Tring, *f.n.*, trɪŋ, tring

Tring, *Herts.*, trɪŋ, tring

Triplow *see* **Thriplow**

Tripp, *f.n.*, trɪp, trip

Trippier, *f.n.*, 'trɪpɪər, tríppi-ĕr

Trispen *Cornwall*, 'trɪspən, tríss-pĕn

Tristram, *C.n. and f.n.*, 'trɪstrəm, trísstrăm

Tritton, *f.n.*, 'trɪtən, tríttŏn
Trocchi, *f.n.*, 'trɒkɪ, trócki
Troedrhiw-fuwch *Mid Glam.*, 'trɔɪdhrɪu'vjux, tróydri-oo-véwch
Troedrhiw-gwair *Gwent*, 'trɔɪdhrɪu'gwaɪər, tróydri-oo-gwír
Troed-yr-aur *Dyfed*, 'trɔɪdər'aɪər, tróydár̈ir
Troed-y-rhiw *Mid Glam.*, 'trɔɪdərɪ'u, tróydări-oó
Trofarth *Clwyd*, 'trouvarθ, tróvaarth
Trollope, *f.n.*, 'trɒləp, tróllŏp
Tron *Edinburgh*, *Glasgow*, trɒn, tronn
Trossachs, The, *Central*, 'trɒsəxs, tróssăchs
Trostre *Gwent*, 'trɒstreɪ, trósstray
Troth, *f.n.*, trɒθ, troth
Trotter, *f.n.*, 'trɒtər, tróttĕr
Trottiscliffe *Kent*, 'trɒzlɪ, trózzli
Troubridge, *f.n.*, 'truːbrɪdʒ, troóbrij
Troughton, *f.n.*, 'trautən, trówtŏn
Troup, *f.n.*, trup, troop
Troway *Derby.*, 'trouɪ, tró-i
Trowbridge *Wilts.*, 'troubrɪdʒ, tróbrij
Trowell, *f.n.*, 'trauəl, trówĕl; 'trouəl, tró-ĕl
Trowell *Notts.*, 'trauəl, trówĕl
Trower, *f.n.*, 'trauər, trówĕr
Trowsdale, *f.n.*, 'trauzdeɪl, t[róuz?]dayl
Trowse *Norfolk*, trous, tróss
Troy, *f.n.*, trɔɪ, troy
Truckle, *f.n.*, 'trʌkl, trúckl
Trudgill, *f.n.*, 'trʌdgɪl, trúd-gill
Trueman, *f.n.*, 'trumən, troómăn
Truesdale, *f.n.*, 'truzdeɪl, troóz--dayl
Trueta, *f.n.*, tru'etə, troo-éttă
Trufitt, *f.n.*, 'trufɪt, troófit
Truim, River, *H'land*, 'truɪm, troó-im
Truman, *f.n.*, 'trumən, troómăn
Trunch *Norfolk*, 'trʌnʃ, trunsh
Truro *Cornwall*, 'truərou, troórō
Truscott, *f.n.*, 'trʌskɒt, trússkŏt; 'trʌskɒt, trússkott
Trusham *Devon*, 'trʌsəm, trússăm; 'trɪsəm, tríssăm
Trustan *Co. Fermanagh*, 'trʌstən, trússtăn
Trusthorpe *Lincs.*, 'trʌsθɔrp, trúss-thorp
Trusthorpe Gowt *Lincs.*, 'trʌsθɔrp 'gaut, trúss-thorp gówt
Trustram, *C.n.*, 'trʌstrəm, trússträm
Truzzi, *f.n.*, 'trʌzɪ, trúzzi
Try, *f.n.*, traɪ, trī
Tryfan *Gwynedd*, 'trʌvən, trúvvăn
Tryon, *f.n.*, 'traɪən, trí-ŏn. *Appropriate also for Baron ~.*

Trysull *Staffs.*, 'trɪsl, treéssl; 'trɪzl, treézl
Trythall, *f.n.*, 'traɪθɒl, trí-thawl
Tschaikov, *f.n.*, 'tʃaɪkɒf, chíkoff
Tschiffely, A. F., *author*, tʃɪ'feɪlɪ, chifáyli
Tschirren, *f.n.*, 'tʃɪrən, chírrĕn
Tubb, *f.n.*, tʌb, tubb
Tuchet-Jesson, *f.n.*, 'tʌtʃɪt 'dʒesən, tútchĕt jéssŏn
Tuchner, *f.n.*, 'tʌknər, túcknĕr
Tuck, *f.n.*, tʌk, tuck
Tucker, *f.n.*, 'tʌkər, túckĕr
Tuckett, *f.n.*, 'tʌkɪt, túckĕt
Tuddenham, *f.n.*, 'tʌdənəm, túddĕnăm
Tudley *Kent*, 'tjudlɪ, téwdli; 'tudlɪ, toódli
Tudhoe *Durham*, 'tʌdou, túddō
Tudhope, *f.n.*, 'tjudəp, téwdŏp
Tudsbery, *f.n.*, 'tʌdzbərɪ, túdz-bĕri
Tudur, *Welsh C.n.*, 'tɪdɪər, tíddeer
Tudweiliog *Gwynedd*, tɪd'waɪljɒg, tidwíl-yog
Tueart, *f.n.*, 'tjuərt, téw-ărt; 'tjuərt, tyóo-ärt
Tue Brook *Merseyside*, 'tju brok, téw broók
Tufano, *f.n.*, tu'fanou, toōfaánō
Tuffin, *f.n.*, 'tʌfɪn, túffin
Tuffnell, *f.n.*, 'tʌfnəl, túffnĕl
Tugendhat, *f.n.*, 'tugənhat, toógĕn-haat
Tuggal *see* **Tughall**
Tughall, *also spelt* **Tuggal,** *Northd.*, 'tʌgl, túggl. **Tuggal** *is an older spelling, used in his title by the late Baron Beveridge of ~.*
Tugwell, *f.n.*, 'tʌgwəl, túgwĕl
Tuite, *f.n.*, tjut, tewt; 'tjuɪt, téw-it
Tuke, *f.n.*, tjuk, tewk
Tuker, *f.n.*, 'tjukər, téwkĕr
Tulchan Lodge *Tayside*, 'tʌlxən, túlchăn
Tulk, *f.n.*, tʌlk, tulk
Tullibardine, Marquess of, ˌtʌlɪ'bardɪn, tullibaárdin
Tulliemet *Tayside*, ˌtʌlɪ'met, tullimét
Tulloch *H'land*, 'tʌləx, túllŏch
Tully Carnet *Belfast*, 'tʌlɪ 'karnɪt, túlli kaárnĕt
Tummel, Loch *and* River, *Tayside*, 'tʌml, túmml
Tunesi, *f.n.*, tju'nesɪ, tewnéssi
Tungate, *f.n.*, 'tʌŋgeɪt, túng-gayt
Tungay, *f.n.*, 'tʌŋgeɪ, túng-gay
Tunnard, *f.n.*, 'tʌnərd, túnnărd
Tunnell, *f.n.*, tə'nel, tŭnéll
Tunstall *Norfolk*, 'tʌnstəl, túnsstawl
Tunstall *Staffs.*, 'tʌnstəl, túnsstäl

Tunstead *Norfolk*, 'tʌnstɪd, túnstĕd

Tuohey, *f.n.*, 'tuɪ, tóo-i

Tuohy, *f.n.*, 'tuɪ, tóo-i

Tupper, *f.n.*, 'tʌpər, túppĕr

Tuppholme, *f.n.*, 'tʌphoʊm, túpp-hōm

Turgis Green *Hants*, 'tɜrdʒɪs 'grin, túrjiss green

Turjansky, *f.n.*, tʊər'jænskɪ, tōōr-yánski

Turl, *f.n.*, tɜrl, turl

Turley, *f.n.*, 'tɜrlɪ, túrli

Turnbull, *f.n.*, 'tɜrnbʊl, túrnbōōl

Turnell, *f.n.*, tər'nel, tŭrnéll

Turner, *f.n.*, 'tɜrnər, túrnĕr

Turnhouse *Lothian*, 'tɜrnhaʊs, túrn-howss

Turnill, *f.n.*, 'tɜrnɪl, túrnil

Turnour, *f.n.*, 'tɜrnər, túrnŭr

Turnour, Cyril, *see* **Tourneur,** Cyril

Turquand, *f.n.*, tɜr'kwænd, turkwánd; 'tɜrkwɒnd, túrkwănd; tɜr'kɒɳ, turkóng

Turrell, *f.n.*, 'tʌrəl, túrrĕl

Turriff *Grampian*, 'tʌrɪf, túrrif

Turvey, *f.n.*, 'tɜrvɪ, túrvi

Turweston *Bucks.*, tər'westən, tŭrwésstŏn

Tusa, *f.n.*, 'tjusə, téwssă

Tushielaw *Borders*, ,tʌʃɪ'lɔ, tushi-láw

Tuson, *f.n.*, 'tjusən, téwssŏn

Tussaud, *f.n.*, 'tusoʊ, tóossō. *Although members of the family themselves use this pronunciation, they expect and accept the popular versions for Madame ∼'s exhibition, q.v.*

Tussaud's, Madame, *waxworks exhibition*, tə'sɔdz, tŭssáwdz; tə'soʊdz, tŭssŏdz

Tustain, *f.n.*, 'tʌsteɪn, tússtayn

Tutaev, *f.n.*, tu'taɪef, tootí-eff

Tutill, *f.n.*, 'tutɪl, tóotil

Tuttiett, *f.n.*, 'tʌtjet, tút-yet

Tuxford *Notts.*, 'tʌksfərd, túcksfŏrd

Tuyrrell, *f.n.*, 'tɪrəl, tírrĕl

Tuzo, *f.n.*, 'tjuzoʊ, téwzō

Twechar *S'clyde*, 'twexər, twéchăr

Tweddel, *f.n.*, 'twedl, twéddl

Tweed, River, *Scotland*, twid, tweed

Tweeddale, Marquess of, 'twiddeɪl, twéed-dayl

Tweedsmuir, Baron, 'twidzmjʊər, twéedz-myōōr

Twentyman, *f.n.*, 'twentɪmən, twéntimăn

Tweseldown *Hants*, 'twizldaʊn, twéezldown

Twidell, *f.n.*, twɪ'del, twidéll; 'twɪdl, twíddl

Twidle, *f.n.*, 'twaɪdl, twídl

Twigworth *Glos.*, 'twɪgwɜrθ, twígwurth

Twiname, *f.n.*, 'twaɪnəm, twínăm

Twine, *f.n.*, twaɪn, twīn

Twineham *W. Sussex*, 'twaɪnəm, twínăm

Twinhoe *Avon*, 'twinoʊ, twínnō

Twining, *f.n.*, 'twaɪnɪɳ, twíning

Twisleton-Wykeham-Fiennes, *f.n.*, 'twɪsltən 'wɪkəm 'faɪnz, twissltŏn wíckăm fínz. *Family name of Baron Saye and Sele.*

Twisly *E. Sussex*, twɪz'laɪ, twizz-lí

Twitchett, *f.n.*, 'twɪtʃɪt, twítchĕt

Twizell *Durham*, 'twaɪzl, twízl

Twohy, *f.n.*, 'tuɪ, tóo-i

Twomey, *f.n.*, 'tumɪ, tóomi

Twomley, *f.n.*, 'twɒmlɪ, twómli

Twyman, *f.n.*, 'twaɪmən, twímăn

Twynholm *D. & G.*, 'twaɪnəm, twínŏm

Twyn-yr-Odyn *S. Glam.*, 'tuɪn ər 'ɒdɪn, tóo-in ŭr óddin

Tyacke, *f.n.*, 'taɪæk, tí-ack

Tyberton *H. & W.*, 'tɪbərtən, tíbbĕrtŏn

Tyburn *W. Midlands*, 'taɪbərn, tíbŭrn

Tycoch Study Centre *Swansea*, 'tikoʊx, teékōch

Ty-croes *Dyfed*, ti'krɔɪs, tee-króyss

Tydd Gote *Lincs.*, 'tɪd 'goʊt, tídd gŏt

Tydd St. Giles *Cambs.*, 'tɪd snt 'dʒaɪlz, tídd sĭnt jílz

Tydd St. Mary *Norfolk*, 'tɪd snt 'mɛərɪ, tídd sĭnt máiri

Tydeman, *f.n.*, 'taɪdɪmən, tídimăn; 'taɪdmən, tídmăn

Tye, *f.n.*, taɪ, tī

Tyersal *W. Yorks.*, 'taɪərsl, tí-ĕrssl

Ty-hyll Bridge *Gwynedd*, ti 'hɪɬ, tee híhl

Tyla-gwyn *Mid Glam.*, ,tʌlə'gwɪn, tullăgwin

Tyldesley, *f.n.*, 'tɪldzlɪ, tíldzli

Tyldesley *Gtr. M'chester*, 'tɪldzlɪ, tíldzli; 'tɪlzlɪ, tíllzli

Tylecote, *f.n.*, 'taɪlkoʊt, tílkōt

Tylee, *f.n.*, 'taɪlɪ, tílee

Tyler, *f.n.*, 'taɪlər, tílĕr

Tylney Hall *Hants*, 'tɪlnɪ, tíllni

Tylorstown *Mid Glam.*, 'taɪlərztaʊn, tílŏrztown

Tylwch *Powys*, 'tʌlʊx, túllōōch

Ty-mawr *Clwyd*, ti'maʊər, teemówr

Tymiec, *f.n.*, 'tɪmɪek, tímmi-eck

Tynan, *f.n.*, 'taɪnən, tínăn

Tynan *Co. Armagh*, 'taɪnən, tínän
Tyndale, William, *translator of the New Testament*, 'tɪndl, tíndl
Tyndrum *Central*, taɪn'drʌm, tīndrúm
Tyne, *Rivers, Lothian, Northd.– Tyne & Wear*, taɪn, tīn
Tynemouth *Tyne & Wear*, 'taɪnmaʊθ, tínmowth; 'tɪnməθ. tínmúth
Tynewydd *Mid Glam.*, ti'newɪð, teené-with
Tyninghame *Lothian*, 'tɪnɪŋhəm, tínning-häm
Tynte, *f.n.*, tɪnt, tint
Tyntesfield *Avon*, 'tɪntsfild, tíntsfeeld
Tynwald, *Manx legislative assembly*, 'tɪnwəld, tínwäld
Tynygongl *Gwynedd*, ˌtɪnə'gɒŋl, tinnăgóng-ĕl
Tyree, *also spelt* Tiree, *S'clyde*, taɪ'ri, tī-reé
Tyrell, *f.n.*, 'tɪrəl, tírrĕl
Tyrella *Co. Down*, tɪ'relə, tĭréllă
Tyrer, *f.n.*, 'taɪərər, tíerĕr
Tyrie, *f.n.*, 'tɪrɪ, tírri
Tyringham, *f.n.*, 'tɪrɪŋəm, tírring-äm
Tyrone *Co. name*, tɪ'roʊn, tirón. *Appropriate also for the Earl of* ~.
Tyrrell, *f.n.*, 'tɪrəl, tírrĕl
Tyrwhitt, *f.n.*, 'tɪrɪt, tírrit
Tyseley *W. Midlands*, 'taɪzlɪ, tízli
Tysilio, *Welsh saint*, tə'sɪljoʊ, tŭssíl-yō
Tysoe, Lower, Middle, *and* Upper, *Warwicks.*, 'taɪsoʊ, tísō
Tyssen, *f.n.*, 'taɪsən, tíssĕn
Tysser, *f.n.*, 'taɪsər, tíssĕr
Tyte, *f.n.*, taɪt, tīt
Tythby, *also spelt* Tithby, *Notts.*, 'tɪðbɪ, títhbi
Tytler, *f.n.*, 'taɪtlər, títlĕr
Tywardreath *Cornwall*, ˌtaɪwər'dreθ, tī-wärdréth
Tywyn *Gwynedd*, 'taʊɪn, tów-in
Tyzack, *f.n.*, 'taɪzæk, tízack; 'tɪzæk, tízzack

U

Ubbelohde, *f.n.*, 'ʌbəloʊd, úbbĕlōd
Ubberley *Staffs.*, 'ʌbərlɪ, úbbĕrli
Uber, *f.n.*, 'jubər, yoóbĕr

Ubley *Avon*, 'ʌblɪ. úbbli
Ubsdell, *f.n.*, 'ʌbzdəl, úbzdĕl
Ubysz, *f.n.*, 'jubɪʃ, yoóbish
Udal, *f.n.*, 'judl, yoódl
Udale, *f.n.*, 'judeɪl, yoódayl; ju'deɪl, yoodáyl
Udall, *f.n.*, 'judl, yoódl; 'judəl, yoódawl; 'judeɪl, yoodál; ju'dæl, yoodál; ju'dɔl, yoodáwl
Udell, *f.n.*, ju'del, yōodéll
Uden, *f.n.*, 'judən, yoódĕn
Udimore *E. Sussex*, 'judɪmər, yoódimor; 'ʌdɪmər, úddimor
Udny *Grampian*, 'ʌdnɪ, úddni
Uffculme *Devon*, 'ʌfkəm, úffkŭm
Ugglebarnby *N. Yorks.*, 'ʌgl-'barnbɪ, úggl-baárnbi
Ugley *Essex*, 'ʌglɪ, úggli
Uglow, *f.n.*, 'ʌgloʊ, úgglō; 'juglou, yoóglō. *The first is usual in Cornwall.*
Ugthorpe *N. Yorks.*, 'ʌgθɔrp, úg-thorp
Uig *H'land*, 'uɪg, oó-ig
Uisgean *Mull*, 'uʃgən, oósh-gän
Uist, North *and* South, *W. Isles*, 'juɪst, yoó-ist; 'uɪst, oó-ist
Ulbster *H'land*, 'ʌlbstər, úlbstĕr
Ulceby *Humberside*, 'ʌlsəbɪ, úlssĕbi; 'ʌlsbɪ, úlssbi
Ulceby *Lincs.*, 'ʌlsbɪ, úlssbi
Ulcombe *Kent*, 'ʌlkəm, úlkŏm
Uldale *Cumbria*, 'ʌldeɪl, úldayl
Uley *Glos.*, 'julɪ, yoóli
Ulgham *Northd.*, 'ʌfəm, úffäm
Ulick, *C.n.*, 'julɪk, yoólick
Ullapool *H'land*, 'ʌləpul, úllăpool
Ulleskelf *N. Yorks.*, 'ʌləskelf, úllĕskelf
Ullesthorpe *Leics.*, 'ʌləsθɔrp, úllĕss-thorp
Ullman, *f.n.*, 'ʊlmən, oólmän
Ullock, *f.n.*, 'ʌlək, úllŏk
Ullswater *Cumbria*, 'ʌlzwɔtər, úlzwawtĕr. *Appropriate also for Viscount* ~.
Ulnes Walton *Lancs.*, 'ʌlzwɔltən, úlzwawltŏn
Ulph, *f.n.*, ʌlf, ulf
Ulva *S'clyde*, 'ʌlvə, úlvă
Ulverston *Cumbria*, 'ʌlvərstən, úlvĕrsston
Umberleigh *Devon*, 'ʌmbərlɪ, úmbĕrli
Umfreville, *f.n.*, 'ʌmfrɪvɪl, úmfrĕvil
Uncles, *f.n.*, 'ʌŋklz, únklz
Underdown, *f.n.*, 'ʌndərdaʊn, úndĕrdown
Underhill, *f.n.*, 'ʌndərhɪl, úndĕr-hil
Underwood, *f.n.*, 'ʌndərwʊd, úndĕrwŏod
Undery, *f.n.*, 'ʌndərɪ, úndĕri

Ungar, *f.n.*, 'ʌŋgər, úng-găr
Ungoed, *Welsh C.n.*, 'ɪŋgɔɪd, íng-goyd
Ungoed, *f.n.*, 'ɪŋgɔɪd, íng-goyd; 'ʌŋgɔɪd, úng-goyd
Uniacke, *f.n.*, 'juːnɪæk, yóoni-ack
Unst *Shetland*, ʌnst, unsst
Unstone *Derby.*, 'ʌnstən, únsstön
Unthank, *f.n.*, 'ʌnθæŋk, únthank
Unthank *Cumbria*, 'ʌnθæŋk, únthank
Unwin, *f.n.*, 'ʌnwɪn, únwin. *Appropriate for George Allen and ~, publishers.*
Upavon *Wilts.*, 'ʌpeɪvən, úppayvŏn
Upend *Cambs.*, 'ʌpend, úppend
Up Exe *Devon*, ʌp eks, úp ecks
Up Holland *Lancs.*, ʌp 'hɒlənd, up hólländ
Upjohn, *f.n.*, 'ʌpdʒɒn, úpjon
Upleadon *H. & W.*, ʌp'liːdən, upléddön
Uplowman *Devon*, ʌp'loʊmən, uplṓmăn
Up Marden *W. Sussex*, ʌp mɑːdən, úp maardĕn
Up Ottery *Devon*, ʌp 'ɒtərɪ, up óttĕri
Uppark *W. Sussex*, 'ʌppɑːk, úp-paark
Upper Benefield *Northants.*, ʌpər 'benɪfiːld, úppĕr bénnifeeld
Upper Broughton *Notts.*, ʌpər 'brɔːtən, úppĕr bráwtön
Upperdine, *f.n.*, 'ʌpərdaɪn, úppĕrdīn
Upper Hardres *Kent*, ʌpər 'hɑːdz, úppĕr haárdz
Upper Haugh *S. Yorks.*, ʌpər 'hɔːf, úppĕr háwf
Upper Heyford, *also sometimes called* **Heyford Warren,** *Oxon.*, ʌpər 'heɪfərd, úppĕr háyförd
Upper Hiendley *W. Yorks.*, ʌpər 'hiːndlɪ, úppĕr heéndli
Upperlands *Co. Derry*, 'ʌpərləndz, úppĕrländz
Upper Shuckburgh *Warwicks.*, ʌpər 'ʃʌkbərə, úppĕr shúckbŭrä
Upper Slaughter *Glos.*, ʌpər 'slɔːtər, úppĕr sláwtĕr
Upper Tean *Staffs.*, ʌpər 'tiːn, úppĕr teén
Upper Wyche *H. & W.*, ʌpər 'wɪtʃ, úppĕr wítch
Uprichard, *f.n.*, juː'prɪtʃɑːd, yooprítchaard; juː'prɪtʃərd, yooprítchärd; ʌp'rɪtʃərd, upprítchärd
Upshire *Essex*, 'ʌpʃaɪər, úp-shīr; 'ʌpʃər, úp-shĕr

Upton, *f.n.*, 'ʌptən, úptŏn
Upton Hellions *Devon*, 'ʌptən 'heliənz, úptŏn hélli-ŏnz
Upware *Cambs.*, 'ʌpwɛər, úpwair
Upwell *Cambs.–Norfolk border*, 'ʌpwel, úpwel
Upwey *Dorset*, 'ʌpweɪ, úpway
Urban, *f.n.*, 'ɜːbən, úrbăn
Urch, *f.n.*, ɜːtʃ, urtch
Urchfont *Wilts.*, 'ɜːtʃfɒnt, úrtchfont
Urdd Gobaith Cymru, *Welsh League of Youth*, 'ɪərð 'gɒbaɪθ 'kʌmrɪ, eérth góbbīth kúmri
Ure, *f.n.*, jʊər, yŏor
Uren, *f.n.*, jʊəˈren, yŏorén
Uridge, *f.n.*, 'jʊərɪdʒ, yŏórij
Urmston *Gtr. M'chester*, 'ɜːmstən, úrmsstön
Urquhart, *f.n.*, 'ɜːxərt, úrchärt; 'ɜːkərt, úrkärt
Urrard House *Tayside*, 'ʌrərd, úrrärd
Urray *H'land*, 'ʌrɪ, úrri
Urswick *Cumbria*, 'ɜːzwɪk, úrzwick; 'ɜːzɪk, úrzick; 'ɒsɪk, óssick
Urwick, *f.n.*, 'ɜːwɪk, úrwick
Ury, *f.n.*, 'jʊərɪ, yŏóri
Usan *Tayside*, 'uːzən, óozăn
Usborne, *f.n.*, 'ʌzbɔːn, úzzborn
Ushaw *Durham*, 'ʌʃə, úsh-ă; 'ʌʃɔ, úsh-aw
Usher, *f.n.*, 'ʌʃər, úsh-ĕr
Usherwood, *f.n.*, 'ʌʃərwʊd, úshĕrwŏod
Usk *Gwent*, ʌsk, ussk. *Appropriate also for ~ Priory.*
Usk, River, *Powys–Gwent*, ʌsk, ussk
Uskmouth *Gwent*, 'ʌskmaʊθ, ússkmowth
Ussleby *Lincs.*, 'ʌslbɪ, ússlbi
Ussher, *f.n.*, 'ʌʃər, úsh-ĕr
Ustinov, *f.n.*, 'justɪnɒf, yoóstinoff; 'ustɪnɒf, oóstinoff. *Peter ~, film producer, actor and playwright, submits to either pronunciation.*
Uswayford *Northd.*, 'ʌzweɪfərd, úzzwayford
Usworth *Tyne & Wear*, 'ʌzwɜːθ, úzzwurth
Uthwatt, *f.n.*, 'ʌθwɒt, úth-wott. *Appropriate also for the Barony of ~.*
Utiger, *f.n.*, 'jutɪgər, yoótigĕr
Utting, *f.n.*, 'ʌtɪŋ, útting
Uttoxeter *Staffs.*, ju'tɒksɪtər, yootóckssĕtĕr; ʌ'tɒksɪtər, uttóckssĕtĕr; 'ʌksɪtər, úckssĕtĕr. *There are other less common variants.*

Uvarov, *f.n.*, juˈvɑrɒf, yoovaʹaroff; ˈjuvərɒf, yoovároff

Uwins, *f.n.*, ˈjuɪnz, yoo-inz

Uxbridge *London*, ˈʌksbrɪdʒ, úcksbrij

Uyeasound *Shetland*, ˈjuəsaʊnd, yoo-ássownd

Uziell, *f.n.*, ˈjuzɪel, yoózi-el

Uzmaston *Dyfed*, ˈʌzməsən, úzzmássŏn

V

Vache, The, *Bucks.*, ðə ˈvætʃ, thĕ vátch

Vachell, *f.n.*, ˈveɪtʃl, váytchl; ˈvætʃl, vátchl

Vachell, Horace Annesley, *author*, ˈhɒrɪs ˈænzlɪ ˈveɪtʃl, hórriss ánzli váytchl

Vacher, *f.n.*, ˈvæʃər, váshĕr. *Appropriate in particular for the printers of ~'s Parliamentary Companion.*

Vaesen, *f.n.*, ˈveɪzən, váyzĕn

Vaila *Shetland*, ˈveɪlə, váylă

Vaillant, *f.n.*, ˈvæljənt, vál-yănt; ˈvaɪjɒŋ, ví-yong

Vaizey, *f.n.*, ˈveɪzɪ, váyzi

Valency, *f.n.*, vəˈlensɪ, vălénssi

Valency, River, *Cornwall*, vəˈlensɪ, vălénssi

Valentin, *f.n.*, ˈvæləntɪn, válĕntin

Valentine, *C.n. and f.n.*, ˈvæləntaɪn, válĕntīn

Valerio, *f.n.*, vəˈlɛərɪoʊ, văláiriō

Valetort, *f.n.*, ˈvælɪtɔrt, válĕtort

Vallance, *f.n.*, ˈvæləns, válănss

Vallancey, *f.n.*, vəˈlænsɪ, valánssi

Vallans, *f.n.*, ˈvæləns, válănss

Vallaquie *see* **Dunrossil of ~**, Viscount

Valle Crucis Abbey *Clwyd*, ˈvælɪ ˈkrusɪs, váli kroóssiss

Vallely, *f.n.*, ˈvæləlɪ, válĕli

Valley *Gwynedd*, ˈvælɪ, váli

Vallier, *f.n.*, ˈvæljeɪ, vál-yay

Vallins, *f.n.*, ˈvælɪnz, válinz

Van Asch, *f.n.*, væn ˈæʃ, van ásh

van Barthold, *f.n.*, væn ˈbɑrtoʊld, van baártōld

Vanbrugh, *f.n.*, ˈvænbrə, vánbră

Vanburgh, *f.n.*, ˈvænbrə, vánbră

Vance, *f.n.*, væns, vanss; vɑns, vaanss

Van Cutsem, *f.n.*, væn ˈkʌtsəm, van kúttsĕm

Vandam, *f.n.*, vænˈdæm, vandám

Van Damm, *f.n.*, væn ˈdæm, van dám

Vanden-Bempde-Johnstone, *f.n.*, ˈvændən ˈbemptɪ ˈdʒɒnstən, vándĕn bémpti jónstŏn. *Family name of Baron Derwent.*

Van den Bergh, *f.n.*, ˈvændən bərg, vándĕnberg

Vandepeer, *f.n.*, ˌvændəˈpɪər, vandĕpéer

van der Beek, *f.n.*, ˌvændərˈbik, vandĕrbéek

van der Burgh, *f.n.*, ˈvændərbərg, vándĕrburg

Vanderbyl, *f.n.*, ˈvændərbaɪl, vándĕrbīl

Van Der Gucht, *f.n.*, ˈvændərgut, vándĕrgoot

Van der Pant, *f.n.*, ˈvændərpænt, vándĕrpant

Vanderplank, *f.n.*, ˈvændərplæŋk, vándĕrplank

Van der Pump, *f.n.*, ˈvændərpʌmp, vándĕrpump

van der Riet, *f.n.*, ˈvændərit, vándĕreet

Vanderspar, *f.n.*, ˈvændərspɑr, vándĕrspaar

van der Sprenkel, *f.n.*, ˌvændər ˈspreŋkl, vandĕr sprénkl

Van der Weyer, *f.n.*, ˌvændər ˈweɪər, vandĕr wáy-ĕr

Vandyck, *f.n.*, vænˈdaɪk, vandík

Van Dyck, *f.n.*, væn ˈdaɪk, van dík

Van Eyssen, *f.n.*, væn ˈaɪsən, van íssĕn

Vange *Essex*, vændʒ, vanj

van Geloven, *f.n.*, ˌvæn gəˈloʊvən, van gĕlóvĕn

van Greenaway, *f.n.*, væn ˈgrinəweɪ, van gréenă-way

van Gyseghem, *f.n.*, væn ˈgaɪzəgəm, van gízĕgĕm

Van Kampen, *f.n.*, væn ˈkæmpən, van kámpĕn

Van Moppes, *f.n.*, væn ˈmɒpɪz, van móppĕz

Vanneck, *f.n.*, vænˈek, vannéck

Van Praagh, *f.n.*, væn ˈprɑg, van praág

Van Riemsdijk, *f.n.*, væn ˈrimzdaɪk, van réemzdík

Vans Colina, *f.n.*, ˌvænz kəˈlinə, vanz kŏléenă

Vansittart, *f.n.*, vænˈsɪtərt, van-síttărt. *Appropriate also for the Barony of ~.*

van Straten, *f.n.*, væn ˈstrɑtən, van straátĕn

van Straubenzee, *f.n.*, ˌvæn strɒˈbenzɪ, van strawbénzi

Van Thal, *f.n.*, væn ˈtɒl, van táwl

Van Wyck, *f.n.*, væn ˈwaɪk, van wík

Varah, *f.n.*, ˈvɑrə, vaáră

Varcoe, *f.n.*, ˈvɑrkoʊ, vaárkō

Varley, *f.n.,* 'vɑrlɪ, va'arlı
Varndell, *f.n.,* vɑrn'del, vaarndéll
Varnel, *f.n.,* vɑr'nel, vaarnéll
Varteg *Gwent,* 'vɑrteg, va'arteg
Vas, *f.n.,* vɑs, vaass
Vasey, *f.n.,* 'veɪzɪ, váyzi
Vaternish *see* **Waternish**
Vatersay *W. Isles,* 'vætərseɪ, vátterssay
Vaughan, *f.n.,* vɔn, vawn
Vaughan Williams, Ralph, *composer,* 'reɪf ,vɔn 'wɪljəmz, ráyf vawn wílyămz
Vaus, *f.n.,* vɔs, vawss
Vautor, Thomas, *16th–17th-c. composer,* 'voutər, vótor
Vaux, *f.n.,* vɒks, vawks; vou, vō; vɒks, vocks
Vaux of Harrowden, Baron, 'vɒks əv 'hæroudən, váwks ŏv hárrō-dĕn
Vauxhall *London, West Midlands,* 'vɒksɔl, vócksawl; 'vɒkshɔl, vócks-hawl
Vavasour, *f.n.,* 'vævəsər, vávvăs-sŭr
Vavasseur, *f.n.,* ,vævə'sɜr, vavvăs-súr
Vayne, *f.n.,* veɪn, vayn
Vaynol *Gwynedd,* 'vaɪnɒl, vínoll
Vaynor *Mid Glam.,* 'veɪnɔr, váynor; 'vaɪnɔr, vínor
Vear, *f.n.,* vɪər, veer
Veasey, *f.n.,* 'vizɪ, véezi
Vedast, saint, 'vidæst, véedasst
Vedrenne, *f.n.,* vɪ'dren, vĕdrén
Veitch, *f.n.,* vitʃ, veetch
Vel, *f.n.,* vel, vell
Velindre *Dyfed,* ve'lɪndreɪ, velíndray; ve'lɪndrə, velíndrĕ. *Cf.* **Felindre.** *The first is the Welsh pronunciation, appropriate for both places of the name in Dyfed, although the steel-works near Newcastle Emlyn is usually known by the second, anglicized, pronunciation.*
Velindre *Powys,* ve'lɪndreɪ, velíndray
Vellenoweth, *f.n.,* 'velənouɪθ, véllĕnō-ĕth; 'velnouθ, vélnōth; ,velə'nauɪθ, vellĕnów-ĕth; 'velənauθ, véllĕnowth; 'velnəθ, vélnŏth
Vementry *Shetland,* 'veməntrɪ, vémmĕntri
Venables, *f.n.,* 'venəblz, vénnăblz
Vendryes, *f.n.,* ven'dris, vendréess
Venediger, *f.n.,* vɪ'nedɪdʒər, vĕnéddijĕr
Veness, *f.n.,* vɪ'nes, vĕnéss
Vennachar, Loch, *Central,* 'venəxər, vénnăchăr

Venner, *f.n.,* 'venər, vénnĕr
Venning, *f.n.,* 'venɪŋ, vénning
Venour, *f.n.,* 'venər, vénnŭr; vɪ'nuər, vĕnóor
Ventham, *f.n.,* 'venθəm, vén-thăm
Ver, River, *Herts.,* vɜr, ver
Verco, *f.n.,* 'vɜrkou, vérkō
Vercoe, *f.n.,* 'vɜrkou, vérkou
Vercow, *f.n.,* vər'kou, vĕrkó
Vercowe, *f.n.,* vər'kou, vĕrkó
Vereker, *f.n.,* 'verɪkər, vérrĕkĕr
Verey, *f.n.,* 'vɪərɪ, véeri
Verinder, *f.n.,* 'verɪndər, vérrindĕr
Verity, *C.n. and f.n.,* 'verɪtɪ, vérriti
Verlander, *f.n.,* vər'lændər, vĕrlándĕr; 'vɜrləndər, vérlăndĕr
Vernède, *f.n.,* vər'neɪd, vĕrnáyd
Verney, *f.n.,* 'vɜrnɪ, vérni
Vernon, *C.n. and f.n.,* 'vɜrnən, vérnŏn
Verrall, *f.n.,* 'verəl, vérrăl
Verrells, *f.n.,* 'verəlz, vérrĕlz
Verschoyle, *f.n.,* 'vɜrskɔɪl, vérsskoyl
Verstappen, *f.n.,* vər'stæpən, vĕrstáppĕn
Vertigan, *f.n.,* 'vɜrtɪgən, vértigăn
Verulam, Earl of, 'verʊləm, vérrŏolăm
Verulamium, *Roman site near St. Albans,* ,verʊ'leɪmɪəm, verrŏoláymiŭm
Veryan *Cornwall,* 'verɪən, vérri-ăn
Vesey, *f.n.,* 'vizɪ, véezi
Vesian, *f.n.,* 'vezɪən, vézzi-ăn
Vesselo, *f.n.,* vɪ'selou, vĕsséllō
Vevers, *f.n.,* 'vivərz, véevĕrz
Veysey, *f.n.,* 'veɪzɪ, váyzi
Vezin, *f.n.,* 'vizɪn, véezin
Via Gellia *Derby.,* 'vaɪə 'dʒelɪə, ví-ă jélli-ă
Vialls, *f.n.,* 'vaɪəlz, ví-ălz; 'vaɪɔlz, ví-awlz
Viant, *f.n.,* 'vaɪənt, ví-ănt
Vibart, *f.n.,* 'vaɪbərt, víbărt
Vidal, *f.n.,* 'vaɪdl, vídl
Videan, *f.n.,* 'vɪdɪən, víddi-ăn
Vidler, *f.n.,* 'vɪdlər, víddlĕr
Vieler, *f.n.,* 'vilər, véelĕr
Vigar, *f.n.,* 'vaɪgər, vígăr; 'vaɪgɑr, vígaar
Vigay, *f.n.,* 'vaɪgeɪ, vígay
Vigers, *f.n.,* 'vaɪgərz, vígĕrz
Viggers, *f.n.,* 'vɪgərz, víggĕrz
Vigne, *f.n.,* vaɪn, vīn
Vignes, *f.n.,* vɪnz, veenz
Vignoles, *f.n.,* 'vɪnjoulz, vín-yōlz; 'vinjoulz, véen-yōlz; 'vɪnjool, vín'joulz, vin-yŏlz; 'vɪnjɒlz, véen-yollz
Vigo Inn *Kent,* 'vaɪgou, vígō
Vigor, *f.n.,* 'vaɪgor, vígor
Vigrow, *f.n.,* 'vɪgrou, véegrō

Vigurs, *f.n.,* 'vaɪgərz, vígŭrz; 'vɪgərz, víggŭrz

Viles, *f.n.,* vaɪlz, vīlz

Villiers, *f.n.,* 'vɪlərz, víllĕrz; 'vɪljərz, víl-yĕrz. *The first is appropriate for the family name of the Earl of Clarendon and of the Earl of Jersey, for Viscount ∼ and for Baron de ∼.*

Vinall, *f.n.,* 'vaɪnl, vínl

Vinaver, *f.n.,* vɪ'nɑvər, vinaávĕr

Vincent, *C.n. and f.n.,* 'vɪnsənt, vínssĕnt

Vincze, *f.n.,* vɪnts, vints

Vine, *f.n.,* vaɪn, vīn

Viner, *f.n.,* 'vaɪnər, vínĕr

Vinerian, *pertaining to Viner,* vaɪ'nɪərɪən, vīnéeri-ăn. *Appropriate for the ∼ common law professorship and fellowships at the University of Oxford.*

Viney Hill *Glos.,* 'vaɪnɪ 'hɪl, víni híll

Vintcent, *f.n.,* 'vɪnsənt, vínssĕnt

Vinter, *f.n.,* 'vɪntər, víntĕr

Vintner, *f.n.,* 'vɪntnər, víntnĕr

Viollet, *f.n.,* 'vaɪələt, ví-ŏlĕt

Vipont, *f.n.,* 'vaɪpɒnt, vípont

Virago Press, *publishers,* vɪ'rɑgoʊ, viraágō

Virginia Water *Surrey,* vər'dʒɪnɪə 'wɒtər, vŭrjínni-ă wáwtĕr

Vivary Park *Taunton,* 'vaɪvərɪ, vívári

Viveash, *f.n.,* 'vaɪvæʃ, vívash

Vivian, *f.n.,* 'vɪvɪən, vívvi-ăn

Vivis, *f.n.,* 'vɪvɪs, véeviss

Vizard, *f.n.,* 'vɪzɑrd, vízzaard

Vizetelly, *f.n.,* ˌvɪzə'telɪ, vizĕtélli

Voce, *f.n.,* voʊs, vōss

Voelcker, *f.n.,* 'voʊlkər, vólkĕr

Vogel, *f.n.,* 'voʊgl, vṓgl

Vogt, *f.n.,* voʊkt, vōkt; voʊt, vōt; vɒt, vott

Vogue Beloth *Cornwall,* 'voʊg bɪ'lɒθ, vṓg bélŏth

Voigt, *f.n.,* vɔɪt, voyt

Voisey, *f.n.,* 'vɔɪzɪ, vóyzi

Volante, *f.n.,* və'læntɪ, vŏlánti

Volckman, *f.n.,* 'vɒlkmən, vóllkmăn

Volk, *f.n.,* vɒlk, vollk; voʊlk, vōlk. *The first is appropriate for ∼'s Railway at Brighton.*

Volze, *f.n.,* voʊlz, vōlz

Von der Heyde, *f.n.,* 'vɒndərhaɪd, vóndĕr-hīd

Von Stranz, *f.n.,* vɒn 'strænz, von stránz

Vores, *f.n.,* vɔrz, vorz

Vortigern, *5th-c. king of the Britons,* 'vɔrtɪgərn, vórtigĕrn

Vos, *f.n.,* vɒs, voss

Vosburgh, *f.n.,* 'vɒsbərə, vóssbŭră

Voss, *f.n.,* vɒs, voss

Vought, *f.n.,* vɒt, vawt

Voules, *f.n.,* voʊlz, vōlz; vaʊlz, vowlz

Vowden, *f.n.,* 'vaʊdən, vówdĕn

Vowles, *f.n.,* voʊlz, vōlz; vaʊlz, vowlz

Voysey, *f.n.,* 'vɔɪzɪ, vóyzi

Vroncysyllte *see* **Froncysyllte**

Vuller, *f.n.,* 'vʊlər, vŏŏlĕr

Vulliamy, *f.n.,* 'vʌljəmɪ, vúl-yämi. *Appropriate for Benjamin Lewis ∼, 18th-c. clock-maker.*

Vychan, *f.n.,* 'vʌxən, vúᴄͪăn

Vyrnwy, Lake *and* River, *Powys,* 'vɜrnʊɪ, vŭrnōō-i

Vyse, *f.n.,* vaɪz, vīz

Vyvyan, *C.n. and f.n.,* 'vɪvɪən, vívvi-ăn

W

Wacey, *f.n.,* 'weɪsɪ, wáyssi

Wach, *f.n.,* wɒtʃ, wotch

Wacher, *f.n.,* 'weɪtʃər, wáytchĕr

Wacton *Norfolk,* 'wæktən, wácktŏn

Waddell, *f.n.,* 'wɒdl, wóddl; wə'del, wŏdéll

Waddesdon *Bucks.,* 'wɒdzdən, wódzdŏn

Waddicor, *f.n.,* 'wɒdɪkər, wóddikor

Waddilove, *f.n.,* 'wɒdɪlʌv, wóddiluv

Waddon *London,* 'wɒdən, wóddŏn

Wade, *f.n.,* weɪd, wayd

Wadebridge *Cornwall,* 'weɪdbrɪdʒ, wáydbrij

Wadeford *Somerset,* 'weɪdfərd, wódfŏrd

Wade-Gery, *f.n.,* 'weɪd 'gɪərɪ, wáyd géeri

Wadenhoe *Northants.,* 'wɒdənhoʊ, wóddĕn-hō

Wadey, *f.n.,* 'weɪdɪ, wáydi

Wadham College *Univ. of Oxford,* 'wɒdəm, wóddăm

Wadsley, *f.n.,* 'wɒdzlɪ, wódzli

Wadsworth, *f.n.,* 'wɒdzwərθ, wódzwŭrth

Waechter, *f.n.,* 'veɪktər, váyktĕr

Waenfawr, *also spelt* **Waunfawr,** *Dyfed,* 'waɪnvaʊər, wínvowr

Wagg, *f.n.,* wæg, wagg

Waghen *see* **Wawne**

Wagner, *f.n.,* 'wægnər, wágnĕr

Wahab, *f.n.,* wɒb, wawb

Waight, *f.n.,* weɪt, wayt

Wainfleet *Lincs.,* 'weɪnflɪt, wáynfleet

Wainwright, *f.n.*, 'weɪnraɪt, wáyn-rīt

Waites, *f.n.*, weɪts, wayts

Waith, *f.n.*, weɪθ, wayth

Waithman, *f.n.*, 'weɪθmən, wáyth-mǎn

Wake, *f.n.*, weɪk, wayk

Wakefield, *f.n.*, 'weɪkfɪld, wáyk-feeld

Wakefield *W. Yorks.*, 'weɪkfɪld, wáykfeeld

Wakeling, *f.n.*, 'weɪklɪŋ, wáykling

Wakering, *Great and Little, Essex,* 'weɪkərɪŋ, wáykěring

Wakes Colne *Essex,* 'weɪks 'koʊn, wáyks kṓn

Wakley, *f.n.*, 'wæklɪ, wáckli; 'weɪklɪ, wáykli. *The first is considered appropriate for Thomas* ∼, *19th-c. surgeon, founder of* '*The Lancet'.*

Walberswick *Suffolk,* 'wɒlbərz-wɪk, wáwlběrzwick

Walcot, *f.n.*, 'wɒlkɒt, wáwlkott

Walcote *Leics.*, 'wɒlkoʊt, wáwl-kōt

Waldegrave, *f.n.*, 'wɒlgreɪv, wáwlgrayv; 'wɒldɪgreɪv, wáwl-děgrayv. *The first is appropriate for Earl* ∼.

Walden, *f.n.*, 'wɒldən, wáwldĕn; 'wɒlldən, wóldĕn

Walder, *f.n.*, 'wɒldər, wáwldĕr

Walderslade *Kent,* 'wɒldərsleɪd, wáwldĕrsslayd

Waldo, *C.n.*, 'wɒldoʊ, wáwldō; 'wɒldoʊ, wólldō

Waldron, *f.n.*, 'wɒldrən, wáwldrŏn

Waleran, Barony of, 'wɒlrən, wáwlrăn

Walesby *Lincs., Notts.*, 'weɪlzbɪ, wáylzbi

Waley, *f.n.*, 'weɪlɪ, wáyli

Walford, *f.n.*, 'wɒlfərd, wáwlfŏrd; wɒllfərd, wólfŏrd

Walhampton *Hants,* 'wɒl'hæmp-tən, wáwl-hámptŏn

Walkden *Gtr. M'chester,* 'wɒkdən, wáwkdĕn

Walke, *f.n.*, wɔk, wawk

Walker, *f.n.*, 'wɔkər, wáwkĕr

Walkerdine, *f.n.*, 'wɔkərdin, wáwkĕrdeen

Walkern *Herts.*, 'wɔkərn, wáw-kĕrn

Walkham, River, *Devon,* 'wɒlkəm, wáwlkăm

Walkley *S. Yorks.*, 'wɔklɪ, wáwkli

Wall, *f.n.*, wɔl, wawl

Walla, *f.n.*, 'wɒlə, wóllă

Wallace, *f.n.*, 'wɒlɪs, wólliss

Wallach, *f.n.*, 'wɒlək, wólláck; 'wɒlə, wóllă

Wallage, *f.n.*, 'wɒlɪdʒ, wóllij

Wallasey *Merseyside,* 'wɒləsɪ, wóllăssi

Waller, *f.n.*, 'wɒlər, wóllĕr; 'wɔlər, wáwlĕr

Walles, *f.n.*, 'wɒlɪs, wólliss

Wallich, *f.n.*, 'wɒlɪk, wóllick

Walliker, *f.n.*, 'wɒlɪkər, wólliker

Wallinger, *f.n.*, 'wɒlɪndʒər, wóllin-jĕr

Wallington *Clwyd, Hants, Herts., London,* 'wɒlɪŋtən, wóllingtŏn

Wallis, *f.n.*, 'wɒlɪs, wólliss

Wallop, *f.n.*, 'wɒləp, wóllŏp

Wallop, Middle, Nether, *and* Over, *Hants,* 'wɒləp, wóllŏp

Wallsend *Tyne & Wear,* 'wɔlz-'end, wáwlzénd

Walmer *Kent,* 'wɒlmər, wáwlmĕr

Walmersley *Gtr. M'chester,* 'wɒmzlɪ, wáwmzli

Walmesley, *f.n.*, 'wɒmzlɪ, wáwm-zli

Walmisley, *f.n.*, 'wɒmzlɪ, wáwm-zli

Walmsley, *f.n.*, 'wɒmzlɪ, wáwmzli

Walne, *f.n.*, wɒn, wawn

Walney, Isle of, *Cumbria,* 'wɒlnɪ, wáwlni

Walond, William, *18th-c. composer and organist,* 'wɒlənd, wóllŏnd

Walpole, *f.n.*, 'wɒlpoʊl, wáwlpōl; 'wɒlpoʊl, wóllpōl. *The first is appropriate for Baron* ∼.

Walpole Highway *Norfolk,* 'wɒlpoʊl 'haɪweɪ, wáwlpōl hí-way; 'wɒlpoʊl 'haɪweɪ, wóllpōl hí-way

Walrond, *f.n.*, 'wɒlrənd, wáwl-rŏnd

Walsall *W. Midlands,* 'wɒlsl, wáwlssl; 'wɒlsɒl, wáwlssawl; 'wɒsl, wáwssl

Walsden *W. Yorks.*, 'wɒlzdən, wáwlzdĕn

Walsh, *f.n.*, wɒlʃ, wawlsh; wɒlʃ, wollsh; welʃ, welsh

Walsham, North *and* South, *Norfolk,* 'wɒlʃəm, wáwl-shăm

Walsingham, Baron, 'wɒlsɪŋəm, wáwlssing-ăm

Walsingham, Great *and* Little, *Norfolk,* 'wɒlzɪŋəm, wáwlzing-ăm

Walsoken *Cambs.*, 'wɒl'soʊkən, wawlssṓkĕn

Walston, *f.n.*, 'wɒlstən, wáwlsstŏn. *Appropriate also for Baron* ∼.

Walsworth, *f.n.*, 'wɒlzwərθ, wáwlzwürth

Walter, *C.n. and f.n.*, 'wɒltər, wáwltĕr; 'wɒltər, wólltĕr

Walters, *f.n.*, 'wɒltərz, wáwltĕrz; 'wɒltərz, wólltĕrz

Waltham, *f.n.*, 'wɒlθəm, wáwl-
-thăm
Waltham *Humberside*, 'wɒlθəm,
wáwl-thăm
Waltham, Great *and* Little, *Essex*,
'wɒltəm, wáwltăm
Waltham, North, *Hants*, 'wɒlθəm,
wáwl-thăm
Waltham Abbey *Essex*, 'wɒlθəm
'æbɪ, wáwl-thăm ábbi
Waltham Cross *Herts.*, 'wɒlθəm
'krɒs, wáwl-thăm króss
Waltham Forest *London*, 'wɒlθəm
'fɒrɪst, wáwl-thăm fórrěst
Waltham-on-the-Wolds *Leics.*,
'wɒlθəm ɒn ðə 'wouldz, wáwl-
-thăm on the wöldz
Waltham St. Lawrence *Berks.*,
'wɒlθəm snt 'lɒrəns, wáwl-thăm
sĭnt lórrěnss
Walthamstow *London*, 'wɒlθəm-
stou, wáwl-thămsstō
Walthew, *f.n.*, 'wɒlθju, wáwl-thew
Walton, *f.n.*, 'wɒltən, wáwltŏn;
'wɒltən, wólltŏn
Walton-le-Dale *Lancs.*, 'wɒltən
lɪ'deɪl, wáwltŏn l dáyl
Walton-on-the-Naze *Essex*,
'wɒltən ɒn ðə 'neɪz, wáwltŏn on
the náyz
Walton-on-Thames *Surrey*,
'wɒltən ɒn 'temz, wáwltŏn on
témz
Walwick *Northd.*, 'wɒlɪk, wóllick;
'wɒlwɪk, wáwlwick
Walwyn, *f.n.*, 'wɒlwɪn, wáwlwin
Wamil Hall *Suffolk*, 'wɒmɪl,
wómmil
Wamphray Water *D. & G.*, 'wɒm-
freɪ, wómfray
Wanborough *Wilts.*, 'wɒnbrə,
wónnbră
Wand, *f.n.*, wɒnd, wonnd
Wandor, *f.n.*, 'wɒndər, wónndŏr
Wands, *f.n.*, wɒndz, wonndz
Wandsworth *London*, 'wɒndz-
wərθ, wónndzwŭrth
Wanhills, *f.n.*, 'wɒnhɪlz, wónn-
-hilz
Wanklyn, *f.n.*, 'wæŋklɪn, wánklin
Wanlip *Leics.*, 'wɒnlɪp, wónn-lip
Wanlockhead *D. & G.*, ,wɒnlɒk-
'hed, wonnlock-héd
Wann, *f.n.*, wɒn, wonn
Wannop, *f.n.*, 'wɒnəp, wónnŏp
Wansbeck, River, *Northd.*,
'wɒnzbek, wónnzbeck
Wansbeck parliamentary divi-
sion *Northd.*, 'wɒnzbek, wónnz-
beck
Wansborough, *f.n.*, 'wɒnzbərə,
wónnzbŭră
Wansbrough, *f.n.*, 'wɒnzbrə,
wónnzbră

Wansey, *f.n.*, 'wɒnzɪ, wónnzi
Wansford *Cambs.*, 'wɒnzfərd,
wónnzförd
Wanstall, *f.n.*, 'wɒnstɒl, wónns-
stawl
Wanstead *London*, 'wɒnsted,
wónnssted
Wantage, *f.n.*, 'wɒntɪdʒ, wónntij
Wantage *Oxon.*, 'wɒntɪdʒ, wónn-
tij
Wantisden *Suffolk*, 'wɒntsdən,
wónntsděn
Wapping *London*, 'wɒpɪŋ, wóp-
ping
Wapping Old Stairs *London*,
,wɒpɪŋ 'ould steərz, wopping
öld stairz
Warbeck, *f.n.*, 'wɔrbek, wáwr-
beck
Warboys *Cambs.*, 'wɔrbɔɪz,
wáwrboyz
Warbstow *Cornwall*, 'wɔrbstou,
wáwrbsstō
Warburg, *f.n.*, 'wɔrbɜrg, wáwr-
burg
Warburg Institute *London*, 'wɔr-
bɜrg, wáwrburg
Warburton, *f.n.*, 'wɔrbərtən,
wáwrbŭrtŏn
Warcop *Cumbria*, 'wɔrkəp, wáwr-
kŏp
Ward, *f.n.*, wɔrd, wawrd
Wardell, *f.n.*, wɔr'del, wawrdéll
Wardhaugh, *f.n.*, 'wɔrdhɒ,
wáwrd-haw
Wardrop, *f.n.*, 'wɔrdrəp, wáwr-
drŏp
Wardy Hill *Cambs.*, 'wɔrdɪ 'hɪl,
wáwrdi hîll
Wareing, *f.n.*, 'weərɪŋ, wáiring
Waren Burn *Northd.*, 'weərən,
wáirěn
Warenford *Northd.*, 'weərənfɔrd,
wáirěn-ford
Waren Mills *Northd.*, 'weərən
'mɪlz, wáirěn millz
Warenton *Northd.*, 'weərəntən,
wáirěntŏn
Wargrave *Berks.*, 'wɔrgreɪv,
wáwr-grayv
Warham, William, *15th–16th-c.*
Archbishop of Canterbury,
'wɒrəm, wórrăm
Waring, *f.n.*, 'weərɪŋ, wáiring
Waringstown *Co. Down*, 'weərɪŋz-
taun, wáiringztown
Wark *Northd.*, wɔrk, wawrk
Warkleigh *Devon*, 'wɔrklɪ, wáwrk-
li
Warkworth, *f.n.*, 'wɔrkwərθ,
wáwrkwŭrth
Warkworth *Northd.*, 'wɔrkwərθ,
wáwrkwŭrth. *Appropriate also*
for Baron ~.

Warleggan, *also spelt* **Warleggon**, *Cornwall*, wɔr'legən, wawr-léggăn

Warley *Staffs., W. Yorks.*, 'wɔrlɪ, wáwrli

Warley, Great *and* Little, *Essex*, 'wɔrlɪ, wáwrli

Warley Common *Essex*, 'wɔrlɪ 'kɒmən, wáwrli kómmŏn

Warlock, *f.n.*, 'wɔrlɒk, wáwrlock

Warman, *f.n.*, 'wɔrmən, wáwrmăn

Warmington *Northants.*, 'wɔrmɪŋtən, wáwrmingtŏn

Warmsworth *S. Yorks.*, 'wɔrmzwɜrθ, wáwrmzwurth

Warmwell *Dorset*, 'wɔrmwel, wáwrmwel

Warncken, *f.n.*, 'wɔrŋkɪn, wáwrnkĕn

Warner, *f.n.*, 'wɔrnər, wáwrnĕr

Warnham, *f.n.*, 'wɔrnəm, wáwrnăm

Warninglid *W. Sussex*, 'wɑrnɪŋlɪd, waárning-lidd

Warnock, *f.n.*, 'wɔrnɒk, wáwrnock

Warr, *f.n.*, wɔr, wawr

Warrack, *f.n.*, 'wɒræk, wórrăck

Warre, *f.n.*, wɔr, wawr

Warrell, *f.n.*, 'wɒrəl, wórrĕl

Warren, *f.n.*, 'wɒrən, wórrĕn

Warrender, *f.n.*, 'wɒrɪndər, wórrĕndĕr

Warrick, *f.n.*, 'wɒrɪk, wórrick

Warrin, *f.n.*, 'wɒrɪn, wórrin

Warsash *Hants*, 'wɔrsæʃ, wáwrssash; 'wɔrzæʃ, wáwrzash

Warschauer, *f.n.*, 'wɒʃər, wóshĕr

Warsop *Notts.*, 'wɔrsɒp, wáwrssop

Warter, *f.n.*, 'wɔrtər, wáwrtĕr

Wartle *Grampian*, 'wɔrtl, wáwrtl

Wartling *E. Sussex*, 'wɔrtlɪŋ, wáwrtling

Warton, *f.n.*, 'wɔrtən, wáwrtŏn

Warwick, *f.n.*, 'wɒrɪk, wórrick

Warwick *Cumbria, Warwicks.*, 'wɒrɪk, wórrick. *Appropriate also for the Earl of ~.*

Wasdale, *also spelt* **Wastdale**, *Cumbria*, 'wɒsdl, wóssdl.
Wastdale *is the ecclesiastical spelling.*

Wasdale Head, *also spelt* **Wastdale Head**, *Cumbria*, 'wɒsdl 'hed, wóssdl héd

Wash, *f.n.*, wɒʃ, wosh

Washbourne, *f.n.*, 'wɒʃbɔrn, wóshborn

Wass, *f.n.*, wɒs, woss

Wasserstein, *f.n.*, 'wæsərstin, wássĕr-steen

Wasson, *f.n.*, 'wɒsən, wóssŏn

Wastdale *see* **Wasdale**

Wastell, *f.n.*, 'wɒstl, wósstl

Wastie, *f.n.*, 'wæstɪ, wássti

Wastwater *Cumbria*, 'wɒstwɔtər, wósstwawtĕr

Watchet *Somerset*, 'wɒtʃɪt, wótchĕt

Watendlath *Cumbria*, wɒ'tendləθ, wotténdláth

Waterden *Norfolk*, 'wɒtərdən, wáwtĕrdĕn

Waterford, Marquess of, 'wɒtərfərd, wáwtĕrfŏrd

Waterlooville *Hants*, ˌwɒtərlu'vɪl, wawtĕrloo-vill

Waterman, *f.n.*, 'wɒtərmən, wáwtĕrmăn

Waternish, *also spelt* **Vaternish**, *H'land*, 'wɒtərnɪʃ, wáwtĕrnish

Waterrow *Somerset*, 'wɒtərou, wáwtĕrō

Waters, *f.n.*, 'wɒtərz, wáwtĕrz

Watford *Herts.*, 'wɒtfərd, wótt-fŏrd

Wath *N. Yorks.*, wɒθ, woth

Wathen, *f.n.*, 'wɒθən, wóthĕn

Watherston, *f.n.*, 'wɒθərstən, wóthĕrstŏn

Wathes, *f.n.*, 'wɒθɪz, wóthĕz

Wath upon Dearne *S. Yorks.*, 'wɒθ əpɒn 'dɜrn, wóth ŭpon dérn; 'wæθ əpɒn 'dɜrn, wáth ŭpon dérn

Watkin, *f.n.*, 'wɒtkɪn, wóttkin

Watkins, *f.n.*, 'wɒtkɪnz, wóttkinz

Watling, *f.n.*, 'wɒtlɪŋ, wóttling

Watling Street, *Roman military road, Kent–N. Wales*, 'wɒtlɪŋ strɪt, wóttling street

Watmough, *f.n.*, 'wɒtmou, wótt-mō

Watney, *f.n.*, 'wɒtnɪ, wóttni

Watrous, *f.n.*, 'wɒtrəs, wóttrŭss

Watson, *f.n.*, 'wɒtsən, wóttssŏn

Watt, *f.n.*, wɒt, wott

Watten *H'land*, 'wɒtən, wóttĕn; 'wætən, wáttĕn

Watters, *f.n.*, 'wɒtərz, wáwtĕrz; 'wɒtərz, wóttĕrz

Watthews, *f.n.*, 'wɒθjuz, wáw-thewz

Wattis, *f.n.*, 'wɒtɪs, wóttiss

Wattisfield *Suffolk*, 'wɒtɪsfɪld, wóttisfeeld

Wattisham *Suffolk*, 'wɒtɪʃəm, wótti-shăm

Watton *Norfolk*, 'wɒtən, wóttŏn

Watts, *f.n.*, wɒts, wotts

Wattstown *Mid Glam.*, 'wɒtstaun, wóttstown

Wauchope, *f.n.*, 'wɒxəp, wóchŏp; 'wɒkəp, wáwkŏp

Waugh, *f.n.*, wɔ, waw; wɒx, woch; wɒf, woff; wɒf, waf, waaf. *The first is appropriate for Auberon,* 'ɔbərən, áwbĕrŏn, *and Evelyn,* 'ivlɪn, éevlin, *authors.*

Waunarlwydd *W. Glam.*, waɪn-'arlʊɪð, wīnaarlōō-ith

Waunfawr *see* **Waenfawr**

Waun-lwydd *Gwent*, waɪn'lʊɪð, wīn-lōō-ith

Waun-pound *Gwent*, waɪn'paʊnd, wīnpównd

Wauthier, *f.n.*, 'voʊtjeɪ, vŏt-yay

Wavell, *f.n.*, 'weɪvl, wáyvl

Wavendon *Bucks.*, 'wævəndən, wávvĕndŏn

Waveney, River, *Norfolk–Suffolk*, 'weɪvənɪ, wáyvĕni

Waverley *Surrey*, 'weɪvərlɪ, wáy-vĕrli. *Appropriate also for Viscount ~*.

Waverton *Ches.*, 'weɪvərtən, wáyvĕrtŏn

Wavertree *Merseyside*, 'weɪvərtrɪ, wáyvĕrtree

Wawne, *also spelt* **Waghen,** *Humberside*, wɒn, wawn

Weacombe *Somerset*, 'wikəm, weékŏm

Weal, *f.n.*, wil, weel

Wealdstone *London*, 'wildstoʊn, weéldsstŏn

Wealeson, *f.n.*, 'wilsən, weélssŏn

Wealleans, *f.n.*, 'wilənz, weélĕnz

Wear, River, *Durham–Tyne & Wear*, wɪər, weer

Weardale *Durham*, 'wɪərdeɪl, weérdayl

Wearde *Cornwall*, wɛərd, waird

Weare Giffard *Devon*, 'wɪər 'dʒɪfərd, weér jíffård

Wearing, *f.n.*, 'wɛərɪŋ, wáiring

Wearn, *f.n.*, wɜrn, wern

Wearne, *f.n.*, wɜrn, wern

Wearne *Somerset*, wɛərn, wairn; wɪərn, weern; wɜrn, wern

Weasenham All Saints *Norfolk*, 'wizənəm ɔl 'seɪnts, weézĕnăm awl sáynts

Weasenham St. Peter *Norfolk*, 'wizənəm snt 'pitər, weézĕnăm sĭnt peétĕr

Weaste *Gtr. M'chester*, wist, weest

Weaverham *Ches.*, 'wivərhæm, weévĕr-ham

Webb, *f.n.*, web, webb

Webber, *f.n.*, 'webər, wébbĕr

Weber, *f.n.*, 'webər, wébbĕr; 'wibər, weébĕr; 'weɪbər, wáybĕr

Webster, *f.n.*, 'webstər, wébsstĕr

Weddell, *f.n.*, 'wedl, wéddl; wɪ'del, wĕdéll

Wedderburn, *f.n.*, 'wedərbɜrn, wéddĕrburn

Wedgewood, *f.n.*, 'wedʒwʊd, wéjwōŏd

Wedgwood, *f.n.*, 'wedʒwʊd, wéjwōŏd. *Appropriate for Josiah and Thomas ~, 18th-c. potters.*

Wednesbury *W. Midlands*, 'wenzbərɪ, wénzbŭri; 'wedʒbərɪ, wéjbŭri

Wednesfield *W. Midlands*, 'wensfild, wénssfeeld; 'wedʒfɪld, wéjfeeld

Weeks, *f.n.*, wiks, weeks

Weelkes, Thomas, *16th-c. organist and composer*, wɪlks, wilks; wiks, weelks. *The first is now more common among Weelkes scholars, who base this on variant spellings in old documents.*

Weem *Tayside*, wim, weem

Wegener, *f.n.*, 'wegənər, wéggĕnĕr

Wegg, *f.n.*, weg, wegg

Wegner, *f.n.*, 'veɪgnər, váygnĕr

Weguelin, *f.n.*, 'wegəlɪn, wéggĕlin

Weidenfeld and Nicolson, George, *publishers*, 'vaɪdənfelt ənd 'nɪklsən, vídĕnfelt ănd nícklssŏn

Weigal, *f.n.*, 'waɪgl, wígl

Weigall, *f.n.*, 'waɪgɔl, wígawl; 'waɪgl, wígl

Weigh, *f.n.*, weɪ, way

Weighell, *f.n.*, 'weɪəl, wáy-ĕl; wil, weel

Weighill, *f.n.*, 'weɪhɪl, wáyhil

Weight, *f.n.*, weɪt, wayt

Weightman, *f.n.*, 'weɪtmən, wáytmăn

Weil, *f.n.*, wil, weel; vaɪl, vīl

Weiland, *f.n.*, 'wɪlənd, weélănd

Wein, *f.n.*, win, ween

Weiner, *f.n.*, 'waɪnər, wínĕr

Weinreich-Haste, *f.n.*, 'waɪnraɪk 'heɪst, wínrīk háyst

Weinstock *f.n.*, 'waɪnstɒk, wín-stock

Weipers, *f.n.*, 'waɪpərz, wípĕrz

Weir, *f.n.*, wɪər, weer

Weis, *f.n.*, wis, weess

Weisdale *Shetland*, 'wizdeɪl, weézdayl

Weisner, *f.n.*, 'wiznər, weéznĕr

Weiss, *f.n.*, vaɪs, vīss

Weist, *f.n.*, wist, weesst

Weitz, *f.n.*, wits, weets

Weitzman, *f.n.*, 'waɪtsmən, wítsmăn

Welbourne, *f.n.*, 'welbɔrn, wél-born

Welch, *f.n.*, weltʃ, weltch; welʃ, welsh

Weldon, *f.n.*, 'weldən, wéldŏn

Wellbeloved, *f.n.*, 'welbɪlʌvd, wélbĕluvd

Weller, *f.n.*, 'welər, wéllĕr

Wellesbourne *Warwicks.*, 'welzbɔrn, wélzborn

Wellesley, *f.n.*, 'welzlɪ, wélzli. *Appropriate also for Viscount ~*.

Wellesz, Egon, *composer and musicologist,* 'eɪgɒn 'velɪs, áygon vélless

Wellingborough *Northants.,* 'welɪŋbərə, wéllingbŭră

Wellington, *f.n.,* 'welɪŋtən, wéllingtŏn

Wellington *Cumbria, H. & W., Salop, Somerset,* 'welɪŋtən, wéllingtŏn. *Appropriate also for the Duke of* ∼.

Wellman, *f.n.,* 'welmən, wélmăn

Wells, *f.n.,* welz, wellz

Wells-Pestell, *f.n.,* 'welz pes'tel, wéllz pestéll

Welltog Island *Gwynedd,* 'weltɒg, wéhltog

Wellwood, *f.n.,* 'welwʊd, wél--wood

Welnetham *see* **Whelnetham**

Welney *Norfolk,* 'welnɪ, wélni

Welsh, *f.n.,* welʃ, welsh

Welshpool *Powys,* 'welʃpul, wélshpool; 'welʃ'pul, wélsh-poól

Welwick *Humberside,* 'welɪk, wéllick

Welwyn *Herts.,* 'welɪn, wéllin

Welwyn Garden City *Herts.,* 'welɪn ˌgɑrdən 'sɪtɪ, wéllin gaardĕn sítti

Wem *Salop,* wem, wemm

Wembley *London,* 'wemblɪ, wémbli

Wemyss *Fife,* wimz, weemz. *Appropriate also for the Earl of* ∼.

Wemyss Bay *S'clyde,* 'wimz 'beɪ, weémz báy

Wendon, *f.n.,* 'wendən, wéndŏn

Wendover *Bucks.,* 'wendoʊvər, wéndōvĕr

Wendron *Cornwall,* 'wendrən, wéndrŏn

Wendy-cum-Shingay *Cambs.,* 'wendɪ kʌm 'ʃɪŋgɪ, wéndi kum shíng-gi

Wenger, *f.n.,* 'weŋər, wéng-ĕr

Wenninger, *f.n.,* 'wenɪndʒər, wénninjĕr

Wensley *N. Yorks.,* 'wenzlɪ, wénzli

Wensleydale *N. Yorks.,* 'wenzlɪdeɪl, wénzlidayl. *Appropriate also for* ∼ *cheese and for the* ∼ *breed of sheep.*

Wensum, River, *Norfolk,* 'wensəm, wénssŭm

Wentworth, *f.n.,* 'wentwərθ, wéntwŭrth; 'wentwɜrθ, wént-wurth

Wentz, *f.n.,* wents, wents

Wentzel, *f.n.,* 'wentsl, wéntssl

Wenvoe *S. Glam.,* 'wenvoʊ, wénvō

Weobley *H. & W.,* 'weblɪ, wébli

Weoley Castle *W. Midlands,* 'wɪəlɪ, weé-ŏli

Werner, *f.n.,* 'wɜrnər, wérnĕr; 'wɔrnər, wáwrnĕr

Werneth *Gtr. M'chester,* 'wɜrnəθ, wérnĕth

Wernher, *f.n.,* 'wɜrnər, wérnĕr

Wernick, *f.n.,* 'wɜrnɪk, wérnick

Wesham *Lancs.,* 'wesəm, wéssăm

Wesil, *f.n.,* 'wesl, wéssl

Weske, *f.n.,* wesk, wesk

Wesker, *f.n.,* 'weskər, wéskĕr

Wesley, *f.n.,* 'weslɪ, wéssli; 'wezlɪ, wézli. *The first is appropriate for John* ∼, *18th-c. evangelist and leader of Methodism, and his brother Charles.*

Wesleyan, *pertaining to John and Charles* **Wesley,** 'weslɪən, wéssli-ăn

Wess, *f.n.,* wes, wess

Westaby, *f.n.,* 'westəbɪ, wéstăbi

Westacott, *f.n.,* 'westəkɒt, wéstă-kot

Westall, *f.n.,* 'westɔl, wéstawl

West Alvington *Devon,* 'west 'ɔlvɪŋtən, wést áwlvingtŏn

West Bradley *Somerset,* 'west 'brædlɪ, wést brádli

West Bromwich *W. Midlands,* 'west 'brɒmɪtʃ, wést brómmitch

Westbrook, *f.n.,* 'westbrʊk, wéstbrook

Westbury-on-Trym *Avon,* 'westbərɪ ɒn 'trɪm, wéstbŭri on trím

West Calder *Lothian,* 'west 'kɔldər, wést káwldĕr

West Challow *Oxon.,* 'west 'tʃæloʊ, wést chálō

Westcott, *f.n.,* 'westkət, wéstkŏt; 'weskət, wéskŏt

Westenra, *f.n.,* 'westənrə, wés-tĕnră

Wester Fearn *H'land,* 'westər 'fɜrn, wéstĕr férn

West Freugh *D. & G.,* 'west 'frux, wést froóch

Westgate, *f.n.,* 'westgeɪt, wést-gayt; 'westgɪt, wéstgit

West Grinstead *W. Sussex,* 'west 'grɪnstɪd, wést grínsstĕd

Westham *E. Sussex,* 'westhæm, wést-ham

West Hartlepool *Cleveland,* 'west 'hɑrtlɪpul, wést haártlipool

West Heslerton *N. Yorks.,* 'west 'heslərtən, wést hésslĕrtŏn

West Hoathly *W. Sussex,* 'west hoʊθ'laɪ, wést hōth-lí

West Horsley *Surrey,* 'west 'hɔrzlɪ, wést hórzli

Westhoughton *Gtr. M'chester,* 'west'hɒtən, wést-háwtŏn

Westleton *Suffolk*, 'wesltən, wéssltŏn

Westley *Suffolk*, 'westlɪ, wéstli

Westley Waterless *Cambs.*, 'westlɪ 'wɔːtərlɪs, wéstli wáwtĕrlĕss

West Lockinge *Oxon.*, 'west 'lɒkɪndʒ, wést lóckinj

West Lothian *Lothian*, 'west 'louðɪən, wést lóthiăn

West Malling *Kent*, 'west 'mɔːlɪŋ, wést máwling

West Meon *Hants.*, 'west 'miːən, wést mée-ŏn

West Mersea *Essex*, 'west 'mɜːzɪ, wést mérzi

Westmeston *E. Sussex*, west-'mestən, westméstŏn

Westminster *London*, 'west-mɪnstər, wéstminstĕr

West Molesey *Surrey*, 'west 'moulzɪ, wést mólzi

Westmorland *former Co. name*, 'westmərlənd, wéstmŏrlănd. *Appropriate also for the Earl of* ~.

Westoby, *f.n.*, 'westəbɪ, wéstŏbi; wes'toubɪ, westóbi

Weston, *f.n.*, 'westən, wéstŏn

Weston Bampfylde *Somerset*, 'westən 'bæmfɪld, wéstŏn bámfeeld

Weston Colville *Cambs.*, 'westən 'koulvɪl, wéstŏn kólvil

Weston Favell *Northants.*, 'westən 'feɪvl, wéstŏn fáyvl

Westoning *Beds.*, 'westənɪŋ, wéstŏning

Weston-super-Mare *Avon*, 'westən ˌsuːpər 'mɛər, wéstŏn soopĕr máir; 'westən ˌsjuːpər 'mɛər, wéstŏn sewpĕr máir; 'westən ˌsjuːpər 'mɛərɪ, wéstŏn sewpĕr máiri

Weston Zoyland *Somerset*, 'westən 'zɔɪlənd, wéstŏn zóyländ

Westray *Orkney*, 'westreɪ, wéstray

Westrope, *f.n.*, 'westroup, wést-rōp

Westruther *Borders*, 'westrʌðər, wéstruthĕr

West Somerton *Norfolk*, 'west 'sʌmərtən, wést súmmĕrtŏn

West Stoughton *Somerset*, 'west 'stɔtən, wést stáwtŏn

West Walton Highway *Norfolk*, 'west 'wɒltən 'haɪweɪ, wést wáwltŏn hí-way; 'west 'wɒltən 'haɪweɪ, wést wólltŏn hí-way

Westward *Cumbria*, west'wɔrd, west-wáwrd

Westwater, *f.n.*, 'westwɒtər, wéstwawtĕr

West Wickham *Cambs.*, 'west 'wɪkəm, wést wíckăm

Westwoodside *Humberside*, 'westwudsaɪd, wéstwŏŏd-sīd

West Wratting *Cambs.*, 'west 'rætɪŋ, wést rátting

West Wycombe *Bucks.*, 'west 'wɪkəm, wést wíckŏm

Wetherby *W. Yorks.*, 'weðərbɪ, wéthĕrbi

Wetton, *f.n.*, 'wetən, wéttŏn

Wetwang *Humberside*, 'wetwæŋ, wétwang

Wevill, *f.n.*, 'wevɪl, wévvil

Wexler, *f.n.*, 'wekslər, wékslĕr

Weybourne *Norfolk*, 'webərn, wébbŭrn

Weybridge *Surrey*, 'weɪbrɪdʒ, wáybrij

Weyman, *f.n.*, 'waɪmən, wímăn. *Appropriate for Stanley J.* ~, *author.*

Weymouth *Dorset*, 'weɪməθ, wáy-mŭth. *Appropriate also for Viscount* ~.

Whaddon *Cambs.*, 'wɒdən, wóddŏn

Whaley Bridge *Derby.*, 'weɪlɪ 'brɪdʒ, wáyli brij

Whalley, *f.n.*, 'hwɒlɪ, whólli; 'hwɔːlɪ, whàwli; 'weɪlɪ, wáyli

Whalley *Lancs.*, 'hwɒlɪ, whàwli

Whalley Range *Gtr. M'chester*, 'wɒlɪ 'reɪndʒ, wólli ráynj

Whalsay *Shetland*, 'hwɔːlseɪ, whàwlssay

Whannel, *f.n.*, 'hwɒnl, whónnl; wɒ'nel, wonnéll

Whaplode *Lincs.*, 'hwɒploud, whóp-lōd

Wharam, *f.n.*, 'hwɛərəm, wháirăm

Wharfe, River, *N. & W. Yorks.*, wɔrf, wawrf

Wharncliffe, Earl of, 'wɔrnklɪf, wórn-kliff

Wharram le Street *N. Yorks.*, 'wɒrəm lə 'striːt, wórrăm lĕ stréet

Wharram Percy *N. Yorks.*, 'wɒrəm 'pɜrsɪ, wórrăm pérssi

Whateley, *f.n.*, 'hweɪtlɪ, wháytli

Whatham, *f.n.*, 'wɒdəm, wóthăm; 'wɒtəm, wóttăm; 'wɒðəm, wóthăm

Whatley, *f.n.*, 'hwɒtlɪ, whóttli

Whatling, *f.n.*, 'hwɒtlɪŋ, whóttling

Whatmore, *f.n.*, 'hwɒtmɔr, whótt-mor

Whatmough, *f.n.*, 'hwɒtmou, whóttmō; 'wɒtmʌf, wóttmuff; 'wɒtmuf, wóttmōōf

Whatsley, *f.n.*, 'wɒtslɪ, wóttsli

Whatstandwell *Derby.*, wɒt-'stændwel, wottstándwel

Whatton, _f.n.,_ 'wɒtən, wóttŏn
Whatton _Notts.,_ 'wɒtən, wóttŏn
Wheadon, _f.n.,_ 'widən, weédŏn
Wheal Rose _Cornwall,_ 'wil 'rouz, weél róz
Wheare, _f.n.,_ hwɛər, whair
Wheatacre _Norfolk,_ 'hwɪtəkər, whíttăkĕr
Wheathampstead _Herts.,_ 'hwet-əmstəd, whéttămsstĕd; 'hwitəm-sted, wheétămssted
Wheatley, _f.n.,_ 'hwitlɪ, wheétli
Wheatstone, _f.n.,_ 'hwitstən, wheétstŏn
Wheeler, _f.n.,_ 'hwilər, wheélĕr
Whelan, _f.n.,_ 'hwilən, wheélăn
Wheldon, _f.n.,_ 'weldən, wéldŏn
Wheldale _W. Yorks.,_ 'weldeɪl, wéldayl
Whelen, _f.n.,_ 'hwilən, wheélĕn
Whelleans, _f.n.,_ 'wilənz, weélĕnz
Whelnetham, _also spelt_ **Welnetham,** _Suffolk,_ wel'niθəm, welneéthăm; 'welnetəm, wélnettăm
Whernside, mt., _Cumbria–N. Yorks.,_ 'wɜrnsaɪd, wérnssíd
Wherstead _Suffolk,_ 'wɜrsted, wérssted
Wherwell _Hants,_ 'hwɜrwel, whér-wel
Wheway, _f.n.,_ 'hwiweɪ, wheéway
Whewell, _f.n.,_ 'hjuəl, héw-ĕl
Whibley, _f.n.,_ 'hwɪblɪ, whíbbli
Whichcote, _f.n.,_ 'hwɪtʃkout, whítch-kôt
Whicher, _f.n.,_ 'wɪtʃər, wítchĕr
Whicker, _f.n.,_ 'wɪkər, wíckĕr
Whiddett, _f.n.,_ wɪ'det, widétt
Whiffen, _f.n.,_ 'wɪfɪn, wiffĕn
Whiffin, _f.n.,_ 'wɪfɪn, wiffin
Whiffing, _f.n.,_ 'wɪfɪŋ, wiffing
Whigham, _f.n.,_ 'hwɪgəm, whíggăm
Whilding, _f.n.,_ 'hwaɪldɪŋ, whílding
Whiligh _E. Sussex,_ 'hwaɪlaɪ, whí-lī
Whincup, _f.n.,_ 'wɪŋkəp, wínkŭp
Whinerey, _f.n.,_ 'hwɪnərɪ, whínnĕri
Whipsnade _Beds.,_ 'hwɪpsneɪd, whíp-snayd
Whissendine _Leics.,_ 'hwɪsəndaɪn, whisséndīn
Whistlefield _S'clyde,_ 'hwɪslfild, whísslfeeld
Whitaker, _f.n.,_ 'hwɪtəkər, whít-tăkĕr. _Appropriate for_ ~'s _Almanac._
Whitbread, _f.n.,_ 'hwɪtbred, whítt-bred
Whitby, _f.n.,_ 'hwɪtbɪ, whíttbi
Whitby _N. Yorks.,_ 'hwɪtbɪ, whíttbi
Whitcher, _f.n.,_ 'wɪtʃər, wítchĕr
Whitchurch Canonicorum _Dorset,_ 'hwɪt-tʃɜrtʃ kə,nɒnɪ'kɔrəm, whít-churtch kănonnikáwrŭm

White, _f.n.,_ hwaɪt, whīt
Whiteabbey _Co. Antrim,_ hwaɪt-'æbɪ, whītábbi
Whiteadder, River, _Borders--Northd.,_ 'hwɪtədər, whíttădĕr
Whitear, _f.n.,_ 'hwɪtɪər, whítti-är
Whitebridge _H'land,_ 'hwaɪtbrɪdʒ, whítbrij
White Colne _Essex,_ 'hwaɪt 'koun, whīt kŏn
Whitefield, _f.n.,_ 'hwɪtfild, whítt-feeld; 'hwaɪtfild, whítfeeld. _The first is appropriate for George_ ~, _18th-c. preacher and evangelist, and hence for the_ ~ _Memorial Church in London._
Whitefield _Gtr. M'chester,_ 'hwaɪt-fild, whítfeeld
White Friargate _Hull,_ 'waɪtfrə-geɪt, wít-frägayt
Whitehall _London,_ 'hwaɪthɒl, whít-hawl; 'hwaɪt'hɒl, whít--háwl
Whitehaugh _Grampian,_ hwaɪt'hɔ, whít-háw
Whitehaven _Cumbria,_ 'hwaɪt-heɪvən, whít-hayvĕn
Whitehead, _f.n.,_ 'hwaɪthed, whít-hed
Whitehead _Co. Antrim,_ hwaɪt-'hed, whīt-héd
Whitehorn, _f.n.,_ 'hwaɪthorn, whít--horn
Whitehough _Derby.,_ 'hwaɪthʌf, whít-huff
Whitehouse, _f.n.,_ 'hwaɪthaus, whít-howss
Whitehouse _Co. Antrim,_ 'hwaɪt-haus, whít-howss
Whiteley, _f.n.,_ 'hwaɪtlɪ, whítli
Whitelock, _f.n.,_ 'hwaɪtlɒk, whít-lock
Whitemoor _Cornwall,_ 'hwaɪtmuər, whítmoōr
Whitemore, _f.n.,_ 'hwaɪtmor, whít-mor
Whiten Head _H'land,_ 'hwaɪtən 'hed, whítĕn héd
Whiteside, _f.n.,_ 'hwaɪtsaɪd, whít-sīd
Whiteslea Lodge _Norfolk,_ 'hwaɪtsli, whítsslee
Whitestone _Devon,_ 'hwɪtstən, whíttstŏn
White Stone _H. & W.,_ 'hwaɪt stoun, whít stŏn
White Waltham _Berks.,_ 'hwaɪt 'wɒlθəm, whít wáwl-thăm; 'hwaɪt 'wɒltəm, whít wáwltăm
Whitfield, _f.n.,_ 'hwɪtfild, whítt-feeld
Whitfield _Kent,_ 'wɪtfild, wíttfeeld
Whithorn _D. & G.,_ 'hwɪthorn, whítt-horn

Whiting, *f.n.*, 'hwaɪtɪŋ, whíting
Whiting Bay *S'clyde*, 'hwaɪtɪŋ 'beɪ, whíting báy
Whitla Hall *Queen's University, Belfast*, 'hwɪtlə, whíttlă
Whitley, *f.n.*, 'hwɪtlɪ, whíttli
Whitlock, *f.n.*, 'hwɪtlɒk, whíttlock
Whitmore, *f.n.*, 'hwɪtmɔr, whíttmor
Whitney, *f.n.*, 'hwɪtnɪ, whíttni
Whitred, *f.n.*, 'hwɪtrɪd, whíttrĕd
Whitrow, *f.n.*, 'wɪtroʊ, wíttrō
Whittaker, *f.n.*, 'hwɪtəkər, whíttăkĕr
Whittenbury, *f.n.*, 'hwɪtənbərɪ, whíttĕnbŭri
Whittingehame *Lothian*, 'hwɪtɪndʒəm, whíttinjăm
Whittingham *Lancs.*, 'hwɪtɪnhəm, whíttin-hăm
Whittingham *Northd.*, 'hwɪtɪndʒəm, whíttinjăm
Whittle, *f.n.*, 'hwɪtl, whíttl
Whittle-le-Woods *Lancs.*, 'hwɪtl lə 'wʊdz, whíttl lĕ wŏōdz
Whittlesford *Cambs.*, 'wɪtlzfərd, wíttlzfŏrd
Whittock, *f.n.*, 'hwɪtək, whíttŏk
Whitton, *f.n.*, 'hwɪtən, whíttŏn
Whitty, *f.n.*, 'hwɪtɪ, whítti
Whitwick *Leics.*, 'hwɪtɪk, whíttick
Whitworth, *f.n.*, 'hwɪtwɜrθ, whítt-wurth
Whoberley *W. Midlands*, 'woʊbərlɪ, wṓbĕrli
Whone, *f.n.*, woʊn, wōn
Whorlow, *f.n.*, 'wɜrloʊ, wúrlō
Whyberd, *f.n.*, 'waɪbərd, wíberd
Whybrow, *f.n.*, 'hwaɪbraʊ, whíbrow
Whyke *W. Sussex*, wɪk, wick
Whyman, *f.n.*, 'waɪmən, wímăn
Whymant, *f.n.*, 'waɪmənt, wímănt
Whymper, *f.n.*, 'hwɪmpər, whímpĕr
Whyte, *f.n.*, hwaɪt, whīt
Whyteleaf *Surrey*, 'hwaɪtlif, whítleef
Whytham, *f.n.*, 'hwaɪtəm, whítăm
Whythorne, Thomas, *16th-c. composer*, 'hwaɪthɔrn, whít-horn. *The name also appears spelt Whithorne.*
Wibaut, *f.n.*, 'viboʊ, véebō
Wibsey *W. Yorks.*, 'wɪpsɪ, wípssi; 'wɪbzɪ, wíbzi
Wichelo, *f.n.*, 'wɪtʃɪloʊ, wítchĕlō
Wichnor *Staffs.*, 'wɪtʃnɔr, wítchnor
Wick *H'land*, wɪk, wick
Wicken, *f.n.*, 'wɪkɪn, wíckĕn
Wicken *Cambs.*, 'wɪkɪn, wíckĕn
Wickhambreaux, *also spelt* **Wickhambreux,** *Kent*, 'wɪkəmbru, wíckămbroo

Wickhambrook *Suffolk*, 'wɪkəmbrʊk, wíckămbrŏŏk
Wickhamford *H. & W.*, 'wɪkəmfɔrd, wíckămfórd
Wickham Market *Suffolk*, 'wɪkəm 'markɪt, wíckăm maárkĕt
Wickham Skeith *Suffolk*, 'wɪkəm 'skiθ, wíckăm skéeth
Wickins, *f.n.*, 'wɪkɪnz, wíckinz
Wicks, *f.n.*, wɪks, wicks
Wickwar *Avon*, 'wɪkwɔr, wíckwawr
Wicor *Hants*, 'wɪkər, wíckŏr
Widecombe *Devon*, 'wɪdɪkəm, wíddĕkŏm
Wideford Hill *Orkney*, 'waɪdfərd, wídfŏrd
Widemouth Bay *Cornwall*, 'wɪdməθ 'beɪ, wídmŭth báy
Wideopen *Tyne & Wear*, 'waɪdoʊpən, wídŏpĕn
Wideson, *f.n.*, 'waɪdsən, wídssŏn
Widgery, *f.n.*, 'wɪdʒərɪ, wíjjĕri
Widlake, *f.n.*, 'wɪdleɪk, wídlayk
Widley *Hants*, 'wɪdlɪ, wídli
Widnall, *f.n.*, 'wɪdnəl, wídnăl
Widnes *Ches.*, 'wɪdnɪs, wídnĕss
Widnesian *native of Widnes*, wɪd'nizɪən, widnéezi-ăn
Wiegold, *f.n.*, 'waɪgoʊld, wígōld
Wieler, *f.n.*, 'wilər, wéelĕr
Wien, *f.n.*, win, ween
Wiesenthal, *f.n.*, 'visəntal, véessĕntaal
Wigan, *f.n.*, 'wɪgən, wíggăn
Wigan *Gtr. M'chester*, 'wɪgən, wíggăn
Wigdor, *f.n.*, 'wɪgdɔr, wígdor
Wigfull, *f.n.*, 'wɪgfəl, wígfŭl
Wiggall, *f.n.*, 'wɪgəl, wíggawl
Wiggins, *f.n.*, 'wɪgɪnz, wígginz
Wigham, *f.n.*, 'wɪgəm, wíggăm
Wight, I. of, waɪt, wīt
Wightman, *f.n.*, 'waɪtmən, wítmăn
Wighton, *f.n.*, 'waɪtən, wítŏn
Wightwick, *f.n.*, 'wɪtɪk, wíttick
Wightwick *W. Midlands*, 'wɪtɪk, wíttick
Wigley, *f.n.*, 'wɪglɪ, wígli
Wigmore, *f.n.*, 'wɪgmɔr, wígmor
Wigoder, *f.n.*, 'wɪgədər, wíggŏdĕr
Wigram, *f.n.*, 'wɪgrəm, wígrăm. *Appropriate also for Baron* ~.
Wigtown *D. & G.*, 'wɪgtaʊn, wígtown; 'wɪgtən, wígtŏn
Wigzell, *f.n.*, 'wɪgzl, wígzl
Wilbarston *Northants.*, wɪl'barstən, wilbaársstŏn
Wilberforce, *f.n.*, 'wɪlbərfɔrs, wílbĕrforss
Wilbraham, *f.n.*, 'wɪlbrəhəm, wílbrăhăm; 'wɪlbrəm, wílbrăm

Wilbraham, Great *and* Little, *Cambs.*, 'wɪlbrəm, wɪlbrăm; 'wɪlbrəhæm, wɪlbrăham

Wilburton *Cambs.*, wɪl'bɜrtən, wɪlbúrtŏn

Wilbye, John, *16th–17th-c. madrigal composer*, 'wɪlbɪ, wɪlbĭ. *A contemporary reference to him as Wilbee seems to discount the view held by some that the second syllable should rhyme with 'high'.*

Wilcox, *f.n.*, 'wɪlkɒks, wĭlkocks

Wild, *f.n.*, waɪld, wīld

Wildash, *f.n.*, 'waɪldæʃ, wīldash

Wilde, *f.n.*, waɪld, wīld

Wildeman, *f.n.*, 'waɪldmən, wīldmăn

Wildenstein Gallery *London*, 'wɪldənstaɪn, wĭldĕnsstīn

Wilder, *f.n.*, 'waɪldər, wíldĕr

Wilderhope *Salop*, 'wɪldərhoup, wĭldĕr-hōp

Wilderspool *Ches.*, 'wɪldərzpul, wĭldĕrzpool

Wilding, *f.n.*, 'waɪldɪŋ, wīlding

Wildman, *f.n.*, 'waɪldmən, wīldmăn

Wilen, *f.n.*, vɪ'leɪn, vɪláyn

Wilenski, *f.n.*, wɪ'lenskɪ, wɪlénskɪ

Wiles, *f.n.*, waɪlz, wīlz

Wiliam, *f.n.*, 'wɪljəm, wíl-yăm

Wilkes, *f.n.*, wɪlks, wĭlks

Wilkie, *f.n.*, 'wɪlkɪ, wílkĭ

Wilkinson, *f.n.*, 'wɪlkɪnsən, wílkinssŏn

Willapark Point *Cornwall*, 'wɪləpɑrk 'pɔɪnt, wĭlăpaark póynt

Willard, *f.n.*, 'wɪlɑrd, wíllaard

Willcocks, *f.n.*, 'wɪlkɒks, wíl-kocks

Willcox, *f.n.*, 'wɪlkɒks, wíl-kocks

Willenhall *W. Midlands*, 'wɪlənhɔl, wĭllĕnhawl

Willes, *f.n.*, wɪlz, willz

Willesden *London*, 'wɪlzdən, wílzdĕn

Willey, *f.n.*, 'wɪlɪ, wílli

Williams, *f.n.*, 'wɪljəmz, wíl-yămz

Williamscot *Oxon.*, 'wɪlskət, wíllsskŏt

Willicomb, *f.n.*, 'wɪlɪkəm, wíllikŏm

Willies, *f.n.*, 'wɪlɪz, wílliz; 'wɪlɪs, wílliss

Willingale, *f.n.*, 'wɪlɪŋgeɪl, wílling-gayl

Willingham, *f.n.*, 'wɪlɪŋəm, wílling-ăm

Willis, *f.n.*, 'wɪlɪs, wílliss

Willison, *f.n.*, 'wɪlɪsən, wíllissŏn

Willmott, *f.n.*, 'wɪlmət, wílmŏt; 'wɪlmɒt, wílmott

Willoughby, *f.n.*, 'wɪləbɪ, wíllŏbi

Willoughby de Broke, Baron, 'wɪləbɪ də 'brʊk, wíllŏbi dĕ brŏŏk

Willoughby de Eresby, Baron, 'wɪləbɪ 'dɪərzbɪ, wíllŏbi deĕrzbi

Wills, *f.n.*, wɪlz, willz

Wills Neck *Somerset*, 'wɪlz 'nek, wíllz néck

Willson, *f.n.*, 'wɪlsən, wíllssŏn

Willum, *f.n.*, 'wɪləm, wíllŭm

Wilmcote *Warwicks.*, 'wɪlmkout, wílmkōt

Wilmslow *Ches.*, 'wɪlmzlou, wílmzlō; 'wɪmzlou, wímzlō

Wilnecote *Staffs.*, 'wɪlnɪkət, wílnĕkŏt; 'wɪŋkət, wínkŏt

Wilpshire *Lancs.*, 'wɪlpʃər, wĭlp-shĕr

Wilshamstead *Beds.*, 'wɪlʃəmstɪd, wíl-shămsstĕd. *Also spelt* Wilstead, *q.v.*

Wilshaw, *f.n.*, 'wɪlʃɔ, wil-shaw

Wilshin, *f.n.*, 'wɪlʃɪn, wíl-shin

Wilson, *f.n.*, 'wɪlsən, wíllssŏn

Wilstead *Beds.*, 'wɪlstɪd, wíllsstĕd. *Also spelt* Wilshamstead, *q.v.*

Wiltshire, *f.n.*, 'wɪlt-ʃər, wĭlt-shĕr

Wiltshire *Co. name*, 'wɪlt-ʃər, wĭlt-shĕr; 'wɪlʃər, wíl-shĕr

Wimbledon *London*, 'wɪmbldən, wímbldŏn

Wimbotsham *Norfolk*, 'wɪmbət-ʃəm, wímbŏt-shăm

Wimhurst, *f.n.*, 'wɪmhərst, wímhurst

Wincanton *Somerset*, wɪn'kæntən, win-kántŏn

Winch, *f.n.*, wɪntʃ, wintch

Winchburgh *Lothian*, 'wɪnʃbərə, wínshbŭră

Winchcombe *Glos.*, 'wɪnʃkəm, wínshkŏm

Winchelsea *E. Sussex*, 'wɪntʃlsɪ, wíntchlssee

Winchelsey, *f.n.*, 'wɪntʃlsɪ, wíntchlssi

Winchester *Hants.*, 'wɪntʃɪstər, wíntchĕstĕr

Winchilsea, Earl of, 'wɪntʃlsɪ, wíntchlssi

Winchwen *W. Glam.*, 'wɪnʃwen, wínsh-wen

Winckless, *f.n.*, 'wɪŋkles, wínkless

Wincle *Ches.*, 'wɪŋkl, wínkl

Wincott, *f.n.*, 'wɪŋkət, wínkŏt

Windeatt, *f.n.*, 'wɪndɪət, wíndi-ăt

Windebank, *f.n.*, 'wɪndɪbæŋk, wíndĕbank

Winder, *f.n.*, 'wɪndər, wíndĕr

Windermere *Cumbria*, 'wɪndərmɪər, wíndĕrmeer

Winders, *f.n.*, 'wɪndərz, wíndĕrz

Windess, *f.n.*, 'wɪndɪs, wíndĕss

Windeyer, *f.n.*, 'wɪndɪər, wíndi-ĕr

Winding, *f.n.*, 'waɪndɪŋ, wínding
Windle, *f.n.*, 'wɪndl, wíndl
Windlesham *Surrey*, 'wɪndlʃəm, wíndl-shăm. *Appropriate also for Baron* ~.
Windley, *f.n.*, 'wɪndlɪ, wíndli
Windram, *f.n.*, 'wɪndrəm, wínd-răm
Windrush, River, *Glos.–Oxon.*, 'wɪndrʌʃ, wíndrush
Windscale *Cumbria*, 'wɪndskeɪl, wíndskayl
Windsor, *f.n.*, 'wɪnzər, wínzŏr
Windsor *Berks.*, 'wɪndzər, wínd-zŏr
Windus, *f.n.*, 'wɪndəs, wíndŭss
Windygates *Fife*, 'wɪndɪɡeɪts, wíndigayts
Wine, *f.n.*, waɪn, wīn
Winearls, *f.n.*, 'wɪnərlz, wínnĕrlz
Wineham *W. Sussex*, waɪn'hæm, wīn-hám
Winestead *Humberside*, 'waɪn-sted, wínsted
Winfrith *Dorset*, 'wɪnfrɪθ, wínfrith
Winfrith Heath *Dorset*, 'wɪnfrɪθ 'hiθ, wínfrith héeth
Winfrith Newburgh *Dorset*, 'wɪn-frɪθ 'njubərɡ, winfrith néwburg
Wing, *f.n.*, wɪŋ, wing
Wing *Bucks.*, wɪŋ, wing
Wingerworth *Derby.*, 'wɪŋərwɜrθ, wing-ĕr-wurth
Winget, *f.n.*, 'wɪŋɪt, wíng-ĕt
Wingham, *f.n.*, 'wɪŋəm, wing-ăm
Wingrove, *f.n.*, 'wɪŋɡrouv, wing--grōv
Winkle, *f.n.*, 'wɪŋkl, wínkl
Winkleigh *Devon*, 'wɪŋklɪ, wínkli
Winlaton *Tyne & Wear*, wɪn-'leɪtən, winláytŏn; 'wɪnlətən, wínlettŏn
Winn, *f.n.*, wɪn, winn
Winnall *Hants.*, 'wɪnl, wínnl
Winsborough, *f.n.*, 'wɪnzbrə, wínzbră
Winser, *f.n.*, 'wɪnzər, wínzĕr
Winsham *Somerset*, 'wɪnsəm, wínssăm
Winshill *Staffs.*, 'wɪnzhɪl, wínz-hil
Winslade, *f.n.*, 'wɪnsleɪd, wínss-layd
Winsor, *f.n.*, 'wɪnzər, wínzŏr
Winspear, *f.n.*, 'wɪnspɪər, wíns-speer
Winstanley, *f.n.*, 'wɪnstənlɪ, wínsstănli; wɪn'stænlɪ, wins-stánli
Winstanley *Gtr. M'chester*, 'wɪnstənlɪ, wínsstănli; wɪn-'stænlɪ, winsstánli
Winstock, *f.n.*, 'wɪnstɒk, wíns-stock
Winter, *f.n.*, 'wɪntər, wíntĕr

Winterbourne Whitechurch *Dorset*, 'wɪntərbɔrn 'hwɪt-tʃɜrtʃ, wíntĕrborn whit-churtch
Winterbotham, *f.n.*, 'wɪntərbɒtəm, wíntĕrbottăm
Winterbottom, *f.n.*, 'wɪntərbɒtəm, wíntĕrbottŏm
Winterflood, *f.n.*, 'wɪntərflʌd, wíntĕrfludd
Winther, *f.n.*, 'wɪntər, wíntĕr
Wintle, *f.n.*, 'wɪntl, wíntl
Wintour, *f.n.*, 'wɪntər, wíntŭr
Wintringham, *f.n.*, 'wɪntrɪŋəm, wíntring-ăm
Winward, *f.n.*, 'wɪnwərd, wínwărd
Winwick *Cambs.*, 'wɪnɪk, wínnick
Wippell, *f.n.*, 'wɪpl, wippl
Wirksworth *Derby.*, 'wɜrkswɔrθ, wírkswûrth
Wirral *Merseyside–Ches.*, 'wɪrəl, wírräl
Wirswall *Ches.*, 'wɜrzwəl, wírzwăl
Wirth, *f.n.*, wɜrθ, wirth
Wisbech *Cambs.*, 'wɪzbitʃ, wíz-beetch
Wisdom, *f.n.*, 'wɪzdəm, wízdŏm
Wise, *f.n.*, waɪz, wīz
Wiseton *Notts.*, 'waɪstən, wísstŏn
Wishart, *f.n.*, 'wɪʃərt, wíshărt
Wishaw *S'clyde, Warwicks.*, 'wɪʃɔ, wíshaw
Wisher, *f.n.*, 'wɪʃər, wíshĕr
Wiske, River, *N. Yorks.*, wɪsk, wisk
Wiskemann, *f.n.*, 'wɪskəmən, wísskĕmăn
Wisley *Surrey*, 'wɪzlɪ, wízzli
Wissington see **Wiston** *Suffolk*
Wistaston *Ches.*, 'wɪstəstən, wísstásstŏn
Wiston *Dyfed*, 'wɪsən, wíssŏn
Wiston *S'clyde*, 'wɪstən, wísstŏn
Wiston, *also spelt* **Wissington**, *Suffolk* 'wɪstən, wísstŏn
Wiston *W. Sussex*, 'wɪstən, wís-stŏn; 'wɪsən, wíssŏn
Wistow *Cambs., Leics., N. Yorks.*, 'wɪstou, wísstō
Wistreich, *f.n.*, 'wɪstraɪk, wísstrík
Wistrich, *f.n.*, 'wɪstrɪtʃ, wísstritch
Witcham *Cambs.*, 'wɪtʃəm, wítchăm
Witchell, *f.n.*, 'wɪtʃl, wítchl
Witham, *f.n.*, 'wɪtəm, wíttăm
Witham *Essex*, 'wɪtəm, wíttăm
Witham, River, *Leics.–Lincs.*, 'wɪðəm, wíthăm
Witham Friary *Somerset*, 'wɪtəm 'fraɪərɪ, wíttăm frí-ări; 'wɪðəm 'fraɪərɪ, wíthăm frí-ări
Withe, *f.n.*, wɪð, with
Withern *Lincs.*, 'wɪðərn, wíthĕrn
Withernsea *Humberside*, 'wɪðərn-sɪ, wíthĕrnssee

Witherow, *f.n.,* 'wıðərou, wíŧ̣ĕrō

Withers, *f.n.,* 'wıðərz, wíŧ̣ĕrz

Witherspoon, *f.n.,* 'wıðərspun, wíŧ̣ĕrsspoon

Withington *Gtr. M'chester,* 'wıðıŋtən, wíŧ̣ıngtŏn

Withnall, *f.n.,* 'wıθnəl, wíthnăl

Withnell *Lancs.,* 'wıθnəl, wíthnĕl

Withy, *f.n.,* 'wıðı, wíŧ̣i

Withycombe Raleigh *Devon,* 'wıðıkəm 'rɔlı, wíŧ̣ikŏm ráwli

Withyham *E. Sussex,* wıðı'hæm, wiŧ̣i-hám; 'wıðıhæm, wíŧ̣i-ham

Witt, *f.n.,* wıt, witt

Wittenbach, *f.n.,* 'wıtənbak, wíttĕnbaak

Wittersham *Kent,* 'wıtərʃəm, wíttĕr-shăm

Wittkower, *f.n.,* 'wıtkouvər, wíttkŏvĕr

Wittle, *f.n.,* 'wıtl, wíttl

Witton Gilbert *Durham,* 'wıtən 'dʒılbərt, wíttŏn jílbĕrt; 'wıtən 'gılbərt, wíttŏn gílbĕrt

Wiveliscombe *Somerset,* 'wıvəlıskəm, wívvĕlisskŏm; 'wılskəm, wílsskŏm

Wivelsfield *E. Sussex,* 'wıvlzfıld, wívvlzfeeld

Wivenhoe *Essex,* 'wıvənhou, wívvĕn-hō

Wivenhoe Cross *Essex,* 'wıvənhou 'krɒs, wívvĕn-hō króss

Wiverton *Notts.,* 'waıvərtən, wívĕrtŏn; 'wɜrtən, wértŏn

Wiveton *Norfolk,* 'wıvtən, wívtŏn; 'wıvıtən, wívvĕtŏn

Woan, *f.n.,* woun, wōn

Wober, *f.n.,* 'woubər, wóbĕr

Woburn *Beds.,* 'woubərn, wóburn; 'wubərn, wóoburn. *The second is used by the family of the Duke of Bedford and is therefore appropriate for* ~ *Abbey and Wild Animal Kingdom. The first is usual in the village.*

Woburn *Co. Down,* 'woubərn, wóbŭrn

Woburn Press, *publishers,* 'woubərn, wóburn

Woburn Sands *Beds.–Bucks. border,* 'woubərn 'sændz, wóburn sándz; 'wubərn 'sændz, wóoburn sándz

Wodehouse, *f.n.,* 'wudhaus, wŏŏd-howss; 'wudəs, wŏŏdŭss. *The first is appropriate for P. G.* ~, *author.*

Wodell, *f.n.,* wɒ'del, woddéll

Wofford, *f.n.,* 'wɒfərd, wóffŏrd

Wofinden, *f.n.,* 'wufındən, wŏŏfíndĕn

Woking *Surrey,* 'woukıŋ, wóking

Wokingham *Berks.,* 'woukıŋəm, wóking-ăm

Wolborough *Devon,* 'wulbərə, wŏŏlbŭră

Woldingham *Surrey,* 'wouldıŋəm, wólding-ăm

Woledge, *f.n.,* 'wulıdʒ, wŏŏlĕj

Wolfe, *f.n.,* wulf, wŏŏlf

Wolfenden, *f.n.,* 'wulfəndən, wŏŏlfĕndĕn

Wolferstan, *f.n.,* 'wulfərstən, wŏŏlfĕrstăn

Wolferton *Norfolk,* 'wulfərtən, wŏŏlfĕrtŏn

Wolff, *f.n.,* wulf, wŏŏlf

Wolfgang, *f.n.,* 'wulfgæŋ, wŏŏlfgang

Wolfhampcote *Warwicks.,* 'wulfəmkət, wŏŏlfămkŏt

Wolfrunian, *native of Wolverhampton,* wul'frunıən, wŏŏlfroonıăn

Wolfsthal, *f.n.,* 'wulfstɑl, wŏŏlfstaal

Wollaston, *f.n.,* 'wuləstən, wŏŏlăsstŏn

Wollaston *Northants.,* 'wuləstən, wŏŏlăstŏn

Wollaton *Notts.,* 'wulətən, wŏŏlătŏn

Wollescote *W. Midlands,* 'wulıskout, wŏŏlĕsskŏt

Wollstonecraft, *f.n.,* 'wulstənkraft, wŏŏlstŏn-kraaft

Wolmer, Viscount, 'wulmər, wŏŏlmĕr

Wolmer, *f.n.,* 'wulmər, wŏŏlmĕr

Wolpert, *f.n.,* 'wulpərt, wŏŏlpĕrt

Wolridge, *f.n.,* 'wulrıdʒ, wŏŏlrij

Wolseley, *f.n.,* 'wulzlı, wŏŏlzli

Wolsey, *f.n.,* 'wulzı, wŏŏlzi

Wolsingham *Durham,* 'wulzıŋəm, wŏŏlzing-ăm

Wolstanton *Staffs.,* wul'stæntən, wŏŏlstántŏn

Wolstenbury Hill *E. Sussex,* 'wulstənbərı, wŏŏlstĕnbŭri

Wolstencroft, *f.n.,* 'wulstənkrɒft, wŏŏlstĕn-kroft

Wolstenholme, *f.n.,* 'wulstənhoum, wŏŏlstĕnhōm

Wolsty *Cumbria,* 'wulstı, wŏŏlsti; 'wustı, wŏŏssti

Wolterton *Norfolk,* 'wultərtən, wŏŏltĕrtŏn

Wolvercote *Oxon.,* 'wulvərkət, wŏŏlvĕrkŏt

Wolverhampton *W. Midlands,* ‚wulvər'hæmptən, wŏŏlvĕr-hámptŏn

Wolverley *H. & W.,* 'wulvərlı, wŏŏlvĕrli

Wolverton, Baron, 'wulvərtən, wŏŏlvĕrtŏn

Wolviston *Cleveland*, 'wɒlvɪstən, wŏolvisstŏn

Wombourn *Staffs.*, 'wɒmbərn, wómbŭrn

Wombridge *Salop*, 'wʌmbrɪdʒ, wúmbrij

Wombwell, *f.n.*, 'wumwəl, woomwĕl; 'wumwəl, woomwĕl; 'wɒmwəl, wómwĕl

Wombwell *S. Yorks.*, 'wumwel, woomwell

Womenswold *Kent*, 'wɪmɪnzwould, wímmĕnzwōld; 'wimzwould, weemzwōld

Womersley, *f.n.*, 'wumərzlɪ, woomĕrzli; 'wɒmərzlɪ, wómmĕrzli

Wonersh *Surrey*, 'wɒnərʃ, wónnersh

Wonnacott, *f.n.*, 'wɒnəkɒt, wónnăkott

Wontner, *f.n.*, 'wɒntnər, wónntnĕr

Wooburn *Bucks.*, 'wubɜrn, wooburn

Wood, Haydn, *composer*, 'heɪdn 'wud, háydn wood

Woodall, *f.n.*, 'wudɔl, woodawl

Woodbridge, *f.n.*, 'wudbrɪdʒ, woodbrij

Woodbridge *Suffolk*, 'wudbrɪdʒ, woodbrij

Woodburn, East *and* West, *Northd.*, 'wudbɜrn, woodburn

Woodchester *Glos.*, 'wutʃɪstər, wootchĕstĕr

Woodforde-Finden, *f.n.*, 'wudfərd 'fɪndən, woodfŏrd fíndĕn

Woodford Halse *Northants.*, 'wudfərd 'hɒls, woodfŏrd hólss

Woodgate, *f.n.*, 'wudgeɪt, wood-gayt

Woodger, *f.n.*, 'wudʒər, woojĕr

Woodget, *f.n.*, 'wudgɪt, wood-gĕt

Woodhall, *f.n.*, 'wudhɔl, wood-hawl

Woodhatch, *f.n.*, 'wudhætʃ, wood-hatch

Woodhouse, *f.n.*, 'wudhaus, wood-howss

Woodiwiss, *f.n.*, 'wudɪwɪs, woodiwiss

Woodland, *f.n.*, 'wudlənd, woodlănd

Woodlesford *W. Yorks.*, 'wudlzfərd, woodlzfŏrd

Woodley, *f.n.*, 'wudlɪ, woodli

Woodliff, *f.n.*, 'wudlɪf, woodliff

Woodman, *f.n.*, 'wudmən, woodmăn

Woodnesborough *Kent*, 'wudnəzbərə, woodnĕzbŭră; 'wunzbərə, woonzbŭră; 'wɪnzbərə, wínzbŭră

Woodnutt, *f.n.*, 'wudnʌt, woodnutt

Woodrooffe, *f.n.*, 'wudrəf, woodrŏf

Woods, *f.n.*, wudz, woodz

Woodstock *Oxon.*, 'wudstɒk, woodstock

Woodvale *Merseyside*, 'wudveɪl, woodvayl

Woodville, *f.n.*, 'wudvɪl, woodvil

Woodward, *f.n.*, 'wudwərd, woodwărd

Woof, *f.n.*, wuf, woof

Woofferton *Salop*, 'wufərtən, woofĕrtŏn

Wookey *Somerset*, 'wukɪ, wooki

Woolam, *f.n.*, 'wuləm, woolăm

Woolard, *f.n.*, 'wulard, woolaard

Woolas, *f.n.*, 'wuləs, woolăss

Woolaston *Glos.*, 'wuləstən, woolăsstŏn

Woolavington *Somerset*, wul-'ævɪŋtən, woolávvingtŏn

Woolbeding *W. Sussex*, 'wulbidɪŋ, woolbeeding

Woolcombe, *f.n.*, 'wulkəm, woolkŏm

Wooldridge, *f.n.*, 'wuldrɪdʒ, wooldrij

Wooler, *f.n.*, 'wulər, woolĕr

Woolf, *f.n.*, wulf, woolf

Woolfardisworthy *nr. Bideford* (*Devon*), *see* **Woolsery**

Woolfardisworthy *nr. Crediton* (*Devon*), wul'fard ɪswərðɪ, woolfaardisswurthi

Woolford, *f.n.*, 'wulfərd, woolfŏrd

Woolhampton *Berks.*, wul'hæmptən, wool-hámptŏn

Woolhouse, *f.n.*, 'wulhaus, wool-howss

Wooll, *f.n.*, wul, wool

Woolland, *f.n.*, 'wulənd, woolländ

Woollard, *f.n.*, 'wulard, woolaard

Woollcombe, *f.n.*, 'wulkəm, woolkŏm

Woolley, *f.n.*, 'wulɪ, wooli

Woolley *Cambs.*, 'wulɪ, wooli

Woolnough, *f.n.*, 'wulnou, woolnō

Woolsery, *formerly spelt* **Woolfardisworthy**, *nr. Bideford* (*Devon*), 'wulzərɪ, woolzĕri

Woolsington *Tyne & Wear*, 'wulzɪŋtən, woolzingtŏn

Woolsthorpe *Lincs.*, 'wulzθɔrp, woolzthorp. *Appropriate for both places of this name in Lincs.*

Woolwich *London*, 'wulɪtʃ, woolitch; 'wulɪdʒ, woolij

Woon, *f.n.*, wun, woon

Woore *Salop*, wɔr, wawr

Woosnam, *f.n.*, 'wuznəm, wooznăm

Wootton, *f.n.*, 'wutən, wootŏn

Wootton Wawen *Warwicks.*, 'wutən 'wɔən, wootŏn wáw-ĕn

Worbarrow Bay *Dorset*, 'wɔr-bærou 'beɪ, wúrbarrŏ báy

Worcester, *f.n.*, 'wustər, wŏosstĕr

Worcester *H. & W.*, 'wustər, wŏosstĕr

Worden, *f.n.*, 'wɔrdən, wáwrdĕn

Wordie, *f.n.*, 'wɜrdɪ, wúrdi

Wordingham, *f.n.*, 'wɜrdɪŋəm, wúrding-ăm

Wordsworth, *f.n.*, 'wɜrdzwɜrθ, wúrdzwurth; 'wɜrdzwərθ, wúrdzwŭrth

Worfield *Salop*, 'wɔrfild, wúrfeeld

Worfolk, *f.n.*, 'wɔrfouk, wúrfŏk

Worger, *f.n.*, 'wɔrgər, wáwrgĕr

Work, *f.n.*, 'wɜrk, wurk

Workington *Cumbria*, 'wɜrkɪŋtən, wúrking-tŏn

Workman, *f.n.*, 'wɜrkmən, wúrk-măn

Worland, *f.n.*, 'wɔrlənd, wáwr-lănd

Worle *Avon*, wɜrl, wurl

Worledge, *f.n.*, 'wɜrlɪdʒ, wúrlĕj

Worley, *f.n.*, 'wɜrlɪ, wúrli

Worlingham *Suffolk*, 'wɜrlɪŋəm, wúrling-ăm. *Appropriate also for Baron ~.*

Worlington, East *and* West, *Devon*, 'wɜrlɪŋtən, wúrlingtŏn

Worlledge, *f.n.*, 'wɜrlɪdʒ, wúrlĕj

Worlock, *f.n.*, 'wɜrlɒk, wáwrlock

Wormald, *f.n.*, 'wɜrmɔld, wúrmáld

Wormegay *Norfolk*, 'wɜrmɪgeɪ, wúrmĕgay

Wormelow *H. & W.*, 'wɜrmɪlou, wúrmĕlŏ

Wormingford *Essex*, 'wɜrmɪŋfərd, wúrmingfŏrd

Wormington, *f.n.*, 'wɔrmɪŋtən, wáwrmingtŏn

Wormit *Fife*, 'wɜrmɪt, wúrmit

Wormleighton *Warwicks.*, 'wɜrm-'leɪtən, wúrm-láytŏn

Wormley *Surrey*, 'wɜrmlɪ, wúrmli

Worn, *f.n.*, wɔrn, wawrn

Worne, *f.n.*, wɔrn, wawrn

Wornum, *f.n.*, 'wɜrnəm, wúrnŭm

Worplesdon *Surrey*, 'wɔrplzdən, wáwrplzdŏn

Worrall, *f.n.*, 'wʌrəl, wúrrăl; 'wɒrəl, wórrăl

Worsall, High *and* Low, *N. Yorks.*, 'wɜrsl, wúrssl

Worsley, *f.n.*, 'wɜrslɪ, wúrssli; 'wɜrzlɪ, wúrzli. *The first, apparently much the more usual, is appropriate for the maiden name of HRH the Duchess of Kent; the second for Baron ~, subsidiary title of the Earl of Yarborough.*

Worsley *Gtr. M'chester*, 'wɜrslɪ, wúrssli

Worsley Mesnes *Gtr. M'chester*, 'wɜrslɪ 'meɪnz, wúrssli máynz

Worsnip, *f.n.*, 'wɜrsnɪp, wúrssnip

Worsnop, *f.n.*, 'wɜrznəp, wúrz-nŏp

Worstead *Norfolk*, 'wusted, wŏossted; 'wustɪd, wŏosstĕd

Worster, *f.n.*, 'wustər, wŏosstĕr

Worsthorne, *f.n.*, 'wɜrsθɔrn, wúrss-thorn

Worswick, *f.n.*, 'wɜrswɪk, wúrss--wick; 'wɜrsɪk, wúrssick

Worth, *f.n.*, wɜrθ, wurth

Wortham *Suffolk*, 'wɜrðəm, wúrthăm

Worthing *W. Sussex*, 'wɜrðɪŋ, wúrthing

Worthington, *f.n.*, 'wɜrðɪŋtən, wúrthingtŏn

Worthley, *f.n.*, 'wɜrθlɪ, wúrthli

Worth Matravers *Dorset*, 'wɜrθ mə'trævərz, wúrth mătrávvĕrz

Worting *Hants*, 'wɜrtɪŋ, wúrting

Wortley, *f.n.*, 'wɜrtlɪ, wúrtli

Wortley *W. Yorks.*, 'wɜrtlɪ, wúrtli

Worton *Wilts.*, 'wɜrtən, wúrtŏn

Wortwell *Norfolk*, 'wɜrtwəl, wúrtwĕl

Wotherspoon, *f.n.*, 'wʌðərspun, wúthĕrspoon; 'wɒðərspun, wóthĕrspoon

Wothespoon, *f.n.*, 'wʌðəspun, wúthĕsspoon; 'wɒðəspun, wóthĕsspoon

Wotton, *f.n.*, 'wutən, wŏotŏn

Wotton-under-Edge *Glos.*, 'wutən 'ʌndrɪdʒ, wŏotŏn úndrĕj; 'wutən ˌʌndər 'edʒ, wŏotŏn undĕr éjj

Woughton *Bucks.*, 'wuftən, wŏof-tŏn

Would, *f.n.*, wud, wŏod

Wouldham *Kent*, 'wuldəm, wŏoldăm

Wrafton *Devon*, 'ræftən, ráfftŏn

Wrangaton *Devon*, 'ræŋətən, ráng--ătŏn

Wrangham, *f.n.*, 'ræŋəm, ráng-ăm

Wrantage *Somerset*, 'rɑntɪdʒ, raántij; 'ræntɪdʒ, rántij

Wrath, Cape, *H'land*, rɔθ, rawth; rɑθ, raath; ræθ, rath; rɒθ, roth

Wrathall, *f.n.*, 'rɒθl, róthl

Wraxhall, *f.n.*, 'ræksl, rácksl

Wray, *f.n.*, reɪ, ray

Wraysbury *see* **Wyardisbury**

Wrea Green *Lancs.*, 'reɪ 'grin, ráy gréen

Wreake, River, *Leics.*, rik, reek

Wreay *Cumbria*, 'rɪə, rée-ă

Wreford, *f.n.*, 'rɪfərd, réefŏrd

Wrekenton *Tyne & Wear*, 'rekɪn-tən, réckĕntŏn

Wrekin, The, *Salop*, 'rıkın, réekin. *Appropriate also for the admin. dist. of Shropshire.*

Wreningham *Norfolk*, 'renıŋəm, rénning-äm

Wrentham *Suffolk*, 'renθəm, rén-thäm

Wrexham *Clwyd*, 'reksəm, récksäm

Wrey, *f.n.*, reı, ray

Wreyland *Devon*, 'reılənd, ráyländ

Wright, *f.n.*, raıt, rīt

Wrighton, *f.n.*, 'raıtən, rítön

Wrigley, *f.n.*, 'rıglı, rĭggli

Wriothesley, *f.n.*, 'raıəθslı, rí--ŏthsli; 'rɒtslı, róttsli; 'rɒtıslı, róttessli; 'rıθlı, rithli; 'rızlı, rizzli. *The name, now historic, was the family name of the Elizabethan Earls of Southampton. The first is the pronunciation used by at least one descendant, the thirteenth Duke of Bedford. To judge by various works of reference, the others were current, singly or severally, in the fifteenth and sixteenth centuries.*

Wrisberg, *f.n.*, 'rısbərg, rĭssberg

Writhlington *Somerset*, 'rıðlıŋtən, ríthlingtŏn

Wrixon, *f.n.*, 'rıksən, rĭcksŏn

Wrobel, *f.n.*, 'roubl, róbl

Wrose *W. Yorks.*, rouz, rōz

Wrotham *Kent*, 'rutəm, róotäm

Wrottesley, *f.n.*, 'rɒtslı, róttsli. *Appropriate also for Baron ~.*

Wrottesley *Staffs.*, 'rɒtslı, róttsli

Wroughton, *f.n.*, 'rɔtən, ráwtön

Wroughton *Wilts.*, 'rɔtən, ráwtön

Wroxall *Warwicks.*, 'rɒksɔl, róck-sawl

Wulfrun Hall *Wolverhampton*, 'wolfrən, woolfrŭn

Wulstan, *C.n. and f.n.*, 'wolstən, woolstän

Wvendth, *f.n.*, wentθ, went-th

Wyatt, *f.n.*, 'waıət, wí-ät

Wyberg, *f.n.*, 'waıbər, wíbĕr

Wyberton *Lincs.*, 'wıbərtən, wĭbbértön

Wyboston *Beds.*, 'waıbəstən, wíbŏstön

Wybrew, *f.n.*, 'waıbru, wíbroo

Wybunbury *Ches.*, 'wımbrı, wímbri

Wychbold *H. & W.*, 'wıtʃbould, witch-bōld

Wych Cross *E. Sussex*, 'wıtʃ 'krɒs, witch króss

Wyche, *f.n.*, waıtʃ, wītch

Wyche, Lower *and* Upper, *H. & W.*, wıtʃ, witch

Wychnor Bridges *Staffs.*, 'wıtʃnɔr 'brıdʒız, witchnor bríjĕz

Wychwood Forest *Oxon.*, 'wıtʃ-wod, witchwŏod

Wycliffe, *also spelt* **Wyclif**, John, *14th-c. religious reformer*, 'wıklıf, wĭckliff

Wycoller *Lancs.*, 'waıkɒlər, wíkoller

Wycombe *Bucks.*, 'wıkəm, wĭcköm

Wyddfa, Yr *Gwynedd*, ər 'uıðvə, ŭr óo-ithvă. *This is the Welsh name for* **Snowdon**.

Wye, River, *Gwent–Glos. border*, waı, wī. *Its Welsh name is* **Gwy**, *q.v.*

Wyfordby *Leics.*, 'waıfərdbı, wífördbi

Wykeham, *f.n.*, 'wıkəm, wĭckäm

Wykeham *N. Yorks.*, 'waıkəm, wíkäm

Wykehamist, *one educated at* **Winchester** *College*, 'wıkəmıst, wíckämist

Wyken *W. Midlands*, 'waıkən, wíkĕn

Wyke Regis *Dorset*, 'waık 'rıdʒıs, wík réejiss

Wykes, *f.n.*, waıks, wīks

Wykey *Salop*, 'waıkı, wíki

Wykham Hall *Banbury*, 'wıkəm, wĭckäm

Wylam *Northd.*, 'waıləm, wíläm

Wyld, *f.n.*, waıld, wīld

Wylde, *f.n.*, waıld, wīld

Wylfa *Gwynedd*, 'wılvə, wĭlvă

Wylie, *f.n.*, 'waılı, wíli

Wyllie, *f.n.*, 'waılı, wíli

Wylye *Wilts.*, 'waılı, wíli

Wymer, *f.n.*, 'waımər, wímĕr

Wymering *Hants*, 'wımərıŋ, wímmĕring

Wymeswold *Leics.*, 'waımz-would, wímzwōld

Wymington *Beds.*, 'wımıŋtən, wímmingtön

Wymondham *Leics.*, 'waıməndəm, wímŏndäm

Wymondham *Norfolk*, 'wındəm, wíndäm

Wymondley, Great *and* Little, *Herts.*, 'waıməndlı, wímŏndli

Wyn, *Welsh C.n.*, wın, win

Wynd, *f.n.*, waınd, wīnd

Wyndham, *f.n.*, 'wındəm, wíndäm

Wyness, *f.n.*, 'waınıs, wínĕss

Wynford, *f.n.*, 'wınfərd, wínförd

Wynn, *f.n.*, wın, winn

Wynne, *f.n.*, wın, winn

Wynward, *f.n.*, 'wınərd, wínnärd

Wynyard, *f.n.*, 'wınjərd, win-yärd

Wynyard *Cleveland*, 'wınjərd, win-yärd

Wyrardisbury, *also spelt* **Wraysbury**, *Berks.*, 'reɪzbəri, ráyzbŭri
Wyre, River, *Lancs.*, 'waɪər, wīr
Wyreside *Lancs.*, 'waɪərsaɪd, wīrssīd
Wyrley, Great *and* Little, *Staffs.*, 'wɜrlɪ, wúrli
Wyrley and Essington Canal *Staffs.*, 'wɜrlɪ ənd 'esɪŋtən, wúrli ănd éssing-tŏn
Wysall *Notts.*, 'waɪsl, wíssll
Wytch Farm *Dorset*, wɪtʃ, witch
Wythall *H. & W.*, 'wɪðɔl, wíthawl
Wytham *Oxon.*, 'waɪtəm, wītăm
Wythburn *Cumbria*, 'waɪðbərn, wíthburn
Wythenshawe *Gtr. M'chester*, 'wɪðənʃə, wíthĕn-shaw
Wythop *Cumbria*, 'wɪðəp, wíthŏp
Wyton, *f.n.*, 'waɪtən, wītŏn
Wyton *Cambs.*, 'wɪtən, wíttŏn
Wyver, *f.n.*, 'waɪvər, wívĕr
Wyvis, Ben, *H'land*, 'wɪvɪs, wívviss; 'wɪvɪs, wéeviss

X

Xavier, *f.n.*, 'zeɪvjər, záyv-yĕr
Xerri, *f.n.*, 'ʃerɪ, shérri
Xiberras, *f.n.*, ˌʃɪbə'rɑs, shib-bĕraáss
Xuereb, *f.n.*, 'ʃweɪrəb, shwáy-rĕb

Y

Yalden, *f.n.*, 'jɔldən, yáwldĕn
Yalding *Kent*, 'jɔldɪŋ, yáwlding
Yallop, *f.n.*, 'jæləp, yálŏp
Yar, River, *I. of Wight*, jɑr, yaar. *Appropriate for both rivers of this name on the I. of Wight.*
Yarborough, Earl of, 'jɑrbərə, yaárbŭră
Yarburgh *Lincs.*, 'jɑrbərə, yaárbŭră
Yare, River, *Norfolk*, jɛər, yeér
Yarmouth *I. of Wight*, 'jɑrməθ, yaármŭth
Yarmouth, Great, *Norfolk*, 'jɑrməθ, yaármŭth
Yarrow *Borders*, 'jærou, yárrō
Yate *Avon*, jeɪt, yayt
Yates, *f.n.*, jeɪts, yayts
Yatton Keynell *Wilts.*, 'jætən 'kenl, yáttŏn kénnl
Yeabsley, *f.n.*, 'jebzlɪ, yébzli
Yeading *London*, 'jedɪŋ, yédding
Yeadon, *f.n.*, 'jidən, yéedŏn; 'jedən, yéddŏn

Yeadon *W. Yorks.*, 'jidən, yéedŏn
Yealand Conyers *Lancs.*, 'jelənd 'kɒnjərz, yélländ kón-yĕrz
Yealm, River, *Devon*, jæm, yamm
Yealmpton *Devon*, 'jæmtən, yámtŏn
Yeaman, *f.n.*, 'jeɪmən, yáymăn; 'jimən, yéemăn
Yeames, *f.n.*, jimz, yeemz; jeɪmz, yaymz
Yearby *Cleveland*, 'jɜrbɪ, yérbi
Yearsley, *f.n.*, 'jɪərzlɪ, yéerzli
Yeates, *f.n.*, jeɪts, yayts
Yeathouse *Cumbria*, 'jethaʊs, yét-howss
Yeatman, *f.n.*, 'jeɪtmən, yáytmăn
Yeats, *f.n.*, jeɪts, yayts
Yeavering *Northd.*, 'jevərɪŋ, yévvĕring
Yeaxlee, *f.n.*, 'jækslɪ, yácksli; 'jekslɪ, yécksli
Yell *Shetland*, jel, yell
Yelland, *f.n.*, 'jelənd, yélländ
Yelland *Devon*, 'jelənd, yélländ
Yelverton *Devon*, 'jelvərtən, yélvĕrtŏn
Yeo, *f.n.*, joʊ, yō
Yeoell, *f.n.*, 'joʊəl, yŏ-ĕl
Yeolmbridge *Cornwall*, 'joʊmbrɪdʒ, yŏmbrij
Yeovil *Somerset*, 'joʊvɪl, yŏvil
Yeowell, *f.n.*, 'joʊəl, yŏ-ĕl
Yerburgh, *f.n.*, 'jɑrbərə, yaárbŭră
Yerbury, *f.n.*, 'jɑrbərɪ, yérbŭri
Yester *Lothian*, 'jestər, yésstĕr
Yetholm, Kirk, *Borders*, kɜrk 'jetəm, kirk yéttŏm
Yevele, Henry **de**, 14th-*c. master-mason and architect*, də 'jivəlɪ, dĕ yéevĕli
Yglesias, *f.n.*, ɪ'gleɪsɪəs, igláyssi-ăss
Yielden *Beds.*, 'jildən, yéeldĕn
Yiend, *f.n.*, jend, yend
Yip, *f.n.*, jɪp, yip
Ynysangharad *Mid Glam.*, ˌʌnɪsæŋ'hærəd, únnissang--hárrăd
Ynys-ddu *Dyfed*, ˌʌnɪs'ðɪ, únniss-thée
Ynys-hir *Mid Glam.*, ˌʌnɪs'hɪər, únniss-heér
Ynys Llanddwyn *Anglesey*, 'ʌnɪs 'ɬænðuɪn, únniss hlánthŏŏ-in
Ynys Môn *Gwynedd*, 'ʌnɪs 'mɒn, únniss máwn. *This is the Welsh name for* **Anglesey.**
Ynysowen *Mid Glam.*, ˌʌnɪs'oʊɪn, únniss-ŏ-ĕn
Ynys Tawe *W. Glam.*, 'ʌnɪs 'taʊeɪ, únniss tów-ay
Ynys Welltog *Gwynedd*, 'ʌnɪs 'weɬtɒɡ, únniss wéhltog
Ynys-wen *Mid Glam.*, ˌʌnɪs'wen, únniss-wén

Ynysybwl *Mid Glam.*, ˌʌnɪsəˈbʊl, unnissăbŏŏl

Yoker *S'clyde*, ˈjoʊkər, yŏkĕr

Yonge, *f.n.*, jʌŋ, yung

Yorath, *f.n.*, ˈjɔːrəθ, yáwrăth

York, *f.n.*, jɔːk, york

York *N. Yorks.*, jɔːk, york

Yorke, *f.n.*, jɔːk, york

Youatt, *f.n.*, ˈjuːət, yoó-ăt

Youde, *f.n.*, jud, yood

Youds, *f.n.*, jaʊdz, yowdz

Youel, *f.n.*, ˈjuəl, yoó-ĕl; ˈjʊəl, yŏŏ-ĕl; jul, yool

Youell, *f.n.*, ˈjuəl, yoó-ĕl; ˈjʊəl, yŏŏ-ĕl; jul, yool

Youens, *f.n.*, ˈjuːɪnz, yoó-ĕnz

Youghal, *f.n.*, jɔl, yawl

Youings, *f.n.*, ˈjuːɪŋz, yoó-ingz

Youldon, *f.n.*, ˈjuldən, yoóldŏn

Youlgrave, *also spelt* **Youlgreave**, *Derby.*, ˈjulɡreɪv, yoólgrayv

Youlton *N. Yorks.*, ˈjultən, yoóltŏn

Youmans, *f.n.*, ˈjumənz, yoómănz

Young, *f.n.*, jʌŋ, yung

Younger, *f.n.*, ˈjʌŋɡər, yúng-gĕr

Younger of Leckie, Viscount, ˈjʌŋɡər əv ˈlɛkɪ, yúng-gĕr ŏv lécki

Younghusband, *f.n.*, ˈjʌŋhʌzbənd, yúng-huzbănd

Youngman, *f.n.*, ˈjʌŋmən, yúng-măn

Younkman, *f.n.*, ˈjʌŋkmən, yúnkmăn

Younson, *f.n.*, ˈjunsən, yoónssŏn

Youseman, *f.n.*, ˈjusmən, yoóssmăn

Yow, *f.n.*, jaʊ, yow

Yoxall, *f.n.*, ˈjɒksl, yócksl

Ypres, Earl of, ipr̩, eepr

Ypres Tower *Rye*, ipr̩, eepr

Yr Wyddfa *Gwynedd*, ər ˈuɪðvə, ŭr oó-ithvă. *This is the Welsh name for* **Snowdon**.

Ysceifiog *Clwyd*, ʌsˈkaɪvjɒɡ, usskív-yog

Yspytty *Dyfed*, ʌsˈpʌtɪ, usspútti

Yspytty Ystwyth *Dyfed*, ʌsˈpʌtɪ ˈʌstwɪθ, usspútti ústwith

Ystalyfera *W. Glam.*, ˌʌstələˈverə, usstălăvérră

Ystrad *Mid Glam.*, ˈʌstrəd, ússtrăd

Ystrad, River, *Clwyd*, ˈʌstrəd, ússtrăd

Ystradfellte *Powys*, ˌʌstrədˈveltei, usstrăd-véhltay

Ystrad Fflur *Dyfed*, ˈʌstrəd ˈflɪər, ússtrăd fleér. *The English form is* **Strata Florida**, *q.v.*

Ystradgynlais *Powys*, ˌʌstrədˈɡʌnlaɪs, usstrăd-gúnlĭss

Ystrad Meurig *Dyfed*, ˈʌstrəd ˈmaɪərɪɡ, ússtrăd mírig

Ystrad Mynach *Mid Glam.*, ˈʌstrəd ˈmʌnəx, ússtrăd múnnă<u>ch</u>

Ystrad Rhondda *Mid Glam.*, ˈʌstrəd ˈrɒnðə, ússtrăd rón<u>th</u>ă

Ystwyth, River, *Powys–Dyfed*, ˈʌstwɪθ, ússtwith

Ythan, River, *Grampian*, ˈaɪθən, íthăn

Ythanbank *Grampian*, ˈaɪθənˈbæŋk, íthăn-bánk

Ythanwells *Grampian*, ˈaɪθənˈwelz, íthăn-wéllz

Yudkin, *f.n.*, ˈjudkɪn, yoódkin

Yuille, *f.n.*, ˈjuɪl, yoó-il

Z

Zaehner, *f.n.*, ˈzeɪnər, záynĕr

Zalud, *f.n.*, ˈzælud, zálood

Zander, *f.n.*, ˈzændər, zándĕr

Zangwill, *f.n.*, ˈzæŋwɪl, záng-wil

Zara, *C.n.*, ˈzɑrə, zááră

Zealley, *f.n.*, ˈziːlɪ, zeéli

Zeal Monachorum *Devon*, ˈzil mɒnəˈkɔrəm, zeél monnăkáwrŭm

Zeals *Wilts.*, zilz, zeelz

Zeeman, *f.n.*, ˈzimən, zeémăn

Zelah *Cornwall*, ˈzilə, zeélă

Zennor *Cornwall*, ˈzenər, zénnŏr

Zerdin, *f.n.*, ˈzɜrdɪn, zérdin

Zetland, *alternative spelling of* **Shetland**, ˈzetlənd, zétlănd. *Appropriate also for the Marquess of* ~.

Zeuner, *f.n.*, ˈzɔɪnər, zóynĕr

Ziegler, *f.n.*, ˈziɡlər, zeéglĕr

Zilliacus, *f.n.*, ˌzɪlɪˈɑkəs, zilli-áákŭss

Ziman, *f.n.*, ˈzaɪmən, zímăn

Zinkeisen, *f.n.*, ˈzɪŋkaɪzən, zínkīzĕn. *Appropriate for Anna* ~, *painter*.

Zinovieff, *f.n.*, zɪˈnɒvɪef, zinnóvvi-eff

Zoffany, John, *18th–19th-c. painter*, ˈzɒfənɪ, zóffăni

Zogolovitch, *f.n.*, zəˈɡɒləvɪtʃ, zŏgólŏvitch

Zoller, *f.n.*, ˈzɒlər, zóllĕr

Zorian, *f.n.*, ˈzɔrɪən, záwri-ăn

Zorza, *f.n.*, ˈzɔrʒə, zórz<u>h</u>ă

Zouch *Notts.*, zɒtʃ, zotch

Zouche, Baron, zuʃ, zoosh

Zuckerman, *f.n.*, ˈzʊkərmən, zŏŏkĕrmăn. *Appropriate for Sir Solly* ~, *scientist*.

Zuill, *f.n.*, jul, yool

Zussman, *f.n.*, ˈzʌsmən, zússmăn

Zwemmer, *f.n.*, ˈzwemər, zwémmĕr

CHANNEL ISLANDS APPENDIX

A

A'Court, *f.n.,* 'eɪkɔrt, áykort
Ahier, *f.n.,* 'ɑjeɪ, a'a-yay
Albiges, *f.n.,* 'ælbɪ'ʒeɪ, albi<u>zh</u>áy
Alderney, 'ɔldərnɪ, áwldĕrni
Alexandre, *f.n.,* ælɪk'zɒndr, alĕkzóndr
Allaire, *f.n.,* 'ælɛər, álair
Allenet, *f.n.,* 'ælɪneɪ, álinay
Alles, *f.n.,* 'ɔleɪ, áwlay
Allez, *f.n.,* 'ɔleɪ, áwlay
Allo, *f.n.,* 'ælou, álō
Amourette, *f.n.,* 'æmʊ'ret, ammōō-rétt
Andrieux, *f.n.,* 'ændrɪʒ, ándree-ö
Anthoine, *f.n.,* ɒn'twɒn, awn-twónn
Aubert, *f.n.,* 'oubɛər, óbair
Aubin, *f.n.,* 'oubɪn, óbin
Audrain, *f.n.,* 'oudrɑ, ódraa
Averty, *f.n.,* ə'vɑrtɪ, ăvérti
Avrill, *f.n.,* 'ævrɪl, ávril

B

Baal, *f.n.,* beɪl, bayl
Babbé, *f.n.,* bæ'beɪ, babbáy
Bailhache, *f.n.,* 'bæləʃ, bálash
Bailiff, *f.n.,* 'beɪlɪf, báylif
Balleine, *f.n.,* 'bæleɪn, bálayn
Bannier, *f.n.,* 'bænjeɪ, bán-yay
Barbé, *f.n.,* bɑr'beɪ, baarbáy
Bataille, *f.n.,* 'bætaɪ, báttī
Batiste, *f.n.,* 'bætɪst, bátteest
Baudains, *f.n.,* 'boudæ, bódan<u>g</u>
Baudet, *f.n.,* 'boudeɪ, bóday
Beaucamps, *f.n.,* 'boukɒn, bókon
Beauchamp, *f.n.,* 'bouʃɔ, bó-shaw
Beaugie, *f.n.,* 'bouʒeɪ, bó<u>zh</u>i-ay
Beaulieu, *f.n.,* 'bouljə, ból-yö
Beauport, *also spelt* **Beau Port,** *Jersey,* 'boupər, bópor; 'boupɔrt, bóport
Bechelet, *f.n.,* 'beʃleɪ, béshlay
Becquet, *f.n.,* 'bekeɪ, béckay
Beghin, *f.n.,* 'begæ, béggan<u>g</u>
Benest, *f.n.,* 'beneɪ, bénnay
Bertaille, *f.n.,* 'bɜrtaɪ, bértī
Berteau, *f.n.,* 'bɜrtou, bértō
Berthelot, *f.n.,* 'bɜrtɪlou, bértēlō
Besnard, *f.n.,* 'beɪnɑrd, báynaard
Besquet, *f.n.,* 'biskweɪ, béesskway
Beuzeval, *f.n.,* 'bɑzvɑl, bózvaal
Bichard, *f.n.,* 'bɪʃɑr, bíshaar

Billot, *f.n.,* 'bɪlou, bíllō
Binet, *f.n.,* 'bɪneɪ, bínnay
Bisset, *f.n.,* 'bɪsɪt, bíssĕt
Bisson, *f.n.,* 'bɪsɒn, bísson; 'bɪsɔ, bíssaw. *The first is a Guernsey pronunciation, the second a Jersey one.*
Blampied, *f.n.,* bləm'peɪ, blămpée-ay; 'blɒmpieɪ, blómpee, blómpee-ay. *The first is a Guernsey pronunciation, the second a Jersey one.*
Bliault, *f.n.,* 'bliou, blée-ō
Blondel, *f.n.,* 'blɒndl, blóndl
Bois, *f.n.,* bwɑ, bwaa
Bonne Nuit *Jersey,* 'bɒn 'nwi, bón nweé
Bouchard, *f.n.,* 'buʃɑrd, bóō-shaard
Boudin, *f.n.,* 'budæ, bóōdan<u>g</u>
Bougeard, *f.n.,* 'buʒɑrd, bóō<u>zh</u>-aard
Bougourd, *f.n.,* 'buguər, bóōgōōr
Bouley *Jersey,* 'bulɪ, bóōli
Bourgaize, *f.n.,* 'buərgeɪz, bóōr-gayz
Brâche, *f.n.,* brɑʃ, braash
Braye *Alderney,* breɪ, bray
Brechou Island, *also spelt* **Brecqhou,** 'breku, bréckoo
Brecqhou, *f.n.,* 'breku, bréckoo
Brehaut, *f.n.,* breɪ'ou, bray-ó
Breuilly, *f.n.,* brui, bróō-ee
Brouard, *f.n.,* 'bruɑrd, bróō-aard
Buesnel, *f.n.,* 'bjunel, béwnel; 'bjuznəl, béwznĕl
Burhou *islet, nr. Alderney,* bə'ru, bŭroó

C

Cabeldu, *f.n.,* 'kæbldu, kábbl-doo
Cabot, *f.n.,* 'kæbou, kábbō
Cadin, *f.n.,* 'kædæ, káddan<u>g</u>
Canichers, Les *and* Upper, *Guernsey,* 'kænɪʃərz, kánnishĕrz
Carey, *f.n.,* 'keərɪ, káiri
Carré, *f.n.,* 'kareɪ, ka'aray
Casquets *rocks, west of Alderney,* 'kæskɪts, kásskĕts
Castel, *f.n.,* 'katel, ka'atel
Castle Cornet *Guernsey,* 'kɑsl 'kɔrnɪt, ka'assl kórnĕt
Cauvain, *f.n.,* 'kouvæ, kóvan<u>g</u>
Chevalier, *f.n.,* ʃɪ'væljeɪ, shĕvál-yay

Cloche, *f.n.*, klɒʃ, klosh
Cohu, *f.n.*, 'koʊju, kṓ-yoo
Colin, *f.n.*, 'kɒlæ, kóllang
Collas, *f.n.*, 'koʊləs, kṓläss
Collenette, *f.n.*, 'kɒlinet, kóllĕ-net
Corbet, *f.n.*, 'kɔrbɪt, kórbĕt
Corbière Point *Jersey*, kɔr'bjɛər, korbyáir
Corbin, *f.n.*, 'kɔrbɪn, kórbin
Cordiere, *f.n.*, 'kɔrdɪɛər, kórdi-air
Corniere, *f.n.*, 'kɔrnɪɛər, kórni-air
Coutanche, *f.n.*, 'kutɒnʃ, koo-tawnsh; 'kutɑ̄ʃ, kṓotaangsh. *The second is also appropriate for the Barony of ~.*

D

Dallain, *f.n.*, 'dælæ, dálang
D'Eauthreau, *f.n.*, 'doʊtroʊ, dṓtrō
De Caen, *f.n.*, də 'kɑ̄, dĕ ka'ang
De Carteret, *f.n.*, də ˌkɑrtə'ret, dĕ kaartĕrétt
Decaux, *f.n.*, də'koʊ, dĕkṓ
De Faye, *f.n.*, də 'feɪ, dĕ fáy
De Garis, *f.n.*, də 'gɑri, dĕ ga'aree
De Gruchy, *f.n.*, də 'grɪʃɪ, dĕ gríshi; də 'gruʃɪ, dĕ grṓoshi; də 'gruʃɪ, dĕ gróoshi
De La Court, *f.n.*, ˌdelə'kɔr, dellåkór
De La Mare, *f.n.*, də lə 'mɛər, dĕ lă máir
De La Perrelle, *f.n.*, ˌdelə 'pɛərel, dellå páirel
De Louche, *f.n.*, də 'luʃ, dĕ lóosh
De Mesquita, *f.n.*, də məs'kitə, dĕ mĕskéetä
De Moulpied, *f.n.*, də mul'pieɪ, dĕ moolpée-ay
De Putron, *f.n.*, də 'pjutrɒn, dĕ péwtron
Derouet, *f.n.*, 'dɛəruei, dáiroo-ay
De Ste Croix, *f.n.*, də sæn 'krwɑ, dĕ san krwáa; de snt 'krɔɪ, dĕ sĭnt króy
De Saumarez, *f.n.*, də 'sɒmərei, dĕ sómmăray
De Sausmarez, *f.n.*, də 'sɒmərei, dĕ sómmăray
Deslandes, *f.n.*, 'deilɒnd, dáylawnd
Desperques, *f.n.*, deɪ'pɜrk, day-pérk
De Veulle, *f.n.*, də 'vɒl, dĕ vṓl
Digard, *f.n.*, 'dɪgɑr, díggaar
Ditot, *f.n.*, 'dɪtoʊ, díttō
Dixcart *Sark*, 'dikɑr, dée̊kaar
Domaille, *f.n.*, 'doʊmaɪl, dṓmīl

Dorey, *f.n.*, dɒrɪ, dórri; 'dɔrɪ, dáwri. *The first is a Guernsey pronunciation, the second a Jersey one.*
Dubras, *f.n.*, doʊ'brɑ, dṓōbra'a
Duchemin, *f.n.*, 'duʃmɪn, dóosh-min
Du Feu, *f.n.*, du 'fɜ, doo fṓ
Du Heaume, *f.n.*, du 'hoʊm, doo hṓm
Du Parcq, *f.n.*, du 'nɑrk, doo pa'ark
Dupré, *f.n.*, du'prei, doopráy
Duquemin, *f.n.*, 'djukmɪn, déwk-min; 'dukmɪn, dóokmin; 'dukmæ, dóokmang. *The first two are Guernsey pronunciations, the third a Jersey one.*
Durell, *f.n.*, du'rel, doo-réll
Dutertre, *f.n.*, du'tɜrtr, dootértr

E

Ecobichon, *f.n.*, ˌekoʊ'biʃɔ, eckṓ-béeshaw
Ecrehou Islands, 'ekrɪhoʊ, éckrĕhō
Egré, *f.n.*, 'egreɪ, égray
Eker, *f.n.*, 'ikər, éekĕr
Enevoldsen, *f.n.*, en'vɒlsən, envóllssĕn
Ereaut, *f.n.*, 'ɛəroʊ, áirō
Esnouf, *f.n.*, 'eɪnuf, áynoof
Etienne, *f.n.*, 'etjen, ét-yen

F

Falla, *f.n.*, 'fælɑ, fálaa
Fauvel, *f.n.*, 'foʊvel, fṓvel
Ferbrashe, *f.n.*, 'fɛərbrʌʃ, fáirbrush
Filleul, *f.n.*, 'fɪljəl, fíl-yöl
Fiott, *f.n.*, 'fioʊ, fée-ō
Fosse, *f.n.*, fɒs, foss
Foullain, *f.n.*, 'fɒlæ, fóllang
Froome, *f.n.*, frum, froom
Frossard, *f.n.*, 'frɒsɑr, fróssaar

G

Gallichan, *f.n.*, 'gælɪʃɔ, gálishaw
Gallienne, *f.n.*, gæ'leɪn, galáyn
Garignon, *f.n.*, 'gærɪnjɔ, gárrin-yaw
Gaudin, *f.n.*, 'goʊdɪn, gṓdin
Gaudion, *f.n.*, 'goʊdɪɒn, gṓdi-on
Gautier, *f.n.*, goʊ'tieɪ, gōtée-ay
Gavet, *f.n.*, 'gæveɪ, gávvay

Gavey, *f.n.*, 'gæveɪ, gávvay
Gibault, *f.n.*, 'ʒɪboʊ, <u>zh</u>íbbō
Girard, *f.n.*, 'ʒɪrɑr, <u>zh</u>írraar
Godel, *f.n.*, 'gɒdel, gáwdel
Gorey *Jersey*, gɔ'ri, gawreé
Gorin, *f.n.*, 'gɔræ, gáwra*ng*
Goubert, *f.n.*, 'gubɛər, goobair
Gouyette, *f.n.*, 'gujet, goó-yet
Grandes Rocques *Guernsey*, 'grænd 'rɒk, gránd róck
Greffier, *f.n.*, 'grefjeɪ, gréff-yay
Greve de Lecq *Jersey*, 'greɪv də 'lek, gráyv dě léck
Grouville, *f.n.*, gru'vɪl, groovíll
Gruchy, *f.n.*, 'gruʃɪ, groóshi. *But cf.* **De Gruchy.**
Guegan, *f.n.*, 'gɪgən, géegăn
Guernsey, 'gɜrnzɪ, gérnzi
Guille, *f.n.*, gil, geel
Guillemette, *f.n.*, 'gɪlmet, gílmet
Guiton, *f.n.*, 'gɪtɔ, gittaw

Jerbourg Point *Guernsey*, 'dʒɜrbɜrg 'pɔɪnt, jérburg póynt
Jerrom, *f.n.*, 'dʒerəm, jérröm
Jersey, 'dʒɜrzɪ, jérzi
Jethou *island nr. Guernsey*, 'dʒetu jéttoo
Jeune, *f.n.*, 3ən, <u>zh</u>ön
Jory, *f.n.*, 'dʒɔrɪ, jáwri
Jouan, *f.n.*, 'ʒuɔ, <u>zh</u>oó-aw
Jouget, *f.n.*, 'ʒugeɪ, <u>zh</u>oógay
Journeaux, *f.n.*, 'ʒɜrnoʊ, <u>zh</u>órnō
Jurat, *f.n.*, 'dʒʊərət, jŏŏrăt

K

Kergozou, *f.n.*, 'kɛərgoʊzu, káirgōzoo
Kerhoat, *f.n.*, 'kɛərhwɑ, káir--hwaa
Keyho, *f.n.*, 'keɪoʊ, káy-ō

H

Hacquoil, *f.n.*, 'hækwɔɪl, háckwoyl
Hamon, *f.n.*, 'hæmɔ̃, hámaa*ng*; 'hæmɒn, hámmon. *The first is a Guernsey pronunciation, the second a Jersey one.*
Hautes Capelles *Guernsey*, 'hoʊt kə'pel, hŏt kăpéll
Heaume, *f.n.*, joʊm, yōm. *But cf.* **Du Heaume.**
Hegerat, *f.n.*, 'hegɑrɑ, héggĕraa
Herissier, *f.n.*, hɛə'rɪsjeɪ, hairíss--yay
Herivel, *f.n.*, 'herɪvel, hérrivel
Herm, hɜrm, herm
Hervé, *f.n.*, 'hɜrvɪ, hérvi
Hervieu, *f.n.*, 'hɛərvju, háirvew
Houguez, *f.n.*, 'hugeɪ, hoógay
Houiellebecq, *f.n.*, 'hulbek, hoólbeck
Hucquet, *f.n.*, 'hukeɪ, hoókay
Huelin, *f.n.*, 'hjulɪn, héwlin

L

Labey, *f.n.*, 'læbɪ, lábbi
La Corbière *Guernsey, Jersey*, ˌlækər'bjeər, lackorbyáir
La Coupée, *f.n.*, lɑ 'kupeɪ, laa koópay
Lainé, *f.n.*, 'leɪneɪ, láynay
La Maseline *Sark*, lɑ 'mæzəlin, laa mázzěleen
La Moye Point *Guernsey, Jersey*, lə 'mɔɪ, lǎ móy
Lamy, *f.n.*, 'læmɪ, lámmi
Langlois, *f.n.*, 'lɒŋleɪ, lóng-lay; 'lɔŋgwɑ, láwn-gwaa. *The first is a Guernsey pronunciation, the second a Jersey one.*
Larbalestier, *f.n.*, lɑr'bɒlestɪeɪ, laarbólesti-ay
Laurens, *f.n.*, 'lɔrɔ, láwraw
La Villiaze *Guernsey*, ˌlɑ vi'jɑz, laa vee-yáaz
Le Bailly, *f.n.*, lə 'baɪɪ, lě bí-ee
Le Bas, *f.n.*, lə 'bɑ, lě báa
Le Blancq, *f.n.*, lə 'blɔ, lě bláw
Le Boutillier, *f.n.*, lə 'butɪljeɪ, lě boótil-yay
Le Breton, *f.n.*, lə 'bretɒn, lě brétton
Le Brun, *f.n.*, lə 'brʌn, lě brúnn
Le Cappelain, *f.n.*, lə 'kæplæ, lě kápla*ng*
Le Chaminant, *f.n.*, lə 'ʃemɪnɔ, lě shémminaw
Le Chanu, *f.n.*, lə 'ʃænu, lě shánnoo
Le Cheminant, *f.n.*, lə 'ʃemɪnɔ̃, lě shémminaa*ng*
Le Clercq, *f.n.*, lə 'klɛər, lě kláir

I

Icart Point *Guernsey*, 'ikɑr, éekaar
Illien, *f.n.*, 'ɪljen, ill-yen
Ingrouille, *f.n.*, ɪn'gruil, in-groó-eel

J

Jamouneau, *f.n.*, ʒæ'munoʊ, <u>zh</u>ammoónō
Jehen, *f.n.*, 'dʒiæn, jée-an; 'ʒiæn. <u>zh</u>ée-an. *The first is a Guernsey pronunciation, the second a Jersey one.*

Le Cocq, *f.n.,* lə 'koʊk, lĕ kṓk; lə 'kɒk, lĕ kóck. *The first is a Guernsey pronunciation, the second a Jersey one.*

Le Cornu, *f.n.,* lə 'kɔrnju, lĕ kórnew

Le Couteur, *f.n.,* lə 'kutər, lĕ kóotĕr

Le Cras, *f.n.,* lə 'krɑ, lĕ kráa

Le Cuirot, *f.n.,* lə 'kwɪroʊ, lĕ kwirrṓ

Le Druillenec, *f.n.,* lə 'druɪlnek, lĕ drṓo-ilneck

Le Fauvic *Jersey,* lə 'foʊvɪk, lĕ fóvick

Le Febvre, *f.n.,* lə 'fɛːbr, lĕ fébbr

Le Feuvre, *f.n.,* lə 'fivər, lĕ féevĕr

Le Fondre, *f.n.,* lə 'fɔndreɪ, lĕ fáwndray

Le Gallais, *f.n.,* lə 'gæleɪ, lĕ gálay

Le Gallez, *f.n.,* lə 'gæleɪ, lĕ gálay

Le Gresley, *f.n.,* lə 'greɪlɪ, lĕ gráyli

Le Gros, *f.n.,* lə 'groʊ, lĕ grṓ

Le Hucquet, *f.n.,* lə 'hukeɪ, lĕ hóokay

Le Huray, *f.n.,* lə hju'reɪ, lĕ hew-ráy

Le Lacheur, *f.n.,* lə 'læʃər, lĕ láshĕr

Le Lievre, *f.n.,* lə 'livər, lĕ léevĕr

Le Machon, *f.n.,* lə 'mæʃə, lĕ máshă

Le Main, *f.n.,* lə 'mæ̃, lĕ máng

Le Maistre, *f.n.,* lə 'meɪtr, lĕ máytr

Le Maître, *f.n.,* lə 'meɪtr, lĕ máytr

Le Marchand, *f.n.,* lə 'marʃɔ, lĕ maárshaw

Le Marquand, *f.n.,* lə 'markɑ̃, lĕ maárkaang; lə 'markə, lĕ maárkă. *The first is a Guernsey pronunciation, the second a Jersey one.*

Le Masurier, *f.n.,* lə mə'soʊəreɪ, lĕ mássŏŏri-ay; lə 'mæzʊəreɪ, lĕ mázŏŏri-ay. *The first is a Guernsey pronunciation, the second a Jersey one.*

Le Messurier, *f.n.,* lə 'meʒərər, lĕ mézhĕrĕr

Le Mesurier, *f.n.,* lə 'mezʊəreɪ, lĕ mézzŏŏri-ay

Le Moisne, *f.n.,* lə 'mwɑn, lĕ mwaán

Le Monnier, *f.n.,* lə 'mɒnjeɪ, lĕ món-yay

Le Montais, *f.n.,* lə 'mɒnteɪ, lĕ móntay

Lenfestey, *f.n.,* len'festɪ, lenfésti

Le Noury, *f.n.,* lə 'nʊərɪ, lĕ nŏŏri

Le Page, *f.n.,* lə 'peɪdʒ, lĕ páyj

Le Pelley, *f.n.,* lə 'peleɪ, lĕ péllay

Le Pennec, *f.n.,* lə 'penek, lĕ pénneck

Le Poidevin, *f.n.,* lə 'pedvɪn, lĕ pédvin; lə 'pɒdvæ̃, lĕ pódvang. *The first is a Guernsey pronunciation, the second a Jersey one.*

Le Prevost, *f.n.,* lə 'prevoʊ, lĕ prévvṓ

Le Quesne, *f.n.,* lə 'keɪn, lĕ káyn

Le Rendu, *f.n.,* lə 'rɒndu, lĕ ráwndoo

Le Riche, *f.n.,* lə 'rɪʃ, lĕ rísh

Le Rossignol, *f.n.,* lə 'rɒsɪnjɒl, lĕ róssin-yol

Le Ruez, *f.n.,* lə 'rueɪ, lĕ róo-ay

Le Sauteur, *f.n.,* lə 'soʊtər, lĕ sótur

Le Sauvage, *f.n.,* lə sɒ'vɑʒ, lĕ sovvaázh

Les Canichers *Guernsey,* leɪ 'kænɪʃərz, lay kánnishĕrz

Les Hanois Lighthouse *Guernsey,* leɪ 'hænwɑ, lay hán-waa

Les Mielles *Guernsey,* leɪ 'mjel, lay myéll

Les Mouriaux *Alderney,* leɪ 'mʊərɪoʊ, lay mŏŏrí-ō

Le Sueur, *f.n.,* lə 'swɜr, lĕ swúr

Les Vauxbelets *Guernsey,* leɪ 'voʊbəleɪ, lay vóbĕlay

Le Tissier, *f.n.,* lə 'tɪsjeɪ, lĕ tíss-yay

Le Tocq, *f.n.,* lə 'tɒk, lĕ tóck

Le Vesconte, *f.n.,* lə 'veɪkɒnt, lĕ váykont

Lihou Island, 'liu, lee-oo

Loveridge, *f.n.,* 'lʌvərɪdʒ, lúv-vĕrij

M

Machon, *f.n.,* 'mæʃɒn, máshon

Mahy, *f.n.,* 'mɑi, maá-ee

Marquand, *f.n.,* 'markɑ̃, maárkaang. *But cf.* **Le Marquand.**

Marquis, *f.n.,* 'markɪ, maárkee

Martel, *f.n.,* 'martel, maártel

Mauger, *f.n.,* 'meɪdʒər, máyjĕr

Mesny, *f.n.,* 'meɪnɪ, máyni

Michel, *f.n.,* 'mɪʃel, míshel

Miere, *f.n.,* 'miɛər, mée-air

Mignot, *f.n.,* 'mɪnjoʊ, mín-yō

Minquiers *reef, south of Jersey,* 'mɪŋkɪz, mínkiz; 'mækjeɪ, máng-kyay

Mollet, *f.n.,* 'mɒleɪ, móllay

Montais, *f.n.,* 'mɒnteɪ, móntay

Mont Orgueil Castle *Jersey,* ˌmɒt ɔr'gɜi, mŏngt orgŏ-i

Morin, *f.n.,* 'mɔræ̃, máwrang

Moulin Huet *Guernsey,* 'mulɪn wet, móolin wet

Mourant, *f.n.,* 'murɔ, móo-raw

N

Neveu, *f.n.*, 'nevju, névvew
Nicholle, *f.n.*, 'nɪkoʊl, nícköl
Noel, *f.n.*, noʊl, nõl
Noirmont Point *Jersey*, 'nwarmõ, nwaarmõng
Noyon, *f.n.*, 'nɔɪjɒn, nóy-yon

O

Oeillet, *f.n.*, 'ɔjeɪ, áw-yay
Ogier, *f.n.*, 'oʊʒɪər, ózheer; oʊ'ʒijeɪ, ōzhee-yay. *The first is a Guernsey pronunciation, the second a Jersey one.*
Orange, *f.n.*, 'ɔrɒnʒ, áwrawnzh
Ouaisne *Jersey*, 'weɪneɪ, wáynay
Ozanne, *f.n.*, oʊ'zæn, ōzánn
Ozouf, *f.n.*, 'oʊzuf, ōzoof

P

Paisnel, *f.n.*, peɪ'nel, paynéll
Pallot, *f.n.*, 'pæloʊ, pálö
Parmentier, *f.n.*,,parmɒn'tɪər, paarmontéer
Perchard, *f.n.*, 'pərʃard, pér-shaard
Perelle, *f.n.*, 'peərel, páirel
Perelle Bay *Guernsey*, 'peərel, páirel
Perrée, *f.n.*, peə'reɪ, pairáy
Petit, *f.n.*, 'petɪ, pétti
Petit Bot *Guernsey*, 'petɪ 'boʊ, pétti bõ
Petit Port *Guernsey*, 'petɪ 'pɔr, pétti pór
Pettiquin, *f.n.*, 'petɪkæ, péttikang
Picot, *f.n.*, 'pɪkoʊ, píckö
Pigeon, *f.n.*, 'pɪʒɒ, péezhaw
Pinchemain, *f.n.*, 'pɪnʃmeɪn, pínshmayn
Pinel, *f.n.*, 'pɪnel, pínnel
Pirouet, *f.n.*, 'pɪroeɪ, pírröö-ay
Pleinmont Point *Guernsey*, 'plaɪmɒn, plímon
Plémont *Jersey*, 'plemɔ, plémmaw
Poingdestre, *f.n.*, 'pɔɪndestər, póyndestér
Poree, *f.n.*, 'pɔreɪ, páwray
Potier, *f.n.*, 'pɒtjeɪ, pót-yay
Priaulx, *f.n.*, 'prioʊ, prée-ō
Procureur, *f.n.*, 'prɒkjʊərər, próck-yŏŏrér

Q

Quellenec, *f.n.*, 'kelɪnek, kéllêneck
Quentin, *f.n.*, 'kwentɪn, kwéntin

Queripel, *f.n.*, 'kerɪpel, kérripel
Quesnard Lighthouse *Alderney*, 'keɪnard, káynaard
Quesnel, *f.n.*, 'keɪnel, káynel
Quevatre, *f.n.*, kɪ'vatr, kěva̱tr
Quinain, *f.n.*, kɪ'neɪn, kináyn
Quinquenel, *f.n.*, 'kæŋkɪnel, kánkinel
Quirot, *f.n.*, 'kwɪroʊ, kwírrō

R

Rabet, *f.n.*, 'ræbeɪ, rábbay
Rabey, *f.n.*, 'reɪbɪ, ráybi
Raimbault, *f.n.*, 'ræmboʊ, rámbō
Rault, *f.n.*, roʊlt, rōlt
Rebourg, *f.n.*, re'bʊərg, reb-bŏŏrg
Rebours, *f.n.*, re'bʊər, rebbŏŏr
Renier, *f.n.*, 'renjeɪ, rén-yay
Renouard, *f.n.*, 'renwar, rénwaar
Renouf, *f.n.*, re'nuf, rennoof; 'renɒf, rénnoff. *The first is a Guernsey pronunciation, the second a Jersey one.*
Richard, *f.n.*, 'rɪʃar, ríshaar
Ricou, *f.n.*, 'rɪku, ríckoo
Rihoy, *f.n.*, 'rɪɔɪ, rée-oy
Rimeur, *f.n.*, 'rɪmɜr, rímmur
Robilliard, *f.n.*, roʊ'bɪlɪərd, rōbílli-árd
Robin, *f.n.*, 'roʊbɪn, róbin
Roche, *f.n.*, roʊʃ, rōsh
Rocquaine Bay, *Guernsey*, roʊ-'keɪn, rōkáyn
Rohais, *f.n.*, 'roʊheɪz, rō-hayz
Romerill, *f.n.*, 'rɒmrɪl, rómril
Rouget, *f.n.*, ru'ʒeɪ, roozháy
Rousseau, *f.n.*, 'rusoʊ, róossō
Roussel, *f.n.*, ru'sel, roosséll
Routier, *f.n.*, 'rutɪeɪ, róoti-ay
Rozel *Jersey*, 'roʊzel, rōzel

S

St. Aubin *Jersey*, snt 'oʊbɪn, sïnt ōbin; snt 'ɔbɪn, sïnt áwbin
St. Brelade *Jersey*, snt brɪ'lad, sïnt brēla̱ad
St. Helier *Jersey*, snt 'helɪər, sïnt hélli-ěr
St. Ouen's *Jersey*, snt 'wɒnz, sïnt wónnz
St. Peter Port *Guernsey*, snt 'pitər 'pɔrt, sïnt pééter pórt
Salsac, *f.n.*, 'sælzæk, sálzack
Sangan, *f.n.*, 'sæŋen, sáng-en
Sark, *f.n.*, sark, saark
Sarre, *f.n.*, sar, saar

Savident, *f.n.,* 'sævɪdɒn, sávvidon
Sebire, *f.n.,* 'sebɪər, sébbeer
Simon, *f.n.,* 'sɪmã, símmaang;
'sɪmɔ, símmaw. *The first is a*
Guernsey pronunciation, the
second a Jersey one.
Sohier, *f.n.,* 'sɔjeɪ, sáw-yay
Surcouf, *f.n.,* 'suərkuf, sóor-
koof
Syvret, *f.n.,* 'sɪvreɪ, sívray

T

Tabel, *f.n.,* 'teɪbel, táybel
Talibard, *f.n.,* 'tælɪbɑr, tálibaar
Tanguy, *f.n.,* 'tæŋɪ, táng-i; 'tæŋgɪ,
táng-gi. *The first is a Guernsey*
pronunciation, the second a
Jersey one.
Tardif, *f.n.,* 'tɑrdɪf, taárdif
Tardivel, *f.n.,* 'tɑrdɪvel, taárdi-
vel
Thoume, *f.n.,* tum, toom
Thoumine, *f.n.,* tu'min, toomeén
Tirel, *f.n.,* 'tɪrel, tírrel
Torode, *f.n.,* 'tɒroʊd, tórrōd
Tostevin, *f.n.,* 'tɒstɪvɪn, tósstĕ-
vin
Tourtel, *f.n.,* 'tuərtel, tŏŏrtel
Touzeau, *f.n.,* 'tuzoʊ, tóozō
Touzel, *f.n.,* 'tuzel, tóozel
Tregear, *f.n.,* trɪ'gɛər, trĕgáir
Trehorel, *f.n.,* 'treɪɔrel, tráy-
-awrel
Troquer, *f.n.,* 'trouker, trókay
Trouteaud, *f.n.,* tru'tou, trootó
Tulié, *f.n.,* 'tulɪ'eɪ, tooli-áy

U

Udle, *f.n.,* 'judl, yóodl
Upper Canichers *Guernsey,* 'ʌpər
'kænɪʃərz, úppĕr kánnishĕrz

V

Vaillant, *f.n.,* 'veɪjə, váy-yă
Vallois, *f.n.,* 'vælwɑ, válwaa
Valpied, *f.n.,* 'vælpɪeɪ, válpi-ay
Vasselin, *f.n.,* 'væslæ, vásslang
Vaudin, *f.n.,* 'voʊdɪn, vṓdin
Vautier, *f.n.,* 'voʊtjeɪ, vŏt-yay
Vazon Bay *Guernsey,* 'vɑzɒn,
vaázon
Vibert, *f.n.,* 'vaɪbərt, víbĕrt;
'vibɛər, véebair
Vidamour, *f.n.,* 'vɪdəmuər, víddă-
mŏŏr
Viel, *f.n.,* 'viel, vée-el
Vining, *f.n.,* 'vɪnɪŋ, vínning
Voisin, *f.n.,* 'vɔɪzɪn, vóyzin

Y

Yvette, *C.n. and f.n.,* i'vet, eevét
Yvonne, *C.n. and f.n.,* i'vɒn,
eevónn

Z

Zabiela, *f.n.,* zæ'bɪlə, zabbíllă